QUANTITATIVE TECHNIQUES AND STATISTICS

QUANTITATIVE TECHNIQUES AND STATISTICS

K.L. SEHGAL
M.Sc. (Maths). M.Stat. (Indian Statistical Institute)
Prof. NSB (formerly NIILM School of Business)
(Retd. Prof. Indian Statistical Institute)

Himalaya Publishing House

• MUMBAI • NEW DELHI • BENGALURU • HYDERABAD • CHENNAI • ERNAKULAM • NAGPUR
• PUNE • AHMEDABAD • LUCKNOW • BHUBANESWAR • INDORE • KOLKATA • GUWAHATI

First Edition : 2011

Published by : Mrs. Meena Pandey for **Himalaya Publishing House Pvt. Ltd.**, "Ramdoot", Dr. Bhalerao Marg, Girgaon, **Mumbai - 400 004.** Phone: 022-23860170/23863863, Fax: 022-23877178 **E-mail: himpub@vsnl.com; Website: www.himpub.com**

Branch Offices :

New Delhi : "Pooja Apartments", 4-B, Murari Lal Street, Ansari Road, Darya Ganj, New Delhi - 110 002. Phone: 011-23270392, 23278631; Fax: 011-23256286

Nagpur : Kundanlal Chandak Industrial Estate, Ghat Road, Nagpur - 440 018. Phone: 0712-2738731, 3296733; Telefax: 0712-2721215

Bengaluru : No. 16/1 (Old 12/1), 1st Floor, Next to Hotel Highlands, Madhava Nagar, Race Course Road, Bengaluru - 560 001. Phone: 080-32919385; Telefax: 080-22286611

Hyderabad : No. 3-4-184, Lingampally, Besides Raghavendra Swamy Matham, Kachiguda, Hyderabad - 500 027. Phone: 040-27560041, 27550139; Mobile: 09848130433

Chennai : No. 85/50, Bazullah Road, T. Nagar, Chennai - 600 017. Phone: 044-28144004/28144005

Pune : First Floor, "Laksha" Apartment, No. 527, Mehunpura, Shaniwarpeth (Near Prabhat Theatre), Pune - 411 030. Phone: 020-24496323/24496333

Lucknow : Jai Baba Bhavan, Church Road, Near Manas Complex and Dr. Awasthi Clinic, Aliganj, Lucknow - 226 024. Phone: 0522-2339329, 4068914; Mobile: 09305302158, 09415349385, 09389593752

Ahmedabad : 114, "SHAIL", 1st Floor, Opp. Madhu Sudan House, C.G. Road, Navrang Pura, Ahmedabad - 380 009. Phone: 079-26560126; Mobile: 09327324149, 09377088847

Ernakulam : 39/104 A, Lakshmi Apartment, Karikkamuri Cross Rd., Ernakulam, Cochin - 622011, Kerala. Phone: 0484-2378012, 2378016; Mobile: 09344199799

Bhubaneswar : 5 Station Square, Bhubaneswar - 751 001 (Odisha). Phone: 0674-2532129, Mobile: 09861046007

Indore : Kesardeep Avenue Extension, 73, Narayan Bagh, Flat No. 302, IIIrd Floor, Near Humpty Dumpty School, Indore - 452 007 (M.P.). Mobile: 09301386468

Kolkata : 108/4, Beliaghata Main Road, Near ID Hospital, Opp. SBI Bank, Kolkata - 700 010, Phone: 033-32449649, Mobile: 09910440956

Guwahati : House No. 15, Behind Pragjyotish College, Near Sharma Printing Press, P.O. Bharalumukh, Guwahati - 781009, (Assam). Mobile: 09883055590, 09883055536

DTP by : Times Printographics

Printed at : New Delhi

Preface

TO THE FIRST EDITION

Business executives and managers need basic knowledge of mathematics tools to be used in quantitative techniques for decision making. As such knowledge of "Basic Mathematics" for all the management students is essential and also this knowledge will be useful for learning other subjects/papers which make use of it .

It gives me great pleasure to present this book for such students and especially for those who have little background of mathematics and statistics. On the basis of my experience of teaching the subject to the students of management, I had observed that majority of students fall in this category. I had restricted myself to basics and as such difficult concepts which are rarely used had been left out. For this reason I had tried to be as simple as possible and added a large number of examples so that students understand the concept and its utility. The examples are arranged in increasing order of difficulty level designs to clarify the concept smoothly. Practice exercises containing large number of questions are inserted in between at appropriate places in the text.

In nut shell an honest effort is made to organize the chapters in the book so that it needs little endeavor on the part of students to learn and comprehend the subjects with ease. On the basis of my long contact and interaction with students of management I had known their weakness, problems and needs. I earnestly feel that this book will overcome their psychological scare and fear of learning basic statistics.

I am thankful to Shri Niraj Pandey, M.D., and Shri V.S. Rawat, Slaes Manager, both from Himalaya Publishing House Pvt. Ltd for their continued persuasion to write this book.

Though I have tried to eliminate errors, however some errors might not have been detected. I shall feel obliged if such errors are brought to my notice I welcome suggestions from teachers and students.

K.L. SEHGAL
Mob : 9312833473
E-mail : kl.sehgal@nsb.in

Contents

1

Introduction : Quantitative Techniques and Statistics

CHAPTER OUTLINE

- Quantitative Techniques
- Statistics
- Applications of Statistics in Management

Socio-economic life of man became increasingly complex with the fast changing technologies and life styles. 'Severe competition', the by-product of globalisation became an unavoidable component in every segment of the economy, especially in administration and business. Decision-making, the core responsibility of policy makers and top managers was once based on subjective matter such as observation, experience and intelligent guess of the decision maker. Now it is shifted to database, which provides accurate base. In today's world of business management a minor mistake in decision-making leads to a heavy loss or complete closure of the business. Such conditions diverted the attention of planners towards quantitative techniques, making it an important tool in decision-making, goal programming and policy framing. Knowledge of quantitative analysis and quantitative techniques is essential to those who wish to develop their career in any economic activity, where competition is a threat.

1.1 CONCEPT OF QUANTITATIVE TECHNIQUES

"Quantity" is the root from which the concept 'quantitative techniques' is developed. The term "quantity" literally means the ability to be measured through measurable units in numbers or symbols, such as weight, length etc. The word "quantity" is derived from the Latin term 'Quantum Libet' which means 'as much as you please'. Thus quantity is something measurable with definiteness. Quantitative is concerned with quantity. It can be explained as the numerical expression of information or fact against qualitative expression. which is a non-numerical statement of a fact. Thus quantitative techniques involve introduction of the clement of quantities such as numbers, symbols and other mathematical expressions.

Example of Qualitative Statement

- You must show good progress in sales in the next month.
- He is expecting 'big amount' for advertising the product.

These two are qualitative expressions.

Example of Quantitative Expression

- You must improve sales by 12% by next month.
- He is expecting ₹ 25,000 for advertising the product.

Examples show that qualitative expression lacks measuring units in numerical form. Quantitative expressions require units of measurement, in numbers, which can also be called data.

Definition of Quantitative Techniques

As the name indicates plural form, it contains more than one technique or tool. Thus the term can be defined as :

1. "Quantitative Techniques may be defined as those techniques which provide the decision maker with a systematic and powerful means of analysis and help, based on quantitative data, in exploring policies for achieving pre-determined goals."

Thus quantitative techniques are numerical descriptions of quantitative process and analysis extensively applied in the study of problems and process of decision-making.

Classification

The term Quantitative Techniques is defined as a group of devices. It implies that different tools or models constitute the branch of quantitative technique. On the basis of the principles applied in the models. the quantitative technique can be broadly classified under three heads :

1. Statistical Quantitative Techniques.
2. Mathematical Quantitative Techniques.
3. Programming or Operations Research Quantitative Techniques.

Statistical Quantitative Techniques

The technique in which the principles, procedures and the formulae of statistics are used, are classified under the statistical quantitative techniques. The techniques are built on statistics, which is the science of quantitative data.

1.2 STATISTICS — INTRODUCTION

Statistics as a science finds its application in technical, scientific and economic fields of modern economy. As a technique, statistics comes very close to man's routine life. Though statistics is a recently developed science, its usage can be traced in ancient socio-political systems of economically developed countries such as Egypt, India, China and Rome.

History

Statistics is as old as human civilization. It was a powerful tool in the hands of kings and rulers to maintain certain essential records. Thus it was popular as 'Science of statecraft'. Proofs arc available about the custom of systematic collection of data about heads of families, military strength, revenue etc. during ancient political administrations. Statistical historians believe that a population census was conducted in 2030 B C in Jedda (Egypt). Proofs of statistics in India are found in ancient literature such as Manusmrithi, Kautilya's Arthasastra and in writings of Megasthenese.

During 15th and 16th centuries statistics developed as a science in association with mathematics. For a few centuries, statistics remained as a part of mathematics because the pioneers of statistics were mathematicians such as Pascal (1623-1662) J. Bermoulli (1654-1705) and De Moiure (1667-1754) etc. After Industrial Revolution there were sudden changes in the socio-economic life. Social scientists and mathematicians started exploring for techniques to measure the effects of changes. Gradually statistics developed into a separate science. Statisticians, economists and mathematicians of 18th and 19th centuries developed statistics as a separate branch of science. Some of prominent statisticians were Ronald A. Fishers (1890-1962), Sir Francis Galton, Karl Pearson (1857-1936), William, S. Gosset (1876-1937), Marshal (1842-1924). Edgeworth and Bowley etc.

During 17th century John Graunt developed Vital Statistics, a systematic study of birth and death rates. Till very recently statistics is applied only for the collection of official information relating to population census and data of government revenue. But modern statistics has found its application in several fields.

Meaning : The term 'statistics' was first used in a book 'Elements of Universal Education', by Baron J.F. Von Bielfeld and translated by Hooper. M.D. Statisticians believe that the term 'statistics' is derived from a word, which may be one of the following, the Latin term status, the Italian world Statista or a German term Statick or the French word Statistique which denotes a political state or an independent nation. The reason for their argument is that the early statistics was confined to the collection of official information and data for analysis by the kings and the administrators.

Modern statistics has multiple meanings. For convenience they can be classified under two needs—Statistics as data in plural form and statistics as method in its singular form. But for a common man statistics is always data.

Definitions : The concept statistics is defined by different authors as data in a plural sense and as a method in singular form. Some are given as below :

1. *Statistics is the science which deals with classification and tabulation of numerical facts as the basis for explanation, description and comparison of phenomenon."*—**Lovin**
2. *"Statistics is the science which deals with the methods of collecting, classifying, presenting, comparing and interpreting numerical data collected to throw some light on any sphere of enquiry."*—**Selligman**
3. *"Statistics may be defined as the science of collection, presentation, analysis and interpretation of numerical data."*—**Croxton and Cowden**

1.3 APPLICATIONS OF STATISTICS IN VARIOUS AREAS OF MANAGEMENT

Statistics in Business and Management. Prior to the Industrial Revolution, when the production was at the handicraft stage, the business activities were very much limited and were confined only to small units operating in their own areas. The owner of the concern personally looked after all the departments of business activity like sales, purchase, production, marketing, finance and so on. But after the Industrial Revolution, the developments in business activities have taken such unprecedented dimensions both in the size and the competition in the market that the activities of most of the business enterprises and firms are confined not only to one particular locality, town or place but to larger areas. Some of the leading houses have the network of their business activities in almost all the leading towns and cities of the country and even abroad. Accordingly it is impossible for a single person (the owner of the concern) to look after its activities and management has become a specialised job. The manager and a team of management executives is imperative for the efficient handling of the various operations like sales, purchase, production, marketing, control, finance, etc., of the business house. It is here that statistical data and the powerful statistical tools of probability, expectation, sampling techniques, tests of significance, estimation theory, forecasting techniques and so on play an indispensable role. According to Wallis and Roberts : *"Statistics may be regarded as a body of methods for making wise decisions in the face of uncertainty."* A refinement over this definition is provided by Prof. Ya-Lun-Chou as follows : *"Statistics is a method of decision making in the face of uncertainty on the basis of numerical data and calculated risks."* These definitions reflect the applications of Statistics in business since modern business has its roots in the accuracy and precision of the estimates and statistical forecasting regarding the future demand for the product, market trends and so on. Business forecasting techniques which are based on the compilation of useful statistical information on lead and lag indicators are very useful for obtaining estimates which serve as a guide to future economic events. Wrong expectations which might be the result of faulty and inaccurate analysis of various factors affecting a particular phenomenon might lead to his disaster.

The studies of *Economic Barometers* (Index Numbers) enable the businessman to have an idea about the purchasing power of money. The statistical tools of demand analysis enable the businessman to strike a balance between supply and demand. [For details, see Statistics in Economics].

The technique of Statistical Quality Control, through the powerful tools of 'Control Charts' and 'Inspection Plans' is indispensable to any business organisation for ensuring that the quality of the manufactured product is in conformity with the consumer's specifications. (For details see Statistics in operations).

Statistical tools are used widely by business enterprises for the promotion of new business. Before embarking upon any production process, the business house must have an idea about the quantum of the product to be manufactured, the amount of the raw material and labour needed for it, the quality of the finished product, marketing avenues for the product, the competitive products in the market and so on. Thus the formulation of a production plan is a must and this cannot be achieved without collecting the statistical information on the above items without resorting to the powerful technique of '*Sample Surveys*'. As such, most of the leading business and industrial concerns have full-fledged statistical units with trained and efficient statisticians for formulating such plans and arriving at valid decisions in the face of uncertainty with calculated risks. These units also carry on research and development programmes for the improvement of the quality of the existing products (in the light of the competitive products in the market), introduction of new products and optimisation of the profits with existing resources at their disposal.

Statistical tools of probability and expectation are extremely useful in *Life Insurance* which is one of the pioneer branches of Business and Commerce to use Statistics since the end of the seventeenth century. (For details see Statistics in Insurance). Use of statistics in various activities/disciplines is described briefly as follows :

1.3.1 Marketing

As per Philip Kotler and Gary Armstrong, marketing "identifies customer needs and wants, determins which target markets the organisations can serve best, and designs appropriate products, services and programmes to serve these markets".

Statistical methods of analysis are helpful in the marketing function of an enterprise through its enormous help in market research, choosing appropriate strategy for organising and evaluation of advertising campaigns. As mentioned earlier, Statistics exists only because of variation in nature and in live data. If all the customers had similar needs and preferences, marketing would have been so easy and routine. Sample surveys are conducted to ascertain customers' responses about their needs and reactions to the various products and services. The sales performances of various offices and individuals are scientifically compared with the help of statistical methods. Statistics is also used for evaluating brand equity of companies.

Use of Statistics is indispensable in forecasting sales, market share and demand for various types of industrial products.

Factor analysis, conjoint analysis and multidimensional scaling are invaluable tools which are based on statistical concepts, for designing of products and services based on customer responses.

1.3.2 Economics

Statistical data and methods render valuable assistance in the proper understanding of the economic problems and the formulation of economic policies. Most economic phenomena and indicators can be quantified and dealt with statistically sound logic.

In fact, Statistics got so much integrated with Economics that it led to development of a new subject called Econometrics which basically deals with economic issues involving use of Statistics.

1.3.3 Finance

Uncertainty is the hallmark of the financial world. All financial decisions are based on 'Expectation" that is best analysed with the help of the theory of probability and statistical techniques. In general, finance is concerned with measuring and managing financial yields and risks, which arise due to uncertainty about returns on an investment. We wonder how many persons would have been interested in studying finance if returns on all investments were fixed and predetermined. In real life, the return on an investment is usually, a random variable, and there is a chance associated with the values that it might take. Statistical methods help in ascertaining risks in quantitative terms as also measuring variation in risk. In financial terminology, Statistics helps in evaluating **VaR**—abbreviation for 'value at risk'. It is one of the best indications of financial risk. Statistics is also used for comparing returns on investments in two or more instruments or companies.

Beta of a stock or equity is a statistical tool for comparing volatility, and is highly useful for selection of portfolio of stocks.

1.3.4 Insurance

Life insurance is essentially based on the concept of probability. The mortality tables on which all life insurance is based, are basically the concept of probability carried over to human life expectancies. The tables predict how many people, alive at a given age, will die that year and each year thereafter. An insurance company combines this information with data on the interest that it will earn from premiums while the customer is alive and the cost of underwriting before determining the premiums for each customer.

1.3.5 Operations

Operations has been defined as the management of systems or processes that create goods and/or provide services. It encompasses the ongoing activities of designing, reviewing and using the operating system to achieve service outputs for customers. Statistics plays a very useful role at the input stage through sampling inspection and inventory management, in the process stage through statistical quality control and six sigma method, and in the output stage through sampling inspection. In fact, it also plays an important role in supply chain management which encompasses the management of components, manufacturing and distribution of a manufactured item.

1.3.6 Human Resource Management or Development

Human Resource Departments are *inter alia entrusted* with the responsibility of evaluating the performances, developing rating systems. evolving compensatory reward and training system. etc. All these functions involve designing forms, collecting, storing, retrieval and analysis of a mass of data. All these functions can be performed efficiently and effectively with the help of Statistics.

□□□

2

Data Measurement, Collection and Classification

CHAPTER OUTLINE

- Variables and Data
- Measurements of Data
- Types of Data—Primary and Secondary
- Abstract of Govt. Publications
- Methods of Collection of Primary Data
- Questionnaire and its Requisites
- Specimen Questionnaires
- Data Classifications
- Ungrouped and Grouped Data
- Frequency Distributions
- Cumulative Frequency Distributions

2.1 VARIABLES

A variable is any measured characteristic or attribute that has different values for different subjects. For example, if the height of 1000 subjects were measured, then height would be a variable. Variables can be *quantitative* or *qualitative* (sometimes called 'categorical variables'). Quantitative variables (or numerical variables) are measured on one of three scales : interval, ratio, or ordinal. Qualitative variables are measured on a nominal (or categorical) scale. If a group of business students were asked to name their favourite browser to browse the web, then the variable would be qualitative. If the time spent on the computer to research a topic were measured, then the variable would be quantitative. Another classification of variables is : (*a*) Discrete variable (*b*) Continuous variable.

(*a*) Discrete variable is one that cannot take on all values within the limits of the variable. For example responses to 5-point rating scale can take on either of the values 1, 2, 3, 4, and 5. The variable cannot have the value 1.3 or 1.31.

In case we are enumerating no. of persons in a family it can take only integral +ve values. Such variables are called discrete.

(*b*) Continuous variables : These are variables which are measurable (not countable) like height, distance, time, weight etc. Such variable can have any value. Height of a person can take any value like 1.3 *m* or 1.31 *m* or 1.317 *m*.

The two classifications are shown diagramatically as below :

2.2 STATISTICAL UNITS AND POPULATION

A well defined and identifiable object or a group of objects on which measurements (qualitative or quantitative) are taken is called statistical unit or simply a unit.

Population : Population is set of all well defined units which are being observed or on which measurements are taken. For example if there are 50 students in a class and measurement is their heights. Then each student is a unit and there are 50 units. The population consists of 50 units (each student is a unit) and variable is height.

2.3 DATA

Set of variable values of all units of a population is called data. If there n units in the population their nature are denoted by $X_1, X_2, X_3, \ldots\ldots, X_n$ where X_i is value of ith unit. The set of values $X_1, X_2 \ldots, X_n$ is called data.

2.3 DATA MEASUREMENT

There are 4 types of measurements used in statistics.

1. Nominal
2. Ordinal
3. Interval
4. Ratio

Nominal Level

The *lowest level of data measurement* is the **nominal level.** Numbers representing nominal level data (the world *level* often is omitted) can be *used only to classify or categorize.*

Employee identification numbers are an example of nominal data. The numbers are used only to differentiate employees and not to take a value statement about them. Many demographic questions in surveys result in data that are nominal because the questions are used for classification only. The following is an example of such a question that would result in nominal data :

Which of the following employment classifications best describes your area of work?

(*a*) Educator

(*b*) Construction worker

(*c*) Manufacturing worker

(*d*) Lawyer

(*e*) Doctor

(*f*) Other

Suppose that, for computing purposes, an educator is assigned a 1, a construction worker is assigned a 2, a manufacturing worker is assigned a 3, and so on. These numbers should be used only to classify respondents. The number 1 does not denote the top classification. It is used only to differentiate an educator (1) from a lawyer (4).

Some other types of variables that often produce nominal-level data are gender, religion, ethnicity, geographic location, and place of birth. Social security numbers, telephone numbers, employee ID numbers, and ZIP code numbers are further examples of nominal data. Statistical techniques that are appropriate for analyzing nominal data are limited. However, some of the more widely used statistics, such as the chi-square statistic, can be applied to nominal data, often producing useful information.

Ordinal Level

Ordinal-level data measurement is higher than the nominal level. In addition to the nominal-level capabilities, ordinal-level measurement can be used to rank or order objects. For example, using ordinal data, a supervisor can evaluate three employees by ranking their productivity with the numbers I through 3. The supervisor could identify one employee as the most productive, one as the least productive, and one as somewhere between by using ordinal data. However, the supervisor could not use ordinal data to establish that the intervals between the employees ranked 1 and 2 and between the employees ranked 2 and 3 are equal; that is, she could not say that the differences in the amount of productivity between workers ranked 1, 2, and 3 are necessarily the same. With ordinal data. the distances or spacing represented by consecutive numbers are not always equal.

Some questionnaire Likert-type scales are considered by many researchers to be ordinal in level. The following is an example of one such scale :

This computer tutorial is :

not helpful	somewhat helpful	moderately helpful	very helpful	extremely helpful
1	2	3	4	5

When this survey question is coded for the computer, only the numbers 1 through 5 will remain, not the adjectives. Virtually everyone would agree that a 5 is higher than a 4 on this scale and that ranking responses is possible. However, most respondents would not consider the differences between not helpful. somewhat helpful, moderately helpful. very helpful, and extremely helpful to be equal.

Mutual funds as investments are sometimes rated in terms of risk by using measures of default risk, currency risk and interest rate risk. These three measures are applied to investments by rating them as having high, medium, and low risk. Suppose high risk is assigned a 3, medium risk a 2, and low risk a 1. If a fund is awarded a 3 rather than a 2, it carries more risk, and so on. However, the differences in risk between categories I, 2, and 3 are not necessarily equal. Thus, these measurements of risk are only ordinal-level measurements. Another example of the use of ordinal numbers in business is the ranking of the top 50 most admired companies in *Fortune* magazine. The numbers ranking the companies are only ordinal in measurement. Certain statistical techniques are specifically suited to ordinal data, but many other techniques are not appropriate for use on ordinal data.

Because nominal and ordinal data are often derived from imprecise measurements such as demographic questions, the categorization of people or objects. or the ranking of items, *nominal* and *ordinal* data are **nonmetric data** and are sometimes referred to as *qualitative data.*

Interval Level

Interval-level data measurement is the *next higher level of data measurement in which the distances between consecutive numbers have meaning and the data are always numerical.* The distances represented by the differences between consecutive numbers are equal; that is, interval data have equal intervals. An example of interval measurement is Fahrenheit temperature. With Fahrenheit temperature numbers. the temperatures can be ranked, and the amounts of heat between consecutive readings, such as 20°, 21°, and 22°, are the same.

In addition, with interval-level data, the zero point is a matter of convention or convenience and not a natural or fixed zero point. Zero is just another point on the scale and does not mean the absence of the phenomenon. For example, zero degrees Fahrenheit is not the lowest possible temperature. Some other examples of interval level data are the percentage change in employment the percentage return on a stock, and the dollar change in stock price.

With interval level data, converting the units from one measurement to another involves multiplying by some factor, a, and adding another factor, b, such that $y = b + ax$. As an example, converting from centigrade temperature to Fahrenheit temperature involves the relationship.

$$\text{Fahrenheit} = 32 + \frac{9}{5}\text{ centigrade}$$

Ratio Level

Ratio-level data measurement is the *highest level of data measurement*. Ratio data *have the same properties as interval data.* but ratio data have an *absolute zero* and *the ratio of two numbers is meaningful*. The notion of absolute zero means that zero is fixed, and *the zero value in the data represents the absence of the characteristic* being *studied* The value of zero cannot be arbitrarily assigned because it represents a fixed point This definition enables the statistician to create *ratios* with the data.

Examples of ratio data are height, weight, time, volume, and Kelvin temperature. With ratio data, a researcher can state that 180 pounds of weight is twice as much as 90 pounds or, in other words, make a ratio of 180:90. Many of the data gathered by machines in industry are ratio data.

Other examples in the business world that are ratio level in measurement are production cycle time, work measurement time, passenger miles, number of trucks sold, complaints per 10,000. and number of employees. With ratio-level data' no b factor is required in converting units from one measurement to another, that is, $y = ax$. As an example. in converting height from yards to feet: 1 yard = 3 feet.

Interval-level and ratio-level data are usually gathered by precise instruments often used in production and engineering processes. in national standardized testing, or in standardized accounting procedures, they are called **metric data** and are sometimes referred to as *quantitative* data.

Many changes continue to occur in the healthcare industry. Because of increased competition for patients among providers and the need to determine how providers can better serve their clientele, hospital administrators sometimes mail a quality satisfaction survey to their patients after the patient is released. The following types of questions are sometimes asked on such a survey.

Example : These questions will result in what level of data measurement?

1. How long ago were you released from the hospital?
2. Which type of unit were you in for most of your stay?
   — Coronary care
   — Intensive care
   — Maternity care
   — Medical unit
   — Pediatric/children's unit
   — Surgical unit
3. In choosing a hospital, how important was the hospital's location?
   (circle one)
   Very Important   Somewhat Important   Not Very Important   Not at All Important
4. How serious was your condition when you were first admitted to the hospital?
   —Critical   —Serious   —Moderate   —Minor
5. Rate the skill of your doctor :
   —Excellent   —Very Good   —Good   —Fair   —Poor
6. On the following scale from one to seven, rate the nursing care :
   1 2 3 4 5 6 7
   ↓ (1) Poor   ↓ (7) Excellent

Solution. Question 1 is a time measurement with an absolute zero and is therefore ratio-level measurement. A person who has been out of the hospital for two weeks has been out twice as long as someone who has been out of the hospital for one week.

Question 2 yields nominal data because the patient is asked only to categorize the type of unit he or she was in. This question does not require a hierarchy or ranking of the type of unit. Questions 3, 4, and 5 are likely to result in ordinal-level data. Suppose a number is assigned the descriptors in each of these three questions. For question 3, "very important" might be assigned a 4, "somewhat important" a 3, "not very important" a 2, and "not at all important" a 1. Certainly, the higher the number, the more important is the hospital's location. Thus, these responses can be ranked by selection. However, the increases in importance from 1 to 2 to 3 to 4 are not necessarily equal. This same logic applies to the numeric values assigned in questions 4 and 5.

Question 6 displays seven numeric choices with equal distances between the numbers shown on the scale and no adjective descriptors assigned to the numbers. Many researchers would declare this to be interval-level measurement because of the equal distance between numbers and the absence of a true zero on this scale. Some researchers might argue that because of the imprecision of the scale and the vagueness of selecting values between "poor" and "excellent" the measurement is only ordinal in level.

2.5 COLLECTION OF DATA

Collection of Data — An Introduction

The collection of data is the first and most important step in the statistical study of any investigation since all calculations and results depend upon quality of the data so collected. There is no exaggeration if we say that the collection of data plays the part of the bricks in the construction of the building of statistical investigation. We know that a building cannot be constructed without the right bricks, similarly we may come to faulty conclusion if the collection of data is not proper. Thus, if there is any defect or deficiency in the collection of data then it will affect the whole investigation and the conclusions derived from these will not be helpful in decision making. Thus, it is most important for the one who collects the data to be alert, conscious, thoughtful, firm and patient so that the data collected by him be faultless and dependable.

Thus, before collecting the data the investigator (the one who collects the data) should know and plan the field of his work and the method of collecting the data.

Types of Data

Statistical data are of two types :

(*i*) Primary data, and (*ii*) Secondary data.

Primary Data

These data are collected by the investigator for the first time for his own use, i.e., there is originality in the whole investigation.

Secondary Data

These are the data which were already collected and published by a previous investigator for a certain investigation and the present investigator simply adopts them for his own purpose.

Hence the data which are collected by an investigator for the first time works out as primary data for him and when this very data is used by another investigator for some investigation then these workout as secondary data.

***Example*:** Data collected from students of a college on their performance in an examination is primary data. If he collects information from the records of the college, it can be said that he is using secondary data. Population census is the primary data. If investigator uses any part of it, such as literacy or income etc. it is secondary data for him.

2.6 METHODS OF COLLECTION OF PRIMARY DATA

The following are some of the popular methods of collecting primary data:

1. Observation : It refers to the method of observing the sample items to understand and collect information. Observation does not require questioning.

***Example*:** Study of man-hours lost near railway crossing when the gate is closed requires continuous observation of number of vehicles and passengers waiting near the gate and the time wasted, Investigator records such necessary information within the given period.

Merits

- This is a simple, easy and cheaper method.
- Original data can be collected.
- Results will be accurate.
- It is the best method for such simple problems where data can be collected through observation.

Demerits

- There is an element of subjectivity in data collection
- Investigator cannot probe into the reasons which may be the determining factors for the study.
- Uniformity is not possible unless total process is rigidly defined.

2. Experimentation: The investigator conducts some experiments on the selected sample items under controlled conditions. The results of the experiment are recorded. This forms the data for the study.

***Example*:** Paddy can be cultivated on small pieces of land A, B, C and D to study its output under different conditions such as; A-using natural manures; B-Water management; C-using fertilizers: D-adopting modern methods. After recording the output of different lands, the investigator assesses the impact of different methods.

Merits

- This method promises more accuracy in the study.

- Reliable data can be collected.
- This is more suitable to the problem with heterogeneous influencing factors.

Demerits

- This is very costly method.
- This is suitable to simple problems with limited scope.
- This is a time consuming method.

3. Interview Method: The investigator identifies the persons who can provide information for the study. He establishes personal contact with them and obtains information through questions and discussions. Investigator prepares a semi-structured questionnaire, which is flexible to evolve maximum information. This method can be advocated when the area of investigation is limited and more accuracy is expected.

Merits

- First hand information can be gathered.
- Promptness is assured in this method.
- Investigator can get expert advice.
- This method gives opportunity to probe into the topic more deeply.
- Sufficient and reliable information can be collected.
- Additional information is also available in this method.

Demerits

- If informants are large in number this method is not suitable.
- This is highly time consuming and expensive method.
- Results of interview depend on the physical and emotional conditions of the interviewer and interviewee.
- Unless the investigator is highly tactful and efficient in communication skills and knowledge *of* the problem under study, the method fails to achieve expected results.
- Personal bias may change the result.

Example: News agencies adopt this method to collect crucial and important news. Press reporters and journalists are best investigators in this type of data collection.

If conditions are favourable and the time and budget of the investigator permits, this is the best method to get reliable and suitable data. To make interview method effective the investigator should possess the skill of conducting, interviews in favourable and unfavourable situations. He should be tactful to communicate with different people with different temperamental characters. He should have sufficient knowledge in the area of problem to ask good questions.

4. Questionnaires to be filled-in by the informants: This method requires the following procedure:

- Investigator prepares a questionnaire with sufficient blank space to answer. It is usually in the form of multiple choice questions or simple alternate questions.

- Necessary directions to fill the questionnaire are to be given wherever it is essential.
- Topic and idea of investigation are to be given along with a note of request to the informants to fill the questionnaire.
- Locate the informants and prepare a list along with their postal address If it is through e-mail. care to be taken to identify addresses.
- Post the questionnaires along with a covering letter in simple and direct language and self-addressed cover with stamps to post the filled questionnaires to the investigator.
- Assurance is to be given that the information supplied by the informants and their identity will not be revealed anywhere, at any time.

Research scholars of universities and institutions adopt this method. To collect information on specific topics and technology or skill based issues, it is the most appropriate method. Ex : opinion study of doctors in A.P. on a new type of fever spread in a district during rainy season.

Merits

- A wide area can be covered.
- This method is cheap and quick.
- Original data can be collected.
- If questionnaire is perfect, high quality data can be collected.
- As the informants are given freedom. the real feelings, opinion and suggestions can he gathered. This advantage is not found in other methods.

Demerits

- This method cannot work with illiterates.
- Due to their busy work, informants may not take trouble to fill-up questionnaire and post it back to the investigator. Thus non-response is the greatest limitation.
- In a majority of cases, they supply half information.
- Sometimes they may give funny and unnecessary answers, because investigator is away from them.
- They may misunderstand and give wrong information.
- This method is not flexible to admit changes according to the requirements.
- It is difficult to test the accuracy of answers.

To make the method effective, investigator should take great care in preparation of the questions and questionnaire. He should make a study and select the most suitable and reliable informants to obtain good quality data. Investigator should take special care to reduce the manual work of informants to a maximum extent by reducing number of questions etc.

5. Questionnaire (Schedule) to be filled in by the Investigator: Under this method investigator or the enumerators appointed by him, fill up the questionnaire. For this data collection, investigator prepares a standard questionnaire with sufficient blank space to record the information. He approaches the informants and explains to them the objectives and the theme of the study. By asking questions he elicits information and records it by himself.

Merits

- Highly reliable data can be collected.
- Maximum information can be obtained by asking supportive questions.
- It is flexible because the investigator can make changes if necessary during data collection.
- Wide area can be covered, because it is simply filling the questionnaire.

Demerits

- This is expensive and time-consuming method.
- Appointed enumerators may not involve in the work and may not get accurate information.
- Some times there may be an element of human bias.
- This method requires special attention of the investigator in selection of informants, preparation of the questionnaire and appointment of enumerators.

2.7 DRAFTING A QUESTIONNAIRE OR A SCHEDULE

A questionnaire or a schedule is a list of questions relating to the problem under investigation. There is no basic difference between a questionnaire and a schedule. A questionnaire is filled by the respondent, while a schedule is filled by the investigator.

The quality of information collected through the filling of a questionnaire depends, to a large extent, upon the drafting of its questions. Hence, it is extremely important that the questions be designed or drafted very carefully and in a tactful manner. Although, there are no hard and fast rules to be followed, but the following general points must always be kept in mind to draft a good questionnaire or schedule.

1. The questions should be simple, unambiguous and precise.
2. The number of questions should be as small as possible. Only those questions which have a direct relevance to the problem be included.
3. The question should be framed in such a manner that their answers are specific and precise.

   The following four type of questions are generally framed in any questionnaire :

   (*a*) *Simple alternative questions* : Such questions are answered by yes/no or right/wrong, etc.

   (*b*) *Multiple choice questions :* In such questions, the possible answers arc printed in the questionnaire and the respondent is supposed to tick any one of them. For example,

   What is your occupation?

   1. Agriculture ☐
   2. Industry ☐

3. Trade ☐
4. Service ☐
5. Any other ☐

(c) *Specific information questions :* Such questions are used to extract specific information like; how many members are there in your family, what is your monthly income, *etc.*

(d) *Open questions :* These types of questions are to be answered by the respondent in his own words. The questions should be such that it is possible to answer them in few words. Care should be taken to avoid answers that use the words like probability, fairly good, *etc.*

4. The questions should be capable of being easily answered by the respondents. The questions that rely too much on the memory of the respondent should be avoided.

5. *Leading questions should be avoided.* For example, the question 'Why do you use a particular brand of blades, say, Erasmic blades' should preferably be framed into two questions.

(*i*) Which blade do you use?

(*ii*) Why do you prefer it?

Gives a smooth shave	☐	Readily available in the market	☐
Gives more shaves	☐	Any other	☐
Price is less (Cheaper)	☐		

6. *Cross Checks.* The questionnaire should be so designed as to provide internal checks on the accuracy of the information supplied by the respondents by including some connected questions at least with respect to matters which are fundamental to the enquiry. For example in a social survey for finding the age of the mother the question 'What is your age"?, can be supplemented by additional questions 'What is your date of birth' or 'What is the age of your eldest child?' Similarly, the question, 'Age at marriage' can be supplemented by the question. The age of the first child'.

7. *Pre-testing the Questionnaire.* From practical point of view it is desirable to try out the questionnaire on a small scale (*i.e.,* on a small cross-section of the population for which the enquiry is intended) before using it for the given enquiry on a large scale. This testing on a small scale (called *pre-test*) has been found to be extremely useful in practice. The given questionnaire can be improved or modified in the light of the drawbacks, shortcomings and problems faced by the investigator in the pre-test. Pre-testing also helps to decide upon the effective methods of asking questions for soliciting the requisite information.

8. *A Covering Letter.* A covering letter from the organisers of the enquiry should be enclosed along with the questionnaire for the following purposes :

(*i*) It should clearly explain in brief the objectives and scope of the survey to evoke the interest of the respondents and impress upon them to render their full co-operation by returning the schedule/questionnaire duly filled in within the specified period.

(*ii*) It should contain a note regarding the operational definitions to the various terms and the concepts used in the questionnaire; units of measurements to be used and the degree of accuracy aimed at.

(*iii*) It should take the respondents in confidence and ensure them that the information furnished by them will be kept completely secret and they will not be harassed in any way later.

(*iv*) In the case of mailed questionnaire method as self-addressed stamped envelope should be enclosed for enabling the respondents to return the questionnaire after completing it.

(*v*) To ensure quick and better response the respondents may be offered awards/ incentives in the form of free gifts, coupons, etc.

(*vi*) A copy of the survey report may b promised to the interested respondents.

9. Mode of tabulation and analysis *viz.*, hand operated, machine tabulation or computerisation should also be kept in mind while designing the questionnaire.

10. Lastly, the questionnaire should be made attractive by proper layout and appealing get up.

2.8. SPECIMEN QUESTIONNAIRES

Given below are specimen questionnaires for illustration.

QUESTIONNAIRE NO. 1

DEPARTMENT OF BUSINESS ADMINISTRATION

Birla Institute of Technology and Science, Pilani (Rajasthan)

Dear/Sir/Madam,

We believe that you are the spokesman for thousands of persons who visit the SUPER BAZAR in Delhi and since we are interested in knowing their preferences we seek your help. We believe that this survey would help in evolving better ways of providing shopping facilities to the consumers. Would you please, therefore, answer the enclosed questionnaire and return it by post? A self-addressed stamped envelope is attached herewith for your convenience.

We assure you that we are in no way connected with the SUPER BAZAR. The information supplied by you will be treated as strictly confidential.

Thanking you,

yours truely

SUPER BAZAR

QUESTIONNAIRE : CONSUMER PREFERENCES

NOTE : Please tick mark (√) in the square where necessary.)

A. General :

Name :

Address : Age:

Occupation

Service ☐ Sex : Male ☐ Female ☐

Business ☐ Married ☐ Unmarried ☐
Other ☐

Number of members in the family *Monthly income in rupees*

1 to 3 ☐ Below ₹ 1,000* ☐
3 to 6 ☐ 1,000—1,500 ☐
Over 6 ☐ 1,500—2,000 ☐
Above 2,000 ☐

B. How many times do you visit Super Bazar in a month?

1-5 ☐ 5-10 ☐ Over 10 ☐

C. Do you prefer any particular day for shopping?

Yes ☐ No ☐

If yes, specify the day you prefer

Sunday ☐ Monday ☐ Tuesday ☐ Wednesday ☐
Thursday ☐ Friday ☐ Saturday ☐

D. Do you buy most of your daily requirements from the Super Bazar?

Yes ☐ No ☐

E. Are you attracted to the Bazar because of

(*i*) reasonable price? Yes ☐ No ☐
(*ii*) reliability of price? Yes ☐ No ☐
(*iii*) no bargaining? Yes ☐ No ☐

I. Do you feel the profit margin charged by the Supper Bazar is reasonable? Yes ☐ No ☐

F. Do you prefer Super Bazar because of :

(*i*) availability of your requirements under one roof? Yes ☐ No ☐
(*ii*) certainty of getting goods? Yes ☐ No ☐
(*iii*) wide selection and choice? Yes ☐ No ☐
(*iv*) availability of goods in short supply? Yes ☐ No ☐
(*v*) availability of quality goods? Yes ☐ No ☐
(*vi*) surety about quality? Yes ☐ No ☐
(*vii*) saving in shopping time? Yes ☐ No ☐

G. Do you find the sales assistants in the Super Bazar :
[Please tick mark (√) only one of the alternatives.]

(*i*) Attentive ☐ Inattentive ☐
(*ii*) Courteous ☐ Rude ☐
(*iii*) Co-operative ☐ Indifferent ☐
(*iv*) Efficient ☐ Inefficient ☐

H. 1. Do you visit the cafe in the Super Bazar while shopping? Yes ☐ No ☐

2. Do you find any difficulty in locating the desired products? Yes ☐ No ☐

3. Do you need parking facilities to make your visit easy? Yes ☐ No ☐

I. Do you visit the Super Bazar because :

(*i*) it is near your home? Yes ☐ No ☐

(*ii*) it is on you way to home? Yes ☐ No ☐

(*iii*) it is centrally located? Yes ☐ No ☐

J. Are you shareholder in the Super Bazar?

1. Are you a attracted by the shareholders' discount? Yes ☐ No ☐

2. Do you prefer sales girls to salesmen? Yes ☐ No ☐

3. Are you satisfied with the packing provided by the Super Bazar? Yes ☐ No ☐

K. Please give you first, second and third preference for visiting the Super Bazar out of the following :

(Please write numbers in the squares.)

Availability of all goods under one roof ☐

Quality ☐ Price ☐

Service ☐ Location ☐

Time-saving ☐ Shareholding interest ☐

QUESTIONNAIRE NO. 2

FACULTY OF MANAGEMENT STUDIES

Executive Development Programme for Senior Government Officers

EVALUATION PROFORMA

Dear Participant.

Will you kindly fill in the enclosed evaluation form? We hope, your response together with our own assessment will contribute to the improvement of our future programmes. I need not stress that frankness will be of great value in this regard. There is no need to disclose your identity. If any points are not covered in this, kindly add the same towards the end.

Tanking you

Yours sincerely,

Course Director

EVALUATION PROFORMA

I. *Objective*

(*a*) The Programme Brochure listed the following as Course Objectives :

(*i*) (*ii*)

(*iii*) (*iv*)

(*b*) What were you objectives/personal motives in attending this Programme?

(*i*) (*ii*)

(*iii*) (*iv*)

(*c*) (*i*) How far do your objectives match with the above-mentioned Course Objectives? (Tick appropriate box.)

Closely related ☐ Somewhat related ☐ Not related ☐

(*ii*) Give reasons if you have ticked the box 'Somewhat related' or 'Not related'.

(*d*) (*i*) How far have the course objectives been realised by this programme? (Tick Column)

Objectives	*Totally*	*Partially*	*Not at all*
Objective (*i*)			
Objective (*ii*)			
Objective (*iii*)			
Objective (*iv*)			

(*ii*) Give reasons if you have ticked the column 'Not at all'.

(*e*) Is there a need to have any other objective(s)?

Yes ☐ No ☐

If yes, mention the objective(s).

(*f*) How far have your own objectives been realised through participation in the programme?

II. *Programme Design*

(*a*) How would you rate the overall design of the programme?

		Excellent	*Very Good*	*Fair*	*Poor*
(*i*)	Areas and subject coverage				
(*ii*)	Conceptual framework				
(*iii*)	Orientation to practical problems				
(*iv*)	Distribution of time among various components of the course				
(*v*)	Any other (Please mention)				

(*b*) Indicate any suggestions for improving the programme design.

Please give your reasons and positive suggestions for the same to make them more effective and meaningful.

III. *On the basis of inputs, please comment as under*

(*a*) Any topics/sessions which you felt were particularly useful and your reasons why you thought it so.

S. No.	*Topics / Sessions*	*Comments*
1.		
2.		
3.		
4.		
etc.		

(*b*) Any topics/sections which you felt were overemphasized or might otherwise have been improved.

S. No.	*Topics / Sessions*	*Comments*
1.		
2.		
and so on		

IV. *Methodology*

(*a*) Which of the following pedagogical methods were effectively employed in the programme :

	Method	*Very Effective*	*Effective*	*Not Effective*
1.	Talks by Faculty			
2.	Talks by Guest Speakers			
3.	Case Discussion			
4.	Exercises			
5.	Group Discussion			
6.	Business Games			
7.	Visual Aids			
8.	Project Work			

(*b*) Have you any suggestions to make regarding the methodology employed in the programme?

V. *Reading Material*

	Useful	Somewhat Useful	Least Useful
(*i*)	☐	☐	☐
	Adequate	Somewhat adequate	Inadequate
(*ii*) Adequacy	☐	☐	☐

VI. *Strengths and Weaknesses*

Kindly identify the strengths and weaknesses of the programme as you perceived them :

Strengths : (Happy features of the programme)

Weakness : (Unhappy features of the programme)

VII. *Please give your Suggestions which may increase the effectiveness of the Programme with reference to :*

(*a*) Selection of participants

(*b*) Volume of work

(*c*) Subject areas to be covered.

VIII. *Briefly state the different ways in which the programme has been beneficial to you.*

IX. *Kindly indicate your feelings about administrative arrangements*

— Layout of Classrooms

— Distribution of Materials

— Lunch-Tea/Coffee

— Any other.

Format of a Questionnaire for assessing preferences of the users of two-wheelers.

QUESTIONNAIRE NO. 3

EVALUATION OF SCOOTER PERFORMANCES

Note : Please put tick mark (√) in the relevant box of each question.

Section A

1. Name : ....
2. Address : ....
3. Age : ....
4. Sex : Male ☐ Female ☐
5. Marital Status : Married ☐ Unmarried ☐ Others ☐
6. Number of children, if married :

   Name ☐ One ☐ Two ☐ More than two ☐
7. Highest educational qualification :

   Under Matric ☐ Matric ☐ Senior Secondary ☐

   Graduate ☐ Post Graduate ☐ Higher ☐
8. Occupation :

   Service ☐ Manufacture ☐ Trade ☐

   Agriculture ☐ Others ☐
9. Annual Income (in ₹) :

   Less than 20,000 ☐ 20,000 – 30,000 ☐ 30,000 – 40,000 ☐

   40,000 – 50,000 ☐ 50,000 – 60,000 ☐ 60,000 and above ☐

Section B

1. What is the brand name of your scooter?

   Bajaj ☐ L.M.L. Vespa ☐ Kinetic Honda ☐

   Vijay Super ☐ Any other ☐

2. How did you know this brand?
   Through advertisement in a newspaper ☐
   Through advertisement in radio ☐
   Through advertisement in television ☐
   Through some friend ☐
   Through some other agency ☐
3. You purchased this scooter because :
   It gives more mileage ☐
   It requires less maintenance ☐
   It is more powerful ☐
   It is more stable ☐
   It has a better after-sales service ☐
   (*You can put tick mark in more than one box.*)
4. You purchased this scooter from :
   Company showroom ☐
   Authorised dealer ☐
   Local dealer ☐
   Others ☐
5. What are the mode of payment?
   On cash down payment ☐
   On Instalment basis ☐
   On Hire-Purchase basis ☐
   Others ☐
6. How old is your scooter?
   Less than 1 year ☐
   1—3 years ☐
   3—5 years ☐
   5—10 years ☐
   10 or more years ☐
7. Are you satisfied with your scooter? yeas ☐ no ☐
8. The maintenance expenditure, per month, of your scooter :
   Less than ₹ 100 ☐ ₹ 100 – 200 ☐ ₹ 200 or more ☐
9. For major repairs, you go to :
   The authorised service station ☐
   The local service station ☐
   Any other workshop ☐
10. If given a chance to purchase a new scooter, would you like to purchase the same scooter? yes ☐ no ☐

QUESTIONNAIRE NO. 4

Questionnaire for Collecting Information(Covering Production, Employment etc.) Relating to an Industrial concern

1. Name of the concern ....
2. (*a*) Name of the Proprietor/Managing Director ....
   (*b*) Qualifications :
   (*i*) Academic ....
   (*ii*) Technical/ Professional ....
3. (*a*) Location (*b*) Telephone Number (*c*) e-mail Address
   (*a*) Location: (*i*) Factory .... (*ii*) Office ....
   (*b*) Telephone Number: (*i*) Factory .... (*ii*) Office ....
   (*c*) e-mail Address: (*i*) Factory .... (*ii*) Office ....
4. Factory Registration Number (with date) ....
5. Total Capital employed/Assets (approximately) ....
6. Number of Shifts ....
7. Whether the machinery used is indigenous?
   Yes ☐ No ☐ Other ☐
8. What is the approximate value of the imported machinery? ....
9. Whether the raw material used is available in domestic market?
   Yes ☐ No ☐
10. From which country is the raw material imported? ....
11. What is the approximate annual consumption of the raw material? ....
12. Expenditure in foreign currency :
    (*i*) Foreign Travel ....
    (*ii*) Technical know-how ....
    (*iii*) Material and goods ....
13. Employment (Pay-roll) :

S. No.	*Categories*	*Working hours per week*	*No. employed*		*Salaries paid in '000 ₹*	
			2001	*2002*	*2001*	*2002*
(*i*)	Management					
(*ii*)	Supervisory/Technical Personnel					
(*iii*)	Skilled workers					
(*iv*)	Unskilled workers					
(*v*)	Non-technical office staff					

14. Production :

S. No.	*Items (Production)*	*Installed Capacity*	*Actual Production*	
			2001	*2002*

15. Market 2001 2002

(*a*) Gross value of sales ('000 ₹) ....

(*b*) Who are :

(*i*) Immediate purchasers ....

(*ii*) End users ....

(*c*) The extent of market is

Local ☐ National ☐ International ☐

(*d*) If the extent of the market is international

(*i*) What are the approximate foreign exchange earnings (annually)?

(*ii*) Which countries are the chief importers of the product?

(*e*) Total Sales ('000 ₹) :

National market : ....

International market : ....

(*f*) Are the present conditions of the market satisfactory/not satisfactory/poor? ......

16. Financial Highlights

Items	*(Rupees '000s)*	
	2001	*2002*
Sales		
Profits		
Dividends		
Capital expenditure		
Fixed assets		
Shareholders' funds		

QUESTIONNAIRE NO. 5

We give below the 1997 Census-Individual Slip which was used for a general purpose survey to collect :

(*i*) Social and cultural data like nationality, religion, literacy, mother tongue, etc. :

(*ii*) Exhaustive economic data like occupation, industry, class of worker and activity, if not working ;

(*iii*) Demographic data like relation to the head of the house, sex, age, marital status, birth place, births and deaths and the fertility of women to assess in particular the performance of the family planning programme.

1971 Census — Individual Slip

1. Name. ....
2. Relationship to the head of the family ....
3. Sex. ....
4. Age. ....
5. Marital status. ....
6. For currently married women only :
   (*a*) Age at marriage ....
   (*b*) Any child born in the last one year ....
7. Birth place :
   (*i*) Place of birth .... (*ii*) Rural or urban ....
   (*iii*) District .... (*iv*) State/country ....
8. Last Residence :
   (*i*) Place of last residence .... (*ii*) Rural/urban ....
   (*iii*) District .... (*iv*) State/country ....
9. Duration of present residence ....
10. Religion ....
11. Schedule Caste or Tribe ....
12. Literacy ....
13. Educational level ....
14. Mother tongue ....
15. Other languages, if any ....
16. Main activity :
    (*a*) Broad category :
    (*i*) Worker (C, AL, HHI, OW)*
    (*ii*) Non-worker (H, ST, R, D.B.I.O)**
    (*b*) Place of work (Name of Village/Town) ....
    (*c*) Name of establishment ....
    (*d*) Name of Industry. Trade, Profession or Service ....
    (*e*) Description of work ....
    (*f*) Class of worker ....
17. Secondary work :
    (*a*) Broad category (C, AL, HHI, OW)
    (*b*) Place of work ....

(*c*) Name of establishment ....

(*d*) Nature of Industry, Trade, Profession or Service ....

(*f*) Class of worker ....

QUESTIONNAIRE NO. 6

A Survey on Saving Habits of Students

Dear Sir/Madam/Friends

As a part of our project work, we are conducting a small study on saving habits of students in our college. You are requested to fill the questionnaire and help us to complete our study.

1. Name/class.
2. Male/Female
3. Income (monthly) ₹ ....
4. (Pocket Money) ₹ ....
5. Do you have a part time job? Yes/No.
   If yes, what is your income?
6. Do you save? Yes/No/Sometimes
7. If yes, what percentage of your income? (*a*) 50% (*b*) 40% (*c*) 30% (*d*) 35% (*e*) 20%
8. For what do you want to save? (*a*) Books (*b*) Studies (*c*) Friends (*d*) Personal (*e*) Unexpected expenditure (*f*) Others
9. Do you parent know about your savings (*a*) Yes (*b*) No. (*c*) May be (*d*) No idea (*e*) Some times.
10. How do you save? (*a*) Bank (*b*) Post Office (*c*) Parents (*d*) Relations (*e*) Nothing like these (*f*) With own cash bag.
11. Do you like to open a bank account? Yes/No
12. Do you think every student should save? (*a*) Yes (*b*) NO (*c*) Not necessary (*d*) Compulsory.
13. Do you think your pocket money is sufficient to save?
14. What is your opinion on saving habits of students in general?

2.9 SECONDARY DATA

Secondary data is a published data by same other agency. If the investigator uses already collected and published data (or unpublished) it is secondary data for him.

Meaning

As the name Secondary Data' indicates, it is used for a second time but not first time. It implies a collected, used and published data. It is defined by W.A. Neiswanger as "A secondary source is a publication reporting data which has been gathered by other authorities and for which others are responsible". Usually data once collected is made available through internal records, reports, personal records etc.

1. Sources of Secondary Data

Sources of secondary data can be broadly classified into two: Published sources and Unpublished sources.

1. **Government Publications:** Various Ministries and Departments of the Government publish data regularly on number of subjects such as national income, exports, foreign exchange reserves, industrial production etc. Some of these are annual others are monthly statistics and some are weekly. Ex. Important publications of the Government of India are Statistical Abstract of India (Annual) Agricultural Statistics etc.
2. **Publications by International Organisations:** International organisations such as United Nations Organization, World Bank, IMF, WTO, WHO etc. collect and publish reliable data on various topics regularly, which is a greatest source of secondary data.
3. **Reports of Committees and Commissions:** Special committees are appointed internationally and nationally by the governments or organizations to conduct special studies. Such committees submit detailed reports which contain valuable data and rich information. Ex. Basele's Committee Report on financial sector reforms, Finance Commission Report etc.
4. **Trading, Banking and Non-Trade Organisations:** In India LIC, ECGC, RBI, SEBI etc. publish monthly and annual reports along with relevant data, which are reliable and useful for any purpose of statistical studies.
5. **Data Published by Chambers of Commerce and Associations:** Chambers of Commerce, Trade Associations, Bankers Associations, Export Promotion Councils etc. collect data and publish regularly.
6. **Journals and News Papers:** News agencies, newspapers, journals etc. also publish annual and monthly reports with supportive data. The Hindu paper publishes annual reports on various topics. Prominent among them are survey of industries, agriculture etc. Economic and Political Weekly publishes monthly and annual reports regularly.
7. **Universities, Research Organizations and other Institutions:** Universities such as Oxford, Andhra, Osmania, Central University, JNU etc. are great source of data collected b`! research scholars on various topics. Research and training institutions such as Indian Institute of Foreign Trade,. Indian Institute of Packaging also publish research data regularly.
8. **Others:** Market surveys, project reports, research papers published by authors, surveys conducted by individuals and institutions are great source of secondary data.
9. **Internet:** Internet became the largest single supplier of the latest information and data on different subjects through web sites.
10. **Books:** Ancient works stored in libraries are great source of information. Even today there are researchers who refer to ancient scriptures for some information.
11. **Institutions :** Every institution big or small, trade or non-trade, maintains internal records where data is recorded regularly. This is a good source of secondary data.

Reports of internal activities, financial statements, progress reports, published annually by institutions are part of internal data.

2. Un-Published Data

All statistics are not published. Research work. reports of internal activities, certain financial data etc. are not published. Documents letters. minutes of meetings, monthly reports etc. are also a good source of data for investigators.

2.10 RELIABILITY OF SECONDARY DATA

Before using the secondary data, the investigator should make the following points clear to obtain quality results from his study. They are:

1. **Whether the data is suitable or not:** The data may be relating to the same area of study but because of time gap or change in the geographical area (Rural and Urban) it may not be suitable for the study.
2. **Adequacy of the Data:** Secondary Data is already collected. Therefore it cannot be increased if necessary. The investigator should make sure whether it is adequate or not before using the data for the study.
3. **Reliability:** It is very essential to check whether the data is genuine and the collected'. agency is trust worthy. Only when he gets satisfactory response to these questions he can use the data.
4. **Period of data:** Change is very rapid in modern days. Obsolete data gives misleading conclusions. Care should be taken to avoid outdated information.
5. **Units of measurement:** Care should be taken to understand the units used in data collection. For Example: Rupees and Dollars, Kilometers and Meters etc. have lot of influence on results.
6. **Context, Purpose and Objective:** When, where and for what the data is collected? It is important to know such information.
7. **Accuracy:** Before using secondary data investigator should study the data to assess its accuracy. By applying a few test checks, he can understand its reliability. For example: A researcher submitted his lengthy report of 400 pages on rural socio-economic problems. One of the tables show that there are 28 bore wells in a village of which only 4 are working. He recommended to the government to undertake immediate repair work for 33 bore wells. This shows that it is not accurate data and hence not reliable.

2.11 ABSTRACT OF GOVT. PUBLICATIONS

1. *Official Publications of Central Government.* The following are various government organisations along with the year of their establishment [given in bracket ( )] which collect, compile and publish statistical data on number of topics of current interest—prices, wages, population, production and consumption, labour, trade, army, etc.

(1) Office of the Registrar General and Census Commissioner of India, New Delhi (1949).

(2) Directorate-General of Commercial Intelligence and Statistics—Ministry of Commerce (1895).

(3) Labour Bureau—Ministry of Labour (1946).

(4) Directorate of Economics and Statistics—Ministry of Agriculture and Irrigation (1948).

(5) The Indian Army Statistical Organisation (I.A.S.O.)—Ministry of Defence (1947).

(6) National Sample Survey Organisation (N.S.S.O.). Department of Statistics. Ministry of Planning (1950).**

(7) Central Statistical Organisation (C.S.O.)—Department of Statistics. Ministry of Planning (1951).

* In India census has been carried out every ten years since 1881. Prior to the establishment of this organisation the census was conducted by a temporary cell in the Ministry of Home Affairs.

** National Sample Survey (N.S.S.) was set up in 1950 in Ministry of Finance. In 1957. N.S.S. was transferred to the Cabinet Secretariate and named National Sample Survey Organisation (N.S.S.O.)

Some of the main publications of the above government agencies are :

(*a*) Monthly Abstract of Statistics; Monthly Statistics of Production of Selected Industries in India; Statistical Pocket Book India; Annual Survey of Industries - General Review; Sample Surveys of Current Interest in India (all published annually); Statistical Systems of India; National Income Statistics — Estimates of Savings in India (1960-61 to 1965-66); National Income Statistics-Estimates of Capital Formation in India (1960-61 to 1965-66) (Ad-hoc publications); all published by the Central Statistical Organisation (C.S.O.) New Delhi.

(*b*) Census data in various census reports; Vital Statistics of India (Annual) Indian Population Bulletin (Biennial) — all published by Registrar-General of India (R.G.I).

(*c*) Various statistical reports on phenomenon relating to socio-economic and demographic conditions, prices, area and yield of different crops as a result of the various surveys conducted in different rounds by National Sample Survey Organisation (N.S.S.O.).

In addition to the above organisations a number of departments in the State and Central Government like Income Tax Department, Directorate General of Supplies and Disposals, Railways, Post and Telegraphs. Central Board of Revenues, Textile Commissioner's Office, Central Excise Commissioner's Office, Iron and Steel Controller's Office and so on, publish statistical reports on current problems and the information supplied by them is, in general, more authentic and reliable than that obtained from other sources on the same subject.

2. *Publications of Semi-Government Statistical Organisations.* Very useful information is provided by the publications of the semi-government statistical organisations some of which are enumerated below :

(*i*) Statistics department of the Reserve Bank of India (Mumbai) which brings out an Annual Report of the Bank. Currency and Finance; Reserve Bank of India Bulletin (monthly) and various monthly and quarterly reports.

(*ii*) Economic department of Reserve Bank of India.

(*iii*) The Institute of Economic Growth, Delhi.

(*iv*) Gokhale Institute of Politics and Economics, Poona.

(*v*) The Institute of Foreign Trade, New Delhi.

Moreover, the statistical material published by the institutions like Municipal and District Boards, Corporations, Block and Panchayat Samitis on Vital Statistics (births and deaths), health, sanitation and other related subjects provides a fairly reliable and useful information.

3. *Publications of Research Institutions.* Individual research scholars, the different departments in the various universities of India and various research organisations and institutes like Indian Statistical Institute (I.S.I.), Kolkata and Delhi; Indian Council of Agricultural Research (I.C.A.R.), New Delhi; Indian Agricultural Statistics Research Institute (I.A.S.R.I.), New Delhi: National Council of Educational Research and Training (N.C.E.R.T.), New Delhi; National Council of Applied Economic Research, New Delhi; The Institute of Applied Man Power Research. New Delhi: The Institute of Labour Research, Mumbai : Indian Standards Institute, New Delhi: and so on publish the findings of their research programmes in the form of research papers, or monographs or journals which arc a constant source of secondary data on the subjects concerned.

4. *Publications of Commercial and Financial Institutions.* A number of private commercial and trade institutions like Federation of Indian Chamber of Commerce and Industries (FICCI). Institute of Chartered Accountants of India, Trade Unions, Stock Exchanges, Bank Bodies, Co-operative Societies, etc. publish reports and statistical material on current economic, business and other phenomena.

5. *Reports of Various Committees and Commissions appointed by the Government. The* report of the Survey and enquiry commissions and committees of the Central and State Governments to find their expert views on some important matters relating to economic and social phenomena like wages, dearness allowance, prices, national income, taxation, land, education, etc. are invaluable source of secondary information. For instance Simon-Kuznet Committee report on National Income in India. Wanchoo Commission report on Taxation, Kothari Commission report on Educational Reforms Pay Commissions Reports, Land Reforms Committee report, Gupta Commission report on Maruti Affairs. etc. arc invaluable sources of secondary data.

2.12 CLASSIFICATION OF DATA

Generally in the beginning of a statistical enquiry we find that the available data are disarranged and in such a great number of details that it becomes difficult to come to any conclusion. So the first and foremost work for the investigator is to decrease the amount of detail and to arrange them in such a form that these may be understood easily and the important features become prominent. For this, the available data is classified into various classes and expressed by means of tables, graphs so that these become simple and intelligible at a first glance.

Definition. The process of arranging the collected material in groups or classes according to their similarity or resemblance is called classification.

Objects of Classification. The objects of classification are as follows:

(*i*) The data becomes simple and easy to interpret, *i.e.*, it helps in forming a mental picture of data without any great mental strain.

(*ii*) It ensures an orderly arrangement of the data according to the attributes.

(*iii*) It helps in comparative study and

(*iv*) It helps in clarifying the points of similarity and dissimilarity.

2.12.1 Methods of Classification

Mass data is a large group of different types of elements collected through various modes and sources. Due to various types of characteristics, data differs from one group to another. Some data such as profits of an organization can be directly measurable. Some groups of data may not have such direct measurement such as sex, education. occupation etc. Depending on the nature of data classification is of different types. The following are the important types of classification modes :

(A) Chronological Classification

Data relating to a point of time or a period of time is chronological data and when such data is classified on the basis of time or a period it can be chronological classification. Such data is directly measurable and is measured in definite units of measurement. Data relating to growth of population, exports and imports, sales, profits etc. are classified under this category. Growth oriented measurements are chronologically classified.

Chronological classification has an advantage of measuring developments over a period of time. It is also convenient to compare changes from one point of (period of) time to another. It is easy to analyse the influence of a particular period over the data through this type of classification. Chronological classification is widely used in government. non-government, trade and non-trade organizations to assess the general performance.

Example :

Performance of Aditya & Company over 5 years

Year	*Sales (000)*	*Expenditure (₹ 000)*	*Profits (₹ 000)*
1999	555	10	85
2000	602	12	102
2001	628	15	115
2002	675	16	148
2003	710	18	162

(B) Geographical Classification

If the data is classified on the basis of area such as region, state or country, it is geographical classification. Geographical classification is used to make a comparative analysis of a particular phenomenon or fact between two countries or states or two areas. it is popularly used by International Organisations such as UNO, World Bank and the governments at various levels such as State, Districts etc.

Example: Results of Intermediate Examinations in Andhra Pradesh May - 2004

District	*A*	*B*	*C*	*D*	*E*	*F*	*G*	*H*	*I*	*J*
Pass %	71.80	66.07	60.72	57.67	55.91	52.86	58.54	46.57	40.60	52.44

Geographical classification is of great help for making comparison of performance of trade or non-trade organizations. It helps to make micro studies of a particular region. This type of classification is convenient for study of a specific problem in a particular area.

(C) Qualitative Classification

This is also known as classification by attributes. Data relating to certain facts, which cannot be measured directly in quantitative terms are called qualitative data or attributes. Example : Religion, marital status, literacy, occupation etc. are the attributes which are present in data. The basis of qualitative classification is presence or absence of such character. Therefore classification can be done on the basis of presence and absence of attributes. There are two types of classification by attributes.

(*a*) **Simple Classification.** When facts are classified into two classes according to one attribute only, then the classification is said to be simple. For example, if we divide (or classify) the consumer population of a state into two groups, say those of males and females then the classification is simple.

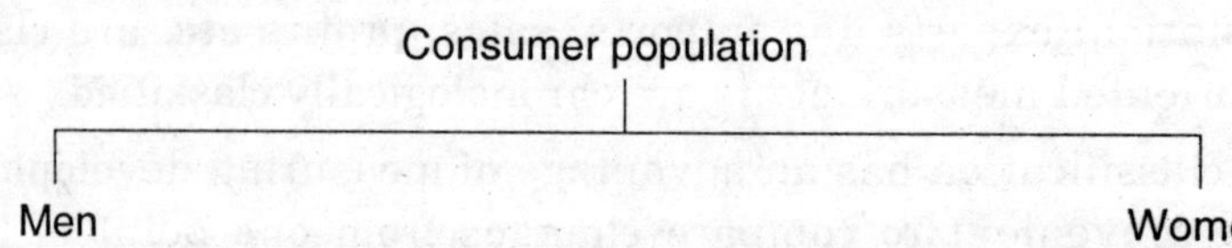

A single attribute may have more than two classes.

Example:

Number of Students in St. Theresa's College 2004-05

S. No.	*Courses*	*No. of Students*
1	Intermediate	150
2	B.A	510
3	B.Sc.	500
4	B.Com.	300
5	P.G.	250
	Total :	3060

(*b*) **Manifold Classification.** When facts are classified according to more than one attribute, or when each class is subdivided into more than two subclasses, then the classification is said to be manifold. For example, if we classify the consumer population of India into men and women, then subdivide into urban and rural and further subdivide according to employment, we find that a no. of subclasses are formed.

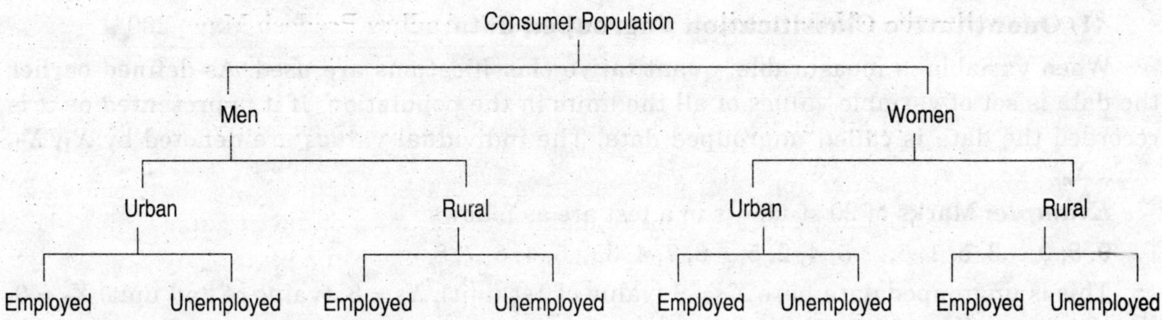

(*i*) Classification according to 2 attributes :

Example: **Number of Employees working in an organisation**

Department	*Permanent*	*Temporary*	*Total*
A Dept	22	20	42
B Dept	18	12	30
C Dept	20	10	30
Total	60	42	102

(*ii*) **Manifold Table :** It is a complex with more than three aspects of data. Accordingly number of columns and rows also increase. Such table contains many sub-divisions to record complex data. They are difficult to construct and also understand. It takes time to interpret the data because it is difficult to apply any technique to measure the values or identify features of the table.

Table Showing the Distribution of Students in a College

Courses	*Class*	*Students*						
		Hostel Students			*Day-Students*			*Total*
		M	*F*	*Total*	*M*	*F*	*Total*	
	I Year	20	4	24	30	10	40	64
B.A.	II Year	15	5	20	25	15	40	60
	III Year	10	3	13	20	7	27	40
	I Year	25	15	40	30	10	40	80
B.Sc.	II Year	20	10	30	17	13	30	60
	III Year	10	5	15	20		25	40
	I Year	8	2	10	18	2	20	30
B.Com.	II Year	6	4	10	10	6	16	26
	III Year	8	4	12	12	6	18	30
Total		122	52	174	182	74	254	430

M = Male, *F* = Female

(1) Quantitative Classification ungrouped data.

When variable is measurable, quantitative classifications are used. As defined earlier the data is set of variable values of all the units in the population. If it is presented as it is recorded the data is called ungrouped data. The individual values are denoted by X_1, X_2, ..., X_n.

***Example*:** Marks of 20 students in a test are as follows:

9, 8, 0, 3, 5, 1, 6, 5, 4, 2, 5, 6, 7, 4, 3, 5, 4, 6, 7, 8

This is ungrouped data here $X_1 = 9$ (value of 1st unit), $X_2 = 8$. (value of 2nd unit) $X_3 = 0$, $X_4 = 3$, ..., $X_{20} = 8$.

(2) Grouped Data : Since the objective of classification is to put the data in a form which is precise and comprehensive so that it is easily understood. This becomes more important when the data is huge. Classification which actually means grouping in case of quantitative variable. There are two types of grouping. The data expressed in groups is known grouping. The data expressed in groups is known as frequency distribution.

(*a*) grouped discrete data/discrete distribution frequency

(*b*) grouped continuous data/continuous frequency distribution

Thus frequency distribution consists of two components;

1. The size of variable or magnitude of a class of variables.

2. The number of times variables repeated in a class which is called frequency.

Definition

1. "A frequency distribution is a table that divides a set of data into a suitable number of classes (categories) showing also the number of items belonging to each class".
   Richard A. Johnson

2. "Frequency distribution is a statistical table which shows the set of all distinct values of the variable arranged in order of magnitude, either individually or in groups, with their corresponding frequencies side by side." *Croxton and Cowden*

(*a*) Grouped discrete data or discrete frequency distribution This distribution is of the form

X Variable value	f frequency		X	f
X_1	f_1		85	12
X_2	f_2	for example	89	15
$\vdots$	$\vdots$		90	4
X_k	f_k		93	3

Frequency, *i.e.*, how many times a value is repeated, is obtained by use of tally-marks.

Tally marks are vertical lines, which indicate the no. of repetitions.

No. of repetitions	1	2	3	4	5	6
Tally marks	|	||	||	||||	𝍸	𝍸 |

In this case "𝍸" indicates 5 repetitions; thus 𝍸 𝍸 shows 2 × 5 repetitions.

Example 1. *Preparing a discrete frequency distribution.*

Prepare discrete frequency distribution for the marks of 20 students in a test.

Marks X = 9, 5, 8, 0, 3, 5, 1, 6, 5, 4, 2, 5, 6, 7, 4, 8, 9, 3, 5, 4

Solution.

X =	0	1	2	3	4	5	9	7	8	9
Tally marks	|	|	|	||	|||	~~||||~~	||	|	||	||
Frequency *f*	1	1	1	2	3	5	2	1	2	2

Method : X_1 is 9, put one tally mark below 9.

X_2 = 8, put one tally mark below 8.

and so on.

Example 2. *Convert the following statement into a discrete series of no. of letters in words of "I love my India because I am an Indian and I belong to this great country."*

Solution : There are 16 words in the statement

Number of letters (*X*) :	1	2	3	4	5	6	7	
Tally marks	|||	||||	|	||	||	||	||	Total
Frequency *f* (no. of words)	3	4	1	2	2	2	2	16

Here *X* values are 1, 4, 5, 7, 1, 2, 2, 6, 3, 1, 6, 2, 4, 5, 7

X = no. of words

(*b*) Continuous Series: In a continuous series observations are expressed in small groups called class-intervals with certain limits. Frequencies in continuous series refer to the group but not to the individual items. As the name indicates, class intervals are in a continuous form from the beginning of the frequency distribution, till the end, within a given range of the data. Continuous series is applied under the following conditions :

When the total number of items and their range is large in number, discrete series or individual series cannot help in analysis, as it is not possible to list out the variables in single column.

i.e., when no. of units is very large individual series or discrete series is not suitable.

Example 3. *To arrange 500 visitors of a library with age group ranging from 6 to 90 years, continuous series is suitable. Such data if grouped in class intervals, it becomes precise and easy to compute any measure. The above data can be arranged in frequency table in the following way.*

Age Group :	*Below 10*	*10-20*	*30-40*	*40-50*	*30-40*	*50-60*	*60-70*	*70-80*	*80-90*
Visitors :	25	35	58	62	100	150	40	30	20

Here 20-30, 30-40, ... are individual classes.

Example 4. *Following marks were obtained by 25 students of a class in Mathematics paper carrying 50 marks. Classify these by taking class-interval of ten marks :*

8, 13, 12, 25, 32, 2, 31, 16, 21, 23, 27, 41, 29, 34, 5, 3
33, 42, 17, 11, 22, 26, 14, 4, 15.

Express this data as frequency distribution using exclusive / continuous classes.

Solution. We have the following five classes by taking the class-interval of ten marks :

0-10, 10-20, 20-30, 30-40 and 40-50.

Now the marks (or observations) falling within the class-interval 0-10 are 8, 2, 5, 3 and 4 *i.e.,* 5 times, the marks falling within the class-interval 10-20 are 13, 12, 16, 17, 11, 14, 15, *i.e.,* 7 times and so on.

The above classes are classified as follows :

Class	*Items (X)*	*Tally marks*	*Frequency*
0-10	8, 2, 5, 3, 4	~~IIII~~	5
10-20	13, 12, 16, 17, 11, 14, 15	~~IIII~~ II	7
20-30	25, 21, 23, 27, 29, 22, 26	~~IIII~~ II	7
30-40	32, 31, 34, 33	IIII	4
40-50	41, 42	II	2
			Total = 25

Here $X_1 = 8$, which falls in class 0—10 which is written below item (X) and are tally mark is given. Then $X_2 = 13$ which falls in 10—20 and so on.

2.13 FORMATION OF CLASSES

There are two methods, of classifying according to class-intervals viz., (*i*) Exclusive method (*ii*) Inclusive method.

(*i*) **Exclusive Method :** In this method, the upper limit of one class is equal to the lower limit of the next class. Any item equal to the upper limit of any class is excluded from that class (*i.e.,* not taken in that class) but included (or taken) in the next class and so it is called the exclusive method. For example, if any student has secured 30 marks in the preceding example, then his marks would have been taken in the class-interval 30—40 and not in 20—30.

The class-intervals in this method for the foregoing example can also be taken as

$[0, 10) = 0$ and below 10 *i.e.,* includes all x such that $0 \leq X < 10$

$[10, 20) = 10$ and below 20 *i.e.,* includes all x such that $10 \leq X < 20$

$[20, 30) = 20$ and below 30 *i.e.,* includes all x such that $20 \leq X < 30$

$[30, 40) = 30$ and below 40 *i.e.,* includes all x such that $30 \leq X < 40$

$[40, 50) = 40$ and below 50 *i.e.,* includes all x such that $40 \leq X < 50$

(*ii*) **Inclusive Method :** In this method, any item equal to the upper limit of any class is included (or taken) in that class and so it is called the inclusive method.

In the foregoing example, if we classify according to this method, then we shall get

Class	*Frequency*
0-9	5
10-19	7
20-29	7
30-39	4
40-49	2
	Total 25

In this case 0—9 includes all X such that $0 \le X \le 9$ and so on.

2.13.1 Changing from inclusive "to exclusive" classes

While discussing problems, the class-intervals given in inclusive method should invariably have to be changed to those in exclusive method. For this, we must find out the difference of the upper limit of any class-interval and the lower limit of the next class-interval of the inclusive method, and let it be 'd' then we add $\frac{d}{2}$ to each upper limit and subtract $\frac{d}{2}$ from each lower limit of inclusive method. Thus the above "inclusive" classes will be change to "exclusive" classes as following.

Class	*f*
– 0.5-9.5	5
9.5-19.5	7
19.5-29.5	7
29.5-39.5	4
39.5-49.5	2

2.14. COMPONENTS OF CONTINUOUS FREQUENCY DISTRIBUTION

1. ***Number of Classes :*** Though there is no hard and fast rule regarding the number of classes to be formed, yet their number should be neither very large no very small. If there are too many classes, the frequency distribution appears to be too fragmented to reveal the pattern of behaviour of characteristics. Fewer classes imply that the width of the class intervals will be broad and accordingly it would include a large number of observations. As will be obvious later that in any statistical analysis, the value of a class is represented by its mid-value and here a class interval with broader width will be representative of a large number of observations. Thus, the magnitude of loss of information due to grouping will be large when there are small number of classes. On the other hand, if the number of observations is small or the distribution of observations is irregular, *i.e.*, not uniform. having more number of classes might result in very small frequencies of same classes, thus, revealing no pattern of behaviour. Therefore, the number of classes depends upon the nature

and the number of observations. If the number of observations is large or the distribution of observations is regular, one may have more number of classes. In practice, the minimum number of classes should not be less than 5 or 6 and in any case there should not be more than 20 classes.

The approximate number of classes can also be determined by Struge's formula : $n = 1 + 3.322 \times \log_{10} N$, where n (rounded to the next whole number) denotes the number of classes and N denotes the total number of observations.

Based on this formula, we have

$$n = 1 + 3.322 \times 2.000 = 7.644 \text{ or } 8, \text{ when } N = 100$$

$$n = 1 + 3.322 \times 2.699 = 9.966 \text{ or } 10, \text{ when } N = 500$$

$$n = 1 + 3.322 \times 4.000 = 14.288 \text{ or } 15, \text{ when } N = 10{,}000$$

$$n = 1 + 3.322 \times 4.699 = 16.610 \text{ or } 17, \text{ when } N = 50{,}000$$

From the above calculations we may not that even the formation of 20 class intervals is very rarely needed.

2. ***Width of a Classes*** : width of a class defined as $U—L$ where U = upper limit and L = lower limit of a class. Thus width of a class 4 to 8 is $8 - 4 = 4$. After determining the number of class intervals, one has to determine their width. The problem of determining the width of a class interval is closely related to the number of class intervals.

As far as possible, all the class intervals should be of equal width. However, there can be situations where it may not be possible to have equal width of all the classes. Suppose that there is a frequency distribution, having all classes of equal width, in which the pattern of behaviour of the observations is not regular, *i.e.*, there are nil or very few observations in some classes while there is concentration of observations in other classes. In such a situation, one may be compelled to have unequal class intervals in order that the frequency distribution becomes regular.

The approximate size of a class interval can be decided by the use of the following formula :

$$\text{Class Interval} = \frac{\text{Largest observation} - \text{Smallest observation}}{\text{Number of classes}} = \frac{\text{Range}}{\text{Number of classes}}$$

$$\text{or using notations, Class Interval} = \frac{L - S}{n}$$

Before taking a final decision on the width of various class intervals, it is worthwhile to consider the following points :

(*a*) It should be convenient to find the mid-value of a class interval.

(*b*) Most of the observations in a class should be uniformly distributed or concentrated around its mid-value.

(*c*) As far as possible, the classes should be of equal width. A frequency distribution of equal class width is convenient to be represented diagrammatically and easy to analyse.

3. ***Class Limits :*** The class limits are the smallest and the largest observation in class. These are respectively known as the lower limit and the upper limit of a class. For frequency distribution, it is necessary to designate these class limits very unambiguously, because the mid-value of a class is obtained by using these limits. As will be obvious later, the mid-value will be used in all the computations about a frequency distribution and the accuracy of these computations will depend upon the proper specification of class limits.

The designation of class limits for various class intervals can be done in two ways : (*i*) Exclusive Method and (*ii*) Inclusive Method which have already been described. Class limits of class in case of exclusive Class 10—20 are 10 and 20.

4. ***Class boundaries :*** When there is a gap between the upper limit of the first class interval and the lower limits of the next class, there is a need to determine the class boundaries, without which some measures cannot be computed.

Example : 9-19, 20-29, 30-9, 40-40 ......

For such class intervals, class boundaries can be determined by using the following formula :

Lower limit of class boundary = Lower limit - 1/2 d.

Upper class boundary = Upper class limit + 1/2 d.

d = common difference between upper limit of the first class and lower limit of the next class .

Example 5. *Determine class boundaries for the given class intervals.*

Classes : 50-54, 55-59, 60-64,65-69, 70-74

Solution.

Classes	*Class boundaries*
50-54	49.5-54.5
55-59	54.5-59.5
60-64	59.5-64.5
65-69	64.5-69.5
70-74	59.5-74.5

Lower Class Boundary = Lower limit – 1/2 d = 50 – 1/2 (1) = 49.5

Upper Class boundary = Upper limit + 1/2 d = 54 + 1/2 (1) = 54.5

5. Mid-value, Mid-points/Class Mark. Once data is classified under class intervals with certain limits, individual items of the series lose their identity. An item is described along with the items in each group (*i.e.,* class interval). To represent the class interval in measuring any technique, its mid point is considered. Therefore in continuous class intervals mid-point has a significant role. Any measure of dispersion or correlation etc. Mid-values or Mid-points or class marks are the middle value of the class-interval. It is defined as the average of two limits of a class interval. It is found by adding upper limit (U) and lower limit (L) and the total is divided by two.

$$\text{Mid-value} = \frac{L + U}{2}$$

Suppose a part of frequency distribution is

Class	f
10-20	8
20-30	12

There are 8 variable values X which have values between 10 and 20 or $10 \leq X < 20$. However we do not know their actual values. Thus we assume that all 8 values are mid value of 10 and 20. *i.e.,* 15.

Example 6. *Given below are the weights (in pounds) of 70 students.*

(i) Construct a frequency distribution when class intervals are inclusive, taking the lowest class as 60-69. Also construct class boundaries.

(ii) Construct a frequency distribution when class intervals are exclusive, taking the lowest class as 60-70.

61, 80, 91, 113, 100, 106, 109, 73, 88, 92, 101, 106, 107, 97, 93, 96, 102, 114, 87, 62, 74, 107, 109, 91, 72, 89, 94, 98, 112, 103, 101, 77, 92, 73, 67, 76, 84, 90, 118, 107, 108, 82, 78, 84, 77, 95, 111, 115, 104, 69, 106, 105, 63, 76, 85, 88, 96, 90, 95, 99, 83, 98, 88, 72, 75, 86, 82, 86, 93, 92.

Solution.

(*i*) Construction of frequency distribution using inclusive class intervals.

Class Intervals	*Tally Marks*	*Frequency*	*Class Boundaries*
60-69	𝍸	5	59.5-69.5
70-79	𝍸 𝍸 𝍷	11	69.5-79.5
80-89	𝍸 𝍸 𝍷𝍷𝍷	14	79.5-89.5
90-99	𝍸 𝍸 𝍸 𝍷𝍷𝍷	18	89.5-99.5
100-109	𝍸 𝍸 𝍸 𝍷	16	99.5-109.5
110-119	𝍸 𝍷	6	109.5-119.5
Total		70	

To determine the class boundaries, we note that measured weights are approximated to the nearest pound. Therefore, a measurement between 69 and 69.5 is approximated as 69 and included in the class interval 60-69. Similarly, a measurement between 69.5 and 70 is approximated as 70 and is included in the class interval 70-79. Thus, the class boundaries are obtained by subtracting 0.5 from the lower limit and adding 0.5 to the upper limit of various classes. These boundaries are shown in the last column of the above table.

(*ii*) The frequency distribution of exclusive type of class intervals can be directly written from the above table as shown below :

Class Intervals	*Frequency*
60-70	5
70-80	11
80-90	14
90-100	18
100-110	16
110-120	6
Total	70

2.15 PROCEDURE TO DETERMINE CLASS INTERVALS FROM MID-VALUE

1. Find the difference between two mid-values, let it be i (which is class interval)
2. Divide the value by *i.e.*, find $\frac{i}{2}$.
3. Add the resulting value to the mid-value to get upper limit of the class and deduct the value from the mid-value to get the lower limit, *i.e.*, find Lower limit $= x - \frac{i}{2}$ and upper limit $= x + \frac{i}{2}$ where x = mid value.
4. These two constitute the first class interval.

Example 7. *Compute class intervals for the given Mid-values.*

Mid-values : *110, 120, 130, 140, 150, 160*

Solution. Difference between mid-values = 120 – 110 = 10 = $i, \frac{i}{2} = \frac{10}{2} = 5$

Thus lower and upper limits of class whose mid value is 110 are 110 – 5 = 105 and 110 + 5 = 115 respectively. Thus the class is 105–115. Similarly we find the other classes. Thus the classes are

105-115, 115-125, 125-135, 135-145, 145-155, 155-165

2.16 RELATIVE OR PERCENTAGE FREQUENCY DISTRIBUTION

If instead of frequencies of various classes their relative or percentage frequencies are written, we have a relative or percentage frequency distribution.

$$\text{Relative frequency of a class} = \frac{\text{Frequency of the class}}{\text{Total Frequency}}$$

Percentage frequency of a class = Relative frequency × 100

These frequencies are shown in the following table.

Example :

Class Interval	*Frequency*	*Relative Frequency*	*Percent frequency*
0-15	15	0.10	10
15-30	26	0.15	15
30-45	32	0.18	18
45-60	35	0.20	20
60-75	28	0.16	16
75-90	20	0.11	11
90-105	18	0.10	10
Total	177	1	100

2.17 FREQUENCY DENSITY

Frequency density in a class is defined as the number of observations per unit of its width. Frequency density gives the rate of concentration of observations in a class :

$$\text{Frequency Density} = \frac{\text{Frequency of the class}}{\text{Width of the class}}$$

Table showing Frequency Density of various class :

Class Intervals	*Frequency*	*Frequency Density*
1.00-1.10	4	$40 = \frac{4}{0.1}$
1.10-1.20	7	$70 = \frac{7}{0.1}$
1.20-1.30	10	100
1.30-1.40	14	140
1.40-1.50	20	200
1.50-1.60	13	130
1.60-1.70	9	90
1.70-1.80	6	60
1.80-1.90	4	40
1.90-2.00	3	30
Total	90	

2.18 CUMULATIVE FREQUENCY DISTRIBUTION

There are two types of cumulative frequency distribution :

(*a*) "Less than" cumulative frequency distribution.

(*b*) "More than" cumulative frequency distribution.

(*a*) **"Less than" frequency distribution.** Frequency less than x means the number of all variable values less than x. Suppose a frequency distribution is given, its "less than" frequency distribution is as follows :

Class	f
10-20	5
20-30	10
30-40	6
Total	21

X less than	f	
10	0 ↓	as there is no value less than 10
20	5 ↓	there are 5 values less than 20
30	10 + 5 = 15	there are 15 values less than 30
40	15 + 6 = 21	

"Less than" Cumulative frequency is the running total of frequencies with cumulative totals of every class-interval.

Similarly, "More than" cumulative frequency represents the total number of values more than and equal to which it relates. More than cumulative distributions are constructed similarly by adding frequencies starting from the last frequency. Using the frequency distribution as below :

Class	*f*
10-20	5
20-30	10
30-40	6

"More than" is obtained as follows :

X more than	*f*
10	21
20	16
30	6 ↑
40	0 ↑

There are 6 values greater than 30 which are in 30-40 starting point (as there is no value greater than 40)

Example 8. *From frequency distribution as given in (1) "More than" and "Less than" cummulative frequency distributions are obtained as given (3) and (2) respectively*

Normal Frequency (1)		*Less than Frequency (2)*		*More than frequency (3)*	
Marks	*Students*	*Marks*	*Students*	*Marks*	*Students*
0-10	5	Less than - 0	0	More than - 0	100
10-20	5	Less than - 10	5	More than - 10	95
20-30	10	Less than - 20	10	More than - 20	90
30-40	16	Less than - 30	20	More than - 30	80
40-50	18	Less than - 40	36	More than - 40	64
50-60	16	Less than - 50	54	More than - 50	46
60-70	11	Less than - 60	70	More than - 60	30
70-80	7	Less than - 70	81	More than - 70	19
80-90	7	Less than - 80	88	More than - 80	12
90-100	5	Less than - 90	95	More than - 90	5
		Less than - 100	100	More than - 100	0

Example 9. *From the following "Less than" cumulative frequency distribution find the frequency distribution.*

X Less than	* Frequency
20	5
30	17
40	25
50	29

* frequency means cumulative frequency.

Solution. Obviously class interval is 10 each in fist class will be 10-20 with frequency 5 and the next class will be 20-30 with frequency = 17 – 5 = 12

Thus the frequency distribution is

Class	*Frequency* *f*
10-20	5
20-30	17 – 5 = 12
30-40	25 – 17 = 8
40-50	29 – 25 = 4

□□□

3

Diagrammatic and Graphical Presentation

CHAPTER OUTLINE

- Utility and Advantages of Diagrammatic Presentation
- Types of Diagrams (line, bar, pie)
- Graphs — Line
- Histograms
- Graphs of Frequency Distributions
- Histogram, Frequency Polygon
- Frequency Curve
- Ogives

3.1 INTRODUCTION

An important function of statistics is the presentation of complex mass of data in a simple way so that it becomes easier to understand. Classification and tabulation are the techniques that help in presenting the data in an intelligible form. But with increase in volume of data, it becomes more and more inconvenient to understand even after its classification and tabulation. Thus, to understand various trends of the data at a glance and to facilitate the comparison of various situations, the data are presented in the form of diagrams and graphs. Diagrammatic presentation and graphic presentation is discussed in this chapter.

3.2 UTILITY AND ADVANTAGES OF DIAGRAMMATIC PRESENTATION

Data presented in the form of diagrams are useful as well as advantageous in many ways, as is obvious from the following :

(*i*) ***Diagrams are attractive and impressive :*** Data presented in the form of diagrams are able to attract the attention of even a common man. It may be difficult for a common man to understand and remember the data presented in the form of figures but diagrams create a lasting impression upon his mind. Due to their attractive and impressive character, the diagrams are very frequently used by various newspapers and magazines for the explanation of certain phenomena. Diagrams are also useful in modern advertising campaign.

(*ii*) ***Diagrams simplify data :*** Diagrams are used to represent a huge mass of complex data in simplified and intelligible from which is easy to understand.

(*iii*) ***Diagrams give more information :*** In addition to the depiction of the characteristics of data the diagrams may bring out other hidden facts and relations which are not possible to know from the classified and tabulated data.

(*iv*) ***Diagrams save time and labour :*** A lot of time is required to study the trend and significance of voluminous data. The same data, when presented in the form of diagrams, can be understood practically in no time.

(*v*) ***Diagrams are useful in making comparisons :*** Many a times the objective of the investigation is to compare two or more situations either with respect to time or places. The task of comparison often be very conventionally done by the use of diagrams.

(*vi*) ***Diagrams have universal applicability :*** Diagrams are used in almost in every field of study like economics, business, administration, social institutions and other fields.

3.3 TYPES OF DIAGRAMS

There are a large number of diagrams which can be used for presentation of data. The selection of a particular diagram depends upon the nature of data, objective of presentation and the ability and experience of the person doing this task. For convenience, few diagrams are described.

(*A*) Line diagram

(*B*) Bar diagrams

- (*i*) Simple Bar Diagram
- (*ii*) Multiple Bar Diagram
- (*iii*) Sub-divided or Component Bar Diagram
- (*iv*) Percentage Sub-divided Bar Diagram

(*C*) Pie diagram

(*A*) ***Line Diagram :*** In case of a line diagram, different values are represented by the length of the line drawn vertically or horizontally. The gap between the successive lines is kept uniform. The comparison of values of various items is done by the length of these lines.

Although the comparison is easy, the diagram is not very attractive. This diagram is used when the number of items is relatively large.

Example 1. *The income of 12 workers on a particular day was recorded as given below. Represent the data line diagram.*

S. No. of workers :	1	2	3	4	5	6	7	8	9	10	11	12
Income (in ₹) :	25	35	30	45	50	55	40	50	60	55	40	35

Solution.

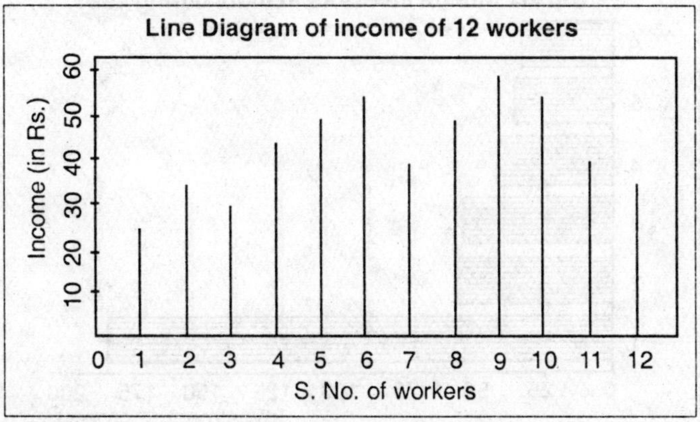

Fig. 1

(*B*) Bar Diagrams.

(*i*) ***Simple Bar Diagram :*** In case of a simple bar diagram, the vertical or horizontal bars, with height proportional to the value of the item, are constructed. The width of a bar is chosen arbitrarily and is kept constant for every bar. Different bars are drawn so that the gap between the successive bars is same. Bar diagrams are particularly suitable for presenting individual series, such as time and spatial series.

Example 2. *Represent the following data by a suitable diagram.*

Years	:	*1987*	*1988*	*1989*	*1990*	*1991*
C.F.A Enrolments	:	*7300*	*9400*	*12100*	*14600*	*16700*

Solution.

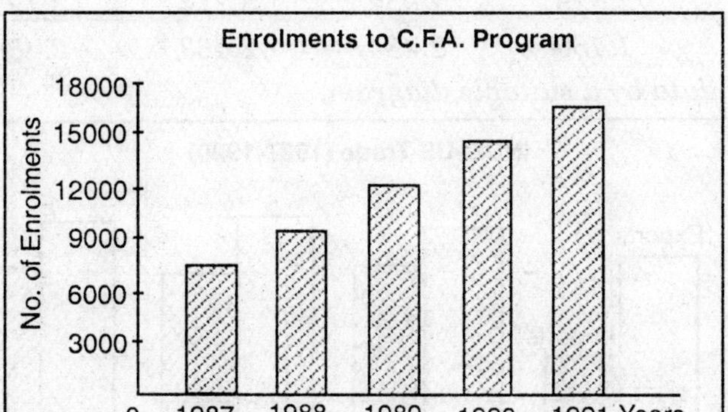

Fig. 2

Example 3. *The following table gives the figures of foreign investment in India by the top six investors during 1991. represent the data by a horizontal bar diagram.*

S. No.	Country	Investment (₹ Crores)	S. No.	Country	Investment (₹ Crores)
1.	U.S.A	185.9	4.	Germany	41.8
2.	Netherlands	55.9	5.	Switzerland	35.5
3.	Japan	52.7	6.	U.K.	32.1

Solution.

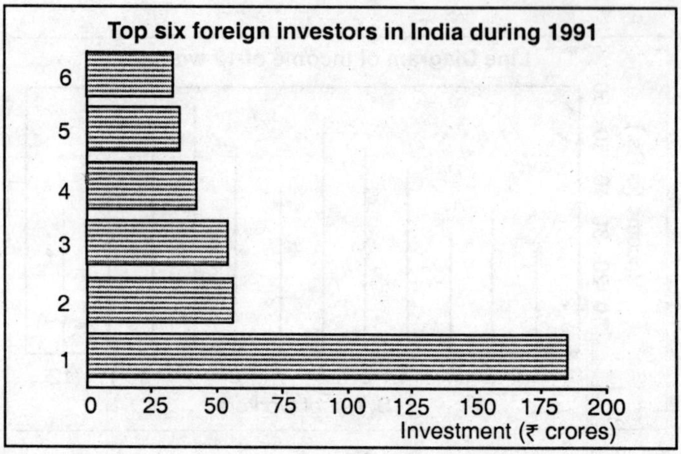

Fig. 3

(*ii*) ***Multiple Bar Diagram :*** This type of diagram, also known as *compound bar diagram,* is used who comparisons are to be shown between two or more sets of data. As set of bars for a period or related phenomena are drawn side by side without gaps while various sets of bars are separated by some arbitrarily chosen constant gap. Different bars are distinguished by different shades of colours. In order that various bars are comparable, it is necessary to draw them on the same scale

Example 4. *The following table gives the figures of Indo-US trade during 1987 to 1990. The figures of Indian export and imports are in $ billion.*

Year	:	*1987*	*1988*	*1989*	*1990*
Export	:	*2.529*	*2.952*	*3.314*	*3.191*
Import	:	*1.460*	*2.484*	*2.463*	*2.486*

Present the above data by a suitable diagram.

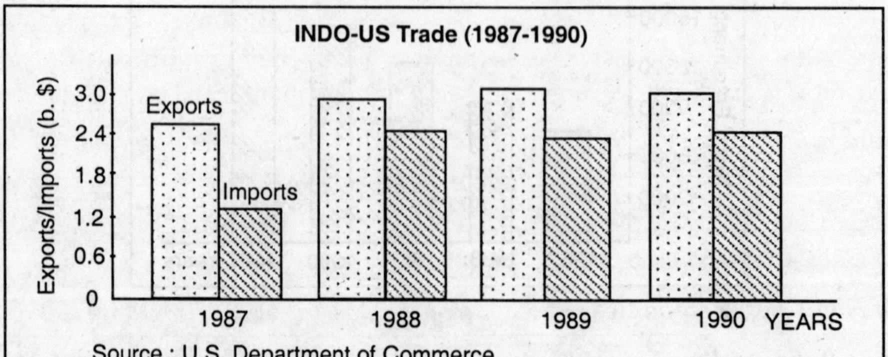

Fig. 4

Example 5. *Represent the following data on faculty-wise distribution of students, by a multiple bar diagram.*

College	*Arts*	*Science*	*Commerce*
A	*1200*	*600*	*500*
B	*1000*	*800*	*650*
C	*1400*	*700*	*800*
D	*750*	*900*	*300*

Solution.

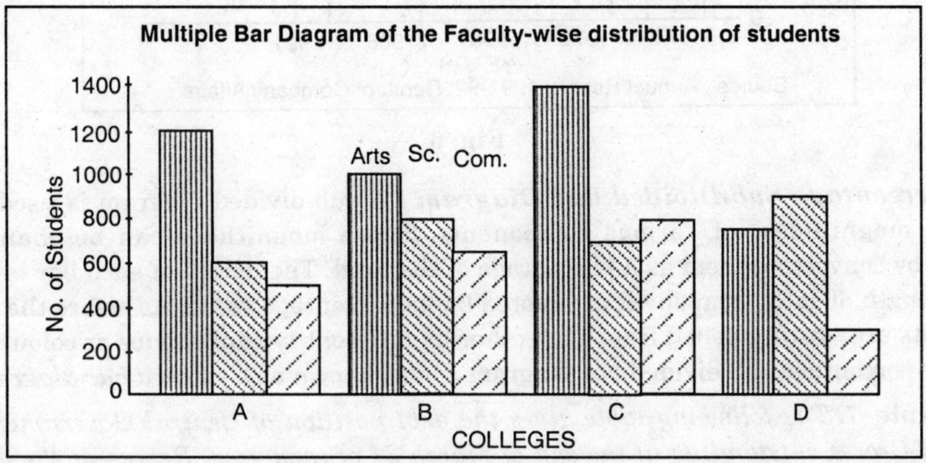

Fig. 5

(*iii*) ***Sub-divided or Component Bar Diagram :*** In case of a sub-divided bar diagram a bar, corresponding to each phenomenon is divided into various components. The portion of each division component denotes its share in the total. For example, the bar corresponding the number of students in a course can be sub-divided into boys and girls. The subdivision into different bars should always be done in the same order and they should be distinguished from each other by using different colours or shades.

Sub-divided bar diagram is useful when it is desired to represent the comparative value of different components of a phenomenon. The main limitation of this diagram is that since various components are not drawn on a common base, they are difficult to compare. This diagram is used if there are few components of a phenomenon.

Example 6. *Represent the following data by a sub-divided bar diagram.*

Years	*1971*	*1976*	*1981*	*1986*	*1991*
No. of Govt. Companies	*322*	*674*	*867*	*1034*	*1170*
No. of Non-Govt. Companies	*31*	*45*	*66*	*133*	*223*
Total	*353*	*719*	*933*	*1167*	*1393*

Solution.

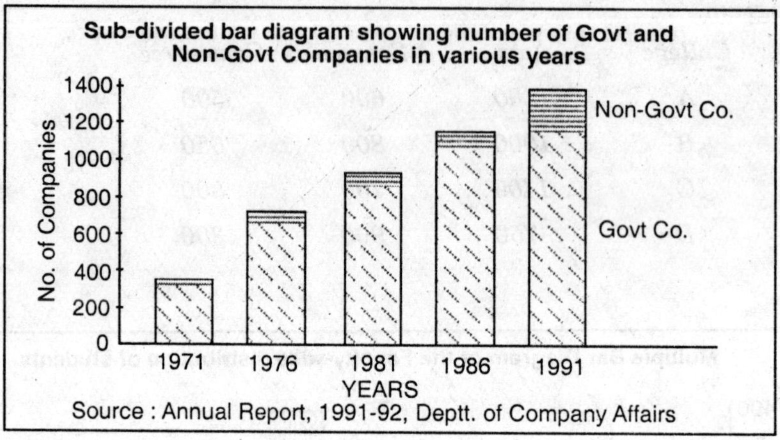

Fig. 6

(*iv*) ***Percentage Sub-Divided bar Diagram :*** A sub-divided diagram is used to show absolute magnitudes of various components. These magnitudes can be changed into relatives by converting them as a percentage of the total. The length of each bar is taken as 100 and length of each component is denoted by its percentage value. As before the different components are distinguished from each other by different type of shades or colours. A sub-divided or percentage sub-divided bar diagram is also known as a *stacked bar diagram.*

Example 7. *The following table gives the debt position of Central Government as the amount (₹ Crores outstanding at the end of March 31 of each year. Represent the data by a percentage sub-divided bar diagram.*

Years	:	*1984-1985*	*1985-86*	*1986-87*	*1987-88*
Internal Debt	:	*58537*	*71039*	*86313*	*98646*
External Debt	:	*16637*	*18153*	*20299*	*23223*
Other Liabilities	:	*38267*	*48422*	*59934*	*74692*
Total	:	*113441*	*137614*	*166546*	*195561*

Solution. The amounts are given in absolute terms, therefore, these are to be converted into percentages in order to show them on a percentage sub-divided bar diagram.

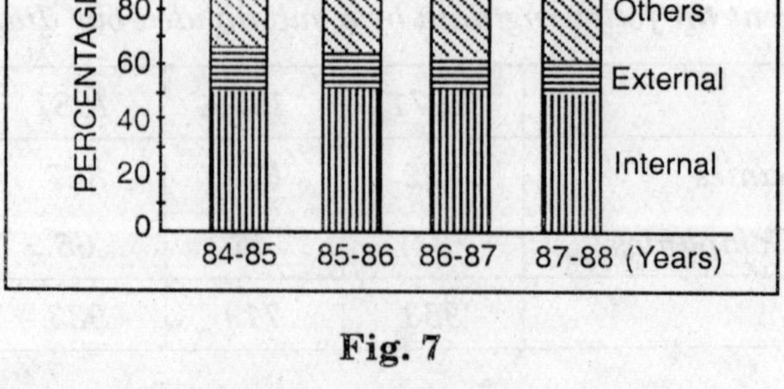

Fig. 7

Years	:	1984-1985	1985-86	1986-87	1987-88
Internal Debt	:	51	52	52	50
External Debt	:	15	13	12	12
Other Liabilities	:	34	35	36	38
Total	:	100	100	100	100

(C) Angular or Pie Diagram. Just as sub-divided and percentage bars are used to represent the total magnitude of its various components, the circle (representing the total) may be divided into various sections or segments *viz.*, sectors representing certain proportion or percentage of the various component parts to the total. Such a sub-divided circle diagram is known as an **angular or pie diagram,** named so because the various segments resemble slices cut from a pie.

Steps for Construction of Pie Diagram

1. Express each of the component values as a percentage of the respective total.

2. Since the angle at the centre of the circle is 360°, the total magnitude of the various components is taken to be equal to 360° and each component part is to be expressed proportionately in degrees. Since 1 per cent of the total value is equal to 360/100 = 3·6°, the percentage of the component parts obtained in step 1 can be converted to degrees by multiplying each of them by 3·6.

3. Draw a circle of appropriate radius using an appropriate scale depending on the space available. If only one category or characteristic is to be used, the circle may be drawn of any radius. However, if two or more sets of data are to be presented simultaneously for comparative studies, then the radii of the corresponding circles are to be proportional to the square roots of their total magnitudes.

4. Having drawn the circle, draw any radius (preferably horizontal). Now with this radius as the base line draw an angle at the centre [with the help of protractor] equal to the degree represented by the first component, the new line drawn at the centre to form this angle will touch the circumference. The sector so obtained will represent the proportion of the first component. From this second line as base, now draw another angle at the centre equal to the degree represented by the 2nd component, to give the sector representing the proportion of the second component. Proceeding similarly, all the sectors representing different component parts can be constructed.

5. Different sectors representing various component parts should be distinguished from one another by using different shades, dottings, colours, etc., or giving them explanatory or descriptive labels either inside the sector (if possible) or just outside the circle with proper identification.

Remarks 1. The degrees represented by the various component parts of a given magnitude can be obtained directly without computing their percentage to the total value as follows :

$$\text{Degree of any component part} = \frac{\text{Component value}}{\text{Total value}} \times 360°.$$

2. Pie diagrams are also called *circular* diagrams.

3. Since the comparison of the pie diagrams is to be made on the basis of the areas of the various sectors which are difficult to be ascertained visually with precision, generally sub-divided or percentage bars or rectangles are preferred to pie diagrams for studying the changes in the total and component parts. Moreover, pie diagrams are difficult to construct as compared with bars or rectangle diagrams. Any way, if the number of component parts is more than 10, pie chart is preferred to bar or rectangle diagram which becomes rather confusing in such a situation.

We give below some illustrations of pie diagrams.

Example 8. *Draw a pie diagram to represent the following data of proposed expenditure by a State Government for the year 1997-98.*

Items	*Agriculture & Rural Development*	*Industries & Urban Development*	*Health & Education*	*Miscellaneous*
Proposed Expenditure (in million ₹)	*4,200*	*1,500*	*1,000*	*500*

Solution.

CALCULATIONS FOR PIE CHART

Items	*Proposed expenditure (in million ₹)*	*Angle at the centre*
(1)	(2)	(3) = $\frac{(2)}{7200} \times 360°$
Agriculture and Rural Development	4,200	$\frac{42}{72} \times 360° = 210°$
Industries and Urban Development	1,500	$\frac{15}{72} \times 360° = 75°$
Health and Education	1,000	$\frac{10}{72} \times 360° = 50°$
Miscellaneous	500	$\frac{5}{72} \times 360° = 25°$
Total	7,200	360°

PIE DIAGRAM REPRESENTING PROPOSED EXPENDITURE BY STATE GOVERNMENT ON DIFFERENT ITEMS FOR 1997-98

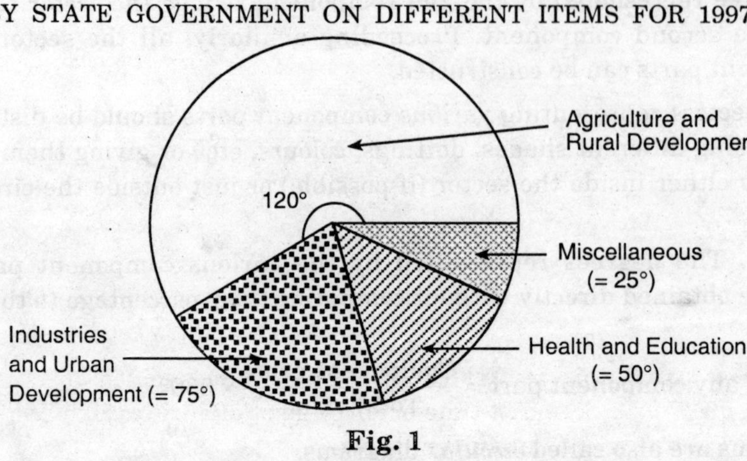

Fig. 1

Example 9. *The following table shows the area in millions of sq. km., of oceans of the world :*

Ocean	*Area (million sq. km.)*
Pacific	*70·8*
Atlantic	*41·2*
Indian	*28·5*
Antarctic	*7·6*
Arctic	*4·8*

Draw a pie diagram to represent the data.

Solution.

CALCULATIONS FOR PIE DIAGRAM

Ocean	*Area (million sq. km.)*	*Angle at the centre*
Pacific	70·8	$\frac{70·8}{152·9} \times 360° = 166·7°$
Atlantic	41·2	$\frac{41·2}{152·9} \times 360° = 97·0°$
Indian	28·5	$\frac{28·5}{152·9} \times 360° = 67·1°$
Antarctic	7·6	$\frac{7·6}{152·9} \times 360° = 17·9°$
Arctic	4·8	$\frac{4·8}{152·9} \times 360° = 11·3°$
Total	152·9	360°

PIE DIAGRAM SHOWING THE AREA (IN MILLIONS OF SQUARE KMS) OF OCEANS OF THE WORLD

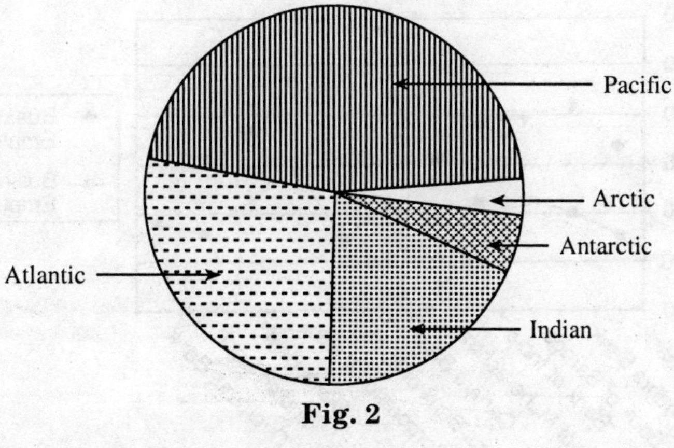

Fig. 2

2.4 GRAPHS

Line Graph

A line graph is a visual presentation of a set of data values joined by straight liens. The data values could be over a period of time or over a set of entities like banks, individuals, etc. A few examples of line graphs are given below.

Example 10. *The following graph gives the productivity of staff i.e., 'Business per Employee' for some of the public sector banks.*

Business per Employee in Some Public Sector Banks

(*₹ in Lakhs*)

Bank	*Business Per Employee 2005-06*	*Business Per Employee 2001-02*
Allahabad Bank	336	153
Andhra Bank	426.75	195.96
Bank of Baroda	396	222.76
Bank of India	381	218.74
Bank of Maharashtra	306.18	191.44
Canara Bank	441.57	214.88
Central Bank of India	240.46	148.77
Corporation Bank	527	290.44
Dena Bank	364	221
Indian Bank	295	156
Indian Overseas Bank	354.73	175.41

Business per Employee in Banks

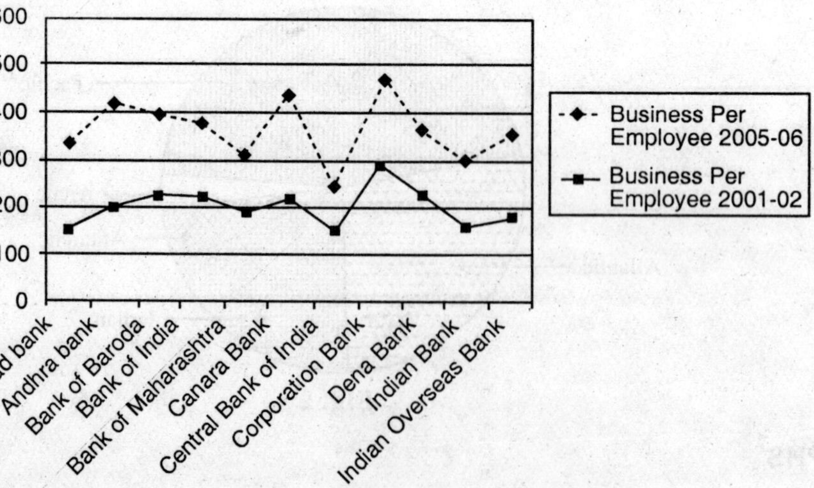

The graph gives variation in 'Business per Employee' among different banks. It also provides a visual comparison of 'Business per Employee' in the two years.

Example 11. *Yet another example of line graph is provided for the following data, which gives the wholesale and consumer price indices for period 1993-94 to 2005-06.*

Year	*Wholesale Price Index*	*Consumer Price Index*
1993-94	100.0	100
1994-95	112.6	107.5
1995-96	121.6	118.3
1996-97	127.2	130.4
1997-98	132.8	152.5
1998-99	140.7	172.5
1999-00	145.3	178.3
2000-01	155.7	185
2001-02	161.3	192.9
2002-03	166.8	200.8
2003-04	175.9	208.3
2004-05	187.3	216.7
2005-06	195.5	225.8

The movement in the above price indices, over the period, is presented with the help of a line graph given below.

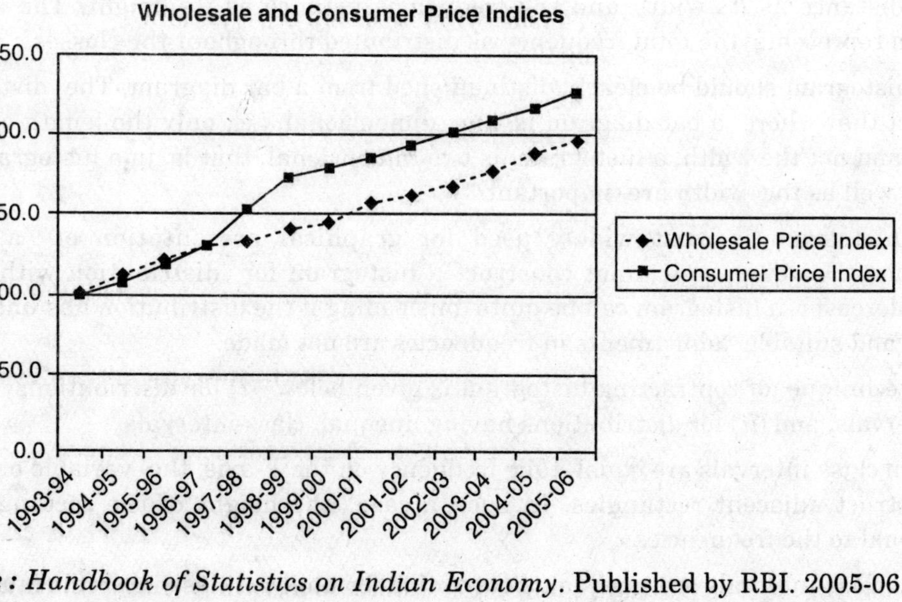

Source : *Handbook of Statistics on Indian Economy*. Published by RBI. 2005-06.

TIME SERIES GRAPHS OR HISTORIGRAMS

A time series is a series of values of a variable recorded at successive intervals of time; *e.g.*, the figures of national income, sale, production, employment, enrolment, *etc.*, at successive points of time. In case of a time series graph, the time is measured along *X*-axis and the other variable along *Y*-axis, such a graph is also termed as *Historigram*. If the actual values of a series are plotted, the resulting graph is called as *Absolute Historigram* while if their indices are plotted, we get an *Index Historigram*. (as in example above)

3.5 GRAPHS OF FREQUENCY DISTRIBUTIONS

A frequency distribution can be presented graphically in any of the following ways :

- Histogram.
- Frequency polygon.
- Smoothed frequency curve, and
- 'Ogives' or cumulative frequency curves.

3.5.1. Histogram

Out of several methods of presenting a frequency distribution graphically, histogram is the most popular and widely used in practice. A histogram is a set of vertical bars whose areas are proportional to the frequencies represented.

While constructing histogram the variable is always taken on the X-axis and the frequencies depending on it on the Y-axis. Each class is then represented by a distance on the scale that is proportional to its class-interval. The distance for each rectangle on the X-axis shall remain the same in case the class-intervals are uniform throughout. If they are different they vary. The Y-axis represents the frequencies of each class which constitute the height of its rectangle. In this manner we get a series of rectangles each having a class-interval distance as its width and the frequency distance as its height. The area of the histogram represents the total frequency as distributed throughout the classes.

The histogram should be clearly distinguished from a bar diagram. The distinction lies in the fact that where a bar diagram is one dimensional, *i.e.,* only the length of the bar is material and not the width, a histogram is two-dimensional, that is, in a histogram both the length as well as the width are important.

The histogram is most widely used for graphical presentation of a frequency distribution. However, we cannot construct a histogram for distribution with open- end classes. Moreover, a histogram can be quite misleading if the distribution has unequal class-intervals and suitable adjustments in frequencies are not made.

The technique of contracting histogram is given below (*i*) for distributions have equal class-intervals, and (*ii*) for distributions having unequal class-intervals.

When class-intervals are equal, take frequency on the Y-axis, the variable on the X-axis and construct adjacent rectangles. In such a case the height of the rectangles will be proportional to the frequencies.

When class-intervals are unequal, a correction for unequal class intervals must be made. The correction consists of finding for each class the frequency density or the relative frequency density or the relative frequency density. The frequency density is the frequency for that class divided by the width of that class. A histogram or frequency density polygon constructed from these density values would have the same general appearance as the corresponding graphical display developed from equal class intervals.

For making the adjustment we take that class which has lowest class-interval and adjust the frequencies of other classes in the following manner. If one class-interval is twice as wide as the one having lowest class- interval we divide the height of its rectangle by two, if it is three times more we divide the height of its rectangle by three, etc., *i.e.*, the heights will be proportional to the ratio of the frequencies of the width of the class.

The following illustration would clearly indicate the manner in which the adjustment has to be made :

Example 12. *Represent the following data by a histogram :*

Marks	*No. of Students*	*Marks*	*No. of Students*
0-10	*8*	*50-60*	*60*
10-20	*12*	*60-70*	*52*
20-30	*22*	*70-80*	*40*
30-40	*35*	*80-90*	*30*
40-50	*40*	*90-100*	*5*

Solution. Since class-intervals are equal throughout no adjustment in frequencies is required.

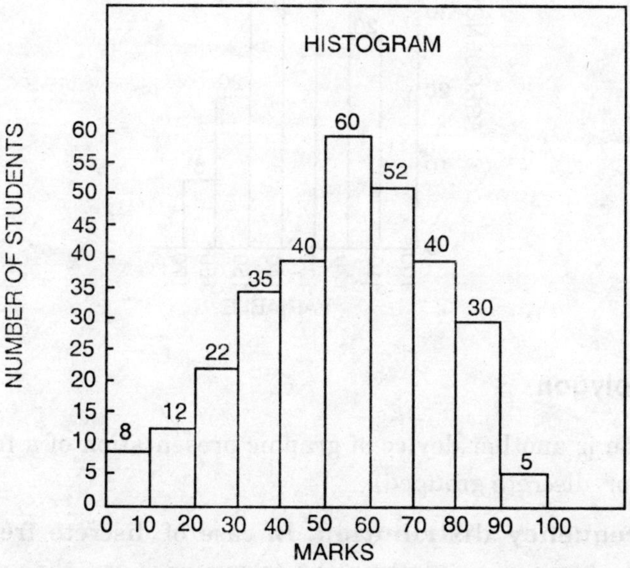

Example 13. *Represent the following data by means of a histogram :*

Weekly Waves (in ₹)	*No. of Workers*	*Weekly Wages (in ₹)*	*No. of Workers*
10-15	*7*	*30-40*	*12*
15-20	*19*	*40-60*	*12*
20-25	*27*	*60-80*	*8*
25-30	*15*		

Solution. Since the class-intervals are unequal, frequencies must be adjusted otherwise the histogram would give a misleading picture. The adjustment is done as follows. The lowest class interval is 5. The frequencies of the class 30-40 shall be divided by two since the class interval is double, frequency of the class 40-60 will be divided by 4 and so on.

Example 14. *Draw the histogram for the following data :*

Variable	*Frequency*	*Variable*	*Frequency*
100-110	*11*	*140-150*	*33*
110-120	*28*	*150-160*	*20*
120-130	*36*	*160-170*	*8*
130-140	*49*		

Solution.

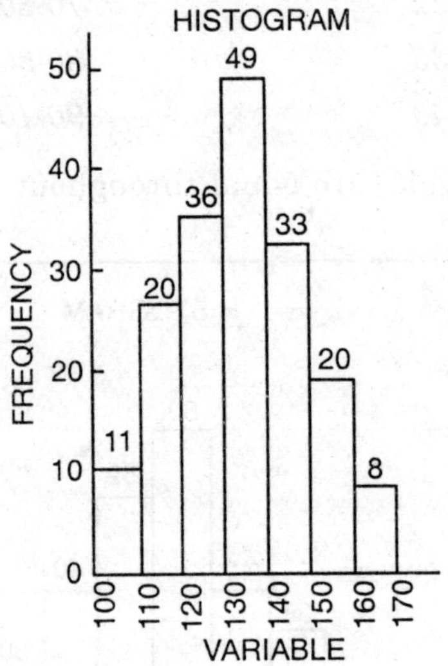

3.5.2. Frequency Polygon

Frequency polygon is another device of graphic presentation of a frequency distribution (continuous grouped or discrete grouped).

(*a*) **Discrete frequency distribution.** In case of discrete frequency distribution, frequency polygon is obtained on plotting the frequencies on the variable axis (*Y*-axis) against the corresponding values of the variable on the horizontal axis (*X*-axis) and joining the points so obtained by straight lines.

Example 15. *The following data show the number of accidents sustained by 313 drivers of a public utility company over a period of 5 years.*

Number of accidents (*x*) :	0	1	2	3	4	5	6	7	8	9	10	11	(= *X*)
Number of drivers (*f*) :	80	44	68	41	25	20	13	7	5	4	3	2	(= *f*)

Draw the frequency polygon.

Solution. See Fig. 1.

(*b*) **Continuous frequency distribution.** In case of grouped continuous frequency distribution, frequency polygon may be drawn in two ways.

Case (*i*) *From histogram.* First draw the histogram of the given frequency distribution as just explained. Now join the mid-points of the tops (upper horizontal sides) of the adjacent rectangles of the histogram by straight line graph. It is necessary to close the polygon at both ends by extending them to the base line such that it meets the *X*-axis at the mid-points of two hypothetical classes, *viz.*, the class before the first class and the class after the last class, at both the ends each with frequency zero.

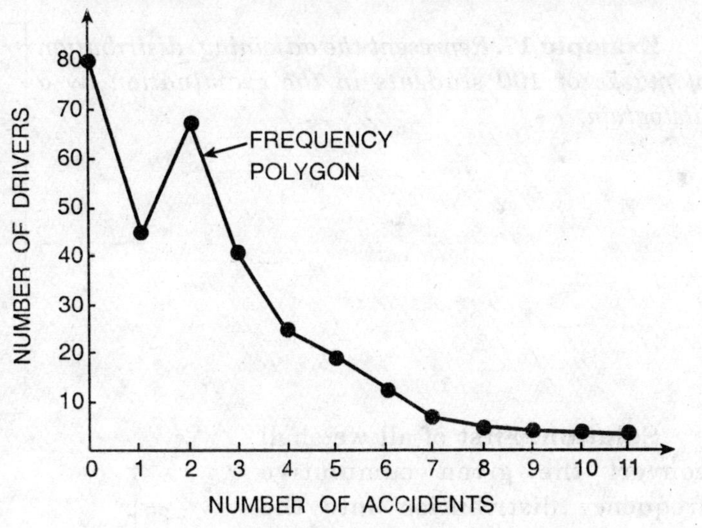

Fig. 1

Example 16. *Draw histogram for the following frequency distribution and hence frequency polygon.*

Class :	*10–20*	*20–30*	*30–40*	*40–50*	*50–60*	*60–70*	*70–80*
Frequency :	*12*	*30*	*35*	*65*	*45*	*25*	*18*

Solution.

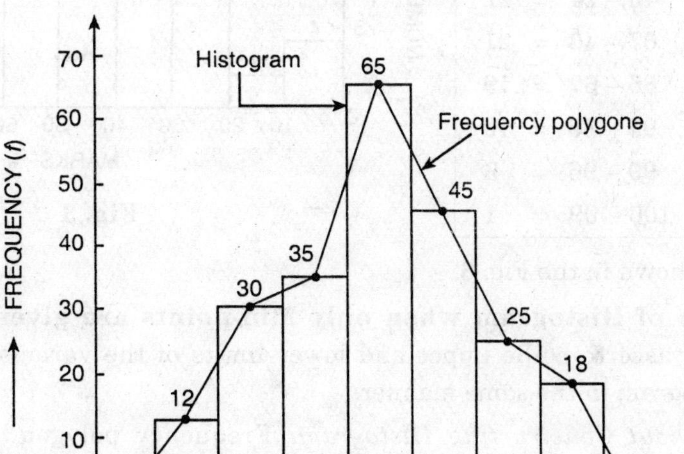

Fig. 2

In this cases two classes 0–10 and 80–90 each with frequency 0 are added. Thus "Histogram" extends from $X = 0$ to $X = 90$ then mid points of upper horizontal lines of rectangles of "Histogram" are joined.

Example 17. *Represent the adjoining distribution of marks of 100 students in the examination by a histogram.*

Marks obtained	*No. of students*
Less than 10	*4*
Less than 20	*6*
Less than 30	*24*
Less than 40	*46*
Less than 50	*67*
Less than 60	*86*
Less than 70	*96*
Less than 80	*99*
Less than 90	*100*

Solution. First of all we shall convert the given cumulative frequency distribution into the frequency distribution of marks as given in the following table.

Marks	*No. of students*
0–10	4
10–20	6 – 4 = 2
20–30	24 – 6 = 18
30–40	46 – 24 = 22
40–50	67 – 46 = 21
50–60	86 – 67 = 19
60–70	96 – 86 = 10
70–80	99 – 96 = 3
80–90	100 – 99 = 1

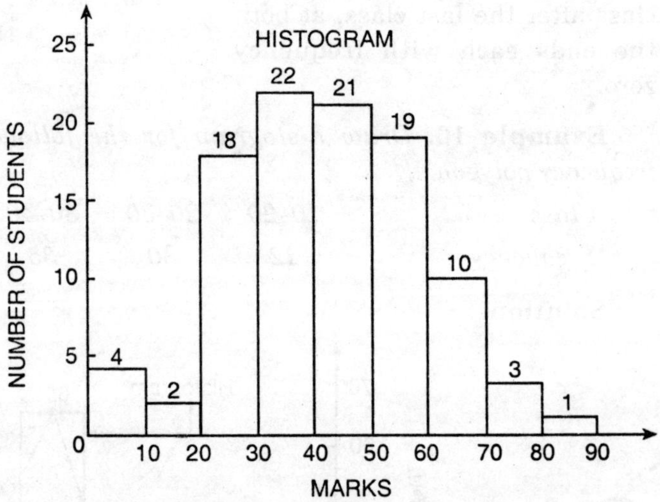

Fig. 3

Histogram is shown in the Fig. 3.

Construction of Histogram when only Mid-points are given. When only mid-points are given, ascertain the upper and lower limits of the various classes and then construct the histogram in the same manner.

Case (*ii*) *Without Constructing Histogram.* Frequency polygon of a grouped or continuous frequency distribution is a straight line graph which can also be constructed directly without drawing the histogram.

This is drawn the same way as it is done for discrete frequency distribution. In this case *X*-values are mid points of the classes (After adding two classes at each end of frequency distribution with zero frequencies). Let $x_1, x_2, x_3, \ldots\ldots, x_k$ are mid values of the classes and $f_1, f_2, \ldots\ldots, f_k$ are their corresponding frequencies where $f_1 = 0$ and $f_k = 0$ (these are frequencies of two hypothetical classes added on each end. Then points (x_1, f_1), (x_2, f_2), ..., (x_k, f_k) are plotted and which are joined by straight lines to get frequency polygon.

Example 18. *Draw frequency polygon of previous example without drawing "Histiogram"*

Solution. After adding two classes the frequency distribution is

Class	*0–10*	*10–20*	*20–30*	*30–40*	*40–50*	*50–60*	*60–70*	*70–80*	*80–90*
f	*0*	*12*	*30*	*35*	*65*	*45*	*25*	*18*	*0*
Mid value (X)	*5*	*15*	*25*	*35*	*45*	*55*	*65*	*75*	*85*

The points (5, 0), (15, 12), (25, 30), (35, 35), (45, 65), (55, 45), (65, 25), (75, 18), (85, 0) are plotted and joined by straight lines to get "frequency polygon" as shown in adjoining figure.

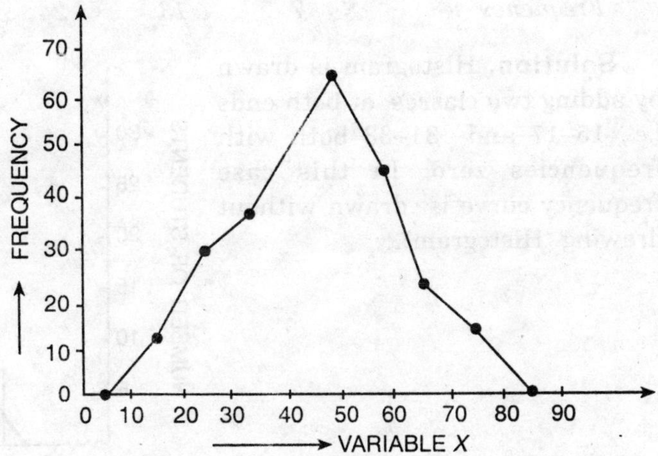

Fig. 4

3.5.3. Frequency Curve

A frequency curve is a smooth free hand curve drawn through the vertices of a frequency polygon. The object of smoothing of the frequency polygon is to eliminate, as far as possible, the random or erratic fluctuations that might be present in the data. The area enclosed by the frequency curve is same as that of the histogram or frequency polygon but its shape is smooth one and not with sharp edges. Frequency curve may be regarded as a limiting form of the frequency polygon as the number of observations (total frequency) becomes very large and the class intervals are made smaller and smaller.

Remarks 1. Smoothing should be done very carefully so that the curve looks as regular as possible and sudden and sharp turns should be avoided. In case of the data pertaining to natural phenomenon like tossing of a coin or throwing of a dice the smoothing can be conveniently done because such data generally give rise to symmetrical curves. However, for the data relating to social, economic or business phenomenon, smoothing cannot be done effectively as such data usually give rise to skewed (asymmetrical) curves. In fact, it is desirable to attempt a frequency curve if we have sufficient reasons to believe that the frequency distribution under study is fairly regular. It is futile to attempt a frequency curve for an irregular distribution. In general, frequency curves should be attempted when the distributions are continuous.

2. We have already seen that a frequency polygon can be drawn with or without a histogram. However, to obtain an ideal frequency curve for a given frequency distribution, it is desirable to proceed in a logical sequence, *viz.*, first draw a histogram, then a frequency polygon and finally a frequency curve, because in the absence of a histogram the smoothing of the frequency polygon cannot be done properly. As discussed in frequency polygon, the frequency curve should also be extended to the base on both sides of the histogram so that the area under the frequency curve represents the total frequency of the distribution.

Example 19. *Draw a frequency curve for the following distribution :*

Age (Yrs.) :	*17–19*	*19–21*	*21–23*	*23–25*	*25–27*	*27–29*	*29–31*
Frequency :	*7*	*13*	*24*	*30*	*22*	*15*	*6*

Solution. Histogram is drawn by adding two classes at both ends *i.e.,* 15–17 and 31–33 both with frequencies zero. In this case frequency curve is drawn without drawing "Histogram".

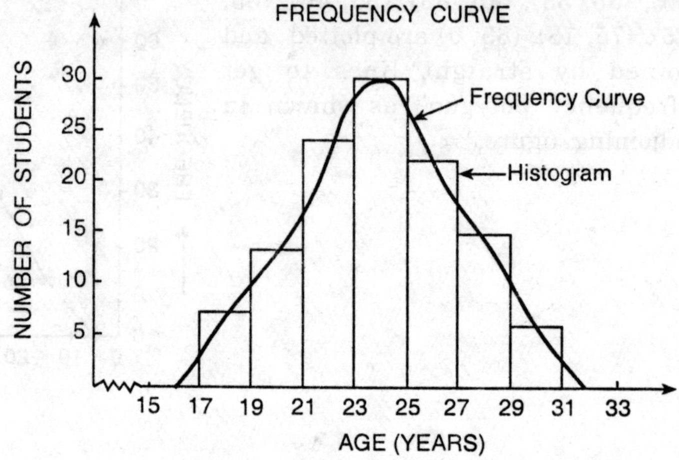

Fig. 1

Example 20. *Given below is the frequency distribution of monthly wages in (₹ 000) of 67 employees of a company. Draw histogram, frequency polygon and frequency curve of the distribution.*

Wages (₹ 000)	*30–40*	*40–50*	*50–60*	*60–70*	*70–80*	*80–90*	*90–100*	*100–110*
No. of employees (Total 67)	*2*	*5*	*8*	*12*	*18*	*15*	*4*	*3*

Solution.

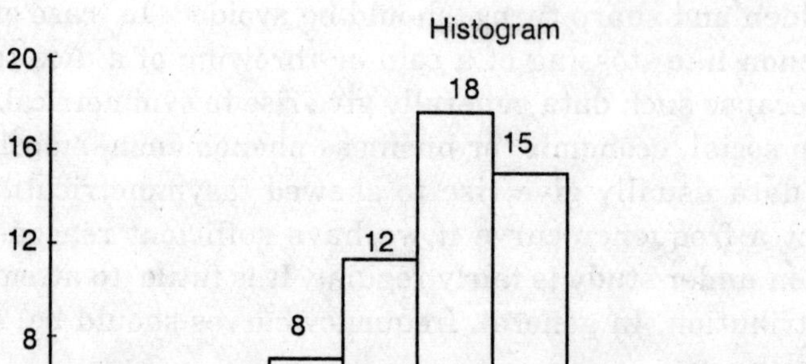

Frequency polygon is obtained by taking mid-points of class intervals which are shown on X-axis and corresponding frequencies on Y-axis. Two points on extreme ends (25, 0) and (115, 0) are added.

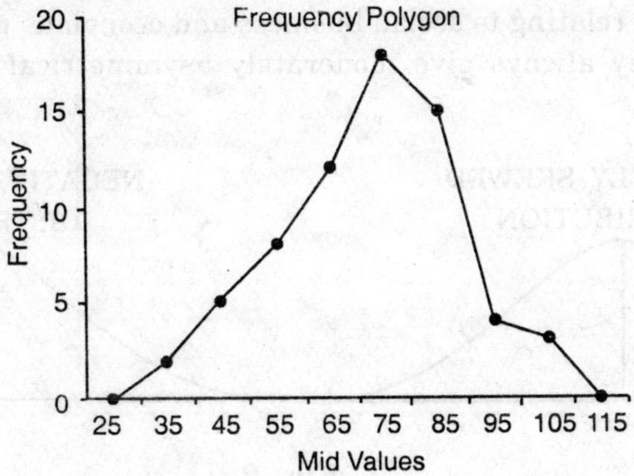

Frequency polygon is replaced by smooth curve which is known as frequency curve.

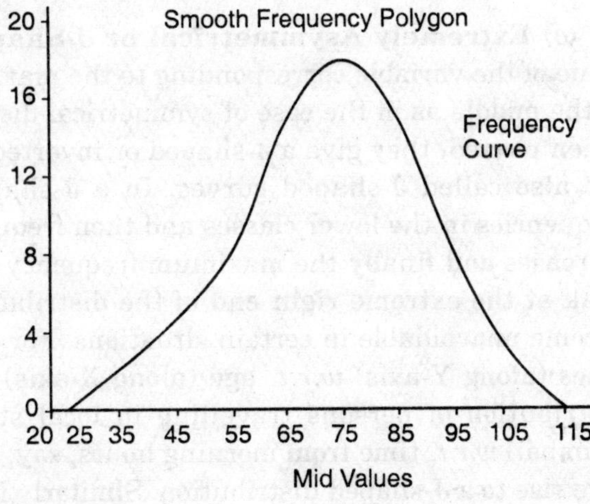

3.6 SOME OF TYPICAL FREQUENCY CURVES

(*a*) Symmetrical curve (like normal curve which we describe in a chapter later).

Normal curve, generally describes the data relating to natural phenomenon like tossing of a coin, throwing of a dice, etc. Most of the data relating to psychological and educational statistics also give rise to normal curve.

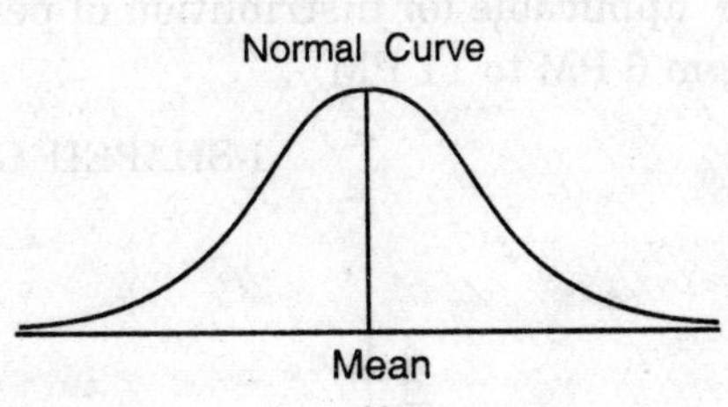

Fig. 1

(*b*) **Moderately Asymmetrical (Skewed) Frequency Curves.** A frequency curve is said to be skewed (asymmetrical) if it is not symmetrical. Such curves are stretched more to one side than to the other. If the curve is stretched more to the right (*i.e.,* it has a longer tail towards the right), it is said to be *positively skewed* and if it is stretched more to the left (*i.e.,* has a longer tail towards the left), it is said to be *negatively skewed.* Thus, in a positively skewed distribution, most of the frequencies are associated with smaller values of the variable and in a negatively skewed distribution most of the frequencies are associated with larger values of the variable. The following figures show positively skewed and negatively skewed distributions.

However, the data relating to social, business and economic phenomena do not conform to normal curve. They always give moderately asymmetrical (slightly skewed) curves discussed below.

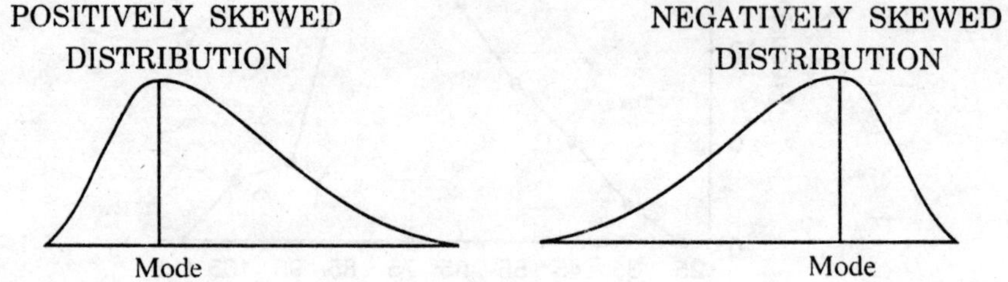

Fig. 2

(*c*) **Extremely Asymmetrical or J-Shaped Curves.** The distributions in which the value of the variable corresponding to the maximum frequency is at one of the ends (and not in the middle as in the case of symmetrical distributions), give rise to highly skewed curves. When plotted, they give a J-shaped or inverted J-shaped curve and accordingly such curves are also called J-shaped curves. In a J-shaped curve, the distribution starts with low frequencies in the lower classes and then frequencies increase steadily as the variable value increases and finally the maximum frequency is attained in the last class thus exhibiting a peak at the extreme right end of the distribution. Such curves are not regular curves but become unavoidable in certain situations. For example, the distribution of mortality (death) rates (along Y-axis) *w.r.t.* age (along X-axis) after ignoring the accidental deaths; or the distribution of persons travelling in local state buses, (*e.g.*, DTC in Delhi or BEST in Mumbai) *w.r.t.* time from morning hours, say, 5 A.M. to peak traffic hours, say, 10 A.M. will give rise to a J-shaped distribution. Similarly in an invested J-shaped curve the frequencies keep on decreasing as X increases (thus maximum is attained in the beginning). This will be applicable for distribution of persons travelling in local state buses in evening hours say from 6 PM to 11 PM

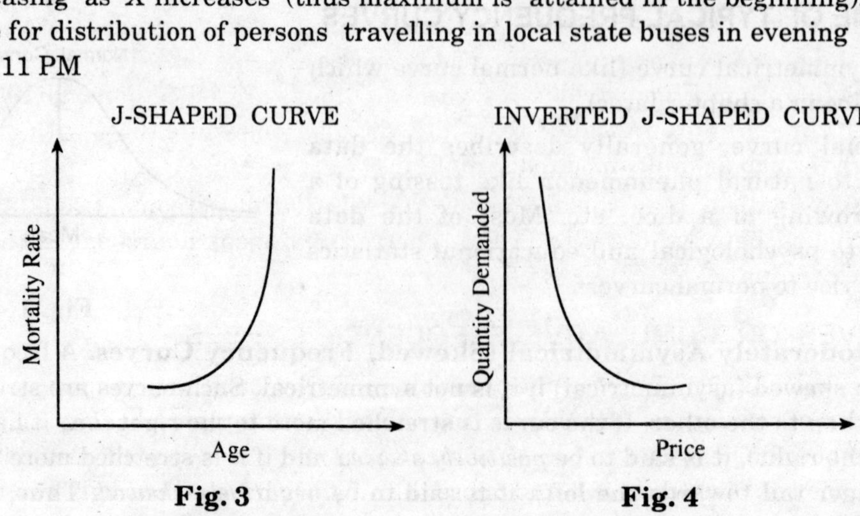

Fig. 3 **Fig. 4**

(*d*) **U-Curve.** The frequency distributions in which the maximum frequency occurs at the extremes (*i.e.,* both ends) of the range and the frequency keeps on falling symmetrically (about the middle), the minimum frequency being attained at the centre give rise to a U-shaped curve. In this type of distribution, most of values are associated with the values of the variable at the extremes *i.e.,* with smaller and larger values whereas smaller frequencies are associated with the intermediate values, the central value having the minimum frequency. The distribution of persons travelling in local state buses between morning and evening peak hours will give, more or less, a U-shaped curve shown in Fig. 5.

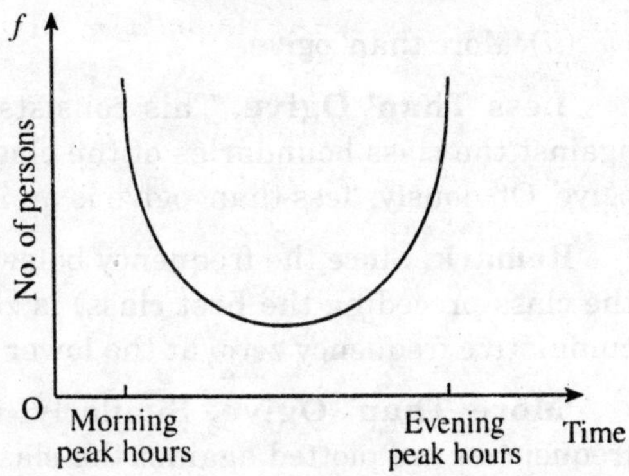

Fig. 5.

(*e*) **Mixed Curves.** Most of the distributions are either symmetrical (as in (*a*)) or near symmetrical (as in '*b*') where it is observed that highest concentration of the frequencies in the centre or near centre. But sometimes, though very rarely, we come across certain distributions in which maximum frequency is attained at two or more points in an irregular manner as shown in Fig. 6.

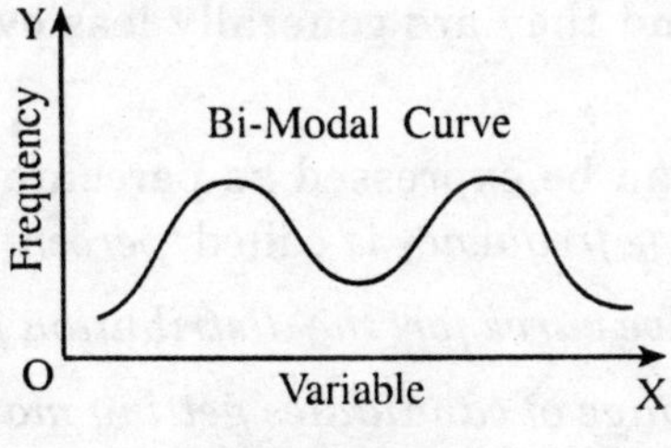

Fig. 6 (*a*)

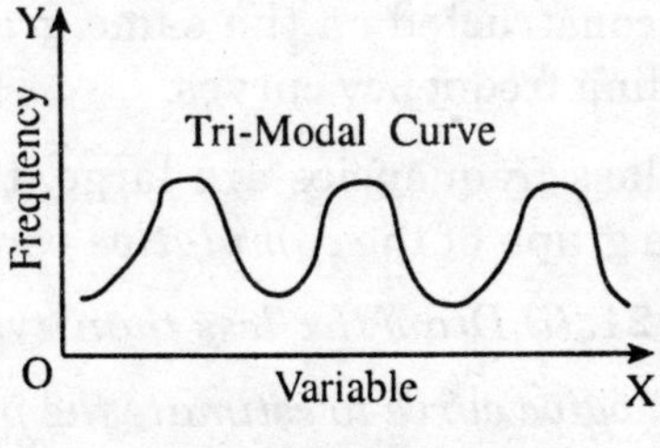

Fig. 6 (*b*)

Such curves are obtained in a distribution where as the value of the variable increases, the frequencies increase and decrease, then again increase and decrease in an irregular manner; the phenomenon may be repeated twice or thrice as shown in the above diagrams or even more than that. The distributions with two humps are called bi-modal distributions and those with three humps are called tri-modal distributions while those with more than three humps are termed as multi-modal distributions.

Fig. 6 (*a*) will display the frequency distribution of persons travelling in buses in different hours between 6 AM to 11 PM. There are to peak hours one in the morning and one in the evening .

3.7 OGIVES OR CUMULATIVE FREQUENCY CURVES

Ogive, pronounced as "ojive", is a graphic presentation of the cumulative frequency (*c.f.*) distribution of *continuous* variable. It consists in plotting the *c.f.* (along the Y-axis) against the class boundaries (along X-axis). Since there are two types of cumulative frequency distributions *viz.,* 'less than' *c.f.* and 'more than' *c.f.* we have accordingly two types of ogives, *viz.,* (*i*) 'Less than' ogive.

(*ii*) 'More than' ogive.

'Less Than' Ogive. This consists in plotting the 'less than' cumulative frequencies against the class boundaries of the classes. The points so obtained are joined by 'less than' ogive. Obviously, 'less than' ogive is an increasing curve, sloping upwards from left to right.

Remark. Since the frequency below the lower limit of the first class (*i.e.,* upper limit of the class preceding the first class) is zero, the ogive curve should start on the left with a cumulative frequency zero at the lower boundary of the first class.

'More Than' Ogive. Similarly, in 'more than' ogive, the 'more than' cumulative frequencies are plotted against the class boundaries of the respective classes. The points so obtained are joined to give 'more than' ogive. 'More than' ogive is a decreasing curve and slopes downwards from left to right.

Remark 1. Ogives are particularly useful for graphic computation of *partition values, viz.*, Median, Quartiles, Deciles, Percentiles, etc. They can also be used to determine graphically the number or proportion of observations below or above a given value of the variable or lying between certain interval of the values of the variable.

2. Ogives can be used with advantage over frequency curves for comparative study of two or more distributions because like frequency curves, for each of the distributions different ogives can be constructed on the same graph and they are generally less overlapping than the corresponding frequency curves.

3. If the class frequencies are large, they can be expressed as percentages of the total frequency. The graph of the *cumulative percentage frequency* is called '*percentile curve*'.

Example 21. *(i) Draw the 'less than' type ogive curve for the distribution given below.*

(ii) Use the ogive curve to estimate the percentage of candidates getting marks 45 or less.

FREQUENCY DISTRIBUTION OF MARKS OF STUDENTS

Marks	*No. of candidates* (*f*)
0–10	2
10–20	3
20–30	6
30–40	11
40–50	12
50–60	15
60–70	10
70–80	7
80–90	4
Total	70

Solution. "Less than" cumulative distribution as obtained from is as follows :

X less than	*c.f.*
0	0
10	2
20	2 + 3 = 5
30	5 + 6 = 11
40	11 + 11 = 22
50	22 + 12 = 34
60	34 + 15 = 49
70	49 + 10 = 59
80	59 + 7 = 66
90	66 + 4 = 70

"Less than" Ogive is obtained by plotting the points (0, 0) (10, 2), (20, 5), ... (90, 70) as obtained in "Less than" cumulative distribution.

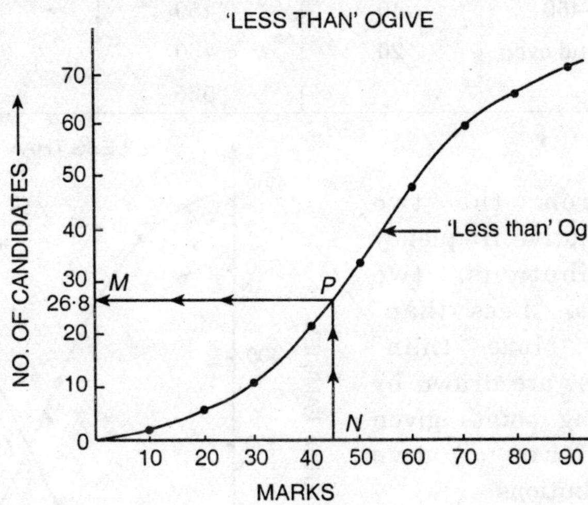

Fig. 1

(*iii*) To estimate the number of candidates getting marks 45 or less, draw a perpendicular to the X-axis (representing marks) at $x = 45$ *i.e.*, from *N* meeting the 'less than' ogive at point P. From P draw a perpendicular PM on the Y-axis (representing number of candidates). Then from the graph OM = 26·8 (approx.) ≃ 27 is the number of candidates getting score 45 or less. Hence, the percentage of candidates getting 45 or less marks is given by :

$$\frac{27}{70} \times 100 = 38{\cdot}57.$$

Example 22. *The following table gives the distribution of monthly income of 600 families in a certain city.*

Monthly Income ('00 ₹)	*Below 75*	*75—150*	*150—225*	*225—300*	*300—375*	*375—450*	*450 and over*
No. of Families	*60*	*170*	*200*	*60*	*50*	*40*	*20*

Draw a 'less than' and a 'more than' ogive curve for the above data on the same graph.

Solution. For drawing the 'less than' and 'more than' ogive we convert the given distribution into 'less than' and 'more than' cumulative frequencies (*c.f.*) as given in the following table.

		"Less than" cumulative frequency		*"More than" Cumulative Frequency*	
Class	*Frequency f*	*X Less than*	*Frequency (c.f.)*	*X more than*	*Frequency (c.f.)*
	0	0	0	0	600
Below 75	60	75	60	75	540
75—150	170	150	230	150	370
150—225	200	225	430	225	170
225—300	60	300	490	300	110

300—375	50	375	540	375	60
375—450	40	450	580	450	20
450 and over	20	450	600	450	0
		525		525	

From the two cumulative frequency distributions, two ogives, "Less than" and "More than" ogives are drawn by plotting points given by the two distributions

X-value of the point of intersection *M* of two ogives is median (which will be discussed later) which is nearly 175.

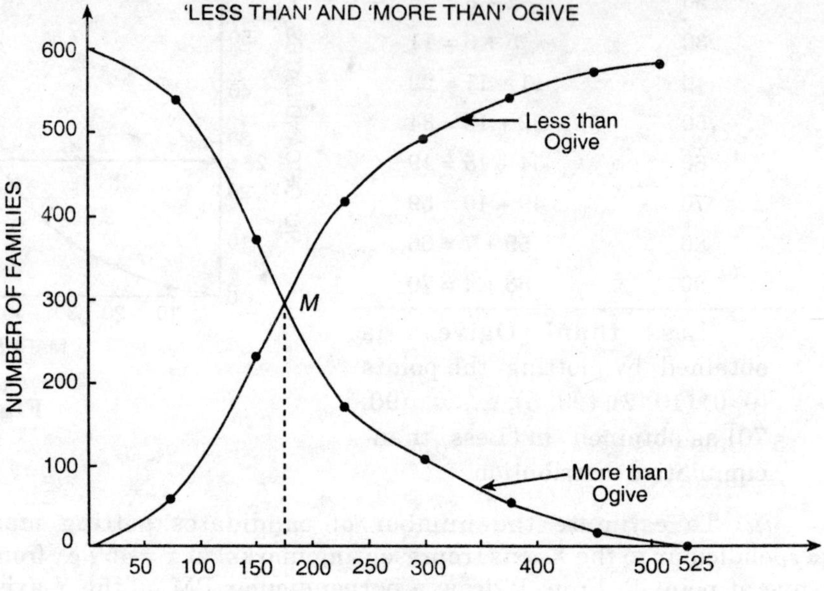

Fig. 2

EXERCISE 3.1

1. Draw histogram and frequency polygon to present the following data :

Income (₹)	100–149	150–199	200–249	250–299
No. of individuals	21	32	52	105
Income (₹)	300–349	350–399	400–449	450–499
No. of Individuals	62	43	18	9

2. From the following data, construct (*i*) Frequency Histogram, (*ii*) Frequency polygon, and (*iii*) Frequency Curve :

Wages groups ('00 ₹)	0-10	10-20	20-30	30-40	40-50	50-60	60-70	70-80	80-90
No. of Workers :	2	4	11	15	25	18	15	4	3

3. The following table gives the scholastic aptitude scrores of the 50 departmental students of a certain department in a certain university :

345	530	556	354	590	395	515	479	494	420
563	444	629	440	485	505	604	490	445	605
402	406	730	506	516	472	475	610	586	523
691	520	465	468	545	624	582	570	578	505
523	575	420	605	527	461	440	585	420	384

(*i*) Construct a frequency distribution table with appropriate class limits and class boundaries. (Take the length of the class equal to 30 units).

(*ii*) Draw histogram to represent the above frequency distribution.

4. The data below give the yearly profits (in thousand rupees) of two companies *A* and *B* :

Profits (in '000 ₹)

Year	*Company A*	*Company B*
1999-00	120	90
2000-01	135	95
2001-02	140	108
2002-03	160	120
2003-04	175	130

[**Ans.** Multiple bar diagram]

Represent the data by means of a suitable diagram.

5. Below is given the frequency distribution of weekly wages of 100 workers in a factory :

Monthly wages (₹)	*No. of workers*	*Monthly wages* (₹)	*No. of workers*
3000-3500	3	5500-6000	10
3500-4000	5	6000-6500	8
4000-4500	12	6500-7000	5
4500-5000	23	7000-7500	3
5000-5500	31		

Draw the ogive for the distribution.

6. Present the following information in a suitable tabular form supplying the figures not directly given :

"In 2002, out of a total 2,000 workers in a factory 1,550 were members of a trade union. The number of women workers employed was 250, out of which 200 did not belong to any trade union."

"In 2003, the number of union workers was 1,725 of which 1,600 ware men. The number of non-union workers was 380 among which 155 were women."

7. The proprietor of Goodwill Tyres Co. kept a record of the number of car tyres of each brand that were sold during 2003-04. He arranged the data as follows :

Brand	*No. of Tyres Sold*
Dunlop	280
Modi	270
Firestone	200

Ceat	190
Goodyear	160
J.K.	100

(*a*) What kind of a distribution is this?

(*b*) Present the data by a suitable diagram/graph.

[**Ans.** Qualitative, sample bar diagram]

8. Draw a suitable diagram to represent the following information :

	Company A	*Company B*
Selling price	12,000	8,000
Raw materials	5,000	6,000
Direct Wages	4,000	3,200
Factory and office on cost	1,000	800

9. A company dealing in 60 products, in the course of establishing an inventory control system, classified products according to price as shown in the frequency table below :

(In hundreds of ₹)	:	3-5	6-8	9-11	12-14	15-17	18-20	21-23
No. of items	:	6	8	10	20	8	5	3

Prepare more than ogive for the distribution on a graph paper. Use this graph to determine 20th and 80th percentiles.

10. Represent the following data by a suitable diagram :

Year	1999	2000	2001	2002	2003	2004
Sale of steel (in thousand tonnes)	8	8.8	9.2	10.2	7.6	12.5

[**Ans.** Simple bar diagram]

11. Represent the following data by a suitable diagram :

Year	1999-2000	2000-01	2001-02	2002-03	2003-04	2004-05
Profit before taxes (₹ lakhs)	28	29.4	30.2	27	32.5	40.6

[**Ans.** Simple bar diagram]

12. Represent the following data by a sub-division bar diagram :

(in lakhs for ₹)

Year	2001-02	2002-03	2003-04
Gross Income	460	482	552
Gross expenditure	400	450	500
Net Income	60	32	22

13. Represent the following information diagrammatically :

Factory	*Wages* (₹)	*Material* (₹)	*Other costs* (₹)	*Profits* (₹)	*No. of Units* (₹)
A	3,000	5,000	1,000	1,000	1,000
B	2,000	3,000	800	500	700

14. Represent the following data of the distribution of expenditure of a company by pie diagram :

	(₹ lakhs)
Raw materials	1,689
Taxes	582
Manufacturing expenses	543
Employees	470
Other expenses	286
Depreciation	94
Dividends	75
Retained income	51
	3,790

□□□

4

Measures of Central Tendency

CHAPTER OUTLINE

4.1 INTRODUCTION

One of the most important objectives of statistical analysis is to get one single value that describes the characteristic of the entire mass of unwieldy data and which has tendency to lie in the centre of data. Such a value is called the central value or an 'average' or the expected value of the variable. The word average is very commonly used in day-to-day conversation. For example, we often talk of average student in a class, average height or life of an Indian, average income, etc. When we say 'he is an average student' what it means is that he is neither very good nor very bad, just a mediocre type of student. However, in statistics the term average has a different meaning.

AVERAGE DEFINED

The word 'average' has been defined differently by various authors. Some important definitions are given below:

- "An average is a single value selected from a group of values to represent them in some way–a value which is supposed to stand for whole group, of which it is a part, as typical of all the values in the group." **—A.E. Waugh**
- "An average is a typical value in the sense that it is sometimes employed to represent all the individual values in a series or of a variable." **—Ya-Lun Chou**
- "An average value is a single value within the range of the data that is used to represent all of the values in the series. Since an average is somewhere within the range of the data, it is also called a measure of central value." **—Croxton & Cowden**

It is clear from the above definitions that an average is a single value that represents a group of values. Such a value is of great significance because it depicts the characteristic of the whole group. Since an average represents the entire data, its value lies somewhere in between the two extremes. *i.e.,* the largest and the smallest items. For this reason an average is frequently referred to as a measure of central tendency.

4.2 OBJECTIVES OF AVERAGING

There are two main objectives of the study of averages:

(*i*) *To get single value that describes the characteristic of the entice group.* Measures of central value, by condensing the mass of data in one single value, enable us to get a bird's-eye view of the entire data. Thus one value can represent thousands, lakhs and even millions of values. For example, it is impossible to remember the individual incomes of millions of earning people of India and even if one could do it there is hardly any use. But if the average income is obtained by dividing the total national income by total population we get one single value that represents the entire population. Such a figure would throw light on the standard of living of an average Indian.

(*ii*) *To Facilitate Comparison.* Measures of central value, by reducing the mass of data to one single figure, enable comparison to be made. Comparisons can be made either at a point of time or over a period of time. For example, we can compare the percentage results of the students of different colleges in a certain examination. say, B.Com. for 2005, and thereby conclude which college is the best or we can compare the pass percentage of the same college for different time periods and thereby conclude as to whether the results are improving or deteriorating. Such comparisons are of immense help in framing suitable and timely policies. For example, if the pass percentage of students in College A in B.Com. was 80 in 2004 and 75 in 2005, the authorities have sufficient reason for investigating the possible cause of the deterioration in results.

REQUISITES OF A GOOD AVERAGE

Since an average is a single value representing a group of values, it is desired that such a value satisfies the following properties:

(*i*) *Easy to Understand.* Since statistical methods are designed to simplify complexity, it is desirable that an average be such that can be readily understood; otherwise, its use is bound to be very limited.

(*ii*) *Simple to Compute.* An average should not only be easy to understand but also simple to compute so that it can be used widely. However, though ease of computation is desirable, it should not be sought at the expense of there advantages, *i.e.,* if in the interest of greater accuracy, use of a more difficult average is desirable, one should prefer that.

(*iii*) *Based on all the Items.* The average should depend upon each and every item of the series so that if any of the items is dropped the average itself is altered. For example, the arithmetic mean of 10, 20, 30, 40, 50, is $\frac{10 + 20 + 30 + 40 + 50}{5} = \frac{150}{5} = 30$. If we drop one item, say, 50, the arithmetic mean would be = 25.

(*iv*) *Not be unduly Affected by Extreme Observations.* Although each and every item should influence the value of the average, none of the items should influence it unduly. If one or two very small or very large items unduly affect the average, *i.e.,* either increase its value or reduce its value, the average cannot be really typical of the entire series. In other words, extremes may distort the average and reduce its usefulness.

(*v*) *Rigidly Defined.* An average should be properly defined so that it has one and only one interpretation. It should preferably be defined by algebraic formula so that if different people compute the average from the same figures they all get the same answer (barring arithmetical mistakes). The average should not depend upon the personal prejudice and bias of the investigator, otherwise the results can be misleading.

(*vi*) *Capable of Further Algebraic Treatment.* We should prefer to have an average that could be used for further statistical computations so that its utility is enhanced. For example, if we are given the data about the average income and number of employees of two or more factories, we should be able to compute the combined average.

(*vii*) *Sampling Stability.* Last, but not the least, we should prefer to get a value which has what the statisticians call 'sampling stability'. This means that if we pick 10 different groups of college students and compute the average of each group, we should expect to get approximately the same value. It does not mean, however, that there can be no difference in the values of different samples. There may be some difference but those samples in which this difference (technically called sampling fluctuation) is less are considered better than those in which this difference is more.

4.3 VARIOUS MEASURE OF CENTRAL TENDENCY

The following are the important measures of central tendency :

- Arithmetic mean; (*i*) simple, and (*ii*) weighted.
- Median
- Mode
- Geometric mean
- Harmonic mean

Besides these, are less important averages like moving average, progressive average, etc. These average have a very limited field of application and are, therefore, not so popular.

4.4 ARITHMETIC MEAN (A.M.)

The most popular and widely used measure of representing the entire data by one value is what most laymen call an 'average' and what the statisticians call the arithmetic mean.

Its value is obtained by adding together all the items and by dividing this total by the number of items. Arithmetic mean may either be

(*i*) simple arithmetic mean, or

(*ii*) weighted arithmetic mean.

4.4.1. Calculation of Simple Arithmetic Mean—Individual Observations (Ungrouped data)

The process of computing mean in case of individual observations (*i.e.*, where frequencies are not given) is very simple. Add together the various values of the variable and divide the total by the number of items. Symbolically :

$$\overline{X} = \frac{X_1 + X_2 + X_3 + \ldots + X_n}{N} \quad \text{or} \quad \overline{X} = \frac{\Sigma X}{N} \; [\Sigma X \text{ is read as sigma } X]$$

Here $\overline{X}$ = Arithmetic Mean, ΣX = Sum of all the values of the variable X, *i.e.*, $X_1, X_2, X_3, \ldots, X_n$; N = Number of observations.

Steps. The formula involves two steps in calculating mean :

(*i*) Add together all the values of the variable X and obtain the total, *i.e.*, ΣX.

(*ii*) Divide this total by the number of the observations, *i.e.*, N.

Example 1. *The following table gives the monthly income of 10 employees in an office.*

Income (₹)	*1,780*	*1,760*	*1,690*	*1,750*	*1,840*	*1,920*	*1,100*	*1,810*	*1,050*	*1,950*

The variable X is income of employee. Calculate the arithmetic mean of incomes.

Solution.

CALCULATION OF ARITHMETIC MEAN

Employee	*Monthly Income (₹) X*	*Employee*	*Monthly Income (₹) X*
1	1,780	6	1,920
2	1,760	7	1,100
3	1,690	8	1,810
4	1,750	9	1,050
5	1,840	10	1,950
		$N = 10$	$\Sigma X = 16,650$

$$\overline{X} = \frac{\Sigma X}{N} \; . \; \Sigma X = 16,650, N = 10$$

$$\overline{X} = \frac{16,50}{10} = 1,665 = \text{Average income of an employee.}$$

4.4.2. Short-Cut Methods for calculating A.M.

There are two short cut methods :

(*i*) Deviation method (*ii*) Step Deviation Method

(*i*) *Deviation Method* : We define another variable d from X variable by subtracting a constant A (called arbitrary constant or assumed mean) which is a convenient number close to guessed or assumed mean.

i.e. $d = X - A$

where d is called deviation from A.

$$d_1 = X_1 - A$$
$$d_2 = X_2 - A$$
$$d_3 = X_3 - A$$
$$\vdots \quad \vdots \quad \vdots$$
$$d_n = X_n - A$$

Thus $\Sigma d = \Sigma X - nA$

Thus $\dfrac{\Sigma d}{n} = \dfrac{\Sigma X}{n} - A = \overline{X} - A$

$$\Rightarrow \quad \overline{X} = A + \frac{\Sigma d}{n} \qquad \ldots(i)$$

This implies if A is subtracted from all values of X to get d. Then A is added back to A.M. of d. Obviously d values become small and hence calculations become simpler.

Example 2. *Calculate A.M. of example of 1 by taking A = 1800*

Solution.

CALCULATION OF ARITHMETIC MEAN

Employee	*Income X*	*d = (X–1800)*
1	1,780	–20
2	1,760	–40
3	1,690	–110
4	1,750	–50
5	1,840	+40
6	1,920	+120
7	1,100	–700
8	1,810	+10
9	1,050	–750
10	1,950	+150
N = 10		*Σd = – 1350*

$$\overline{X} = A + \frac{\Sigma d}{N}$$

$$A = 1800, \Sigma d = -1350. N = 10$$

$$\overline{X} = 1800 - \frac{1,350}{10} = 1,800 - 135 = 1,665.$$

Hence the average income is ₹ 1,665.

(*ii*) *Step Variation Method*. If we find deviations from *A, i.e.,* $d = X - A$ has some common factor we may divide d *by* C (where C is common factor of d values) and denote it by d', *i.e.,* $d' = \dfrac{d}{C} = \dfrac{X - A}{C}$. Thus we get another variable d' which is much smaller than d values. Thus

$$d_1' = \frac{X_1 - A}{C} = \frac{d_1}{C}$$

$$d_2' = \frac{X_2 - A}{C} = \frac{d_2}{C}$$

$$\vdots$$

$$d_n' = \frac{X_n - A}{C} = \frac{d_n}{C}$$

$$\Sigma d' = \frac{1}{C}[\Sigma d]$$

$$= \frac{1}{C}(\Sigma X - nA) \text{ from } (i)$$

$$\Rightarrow \quad \frac{\Sigma d'}{n} = \frac{1}{C}\left(\frac{\Sigma X}{n} - A\right) \text{ (dividing both sides by } n)$$

$$\Rightarrow \quad \frac{C\Sigma d'}{n} = \overline{X} - A$$

$$\Rightarrow \quad \boxed{\overline{X} = A + C\frac{\Sigma d'}{n}} \qquad \ldots(ii)$$

Thus to get $\overline{X}$, $\bar{d}'$ is multiplied by C and then A is added it. (as d' is obtained by dividing d by C and d is obtained by subtracting A from X).

Example 3. *Find A.M. of example I by using*

$$d' = \frac{X - 1800}{10} \text{ [as we see all d's in example 2 are divisible by 10]}$$

Solution.

X	$d = X - 1800$	$d' = \frac{X - 1800}{10}$
1780	–20	–2
1760	–40	–4
1690	–110	–11
1750	–50	–5
1840	40	4
1920	120	12
1100	–700	–70
1810	10	1
1050	–750	750
1950	150	15
		$-135 = \Sigma d'$

$$\overline{X} = A + C\frac{\Sigma d'}{n}$$

$$= 1800 + 10\left(\frac{-135}{10}\right) \qquad [A = 1800, C = 10]$$

$$= 1665$$

4.4.2. Arithmetic Mean in case of discrete frequency distribution

(i) Direct Method

If X_1 has frequency f_1 then total of all these values of X_1 repeated f_1 times is equal to f_1X_1. Thus fX = Total of a class where X values are repeated f time.

Thus $\Sigma X = f_1X_1 + f_2X_2 + f_2X_2 + \text{.........} + f_kX_k$

and n = Total no. of units $= f_1 + f_2 + \ldots + f_k$

$$\text{Thus} \quad \overline{X} = \frac{\Sigma X}{n} = \frac{\Sigma fX}{\Sigma f}$$

Format of calculation will be as follows :

X	f	fX
X_1	f_1	f_1X_1
X_2	f_2	f_2X_2
X_3	f_3	f_3X_3
	$\Sigma f = n$	$\Sigma X = \Sigma fX$

$$\text{Thus } \overline{X} = \frac{\Sigma fX}{\Sigma f}$$

Example 4. *From the following data of the marks obtained by 60 students of a class. Calculate the arithmetic mean :*

Marks	*No. of Students*	*Marks*	*No. of Students*
20	8	50	10
30	12	60	6
40	20	70	4

Solution. Let the marks be denoted by X and the number of students by f.

CALCULATION OF ARITHMETIC MEAN

Marks X	*No. of students* f	fX
20	8	160
30	12	360
40	20	800
50	10	500
60	6	360
70	4	280
	$n = 60 = \Sigma f$	$\Sigma fX = 2{,}460$

$$\overline{X} = \frac{\Sigma fX}{n} = \frac{2{,}460}{60} = 41$$

Hence the average marks = 41.

Short-Cut Method.

(i) Deviation Method: As in case of ungrouped data we have $\overline{X} = A + \frac{\Sigma d}{n}$ where $d = X - A$.

Same way in case of discrete frequency distribution we have

$$\boxed{\overline{X} = A = \frac{\Sigma fd}{\Sigma f}}$$

Example 5. *Calculate A.M. by deviation method of data given in example 1.*

Solution.

CALCULATION OF ARITHMETIC MEAN

Marks X	*No. of Students* f	*(X – 40)* $= d$	*fd*
20	8	– 20	– 160
30	12	– 10	– 120
40	20	0	0
50	10	+ 10	+ 100
60	6	+ 20	+ 120
70	4	+ 30	+ 120
	$N = 60$		$\Sigma fd = 60$

$$\overline{X} = A + \frac{\Sigma fd}{N} = 40 + \frac{60}{60} = 40 + 1 = 41$$

(ii) Step Deviation Method : As in case of example above d values are divisible by a common factor 10. We divide these values by to make them still smaller so that calculations become easier.

Thus we use step deviation method *i.e.*, $d' = \frac{X - A}{C}$ then (as found earlier)

$$\boxed{\overline{X} = A + C\,\frac{\Sigma fd'}{\Sigma f}}$$

Example 6. *Use "Step deviation" Method to find A.M. of data given in example 1.*

Solution.

X	f	$d = X - 40$	$d' = \frac{X-40}{10}$	fd'
20	8	– 20	– 2	– 16
30	12	– 10	– 1	– 12
40	20	0	0	0
50	10	10	1	10
60	6	20	2	12
70	4	30	3	12
	$\Sigma f = 60 = n$			$\Sigma fd' = 6$

$$\overline{X} = A + C\frac{\Sigma fd'}{\Sigma f} \qquad [A = 40, C = 10]$$

$$= 40 + 10\frac{6}{60} = 40 + 1 = 41$$

which is same as obtained in example 1 and 2.

4.4.3. Calculation of Arithmetic Mean—Continuous Grouped Data

In continuous series, arithmetic mean may be computed by applying any of the following method :

(*i*) Direct method.

(*ii*) Short-cut methods.

Direct Method. When direct method is used

$$\overline{X} = \frac{\Sigma fm}{N} = \frac{\Sigma fX}{\Sigma f}$$

where m/X is mid-points of various classes; f = the frequency of each class : N = the total frequency.

[We assume all the variable value, lying in the particular interval have same value m where m is mid value of the class. Thus continuous frequency distribution changes to discrete frequency distribution with X values equal to m.]

Example 7. *From the following data compute arithmetic mean by direct method:*

Marks	*0-10*	*10-20*	*20-30*	*30-40*	*40-50*	*50-60*
No. of students	*5*	*10*	*25*	*30*	*20*	*10*

Solution.

CALCULATION OF ARITHMETIC MEAN BY DIRECT METHOD

Marks	*Mid-point* m/X	*No. of Students* f	fm/fX
0–10	5	5	25
10–20	15	10	150
20–30	25	25	625
30–40	35	30	1,050
40–50	45	20	900
50–60	55	10	550
		$N = 100$	$\Sigma fm = 3{,}300$ or ΣfX

$$\overline{X} = \frac{\Sigma fm}{N} = \frac{3{,}300}{100} = 33.$$

Short-Cut Method. *i.e.,* Deviation or step deviation methods are same way used as for discrete frequency distribution, *i.e.,* using $d = X—A$ $(= m - A)$ or $d' = \frac{X-A}{C}\left(\text{or } \frac{m-A}{C}\right)$. In this case X is found as mid mark of the class.

$\overline{X} = A + \frac{\Sigma fd}{\Sigma f}$ or $\overline{X} = A + C\frac{\Sigma fd'}{\Sigma f}$. The above example is solved by both the methods.

(*i*) **Deviation Method.**

Class	*f*	*X* *mid point*	*d* $= X - 35$	*fd*
0–10	5	5	– 30	– 150
10–20	10	15	– 10	– 200
20–30	25	25	– 10	– 250
30–40	30	35	0	0
40–50	20	45	10	200
50–60	10	55	20	200
	100 $= \Sigma f$			– 200 $= \Sigma fd$

$$\overline{X} = A + \frac{\Sigma fd}{\Sigma f} = 35 - \frac{200}{100} = 33.$$

Step Deviation Method

In order to simplify the calculations, we can divide the deviations by class intervals. *i.e.*, calculate $(m - A)/i$ and then multiply by i in the formula for getting mean. The formula becomes:

$$\overline{X} = A + \frac{\Sigma fd}{N} \times i$$

In case A is one of X values and i = class interval in case class intervals are same for all classes.

It may be pointed out that when class intervals are unequal we can simplify calculations by taking a common factor. In such a case, we should use $(m - A)/C$ instead of $(m - A)/i$ while making calculations where C is common factor.

Example 8. *From the data of Example 7 compute arithmetic mean by step deviation method.*

Solution.

CALCULATION OF ARITHMETIC MEAN

Marks	*Mid-point 'm'*	*No. of Students f*	*(m - 35) d*	*(m - 35)/10 = d'*	*fd'*
0–10	5	5	–30	–3	–15
10–20	15	10	–20	–2	–20
20–30	25	25	–10	–1	–25
30–40	35	30	0	0	0
40–50	45	20	+10	+1	+20
50–60	55	10	+20	+2	+20
		$N = 100 = \Sigma f$			$\Sigma fd' = -20$

$$\overline{X} = A + \frac{\Sigma fd'}{N} \times i = 35 - \frac{20}{100} \times 10 = 35 - 2 = 33.$$

[**Note :** In case [c = class interval than d' values will be like –3, –2, –1, 0, 1, 2. always, 0 value will correspond when A = one of X values].

Correcting Incorrect A.M. It sometimes happens that due to an oversight or mistake in copying, certain wrong items are taken while calculating mean. The problem is how to find out the correct mean. The process is very simple. From incorrect ΣX deduct wrong items and add correct items and then divide the correct ΣX by the number of observations. The result, so obtained, will give the value of correct mean.

Example 9. *The mean marks of 100 students were found to be 40. Later on, it was discovered that a score of 53 was misread as 83. Find the correct mean corresponding to the correct score.*

Solution. We are given $N = 100, \overline{X} = 40$ (incorrect)

Since $\overline{X} = \frac{\Sigma X}{N}$

Incorrect $\Sigma X = N\overline{X} = 100 \times 40 = 4000$

Correct ΣX = Incorrect ΣX – wrong item + correct item

$= 4000 - 83 + 53 = 3970$

$\therefore$ Correct $\overline{X} = \frac{\text{correct } \Sigma X}{N} = \frac{3970}{100} = 39.7$

Hence the correct average = 39.7.

4.6 PROPERTIES OF A.M.

1. The sum of the deviations of the items from the arithmetic mean (taking signs into account) is always zero, *i.e.*, $\Sigma (X - \overline{X}) = 0$. This would be clear from the following example:

Proof Now $\overline{X} = \frac{\Sigma X}{n} \Rightarrow \Sigma X = n\overline{X}$ we had already shown that $\Sigma (X - A)\ \Sigma X - nA$. Now if $A = \overline{X}$, then $\Sigma(X - \overline{X}) = \Sigma X - n\overline{X} = n\overline{X} - n\overline{X} = 0$.

Verification. Verify this by taking X values as 5, 10, 13, 17, 15.

Now

X	$X - 12 = X - \overline{X}$
5	– 7
10	– 2
13	1
17	5
15	3

$\Sigma X = 60$ $\quad \Sigma(X - 12) = 0$ *i.e.*, $\Sigma X - \overline{X} = 0$.

$\overline{X} = 12$

2. The sum of the squared deviations of the items from arithmetic mean is minimum, that is, less than the sum of the squared deviations of the items from any other value. The following example would verify the point :

Proof of this may be provided in next chapter (measures of dispersion).

Verification : It is done for the above example

X	$X-\overline{X}=X-12$	$(X-\overline{X})^2$	$X-13$	$(X-13)^2$	$(X-11)$	$(X-11)^2$
5	−7	49	−8	64	−6	36
10	−2	4	−3	9	−1	1
13	1	1	0	0	2	4
17	5	25	4	16	6	36
15	3	9	2	4	4	16
$\Sigma X = 60$		88		93		93
$\overline{X} = 12$		$=\Sigma(X-\overline{X})^2$		$=\Sigma(X-13)^2$		$\Sigma(X-11)^2$

Thus it is seen that $\Sigma(X-\overline{X})^2 = \Sigma(X-12)^2 = 88$

and $\Sigma(X-13)^2 = 93$

$\Sigma(X-11)^2 = 93$

Thus it is verified that $\Sigma(X-12)^2 = \Sigma(X-\overline{X})^2$ is minimum.

4.7. Combined mean of two groups, from the means of two groups. Let Mean of group of n_1 units be $\overline{X}_1$ and mean of other groups of n_2 units be $\overline{X}_2$ then combined mean of two groups be $\overline{X}_{12}$ which is given as follows :

$$\overline{X}_{12} = \frac{n_1\overline{X}_1 + n_2\overline{X}_2}{n_1 + n_2}$$

Proof. We know $\Sigma X = n\overline{X}$ (for any group)

Thus sum of values of 1st group $= n_1\overline{X}_1$

Thus sum of values of 2nd group $= n_2\overline{X}_2$

Sum of values of both groups $= n_1\overline{X}_1 + n_2\overline{X}_2$

no. of units in both groups $= n_1 + n_2$

thus mean of both groups together is $\overline{X}_{12}$,

$$\text{where } \overline{X}_{12} = \frac{n_1\overline{X}_1 + n_2\overline{X}_2}{n_1 + n_2}$$

Similarly

If we have to find out the combined mean of three sub-groups the above formula can be extended as follows :

$$\overline{X}_{123} = \frac{N_1\overline{X}_1 + N_2\overline{X}_2 + N_3\overline{X}_3}{N_1 + N_2 + N_3}$$

Example 10. *The mean height of 25 male workers in a factory is 61 inches and the mean height of 35 female workers in the same factory is 58 inches. Find the combined mean height of 60 workers in the factory.*

Solution. $$\overline{X}_{12} = \frac{N_1\overline{X}_1 + N_2\overline{X}_2}{N_1 + N_2}$$

$N_1 = 25$, $\overline{X}_1 = 61$, $N_2 = 35$, $\overline{X}_2 = 58$

$$\overline{X}_{12} = \frac{(25 \times 61) + (35 \times 58)}{25 + 35} = \frac{1525 + 2030}{60} = \frac{3555}{60} = 59.25.$$

Thus the combined mean height of 60 workers is 59.25 inches.

4.8 WEIGHTED ARITHMETIC MEAN

In case of frequency distribution $\overline{X} = \frac{\Sigma fX}{\Sigma f}$

That means that X values of weighted with their frequencies. There are situation where certain values are to be weighted (in this case weight implies relative importance, that means some values will have larger weights than other). For example in school examinations such as periodic, half yearly and annual are held and performance in these examinations are given different weights to get one value, which we call weighted mean which is denoted as $\overline{X}_w$ (weighted mean) and it is defined as

$$\overline{X}_w = \frac{\Sigma WX}{\Sigma W}$$

Example 11. *A train runs for 3 hours at speed of 30 km/hr, 2 hours at a speed of 40 km/hr and 6 minutes at speed of 10 km/hr. Find the average speed.*

Solution. It trains runs at a speed for a longer period, it should have larger weight to find average speed. Thus time is taken as weight

Speed X	*Time (hours)* W	*WX*
30	3	90
40	2	80
10	$\frac{1}{10}$	1
	$\frac{51}{10} = \Sigma W$	$171 = \Sigma WX$

Thus $\overline{X}_w = \frac{\Sigma WX}{\Sigma W}$

$= \frac{171}{51/10}$

$= \frac{1710}{51} = 33.5$

4.9 SECOND MEASURE OF CENTRAL TENDENCY—MEDIAN

Median

The median of a distribution is the value of the variable that divides it into two equal parts so that one half of the data has values less than the median while the other half has values greater than the median. Median may be defined as the middle or central value of the variable when values are arranged in the order of magnitude. In other words, median is defined as that value of the variable that divides the group into two equal parts, one part comprising all values greater and the other all values lesser than the median.

Median is generally denoted by M_e or M_d.

Example 12. *Find median of the following variable values.*

X values : *15, 18, 11, 12, 14, 15, 20.*

Solution. Arrange the variable values in ascending order

X values are 11, 12, 14, 15, 15, 18, 20
↓
Central unit (4th unit)

Thus there are 7 values and 4th unit is central unit, median = M_e = value of 4th unit = 15.

4.10 DETERMINATION OF MEDIAN

(a) When individual observations are given (ungrouped data)

The following steps are involved in the determination of median :

(*i*) The given observations are arranged in either ascending or descending order of magnitude.

(*ii*) Given that there are n observations, the median is given by:

1. The size of $\left(\frac{n+1}{2}\right)$th observations, when n is odd.

2. The mean of the sizes of $\frac{n}{2}$th and $\left(\frac{n}{2}+1\right)$th observations, when n is even.

Example 13. *Find median of the following observations :*

20, 15, 25, 28, 18, 16, 30.

Solution.

Writing the observations in ascending order, we get 15, 16, 18, 20, 25, 28, 30.

Since $n = 7$, *i.e.*, odd, the median is the size of $\left(\frac{7+1}{2}\right)$ th, *i.e.*, 4th observation.

Hence, median, denoted by $M_d = 20$.

Note : The same value of M_d will be obtained by arranging the observations in descending order of magnitude.

Example 14. *Find median of the data : 245, 230, 265, 236, 220, 250.*

Solution. Arranging these observations in ascending order of magnitude, we get 220, 230, 236, 245, 250, 265. Here $n = 6$, *i.e.*, even.

∴ Median will be arithmetic mean of the size of $\frac{6}{2}$th, *i.e.*, 3rd and $\left(\frac{6}{2}+1\right)$th, *i.e.*, 4th observations. Hence $M_d = \frac{236+245}{2} = 240.5$.

Remarks:

Consider the observations: 13, 16, 16, 17, 17, 18, 19, 21, 23. On the basis of the method given above, their median is 17.

According to the above definition of median, "half (*i.e.*, 50%) of the observations should be below 17 and half of the observations should be above 17". Here we may note that only 3 observations are below 17 and 4 observations are above it and hence, the definition of median given above is some what ambiguous. In order to avoid this ambiguity, the median of a distribution may also be defined in the following way :

Median of a distribution is that value of the variate such that at least half of the observations are less than or equal to it and at least half the observations are greater than or equal to it.

Based on this definition, we find that there are 5 observations which are less than or equal to 17 and there are 6 observations which are greater than or equal to 17. Since $n = 9$, the numbers 5 and 6 are both more than half, *i.e.*, 4.5. Thus, median of the distribution is 17.

Example 15. *Data below relates to the monthly salaries of 10 employees (in thousand rupees). Compute the median salary of the employees.*

Monthly salaries of employees

Employee	*1*	*2*	*3*	*4*	*5*	*6*	*7*	*8*	*9*	*10*
Salary	*120*	*135*	*135*	*128*	*148*	*136*	*138*	*151*	*153*	*150*

Solution. To compute the median, we first arrange the data in ascending order.

120, 128, 132, 135, 136, 138, 148, 150, 151, 153

This data series contains 10 items. As the number of observations in this data series is even, median will be the average of $\frac{n}{2}$th term and $\left(\frac{n}{2}+1\right)$th term, that is, average of $\frac{10}{2}$th term and $\left(\frac{10}{2}+1\right)$th term. Hence, median will be the average of the 5th and 6th term.

So, median $(M_d) = \frac{136 + 138}{2} = 137$

Thus, the median salary is ₹ 137,000.

4.10.1. Computation of Median for a Discrete Frequency Distribution

In the case of a discrete series, median can be calculated by using the following steps:

1. Arrange the data in ascending or descending order of magnitude.
2. Obtain cumulative frequencies
3. Size of $\left(\frac{N+1}{2}\right)$th item must be determined, when N is the total of all the frequency, that is, $\sum_{i=1}^{n} f_i = N$.
4. The value for which cumulative frequency includes $\left(\frac{N+1}{2}\right)$th item is taken as the median.

Example 16. *Calculate the median for the values and frequencies given below.*

Values and frequencies for Example 3.14

Value	*2*	*3*	*4*	*5*	*6*	*7*	*8*	*9*	*10*	*11*	*12*
Frequency	*2*	*3*	*8*	*10*	*12*	*16*	*10*	*8*	*6*	*5*	*6*

Solution.

We rewrite the frequency distribution in normal form.

X	f	*Cumulative Frequency*	Position of observations in this class
2	2	2	first two
3	3	2 + 3 = 5	3rd to 5th
4	8	5 + 8 = 13	6th to 13th
5	10	13 + 10 = 23	14th to 23rd
6	12	23 + 16 = 51	24th to 35th
7	16	35 + 16 = 51	36th to 51st
8	10	51 + 10 = 61	
9	8	61 + 8 = 69	
10	6	69 + 6 = 75	
11	5	75 + 5 = 80	
12	6	80 + 6 = 86 = n	

Thus there are $n = 86$ (no. of observations) which is even. Thus central values are 43rd and 44th and both these units have X value as 7.

[In the column indicating position of variable values we find that all values between 36th to 51st value are 7, *i.e.*, $X_{36} = X_{37} = \ldots\ldots = X_{51} = 7$]

Thus $X_{43} = 7, X_{44} = 7.$

and $M_d = \frac{X_{43} + X_{44}}{2} = \frac{7 = 7}{2} = 7.$

[**Note :** In actual practice the column showing position of different value need not be drawn].

Example 17. *Locate median of the following frequency distribution :*

Variable (X) :	*10*	*11*	*12*	*13*	*14*	*15*	*16*
Frequency (f) :	*8*	*15*	*25*	*20*	*12*	*10*	*5*

Solution.

X :	10	11	12	13	14	15	16
f :	8	15	25	20	12	10	5
c.f. :	8	23	48	68	80	90	95

Here $N = 95$, which is odd. Thus, median is size of $\left[\frac{95+1}{2}\right]^{th}$ *i.e.*, 48th observation. From the table 48th observation is 12, $\therefore M_d = 12$.

Alternative Method

$\frac{N}{2} = \frac{95}{2} = 47.5$. Looking at the frequency distribution we note that there are 48 observations which are less than or equal to 12 and there are 72 (*i.e.*, 95 – 23) observations which are greater than or equal to 12. Hence, median is 12.

Example 18. *Locate median of the following frequency distribution :*

X	:	0	1	2	3	4	5	6	7
f	:	7	14	18	36	51	54	52	20

Solution.

X	f.	$c.f.$
0	7	7
1	14	21
2	18	29
3	36	75
4	51	126
5	54	180
6	52	232
7	20	$252 = N$

Here $N = 252$, *i.e.*, even.

Now $\frac{N}{2} = \frac{252}{2} = 126$ and $\frac{N}{2} + 1 = 127$. Now $X_{126} = 4$ and $X_{127} = 5$

$\therefore \quad M_d = \frac{4+5}{2} = 4.5$

4.10.2. Determination of Median for a Continuous Frequency Distribution

As in a discrete frequency distribution, in case of a continuous series also cumulative frequencies are calculated. As a next step the size of N/2th item is computed (N being the total frequency). Then, the median class in the cumulative frequencies column where the size of N/2th item falls is located. Then, the following formula is applied to calculate median:

$$\text{Median} = L + \frac{(N/2) - c}{f} \times i$$

where L is the lower limit of the median class, N the sum of the frequencies, c the cumulative frequency of the class preceding the median class, and i the width of the median class.

This formula is used irrespective of whether N is odd or even.

Example 19. *Delta Tiers employed 159 employees for a factory located at Kanpur. The company's management is worried about the high absenteeism rate in the organization. Before taking any corrective action, the management has decided to calculate the median leaves availed by the employees. Table below shows vacations availed in a year and the number of employees who availed vacations. Compute median from the data.*

Vacations availed in a year and the number of employees who availed vacation

Vacations availed in a year	*0-10*	*10-20*	*20-30*	*30-40*	*40-50*	*50-60*	*60-70*	*70-80*
Number of employees	*2*	*18*	*30*	*45*	*35*	*20*	*6*	*3*

Solution. For computing the median, for a continuous frequency distribution we have to compute cumulative frequencies as shown below.

Vacations availed	Number of employees (f)	Cumulative frequency (cf)
0-10	2	2
10-20	18	20
20-30	30	50
30-40	45	95 ← 79.5 liens in this class (median class)
40-50	35	130
50-60	20	150
60-70	6	156
70-80	3	159
	$\sum_{i=1}^{n} f_i = N = 156$	

$\frac{N}{2} = \frac{159}{2} = 79.5$, which falls in the class 30-40 (see the row of the cumulative frequency 95 which contains 51st to 95th units and hence 79.5 lies in it). Hence the median class is 30-40 .

L = lower limit of median class = 30

f = frequency of median class = 45

c = total of all frequencies preceding median class = 50

i = width of class interval of median class = 10

$$\text{Median } = L + \frac{\left(\frac{N}{2}\right) - c}{f} \times i$$

$$= 30 + \frac{\left(\frac{159}{2}\right) - 50}{45} \times 10 = 30 + \frac{79.5 - 50}{45} \times 10$$

$$= 30 + \left(\frac{29.5}{45} \times 10\right) = 30 + \frac{395}{45} = 30 + \frac{59}{9}$$

$$= 30 + 6.55 = 36.55$$

[Note : To compute median for continuous grouped frequency distribution, the classes has to be exclusive, *i.e.*, continuous. In case these are inclusive or discontinuous, these are to be changed to exclusive classes first].

Example 20. *The following table gives the distribution of marks by 500 students in an examination. Obtain median of the given data.*

Marks :	*0-9*	*10-19*	*20-29*	*30-39*	*40-49*	*50-59*	*60-69*	*70-79*
No. of Students :	*30*	*40*	*50*	*48*	*24*	*162*	*132*	*14*

Solution. Since the class intervals are inclusive, therefore, it is necessary to convert them into class boundaries.

Class Intervals	*Class Boundaries*	*Frequency*	*'Less than' type c.f.*	
0-9	– 0.5-9.5	30	30	
10-19	9.5-19.5	40	70	
20-29	19.5-29.5	50	120	
30-39	29.5-39.5	48	168	
40-49	39.5-49.5	24	192	
50-59	49.5-59.5	162	354	⟵ median class.
60-69	59.5-69.5	132	486	
70-79	69.5-79.5	14	500	

Since $\frac{N}{2} = 250$, the median class is 49.5 - 59.5 and, therefore, L = 49.5, $h = 10$, $f = 162$, C = 192.

Thus, $M_d = 49.5 + \frac{250 + 192}{162} \times 10 = 53.08$ marks.

4.10.3. Determination of Median When 'greater than' type cumulative frequencies are given

In case "greater than" or "more than" cumulative frequency distribution is known, median is obtained without changing it to "less than" cumulative frequency distribution, by slightly changing the formula, as follows.

$$M_d = U_m - \frac{N/2 - C}{f_m} \times h$$

where U_m = Upper limit of median class

C = cumulative frequency of the class which follows median class.

f_m = frequency of median class

h = width of median class

Median class is obtained in which $\frac{N}{2}$ lies in *c.f.* The method is explained in the example given below.

Example 21. *Find the median of the following data :*

Age grater than (in yrs)	:	0	10	20	30	40	50	60	70
No. of Persons	:	130	218	200	165	123	73	28	8

Solution.

Note that it is *'greater than'* type frequency distribution.

Class Intervals	*Greater than c. f.*	*Frequency*
0-10	230	12
10-20	218	18
20-30	200	35
30-40	165	42

40-50	123 ⟵ Median Class	50 ← f_m
50-60	73	45
60-70	28	20
70 and above	8	8

[In class 40–50, all values between 74th & 123rd are included, in case values are arranged in descending order]

Since $\frac{N}{2} = \frac{230}{2} = 115$, the median class is 40 - 50.

Using the formula, $M_d = U_m - \frac{\frac{N}{2} - C}{f_m} \times h$

$$= 50 - \frac{115 - 73}{50} \times 10 = 41.6 \text{ years}$$

C = cumulative frequency of next class to median class, *i.e.*, 50 – 60 class = 73

Example 22. *The following table gives the daily profits (in ₹) of 195 shops of a town. Calculate mean and median.*

Profits :	*50-60*	*60-70*	*70-80*	*80-90*	*90-100*	*100-110*	*110-120*	*120-130*	*130-140*
No. of shops :	*15*	*20*	*32*	*35*	*33*	*22*	*20*	*10*	*8*

Solution.

The calculations of $\overline{X}$ and M_d are shown below :

Class Intervals	*f*	*Mid - value (X)*	$u = \frac{X - 95}{10}$	*fu*	*Less than c. f.*
50–60	15	55	– 4	– 60	15
60–70	20	65	– 3	– 60	35
70–80	32	75	– 2	– 64	67
80–90	35	85	– 1	– 35	102
90–100	33	95	0	0	135
100–110	22	105	1	22	157
110–120	20	115	2	40	177
120–130	10	125	3	30	187
130–140	8	135	4	32	195
Total	195	–		– 95	

$$\overline{X} = A + \frac{\Sigma fu}{N} \times h = 95 - \frac{95}{195} \times 10 = ₹\ 90.13$$ [*u* has replaced *d′*)

Since $\frac{N}{2} = \frac{195}{2} = 97.5$, the median class is 80–90.

$$M_d = 80 + \frac{97.5 - 67}{35} \times 10 = ₹\ 88.71$$

Median through Ogive

(*A*) **Use of Ogive.** Let graph of less than ogive be as shown in the figure. Let me explain how do we use it. Suppose we want to know, "How many units have values less than a given value X_1". Assuming X_1 lies between 30 and 40 as shown in figure. Draw a line through X_1 parallel to *y*-axis which cuts "less than" ogive at *A*. Through *A* draw *AB* parallel to *x*-axis to cut *Y*-axis at *B*. Let *y*-coordinate of *B* be *m*. Then it indicates that there are *m* values less than X_1. Similarly of we want to know the value of *X* such that number of units less than this value is given '*k*'. Let us take value '*k*' at a point *C* on *y*-axis. Draw *CD* parallel to *x*-axis to cut "*Less than*" ogive at *D*. Through *D* draw a line parallel to *y*-axis to cut *X*-axis at X_2. Then we know that no. of units having values less than X_2 are '*k*'.

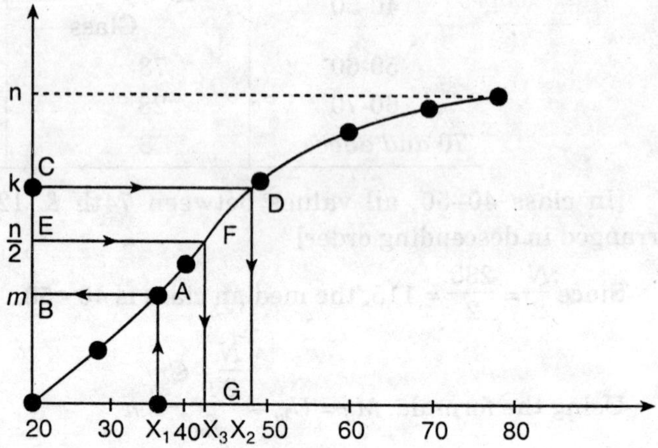

(*B*) How to find median from "*less than*" ogive. We have to find that value such that $\frac{n}{2}$ units have values less than or equal to it. (As median is a value such that $\frac{n}{2}$ units have values less than or equal to it. Thus we take $\frac{n}{2}$ value at *E* on *y*-axis. Draw EF parallel to *X*-axis which cuts "less than" ogive at *F*. From F draw a line parallel to *y*-axis to cut *X*-axis at *G*. Then *x* co-ordinate of *G* gives value of median which is X_3.

Example 23. *The following table gives the wages of the workers in a certain factory:*

Daily wages (₹)	*No. of worker*	*Daily wages* (₹)	*No. of workers*
20–25	21	60–65	36
25–30	29	65–70	45
30–35	19	70–75	27
35–40	39	75–80	48
40–45	43	80–85	21
45–50	94	85–90	12
50–55	73	90–95	5
55–60	68		

(1) Draw "less than" ogive and find median from it.

(2) Find the number of workers getting wages between ₹ 57 and ₹ 77.

Solution. In order to find out the number of workers getting wages between ₹ 57 and ₹ 77 we will draw "less than" ogive.

Daily wages (₹)	*No. of worker*	*Daily wages (₹)*	*No. of workers*
Less than 20	0		
Less than 25	21	Less than 65	422
Less than 30	50	Less than 70	467
Less than 35	69	Less than 75	494
Less than 40	108	Less than 80	542
Less than 45	151	Less than 85	563
Less than 50	245	Less than 90	575
Less than 55	318	Less than 95	580
Less than 60	386		

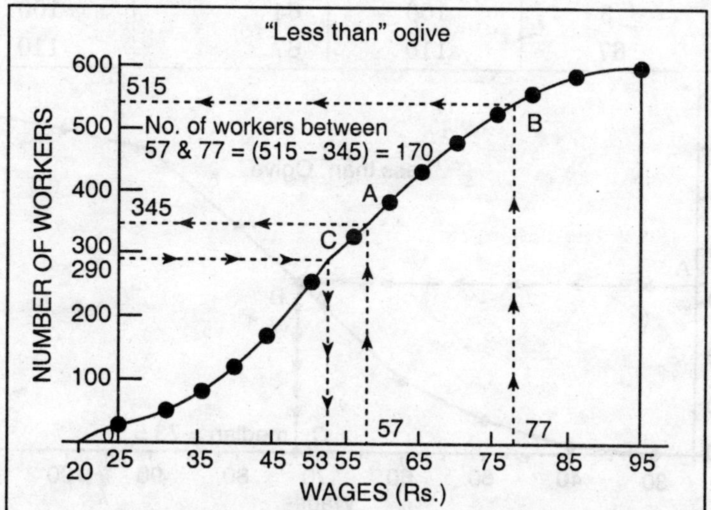

We wish to find the no. of workers getting wages between 57 and 77. As shown in figure lines parallel to y-axis through $X = 57$ and $X = 77$ are drawn to cut "less than" ogive at A and B. Y-coordinate of points A and B are found to be 345 and 515 respectively. Thus no. of workers getting wages between 57 and 77 are :

= no. of workers getting wages less than 77– no. of workers getting wages less than 57.

= 515 – 345 = 170

Now in order to get median from this we find $\frac{n}{2} = \frac{580}{2} = 290$. Now we have to X corresponding to *c.f.* = 290. A point showing $Y = 290$ (at y-axis) is taken and a line parallel to X-axis is drawn to cut ogive at C. X-coordinate of C is found to be roughly equal to 53 (as shown is figure).

Thus median of the data = 53.

Example 24. *From the given frequency distribution find (i) Median from "less than" ogive (ii) Median using both the ogives. (iii) median through formula.*

Solution. Two cumulative frequency distributions, "less than" and "more than", are as follows :

Wages (₹)	*Number of Employee*	*Less than Cumulative Frequency*		*More than Cumulative Frequency*	
		X less than	*f*	*X More than*	*f*
30–40	2	30	0	30	67
40–50	5	40	2	40	62
50–60	8	50	7	50	54
60–70	12	60	15	60	42
70–80	18	70	27	70	24
80–90	15	80	45 ← Median Class	80	9
90–100	4	90	60	90	5
100–110	3	100	64	100	2
Total	67	110	67	110	0

(*i*)

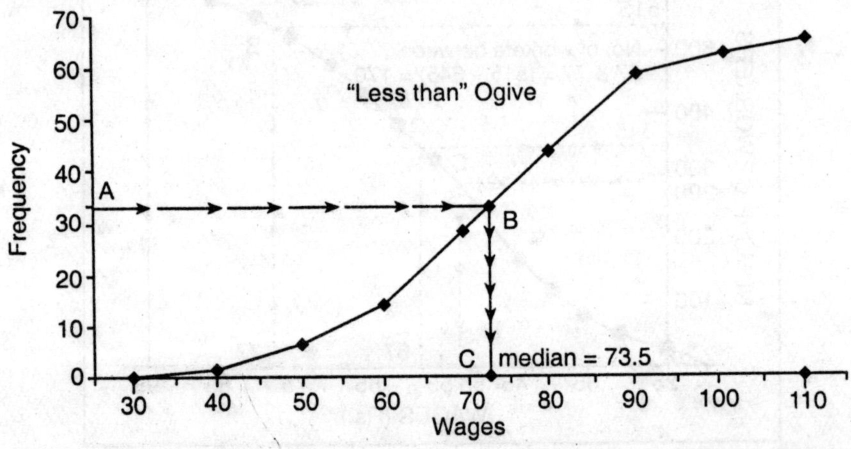

(*i*) **"Less than" Ogive.** To find median find $\frac{n}{2} = \frac{67}{2} = 33.5$. Take A with $y = 33.5$. Draw AB parallel to X-axis and then BC parallel to Y-axis Median = X-coordinate of C = 73.5 (approximately).

(*ii*)

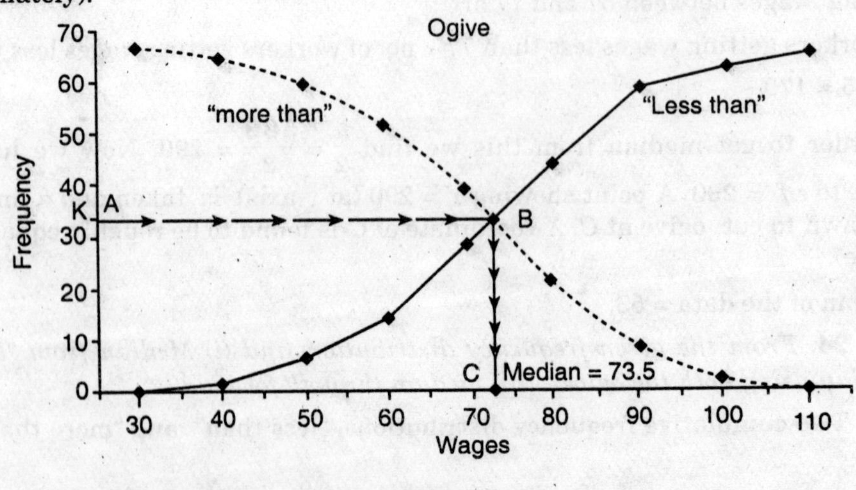

Both the ogives are drawn on the same graph. Median is X-coordinates of point of intersection of two ogives. (As this is value of X, frequencies below this and above this value are same and which is equal to k, thus k must be equal to $\frac{n}{2}$. Median is at C.

(*iii*) $\frac{n}{2} = 33.5$ lies in class 70–80, (obtained from *c.f.*)

Thus

$$M_d = L + \frac{\frac{n}{2} - C}{f} \times i$$

$$= 70 + \frac{33.5 - 27}{18} \times 10$$

$$= 70 + \frac{65}{18} = 70 + 3.61 = 73.61$$

4.11 PROPERTIES OF MEDIAN

1. It is a positional average.
2. It can be shown that the sum of absolute deviations is minimum when taken from median. This property implies that median is centrally located.

4.12 MERITS AND DEMERITS OF MEDIAN

Merits

1. It is easy to understand and easy to calculate, especially in series of individual observations and ungrouped frequency distributions. In such cases it can even be located by inspection.
2. Median can be determined even when class intervals have open ends or not of equal width.
3. It is not much affected by extreme observations. It is also independent of range or dispersion of the data.
4. Median can also be located graphically.
5. It is centrally located measure of average since the sum of absolute deviation is minimum when taken from median.
6. It is the only suitable average when data are qualitative and it is possible to rank various items according to qualitative characteristics.
7. Median conveys the idea of a typical observation.

Demerits

1. In case of individual observations, the process of location of median requires their arrangement in the order of magnitude which may be a cumbersome task, particularly when the number of observations is very large.
2. It, being a positional average, is not capable of being treated algebraically.
3. In case of individual observations, when the number of observations is even, the median is estimated by taking mean of the two middle-most observations, which is not an actual observation of the given data.

4. It is not based on the magnitudes of all the observations. There may be a situation where different sets of observations give same value of median. For example, the following two different sets of observations, have median equal to 30.

   Set 1 : 10, 20, 30, 40, 50 and Set II : 15, 25, 30, 60, 90.

5. In comparison to arithmetic mean, it is much affected by the fluctuations of sampling.
6. The formula for the computation of median, in case of grouped frequency distribution, is based on the assumption that the observations in the median class are uniformly distributed. This assumption is rarely met in practice.
7. Since it is not possible to define weighted median like weighted arithmetic mean, this average is not suitable when different items are of unequal importance.

4.13 USES

1. It is an appropriate measure of central tendency when the characteristics are not measurable but different items are capable of being ranked.
2. Median is used to convey the idea of a typical observation of the given data.
3. Median is the most suitable measure of central tendency when the frequency distribution is skewed. For example, income distribution of the people is generally positively skewed and median is the most suitable measure of average in this case.
4. Median is often computed when quick estimates of average are desired.
5. When the given data has class intervals with open ends, median is preferred as a measure of central tendency since it is not possible to calculate mean in this case.

4.14 OTHER PARTITION OR POSITIONAL MEASURES

Though these *are not measures of central tendency*, but since these are similar to median, hence are discussed here.

Median of a distribution divides it into two equal parts. It is also possible to divide it into more than two equal parts. The values that divide a distribution into more than two equal parts are commonly known as partition values or *fractiles*. Some important partition values are discussed in the following sections.

4.14.1. Quartiles

The values of a variable that divide a distribution into four equal parts are called quartiles. Since three values are needed to divide a distribution into four parts, there are three quartiles, *viz.* Q_1, Q_2 and Q_3 known as the first, second and third quartile respectively.

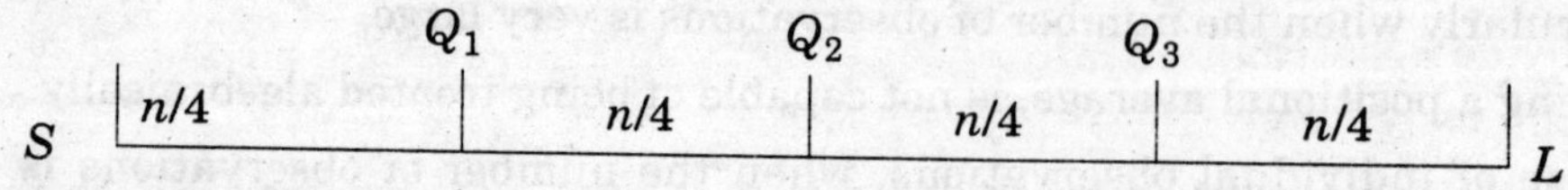

Let the observations be arranged in ascending order and S and L be the smallest and larger values respectively.

For a discrete distribution, the first quartile (Q_1) is defined as that value of the variate such that at least 25% of the observations are less than or equal to it and at least 75% of the observations are greater than or equal to it.

For continuous variable Q_1 is a value such that $\frac{n}{4}$ units (25% of all values) have values less that it and $\frac{3n}{4}$ units have values more than it. Same way Q_3 is a value such that $\frac{3n}{4}$ units have values less than it and $\frac{n}{4}$ units have values less than it. Obviously Q_2 = median.

For a continuous or grouped frequency distribution, Q_1 is that value of the variate such that the area under the histogram to the left of the ordinate at Q_1 is 25% and the area to its right is 75%. The formula for the computation of Q_1 can be written by making suitable changes in the formula of median.

For a grouped frequency distribution, Q_3 is that value of the variate such that area under the histogram to the left of the ordinate at Q_3 is 75% and the area to its right is 25%. The formula for

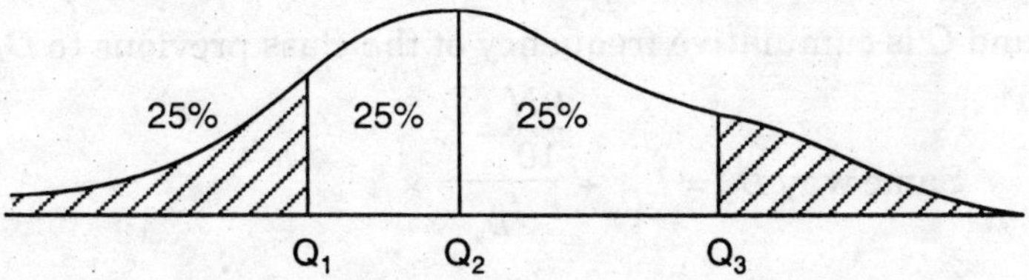

First Quartile class is that class in which $\frac{n}{4}$ lies in the cumulative frequency distribution.

$$Q_1 = L_{Q_1} + \frac{\left(\frac{N}{4} - C\right)}{f_{Q_1}} \times h,$$

Here L_{Q_1} is lower limit of the first quartile class, h is its width, f_{Q_1} is its frequency and C is cumulative frequency of class preceding the first quartile class.

Same way Q_3 (third quartile) class is the class in which $\frac{3n}{4}$ lies in *c.f.* of that class.

Formula for computation of Q_3 can be written as

$$Q_3 = L_{Q_3} + \frac{\left(\frac{3N}{4} - C\right)}{f_{Q_3}} \times h,$$ where the symbols have their usual meaning.

where L_{Q_3}, f_{Q_3}, h are lower limit, frequency and class width of Q_3 class and C is *c.f.* of previous class of the Q_3 class.

4.14.2. Deciles

Deciles divide a distribution into 10 equal parts and there are, in all, 9 deciles denoted as D_1, D_2, ... D_9 respectively.

For a discrete distribution, the i th decile D_i is that value of the variate such that at least $(10i)$% of the observation are less than or equal to it and at least $(100 - 10i)$% of the observations are greater than or equal to it (i = 1, 2, ... 9).

For a continuous or grouped frequency distribution, D_i is that value of the variate such that the area under the histogram to the left of the ordinate at D_i is $(10i)\%$ and the area to its right is $(100 - 10i)\%$. The formula for the i th decile can be written as

$$D_i = L_{D_i} + \frac{\left(\frac{iN}{10} - C\right)}{f_{D_i}} \times h \ (i = 1, 2, \ldots\ldots 9)$$

e.g. D_4 is value such that 40% values are less than it and remaining 60% values are greater than it.

Now $D_4 = L_{D_4} + \frac{\frac{4N}{10} - C}{f_{D_4}} \times h$. First we locate D_4 class, *i.e.*, the class in which $\frac{4N}{10}$ lies under *c.f.* and then we find L_{D_4}, f_{D_4} and h, *i.e.*, lower limit, frequency and class width of that class and C is cumulative frequency of the class previous to D_4 class.

Same way $D_9 = L_{D_9} + \frac{\frac{9N}{10} - C}{f_{D_9}} \times h$

4.14.3. Percentiles

Percentiles divide a distribution into 100 equal parts and there are, in all, 99 percentiles denoted as P_1..... P_2..... P_{25}..... P_{40}..... P_{60}..... P_{99} respectively.

For a discrete distribution, the k th percentile P_k is that value of the variate such that at least $k\%$ of the observations are less than or equal to it and at least $(100 - k)\%$ of the observations are greater than or equal to it.

For a grouped frequency distribution, P_k is that value of the variate such that the area under the histogram to the left of the ordinate at P_k is $k\%$ and the area to its right is $(100 - k)\%$. The formula for the k th percentile can be written as

$$P_k = L_{P_k} + \frac{\left(\frac{kN}{100} - C\right)}{f_{P_k}} \times h. \ (k = 1, 2, \ldots\ldots 99)$$

e.g. $$P_{20} = L_{P_{20}} + \frac{\frac{20N}{100} - C}{f_{P_{20}}} \times h$$

[**Note :** $P_{20} = D_2$, $Q_1 = P_{25}$, $Q_3 = P_{75}$, $M_d = P_{50} = Q = D_5$

Meaning of $P_{20} \Rightarrow$ 20% of values are less than P_{20}

as meaning of $Q_1 \Rightarrow$ 25% of values are less than Q_1]

Example 25. *Locate Median, Q_1, Q_3, D_4, D_7, P_{15}, and P_{60} from the following data :*

Daily Profit (in ₹) :	75	76	77	78	79	80	81	82	83	84	85
No. of Shops :	15	20	32	35	33	22	20	10	8	3	2

Solution. Change the above frequency distribution to "less than" cumulative above frequency distribution to

X Profit	f	cf
75	15	15
76	20	35
77	32	67
78	35	102
79	33	135
80	22	157
81	20	177
82	7	184

Q_1 class $\left(\text{as } \frac{n}{4} = 46 \text{ lies in thus class}\right)$ (row 77)

92th unit, Median class (row 78)

Q_3 class for $\frac{3n}{4} = 138$ (row 80)

(*i*) To find Median, Now $\frac{n}{2} = \frac{184}{2} = 92$, which lines in class corresponding to *c.f.* = 102.
Now $X_{92} = 78$ [all units with positions 68th to 102nd all have values 78]

(*ii*) To find $Q_1 \rightarrow$ find $\frac{n}{4} = \frac{184}{4} = 46$. Now $X_{46} = 77 \therefore Q_1 = 77$

(*iii*) To find $Q_3 \rightarrow$ find $\frac{3n}{4} = 3\left(\frac{n}{4}\right) = 3(46) = 138$ and $X_{138} = 80$

(*iv*) For D_4 find $\frac{4n}{10} = \frac{4\,(184)}{10} = 73.6$ which is in class corresponding to *c.f.* of 102 (which lies in between X_{73} and X_{74}. However both are equal to 78. $\Rightarrow D_4 = 78$.

(*v*) To find D_7, first we find $\frac{7N}{10} = \frac{7 \times 184}{10} = 128.8$. Thus D_7 lies between values of X_{128} and X_{129} and both have same value 79. Hence $D_7 = 79$.

(*vi*) To find P_{15}. Find $\frac{15}{100} n = \frac{15}{100} \times 184 = 27.60$.
Thus P_{15} lies between X_{27} and X_{28} and both have same value as 76. Hence $P_{15} = 76$.

(*vii*) To find $P_{60} \rightarrow$ find $\frac{60}{100} n = \frac{60 \times 184}{100} = 110.4$. Thus P_{60} lies between X_{110} and X_{111} and both have value 79. Hence $P_{60} = 79$.

Example 26. *From the given frequency distribution find D_3, Q_1, Q_3, P_{15}, P_{72}*

Marks	*No. of students*	*Marks*	*No. of students*
0–9	*9*	*50–59*	*102*
10–19	*42*	*60–69*	*71*
20–29	*61*	*70–79*	*23*
30–39	*140*	*80–89*	*2*
40–49	*250*		

Solution. The classes are not exclusive (not continuous) so we make them exclusive (continuous) and find *c.f.*

Marks	Frequency	Cumulative Frequency	
0.5–9.5	9	9	
9.5–19.5	42	51	
19.5–29.5	61	112	P_{15} class
29.5–39.5	140	252	Q_1 class, D_3 class
39.5–49.5	250	502	
49.5–59.5	102	604	Q_3 class, P_{72} class
59.5–69.5	71	675	
69.5–79.5	23	698	
79.5–89.5	3	700	

(1) To find $D_3 \to$ find $\frac{3n}{10} = \frac{3}{10}(700) = 210$ (in *c.f.* column 210 lies in 29.5 – 39.5 class. D_3 lies in this class. $D_3 = 29.5$, $f_{D_3} = 140$, $h = 10$ $C = 112$ (*c.f.* of previous class).

Now
$$D_3 = L_{D_3} + \frac{\frac{3n}{10} - C}{f_{D_3}} \times h$$

$$= 29.5 + \frac{210 - 112}{140} \times 10 = 29.5 + \frac{98}{14} = 29.5 + 7$$

$$= 36.5.$$

(*ii*) To find $Q_1 \to$ find $\frac{n}{4} = \frac{700}{4} = 175$ which lies in class 29.5 – 39.5 (according to *c.f.* column) Q_1 lies in this class. Thus $L_{Q_1} = 29.5$, $f_{Q_1} = 140$, $h = 10$, $C = 112$

$$\therefore \quad Q_1 = L_{Q_1} + \frac{\frac{n}{4} - C}{f_{Q_1}} . h$$

$$= 29.5 + \frac{175 - 112}{140} \times 10 = 29.5 + \frac{63}{14} = 29.5 + 4.5$$

$$= 34.$$

(*iii*) To find $Q_3 \to$ Find $\frac{3n}{4} = \frac{3}{4} \times 700 = 525$. Now X_{525} lies in 49.5 – 59.5 class (according to *c.f.* column)

Now $L_{Q_3} = 49.5$, $f_{Q_3} = 102$, $h = 10$; $C = 502$

$$Q_3 = L_{Q_3} + \frac{\frac{3n}{4} - C}{f_{Q_3}} h$$

$$= 49.5 + \frac{525 - 502}{102} \times 10 = 49.5 + \frac{230}{102} = 49.5 + 2.3$$

$$= 51.8$$

(*iv*) To find $P_{15} \to$ find $\frac{15}{100} n = \frac{15}{100} \times 700 = 105$ which lies in class 19.5 – 29.5 with *c.f.* as 112.

Now $L_{P_{15}} = 19.5, f_{P_{15}} = 61, C = 51, h = 10$

$$P_{15} = L_{P_{15}} + \frac{\frac{15}{100}n - C}{f_{P_{15}}} \times h = 19.5 + \frac{105 - 51}{61} \times 10$$

$$= 19.5 + \frac{540}{61} = 19.5 + 8.9 = 28.4$$

(*v*) To find $P_{72} \rightarrow$ find $\frac{72}{100}n = \frac{72}{100} \times 700 = 504$, using *c.f.* column X_{504} lies in class 49.5 – 59.5. P_{72} lies in this class. $L_{P_{72}} = 49.5$ $C = 502, f_{P_{72}} = 102, h = 10$.

$$P_{72} = L_{P_{72}} + \frac{\frac{72}{100}n - C}{f_{P_{72}}} \times h$$

$$= 49.5 + \frac{504 - 502}{102} \times 10 = 49.5 + \frac{20}{102} = 49.5 + .2$$

$$= 49.7.$$

4.15. POSITIONAL MEASURES GRAPHICALLY—USING "LESS THAN" OGIVE

Draw "less than" ogive by taking X values on X-axis and *c.f.* on Y axis. For a given *c.f.*, X values can be found out from that ogive. For any positional measure *c.f.* is known.

For example to find P_{20}, *c.f.* $= \frac{20}{100}n$ and corresponding to this *c.f.* X value is P_{20}.

Similarly to find D_3, *c.f.* $= \frac{3}{10}n$, find X corresponding to this and that $X = D_3$ and so on.

Example 27. Find P_{27} , Q_3, D_2 and P_{84} graphically using "less than" ogive of the distribution of wages of 67 workers.

Wages	*30-40*	*40-50*	*50-60*	*60-70*	*70-80*	*80-90*	*90-100*	*100-110*
f *no. of workers*	2	5	8	12	18	15	4	3

Less than Cumulative Frequency	
X less than	*f*
30	0
40	2
50	7
60	15
70	27
80	45
90	60
100	64
110	67

(*i*) To find $P_{27} \rightarrow$ find $\frac{27}{100}n = \frac{27 \times 67}{100} = 18.09 = 18$ approx. We take 18 on *Y*-axis at *A* and corresponding to *c.f.* = 18, *X* = 62.5 (at *B*) $\Rightarrow P_{27} = 62.5$.

(*ii*) To find Q_3, find $3\frac{n}{4} = 3 \times \frac{67}{4} = 50.25$, $\frac{3n}{4} = 50.25$ is taken on *c.f.* line *i.e.*, *Y*-axis at *C*. Now corresponding this *c.f.* *X* is given by point *D* where *X* = 84 nearly. Thus $Q_3 = 84$.

(*iii*) To find $D_2 \rightarrow$ find $\frac{2}{10}n = \frac{2}{10}(67) = 13.4 = c.f.$ which is at *E*. Corresponding this *c.f.* of 13.4, *X* value is at *F* which is nearly 58.5. Thus $D_2 = 58.5$.

(*iv*) To find $P_{89} \rightarrow$ find $\frac{89}{100}n = \frac{89}{100} \times 67 = 59.6$, this *c.f.* = 59.6 is at *G* (*Y*-axis). Corresponding to this *G*, *X* is given at *H* which is nearly 60. Thus $P_{89} = 90$ (nearly) $\Rightarrow$ 89% of workers are getting less than ₹ 90.

"Less than" Ogive

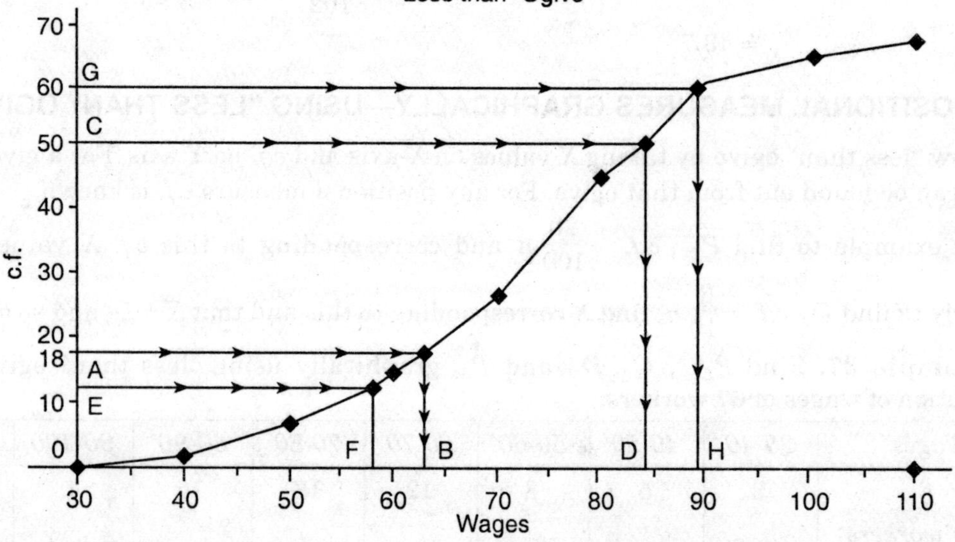

4.16. MODE

Mode is that value of the variate which occurs maximum number of times in a distribution and around which other items are densely distributed. In the words of Croxton and Cowden, *"The mode of a distribution is the value at the point around which the items tend to be most heavily concentrated. It may be regarded the most typical of a series of values."* Further, according to A.M. Tuttle, *"Mode is the value which has the greatest frequency density in its immediate neighbourhood."*

If the frequency distribution is regular, then mode is determined by the value corresponding to maximum frequency. The may be a situation where concentration of observations around a value having maximum frequency is less than the concentration of observations around some other value. In such a situation, mode cannot be determined by the use of maximum frequency criterion. Further, there may be concentration of observations around more than one value of the variable and, accordingly, the distribution is said to be bi-modal or multi-modal depending upon whether it is around two or more than two values.

The concept of mode, as a measure of central tendency, is preferable to mean and median when it is desired to know the most typical value, *e.g.*, the most common size of shoes, the most common size of a ready-made garment, the most common size of income, the most common size of pocket expenditure of a college student, the most common size of a family in a locality, the most common duration of viral-fever, the most popular candidate in an election, *etc*.

Examine the following statements :

(*i*) average size of the shoe sold in a shop is 7,

(*ii*) average height of an Indian (male) is *5 feet 6 inches* (1. 68 metres *approx.*),

(*iii*) average collar size of the shirt sold in a ready-made garment shop is 35 cms,

(*iv*) average student in a professional college spends ₹ 2,500 per month; the average referred to is neither mean nor median but mode, the most frequent value in the distribution. For example, by the first statement we mean that there is maximum demand for the shoe of size No. 7.

4·17. DETERMINATION OF MODE

To find the data has to be in grouped form, *i.e.*, either discrete on continuous frequency distribution. All individual and distinct values will not have any mode unless they are put in frequency distribution form in case of discrete frequency.

Example 28. *Compute mode of the following data :*

3, 4, 5, 10, 15, 3, 6, 7, 9, 12, 10, 16, 18,
20, 10, 9, 8, 19, 11, 14, 10, 13, 17, 9, 11

Solution. Writing this in the form of a frequency distribution, we get

Values	3	4	5	6	7	8	9	10	11	12	13	14	15	16	17	18	19	20
Frequency	2	1	1	1	1	1	3	4	2	1	1	1	1	1	1	1	1	1

∴ Mode = 10 (as it has maximum frequency 4).

Remarks:

(*i*) If the frequency of each possible value of the variable is same, there is no mode.

(*ii*) If there are two values having maximum frequency, the distribution is said to be bi-modal.

Example 29. *Compute mode of the following distribution:*

X	5	10	15	20	25	30	35	40
f	2	4	6	10	15	9	5	4

Solution. The given distribution is fairly regular. Therefore, the mode can be determined just by inspection. Since for X = 25 the frequency is maximum, mode = 25.

4.16.2. Mode in case of continuous frequency distribution

(*A*) Requirements of frequency distribution for finding mode.

(1) The classes should be continuous (exclusive)

(2) Class intervals should be equal

(B) Calculation of Mode — Grouped Data Continuous

In the case of grouped data, the following formula is used for calculating mode :

$$M_0 = L + \frac{\Delta_1}{\Delta_1 + \Delta_2} \times i \qquad \text{...(i)}$$

where, L = Lower limit of the modal class. (the class which has maximum frequency)

Δ_1 = The difference between the frequency of the modal class and the frequency of the pre-modal class, *i.e.,* preceding class.

Δ_2 = The difference between the frequency of the modal class and the frequency of the post-modal class, *i.e.,* succeeding class.

i = The size of the modal class.

Another form of this formula is :

$$M_0 = L + \frac{f_1 - f_0}{2f_1 - f_0 - f_2} \times i \quad , \quad \Delta_1 = f_1 - f_0, \Delta_2 = f_1 - f_2 \qquad \text{...(ii)}$$

where L = Lower limit of the modal class.

f_1 = Frequency of the modal class.

f_0 = Frequency of the class preceding the modal class.

f_2 = Frequency of the class succeeding the modal class.

While applying the above formula for calculating mode, it is necessary to see that the class intervals are *uniform* throughout. If they are unequal, they should first be made equal on the assumption that the frequencies are equally distributed throughout the class, otherwise we will get misleading results.

A distribution having only one mode is called *unimodal.* If it contains more than one mode, it is called *bimodal* or *multimodal*. In the latter case, the value of mode cannot be determined by the above formula and hence mode is *ill-defined* when there is more than one value of mode.

Where mode is ill-defined, its value may be ascertained by the following approximate formula based upon the relationship between mean, median and mode.

Mode = 3 Median – 2 Mean ...(iii)

(C) When is mode all-defined

Mode is generally not used as measure of central tendency in case of frequency distributions of following type.

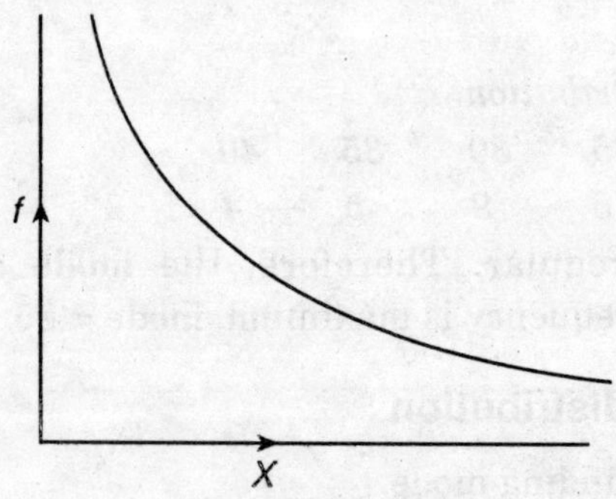

Fig. 1

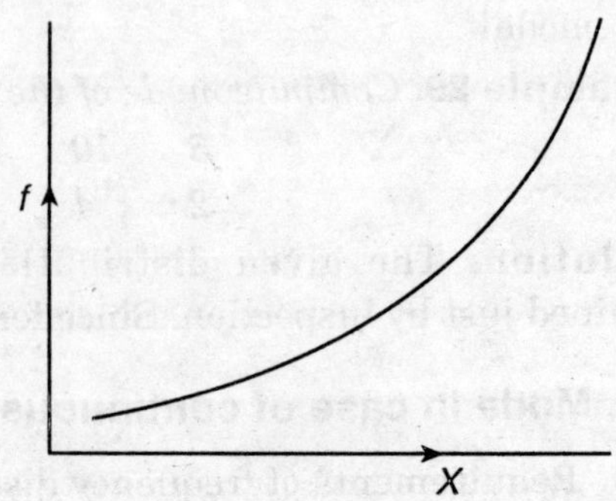

Fig. 2

In case of frequency distributions in Fig. 1 and Fig. 2 the modal class is at either end of the distribution. Thus mode does not lie in the centre of the distribution.

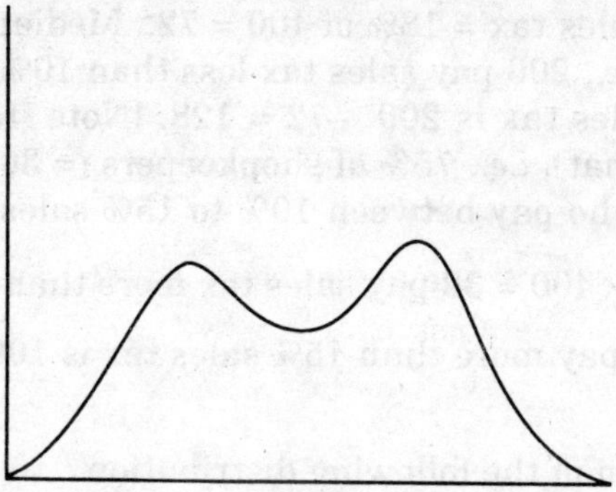

Fig. 3

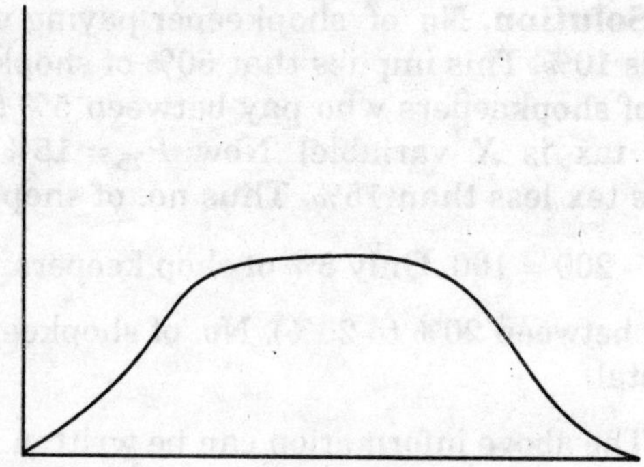

Fig. 4

In case of figures 3 and 4 mode is not distinct.

(*D*) **Distinct Mode.** Mode is distinct in case of frequency distribution with a distinct modal class which is represented as shown in Fig. 5.

Frequencies around modal class are much less compared to frequency of modal class.

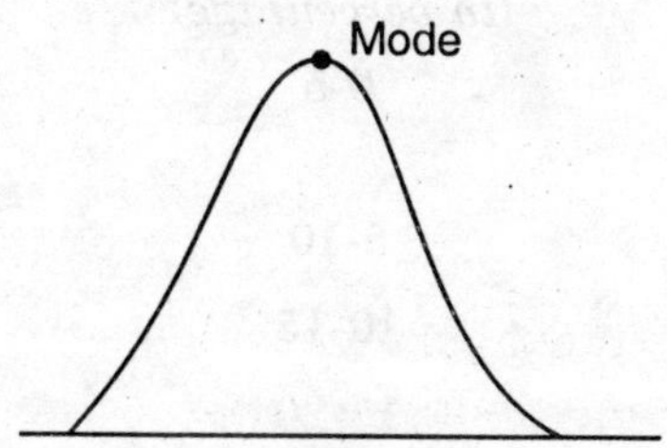

Fig. 5

Example 30. *Compute modal daily expenditure of 100 tourists in Tirumala.*

Expenditure	*0-10*	*10-20*	*20-30*	*30-40*	*40-50*	*50-60*	*60-70*	*70-80*	*80-90*	*90-100*
Tourists	*3*	*5*	*7*	*10*	*12*	*20*	*12*	*6*	*3*	*2*

Solution.

Expenditure ₹	*Tourists*	
0-10	3	
10-20	5	
20-30	7	
30-40	10	
40-50	12 $= f_0$	
50-60	20 $= f_1$	← modal class
60-70	12 $= f_2$	
70-80	6	
80-90	3	
90-100	2	

By observation it is noticed that the series is regular and uniform. Therefore by inspection modal class can be located. It is 50-60

$$M_0 = L + \frac{f_1 - f_0}{2f_1 - f_0 - f_2} \times i$$

$$= 50 + \frac{20 - 12}{2(20) - 12 - 12} \times 10$$

$$M_0 = 50 + 5 = 55$$

Example 31. *The rate of sales tax as a percentage of sales, paid by 400 shopkeepers of a market during an assessment year ranged from 0 to 25%. The sales tax paid by 18% of them was not greater than 5%. The median rate of sales tax was 10% and 75th percentile rate of sales tax was 15%. If only 8% of the shopkeepers paid sales tax at a rate greater than 20% but* *not greater than 25%, summarise the information in the form of a frequency distribution taking intervals of 5%. Also find the modal rate of sales tax.*

Solution. No. of shopkeeper paying upto 5% sales tax = 18% of 400 = 72. Median sales tax is 10%. This implies that 50% of shopkeepers, *i.e.,* 200 pay sales tax less than 10%. Thus no. of shopkeepers who pay between 5% to 10% sales tax is 200 – 72 = 128. [Note rate of sale tax is X variable] Now P_{75} = 15% (sales that), *i.e.,* 75% of shopkeepers (= 300) pay sales tax less than 15%. Thus no. of shopkeepers who pay between 10% to 15% sales tax is 300 – 200 = 100. Only 8% of shop keepers, *i.e.,* $\frac{8}{100} \times 400 = 32$ pay sales tax more than 20%% (*i.e.,* between 20% to 25%). No. of shopkeepers who pay more than 15% sales tax is 100 (25% of total).

The above information can be written in the form of the following distribution :

Class Intervals (in percentage)	*No. of shopkeepers*
0-5	$\frac{18}{100} \times 400 = 72 \quad = f_0$
5-10	$200 - 72 = 128 \quad = f_1$ (maximum frequency)
10-15	$300 - 200 = 100 \quad = f_2$
15-20	$100 - 32 = 68$
20-25	$\frac{8}{100} \times 400 = 32$

By inspection, the modal class is 5-10.

$$\therefore M_0 = 5 + \frac{128 - 72}{(128 - 72) + (128 - 100)} \times 5 = 8.33\%$$

Using $M_0 = L + \frac{\Delta_1}{\Delta_1 + \Delta_2} \cdot i$

Example 32. *Calculate mode of the following distribution :*

Weights (lbs.)	:	*below* 100	*below* 110	*below* 120	*below* 130	*below* 140
No. of Students	:	4	6	24	46	67
Weights (lbs.)	:	*below* 150	*below* 160	*below* 170	*below* 180	
No. of Students	:	86	96	99	100	

Solution. Rewriting the above distribution in the form of a frequency distribution with class limits, we get

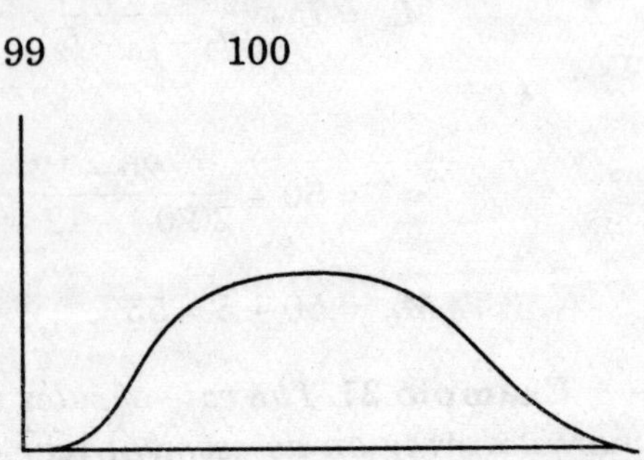

This frequency distribution by inspection is of the form as shown. In this modal class is not distinct, as frequencies near modal class are almost of the same magnitude (18, 22, 21, 19)

Therefore we use $M_0 = 3\, M_e - 2\overline{X}$

Class	f	Mid value X	$d' = \frac{X - 135}{10}$	fd'	cf	
90–100	4	95	–4	–16	4	
100–100	2	105	–3	–6	6	
110–120	18	115	–2	–36	24	
120–130	22	125	–1	–22	46	
130–140	21	135	0	0	67	← Median Class
140–150	19	145	1	19	86	
150–160	10	155	2	20	96	
160–170	3	165	3	9	99	
170–180	1	175	4	4	100	
	$100 = \Sigma f$			$-28 = \Sigma fd'$		

$$\overline{X} = A + \frac{\Sigma fd'}{\Sigma f} \cdot c = 135 + \frac{-28}{100} \times 10$$

$$= 132.82\ (lbs)$$

$$M_e = L_{M_e} + \frac{\frac{n}{2} - c}{f_{M_e}} \times i \qquad (i = \text{class interval})$$

$$= 130 + \frac{50 - 46}{21} \times 10 = 130 + \frac{40}{21} = 130 + 1.9$$

$$= 131.9\ (lbs)$$

Now M_0 = Mode = $3\,M_e - 2\,\overline{X}$

$= 3(131.9) - 2(132.2)$

$= 131.3\ (lbs)$

4.16.3. Mode—Graphically (using histogram)

In a frequency distribution the value of mode can also be determined graphically. The steps in calculation are :

1. Draw a histogram of the given data.

2. Draw two lines diagonally on the inside of the modal class bar, starting from each upper corner of the bar to the upper corner of the adjacent bar.

3. Draw a perpendicular line from the intersection of the two diagonal lines to the X-axis (horizontal scale) which gives us modal value.

The method is illustrated by the example which follows :

Example 33. *The daily profits in rupees of 100 shops are given as follows:*

Profits (in ₹ lakhs)	*No. of shops*	*Profits (in ₹ lakhs)*	*No. of shops*
0–100	*12*	*300–400*	*20*
100–200	*18*	*400–500*	*17*
200–300	*27*	*500–600*	*6*

Draw the histogram and thence find the modal value. Check this value by direct calculation.

Solution. *Direct calculation :*

Mode lies in the class 200—300, $f_0 = 18, f_1 = 27, f_2 = 20$

$$\text{Mode} = L + \frac{\Delta_1}{\Delta_1 + \Delta_2} \times i = 200 + \frac{9}{9+7} \times 100 = 256.25 \quad [\Delta_1 = f_1 - f_0 = 9,\ \Delta_2 = f_1 - f_2 = 7]$$

From the above diagram, the modal value is also 256. Hence by both the methods we get the same value of mode.

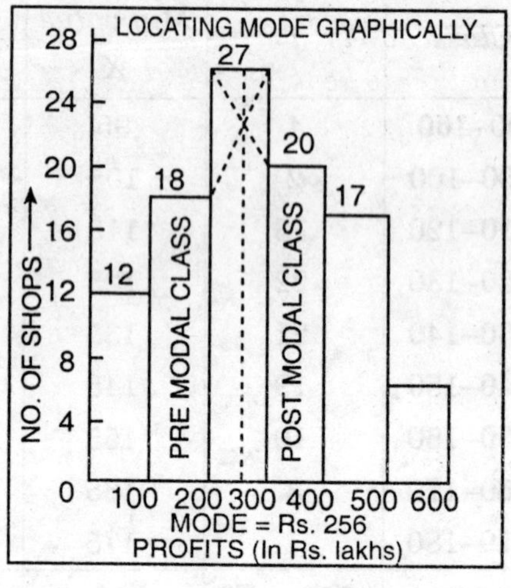

4.16.4. Merits and Demerits of Mode

Merits

1. It is easy to understand and easy to calculate. In many cases it can be located just by inspection.
2. It can be located in situations where the variable is not measurable but categorisation or ranking of observations is possible.
3. Like mean or median, it is not affected by extreme observations. It can be calculated even if the extreme observations are not known.
4. It can be determined even if the distribution has open end classes.
5. It can be located even when the class intervals are of unequal width provided that the width of modal and that of its preceding and following classes are equal.
6. It is a value around which there is more concentration of observations and hence the best representative of the data.

Demerits

1. It is not based on all the observations.
2. It is not capable of further mathematical treatment.
3. In central cases mode is not rigidly defined and hence, the important requisite of a good measure of central tendency is not satisfied.
4. It is much affected by the fluctuations of sampling.
5. It is not easy to calculate unless the number of observations is sufficiently large and reveal a marked tendency of concentration around a particular value.
6. It is not suitable when different items of the data are of unequal importance.
7. It is an unstable average because, mode of a distribution depends upon the choice of width of class intervals.

4.17 MORE PROBLEMS ON A.M., MEDIAN AND MODE

Example 34. *The following distribution is with regard to weight in grams of mangoes of a given variety, mangoes of weight less than 443 grams be considered unsuitable for foreign* *market. What is the percentage of total yield suitable for it? Assume the given frequency distribution to be typical of the variety:*

Weight in gms	*No. of mangoes*	*Weight in gms*	*No. of mangoes*
410–419	*10*	*450–459*	*45*
420–429	*20*	*460–469*	*18*
430–439	*42*	*470–479*	*7*
440–449	*54*		

Draw an ogive of 'more than' type of the above data and deduce how many mangoes will be more than 443 grams.

Solution. Mangoes weighing more than 443 gms. are suitable for foreign market. Number of mangoes with weights more than 443 gms. lie in the last four classes. Number of mangoes weighing between 444 grams and 449 grams would be :

$$\frac{6}{10} \times 54 = \frac{324}{10} = 32.4$$

Total number of mangoes weighing more than 443 gms. = 32.4 + 45 + 18 + 7 = 102.4

$$\text{Percentage} = \frac{102.4}{196} \times 100 = 52.25$$

Therefore, the percentage of the total mangoes suitable for foreign market is 52.25.

OGIVE BY MORE THAN METHOD

Weight more than (gms.)	*No. of mangoes*
410	196
420	186
430	166
440	124
450	70
460	25
470	7

From the graph, it can be seen that there are 103 mangoes whose weight will be more than 443 gms. and are suitable for foreign market.

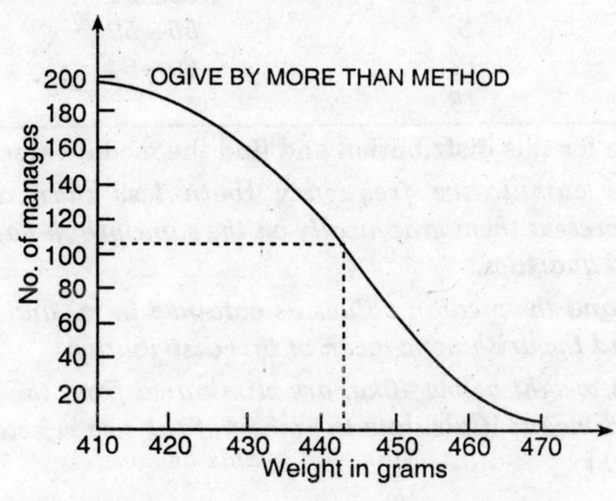

Example 35. *The following table gives the incomplete income distribution of 300 workers of a firm, where the frequencies of the classes 3000-4000 and 5000-6000 are missing. If the mode of the distribution is ₹ 4428.57, find the missing frequencies.*

Monthly Income (₹)	*No. of Workers*
1000-2000	*30*
2000-3000	*35*
3000-4000	*?*
4000-5000	*75*
5000-6000	*?*
6000-7000	*30*
7000-8000	*15*
Total	*300*

Solution. Let the frequency of the class 3000-4000 be f_1. Then the frequency of the class 5000-6000 will be equal to $300 - 30 - 35 - f_1 - 75 - 30 - 15 = 115 - f_1$. It is given that mode = 4428.57, therefore, modal class 4000-5000.

Thus, $L_m = 4000$, $\Delta_1 = 75 - f_1)$ $\Delta_2 = 75 - (115 - f_1) = f_1 - 40$ and $h = 1000$.

Using the formula for finding mode, *i.e.*,

$$M_0 = L + \frac{\Delta_1}{\Delta_1 + \Delta_2} i$$

$$4428.57 = 4000 + \frac{75 - f_1}{75 - f_1 + f_1 - 40} \times 1000$$

or $428.57 = \dfrac{75 - f_1}{35} \times 1000$ or $14.999 = 75 - f_1$

or $f_1 = 75 - 15 = 60$ (taking 14.999 = 15).

Also $f_2 = 115 - 60 = 55$

[f_2 = frequency of class 5000 – 6000]

Monthly Income (₹) *X*	*Frequency* *f*	
1000 – 2000	30	
2000 – 3000	35	
3000 – 4000	f_1	
4000 – 5000	75	← modal class
5000 – 6000	$115 - f_1$	
6000 – 7000	30	
7000 – 800	15	
	Total 300	

Example 36. *Below is given the frequency distribution of weights of a group of 60 students of a class in a school :*

Weight in kg.	*Number of students*	*Weight in kg.*	*Number of students*
30-34	*3*	*50—54*	*14*
35-39	*5*	*55—59*	*6*
40-44	*12*	*60—64*	*2*
45-49	*18*		

(*a*) Draw histogram for this distribution and find the modal value.

(*b*) (*i*) *Prepare the cumulative frequency (both less than and more than types) distribution, and (ii) represent them graphically on the same graph paper. Hence, find the (iii) median, (iv) 1st and 3rd quartiles.*

(*c*) *With the modal and the median values as obtained in (a) and (b), use an appropriate empirical formula to find the arithmetic mean of this distribution.*

(*d*) *If students with weight below 40kg. are eliminated from the frequency distribution, what will be the revised mean? [Calculate the mean of the two rejected classes only and use the result obtained in (c).]*

Solution. (*a*) To draw the histogram and cumulative frequency curves (both less than and more than types) we first convert the distribution into continuous class intervals as given in the adjoining table.

Weight in kgs.	*Number of students (f)*	*Less than c.f.*	*More than c.f.*
29.5–34.5	3	3	60
34.5–39.5	5	8	57
39.5–44.5	12	20	52
44.5–49.5	18	38	40
49.5–54.5	14	52	22
54.5–59.5	6	58	8
59.5–64.5	2	60	2

(*a*) *Histogram.* Histogram is obtained on erecting rectangles on the class intervals with heights proportional to the corresponding class frequencies.

Mode = OP = 48.

(*b*) (*i*) The 'less than' and 'more than' cumulative frequency distributions are given in the Table in Part (*a*)

(*ii*) The 'less than' and 'more than' (ogives) are drawn in the Fig. below.

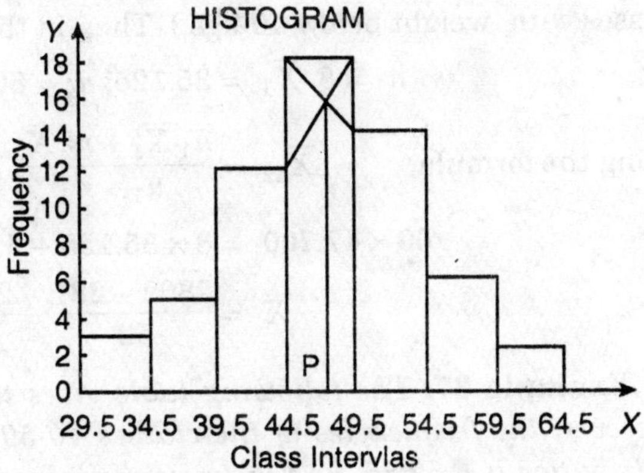

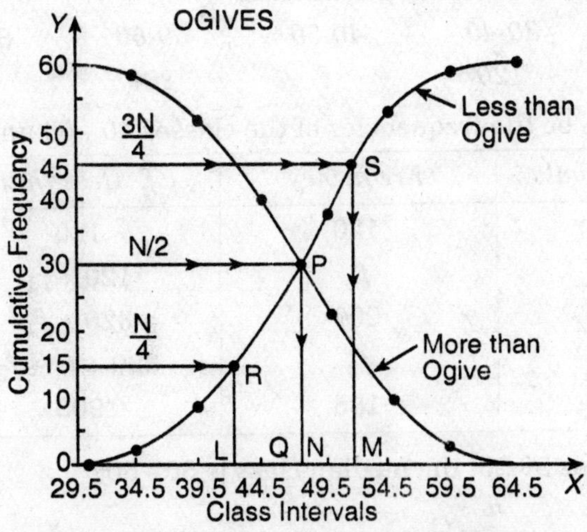

(*iii*) From the point of intersection P of the two curves (ogives), draw perpendicular on X-axis meeting X-axis at Q. Then OQ = 47.8 kgs. gives the median weight.

(*iv*) Draw lines parallel to X-axis at frequency equal to $\frac{N}{4} = 15$ and $\frac{3N}{4} = 45$ meeting the less than ogive at points R & S respectively. From R & S draw perpendiculars to X-axis meeting OX at L, M respectively. Then $Q_1 = OL = 42.9$ kgs. and $Q_3 = OM = 51.75$ kgs.

(c) The empirical relation between mean, median and mode is given by :

$$M_0 = 3Md - 2M \Rightarrow M = \frac{3Md - M_0}{2} = \frac{3 \times 47.8 - 48}{2}$$

$$\therefore \quad \text{Mean } (M) = \frac{143.4 - 48}{2} = \frac{95.4}{2} = 47.700 \text{ kgs.}$$

(d) Let $\overline{X}_1$ be the mean of the two classes with weight below 40 kgs.

Weight in kgs.	Mid-value (X)	(f)	fX
30—34	32	3	96
35—39	37	5	185
		$\Sigma f = 8 = n_1$, (say)	$\Sigma fX = 281$

$$\therefore \overline{X}_1 = \frac{\Sigma fX}{\Sigma f} = \frac{281}{8} = 35.125 \text{ kgs.}$$

Let $\overline{X}_2$ be the mean of the distribution obtained on eliminating the first two classes (*i.e.*, classes with weight below 40 kgs.). Then in the usual notations, we have

$$n_1 = 8, \overline{X}_1 = 35.125; n_2 = 60 - 8 = 52, \overline{X}_2 = ?, \overline{X}_{12} = 47.700 \quad \text{[From Part (c)]}$$

Using the formula, $\overline{X}_{12} = \dfrac{n_1 \overline{X}_1 + n_2 \overline{X}_2}{n_1 + n_2}$, we get

$$60 \times 47.700 = 8 \times 35.125 + 52 \overline{X}_2 \Rightarrow 2862 = 281 + 52 \overline{X}_2$$

$$\therefore \quad \overline{X} = \frac{2862 - 281}{52} = \frac{2581}{52} = 49.635 \text{ kgs.}$$

Example 37. *The following table gives the distribution of daily wage of 900 workers. However, the frequencies of the classes 40-50 and 60-70 are missing. If the median of the distribution is ₹ 59.25, find the missing frequencies.*

Wages (₹) :	*30-40*	*40-50*	*50-60*	*60-70*	*70-80*
No. of Workers :	*120*	*?*	*200*	*?*	*185*

Solution. Let f_1 and f_2 be the frequencies of the classes 40 - 50 and 60 - 70 respectively.

Class Intervals	*Frequency*	*c.f. (less than)*
30 - 40	120	120
40 - 50	f_1	$120 + f_1$
50 - 60	200	$320 + f_1$
60 - 70	f_2	$320 + f_1 + f_2$
70 - 80	185	900

Since median is given as 59.25, the median class is 50 - 60.

Therefore, we use $M_e = L_m + \dfrac{\frac{n}{2} - C}{f_m} i$

$$59.25 = 50 + \frac{450 - (120 + f_1)}{200} \times 10 = 50 + \frac{330 - f_1}{20}$$

or $9.25 \times 20 = 330 - f_1$ or $f_1 = 330 - 185 = 145$

Further, $f_2 = 900 - (120 + 145 + 200 + 185) = 250.$

Example 38. *Find median of the following distribution:*

Mid - Values	:	*1500*	*2500*	*3500*	*4500*	*5500*	*6500*	*7500*
Frequency	:	*27*	*32*	*65*	*78*	*58*	*32*	*8*

Solution. Since the mid-values are equally spaced, the difference between their two successive values will be the width of each class interval. This width is 1,000. On subtracting and adding half of this, *i.e.*, 500 to each of the mid-values, we get the lower and the upper limits of the respective class intervals. After this, the calculation of median can be done in the usual way.

Mid-values	*Class Intervals*	*Frequency*	*c.f. (less than)*
1500	1000 - 2000	27	27
2500	2000 - 3000	32	59
3500	3000 - 4000	65	124
4500	4000 - 5000	78	202
5500	5000 - 6000	58	260
6500	6000 - 7000	32	292
7500	7000 - 8000	8	300

Since $\frac{N}{2} = 150$, the median class is 4,000 – 5,000.

Hence $M_d = 4{,}000 + \frac{150 - 124}{78} \times 1{,}000 = 4{,}333.33.$ $\left[M_e = L_m + \frac{\frac{n}{2} - c}{f_m} i\right]$

Example 39. *The following are the marks obtained by students in a class test. Find the modal marks.*

Marks	*Students*	*Marks*	*Students*
32–35	*10*	*48–51*	*51*
36–39	*37*	*52–55*	*35*
40–43	*65*	*56–59*	*18*
44–47	*80*	*60–63*	*4*

Solution. It is clear from the data that the mode lies in the class 44–47. But the real limit of this class is 43.5–47.5

$$\text{Mode} = L + \frac{\Delta_1}{\Delta_1 + \Delta_2} \times i$$

$L = 43.5, \Delta_1 = (80 - 65) = 15, \Delta_2 = (80 - 51) = 29, i = 4$

$$\text{Mode} = 43.5 + \frac{15}{15 + 29} \times 4$$

$= 43.5 + 1.364 = 44.864$ or 44.9

Example 40. *From the following data on the weight of 122 persons determine the modal weight:*

Weight (in lbs.)	*No. of persons*	*Weight (in lbs)*	*No. of persons*
100–110	*4*	*140–150*	*33*

110–120	*6*	*150–160*	*17*
120–130	*20*	*160–170*	*8*
130–140	*32*	*170–180*	*2*

Solution. By inspection it is difficult to say which is the modal class. As frequencies of 2 classes 130-140 and 140-150 and 32 and 33 which are of the same magnitude.

Hence mode has to be determined indirectly by applying the formula:

Mode = 3 Median – 2 Mean.

Median = Size of $\frac{N}{2}$th item = Size of $\frac{122}{2}$ = 61st item

Hence median lies in the class 130—140

$$\text{Median} = L + \frac{N/2 - c.f.}{f} \times i$$

$L = 130, N/2 = 61, c.f. = 30, f = 32, i = 10.$

$$\text{Median} = 130 + \frac{61 - 30}{32} \times 10 = 130 + \frac{310}{32} = 139.69$$

Calculation of mean:

CALCULATION OF MEAN

Weight (in lbs)	*m*	*No. of persons* *f*	$d' = \frac{m - 135}{10}$	*fd'*
100–110	105	4	– 3	– 12
110–120	115	6	– 2	– 12
120–130	125	20	– 1	– 20
130–140	135	32	0	0
140–150	145	33	+ 1	+ 33
150–160	155	17	+ 2	+ 34
160–170	165	8	+ 3	+ 24
170–180	175	2	+ 4	+ 8
		N = 122		*Σfd'* = 55

$$\overline{X} = A + \frac{\Sigma fd'}{N} \times i$$

$A = 135, \Sigma fd' = 55, N = 122, i = 10$

$$\overline{X} = 135 + \frac{55}{122} \times 10 = 135 + 4.51 = 139.51$$

Mode = 3 Median – 2 Mean.

Mode = (3 × 139.69) – (2 × 139.51) = 419.07 – 279.02 = 140.05

Hence modal weight is 140.05 lb.

Example 41. *Calculate mean, median and mode for the following data pertaining to marks in Statistics out of 140 marks for 80 students in a class :*

Marks more than :	*0*	*20*	*40*	*60*	*80*	*100*	*120*
No. of Students :	*80*	*76*	*50*	*28*	*18*	*9*	*3*

Solution. CALCULATION OF MEAN, MEDIAN AND MODE

Marks	*No. of Students* *f*	*m.p.* X	*(X – 70)/20* *d*	*fd*	*c.f.*
0–20	4	10	– 3	– 12	4
20–40	26	30	– 2	– 52	30
40–60	22	50	– 1	– 22	52
60–80	10	70	0	0	62
80–100	9	90	+ 1	+ 9	71
100–120	6	110	+ 2	+ 12	77
120–140	3	130	+ 3	+ 9	80
	$N = 80$			$\Sigma fd = -56$	

Mean : $\overline{X} = A + \frac{\Sigma fd}{N} \times i = 70 - \frac{56}{80} \times 20 = 70 - 14 = 56$

Median : Med = Size of $\frac{N}{2}$ th observation = $\frac{80}{2}$ = 40th observation Median lies in the class 40-60.

Median lies in the class 40-60

$$\text{Med} = L + \frac{N/2 - c.f.}{f} \times i = 40 + \frac{40 - 30}{22} \times 20 = 40 + 9.09 = 49.09$$

Mode : Since the highest frequency is 26, mode lies in the class 20-40.

$$M_0 = L + \frac{\Delta_1}{\Delta_1 + \Delta_2} \times i = 20 + \frac{22}{22 + 4} \times 20 = 20 + 16.92 = 36.92$$

Example 42. *Calculate the median and mode for the distribution of the weights of 150 students from the data given below :*

Weight (in kg) :	*30–40*	*40–50*	*50–60*	*60–70*	*70–80*	*80–90*
Frequency :	*18*	*37*	*45*	*27*	*15*	*8*

Solution. CALCULATION OF MEDIAN AND MODE

Weight (kg)	*f*	*c.f.*
30–40	18	18
40–50	37	55
50–60	45	100
60–70	27	127
70–80	15	142
80–90	8	150
	$N = 150$	

Median = $\frac{N}{2}$th item = observation = $\frac{150}{2}$ = 75th observation; which lies in class 50—60, under *c.f.*

Median lies in the class 50–60.

$$\text{Median} = L + \frac{N/2 - C_b}{f} \times i = 50 + \frac{75-55}{45} \times 10 = 50 + 4.444 = 54.44$$

Mode : Since highest frequency is 45, mode lies in the class 50–60.

$$\text{Mode} = L + \frac{\Delta_1}{\Delta_1 + \Delta_2} \times i = 50 + \frac{8}{8+18} \times 10 = 50 + 3.08 = 53.08$$

Example 43. *Following distribution gives the pattern of overtime work per week done by 100 employees of a company. Calculate median, first quartile, and 7th decile.*

Overtime hours	:	*10–15*	*15–20*	*20–25*	*25–30*	*30–35*	*35–40*
No. of employees	:	*11*	*20*	*35*	*20*	*8*	*6*

Solution. CALCULATION OF MEDIAN Q_1 and D_7

Overtime (hrs.)	*f*	*c.f.*
10–15	11	11
15–20	20	31
20–25	35	66
25–30	20	86
30–35	8	94
35–40	6	100
	N = 100	

for Median, $\frac{N}{2}$th observation = $\frac{100}{2}$ = 50th observation

Median lies in the class 20–25.

$$\text{Median} = L + \frac{N/2 - C}{f} \times i = 20 + \frac{50-30}{35} \times 5 = 20 + 2.714 = 22.714$$

for Q_1, $\frac{N}{4}$th observation = $\frac{100}{4}$ = 25th observation

Q_1 lies in the class 15–20.

$$Q_1 = L + \frac{N/4 - C}{f} \times i = 15 + \frac{25-11}{20} \times 5 = 15 + 3.5 = 18.5$$

for D_7, $\frac{7N}{10}$th observation = $\frac{7 \times 100}{20}$ = 70th observation

D_7 lies in the class 25–30.

$$D_7 = L + \frac{7N/10 - C}{f} \times 5 = 25 + \frac{70-66}{20} \times 5 = 25 + 1 = 26.$$

Example 44. (*a*) *Find the missing frequency from the following data :*

Marks:	*0-10*	*10-20*	*20-30*	*30-40*	*40-50*	*50-60*
No. of Students	*5*	*15*	*20*	—	*20*	*10*

The arithmetic mean is 34 marks.

Solution. Let the missing value be X

FINDING MISSING FREQUENCY

Marks	*f*	*m*	*fm*
0–10	5	5	25
10–20	15	15	225
20–30	20	25	500
30–40	X	35	$35X$
40–50	20	45	900
50–60	10	55	550
	$N = 70 + X$		$\Sigma fm = 2200 + 35X$

$$\overline{X} = \frac{\Sigma fm}{N}$$

$$34 = \frac{2200 + 35X}{70 + X}$$

$$34\,(70 + X) = 2200 + 35X$$

$$2380 + 34X = 2200 + 35\,X \text{ or } X = 180$$

Hence the missing frequency is 180.

Example 45. *The median and mode of the following wage distribution are known to be ₹ 33.5 and ₹ 34 respectively. Three frequency values from the table are, however, missing Find these missing values.*

Daily wages in ₹	*Frequencies*
0–10	*10*
10–20	*10*
20–30	*?*
30–40	*?*
40–50	*?*
50–60	*6*
60–70	*4*
	230

Solution. Let the missing frequencies be:

20–30	x
30–40	y
40–50	$230–30 - x - y$

Since median and mode are 33.5 and 34 they both lie in the class 30–40.

$$\text{Med} = L + \frac{N/2 \; - c.f.}{f} \times i$$

Med = 33.5, $L = 30$, $N/2 = 115$, $c.f. = 20 + x$, $f = y$, $i = 10$

$$33.5 = 30 + \frac{115 - (20 + x)}{y} \times 10 = 30 + \frac{115 - 20 - x}{y} \times 10$$

$= 30 + \frac{95 - x}{y} \times 10$

$33.5y = 30y + 950 - 10x$

$3.5y = 950 - 10x$ ...(i)

$\text{Mode} = L + \frac{\Delta_1}{\Delta_1 + \Delta_2} \times i$

Mode = 34, $L = 30$; $\Delta_1 = (y - x)$; $\Delta_2 = [y - (230 - 30\ \ x - y]$; $i = 10$

$34 = 30 + \frac{y - x}{y - x + 2y - 200 + x} \times 10 = 30 + \frac{y - x}{3y - 200} \times 10$

$4 = \frac{10y - 10x}{3y - 200}$

$12y - 800 = 10y - 10x$ ...(ii)

$2y + 10x = 80$

or

Multiplying Eqn. (i) by 10

$$\begin{aligned} 3.5y + 10x &= 950 \\ 2y + 10x &= 800 \\ - \quad - \quad &\ \ - \\ \hline 1.5y &= 150 \\ y &= 100 \end{aligned}$$

Substituting the value of y in Eqn. (i),

$$\begin{aligned} 3.5 \times 100 + 10x &= 950 \\ 35 + x &= 95 \\ x &= 60 \end{aligned}$$

Thus the missing frequencies are:

Class intervals	*Frequencies*
20–30	$x = 60$
30–40	$y = 100$
40–50	$200 - 60 - 100 = 40$

Example 46. *Draw a percentile curve for the following distribution of marks obtained by 700 students at an examination.*

Marks	*0–10*	*10–19*	*20–29*	*30–39*	*40–49*
No. of Students	*9*	*42*	*61*	*140*	*250*
Marks	*50–59*	*60–69*	*70–79*	*80–89*	
No. of Students	*102*	*71*	*23*	*2*	

Find from the graph

(i) the marks at the 20th percentile, and

(ii) the percentile equivalent to a mark of 65.

Solution. A percentile curve is obtained on expressing the 'less than' cumulative frequencies as percentage of the total frequency and then plotting these cumulative percentage frequencies (P) against the upper limit of the corresponding class boundaries (x). These points are then joined by a smooth freehand curve.

COMPUTATION OF CUMULATIVE PERCENTAGE FREQUENCY DISTRIBUTION

Marks	*Frequency (f)*	*'Less than' c.f.*	*Percentage 'Less than' c.f. (P)*
– 9.5	9	9	1.3
9.5–19.5	42	51	7.3
19.5–29.5	61	112	16.0
29.5–39.5	140	252	36.0
39.5–49.5	250	502	71.7
49.5–59.5	102	604	86.3
59.5–69.5	71	475	96.4
69.5–79.5	23	498	99.7
79.5–89.5	2	700	100.0

Percentage 'less than' $c.f.$

$$= \frac{\text{'Less than' } c.f.}{\text{Total frequency}} \times 100$$

$$= \frac{c.f.}{700} \times 100 = \frac{c.f.}{7}$$

(*i*) To find marks (x) corresponding to the 20th percentile, at $P = 20$, draw a line parallel to X-axis, meeting the percentile curve at A. Draw AM perpendicular to X-axis, meeting X-axis at M. Then $OM = 31.5$, gives the marks at the 20th percentile.

(*ii*) To find percentile equivalent to mark $x = 65$, at $x = 65$, draw perpendicular to X-*axis* meeting the percentile curve at B. From B draw a line parallel to X-axis meeting the Y-axis at N. Then $ON = 92$, is the percentile equivalent to score of 65.

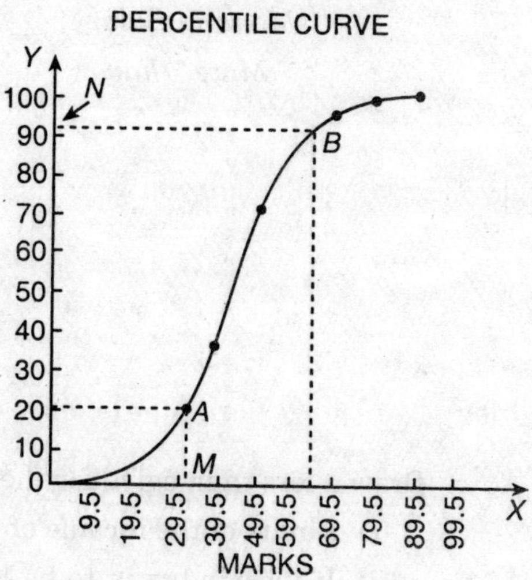

EXERCISE 4.1

1. Calculate Mean, Median and Mode for the data given below :

X	0.5	1.2	0.9	1.0	0.6	0.8	1.8	0.9	2.2	1.1

(AM = 1.1, M_d = 0.95, Mo = 0.9)

2. Calculate Mean, Median and Mode for the information given below.

Class Interval	0-4	5-9	10-14	15-19	20-24	25-29	30-34	35-39	40-44
Frequency	8	10	11	13	25	13	10	5	5

(AM = 21.15, M = 21.1, Mo = 22)

3. Compute median from the following data:

X :	10–19	20–29	30–39	40–49	50–59	60–69
f :	12	19	31	27	16	8

[$Md = 37.73$]

4. Calculate the value of mode from the following distribution.

Rent (in ₹)	*No. of Houses*	*Rent (in ₹)*	*No. of Houses*
15–25	8	55–65	40
25–35	10	65–75	20
35–45	15	75–85	15
45–55	25	85–95	7

[$Mo = 59.29$]

5. The monthly salary distribution of 250 families in a certain locality in Agra is given below :

Monthly Salary		*No. of families*
More than	0	250
" "	500	200
" "	1000	120
" "	1500	80
" "	2000	55
" "	2500	30
" "	3000	15
" "	3500	5

Draw a less than ogive for the data given above and hence find out

(*i*) Limits of the income of middle 50% of the families; and

(*ii*) If income-tax is to be levied on families whose income exceeds ₹ 1,800 p.m., find percentage of families which will be paying income-tax.

[(*i*) $Q_3 = 1,850$, $Q_1 = 578$; 578 — 1850; (*ii*) 26%]

6. Calculate mean, median and mode from the following data:

Marks		*Number of students*
More than	0	80
" "	20	76
" "	40	50
" "	60	28
" "	80	18
" "	100	9
" "	120	3

[$\overline{X} = 56$, $Md = 49.09$, $Mo = 45$]

7. Find mean and median for the following data:

Age	: Below 10	20	30	40	50	60	70	80
No. of persons :	5	25	60	105	180	250	275	320

[$\bar{X}$ = 46.875, Md = 47.33]

8. The following table gives the daily wages (in rupees) in a certain commercial organisation :

Daily wages (₹)	30–32	32–34	34–36	36–38	38–40
No. of Workers	2	9	25	30	49
Daily wages (₹)	40–42	42–44	44–46	46–48	48–50
No. of Workers	62	39	20	11	3

Calculate from the above data :

(*i*) the median and the third quartile wages; and

(*ii*) the number of wage-earners receiving between ₹ 37 and ₹ 45.

[(*i*) Med. 40.32; Q_3 = 42.54, (*ii*) 175]

9. An incomplete distribution is given below :

Variable :	10–20	20–30	30–40	40–50	50–60	60–70	70–80	Total
Frequency :	12	30	?	65	?	25	18	229

You are told that the median value is 46. Using the median formula, fill up the missing frequencies and calculate the arithmetic mean of the completed table.

[Freq. corresponding to 30 – 40 is 33.5; and corresponding to 50 – 60 is 45.5; and X = 45.87]

10. The following table gives the daily wages (in rupees) in a certain commercial organisation :

Daily wages (₹)	30–32	32–34	34–36	36–38	38–40
No. of Workers	2	9	25	30	49
Daily wages (₹)	40–42	42–44	44–46	46–48	48–50
No. of Workers	62	39	20	11	3

Calculate form the above data :

(*i*) the median and the third quartile wages; and

(*ii*) the number of wage-earners receiving between ₹ 37 and ₹ 45.

[(*i*) Med. 40.32; Q_3 = 42.54, (*ii*) 175]

11. Define percentile Find the 45th and 57th percentiles for the following data on marks obtained by 100 students :

Marks	20–25	25–30	30–35	35–40	40–45	45–50
No. of Students	10	20	20	15	15	20

[**Ans.** P_{45} = 33.75 ; P_{57} = 37.33]

12. Calculate median, first quartile and eighty-fifth percentile of the following data incomes :

Income in '00 ₹ :	0–5	5–10	10–15	15–20	20–25	25–30	30–35	35–40
No. of families :	75	250	350	192	68	35	24	6

[**Ans.** Median = ₹ 1250; Q_1 = ₹ 850; P_{85} = ₹ 1956.]

13. Find :

(*a*) the 2nd decile, (*b*) the 4th decile, (*c*) the 90th percentile, and (*d*) the 68 percentile for the data given below, interpreting clearly the significance of each.

Age of Head of Family (years)	*Number (in millions)*	*Age of Head of Family (years)*	*Number (in millions)*
Under 25	2.22	55—64	6.63
25—29	4.05	65—74	4.16
30—34	5.08	75 and over	1.66
45—54	9.47		Total 43.72

[**Ans.** D_2 = 31.94 years, D_4 = 40.38 years, P_{90} = 67.98 years, P_{68} = 52.87 years.]

14. Find the semi inter-quartile range for the following distribution :

Daily Income (in ₹)	*No. of families*	*Daily Income (in ₹)*	*No. of families*
0—75	14	200—250	334
75—100	52	250—350	443
100—150	200	350—550	218
150—200	239	250—800	225

Find also the median and find its difference from the average of two quartiles.

[**Ans.** $\frac{1}{2}(Q_3 + Q_1)$ = ₹ 237.92; Median = ₹ 255.30; $Md - \frac{1}{2}(Q_1 + Q_3)$ = ₹ 17.38.]

15. Find the (*i*) Lower quartile, (*ii*) upper quartile, (*iii*) 7th decile, and (*iv*) 60th percentile, for the following frequency distribution :

Wages (₹) :	30–40	40–50	50–60	60–70	70–80	80–90	90–10
No. of Persons :	1	3	11	21	43	32	9

[**Ans.** (*i*) ₹ 67.14, (*ii*) ₹ 83.44, (*iii*) ₹ 81.56, (*iv*) ₹ 78.37.]

16. Draw an ogive for the data given below and show how can the value of median be read off from this graph. Verify your result.

Class Interval :	0–5	5–10	10–15	15–20	20–25	25–30
Frequency :	5	10	15	8	7	5

[**Ans.** Median = 13.5 (approx.); By formula, Md = 13.33.]

17. Draw a 'less than ogive' from the following data and hence find out the value of lower quartile.

Class Interval :	0–5	5–10	10–20	20–30	30–40	40–50
Frequency :	5	7	15	20	8	5

[**Ans.** Q_1 = 12.]

18. The following table gives the distribution of the wages of 65 employees in a factory :

Wages in ₹ (Equal to or more than)	50	60	70	80	90	100	110	120
Number of Employees	65	57	47	31	17	7	2	0

Draw a 'less than' ogive curve from the above data, and estimate the number of employees earning at least ₹ 63 but less than ₹ 75.

[**Ans.** 15]

19. Draw a less than cumulative frequency curve of the following distribution and find the limits for the central 60% of the distribution from the graph.

x (less than) :	5	10	15	20	25	30	35	40	45
Frequency :	2	11	29	45	69	83	90	96	100

[**Ans.** 13 to 29.8]

20. Following is the distribution of marks in law obtained by 50 students :

Marks (more than) :	0	10	20	30	40	50
No. of students :	50	46	40	20	10	3

Draw on ogive curve on a graph paper. Also calculate the median marks.

21. Construct a frequency table for the following data regarding annual profits, in thousands of rupees in 50 firms, taking 25–34, 35–44, etc., as class intervals.

28	35	61	29	36	48	57	67	69	50
48	40	47	42	41	37	51	62	63	33
31	31	34	40	38	37	60	51	54	56
37	46	42	38	61	59	58	44	39	57
38	44	45	45	47	38	44	47	47	64

Construct a less than ogive and find :

(*i*) Number of firms having profit between ₹ 37,000 and ₹ 58,000.

(*ii*) Profit above which 10% of the firms will have their profits.

(*iii*) Middle 50% profit group.

[**Ans.** (*i*) 30, (*ii*) ₹ 62,000, (*iii*) ₹ 39,000 to ₹ 56,000.]

22. (*a*) Find out the value of median for the following data :

Weight in lbs. :	60–64	65–74	75–79	80–84	85–94	95–99	100–104
No. of students :	10	39	35	20	26	9	6

(*b*) Calculate the median from the following data :

Weight (in gms.) :	410—419	420—429	430—439	440—449	450—459	460—469	470—479
No. of Apples :	14	20	42	54	45	18	7

[**Ans.** (*a*) Median = 77.86 *lbs.* (*b*) Median = 443.94 gms]

23. Calculate Median and Arithmetic Mean from the following series :

05 men get less than ₹ 5 ; 30 men get less than ₹ 20

12 men get less than ₹ 10 ; 36 men get less than ₹ 25

22 men get less than ₹ 15 ; 40 men get less than ₹ 30

[**Ans.** Arithmetic Mean = 14.375; Median = 14.]

24. From the following distribution of hourly earnings, calculate :

(*i*) the most usual wage and (*ii*) the percentage of persons earning more than ₹ 31.50.

25—26	25	31—	340
26—	70	32—	130
27—	210	33—	90
28—	275	34—	55
29—	430	35—36	25
30—	550	Total	2,200

Also find :

(*iii*) the mean wage ; (*iv*) the median wage,

(*v*) the percentage of persons earning less than ₹ 27.50 per hour,

(*vi*) the percentage of persons earning between ₹ 28.50 and ₹ 31.50 per hour,

(*vii*) the hourly wage limits for the central 50% of the wage earners,

[**Ans.** (*i*) Modal hourly wage = ₹ 30.36.

(*ii*) Percentage of persons earning more than ₹ 31.50 pr hour is :

$$\left[\left(\frac{1}{2} \times 340\right) + 130 + 90 + 5 + 25\right] \times \frac{100}{2200} = 21.364$$

(*iii*) ₹ 30.14, (*iv*) ₹ 30.16, (*v*) 9.09%, (*vi*) 38.30%, (*vii*) ₹ 28.89 to ₹ 31.26.]

25. The following table gives the distribution of marks secured by some students in a certain examination :

Marks :	0–20	21–30	31–40	41–50	51–60	61–70	71–80
No. of Students :	42	38	120	84	48	36	31

Find: (*i*) Median marks.

(*ii*) The percentage of failure if minimum for a pass is 35 marks.

[**Ans.** (*i*) Md = 40.46 (*ii*) 31.58%.]

26. (*a*) Draw a less than cumulative frequency curve for the following distribution. Read the median from the graph and verify your result by the mathematical formula. Also obtain the limits of monthly income of central 50% of the employees :

Monthly Income (₹)	*No. of Employees*
Below 2000	3
2000—2200	7
2200—2400	25
2400—2600	30
2600—2800	24
2800—3000	9
3000 and above	2

[Med = 50 , Q_1 = 2320 , Q_3 = 2683.33 ,$Q_3 - Q_1$ = 363.33]

27. Calculate mean and median for the following data :

Profits (₹ Lakhs)	*Frequency*	*Profits (₹ Lakhs)*	*Frequency*
10–20	4	10–60	124
10–30	16	10–70	137
10–40	56	10–80	146
10–50	97	10–90	150

[$\overline{X}$ = 46.33 , Med. = 44.63]

28. The mean age of a combined group of men and women is 25 years. If the mean age of the group of men is 26 and that of the group of women is 21, find out the percentage of men and women in the group.

[**Ans.** Men 80% and women 20%]

29. You are given below a distribution of income per month. Calculate the most suitable average giving reasons for your choice:

Income (₹)		*Frequency*
Less than 100	...	40
100—200	...	89
200—300	...	148
300—400	...	64
400 and above	...	39

[Since it is an open end distribution, median would be more appropriate. Med. = 241.22]

4.18. GEOMETRIC MEAN (G.M.)

Geometric mean is another useful average which is specifically helpful to find averages of growth rates of population, prices, national income, depreciation rate, compound interest rates etc.

Geometric Mean—Defined

G.M. is n'th root of product of *n* variable values

Geometric Mean = $\sqrt[n]{X_1 X_2 \ldots X_n}$. Where *n* is number of items and $X_1 X_2$ are variables. If there are two numbers its square root is considered to determine Geometric Mean.

Example: If two numbers are 25 and 100, the GM will be $\sqrt{(5)^2 \times (10)^2} = 5 \times 10 = 50$

If there are 3 numbers, the cube root is the Geometric Mean. Calculation of geometric mean of two or 3 items is simple in the above method. If items are more, geometric mean cannot be calculated in the above procedure. Calculations are simplified if logarithms are used to calculate G.M.

$$G.M. = (X_1 X_2 X_3 \ldots\ldots X_n)^{1/n}$$

$$\log (G.M.) = \frac{1}{n} \log (X_1 X_2 \ldots\ldots X_n)$$

$$= \frac{1}{n} [\log X_1 + \log X_2 + \ldots\ldots + \log X_n]$$

$$= \frac{1}{n} \Sigma \log X = \frac{\Sigma \log X}{n}$$

$\Rightarrow$ logarithm of $GM = A.M.$ of logarithms of variable values.

or $GM = \text{Antilogarithm} \left(\frac{\Sigma \log X}{n} \right)$

Example 47. *The following are the numbers of the complaints received in 10 counters. Calculate GM.*

Complaints: 25 150 120 58 9 8 13 66 35 10

Solution:

X	$\log X$
25	1.3979
150	2.1761
120	2.0792
58	1.7634
9	0.9542
8	0.9031
13	1.1139
66	1.8195
35	1.5441
10	1.0000
	14.7514 $= \Sigma \log X$

$$\text{G.M.} = \text{Antilog of} \frac{\Sigma \log X}{N}$$

$$\text{G.M.} = \text{Antilog} \left(\frac{14.7514}{10} \right) = \text{Antilog } (1.47514)$$

$$\text{G.M.} = 29.86$$

4.18.1 Calculation of Geometric Mean Under Discrete Series

The following procedure is necessary to calculate Geometric Mean under discrete series:

1. Obtain logarithms to the values in the observation series $\log X$.
2. Multiply each '$\log X$' with respective frequencies and find its total $\Sigma f \log X$.
3. Find the total of frequencies, Σf.
4. Formula: Geometric Mean = Antilog of $\frac{\Sigma f \log X}{\Sigma f}$.

Example 48. *Calculate Geometric Mean of the information given below:*

X	2	3	4	5	6	7	8	9
f	6	10	18	22	16	12	8	8

Solution:

X	f	$\log X$	$f \log X$
2	6	0.3010	1.8060
3	10	0.4771	4.7710
4	18	0.6021	10.8378
5	22	0.6990	15.3780

$$\text{G.M.} = \text{Antilog of} \frac{\Sigma f \log X}{\Sigma f}$$

$$\text{G.M.} = \text{Antilog of} \frac{70.2436}{100}$$

6	16	0.7782	12.4512
7	12	0.8451	10.1412
8	8	0.9031	7.2248
9	8	0.9542	7.6336
	100		70.2436

G.M. = Antilog of 0.702436 = 5.040

Example 49. *Calculate Geometric Mean of the information given below:*

X	*8*	*9*	*10*	*11*	*12*	*13*	*14*
f	*1*	*8*	*6*	*10*	*8*	*5*	*2*

Solution:

X	*f*	log *X*	*f* log *X*
8	1	0.9031	0.9031
9	8	0.9542	7.6336
10	6	1.0000	6.0000
11	10	1.0414	10.4140
12	8	1.0792	8.6336
13	5	1.1139	5.5695
14	2	1.1461	2.2922
	40		41.4460

$$\text{G.M.} = \text{Antilog of } \frac{\Sigma f \log X}{\Sigma f}$$

$$\text{G.M.} = \text{Antilog of } \frac{41.4460}{40}$$

G.M. = Antilog of 1.03615 = **10.86**

4.18.2 Calculation of Geometric Mean Under Discrete Series

Procedure:

1. Calculate mid values of the class intervals and denote them '*X*' or '*m*'
2. Find out logarithms of mid-values, 'log *X*'
3. Multiply the logs of mid values with respective frequency and denote it by *f* log *X*
4. Find the sum of products Σ *f* log *X*
5. Find the total of frequencies, Σ*f*
6. Substitute the values in the formula to obtain Geometric Mean:

$$\text{G. M.} = \text{Antilog of } \frac{\Sigma f \log X}{\Sigma f}$$

Example 50. *Calculate the average age of walkers in a colony by using Geometric Mean.*

Age X	*10-20*	*20-30*	*30-40*	*40-50*	*50-60*	*60-70*
Walkers f	*5*	*12*	*28*	*35*	*15*	*5*

Solution:

Class	*f*	*X*	log *X*	*f* log *X*
10-20	5	15	1.1761	5.8805
20-30	12	25	1.3979	16.7748

$$\text{G.M.} = \text{Antilog of } \frac{\Sigma f \log X}{\Sigma f}$$

30-40	28	35	1.5441	43.2348
40-50	35	45	1.6532	57.8620
50-60	15	55	1.7404	26.1060
60-70	5	65	1.8129	9.0645
	100			158.9226

$$\text{G.M.} = \text{Antilog of } \frac{158.9226}{100}$$

G.M. = Antilog of 1.589226 = 38.84

Example 51. *Calculate the Geometric Mean of the following data.*

Class	*0-6*	*6-12*	*12-18*	*18-24*	*24-30*	*30-36*
Frequency f	*2*	*8*	*15*	*10*	*10*	*5*

Solution:

Class	f	X	$\log X$	$f \log X$
0-6	2	3	0.4771	0.9542
6-12	8	9	0.9542	7.6336
12-18	15	15	1.1761	17.6415
18-24	10	21	1.3222	13.2220
24-30	10	27	1.4314	14.3140
31-36	5	33	1.5185	7.5925
	50			61.3578

$$\text{G.M.} = \text{Antilog of } \frac{\Sigma f \log X}{\Sigma f}$$

$$\text{G.M.} = \text{Antilog } \frac{61.3378}{50}$$

G.M. = Antilog of 1.2271 = 16.87

4.18.3. Weighted Geometric Mean

In weighted geometric mean weights are given to the variables. The procedure is the same as followed in the discrete series. (as in case of weighted A.M.)

$$\text{G. M} = \text{Antilog of } \frac{\Sigma W \log X}{\Sigma W}$$

Where Σ W log X is the total of products of weights multiplied with respective variables

Σ W is total of weights.

Example 52. *Calculate the Geometric Mean of the following data.*

Items	*Food*	*Clothings*	*House*	*Fuel*	*Health*	*Others*
Index	*285*	*210*	*100*	*150*	*120*	*160*
Weights	*45*	*10*	*15*	*10*	*20*	*5*

Solution:

Items	X	W	Log X	$W \log X$
Food	285	45	2.4548	110.446
Clothing	210	10	2.3222	23.2220
House	100	15	2.0000	30.0000
Fuel	150	10	2.1761	21.7610
Health	120	15	2.0792	31.1880
Others	160	5	2.2041	11.0205
		100		227.6375

$$\text{G.M.} = \text{Antilog of } \frac{\Sigma W \log X}{\Sigma W}$$

$$\text{G.M.} = \text{Antilog of } \frac{227.6375}{100}$$

G.M. = Antilog of 2.276375 = **188.9**

Example 53. *Calculate the Geometric Mean of prices using quantities as weights.*

Items	*A*	*B*	*C*	*D*	*E*	*F*
Price	*155*	*68*	*95*	*262*	*71*	*80*
Quantity	*5*	*15*	*10*	*20*	*15*	*5*

Solution:

Items	Price X	Quantity W	Log X	W log X
A	155	5	2.1903	10.9515
B	68	15	1.8325	27.4875
C	95	10	1.9777	19.7770
D	262	20	2.4183	48.3660
E	71	15	1.8513	27.7695
F	80	5	1.9031	9.5155
		70		143.8670

$$\text{G.M.} = \text{Antilog of } \frac{\Sigma W \log X}{\Sigma W}$$

$$\text{G.M.} = \text{Antilog of } \frac{143.8670}{70}$$

G.M. = Antilog of 2.0552 = **113.6**

4.18.4 Properties of Geometric Mean

1. If geometric mean is placed in the place of each value of observations of a series, the product of values will be the same as the product of original values.

   For Example : GM of 16, 32, 64 = 32

   $16 \times 32 \times 64 = 32 \times 32 \times 32 = 32{,}768$

2. Sum of deviations of logs of observations from the logs of geometric mean is zero.
3. if geometric mean and number of items of two or more series are given, combined geometric mean can be computed.
4. If geometric mean and number of items are known, the product of values can be calculated.

4.18.5 Merits of Geometric Mean

1. Geometric Mean is the most suitable technique to study the average changes in the growth ratio or percentage of economic indicators such as GNP, Population, Price Index etc.
2. Geometric Mean is a rigidly defined average. If avoids the trouble of different interpretations.
3. Geometric Mean is a good representative of the series because it is based on all the items of the series.
4. It is less affected by extreme values.
5. Geometric Mean is a suitable measure when large weights are to be given to small values.
6. Geometric Mean is suitable for further mathematical treatment.
7. It is useful for finding the compound rates of change.
8. Geometric Mean widely applied in the construction of Index Numbers.

4.18.6 Demerits

1. Geometric Mean is difficult to understand and calculate. It requires the knowledge of logarithms.
2. The process of computation is lengthy, specially when the data is large with higher values of frequency.
3. It cannot be calculated without the aid of logarithm tables, calculators etc.
4. Geometric Mean cannot be used if any of the value in the series is '0' (Zero) or negative.
5. In many cases, Geometric Mean is not an actual value of the series.
6. If some of the values in the series are not known Geometric Mean cannot be calculated.

4.18.7 Use of Geometric Mean to find Average of compound interest rates

Suppose a bank pays compound rates of interest of r_1, r_2, r_3 for three years. Average of these rates is a rate r which applied uniformly for 3 years is equivalent to the different rates. Thus amount received after 3 years in 2 cases should be same.

Let A_3 be the amount after 3 years in two cases. Using compound interest formula.

$$A_3 = P\left(1+\frac{r_1}{100}\right)\left(1+\frac{r_2}{100}\right)\left(1+\frac{r_3}{100}\right) = P\left(1+\frac{r}{100}\right)^3 \quad \text{...(1)}$$

$$\Rightarrow \left(\frac{100+r_1}{100}\right)\left(\frac{100+r_2}{100}\right)\left(\frac{100+r_3}{100}\right) = \frac{(100+r)^3}{(100)^3}$$

$$\Rightarrow (100+r)^3 = (100+r_1)(100+r_2)(100+r_3) \quad \text{...(2)}$$

$$\Rightarrow (100+r)^3 = X_1\ X_2\ X_3\ [\text{where } 100+r_1 = X_1,\ 100+r_2 = X_2 \text{ and so on}]$$

$$\Rightarrow (100+r) = (X_1\ X_2\ X_3)^{\frac{1}{3}}$$

$$= \text{G.M. of } X_1, X_2 \text{ and } X_3$$

$$r = (\text{G.M. of } X_1, X_2 \text{ and } X_3) - 100 \quad \text{...(3)}$$

r is average interest rate.

Steps to calculate average interest rate

1. Add 100 to each interest rate (where r is a variable) to get another variable X.
2. Find G.M. of these X variable values.
3. Subtract 100 from the G.M. of X values to get average interest rate.

Example 54. *The price of a good increased by 5%, 8% and 77% for the years 2004, 2005 and 2006 respectively. Find the average increase in price.*

Solution. Though we are required to find average price increase, in this case we have to use G.M. to find average as it is most appropriate.

% Rise r	$X = 100 + r$	$\log X$
5	105	2.0212
8	108	2.0334
77	177	2.2480
		$\Sigma \log X = 6.3026$

$$\text{G.M.} = \text{A.L.}\left(\frac{\Sigma \log X}{N}\right) = A.L.\left(\frac{6.3026}{3}\right) = A.L.\ 2.1009 = 126.2$$

The average increase from 2002 to 2004 = r = G.M. (X) – 100

= 126.2 – 100 = 26.2% or approx. 26%

Example 55. *Find are average rate of increase in population which in the first decade has increased by 20%, in the second decade by 30% and in the third decade by 40%.*

Solution. CALCULATION OF GEOMETRIC MEAN

Decade	*% Rise r*	*X = 100 + r*	*log X*
1st	20	120	2.0792
2nd	30	130	2.1139
3rd	40	140	2.1461
			$\Sigma \log X = 6.3392$

$$\text{G.M.} = \text{A.L.}\left(\frac{\Sigma \log X}{N}\right) = A.L.\left(\frac{6.3392}{3}\right) = A.L.\ (2.1131) = 129.7$$

Thus the average rate of increase in population is (129.7 – 100) = 29.7 per cent per decade.

4.18.8 G.M. to find average depreciation rate

If d is depreciation rate per annum and P is present value of an asset, its value after a year $A_1 = P\left(1 - \frac{d}{100}\right)$ $\left[\text{as in case of growth rate } A_1 = P\left(1 + \frac{r}{100}\right)\right]$ Thus d may be taken as negative growth which decreases value of an asset.

Let d_1, d_2, d_3 be depreciation rates for 3 years and d be its average depreciation rate and A_3 is depreciated value after 3 years than $A_3 = P\left(1 - \frac{d_1}{100}\right)\left(1 - \frac{d_2}{100}\right)\left(1 - \frac{d_3}{100}\right)$ $= \left(1 - \frac{d}{100}\right)^3$

(refer to equation (1) of previous article)

Thus $\quad 100 - d = [(100 - d_1)(100 - d_2)(100 - d_3)]^{\frac{1}{3}}$

$\quad 100 - d = (X_1 X_2 X_3)^{\frac{1}{3}}$ [where $X = 100 - d$]

$\quad = \text{G.M. of } X_1, X_2, X_3$

$\therefore \quad d = 100 - \text{G.M. of } X_1, X_2, X_3$

Steps to find average depreciation rate

1. Let $X = 100 - d$ (a new variable X is defined)
2. Find G.M. of these X values.
3. Subtract G.M. from 100 to get average depreciation rate.

Example 56. *A machine is assumed to depreciate at the rate of 35.5% p.a. in value in the first year, 22.5% value in the second year and @ 9.5%, p.a. in value in the third year, each percentage being computed on the diminishing value. What is the average percentage depreciation for the three years.*

Solution.

Year	*r*	X = 100 – *r*	Log *X*
I	35.5	100 – 35.5 = 64.5	1.8096
II	22.5	100 – 22.5 = 77.5	1.8893
III	9.5	100 – 9.5 = 90.5	1.9566
			$\Sigma \log X = 5.6555$

$$\text{G.M.} = A.L.\left(\frac{\Sigma \log X}{N}\right) = A.L.\left(\frac{5.6555}{3}\right)$$

$$= A.L.\ 1.8852 = 76.78$$

The average rate of depreciation charged for three years is therefore = 100 – G.M. = 100 – 76.78

Average depreciation rate = 23.22%.

Example 57. *If the price of a commodity doubles in a period of 4 years, what is the average increase per year*

Solution.

Average increase per year is to be calculated by Geometric mean. Using compound interest formula.

$$A_n = P(1 + r)^n = 2P$$

Since $A_n = 2P$ in 4 years, $n = 4$

$$\Rightarrow \quad 2 = \left(1 + \frac{r}{100}\right)^4$$

Using logarithms

$\log 2 = 4 \log (1 + r')$ where $r' = \dfrac{r}{100}$

$0.3010 = 4 \log (1 + r')$

$\log (1 + r') = \dfrac{0.3010}{4}$

$\log (1 + r') = 0.07525$

$1 + r' = 1.19$ [using antilogarithm]

$r' = 1.19 - 1 = 0.19$

Hence average increase per year = 19%

Example 58. *The annual rate of growth of output of a factory in five years is 5.0, 6.5, 4.5, 8.5, and 7.5 per cent respectively. What is the compound rate of growth of output per annum for the period.*

Solution: Calculation of Geometric Mean. (Ave. of growth rates)

Year	*% Rise r*	*X = 100 + r*	*log X*
I	5.0	105.0	2.0212
II	6.5	106.5	2.0273
III	4.5	104.5	2.0191
IV	8.5	108.5	2.0354
V	7.5	107.5	2.0314
			$\Sigma \log X = 10.1344$

$$\text{G.M.} = A.L. \left(\frac{\Sigma \log X}{N}\right) = A.L. \left(\frac{10.1344}{5}\right)$$

$$= A.L. (2.02688) = 106.4$$

Thus the average rate of growth is 6.4% per year [r = (G.M. – 100)%]

4.19 HARMONIC MEAN

Harmonic Mean is an average with very specific application. Thus it is not a popular average.

H.M. is used to find averages of rates such as

1. Speed is kilometers per hour $= \dfrac{\text{Distance in kms}}{\text{Time in hours}}$
2. Price is ₹ per unit $= \dfrac{\text{Value in ₹}}{\text{quantity}}$
3. Interest is ₹ per annum (on ₹ 100) $= \dfrac{\text{Total interest (on ₹ 100)}}{\text{Time}}$
4. Typing rate is letters per hour $= \dfrac{\text{No. of letters in time } t}{\text{Time } t}$

4.19.1 Harmonic Mean – Defined

Harmonic Mean is defined as reciprocal of arithmetic mean of the reciprocals of values. It is denoted by H.M.

Reciprocal: Reciprocal of a number is that value which is obtained by dividing 'I' by the value.

Example Reciprocal of 15 is 1/15, 500 is 1/500, 1215 is 1/1215

Calculation of reciprocals is facilitated by reciprocal tables,

$$\text{Harmonic Mean} = \text{Reciprocal of} \frac{\frac{1}{X_1} + \frac{1}{X_2} \cdots \frac{1}{X_n}}{n} = \frac{n}{\frac{1}{X_1} + \frac{1}{X_2} + \ldots + \frac{1}{X_n}} = \frac{n}{\Sigma \frac{1}{X}}$$ to here X_1, X_2, X_3 ... are values in the series and n is number of variable values

4.19.2 Calculation of Harmonic Mean Under Individual Series

Procedure :

1. Find the reciprocals of values of the observations

2. Find the total of Reciprocals, Σ Rec X. = $\Sigma \frac{1}{X}$ [Rec. stands for reciprocal]
3. Substitute values in the formula.

$$\text{H. M} = \text{Reciprocal of } \frac{\Sigma \text{ Rec } X}{N} = \frac{N}{\Sigma 1/X}$$

HM = Harmonic Mean

N = Number of Items

Σ Rec. X = total of reciprocals of 'X' series

Example 59. *Calculate Harmonic Mean of the given data.*

X	6	7	8	9	10	11	12	13	14	15

Solution :

X	$\frac{1}{X}$
6	0.16667
7	0.1429
8	0.12500
9	0.11111
10	0.10000
11	0.09091
12	0.08333
13	0.07692
14	0.07143
15	0.06667
	1.03496 $= \Sigma \frac{1}{X}$

$$\text{H.M.} = \frac{N}{\Sigma \frac{1}{X}}$$

$$\text{H.M.} = \frac{10}{1.03496}$$

H.M. = 9.672

4.19.3 Calculation of HM under Discrete Series

Procedure:

1. Find out Reciprocals of the variables and denote them by $\frac{1}{X}$.
2. Multiply the reciprocal with respective frequency *i.e.,* find $\frac{f}{X}$
3. Obtain the total of these products = $\Sigma f/x$
4. Find out the sum of frequencies Σf. Apply the formula to obtain Harmonic Mean.

$$\text{H.M} = \frac{\Sigma f}{\Sigma f/x}$$

Example 60. *From the following data compute the value of harmonic mean:*

Marks	10	20	25	40	50
No. of students	20	30	50	15	5

Solution. CALCULATION OF HARMONIC MEAN

Marks *X*	*f*	(*f* /*X*)
10	20	2.000
20	30	1.500
25	50	2.000
40	15	0.375
50	5	0.100
	$N = 120$	$\Sigma (f/X) = 5.975$

$$\text{H.M.} = \frac{N}{\Sigma(f / X)} = \frac{120}{5.975} = 20.08$$

4.19.4 Calculation of Harmonic Mean — Continuous Series

For calculating harmonic mean in continuous series the procedure is the same as applied to discrete series. The only difference is that here we take the reciprocal of the mid-points.

Example 61. *From the following data compute the value of Harmonic mean:*

Class interval:	*10-20*	*20-30*	*30-40*	*40-50*	*50-60*
Frequency	*4*	*6*	*10*	*7*	*3*

Solution: CALCULATION OF HARMONIC MEAN

Class interval	*Mid–points* *m*	*Frequency* *f*	*f* / *m*
10–20	15	4	0.267
20–30	25	6	0.240
30–40	35	10	0.286
40–50	45	7	0.156
50–60	55	3	0.055
		$N = 30$	$\Sigma (f / m) = 1.004$

$$\text{H.M.} = \frac{N}{\Sigma(f / m)} = \frac{30}{1.004} = 29.88$$

4.19.5 Merits and Demerits of Harmonic Mean

Merits

1. It is a rigidly defined average.
2. It is based on all the observations.
3. It gives less weight to large items and vice-versa.
4. It is capable of further mathematical treatment.
5. It is suitable in computing average rate under certain conditions.

Demerits

1. It is not easy to compute and is difficult to understand.
2. It may not be an actual item of the given observations.
3. It cannot be calculated if one or more observations are equal to zero.
4. It may not be representative of the data if small observations are given correspondingly small weights.

4.19.6. Use of H.M.—Average of rates—Choice between H.M. and A.M.

In case we are required to get average of rates (given rates is X variable) and given one quantity out of two, ratio of which is rate will be used as weight (or frequency). For example in case we are required to find average of speeds (speeds is X variable) and speed is ratio of $\frac{\text{distance}}{\text{time}}$ and one of two variables either distance or time values related to given speeds are given which will be used as weight or frequency (f). If numerator variable is given we use H.M. to find *av.* of rates and if denominator variable values are given then to find average rate, A.M. is used.

Thus if speeds and corresponding distances are given than average speed is found by using H.M., where X variable is different speeds and distances given are used as f or w.

And different speeds (X variable) and time duration of these speeds (w or f) then average speed is found using A.M. Thus average of rates will be either weighted AM or HM.

Example 62. *A train travels 50 kms at a speed of 40 kms / hour, 60 kms at a speed of 50 kms / hour and 40 kms at speed of 60 kms / hour. Calculate the weighted harmonic mean of the speed of the train taking distance traveled as weights. Verify that this harmonic mean represents an appropriate average of the speed train.*

Solution.

X *Speed*	W *distance*	$\frac{W}{X}$
40	50	1.25
50	60	1.20
60	40	0.67
	$\Sigma W = 150$	$\Sigma \frac{W}{X} = 3.12$

$$HM = \frac{\Sigma W}{\Sigma \frac{W}{X}} = \frac{150}{\frac{50}{40} + \frac{60}{50} + \frac{40}{60}} = \frac{150}{1.25 + 1.20 + 0.67} = \frac{150}{3.12}$$

$= 48.13$ kms/hour

Verification :

$$\text{Average speed} = \frac{\text{Total distance travelled}}{\text{Total time taken}}$$

We note that the numerator of Equation (1) gives the total distance travelled by train. Further, its denominator represents total time taken by the train in travelling 150 kms, since $\frac{50}{40}$ is time taken by the train in travelling 50 kms at a speed of 40 kms/hour.

Similarly $\frac{60}{50}$ and $\frac{40}{60}$ are time taken by the train in travelling 60 kms and 40 kms at the speeds of 50 kms./hour and 60 kms/hour respectively Hence, weighted harmonic mean is most appropriate average in this case.

Example 63. *Ram goes from his house to office on a cycle at a speed of 12 kms / hour and returns at a speed of 14 kms / hour. Find his average speed.*

Solution. Since the distance d of travel at various speeds are equal, the average speed of Ram will be given by the harmonic mean of the given speeds.

$$\text{Average speed} = \frac{2d}{\frac{d}{12}+\frac{d}{14}} = \frac{2}{0.1547} = 12.92 \text{ kms/hour}$$

Example 64. *Peter traveled by a car for four days. He drove 10 hours each day. He drove first day at the rate of 45 kms / hour, second day at the rate of 40 kms / hour, third day at the rate of 38 kms / hour and fourth at the rate of 37 kms / hour. What was his average speed.*

Solution. Since the rate to be averaged is speed $\left(=\frac{\text{distance}}{\text{time}}\right)$ and the weights are given in terms of time therefore AM will be appropriate. Further, since Peter travelled for equal number of hours on each of the four days, simple AM will be calculated.

$$\therefore \text{Average speed} = \frac{45+40+38+37}{4} = 40 \text{ kms/hour}$$

Aliter

$$\text{Av. Speed} = \frac{\Sigma WX}{\Sigma W} \text{ (using } AM)$$

$$= \frac{1600}{40}$$

$$= 40 \text{ kms/hr.}$$

X *Speed*	W *Time*	WX
45	10	450
40	10	400
38	10	380
37	10	370
	$40 = \Sigma W$	1600

Example 65. *An individual purchases three qualities of pencils. The relevant data are given below:*

Quality	*Price per pencil (₹)*	*Money Spent (₹)*
A	*1.00*	*50*
B	*1.50*	*30*
C	*2.00*	*20*

Calculate average price per pencil.

Solution. In this case price (X-variable) $= \frac{\text{money spent}}{\text{quantity}}$. Given with price variable is the money spent (the numerator of the rate price) as such average price will be found using H.M.

Average price = weighted HM

$$= \frac{\Sigma W}{\Sigma W/X}$$

$$= \frac{100}{80} = 1.25$$

X *(price)*	W *(money)*	$\frac{W}{X}$
1.00	50	50
1.50	30	20
2.00	20	10
	$\Sigma W = 100$	$80\ \Sigma W/X$

Example 66. *In a certain factory, a unit of work is completed by A in 4 minutes, by B in 5 minutes, by C in 6 minutes by D in 10 minutes and by E in 12 minutes. What is their average rate of working? What is the average number of units of work completed per minute? At this rate, how many units of work each of them, the average, will complete in a six hour day? Also find the total units of work completed.*

Solution. Here the rate to be averaged is time taken to complete a unit of work, *i.e.*, $\frac{\text{time}}{\text{units of work done}}$. Since we have to determine the average with weights as time, therefore, *HM* of the rates will give appropriate average.

Thus, the average rate of working (per person) = $\frac{5}{\frac{1}{4}+\frac{1}{5}+\frac{1}{6}+\frac{1}{10}+\frac{1}{12}}$ = 6.25 minutes/unit.

The average number of units of work completed per minute = $\frac{1}{6.25}$ = 0.16.

The average number of units of work completed by each person = 0.16 × 360 [6 hours = 360 mts]
= 57.6.

Total units of work completed by all the five persons = 57.6 × 5 = 288.0.

Example 67. *A scooterist purchased petrol at the rate of ₹ 14, 15.50 and 16 per litre during three successive years. Calculate the average price of petrol (i) if he purchased 150, 160 and 170 litres of petrol in the respective years and (ii) if he spent ₹ 2,200,2,500 and 2,600 on petrol in the three years.*

Solution. The rate *i.e.* price is to be averaged is expressed as $\frac{\text{money}}{\text{quantity (litre)}}$

(*i*) Since quantities of petrol purchased (Denominator) are known. Average price will be found using A.M.

(*ii*) In this case money spent (numerator) for different prices is known as such H.M. is appropriate average.

(*i*) *AM*

Price	*Quantity*	*WX*
14	150	2100
15.5	160	2480
16	170	2720
	480 Σ W	7300 Σ WX

Av. price = $\bar{X} = \frac{\Sigma WX}{\Sigma W} = \frac{7300}{480}$

= 15.21 (₹/litre)

(*ii*) *HM*

Price X	*Value W*	*W/X*
14	2200	157.14
15.5	2500	161.29
16	2600	162.50
	7300 ΣW	480.93 Σ W/X

Average price = HM

$= \frac{\Sigma W}{\Sigma W/X}$

$= \frac{7300}{480.93}$

= 15.18 (₹/litre)

Example 68. *The amount of interest paid on each of the three different sums of money yielding 10%, 12% and 15% simple interest per annum are equal. What is the average yield per cent of sum invested?*

Solution. Since the amount of simple interest per annum is given and is equal, the appropriate average is harmonic mean.

We have $\text{Int} = P \dfrac{r}{100} t$

$$\frac{r}{100} = \frac{\text{Int}}{P} \quad [t = 1 \text{ as rate is per annum}]$$

In this case, rate is ratio of interest and principal and we know that interest is same (given) Thus rate and numerator of rate is known. Hence H.M. is appropriate to find average rate of interest. Let equal interest be A.

Rate % X	*Interest* W	*W/X*
10	A	$\frac{A}{10}$
12	A	$\frac{A}{12}$
15	A	$\frac{A}{15}$
	3A = Σw	

$$\text{H.M} = \frac{\Sigma W}{\Sigma W/X} = \frac{3A}{\frac{A}{10} + \frac{A}{12} + \frac{A}{15}}$$

$$= \frac{3}{\frac{6+5+4}{60}} = \frac{180}{15} = 12\%$$

Example 69. *A person walks 9 hours at a speed of 3 kms per hour and again walks 8 hours at a speed of 4 kms per hour. Find the average speed per hour by using appropriate average.*

Solution. In this case rate = speed = $\dfrac{\text{Distance}}{\text{Time}}$. Since speeds ($X$) and associated time (the denominator of rate) is given, A.M. is the appropriate average

$$\text{AM} = \overline{X} = \frac{\Sigma WX}{\Sigma W}$$

$$= \frac{59}{17} = 3.47 \text{ (kms/hr)}$$

Speed X	*Time* W	*WX*
3	9	27
4	8	32
	17 = ΣW	59 = ΣWX

4.20 RELATIONSHIP AMONG AM, GM AND HM

If all the observations of a variable are same, all the three measures of central tendency coincide, *i.e.*, $AM = GM = HM$. Otherwise, we have $AM > GM > HM$.

Example 70. *Show that for any two positive numbers a and b,* $AM \geq GM \geq HM$.

Solution. The three averages of a and b are :

$$AM = \frac{a+b}{2},\ GM = \sqrt{ab} \text{ and } HM = \frac{2}{\frac{1}{a} + \frac{1}{b}} = \frac{2ab}{a+b}.$$

Since the sequence of the difference between a and b is always a non-negative number, we can write

$$(a - b)^2 \geq 0 \text{ or } a^2 + b^2 - 2ab \geq 0 \text{ or } a^2 + b^2 > 2ab.$$

Adding $2ab$ to both sides, we have

$$a^2 + b^2 + 2ab \geq 4ab \text{ or } (a + b)^2 \geq 4ab$$

or $$\frac{(a + b)^2}{4} \geq ab \text{ or } \frac{a + b}{2} \geq \sqrt{ab} \qquad ...(1)$$

$\Rightarrow$ $$AM \geq GM \qquad ...(2)$$

Divide both sides of inequality (1) by $\frac{a + b}{2}$, to get $1 \geq \frac{2\sqrt{ab}}{a + b}$

Multiply both sides by $\sqrt{ab}$, to get $\sqrt{ab} \geq \frac{2ab}{a + b}$

$\Rightarrow$ $$GM \geq HM \qquad ...(3)$$

Combining (2) and (3), we can write

$$AM \geq GM \geq HM$$

Note : The quality sign will hold when $a = b$. The above result can also be generalised for n positive numbers.

Example 71. *For any two positive numbers, show that* $GM = \sqrt{AM \times HM}$.

Solution. If a and b are two positive numbers, then

$$AM = \frac{a + b}{2}, \; GM = \sqrt{ab} \text{ and } HM = \frac{2\,ab}{a + b}$$

Now $$AM.\,HM = \frac{a + b}{2} \cdot \frac{2ab}{a + b} = ab = (GM)^2$$

or $GM = \sqrt{AM \times HM}$. Hence the result.

Example 72. *(a) If AM of two observations is 15 and their GM is 9, find their HM and the two observations.*

(b) Comment on the following :

The AM of 20 observations is 25, GM = 20 and HM = 21.

Solution.

(*a*) $\sqrt{AM \times HM} = GM$

$\therefore \sqrt{15 \times HM} = 9$ or $15 \times HM = 81$. Thus, $HM = 5.4$.

Let the two observations be X_1 and X_2. We are given that $\frac{X_1 + X_2}{2} = 15$

or $$X_1 + X_2 = 30 \qquad ...(1)$$

Also $\sqrt{X_1 . X_2} = 9$ or $X_1 X_2 = 81$

We can write $(X_1 - X_2)^2 = (X_1 + X_2)^2 - 4X_1X_2$

$$= 900 - 4 \times 81 = 576$$

or $$X_1 - X_2 = 24 \qquad ...(2)$$

Adding (1) and (2), we get

$$2X_1 = 54, \; \therefore X_1 = 27. \text{ Also } X_2 = 3$$

(*b*) The statement is wrong because *HM* cannot be greater than *GM*.

EXERCISE 4.1

1. (*a*) A motor car covered a distance of 50 miles four times. The first time at 50 m.p.h. second at 20 m.p.h., the third at 40 m.p.h. and the fourth at 25 m.p.h. Calculate average speed and explain the choice of the average.

   (*b*) A man gets three annual raises in salary. At the end of the first year, he gets increase of 4%, at the end of second, an increase of 6% on his salary as it was at end of the year, and at the end of the third year, and increase of 9% on his salary as was at the end of the third year. What is the average percentage increase?

   (*c*) A machine is assumed to depreciate 40 per cent in value in the first year, 25% in the second year and 10% per annum for the next three years, each percentage being calculated on the diminishing value. What is the average percentage depreciation for five years?

   [**Ans.** (*a*) 29.63, (*b*) 6.3%, (*c*) 20.02%]

2. (*a*) Mr. A spends ₹ 100 for apples costing ₹ 10 per kilogram and another ₹ 100 for apples costing ₹ 8 per kilogram. What is the average price per kilogram?

   (*b*) A company expects the sale of its products to increase by 50% in the following year. By what percentage should it increase the selling price in order to double its gross revenue?

   (*c*) Three men take 12, 8, 6 hours respectively to husk an acre of corn. Determine the average number of hours to husk an acre.

   (*d*) In a moderately skewed distribution arithmetic mean = 24.6 and the mode = 16.1 Find the value of the median and explain the reason for the method employed.

   [**Ans.** (*a*) 4.44. (*c*) $\overline{X}$ = 8.67. (*d*) 25.1]

3. (*a*) From the information given below, find :

   (*i*) Which factory pays larger amount as daily wages?

   (*ii*) What is the average daily wage for the workers of two factories?

	Factory A	*Factory B*
No. of wage earners	250	200
Average daily wages	₹ 12.0	₹ 13.8

   (*b*) A cyclist covers his first three kms at an average speed of 8 km. per hour, another two km. at 9 kms. per hour and the last two km. at 2 kms. per hour. Find the average speed for the entire journey.

   (*c*) The average weight of a group of 25 boys was calculated to be 78.4 lb. It was later discovered that weight of one boy was misread as 69 lb. instead of the correct value 96 lb. Calculate the correct average.

   [**Ans.** (*a*) X_{12} = 12.8, (*b*) 4.3km., (*c*) 79.5]

4. (*a*) A person purchases one kilogram of cabbage from each of the four places at the rate of 20 kg., 16 kg., 12 kg. and 10 kg. per 100 rupee respectively. On the average how many kg. of cabbage has he purchased per 100 rupees?
[**Ans.** 13.5 kg.]

(*b*) If you spend ₹ 100 per week on apples and the price of apples for three weeks is ₹ 25, ₹ 20 and ₹ 10 per kilogram, what is the average price of apples for you?
[**Ans.** ₹ 15.79 per kg.]

(*c*) If a person spends ₹ 600 on books priced ₹ 40 each, ₹ 600 on books priced ₹ 50 each and ₹ 600 on books priced ₹ 60 each, can it be said that the average price of the books purchased by him is ₹ 50 ? Why ?
[**Ans.** No. Average price = ₹ 48.70 (Weighted Harmonic Mean).]

5. (*a*) In a certain office a letter is typed by *A* in 4 minutes. The same letter is typed by *B, C* and *D* in 5, 6, 10 minutes respectively. What is the average time taken is completing one letter ? How many letters do you expect to be typed in one day comprising of 8 working hours.
[**Ans.** H.M. = 5.58 minutes per letter ; Letters typed in 8 hours (480 minutes) = $\frac{480}{5.58} = 86.$]

6. A man travels from Agra to Dehradun covering 204 miles at a mileage rate of 10 miles per gallon of petrol and via Ghaziabad with an additional journey of 40 miles at the rate of 15 miles per gallon. Find the average mileage per gallon.
[**Ans.** 10.58 miles per gallon.]

7. The consumption of petrol by a motor was a gallon for 20 miles while going up from plains to hill station and a gallon for 24 miles while coming down. What particular average would you consider appropriate for finding the average consumption in miles per gallon for up and down journey, and why ?
[**Ans.** Harmonic Mean = 21.82 m.p. gallon.]

8. A man having to drive 90 kilometres wishes to achieve an average speed of 30 kilometres per hour. For the first half of the journey he averages only 20 km. p.h. What must be his average for the second half of the journey if his overall average is to be 30 km. p.h.
[**Ans.** 60 km. p.h.]

9. An investor buys ₹ 1,500 worth of shares in a company each month. During the first four months he bought the shares at a price of ₹ 10, ₹ 15, ₹ 20 and ₹ 30 per share. What is the average price paid for the shares bought during these four months? Verify your result.
[**Ans.** ₹ 16.]

10. During a period of decline in stock market prices, a stock sold at ₹ 50 per share on one day, ₹ 40 on the next day and ₹ 25 on the third.

(*i*) If an investor bought 100, 120 and 180 shares on the respective three days, find the average price paid per share.

(*ii*) In an investor bought ₹ 1000 worth of shares on each of the three days, find the average price paid per share.

[**Ans.** (*i*) AM = 35.75 (*ii*) HM = 35.29]

11. The annual rates of growth achieved by a nation for 5 years are 5.0, 7.5, 2.5, 5.0 and 10 per cent respectively. What is the compound rate of growth for the 5 year period?

    [**Ans.** 6%]

12. A man gets three annual increases in salary. At the end of the first year he gets an increase of 4% at the end of second year an increase of 6% on his salary as it was at the end of the first year, and at the end of the third year an increase of 9% on his salary as it was at the end of the second year. What is the average percentage increase?

    [**Ans.** 6.7]

13. A machine is assumed to depreciate 44 per cent in value in the first year, 25% in the second year and 10% per annum for the next three years, each percentage being calculated on the diminishing value. What is the average percentage depreciation for the five years?

    [**Ans.** 21.07%]

14. A certain store made weekly profits of ₹ 5,000, ₹ 10,000 and ₹ 80,000 in 2002. 2003 and 2004 respectively. Determine the average rate of growth of this store's profits.

    [**Hint :** It increased from 5000 to 80,000 in 2 years ⇒ $80,000 = 5000\left(1+\frac{r}{100}\right)^2$]

    [**Ans.** 266.6]

15. A economy grows at the rate of 2% in the first year, 2.5% in the second year, 3% in the third year, fourth year and 10% in the fifth year. What is the compound rate of growth of the economy for year period?

16. The number of bacteria in a certain culture was found to be 4×10^6 at noon of one day. At noon the number was 4×10^6. If the number increased at a constant rate per hour, how many bacteria at the intervening mid-night?

□□□

5

Measures of Variation

CHAPTER OUTLINE

- Definition
- Different Methods of Dispersion
- Operation on Dispersion
  (Correction, Combined Dispersion)
- Applications of Dispersion

5.1 INTRODUCTION

The various measures of central tendency discussed in the previous chapter give us one single value that represents the entire data. But the average alone cannot adequately describe a set of observations, unless all the observations are alike. It is necessary to describe the variability of dispersion of the observations. Also in two or more distributions the average value may be the same but still there can be wide disparities in the formation of the distributions. This is explained by the following simple example — Two small groups each having 3 students whose score are as follows:

Group A	49,50,51
Group B	20,50,80

Diagramatically these are represented as

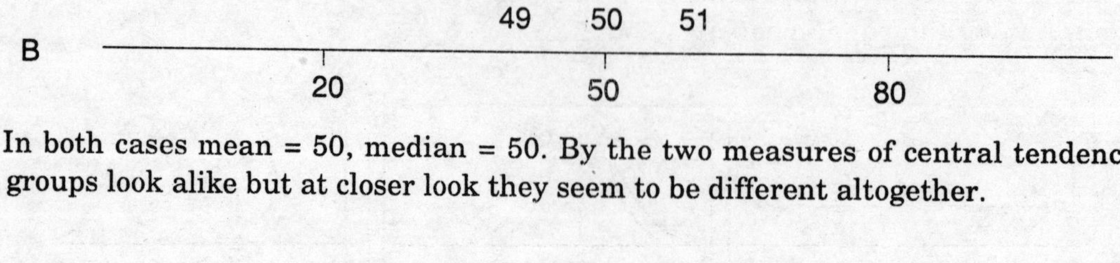

In both cases mean = 50, median = 50. By the two measures of central tendency these two groups look alike but at closer look they seem to be different altogether.

Another example : The wages of 5 workers in the three factories *A*, *B* and *C* are given below :

	Factory A *wages* (₹)	*Factory B* *wages* (₹)	*Factory C* *wages* (₹)
	2300	2310	2380
	2300	2300	2210
	2300	2304	2220
	2300	2306	2200
	2300	2280	2490
Total :	11,500	11,500	11,500
$\overline{X}$:	2,300	2,300	2,300

The above data pertains to five workers each in three different factories. Since the average wage is the same in all factories, one is likely to conclude that the factories are alike in their wage structure, but a close examination shall reveal that the wage distribution in the three factories differs widely from one another. In factory *A*, each and every worker is perfectly represented by the arithmetic mean, *i.e.*, average wage or, in other words, none of the workers of factory *A* deviates from the arithmetic mean and hence there is no variation. In factory *B*, only one worker is perfectly represented by the arithmetic mean, the other workers vary from the mean but the variation is very small as compared to the workers of factory *C*. Thus we find there is no variation in the wages of workers in factory *A*, there is very little variation in factory *B* but the wages of workers of factory *C* differ most widely. For the student of social sciences, the mean wage is not so important as to know how these wages are distributed. Are there a large number receiving the mean wage or are there a few with enormous wages and millions with wages far below the mean? The following three diagrams (given on next page) represent frequency distribution with some of the characteristics we wish to emphasise :

Measures of variation help us in studying another important characteristic of a distribution, *i.e.*, the extent to which the observations vary from one another from some average value. The significance of the measure of variation can best be appreciated from the above two examples :

The following three diagrams represent frequency distributions with some of the characteristics we wish to emphasise :

The two curves in diagram (*a*) represent two distributions with the same mean $\overline{X}$, but with different variations. The two curves in Diagram (*b*) represents two distributions with equal means and unequal variations. Diagram (*c*) represent two distributions with the same variations but with unequal means, $\overline{X}_1$, and $\overline{X}_2$.

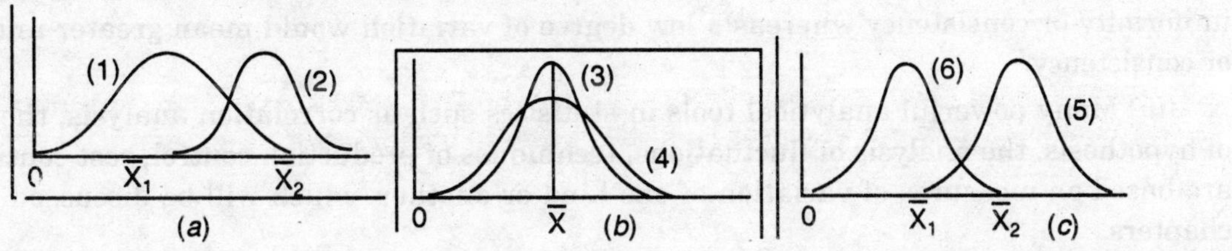

Fig. (a) shows two distributions with different means with different dispersions. Distribution (1) has larger dispersion.

In Fig. (b) Distributions (3) and (4) have same means but (4) has larger dispersion.

In Fig. (c) distributions (5) and (6) both have same dispersion but different means.

The measures of central tendency are, therefore, insufficient. They must be supported and supplemented with other measures. In this chapter, we shall be especially concerned with the measures of variation (or spread, or dispersion). A measure of variation is designed to state the extent to which the individual measures differ on an average from the mean. In measuring variation, we shall be interested in the amount of the variation or its *degree* but not in the *direction.* For example, a measure of 6 centimetres below the mean has just as much variation as a measure of 6 centimetres above the mean.

5.2 SIGNIFICANCE OF MEASURING VARIATION

Measures of variation are needed for four basic purposes:

(*i*) To determine the reliability of an average;

(*ii*) To serve as a basis for the control of the variability;

(*iii*) To compare two or more series with regard to their variability; and

(*iv*) To facilitate the use of other statistical measures.

A brief explanation of these points is given below:

(*i*) Measures of variation point out as to how far a sample average is representative of the entire data. When variation is small, this average is a typical value in the sense that it closely represents the individual value and it is reliable in the sense that it is good estimate of the average in the corresponding universe. On the other hand, when variation is large, the sample average is not so typical, and unless the sample is very large, the average may be quite unreliable.

(*ii*) Another purpose of measuring variation is to determine nature and cause of variation in case it is found to be large in order to control the variation itself. In matters of health, variation in body temperature, pulse beat and blood pressure are the basic guides to diagnosis. Prescribed treatment is designed to control their variation. In industrial production, efficient operation requires control of quality variation, the causes of which are sought through inspection and quality control programmes. Thus measurement of variation is basic to the control of cause of variation. In engineering problems, measures of variation are often specially important. In social sciences, a special problem requiring the measurement of variability is the measurement of "inequality" of the distribution of income and wealth, etc.

(*iii*) Measures of variation enable comparison to be made of two or more series with regard to their variability. The study of variation may also be looked upon as a means of determining uniformity or consistency. A high degree of variation would mean little uniformity or consistency whereas a low degree of variation would mean greater uniformity or consistency.

(*iv*) Many powerful analytical tools in statistics such as correlation analysis, the testing of hypothesis, the analysis of fluctuations, techniques of production control, cost control, etc., are based on measures of variation of one kind or another, which will be discussed in later chapters.

5.3 PROPERTIES OF A GOOD MEASURE OF VARIATION

A good measure of variation should possess, as far as possible, the following properties :

(i) It should be simple to understand.

(ii) It should be easy to compute.

(iii) It should be rigidly defined.

(iv) It should be based on each and every observation of the distribution.

(v) It should be amenable to further algebraic treatment.

(vi) It should have sampling stability.

(vii) It should not be unduly affected by extreme observations.

5.4 METHODS OF STUDYING VARIATION

The following are the important methods of studying variation :

I. The Range,

II. The Interquartile Range or Quartile Deviation,

III. The Average Deviation or Mean Deviation,

IV. The Standard Deviation.

5.5 ABSOLUTE AND RELATIVE MEASURES OF VARIATION

Measures of variation may be either absolute or relative. Absolute measures of variation are expressed in the same statistical unit in which the original data are given such as rupees, kilograms, tonnes, etc. These values may be used to compare the variation in two or more than two distributions provided the variables are expressed in the same units and have almost the same average value. In case the two sets of data are expressed in different units, such as quintals of sugar *versus* tonnes of sugarcane or if the average value is very different, such as manager's salary *versus* worker's salary, the absolute measures of variation are not comparable. In such cases measures of relative variation should be used.

A measure of relative variation is the ratio of a measure of absolute variation to an average. It is sometimes called a coefficient of variation, because "coefficient" means a pure number that is independent of the unit of measurement. It should be remembered that while computing the relative variation the average used as base should be the same one from which the absolute deviations were measured. This means that the arithmetic mean should be used with the standard deviation and either the arithmetic mean or median with the average deviation. "Coefficient" is taken to make the "measure" independent of units of measurement.

5.6 RANGE

Range is the simplest method of studying variation. It is defined as the difference between the value of the smallest observation and the value of the largest observation included in the distribution. Symbolically,

$$\text{Range} = L - S$$

L = Largest value, and

S = Smallest value

The relative measure corresponding to range, called the **COEFFICIENT OF RANGE**, is obtained by applying the following formula :

$$\text{Coefficient of Range} = \frac{L - S}{L + S}$$

Example 1. *The following are the prices of shares of a company from Monday to Saturday :*

Day	*Price (₹)*	*Day*	*Price (₹)*
Monday	*200*	*Thursday*	*160*
Tuesday	*210*	*Friday*	*220*
Wednesday	*208*	*Saturday*	*250*

Calculate range and coefficient of range.

Solution.

$$\text{Range} = L - S$$

$$L = 250 \text{ and } S = 160$$

$$\text{Range} = 250 - 160 = ₹\ 90$$

$$\text{Coefficient of Range} = \frac{L - S}{L + S} = \frac{250 - 160}{250 + 160} = \frac{90}{410} = 0.129$$

In a frequency distribution, range is calculated by taking the difference between the lower limit of the lowest class and the upper limit of the highest class.

Example. 2. *Calculate coefficient of range from the following data :*

Profits (₹ lakhs)	*No. of Cos.*	*Profits (₹ lakhs)*	*No. of Cos.*
10–20	*8*	*40–50*	*8*
20–30	*10*	*50–60*	*4*
30–40	*12*		

Solution. Coefficient of Range $= \frac{L - S}{L + S} = \frac{60 - 10}{60 + 10} = \frac{50}{70} = 0.714$

5.7 MERITS AND DEMERITS OF RANGE

Merits

1. It is easy to understand and easy to calculate.
2. It gives a quick measure of variability.

Demerits

1. It is not based on all the observations.
2. It is based only on extreme observations.
3. It gives rough idea of spread of observations.
4. It does not give any idea about the pattern of the distribution. There can be two distribution with the same range but different patterns of distribution.
5. It is very much affected by fluctuations of sampling.
6. It is not capable of being treated mathematically.
7. It cannot be calculated for a distribution with open end classes.

5.8 USES OF RANGE

Inspite of many serious demerits, it is useful in the following situations :

1. It is used in the preparation of control charts for controlling the quality of manufactured items.
2. It is also used in the study of fluctuations of, say, price of a commodity, temperature of a patient, amount of rainfall in a given period, etc.

5.9 INTER QUARTILE RANGE

Interquartile Range is an absolute measure of dispersion given by the difference between third quartile (Q_3) and first quartile (Q_1).

Symbolically, Interquartile range = $Q_3 - Q_1$.

The range of a distribution is not a satisfactory measure, particularly, when it contains extreme values. The presence of a very high and a very low observation unduly increases the range of distribution. To avoid this difficulty, interquartile range is used as measure of dispersion. Interquartile range is the range of middle 50% of observations as Q_1 is smallest value and Q_3 is largest value of middle 50% units (as shown in figure below. If the observations of a distribution are more densely concentrated around median, interquartile range will be less than half of the range. Further, if they do not have any concentration around median then corresponding interquartile range will be wide and will tend to be equal to half of the range.

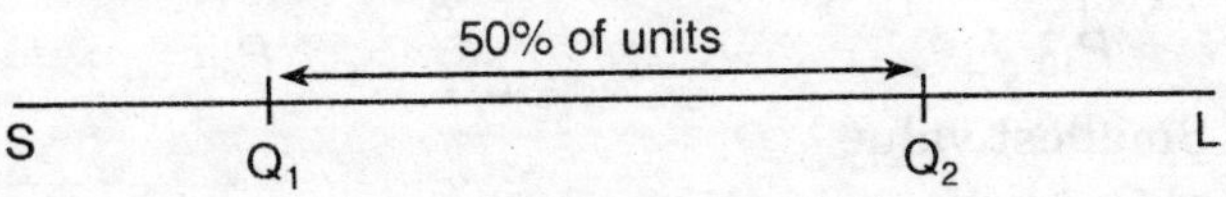

5.9.1. Quartile Deviation or Semi-Interquartile Range

Half of the interquartile range is called the quartile deviation or semi-interquartile range. Symbolically Q.D. = $\dfrac{Q_3 - Q_1}{2}$

The value of *Q.D.* gives the average magnitude by which the two quartiles deviate from median. If the distribution is approximately symmetrical, then $M_d \pm Q.D.$ will include about 50% of the observations and, thus, we can write $Q_1 = M_d - Q.D.$ *and* $Q_3 = M_d + Q.D.$

Further, a low value of *Q.D.* indicates a high concentration of central 50% observations and *vice-versa*.

Quartile deviation is an absolute measure of dispersion. The corresponding relative measure is known as coefficient of quartile deviation defined as

$$\text{Coefficient of Q.D.} = \frac{\dfrac{Q_3 - Q_1}{2}}{\dfrac{Q_3 + Q_1}{2}} = \frac{Q_3 - Q_1}{Q_3 + Q_1}$$

5.9.2. Merits and Limitations of Quartile Deviation

Merits. (*i*) In certain respects it is superior to range as a measure of variation. (*ii*) It has a special utility in measuring variation is case of open-end distributions or one in which the data may be ranked out measured quantitatively. (*iii*) It is also useful in erratic or highly skewed distributions, where the other measures of variation would be affected by extreme values. The quartile deviation is not affected by the presence of extreme values.

Limitations. (*i*) Quartile deviation ignores 50% items, *i.e.*, the smaller 25% and the larger 25%. As the value of quartile deviation does not depend upon every observation it cannot be regarded as a good method of measuring variation. (*ii*) It is not capable of mathematical manipulation. (*iii*) Its value is very much affected by sampling fluctuations. (*iv*) It is in fact not a measure of variation as it really does not show the scatter around an average but rather a distance on a scale, *i.e.*, quartile deviation is not itself measured from an average, but it is a positional average.

Consequently, some statisticians speak of quartile deviation as measure of *partition* rather than as a measure of variation. If we really desire to measure variation is the sense of showing the scatter around an average, we must include the deviation of each and every observation from an average in the measurement.

Because of the above limitations, quartile deviation is rarely used in practice.

5.10. INTER PERCENTILE RANGE , DERIVATION AND ITS COEFFICIENT

In case of *Q.D.* 50% of observations are ignored which is very large and hence to do away. this drawback we ignore only 20% of the observations (10% on either end). Thus interpercentile range.

S = Smallest value

L = Largest value

is defined as range of middle 80% units, *i.e.*,

Inter percentile range = $P_{90} - P_{10}$

Analogous to quartile deviation in this case also define percentile deviation (*P.D.*) and coefficient of *P.D.*

$$\text{Percentile Derivation } (P.D.) = \frac{P_{90} - P_{10}}{2}$$

$$\text{Coefficient of percentile deviation} = \frac{P_{10} - P_{10}}{P_{90} + P_{10}}$$

Thus theoretically *P.D.* Should be a better measure than *Q.D.* (as it is based on 80% of observation) but in practice it is not commonly used.

Example 3. *Find the quartile deviation, percentile deviation and their coefficients from the following data:*

Age (in years)	:	15	16	17	18	19	20	21
No. of Students	:	4	6	10	15	12	9	4

Solution.

TABLE FOR THE CALCULATION OF Q.D. AND P.D.

Age (X)	*No. of Students (f)*	*Less than c.f.*
15	4	4
16	6	10 ← 6th unit

17	10	20 ←15th unit
18	15	35
19	12	47 ←45th unit
20	9	56 ←54th unit
21	4	60

We have, $\frac{N}{4} = \frac{60}{4} = 15$ $\therefore$ $Q_1 = 17$ (by inspection)

$\frac{3N}{4} = \frac{3 \times 60}{4} = 45$ $\therefore$ $Q_3 = 19$ (by inspection)

$\frac{10N}{100} = \frac{10 \times 60}{100} = 6$ $\therefore$ $P_{10} = 16$ (by inspection)

$\frac{90N}{100} = \frac{90 \times 60}{100} = 54$ $\therefore$ $P_{90} = 20$ (by inspection)

Thus, $Q.D. = \frac{19 - 17}{2} = 1$ year and $P.D. = \frac{20 - 16}{2} = 2$ years

Also, Coefficient of $Q.D. = \frac{19 - 17}{19 + 17} = 0.056$

and Coefficient of $P.D. = \frac{20 - 16}{20 + 16} = 0.11$

Example 4. *Compute the quartile deviation, percentile deviation and their coefficients from the following distribution :*

Weekly wages (in ₹)	:	*0–100*	*100–200*	*200–300*	*300–400*
No. of workers	:	*12*	*18*	*35*	*42*
Weekly wages (in ₹)	:	*400–500*	*500–600*	*600–700*	*700–800*
No. of workers	:	*50*	*54*	*20*	*8*

Solution.

TABLE FOR THE CALCULATION OF Q.D. AND P.D.

Weekly Wages	*Frequency*	*Less than c.f.*
0–100	12	12
100–200	18	30 ←P_{10} class
200–300	35	65 ←Q_1 class
300–400	42	107
400–500	50	157
500–600	45	202 ←Q_3 class
600–700	20	222 ←P_{90} class
700–800	8	230

Calculation of Q_1

Since $\frac{N}{4} = \frac{230}{4} = 57.5$, $\therefore$ Q_1 lies in the interval 200 - 300.

$\therefore$ $L_{Q_1} = 20, f_{Q_1} = 35, h = 100$ and $C = 30$

Hence, $Q_1 = 200 + \frac{57.5 - 30}{35} \times 100 = ₹\ 278.57$

Calculation of Q_3

Since $\frac{3N}{4} = \frac{3 \times 230}{4} = 172.5$, Q_3 lies in the interval 500 – 600.

$\therefore \quad L_{Q_3} = 500, f_{Q_3} = 45, h = 100$ and $C = 157$

$$Q_3 = 500 + \frac{172.5 - 157}{45} \times 100 = ₹\ 534.44$$

Further, $Q.D. = \frac{534.44 - 278.57}{2} = ₹\ 127.94$

and coefficient of $Q.D. = \frac{534.4 - 278.57}{534.44 + 278.57} = 0.315$

Calculation of P_{10}

Since $\frac{10N}{100} = \frac{10 \times 230}{100} = 23$, P_{10} lies in the interval 100 – 200.

$\therefore \quad L_{P_{10}} = 100, f_{P_{10}} = 18, h = 100$ and $C = 12$

$\therefore \quad P_{10} = 100 + \frac{23 - 12}{18} \times 100 = 161.11$

Calculation of P_{90}

Since $\frac{90N}{100} = \frac{90 \times 230}{100} = 207$, P_{90} lies in the interval 600 – 700.

$L_{P_{90}} = 600, f_{P_{90}} = 20, h = 100, C = 202$

$P_{90} = 600 + \frac{207 - 202}{20} \times 100 = 600 + 25 = 625$

P.D. L percentile deviation $= \frac{P_{90} - P_{10}}{2} = \frac{625 - 161.11}{2}$

$= 231.95$ (₹)

Coefficient of *P.D.* $= \frac{625 - 161.11}{625 + 161.11} = 0.59.$

5.11. THE AVERAGE DEVIATION/MEAN DEVIATION (A.D./M.D.)

The three methods of variation discussed above, namely, range percentile and quartile deviations, are not measures of variation in the strict sense of the term because they do not show the scatterness around an average. However, to study the formation of a distribution we should take the deviations from an average. The two other measures, namely, the average deviation and the standard deviation, help us in achieving this goal.

Average deviation is obtained by calculating the absolute deviations of each observation from median (or mean), and then averaging these deviations by taking their arithmetic mean. The formula for average deviation may be written as :

Mean deviation from median = M.D._{Md} or $\text{A.D.}_{(\text{Med.})} = \frac{\Sigma \mid X - \text{Med.} \mid}{N}$

In case deviations are taken from mean the formula shall be written as :

$$M.D._{\overline{X}} \text{ or } A.D._{\overline{(X)}} = \frac{\Sigma \mid X - \overline{X} \mid}{N}$$

The relative measure corresponding to the mean deviation. called the coefficient of mean deviation, is obtained by dividing mean deviation be the particular average used in computing mean deviation. Thus, if mean deviation has been computed from median, the coefficient of mean deviation shall be obtained by dividing mean deviation be median.

$$\text{Coefficient of M.D. from median} = \frac{\text{M.D. from median}}{\text{Median}}$$

If mean has been used while calculating the value of mean deviation, in such a case coefficient of mean deviation shall be obtained by dividing mean deviation from mean by mean.

$$\text{Coefficient of } M.D._{\overline{X}} = \frac{\text{M.D. from mean}}{\text{Mean}}$$

Example 5. *Calculate the mean deviation and its coefficient of the two income groups of five and seven members given below :*

I (₹) :	*4,000*	*4,200*	*4,400*	*4,600*	*4,800*		
II (₹) :	*3,000*	*4,000*	*4,200*	*4,400*	*4,600*	*4,800*	*5,800*

Solution.

CALCULATION OF MEAN DEVIATION

Group I	*Absolute Deviations from median 4400 = |D |*	*Group II*	*Deviation from median 4400 = | D |*
4,000	400	3,000	1,400
4,200	200	4,000	400
4,400	0	4,200	200
4,600	200	4,400	0
4,800	400	4,600	200
		4,800	400
		5,800	1,400
$N = 5$	$\Sigma D = 1200$	$N = 7$	$\Sigma \mid D \mid = 4,000$

Mean Deviation : Group I: $M.D. = \frac{\Sigma \mid D \mid}{N}$

$$\left[\text{Median} = \text{Size of } \frac{N+1}{2} \text{ th item} = \left(\frac{5+1}{2}\right) \text{ size of 3rd item} = 4400 \right]$$

$$M.D. = \frac{1,200}{5} = 240$$

This means that the average deviation of the individual incomes from the median income is ₹ 240.

Mean Deviation ; Group II

$$\text{Median} = \text{Size of } \frac{N+1}{2} \text{ th item} = \left(\frac{7+1}{2}\right) \text{th item} = \text{size of the item} = 4400$$

$$\Sigma \mid D \mid = 4{,}000, N = 7$$

$$\therefore \quad \text{M.D.} = \frac{4{,}000}{7} = 571.43.$$

Note. If we were to compute coefficient of mean deviation we shall divide mean deviation by median. Thus for the first group :

$$\text{Coefficient of M.D.} = \frac{240}{4{,}400} = 0.054$$

and for the second group

$$\text{Coefficient of M.D.} = \frac{571.43}{4{,}400} = 0.130.$$

5.11.1. Calculation of Mean Deviation from discrete frequency distribution

Discrete Series. In discrete series the formula for calculating mean deviation is

$\text{M.D.} = \frac{\Sigma f \mid D \mid}{N}$ (by the same logic as given before)

$\mid D \mid$ denotes deviation from median or mean

Steps.

(*i*) Calculate the median of the series.

(*ii*) Take the deviations of the items from median or mean ignoring signs and denote them by $\mid D \mid$.

(*iii*) Multiply these deviations by the respective frequencies and obtain the total $\Sigma f \mid D \mid$.

(*iv*) Divide the total obtained in Step (*iii*) by the number of observations. This gives us the value of mean deviation from median.

Example 6. (*a*) *Calculate mean deviation from the following series :*

X	*10*	*11*	*12*	*13*	*14*
f	*3*	*12*	*18*	*12*	*3*

Solution. CALCULATION OF MEAN DEVIATION

	f	*c.f.*	$\mid D \mid = \mid X - 12 \mid$	$f \mid D \mid$
10	3	3	2	6
11	12	15	1	12
12	18	33	0	0
13	12	45	1	12
14	3	48	2	6
		$N = 48$		$\Sigma f \mid D \mid = 36$

$N = 48.\ \frac{N}{2} = 24$ Median = size of 24th item = 12

$$\text{M.D. (from Median)} = \frac{\Sigma f\,|D|}{N} = \frac{36}{48} = 0.75$$

$$\text{Coefficient of } M.D_{M_d} = \frac{M.D_{M_d}}{Md} = \frac{0.75}{12} = 0.0625$$

Example 6. (*b*) *Calculate the mean deviation from the mean for the following data:*

Size	:	2	4	6	8	10	12	14	16
Frequency	:	2	2	4	5	3	2	1	1

Solution. CALCULATION OF MEAN DEVIATION FROM MEAN

X	f	fX	$\lvert X-\overline{X}\rvert = [X-8] = \lvert D\rvert$	$f\lvert D\rvert$
3	3	4	6	12
4	2	8	4	8
6	4	24	2	8
8	5	40	0	0
10	3	30	2	6
12	2	24	4	8
14	1	14	6	6
16	1	16	8	8
	$N = 20$	$\Sigma fX = 160$		$\Sigma f\lvert D\rvert = 56$

$$\overline{X} = \frac{\Sigma fX}{N} = \frac{160}{20} = 8$$

$$M.D._{\overline{X}} = \frac{\Sigma f\,|D|}{N} = \frac{56}{20} = 2.8.$$

$$\text{Coefficient of } M.D._{\overline{X}} = \frac{M.D._{(\overline{X})}}{\overline{X}} = \frac{2.8}{8} = 0.35$$

5.11.2. Calculation of Mean Deviation — Continuous Series

For calculating mean deviation in continuous series the procedure remains the same as discussed above. The only difference is that here we have to obtain the mid-point of the various classes and take deviations of these points from median. The formula is same, *i.e.,*

$$\text{M.D.} = \frac{\Sigma f\,|D|}{N}.$$

Example 7. (*a*) *Find the median and mean deviation of the following data :*

Size	*Frequency*	*Size*	*Frequency*
0–10	*7*	*40–50*	*16*
10–20	*12*	*50–60*	*14*
20–30	*18*	*60–70*	*8*
30–40	*25*		

[*B.Com. Mysore Univ. 19...*]

Solution.

CALCULATION OF MEDIAN AND MEAN DEVIATION

Size	*f*	*c.f.*	*m.p. X*	$\lvert X-35.2\rvert = \lvert D\rvert$	$f\lvert D\rvert$
0–10	7	7	5	30.2	211.4
10–20	12	19	15	20.2	242.4
20–30	18	37	25	10.2	183.6
30–40	25	62	35	0.2	5.0
40–50	16	78	45	9.8	156.8
50–60	14	92	55	19.8	277.2
60–70	8	100	65	29.8	238.4
	$N = 100$				$\Sigma f\lvert D\rvert = 1314.8$

To find median find $\frac{N}{2} = \frac{100}{2} = 50.$

Thus median class is 30—40

Now $L_{M_d} = 30$ $f_{M_d} = 25$, $C = 37$, $h = 10$

$$\text{Thus } M_d = 30 + \frac{50-37}{25} \times 10 = 30 + \frac{170}{25} = 30 + 5.2 = 35.2$$

$$\text{Mean deviation from median} = M.D._{M_d} = \frac{\Sigma f\mid D\mid}{\Sigma f} = \frac{1314.8}{100} = 13.148$$

5.11.3. Merits and Demerits of Mean Deviation

Merits

1. It is easy to understand and easy to compute.
2. It is based on all the observations.
3. It is less affected by extreme observations *vis-a-vis* range or standard deviation (to be discussed) in the next section.
4. It is not much affected by fluctuations of sampling.

Demerits

1. It is not capable of further mathematical treatment. Since mean deviation is the arithmetic mean of absolute values of deviations, it is not very convenient to be algebraically manipulated. Thus there was need of some measure which is capable of being subjected to further mathematical treatment which is "Standard Deviation" discussed in next section.

5.12. STANDARD DEVIATION

Standard deviation usually denoted by the letter σ (small sigma) of the Greek alphabet was first suggested by. Karl Pearson as a measure of dispersion in 1893. It is defined as the positive square root of the arithmetic mean of the squares of the deviations of the given observations from their arithmetic mean. Thus if $X_1, X_2 ...., X_n$ is a set of n observations then its standard deviation is given by :

$$\sigma = \sqrt{\frac{1}{n}\Sigma(X-\overline{X})^2} \qquad ...(5.16)$$

where $\overline{X} = \frac{1}{n} \Sigma X$, is the arithmetic mean of the given values. ...(5.16*a*)

Steps for Computation of Standard Deviation

1. Compute the arithmetic mean $\overline{X}$ by the formula (5.16*a*).
2. Compute the deviation $(X - \overline{X})$ of each observation from arithmetic mean *i.e.,* obtain
$$X_1 - \overline{X}, X_2 - \overline{X}, \ldots, X_n - \overline{X}.$$
3. Square each of the deviations obtained in step 2 *i.e.,* compute $(X_1 - \overline{X})^2, (X_2 - \overline{X})^2, \ldots, (X_n - \overline{X})^2$.
4. Find the sum of the squared deviations in step 3 given by :
$$\Sigma(X - \overline{X})^2 = (X_1 - \overline{X})^2 + (X_2 - \overline{X})^2 + \ldots + (X_n - \overline{X})^2.$$
5. Divide this sum in step 4 by n to obtain $\frac{1}{n} \Sigma (X - \overline{X})^2$.
6. Take the positive square root of the value of obtained in step 5.
7. The resulting value gives the standard deviation of the distribution.

Example 8. *Find standard deviations of numbers 15, 10, 18, 8, 4.*

Solution.

X	$(X - \overline{X}) = (X - 11)$	$(X - \overline{X})^2$
15	4	6
10	– 1	1
18	–7	49
8	– 3	9
4	– 7	49
$\Sigma X = 55$ $\overline{X} = 11$		$124 = \Sigma(X - \overline{X})^2$

Thus
$$\sigma = \sqrt{\frac{\Sigma (X - \overline{X})^2}{n}}$$
$$= \sqrt{\frac{124}{5}} = \sqrt{24.8}$$
$$= 4.99$$

Variance (= σ^2) square of standard deviation is called variance *i.e.,* σ^2. In practice we are finding first $\frac{\Sigma(X - \overline{X})^2}{n} = \sigma^2$ and getting + ve square root of this.

Thus $\sigma^2 = \frac{\Sigma (X - \overline{X})^2}{n}$. In the above example σ^2 (variance) = 28.8.

5.12.1. Variance in case of graphed data

(*i*) Discrete (*ii*) Continuous is defined as $\frac{\Sigma f (X - \overline{X})^2}{\Sigma f}$ where X is given in case of discrete frequency distribution and X is mid-mark of class in case of grouped continuous data.

5.12.2. Another formula to find variance

We find that $\frac{\Sigma(X-\overline{X})^2}{n} = \frac{\Sigma X^2}{n} - \left(\frac{\Sigma X}{n}\right)^2$

[Proof : $\Sigma(X-\overline{X})^2 = \Sigma\,(X^2 - 2\,X\overline{X} + \overline{X}^2)$

$= \Sigma X^2 - 2\overline{X}\,\Sigma X + n\overline{X}^2$ [$\overline{X}^2$ is a constant is added n times]

$= \Sigma X^2 - 2\overline{X}\,(n\overline{X}) + n\,\overline{X}^2$

$= \Sigma X^2 - 2n\,\overline{X}^2 + n\,\overline{X}^2$

$= \Sigma X^2 - n\overline{X}^2 = \Sigma X^2 - n\left(\frac{\Sigma X}{n}\right)^2 = \Sigma X^2 - \frac{(\Sigma X)^2}{n}$

Thus $\frac{\Sigma\,(X-\overline{X})^2}{n} = \frac{\Sigma X^2}{n} - \frac{(\Sigma X)^2}{n^2} = \frac{\Sigma X^2}{n} - \left(\frac{\Sigma X}{n}\right)^2$]

In case $\overline{X}$ is not a whole number and is a typical fraction then finding $X - \overline{X}$ and $(X - \overline{X})^2$ is cumbersome, thus in place of $\frac{\Sigma(X-\overline{X})^2}{n}$. We may use $\sigma^2 = \frac{\Sigma X^2}{n} - \left(\frac{\Sigma X}{n}\right)^2$

Example 9. *We apply this method on example already solved, i.e., to find σ^2 for numbers 15, 10, 18, 8, 4.*

Solution.

X	X^2
15	225
10	100
18	324
8	64
4	16
$\Sigma X = 55 = n = 5$	729

$$\sigma^2 = \frac{\Sigma X^2}{n} - \left(\frac{\Sigma X}{n}\right)^2$$

$$= \frac{729}{5} - \left(\frac{55}{5}\right)^2$$

$$= 145.8 = 121 = 24.8$$

Thus we see $\frac{\Sigma\,(X-\overline{X})^2}{n} = \frac{\Sigma X^2}{n} - \left(\frac{\Sigma X}{n}\right)^2$ ...(1)

5.12.3. Short-Cut Methods

(*i*) Deviation Method (*ii*) Step deviation Method

(1) *Deviation Method :* As already explained in case of funding mean we change the variable X to d by conversion $d = X - A$.

Thus transformation is called "shift of origin" as zero of new variable starts at A as when $X = A$, $d = X - A = 0$.

$d = X - A$ ...(1)

$\Sigma d = \Sigma X - n\,A$

$\overline{d} = \overline{X} - A$ (Dividing by n) ...(2)

Subtracting (2) from (1) we get

$$d - \bar{d} = X - \bar{X}$$

$\Rightarrow$ $$\Sigma(d - \bar{d})^2 = \Sigma(X - \bar{X})^2$$

$\Rightarrow$ $$\frac{\Sigma(d - \bar{d})^2}{n} = \frac{\Sigma(X - \bar{X})^2}{n}$$

$\Rightarrow$ $$\boxed{\sigma_d^2 = \sigma_x^2} \quad ...(3)$$

$\Rightarrow$ Change of origin does not change the variance or we say variance is independent of shift of origin.

Thus $$\sigma_x^2 = \frac{\Sigma(d - \bar{d})^2}{n} = \frac{\Sigma d^2}{n} - \left(\frac{\Sigma d}{n}\right)^2$$ —[refer 5.12.2]

In case of grouped data we use the same formula after incorporating f in it.

i.e., $\sigma_x^2 = \sigma_d^2 = \frac{\Sigma f d^2}{\Sigma f} = \left(\frac{\Sigma f d}{\Sigma f}\right)^2$ in both types of grouped data, *i.e.*, grouped discrete or continuous distributions.

Example 10. *Find variance of 15, 10, 18, 8, 4 using "deviation method" with A = 12.*

Solution.

X	$d = X - 12$	d^2
15	3	9
10	– 2	4
18	6	36
8	– 4	16
4	– 8	64
	– 5 Σd	129 $= \Sigma d^2$

$$\sigma_x^2 = \sigma_d^2 = \frac{\Sigma d^2}{n} - \left(\frac{\Sigma d}{n}\right)^2$$

$$= \frac{129}{5} - \left(\frac{-5}{5}\right)^2$$

$$= \frac{124}{5} = 24.8$$

Same as obtained in examples 8 and 9)

Example 11. *Complete a table showing the frequencies with which words of different numbers of letters occur in the extract reproduced below (omitting punctuation marks) treating as the variable the number of letters in each word, and obtain the mean and standard deviation of the distribution :*

"Her eyes were blue : blue as autumn distance — blue as the blue we see, between the retreating mouldings of hills and woody slopes on a sunny September morning : a misty and shady blue, that had no beginning or surface, and was looked into rather than at."

Solution. Here we take the variable (X) as the number of letters in each word in the extract given above. We find that in the extract given above there are words with number of letters ranging from 1 to 10. Hence, the variable X takes the values from 1 to 10. The frequency distribution is easily obtained by using 'tally marks' as given in the following Table.

$$\text{Mean} = A + \frac{\Sigma fd}{N} = 6 + \left(\frac{-76}{46}\right)$$

$$= 6 - 1.65 = 4.35$$

$$\sigma^2 = \frac{1}{N} fd^2 - \left(\frac{1}{N}\Sigma fd\right)^2$$

$$= \frac{345}{46} - (-1.65)^2$$

$$= 7.6956 - 2.7225$$

$$= 4.9731$$

$$\Rightarrow \sigma = \sqrt{4.9731} = 2.23$$

No. of letters in a word (X)	Frequency (f)	d = X − A = X − 6	fd	fd²
1	2	−5	−10	50
2	8	−4	−32	128
3	9	−3	−27	81
4	10	−2	−20	40
5	5	−1	−5	5
6	4	0	0	0
7	3	1	3	3
8	1	2	2	4
9	3	3	9	27
10	1	4	4	16
Total	$N = \Sigma f = 46$		$\Sigma fd = -76$	$\Sigma fd^2 = 354$

[**Note :** fd^2 its computed by multiplying fd and d]

5.12.4. Step deviation method

As already described we use transformation $u = \frac{X-A}{C}$ where C is common factor of d *values* (in place of d' earlier used, value u is used for convenience)

In this case $$u = \frac{X-A}{C} \quad \text{...(4)}$$

$$\bar{u} = \frac{1}{c}(\bar{X} - A) \quad \text{...(5)}$$

$$u - \bar{u} = \frac{1}{c}(X - \bar{X})$$

$$\Rightarrow \frac{\Sigma(u - \bar{u})^2}{n} = \frac{1}{C^2}\frac{\Sigma(X - \bar{X})^2}{n}$$

$$\Rightarrow \sigma_u^2 = \frac{1}{C^2}\sigma_x^2$$

$$\Rightarrow \boxed{\sigma_x^2 = C^2\sigma_u^2} \quad \text{...(6)}$$

5.12.5 Change of scale (Step deviation method)

$u = \frac{X-A}{C}$ is called shift of origin and change of scale, division by C amounts to change of scale). Now we see that change of scale changes variance of X. Thus we say that the variance is independent of shift of origin and dependent of change of scale.

Thus $$\sigma_x^2 = C^2\sigma_u^2$$

$$= C^2\left[\frac{\Sigma u^2}{n} - \left(\frac{\Sigma u}{n}\right)^2\right] \text{ or } C^2\left[\frac{\Sigma f u^2}{\Sigma f} - \left(\frac{\Sigma fu}{\Sigma f}\right)^2\right] \quad \text{...(7)}$$

according to it ungrouped data or grouped data.

Example 12. *Calculate the mean and standard deviation from the following data :*

Value :	*90–99*	*90–89*	*70–79*	*60–69*	*50–59*	*40–49*	*30–39*
Frequency :	*2*	*12*	*22*	*22*	*14*	*4*	*1*

Solution.

CALCULATIONS FOR MEAN AND S.D.

Class	*Mid-value* (*x*)	*Frequency* (*f*)	$d = \frac{x - 64.5}{10}$	*fd*	fd^2
90–99	94.5	2	3	6	18
80–89	84.5	12	2	24	48
70–79	74.5	22	1	22	22
60–69	64.5	20	0	0	0
50–59	54.5	14	–1	–14	14
40–49	44.5	4	–2	–8	16
30–39	34.5	1	–3	–3	9
Total		$N = 75$		$\Sigma fd = 27$	$\Sigma fd^2 = 127$

$$\text{Mean } = A + \frac{C\Sigma fd}{N} = 64.5 + \frac{10 \times 27}{75} = 64.5 + 3.6 = 68.1$$

$$\text{S.D.} = C.\sqrt{\frac{\Sigma fd^2}{N} - \left(\frac{\Sigma fd}{N}\right)^2} = 10 \times \sqrt{\frac{127}{75} - \left(\frac{27}{75}\right)^2} = 10 \times \sqrt{1.6933 - 0.1296}$$

$$= 10 \times \sqrt{1.5637} = 10 \times 1.2505 = 12.505.$$

Example 13. *The arithmetic mean and the standard deviation of a set of 9 items are 43 and 5 respectively. If an item of value 63 is added to the set, find the mean and standard deviation of 10 items.*

Solution. We are given : $n = 9, \bar{x} = 43$ and $\sigma = 5$.

$$\bar{x} = \frac{\Sigma x}{n} \Rightarrow \Sigma x = n\,\bar{x} = 9 \times 43 = 387$$

Also $$\sigma^2 = \frac{\Sigma x^2}{n} - (\bar{x})^2 \Rightarrow \Sigma x^2 = n(\sigma^2 + \bar{x}^2)$$

$\therefore$ $$\Sigma x^2 = 9(25 + 43^2) = 9(25 + 1849) = 9 \times 1874 = 16866$$

If a new item 63 is added, then number of terms becomes 10.

$$\text{New } (\Sigma x) = \text{old } \Sigma x + 63 = 387 + 63 = 450$$

$\therefore$ $$\text{New mean } = \frac{450}{10} = 45$$

$$\text{New } (\Sigma x^2) = \text{old } \Sigma x^2 + 63^2 = 16866 + 3969 = 20835$$

$$\text{New } s.d. = \sqrt{\frac{\text{New } (\Sigma x^2)}{10} - (\text{New mean})^2} = \sqrt{\frac{20835}{10} - (45)^2}$$

$$= \sqrt{2083.5 - 2025} = \sqrt{58.5} = 7.65.$$

[Note : If all values of X are same and in that case $\sigma^2 = 0$ as let $X_1 = X_2 = \ldots\ldots\ldots = X_n = k$ (a constant) then $\bar{X} = k$. Thus $\Sigma(X - \bar{X})^2 = 0 \Rightarrow \sigma^2 = 0$]

Example 14. *Twenty passengers were found ticketless on a bus. The sum of squares and the S.D. of the amount found in their pockets were ₹ 2,000.00 and ₹ 6.00 respectively. If the total fine imposed on these passengers is equal to the total amount recovered from them and fine imposed is uniform, what is the amount each one of them has to pay as fine ? What difficulties do you visualize if such a system of penalty were imposed ?*

Solution. Let x_i, $i = 1, 2, ..., 20$ be the amount (in ₹) found in the pocket of the ith passenger. Then we are given :

$$n = 20, \sum_{i=1}^{20} x_i^2 = ₹\ 2,000 \text{ and s.d.}(\sigma) = ₹\ 6$$

The total fine imposed on the ticketless passengers is given to be equal to the total amount recovered from them.

$$\therefore \qquad \text{Total fine imposed on the 20 passengers} = \sum_{i=1}^{20} x_i.$$

Further, since the fine imposed is uniform among all the 20 passengers,

$$\therefore \qquad \text{Fine to be paid by each passenger} = \frac{1}{20} \sum_{i=1}^{n} x_i = \bar{x}$$

$$\text{We have : } \sigma^2 = \frac{1}{n} \Sigma x_i^2 - \bar{x}^2 \quad \Rightarrow \quad \bar{x}^2 = \frac{1}{20} \Sigma x_i^2 - \sigma^2$$

$$\therefore \qquad \bar{x}^2 = \left(\frac{2000}{20} - 6^2 \right) = (100 - 36) = 64, \quad \Rightarrow \quad \bar{x} = 8\ (₹)\ [\text{From } (i)]$$

Hence, using (ii), the fine paid by each of the passengers is ₹ 8.

If among these ticketless passengers, there are a few rich persons with large sums of money in their pockets, then an obvious shortcoming of this system of imposing penalty is that the poor persons have to pay higher penalty.

Example 15. *Find the standard deviation for the following distribution:*

X :	*4.5*	*14.5*	*24.5*	*34.5*	*44.5*	*54.5*	*64.5*
f :	*1*	*5*	*12*	*22*	*17*	*9*	*4*

Solution. CALCULATION OF STANDARD DEVIATION

X	f	(X–34.5)/10 d	fd	fd^2
4.5	1	– 3	– 3	9
14.5	5	– 2	– 10	20
24.5	12	– 1	– 12	12
34.5	22	0	0	0
44.5	17	+ 1	+ 17	17
54.5	9	+ 2	+ 18	36
64.5	4	+ 3	+ 12	36
	$N = 70$		$\Sigma fd = 22$	$\Sigma fd^2 = 130$

$$\sigma = \sqrt{\frac{\Sigma fd^2}{N} - \left(\frac{\Sigma fd}{N}\right)^2} \times c$$

Here $\Sigma fd^2 = 130$, $\Sigma fd = 22$, $c = 10$, $N = 70$

Substituting the values

$$\sigma = \sqrt{\frac{130}{70} - \left(\frac{22}{70}\right)^2} \times 10 = \sqrt{1.857 - 1} \times 10$$

$$= \sqrt{1.757} \times 10 = 1.326 \times 10 = 13.26$$

5.13 COEFFICIENT OF VARIATION AND CONSISTENCY

The standard deviation discussed so far is an absolute measure of variation. The corresponding relative measure is known as the *coefficient of variation.* This measure developed by Karl Pearson is the most commonly used measure of relative variation. It is used in such problems where we want to compare the variability of two or two or more than two series. That series (or groups) for which the coefficient of variation is greater is said to be more variable or conversely less consistent, less uniform, less stable or less homogeneous. On the other hand, the series for which coefficient of variation is less is said to be less variable or more consistent, more uniform, more stable or more homogeneous. Coefficient of variation denoted by C.V. is obtained as follows :

$$C.V. = \frac{\sigma}{\bar{X}} \times 100$$

It may be pointed out that although any measure of variation can be used in conjunction with any average in computing relative variation, statisticians, in fact, almost always use the standard deviation as the measure of variation and the arithmetic mean as the average. Coefficient of variation is more useful when the two distributions are entirely different and the units of measurement are also different. When the relative variation is stated in terms of the arithmetic mean and the standard deviation, the resulting percentage is known as the coefficient of variation or coefficient of variability.

Example 16. *Suppose that samples of polythene bags from two manufacturers A and B are tested by a prospective buyer for bursting pressure, with the following results :*

Bursting pressure (lbs)	*Number of bags* A	B
5.0–9.9	2	9
10.0–14.9	9	11
15.0–19.9	29	18
20.0–24.9	54	32
25.0–29.9	11	27
30.0–34.9	5	13
	110	110

Which set of bags has the highest average bursting pressure? Which has more uniform pressure? If prices are same, which manufacturer's bags would be preferred by the buyer? Why?

Solution. For determining which set of bags has the highest average bursting pressure, calculate arithmetic mean and for finding out which has more uniform pressure compute coefficient of variations.

Manufacturer A :

CALCULATION OF MEAN AND STANDARD DEVIATION

Bursting pressure (lbs)	*m.p.* *X*	*f*	*(X – 17.45)/5* *d*	*fd*	*fd²*
4.95–9.95	7.45	2	– 2	– 4	8
9.95–14.95	12.45	9	– 1	– 9	9
14.95–19.95	17.45	29	0	0	0
19.95–24.95	22.45	54	+ 1	+ 54	54
24.95–29.95	27.45	11	+ 2	+ 22	44
29.95–34.95	32.45	5	+ 3	+ 15	45
		N = 110		Σ*fd* = 78	Σ*fd*² = 160

$$\overline{X} = A + \frac{\Sigma fd}{N} \times C = 17.45 + \frac{78}{110} \times 5 = 17.45 + 3.55 = 21$$

$$\sigma = \sqrt{\frac{\Sigma fd^2}{N} - \left(\frac{\Sigma fd}{N}\right)^2} \times C = \sqrt{\frac{160}{110} - \left(\frac{78}{110}\right)^2} \times 5$$

$$= \sqrt{1.455 - 0.503} \times 5 = \sqrt{0.952} \times 5 = 0.976 \times 5 = 4.879$$

$$C.V. = \frac{\sigma}{\overline{X}} \times 100 = \frac{4.879}{21} \times 100 = 23.23\%.$$

Manufacturer B :

CALCULATION OF MEAN AND STANDARD DEVIATION

Bursting pressure (lbs.)	*m.p.* *X*	*f*	*(X–17.45)/5* *d*	*fd*	*fd²*
4.95–9.95	7.45	9	– 2	– 18	36
9.95–14.95	12.45	11	– 1	– 11	11
14.95–19.95	17.45	18	0	0	0
19.95–24.95	22.45	32	+ 1	+ 32	32
24.95–29.95	27.45	27	+ 2	+ 54	108
29.95–34.95	32.45	13	+ 3	+ 39	117
		N = 110		Σ*fd* = 96	Σ*fd*² = 304

$$\overline{X} = A + \frac{\Sigma fd}{N} \times C = 17.45 + \frac{96}{110} \times 5 = 21.81$$

$$\sigma = \sqrt{\frac{\Sigma fd^2}{N} - \left(\frac{\Sigma fd}{N}\right)^2} \times C = \sqrt{\frac{304}{110} - \left(\frac{96}{110}\right)^2} \times 5$$

$$= \sqrt{2.764 - 0.762} \times 5 = 1.4149 \times 5 = 7.0745$$

$$C.V. = \frac{\sigma}{\overline{X}} \times 100 = \frac{7.0745}{21.81} \times 100 = 32.44\%$$

Since the average bursting pressure is higher for manufacturer B, hence the bags of manufacturer B have a higher bursting pressure. The bags of manufacturer A have more uniform pressure since the coefficient of variation is less for manufacturer A. If prices are the same, the bags of manufacturer A should be preferred by the buyer because they have more uniform pressure.

5.14 COMBINED VARIANCE OF TWO GROUPS

Combined standard deviation. Just as it is possible to compute combined mean of two or more than two groups, similarly we can also compute combined standard deviation of two or morc groups. Combined standard deviation is denoted by σ_{12} and is computed as follows:

$$\sigma_{12} = \sqrt{\frac{N_1\sigma_1^2 + N_2\sigma_2^2 + N_1 d_1^2 + N_2 d_2^2}{N_1 + N_2}} = \sqrt{\frac{N_1(\sigma_1^2 + d_1^2) + N_2(\sigma_2^2 + d_2^2)}{N_1 + N_2}}$$

σ_{12} = combined standard deviation of both groups; σ_1 = standard deviation of first group

σ_2 = standard deviation of second group.

$$d_1 = |\overline{X}_1 - \overline{X}_{12}|\,;\ d_2 = |\overline{X}_2 - \overline{X}_{12}|$$

where $\overline{X}_{12}$ (combined mean of 2 groups) $= \dfrac{n_1\overline{X}_1 + n_2\overline{X}_2}{n_1 + n_2}$

we may write in terms of combined variance

$$\boxed{\sigma_{12}^2 = \frac{N_1(\sigma_1^2 + d_1^2) + N_2(\sigma_2^2 + d_2^2)}{N_1 + N_2}}$$

Example 17. *The numbers examined, the mean weight and the standard deviation in each group of examination and two medical examiners are given below. Find the mean weight and standard deviation of both groups taken together.*

Medical	*Number examined*	*Mean weights (lbs.)*	*Standard deviation (lbs.)*
A	50	113	6.5
B	60	120	8.2

Solution. $\overline{X}_{12} = \dfrac{N_1\overline{X}_1 + N_2\overline{X}_2}{N_1 + N_2}$

$$N_1 = 50,\ N_2 = 60,\ \overline{X}_1 = 113,\ \overline{X}_2 = 120$$

$$\overline{X}_{12} = \frac{(50 \times 113) + (60 \times 120)}{50 + 60} = \frac{5650 + 7200}{110} = \frac{12850}{110} = 116.82$$

$$\sigma_{12} = \sqrt{\frac{N_1\sigma_1^2 + N_2\sigma_2^2 + N_1 d_1^2 + N_2 d_2^2}{N_1 + N_2}}$$

$$N_1 = 50,\ \sigma_1 = 6.5,\ N_2 = 60,\ \sigma_2 = 8.2$$

$$d_1 = |\overline{X}_1 - \overline{X}_{12}| = |113 - 116.82| = 3.82$$

$$d_2 = |\overline{X}_2 - \overline{X}_{12}| = |120 - 116.82| = 3.18$$

Substituting the values, $\sigma_{12} = \sqrt{\dfrac{50(6.5)^2 + 60(8.20)^2 + 50(3.82)^2 + 60(3.18)^2}{50 + 60}}$

$$= \sqrt{\dfrac{2112.5 + 4034.4 + 729.62 + 606.744}{110}}$$

$$= \sqrt{\dfrac{7483.264}{100}} = \sqrt{68.03} = 8.25$$

5.14.1. The above formula can be extended to find out the standard deviation of three or more groups. For example, combined standard deviation of three groups would be :

$$\sigma_{123} = \sqrt{\dfrac{N_1\sigma_1^2 + N_2\sigma_2^2 + N_3\sigma_3^3 + N_1d_1^2 + N_2d_2^2 + N_3d_3^2}{N_1 + N_2 + N_3}}$$

where $\quad d_1 = |\overline{X} - \overline{X}_{123}|;\ d_2 = |\overline{X}_2 - \overline{X}_{123}|;\ d_3 = |\overline{X}_3 - \overline{X}_{123}|.$

or $\quad \sigma_{123}^2 = \dfrac{N_1(\sigma_1^2 + d_1^2) + N_2(\sigma_2^2 + d_2^2) + N_3(\sigma_3^2 + d_3^2)}{N_1 + N_2 + N_3}$

Example 18. *The number of workers employed, the mean wage (in ₹) per month and standard deviation (in ₹) in each section of a factory are given below. Calculate the mean wages and standard deviation of all workers taken together.*

Section	*No. of workers employed*	*Mean wage (₹)*	*Standard deviation (₹)*
A	*50*	*113*	*6*
B	*60*	*120*	*7*
C	*90*	*115*	*8*

Solution. $\overline{X}_{123} = \dfrac{N_1\overline{X}_1 + N_2\overline{X}_2 + N_3\overline{X}_3}{N_1 + N_2 + N_3}$

$$= \dfrac{(50 \times 113) + (60 \times 120) + (90 \times 115)}{50 + 60 + 90}$$

$$= \dfrac{5650 + 7200 + 10350}{20} = \dfrac{23200}{200} = ₹\ 116.$$

Combined variance of three series :

$$\sigma_{123}^2 = \dfrac{N_1(\sigma_1^2 + d_1^2) + N_2(\sigma_2^2 + d_2^2) + N_3(\sigma_3^2 + d_3^2)}{N_1 + N_2 + N_3}$$

$d_1 = |\overline{X}_1 - \overline{X}_{123}|$ or $|113 - 116| = 3$

$d_2 = |\overline{X}_2 - \overline{X}_{123}|$ or $|120 - 116| = 4$

$d_3 = |\overline{X}_3 - \overline{X}_{123}|$ or $|115 - 116| = 1$

$\sigma_{123}^2 = \dfrac{50(6^2 + 3^2) + 60(7^2 + 4^2) + 90(8^2 + 1^2)}{50 + 60 + 90} = \dfrac{12000}{200} = 60$

$\sigma_{123} = \sqrt{60} = 7.74.$

Example 19. *In two factories A and B engaged in the same industry, the average monthly wages and standard deviations are as follows :*

Factory	*Average Monthly Wages (₹)*	*S.D. of Wages (₹)*	*No. of Wage Earners*
A	4600	500	100
B	4900	400	80

(i) Which factory A or B pays larger amount as monthly wages?

(ii) Which factory shows greater variability in the distribution of wages?

(iii) What is the mean and standard deviation of all the workers in two factories taken together?

Solution. (*i*) **For finding out which factory A or B pays larger amount as monthly wages; we have to compare the total wages.**

Factory A : Total wage bill = 4600 × 100 = ₹ 4,60,000 [as $\Sigma X = n\overline{X}$]

Factory B : Total wage bill = 4900 × 80 = ₹ 3,92,000

Hence factory A pays larger amount as monthly wages.

(*ii*) **For determining which factory shows greater variation in the distribution of wages, we have to compare coefficient of variation.**

$$C.V. \text{ (factory } A) = \frac{\sigma}{\overline{X}} \times 100 = \frac{500}{4600} \times 100 = 10.87$$

$$C.A. \text{ (factory } B) = \frac{\sigma}{\overline{X}} \times 100 = \frac{400}{4900} \times 100 = 8.16$$

Since coefficient of variation is higher in factory *A*, **hence factory** *A* **shows greater variability in the distribution of wages.**

(iii) Combined mean :

$$\overline{X}_{12} = \frac{N_1\overline{X}_1 + N_2\overline{X}_2}{N_1 + N_2}$$

$$= \frac{(100 \times 4600) + (80 \times 4900)}{100 + 80} = \frac{460000 + 392000}{180}$$

$$= \frac{852000}{180} = ₹\ 4,733.33$$

Combined Standard Deviation : $\sigma_{12} = \sqrt{\dfrac{N_1\sigma_1^2 + N_2\sigma_2^2 + N_1 d_1^2 + N_2 d_2^2}{N_1 + N_2}}$

$$N_1 = 100, \sigma_1 = 500, N_2 = 80, \sigma_2 = 400, d_1 = |\overline{X}_2 - \overline{X}_{12}|$$

$$d_1 = |4600 - 4733.33| = 133.33,\ d_2 = |\overline{X}_2 - \overline{X}_{12}| = |4900 - 4733.33| = 166.67$$

$$\sigma_{12} = \sqrt{\frac{100(50)^2 + 80(400)^2 + 100(133.33)^2 + 80(166.67)^2}{100 + 80}}$$

$$= \sqrt{\frac{25000000 + 1200000 + 1777688.89 + 2222311.11}{180}}$$

$$= \sqrt{\frac{42192486.335}{180}} = 484.15$$

Hence combined *standard deviation is ₹ 484.15.*

Example 20. *Daily wages per employee and the variance of the wages per employee for two factories are given below :*

	Factory A	*Factory B*
Number of employees	*50*	*100*
Average daily wages per employee (₹)	*120*	*85*
Variance of the daily wages per employee (₹)	*9*	*16*

In which factory is there greater variation in the distribution of daily wages per employee?

Solution. *Variation in the distribution of wages*

Factory A

$$C.V. = \frac{\sigma}{\overline{X}} \times 100$$

$$\sigma = \sqrt{9} = 3, \overline{X} = 120$$

$$C.V. = \frac{3}{120} \times 100 = 2.5$$

Factory B

$$C.V. = \frac{\sigma}{\overline{X}} \times 100$$

$$\sigma = \sqrt{16} = 4, \overline{X} = 85$$

$$\therefore \; C.V. = \frac{4}{85} \times 100 = 4.7$$

The coefficient of variation is greater for factory B, hence there is greater variation in the distribution of wages per employee in factory B.

5.15. CORRECTING INCORRECT VALUE OF STANDARD DEVIATION

Mistakes in calculations are always possible. Sometimes it so happens that while calculating mean and standard deviation we unconsciously copy out observations wrongly. For example, an observation 21 may be taken as 12. Similarly, one observation 127 may be taken as only 27. In such cases if the entire calculations are done again, it would become too difficult a task. By adopting a very simple procedure we can correct the incorrect values of mean and standard deviation. For obtaining correct mean we find out correct ΣX by deducting from the incorrect ΣX the wrong observations and adding to it the correct observations. Similarly, for calculating correct standard deviation we obtain the value of correct ΣX^2. The following illustration shall clarify the procedure :

Example 21. *The mean and standard deviation of a set of 100 observations were worked out as 40 and 5 respectively by a computer which by mistake took the value 50 in place of 40 for one of the observations. Find the correct mean and variance*

Solution. $\overline{X} = \frac{\Sigma X}{N}, \; N\overline{X} = \Sigma X, N = 100, \overline{X} = 40$

$$\therefore \quad \Sigma X = 100 \times 4 = 4{,}000$$

But this is not the correct ΣX because one observation has been taken as 50 instead of 40.

$\therefore$ Correct $\Sigma X = 4{,}000 - 50 + 40 = 3{,}990$

$$\text{Correct Mean} = \frac{3{,}990}{100} = 39.9$$

$$\text{Variance} = \frac{\Sigma X^2}{N} - (\overline{X})^2$$

$$\text{Variance} = \sigma^2 = (5)^2 = 25, N = 100.$$

$$25 = \frac{\Sigma X^2}{100} - (40)^2 \text{ or } 2{,}500 = \Sigma X^2 - 1{,}60{,}000$$

$$\text{Incorrect } \Sigma X^2 = 1{,}60{,}000 + 2{,}500 = 1{,}62{,}500$$

$$\text{Correct } \Sigma X^2 = 1{,}62{,}500 - (50)^2 + (40)^2 = 1{,}62{,}500 - 2{,}500 + 1{,}600 = 1{,}61{,}600$$

$$\text{Correct variance} = \frac{\text{Correct } \Sigma X^2}{N} - (\textit{Correct } \overline{X})^2$$

$$= \frac{1{,}61{,}600}{100} - (39.9)^2 = 1{,}616 - 1{,}592.01 = 23.99$$

Thus correct mean = 39.9 and the correct variance = 23.99.

5.16 MERITS AND LIMITATIONS OF STANDARD DEVIATION

Merits. (*i*) The standard deviation is the best measure of variation because of its mathematical characteristics. It is based on every item of the distribution. Also it is amenable to algebraic treatment and is less affected by fluctuations of sampling than most other measures of variation.

(*ii*) It is possible to calculate the combined standard deviation of two or more groups. This is not possible with any other measure.

(*iii*) For comparing the variability of two or more distributions coefficient of variation is considered to be most appropriate and this measure is based on mean and standard deviation.

(*iv*) Standard deviation is most prominently used in further statistical work. For example, in comparing skewness, correlation, etc., use is made of standard deviation. It is a key-note in sampling and provides a unit of measurement for the normal distribution.

Limitations. (*i*) As compared to other measures it is difficult to compute. However, it does not reduce the importance of this measure because of the high degree of accuracy of result it gives.

(*ii*) It gives more weight to extreme values and less to those which are near the mean. It is because of the fact that the squares of the deviations which are big in size would be proportionately greater than the squares of those deviations which are comparatively small. The deviations 2 and 8 are in ratio of 1 : 4 but their squares, *i.e.*, 4 and 64, would be in the ratio 1 : 16.

5.17 RELATION BETWEEN Q.D., M.D. AND S.D.

In case of near symmetrical distributions following is the relationship (approximate) between the three quantities.

$$Q.D. = \frac{2}{3}\sigma, \quad M.D. = \frac{4}{5}\sigma$$

Thus, $$Q.D. = \frac{5}{6} M.D.$$

5.18 MORE SOLVED EXAMPLES

Example 22. *You are given the frequency distribution of 292 workers of a factory according to their average weekly income. Calculate quartile deviation and its coefficient from the following data :*

Weekly Income (₹)	*No. of workers*	*Weekly Income (₹)*	*No. of workers*
Below 1350	*8*	*1450–1470*	*22*
1350–1370	*16*	*1470–1490*	*15*
1370–1390	*39*	*1490–1510*	*15*
1390–1410	*58*	*1510–1530*	*9*
1410–1430	*60*	*1530 & above*	*10*
1430–1450	*40*		

Solution.

CALCULATION OF QUARTILE DEVIATION

Weekly Income (₹)	*No. of workers* *f*	*c.f.*
Below 1350	8	8
1350–1370	16	24
1370–1390	39	63
1390–1410	58	121 ←Q_1 *class*
1410–1430	60	181 ←*Median class*
1430–1450	40	221 ←Q_3 *class*
1450–1470	22	243
1470–1490	15	258
1490–1510	15	273
1510–1530	9	282
1530 & above	10	292
	$N = 292$	

$\frac{N}{2}$ th observation $= \frac{292}{2} = 146$th observation

Median lies in the class 1410 – 1430, $Me = L_{Me} + \frac{\frac{n}{2} - C}{f_{Me}} \times i$

$$Me = 1410 + \frac{146 - 121}{60} \times 20 = 1410 + 8.33 = 1418.33$$

To find Q_1, Find $\frac{N}{4} = \frac{292}{4} = 73$ [see under *c.f.* column]

Q_1 lies in the class 1390–1410.

$$Q_1 = L + \frac{N/4 - C}{f} \times i = 1390 + \frac{73 - 63}{58} \times 20 = 1390 + 3.448 = 1393.448$$

To find Q_3, Find $\frac{3N}{4} = 3(73) = 219 \Rightarrow Q_3$ lies in the class 1430 – 1450.

$$Q_3 = L + \frac{3N/4 - C}{f} \times i = 1430 + \frac{219 - 181}{40} \times 20 = 1430 + 19 = 1449$$

$$\text{Coef. of } Q.D. = \frac{Q_3 - Q_1}{Q_3 + Q_1} = \frac{1449 - 1393.448}{1393.448} = \frac{55.552}{2842.448} = 0.020.$$

Example 23. *Calculate the mean deviation and its coefficient from the following data :*

Class	*Frequency*	*Class*	*Frequency*
0–10	*5*	*40–50*	*20*
10–20	*8*	*50–60*	*14*
20–30	*12*	*60–70*	*12*
30–40	*15*	*70–80*	*6*

Solution. Since nothing is special we will calculate mean deviation from median :

CALCULATION OF MEAN DEVIATION

Class	*Frequency* *f*	*c.f.*	*m.p.* X	| *X–43* | = |*D*|	*f* |*D*|
0–10	5	5	5	38	190
10–20	8	13	15	28	224
20–30	12	25	25	18	216
30–40	15	40 Median	35	8	120
40–50	20	60 class	45	2	40
50–60	14	74	55	12	168
60–70	12	86	65	22	264
70–80	6	92	75	32	192
	$N = 92$				$\Sigma f\,\lvert D\rvert = 1414$

$$\frac{N}{2} = \frac{92}{2} = 46$$

Median lies in the class 40—50.

$$\text{Med.} = L + \frac{N/2 - C}{f} \times i$$

$$L = 40,\ N/2 = 46,\ C = 40,\ f = 20,\ i = 10$$

$$\therefore \quad \text{Med.} = 40 + \frac{46 - 40}{20} \times 10 = 40 + 3 = 43$$

$$\text{M.D.} = \frac{\Sigma f\,\lvert D \rvert}{N} = \frac{1414}{92} = 15.37$$

$$\text{Coeff. of M.D.} = \frac{\text{M.D. from median}}{\text{Median}} = \frac{15.37}{43} = 0.357.$$

Example 24. *Calculate standard deviation for the following distribution of net profits earned by a group of companies.*

Profits ('000 ₹)	*20–30*	*30–40*	*40–50*	*50–60*	*60–70*	*70–80*	*80–90*	*90–100*
No. of Cos.	*30*	*58*	*62*	*85*	*112*	*70*	*57*	*26*

Solution.

CALCULATION OF STANDARD DEVIATION

Profits ('000 ₹)	*m.p.* m.	*No. of Cos.* f	*(m–55)/10* d	*fd*	*fd*^{2}
20–30	25	30	– 3	– 90	270
30–40	35	58	– 2	–116	232
40–50	45	62	– 1	– 62	62
50–60	55	85	0	0	0
60–70	65	112	+ 1	+ 112	112
70–80	75	70	+ 2	+ 140	280
80–90	85	57	+ 3	+ 171	513
90–100	95	26	+ 4	+ 104	416
		$N = 500$		$\Sigma fd = 259$	$\Sigma fd^2 = 1885$

$$\sigma = \sqrt{\frac{\Sigma fd^2}{N} - \left(\frac{\Sigma fd}{N}\right)^2} \times C$$

$$\Sigma fd^2 = 1885,\ \Sigma fd = 259,\ N = 500$$

$$\sigma = \sqrt{\frac{1885}{500} - \left(\frac{259}{500}\right)^2} \times 10 = \sqrt{3.77 - .268} \times 10$$

$$= \sqrt{3.502} \times 10 = 1.871 \times 10 = 18.71.$$

Example 25. *The arithmetic mean and standard deviation of a series of 20 items were calculated by a student as 20 cm and 5 cm. respectively. But while calculating them an item 13 was misread as 30. Find the correct arithmetic mean and standard deviation.*

Solution. *Calculation of correct mean*

$$\overline{X} = \frac{\Sigma X}{N} \text{ or } N\overline{X} = \Sigma X$$

$$N = 20, \overline{X} = 20$$

Incorrect $\Sigma X = 20 \times 20 = 400$

Correct $\Sigma X = 400 - 30 + 13 = 383$

Correct $\overline{X} = \frac{383}{20} = 19.15$

Calculation of correct standard deviation :

$$\sigma^2 = \frac{\Sigma X^2}{N} - (\overline{X})^2$$

$$5^2 = \frac{\Sigma X^2}{20} - (20)^2$$

$$25 \times 20 = \Sigma X^2 - 400 \times 20 \text{ or } \Sigma X^2 = 8500 \text{ (incorrect)}$$

Correct $\Sigma X^2 = 8500 - (30)^2 + (13)^2 = 8500 - 900 + 169 = 7769.$

Correct $\sigma = \sqrt{\frac{\text{Correct } \Sigma X^2}{N} - (\text{Correct } \overline{X})^2}$

$$= \sqrt{\frac{7769}{20} - (19.15)^2} = \sqrt{388.45 - 366.72} = \sqrt{21.73} = 4.66$$

Thus correct mean is 19.15 and correct standard deviation is 4.66.

Example 26. *Find the coefficient of variation from the following data:*

Weekly Wages	*No. of Workers*	*Weekly Wages*	*No. of Workers*
Up to ₹ 300	*12*	*Up to ₹ 700*	*157*
" " " 400	*30*	*" " " 800*	*202*
" " " 500	*65*	*" " " 900*	*222*
" " " 600	*107*	*" " " 1000*	*230*

Solution:

Cum. frequency distribution is given which is converted to original frequency distribution.

FINDING COEFFICIENT OF VARIATION

Weekly Wages (₹)	*m.p.* X.	*No. of Workers* *f*	*(X–550)/100* *d*	*fd*	*fd*^{2}
200–300	250	12	– 3	– 36	108
300–400	350	18 (30 – 12)	– 2	– 36	72
400–500	450	35 (65 – 30)	– 1	– 35	35
500–600	550	42	0	0	0
600–700	650	50	+ 1	+ 50	50
700–800	750	45	+ 2	+ 90	180
800–900	850	20	+ 3	+ 60	180
900–1000	950	8	+ 4	+ 32	128
		$N = 230$		$\Sigma fd = 125$	$\Sigma fd^2 = 753$

$$\text{C.V.} = \frac{\sigma}{\overline{X}} \times 100$$

$$\overline{X} = A + \frac{\Sigma fd}{N} \times C = 550 + \frac{125}{230} \times 100$$

$$= 550 + 54.35 = 604.35$$

$$\sigma = \sqrt{\frac{\Sigma fd^2}{N} - \left(\frac{\Sigma fd}{N}\right)^2} \times C = \sqrt{\frac{753}{230} - \left(\frac{-125}{230}\right)^2} \times 100$$

$$= \sqrt{3.274 - .295} \times 100 = 1.726 \times 100 = 172.6$$

$$\text{C.V.} = \frac{172.6}{604.35} \times 100 = 28.56 \text{ per cent.}$$

Example 27. *Determine the interquartile range and percentile range of the following distribution :*

Class Intervals :	*11–13*	*13–15*	*15–17*	*17–19*	*19–21*	*21–23*	*23–25*
Frequency :	*8*	*10*	*15*	*20*	*12*	*11*	*4*

Solution.

Class Intervals	Frequency	Less than c.f.	
11–13	8	8	←P_{10} class
13–15	10	18	
15–17	15	33	←Q_1 class
17–19	20	53	
19–21	12	65	←Q_3 class
21–23	11	76	←P_{90} class
23–25	4	80	

(*a*) Calculation of Interquartile Range

Calculation of Q_1

Since $\frac{N}{4} = \frac{80}{4} = 20$, the first quartile class is 15 – 17

$\therefore\ l_{Q_1} = 15, f_{Q_1} = 15, i = 2$ and $C = 18$

Hence, $Q_1 = 15 + \frac{20 - 18}{15} \times 2 = 15.27$

Calculation of Q_3

Since $\frac{3N}{4} = \frac{3 \times 80}{4} = 60$, the third quartile class is 19 – 21

$\therefore\ l_{Q_3} = 19, f_{Q_3} = 12, i = 2$ and $C = 53$

Hence, $Q_3 = 19 + \frac{60 - 53}{12} \times 2 = 20.17$

Thus, the interquartile range = 20.17 – 15.27 = 4.90 $[Q_3 - Q_1]$

(*b*) Calculation of Percentile Range

Calculation of P_{10}

Since, $\frac{10N}{100} = \frac{10 \times 80}{100} = 8$, P_{10} lies in the class interval 11 – 13

$\therefore\ L_{P_{10}} = 11, f_{P_{10}} = 8, i = 2$ and $C = 0$

Hence, $P_{10} = 11 + \frac{8-0}{8} \times 2 = 13$

Calculation of P_{90}

Since $\frac{90N}{100} = \frac{90 \times 80}{100} = 72$, P_{90} lies in the class interval 21 – 23

$\therefore\ L_{P_{90}} = 21, f_{P_{90}} = 11, i = 2$ and $C = 65$

Hence, $P_{90} = 21 + \frac{72 - 65}{11} \times 2 = 22.27$

Thus , the percentile range = $P_{90} - P_{10}$ = 22.27 – 13.0 = 9.27.

Example 28. *Find mean and standard deviation of the following observations:*

X :	*1*	*2*	*4*	*6*	*8*	*9*

Transform the above observations such that the mean of transformed observations becomes double of the mean of X, standard deviation remaining unchanged.

Solution:

CALCULATION OF MEAN AND STANDARD DEVIATION

X	$x = (X - 5)$	x^2
1	– 4	16
2	– 3	9
4	– 1	1
6	+ 1	1
8	+ 3	9
9	+ 4	16
$\Sigma X = 30$		$\Sigma x^2 = 52$

Mean : $\overline{X} = \frac{\Sigma X}{N} = \frac{30}{6} = 5$ and let $x = X - \overline{X}$

Standard deviation : $\sigma = \sqrt{\frac{\Sigma x^2}{N}} = \sqrt{\frac{52}{6}} = \sqrt{8.67} = 2.94$ $\left[\text{As } \sigma^2 = \frac{\Sigma(X - \overline{X})^2}{n} = \frac{\Sigma x^2}{n}\right]$

(ii) Standard deviation is affected by change of scale but not by change of origin and mean is affected by both. Thus changing the origin of X series by adding 5 (*i.e.* mean value of X), so that mean becomes double while standard deviation remains unchanged.

$X_1 (= X + 5)$	$d = X_1 - \overline{X}_1$	$(X_1 - \overline{X}_1)^2$
6	– 4	16
7	– 3	9
9	– 1	1
11	+ 1	1
13	+ 3	9
14	+ 4	16
$\Sigma X_1 = 60$	$\Sigma d = 0$	$52 = \Sigma(X_1 - X_1)^2$

Mean : $\overline{X}_1 = \frac{\Sigma X_1}{N} = \frac{60}{6} = 10 = 2\overline{X}$

$$\sigma^2_{X_1} = \frac{\Sigma(X_1 - \overline{X})^2}{n} = \frac{52}{6} = 8.67$$

$$\sigma_{X_1} = \sqrt{8.67} = 2.94 = \sigma_X$$

Now X values are 6,7, 9, 11, 13, 14 whose mean is double of original X values, but standard of both set of values is same.

Example 29. *(i) Coefficient of variation of two series is 60% and 80% Their standard deviations are 24 and 20. What are their arithmetic means?*

(ii) If quartile deviation of a group is 16, what would be the most likely value of variance of that group.

(iii) If the first quartile is 142 and the semi-interquartile range is 18, find the median (assuming the distribution to be symmetrical).

Solution : (*i*) C.V. $= \frac{\sigma}{\overline{X}} \times 100$ (*in percentage*)

first series : $60 = \frac{24}{\overline{X}} \times 100 \Rightarrow \overline{X} = 40$

second series : $80 = \frac{20}{\overline{X}} \times 100 \Rightarrow \overline{X} = 25$

(*ii*) $Q.D. = \frac{2}{3}\sigma$

$$16 = \frac{2}{3}\sigma \Rightarrow \sigma = \frac{16 \times 3}{2} = 24$$

variance $= \sigma^2 = (24)^2 = 576$

(*iii*) Semi-interquartile range or $Q.D. = \frac{Q_3 - Q_1}{2}$

$$18 = \frac{Q_3 - 142}{2}$$

$36 + 142 = Q_3 \Rightarrow Q_3 = 178$

In a symmetrical distribution, median is equidistant from two quartiles

i.e. $Q_3 - Md = Md - Q_1$

$$M_d = \frac{Q_3 + Q_1}{2} = \frac{178 + 142}{2} = 160$$

Example 30. *Compute standard deviation and its coefficient from the following data:*

Class	5–10	10–15	15–20	20–30	30–40	40–50	50–60	60–70
f	11	9	3	8	4	12	17	31

Solution.

COMPUTATION OF STANDARD DEVIATION AND ITS COEFFICIENT

Class	m.p. X	f	(X–25)/5 = d	$u = \left(\frac{X-25}{2.5}\right)$	fu	fu^2
5–10	7.5	11	– 3.5	– 7	– 77	539
10–15	12.5	9	– 2.5	– 5	– 45	225
15–20	17.5	3	– 1.5	– 3	– 9	27
20–30	25.0	8	0	0	0	0
30–40	35.0	4	+ 2.0	4	16	64
40–50	45.0	12	+ 4.0	8	96	768
50–60	55.0	17	+ 6.0	12	204	2448
60–70	65.0	31	+ 8.0	16	496	7936
		$N = 95 = \Sigma f$			$\Sigma fu = 681$	$12007 = \Sigma fu^2$

$$\overline{X} = A + \frac{\Sigma fu}{N} \times C$$

Since class intervals are unequal in this question, we would use C instead in i in the formula. We have

$$\overline{X} = 25 + \frac{681}{95} \times 2.5 = 25 + 17.89 = 42.92$$

$$\sigma_x^2 = \left[\frac{\Sigma fu^2}{\Sigma f} - \left(\frac{\Sigma fu}{\Sigma f}\right)^2\right] C^2$$

$$= (126.39 - 51.39)(2.5)^2$$

$$\sigma_x = \sqrt{75.00} \times 2.5 = 8.66 \times 2.5 = 21.65$$

$$C.V._{(x)} = \frac{\sigma}{\overline{X}} 100 = \frac{21.65}{42.92} \times 100 = 50.44\%$$

Example 31. *Calculate standard deviation and coefficient of variation from the datu given below:*

Mid-points :	5	15	25	35	45	55	65	75
Frequency :	5	8	7	12	28	20	10	10

Solution.

CALCULATION OF STANDARD DEVIATION AND COEFFICIENT OF VARIATION

X	$(X-45)/10 = d$	f	fd	fd^2
5	– 4	5	– 20	80
15	– 3	8	– 24	72
25	– 2	7	– 14	28
35	– 1	12	– 12	12
45	0	28	0	0
55	+ 1	20	+ 20	20
65	+ 2	10	+ 20	40
75	+ 3	10	+ 30	90
		$N = 100$	$\Sigma fd = 0$	$\Sigma fd^2 = 342$

$$\sigma_x = \sqrt{\frac{\Sigma fd^2}{N} - \left(\frac{\Sigma fd}{N}\right)^2} \times i$$

$$\Sigma fd^2 = 342, \ \Sigma fd = 0, N = 100, i = 10$$

$$\sigma = \sqrt{\frac{342}{100} - \left(\frac{0}{100}\right)^2} \times 10 = \sqrt{3.42} \times 10 = 1.849 \times 10 = 18.49.$$

$$\text{C.V.} = \frac{\sigma}{\overline{X}} \times 100$$

$$\overline{X} = A + \frac{\Sigma fd}{N} \times i$$

$$A = 45, \Sigma fd = 0, N = 100, i = 10$$

$$\overline{X} = 45 + \frac{0}{100} \times 10 = 45$$

$$\text{C.V.} = \frac{18.49}{45} \times 100 = 41.09 \text{ per cent.}$$

Example 32. *Verify the correctness of the following statement :*

A batsman scored 60 runs per inning against Pakistan and standard deviation was 12. And against Australia his average and standard deviation ware 50 and 9 runs respectively. Was the batsman's performance less consistent against Pakistan?

Solution. The information contained in the question can be written in the following form:

	Pakistan	*Australia*
$\overline{X}$	60	50
σ	12	9

Since the average runs are lower in case of Australia, it is correct to say that his performance was worse against Australia. For finding out answer to consistency in batting we have to compare the coefficient of variation.

Pakistan

$$C.V. = \frac{\sigma}{\overline{X}} \times 100 = \frac{12}{60} \times 100 = 20\%$$

Australia

$$C.V. = \frac{\sigma}{\overline{X}} \times 100 = \frac{9}{50} \times 100 = 18\%$$

Since coefficient of variation is less against Australia there was greater consistency in his batting against Australia. Hence the statement given in the question about consistency is right.

Example 33. *An algebra test was given to 400 high school children of whom 150 were boys and 250 girls. The results were as follows :*

$$n_1 = 150 \qquad n_2 = 250$$
$$\overline{X}_1 = 72 \qquad \overline{X}_2 = 73$$
$$\sigma_1 = 7.0 \qquad \sigma_2 = 6.4$$

Find the mean and the standard deviation of combined group.

Solution.

$$\overline{X}_{12} = \frac{n_1\overline{X}_1 + n_2\overline{X}_2}{n_1 + n_2}$$

$$n_1 = 150,\ \overline{X}_1 = 72,\ n_2 = 250,\ \overline{X}_2 = 73$$

$$\therefore \quad \overline{X}_{12} = \frac{(150 \times 72) + (250 \times 73)}{150 + 250} = \frac{10800 + 18250}{400} = \frac{29050}{400} = 72.625$$

$$\sigma_{12} = \sqrt{\frac{n_1\sigma_1^2 + n_2\sigma_2^2 + n_1d_1^2 + n_2d_2^2}{n_1 + n_2}}$$

$$\sigma_1 = 7,\ \sigma_2 = 6.4,\ d_1 = |\ \overline{X}_1 - \overline{X}_{12}\ | = |\ 72 - 72.625\ | = 0.625$$

$$d_2 = |\ \overline{X}_2 - \overline{X}_{12}\ | = 73 - 72.625 = 0.375$$

$$\sigma_{12} = \sqrt{\frac{150(7)^2 + 250(6.4)^2 + 150(.625)^2 + 250(.375)^2}{400}}$$

$$= \sqrt{\frac{7350 + 10240 + 58.594 + 35.156}{400}} = \sqrt{\frac{17683.7}{400}} = 6.65$$

Thus the combined mean was ₹ 72.63 and standard deviation 6.65.

Example 34. *Calculate coefficient of quartile deviation and coefficient of variation from the following data :*

Marks	*No. of Students*
Below 20	*8*
" 40	*20*
" 60	*50*
" 80	*70*
" 100	*80*

Solution.

We are given cum. freq. distribution which is converted to original freq. distribution.

CALCULATION OF COEFF. OF Q.D. AND COEFF. OF VARIATION

Marks	*m.p.* .. *m*	*No. of Students* *f*	(*m*–50)/20 *d*	*fd*	*fd*²	*c.f.*	
0–20	10	8	– 2	– 16	32	8	
20–40	30	12	– 1	– 12	12	20	← Q_1 class
40–60	50	30	0	0	0	50	
60–80	70	20	+ 1	+ 20	20	70	← Q_3 class
80–100	90	10	+ 2	+ 20	40	80	
		N = 80		Σ *fd* = 12	Σ*fd*² = 104		

$$\text{C.V.} = \frac{\sigma}{\overline{X}} \times 100$$

$$\overline{X} = A + \frac{\Sigma fd}{N} \times i = 50 + \frac{12}{80} \times 20 = 50 + 3 = 53 \qquad [A = 50,\ i = 20]$$

$$\sigma = \sqrt{\frac{\Sigma fd^2}{N} - \left(\frac{\Sigma fd}{N}\right)^2} \times i = \sqrt{\frac{104}{80} - \left(\frac{12}{80}\right)^2} \times 20$$

$$= \sqrt{1.3 - 0.0225} \times 20 = 1.1303 \times 20 = 22.606$$

$$\text{C.V.} = \frac{22.606}{53} \times 100 = 42.65 \text{ per cent}$$

$$\text{Coeff. of Q.D.} = \frac{Q_3 - Q_1}{Q_3 + Q_1}$$

For Q_1, find $\frac{N}{4} = \frac{80}{4} = 20$

Q_1 lies in the class 20—40

$$Q_1 = L + \frac{N/4 - c.f.}{f} \times i = 20 + \frac{20 - 8}{12} \times 20 = 20 + 20 = 40$$

For Q_3 , Find $\frac{3N}{4} = \frac{3\,(80)}{4} = 60$

Q_3 lies in the class 60—80

$$Q_3 = L + \frac{3N/4 - c.f.}{f} \times i = 60 + \frac{60 - 50}{20} \times 20 = 60 + 10 = 70$$

$$\text{Coeff. of Q.D.} = \frac{70 - 40}{70 + 40} = \frac{30}{110} = 0.273.$$

Example 35. *The mean weight of 150 students is 60 kg. The mean weight of boys is 70 kg. with a standard deviation of 10 kg. For the girls, the mean weight is 55 kg and the standard deviation is 15 kg. Find the number of boys and the combined standard deviation.*

Solution.

$$\overline{X}_{12} = \frac{N_1\overline{X}_1 + N_2\overline{X}_2}{N_1 + N_2}$$

Given $\overline{X}_{12} = 60, \overline{X}_1 = 70, \overline{X}_2 = 55, N_1 + N_2 = 150$

We have to determine the number of boys

Hence N_2 will be the number of girls

$$N_2 = (150 - N_1)$$

Putting the values

$$60 = \frac{N_1\,70 + (150 - N_1)\,55}{150}$$

$$9000 = 70N_1 + 82509 - 55N_1$$

or $\quad 15N_1 = 9000 - 8250 = 750$ or $N_1 = 750/15 = 50$

Hence $\quad N_2 = 150 - 50 = 100$

Thus, the number of boys and girls is 50 and 100 respectively.

Combined Standard Deviation

$$\sigma_{12} = \sqrt{\frac{N_1\sigma_1^2 + N_2\sigma_2^2 + N_1d_1^2 + N_2d_2^2}{N_1 + N_2}}$$

$$N_1 = 50,\ \sigma_1 = 10,\ N_2 = 100,\ \sigma_2 = 15$$

$$d_1 = |\,\overline{X}_1 - \overline{X}_{12}\,| = |\,60 - 70\,| = 10,\ d_2 = |\,\overline{X}_2 - \overline{X}_{12}\,| = |\,55 - 60\,| = 5$$

$$\sigma_{12} = \sqrt{\frac{50(10)^2 + 100(15)^2 + 50(10)^2 + 100(5)^2}{50 + 100}}$$

$$\sigma_{12} = \sqrt{\frac{5000 + 22500 + 5000 + 2500}{150}} = \sqrt{\frac{35{,}000}{150}} = 15.28.$$

Example 36. *The Shareholders Research Center of India has conducted recently a research-study on price behaviour of three leading industrial shares, A, B and C for the period 1989 to 1995, the results of which are published as follows in its Quarterly Journal :*

Share	*Average Price*	*Standard Deviation*	*Current Selling Price*
A	*18.0*	5.4	*36.00*
B	*22.5*	4.5	*34.75*
C	*24.0*	6.0	*39.00*

The above figures are given in ₹

(a) Which share, in your opinion, appear to be more stable in value?

(b) If you are the holder of all the three shares, which one would you like to dispose of at present, and why?

Solution. (*a*) For finding out which share is more stable in value, we have to compare the coefficients of variation of shares *A*, *B* and *C*.

Share A :

$$C.V. = \frac{\sigma}{\overline{X}} \times 100$$

$$\overline{X} = 18.0, \; \sigma = 5.4$$

$$C.V. = \frac{5.40}{18} \times 100 = 30\%$$

Share B :

$$\overline{X} = 22.5, \; \sigma = 4.5$$

$$C.V. = \frac{4.5}{22.50} \times 100 = 20\%$$

Section C :

$$\overline{X} = 24.0, \; \sigma = 6.0$$

$$C.V. = \frac{6.00}{24.00} \times 100 = 25\%$$

Since coefficient of variation is less for share *B*, hence share *B* is more stable in value.

(*b*) I would like to dispose of shares *A*, since their coefficient of variation is highest, meaning thereby that there is maximum variation in prices. And incidently it is giving maximum profit per share (36.0 – 18.0 = 18.00) at the moment.

Example 37. *Mean and coefficient of standard deviation of 100 items are found by a student as 50 and 0.1. If at the time of calculation two items are wrongly taken as 40 and 50 instead of 60 and 30, find the correct mean and standard deviation.*

Solution. Coefficient of standard deviation $= \dfrac{\sigma}{\overline{X}}$ $\left[\text{But } C.V. = \dfrac{\sigma}{\overline{X}} \times 100\right]$

$$0.1 = \frac{\sigma}{50}$$

$\therefore \quad \sigma = 5$ (incorrect) $\qquad \overline{X} = 50$ (incorrect)

$$\overline{X} = \frac{\Sigma X}{100}$$

$$50 = \frac{\Sigma X}{100} \quad \text{or} \quad \Sigma X = 5000 \text{ (incorrect)}$$

$$\text{Correct } \Sigma X = \text{Incorrect } \Sigma X - \text{wrong items} + \text{correct items}$$

$$= 5000 - 40 - 50 + 60 + 30 = 5000$$

$$\text{Correct } \overline{X} = \frac{\text{Correct } \Sigma X}{N} = \frac{5000}{100} = 50$$

$$\sigma = \sqrt{\frac{\Sigma X^2}{N} - (\overline{X})^2}$$

$$5 = \sqrt{\frac{\Sigma X^2}{100} - (50)^2}$$

Squaring, $25 = \frac{\Sigma X^2}{100} - 2500$ (incorrect)

$$2525 \times 100 = \Sigma X^2 = 252500 \text{ (incorrect)}$$

Correct ΣX^2 = Incorrect ΣX^2 – wrong item's square + correct item's square

$$= 252500 - (40)^2 - (50)^2 + (60)^2 + (30)^2$$

$$= 252500 - 1600 - 2500 + 3600 + 900 = 252900$$

Correct $\sigma = \sqrt{\frac{\text{Correct } \Sigma X^2}{N} - (\text{correct } \overline{X})^2}$

$$= \sqrt{\frac{252900}{100} - (50)^2} = \sqrt{29} = 5.4.$$

EXERCISE 5.1

1. Calculate quartiles, median and coefficient of quartile deviation from the following data:

Income group (₹)	*No. of workers*	*Income group* (₹)	*No. of workers*
Below–350	8	450–470	22
350–370	16	470–490	15
370–390	39	490–510	15
390–410	53	510–530	9
410–430	60	530 & above	10
430–450	40		

[**Ans.** Q_1 = 393.302, Q_3 = 449.625, Med = 419.167, Coeff of Q.D. = 0.0668]

2. Calculate the quartile deviation for the following data and verify it graphically:

Class interval:	8–12	12–16	16–20	20–24	24–28
Frequency:	5	12	20	10	3

[Q.D. = 2.8]

3. Calculate the coefficient of variation from the following data:

Income (₹)	*No. of families*	*Income* (₹)	*No. of families*
Less than 5000	8	Less than 8000	50
Less than 6000	20	Less than 9000	58
Less than 7000	38	Less than 10000	60

[C.V. = 19.8]

4. The following data pertain to two workers doing the same job in a factory:

	Worker A	*Worker B*
Mean time of completing the job (minutes)	40	42
Standard deviation (minutes)	8	6

Who is the more consistent worker ?

[C.V. (*A*) = 20, C.V. (*B*) = 14.29: *B* is more consistent]

5. Compute coefficient of variation from the following table :

Weekly Income (in ₹)	*No. of employees*	*Weekly Income (in ₹)*	*No. of employees*
1300–1399	30	1700–1799	60
1400–1499	46	1800–1899	50
1500–1599	58	1900–1999	20
1600–1699	76		

6. The following table gives the fluctuations in the prices of shares of two companies *A* and *B*. Find out which of them shows greater variability. Comment on the result.

Price (in ₹)	*Price (in ₹)*		
Share A	*Share B*	*Share A*	*Share B*
318 2,542	324	2,545	
322 2,522	315	2,530	
325 2,534	308	2,556	
312 2,532	319	2,530	

[Share *A* : C.V. = 1.75; Share *B* : C.V. = 0.42]

7. Find mean and standard deviation of the following distribution:

Age (in years)	*No. of Persons*
less than 20	0
less than 25	170
less than 30	280
less than 35	360
less than 40	405
less than 45	445
less than 50	480

[$\overline{X}$ = 30.21 year σ_x = 7.94 year]

8. A sample of 90 values has mean 55 and standard deviation 3. A second sample of 110 values has mean 60 and standard deviation 2. Find the mean and standard deviation of the combined sample of 200 values.

[$\overline{X}_{12}$ = 57.75, σ_{12} = 3.526.]

9. Calculate standard deviation and its coefficient of variation from the following data :

Measurements :	0–5	5–10	10–15	15–20	20–25
Frequency :	4	1	10	3	2

[$\overline{X}$ = 12, σ = 5.89, C.V. = 49%]

10. Lives of two models of refrigerators in a recent survey are :

Life	*No. of refrigerators*	
(No. of years)	*Model A*	*Model B*
0–2	5	2
2–4	16	7
4–6	13	12
6–8	7	19
8–10	5	9
10–12	4	1

What is the average life of each of these refrigerators ? Which model has greater uniformity ?

[Model A : $\overline{X}$ = 5.12, C.V. = 54.9; Model B: $\overline{X}$ = 6.16, C.V. = 36.2]

11. From the following data compute the coefficient of variation of yield per hectare:

Yield ('00 kg./hectare)	5—10	10—15	15—20	20—25	25—30
No. of fields	40	56	75	41	18

[C.V. = 36%]

12. A student obtained the mean and standard deviation of 100 observations as 40 and 5.1 respectively. It was later found that one observation was wrongly copied as 50, the correct figure being 40. Find the correct mean and standard deviation.

[$\overline{X}$= 39.9 ; σ = 5]

13. A factory produces two types of electric lamps *A* and *B*. In an experiment relating to their life, the following results were obtained :

Length of life (*in hours*)	*No. of lamps* A	*No. of lamps* B
500–700	5	4
700–900	11	30
900–1,100	26	12
1,100–1,300	10	8
1,300–1,500	8	6

Compare the variability of the life of the two types using coefficient of variation.

[CV_A = 21.64; CV_B = 23.41]

14. In the factories *A* and *B* engaged in the same industry, the average weekly wages and standard deviations are as follows:

Factory	*Average weekly wage* (₹)	*S.D. of wages* (₹)	*No. of wage earners*
A	460	50	100
B	490	40	80

(*i*) Which factory A or B pays larger amount as weekly wages?

(*ii*) Which factory shows greater variability in the distribution of wages?

(*iii*) What is the mean and standard deviation of all the workers in two factories taken together?

[(*i*) *A*, (*ii*) *A*, (*iii*) $\overline{X}_{12}$ = 473.33. σ_{12} = 48.19]

15. Calculate Quartile deviation and coefficient of quartile deviation from the following data:

Daily wages	*No. of workers*	*Daily wages*	*No. of workers*
50–60	8	90–100	18
60–70	13	100–110	12
70–80	30	110–120	9
80–90	35	120–130	5

[Q.D. = 17.945, Coeff. of Q.D. = 0.22875]

16. The mean and standard deviation of series of seventeen items are 25 and 5 respectively. While calculating these measures, a measurement 53 was wrongly read as 35. Correct this error and find out the correct standard deviation.

[Correct : $\overline{X}$ = 26.06, σ = 81]

17. Find out who is better and consistent from the following data:

Batsman *A* :	10	12	80	70	60	100	0	4
Batsman *B* :	8	9	7	10	5	9	10	8

	A	*B*
$\overline{X}$	42	8.25
C.V.	88.48	18.92

18. The mean and standard deviation of 15 items were found to be 8 and 2 respectively. On checking, it was discovered that one item 11 had been misread as 5. Calculate the correct mean and standard deviation.

[$\overline{X}$ = 8.4, σ = 1.96]

19. Find out in which company the wages are more variable:

Wages (in ₹)	*No. of workers* Company *A*	Company *B*
3000–4000	15	29
4000–5000	20	52
5000–7000	32	40
7000–9000	42	58
9000–10000	15	31
10000–11000	6	10

[Company *B* : C.V. = 33.45%]

20. During the 10 weeks of a session, the marks scored by two candidates, Jayanth and Vasanth, taking the computer programme course are given below:

Jayanth	:	58	59	60	54	65	66	52	75	69	62
Vasanth	:	87	89	78	71	73	84	65	66	56	46

(*a*) Who is the better scorer : Jayanth or Vasanth?

(*b*) Who is more consistent?

[*Jayanth* ; $\overline{X}$ = 61 ; *C.V.* = 11.89 : *Vasanth*, $\overline{X}$ = 71.5, *C.V.* = 18.29 (*a*) Vasant (*b*) Jayant]

21. From some financial statistics, it is found that the monthly average of electricity charges was ₹ 2,460 and S.D. ₹ 120. The monthly average of direct wages was ₹ 42,000 and S.D. ₹ 1,200. State, which is more variable ?

22. Based on the frequency distribution given below, compute the following statistical measures to characterise the distribution :

(*i*) Coefficient of variation, (*ii*) Inter-quartile range, (*iii*) Modal value.

Annual tax paid (₹ Thousand)	*No. of Managers*	*Annual tax paid (₹ Thousand)*	*No. of Managers*
5–10	18	25–30	20
10–15	30	30–35	12
15–20	46	35–40	6
20–25	28		

[C.V. = 40.16, (*ii*) 10.97, (*iii*) 17.35]

23. After settlement, the average weekly wage in a factory had increased from ₹ 80 to 120 and standard deviation had increased from ₹ 10 to 15. The wages have become higher and more uniform, after settlement. Comment.

[Wages increased but they are not more uniform as C.V. = 12.5% both cases]

24. For a group containing 100 observations, the arithmetic mean and standard deviation are 8 and $\sqrt{10.5}$. For 50 observations selected from these 100 observations, the mean and standard deviation are 10 and 2 respectively. Find the mean and standard deviation of the other half.

[Mean = 6, σ = 3]

25. The mean, standard deviation and range of a symmetrical distribution of weights of a group of 20 are 40 kgs, 5 kgs and 6 kgs, respectively. Find the mean and standard deviation of the group lightest and the heaviest boys are excluded.

[**Hint :** Since mean = 40 *kg* and range of 6. Hence weights vary between 37 and 43 as distribution is symmetrical as range = 6, smallest value = $4 - \frac{6}{2}$ and largest value is $40 + \frac{6}{2}$]

[New $\overline{X}$ = 40 and σ = 5.17]

26. The mean and standard deviation of 200 items are found to be 60 and 20 respectively. If at the time of calculations, two items were wrongly recorded as 3 and 67 instead of 13 and 17, find the correct mean and standard deviation. What is the correct value of the coefficient of variation?

[Correct $\overline{X}$ = 59.8, σ = 20.09, C.V. = 33.60%]

27. Prices of a particular item in 10 years in two cities are given below, which city has more stable prices?

City A	:	55	54	52	53	56	58	52	50	51	49
City B	:	108	107	105	105	106	107	104	103	104	101

[C.V. (A) = 4.99, C.V. (B) = 1.97]

28. Calculate the coefficient of variation of the following two series and show which series is more variable :

Weight in kg.	:	0–10	10–20	20–30	30–40	40–50	50–60	60–70
Class $A : f$	:	1	2	9	8	5	4	1
Class $B : f$	:	1	3	7	8	7	3	1

[C.V. = 39 for both the series]

29. Calculate the mean and standard deviation of the following distribution:

Age (Years)	:	25–30	30–35	35–40	40–45	45–50	50–55
No of workers	:	70	51	47	31	29	22

[X = 36.78 : σ = 8.19]

30. Find the mode, median, lower quartile (Q_1) and upper quartile (Q_3) and Coeff. of Q.D. from following data :

Wages	:	0–10	10–20	20–30	30–40	40–50
No. of workers	:	22	38	46	35	20

[Mode = 24.21; Med. = 24.46,
Q_1 = 14.803; Q_3 = 24.21
Coeff. of Q.D. = 0.396]

□□□

6

Skewness, Moments and Kurtosis

CHAPTER OUTLINE

- Skewness
- Positional Measures of Skewness
- Moments
- Skewness Based on Moments
- Kurtosis and is Measurement

6.1 INTRODUCTION

The measure of central tendency and variation discussed in previous chapters do not reveal the entire story about a frequency distribution. Two distributions may have the same mean and standard deviation but may differ in their shape of the distribution. Further description of their characteristics is necessary that is provided by measures of skewness and kurtosis.

The term 'skewness' refers to lack of symmetry or departure from symmetry, *e.g.*, when a distribution is not symmetrical (or is asymmetrical) it is called a skewed distribution. The measures of skewness indicate the difference between the manner in which the observations are distributed in a particular distribution compared with a symmetrical (or normal) distribution. The concept of skewness gain importance from the fact that statistical theory is often based upon the assumption of the normal distribution. A measure of skewness is, therefore, necessary in order to guard against the consequence of this assumption.

In a symmetrical distribution the values of mean, median and mode are alike. In a skewed distribution, these values differ. If the value of mean is greater than the mode, skewness is said to be positive. On the other hand, if the value of mode is greater than mean, skewness is said to be negative. The following diagrams would clarify the meaning of skewness.

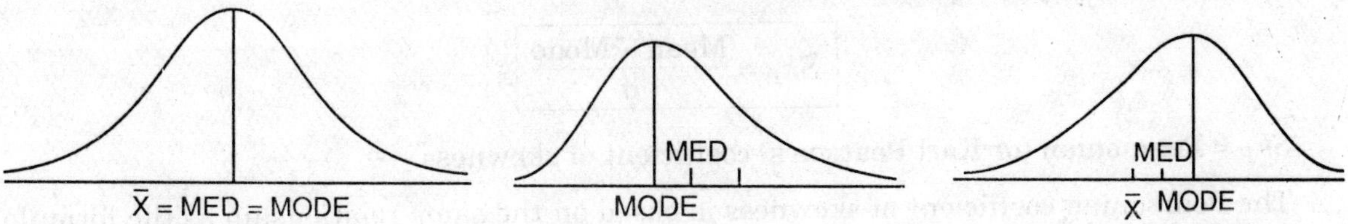

(*a*) Symmetrical Distribution (*b*) Positively Skewed Distribution (*c*) Negatively Skewed Distribution

It is clear from the (*a*), (*b*) and (*c*) diagrams that

1. In a symmetrical distribution, the values of mean, median and mode are alike.

2. In a positively skewed distribution, mean is greater than the mode and the median lies somewhere in between mean and mode. A positively skewed distribution contains some values that are much larger than the majority of other observations.

3. In a negatively skewed distribution, mode is greater than the mean and the median lies in between mean and mode. The mean is pulled towards the low-valued items (that is, to the left). A negative skewed distribution contains some values that are much smaller than the majority of observations.

In moderately asymmetrical distributions, the interval between the mean and the median approximately one-third of the interval between the mean and the mode. It is this relationship that provide a means of measuring the degree of skewness in particular cases, *i.e.* when a mode is ill defined.

6.2 DIFFERENCE BETWEEN VARIATION AND SKEWNESS

The following two points of difference between variation and skewness should be carefully noted :

1. Variation tells us about the amount of the variation. Skewness tells us about the direction of variation.

2. In business and economic series, measures of variation have greater practical applications that measures skewness.

6.3 MEASURES OF SKEWNESS

Measures of skewness can be both absolute as well as relative. Since in a symmetrical distribution mean, median and mode are identical, the more the mean moves away from the mode, the larger the asymmetry or skewness. The distance between the mean and the mode is Karl Pearson's basis of measuring skewness. However, a measure of absolute skewness cannot be used for purposes of comparisons because the same amount of skewness has different meanings in distribution with small variation and distributions with large variation. In order to make valid comparison between the skewness in two or more distributions, we have to eliminate the distributing influence of variation. Such elimination accomplished by dividing the absolute skewness by standard deviation. The following are important methods of measuring relative skewness :

6.3.1. Karl Pearson's Coefficient of Skewness

The method is most frequently used for measuring skewness. The formula for measuring coefficient of skewness is as follows :

$$Sk_P = \frac{\text{Mean} - \text{Mode}}{\sigma}$$

Sk_P = Pearsonian (or Karl Pearson's) coefficient of skewness.

The Pearsonian coefficient of skewness is based on the same relationship as the formula for empirical mode. The diffraction of skewness is determined by observing whether the mean is greater than the mode (positive skewness) or less than the mode (negative skewness). The extent of departure from symmetry is ascertained by observing the extent to which the mean is pulled away from the mode. The extent of departure is expressed in standard units in order to obtain a measure that is *independent* of unit of measurement.

The value of this coefficient would be zero in a symmetrical distribution. If mean is greater than mode, coefficient of skewness would be positive, otherwise negative. In practice, the value of this coefficient usually lies between ±1 for moderately skewed distribution.

If the mode is 'ill-defined' that above formula has to be modified. In such a case the following approximate formula is used :

$$Sk_P = \frac{3\,(\text{Mean} - \text{Median})}{\sigma}$$

6.3.2. Other Measures Based on Positional Measures

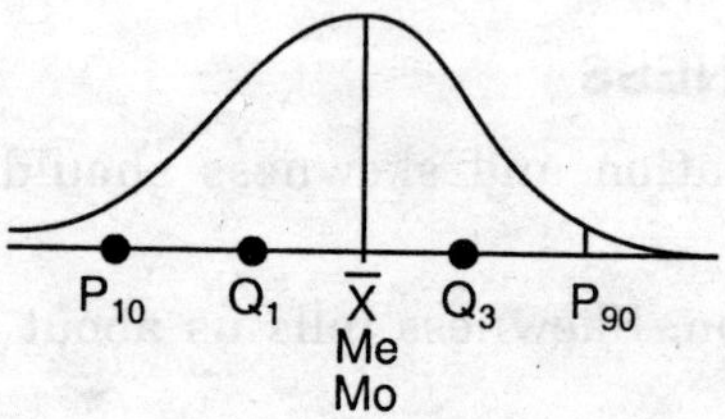

Fig. (*a*)

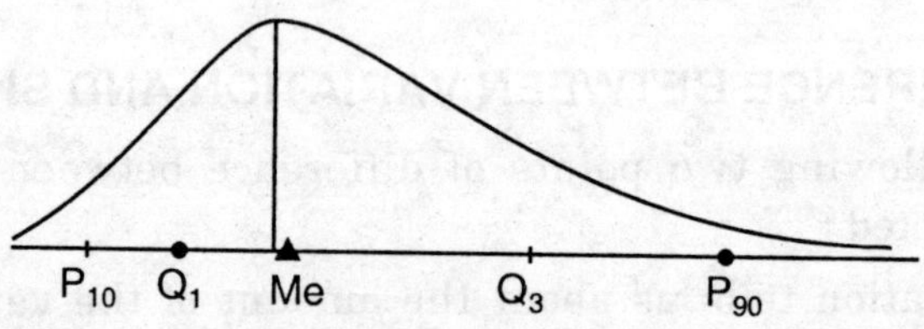

Fig. (*b*)

Fig. (*a*) shows symmetrical distribution in which $\overline{X} = M_e = M_o$. Also M_e lies exactly in the centre of Q_1 and Q_3 *i.e.* $M_e - Q_1 = Q_3 - M_e \Rightarrow Q_1 + Q_3 - 2\,M_e = 0$. Same way M_e lies exactly in between P_{10} and $P_{90} \Rightarrow M_e - P_{10} = P_{90} - M_e \Rightarrow P_{10} + P_{90} - 2M_e = 0$.

Fig. (*b*) shows +vely skewed distribution. In this case $Q_3 - M_e > M_e - Q_1$

$\Rightarrow Q_1 + Q_3 - 2M_e > 0$

Same way $P_{90} - M_e > M_e - P_{10}$

$\Rightarrow P_{90} + P_{10} - 2M_e > 0$

[Incase of –vely skewed the same conditions become $Q_1 + Q_3 - 2M_e < 0$ and

$P_{90} + P_{10} - 2M_e < 0$]

Based on these properties we define other two relative measures as follows :

(A) *Bowley's Coefficient of Skewness.* This method is based on quartiles. The formula for calculating coefficient of skewness is :

$$Sk_B = \frac{(Q_3 - Q_2) - (Q_2 - Q_1)}{Q_3 - Q_1} = \frac{Q_3 + Q_1 - 2\text{Med.}}{Q_3 - Q_1}$$

$Q_3 + Q_1 - 2Me$ is divided by $Q_3 - Q_1$ in order to make the measure independent of units (that is why it is called coefficient).

The value of this coefficient will be zero if it is a symmetrical distribution. If the value is greater than zero, it is positively skewed and if the value is less than zero, it is negatively skewed distribution.

Sk_B = Bowley's coefficient varies between ±1 for moderately skewed distribution.

This method is particularly useful in case of open-end distributions and where extreme values are present. Also when positional measures are called for, skewness should be measured by the Bowley's method.

(B) *Kelly' Coefficient of Skewness.* Another measure of skewness devised by Kelly is based on percentiles and deciles.

The formula for calculating coefficient of skewness is given below :

$$Sk_K = \frac{P_{90} + P_{10} - 2Me}{P_{90} - P_{10}} \qquad \text{(based on percentiles)}$$

$$Sk_K = \frac{D_9 + D_1 - 2Me}{D_9 - D_1} \qquad \text{(based on deciles) [as } P_{90} = D_9]$$

Sk_K = Kelly's coefficient of skewness.

It is clear from this formula that to calculate coefficient of skewness we have to determine the value of 10th, 50th and 90th percentiles. However, this method is not very popular in practice.

It should be noted that three different formulae of calculating skewness are based on different assumptions and hence the answer obtained from the same question by different method may differ.

It may be pointed out that measures of coefficient of skewness are used mainly for making comparison between two or more distributions. As a description of one distribution alone, the interpretation of a measure of skewness is vague as 'slight skewness', 'marked skewness', or 'moderate skewness' :

Example 1. *The following data relate to the profits of 1,000 companies :*

Profits (₹ lakhs)	*No. of companies*	*Profits (₹ lakhs)*	*No. of companies*
100–120	*17*	*180–200*	*327*
120–140	*53*	*200–220*	*208*
140–160	*199*	*220–240*	*2*
160–180	*194*		

Calculate the coefficient of skewness and comment on its value.

Solution. CALCULATION OF COEFFICIENT OF SKEWNESS

Profits (*₹ lakhs*)	*m.p.* *X*	*f*	*(X-170)/20* *d*	*fd*	fd^2
100–120	110	17	–3	–51	153
120–140	130	53	–2	–106	212
140–160	150	199	–1	–199	199
160–180	170	194	0	0	0
180–200	190	327	+1	+327	327
200–220	210	208	+2	+416	832
220–240	230	2	+3	+6	18
		N = 1,000		$\Sigma fd = 393$	$\Sigma fd^2 = 1{,}741$

$$Sk_P = \frac{\text{Mean} - \text{Mode}}{\sigma} \qquad (m.p. = \text{mid-point})$$

Calculation of Mean : $\bar{X} = A + \frac{\Sigma fd}{N} \times i = 170 + \frac{393}{1000} \times 20 = 170 + 7.86 = 177.86$

Calculation of Mode : By inspection mode lies in the class 180—200.

$$\text{Mode} = L + \frac{\Delta_1}{\Delta_1 + \Delta_2} \times i = 180 + \frac{133}{133 + 119} \times 20 = 180 + 10.56 = 190.56$$

$$\Delta_1 = 327—194 = 133, \qquad \Delta_2 = 327 - 208 = 119$$

Calculation of Standard Deviation :

$$\sigma = \sqrt{\frac{\Sigma fd^2}{N} - \left(\frac{\Sigma fd}{N}\right)^2} \times i = \sqrt{\frac{1741}{1000} - \left(\frac{393}{1000}\right)} \times 20$$

$$= \sqrt{1.74 - 0.15} \times 20 = 1.26 \times 20 = 25.2$$

$$Sk_P = \frac{177.86 - 190.56}{25.2} = -0.504$$

The mode is greater than the mean by an amount equal to about 50.4 per cent of the value of standard deviation. It is moderate negatively skewed distribution.

Example 2. *Find Bowley's coefficient of skewness for the following frequency distribution :*

No. of children per family	*0*	*1*	*2*	*3*	*4*	*5*	*6*
No. of families	*7*	*10*	*16*	*25*	*18*	*11*	*8*

Solution. CALCULATION OF BOWLEY'S COEFFICIENT OF SKEWNESS

No. of children per family *X*	*No. of families* *f*	*c.f.*
0	7	7
1	10	17
2	16	33
3	25	58
4	18	76
5	11	87
6	8	95

$$Sk_B = \frac{Q_3 + Q_1 - 2\text{ Med.}}{Q_3 - Q_1}$$

$$Q_1 = \text{Size of } \frac{N+1}{4}\text{th item} = \frac{95+1}{4} = 24\text{th item, Hence } Q_1 = 2$$

$$Q_3 = \text{Size of } \frac{3(N+1)}{4}\text{th item} = \frac{3 \times 96}{4} = 72\text{th item}$$

Size of 72th item is 4, Hence $Q_3 = 4$

$$\text{Med.} = \text{Size of } \frac{N+1}{2}\text{th item} = \frac{96}{2} = 48\text{th item.}$$

Size of 48th item is 3. Hence median = 3

$$Sk_B = \frac{4 + 2 - 2(3)}{4-2} = \frac{0}{2} = 0.$$

Example 3. *You are given the position in a factory before and after the settlement of an industrial dispute. Comment on the gains or losses from the point of view of workers and that of management.*

	Before	***After***
No. of workers	*2,400*	*2,350*
Mean wages (₹)	*45.5*	*47.5*
Median wages (₹)	*48.0*	*45.0*
Standard Deviation (₹)	*12.0*	*10.0*

Solution

The following comments can be made on the basis of the information given :

(*i*) By comparing the total wages bill we can comment on the increase or decrease in the level of wages.

Total wage bill *before* the settlement of dispute = 2,400 × 46.5 = ₹ 1,09,200

Total wage bill *after* the settlement of dispute = 2,350 × 47.5 = ₹ 1,11,625.

Hence, the total wages bill has gone up after the settlement of dispute even though the number of workers has decreased from 2,400 to 2,350. This means that the average wage is now higher. This is definitely a gain to the workers.

Conversely, we cannot say that increased wage bill is necessarily a loss to management because it is results in greater efficiency of workers and, therefore, higher productivity, it would be a positive gain to management also.

(*ii*) Median before settlement of the dispute was 48 and after settlement it is 45. This means that formerly 50% of workers used to get wages below ₹ 48 and now 50% are getting below ₹ 45. Thus there is reduction of salaries of those getting less salary.

(*iii*) By comparing the coefficient of variation before and after the settlement of dispute we can comment on the distribution of wages.

Coefficient of variation *before* the settlement of dispute

$$\text{C.V.} = \frac{\sigma}{\overline{X}} \times 100, \text{ where } \sigma = 12, \overline{X} = 45.5$$

$$\therefore \quad \text{C.V.} = \frac{12}{45.5} \times 100 = 26.37$$

Coefficient of variation *after* the settlement of dispute $\sigma = 12, \overline{X} = 47.5$

$$\therefore \quad \text{C.V.} = \frac{10}{47.5} \times 100 = 21.05$$

Since the value of the coefficient of variation has decreased from 26.27 to 21.05 there is sufficient evidence to conclude that wages are more uniformly distributed after the settlement of dispute or, in other words, there is lesser inequality in the distribution of wages after the dispute is settled.

(*iv*) By comparing skewness we can comment upon the nature of the distribution.

Coefficient of skewness *before* the settlement of dispute

$$Sk_P = \frac{3(\overline{X} - \text{Med.})}{\sigma} = \frac{3(45.5 - 48)}{12} = -0.625$$

Coefficient of Skewness *after* the settlement of dispute

$$Sk_P = \frac{3(47.5 - 45)}{10} = \frac{7.5}{10} = +0.75$$

Thus, the distribution is positively skewed after the settlement of dispute whereas it was negatively skewed before the settlement of dispute. This suggests that the number of workers getting low wages has increased considerably and that of workers getting high wages fallen, though the actual wage of workers has increased.

Example 4. *You are given the weekly wages of 30 workers working in a factory*

Weekly wages (₹)

350.4	*375.8*	*380.2*	*420.7*
469.2	*392.6*	*420.0*	*460.2*
578.3	*492.4*	*536.4*	*625.2*
633.2	*475.3*	*375.4*	*608.2*
592.9	*576.5*	*517.2*	*594.5*
462.7	*42.8*	*479.2*	*588.6*
572.5	*517.9*	*537.6*	*493.4*
708.5	*727.9*		

Form a frequency distribution of the above data taking the first class as 300–400 and from the frequency distribution so formed, calculate Karl Pearson's coefficient of skewness.

Solution.

FORMATION OF FREQUENCY DISTRIBUTION

Weekly wages	*Tally bars*	*Frequency*
300–400	𝍸	5
400–500	𝍸 𝍸	10
500–600	𝍸 𝍸	10
600–700	|||	3
700–800	||	2

Since it is a bimodal series the following formula for calculating skewness shall be applied :

$$Sk_P = \frac{3\,(\text{Mean} - \text{Median})}{\sigma}$$

CALCULATION OF COEFFICIENT OF SKEWNESS

Weekly wages (₹)	m.p. m	f	$(m\text{-}550)/100$ d	fd	fd^2	c.f.
300–400	350	5	–2	–10	20	5
400–500	450	10	–1	–10	10	15
500–600	550	10	0	0	0	25
600–700	650	3	+1	+3	3	28
700–800	750	2	+2	+4	8	30
		$N = 30$		$\Sigma fd = -13$	$\Sigma fd^2 = 41$	

Mean : $\overline{X} = A + \frac{\Sigma fd}{N} \times i$

$A = 550, \Sigma fd = -13, N = 30, i = 100$

$\overline{X} = 550 - \frac{13}{30} \times 100 = 550 - 43.33 = 506.67$

Median : Med $=$ Size of $\frac{N}{2}$th item $= \frac{30}{2} = 15$th item.

Median lies in the class 400—500

$$\text{Med} = L + \frac{N/2 - c.f.}{f} \times i$$

$L = 400, N/2 = 15, c.f. = 5, f = 10, i = 100$

$$\text{Med} = 400 + \frac{15-5}{10} \times 100 = 400 + 100 = 500$$

Standard Deviation : $\sigma = \sqrt{\frac{\Sigma fd^2}{N} - \left(\frac{\Sigma fd}{N}\right)^2} \times i$

$\Sigma fd^2 = 41, N = 30, \Sigma fd = -13, i = 100$

$$\sigma = \sqrt{\frac{41}{30} - \left(\frac{-13}{30}\right)^2} \times 100 = \sqrt{1.367 - .188} \times 100$$

$$= \sqrt{1.179} \times 100 = 1.0858 \times 100 = 108.58$$

$\therefore$ Coeff. of $Sk = \frac{3(506.67 - 500)}{108.58} = \frac{20.01}{108.58} = 0.184.$

Example 5. *Calculate the Kelly's coefficient of skewness from the following data :*

Wages (₹)	*No. of Workers*	*Wages (₹)*	*No. of Workers*
800–900	*10*	*1200–1300*	*160*
900–1000	*33*	*1300–1400*	*80*

1000–1100	*47*	*1400–1500*	*60*
1100–1200	*110*		

Solution.

CALCULATION OF P_{10}, P_{50} AND P_{90}

Class Intervals	*No. of Workers (f)*	*Less than (c.f.)*
800–900	10	10
900–1000	33	43
1000–1100	47	90
1100–1200	110	200
1200–1300	160	360
1300–1400	80	440
1400–1500	60	500
Total	500	

(*i*) Since $\frac{10}{100}N = \frac{10 \times 500}{100} = 50$, P_{10} lies in the interval 1000–1100.

Thus, $L_{P_{10}} = 1000, C = 43, f_{P_{10}} = 47, i = 100$

Hence, $P_{10} = 1000 + \frac{50-43}{47} \times 100 =$ ₹ 1014.89

$$P_{10} = L_{P_0} + \frac{\frac{10n}{100} - C}{f_{P_{10}}} i$$

(*ii*) Since $\frac{50}{100}N = 250$, P_{50} lies in the interval 1200–1300.

Thus, $L_{P_{50}} = 1200, C = 200, f_{P_{50}} = 160, i = 100$

Hence, $P_{50} = 1200 + \frac{250-200}{160} \times 100 =$ ₹ 1231.25 = Median

(*iii*) Since $\frac{90}{100}N = 450$, P_{90} lies in the class 1400–1500.

Thus, $L_{P_{90}} = 1400, \; C = 440, f_{P_{90}} = 60, i = 100$

Hence, $P_{90} = 1400 + \frac{450-440}{60} \times 100 =$ ₹ 1416.67

$$Sk_k = \frac{1416.67 + 1014.89 - 2 \times 1231.25}{1416.67 - 1014.89} = \frac{-30.94}{401.78} = -0.08 \qquad \left[Sk_K = \frac{P_{90} + P_{10} - 2\,Me}{P_{90} - P_{10}} \right]$$

Example 6. *Calculate Karl Pearson's co-efficient of skewness from the following data* :

Size	:	*1*	*2*	*3*	*4*	*5*	*6*	*7*
Frequency	:	*10*	*18*	*30*	*25*	*12*	*3*	*2*

Solution.

COMPUTATION OF MEAN, MODE AND S.D.

Size (x)	Frequency (f)	f.x	$f.x^2$
1	10	10	10
2	18	36	72
3	30	90	270
4	25	100	400
5	12	60	300
6	3	18	108
7	2	14	98
Total	$N = 100$	$\Sigma fx = 328$	$\Sigma fx^2 = 1258$

$$\text{Mean } (M) = \frac{\Sigma fx}{N} = \frac{328}{100} = 3.28$$

$$\text{S.D. } (\sigma) = \sqrt{\frac{\Sigma fx^2}{N} - \left(\frac{\Sigma fx}{N}\right)^2}$$

$$= \sqrt{\frac{1258}{100} - \left(\frac{328}{100}\right)^2}$$

$$= \sqrt{12.58 - 10.7584} = \sqrt{1.8216}$$

$$= 1.3497$$

Since the maximum frequency is 30, corresponding value of x *viz.*, 3 is the mode. Thus Mode $(Mo) = 3$.

Karl Pearson's Coefficient of Skewness is given by

$$Sk = \frac{M - Mo}{\sigma} = \frac{3.28 - 3.00}{1.3497} = \frac{0.28}{1.3497} = 0.2075$$

Hence, the distribution is slightly positively skewed.

Example 7. *A distribution of wages paid to workers would show that, although a few reach very high levels, most workers are at lower level of wages. If you were an employer, resisting worker's claim for an increase of wages, which average would suit your case? Do you think your argument will be different if you are a trade union leader ? Explain.*

Solution. The distribution of wages paid to the workers would show that, although a few reach very high levels, most workers are at lower level of wages. This implies that the distribution of wages of workers in the factory is positively skewed so that

$$\text{Mean} > \text{Median} > \text{Mode} \quad \Rightarrow \quad \text{Mode} < \text{Median} < \text{Mean}.$$

Since mode is the least of the three averages mean, median and mode, the average that will suit the employer most (to resist workers claim for higher wages) will be *mean*.

By similar argument, since mode is the smallest of the three averages, it will suit most to the trade union leader.

Example 8. *If the income distribution in a particular region is symmetric, then will the symmetry be affected if income of everyone is increased :*

(i) by ₹ 100 ?

(ii) by a certain proportion ?

(iii) What happens to the symmetry of the income distribution if the income of everyone becomes square of what it is now ?

Solution. Since the income distribution in a 'particular region' is given to be symmetrical, its mean, median and mode coincide, *i.e.,*

$$\text{Mean} = \text{Median} = \text{Mode} \qquad \ldots(*)$$

(*i*) If the income of each individual is increased by ₹ 100, the values of each of mean, median and mode will go up by ₹ 100. Hence using the values of mean, median and mode for the new distribution will also be equal, *i.e.*, the new distribution will also be symmetrical. In other words, the symmetry of the given distribution will not be affected.

(*ii*) If the income of each individual is increased by a certain proportion, the values of each of mean, median and mode will go up by the same proportion. Hence, as discussed in part (*i*), the new distribution also remains symmetrical, *i.e.*, the symmetry of the given distribution is not affected in this case also.

(*iii*) If the income of each individual is squared, a symmetrical distribution would become positively skewed. Let us consider the following symmetrical distribution :

X	1	2	3	4	5	6	7
f	5	8	12	20	12	8	5
$Y = X^2$	1	4	9	16	25	36	49

Let $Y = X^2$.

On drawing the frequency curves of the distributions of X and Y we shall see that the distribution of X is symmetrical and that of Y is positively skewed, *i.e.*, frequency curve is stretched more to the right than to the left. As mode is 9 and mean will be larger than 9.

Example 9. *Consider the following distributions :*

	Distribution A	*Distribution B*
Mean	*100*	*90*
Median	*90*	*80*
Standard Deviation	*10*	*10*

(i) Show that distribution A has the small degree of the variation as distribution B.

(ii) Both distributions have the same degree of skewness. True/False? Comment, giving reasons.

Solution.

(*i*) $$\text{C.V. for distribution } A = 100 \times \frac{\sigma_A}{\bar{X}_A} = 100 \times \frac{10}{100} = 10.00$$

$$\text{C.V. for distribution } B = 100 \times \frac{\sigma_B}{\bar{X}_B} = 100 \times \frac{10}{90} = 11.11$$

Since C.V. (B) > C.V. (A), the distribution B is more variable than the distribution A.

(*ii*) Karl Pearson's coefficient of skewness for the distributions A and B is given by :

$$Sk\,(A) = \frac{3(M - Md)}{\sigma} = \frac{3(100 - 90)}{10} = 3 \;;\; Sk\,(B) = \frac{3(90 - 80)}{10} = 3$$

Since $Sk(A) = Sk(B) = 3$, the statement that both the distributions have the same degree of skewness is true.

Example 10. *Pearson's coefficient of skewness for a distribution is 0.4 and coefficient of variation is 30%. Its mode is 88. Find the mean and the median.*

Solution. We are given : $Sk_P = 0.4$, $C.V. = 30\%$, $Mo = 88$

The formula for coefficient of variation is

$$C.V. = \frac{\sigma}{\overline{X}} \times 100$$

$$30 = \frac{\sigma}{\overline{X}} \times 100 \quad \text{or} \quad \frac{\sigma}{\overline{X}} = \frac{3}{10} \qquad ...(i)$$

Now from the formula of coefficient of skewness, we can determine the value of standard deviation

$$Sk_P = \frac{\overline{X} - Mo}{\sigma}$$

$$0.4 = \frac{\overline{X}}{\sigma} - \frac{88}{\sigma} \Rightarrow \quad 0.4 = \frac{10}{3} - \frac{88}{\sigma}$$

$$\frac{88}{\sigma} = \frac{88}{30} \quad \text{or} \quad \sigma = 30$$

Substituting the value of σ in (*i*)

$$\frac{30}{\overline{X}} = \frac{3}{10} \quad \text{or} \quad \overline{X} = 100$$

The value of median can now be determined from the formula

$$\text{Mode} = 3 \text{ Median} - 2 \text{ Mean}$$

$$88 = 3\,Md - 2 \times 100$$

$$Md = \frac{288}{3} = 96$$

Hence the mean and median are 100 and 96 respectively.

Example 11. *Pearson's measure of skewness of a distribution is 0.5. Its median and mode are respectively 42 and 36. Find the Coefficient of Variation.*

Solution. We are given : Median = 42, Mode = 36 ...(*)

and Pearson's coefficient of skewness = 0.5

$$\Rightarrow \quad Sk = \frac{\text{Mean} - \text{Mode}}{\sigma} = 0.5 \qquad ...(**)$$

To find *s.d.* (σ), we shall first find the value of mean, by using the empirical relationship between mean, median and mode for a moderately asymmetrical distribution *viz.*,

$$\text{Mode} = 3 \text{ Median} - 2 \text{ Mean} \quad \Rightarrow \quad \text{Mean} = \frac{3 \text{ Median} - \text{Mode}}{2}$$

$$\therefore \quad \text{Mean} = \frac{3 \times 42 - 36}{2} = \frac{126 - 36}{2} = \frac{90}{2} = 45$$

Substituting in (**), we get

$$(s.d.)\ \sigma = \frac{\text{Mean} - \text{Mode}}{0.5} = \frac{45 - 36}{0.5} = \frac{9}{0.5} = 18$$

$$\text{Coefficient of Variation (C.V.)} = \frac{100 \times \sigma}{\text{Mean}} = \frac{100 \times 18}{45} = 40$$

Hence, C.V. is 40.

Example 12. *The sum of 50 observations is 500 and the sum of their squares is 6,000 and median is 12. Compute the coefficient of variation and the coefficient of skewness.*

Solution. In the usual notations, we are given :

$$n = 50\ ,\ \Sigma x = 500 \quad \text{and} \quad \Sigma x^2 = 6{,}000\ ;\ \text{Median} = 12$$

$$\therefore \quad \text{Mean } (\bar{x}) = \frac{\Sigma x}{n} = \frac{500}{50} = 10$$

$$\sigma^2 = \frac{\Sigma x^2}{n} - \bar{x}^2 = \frac{6{,}000}{50} - 100 = 20 \quad \Rightarrow \sigma = \sqrt{20} = 4.47$$

$$\text{Coefficient of Variation (C.V.)} = \frac{100\ \sigma}{\bar{X}} = \frac{100 \times 4.47}{10} = 44.7$$

Karl Pearson's coefficient of skewness is given by :

$$Sk = \frac{3(\text{Mean} - \text{Median})}{\sigma} = \frac{3(10 - 12)}{4.47} = \frac{-6}{4.47} = -1.34.$$

Example 13. *The following information was obtained from the records of a factory relating to the wages.*

	₹
Arithmetic Mean	*56.80*
Median	*59.50*
S.D.	*12.40*

Give as much information as you can about the distribution of wages.

Solution. We can obtain the following information from the above data :

(*i*) Since Md = ₹ 59.50, we conclude that 50% of the workers in the factory obtain the wages below ₹ 59.50.

(*ii*) $$\text{C.V.} = \frac{100\ \sigma}{M} = \frac{100 \times 12.40}{56.80} = 21.83 \qquad [M = \text{Mean}]$$

(*iii*) Karl Pearson's coefficient of skewness is given by :

$$Sk = \frac{3(M - Md)}{\sigma} = \frac{3(56.80 - 59.50)}{12.40} = \frac{3 \times (-2.70)}{12.40} = \frac{-8.1}{12.4} = -0.65$$

It is negatively skewed which indicates presence of much smaller values compared to many others.

Example 14. *Calculate coefficient of skewness based on quartiles and median from the following data :*

Variable	*Frequency*	*Variable*	*Frequency*
0–10	12	40–50	22
10–20	16	50–60	15
20–30	26	60–70	7
30–40	38	70–80	4

Solution. The Bowley's coefficient of skewness given by the following formula is based on quartiles and median :

$$Sk_B = \frac{Q_3 + Q_1 - 2\ \text{Med.}}{Q_3 - Q_1}$$

CALCULATION OF BOWLEY'S COEFFICIENT OF SKEWNESS

Variable	*f*	*c.f.*
0–10	12	12
10–20	16	28
20–30	26	54 ← Q_1 class
30–40	38	92 ← *Me* class
40–50	22	114 ← Q_3 class
50–60	15	129
60–70	7	136
70–80	4	140

Q_1 = Size of $\frac{N}{4}$th item = $\frac{140}{4}$ = 35th item. It lies in the class 20—30.

$$Q_1 = L + \frac{N/4 - c.f.}{f} \times i$$

$L = 20, N/4 = 35, c.f. = 28, f = 26, i = 10$

$$Q_1 = 20 + \frac{35 - 28}{26} \times 10 = 20 + 2.69 = 22.69$$

Q_3 = Size of $\frac{3N}{4}$th item = $\frac{3 \times 140}{4}$ = 105th item. It lies in the class 40—50.

$$Q_3 = L + \frac{3N/4 - c.f.}{f} \times i$$

$L = 40, 3N/4 = 105, c.f. = 92, f = 22, i = 10$

$$Q_3 = 40 + \frac{105 - 92}{22} \times 10 = 40 + 5.91 = 45.91$$

Med. = Size of $\frac{N}{2}$th item = $\frac{140}{2}$ = 70th item. It lie sin the class 30—40.

$$\text{Med.} = L + \frac{N/2 - c.f.}{f} \times i$$

$L = 30, N/2 = 70, c.f. = 54, f = 38, i = 10$

$$\text{Med.} = 30 + \frac{70 + 54}{38} \times 10 = 30 + 4.21 = 34.21$$

$$\text{Coeff. of } Sk = \frac{45.91 + 22.69 - 2\,(34.21)}{45.91 - 22.69} = \frac{68.6 - 68.42}{23.22} = 0.008.$$

Example 15. *In a frequency distribution the coefficient of skewness based upon quartiles is 0.6. If the sum of upper and lower quartiles is 100 and median is 38, find the values of upper and lower quartiles.*

Solution. It is given that $Q_3 + Q_1 = 100$, $M_d = 38$ and $S_{K_B} = 0.6$

Substituting these values in Bowley's formula, we get

$$0.6 = \frac{100 - 2 \times 38}{Q_3 - Q_1} \Rightarrow Q_3 - Q_1 = 40$$

Adding the equations $Q_3 + Q_1 = 100$ and $Q_3 - Q_1 = 40$, we get

$$2Q_3 = 140 \quad \text{or} \quad Q_3 = 70$$

Also $\qquad Q_1 = 30 \; (\because \; Q_1 + Q_3 = 100)$

Example 16. *You are given the position in a factory before and after the settlement of an industrial dispute. Comment on the gains or losses from the point of view of workers and that of management :*

	Before	***After***
No. of workers	*3,000*	*2,950*
Mean wage (₹)	*2,220*	*2,280*
Median wage (₹)	*2,250*	*2,225*
Standard deviation (₹)	*300*	*260*

Solution. The following comments can be made on the basis of information given :

(*i*) By comparing the total wage bill, we can comment on the increase or decrease in the level of wages.

	Before	*After*
Total wage bill :	3,000 × 2,220 = ₹ 66,60,000	2950 × 2280 = ₹ 67,26,000

Hence the total wage bill has gone up after the settlement of dispute even though the number of workers has decreased from 3,000 to 2,950. This means that average wage is now better. This is definitely a gain to the workers. Conversely, we cannot say that increased wage bill is a loss to management because if it results in greater efficiency of workers and, therefore, higher productivity, it would be a gain to management also.

(*ii*) Median wage before settlement of the dispute was ₹ 2,250 and after settlement is ₹ 2,225. This means that formerly 50% of workers used to get wage below ₹ 2,250 and now after the settlement of dispute they get below ₹ 2,225. Though the average has increased and 50% of workers getting less than average, this fact goes against the workers.

(*iii*) By comparing the coefficient of variation, we can comment on the distribution pattern of wages.

	Before	*After*
Coefficient of variation :	$\frac{300}{2220} \times 100 = 13.51$	$\frac{260}{2280} \times 100 = 11.40$

Since the coefficient of variation has decreased from 13.51 to 11.40, there is sufficient evidence to conclude that wages are more uniformly distributed after the settlement of dispute, or, in other words, there is lesser inequality in the distribution of wages after the dispute is settled.

(*iv*) By comparing skewness we can comment on the nature of the distribution

	Before	*After*
Coefficient of skewness :	$\frac{3\,(2220 - 2250)}{300} = -0.3$	$\frac{3(2280 - 2225)}{260} = +0.635$

The distribution was negatively skewed before the settlement and is positively skewed after the settlement. This indicates that a few workers are getting much more than the mean.

Example 17. *The table gives the distribution of daily wages of 500 workers in a factory.*

Daily wages (₹)	*No. of workers*
Below 200	*10*
200–250	*25*
250–300	*145*
300–350	*220*
350–400	*70*
400 and above	*30*

(i) Obtain the limits of daily wages of central 50 per cent of the observed workers.

(ii) Calculate Bowley's Coefficient of Skewness.

Solution.

CALCULATION OF LIMITS OF CENTRAL 50% OF WORKERS AND BOWLEY'S COEFFICIENT

Daily wages (₹)	*f*	*c.f.*
Below 200	10	10
200–250	25	35
250–300	145	180
300–350	220	400
350–400	70	470
400 and above	30	500

For obtaining the limits of central 50% of the workers, calculate Q_1 and Q_3 as Q_1 is smallest and Q_3 the largest value of middle 50% units.

for Q_1 find $\frac{N}{4} = \frac{500}{40} = 125$

Q_1 lies in the class 250—300.

$$Q_1 = L + \frac{N/4 - c.f.}{f} \times i = 250 + \frac{125 - 35}{145} \times 50 = 250 + 31.03 = 281.03$$

for Q_3 find $\frac{3N}{4} = \frac{3 \times 500}{40} = 375$

Q_3 lies in the class 300—350.

$$Q_3 = L + \frac{3N/4 - c.f.}{f} \times i = 300 + \frac{375 - 180}{220} \times 50 = 300 + 44.32 = 344.32$$

Hence the daily wages of central 50% of workers lie between ₹ 281.03 and ₹ 344.32.

(ii) Bowley's Coefficient of Skewness

$$Sk_B = \frac{Q_3 + Q_1 - 2\text{ Med.}}{Q_3 - Q_1}$$

for Med. $\frac{N}{2} = \frac{500}{2} = 250$

Median lies in the class 300-350.

$$\text{Med.} = L + \frac{N/2 - c.f.}{f} \times i = 300 + \frac{250 - 180}{220} \times 50 = 300 + 15.9 = 315.9$$

$$Sk_B = \frac{344.32 + 281.03 - 2(315.9)}{344.32 - 281.03} = \frac{-6.45}{63.29} = -0.102$$

The negative coefficient –0.102 indicates that the distance between Q_3 and Q_2 is smaller than that between Q_2 and Q_1. Thus the distribution is skewed to the left or there are more smaller values on the X-scale.

6.4. MOMENTS AND SKEWNESS

There are 3 types of moments which are defined as follows :

(A) Moments about origin/zero (Raw Moments)

1st moment about zero $= \frac{\Sigma X}{n}$ or $\frac{\Sigma fX}{\Sigma f} = m_1$

(which is infact mean)

2nd moment about zero $= \frac{\Sigma X^2}{n}$ or $\frac{\Sigma fX^2}{\Sigma f} = m_2$

3rd moment about zero $= \frac{\Sigma X^3}{n} = \frac{\Sigma X^3}{\Sigma f} = m_3$ and so on.

(B) Moments about any constant A

[in above expressions X is replaced by $X - A = d$ = deviation from A]

$\mu_1' =$ 1st moment about $A = \frac{\Sigma(X - A)}{n}$ or $\frac{\Sigma f(X - A)}{\Sigma f}$ or $\frac{\Sigma fd}{\Sigma f}$ or $\frac{\Sigma d}{n}$

(depending on whether it is ungrouped or grouped data)

$\mu_2' =$ 2nd moment about $A = \frac{\Sigma d^2}{n}$ or $\frac{\Sigma fd^2}{\Sigma f}$ or $\frac{\Sigma(X - A)^2}{n}$ or $\frac{\Sigma f(X - A)^2}{\Sigma f}$

$\mu_3' =$ 3rd moment about $A = \frac{\Sigma d^3}{n}$ or $\frac{\Sigma fd^3}{\Sigma f}$ or $\frac{\Sigma (X - A)^3}{n}$ or $\frac{\Sigma f(X - A)^3}{\Sigma f}$ and so on.

(C) Moments about mean (Central Moments)

(In this case A is replaced by $\overline{X}$) and the 1st, 2nd, 3rd and 4th central moments are denoted by μ_1, μ_2, μ_3 and μ_4 respectively and are defined as follows :

For ungrouped data :

$$\mu_1 = \frac{\Sigma (X - \overline{X})}{N} = 0 \text{ (always)} \qquad \mu_2 = \frac{\Sigma (X - \overline{X})^2}{N}$$

$$\mu_3 = \frac{\Sigma (X-\overline{X})^3}{N}; \qquad \mu_4 = \frac{\Sigma (X-\overline{X})^4}{N}$$

For grouped data :

$$\mu_1 = \frac{\Sigma f (X-\overline{X})}{N}; \qquad \mu_2 = \frac{\Sigma f (X-\overline{X})^2}{N}$$

$$\mu_3 = \frac{\Sigma f (X-\overline{X})^3}{N}; \qquad \mu_4 = \frac{\Sigma f (X-\overline{X})^4}{N} \qquad [\text{where } \Sigma f = N]$$

We can extend the moments to higher power in the similar way. But in practice the first four moments suffice.

The first moment about the origin tells us about the mean, the second moment about variance, the third moment about skewness and the fourth moment about the kurtosis.

Thus in general moments, in short, are defined as

For Ungrouped Data

The rth moment of a variable X about the arithmetic mean $\overline{X}$ is given by :

$$\mu_r = \frac{1}{N} \Sigma (X-\overline{X})^r \text{ central moments}$$

The rth moment of a variable X about any arbitrary point A is given by :

$$\mu_r' = \frac{1}{N} \Sigma (X - A)^r = \frac{1}{N} \Sigma d^r$$

For Grouped Data

$$\mu_r = \frac{1}{N} \Sigma f (X-\overline{X})^r$$

and $$\mu_r' = \frac{1}{N} \Sigma f (X-A)^r = \frac{1}{N} \Sigma f d^r$$

For different values of r, we shall get different moments. Thus if we put $r = 1$, we will get first moment, if we put $r = 2$, we will get second moment, and so on.

Moments about Arbitrary Point

We generally need central moments for analysing the data, *i.e.*,

$$\mu_r = \frac{\Sigma (X-\overline{X})^r}{N} \text{ or } \frac{\Sigma f (X-\overline{X})^r}{\Sigma f} = \frac{\Sigma f x^r}{\Sigma f} \text{ (where } x = X-\overline{X})$$

However, when actual mean is in fraction, moments are first calculated about an arbitrary origin and then converted to moments about the actual mean. When deviations are taken from arbitrary point, the formulae are (as already mentioned).

$$\mu_1' = \frac{\Sigma (X-A)}{N} \qquad \mu_2' = \frac{\Sigma (X-A)^2}{N}$$

$$\mu_3' = \frac{\Sigma (X-A)^3}{N} \qquad \mu_4' = \frac{\Sigma (X-A)^4}{N}$$

μ_1', μ_2', etc., denote first, second moment, etc., about an arbitrary point 'A'.

In a frequency distribution, to simplify calculations we can take a common factor i but in that case the various moments have to be multiplied by i, i^2, i^3 and i^4 respectively, *i.e.*, if $d' = \frac{X-A}{i}$ is taken $(X - A) = id'$, we get

$$\mu_1' = \frac{\Sigma f(X-A)}{N} = \frac{\Sigma fd}{\Sigma f} = \frac{\Sigma fd'}{N} \times i$$

$$\mu_2' = \frac{\Sigma f(X-A)^2}{N} = \frac{\Sigma fd^2}{\Sigma f} = \frac{\Sigma fd'^2}{\Sigma f} \cdot i^2$$

$$\mu_3' = \frac{\Sigma f(X-A)^3}{N} \quad \text{or} \quad \frac{\Sigma fd'^3}{N} \times i^3 \qquad [N = \Sigma f]$$

$$\mu_4' = \frac{\Sigma f(X-A)^4}{N} \quad \text{or} \quad \frac{\Sigma fd'^4}{N} \times i^4$$

Finding Central Moments from Moments about Arbitrary Point

With the help of following relationships, moments about an arbitrary point can be converted to moments about mean :

$$\mu_1 = 0 \qquad \text{[always]}$$

$$\mu_2 = \mu_2' - (\mu_1')^2$$

$$\mu_3 = \mu_3' - 3\mu_1'\mu_2' + 2(\mu_1')^3$$

$$\mu_4 = \mu_4' - 4\mu_1'\mu_3' + 6\mu_2'\mu_1'^2 - 3\mu_1'^4$$

result taken without proof.

6.5 KARL PEARSON'S BETAS (β's) AND GAMMAS (γ's) COEFFICIENTS BASED ON CENTRAL MOMENTS

Betas $\beta_1 = \frac{\mu_3^2}{\mu_2^3}$, $\beta_2 = \frac{\mu_4}{\mu_2^2} = \frac{\mu_4}{\sigma^4}$ [as $\mu_2 = \sigma^2$]

Gammas $\gamma_1 = \frac{\mu_3}{(\mu_2)^{3/2}} = \pm\sqrt{\beta_1}$, $\gamma_2 = \beta_2 - 3$

(+ sign is taken if μ_3 is +ve and – sign is taken if μ_3 is –ve.)

All these coefficients are pure numbers (*i.e.* the values are independent of units of measurement of the variable).

6.5.1. Significance of Gammas

$$\gamma_1 \text{ (Gamma one)} = \frac{\mu_3}{(\mu_3)^{3/2}} = \frac{\mu_3}{(\sigma^2)^{3/2}} = \frac{\mu_3}{\sigma^3}$$

γ_1 measures skewness [sometimes β_1 is referred to as measure of **skewness or moment coefficient of skewness**, but it does not give direction of skewness as it will be always +ve]

$$\gamma_2 \text{ (Gamma two)} = \frac{\mu_4}{\sigma_2^2} - 3$$

measures "Kurtosis" which is explained in a section later, in this chapter.

Example 18. *From the following data, calculate moments about assumed mean 25 and convert them into central moments :*

X	:	0–10	10–20	20–30	30–40
f	:	1	3	4	2

Solution. CALCULATIONS FOR MOMENTS ABOUT THE POINT $X = 25$

Class	Mid-value (X)	f	$d = \frac{x-25}{10}$	fd	fd^2	fd^3	fd^4
0–10	5	1	–2	–2	4	– 8	16
10–20	15	3	–1	–3	3	–3	3
20–30	25	4	0	0	0	0	0
30–40	35	2	1	2	2	2	2
Total		$N = \Sigma f = 10$		$\Sigma fd = -3$	$\Sigma fd^2 = 9$	$\Sigma fd^3 = -9$	$\Sigma fd^4 = 21$

Moments about the Point X = 25

$$\mu_1' = i \cdot \frac{\Sigma fd}{N} = \frac{10 \times (-3)}{10} = -3 \qquad \mu_3' = \frac{i^3 \times \Sigma fd^3}{N} = \frac{10^3 \times (-9)}{10} = -900$$

$$\mu_2' = i^2 \cdot \frac{\Sigma fd^2}{N} = \frac{10^2 \times 9}{10} = 90 \qquad \mu_4' = \frac{i^4 . \Sigma fd^4}{N} = \frac{10^4 \times 21}{10} = 21{,}000$$

Central Moments (Moments About Mean)

$$\mu_1 = 0$$

$$\mu_2 = \mu_2' - \mu_1'^2 = 90 - 9 = 81 = \sigma^2$$

$$\mu_3 = \mu_3' - 3\mu_2'\mu_1' + 2\mu_1'^3$$
$$= -900 - 3 \times 90 \times (-3) + 2\,(-3)^3$$
$$= -900 + 810 - 54 = -144$$

$$\mu_4 = \mu_4' - 4\mu_3'\mu_1' + 6\mu_2'\,\mu_1'^2 - 3\mu_1'^4$$
$$= 21{,}000. - 4 \times (-900) \times (-3) + 6 \times 90 \times (-3)^2 - 3 \times (-3)^4$$
$$= 21{,}000 - 10{,}800 + 4{,}860 - 243$$
$$= 14{,}817$$

Example 19. *The first three moments of a distribution about the value 67 of the variable are 0·45, 8·73 and 8·91. Calculate the second and third central moments, and the moment coefficient of skewness. Indicate the nature of the distribution.*

Solution. In the usual notations we are given :

$$A = 67, \quad \mu_1' = 0{\cdot}45, \quad \mu_2' = 8{\cdot}73 \quad \text{and} \quad \mu_3' = 8{\cdot}91$$

The second and third central moments are given by :

$$\mu_2 = \mu_2' - \mu_1'^2 = 8{\cdot}73 - (0{\cdot}45)^2 = 8{\cdot}73 - 0{\cdot}2025 = 8{\cdot}5275$$

$$\mu_3 = \mu_3' - 3\,\mu_2'\,\mu_1' + 2\mu_1'^3 = 8{\cdot}91 - 3 \times 8{\cdot}73 \times 0{\cdot}45 + 2 \times (0{\cdot}45)^3$$
$$= 8{\cdot}91 - 11{\cdot}7855 + 0{\cdot}18225 = -2{\cdot}6933$$

Hence, the variance of the distribution is

$$\sigma^2 = \mu_2 = 8{\cdot}5275 \quad \Rightarrow \quad \sigma(\text{s.d.}) = \sqrt{8{\cdot}5275} = 2{\cdot}9202$$

Since μ_3 is negative, the given distribution is negatively skewed. In other words, the frequency curve has a longer tail towards the left. Karl Pearson's moment coefficient of skewness is given by :

$$\gamma_1 = \frac{\mu_3}{\mu_2^{3/2}} = \frac{\mu_3}{\mu_2\sqrt{\mu_2}} = \frac{-2{\cdot}6933}{8{\cdot}5275 \times 2{\cdot}9202} = \frac{-2{\cdot}6933}{24{\cdot}9020} = -0{\cdot}1082$$

$$\Rightarrow \qquad \beta_1 = \frac{\mu_3^2}{\mu_2^3} = (-0{\cdot}1082)^2 = 0{\cdot}0117$$

Since γ_1 and β_1 are approximately zero, the given distribution is approximately symmetrical.

Example 20. *The first three moments of a distribution about the value 1 are 2, 25 and 80. Find its mean, standard deviation and the moment-measure of skewness.*

Solution. $\mu_1' = 2, \mu_2' = 25, \mu_3' = 80, A = 1$

Mean : $\overline{X} = \mu_1' + A = 2 + 1 = 3$ $\left[\overline{X} = A + \frac{\Sigma d}{n} = A + \mu_1'\right]$

Standard deviation : $\mu_2 = \mu_2' - \mu_1'^2 = 25 - (2)^2 = 21$ $[\mu_2 = \sigma^2]$

$$\sigma = \sqrt{\mu_2} = \sqrt{21} = 4.583$$

$$\mu_3 = \mu_3' - 3\mu_1'\mu_2' + 2(\mu_1')^3 = 80 - 3 \times 2 \times 25 + 2(2)^3 \text{ or } \mu_3 = 80 - 150 + 16 = -54$$

Moment-measure of skewness : $\gamma_1 = \frac{\mu_3}{\sigma^3} = \frac{(-54)}{(4.583)^3} = -54 = -0.561$

Example 21. *From the following data calculate first four moments and also find the value of* γ_1:

Monthly Profits (in lakh ₹)	*No. of Companies*	*Monthly Profits (in lakh ₹)*	*No. of Companies*
Less than 7.5	*4*	*22.5–27.5*	*16*
7.5–12.5	*10*	*27.5–32.5*	*12*
12.5–17.5	*20*	*32.5–37.5*	*2*
17.5–22.5	*36*		

Solution.

CALCULATION OF MOMENTS

Monthly Profits (in lakh ₹)	*m.p.* X	*f*	*(X – 20)/5* *d*	*fd*	*fd²*	*fd³*	*fd⁴*
Less than 7.5	5	4	–3	–12	36	–108	324
7.5–12.5	10	10	–2	–20	40	–80	160
12.5–17.5	15	20	–1	–20	20	–20	20
17.5–22.5	20	36	0	0	0	0	0
22.5–27.5	25	16	+1	+16	16	+16	16
27.5–32.5	30	12	+2	+24	48	+96	192
32.5–37.5	35	2	+3	+6	18	+54	162
		$N = 100$		$\Sigma fd = -6$	$\Sigma fd^2 = 178$	$\Sigma fd^3 = -42$	$\Sigma fd^4 = 874$

Moments about arbitrary origin 20 :

$$\mu_1' = \frac{\Sigma fd}{N} \times i = \frac{-6}{100} \times 5 = -0.3; \ \mu_2' = \frac{\Sigma fd^2}{N} \times i^2 = \frac{178}{100} \times 25 = 44.5;$$

$$\mu_3' = \frac{\Sigma fd^3}{N} \times i^3 = \frac{-42}{100} \times 125 = -52.5; \ \mu_4' = \frac{\Sigma fd^4}{N} \times i^4 = \frac{874}{100} \times 625 = 5462.5$$

Moments about mean

$$\mu_2 = \mu_2' - (\mu_1')^2$$
$$= 44.5 - (-0.3)^2 = 44.5 - 0.09 = 44.41$$
$$\mu_3 = \mu_3' - 3\mu_1'\mu_2' + (\mu_1')^3$$
$$= -52.5 - 3\,(-0.3 \times 44.5) + 2\,(-0.3)^3$$
$$= -52.5 + 40.05 - .054 = -\ 12.504$$
$$\mu_4 = \mu_4' - 4\mu_4'\mu_3' + 6\mu_2'\mu_1'^2 - 3\mu_1'^4$$
$$= 5462.5 - 4\,(-0.3 \times -52.5) + 6(44.5)\,(-0.3)^2 - 3\,(-0.3)^4$$
$$= 5462.5 - 63 + 24.03 - .0243 = 5423.5057$$

$$\gamma_1 = \frac{\mu_3}{\sigma^3} = \frac{-12.504}{(6.6641)^3} = \frac{12.504}{295.954} = -00422.$$

6.6 KURTOSIS

Study of complete features of data under a particular frequency distribution is essential during quantitative analysis. One such features is the degree of peakedness of the distribution, which is not measured by averages or dispersion or skewness. Measure of convexity of frequency distribution is required for some of the managerial decisions. 'Kurtosis' is such a technique that measures the extent of peakedness or flatness in the distribution.

6.6.1. Concept of Kurtosis

Kurtosis is a quantitative technique that measures the extent to which a unimodal frequency curve is peaked. The term 'Kurtosis' is derived from a Greek word which means bulginess. As a quantitative tool it refers to the degree of flatness or peakedness in the frequency distribution. The degree of kurtosis of a distribution is measured in relation to the peakedness of normal curve. The measure helps to identify the shape and nature of the bulginess, usually the middle part of the frequency distribution :

Definitions :

- "A measure of Kurtosis indicates the degree to which a curve of frequency distribution is peaked or flat topped." —*Croxton & Cowden*
- "The degree of Kurtosis of a distribution is measured relative to the peakedness of a normal curve." —*Simpson & Kafka*

From the definitions given by different authors it is clear that the Kurtosis help us to identify the shape, nature and extent of hump in a distribution. Two frequency distributions may exhibit same degree of dispersion and skewness. But one series may differ in peakedness in the distribution compared to other, which shows that the features of data are not same. Thus Kurtosis describes that particular feature *i.e.* it indicates whether the curve of a frequency distribution is flat or peaked compared to a normal curve which is neither flat nor peaked.

6.6.2. Types of Curves

Karl Pearson described 3 types of curves of Kurtosis. They differ in the convexity of the shape of the frequency curve. They are :

1. **Leptokurtic Curve :** A curve having more peaked shape than normal curve is called leptokurtic curve. In the diagram A is example of leptokurtic curve. They usually have negative Kurtosis.
2. **Mesokurtic Curve :** Meso means the middle. Therefore Mesokurtic curve is neither flat not Peaked. The shape of its curve is considered as normal and such curves have normal Kurtosis. Example : Curve B of the diagram.
3. **Platykurtosis :** The curve which is flattened than normal curve is known as platykurtic. Such curves exhibit negative Kurtosis.

These three curves differ widely with regard the presence of Kurtosis though all of them are nearly symmetrical *i.e.* the peakedness at a point.

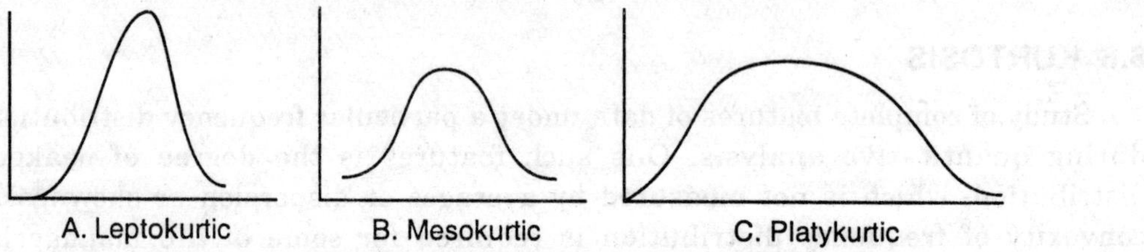

A. Leptokurtic Sharp-peaked; B. Mesokurtic Not so sharp (normal curve); C. Platykurtic Plateau type

Measures of Kurtosis

Measure of Kurtosis is based on central moments. It is based on second and fourth moments. Karl Pearson has developed a formula to measure kurtosis, *i.e.,* β_2 (Beta Two) and γ_2 (Gamma two). The measure of Kurtosis based upon the fourth and second central moments is denoted by β_2.

Measure of Kurtosis (β_2) = $\dfrac{\mu_4}{\mu_2^{\,2}} = \dfrac{\text{Fourth moment}}{(\text{Second moment})^2}$ (Or) $\dfrac{\mu_4}{\sigma^4}$ [as $\mu_2 = \sigma^2$]

Description : The degree of kurtosis of a distribution is measured relative to the peakedness of a normal curve.

In a normal distribution $\beta_2 = 3$

In a Platy kurtic distribution $\beta_2 < 3$ (β_2 less than 3)

In a Lepto-Kurtic distribution $\beta_2 > 3$ (β_2 is greater than 3)

Measure of Kurtosis is also measured by γ_2 where $\gamma_2 = \beta_2 - 3$

If γ_2 or $\beta_2 - 3 = 0$ then the curve is mesokurtic.

If γ_2 is positive, the curve is lepto-kurtic

If γ_2 is negative, the curve is platy kurtic

Measurement of kurtosis whether on the basis of β_2 or γ_2 are equivalent. Any one of the measure may be used.

Example 22. *Compute Kurtosis and find out which type of distribution is it ?*

X	2	5	8	12	13	15	16	18	20	21

Solution

	X	d = (X – 13)	d^2	d^3	d^4
	2	–11	121	–1331	14641
	5	–8	64	–512	4096
	8	–5	25	–125	625
	12	–1	1	–1	1
	13	0	0	0	0
	15	2	4	8	16
	16	3	9	27	81
	18	5	25	125	625
	20	7	49	343	2401
	21	8	64	512	4096
Total	130	0	362	–954	26582

$\Sigma X = 130 \quad n = 10 \quad \overline{X} = \dfrac{130}{10} = 13$

$d = X - \overline{X} = X - 13$

First Central Moment $\mu_1 = \dfrac{\Sigma d}{N} = \dfrac{0}{10} = 0$

Second Central Moment $\mu_2 = \dfrac{\Sigma d^2}{N} = \dfrac{362}{10} = 36.2$

Third Central Moment $\mu_3 = \dfrac{\Sigma d^3}{N} = \dfrac{-954}{10} = -95.4$

Fourth Central Moment $\mu_4 = \dfrac{\Sigma d^4}{N} = \dfrac{26582}{10} = 2658.2$

Measure of Kurtosis $(\beta_2) = \dfrac{\mu_4}{\mu_2^2} = \dfrac{2658.2}{(36.2)^2} = 2.03$

$(\beta_2 < 3)$

Therefore it is Platy Kurtic Distribution.

Example 23. *Compute measure of Kurtosis for the information given below :*

X	5	6	8	10
f	2	4	2	2

Solution :

X	*f*	*fx*	*dx*	*fdx*	*fdx*^{2}	*fdx*^{3}	*fdx*^{4}
5	2	10	–2	–4	8	–16	32
6	4	24	–1	–4	4	–4	4
8	2	16	1	2	2	2	2
10	2	20	3	6	18	54	162
	10	70		0	32	36	200

$\overline{X} = \frac{\Sigma fx}{\Sigma f} = \frac{70}{10} = 7$ Let $dx = X - \overline{X} = X - 7$

[**Note :** $fdx^2 = (fdx)\, dx$, $fdx^3 = (fdx^2)\, dx$, $fdx^4 = (fdx^3)\, dx$]

Central moments.

First Moment $\mu_1 = \frac{\Sigma fdx}{\Sigma f} = \frac{0}{10} = 0$ [as $dx = (X - \overline{X})$]

Second Moment $\mu_2 = \frac{\Sigma fdx^2}{\Sigma f} = \frac{32}{10} = 3.2$

Third Moment $\mu_3 = \frac{\Sigma fdx^3}{\Sigma f} = \frac{36}{10} = 3.6$

Fourth Moment $\mu_4 = \frac{\Sigma fdx^4}{\Sigma f} = \frac{200}{10} = 20$

Measure of Kurtosis $(\beta_2) = \frac{\mu_4}{\mu_2^2} = \frac{20}{(3.2)^2} = 1.95$

$\beta_2 < 3$

Therefore is Platy Kurtric distribution.

Example 24. *Calculate the first four moments about the mean for the following data and comment on the nature of the distribution :*

x :	*1*	*2*	*3*	*4*	*5*	*6*	*7*	*8*	*9*
f :	*1*	*6*	*13*	*25*	*30*	*22*	*9*	*5*	*2*

Solution. CALCULATIONS FOR MOMENTS

x	*f*	*d* = *x* – 5	*fd*	*fd*^{2}	*fd*^{3}	*fd*^{4}
1	1	– 4	– 4	16	– 64	256
2	6	–3	–18	54	–162	486
3	13	–2	–26	52	–104	208
4	25	–1	–25	25	–25	25
5	30	0	0	0	0	0
6	22	1	22	22	22	22
7	9	2	18	36	72	144
8	5	3	15	45	135	405
9	2	4	8	32	128	512
	$\Sigma f = 113$	$\Sigma d = 0$	$\Sigma fd = -10$	$\Sigma fd^2 = 282$	$\Sigma fd^3 = 2$	$\Sigma fd^4 = 2058$

Moments About the Point $x = 5$

$d = x - A = x - 5, (A = 5) ; N = \sum f = 113$

$$\mu_1' = \frac{\sum fd}{N} = \frac{-10}{113} = -0{\cdot}0885$$

$$\mu_2' = \frac{\sum fd^2}{N} = \frac{282}{113} = 2{\cdot}4956$$

$$\mu_3' = \frac{\sum fd^3}{N} = \frac{2}{113} = 0{\cdot}0177$$

$$\mu_4' = \frac{\sum fd^4}{N} = \frac{2058}{113} = 18{\cdot}2124$$

$\therefore$ Mean $= A + \mu_1' = 5 + (-0{\cdot}0885) = 4{\cdot}9115$ $\quad \left[\overline{X} = A + \frac{\sum d}{n}\right]$

Central Moments About Mean

$\mu_1 = 0$

$\mu_2 = \mu_2' - \mu_1'^2 = 2{\cdot}4956 - (-0{\cdot}0885)^2$

$= 2{\cdot}4956 - 0{\cdot}0078 = 2{\cdot}4878$

$\mu_4 = \mu_4' - 4\mu_3'\mu_1' + 6\mu_2'\mu_1'^2 - 3\mu_1'^4$

$= 18{\cdot}2124 - 4 \times (0{\cdot}0177) \times (-0{\cdot}0885)$

$+ 6 \times 2{\cdot}4956 \times (-0{\cdot}0885)^2$

$- 3(0{\cdot}0885)^4$

$= 18{\cdot}2124 + 0{\cdot}00626 + 0{\cdot}11728$

$- 0{\cdot}000184$

$= 18{\cdot}3357$

$\mu_3 = \mu_3' - 3\mu_2'\mu_1' + 2\mu_1'^3$

$= 0{\cdot}0177 - 3 \times 2{\cdot}4956 \times (-0{\cdot}0885)$

$+ 2 \times (-0{\cdot}0885)^3$

$= 0{\cdot}0177 + 0{\cdot}66258 - 0{\cdot}001386$

$= 0{\cdot}6789$

Moment Coefficients of Skewness

$$\beta_1 = \frac{\mu_3^2}{\mu_2^3} = \frac{(0{\cdot}6789)^2}{(2{\cdot}4878)^3} = \frac{0{\cdot}4609}{15{\cdot}3974} = 0{\cdot}0299$$

$$\gamma_1 = \frac{\mu_3}{\mu_2^{3/2}} = \frac{\mu_3}{\mu_2\sqrt{\mu_2}} = \frac{0{\cdot}6789}{3{\cdot}9239} = 0{\cdot}173$$

or $\gamma_1 = \sqrt{\beta_1} = +\sqrt{0{\cdot}0299} = +0{\cdot}173$ $\quad$ ($\because \mu_3$ is positive)

Kurtosis

$$\beta_2 = \frac{\mu_4}{\mu_2^2} = \frac{18{\cdot}3357}{(2{\cdot}4878)^2} = \frac{18{\cdot}3357}{6{\cdot}1891} = 2{\cdot}9626$$

$\Rightarrow \gamma_2 = \beta_2 - 3 = -0{\cdot}0373.$

Interpretation

Since $\gamma_1 = 0{\cdot}173$, the given distribution is *slightly positively skewed.*

Since $\beta_2 = 2{\cdot}9626 \simeq 3$, the given distribution is more or less normal or meso-kurtic.

Example 25. *Calculate the first four moments about the mean from the following data. Also calculate the value of β_1 and β_2.*

Marks	*No. of students*
0–10	5
10–20	12
20–30	18

30–40	*40*
40–50	*15*
50–60	*7*
60–70	*3*

Solution.

CALCULATION OF MOMENTS ABOUT MEAN, β_1 AND β_2

Marks	*f*	*m.p.* *m*	*(m – 35) / 10* *d*	*fd*	*fd²*	*fd³*	*fd⁴*
0–10	5	5	–3	–15	45	–135	405
10–20	12	15	–2	–24	48	–96	192
20–30	18	25	–1	–18	18	–18	18
30–40	40	35	0	0	0	0	0
40–50	15	45	+1	+15	15	+15	15
50–60	7	55	+2	+14	28	+56	112
60–70	3	65	+3	+9	27	+81	243
	$N = 100$			$\Sigma fd = -19$	$\Sigma fd^2 = 181$	$\Sigma fd^3 = -97$	$\Sigma fd^4 = 985$

$$\mu_1' = \frac{\Sigma fd}{N} \times i = \frac{-19}{100} \times 10 = -1.9$$

$$\mu_2' = \frac{\Sigma fd^2}{N} \times i^2 = \frac{181}{100} \times 100 = 181$$

$$\mu_3' = \frac{\Sigma fd^3}{N} \times i^3 = \frac{-97}{100} \times 1000 = -970$$

$$\mu_4' = \frac{\Sigma fd^4}{N} \times i^4 = \frac{985}{100} \times 10000 = 98500$$

$$\mu_2 = \mu_2' - (\mu_1')^2$$

$$= 181 - (-1.9)^2 = 181 - 3.61 = 177.39$$

$$\mu_3 = \mu_3' - 3\mu_1'\mu_2' + 2\mu_1'^3$$

$$= -970 - 3\,(-1.9)\,(181) + 2\,(-1.9)^3$$

$$= 970 + 1031.7 - 13.718 = 47.982$$

$$\mu_4 = \mu_4' - 4\mu_1'\mu_3' + 6\mu_1'^2\mu_2' - 3\mu_1'^4$$

$$= 98500 - 4\,(-1.9)\,(-970) + 6\,(-1.9)^2\,181 - 3\,(-1.9)^4$$

$$= 98500 - 7372 + 3920.46 - 39.096 = 95009.364$$

$$\beta_1 = \frac{\mu_3^2}{\mu_2^3} = \frac{(47.982)^2}{(177.39)^3} = \frac{2302.27}{5581968.75} = 0.0004$$

$$\beta_2 = \frac{\mu_4}{\mu_2^2} = \frac{95009.364}{(177.39)^2} = \frac{95009.364}{31467.212} = 3.02$$

Example 26. *Analyse the frequency distribution by the method of moments :*

X :	2	3	4	5	6
f :	1	3	7	3	1

Solution

CALCULATION OF FIRST FOUR MOMENTS

X	f	fX	x $(X-\overline{X})$ $\overline{X}=4$	fx	fx^2	fx^3	fx^4
2	1	2	− 2	− 2	4	− 8	16
3	3	9	− 1	− 3	3	− 3	3
4	7	28	0	0	0	0	0
5	3	15	+ 1	+ 3	3	+ 3	3
6	1	6	+ 2	+ 2	4	+ 8	16
	$N = 15$	$60 = \Sigma fX$		$\Sigma fx = 0$	$\Sigma fx^2 = 14$	$\Sigma fx^3 = 0$	$\Sigma fx^4 = 38$

$$\overline{X} = \frac{\Sigma fX}{\Sigma f} = \frac{60}{15} = 4$$

$$\mu_1 = \frac{\Sigma f(X-\overline{X})}{N} \text{ or } \frac{\Sigma fx}{N} = \frac{0}{15} = 0 \qquad \mu_3 = \frac{\Sigma fx^3}{N} = 0$$

$$\mu_2 = \frac{\Sigma fx^2}{N} = \frac{14}{15} = 0.9333; \qquad \mu_4 = \frac{fx^4}{N} = \frac{38}{15} = 2.533$$

$$\sigma = \sqrt{\text{Variance}} = \sqrt{\mu_2} = \sqrt{0.933} = 0.966$$

$$\beta_1 = \frac{\mu_3^{\,2}}{\mu_2^{\,3}} = \frac{0}{(0.933)^3} = 0$$

In a symmetrical distribution β_1 is zero; hence the distribution is symmetrical.

$$\beta_2 = \frac{\mu_4}{\mu_2^{\,2}} = \frac{2.533}{(0.933)^2} = \frac{2.533}{0.87} = 2.91$$

Since the value of β_2 is less than three, the distribution is platykurtic.

Example 27. *The following data are given to an economist for the purpose of economic analysis. The data refer to the length of a certain type of batteries.*

$n = 100$, $\Sigma fd = 50$, $\Sigma fd^2 = 1970$, $\Sigma fd^3 = 2948$ and $\Sigma fd^4 = 86752$, in which $d = (X - 48)$.

Do you think that the distribution is platykurtic ?

Solution. In order to ascertain whether the distribution is platykurtic or not we have to calculate the value of β_2.

$$\beta_2 = \frac{\mu_4}{\mu_2^{\,2}}$$

$$\mu_1' = \frac{\Sigma fd}{N} = \frac{50}{100} = .5$$

$$\mu_2' = \frac{\Sigma fd^2}{N} = \frac{1970}{100} = 19.70$$

$$\mu_3' = \frac{\Sigma fd^3}{N} = \frac{2948}{100} = 29.48$$

$$\mu_4' = \frac{\Sigma fd^4}{N} = \frac{86752}{100} = 867.52$$

$$\mu_2 = \mu_2' - (\mu_1')_2 = 19.70 - (0.5)^2 = 19.70 - .25 = 19.45 = \sigma^2$$

$$\mu_3 = \mu'_3 - 3\mu_1'\mu_2' + 2\mu_1'^3$$

$$= 29.48 - 3(0.5)\,(19.70) + 2\,(0.5)^3$$

$$= 29.48 - 29.55 + 0.25 = 0.18$$

$$\mu_4 = \mu_4' - 4\mu_1'\mu_3' + 6\mu_2'(\mu_1')^2 - 3(\mu_1')^4$$

$$\mu_4 = 867.52 - 4\,(0.5)\,(29.48) + 6\,(19.70)\,(0.5)^2 - 3\,(0.5)^4$$

$$= 867.52 - 58.96 + 29.55 - 0.1875 = 837.9225$$

$$\beta_2 = \frac{837.9225}{(19.45)^2} = \frac{837.9225}{378.3025} = 2.215$$

Since the value of β_2 is less than 3, the distribution is platykurtic.

Example 28. *For a distribution mean is 10, standard deviation is 4, $\beta_1 = 1$ and $\beta_2 = 4$. Obtain the first four central moments.*

Solution. $\overline{X} = 10$; $\sigma = 4l$; $\sqrt{\beta_1} = 1$; $\beta_2 = 4$

$$\mu_2 = \sigma^2 = (4)^2 = 16$$

$$\beta_1 = \frac{\mu_3^2}{\mu_2^3}$$

$$1 = \frac{\mu_3^2}{(16)^3}$$

$$\mu_3^2 = 4096$$

$$\mu_3 = \sqrt{4096} = \pm 64$$

$$\beta_2 = \frac{\mu_4}{\mu_2^2}$$

$$4 = \frac{\mu_4}{(16)^2}$$

$$\mu_4 = 4 \times 256 = 1024$$

$$\mu_1 = 0,\ \mu_2 = 16,\ \mu_3 = \pm 64,\ \mu_4 = 1024$$

Example 29. *For a distribution the first four moments about zero are 1, 7, 38 and 155 respectively. (i) Compute the moment coefficient of skewness and kurtosis. (ii) Is the distribution mesokurtic ? Give reason.*

Solution. (*i*) We are given that : $m_1 = 1$, $m_2 = 7$, $m_3 = 38$, $m_4 = 155$

We have to find moments about mean.

We have

$$\mu_2 = \mu_2' - \mu_1'^2 \qquad \ldots(1)$$

In place of μ_2' and μ_1' we may write m_2 and m_1 respectively.

as (1) holds good whatever the value of A and will hold good even if $A = 0$, when $A = 0$, μ_1' and μ_2' becomes m_2 and m_1 respectively (moments about zero). Thus $\mu_2' - \mu_1'^2 = m_2 - m_1^2$ and so on.

$$\mu_2 = \mu_2' - \mu_1'^2$$

$$\mu_2 = m_2 - m_1^2$$

$$= 7 - (1)^2 = 6$$

As $\mu_3 = \mu_3' - 3\mu_2'\mu_1' + 2\,\mu_1'^3$

Thus, $\mu_3 = m_3 - 3m_1m_2 + 2m_1^3$

$$= 38 - 3(1)(7) + 2(1)^3$$

$$= 38 - 21 + 2 = 19$$

Similarly,

$$\mu_4 = m_4 - 4m_3m_1 + 6m_2m_1^2 - 3m_1^4$$

$$= 155 - (4)(1)(38) + 6(7)(1)^2 - 3(1)^4$$

$$= 155 - 152 + 42 - 3 = 42$$

$$\text{Moment coefficient of skewness} = \beta_1 = \frac{\mu_3^2}{\mu_2^3} = \frac{(19)^2}{(6)^3} = \frac{361}{216} = 1.67$$

$$\text{Moment coefficient of Kurtosis} = \beta_2 = \frac{\mu_4}{\mu_2^2} = \frac{(19)^2}{(6)^3} = \frac{42}{36} = 1.167$$

(*ii*) No, the distribution is not mesokurtic because the value of β_2 is less than 3. It is platykurtic.

Example 30. *In a frequency distribution, the co-efficient of skewness based on quartiles is 0.5. If the sum of the upper and lower quartiles is 28 and the median is 11, find the values of lower and upper quartiles.*

Solution. The coefficient of skewness based on quartiles is calculated by Bowley's method :

$$Sk_B = \frac{Q_3 + Q_1 - 2\text{ Med.}}{Q_3 - Q_1}$$

$Sk_B = 0.5$, $Q_3 + Q_1 = 28$, Median = 11, let $Q_3 - Q_1 = x$

Putting the values in the above formula :

$$0.5 = \frac{28 - 2(11)}{x} = \frac{6}{x}$$

$$0.5x = 6;\ x = \frac{6}{0.5} = 12 = Q_3 - Q_1$$

$$Q_3 + Q_1 = 28 \qquad \ldots(i)$$

$$Q_3 - Q_1 = 12 \qquad \ldots(ii)$$

Adding (*i*) and (*ii*)

$$2Q_3 = 40 \quad \text{or} \quad Q_3 = 20$$

$$Q_1 = 28 - Q_3$$

$$= 28 - 20 = 8$$

$\therefore$ $Q_3 = 20$ and $Q_1 = 8$.

EXERCISE 6.1

1. Calculate Bowley's coefficient of skewness for the data given below :

Weight (in lbs.)	*Number of students*	*Weights (in lbs.)*	*Number of students*
Below 99	1	150–159	65
100–109	14	160–169	34
110–119	66	170–179	12
120–129	122	180–189	5
130–139	145	190–199	2
140–149	121	2000 and over	2

[0.025]

2. From the information given below calculate Karl Pearson's coefficient of skewness and also quartile coefficient of skewness :

Measure	*Place A*	*Place B*
Mean	150	140
Median	142	155
S.D.	30	55
Third Quartile	195	260
First Quartile	62	80

[For *A*, $Sk_P = 0.8$, $Sk_B = -0.203$; for *B*, $Sk_P = -0.82$, $Sk_B = 0.167$]

3. Calculate Bowley's coefficient of skewness from the following data :

Profits (₹ lakhs)	*No. of Companies*
Below 20	8
Below 40	28
Below 60	78
Below 80	90
Below 100	100

[Coeff. of *Sk* = –0.083]

4. Calculate the quartile coefficient of skewness for the following distribution :

Class	1–5	6–10	11–15	16–20	21–25	26–30	31–35
Frequency	3	4	68	30	10	6	2

[0.262]

5. Calculate Karl Pearson's coefficient of Skewness for the data given below :

X	0	1	2	3	4	5	6	7
F	12	27	29	19	8	4	1	0

[Coeff. of *Sk* = 0]

6. Calculate coefficient of skewness using the mean, mode and standard deviation from the following data :

Marks (less than) :	20	30	40	50	60	70	80
Number of Students :	10	25	40	65	80	95	100

[–0.089]

7. Find Bowley's coefficient of skewness for the following data :

Salary (in ₹)	*No. of Persons*	*Salary (in ₹)*	*No. of Persons*
5000–6000	10	9000–10000	25
6000–7000	28	10000–11000	18
7000–8000	40	11000–12000	9
8000–9000	64	12000–13000	6

[–0.033]

8. Calculate the first four moments about the mean from the following data. Also calculating the value of β_1 and β_2.

Marks :	0–10	10–20	20–30	30–40	40–50	50–60	60–70
Number of Students :	5	12	18	40	15	7	3

[(*i*) $\beta_1 = 0.02$, (*ii*) $\beta_2 = 3$]

9. Pearson's coefficient of skewness for a distribution is 0.4 and coefficient of variation is 30%. Its mode is 88. Find the mean and the median.

[Mean = 100, Med. = 96]

10. (*i*) Calculate mode and median from the following information :

Karl Pearson's coeff. of *Sk* = + 0.32

Standard deviation = 6.5

Arithmetic mean = 29.6

[Mode = 26.52, Med. = 28.57]

11. The first four moments of distribution about the value 4 are –1.5, 17, –30 and 108. Find : (*i*) Coefficient of variation (*ii*) β_1 (*iii*) First three moments about origin (zero).

[C.V. = 172, $\beta_1 = 0.49$]

12. The following table gives the length of life (in hours) of 400 T.V. picture tubes :

Length of Life (in hours)	*Number of Picture tubes*	*Length of Life (in hours)*	*Number of Picture tubes*
4000–4199	12	5000–5199	55
4200–4399	30	5200–5399	36
4400–4599	65	5400–5599	25
4600–4799	78	5600–5799	9
4800–4999	90		

Compute mean, standard deviation and coefficient of skewness. Comment on the values obtained.

[$\overline{X} = 4845.5$, $\sigma = 365.9$, Coeff. of *Sk* = –0.014]

13. From the following data; calculate the first four moments about mean and also find out the skewness and kurtosis of the distribution :

$N = 10, \Sigma fd = 60, \Sigma fd^2 = 1{,}200, \Sigma fd^3 = 18{,}000, \Sigma fd^4 = 3{,}60{,}000$ in which $d = (x - 25)$.

[$\mu_2 = 84, \mu_3 = 72, \mu_4 = 14{,}832, \beta_1 = 0.0087, \beta_2 = 2.102$]

14. Given the following data, compute the moment coefficient of skewness and comment on the result :

X	2	3	7	8	10

[$\gamma_1 = -0.129$; negatively skewed distribution]

15. The first four moments of a distribution about the value 5 are equal to 2, 20, 40 and 50. Obtain the mean, variance, $\sqrt{\beta_1}$ and β_2 for the distribution.

[$\overline{X} = 7, \sigma^2 = 16, \sqrt{\beta_1} = -11, \beta_2 = 0.633$]

16. The first three moments of a distribution about the value 3 of the variable are 2, 1 and 30 respectively. What are the mean, variance and γ_1 of such a distribution ?

[$\overline{X} = 5, \mu_2 = 6, \gamma_1 = -0.952$]

17. Calculate the first four moments and find the value of β_1 and β_2 from the data given below :

Marks :	0–20	20–40	40–60	60–80	80–100
Number of Students :	8	12	20	6	4

[$\beta_1 = 0.0486$; $\beta_2 = 2.563$]

18. Calculate the first four moments about the mean and also the value of β_2 from the following data :

m :	0	1	2	3	4	5	6	7	8
f	1	8	20	156	170	56	28	8	1

[$\mu_2 = 1.294$; $\mu_3 = 0.642$; $\mu_4 = 6.582$; $\beta_2 = 3.931$]

19. From the following data, compute quartile deviation and the coefficient of skewness :

Size :	5–7	8–10	11–13	14–16	17–19
Frequency :	14	24	38	20	4

[Q.D. = 1.773, $Sk_B = 0.111$]

20. Find the standard deviation and kurtosis of the following series by the method of moment.

Class interval :	0–10	10–20	20–30	30–40	40–50
Frequency :	10	20	40	20	10

[**Ans.** $\sigma = \sqrt{120} = 10.95$; $\beta_2 = 2.5$]

21. Calculate the first four moments about the mean from the following data. Also calculate the values of β_1 and β_2.

Marks :	0–10	10–20	20–30	30–40	40–50	50–60	60–70
No. of Students :	5	12	18	40	15	7	3

[**Ans.** $\mu_1 = 0, \mu_2 = 177.39, \mu_3 = 47.982, \mu_4 = 95009.36$; $\beta_1 = 0.0004 = 0, \beta_2 = 3.0019 = 3$]

Distribution is symmetric and mesokurtic.

22. For the following distribution, calculate the first four central moments and two beta co-efficients :

Class Interval	20–30	30–40	40–50	50–60	60–70	70–80	80–90
Frequency	5	14	20	25	17	11	8

[**Ans.** $\mu_1 = 0$, $\mu_2 = 254$, $\mu_3 = 540$, $\mu_4 = 1{,}49{,}000$; $\beta_1 = 0{\cdot}0178$, $\beta_2 = 2{\cdot}3095$.]

23. Find the second, the third and the fourth central moment of the frequency distribution given in the adjoining table. Hence find (*i*) a measure of skewness and (*ii*) a measure of kurtosis, of the given distribution.

Class Limits	*Frequency*
100—104·9	7
105—109·9	13
110—114·9	25
115—119·9	25
120—124·9	30

[**Ans.** $\mu_2 = 38{\cdot}09$, $\mu_3 = -110{\cdot}772$, $\mu_4 = 3229{\cdot}71$
$\gamma_1 = -0{\cdot}4712$, $\beta_1 = 0{\cdot}2220$, $\beta_2 = 2{\cdot}2261$

24. Distinguish between "Skewness" and "Kurtosis" and bring out their importance in describing frequency distributions.

25. "Averages, dispension, skewness and kurtosis are complementary to one another in understanding a frequency distribution." Elucidate.

26. Explain the terms Skewness and Kurtosis used in connection with the frequency distribution of a continuous variable. Give the different measures of skewness (any three of the measures to be given) and kurtosis.

27. Define skewness and describe briefly the various tests of skewness.

28. Explain briefly how the measures of skewness and kurtosis can be used in describing a frequency distribution.

29. What do you mean by 'skewness'? How is skewness different from kurtosis?

30. Explain the relation between the central moments and raw moments of a frequency distribution and hence express the first four central moments in terms of the raw moments.

31. What are the raw and central moments of a distribution? Show that the central moments are invariant under change of origin but not of scale.

32. Why do we calculate, in general, only the first four moments about mean, of a distribution and not the higher moments?

33. Define moments. How are moments useful in analysing a frequency distribution?

□□□

7

Correlation

CHAPTER OUTLINE

- Definition of Correlation
- Scatter Diagram
- Kari Pearson's Coefficient of Linear Correlation
- Properties of Coefficient of Correiation
- Probable Error of *r*
- Correlation in Bivariate Frequency Distribution
- Merits and Limitations of Coefficient of Correlation
- Spearman's Rank Correlation

So far we have considered distributions relating to a single characteristics. Such distributions are known as *Univariate Distribution*. When various units under consideration are observed simultaneously, with regard to two characteristics, we get a *Bivariate Distribution*. For example, the simultaneous study of the heights and weights of students of a college. For such data also, we can compute mean, variance skwness etc. for each individual characteristics. In addition to this, in the study of a bivariate distribution, we are also interested in knowing whether there exists some relationship between two characteristics or in other words, how far the two variables, corresponding to two characteristics, tend to move together in same or opposite directions i.e. how far they are associated.

The knowledge of this type of relationship is useful for predicting the value of one variable given the value of the other. It also helps in understanding and analysis of various economic and business problems. It should be noted here that statistical relations are different from the exact mathematical relations. Given a statistical relation $Y = a + bX$, between two variables X and Y, we can only get a value of Y that we expect on the average for a given value of X. The study of relationship between two or more variable can be divided into two broad categories:

(*i*) To determine whether there exists some sort of association between the variables. If so, what is the degree of association or the magnitude of correlation between the two.

(*ii*) To determine the most suitable form of the relationship between the variables given that they correlated.

The first category relates to the study of *'Correlation'* which will be discussed in this chapter and the second related to the study of *'Regression'*, to be discussed in next chapter.

7.1 DEFINITION OF CORRELATION

The statistical tool with the help of which these relationships between two or more than two variables is studied is called **correlation**. The measure of correlation called the coefficient of correlation (denoted by the symbol r) summarizes in one figure the direction and degree of correlation. Thus correlation analysis refers to the techniques used in measuring the closeness of the relationship between the variables. A very simple definition of correlation is that given by A.M. Tuttle. He defines correlation as : "An analysis of the covariation of two or more variable is usually called *correlation*."

In case the two variables increase or decrease simultaneously we say that +ve correlation exist, *i.e.,* both the variables more in the same direction. For example if we study market price and supply of a good we find that if price increase supply will also increase and if price decreases, supply will move in the same direction, *i.e.,* will decrease. Same way if we have data on incomes and expenditure of many families we will find that expenditure of families with higher income will also be higher. Thus both variables will move in the same direction—(It may be noted in both the examples there exists cause and effect relationship).

Similarly there exist –ve correlation in two variables if they move in opposite direction *i.e.,* if one variable increases the other will tend to decrease and vice versa, *e.g.,* If we have data on prices and demands of a good we find they move in opposite directions.

Correlation does not specify if one variable changes by a certain amount by what amount the other variable will change. It only specify whether it will increase or decrease but does not specify changes in values.

7.2 SIGNIFICANCE OF THE STUDY OF CORRELATION

The study of correlation is of immense use in practical life because of the following reasons :

1. Most of the variables show some kind of relationship between price and supply, income and expenditure, etc. With the help of correlation analysis we can measure in one figure the degree of relationship existing between the variables.

2. Once we know that two variables are closely related, we can estimate the value of one variable given the value of another. This is done with the help of regression analysis which is discussed in the next chapter.

In business, correlation analysis enables the executive to estimate costs, sales, price and other variables on the basis of some other series with which these costs, sales, or prices may be functionally related. Some of the guesswork can be removed from decisions when the relationship between a variable to be estimated and the one or more other variables on which it depends are close and reasonably invariant.

7.3 CORRELATION AND CAUSATION

Correlation analysis helps us in determining the degree of relationship between two or more variables—it does not tell us anything about cause-effect relationship. Even a high degree of correlation does not necessarily mean that a relationship of cause and effect exists between the variables or, simply stated, correlation does not necessarily imply causation or functional relationship though the existence of causation always implies correlation. By itself it establishes only *covariation.* The explanation of significant degree of correlation may be any one, or a combination of the following factors :

1. *The correlation may be due to pure chance, especially in a small sample.* We may get a high degree of correlation between two variables in the sample but in the universe, there may not be any relationship between the variables at all. This is especially so in case of small samples. Such a correlation may arise either because of pure random sampling variation or because of the bias of the investigator in selecting the sample. The following example shall illustrate the point :

Advertisement expenditure (*₹ lakhs*)	*Sales.* (*₹ crores*)
25	120
35	140
45	160
55	180
65	200

The above data show a perfect positive relationship between advertisement expenditure and sales, *i.e.*, as the advertisement expenditure is increasing, the sales are also increasing and the ratio of changes between the two variable is the same. However, such a situation is rare in practice.

2. *Both the correlated variables may be influenced by one or more other variables.* It is just possible that a high degree of correlation between the variables may be due to the same cause affecting either variable or different causes affecting each with the same effect. For example, a high degree of correlation between the yield per acre of rice and tea may be due to the fact that both are related to the amount of rainfall. But none of the two variables is the cause of the other.

Another example if we have data on the number of traffic policemen deployed and the number of road accident over last 20 years in Delhi. Since the number of vehicles are increasing on the road so policeman required to man traffic is increasing and the no. of accidents over the period is also increasing. Now if we find correlation as both the variables are increasing we will find high +ve correlation between the two variable giving the impression that policemen cause accidents and if policemen are reduced the number of accidents will decrease which does not make sense. Thus the two variables are increasing simultaneously and they will show positive correlation from over one variable is not the cause of other.

7.4 SCATTER DIAGRAM

Let we have n pains of values of variable X and Y which when represented by points (X_1, Y_1), (X_2, Y_2), (X_3, Y_3), ..., (X_n, Y_n) and are plotted on a graph as shown in Fig. 1.

Sr. No.	X	Y
1	X_1	Y_1
2	X_2	Y_2
3	X_3	Y_3
⋮	⋮	⋮
n	X_n	Y_n

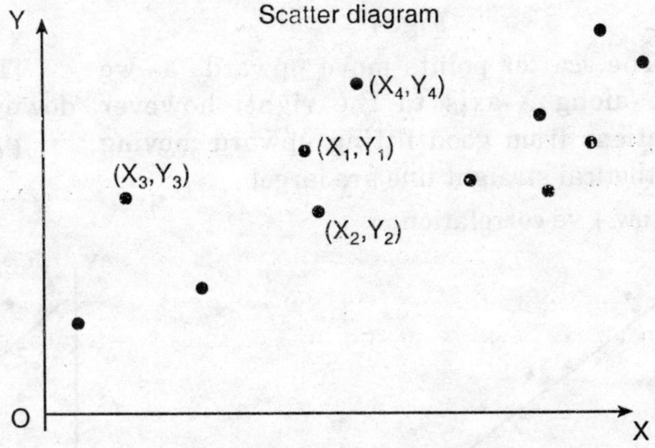

Fig. 1

Scatter diagram is set of points shown with cartesian axes, X-axis and Y-axis, as shown in Fig. 1.

Correlation using scatter diagrams. Different types of diagrams of scatter points along with conclusions regarding correlation are given below :

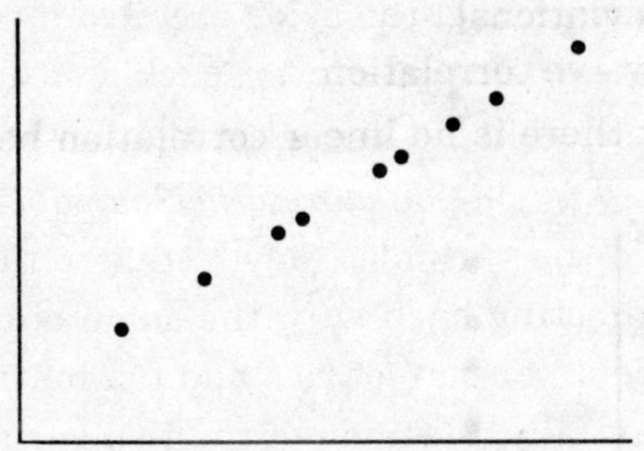

Fig. 2

[Scatter points lie on upward sloping straight line] perfect +ve correlation

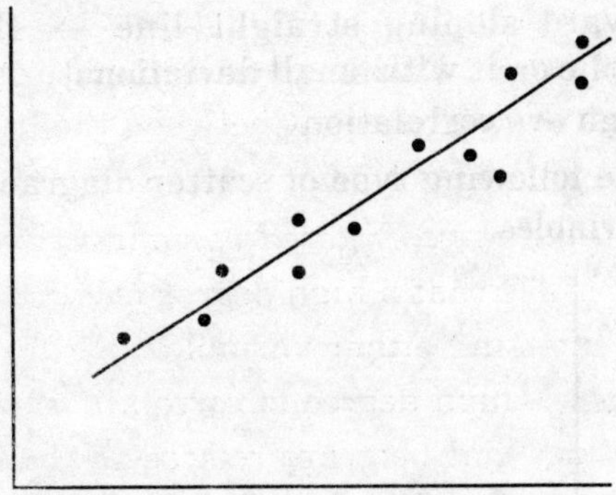

Fig. 3

[Scatter points are very close to hypothetical straight line with small deviations] High +ve correlation

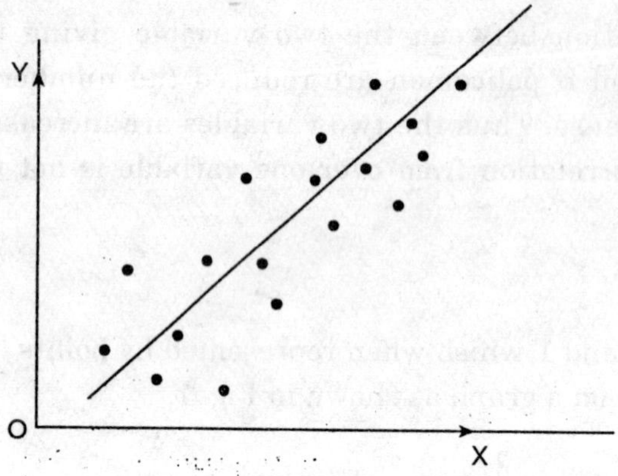

Fig. 4

[The scatter points move upwards as we move along X-axis to the right] however deviations from good fitting upward moving hypothetical straight line are large]

Low + ve correlation

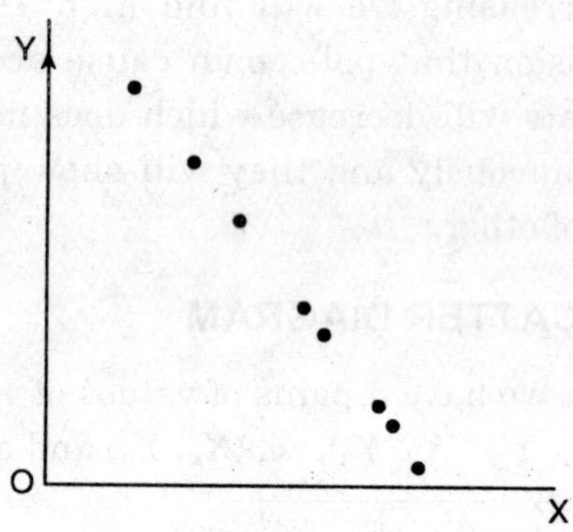

Fig. 5

[The scatter points seem to lie on a downward sloping straight line]

Perfect –ve correlation

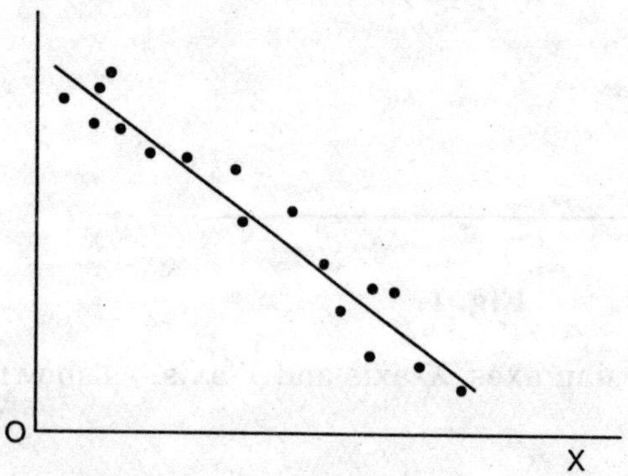

Fig. 6

[The scatter points are very close to a downward sloping straight line → they almost lie on it with small deviations]

High –ve correlation

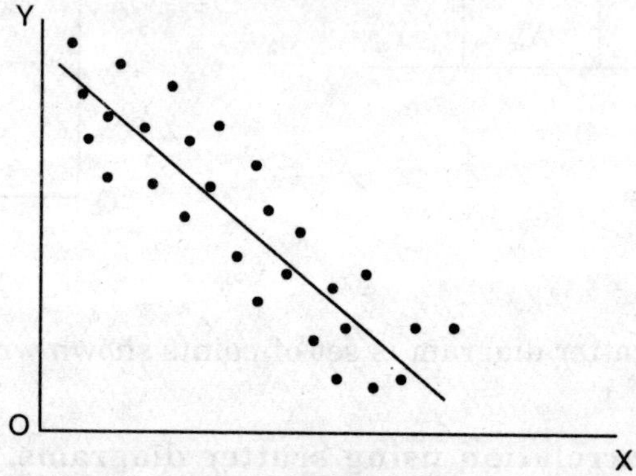

Fig. 7

[The scatter points move around a downward sloping straight line with little large deviations]

Low –ve correlation

The following type of scatter diagrams show that there is no linear correlation between two variables.

Fig. 8(*a*)

Fig. 8(*b*)

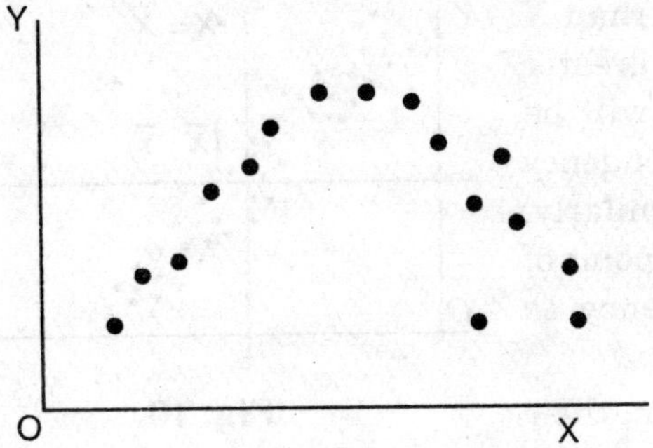

Fig. 8(*c*)

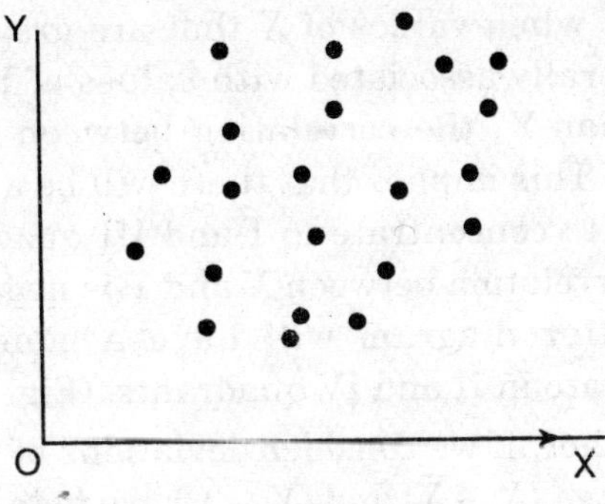

Fig. 8(*d*)

7.4.1. Merits and Limitations of the Method

Merits : 1. It is a simple and non-mathematical method of studying correlation between the variables. As such it can be easily understood and a rough idea can very quickly be formed as to whether or not the variables are related.

2. It is not influenced by the size of extreme values whereas most of the mathematical methods of finding correlation are influenced by extreme values.

3. Making a scatter diagram usually is the first step in investigating the relationship between the variables.

Limitations. By applying this method we can get an idea about the direction of correlation and also whether it is high or low. But we cannot establish the exact degree of correlation between the variables as is possible by applying the mathematical method.

7.5 KARL PEARSON'S COEFFICIENT OF CORRELATION

7.5. One of mathematical methods of measuring correlation, the Karl Pearoson's method, popularly known as Pearsonian coefficient of correlation, is most widely used in practice. The coefficient of correlation is denoted by the symbol r. It is one of the very few symbols that is used universally for describing the degree and direction of relationship between two variables.

7.5.1. Covariance

Let us assume, again, that we have data on two variables X and Y denoted by the pairs (X_i, Y_i), $i = 1, 2, ...n$. Further, let the scatter diagram of the data be as shown in figure 9.

Let $\overline{X}$ and $\overline{Y}$ be the arithmetic means of X and Y respectively. Draw two lines $X = \overline{X}$ and $Y = \overline{Y}$ on the scatter diagram. These two lines, intersect at the point $(\overline{X}, \overline{Y})$ and are mutually perpendicular, divide the whole diagram into four parts, termed as I, II, III and IV quadrants, as shown.

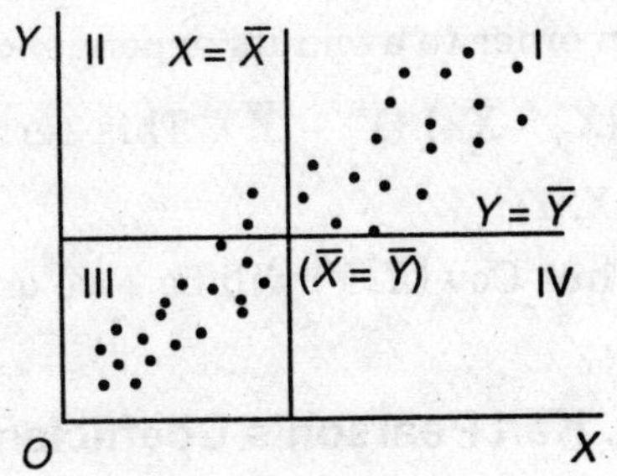

Fig. 9

As mentioned earlier, the correlation between X and Y will be positive if low (high) values of X are associated with low (high) values of Y. In terms of the above figure, we can say that when values of X that are greater (less) than $\overline{X}$ are generally associated with values of Y that are greater (less) than $\overline{Y}$, the correlation between X and Y will be positive. This implies that there will be a general tendency of point to concentrate in I and III quadrants. Similarly, when correlation between X and Y is negative, the point of the scatter diagram will have a general tendency to concentrate in II and IV quadrants. (Fig. 10)

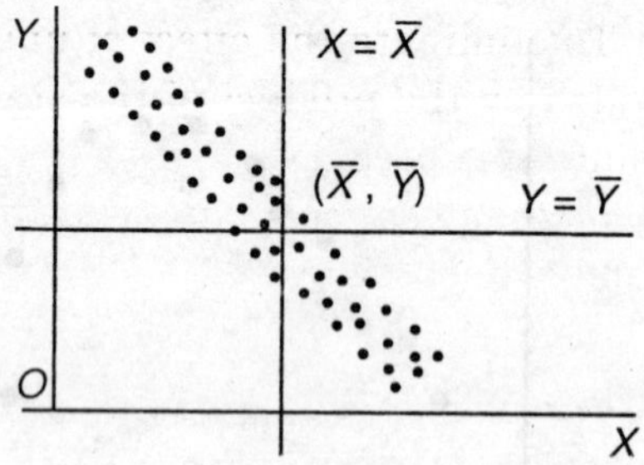

Fig. 10

Further, if we consider deviations of values from their means, *i.e.*, $(X_i - \overline{X})$ and $(Y_i - \overline{Y})$, we note that :

(*i*) Both $(X_i - \overline{X})$ and $(Y_i - \overline{Y})$ will be positive for all points in quadrant *I*.

(*ii*) $(X_i - \overline{X})$ will be negative and $(Y_i - \overline{Y})$ will be positive for all points in quadrant II.

(*iii*) Both $(X_i - \overline{X})$ and $(Y_i - \overline{Y})$ will be negative for all points in quadrant III.

(*iv*) $(X_i - \overline{X})$ will be positive and $(Y_i - \overline{Y})$ will be negative for all points in quadrant IV.

It is obvious from the above that the product of deviations, *i.e.*, $(X_i - \overline{X})(Y_i - \overline{Y})$ will be positive for points in quadrant I and III and negative for points in quadrants II and IV.

Since, for positive correlation, the points will tend to concentrate more in I and III quadrants than in II and IV, the sum of positive products of deviations will outweigh the sum of negative products of deviations. Thus, $\Sigma(X_i - \overline{X})(Y_i - \overline{Y})$ will be positive for all the n observations.

Similarly, when correlation is negative, the points will tend to concentrate more in II and IV quadrants than in I and III. Thus, the sum of negative products of deviations will outweigh the sum of positive products and hence $\Sigma(X_i - \overline{X})(Y_i - \overline{Y})$ will be negative for all the n observations.

Further , if there is no correlation, the sum of positive products of deviations will be equal to the sum of negative products of deviations such that $\Sigma(X_i - \overline{X})(Y_i - \overline{Y})$ will be equal to zero.

On the basis of the above, we can consider $\Sigma(X_i - \overline{X})(Y_i - \overline{Y})$ as an absolute measure of correlation. This measure, like other absolute measures of dispersion, skewness, *etc.*, will depend upon (*i*) the number of observations and (*ii*) the units of measurements of the variables.

In order to avoid its dependence on the number of observations, we take its average, *i.e.*, $\frac{1}{n}\Sigma(X_i - \overline{X})(Y_i - \overline{Y})$. This term is called *covariance* in statistics and is denoted as *Cov* (X, Y).

Thus Cov (X, Y) will be + ve or – ve according as correlation between X and Y is + ve or – ve.

7.5.2. Karl Pearson's Coefficient of Correlation

As seen above cov $(X, Y) = \dfrac{\Sigma(X - \overline{X})(Y - \overline{Y})}{n}$ may be taken as absolute measure of correlation which is dependent on units of measurement of X and Y both. Also σ_x and σ_y have same units of measurements as of X and Y respectively.

To eliminate the effect of units of measurement of the variables, the covariance term is divided by the product of the standard deviation of X and the standard deviation of Y. The resulting expression is known as the Karl Pearson's *coefficient of linear correlation* or the *product moment correlation coefficient* or simply the *coefficient of correlation, between* X and Y and is denoted by r_{XY}

$$r_{XY} = \frac{Cov\,(X, Y)}{\sigma_X\,\sigma_Y} = \frac{\Sigma(X-\overline{X})\,(Y-\overline{Y})}{n\,\sigma_x\,\sigma_y} \quad ...(1)$$

or

$$r_{XY} = \frac{\frac{1}{n}\Sigma\,(X_i-\overline{X})\,(Y_i-\overline{Y})}{\sqrt{\frac{1}{n}\Sigma\,(X_i-\overline{X})^2}\ \sqrt{\frac{1}{n}\Sigma(Y_i-\overline{Y})^2}} \quad ...(2)$$

Cancelling $\frac{1}{n}$ from the numerator and the denominator, we get

$$r_{XY} = \frac{\Sigma\,(X_i-\overline{X})\,(Y_i-\overline{Y})}{\sqrt{\Sigma(X_i-\overline{X})^2}\ \sqrt{\Sigma\,(Y_i-\overline{Y})^2}} \quad ...(3)$$

Consider $\Sigma(X_i\,\overline{X})\,(Y_i-\overline{Y}) = \Sigma(X_i-\overline{X})\,Y_i - \overline{Y}\,\Sigma(X_i-\overline{X})$

$= \Sigma X_i\,Y_i - \overline{X}\,\Sigma Y_i$ (second term $\Sigma X_i - \overline{X}) = 0]$

$= \Sigma X_i Y_i - n\,\overline{X}\,\overline{Y}\ (\Sigma Y_i = n\overline{Y})$

Similarly we can write $\Sigma(X_i-\overline{X})^2 = \Sigma X_i^2 - n\overline{X}^2$

and $\Sigma(Y_i-\overline{Y})^2 = \Sigma Y_i^2 - n\overline{Y}^2$

Substituting these values in equation 3), we have

$$r_{XY} = \frac{\Sigma X_i Y_i - n\overline{X}\overline{Y}}{\sqrt{[\Sigma X_i^2 - n\overline{X}^2]}\ \sqrt{[\Sigma Y_i^2 - n\overline{Y}^2]}} \quad ...(4)$$

$$r_{XY} = \frac{\Sigma X_i Y_i - n\,.\,\frac{\Sigma X_i}{n}\times\frac{\Sigma Y_i}{n}}{\sqrt{\Sigma X_i^2 - n\left(\frac{\Sigma X_i}{n}\right)^2}\ \sqrt{\Sigma Y_i^2 - n\left(\frac{\Sigma Y_i}{n}\right)^2}}$$

$$= \frac{\Sigma X_i Y_i - \frac{(\Sigma X_i)\,(\Sigma Y_i)}{n}}{\sqrt{\Sigma X_i^2 - \frac{(\Sigma X_i)^2}{n}}\ \sqrt{\Sigma Y_i^2 - \frac{(\Sigma Y_i)^2}{n}}} \quad ...(5)$$

On multiplication of numerator and denominator by n; we can write

$$r_{XY} = \frac{n\Sigma X_i Y_i - (\Sigma X_i)(\Sigma Y_i)}{\sqrt{n\Sigma X_i^2 - (\Sigma X_i)^2}\ \sqrt{n\Sigma Y_i^2 - (\Sigma Y_i)^2}} \quad ...(6)$$

Further, if we assume $x_i = X_i - \overline{X}$ and $y_i = Y_i - \overline{Y}$, equation (2), given above, can be written as

$$r_{XY} = \frac{\frac{1}{n}\Sigma x_i y_i}{\sqrt{\frac{1}{n}\Sigma x_i^2}\sqrt{\frac{1}{n}\Sigma y_i^2}} \quad ...(7)$$

or $$r_{XY} = \frac{\Sigma x_i y_i}{\sqrt{\Sigma x_i^2}\sqrt{\Sigma y_i^2}} \quad ...(8)$$

or $$r_{XY} = \frac{\Sigma x_i y_i}{n\,\sigma_x\,\sigma_y} \quad ...(9)$$

Thus working formulae are as follows :

$$r_{XY} = \frac{\text{cov.}(X, Y)}{\sigma_x\,\sigma_y} \quad \text{[by definition]} \quad ...(i)$$

$$= \frac{\Sigma x, y}{n\,\sigma_x\,\sigma_y} \quad [\text{where } x = X - \overline{X}, y = Y - \overline{Y}] \quad ...(ii)$$

$$= \frac{\Sigma xy}{\sqrt{\Sigma x^2\,\Sigma y^2}} \quad ...(iii)$$

$$= \frac{n\,\Sigma XY - \Sigma X\,\Sigma Y}{\sqrt{n\,\Sigma X^2 - (\Sigma X)^2}\sqrt{n\Sigma Y^2 - (\Sigma Y)^2}} \quad ...(iv)$$

7.5.3. Short-cut Methods

It can be shown (proof is not given)

that if $u = X - A$ and $v = Y - B$ (deviation method)

or if $u = \frac{X - A}{C}$ and $v = \frac{Y - B}{D}$ (step deviation method)

in both cases $$r_{XY} = \frac{n\,\Sigma uv - \Sigma u\,\Sigma v}{\sqrt{n\,\Sigma u^2 - (\Sigma u)^2}\sqrt{n\,\Sigma v^2 - (\Sigma v)^2}} \quad ...(v)$$

In practice formula (*v*) is most convenient to use.

[Note : Relation (*v*) gives that $r_{XY} = r_{uv}$, this implies that *r* does not change because of shift of origin or change of scale. As $\mu = \frac{X - A}{C}$ involves both shift of origin and change of scale].

Example 1. *Find Karl Pearson's coefficient of correlation from the following data (by direct method)*

X	9	8	7	6	5	4	3	2	1
Y	15	16	14	13	11	12	10	8	9

Solution.

CALCULATION OF CORRELATION COEFFICIENT (DIRECT METHOD)

X	X^2	*Y*	Y^2	*XY*
9	81	15	225	135
8	64	16	256	128

7	49	14	196	98
6	36	13	169	78
5	25	11	121	55
4	16	12	144	48
3	9	10	100	30
2	4	8	64	16
1	1	9	81	9
$\Sigma X = 45$	$\Sigma X^2 = 285$	$\Sigma Y = 108$	$\Sigma Y^2 = 1{,}356$	$\Sigma XY = 597$

$$r = \frac{N\Sigma XY - (\Sigma X)(\Sigma Y)}{\sqrt{N\Sigma X^2 - (\Sigma X)^2}\cdot\sqrt{N\Sigma Y^2 - (\Sigma Y)^2}}$$

$N = 9, \Sigma XY = 597, \Sigma X = 45, \Sigma Y = 108, \Sigma X^2 = 285, \Sigma Y^2 = 1{,}356$

$$r = \frac{9 \times 597 - 45 \times 108}{\sqrt{9 \times 285 - (45)^2}\ \sqrt{9 \times 1356 - (108)^2}}$$

$$r = \frac{5373 - 4860}{\sqrt{2565 - 2025}\ \sqrt{12{,}204 - 11{,}664}}$$

$$r = \frac{513}{\sqrt{540 \times 450}} = \frac{513}{540} = +0.95.$$

Example 2. *The following table gives indices of industrial production and registered unemployed (in hundred thousand). Calculate the coefficient of correlation for the two variables. (Using actual means).*

Year	:	*1991*	*1992*	*1993*	*1994*	*1995*	*1996*	*1997*	*1998*
Index of Production	:	*100*	*102*	*104*	*107*	*105*	*112*	*103*	*99*
number Unemployed	:	*15*	*12*	*13*	*11*	*12*	*12*	*19*	*26*

Solution.

CALCULATION OF KARL PEARSON'S CORRELATION COEFFICIENTS

Year	*Production* X	$(X-\overline{X}) = (X-104) = x$	x^2	*Unemployed* Y	$(Y-\overline{Y}) = (Y-15) = y$	y^2	xy
1991	100	– 4	16	15	0	0	0
1992	102	– 2	4	12	– 3	9	+ 6
1993	104	0	0	13	– 2	4	0
1994	107	+ 3	9	11	– 4	16	– 12
1995	105	+ 1	1	12	– 3	9	– 3
1996	112	+ 8	64	12	– 3	9	– 24
1997	103	– 1	1	19	+ 4	16	– 4
1998	99	– 5	25	26	+ 11	121	– 55
	$\Sigma X = 832$	$\Sigma x = 0$	$\Sigma x^2 = 120$	$\Sigma Y = 120$	$\Sigma y = 0$	$\Sigma y^2 = 184$	$\Sigma xy = -92$

$n = 8, \overline{X} = \dfrac{832}{8} = 104, \overline{Y} = \dfrac{120}{8} = 15$

We have $r = \dfrac{\Sigma xy}{\sqrt{\Sigma x^2 \, \Sigma y^2}}$

$$x = (X - \overline{X}) \; ; \; y = (Y - \overline{Y})$$

$$\Sigma xy = -92, \Sigma x^2 = 120, \Sigma y^2 = 184$$

$$r = \frac{-92}{\sqrt{120 \times 184}} = -0.619$$

Example 3. *Calculate Pearson's coefficient of correlation between the indices of wages and cost of living from the following data:*

Daily Wages	:	*100*	*101*	*102*	*102*	*100*	*99*	*97*	*98*	*96*	*95*
Cost of living	:	*98*	*99*	*99*	*97*	*95*	*92*	*95*	*94*	*90*	*91*

Solution. Let us denote the weight by X and cost of living index by Y.

CALCULATION OF KARL PEARSON'S COEFFICIENT OF CORRELATION

X	$(X - \overline{X}) = (X - 99) = x$	x^2	Y	$(Y - \overline{Y}) = (Y - 95) = y$	y^2	xy
100	+ 1	1	98	+ 3	9	+ 3
101	+ 2	4	99	+ 4	16	+ 8
102	+ 3	9	99	+ 4	16	+ 12
102	+ 3	9	97	+ 2	4	+ 6
100	+ 1	1	95	0	0	0
99	0	0	92	– 3	9	0
97	– 2	4	95	0	0	0
98	– 1	1	94	– 1	1	+ 1
96	– 3	9	90	– 5	25	+ 15
95	– 4	16	91	– 4	16	+ 16
$\Sigma X = 990$	$\Sigma x = 0$	$\Sigma x^2 = 54$	$\Sigma Y = 950$	$\Sigma y = 0$	$\Sigma y^2 = 96$	$\Sigma xy = 61$

$\overline{X} = \dfrac{\Sigma X}{n} = \dfrac{990}{10} = 99, \quad \overline{Y} = \dfrac{\Sigma Y}{n} = \dfrac{950}{10} = 95$

$$r = \frac{\Sigma xy}{\sqrt{\Sigma x^2 \times \Sigma y^2}} = \frac{61}{\sqrt{54 \times 96}} = 0.847$$

Example 4. *The following data relate to the age of 10 employees and the number of days which they reported sick in a month :*

Age	:	*20*	*30*	*32*	*35*	*40*	*46*	*52*	*55*	*58*	*62*
Sick days	:	*11*	*12*	*10*	*13*	*14*	*16*	*15*	*17*	*18*	*19*

Calculate Karl Pearson's coefficient of correlation and interpret its value.

CALCULATION OF CORRELATION COEFFICIENT

Age X	(X – 43) = d_x	d_x^2	Sick days Y	(Y – 14) = d_y	d_y^2	d_xd_y
20	– 23	529	11	– 3	9	+ 69
30	– 13	169	12	– 2	4	+ 26
32	– 11	121	10	– 4	16	+ 44
35	– 8	64	13	– 1	1	+ 8
40	– 3	9	14	0	0	0
46	+ 3	9	16	+ 2	4	+ 6
52	+ 9	81	15	+ 1	1	+ 9
55	+ 12	144	17	+ 3	9	+ 36
58	+ 15	225	18	+ 4	16	+ 60
62	+ 19	361	19	+ 5	25	+ 45
$\Sigma X = 430$	$\Sigma d_x = 0$	$\Sigma d_x^2 = 1712$	$\Sigma Y = 145$	$\Sigma d_y = 5$	$\Sigma d_y^2 = 85$	$\Sigma d_xd_y = 353$

$$r = \frac{N\Sigma d_xd_y - \Sigma d_x \Sigma d_y}{\sqrt{N\Sigma d_x^2 - (\Sigma d_x)^2}\sqrt{N\Sigma d_y^2 - (\Sigma d_y)^2}} = \frac{10 \times 353 - (0)(-5)}{\sqrt{10 \times 1712 - (0)^2}\sqrt{10 \times 85 - (-5)^2}}$$

$$= \frac{3530}{\sqrt{17120}\sqrt{825}} = \frac{3530}{130.85 \times 28.72} = 0.939$$

Thus, there is a very high degree of positive correlation between age and sick days taken. Hence, we can conclude that as the age of an employee increases, he is liable to be sick more often than others.

Example 5. *Compute Karl Pearson's coefficient of correlation between per capita National Income and per capita Consumer Expenditure from the data given below:*

Year	*1995*	*1996*	*1997*	*1998*	*1999*	*2000*	*2001*	*2002*	*2003*	*2004*
Per capita National Income	*249*	*251*	*248*	*252*	*258*	*269*	*271*	*272*	*280*	*275*
Per capita consumer expenditure	*237*	*238*	*236*	*240*	*245*	*255*	*254*	*252*	*258*	*251*

Solution. Let per capita national income be denoted by X and consumer expenditure by Y.

CALCULATION OF KARL PEARSON'S CORRELATION COEFFICIENT

Year	X	(X – 260) d_x	d_x^2	Y	(Y – 240) d_y	d_y^2	d_xd_y
1995	249	– 11	121	237	– 3	9	+ 33
1996	251	– 9	81	238	– 2	4	+ 18
1997	248	– 12	144	236	– 4	16	+ 48
1998	252	– 8	64	240	0	0	0

1999	258	– 2	4	245	+ 5	25	– 10
2000	269	+ 9	81	255	+ 15	225	+ 135
2001	271	+ 11	121	254	+ 14	196	+ 154
2002	272	+ 12	144	252	+ 12	144	+ 144
2003	280	+ 20	40	258	+ 18	324	+ 360
2004	375	+ 15	225	251	+ 11	121	+ 165
N = 10	ΣX = 2,625	$\Sigma d_x = 25$	Σd_x^2 = 1,385	ΣY = 2,466	$\Sigma d_y = 66$	Σd_y^2 = 1,064	$\Sigma d_x d_y$ =1,047

$$r = \frac{\Sigma d_x d_y - \dfrac{\Sigma d_x \times \Sigma d_y}{N}}{\sqrt{\Sigma d_x^2 - \dfrac{(\Sigma d_x)^2}{N}} - \sqrt{\Sigma d_y^2 - \dfrac{(\Sigma d_y)^2}{N}}}$$

$$= \frac{1047 - \dfrac{25 \times 66}{10}}{\sqrt{1385 - \dfrac{(25)^2}{10}}\sqrt{1064 - \dfrac{(66)^2}{10}}}$$

$$= \frac{1047 - 165}{\sqrt{1385 - 62.5}\sqrt{1064 - 435.6}} = \frac{882}{\sqrt{1322.5}\sqrt{628.4}}$$

$$\log r = \log 882 - \frac{1}{2}(\log 1322.5 + \log 628.4)$$

$$= 2.9455 - 1/2\ (3.1216 + 2.7983)$$

$$= 2.9455 - 2.9599 = - 0.0144$$

$$r = \text{AL } \bar{1}.9856 = + 0.967$$

Example 6. *The following table gives the distribution of the total population and those who are wholly or partially blind among them. Find out if there is any relation between age and blindness.*

Age	*No. of persons (in thousands)*	*Blind*	*Age*	*No. of persons (in thousands)*	*Blind*
0–10	*100*	*55*	*40–50*	*24*	*36*
10–20	*60*	*40*	*50–60*	*11*	*22*
20–30	*40*	*40*	*60–70*	*6*	*18*
30–40	*36*	*40*	*70–80*	*3*	*15*

Solution. Correlation is to be found between age and blindness (not no. of blind). However, blindness/depends on no. of blinds and the population. Incidence of blindness will be measured by no. of blind/thousand or blind per 1 lakh etc. In these 8 units blindness is no. of blinds/lakh.

For facilitating comparison we must determine the number of blinds in terms of a common denominator, say, 1 lakh. The first figure would remain as it is because 55 persons are blind out of 100 thousand, *i.e.* 1 lakh. The second value would be obtained as follows:

Out of 60,000 persons number of blinds = 40

Out of 1,00,000 persons number of blinds = $\frac{40}{60{,}000} \times 1{,}00{,}000 = 67$

In a similar manner other values can be obtained.

Age	*Mid-points* X	(X–35)/10 = d_x	d_x^2	*Blind Persons per lakh* Y	(Y – 185) = d_y	d_y^2	d_xd_y
0–10	5	– 3	9	55	– 130	16,900	+ 390
10–20	15	– 2	4	67	– 118	13,924	+ 236
20–30	25	– 1	1	100	– 85	7,225	+ 85
30–40	35	0	0	111	– 74	5,476	0
40–50	45	+ 1	1	150	– 35	1,225	– 35
50–60	55	+ 2	4	200	+ 15	225	+ 30
60–70	65	+ 3	9	300	+ 115	13,225	+ 345
70–80	75	+ 4	16	500	+ 315	99,225	+ 1,260
		$\Sigma d_x = 4$	$\Sigma d_x^2 = 44$	—	$\Sigma d_y = +3$	Σd_y^2 =1,57,425	Σd_xd_y = 2,311

$$r = \frac{N\,\Sigma d_x\,d_y - \Sigma d_x\,\Sigma d_y}{\sqrt{N\,\Sigma d_x^2 - (\Sigma dx_x)^2}\,\sqrt{N\Sigma d_y^2 - (\Sigma d_y)^2}}$$

$N = 8,\ \Sigma d_x\,d_y = 2{,}311,\ \Sigma d_x = 4,\ \Sigma d_y = 3,\ \Sigma d_x^2 = 44,\ \Sigma d_y^2 = 1{,}57{,}425$

Substituting these values

$$r = \frac{8\,(2311) - 4(3)}{\sqrt{8\,(44) - 4^2}\,\sqrt{8\,(157425\,) - 3^2}}$$

$$= \frac{18488 - 12}{\sqrt{336}\,\sqrt{1259391}} = 0.898$$

[⇒ Use of shift of Origin and change of scale.

As already mentioned coefficient of correlation is independent of shift of origin and change of scale *i.e.*, if

$$u = \frac{X - A}{C},\ v = \frac{Y - B}{D}$$

Then $r\,(X, Y) = r_{(uv)}$ [See 7.5.3]]

Example 7. *Calculate coefficient of correlation from the following data:*

X	*100*	*200*	*300*	*400*	*500*	*600*	*700*
Y	*30*	*50*	*60*	*80*	*100*	*110*	*130*

Solution.

X	$u = \frac{X-400}{100}$	u^2	*Y*	$v = \frac{Y-70}{10}$	v^2	*u v*
100	– 3	9	30	– 4	16	12
200	– 2	4	50	– 2	4	4

300	– 1	1	60	– 1	1	1
400	0	0	80	1	1	0
500	1	1	100	3	9	3
600	2	4	110	4	16	8
700	3	9	130	6	36	18
	0	28		7	83	46
	Σu	Σu^2		Σv	Σv^2	Σuv

$$r_{XY} = r_{uv} = \frac{n\ \Sigma uv - \Sigma u\ \Sigma v}{\sqrt{n\ \Sigma u^2 - (\Sigma u)^2}\ \sqrt{n\ \Sigma v^2 - (\Sigma v)^2}}$$

$$= \frac{7\ (46) - 0\ (7)}{\sqrt{7\ (28) - 0^2}\ \sqrt{7\ (83) - (7)^2}}$$

$$= \frac{322}{\sqrt{196}\ \sqrt{532}} = 0.997$$

Example 8. *If covariance between X and Y variables is 10 and the variances of X and Y are respectively 16 and 9, find the coefficient of correlation.*

Solution.

Covariance of X and $Y = \frac{\Sigma xy}{N} = 10$

Variance of $X = 16$ $\quad \therefore\ \sigma_x = \sqrt{16} = 4$

Variance of $Y = 9$ $\quad \therefore\ \sigma_y = \sqrt{9} = 3$

$$r = \frac{\text{Cov}\ (X, Y)}{\sigma_x\ \sigma_y}$$

Substituting values, $r = \frac{10}{4 \times 3} = +\ 0.833.$

Example 9. *The coefficient of correlation between two variates X and Y is 0.64. Their covariance is 16. The variance of X is 9. Find the standard deviation of Y series.*

Solution.

$$\sigma_x^2 = 9,\ \sigma_x = 3$$

$$r = \frac{\text{Cov}\ (X, Y)}{\sigma_x\ \sigma_j} \Rightarrow 0.64 = \frac{16}{3 \times \sigma_y} \Rightarrow \sigma_y = \frac{16}{3 \times .64} = \frac{1600}{3 \times 64}$$

$$\sigma_y = \frac{25}{3} = 8.33$$

Example 10. *A computer while calculating the correlation coefficient between two variables X and Y obtained the following constants.*

$N = 30$, $\Sigma X = 12\theta$, $\Sigma X^2 = 600$, $\Sigma Y = 90$, $\Sigma Y^2 = 250$, $\Sigma XY = 356$

It was, however, later discovered at the time of checking that it had copied down two pairs of observations as:

X	*Y*
8	*10*
12	*7*

While the correct values were —

X	Y
8	12
10	8

Obtain the corrected values of the correlation coefficient between X and Y.

Solution.

Correct $\Sigma X = 120 - 8 - 12 + 8 + 10 = 118$

Correct $\Sigma Y = 90 - 10 - 7 + 12 + 8 = 93$

Correct $\Sigma X^2 = 600 - (8)^2 - (12)^2 + (8)^2 + (10)^2 = 600 - 64 - 144 + 64 + 100 = 556.$

Correct $\Sigma Y^2 = 250 - (10)^2 - (7)^2 + (12)^2 + (8)^2 = 250 - 100 - 49 + 144 + 64 = 309.$

Correct $\Sigma XY = 356 - (8 \times 10) - (12 \times 7) + (8 \times 12) + (10 \times 8)$

$= 356 - 80 - 84 + 96 + 80 = 368$

Correct $r = \dfrac{n\,\Sigma XY - \Sigma X\,\Sigma Y}{\sqrt{n\,\Sigma X^2 - (\Sigma X)^2}\sqrt{n\,\Sigma Y^2 - (\Sigma Y)^2}}$

$$= \frac{30(368) - 118\,(93)}{\sqrt{30\,(556) - (118)^2}\sqrt{30\,(309) - (93)^2}}$$

$$= \frac{11040 - 10974}{\sqrt{16680 - 13924}\sqrt{9270 - 8649}}$$

$$= \frac{66}{\sqrt{2756}\sqrt{621}} = 0.055$$

Example 11. *Given $r = 0.8$, $\Sigma xy = 60$, $\sigma_y = 2.5$ and $\Sigma x^2 = 90$, find the number of items (x and y are deviations from arithmetic mean).*

Solution. We are given

$\Sigma x^2 = 90,\ r = 0.8,\ \sigma_y = 2.5,\ \Sigma xy = 60$

$$r = \frac{\Sigma xy}{N\sigma_x\sigma_y}$$

$$0.8 = \frac{60}{N\left(\sqrt{\frac{\Sigma x^2}{N}}\right)2.5}$$

$$0.8 = \frac{60}{2.5\,N\sqrt{\frac{90}{N}}}$$

$$0.8 \times 2.5\sqrt{90\,N} = 60$$

$$2\sqrt{90\,N} = 60$$

Squaring both sides $90\,N = 900$

$\Rightarrow N = 10$

Example 12. *From the following table, compute the coefficient of correlation between Savings Bank Deposits and Strikes and Lockouts over a period of seven years.*

Saving bank Deposit (lakhs of ₹). :	*51*	*54*	*56*	*59*	*65*	*60*	*70*
Strikes & Lockouts :	*38*	*44*	*33*	*36*	*33*	*23*	*13*

Solution. Let deposits be denoted by X and strikes and lockout by Y.

CALCULATION OF CORRELATION COEFFICIENT

X	$(X-60)$ d_x	d_x^2	Y	$(Y-30)$ d_y	d_y^2	d_xd_y
51	− 9	81	38	+ 8	64	− 72
54	− 6	36	44	+ 14	196	− 84
56	− 4	16	33	+ 3	9	− 12
59	− 1	1	36	+ 6	36	− 6
65	+ 5	25	33	+ 3	9	+ 15
60	0	0	23	− 7	49	0
70	+ 10	100	13	− 17	289	− 170
$\Sigma X = 415$	$\Sigma d_x = -5$	$\Sigma d_x^2 = 259$	$\Sigma Y = 220$	$\Sigma d_y = +10$	$\Sigma d_y^2 = 652$	$\Sigma d_xd_y = -329$

$$r = \frac{N\,\Sigma d_xd_y - \Sigma d_x \Sigma d_y}{\sqrt{N\Sigma d_x^2 - (\Sigma d_x)^2}\,\sqrt{N\Sigma d_y^2 - (\Sigma d_y)^2}}$$

$$= \frac{7(-329) - (-5)(10)}{\sqrt{7(259) - (-5)^2}\,\sqrt{7(652) - (10)^2}}$$

$$= \frac{-2253}{\sqrt{1788}\,\sqrt{4464}} = \frac{-2253}{\sqrt{1788 \times 4464}}$$

$$= -0.85$$

Example 13. *Calculate Correlation coefficient from the following :*

$$n = 10, \Sigma X = 140, \Sigma Y = 150, \Sigma(X-10)^2 = 180$$
$$\Sigma(Y-15)^2 = 215, \ \Sigma(X-10)(Y-15) = 60.$$

Solution. Let $dx = X - 10$, $dy = Y - 15$

We are given $\Sigma d_x^2 = 180, \Sigma d_y^2 = 215, \Sigma d_xd_y = 60$

We have $$r = \frac{n\,\Sigma d_xd_y - \Sigma d_x\,\Sigma d_y}{\sqrt{n\,\Sigma d_x^2 - (\Sigma d_x)^2}\,\sqrt{n\,\Sigma dy^2 - (\Sigma dy)^2}}$$

Only quantities which are needed are Σd_x and Σd_y.

We know $d_x = X - 10 \Rightarrow \Sigma d_x = \Sigma X - n(10)$

$= 140 - 10(10) = 40$

also $d_y = Y - 15 \Rightarrow \Sigma d_y = \Sigma y - 15n = 150 - 150 = 0.$

Using all the values we find r as follows :

$$r = \frac{10(60) - 0}{\sqrt{10(180) - (40)^2}\,\sqrt{10(215) - 0^2}} = \frac{600}{\sqrt{200 \times 2150}}$$

$$= \frac{600}{\sqrt{430000}} = \frac{6}{\sqrt{43}} = \frac{6}{6.56} = 0.915.$$

7.6 COEFFICIENT OF CORRELATION AND PROBABLE ERROR

It is assumed that 'r' is obtained on the basis of a sample of n units taken from a large normal population, as such computed value of r varies from sample to sample . If r *is* based on whole population (but not on the basis of sample) it is referred as ρ (pronounced as rho)

The probable error of the coefficient of correlation helps in interpreting its value. With the help of probable error it is possible to determine the reliability of the value of the coefficient in so far as it depends on the conditions of random sampling. The probable error of the coefficient of correlation is obtained as follows :

$$P.E.(r) = 0.6745 \frac{1 - r^2}{\sqrt{n}}$$

where r is the coefficient of correlation and n the number of pairs of observations.

- If the value of r is less than the probable error then there is no evidence of correlation, *i.e.,* the value of r is not at all significant. *i.e.,* if $r < P.E.(r)$
- If the value of r is more. than six times the probable error, the coefficient of correlation is practically certain, *i.e.,* the value of r is significant. [when $r > 6\,PE(r)$]
- When $PE\,(r) < r < 6\,Pe\,(r)$, in that case we cannot say confidently about the significance of r i.e., whether r is meaningful or not.

By adding and subtracting the value of probable error from the coefficient of correlation we get respectively the upper and lower limits within which coefficient of correlation of the population can be expected to lie. Symbolically,

$$\rho = r \pm P.E.$$

where ρ (rho) denotes correlation in the population.

Let us compute probable error, assuming a coefficient of correlation of 0.80 and a sample of 16 pairs of items. We will have

$$P.E. = 0.6745 \frac{1 - (8)^2}{\sqrt{16}} = .06$$

The limits of the correlation in the population would be $r \pm P.E.$, *i.e.,* 0.8 ± 0.06 or from 0.74 to 0.86

Example 14. If $r = 0.6$ and $n = 64$, find out the probable error of the coefficient of correlation and determine the limits for population correlation coefficient ρ.

Solution. $$P.E._r = 0.6745 \frac{1 - r^2}{\sqrt{n}}$$

$$r = 0.6 \text{ and } n = 64$$

$$P.E._r = 0.6745 \frac{1 - (0.6)^2}{\sqrt{(64)}} = \frac{0.6745 \times 0.64}{8} = 0.054.$$

Limits of population correlation = $0.6 \pm 0.054 = 0.546$ to 0.654.

7.7. COEFFICIENT OF DETERMINATION

We have n pairs of (X, Y) values. In case we consider only Y values which has σ_y^2. variance. This variability in Y values has two components (1) which is due to changes (variability) in X as X and Y are correlated, hence if X varies Y also varies with it. This part of variability (variance) is known as explained valuation. (2) The variable Y otherwise has some variability which is not due to X but its own or may be because of other factors (*i.e.*, which is not due to X). This part of variance is called unexplained variance.

This has been found out (proof is beyond scope of this book) that $\frac{\text{Explained variance}}{\text{Total variance}} = r^2$.

One very convenient and useful way of interpreting the value of coefficient of correlation between two variables is to use square of coefficient of correlation, which is called coefficient of determination. The coefficient of determination thus equals r^2. If the value of $r = 0.9$, r^2 will be 0.81 and this would mean that 81 per cent of the variation in the dependent variable Y has been explained by the independent variable X. The maximum value of r^2 is unity because it is possible to explain all of the variation in Y, but it is not possible to explain more than all of it.

The coefficient of determination (r^2) is defined as the ratio of the explained variance to the total variance.

$$\text{Coefficient of determination} = \frac{\text{Explained Variation}}{\text{Total Variance}}$$

The ratio of unexplained variance to total variance is frequently called *coefficient of non-determination.*

$$\Rightarrow r^2 \le 1$$

Since explained variance is less than or equal to total variance $\Rightarrow -1 \le r \le 1$.

7.8 INTERPRETING THE COEFFICIENT OF CORRELATION

The coefficient of correlation measures the degree of relationship between two variables. As the reliability of estimates depends upon the closeness of the relationship, it is imperative that utmost care be taken while interpreting the value of coefficient of correlation otherwise fallacious conclusions be drawn.

Unfortunately, the interpretation of the coefficient of correlation depends very much on experience. The full significance of r will only be grasped after working out a number of correlation problems and seeing the kind of data that give rise to various values of r. The investigator must know his data thoroughly in order to avoid errors of interpretation. He must be familiar, or become familiar, with all the relationships and theory which bear upon the data and should reach a conclusion based on logical reasoning and intelligent investigation on significantly related matters. However, the following general guidelines are given which would help in interpreting the value of r.

1. When $r = +1$, it means there is perfect positive correlation between the variables.

2. When $r = -1$, it means there is perfect negative correlation between the variables.

3. When $r = 0$, it means there is no correlation between the variables, *i.e.*, the variable are uncorrelated.

4. The closer r is to $+1$ or -1, the closer the relationship between the variables and the closer r is to 0, the less closer the relationship. Beyond this is not safe to go. The full interpretation of r depends upon circumstances, one of which is the size of the sample. All

that can really be said that when estimating the value of one variable from the value of another; the higher the value of r, the better the estimate.

5. The closeness of the relationship is not proportional to r. If the value of r is 0.8, it does not indicate a relationship twice as close as that of 0.4. Now when $r = 0.8$, $r^2 = .64 \Rightarrow$ the relationship explains 64% of variance of one variable because of other variable. And when $r = 0.4$, $r^2 = 0.16 \Rightarrow$ only 16% of variance is explained.

In case of $r = 0.8$, quite substantial variations are explained by the other variable whereas in case of $r = 0.4$, a very small variations of one variable are explained and as such $r = 0.4$ is very weak correlation.

7.9 RANK CORRELATION COEFFICIENT

The Karl Pearson's method is based on the assumption that the population being studied is normally distributed. When it is known that the population is not normal, or when the shape of the distribution is not known, there is need for a measure of correlation that involves no assumption about the parameters of the population.

It is possible to avoid making any assumption about the populations being studied by ranking the observations according to size and basing the calculations on the ranks rather than upon the original observations. It does not matter which way the items are ranked, item number one may be the largest or it may be the smallest. Using ranks rather than actual observations correlation in ranks is measured which is known as the coefficient of rank correlation.

This method of finding out covariability or the lack of it between two variables was developed by the British psychologist, Charles Edward Spearman in 1904. This measure is especially useful when quantitative measures for certain factors (such as in the evaluation of leadership ability or the judgment of female beauty) cannot be fixed, but the individuals in the group can be arranged in order thereby obtaining of each individual a number indicating his (her) rank in the group. Spearman's rank correlation coefficient is defined as:

$$R = 1 - \frac{6\sum D^2}{n^3 - n}$$

where R denotes rank coefficient of correlation and D refers to the difference of ranks between paired items in two series.

The value of this coefficient, interpreted in the same way as Karl Pearson's correlation coefficients, ranges between + 1 and – 1. When R is + 1 there is complete agreement in the order of the ranks and the ranks are in the same direction. When R is – 1 there is complete disagreement in the order of the ranks and they are in opposite direction. This shall be clear from the following:

R_1	R_2	D $(R_1 - R_2)$	D^2	R_1	R_2	D $(R_1 - R_2)$	D^2
1	1	0	0	1	3	– 2	4
2	2	0	0	2	2	0	0
3	3	0	0	3	1	2	4
			$\sum D^2 = 0$				$\sum D^2 = 8$

$$R = 1 - \frac{6\Sigma D^2}{n^3 - n} \qquad R = 1 - \frac{6\Sigma D^2}{n^3 - n}$$

$$= 1 - \frac{6 \times 0}{3^3 - 3} = 1 - 0 = 1 \qquad = 1 - \frac{6 \times 8}{3^3 - 3} = 1 - 2 = -1$$

[R_1 and R_2 indicated ranks in two groups]

7.9.1. Features of Spearman's Correlation Ceofficient

1. Spearman's correlation coefficient is distribution-free or non-parametric because no such assumptions are made about the form of population from which sample observations are drawn.

2. The Spearman's correlation coefficient is just like Karl Pearson's correlation coefficient between the ranks. Hence it can be interpreted in the same manner as Pearsonian correlation coefficient.

7.9.2. In rank correlation we may have three types of problems

A. Where ranks are given.
B. Where ranks are not given.
C. When ranks are equal.

A. Where ranks are given

Where actual ranks are given to us the steps required for computing rank correlation are:

(*i*) Take the difference of the two ranks, *i.e.*, $(R_1 - R_2)$ and denote these differences by D.
(*ii*) Square these differences and obtain the total ΣD^2.
(*iii*) Apply the formula

$$R = 1 - \frac{6\Sigma D^2}{n^3 - n}$$

Example 15. *Seven methods of imparting business education were ranked by the MBA students of two Universities as follows:*

Method of teaching	*I*	*II*	*III*	*IV*	*V*	*VI*	*VII*
Ranks by students of 'Univ. A'	2	1	5	3	4	7	6
Ranks by students of 'Univ. B'	1	3	2	4	7	5	6

Calculate rank correlation coefficient and comment on its value.

Solution. Let rank by students of Univ. A be denoted by R_A and that of Univ. B by R_B.

CALCULATION OF RANK CORRELATION COEFFICIENT

Method of Teaching	R_A	R_B	$(R_A - R_B)^2$ D^2
I	2	1	1
II	1	3	4
III	5	2	9
IV	3	4	1

V	4	7	9
VI	7	5	4
VII	6	6	0
			$\Sigma D^2 = 28$

$$R = 1 - \frac{6\Sigma D^2}{n^3 - n} = 1 - \frac{6 \times 28}{7^3 - 7} = 1 - 0.5 = 0.5$$

There is a moderate degree of positive correlation between the ranks given by students of Univ. *A* and Univ. *B*.

Example 16. *Two judges in a beauty competition rank the 12 entries as follows:*

X	*1*	*2*	*3*	*4*	*5*	*6*	*7*	*8*	*9*	*10*	*11*	*12*
Y	*12*	*9*	*6*	*10*	*3*	*5*	*4*	*7*	*8*	*2*	*11*	*1*

What degree of agreement is there between the judgments of the two judges?

Solution.

CALCULATION OF RANK CORRELATION COEFFICIENT

X R_1	Y R_2	$(R_1 - R_2)$ D	D^2
1	12	– 11	121
2	9	– 7	49
3	6	– 3	9
4	10	– 6	36
5	3	+ 2	4
6	5	+ 1	1
7	4	+ 3	9
8	7	+ 1	1
9	8	+ 1	1
10	2	+ 8	64
11	11	+ 0	0
12	1	+ 11	121
			$\Sigma D^2 = 416$

$$R = 1 - \frac{6\Sigma D^2}{n^3 - n}. \text{ Here } \Sigma D^2 = 416, N = 12.$$

Substituting the values, $R = 1 - \frac{6 \times 416}{12^3 - 12} = 1 - \frac{2496}{1716} = 1 - 1.454 = -0.454$

Since R is – ve ⇒ These is no agreement between judgements of the two judges.

Example 17. *Ten competitors in a beauty contest are ranked by three judges in the following order:*

1st Judge	*1*	*6*	*5*	*10*	*3*	*2*	*4*	*9*	*7*	*8*
2nd Judge	*3*	*5*	*8*	*4*	*7*	*10*	*2*	*1*	*6*	*9*
3rd Judge	*6*	*4*	*9*	*8*	*1*	*2*	*3*	*10*	*5*	*7*

Use the rank correlation coefficient to determine which pair of judges has the nearest approach to common tastes in beauty.

Solution. In order to find out which pair of judges has the nearest approach to common tastes in beauty we compare Rank Correlation between the judgements of :

(*i*) 1st Judge and 2nd Judge

(*ii*) 2nd Judge and 3rd Judge, and

(*iii*) 1st Judge and 3rd Judge.

COMPUTATION OF RANK CORRELATION

Rank by 1st Judge R_1	*Rank by 2nd Judge* R_2	*Rank by 3rd Judge* R_3	$(R_1 - R_2)^2$ D^2	$(R_2 - R_3)^2$ D^2	$(R_1 - R_3)$ D^2
1	3	6	4	9	25
6	5	4	1	1	4
5	8	9	9	1	16
10	4	8	36	16	4
3	7	1	16	36	4
2	10	2	64	64	0
4	2	3	4	1	1
9	1	10	64	81	1
7	6	5	1	1	4
8	9	7	1	4	1
$N = 10$			$\Sigma D^2 = 200$	$\Sigma D^2 = 214$	$\Sigma D^2 = 60$

Rank correlation between the judgements of 1st and 2nd Judges:

$$R = 1 - \frac{6\Sigma D^2}{n^3 - n}$$

$$\Sigma D^2 = 200, \; n = 10$$

Here we have directly calculated D^2 because D's are not required in applying the formula.

$$\therefore \underset{(I \text{ and } II)}{R} = 1 - \frac{6 \times 200}{10^3 - 10} = 1 - \frac{1200}{990} = 1 - 1.212 = -0.212$$

Rank correlation between the judgement of 2nd and 3rd judges :

$$\underset{(II \text{ and } III)}{R} = 1 - \frac{6\Sigma D^2}{n^3 - n}$$

$$\Sigma D^2 = 214, \; n = 10 \; \therefore R = 1 - \frac{6 \times 214}{10^3 - 10} = 1 - 1.297 = -0.297$$

Rank correlation between judgements of 1st and 3rd judges :

$$\underset{(I \text{ and } III)}{R} = 1 - \frac{6\Sigma D^2}{n^3 - n}$$

$$\Sigma D^2 = 60, n = 10$$

$$R = 1 - \frac{6 \times 60}{10^3 - 10} = 1 - \frac{360}{990} = 0.636.$$

Since coefficient of correlation is maximum in the judgement of the first and third judges, we conclude that they have the nearest approach to common tastes in beauty.

7.9.3. B. Where ranks are not given

When we are given the actual data and not the ranks, it will be necessary to assign the ranks. ranks can be assigned by taking either the highest value as 1 or the lowest value as 1. But whether we start with the lowest value or the highest value we must follow the same method in case of both the variables.

Example 18. *Calculate Spearman's coefficient of rank correlation for the following data:—*

X	*53*	*98*	*95*	*81*	*75*	*61*	*59*	*55*
Y	*47*	*25*	*32*	*37*	*30*	*40*	*39*	*45*

Solution.

CALCULATION OF RANK CORRELATION COEFFICIENT

X	R_1	Y	R_2	$(R_1 - R_2)^2$ D^2
53	1	47	8	49
98	8	25	1	49
95	7	32	3	16
81	6	37	4	4
75	5	30	2	9
61	4	40	6	4
59	3	39	5	4
55	2	45	7	25
				$\Sigma D^2 = 160$

$$R = 1 - \frac{6\Sigma D^2}{N^3 - N}; \Sigma D^2 = 160, N = 8$$

$$R = 1 - \frac{6 \times 160}{8^3 - 8} = 1 - \frac{960}{504} = 1 - 1.905 = -0.905$$

Example 19. *Calculate the coefficient of correlation from the following data by the Spearman's Rank difference method :*

Price of Tea (₹)	*Price of Coffee (₹)*	*Price of Tea (₹)*	*Price of Coffee (₹)*
75	*120*	*60*	*110*
88	*134*	*80*	*140*
95	*150*	*81*	*142*
70	*115*	*50*	*100*

Solution.

CALCULATION OF SPEARMAN'S CORRELATION COEFFICIENT

Price of Tea (₹)	R_1	*Price of Coffee* (₹)	R_2	$(R_1 - R_2)^2$ D^2
75	4	120	4	0
88	7	134	5	4
95	8	150	8	0
70	3	115	3	0
60	2	110	2	0
80	5	140	6	1
81	6	142	7	1
50	1	100	1	0
				$\Sigma D^2 = 6$

$$R = 1 - \frac{6\Sigma D^2}{N^3 - N} = 1 - \frac{6 \times 6}{8^3 - 8}$$

$$= 1 - \frac{36}{512 - 8} = 1 - 0.071 = +0.929$$

7.9.4. (*c*) Equal Ranks/tie in ranks

In some cases it may be found necessary to rank two or more individuals or entries as equal. In such a case it is customary to give each individual an average rank. Thus, if two individuals are ranked equal at fifth place, they are each given the rank $\frac{5+6}{2}$, that is 5.5, and the next item is given rank 7th. While if three are ranked at fifth place. They all are given the rank $\frac{5+6+7}{3} = 6$. And the next item will be assigned rank 8th. In other words, where two or more items are to be ranked equal, the rank assigned for purposes of calculating coefficient of correlation is the average of the ranks which these individuals would have got had they differed slightly from each other.

Where equal ranks are assigned to some entries an adjustment in the above formula for calculating the rank coefficient of correlation is made.

The adjustment consists of adding $\frac{1}{12}(m^3 - m)$ to the value of ΣD^2, where m stands for the number of items whose ranks are common. If there are more than one such group of items with common rank, this value is added as many times as the number of such groups. The formula can thus be written

$$R = 1 - \frac{6\left\{\Sigma D^2 + \frac{1}{12}(m^3 - m) + \frac{1}{12}(m^3 - m) + \cdots\right\}}{N^3 - N}$$

Example 20. *Obtain the rank correlation coefficient between the variables X and Y from the following pairs of observed values.*

X :	*50*	*55*	*65*	*50*	*55*	*60*	*50*	*65*	*70*	*75*
Y :	*110*	*110*	*115*	*125*	*140*	*115*	*130*	*120*	*115*	*160*

Solution. For finding ranks correlation coefficient first rank two various values. Taking lowest as 1 and next higher as 2, etc..

X	*Rank X* R_1	Y	*Rank Y* R_2	$(R_1 - R_2)^2$ D^2
50	2	110	1.5	0.25
55	4.5	110	1.5	9.00
65	7.5	115	4	12.25
50	2	125	7	25.00
55	4.5	140	9	20.25
60	6	115	4	4.00
50	2	130	8	36.00
65	7.5	120	6	2.25
70	9	115	4	25.00
75	10	160	10	00.00
				$\Sigma D^2 = 134$

It may be noted that in series X, 50 is repeated thrice ($m = 3$), 55 is repeated twice ($m = 2$), 65 has been repeated twice ($m = 2$). In series Y, 110 has been repeated twice ($m = 2$) and 115 is repeated thrice ($m = 3$)

$$R = 1 - \frac{6\left\{\Sigma D^2 + \frac{1}{12}(m^3 - m) + \frac{1}{12}(m^3 - m) + \frac{1}{12}(m^3 - m) + \frac{1}{12}(m^3 - m) + \frac{1}{12}(m^3 - m)\right\}}{N^3 - N}$$

$$R = 1 - \frac{6\left\{134 + \frac{1}{12}(3^3 - 3) + \frac{1}{12}(2^3 - 2) + \frac{1}{12}(2^3 - 2) + \frac{1}{12}(2^3 - 2) + \frac{1}{12}(3^3 - 3)\right\}}{10^3 - 10}$$

$$= 1 - \frac{6\,[134 + 2 + .5 + 5 + .5 + 2]}{990}$$

$$= 1 - \frac{6\,(139.5)}{990} = 1 - \frac{837}{990} = 1 - .845 = 0.155.$$

Example 21. *The coefficient of rank correlation of the marks obtained by 10 students in statistics accountancy was found to be 0.8. It was later discovered that the difference in ranks in the two subjects obtained by one of the student was wrongly taken as 7 instead of 9. Find the correct coefficient of rank correlation.*

Solution.

$$R = 1 - \frac{6\Sigma D^2}{N^3 - N}; \text{ Here, } R = 0.8, N = 10$$

$$0.8 = 1 - \frac{6\Sigma D^2}{10^3 - 10} = 1 - \frac{6\Sigma D^2}{990}$$

or $$\frac{6\Sigma D^2}{990} = 0.2$$

$$6\Sigma D^2 = 198 \qquad \therefore \Sigma D^2 = 33$$

But this is not correct ΣD^2

Correct $\Sigma D^2 = 33 - (7)^2 + (9)^2 = 33 - 49 + 81 = 65$

$$R = 1 - \frac{6 \times 65}{990} = 1 - \frac{390}{990} = 1 - 0.394 = 0.606$$

The correct value of the rank correlation coefficient in this case is 0-.606.

Example 22. *The coefficient of rank correlation between debenture prices and share prices is found to be 0.143. If the sum of squares of the differences in rank is given to be 48, find the value of N.*

Solution.
$$R = 1 - \frac{6\Sigma D^2}{N^3 - N}$$

where $R = 0.143, \Sigma D^2 = 48$

$$0.143 = 1 - \frac{6 \times 48}{N^3 - N}$$

$$\frac{288}{N^3 - N} = 0.857 \text{ or } 0.857\,(N^3 - N) = 288$$

$$(N^3 - N) = \frac{288}{0.857} = 336$$

$N^3 - N = N\,(N^2 - 1) = N\,(N - 1)\,(N + 1) = (N - 1)\,(N)\,(N + 1)$

which is product of 3 consecutive numbers hence we break 336 into 3 factors of consecutive numbers as $336 = 6 \times 7 \times 8$

$\Rightarrow (N - 1)\,N\,(N + 1) = 6 \times 7 \times 8$

$\Rightarrow N = 7.$

Example 23. In a question on correlation the value of r is .917 and its probable error is 0.034 What was the value of N ?

Solution.

$$P.E_r = 0.6745 \times \frac{1 - r^2}{\sqrt{N}}$$

We are given $P.E_r = 0.034$, $r = .917$

Substituting the values

$$.034 = 0.6745 \times \frac{1 - .841}{\sqrt{N}}$$

$$.034 = \frac{.6745 \times .159}{\sqrt{N}}$$

$$.034\sqrt{N} = .1072 \Rightarrow N = 10 = \text{no. of pairs.}$$

Example 24. *A student calculates the value of r as + 0.72 for a question comprising 5 pairs of observations and concludes that there is high degree of correlation between the variables. Do you justify his conclusion.*

Solution. The value of r can be interpreted by calculating probable error. If r is more than 6 times the probable error, it is considered significant.

$$PE_r = .6745 \times \frac{1 - r^2}{\sqrt{N}} = .6745 \times \frac{-1\,(.72)^2}{\sqrt{5}}$$

$$= \frac{6745 \times .4816}{2.236} = 0.145$$

$$\frac{r}{P.E_r} = \frac{.72}{0.145} = 4.97$$

Since r is less than 6 times the probable error it cannot be regarded as significant.

7.10 MERITS AND LIMITATIONS OF THE RANK METHOD

Merits 1. Where the data are of a qualitative nature like honesty, efficiency, intelligence, etc., this method can be used with great advantage. For example, the workers of two factories can be raked in order of efficiency and the degree of correlation established by applying the method.

2. This is the only method that can be used where we are given the ranks and not the actual data.

3. Even where actual data are given, rank method can be applied for ascertaining rough degree of correlation.

Limitation 1. This method cannot be used for finding out correlation in a grouped frequency distribution.

2. Where the number of observations exceed 30, the calculations become quite tedious and require a lot of time. Therefore, this method should not be applied where N is exceeding 30 unless we are given the ranks and not the actual values of the variable.

EXERCISE 7.1

1. The following table gives the distribution of the total population and those who are totally or partially blind among them. Find out if there is any relation between age and blindness.

Age (years)	:	0–10	10–20	20–30	30–40	40–50	50–60	60–70	70–80
No. of Persons ('000)	:	100	60	40	36	24	11	6	3
Blind	:	55	40	40	40	36	22	18	15

Hint. Here we shall find the correlation coefficient between age (X) and the numbed of blinds per lakh (Y) as given in the following table.

X	5	15	25	35	45	55	65	75
Y	55	67	100	111	150	200	300	500

[**Ans.** $r = 0.8982$.]

2. With the following data in 6 cities, calculate the coefficient of correlation by Pearson's method between the density of population and the death rate.

Cities	*Area in square miles*	*Population (in '000)*	*No. of deaths*
A	150	30	300
B	180	90	1440
C	100	40	560
D	60	42	840

E	120	72	1224
F	80	24	312

[**Hint.** Find r between, Density $= \frac{\text{Population}}{\text{Area}}$; and Death Rate $= \frac{\text{No. of deaths}}{\text{Population}} \times$ 1000.]

[**Ans.** $r = 0.9876$.]

3. The coefficient of rank correlation between marks in Statistics and marks in Mathematics obtained by a certain group of students is 0.8. If the sum of the squares of the differences in ranks is given to be 33, find the number of students in the group.

[**Ans.** $n = 10$.]

4. If the rank correlation coefficient is 0.6 and the sum of the squares of differences of ranks is 66, then the number of pairs is

(*i*) 8, (*ii*) 9, (*iii*) 10, (*iv*) 11.

[**Ans.** (*iii*).]

5. Coefficient of correlation between debenture prices and share prices is found to be 0.143. If the sum of the squares of differences in ranks is given to be 48, find the value of n.

[**Ans.** $n = 7$.]

6. The coefficient of rank correlation of the marks obtained by 10 students in biology and chemistry was found to be 0.8. It was later discovered that the difference in ranks in the two subjects obtained by one of the students was wrongly taken as 7 instead of 9. Find the correct value of coefficient of rank correlation.

[**And.** Correct value of $\rho = 0.6061$.]

7. The coefficient of rank correlation of the marks obtained by 10 students in Statistics and Accountancy was found to be 0.2. It was later discovered that the difference in ranks in the two subjects obtained by one of the student was wrongly taken as 9 instead of 7. Find the correct value of coefficient of rank correlation.

[**Ans.** Correct (ρ) = 0.3939.]

8. Mention the correct answer.

The ranks according to two attributes in a sample are given below :

R_1	:	1	2	3	4	5
R_2	:	5	4	3	2	1

The rank correlation between them is :

0, +1, –1, None of these.

[**Ans.** $\rho = -1$.]

9. The following data relate to the marks obtained by 10 student of a class in Statistics and Costing :

Marks in Statistics	:	30	38	28	27	28	23	30	33	28	35
Marks in Costing	:	29	27	22	29	20	29	18	21	27	22

Obtain the rank correlation coefficient.

[**Ans.** $\rho = -0.3515$.]

10. Find the coefficient of rank correlation between the marks obtained in Mathematics (x) and those in Statistics (y) by 10 students of certain class out of a total of 50 marks in each subject.

Students No. :	1	2	3	4	5	6	7	8	9	10
x :	12	18	32	18	25	24	25	40	38	22
y :	16	15	28	16	24	22	28	36	34	19

[**Ans.** $\rho = 0.95$.]

11. From the following data, calculate the coefficient of rank correlation between x and y.

x :	32	35	49	60	43	37	43	49	10	20
y :	40	30	70	20	30	50	72	60	45	25

[**Ans.** $\rho = -0.0758$.]

12. Calculate Spearman's coefficient of rank correlation for the following data :

X :	57	16	24	65	16	16	9	40	48	33
Y :	19	6	9	20	4	15	6	24	13	13

$$\left[\textbf{Ans. } \rho = 1 - \frac{6(41 + 2 + 0.5 + 0.5)}{10 \times 990} = 0.7333.\right]$$

13. The following are the marks obtained by a group of students in two papers. Calculate the rank coefficient of correlation.

Economics :	78	36	98	25	75	82	92	62	65	39
Statistics :	84	51	91	69	68	62	86	58	35	49

[**Ans.** $\rho = 0.6121$.]

14. Calculate Spearman's coefficient of rank correlation for the following data of scores in psychological tests (x) and arithmetical ability (y) of 10 children.

Child :	*A*	*B*	*C*	*D*	*E*	*F*	*G*	*H*	*I*	*J*
x :	105	104	102	101	100	99	98	96	93	92
y :	101	103	100	98	95	96	104	92	97	94

[**Ans.** $\rho = 0.6$.]

15. Calculate rank correlation coefficient between the two series X and Y, given below :

X :	70	65	71	62	58	69	78	64
Y :	91	76	65	83	90	64	55	48

Also comment on the result.

[**Ans.** $\rho = -0.3095$; X and Y are moderately negatively correlated.]

16. How do you modify Spearman's rank correlation formula for tied ranks ? Compute the Coefficient of Rank Correlation between X and Y from the data given below :

x :	8	10	7	15	3	20	21	5	10	14	8	16	22	19	6
y :	3	12	8	13	20	9	14	11	4	16	15	10	18	23	25

$$\left[\textbf{Ans. } \rho = 1 - \frac{6 \times (539 + 0.5 + 0.5)}{12 \times 224} = 0.0.357.\right]$$

17. You are given the following information relating to a frequency distribution comprising of 10 observations.

$\overline{X} = 5.5$, $\overline{Y} = 4.0$, $\Sigma X^2 = 385$, $\Sigma Y^2 = 192$ $\Sigma(X + Y)^2 = 947$.

Find r_{XY}.

[Hint. Use $\Sigma(X + Y)^2 = \Sigma X^2 + \Sigma Y^2 + 2\,\Sigma XY$ and find $\Sigma XY = 185$.

[Ans. $r(X, Y) = -0.681$.]

18. A computer while calculating the correlation coefficient between the variables X and Y obtained the following results :

$N = 30, \Sigma X = 120, \Sigma X^2 = 600, \Sigma Y = 90, \Sigma Y^2 = 250, \Sigma XY = 356$

It was, however, later discovered at the time of checking that it had copied down two pairs of observations as :

X	Y		X	Y
8	10	while the correct values were,	8	12
12	7		10	8

Obtain the correct value of the correlation coefficient between X and Y.

[Ans. $r = 0.149$]

19. From the following data, compute the coefficient of correlation between X and Y :

	X series	*Y series*
Arithmetic Mean	15	28
Sum of squares of deviations from Arithmetic mean	144	225

Summation of products of deviations of x and y series from their respective means = 20, Number of pairs = 10.

[$r = 0.11$]

20. Calculate Karl Pearson's coefficient of correlation between imports and exports from the data given below:

Imports :	42	44	58	55	89	98	66
Exports :	56	49	53	58	65	76	58

[$r = 0.9094$]

21. Find correlation coefficient between 2 variables as under.

Year	*1995*	*1996*	*1997*	*1998*	*1999*	*2000*	*2001*	*202*	*2003*	*2004*	*2005*
Index of Money in Circulation	110	120	125	128	132	140	145	148	150	152	154
Index of cost of living	105	108	110	112	108	130	130	132	134	135	136

[$r = 0.92$]

22. (*a*) The coefficient of rank correlation of a bivariate data is 1. Does it imply perfect correlation between the variables? Give reasons for your answer.

(*b*) If the product moment coefficient of correlation is 0, does it mean that the variances are independent?

23. Seven methods of imparting business education were ranked by the M.A. students of two universities as follows:

Method of teaching	I	II	III	IV	V	VI	VII
Rank by students of Univ. '*A*'	2	1	5	3	4	7	6
Rank by students of Univ. '*B*'	1	3	2	4	7	5	6

Calculate rank correlation co-efficient and comment on its value.

[+ 0. 5]

24. Calculate coefficient of correlation between *X* and *Y* series from the following data:

	Series	
	X	*Y*
No. of observations	15	15
Mean	25	18
Square of deviations from mean	136	138
Summation of product deviations of *X* and *Y* series from their means	122	

[$r = 0.891$]

25. (*a*) Calculate the number or items for which $r = 0.5$, $\Sigma xy = 60$, $\sigma_y = 4$ and $\Sigma x^2 = 90$, where x and y denote deviation from respective means.

(*b*) The coefficient of correlation between two varieties *X* and *Y* is 0.42. Their covariance is 10.5. The variance of *X* is 16, find the standard deviation of *Y* series.

(*c*) If covariance between *X* and *Y* variables is 18.6 and variances of *X* and *Y* are respectively 20.2 and 23.7, find the coefficient of correlation between them.

[(*a*) $N = 10$, (*b*) $\sigma_y = 6.25$, (*c*) $r = 0.85$]

26. Ten competitors in a beauty contest are ranked by three judges as follows :

		Competitors									
Judges	:	1	2	3	4	5	6	7	8	9	10
A	:	6	5	3	10	2	4	9	7	8	1
B	:	5	8	4	7	10	2	1	6	9	3
C	:	4	9	8	1	2	3	10	5	7	6

Discuss which pair of judges has the nearest approach to common tastes of beauty.

[**Ans.** $\rho_{ab} = \rho_{ac} = 0.04$, $\rho_{bc} = -0.3$]

Pair of judges *A* and *B* or *A* and *C* have the nearest approach to common tastes in beauty.]

27. Quotations of index number of equity share prices of a certain joint stock company and of prices of preference shares are given below:

Years	:	1991	1992	1993	1994	1995	1996	1997
Equity Shares	:	97.5	99.4	98.6	96.2	95.1	98.4	97.1
Preference Shares	:	75.1	75.9	77.1	78.2	79.0	74.8	76.2

Use the method of rank correlation to determine the relationship between equity share and preference share prices.

[Ans. $\rho = -0.6071$.]

28. For the following data, calculate the Coefficient of Rank Correlation.

x	:	80	91	99	71	61	81	70	59
y	:	123	135	154	110	105	134	121	106

[Ans. $\rho = 0.9524$.]

29. From the data given below, calculate the coefficient of rank correlation between X and Y:

X	:	78	89	97	69	59	79	68	57
Y	:	125	137	156	112	107	136	123	108

[Ans. $\rho = 09524$.]

□□□

8

Regression Analysis

CHAPTER OUTLINE

- Regression and Correlation
- Linear Regression Equations, Regression Lines
- Properties of Regression Lines
- Properties of Regression Coefficients
- Standard Error of Estimate

INTRODUCTION

After having established the fact that two variables are closely related, we may be interested in estimating (predicting) the value of one variable given the value of another. For example, if we know that advertising and sales are correlated, we may find out the expected amount of sales for a given advertising expenditure or the required amount of expenditure for achieving a fixed sales target. *The statistical tool with the help of which we are in a position to estimate (or predict) the unknown values of one variable from known values of another variable through a mathematical function is called* **regression.** With the help of regression analysis, we are in a position to find out the *average probable* change in one variable given a certain amount of change in another.

The dictionary meaning of the term 'regression' is the act of returning or going back. The term 'regression' was first used in 1877 by Francis Galton while studying the relationship between the height of fathers and sons. His study of heights of about one thousand fathers and sons revealed a very interesting relationship, *i.e.,* tall fathers tend to have tall sons and short fathers, short sons; but the average height of the sons of a group of tall fathers is less than that of the tall fathers and the average height of the sons of a group of short fathers is greater than that of the short fathers. The line describing this tendency to regress or going back was called by Galton a 'Regression Line'. The term is still used to describe that line drawn for a group of points to represent the trend present, but it no longer necessarily carries the original implication that Galton intended. These days there is a growing tendency of the modern writers to use the term *estimating line or predicting line* instead of *regression line.*

Regression analysis is a branch of statistical theory that is widely used in almost all the scientific disciplines. In economics it is the basic technique for measuring or estimating the relationship among economic variables that constitute the essence of economic theory and economic life. For example, if we know that two variables price (X) and demand (Y) are closely related we can find out the most probable value of X for a given value of Y or the most probable value of Y for a given value of X. Similarly, if we know that the amount of tax and the rise in the price of a commodity are closely related, we can find out the expected price for a certain amount of tax levy. The regression analysis helps in three important ways:

1. It provides estimates of values of the dependent variables form values of independent variables. The device used to accomplish the estimation procedure is the regression which describes the average relationship existing between X and Y variables.

2. The second goal of regression analysis is to obtain a measure of the error involved in using the regression line as a basis for estimations. For this purpose, the standard error of estimate is calculated. If the line fits the data closely, that is, if there is relatively little scatter of the observations around the regression line, good estimate can be made of Y variable. On the other hand, if there is a great deal of scatter of the observations around the fitted regression line, the line will not produce accurate estimates of the dependent variable.

3. With the help of regression analysis, we can obtain a measure of the degree of association or correlation that exists between the two variables. The coefficient of determination calculated for this purpose measures the strength of the relationship that exists between the variables. It assesses the proportion of variance that has been accounted for by the regression equation.

The tool of regression analysis can be extended to three or more variables. But in this text we shall confine ourselves to the problems of two variables only, *i.e.,* simple regression.

8.1. Difference between Correlation and Regression Analysis

There are two important points of difference between correlation and regression analysis:

1. Whereas correlation coefficient is a measure of degree of relationship between X and Y, the objective of regression analysis is to study the *'nature of relationship'* between the variables.

2. The cause and effect relation is clearly indicated through regression analysis than by correlation. Correlation is merely a tool of ascertaining the degree of relationship between two variables and, there fore, we cannot say that one variable is the cause and the other the effect.

8.2. Regression Equations

If we take the case of two variables we shall have two regression relations as the regression equation of X on Y and regression equation of Y on X. The regression equation of Y on X gives the most probable values of Y for given values of X and same way, the regression equation of X on Y gives the most probable value of X for given value of Y. The regression written as $Y = f(x)$ gives value of Y for a given value of X. X is independent variable and Y is dependent variable. Such relations re called regression of Y on X. Similarly $X = f(y)$ relations are called regression of X on Y.

Some examples of regressions equations are :

Y on X	X on Y
1. Linear Equation $Y = a + bX$ (example $Y = 20 + 2X$)	1. $X = a + bY$ [e.g. $X = 30 - 2y$]
2. Quadratic equation $Y = a + bX + cX^2$ [e.g. $Y = 20 + 2X - 2X^2$)	2. $X = a + bY + cY^2$ [e.g. $X = 30 + 3Y + 2Y^2$]
3. Exponential equation $Y = a\,b^X$ [e.g., $Y = 3(2.1)^X$]	3. $X = ab^Y$ e.g. $X = 2(5^Y)$

8.2.1. Use of regression equation

Regression equation is used to find most probable value of an unknown variable (called dependent variable) for a given value of another variable (called independent variable). *e.g.* if value of Y is to be found out for a given X then we use Y on X regression equation (X is independent & Y is dependent) and Y is obtained by substituting that value of X in that regression equation. *e.g.*, if we required to find Y when $X = 5$ and assume that regression equation of Y on X is

$$Y = 20 + 3x - X^2 \text{ then}$$

$$\hat{Y}(x = 5) = 20 + 3(5) - (5)^2 = 10$$

Value of Y obtained from regression equation is also referred as estimated value of Y and is denoted by $\hat{Y}$ (Y – cap) or Y_e.

8.3. LINEAR AND NON-LINEAR REGRESSION

If the given bivariate data are plotted on a graph, the points so obtained on the scatter diagram will more or less concentrate round a curve, called the '*curve of regression*'. Often such a curve is not distinct and is quite confusing and sometimes complicated too. The mathematical equation of the regression curve, usually called the *regression equation,* enables us to study the average change in the value of the dependent variable for any given value of the independent variable.

If the regression curve is a straight line, we say that there is *linear regression* between the variables under study. The equation of such a curve is the equation of a straight line, *i.e.,* a first degree equation in the variables x and y. In case of linear regression the values of the dependent variable increase by a constant absolute amount for a unit change in the value of the independent variable. However, if the curve of regression is not a straight line, the regression is termed as *curved or non-linear regression.* The regression equation will be a functional relation between x and y involving terms in x and y of degree higher than one. *i.e.,* involving terms of the type x^2, y^2, xy, etc. However, in this chapter we shall confine our discussion to linear regression between two variables only.

8.4. LINES OF REGRESSION/LINEAR REGRESSION EQUATIONS

Line of regression is the line which gives the best estimate of one variable for any given value of the other variable. In case of two variables x and y, we shall have two lines of regression; one of y on x and the other of x on y.

Definition. *Line of regression of y on x is the line which gives the best estimate for the value of y for any specified value of x.*

Similarly, *line of regression of x on y is the line which gives the best estimate for the value of x for any specified value of y.*

The two liens of regression are (*a*) Y on X and (*b*) X on Y.

8.4.1 (*a*) Regression Equation of *Y* on *X*

The regression equation of Y on X is expressed as follows :

$$Y_e = a + bX$$

Where Y_e is the dependent variable to be estimated for the independent variable.

In this equation a and b are two unknown constants (fixed numerical values) which determine the position of the line completely. The constants are called the parameters of the line. If the value of either or both of them is changed, another line is determined. The parameter 'a' determines the *level* of the fitted line (*i.e.*, the distance of the line directly above or below the origin). The parameter 'b' determines the *slope* of the line, *i.e.*, the change in Y per unit change in X.

If the values of the constants 'a' and 'b' are obtained, the line is completely determined. But the question is how to obtain these values. The answer is provided by the *method of least squares method which is explained in a section later.*

The average relationship between X and Y can be adequately described by a linear equation $Y = a + bX$ whose geometrical presentation is a straight line as in the diagram that follows :

As is clear form the above diagram, the height of the line tells the average value of Y at a fixed value of X. When $X = 0$, the average value of Y is equal to a. The value of a is called the Y intercept, since it is the point at which the straight line crosses the Y-axis. The slope of the line is measured by b, which gives the average amount of change of Y per unit change in the value of X. The sign of b also indicates the type of relationship between Y and X.

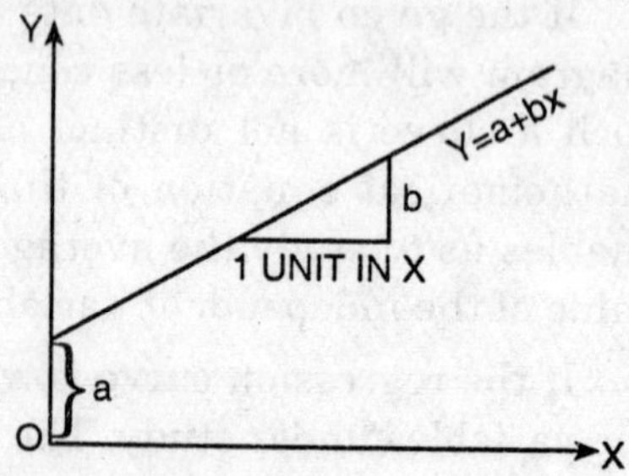

8.4.2(*b*) Regression equation of X on Y

Regression equation is of the type

$$X = a + bY$$

In this case x-intercept is a, *i.e.*, the line cuts X-axis at a distance if a from origin or the value of X is a when $Y = 0$ and b *gives average change* in X per unit change in the value of Y. Graphically the relation is represented below.

In this case $OA = a = x$-intercept (*i.e.*, value of X when $Y = O$) and each unit of Y (= BC) X on average changes by b units (= DC). Again a and b are two parameters which determines the position of straight line. In this case slope of straight line is $\frac{1}{b}$ (as defined by co-ordinate geometry)

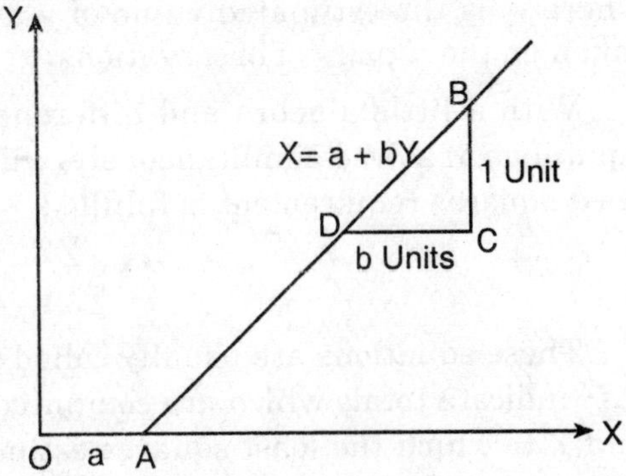

Least Square Method

For determination of parameters a and b of a linear recession, we use least square method.

8.5 "LEAST SQUARE METHOD" WHICH IS EXPLAINED AS UNDER

Observed Values	
X	Y
x_1	y_1
x_2	y_2
⋮	⋮
x_n	y_n

Let $(x_1, y_1), (x_2, y_2), \ldots, (x_n, x_n)$, be n pairs of observations on the two variables x and y under study.

And let $$y = a + bx \qquad \ldots(1)$$

be the line of regression (best fit) of y on x.

For any given point P_i (x_i, y_i,) in the scatter diagram, the error of estimate or residual as given by the line of best fit is $P_i H_i$. Now, the x-coordinate of H_i is same as that of P_i, *viz.*, x_i and since H_i (x_i) lies on the line (1), the y-coordinate of H_i, *i.e.*, $H_i M$ is given by ($a + bx_i$). Hence, the error of estimate of P_i is given by

$$P_i H_i = P_i M - H_i M$$
$$= y_i - (a + bx_i)$$

This is the error (parallel to the y-axis) for the i th point. We will have such errors for all the points on scatter diagram. For the points which lie above the line, the error would be positive and for the points which lie below the line, the error would be negative.

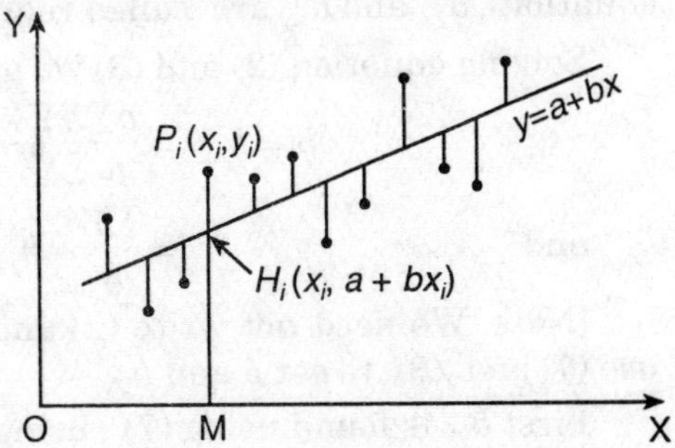

Fig. 1

Since Y_i is observed value for a given x_i, as obtained, and estimated value y_{ei} from the relation $y = a + bx$ is $a + b\,x_i$. The difference between the two *i.e.*, y_{ei} and y_i is the error of estimation. Criteria applied to make the error small is that find a, b of the relation $y = a + bx$. Such that sum of squares of errors is least. This method used to determine a and b (or to find the straight line of best fit) is known as "Least Square Method".

According to the principle of least squares, we have to determine the constants a and b in (1) so that the sum of the squares of the errors of estimates is minimum. In other words, we have to minimise

$$E = \sum_{i=1}^{n} P_i H_i^2 = \sum_{i=1}^{n} (y_i - a - bx_i)^2$$

subject to variations in a and b.

We may also write E as :

$$E = \Sigma(y - y_e)^2 = \Sigma(y - a - bx)^2 \quad ...(1)$$

where y_e is the estimated value of y as given by for given value of x and summation (Σ) is taken on the n pairs of observations.

With a little algebra and differential calculus, it can be shown that the following two equations, if solved simultaneously, will yield values of the parameters a and b such that the least squares requirement is fulfilled.

$$\Sigma Y = na + b\Sigma X \quad ...(2)$$

$$\Sigma XY = a\Sigma X + b\Sigma X^2 \quad ...(3)$$

These equations are usually called the *normal equations.* In the equations $\Sigma X, \Sigma Y, \Sigma XY, \Sigma X^2$ indicate totals which are computed from the observed pairs of values of two variables X and Y to which the least squares estimating line is to be fitted and n is the total number of observed pairs of values.

(B) Regression Equation of *X* on *Y*

The regression equation of X on Y is expressed as follows:

$$X = a + bY \qquad = a + b_{xy}\, Y \quad ...(4)$$

To determine the values of a and b the following two normal equations are to be solved simultaneously :

$$\Sigma Y = na + b\Sigma Y \quad ...(5)$$

$$\Sigma XY = a\Sigma X + b\Sigma Y^2 \quad ...(6)$$

[Note : a and b of relation (1) and (4) are not the same. Some time we distinguish two b's by expressing them as b_{yx} (b of Y on X regression equation) and b_{xy} (b of X on Y regression equation), b_{yx} and b_{xy} are called regression coefficients.]

Solving equation (2) and (3) we get

$$b = b_{yx} = \frac{n\Sigma XY - \Sigma X\,\Sigma Y}{n\,\Sigma X^2 - (\Sigma X)^2} \quad ...(7)$$

and

$$a = \frac{\Sigma Y}{n} - b_{yx}\frac{\Sigma X}{n} = \overline{Y} - b_{yx}\,\overline{X} \quad ...(8)$$

[Note. We need not write (2) and (3) and then solve for a & b (or b_{yx}), instead directly use (7) and (8) to get a and b_{yx}.

First b_{yx} is found using (7) , using this value of b_{yx} in (8) we get a].

Similarly if we are getting regression equation of X on Y similar relations are found just by interchange of Y and X in all relations found for Y on X.

For example

Y on *X*	*X* on *Y*
$Y = a + bX$	$X = a + bY$
normal equations	
$\Sigma Y = na + b\Sigma X$ $\Sigma XY = a\,\Sigma X + b\Sigma X^2$	$\Sigma X = na + b\Sigma Y$ $\Sigma XY = a\,\Sigma Y + b\,\Sigma Y^2$
$b_{yx} = \frac{n\,\Sigma XY - \Sigma X\,\Sigma Y}{n\,\Sigma X^2 - (\Sigma X)^2}$	$b_{xy} = \frac{n\Sigma XY - \Sigma X\,\Sigma Y}{n\,\Sigma Y^2 - (\Sigma Y)^2}$
$a = \overline{Y} - b_{yx}\,\overline{X}$	$a = \overline{X} - b_{xy}\,\overline{Y}$

Example 1. *Calculate the regression equations of X on Y and Y on X from the following data :*

X	:	*1*	*2*	*3*	*4*	*5*
Y	:	*2*	*5*	*3*	*8*	*7*

Solution. CALCULATION OF REGRESSION EQUATIONS

X	Y	X^2	Y^2	XY
1	2	1	4	2
2	5	4	25	10
3	3	9	9	9
4	8	16	64	32
5	7	25	49	35
$\Sigma X = 15$	$\Sigma Y = 25$	$\Sigma X^2 = 55$	$\Sigma Y^2 = 151$	$\Sigma XY = 88$

Y on *X*

$$\left[\begin{array}{l}\Sigma Y = na + b\Sigma X \\ \Sigma XY = a\Sigma X + b\Sigma X^2\end{array}\right.$$

i.e.,

$$\left[\begin{array}{l}25 = 5a + 5b \\ 88 = 15a + 55b\end{array}\right.$$

Solving

$$\text{or} \left[\begin{array}{l}75 = 15a = 15b \\ 88 = 15a = 55b\end{array}\right.$$

Which gives

$b = 1.3, a = 1.1$

or

$$b_{yx} = \frac{n\Sigma XY - \Sigma X\,\Sigma Y}{n\Sigma X^2 - (\Sigma X)^2}$$

$$= \frac{5(88) - 15\,(25)}{5\,(55) - (15)^2}$$

$$= \frac{65}{50}$$

$$= 1.3$$

$$a = \frac{\Sigma Y}{n} - b\,\frac{\Sigma X}{n}$$

$$= \frac{25}{5} - 1.3\left(\frac{15}{5}\right)$$

$$= 1.1$$

X on *Y*

$$\Sigma X = na + b\Sigma Y$$

$$\Sigma XY = a\,\Sigma Y + b\Sigma Y^2$$

i.e.,

$$15 = 5a + 25b$$

$$88 = 25a = 151b$$

$$\left[\begin{array}{l}75 = 25a + 125b \\ 88 = 25a + 151\,b\end{array}\right.$$

which gives

$b = 0.5, a = 0.5$

or

$$b_{xy} = \frac{n\Sigma XY - \Sigma X\,\Sigma Y}{n\,\Sigma Y^2 - (\Sigma Y)^2}$$

$$= \frac{5(88) - 15(25)}{5\,(151) - 15\,(25)^2}$$

$$= \frac{65}{130}$$

$$= 0.5$$

$$a = \frac{\Sigma X}{n} - b\,\frac{\Sigma Y}{n}$$

$$= \frac{15}{5} - 0.5\,\frac{25}{5}$$

$$= 3 - 2.5$$

$$= 0.5$$

Thus, $Y = a + bX$	$X = a + bY$
$= 1.1 + 1.3\,X$	$= 0.5 + 0.5\,Y.$

Example 2. *Obtain the two regression equations for X and Y from the following data:*

X	:	*10*	*9*	*7*	*8*	*11*
Y	:	*6*	*3*	*2*	*4*	*5*

Solution.

CALCULATION TABLE

X	Y	XY	X^2	Y^2
10	6	60	100	36
9	3	27	81	9
7	2	14	49	4
8	4	32	64	16
11	5	55	121	25
45	20	188	415	90

(*a*) Regression of *Y* on *X*

$$b_{yx} = \frac{n\,\Sigma XY - (\Sigma X)(\Sigma Y)}{n\Sigma X^2 - (\Sigma X)^2} = \frac{5 \times 188 - 45 \times 20}{5 \times 415 - (45)^2} = 0.8$$

Also, $\overline{X} = \frac{45}{5} = 9$ and $\overline{Y} = \frac{20}{5} = 4$

Now $a = \overline{Y} - b\overline{X} = 4 - 0.8 \times 9 = -3.2$

$\therefore$ Regression of *Y* on *X* is $Y_C = 3.2 + 0.8X$

(*b*) Regression of *X* on *Y*

$$b_{xy} = \frac{n\Sigma XY - (\Sigma X)(\Sigma Y)}{n\Sigma Y^2 - (\Sigma Y)^2} = \frac{5 \times 188 - 45 \times 20}{5 \times 90 - (20)^2}$$

Also, $a = \overline{X} - \overline{Y} = 9 - 0.8 \times 4 = 5.8$

$\therefore$ The regression of *X* on *Y* is $X_C = 5.8 + 0.8Y$

8.5.1. Short-cut Method

In case we use d_x or $u = X - A$ and dy or $v = Y - B$, in that it can be established (Proof omitted)

that $b_{yx} = b_{vu}$

i.e., $$b_{yx} = \frac{n\Sigma XY - \Sigma X\,\Sigma Y}{n\Sigma X^2 - (\Sigma X)^2} = \frac{n\,(uv) - \Sigma\,u\,\Sigma v}{n\,\Sigma\,u^2 - (\Sigma u)^2}$$

however $a = \overline{Y} - b_{yx}\,\overline{X}$

Same way for *X* on *Y* $$b_{xy} = \frac{n\,\Sigma XY - \Sigma X\,\Sigma Y}{n\,\Sigma Y^2 - (\Sigma Y)^2} = \frac{n\,\Sigma uv - \Sigma u\,\Sigma v}{n\,\Sigma v^2 - (\Sigma v)^2}$$

and $a = \overline{X} - b_{xy}\,\overline{Y}$

Example 3. *From the data given below, find:*

(a) The two regression equations.

(b) The most likely marks in statistics when marks in economics are 30.

Marks in Eco.	:	25	28	35	32	31	36	29	38	34	32
Marks in Stat.	:	43	46	49	41	36	32	31	30	33	39

Solution.

Marks in Eco. (*X*)	*Marks in Stat.* (*Y*)	$u = X - 31$	$v = Y - 41$	uv	u^2	v^2
25	43	– 6	2	– 12	36	4
28	46	– 3	5	– 15	9	25
35	49	4	8	32	16	64
32	41	1	0	0	1	0
31	36	0	– 5	0	0	25
36	32	5	– 9	– 45	25	81
29	31	– 2	– 10	20	4	100
38	30	7	– 11	– 77	49	121
34	33	4	– 8	– 24	9	64
32	39	1	– 2	– 2	1	4
Total		10	– 30	– 123	150	488

From the table, we have

$$\overline{X} = 31 + \frac{10}{10} = 32 \text{ and } \overline{Y} = 41 - \frac{30}{10} = 38 \quad \left[\overline{X} = A + \frac{\Sigma dx}{n}\right]$$

(*a*) The lines of regression

(*i*) Regression of *Y* on *X*

$$b = \frac{n \Sigma uv - (\Sigma u)(\Sigma v)}{n \Sigma u^2 - (\Sigma u)^2} = \frac{-1230 + 330}{1500 - 100} = -0.64$$

$$a = \overline{Y} - b\overline{X} = 38 + 0.64 \times 32 = 59.26$$

∴ Regression equation is

$$Y_C = 59.26 - 0.66X$$

(*ii*) Regression of *X* on *Y*

$$b_{xy} = \frac{n \Sigma uv - (\Sigma u)(\Sigma v)}{n \Sigma v^2 - (\Sigma v)^2} = \frac{-1230 + 300}{4880 - 900} = -0.23$$

$$a = \overline{X} - b_{xy}\overline{Y} = 32 + 0.23 \times 38 = 40.88$$

∴ Regression equation is (*X* on *Y*)

$$X_C = 40.88 - 0.23Y$$

(*iii*) Marks in Economics = 30 = *X*, we need find marks in Stats. (*i.e.*, *Y*). This is obtained by using *Y* on *X*.

$$Y_e = 59.26 - 0.66X$$

When $X = 30$, $Y_C = 59.26 - 0.64\ (30)$

$$= 40$$

8.6. OTHER FORM OF REGRESSION EQUATIONS

we have

$$Y = a + bX \qquad [Y \text{ on } X]$$

$$Y = \overline{Y} - b\overline{X} + bX \qquad [\text{as } a = \overline{Y} - b\,\overline{X}]$$

$$\Rightarrow \quad Y - \overline{Y} = b_{yx}(X - \overline{X}) \qquad \text{...(9)}$$

Thus one can write the regression equation without finding a.

Also

$$b_{yx} = \frac{n\Sigma XY - \Sigma X \Sigma Y}{n\Sigma X^2 - (\Sigma X)^2}$$

$$= \frac{\frac{\Sigma XY}{n} - \frac{\Sigma X}{n}\frac{\Sigma Y}{n}}{\frac{\Sigma X^2}{n} - \left(\frac{\Sigma X}{n}\right)^2} \quad [\text{dividing each term by } n^2] \qquad \text{...(10)}$$

$$= \frac{\frac{\Sigma(X-\overline{X})(Y-\overline{Y})}{n}}{\frac{\Sigma(X-\overline{X})^2}{n}} \qquad \text{...(11)}$$

$$= \frac{\Sigma(X-\overline{X})(Y-\overline{Y})}{\Sigma(X-\overline{X})^2} = \frac{\Sigma xy}{\Sigma x^2} \qquad \text{...(12)}$$

$$[\text{where } x = X - \overline{X},\ y = Y - \overline{Y}]$$

We have established $\frac{\Sigma(X-\overline{X})^2}{n} = \frac{\Sigma X^2}{n} - \left(\frac{\Sigma X}{n}\right)^2$

and $\frac{\Sigma(X-\overline{X})(Y-\overline{Y})}{n} = \frac{\Sigma XY}{n} - \frac{\Sigma X}{n}\frac{\Sigma Y}{n}$

The same way if it is X on Y then from (9) we get

$$X - \overline{X} = b_{xy}(Y - \overline{Y}) \qquad [\text{by interchanging } X \text{ and } Y] \qquad \text{...(13)}$$

Thus two regression equations are

$$Y - \overline{Y} = b_{yx}(X - \overline{X}) \text{ .... } Y \text{ on } X$$

$$X - \overline{X} = b_{xy}(Y - \overline{Y}) \text{ .... } X \text{ on } Y.$$

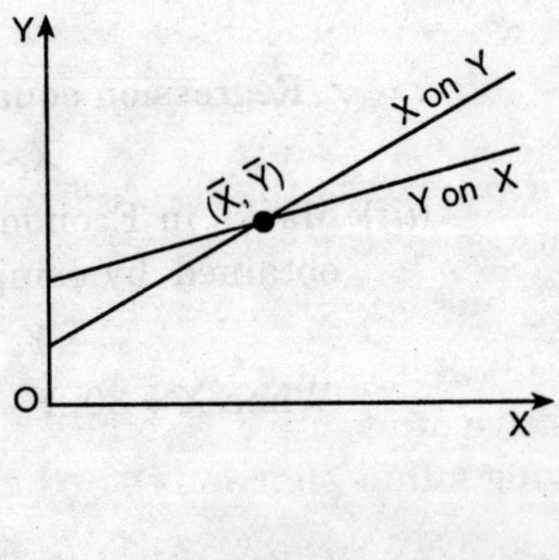

Further (9) and (13) indicate that both the regression lines pass through the point $(X = \overline{X}, Y = \overline{Y})$ *i.e.*, $(\overline{X}, \overline{Y})$ [as $X = \overline{X}$ and $Y = \overline{Y}$ satisfy both the equations].

This property is depicted in attached figures, the point of intersection of two regression lines is $(\overline{X}, \overline{Y})$. Thus $\overline{X}$ and $\overline{Y}$ can be obtained by solving the two equations.

8.7. PROPERTIES OF REGRESSION COEFFICIENTS

We had established that in (11)

$$b_{yx} = \frac{\frac{\Sigma (x-\overline{X})(Y-\overline{Y})}{n}}{\frac{\Sigma (X-\overline{X})^2}{n}}$$

$$= \frac{\text{Cov. }(X, Y)}{\sigma_x^2} \quad \text{[already defined]} \quad \text{...(14)}$$

$$= \frac{\text{Cov. }(X, Y)}{\sigma_x \sigma_y} \frac{\sigma_y}{\sigma_x} \quad \text{[writing (14) in other form]}$$

$$b_{yx} = r \frac{\sigma_y}{\sigma_x} \quad \text{...(15)}$$

Same way $b_{xy} = r \frac{\sigma_x}{\sigma_y}$ [interchanging X and Y) ...(16)

Thus we have $b_{yx}\, b_{xy} = r \frac{\sigma_y}{\sigma_x} r \frac{\sigma_y}{\sigma_x}$ *i.e.*, $b_{yx}\, b_{xy} = r^2$ ...(17)

We also know that $-1 \le r \le 1$

$\Rightarrow$ $0 \le r^2 \le 1$ [r^2 cannot be – ve and it have to less than 1]

$\Rightarrow$ $0 \le b_{yx}\, b_{xy} \le 1$

Thus b_{xy} and b_{xy} both have same signs and also

$b_{xy}\, b_{xy} \le 1$ [Thus both b_{yx} and b_{xy} cannot be greater than 1]

Also $b_{yx} = r \frac{\sigma_y}{\sigma_x}$, $b_{xy} = r \frac{\sigma_x}{\sigma_y}$

Now σ_x and σ_y cannot be – ve, hence b_{yx}, b_{xy} and r all have same sign.

Thus $r = \pm \sqrt{b_{yx}\, b_{xy}}$ from (17)

[It will have + ve sign if b_{yx} and b_{xy} both are + ve and

It will have – ve sign if b_{yx} and b_{xy} both are – ve]

The results are summarised as follows.

Properties of the Regression Coefficients

(1) The coefficient of correlation is the geometric mean of the two regression coefficients. Symbolically :

$$r = \pm \sqrt{b_{xy} \times b_{yx}}$$

Proof. $b_{xy} = r \frac{\sigma_x}{\sigma_y}$; $b_{yx} = r \frac{\sigma_y}{\sigma_x}$

$\therefore$ $b_{xy} \times b_{yx} = r \frac{\sigma_x}{\sigma_y} \times r \frac{\sigma_y}{\sigma_x} = r^2.$

(2) If one of the regression coefficients is greater than unity, the other must be less than unity, since the value of the coefficient of correlation cannot exceed unity. For example, if b_{xy} = 1.2 and b_{yx} = 1.4, r would be $\sqrt{1.2 \times 1.4}$ = 1.29 which is not possible.

(3) Both the regression coefficients will have the same sign, *i.e.*, they will be either positive or negative. In other words, it is not possible that one of the regression coefficients is having minus sign and the other plus sign.

(4) The coefficient of correlation will have the same sign as that of regression coefficients, *i.e.*, if regression coefficients have a negative sign, r will also have negative sign and if the regression coefficients have a positive sign, r would also be positive. For example,

if $b_{xy} = -0.2$ and $b_{yx} = -0.8$

$$r = -\sqrt{0.2 \times 0.8} = -0.4$$

(5) The average value of the two regression coefficients would be greater than the value of coefficient of correlation. In symbols $(b_{xy} + b_{yx})/2 > r$. For example, if $b_{xy} = 0.8$ and $b_{yx} = 0.4$, the average of the two values would be $(0.8 + 0.4)/2 = 0.6$ and the value of r would be \r(0.8 × 0.4) = 0.566 which is less than 0.6.

(6) Regression coefficients are independent of change of origin but not scale without proof.

Example 4. *On the basis of figures recorded below for 'Supply' and 'Price' for nine years, calculate the regression coefficients and the value of r :*

Year	:	*1995*	*1996*	*1997*	*1998*	*1999*	*2000*	*2001*	*2002*	*2003*
Supply	:	*80*	*82*	*86*	*91*	*83*	*85*	*89*	*96*	*93*
Price	:	*145*	*140*	*130*	*124*	*133*	*127*	*120*	*110*	*116*

Solution. Let the price be denoted by Y and supply by X.

CALCULATION OF REGRESSION COEFFICIENTS

Year	*Supply* X	$(X–90)$ d_x	d_x^2	*Price* Y	$(Y–127)$ d_y	d_y^2	d_xd_y
1995	80	– 10	100	145	+ 18	324	– 180
1996	82	– 8	64	140	+ 13	169	– 104
1997	86	– 4	16	130	+ 3	9	– 12
1998	91	+1	1	124	– 3	9	– 3
1999	83	– 7	49	133	+ 6	36	– 42
2000	85	– 5	25	127	0	0	0
2001	89	– 1	1	120	– 7	49	+ 7
2002	96	+ 6	36	110	– 17	289	– 102
2003	93	+ 3	9	116	– 11	121	– 33
$N = 9$	$\Sigma X = 785$	$\Sigma d_x = -25$	$\Sigma d_x^2 = 301$	$\Sigma Y = 1{,}145$	$\Sigma d_y = +2$	$\Sigma d_y^2 = 1{,}006$	$\Sigma d_xd_y = -469$

$$b_{xy} = \frac{N\Sigma d_xd_y - \Sigma d_x\,\Sigma d_y}{N\Sigma d_x^2 - (\Sigma d_x)^2}$$

$$= \frac{9 \times (-469) - (-25)(2)}{9 \times 301 - (-25)^2} = \frac{-4221 + 50}{2709 - 625} = -\frac{4171}{2084} = -2.001$$

$$b_{xy} = \frac{N\Sigma d_x\,d_y - \Sigma d_x\,\Sigma d_y}{N\Sigma d_y^2 - (\Sigma d_y)^2}$$

$$= \frac{9 \times (-469) - (-25)(2)}{9 \times 1006 - (-2)^2} = \frac{-4221 + 50}{9054 - 4} = -0.461$$

$$r = \pm\sqrt{b_{yx} \times b_{xy}} = -\sqrt{2.001 \times 461} = -0.96.$$

[as b_{xy} and b_{yx} both are –ve]

It is a case of very high degree of negative correlation.

Example 5. *The following data relate to advertising expenditure (in lakhs of rupees) and their corresponding sales (in crores of rupees) :*

Advertising Expenditure	:	*10*	*12*	*15*	*23*	*20*
Sales	:	*14*	*17*	*23*	*25*	*21*

Estimate (i) the sales corresponding to advertising expenditure of ₹ 30 lakhs and (ii) the advertising expenditure for a sales target of ₹ 35 crores.

Solution. Let advertising expenditure be denoted by X and sales by Y.

CALCULATION OF REGRESSION EQUATIONS

X	$(X-16)$ $(X-\overline{X})$ x	x^2	Y	$(Y-20)$ $(Y-\overline{Y})$ y	y^2	xy
10	– 6	36	14	– 6	36	+ 36
12	– 4	16	17	– 3	9	+ 12
15	– 1	1	23	+ 3	9	– 3
23	+ 7	49	25	+ 5	25	+ 35
20	+ 4	16	21	+ 1	1	+ 4
$\Sigma X = 80$	$\Sigma x = 0$	$\Sigma x^2 = 118$	$\Sigma Y = 100$	$\Sigma y = 0$	$\Sigma y^2 = 80$	$\Sigma xy = +84$

$\overline{X} = \frac{80}{5} = 16 \qquad \overline{Y} = 20$

(*i*) Regression equation of Y on X : $Y - \overline{Y} = b_{yx}(X - \overline{X})$

$$b_{yx} = \frac{\Sigma xy}{\Sigma x^2} = \frac{84}{118} = 0.712$$

$$Y - 20 = .712\,(X - 16)$$

$$Y - 20 = .712X - 11.392 \text{ or } Y = 8.608 + 0.712X$$

$$Y_{(x=30)} = 8.608 + 0.712\,(30) = 8.608 + 21.36 = 29.968$$

Thus the likely sales corresponding to advertising expenditure of ₹ 30 lakhs is ₹ 29.968 crores.

(*ii*) *Regression equation of X on Y* : $X - \overline{X} = b_{xy}(Y - \overline{Y})$

$$b_{xy} = \frac{\Sigma xy}{\Sigma y^2} = \frac{84}{80} = 1.05$$

$$X - 16 = 1.05\,(Y - 20)$$

$$X = -5 + 1.05\,Y$$

$$X_{(y=35)} = -5 + 1.05(35) = -5 + 36.75 = 31.75.$$

Thus, the advertising expenditure for a sales target of ₹ 35 crores is ₹ 31.75 lakhs.

Example 6. *You are given the following information:*

	Price (₹)	*Amount demanded ('000 units)*
Arithmetic mean	*10*	*35*
Standard deviation	*2*	*5*
Correlation of Coefficient	*r = + 0.8*	

Obtain the regression equation of amount demanded on price and estimate the likely demand when price = ₹ 12.5. *[B.A. (H) Econ., Delhi Univ., 1994]*

Solution. Let the price be denoted by X and amount demanded by Y. The regression equation of amount demanded (Y) on price (X) will be :

$$Y - \overline{Y} = r\frac{\sigma_y}{\sigma_x}(X - \overline{X}) \quad \left(\text{as } b_{yx} = r\frac{\sigma_y}{\sigma_x}\right)$$

$$\overline{Y} = 35, \sigma_y = 5, \overline{X} = 10, \sigma_y = 2, r = 0.8$$

$$Y - 35 = 0.8 \times \frac{5}{2}(X - 10)$$

$$Y - 35 = 2(X - 10)$$

$$Y - 35 = 2X - 20$$

$$Y = 2X + 15$$

The estimated value of $\overline{Y}$ when $X = 12.5$

$$Y = 2(12.5) + 15$$

$$= 25 + 15 = 40$$

Thus, $Y = 40$ ('000 units)

Example 7. *From the following data on age of husbands and age of their wives, determine the two regression lines and estimate the husband's age when wife's age is 16.*

Husband's age	36	23	27	28	28	29	30	31	38	35
Wife's age	28	18	20	22	27	21	29	27	29	28

Solution. Let age of husbands be denoted by X and that of wives by Y.

CALCULATION OF REGRESSION EQUATIONS

X	$(X-30)$ d_x	d_x^2	Y	$(X-27)$ d_y	$d_{\bar{y}}^2$	$d_x d_y$
36	+ 6	36	28	+ 1	1	6
23	− 7	49	18	− 9	81	63
27	− 3	9	20	− 7	49	21
28	− 2	4	22	− 5	25	10
28	− 2	4	27	0	0	0
29	− 1	1	21	− 6	36	6
30	0	0	29	+ 2	4	0
31	+ 1	1	27	0	0	0
38	+ 8	64	29	+ 2	4	16
35	+ 5	25	28	+ 1	1	5
$\Sigma X = 205$	$\Sigma d_x = 5$	$\Sigma d_x^2 = 193$	$\Sigma Y = 249$	$\Sigma d_y = -21$	$\Sigma d_y^2 = 201$	$\Sigma d_x d_y = 127$

Regression equation of Y on X

$$Y - \overline{Y} = b_{yx}(X - \overline{X})$$

$$\overline{Y} = \frac{\Sigma Y}{N} = \frac{249}{10} = 24.9; \overline{X} = \frac{\Sigma X}{N} = \frac{305}{10} = 30.5$$

$$b_{yx} = \frac{N \Sigma d_x d_y - \Sigma d_x \Sigma d_y}{n \Sigma d_x^2 - (\Sigma d_x)^2} = \frac{10\,(127) - 5(-21)}{10(193) - (5)^2}$$

$$= \frac{1270 + 105}{1930 - 25} = \frac{1375}{1905} = 0.722$$

Y on *X* is

$$Y - 24.9 = 0.722\,(X - 30.5) \text{ [using } Y - \overline{Y} = b_{yx}\,(X - \overline{X})]$$

$$Y = 0.722 \times + 2.88$$

for X and Y

$$b_{xy} = \frac{n \Sigma d_x\, d_y - \Sigma d_x\, d_y}{n\, \Sigma d_y^2 - (\Sigma d_y)^2} = \frac{1375}{1569} = 0.876$$

$$X - 30.5 = 0.876\,(Y - 24.9)$$

$$X - 30.5 = 0.876\,Y - 21.81$$

$$X = 0.876\ \ Y - 21.81 + 30.5$$

$$= 0.876\,Y + 8.69$$

When $Y = 16$, X will be

$$X = 0.876\,(16) + 8.69$$

$$= 14.016 + 8.69$$

$$= 22.706 \text{ or } 23$$

8.8 STANDARD ERROR (S.E.) OF ESTIMATE

As already mentioned estimated values $\hat{Y}$, Y_c or Y_e are most probable value of *Y* for a given *X*. In actual real data for the same *X* observed values of *Y* may differ. Thus $\hat{Y}$, Y_c, Y_e is a sort of average value which can be obtained for a given *X*.

As we find it necessary to supplement an average with a measure of dispersion or variation, so in order to see how good or representative the regression line is, we look for a measure of variation about it. If we have a wide scatter or variation of the dots about the regression line, then it would have to be considered a poor representative of the relationship. The more closely the dots cluster around the line, the more representative it is and the better the estimate based on the equation for this line. And if the dots should all lie on the regression line a (hypothetical situation), then there is no variation abut the line and the correlation is perfect.

The variation about the line of average relationship can be measured in the manner similar to the measuring of the variation of the items about an average. Thus, we use here a measure of variation similar to the standard deviation—**the standard error of estimate** when we get standard deviation of an estimate it is referred to as "Standard Error" of estimate.

The measure of variation of the observations around the computed regression line is referred to as the standard error of estimate. Just as the standard deviation is a measure of the scatter of observations in a frequency distribution around the mean of that distribution, the standard error of estimate is a measure of the scatter of the observed values of Y around the corresponding computed values of Y on the regression line. It is computed as a standard deviation, being also a square root of the mean of the squared deviation. But the deviations here are not the deviations of the items from the arithmetic mean ; they are rather the vertical distances of every dot from the line of average relationship.

The deviation of each dot from the regression line is symbolised by $Y - Y_c$. Thus the square root of mean of the squared deviation is written as S_{yx} *i.e.*, standard error of $\hat{Y}$ from Y on X

$$SE(\hat{Y}) = S_{yx} = \sqrt{\frac{\Sigma (Y - Y_c)^2}{N - 2}}$$

This formula is not convenient from the computational point of view because it requires the computation of Y_c, *i.e.*, estimated values of Y. *A* more convenient formula is given below :

$$S_{yx} = \sqrt{\frac{\Sigma Y^2 - a\Sigma Y + b\Sigma YX}{N - 2}}$$

where $S_{y.x}$ denote the S.E. of estimate of y obtained from Y on X.

Similarly, we can calculate S_{xy}

$$S_{x.y} = \sqrt{\frac{\Sigma (X - X_c)^2}{N - 2}} \quad \text{[Standard Error of } \hat{X} \text{ obtained from } X \text{ on } Y]$$

or
$$S_{x.y} = \sqrt{\frac{\Sigma X^2 - a\Sigma X + b\Sigma XY}{N - 2}}$$

The standard error of estimate can very easily be calculated with the help of the following formula

$$S_{x.y} = S_y \sqrt{1 - r^2} = \sigma_y \sqrt{1 - r^2} ;$$

$$S_{y.x} = S_x \sqrt{1 - r^2} \text{ or may write } S_{yx} = \sigma_x \sqrt{1 - r^2}$$

The standard error of estimate measures the accuracy of the estimated figures. The smaller the *S.E.* of standard error of estimate, the closer will be dots to the regression line and the better the estimate based on the equation for this line. If standard error of estimate is zero, then there is no variation above the line and the correlation will be perfect. Thus with the help of standard error of estimate it is possible for us to ascertain how good and representative the regression line is as a description of the average relationship between two series.

Example 8. *Given the following bivariate data :*

X :	− *1*	*5*	*3*	*2*	*1*	*1*	*7*	*3*
Y :	− *6*	*1*	*0*	*0*	*1*	*2*	*1*	*5*

(a) Fit a regression line of Y on X and predict Y if X = 10.

(b) Fit a regression line of X on Y and predict X if Y = 2.5.

Solution.

FITTING REGRESSION EQUATIONS

X	$(X-3)$ d_x	d_x^2	Y	$(Y-2)$ d_y	d_y^2	d_xd_y
– 1	– 4	16	– 6	– 8	64	+ 32
5	+ 2	4	+ 1	– 1	1	– 2
3	0	0	0	– 2	4	0
2	– 1	1	0	– 2	4	+ 2
1	– 2	4	+ 1	– 1	1	+ 2
1	– 2	4	+ 2	0	0	– 0
7	+ 4	16	+ 1	– 1	1	– 4
3	0	0	+ 5	+ 3	9	0
$\Sigma X = 21$	$\Sigma d_x = -3$	$\Sigma d_x^2 = 45$	$\Sigma Y = 4$	$\Sigma d_y = -12$	$\Sigma d_y^2 = 84$	$\Sigma d_xd_y = 30$

(*a*) Y on X; $\quad Y - \overline{Y} = b_{yx}\ (X - \overline{X})$

$$b_{yx} = \frac{N\Sigma d_xd_y - \Sigma d_x \Sigma d_y}{N\Sigma d_x^2 - (\Sigma d_x)^2} = \frac{(8)(30) - (-3)(-12)}{(8)(45) - (-1)^2}$$

$$= \frac{240 - 36}{360 - 1} = \frac{204}{359} = 0.568$$

$$\overline{Y} = \frac{\Sigma Y}{N} = \frac{4}{8} = 0.5;\ \overline{X} = \frac{\Sigma X}{N} = \frac{21}{8} = 2.625$$

$$Y - 0.5 = .568\ (X - 2.625)$$

$$Y = .568X - 0.991$$

when $\quad X = 10,\ Y = 5.68 - 0.99$

$$= 4.69.$$

(*b*) X on Y; $\quad X - \overline{X} = b_{xy}\ (Y - \overline{Y})$

$$b_{xy} = \frac{N\Sigma\ d_xd_y - \Sigma d_x \Sigma d_y}{N\Sigma d_y^2 - (\Sigma d_y)^2}$$

$$= \frac{(8)(30) - (-3)(-12)}{(8)(84) - (-12)^2} = \frac{204}{528} = 0.386$$

$$X - 2.625 = .386\ (Y - .5)$$

$$X = .386\ Y + 2.432$$

If $\quad Y = 2.5$, X shall be

$$X = .386\ (2.5) + 2.432 = 3.397.$$

Example 9. *In a partially destroyed laboratory record of an analysis of correlation data, the following results only are legible:*

Variance of $X = 9$

Regression equations $\quad 8X - 10Y + 66 = 0$

$$40X - 10Y = 214$$

Find on the basis of the above information

(i) The mean values of X and Y

(ii) Coefficient of correlation between X and Y, and

(iii) Standard deviation of Y.

(iv) Also calculate the standard error of estimate of regression of Y on X and X on Y.

Solution. (*i*) The Mean values of X and Y are also obtained by solving the equations

$$8X - 10Y = -66 \quad (i)$$
$$40X - 18Y = 214 \quad (ii)$$

Multiplying eq. (*i*) by 5

$$40X - 50Y = -330$$
$$40X - 18Y = 214$$
$$- \quad + \quad -$$
$$-32Y = -544$$

$$Y = 17 \text{ or } \overline{Y} = 17$$

Substituting the value of Y in eq. (*i*)

$$8X - 10 \times 17 = -66 \qquad X = \overline{X} = 13$$

(*ii*) For finding out the correlation coefficient, we will have to find out the regression coefficients. Since we don't know which of the two regression equations is the equation of X on Y, we make an assumption. Let us take eq. (*i*) as the regression equation of X on Y and (*ii*) be Y on X

$$8X = -66 + 10Y \quad \text{..... from } (i)$$

$$X = -\frac{66}{8} + \frac{10}{8}Y$$

$$\Rightarrow \qquad b_{xy} = \frac{10}{8} = 1.25$$

From eq. (*ii*) we can calculate b_{yx}, by writing in the form $Y = a + bX$

$$40X - 18Y = 214$$

or

$$18Y = 214 - 40X$$

$$Y = -\frac{214}{18} + \frac{40}{18}X$$

$$b_{yx} = \frac{40}{18}$$

Since product of both the regression coefficients exceeds 1 which is not possible thus our assumption is wrong. Hence the first equation is of Y on X. From eq. (*i*)

$$-10Y = -8X - 66$$

$$Y = \frac{8}{10}X + 6.6$$

$$b_{yx} = \frac{8}{10}$$

From eq. (*ii*) $$b_{xy} = \frac{18}{40}$$

$$r = \sqrt{\frac{8}{10} \times \frac{18}{40}} = \sqrt{0.36} = 0.6$$

(*iii*) $$\sigma_x = \sqrt{9} = 3$$

$$b_{xy} = r\frac{\sigma_x}{\sigma_y}$$

$$45 = .6\frac{3}{\sigma_y}$$

$$45\sigma_y = 1.8 \text{ or } \sigma_y = \frac{1.8}{.45} = 4$$

Hence standard deviation of Y is 4.

(*iv*) $$S_{yx} = \sigma_y\sqrt{1 - r^2}$$

$$\sigma_y = 4, r = 0.6$$

$$S_{yx} = 4\sqrt{1 - (0.6)^2} = 4 \times 0.8 = 3.2$$

$$S_{xy} = \sigma_x\sqrt{1 - r^2}$$

$$\sigma_x = 3, r = 0.6$$

$$S_{xy} = 3\sqrt{1 - (0.6)^2} = 3 \times 0.8 = 2.4$$

Example 10. *For 50 students of a class the regression equation of marks in Statistics (X) on the marks in Accountancy (Y) is 3Y – 5X + 180 = 0. The mean marks of Accountancy is 44 and variance of marks in Statistics is 9/16th of the variance of marks in Accountancy. Find the mean marks of Statistics and the coefficient of correlation between marks in two subjects.*

Solution. X represents marks in Statistics and Y marks in Accountancy.

X on Y is

$$3Y - 5X + 180 = 0$$

$$\Rightarrow 5X = 3Y + 180$$

$$\Rightarrow X = 0.6\,Y + 36$$

(*i*) when $Y = 44$, X will be

$$X = 0.6\,(44) + 36$$

$$= 26.4 + 36 = 62.4$$

The mean marks in statistics is 62.4. (as when $Y = \overline{Y}$ then $X = \overline{X}$)

(*ii*) $$X = 0.6\,Y + 36 \quad \text{[found above]}$$

$$b_{xy} = 0.6$$

$$\sigma_x^2 = \frac{9}{16}\sigma_y^2 \text{ (given)}$$

$$\Rightarrow \frac{\sigma_x^2}{\sigma_y^2} = \frac{9}{16}$$

$$\Rightarrow \qquad \frac{\sigma_x}{\sigma_y} = \sqrt{\frac{9}{16}} = \frac{3}{4}$$

Now $$b_{xy} = r\frac{\sigma_x}{\sigma_y}$$

$$0.6 = r\frac{3}{4}$$

$$r = \frac{0.6 \times 4}{3} = \frac{2.4}{3} = 0.8$$

The coefficient of correlation between marks in two subjects is 0.8.

Example 11. *You are given the following data:*

	X	*Y*
Arithmetic Mean	*36*	*85*
Standard Deviation	*11*	*8*

Correlation coeff. between X and Y = 0.66

(i) Find the two Regression Equations

(ii) Estimate the value of X when Y = 75.

Solution.

(i) Regression Equation of X on Y

$$X - \overline{X} = r\frac{\sigma_x}{\sigma_y}(Y - \overline{Y}) \qquad \ldots\ldots\ldots \left[\text{as } b_{xy} = r\frac{\sigma_x}{\sigma_y}\right]$$

$$\overline{X} = 36, r = 0.66, \sigma_x = 11, \sigma_y = 8, \overline{Y} = 85$$

$$X - 36 = 66\frac{11}{8}(Y - 85)$$

$$X - 36 = .9075\,(Y - 85)$$

$$X = .9075\,Y - 77.1375 + 36$$

$$X = .9075\,Y - 41.1375$$

To get Y on X

$$b_{yx} = \frac{r\,\sigma_y}{\sigma_x} = .66 \times \frac{8}{11} = .48$$

$$Y - \overline{Y} = b_{yx}(X - \overline{X})$$

$$Y - 85 = .48\,(X - 36)$$

$$X = .48X + 67.72$$

(ii) Putting $Y = 70$ in X on Y *i.e.*, $X_c = .90754\,Y - 41.1375$

$$X_c = (.9075)(70) - 41.1375$$

$$= 26.925$$

Example 12. *The following data give the ages and blood pressure of 10 women:*

Age (X)	:	56	42	36	47	49	42	60	72	63	55
Blood Pressure (Y)	:	147	125	118	128	145	140	155	160	149	150

(i) Find the correlation coefficient between X and Y.

(ii) Determine the least square regression equation of Y on X.

(iii) Estimate the blood pressure of a woman whose age is 45 years.

Solution.

CALCULATION OF CORRELATION COEFFICIENT

Age X	$(X-49)$ d_x	d_x^2	*Blood pressure* Y	$(Y-145)$ d_y	d_y^2	d_xd_y
56	+ 7	49	147	+ 2	4	+ 14
42	− 7	49	125	− 20	400	+ 140
36	− 13	169	118	− 27	729	+ 351
47	− 2	4	128	− 17	289	+ 34
49	0	0	145	0	0	0
42	− 7	49	140	− 5	25	+ 35
60	+ 11	121	155	+ 10	100	+ 110
72	+ 23	529	160	+ 15	225	+ 345
63	+ 14	196	149	+ 4	16	+ 56
55	+ 6	36	160	+ 5	25	+ 30
$\Sigma X = 522$	$\Sigma d_x = 32$	$\Sigma d_x^2 = 1202$	$\Sigma Y = 1417$	$\Sigma d_y = -33$	$\Sigma d_y^2 = 1813$	$\Sigma d_xd_y = 1115$

(*i*) Coefficient of correlation is given by

$$r = \frac{N\,\Sigma d_x\,d_y - \Sigma d_x\,\Sigma d_y}{\sqrt{N\,\Sigma d_x^2 - (\Sigma d_x)^2}\,\sqrt{N\,\Sigma d_y^2 - (\Sigma d_y)^2}} = \frac{10(1115) - (32)(-33)}{\sqrt{10(1202) - (32)^2}\,\sqrt{10(1813) - (-33)^2}}$$

$$= \frac{11150 + 1056}{\sqrt{12020 - 1024}\,\sqrt{18130 - 1089}} = \frac{12206}{13689} = 0.892$$

There is a high degree of positive correlation between age and blood pressure.

(*ii*) The least square regression equation of *Y* on *X* is given by

$$Y - \overline{Y} = b_{yx}(X - \overline{X})$$

$$\overline{X} = \frac{\Sigma X}{N} = \frac{522}{10} = 52.2;\ \overline{Y} = \frac{\Sigma Y}{N} = \frac{1417}{10} = 141.7$$

and $$b_{yx} = \frac{N\Sigma d_xd_y - \Sigma d_x\,\Sigma d_y}{N\Sigma d_x^2 - (\Sigma d_x)^2} = \frac{10(1115) - 32\,(-33)}{10(1202) - (32)^2} = \frac{12206}{10996} = 1.11$$

Substituting these values in the above equation, we have

$$Y - 141.7 = 1.11(X - 52.2)$$

or $$Y = 1.11X + 141.7 - 57.942 = 83.758 + 1.11X$$

This is the required least square regression equation of Y on X.

(*iii*) When $X = 45$, then

$$Y = 83.758 + 1.11(45) = 83.758 + 49.95 = 133.708$$

Hence, the most likely blood pressure of a woman of 45 years is 134.

Example 13. *The following results were worked out from scores in statistics and mathematics in a certain examination:*

	Scores in Statistics (X)	*Scores in Mathematics (Y)*
Mean	*39.5*	*47.5*
Standard Deviation	*10.8*	*17.8*

Karl Pearson's correlation coefficient between X and Y = 0.42. Find both the regression lines. Use these lines to estimate the value of Y when X = 50 and the value of X when Y = 30.

Solution.

(*a*) Regression of Y on X

Regression coefficient $b_{yx} = r\dfrac{\sigma_Y}{\sigma_X} = 0.72 \times \dfrac{17.8}{10.8} = 0.69$

and $a = \overline{Y} - b\overline{X} = 47.5 - 0.69 \times 39.5 = 20.24$

$\therefore$ The line of regression of Y on X is $Y_C = 20.24 + 0.69X$,

and the predicted value of Y when $X = 50$, is given by

$Y_C = 20.24 + 0.69 \times 50 = 54.74.$

(*b*) Regression of X on Y

Regression coefficient $b_{xy} = r \,.\, \dfrac{\sigma_X}{\sigma_Y} = 0.42 \times \dfrac{10.8}{17.8} = 0.25$

and $a = \overline{X} - b_{xy}\,\overline{Y} = 39.5 - 0.25 \times 47.5 = 27.62$

$\therefore$ The line of regression of X on Y is $X_C = 27.62 + 0.25Y$

and the predicted value of X when $Y = 30$ less is given by

$X_C = 27.62 + 0.25 \times 30 = 35.12$

Example 14. *For a bivariate data, you are given the following information:*

$$\Sigma (X - 58) = 46 \qquad \Sigma (X - 58)^2 = 3086$$
$$\Sigma (Y - 58) = 9 \qquad \Sigma (Y - 58)^2 = 483$$
$$\Sigma (X - 58)(Y - 58) = 1095.$$

Number of pairs of observations = 7. You are required to determine (i) the two regression equations and (ii) the coefficient of correlation between X and Y.

Solution. Let $u = X - 58$ and $v = Y - 58$. In terms of our notations, we are given $\Sigma u = 46$, $\Sigma u^2 = 3086$, $\Sigma v = 9$, $\Sigma v^2 = 483$, $\Sigma uv = 1095$ and $n = 7$.

Now $\overline{X} = 58 + \dfrac{46}{7} = 64.7$ and $\overline{Y} = 58 + \dfrac{9}{7} = 59.29$

(*a*) For regression equation of Y on X, we have

$$b_{yx} = \frac{7 \times 1095 - 46 \times 9}{7 \times 3086 - (46)^2} = 0.37$$

and $a = \overline{Y} - b\overline{X} = 59.29 - 0.37 \times 64.57 = 35.40$

$\therefore$ The line of regression of Y on X is given by

$$Y_C = 35.40 + 0.37X$$

(*b*) For regression equation of X on Y, we have

$$b_{xy} = \frac{7 \times 1095 - 46 \times 9}{7 \times 483 - (9)^2} = 2.20$$

and $a = \overline{X} - b_{xy}\,\overline{Y} = 64.57 - 2.2 \times 59.29 = -65.87$

$\therefore$ The line of regression of X on Y is given by

$$X_C = -65.87 + 2.2Y$$

(*c*) The coefficient of correlation

$$r = \pm\sqrt{b_{xy}\, b_{yx}} = \sqrt{0.37 \times 2.2} = 0.90$$ [+ sign is used as b_{yx} and b_{xy} are + ve]

Example 15. *Find the means of X and Y variables and the coefficient of correlation between them from the following two regression equations:*

$$3Y - 2X - 10 = 0$$
$$2Y - X - 50 = 0$$

Solution.

(*a*) *The means of X and Y*

We know that both the lines of regression intersect at the point $(\overline{X}, \overline{Y})$. The simultaneous solution of the given equations will give the mean values of X and Y as

$\overline{X} = 130$ and $\overline{Y} = 90$ respectively.

(*b*) *Correlation Coefficient*

Let us assume that the first equation be regression of Y on X. Rewriting this equations as $3Y = 2X + 10$ or $Y = \frac{2}{3}X + \frac{10}{3}$.

$\therefore$ The corresponding regression coefficient $b_{yx} = \frac{2}{3}$

Further, assuming the second equation as regression of X on Y, we can rewrite this equation as $X = 2Y - 50$.

$\therefore$ The regression coefficient, $b_{xy} = 2$

Since $b_{xy}\, b_{yx} = \frac{2}{3} \cdot 2 = \frac{4}{3} > 1$, therefore, our assumptions regarding the two regression lines are wrong. Now we reverse these assumptions and assume that the first equation is regression of X on Y and second the regression of Y on X.

The first equation can be rewritten as

$$X = \frac{3}{2}Y - 5 \quad \Rightarrow \quad b_{xy} = \frac{3}{2}$$

and 2nd equation is (Y on X) rewritten as

$$Y = \frac{1}{2}X + 25 \quad \Rightarrow \quad b_{yx} = \frac{1}{2}$$

Now $b_{yx}\, b_{xy} = \frac{1}{2} \cdot \frac{3}{2} = \frac{3}{4}$ (which is less than 1)

Thus $r = +\sqrt{b_{yx}\, b_{xy}}$ (as b_{yx} and b_{xy} both are + ve)

$$= +\sqrt{\frac{3}{4}} = \frac{\sqrt{3}}{2} = .87$$

Example 16. *Find the regression equation of capacity utilisation on production from the following data:*

	Average	*Standard deviation*
Production (in lakh units)	*35.6*	*10.5*
Capacity utilisation (in percentage)	*84.8*	*8.5*

$r = 0.62$

Estimate the production when the capacity utilisation is 70 per cent.

(MBA, Pune Univ., 1998; MBA, DU, 2003)

Solution. Let production be denoted by the variable X and capacity utilisation by Y. Then the regression equation showing the regression equation of capacity utilisation of production will be given by the following formula :

$$Y - \overline{Y} = b_{yx}(X - \overline{X})$$

where $b_{yx} = r\frac{\sigma_y}{\sigma_x} = 0.62 \times \frac{8.5}{10.5} = \frac{5.27}{10.5} = 0.5019$

and $\overline{X} = 35.6;\ \overline{Y} = 84.8$

Substituting all these values in the above equation, we get

$$Y - 84.8 = 0.5019\,(X - 35.6)$$

or $Y = 84.8 + 0.5019\,X - 17.8676$ or $Y = 66.9324 + 0.5019X$

which is the required regression of capacity utilisation on production.

To estimate the production, we shall have to find the regression equation of X on Y, *i.e.*,

$$X - \overline{X} = b_{xy}(Y - \overline{Y})$$

where $b_{xy} = r\frac{\sigma_x}{\sigma_y} = 0.62 \times \frac{10.5}{8.5} = \frac{6.51}{8.50} = 0.7659$

Substituting the values, we have

$$(X - 35.6) = 0.7659\,(Y - 84.8)$$

or $X = 35.6 + 0.7659\,Y - 64.9483$

$= -29.3483 + 0.7659\,Y$

when $Y = 70$, $X = -29.3483 + 0.7659\,(70)$

$X = -29.3483 + 53.613 = 24.2647$ lakh units.

Hence the estimated production is 24,26,470 units when the capacity utilisation 70 per cent.

Example 17. For a given set of bivariate data, the following results were obtained:

$\overline{X} = 53,\ \overline{Y} = 28,\ b\,(Y \text{ on } X) = -1.5,\ b\,(X \text{ on } Y) = -0.2.$

Find: (i) The two regression equations.

(ii) the coefficient of correlation

(iii) The most probable value of Y when $X = 60$.

(iv) The most probable value of X when $Y = 20$.

Solution. (i) Regression Eq. of X on Y

$$X - \overline{X} = b_{xy}(Y - \overline{Y})$$

$$X - 53 = -0.2(Y - 28)$$

$$X - 53 = -0.2Y + 5.6$$

$$X = 53 + 5.6 - 0.2Y$$

$$X = 58.6 - 0.2Y$$

Regression Eq. of Y on X

$$Y - \overline{Y} = b_{yx}(X - \overline{X})$$

$$Y - 28 = -1.5(X - 53)$$

$$Y - 28 = -1.5X + 79.5$$

$$Y = 28 + 79.5 - 1.5X$$

$$Y = 107.5 - 1.5X$$

(ii) Coefficient of Correlation :

$$r = \pm\sqrt{b_{xy} \times b_{yx}} = \pm\sqrt{(-0.2)\times(-1.5)} = -0.548 \text{ (as } b_{yx} \text{ and } b_{xy} \text{ both are –ve)}$$

(iii) Regression Eq. of Y on X : $Y = 107.5 - 1.5X$

When $X = 60$; $Y = 10.5 - 1.5(60)$

$= 107.5 - 90 = 17.5$

(iv) Regression Eq. of X on Y : $X = 58.6 - 0.2Y$

when $Y = 20$; $X = 58.6 - 0.2(20)$

$= 58.6 - 4 = 54.6$

Example 18. *To study the relationship between Expenditure on accommodation, ₹X and Expenditure on food and entertainment, ₹Y, and enquiry into 50 families gave the following results:*

$\Sigma X = 8500$ $\Sigma Y = 9600$

$\sigma_x = 60$ $\sigma_y = 20$ $r = 0.6$

Estimate the expenditure on food and entertainment when expenditure on accommodation is ₹200.

Solution. The required answer can be obtained by the regression equation of Y on X expressed by:

$$Y - \overline{Y} = r\frac{\sigma_y}{\sigma_x}(X - \overline{X}) \qquad \left[b_{yx} = r\frac{\sigma_y}{\sigma_x}\right]$$

$$\overline{Y} = \frac{9600}{50} = 192, \quad r = 0.6, \quad \sigma_y = 20$$

$$\sigma_x = 60, \overline{X} = \frac{8500}{50} = 170$$

$$Y - 192 = .6\frac{20}{60}\ (X - 170)$$

$$Y - 192 = .2\ (X - 170)$$

$$Y - 192 = .2\,X - 34$$

When X is 200, the value of Y will be

$$Y = 158 + 0.2\,(200) = 198$$

Hence the estimated expenditure on food and entertainment is ₹ 198 when expenditure on accommodation is ₹ 200.

Example 19. *The personnel manager of an electronic manufacturing company devises a manual dexterity test for job applicants to predict their production rating in the assembly department. In order to do this he selects a random sample of 10 applicants. They are given the test and later assigned a production rating. Results are as follows:*

Worker	:	*A*	*B*	*C*	*D*	*E*	*F*	*G*	*H*	*I*	*J*
Test Score	:	*53*	*36*	*88*	*84*	*86*	*64*	*45*	*48*	*39*	*69*
Production Rating	:	*45*	*43*	*89*	*79*	*84*	*66*	*49*	*48*	*43*	*76*

Fit a linear least square regression equation of production rating on test score.

(MBA, Delhi Univ., 2002)

Solution. Let test score be denoted by X and production rating by Y. We have to fit a regression equation of Y on X.

FITTING REGRESSION EQUATION OF Y ON X

Worker	X	$(X-61)$ d_x	d_x^2	Y	$(Y-62)$ d_y	d_xd_y
A	53	− 8	64	45	− 17	+ 136
B	36	− 25	625	43	− 19	+ 475
C	88	+ 27	729	89	+ 27	+ 729
D	84	+ 23	529	79	+ 17	+ 391
E	86	+ 25	625	84	+ 22	+ 550
F	64	+ 3	9	66	+ 4	+ 12
G	45	− 16	256	49	− 13	+ 208
H	48	− 13	169	48	− 14	+ 182
I	39	− 22	484	43	− 19	+ 418
J	69	+ 8	64	76	+ 14	+ 112
	$\Sigma X = 612$	$\Sigma d_x = 2$	$\Sigma d_x^2 = 3554$	$\Sigma Y = 622$	$\Sigma d_y = 2$	$\Sigma d_xd_y = 3213$

Regression Equation of Y on X : $Y - \overline{Y} = b_{yx}\,(X - \overline{X})$

$$b_{yx} = \frac{N\Sigma d_xd_y - \Sigma d_x\Sigma d_y}{N\Sigma d_x^2 - (\Sigma d_x)^2} = \frac{10 \times 3213 - 2 \times 2}{10 \times 3554 - (2)^2} = \frac{32130 - 4}{35536} = \frac{32126}{35536}$$

$$= +\ 0.904$$

$$\overline{Y} = \frac{\Sigma Y}{N} = \frac{622}{10} = 62.2; \overline{X} = \frac{\Sigma X}{N} = \frac{612}{10} = 61.2$$

Hence $Y - 62.2 = 0.904\,(X - 61.2)$

$Y = .904X - 55.325 + 62.2$

$Y = 6.875 + 0.904X$ is the required regression equation to predict production rating on test score.

EXERCISE 8.1

1. (*a*) What are regression coefficients? State the properties of a regression coefficient.

(*b*) What are regression coefficients? State the properties of regression coefficients.

2. (*a*) What are the properties of regression coefficients?

(*b*) What is regression? How is it different from correlation?

3. (*a*) Write the properties of regression coefficient.

(*b*) Comment : "Correlation signifies a cause and effect relationship in all situations but regression does not."

4. (*a*) In order to find the correlation coefficient between two variables X and Y from 12 pairs of observations, the following calculations were made :

$\Sigma X = 30$; $\Sigma X^2 = 670$; $\Sigma Y = 5$; $\Sigma Y^2 = 285$; $\Sigma XY = 344$.

On subsequent verification it was discovered that the pair ($X = 11$, $Y = 4$) was copied wrongly, the correct values being $X = 10$, $Y = 14$.

After making necessary correction, find :

(*a*) the two regression coefficients

(*b*) the two regression equations

(*c*) the correlation coefficient.

(*b*) Calculate the (*i*) two regression coefficients, (*ii*) coefficient of correlation, and (*iii*) the two regression equations from the following information :

$N = 10$, $\Sigma X = 350$, $\Sigma Y = 310$, $\Sigma(X - 35)^2 = 162$,

$\Sigma(Y - 31)^2 = 222$, $\Sigma(X - 35)(Y - 31) = 92$.

[**Ans.** (*a*) $b_{yx} = 0.694$, $b_{xy} = 0.898$; (*b*) $X = 0.898Y + 1.295$, $Y = 0.694X - 0.427$; (*c*) $r = 0.79$]

5. (*a*) A panel of judges A and B graded seven debators and independently awarded the following marks :

Debator	1	2	3	4	5	6	7
Marks of A	40	34	28	30	44	38	31
Marks of B	32	39	26	30	38	34	28

An eighth debator was awarded 36 marks by Judge A while Judge B was not present. If Judge B was also present, how many marks would you expect him to award to eighth debator assuming same degree of relationship exists in judgement?

[**Ans.** 33]

(b) The line of regression of marks in Statistics (X) on marks in Accountancy (Y) for a class of 80 students is

$$3Y - 5X + 180 = 0$$

Average marks in Accountancy are 44 and variance of marks in Statistics is 9/16th of variance of marks in Accountancy. Find :

(i) The average marks in Statistics; and

(ii) Coefficient of correlation between marks in Statistics and marks in Accountancy.

[**Ans.** (i) $\overline{X} = 62.4$, (ii) $r = 0.8$]

6. (a) "The regression line gives only a 'best estimate' of the quantity in question. We may assess the degree of uncertainty in this estimate by calculating a quantity known as the Standard Error of Estimate...." Elucidate.

(b) What do you mean by Standard Error (S.E.) of an estimate ? Give expressions for the S.E. of estimate of y for given x and S.E. of estimate of x for given y, assuming linear regression between x and y.

7. (a) Is it correct to say that the greater the value of correlation coefficient, the better will be the estimates as obtained through regression analysis ? Explain with reasons.

(b) What is meant when it is said that the smaller the standard error of estimate, the better the regression line 'fits' the data ? How is the standard error of estimated related to the possible usefulness of a regression line ?

8. Explain the concept of standard error of estimate of the linear regression of Y on X. Can you express it in terms of correlation coefficient ? What is the standard error of estimating Y from X if $r = 1$?

9 The correlation coefficient between the variables x and y is $r = 0.6$. If $\sigma_x = 1.50$, $\sigma_y = 2.00$, $\overline{x} = 10$ and $\overline{y} = 20$, find the equations of the regression lines:

(i) y on x; (ii) x on y.

[**Ans.** $y = 0.8x + 12$; $x = 0.45y + 1$.]

10. An enquiry into 50 families to study the relationship between Expenditure on Accommodation, (₹ X) and Expenditure on Food and Entertainment (₹ Y) gave the following results:

$$\Sigma X = 8500, \quad \Sigma Y = 9600, \quad \sigma_x = 60, \quad \sigma_y = 20, \quad r = 0.6.$$

Estimate the expenditure on Food and Entertainment when expenditure on Accommodation is ₹ 200.

[**Ans.** ₹ 198.]

11. For a bivariate data the mean value of X is 20 and the mean value of Y is 45. The regression coefficient of Y on X is 4 and that of X on Y is 1/9. Find

(i) The coefficient of correlation.

(ii) The standard deviation of X if the standard deviation of Y is 12.

(*iii*) Also write down the equations of regression lines.

[**Ans.** (*i*) 0.67, (*ii*) $\sigma_x = 2$, (*iii*) Regression = *ns* of *y* on *x* and *x* on *y* are respectively : $y = 4x - 35$, $9x = y + 135$.]

12. There are two series of index numbers, *P* for price index and *S* for stock commodities. The mean and standard deviation of *P* are 100 and 8 respectively and of *S* are 103 and 4.

The correlation coefficient between the two series is 0.4. With these data work out a linear equation to read off values of *P* for various values of *S*. What are the assumptions involved in your procedure ?

Can the same equation be used to read off the values of *S* for different values of *P* ? If not, state why not, and give the appropriate equation.

[**Ans.** $P = 0.8S + 17.6$; No; $S = 0.2P + 83$.]

13. Following data give the test scores and sales made by nine salesmen during a certain period:

Test scores	14	19	24	21	26	22	15	20	19
Sales ('000 ₹)	31	36	48	37	50	45	33	41	39

Calculate the coefficient of correlation between the test scores and the sales. Does it indicate that the termination of services of low test scores is justified? If the firm wants a minimum sales volume of ₹ 30,000 what is the minimum test score that will ensure continuation of service?

[$r = 0.947$; $X = 0.5578\,(30) - 2.312 = 14.42$]

14. A survey was conducted to study the relationship between expenditure on accommodation (*X*) and expenditure on food and entertainment (*Y*) and the following results were obtained:

	Mean	S.D.
Expenditure on accommodation	₹ 173	63.15
Expenditure on food and entertainment	₹ 47.8	22.98

Coefficient of correlation = +0.57

Write down the equation of regression of *Y* on *X* and estimate the expenditure on food and entertainment, if the expenditure on accommodation is ₹ 200.

Ans. [$Y = 0.207\,X + 11.99$; $Y_{200} = 53.39$]

15. (*a*) For a bivariate data $X = 20$, $Y = 25$, $\sigma_x = 5$, $\sigma_y = 8$ and $r = 0.7$. Find the regression equation of *X* on *Y* and estimate the value of *X* when *Y* is 30.

[$X = 0.43754 + 9.062$; $X_{30} = 22.187$]

(*b*) Given the two regression coefficients, *X* on *Y*, 1.5 and *Y* on *X*, 0.2, find the correlation coefficient.

Ans. [$r = 0.548$]

16. For a bivariate data, you are given the following information :

$$\Sigma\,(X - 58) = 46$$
$$\Sigma\,(X - 58)2 = 3086$$

$$\Sigma (Y - 58) = 9$$
$$\Sigma (Y - 58)^2 = 483$$
$$[\Sigma (X - 58) (Y - 58) = 1095]$$

Number of pairs of observation = 7.

You are required to determine (*i*) the two regression equations and (*ii*) the coefficient of correlation between *X* and *Y* series.

Ans. [$Y = 35.399 + 0.37 X$; $X = - 65.87 + 2.24$, $r = + 0.902$]

17. A financial manager speculates about the relationship between family incomes and their allocation for investment. The following table presents the results of a survey of 8 randomly selected families :

Annual Income (in '000 ₹) :	8	12	9	24	13	37	10	16
Percent allocation for investment :	36	25	33	15	28	19	20	22

(*a*) Develop a regression equation that best describes this data.

(*b*) Estimate the per cent allocation for investment of family earning ₹ 25,000 annually.

Ans. [(*a*) $Y = 0.576X + 14.814$ (*b*) 29.214]

18. Given the following information :

	X ₹	*Y* ₹
Arithmetic average :	6	8
Standard deviation :	5	40/3

Coefficient of correlation between *X* and *Y* = 8/15.

19. For 50 students of a class, the regression equation of marks in Statistics (x) on marks in Accountancy (y) is $3y - 5x + 180 = 0$. The mean marks in Accountancy is 44 and variance of marks in Statistics is 9/16th of the variance of marks in Accountancy. Find the mean marks in Statistics and coefficient of correlation between marks in two subjects.

[**Ans.** $\bar{x} = 62.4$; $r_{xy} = 0.8$.]

20. For fifty students of a class, the regression equation of marks in Statistics (y) on the marks in Accountancy (x) is $4y - 5x - 8 = 0$. Average marks in Accountancy are 40. The ratio of the standard deviations $\sigma_y : \sigma_x$ is 5 : 2. Find the average marks in Statistics and the coefficient of correlation between the marks in two subjects.

[**Ans.** $\bar{y} = 52$, $r_{xy} = 0.5$.]

21. The regression equation of profits (*X*) on sales (*Y*) of a certain firm is $3Y - 5X + 108 = 0$. The average sales of the firm were ₹ 44,000 and the variance of profits is 9/16th of the variance of sales. Find the average profits and the coefficient of correlation between sales and profits.

[**Ans.** $\bar{x}$ = ₹ 26,421.60 ; $r_{xy} = 0.8$.]

22. (*a*) What is meant by simply linear regression model? Under what assumptions are the parameters of the model estimated?

(*b*) The following random sample gives the number of hours of study (X) and grades (Y) in an examination for students:

X :	3	3	4	4	4	5	5	6	6	7	8
Y :	40	55	55	60	75	70	75	90	80	75	85

Fit a regression line of Y on X to the data.

Ans. [$Y = 7.5X + 31.59$]

23. Given $X = 68$, $Y = 150$, $\sigma_x = 2.5$, $\sigma_y = 20$ and correlation coefficient between X and Y as + 0.6, estimate the value of Y when X is 60.

Ans. [$Y_{60} = 111.6$]

24. The following figures relate to advertising expenditure and sales:

Adv. Exp. (₹ lakhs)	60	62	65	70	73	75	71
Sales (₹ crores)	10	11	13	15	16	19	14

Estimate (*i*) the sales for advertising expenditure of ₹ 90 lakhs and (*ii*) the advertising expenditure for a sales target of ₹ 25 crores.

Ans. [$X_{25} = 87.64$, $Y_{90} = 25.22$ crores]

25. In a partially destroyed record the following data are available:

Variance of $X = 25$,

Regression equation of X on Y; $5X - Y = 22$,

Regression equation Y on X; $64\,X - 45Y = 24$.

Find:

(*i*) Mean values of X and Y.

(*ii*) Standard deviation of Y,

(*iii*) Coefficient of correlation between X and Y.

Ans. [$\overline{X} = 6$, $\overline{Y} = 8$, $\sigma_y = 13.325$, $r = + 0.533$]

26. In a partially destroyed laboratory record of an analysis of correlation data, the following results are only legible :

Variance of $X = 9$, Regression equations :

$$4X - 5Y + 33 = 0$$

$$20X - 9Y' - 107 = 0$$

Find (*i*) The mean values of X on Y (*ii*) The standard deviation of Y (*iii*) The correlation coefficient.

Ans. [$\overline{X} = 13$, $\overline{Y} = 17$, $r = 0.6$, $\sigma_y = 0.667$]

27. The following data about the sales and advertisement expenditure of a firm is given below:

	Sales (₹ crores)	*Advertisement expenditure (₹ crores)*
Mean	40	6
S.D.	10	1.5

Coefficient of correlation, $r = 0.9$.

(*i*) **Estimate the likely sales for a proposed advertisement expenditure of ₹ 10 crores.**

(*ii*) **What should be advertisement expenditure if the firm proposes a sales target of 60 crores of rupees?**

Ans. **[(*i*) 64 crores (*iii*) 8.7 crores]**

28. **The age and blood pressure of 10 women are :**

Age	:	**56**	**42**	**36**	**47**	**49**	**42**	**60**	**72**	**63**	**55**
Blood pressure	:	**147**	**125**	**118**	**128**	**145**	**140**	**155**	**164**	**149**	**150**

(*a*) **Find the correlation coefficient between age and blood pressure.**

(*b*) **Determine the least square regression equation of blood pressure on age.**

(*c*) **Estimate the blood pressure of a woman whose age is 45 years.**

□□□

9

Index Numbers

CHAPTER OUTLINE

- Introduction
- Uses of Index Numbers
- Problems in the Construction of Index Numbers
- Methods of Constructing Index Numbers
- Quantity or Volume Index Numbers
- Value Index Numbers
- Tests of Adequacy of Index Number Formulae
- The Chain Index Numbers
- Base Shifting, Splicing and Deflating the Index Numbers
- Consumer Price Index Numbers
- Index Number of Industrial Production
- Miscellaneous Illustrations

9.1. INTRODUCTION

In very simple word if we express any variable value (current value) as a per cent of a given fixed value (base value), the result is known as "Index Number". Suppose current value is 27 and base fixed value is 20. Then 27 can be expressed as per cent of 20 as $\frac{27}{20} \times 100$ = 135. Thus index number of 27 (with base value = 20) is 135. If we have set of variable values (X-values) which are to be expressed as index numbers, it is shown as follows :

X	*Index No. (Base = 20)*
18	$\frac{18}{20} \times 100 = 90$
20	$\frac{20}{20} \times 100 = 100$
23	$\frac{23}{20} \times 100 = 115$
27	$\frac{27}{20} \times 100 = 135$
40	$\frac{40}{20} \times 100 = 200$

Index numbers are indicators which reflect the relative changes in the level of a certain phenomenon in any given period (or over a specified period of time) called the *current period* with respect to its values in some fixed period, called the *base period* selected for comparison. The phenomenon or variable under consideration may be :

(*i*) The price of a particular commodity like steel, gold, leather, etc., or a group of commodities like consumer goods, cereals, milk and milk products, cosmetics, etc.

(*ii*) Volume of trade, factory production, industrial or agricultural production, imports or exports, stocks and shares, sales and profits of a business house and so on.

(*iii*) The national income of a country, wage structure of workers in various sectors, bank deposits, foreign exchange reserves, cost of living of persons of a particular community, class or profession and so on.

Definition. "*Index numbers are statistical devices designed to measure the relative change in the level of a variable or a group of variables with respect to time, geographical location or other characteristics such as income, profession, etc.*" In other words, index numbers are specialised type of rates, ratios, percentages which give the general level of magnitude of a group of distinct but related variables in two or more situations.

For example, suppose we are interested in studying the general change in the price level of consumer goods, *i.e.,* goods or commodities consumed by the people belonging to a particular section of society, say, low income group or middle income group or labour class and so on. Obviously these changes are not directly measurable as the price quotations of the various commodities are available in different units, *e.g.,* cereals (wheat, rice, pulses, etc.), are quoted in ₹ per quintal or kg.; water in ₹ per gallon; milk, petrol, kerosene, etc., in ₹ per litre; cloth in ₹ per metre and so on.

Further, the prices of some of the commodities may be increasing while those of others may be decreasing during the *two* periods and the rates of increase or decrease may be different for different commodities. *Index number* is a statistical device which enables us to arrive at a single representative figure which gives the general level of the price of the phenomenon (commodities) in an extensive group. According to Wheldon :

"Index number is a statistical device for indicating the relative movements of the data where measurement of actual movements is difficult or incapable of being made."

9.2. INTERPRETATION

If index number is 120, it implies that variable has increased by 20% from the base value of 100, or the variable value is 1.20 times the base value. Similarly if we say the price index is 80, this means that prices has decreased in the current year by 20% from the base year or prices now are 0.80 times what they were in base year.

9.3. USES OF INDEX NUMBERS

The first index number was constructed by an Italian, Mr. Carli, in 1764 to compare the changes in price for the year 1750 (current year) with the price level in 1500 (base year) in order to study the effect of discovery of America on the price level in Italy. Though originally designed to study the general level of prices or accordingly purchasing power of money, today index numbers are extensively used for a variety of purposes in economics, business, management, etc., and for quantitative data relating to production, consumption, profits, personnel and financial matters, etc., for comparing changes in the level of phenomenon for two periods, places, etc. In fact, there is hardly any field of quantitative measurements where index numbers are not constructed. They are used in almost all sciences — natural, social and physical. The main uses of index numbers can be summarised as follows :

1. *Index Numbers as Economic Barometers.* Index numbers are indispensable tools for the management personnel of any government organisation or individual business concern and in business planning and formulation of executive decisions. The indices of prices (wholesale and retail), output (volume of trade, import and export, industrial and agricultural production) and bank deposits, foreign exchange and reserves, etc., throw light on the nature of, and variation in, the general economic and business activity of the country. A careful study of these indices gives us a fairly good appraisal of the general trade, economic development and business activity of the country. In the words of G. Simpson and F. Kafka :

"Index numbers are today one of the most widely used statistical devices...They are used to take the pulse of the economy and they have come to be used as indicators of inflationary or deflationary tendencies."

Like barometers which are used in Physics and Chemistry to measure atmospheric pressure, index numbers are rightly termed as *'economic barometers'* or *'barometers of economic activity'* which measure the pressure of economic and business behaviour.

2. *Index Numbers Help in Studying Trends and Tendencies.* Since the index numbers study the relative changes in the level of a phenomenon at different periods of time, they are specially useful for the study of the general trend for a group phenomena in a time series data. The indices of output (industrial and agricultural production), volume of trade, import and export, etc., are extremely useful for studying the changes in the level of phenomenon due to the various components of a time series, *viz.,* secular trend, seasonal and cyclical variations and irregular components and reflect upon the general trend of production and business activity. As a measure of average change in extensive group, the index numbers can

be used to forecast future events. For instance, if a businessman is interested in establishing a new industry, the study of the trend of changes in the prices, wages and incomes in different industries is extremely helpful to him to frame a general idea of the comparative courses which the future holds for different undertakings.

3. *Index Numbers Help in Formulating Decisions and Policies.* Index numbers of the data relating to prices, production, profits, imports and exports, personnel and financial matters are indispensable for any organisation in efficient planning and formulation of executive decisions. For example, the cost of living index numbers are used by the government and the industrial and business concerns for the regulation of dearness allowance (D.A.) or grant of bonus to the workers so as to enable them to meet the increased cost of living from time to time. The excise duty on the production or sales of a commodity is regulated according to the index numbers of the consumption of the commodity from time to time. Similarly, the indices of consumption of various commodities help in the planning of their future production. Although index numbers are now widely used to study the general economic and business conditions of the society, they are also applied with advantage by sociologists (population indices), psychologists (I.Q.'s), health and educational authorities, etc., for formulating and revising their policies from time to time.

9.4. TYPES OF INDEX NUMBERS

Index numbers may be broadly classified into various categories depending upon the type of the phenomenon or variable in which the relative changes are to be studied. Although index numbers can be constructed for measuring relative changes in any field of quantitative measurement, we shall primarily confine the discussion to the data relating to economics and business, *i.e.,* data relating to prices, production (output) and consumption. In this context index numbers may be broadly classified into the following three categories :

1. Price Index Numbers. The price index numbers measure the general changes in the prices. They are further sub-divided into the following classes :

(*a*) **Wholesale Price Index Numbers.** The wholesale price index numbers reflect the changes in the general price level of a country. The official general purpose index number of wholesale prices in India was first compiled by the Economic Adviser, Ministry of Commerce and Industry (now the Ministry of Commerce) in 1947 (with year ending August 1939 as base year).

(*b*) **Retail Price Index Numbers.** These indices reflect the general changes in the retail prices of various commodities such as consumption goods, stocks and shares, bank deposits, government bonds, etc. In India, these indices are constructed by Labour Ministry in the form of Labour Bureau Index Number of Retail Prices—Urban Centres and Rural Centres.

Consumer Price Index, commonly known as the Cost of Living Index is a specialised kind of retail price index and enables us to study the effect of changes in the prices of a basket of goods or commodities on the purchasing power or cost of living of a particular class or section of the people like labour class, industrial or agricultural worker, low income or middle income class, etc. In India, cost of living index numbers are available for (*i*) Central Government employees, (*ii*) middle class people, and (*iii*) working class.

2. Quantity Index Numbers. Quantity index numbers study the changes in the volume of goods produced (manufactured), consumed or distributed, like the indices of agricultural production, industrial production, imports and exports, etc. They are extremely helpful in studying the level of physical output in an economy.

3. Value Index Numbers. These are intended to study the change in the total value (price multiplied by quantity) of production such as indices of retail sales or profits or inventories. However, these indices are not as common as price and quantity indices.

9.5. METHODS OF CONSTRUCTION OF INDEX NUMBERS

The methods are put in two broad categories

1. Aggregative Method

2. Relative Method

Each category again has been divided into simple or weighted as shown in the diagram below :

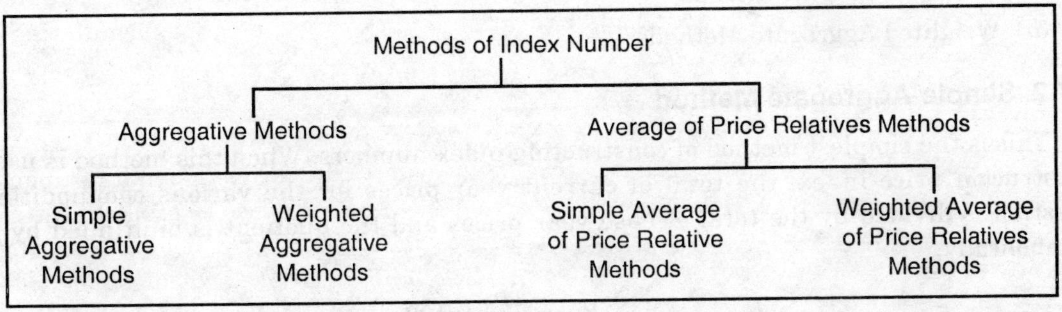

In addition to this, a particular method would depend upon the type of average used. Although geometric mean is more suitable for averaging ratios, arithmetic mean is often preferred because of its simplicity with regard to computation and interpretation.

9.6. NOTATIONS AND TERMINOLOGY

Before writing various formulae of index numbers, it is necessary to introduce certain notations and terminology for convenience.

Base Year: The year from which comparisons are made is called the base year. It is commonly denoted by writing '0' as a subscript of the variable.

Current Year: The year under consideration for which the comparisons are to be computed is called the current year. It is commonly denoted by writing '1' as a subscript of the variable.

Let there be n items in a group which are numbered from 1 to n. Let p_{0i} denote the price of the i th item in base year and p_{1i} denote its price in current year, where $i = 1,2,......n$. In a similar way q_{0i} and q_{1i} will denote the quantities of the i th item in base and current years respectively.

Using these notations, we can write an expression for price relative of the i th item as $P_i = \frac{p_{1i}}{p_{0i}} \times 100$ and quantity relative of the i th item as $Q_i = \frac{q_{1i}}{q_{0i}} \times 100$.

Further, P_{01} will be used to denote the price index number of period '1' as compared with the prices of period '0'. Similarly, Q_{01} and V_{01} would denote the quantity and the value index numbers respectively of period '1' as compared with period '0'.

Thus $P_{2001,\ 2004}$ stands for price index of year 2004 with 2001 as base year, same way $Q_{2003,\ 2005}$ stands for quantity index of a variable or group of variables for the year 2005 with base year 2003. Also generally we write ΣP_0 for ΣP_{0i} (sum of prices of base year for all items in the group.)

9.7 PRICE INDEX NUMBERS

These are two broad categories of numbers :

(A) Aggregative (B) Price Relative

9.7.1. (A) Aggregative Methods

Again under this category there are two classes of methods :

(*a*) Simple Aggregate Method

(*b*) Weighted Aggregate Methods

9.7.2. Simple Aggregate Method

This is the simplest method of constructing index numbers. When this method is used to construct a price index, the total of current year prices for the various commodities in question is divided by the total of base year prices and the quotient is multiplied by 100. Symbolically,

$$P_{01} = \frac{\Sigma p_1}{\Sigma p_0} \times 100$$

Where Σp_1 = Total of current year prices for various commodities, and

Σp_0 = Total of base year prices for various commodities.

This method of constructing the index is very simple and the steps required in computation are :

(*i*) Add the current year prices for various commodities, *i.e.*, obtain Σp_1.

(*ii*) Add the base year prices for the same commodities, *i.e.*, obtain Σp_0.

(*iii*) Divide Σp_i by Σp_0 and multiply the quotient by 100.

Example 1. *From the following data construct an index number for 2005 taking 2004 as base :*

Commodity and Unit	*Price (₹) 2004*	*Price (₹) 2005*
Butter (kg.)	110.00	120.00
Cheese (kg.)	75.00	80.00
Milk. (lt.)	13.00	13.00
Bread (1)	9.00	9.00
Eggs (Doz.)	18.00	20.00
Ghee (1 tin)	850.00	860.00

Solution.

CONSTRUCTION OF PRICE INDEX

Commodity and unit	*Price (₹) 2004* p_0	*Price (₹) 2005* p_1
Butter (kg.)	110.00	120.00
Cheese (kg.)	75.00	80.00
Milk. (lt.)	13.00	13.00
Bread (1)	9.00	9.00
Eggs (Doz.)	18.00	20.00
Ghee (1 tin)	850.00	860.00
	$\Sigma p_0 = 1075.00$	$\Sigma p_1 = 1102.00$

$$p_{01} = \frac{\Sigma p_1}{\Sigma p_0} \text{ x } 100 = \frac{1102}{1075} \times 100 = 102.51$$

This means that as compared to 2004, in 2005 there is a net increase in price of commodities included in the index to the extent of 2.51%.

Example 2. *From the following data construct price index for 2003 with base 2002 (using simple aggregate method) :*

Items	*A*	*B*	*C*	*D*	*E*
Prices (2002)	*50*	*40*	*80*	*110*	*20*
Prices (2003)	*70*	*60*	*90*	*120*	*20*

Solution.

CONSTRUCTION OF PRICE INDEX

Commodity	*Price in 2002* P_0	*Price in 2003* P_1
A	50	70
B	40	60
C	80	90
D	110	120
E	20	20
	$\Sigma P_0 = 300$	$\Sigma P_1 = 360$

$$P_{01} = \frac{\Sigma P_1}{\Sigma P_0} \times 100 = \frac{360}{300} \times 100 = 120$$

This means that as compared to 2002, in 2003 there is a net increase in the prices of commodities included in the index to the extent of 20%.

9.7.3. Limitations of the Method

(1) No consideration is given to the relative importance of the commodities. The unit by which each item happens to be priced introduces an implicit weight. This concealment is undesirable and severely, restricts the usefulness of an index number arrived at through the

method of simple aggregate of actual prices. Price changes of those items which are consumed in large quantities are more important than those which are consumed in small quantities.

(2) The units used in the price or quantity quotations can exert a big influence on the value of the index.

This is illustrated as follows :

This index is based on the assumption that the various terms and their prices are quoted in the same unit. If the unit of measurement is different for different items, the index shall produce vastly divergent results. To illustrate, let us consider the problem of calculating an index comparing the 2003 cost of construction with that of 2002, and let us include only two items, the cost of labour and the price of cement.

	2002 P_0	2003 P_1
Average hourly wage to be paid to construction workers	₹ 2.50	₹ 2.80
Price of cement per bag	₹ 60	₹ 65

Now $\Sigma P_1 = 67.8, \quad \Sigma P_0 = 62.5$

$$P_{01} = \frac{67.8}{62.5} \times 100 = 108.48 \text{ per cent.}$$

Now suppose instead of hourly wage we take the weekly wage. Taking a week of 50 hours we can rewrite the figures as :

	2002	*2003*
Average weekly wage	₹ 125	₹ 140
Price of cement per bag	₹ 60	₹ 65

Now $\Sigma P_1 = 205, \ \Sigma P_0 = 185$

$$\therefore \quad P_{01} = \frac{205}{185} \times 100 = 110.81 \text{ per cent.}$$

One can see at once that when we used weekly wage instead of hourly wage our index increased from 108.48 to 110.81. Manipulations are thus possible to suit one's requirements by quoting per kg rather than per pound or per quintal, and so on. Any index whose value can be manipulated in this manner can hardly be used as an objective measure. Moreover, equal importance is given to all the items which is wrong. It is for these reasons that the simple aggregative index has never gained any great degree of acceptance.

9.7.4. Weighted Aggregative Index Numbers

These index numbers are of the simple aggregative type with the fundamental difference that weights are assigned to the various items included in the index. There are various methods of assigning weights and consequently a large number of formulae for constructing index numbers have been devised.

In general we express $P_{01} = \dfrac{\Sigma wP_1}{\Sigma wP_0}$ ...(1)

According to suggested weights we have the following price indices. These carry the names of persons who had suggested the different methods.

1. Laspeyres method,

2. Paasche method,
3. Dorbish and Bowley's method,
4. Fisher's Ideal method,
5. Marshall-Edgeworth method, and
6. Kelly's method.

1. Laspeyres Method. In this method the basc year quantities are taken as weights. The formula for constructing index is :

$$P_{01}^{La} = \frac{\Sigma p_1 q_0}{\Sigma p_0 q_0} \times 100 \quad [i.e. \quad w = q_0]$$

P_{01}^{La} indicates price index using Laspeyres method.

Steps. (*i*) Multiply the base year prices of various commodities with base year weights and obtain $\Sigma p_1 q_0$.

(*ii*) Multiply the base year prices of various commodities with base year weights and obtain $\Sigma q_0 q_0$.

(*iii*) Divide $\Sigma p_1 q_0$ by $\Sigma p_0 q_0$ and multiply the quotient by 100. This gives us the price index.

Laspeyres index attempts to answer the question: "What is the change in aggregate value of the base period list of goods when valued at given period prices?" The index is very widely used in practical work.

2. Paasche Method. In this method the *current year* quantities are taken as weights. The formula for constructing the index is :

$$P_{01}^{Pa} = \frac{\Sigma p_1 q_1}{\Sigma p_0 q_1} \times 100 \quad [i.e. \quad w = q_1, \text{ quantity in current year}]$$

P_{01}^{Pa} indicates price index using Paasche method.

Steps. (*i*) Multiply the current year prices of various commodities with current year weights and obtain $\Sigma p_1 q_1$.

(*ii*) Multiply the base year prices of various commodities with current year weights and obtain $\Sigma p_0 q_1$.

(*iii*) Divide $\Sigma p_1 q_1$ by $\Sigma p_0 q_1$ and multiply the quotient by 100.

In general this formula answers the question: "What would be the value of the given period list of goods when valued at base period prices?"

Comparison of Laspeyres and Paasche methods. From a practical point of view, Laspeyres index is often preferred to Paasche's for the simple reason that in Laspeyres index weights (q_0) are the base year quantities and do not change from one year to the next. On the other hand, the use of Paasche index requires the continuous use of new quantity weights for each period considered and in most cases these weights are difficult and expensive to obtain.

An interesting property of Laspeyres and Paasche indices is that the former is generally expected to *overestimate,* or to leave an upward bias, whereas the latter tends to *underestimate, i.e.,* show a downward bias. When the prices increase, there is usually a reduction in the consumption of those items for which the increase has been the most pronounced, and, hence, by using base year quantities we will be giving too much weight to the prices that have increased most and the numerator of the Laspeyres index will be too large. When the prices go down, consumers often shift their preference to those items which have declined the most and hence, by using base period weights in the numerator of the Laspeyres index we shall not be giving sufficient weight to the prices that have gone down the most and the numerator will again be too large. Similarly because people tend to spend less on goods when their prices are rising the use of the Paasche or current weighting produces an index which tends to underestimate the rise in prices, *i.e.*, it has a downward bias. But the above arguments do not imply that Laspeyres index must necessarily be larger than the Paasche index.

Unless drastic changes have taken place between the base year and the given year, the difference between the Laspeyres and Paasche's will generally be small and either could serve as a satisfactory measure. In practice, however, the base year weighted Laspeyres type index remains the most popular for reasons of its practicability. The Paasche type index can only be constructed when up-to-date data for the weights are available. Furthermore, the price index of a given year can be compared only with the base year. For example, let P_{97} = 100, P_{98} = 130, and P_{99} = 140. Then P_{98} and P_{99} are using different weights and cannot be compared with each other. If these indices had been obtained by the Laspeyres formula, they could by compared because in that case the weights are the same base year weights (q_0). For these reasons, in practice the Paasche formula is usually not used and the Laspeyres type index remains most popular for reasons of its practicability.

3. Dorbish and Bowley's Method. Dorbish and Bowley have suggested simple arithmetic mean of the two indices (Laspeyres and Paasche) mentioned above so as to neutralise the biases (overestimation and underestimation of two methods). The formula for constructing the index is:

$$P_{01}^{DB} = \frac{L + P}{2}$$

where L = Laspeyres Index, P = Paasche Index

$$P_{01} = \frac{\dfrac{\Sigma p_1 q_0}{\Sigma p_0 q_0} + \dfrac{\Sigma p_1 q_1}{\Sigma p_0 q_1}}{2} \times 100$$

4. Fisher's 'Ideal' Method. Prof. Irving Fisher has given a number of formulae for constructing index number and of these he calls one as the 'ideal' index. The Fisher's Ideal Index is given by the formula.

$$P_{0I}^{Fi} = \sqrt{\frac{\Sigma p_1 q_0}{\Sigma p_0 q_0} \times \frac{\Sigma p_1 q_1}{\Sigma p_0 q_1}} \times 100$$

or $$P_{01} = \sqrt{L \times P}$$

Fisher's Ideal Index is the geometric mean of the Laspeyres and Paasche indices. (G.M. is more stable than A.M.)

The above formula is known as 'Ideal' because of the following reasons:

(*i*) It is based on the geometric mean which is theoretically considered to be the best average for constructing index numbers.

(*ii*) It takes into account both current year as well as base year prices and quantities.

(*iii*) It satisfies both the time reversal test as well as the factor reversal test as suggested by Fisher (which will be discussed later).

(*iv*) It is free from bias. The two formulae (Laspeyres' and Paasche's) that embody the opposing types and weight biases are, in the ideal formula, crossed geometrically, *i.e.*, by an averaging process that of itself has no bias. The result is the complete cancellation of biases of the kinds revealed by time reversal and factor reversal tests.

It is not, however, a practical index to compute because it is excessively laborious. The data, particularly or the Paasche segment of the index, are not readily available. In practice, statisticians will continue to rely upon simple, although perhaps less exact, index number formulae.

(*v*) *Marshall and Edgeworth's Index*

This index number uses arithmetic mean of base and current year quantities.

$$P_{01}^{ME} \frac{\Sigma p_1 \left(\frac{q_0 + q_1}{2}\right)}{\Sigma p_0 \left(\frac{q_0 + q_1}{2}\right)} \times 100 = \frac{\Sigma p_1 (q_0 + q_1)}{\Sigma p_0 (q_0 + q_1)} \times 100 = \frac{\Sigma p_1 p_0 + \Sigma p_1 q_1}{\Sigma p_0 q_0 + \Sigma p_0 q_1} \times 100$$

$$\left[\text{In this case } W = (q_0 + q_1) \text{ in } \frac{\Sigma w p_1}{\Sigma w p_0} \times 100\right]$$

(*vi*) *Kelly's Fixed Weights Aggregative Index*

The weights, in this index number, are quantities which may not necessarily relate to base or current year. The weights, once decided, remain fixed for all periods. The main advantage of this index over Laspeyres's index is that weights do not change with change of base year. Using symbols, the Kelly's Index can be written as

$$P_{01}^{Ke} = \frac{\Sigma p_1 q}{\Sigma p_0 q} \times 100 = \frac{\Sigma p_i w}{\Sigma p_0 w} \times 100$$

Example 3. *Calculate the weighted aggregative price index for 1990 from the following data:*

Item	*Price in 1971*	*Price in 1990*	*Weights*
A	8	9.5	5
B	12	12.5	1
C	6.5	9	3
D	4	4.5	6
E	6	7	4
F	2	4	3

Solution.

CALCULATION TABLE

Item	*Price in 1971* (p_0)	*Price in 1990* (p_1)	*Weights* (w)	p_0w	p_1w
A	8	9.5	5	40.0	47.5
B	12	12.5	1	12.0	12.5

C	6.5	9	3	19.5	27.0
D	4	4.5	6	24.0	27.0
E	6	7	4	24.0	28.0
F	2	4	3	6.0	12.0
Total				125.5	154.0

$$\therefore \text{ Price Index (1971 = 100)} = \frac{\Sigma p_1 w}{\Sigma p_o w} \times 100 = \frac{154.0}{125.5} = 122.7.$$

Note: The term within bracket, *i.e.*, 1971 = 100, indicates that base year is 1971.

Example 4. *For the data given in the following table, compute*

(i) Laspeyres's Price Index

(ii) Paasche's Price Index

(iii) Fisher's Ideal Index

(iv) Dorbish and Bowley's Price Index

(v) Marshall and Edgeworth's Price Index

Commodity	p_0	q_1	p_1	q_1
A	10	30	12	50
B	8	15	10	25
C	6	20	6	30
D	4	10	6	20

Solution.

CALCULATION TABLE

Commodity	p_0	q_0	p_1	q_1	p_0q_0	p_1q_0	p_0q_1	p_1q_1	q_0q_1
A	10	30	12	50	300	360	500	600	1500
B	8	15	10	25	120	150	200	250	375
C	6	20	6	30	120	120	180	180	600
D	4	10	6	20	40	60	80	120	200
					580 Σp_0q_0	690 Σp_1q_0	960 Σp_0q_1	1150 Σp_1q_1	

The calculation of various price index numbers are done as given below:

$$(i)\ P_{01}^{La} = \frac{\Sigma p_1q_0}{\Sigma p_0q_0} \times 100 = \frac{690}{580} = 118.97$$

$$(ii)\ P_{01}^{Pa} = \frac{\Sigma p_1q_1}{\Sigma p_0q_1} \times 100 = \frac{1150}{960} \times 100 = 119.79$$

$$(iii)\ P_{01}^{Fi} = \sqrt{\frac{\Sigma p_1q_0}{\Sigma p_0q_0} \times \frac{\Sigma p_1q_1}{\Sigma p_0q_1}} \times 100 = \sqrt{\frac{690}{580} \times \frac{1150}{960}} \times 100 = 119.38$$

$$(iv)\ P_{01}^{DB} = \frac{1}{2}\left(\frac{\Sigma p_1q_0}{\Sigma p_0q_0} + \frac{\Sigma p_1q_1}{\Sigma p_0q_0}\right) \times 100 = \frac{1}{2}\left[\frac{690}{580} + \frac{1150}{960}\right] \times 100 = 119.4$$

(v) $P_{01}^{ME} = \left(\dfrac{\Sigma p_1q_0 + \Sigma p_1q_1}{\Sigma p_0q_0 + \Sigma p_0q_1}\right) \times 100 = \dfrac{690 + 1150}{580 + 960} \times 100 = 119.48$

Example 5. *Construct index numbers of price from the following data by applying :*

1. *Laspeyres' method,*
2. *Paasche's method,*
3. *Bowley's method,*
4. *Fisher's method, and*
5. *Marshall-Edgeworth method.*

Commodity	*2004*		*2005*	
	Price	*Quantity*	*Price*	*Quantity*
A	2	8	4	6
B	5	10	6	5
C	4	14	5	10
D	2	19	2	13

Solution.

CALCULATION OF VARIOUS INDICES

Commodity	*2004*		*2005*					
	Price p_0	*Quantity* q_0	*Price* p_1	*Quantity* q_1	p_1q_0	p_0q_0	p_1q_1	p_0q_1
A	2	8	4	6	32	16	24	12
B	5	10	6	5	60	50	30	25
C	4	14	5	10	70	56	50	40
D	2	19	2	13	38	38	26	26
					$\Sigma p_1q_0 = 200$	$\Sigma p_0q_0 = 160$	$\Sigma p_1q_1 = 130$	$\Sigma p_0q_1 = 103$

1. *Laspeyres Method :* $P_{01} = \dfrac{\Sigma p_1q_0}{\Sigma p_0q_0} \times 100 = \dfrac{200}{160} \times 100 = 125.$

2. *Paasche's Method :* $P_{01} = \dfrac{\Sigma p_1q_1}{\Sigma p_0q_1} \times 100 = \dfrac{130}{103} \times 100 = 126.21.$

3. *Bowley's Method :* $P_{01} = \dfrac{\dfrac{\Sigma p_1q_0}{\Sigma p_0q_0} + \dfrac{\Sigma p_1q_1}{\Sigma p_0q_1}}{2} \times 100 = \dfrac{\dfrac{200}{160} + \dfrac{130}{103}}{2} \times 100$

$= \dfrac{1.25 + 1.2621}{2} \times 100 = \dfrac{2.5121}{2} \times 100 = 125.605$

or $P_{01} = \dfrac{L + P}{2} = \dfrac{125 + 126.21}{2} = 125.605.$

4. *Fisher's Ideal Method :* $P_{01} = \sqrt{\dfrac{\Sigma p_1q_0}{\Sigma p_0q_0} \times \dfrac{\Sigma p_1q_1}{\Sigma p_0q_1}} \times 100 = \sqrt{\dfrac{200}{160} \times \dfrac{130}{103}} \times 100$

$= \sqrt{1.578} \times 100 = 1.256 \times 100 = 125.6.$

5. *Marshall-Edgeworth Method* : $P_{01} = \frac{\Sigma(q_0 + q_1)p_1}{\Sigma(q_0 + q_1)p_0} \times 100 = \frac{\Sigma p_1q_0 + \Sigma p_1q_1}{\Sigma p_0q_0 + \Sigma p_0q_1} \times 100$

$$= \frac{200 + 130}{160 + 103} \times 100 = \frac{330}{263} \times 100 = 125.475.$$

Example 6. *Construct Laspeyres's, Paasche's and Fisher's indices from the following data:*

Item	1986		1987	
	Price (₹)	Expenditure (₹)	Price (₹)	Expenditure (₹)
1	10	60	15	75
2	12	120	15	150
3	18	90	27	81
4	8	40	12	48

Solution.

Note that expenditure, instead of quantities, are given for the two years.

But expenditure = V (value) = pq

Now $V_0 = p_0q_0 \Rightarrow q_0 = \frac{V_0}{p_0}$

$V_1 = p_1q_1 \Rightarrow q_1 = \frac{V_1}{p_1}$

Item	1986			1987				
	Price (p_0)	Expenditure (V_0) = p_0q_0	$q_0 = V_0/p_0$	Price (p_1)	Expenditure (V_1) = p_1q_1	$q_1 = V_1/p_1$	p_0q_1	p_1q_0
1	10	60	6	15	75	5	50	90
2	12	120	10	15	150	10	120	150
3	18	90	5	27	81	3	54	135
4	8	40	5	12	48	4	32	60
Total		310			354		256	435

From the above table, we can write

(*i*) $P_{01}^{La} = \frac{\Sigma p_1q_0}{\Sigma p_0q_0} \times 100 = \frac{435}{310} \times 100 = 140.32$

(*ii*) $P_{01}^{Pa} = \frac{\Sigma p_1q_1}{\Sigma p_0q_1} \times 100 = \frac{354}{256} \times 100 = 138.28$

(*iii*) $P_{01}^{Fi} = \sqrt{\frac{\Sigma p_1q_0}{\Sigma p_0q_0} \times \frac{\Sigma p_1q_1}{\Sigma p_0q_1}} \times 100 = \sqrt{\frac{435}{310} \times \frac{354}{256}} \times 100 = 139.30.$

Example 7. *Given that $\Sigma p_1q_1 = 250$, $\Sigma p_0q_0 = 150$, Paasche's index number = 150 and Dorbish - Bowley's index number = 145, find out (i) Fisher's ideal index number; and (ii) Marshall-Edgeworth's index number.*

Solution Paasche's index $= \frac{\Sigma p_1q_1}{\Sigma p_0q_1} \times 100$

$$150 = \frac{250}{\Sigma p_0 q_1} \times 100\ ;\ \Sigma p_0 q_1 = \frac{500}{3}$$

$$\text{Dorbish-Bowley's index} = \frac{\dfrac{\Sigma p_1 q_0}{\Sigma p_0 q_0} + \dfrac{\Sigma p_1 q_1}{\Sigma p_0 q_1}}{2} \times 100$$

$$145 = \frac{\dfrac{\Sigma p_1 q_0}{150} + \dfrac{250 \times 3}{500}}{2} \times 100$$

$$\Sigma p_1 q_0 = \left(\frac{145}{50} - \frac{750}{500}\right) \times 150 = 210$$

$$(i)\ \text{Fisher's ideal index} = \sqrt{\frac{\Sigma p_1 q_0}{\Sigma p_0 q_0} \times \frac{\Sigma p_1 q_1}{\Sigma p_0 q_1}} \times 100 = \sqrt{\frac{210}{150} \times \frac{250 \times 3}{500}} \times 100$$

$$= \sqrt{2.1} \times 100 = 144.91$$

$$(ii)\ \text{Marshall-Edgeworth's index} = \frac{\Sigma p_1 q_0 + \Sigma p_1 q_1}{\Sigma p_0 q_0 + \Sigma p_0 q_1} \times 100 = \frac{210 + 250}{150 + \dfrac{500}{3}} \times 100$$

$$= \frac{138000}{950} = 145.26.$$

9.8. (B) PRICE INDICES BASED ON PRICE RELATIVES

A price relative is the ratio of the price of a single commodity in a given period to its price in another period called the base period or reference period. If p_0 and p_x denote the commodity price during the base period and given period respectively, then by definition:

$$P_i = \text{Price relative of } i\text{th item} = \frac{P_{1i}}{P_{0i}} \times 100$$

In fact price relative of ith item is price index of ith item.

9.8.1. Simple Average of Price Relatives Method

When this method is used to construct a price index, first of all price relatives are obtained for the various items included in the index and then average of these relatives is obtained using any one of the measures of central value, *i.e.,* arithmetic mean, median, mode, geometric mean or harmonic mean. When arithmetic mean is used for averaging the relatives, the formula for computing the index is

$$P_{01} = \frac{\Sigma \left(\dfrac{p_1}{p_0} \times 100\right)}{N}$$

where N refers to the number of items (commodities) whose price relatives are thus averaged.

Although any measure of central value can be used to obtain the overall index, price relatives are generally averaged either by the arithmetic or the geometric mean. When geometric mean is used for averaging the price relatives the formula for obtaining the index becomes

$$\log P_{0i} = \frac{\Sigma \log \left[\frac{p_1}{p_0} \times 100\right]}{N} \quad \text{or} \quad \frac{\Sigma \log P}{N} \quad \text{where } P = \frac{p_1}{p_0} \times 100$$

OR

$$P_{01} = \text{antilog}\left(\frac{\Sigma \log \left(\frac{p_1}{p_0} \times 100\right)}{N}\right) = \text{antilog}\,\frac{\Sigma \log P}{N}$$

Example 8. *From the following data construct an index or 2004 taking 2003 as base by the average of relatives method using (a) arithmetic mean, and (b) geometric mean for averaged relatives.*

Commodities	*Price in 2003*	*Price in 2004*
A	*50*	*70*
B	*40*	*60*
C	*80*	*90*
D	*110*	*120*
E	*20*	*20*

Solution.

(*a*) INDEX NUMBER USING ARITHMETIC MEAN OF PRICE RELATIVES

Commodity	*Price in 2003* (₹) p_0	*Price in 2004* (₹) p_1	*Price Relatives* $\frac{p_1}{p_0} \times 100 = P$
A	50	70	140.0
B	40	60	150.0
C	80	90	112.5
D	110	120	109.1
E	20	20	100.0
			$\Sigma \frac{p_1}{p_0} \times 100 = 611.6 = \Sigma P$

$$P_{01} = \frac{\Sigma \frac{p_1}{p_0} \times 100}{N} = \frac{611.6}{5} = 122.32$$

(*b*) INDEX NUMBER USING GEOMETRIC MEAN OF PRICE RELATIVES

Commodities	*Price in 2003* p_0	*Price in 2004* p_1	*P*	*Log P*
A	50	70	140.0	2.1461
B	40	60	150.0	2.1761

C	80	90	112.5	2.0512
D	110	120	109.1	2.0378
E	20	20	100.0	2.0000
				$\Sigma \log P = 10.4112$

$$P_{01} = \text{Antilog}\left[\frac{\Sigma \log P}{N}\right] = \text{Antilog}\left[\frac{10.4112}{5}\right] = \text{Antilog } 2.0822 = 120.9$$

Although arithmetic mean and geometric mean have both been used, the arithmetic mean is often preferred because it is easier to compute and much better known. Some economists, notably F.Y. Edgeworth, preferred to use the median which is not affected by extreme values. Since the argument is important only when an index is based on a very small number of commodities, it generally does not carry much weight and the median is seldom used in actual.

Example 9. *Given below are the prices of 5 items in 1985 and 1990. Compute the simple price index number of 1990 taking 1985 as base year. Use (a) arithmetic mean and (b) geometric mean.*

Item	*Price in 1985 (₹/unit)*	*Price in 1990 (₹/unit)*
1	*15*	*20*
2	*8*	*7*
3	*200*	*300*
4	*60*	*110*
5	*100*	*130*

Solution.

CALCULATION TABLE

Item	*Price in 1985* (P_{0i})	*Price in 1990* (P_{0i})	*Price Relative* $P_i = \frac{p_{1i}}{p_{0i}} \times 100$	$\log P_i$
1	15	20	133.33	2.1249
2	8	7	87.50	1.9420
3	200	300	150.00	2.1761
4	60	110	183.33	2.2632
5	100	130	130.00	2.1139
Total			684.16	10.6201

$\therefore$ Index number, using A.M., is $P_{01} = \frac{684.16}{5} = 136.83$

and Index number, using G.M., is $P_{01} = \text{Antilog}\left[\frac{10.6201}{5}\right] = 133.06$

Example 10. *Calculate Price Index for 1995 and 1996 using 1990 as base year from the following data :*

Commodity	*Prices (₹ per unit)*		
	1990	*1995*	*1996*
A	*5*	*6*	*4*
B	*7*	*10*	*7*
C	*8*	*12*	*6*
D	*20*	*17*	*16*
E	*500*	*550*	*540*

Solution.

CALCULATIONS FOR PRICE INDICES

Commodity	*Prices*			*Price Relatives*	
	1990 p_0	*1995* p_1	*1996* p_2	*For 1995* $(p_1/p_0)\times 100$	*For 1996* $(p_2/p_0)\times 100$
A	5	6	4	120·00	80·00
B	7	10	7	142·86	100·00
C	8	12	6	150·00	75·00
D	20	17	16	85·00	80·00
E	500	550	540	110·00	108·00
Total				607·86	443·00

$$\text{Price index for 1995} = \frac{1}{5}\sum\left(\frac{p_1}{p_0}\times 100\right) = \frac{607{\cdot}86}{5} = 121{\cdot}57$$

$$\text{Price index for 1996} = \frac{1}{5}\sum\left(\frac{p_2}{p_0}\times 100\right) = \frac{443{\cdot}00}{5} = 88{\cdot}6$$

9.8.2. Weighted Average of Price Relatives (using A.M.)

The shortcoming of Simple Average of Relatives Method which assumes that all the relatives are equally important is overcome in this method which consists in assigning appropriate weights to the relatives according to the relative importance of the different commodities in the group. Thus, the index for the whole group is obtained on taking the *weighted* average, usually A.M. or G.M. of the price-relatives. Thus, based on weighted A.M., the price index is given by :

$$P_{01}\,(\text{A.M.}) = \frac{\sum\left[W\left(\frac{p_1}{p_0}\times 100\right)\right]}{\sum W} = \frac{\sum WP}{\sum W}$$

where W is the weight attached to the price-relative P.

9.8.3. Price Relatives and Laspyre's Method & Paasche's Method

In the usual notations, we have :

$$P_{01}{}^{La} = \frac{\sum p_1q_0}{\sum p_0q_0}\times 100 = \frac{\sum\left[\left(\frac{p_1}{p_0}\times 100\right)p_0\,q_0\right]}{\sum p_0q_0} = \frac{\sum PW}{\sum W} \quad \ldots(*)$$

where $P = \frac{p_1}{p_0} \times 100$, is the price-relative of the commodity

and $W = p_0 q_0$, is the value of the commodity in the base year,

the summation being taken over different commodities.

From (*), we conclude that *Laspeyre's price index is the weighted mean of the price-relatives, the corresponding weights being the values of the commodities in the base year.*

Similarly, Paasche's price index number is given by :

$$P_{01}^{Pa} = \frac{\Sigma p_1 q_1}{\Sigma p_0 q_1} \times 100 = \frac{\Sigma \left[\left(\frac{p_1}{p_0} \times 100 \right) p_0 q_1 \right]}{\Sigma p_0 q_1} = \frac{\Sigma WP}{\Sigma W} \quad \ldots(**)$$

where $P = \frac{p_1}{p_0} \times 100$ and $W = p_0 q_1$.

Hence, *Paasche's price index can be expressed as the weighted mean of the price-relatives, the corresponding weights being $w = p_0 q_1$ i.e., the values obtained on taking the current year quantities at the base year prices.*

Example 11. *The following table gives the prices of some food items in the base year and current year and the quantities sold in the base year. Calculate the weighted index number by using the weight base year quantities for price-relatives.*

Items	*Base Year Quantities (Units)*	*Base Year Price (in ₹)*	*Current Year Price (in ₹)*
A	*7*	*18·00*	*21·60*
B	*6*	*3·00*	*4·65*
C	*16*	*7·50*	*9·00*
D	*21*	*2·50*	*2·25*

[*C.A. (Foundation), May 1999*]

Solution.

CALCULATIONS FOR PRICE I. NO. USING PRICE RELATIVES

Items	*Base Year Quantities Weights (W)*	*Prices in Rupees*		*Price Relatives*	
		Base Year (p_0)	*Current Year* (p_1)	$P = \frac{p_1}{p_0} \times 100$	*WP*
A	7	18·00	21·60	120	840
B	6	3·00	4·65	155	930
C	16	7·50	9·00	120	1920
D	21	2·50	2·25	90	1890
	$\Sigma W = 50$				$\Sigma WP = 5580$

Price index number for the current year (Base Year = 100), using weighted average of price-relatives is given by :

$$P_{01} \text{ (Weighted A.M.)} = \frac{\Sigma WP}{\Sigma W} = \frac{5580}{50} = 111{\cdot}6.$$

Example 12. *A departmental store sells stereo systems, television sets and radios. The percentage distribution of the total sales volume (in rupees) is estimated as 30 per cent stereos, 50 per cent televisions and 20 per cent radios. The prices of one stereo, one television and one radio in 1990 were ₹ 20,000, ₹ 15,000 and ₹ 500 respectively while their respective prices in 1995 were ₹ 25,000, ₹ 20,000 and ₹ 800.*

A weighted price index for 1995 with base 1990 is to be computed.

(i) Which index number formula is appropriate, why?

(ii) Compute the index.

Solution. (*i*) The most appropriate index number formula in this case is the weighted average of the price-relatives, the weights being the percentage distribution of total sales volume (in ₹) for different commodities. For the calculation of this index number, we need only the prices of the various commodities (stereos, televisions and radios in this case) in different years. This approach also gives due weightage to each commodity, assuming that the sectoral distribution did not change during this period.

(*ii*) CALCULATIONS FOR INDEX NUMBER

Commodity	*Price (in ₹) per unit*		*Weights (W)*	*Price Relative*	
	1990 (p_0)	*1995 (p_1)*	*(Share in total sales)*	$P = \frac{p_1}{p_0} \times 100$	*WP*
Stereo	20,000	25,000	30	125·00	3,750
Television	15,000	20,000	50	133·33	6666·66
Radio	500	800	20	160·00	3200
			$\Sigma W = 100$		$\Sigma WP = 13616{\cdot}66$

Hence, the weighted price index for 1995 with base 1990, is given by :

$$P_{01} = \frac{\Sigma WP}{\Sigma W} = \frac{13616{\cdot}66}{100} = 136{\cdot}17.$$

9.8.4. Weighted Geometric Mean of Price Relatives

Formula for simple geometric mean is modified for weighted geometric mean as follows :

$$\text{G.M. of price relatives} = AL\left(\frac{\Sigma w \log P}{\Sigma w}\right)$$

However, as already mentioned A.M. of price relative is used as it is convenient to compute.

9.9. QUANTITY INDEX NUMBERS

Quantity indices are similar to price indices and are written as Q_{01} (0 and 1 have usual meaning).

In constructing quantity index numbers, the problems confronting the statistician are analogous to those involved in price indices. We measure changes in quantities, and when we weigh we use prices or values as weights. Quantity indices can be obtained easily by changing p to q and q to p in the various formulae discussed above.

A quantity index number measures the change in quantities in current year as compared with a base year. The formulae for quantity index numbers can be directly written from price index numbers simply by interchanging the role of price and quantity. Similar to a price relative, we can define a quantity relative as

$$Q = \frac{q_1}{q_0} \times 100 \quad \left[\text{as } P = \frac{p_1}{p_0} \times 100\right]$$

Various formulae for quantity index numbers are as given below :

(*i*) Simple aggregative index $Q_{01} = \frac{\Sigma q_1}{\Sigma q_0} \times 100 \quad \left[\text{as } P_{01} = \frac{\Sigma p_1}{\Sigma p_0} \times 100\right]$

(*ii*) Simple average of quantity relatives

(*a*) Taking A.M. $Q_{01} = \frac{\frac{\Sigma q_1}{\Sigma q_0} \times 100}{n} = \frac{\Sigma Q}{n} \quad \left[P_{01} = \frac{\Sigma P}{n}\right]$

(*b*) Taking G.M. $Q_{01} = Antilog \left[\frac{\Sigma \log Q}{n}\right] \quad \left[\text{as } P_{01} = AL\left(\frac{\Sigma \log P}{n}\right)\right]$

(*iii*) Weighted aggregative index

(*a*) $Q_{01}^{La} = \frac{\Sigma q_1 p_0}{\Sigma p_0 q_0} \times 100$ (base year prices are taken as weights) $\left[\text{as } P_{01}^{La} = \frac{\Sigma p_1 q_0}{\Sigma p_0 q_0} \times 100\right]$

(*b*) $Q_{01}^{Pa} = \frac{\Sigma p_1 p_1}{\Sigma q_0 p_1} \times 100$ (current year prices are taken as weights) $\left[\text{as } P_{01}^{Pa} = \frac{\Sigma p_1 q_1}{\Sigma p_0 q_1} \times 100\right]$

(*c*) $Q_{01}^{Fi} = \sqrt{\frac{\Sigma q_1 p_0}{\Sigma q_0 p_0} \times \frac{\Sigma q_1 p_1}{\Sigma q_0 p_1}} \times 100 \quad \left[\text{as } P_{01}^{F1} \sqrt{\frac{\Sigma p_1 q_0}{\Sigma p_0 q_0} \times \frac{\Sigma p_1 q_1}{\Sigma p_0 q_1}} \times 100\right]$

Other aggregative formulae can also be written in a similar way.

(*iv*) Weighted average of quantity relatives

(*a*) Taking A.M. $Q_{01} = \frac{\Sigma WQ}{\Sigma w} \quad \left[\text{as } P_{01} = \frac{\Sigma wP}{\Sigma w}\right]$

(*b*) Taking G.M. $Q_{01} = Antilog \left[\frac{\Sigma w \log Q}{\Sigma w}\right] \quad \left[\text{as } P_{01} = AL\left[\frac{\Sigma w \log P}{\Sigma w}\right]\right]$

Like weighted average of price relatives, values are taken as weights.

Example 13. *From the following data, compute a quantity index:*

Commodity	*Quantity*		*Price in*
	2002	*2003*	*2002*
A	30	25	30
B	20	30	40
C	10	15	20

Solution.

COMPUTATION OF QUANTITY INDEX

Commodity	q_0	q_1	p_0	q_1p_0	q_0p_0
A	30	25	30	750	900
B	20	30	40	1,200	800
C	10	15	20	300	200
				$\Sigma q_1p_0 = 2{,}250$	$\Sigma q_0p_0 = 1{,}900$

$$Q_{01} = \frac{\Sigma q_1p_0}{\Sigma q_0p_0} \times 100 = \frac{2{,}250}{1{,}900} \times 100 = 118.42$$

[As p_0 values are given we can use only Laspyre's method]

Thus compared to 2002 the quantity index has gone up by 18.42 per cent in 2003.

Example 14. *Compute by Fisher's Index Formula the quantity index from the data given below :*

Commodity	*Price*	*Total value*	*Price*	*Total value*
A	10	100	8	96
B	16	96	14	98
C	12	36	10	40

[*B.Com, Punjab Univ., 1994*]

Solution. Since we are given the value and the price we can obtain quantity figure by dividing value figures by price for each commodity. We can then apply Fisher's Ideal Formula.

COMPUTATION OF QUANTITY INDEX BY FISHER'S METHOD

Commodity	p_1	q_0	p_1	q_1	q_1p_0	q_0p_0	q_1p_1	q_0p_1
A	10	10	8	12	120	100	96	82
B	16	6	14	7	112	96	98	84
C	12	3	10	4	48	36	40	30
					Σq_1p_0 = 280	Σq_0p_0 = 232	Σq_1p_1 = 234	Σq_0p_1 = 194

$$Q_{01}^{Fi} = \sqrt{\frac{\Sigma q_1p_0}{\Sigma q_0p_0} \times \frac{\Sigma q_1p_1}{\Sigma q_0p_1}} \times 100$$

$$= \sqrt{\frac{280}{232} \times \frac{234}{194}} \times 100$$

$$= \sqrt{1.45574} \times 100 = 1.2065 \times 100 = 120.65$$

[We know $P_{01}^{Fi} = \sqrt{\frac{\Sigma p_1q_0}{\Sigma p_0q_0} \times \frac{\Sigma p_1q_1}{\Sigma p_0q_1}} \times 100$ (by interchange of p and q we get)

paid q we get $Q_{01}^{Fi} = \sqrt{\frac{\Sigma q_1p_0}{\Sigma q_0p_0} \times \frac{q_1p_1}{q_0p_1}} \times 100$]

9.10. VALUE INDEX NUMBERS

The value of a single commodity is the product of its price and quantity. Thus a value index V is the sum of the values of a given year divided by the sum of the values of the base year. The formula, therefore, is

$$V_{01} = \frac{\Sigma p_1 q_1}{\Sigma p_0 q_0} \times 100, \; V_{01} = \text{Value index}$$

where $\Sigma p_1 q_1$ = Total value of all commodities in the given period, and

$\Sigma p_0 q_0$ = Total value of all commodities in the base period.

Since in most cases the value figures are given the formula can be stated more simply

$$V_{01} = \frac{\Sigma V_1}{\Sigma V_0} \times 100$$

As V stands for value which is in terms of money, no weights are required.

9.11. PRE-REQUISITES OF GOOD INDEX NUMBER TESTS OF ADEQUACY OF INDEX NUMBER FORMULAE

A number of formulae have been given for the construction of index numbers. However, each one of them suffers from one or the other type of drawbacks. It was, therefore, suggested that a satisfactory index number formula should satisfy certain mathematical criteria. These mathematical criteria, also known as tests of adequacy of index numbers, are given below:

1. *Unit Test*: This test requires that an index number formula should be independent of the units of measurement of the variables, *i.e.*, its value should not change with change in units of measurement. This test is satisfied by all index numbers except simple aggregate formula.

   Thus has been illustrated in 9.7.3 that simple aggregate method is affected by the units of measurement of the variables. However, in all other methods, it is weighted by quantity which gives it value at one price or other and hence is not affected. In case of price relative since it is ratio of two prices (of base year and current year) becomes independent of units of measurement. Thus only simple aggregate method does not satisfy this criteria.

2. *Time Reversal Test*: This test is devised on the analogy of a single commodity case. In case of a single commodity if p_0 is its price in period '0' and p_1 is its price in period '1', then the change in price in period '1' as compared with the price of period '0' is given by $\frac{p_1}{p_0}$. Similarly, change in price in period '0' as compared with price of period '1' is given by $\frac{p_0}{p_1}$ which is reciprocal of $\frac{p_1}{p_0}$.

   It may be noted that this property holds good only when $P_{01} = \frac{p_1}{p_0}$ and $P_{10} = \frac{p_0}{p_1}$ which are in relative terms [these are not shown as per cent, *i.e.*, we do not write $P_{01} = \frac{p_1}{p_0} \times 100$ and $P_{10} = \frac{p_0}{p_1} \times 100$].

Generalising this to the case of more than one commodity the index number P_{01} measures the change in price in period '1' as compared with the price of period '0' and the index number P_{10} measures the change in price in period '0' as compared with the price of period '1'. By analogy with one commodity case, the time reversal test requires that the condition $P_{01} = \frac{1}{P_{10}}$ or $P_{01} \times P_{10} = 1$ should be satisfied.

Thus, according to time reversal test the product of an index number with another index number, obtained by reversing of time, should be equal to unity.

Suppose $P_{3,5} = 2$ (in relative terms), *i.e.*, prices in year 5 are twice the prices in year 3 then $P_{5,3}$ (prices in year 3 compared to year 5) should be $\frac{1}{2}$ logically. We will check whether a particular method just satisfy this condition or not. If price index for a year = 125. Then P_{01} = 1.25 (in relative terms) then P_{10} should be = $\frac{1}{1.25} = \frac{100}{125}$ = .8 (according to time reversal test). In terms of index number P_{10} = 80.

How to get P_{10} from P_{01}: We just interchange 0 and 1 in the formula for P_{01} to get P_{10}, *e.g.*,

$$P_{01}^{La} = \frac{\Sigma p_1 q_0}{\Sigma p_0 q_0} \Rightarrow P_{10}^{La} = \frac{\Sigma p_0 q_1}{\Sigma p_1 q_1} \text{ (in relative terms)}$$

This test is not satisfied by the Laspeyres's and Paasche's index numbers. This is obvious as shown below. We can write the Laspeyres's index as

$$P_{01} = \frac{\Sigma p_1 q_0}{\Sigma p_0 q_0} \quad \text{(omitting multiplication by 100)}$$

On reversing the timings, *i.e.*, replacing 1 by 0 and 0 by 1, we have $P_{10} = \frac{\Sigma p_0 q_1}{\Sigma p_1 q_1}$. Since $P_{01} \times P_{10} \neq 1$, the Laspeyres's index does not satisfy time reversal test. Similarly, it can be shown that Paasche's index does not satisfy time reversal test.

This test is satisfied by Fisher's Ideal Index. We write

$$P_{01}^{F} = \sqrt{\frac{\Sigma p_1 q_0}{\Sigma p_0 q_0} \times \frac{\Sigma p_1 q_1}{\Sigma p_0 q_1}} \text{ and } P_{10}^{F} = \sqrt{\frac{\Sigma p_0 q_1}{\Sigma p_1 q_1} \times \frac{\Sigma p_0 q_0}{\Sigma p_1 q_0}}$$

$$P_{01}^{F} \times P_{10}^{F} = \sqrt{\frac{\Sigma p_1 q_0}{\Sigma p_0 q_0} \times \frac{\Sigma p_1 q_1}{\Sigma p_0 q_1} \times \frac{\Sigma p_0 q_1}{\Sigma p_1 q_1} \times \frac{\Sigma p_0 q_0}{\Sigma p_1 q_0}} = 1$$

It can also be shown that Marshall-Edgeworth's, simple aggregate and Kelly's indices also satisfy the time reversal test.

Example 15. *Show that simple Geometric Mean of price relative method satisfies time reversal test.*

Solution. For the index number based on simple G.M. of price-relatives, we have :

$$P_{01}\text{ (G.M.)} = \left[\left(\Pi \frac{p_1}{p_0} \right) \right]^{1/n} \quad \text{and} \quad P_{10}\text{ (G.M.)} = \left[\left(\Pi \frac{p_0}{p_1} \right) \right]^{1/n}$$

$$P_{01}\,(\text{G.M.}) \times P_{10}\,(\text{G.M.}) = \left[\Pi\left(\frac{p_1}{p_0}\right)\right]^{1/n} \times \left[\Pi\left(\frac{p_0}{p_1}\right)\right]^{1/n} = \left[\Pi\left(\frac{p_1}{p_0}\right) \times \Pi\left(\frac{p_0}{p_1}\right)\right]^{1/n} = 1$$

Hence, the simple geometric mean of price-relatives formula satisfies time reversal test. Similarly, the test can be verified for the weighted geometric mean of price-relatives index with fixed weights.

Example 16. *If Laspeyre's price index is equal to Paasche's price index, then show that both follow time reversal test.*

Solution. If Laspeyre's price index number is equal to Paasche's price index number, then in the usual notations, we have :

$$P_{01}^{La} = P_{01}^{Pa} \qquad \Rightarrow \qquad \frac{\sum p_1 q_0}{\sum p_0 q_0} \times 100 = \frac{\sum p_1 q_1}{\sum p_0 q_1} \times 100$$

$$\Rightarrow \qquad (\sum p_1 q_0)(\sum p_0 q_1) = (\sum p_1 q_1)(\sum p_0 q_0), \qquad \ldots(*)$$

the summation being taken over different commodities.

Without factor 100, we have :

$$P_{01}^{La}\,P_{10}^{La} = \frac{\sum p_1 q_0}{\sum p_0 q_0} \times \frac{\sum p_0 q_1}{\sum p_1 q_1}$$

$$= 1 \qquad \text{[From (*)]}$$

Therefore, Laspeyre's price index satisfies the time reversal test.

Without factor 100, we have :

$$P_{01}^{Pa}\,P_{10}^{Pa} = \frac{\sum p_1 q_1}{\sum p_0 q_1} \times \frac{\sum p_0 q_0}{\sum p_1 q_0}$$

$$= 1 \qquad \text{[From (*)]}$$

Therefore, Paasche's price index satisfies the time reversal test.

Hence, *if Laspeyre's price index is equal to Paasche's price index, then both of these index numbers satisfy the time reversal test.*

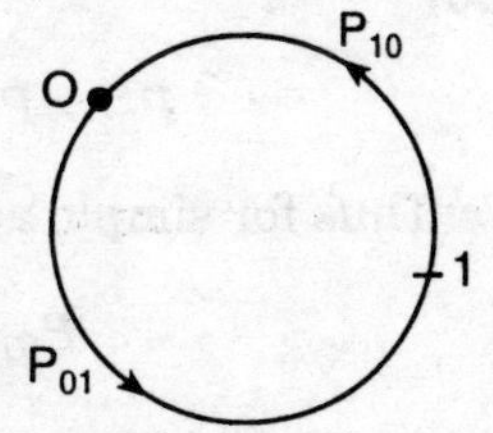

3. Circular Test. Circular test, first suggested by Westergaard, is an extension of time reversal test for more than two periods and is based on the shiftability of the base period. This requires the index to work in a circular manner and this property enables us to find the index numbers from period to period without referring back to the original base each time. For three periods *a, b, c,* the test requires :

$$P_{ab} \times P_{bc} \times P_{ca} = 1, \; a \neq b \neq c$$

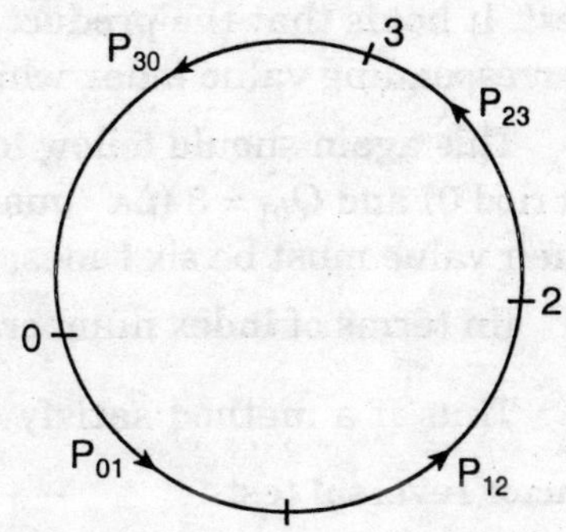

where P_{ij} is the price index (without factor 100) for period '*j*' with period '*i*' as base. In the usual notations, can be stated as :

$$P_{01} \times P_{12} \times P_{20} = 1$$

also $P_{01}\,P_{12}\,P_{23}\,P_{30} = 1$

As we can depict this by taking periods 0, 1, 2, 3 on a circle that is why it is called circular test.

We may also write this from logic that

that $$P_{01}\,P_{12} = P_{02} \text{ (why ?)}$$

Suppose $P_{01} = 2$ (prices in period 1 have doubled from period 0) and $P_{12} = 3$ (prices in period 2 are 3 times the prices in period 1) then obviously prices in period 2 should be 2 × 3 = 6 times the prices in period 0 that is P_{02} = 6 (should be). If this relation is indicated by a particular formula then it is said that the formula follows circular test.

For instance

$$P_{01}^{La} \times P_{12}^{La} \times P_{20}^{La} = \frac{\sum p_1q_0}{\sum p_0q_0} \times \frac{\sum p_2q_1}{\sum p_1q_1} \times \frac{\sum p_0q_2}{\sum p_2q_2} \neq 1.$$

Hence, Laspeyre's index does not satisfy the circular test. Similarly, it can be verified that none of Paasche's, M.E.'s, and Fisher's indices satisfies this test. In fact, circular test is not satisfied by any of the weighted aggregative formulae with changing weights, *i.e.*, if the weights used in the construction of index numbers P_{01}, P_{12} and P_{20} change. This test is satisfied *only* by the index number formulae based on :

(*i*) Simple geometric mean of the price relatives,

(*ii*) Kelly's fixed base method, and

(*iii*) Simple aggregate method.

For example, for the index numbers based on simple geometric mean of price-relatives, we have :

$$P_{01} \times P_{12} \times P_{20} = \left[\Pi\left(\frac{p_1}{p_0}\right)\right]^{1/n} \times \left[\Pi\left(\frac{p_2}{p_1}\right)\right]^{1/n} \times \left[\Pi\left(\frac{p_0}{p_2}\right)\right]^{1/n}$$

$$= \left[\Pi\left(\frac{p_1}{p_0}\right) \times \Pi\left(\frac{p_2}{p_1}\right) \times \Pi\left(\frac{p_0}{p_2}\right)\right]^{1/n} = 1.$$

Hence circular test holds in this case.

Similarly, the index number based on Kelly's fixed weight formula gives (without factor 100)

$$P_{01} \times P_{12} \times P_{20} = \frac{\Sigma Wp_1}{\Sigma Wp_0} \times \frac{\Sigma Wp_2}{\Sigma Wp_1} \times \frac{\Sigma Wp_0}{\Sigma Wp_2} = 1.$$

Thus for simple aggregate method

$$P_{01}\, P_{12}\, P_{20} = \frac{\Sigma p_1}{\Sigma p_0}, \frac{\Sigma p_2}{\Sigma p_1} \frac{\Sigma p_0}{\Sigma p_2} = 1.$$

4. Factor Reversal Test. Another test suggested by Fisher is known as factor reversal test. It holds that the product of a price index and the quantity index should be equal to the corresponding value index which means that $P_{01}\, Q_{01} = V_{01}$ (all in relative terms).

This again should follow logic that if $P_{01} = 2$ (prices have doubled in period 1 compared to period 0) and $Q_{01} = 3$ (*i.e.* quantities used are 3 times in period 1 compared to period 0) then their value must be six times, *i.e.*, if $P_{01} = 2$, $Q_{01} = 3$ then $V_{01} = 6$ (logically).

[In terms of index numbers (with factor 100) $P_{01} = 200$, $Q_{01} = 300$ then $V_{01} = 600$]

Thus if a method satisfy the criteria $P_{01}\, Q_{01} = V_{01} = \frac{\Sigma p_1q_1}{\Sigma p_0q_0}$, then it is said to satisfy factor reversal test.

Example 17. *The factor reversal test is satisfied only by the Fisher's Ideal Index.*

Solution. $$P_{01} = \sqrt{\frac{\Sigma p_1q_0}{\Sigma p_0q_0} \times \frac{\Sigma p_1q_1}{\Sigma p_0q_1}}$$

Changing p to q and q to p

$$Q_{01} = \sqrt{\frac{\Sigma q_1 p_0}{\Sigma q_0 p_0} \times \frac{\Sigma q_1 p_1}{\Sigma q_0 p_1}}$$

$$P_{01} \times Q_{01} = \sqrt{\frac{\Sigma p_1 q_0}{\Sigma p_0 q_0} \times \frac{\Sigma p_1 q_1}{\Sigma p_0 q_1} \times \frac{\Sigma q_1 p_0}{\Sigma q_0 p_0} \times \frac{\Sigma q_1 p_1}{\Sigma q_0 p_1}}$$

$$= \sqrt{\frac{(\Sigma p_1 q_1)^2}{(\Sigma p_0 q_0)^2}} = \frac{\Sigma p_1 q_1}{\Sigma p_0 q_0} = V_{01}$$

Example 18. *If Laspeyre's price index is equal to Paasche's price index, then both follow factor reversal list.*

Solution. If Laspeyre's price index is equal to Paasche's price index, then in the usual notations, we have :

$$P_{01}{}^{La} = P_{01}{}^{Pa} \Rightarrow \frac{\Sigma p_1 q_0}{\Sigma p_0 q_0} \times 100 = \frac{\Sigma p_1 q_1}{\Sigma p_0 q_1} \times 100 \Rightarrow (\Sigma p_1 q_0)(\Sigma p_0 q_1) = (\Sigma p_0 q_0)(\Sigma p_1 q_1), \quad ...(**)$$

the summation being taken over different commodities.

$$P_{01}{}^{La} = \frac{\Sigma p_1 q_0}{\Sigma p_0 q_0} \text{ (Without factor 100)}$$

$$Q_{01}{}^{La} = \frac{\Sigma p_0 q_1}{\Sigma p_0 q_0} = \frac{\Sigma p_1 q_1}{\Sigma p_1 q_0} \quad \text{[From (**)]}$$

$$\therefore P_{01}{}^{La} \,.\, Q_{01}{}^{La} = \frac{\Sigma p_1 q_0}{\Sigma p_0 q_0} \times \frac{\Sigma p_1 q_1}{\Sigma p_1 q_0} = \frac{\Sigma p_1 q_1}{\Sigma p_0 q_0} = V_{01}$$

$\Rightarrow$ Laspeyre's price index satisfies the factor reversal test.

$$P_{01}{}^{Pa} = \frac{\Sigma p_1 q_1}{\Sigma p_0 q_1} \text{ (Without factor 100)}$$

$$Q_{01}{}^{Pa} = \frac{\Sigma p_1 q_1}{\Sigma p_1 q_0} = \frac{\Sigma p_0 q_1}{\Sigma p_0 q_0} \quad \text{[From (**)]}$$

$$\therefore P_{01}{}^{Pa} \,.\, Q_{01}{}^{Pa} = \frac{\Sigma p_1 q_1}{\Sigma p_0 q_1} \times \frac{\Sigma p_0 q_1}{\Sigma p_0 q_0} = \frac{\Sigma p_1 q_1}{\Sigma p_0 q_0} = V_{01}$$

$\Rightarrow$ Paasche's price index satisfies the factor reversal test.

Hence, *if Laspeyre's price index is equal to Paasche's price index, then both of these index numbers satisfy the factor reversal test.*

Example 19. *Show with the help of the following data that the Time and Factor Reversal Tests are satisfied by Fisher's Ideal Formula for index number construction.*

Commodity	*Base Year Price (₹)*	*Base Year Quantity (kg.)*	*Current Year Price (₹)*	*Current year Quantity (kg.)*
A	*6*	*50*	*10*	*56*
B	*2*	*100*	*2*	*120*
C	*4*	*60*	*6*	*61*
D	*8.5*	*30*	*12*	*24*
E	*8*	*40*	*16*	*22*

(MBA, Madurai Kamaraj, 2001)

Solution.

COMPUTATIONS FOR TIME REVERSAL TEST AND FACTOR REVERSAL TEST

Commodity	*Base Year Price (₹)* P_0	*Base Year Quantity (kg.)* q_0	*Current Year Price (₹)* p_1	*Current year Quantity (kg.)* q_1	p_1q_0	p_0q_0	p_1q_1	p_0q_1
A	6	50	10	56	500	300	560	336
B	2	100	2	120	200	200	240	240
C	4	60	6	61	360	240	366	244
D	8.5	30	12	24	360	255	288	204
E	8	40	16	22	640	320	352	176
					$\Sigma p_1q_0 =$ 2,060	$\Sigma p_0q_0 =$ 1,315	$\Sigma p_1q_1 =$ 1,806	$\Sigma p_0q_1 =$ 1,200

Time reversal test is satisfied when : $P_{01} \times P_{10} = 1$

$$P_{01}^F = \sqrt{\frac{\Sigma p_1q_0}{\Sigma p_0q_0} \times \frac{\Sigma p_1q_1}{\Sigma p_0q_1}} \text{ and } P_{10}^F = \sqrt{\frac{\Sigma p_0q_1}{\Sigma p_1q_1} \times \frac{\Sigma p_0q_0}{\Sigma p_1q_0}}$$

Substituting the values $P_{01}^F \times P_{10}^F = \sqrt{\frac{2,060}{1,315} \times \frac{1,806}{1,200} \times \frac{1,200}{1,806} \times \frac{1,315}{2,060}} = \sqrt{1} = 1.$

Hence time reversal test is satisfied.

Factor reversal test is satisfied when $P_{01} \times Q_{01} = \frac{\Sigma p_1q_1}{\Sigma p_0q_0}$

$$P_{01}^F = \sqrt{\frac{\Sigma p_1q_0}{\Sigma p_0q_0} \times \frac{\Sigma p_1q_1}{\Sigma p_0q_1}} \text{ and } Q_{01}^F = \sqrt{\frac{\Sigma q_1p_0}{\Sigma q_0p_0} \times \frac{\Sigma q_1p_1}{\Sigma q_0p_1}}$$

Hence $P_{01}^F \times Q_{01}^F = \sqrt{\frac{2,060}{1,315} \times \frac{1,806}{1,200} \times \frac{1,200}{1,315} \times \frac{1,806}{2,060}}$

$= \frac{1,806}{1,315}$ which is also the value of $\frac{\Sigma p_1q_1}{\Sigma p_0q_0}$

Hence Fisher's Ideal Index satisfies the factor reversal test.

9.12 THE CHAIN INDEX NUMBERS

In the fixed base method discussed so far the base remains the same throughout the series of the index. This method, though convenient, has certain limitations. As time elapses conditions which were once important become less significant and it becomes more difficult to compare accurately present conditions with those of a remote period. New items may have to be included and old ones may have to be deleted in order to make the index more representative. In such cases it may be desirable to use the chain base method. When this method is used the comparisons are not made with a fixed base : rather the base for any year is preceding year. For example, for 2003, 2002 will be the base ; for 2004, 2003 will be the base and so on. When index number for a year is found with previous year as base year, such index numbers are called "Link relatives" (sometimes these are also referred as chain base index numbers). Actually these "link relatives" will be like P_{01}, P_{12}, P_{23}, ... where 0, 1, 2, 3, ... are consecutive years (and not different periods). If, however, it is desired to associate these relatives to a common base, the results may be chained to obtain chain indices. Thus in its simplest form, the chain index is one in which the figures for each year (or sub-period thereof) are first expressed as percentages of the preceding year. These percentages are then chained together by successive multiplication to form a chain index (using circular test).

Steps in Constructing Chain Index

(*i*) Express the figures for each year as percentages of the preceding year. The results so obtained are called link relatives.

(*ii*) Chain together these percentages by successive multiplication to form a chain index. Chain index of any year is link relative of that year multiplied by chain index of previous year divided by 100. In the form of formula :

Chaining or linking these link relatives are based on circular test. We assume that circular test hold good for the method used to find link relatives.

i.e. $P_{02} = P_{01} P_{12}$

$P_{03} = P_{02} P_{23}$ [P_{02} is index no. for base 0, P_{23} is link relative]

$P_{04} = P_{03} . P_{34}$

$P_{05} = P_{04} P_{45}$

[Remember that P_{01}, P_{23}, P_{02} ...... all are in relative terms, *i.e.*, after omitting factor 100]

If we want to change them in % form then

$P_{02} = (P_{01} P_{12})$ 100 [introducing factor 100 for P_{02}]

$$P_{02} = \frac{(P_{01} \times 100)(P_{12} \times 100)}{100} = \frac{P_{01} P_{12}}{100}$$

Now all P_{02}, P_{01}, P_{12} are index numbers with base 100. Thus

$$\text{Chain Index} = \frac{\text{Current year link relative} \times \text{Previous year chain index}}{100}$$

The link relatives obtained in step (*i*) facilitate comparison from one year to another, *i.e.*, between closely situated periods in which the q 's are not likely to have changed much. The chain indices obtained in step (*ii*) by a process of chaining binary comparisons facilitate long-term comparisons.

Chain relatives differ from fixed-base relatives in computation. Chain relatives are computed from link relatives whereas fixed based relatives are computed directly from the original data. The results obtained by the two different methods should be the same, provided the method for computing link relatives follows circular test, but they may differ from each other slightly . Since the process of computing chain relatives is quite complicated and the results are same as the fixed-base relatives obtained from the original data, chain relatives should be used when the original data are not available but the link relatives are.

Year	*Line Relative*	*Chain Base Index Numbers (Fixed Base 0)*
0	100	100
1	P_{01}	P_{01}
2	P_{12}	$\frac{P_{01} P_{12}}{100} \rightarrow P_{02}$
3	P_{23}	$\frac{P_{02} P_{23}}{100} \rightarrow P_{03}$
4	P_{34}	$\frac{P_{03} P_{34}}{100} \rightarrow P_{04}$

Format for finding chain Indices (Fixed base chain index numbers) P_{01}, P_{02}, P_{03} ...... on the basis of link relatives (Link relatives are themselves index numbers found using any of the methods) is explained as above :

Example 20. *From the following data of the wholesale prices of wheat for the ten years. construct index numbers taking 1995 as base. Also find the link relatives and chain base indices.*

Year	*Price of wheat (₹ per 10 kg.)*
1995	50
1996	60
1997	62
1998	65
1999	70

Solution.

CONSTRUCTION OF INDEX NUMBERS TAKING 1995 AS BASE

Year	*Price of wheat*	*Index Number (1995 = 100)*
1995	50	100
1996	60	$\frac{60}{50} \times 100 = 120$
1997	62	$\frac{62}{60} \times 100 = 124$
1998	65	$\frac{65}{50} \times 100 = 130$
1999	70	$\frac{70}{50} \times 100 = 140$

This means that from 1995 to 1996 there was a 20 per cent increase; from 1995 to 1997 there was 24 per cent increase, we are interested in finding out increase from 1995 to 1996, from 1996 to 1997, from 1997 to 1998, we shall have to compute the chain indices.

CALCULATION OF LINK RELATIVES

Year	Price of wheat	Link Relatives	Chain Base Index number
1995	50	100.0	= 100
1996	60	$\frac{60}{50}\times 100 = 120.0$	= 120
1997	62	$\frac{62}{60}\times 100 = 103.3$	$\frac{120 \times 103.3}{100} = 124$
1998	65	$\frac{65}{62}\times 100 = 104.8$	$\frac{124 \times 104.8}{100} = 130$
1999	70	$\frac{70}{65}\times 100 = 107.7$	$\frac{130 \times 107.7}{100} = 140$

[**Note :** Fixed base indices and chain base indices are exactly same and it happen because this method follows circular test. As $P_{01} = \frac{p_1}{p_0}$, $P_{12} = \frac{p_2}{p_1}$ as $P_{01} P_{12} = \frac{p_1}{p_0} \cdot \frac{p_2}{p_1} = \frac{p_2}{p_0} = P_{02}$].

Example 21. *Calculate the fixed base index number and chain base index numbers from the following data. Are the two results same? If not, why ?*

Commodity	*Price (in hundred rupees)*				
	2000	*2001*	*2002*	*2003*	*2004*
I	*2*	*3*	*5*	*7*	*8*
II	*8*	*10*	*12*	*14*	*18*
III	*4*	*5*	*7*	*9*	*12*

Solution. Since base year is not specified the first year in order of time, *i.e.,* 2000 is taken as base. As no weights are given the appropriate method for calculating fixed base numbers is the simple average of price relatives. (other possibility is simple aggregate method only).

FIXED BASE INDEX NUMBERS

Commodity	*Price (in hundred rupees)*				
	2000	*2001*	*2002*	*2003*	*2004*
I	100	$\frac{3}{2}\times 100 = 150$	$\frac{5}{2}\times 100 = 250$	$\frac{7}{2}\times 100 = 350$	$\frac{8}{2}\times 100 = 400$
II	100	$\frac{10}{8}\times 100 = 125$	$\frac{12}{8}\times 100 = 150$	$\frac{14}{8}\times 100 = 175$	$\frac{18}{8}\times 100 = 225$
III	100	$\frac{5}{4}\times 100 = 125$	$\frac{7}{4}\times 100 = 175$	$\frac{9}{4}\times 100 = 225$	$\frac{12}{4}\times 100 = 300$
Total	300	400	575	750	925
Fixed base Index No.	100	133.3	191.7	250.0	308.3

CHAIN BASE INDEX NUMBERS CHAINED TO 2000

Commodity	2000	2001	2002	2003	2004
	Percentage based on preceding year (Link relatives)				
I	100	150	$\frac{5}{3} \times 100 = 166.7$	$\frac{7}{5} \times 100 = 140.00$	$\frac{8}{7} \times 100 = 114.3$
II	100	125	120.0	116.67	128.6
III	100	125	140.0	128.60	133.3
Total of Link Relatives	300	400	426.7	385.3	376.2
Average	100	$133.33 = P_{01}$	$142.23 = P_{12}$	$128.43 = P_{23}$	$125.40 = P_{34}$
Chain indices	100	133.33 P_{01}	189.64 P_{02}	240.55 P_{03}	305.41 P_{04}

On comparison we find that except for first two years, the series of index numbers obtained by fixed base and chain base method are different. It is because simple average of price relative method which has been used to find link relatives does not satisfy circular test (which is assumed to hold good to find chain indices).

e.g. $$P_{02} = \frac{P_{01} P_{12}}{100} = \frac{133.33 \times 142.23}{100} = 189.64$$

$$P_{03} = \frac{P_{02} P_{23}}{100} = \frac{189.64 \times 128.43}{100} = 240.55$$

$$P_{04} = \frac{P_{03} P_{34}}{100} = \frac{240.55 \times 125.40}{100} = 305.41$$

Example 22. *From the following prices of three commodities for the year 1983 to 1986, find chain base index numbers chained to 1983 for the group.*

Item	*1983*	*1984*	*1985*	*1986*
I	*4*	*6*	*8*	*10*
II	*16*	*20*	*24*	*30*
III	*8*	*10*	*16*	*20*

Solution. Since only prices are known only two unweighted methods can be used (1) Sample Aggregate method, (2) Simple average of price relative method. Since price relative method is better to apply, it is used to find link relatives.

PRICE LINK RELATIVES

LR → *Group ↓*	*1983*	*1984*	*1985*	*1986*
I	100	$\frac{6}{4} \times 100 = 150$	$\frac{8}{6} \times 100 = 133.3$	$\frac{10}{8} \times 100 = 125$
II	100	$\frac{20}{16} \times 100 = 125$	$\frac{24}{20} \times 100 = 120$	$\frac{30}{24} \times 100 = 125$
III	100	$\frac{10}{8} \times 100 = 15$	$\frac{16}{10} \times 100 = 160$	$\frac{20}{16} \times 100 = 125$
Total	300	400	413.3	375

Link relatives = CBI	$\frac{300}{3} = 100$	$\frac{400}{3} = 133.3$	$\frac{413.3}{3} = 137.8$	$\frac{375}{3} = 125$
Chained Index	100	133.3	$\frac{137.8 \times 133.3}{100} = 183.7$	$\frac{183.7 \times 125}{100} = 229.6$

Example 23. *From the chain base index numbers given below, prepare fixed base index numbers :*

1999	*2000*	*2001*	*2002*	*2003*
80	*110*	*120*	*90*	*140*

Solution.

COMPUTATION OF FIXED BASE INDEX NUMBERS

Year	*Chain base index number*	*Fixed base index number (Base 1998)*
1999	80	80.0
2000	110	$\frac{110 \times 80}{100} = 88.00$
2001	120	$\frac{120 \times 88}{100} = 105.60$
2002	90	$\frac{90 \times 105.6}{100} = 95.04$
2003	140	$\frac{140 \times 75.04}{100} = 133.06$

*In this case base is 1998 as 1st link relative (chain base index number) is for year 1999, *i.e.* $P_{1998\text{-}1999} = 80$.

9.12.1 Merits of the Chain Base Method

The merits of this method are given below :

1. The chain base method has a great significance in practice because in economic and business data, we are more often concerned with making comparisons with the previous period and not with any distant past. The link relatives obtained by chain base method serve this purpose.

2. Chain base method permits the introduction of new commodities and the detection of old ones without necessitating either the recalculation of entire series or other drastic changes. Because of this flexibility, chain index is used in many types of indices such as the consumer price index and the wholesale price index.

3. Weights can be adjusted as frequently as possible. This flexibility is of great significance in many types of index numbers.

4. Index numbers calculated by the chain base method are free to a greater extent from seasonal variations than those obtained by the other method.

Limitations of the Chain Index. The main limitation of the chain index is that while the percentages of previous year figures give accurate comparisons of year-to-year changes, the long-range comparisons of chained percentages are not strictly valid. However, when the index number user wishes to make year-to-year comparisons, as is so often done by the businessman, the percentages of the preceding year provide a flexible and useful tool.

As mentioned earlier "Fixed Base Index" numbers obtained by link relatives or chain base indices are strictly applicable when circular test is applicable to the method used to find chain base indices.

9.13 BASE SHIFTING, SPLICING AND DEFLATING THE INDEX NUMBERS

(A) Base Shifting

For a variety of reasons, it frequently becomes necessary to change the reference base of an index number series from one time period to another without returning to the original raw data and recomputing the entire series. This change of reference base period is usually referred to as "*shifting the base* ". There are two important reasons for shifting the base:

1. The previous base has become too old and is almost useless for purposes of comparison. By shifting the base it is possible to state the series in terms of a more recent time period.

2. It may be desired to compare several index number series which have been computed on different base periods; particularly if the several series are to be shown on the same graph, it may be desirable for them to have the same base period. This may necessitate a shift in the base period.

Mathematically speaking, this method is strictly applicable only if the index numbers satisfy the circular test. However, for many types of index numbers the method, fortunately, yields results which in practice are close enough to those which would be obtained theoretically.

We may use simple unitary method to change indices with a different base, *e.g.,* if index numbers of 4 year are (Base 1998).

2001	*2002*	*2003*	*2004*
150	160	200	240

Suppose base is shifted to 2003 which is to be taken as 100.

When it was 200 (for 2003) then for 2002 it is 160.

When it is 100 (a for 2003) then for 2002 it is $\frac{160}{200} \times 100 = 80$.

On this basis we may change index numbers of other years by comparing those with 200 (of 2003).

if it is 200 for 2003, index no. for year 2001 is 150.

if it is 100 for 2003, index no. for year 2001 is $\frac{150}{200} \times 100 = 75$.

Example 24. *The following are the index numbers of prices (1994 = 100) :*

Year	*Index*	*Year*	*Index*
1994	*100*	*1999*	*410*
1995	*110*	*2000*	*400*

1996	*120*	*2001*	*380*
1997	*200*	*2002*	*370*
1998	*400*	*2003*	*340*

Shift the base form 1994 to 2000 and recast the index numbers.

Solution.

INDEX NUMBERS WITH 1994 AS BASE (1994 = 100)

Year	*Index Numbers (1994 = 100)*	*Index Numbers (2000 = 100)*
1994	100	$\frac{100}{400} \times 100 = 25.0$
1995	110	$\frac{110}{400} \times 100 = 27.5$
1996	120	$\frac{120}{400} \times 100 = 30.0$
1997	200	$\frac{200}{400} \times 100 = 50.0$
1998	400	$\frac{400}{400} \times 100 = 100.0$
1999	410	$\frac{410}{400} \times 100 = 102.5$
2000	400	$\frac{400}{400} \times 100 = 100.0$
2001	380	$\frac{380}{400} \times 100 = 95.0$
2002	370	$\frac{370}{400} \times 100 = 92.5$
2003	340	$\frac{340}{400} \times 100 = 85.0$

The new series with 2000 as base is obtained very easily by dividing each entry of the first column by 400, *i.e.,* the values of the index for 2000 and multiplying the ratio by 100. Thus

$$\text{Index number for 1994} = \frac{\text{Index number for 1994}}{\text{Index number for 2000}} \times 100 = \frac{100}{400} \times 100 = 25$$

$$\text{Index number for 1995} = \frac{\text{Index number for 1995}}{\text{Index number for 2000}} \times 110 = \frac{110}{400} \times 100 = 27.5$$

In a similar manner other indices can also be obtained.

B. Splicing

The problem of combining two or more overlapping series of index numbers into one continuos series is called splicing. The need for splicing arises for securing continuity in comparison. It happens quite often that an index is discontinued because its base has become too old. A new index series may be started with same items and some recent year as base. If it is desired to connect the new index number series with that of one discontinued. The second series will be merged (spliced) with the first one so as to make the first series continuous. The process of splicing is very simple and akin to that used in shifting the base as can be seen from the following illustration.

Example 25. *The index A given was started in 1995 and continued to 2001, in which year another index B was started. Splice the index B to index A so that a continuous series of index umber, from 1995 up to-date may be available.*

Year	*Index A*	*Year*	*Index A*	*Index B*
1995	*100*	*2000*	*138*	
1996	*110*	*2001*	*150*	*100*
1997	*112*	*2002*		*120*
1998	*120*	*2003*		*140*
1999	*125*	*2004*		*130*

Solution.

INDEX B SPLICED TO INDEX A

Year	*Index A*	*Index B*	*Index B spliced to Index A 1995 as base*
1995	100		100
1996	110		110
1997	112		112
1998	120		120
1999	125		125
2000	138		138
2001	150	100	150
2002		120	$\frac{150}{100} \times 120 = 180$
2003		140	$\frac{150}{100} \times 140 = 210$
2004		130	$\frac{150}{100} \times 130 = 195$

The spliced index now refers to 1995 as base and we can make a continuous comparison of index numbers from 1995 onwards.

Since *B* is spliced to *A* that means *A* series with base 1995 = 100 is made continuous upto 2004 (which now extends upto 2001 only), simple unitary method is used to change indices of *B* series to *A* series. Now *A* series exists upto year 2001. Now indices of *B* series for years 2002 to 2004 (Base 2001 = 100) are to be changed to base 1995 = 100.

Now we have index numbers for year 2001 are 150 and 100 in series A and B respectively. This implies

100 of series B = 150 of series A

For 2002, 120 of series $B = \frac{150}{100} \times 120 = 180$ of series A

same way we find index numbers of series B equivalent to index number in A as shown in the table. There is no change needed for years 1995 to 2001 (series A).

[**Note :** Again mathematically this method is applicable only if method of finding index numbers in the two series satisfies circular test].

Example 26. *Given the following values :*

	A	B
1964	$\sum p_0 q_0 =$ ₹ *10*	
1965	$\sum p_1 q_0 =$ ₹ *12*	
1966	$\sum p_2 q_0 =$ ₹ *15*	
1967	$\sum p_3 q_0 =$ ₹ *20*	$\sum p_3 q_3 =$ ₹ *25*
1968		$\sum p_4 q_3 =$ ₹ *30*
1969		$\sum p_5 q_3 =$ ₹ *40*
1970		$\sum p_6 q_3 =$ ₹ *45*

(i) Calculate two price indices : A with q_0 as weights and B with q_3 as weights.

(ii) Splice the two series so as to make, 'A' a continuous series.

(iii) 'B' a continuous series.

Solution.

INDEX NUMBER SERIES B SPLICED TO SERIES A

Year (1)	Year	*INDEX NUMBER SERIES* A (q_0 *as weights*) (*Base 1964*) (2)	B (q_3 *as weights*) (*Base 1967*) (3)	*Index No. Series 'B' Spliced to Series 'A'* (*Base 1964*) (4) $= \frac{200}{100} \times (3)$	*Series 'A' spliced to series 'B'* (*Base 1967*)
1964	0	100		100	$\frac{100}{200} \times 100 = 50$
1965	1	$\frac{12}{10} \times 100 = 120$		120	$\frac{100}{200} \times 120 = 60$
1966	2	$\frac{15}{10} \times 100 = 150$		150	$\frac{100}{200} \times 150 = 75$
1967	3	$\frac{20}{10} \times 100 = 200$	100	200	100
1968	4		$\frac{30}{25} \times 100 = 120$	$\frac{200}{100} \times 120 = 240$	120

1969	5		$\frac{40}{25}\times 100 = 160$	$\frac{200}{100}\times 160 = 320$	160
1970	6		$\frac{45}{25}\times 100 = 180$	$\frac{200}{100}\times 180 = 360$	180

(1) Index numbers for series A with q_0 as weights (Base 1964 = 100) are given in column (2) of the above table and the index numbers for series B with q_3 as weights (Base 1967 = 100) are given in column (3) of the above table.

For series A, q_0 stands for the year 1964, thus its base is 1964 and 3 stands for year 1967. For year from 1967 to 1970 weight used is for year 1967. Thus for series B base year is 1967.

To make 'B' continuous, it already exist for years 1967 to 1970. Thus "Index Numbers" of years 1964, 1965 and 1966 of series A (Base 1964) to index numbers of series B with base 1967.

Again we use unitary method that 200 of 'A' is equivalent to 100 of 'B' (year 1967)

$$100 \text{ of } 'A' = \frac{100}{200}\times 100 = 50$$

C. Deflating

Deflating means removing effect of prices from a variable, which has price as its component. Sales of a company, in money terms, has two components price and quantity. Thus if price effect is to be removed from sales, we use the relation.

$$Q_{01} = \frac{V_{01}}{P_{01}}\times 100$$

$$Q_{01} = \frac{V_{01}}{\text{price index}}\times 100$$

9.14 DEFLATING AND PURCHASING POWER OF A RUPEE

Deflating means removing effect of prices from a variable which has price as one of its component. Sales of a company, in money terms, has two components price and quantity. Thus, if we want to know changes in quantity, given sales, we have to remove contribution of price changes. If V is value of sales. Suppose price index is 160 that means price is now 1.6 times and V is the value (sales). Had there been no change in price the sales would have been $\frac{V}{1.6}$ (sales value after price effect is removed) $\frac{V}{1.6}$ is called deflated sales.

$$\text{Now deflated sales} = \frac{V}{1.6}$$

$$= \frac{V}{160}\times 100$$

$$= \frac{V}{\text{price index}}\times 100$$

$$\boxed{\text{Deflated sales} = \frac{\text{Sales in value terms}}{\text{price index}}\times 100}$$

Purchasing Power of a Rupee

Same way if price index is 160 if we were able to purchase Q units with a rupee (when index was 100), today we will be able to buy $\frac{Q}{1.6}$ units that is purchasing power of a rupee now = $\frac{1}{1.6}$ times what it was when index was 100.

Purchasing power of a rupee $= \frac{1}{1.6} = \frac{1}{160} \times 100$ in general thus purchasing power of a rupee $= \frac{1}{\text{Price Index}} \times 100$.

Same way purchasing power of money wage (or salary) one gets is called real wage. Thus

$$\text{Real Wage} = \frac{\text{Present money wage}}{\text{Index number}} \times 100$$

Example 27. *From the following table showing monthly wages of workers from 1997 to 2004. Construct the Real Wages Index Numbers :*

Year	*1997*	*1998*	*1999*	*2000*	*2001*	*2002*	*2003*	*2004*
Wages:	*150*	*170*	*200*	*250*	*320*	*360*	*380*	*400*
Price Indices:	*100*	*150*	*250*	*300*	*350*	*380*	*350*	*360*

How much is the worth of one rupee of 1997 in subsequent years?

Solution.

Year	*Wages (₹)*	*Price Index*	*Real Wages*	*Real wage indices Base 1997*
1997	150	100	$\frac{150}{100} \times 100 = 150$	100
1998	170	150	$\frac{170}{150} \times 100 = 113.3$	$\frac{113.33}{150} \times 100 = 75.55$
1999	200	250	$\frac{200}{250} \times 100 = 80.00$	$\frac{80}{150} \times 100 = 53.33$
2000	250	300	$\frac{250}{300} \times 100 = 83.33$	$\frac{83.33}{150} \times 100 = 55.55$
2001	320	350	$\frac{320}{350} \times 100 = 91.43$	$\frac{91.43}{150} \times 100 = 60.95$
2002	360	380	$\frac{360}{380} \times 100 = 94.74$	$\frac{94.74}{150} \times 100 = 63.16$
2003	380	350	$\frac{380}{350} \times 100 = 108.57$	$\frac{108.57}{150} \times 100 = 72.38$
2004	400	360	$\frac{400}{360} \times 100 = 111.11$	$\frac{111.11}{150} \times 100 = 74.07$

The purchasing power of rupee in 2004 as compared to 1997 is $\frac{100}{360}$ = ₹ 0.278 = 28 paise.

The purchasing power of consumer rupee has decreased by 72% from base period 1997 to 2004. It implies a ₹ 1 of 1997 is worth only 28 paise in 2004.

There has been increase in money wages by more than double over the period 1997 to 2004. However, the real wages index has declined to 74.07. Hence, the workers are worse off in 2004.

[**Note :** The method discussed above is frequently used to deflate individual values, value series or value indices. Its special use in problems dealing with such diversified variables as rupee sales, rupee inventories of manufacturer's, wholesaler's and retailer's incomes, wages and the like.]

9.15 GROSS DOMESTIC PRODUCT AT CONSTANT AND CURRENT PRICES

G.D.P. at constant price changes only with quantities and it will not have any price effect. Thus ratios of G.D.P. (constant price) of two years will be ratios of quantities for those 2 years.

Also if we have G.D.P. (constant price) and G.D.P. (current prices) for a particular year then price index $= \frac{\text{G.D.P. at current price}}{\text{G.D.P. at constant price}} \times 100$

G.D.P. at current price = G.D.P. at constant price $\times \frac{P_{01}}{100}$, *i.e.*, if current year price index is 160, then G.D.P. at current price = G.D.P. at constant price × 1.6.

Example 28. *Given the following information on the Gross Domestic Product (in ₹ crores) at the constant (1980-81) prices and at current price for five years. Calculate the series of price index numbers and of quantity index numbers for each of the five years with 1980-81 as base year.*

	G.D.P. at constant (1980 - 81) Prices	*G.D.P. at current Prices*
1980 - 81	*200*	*200*
1981 - 82	*150*	*240*
1982 - 83	*125*	*350*
1983 - 84	*120*	*360*
1984 - 85	*160*	*400*

Solution.

CALCULATION OF PRICE AND QUANTITY INDEX NUMBERS

Year	*G.D.P. at constant Prices*	*G.D.P. at current Prices*	*Quantity Index Number Series*	*Price Index Number Series*
1980-81	200	200	100	$\frac{200}{200} \times 100 = 100$
1981-82	150	240	$\frac{150}{200} \times 100 = 75$	$\frac{240}{150} \times 100 = 160$
1982-83	125	350	$\frac{125}{200} \times 100 = 62.5$	$\frac{350}{125} \times 100 = 280$
1983-84	120	360	$\frac{120}{200} \times 100 = 60$	$\frac{360}{120} \times 100 = 300$
1984-85	160	400	$\frac{160}{200} \times 100 = 80$	$\frac{400}{160} \times 100 = 250$

$$\text{as Price Index} = \frac{\text{Output at current Prices}}{\text{Output at constant Prices}} \times 100.$$

Example 29. *Given the following data:*

Year	*Average Weekly take - home wages (₹)*	*Consumer Price Index (₹)*
1968	*109.50*	*112.8*
1969	*112.20*	*118.2*
1970	*116.40*	*127.4*
1971	*125.08*	*138.2*
1972	*135.40*	*143.5*
1973	*138.10*	*149.8*

(*i*) What was the real weekly wage for each year?

(*ii*) In which year did the employees had the greatest buying power?

(*iii*) What percentage increase in the average weekly wages for the year 1973 is required to provide the same buying power that the employees enjoyed in the year in which they had the highest real wages?

Solution.

(*i*) Calculation of Real Wages

Year	*Money wages*	*Consumer Price Index*	*Real wages*
1968	109.50	112.8	$\frac{109.50}{112.8} \times 100 = 97.07$
1969	112.20	118.2	$\frac{112.20}{118.2} \times 100 = 94.92$
1970	116.40	127.4	$\frac{116.40}{127.4} \times 100 = 91.37$
1971	125.08	138.2	$\frac{125.08}{138.2} \times 100 = 90.51$
1972	135.40	143.5	$\frac{135.4}{143.5} \times 100 = 94.36$
1973	138.10	149.8	$\frac{138.10}{149.8} \times 100 = 92.19$

(*ii*) From the above table, it is obvious that the real wages of the workers were highest in 1968. Thus, the employees had the greatest buying power in 1968.

(*iii*) Money wages should increase proportional to price index numbers for a given purchasing power. Money wages in 1973 should be by a factor $\frac{149.8}{112.8}$.

Money wages in 1973 be $109.540 \times \frac{149.8}{112.8} = 145.42$

Thus, the required increase in weekly wages = 145.42 – 138.10 = ₹ 7.32 is required.

Or the percentage increase in weekly wages of 1973 = $\frac{7.32}{138.10} \times 100 = 5.3\%$.

9.16. CONSUMER PRICE INDEX NUMBERS

9.16.1. Meaning and Need

The consumer price index numbers, also known as cost of living index numbers, are generally intended to represent the average change over time in the prices paid by the ultimate consumer of a specified basket of goods and services. The need for constructing consumer price indices arises because the general index numbers fail to give an exact idea of the effect of the change in the general price level on the cost of living of different classes of people, since a given change in the level of prices affects different classes of people in different manners. Different classes of people consume different types of commodities and even these same type of commodities are not consumed in the same proportion by different classes of people. For example, the consumption pattern of rich, poor and middle class people varies widely. Not only this, the consumption habits of the people of the same class differ from place to place. For example, the mode of expenditure of a lower division clerk living in Delhi may differ widely from that of another clerk of the same category living in, say, Chennai. The consumer price index helps us in determining the effect of rise and fall in prices of different classes of consumers living in different areas. The construction of such an index is of great significance because very often the demand for a higher wage is base on the cost of living index and the wages and salaries in most countries are adjusted in accordance with the consumer price index.

It should be carefully noted that the cost of living index does not measure the actual cost of living nor the fluctuations in the cost of living due to causes other than the change in the price level; its objects is to find out how much the consumers of a particular class have to pay more for a certain basketful of goods and services in a given period compared to the base period.

9.16.2. Utility of the Consumer Price Indices

The Consumer Price Indices are of great significance as can be seen from the following :

(1) The most common use of these indices is in wage negotiations and wage contracts. Automatic adjustments of wage or dearness allowance component of wages are governed in many countries by such indices.

(2) At Government level, the index numbers are used for wage policy, price policy, rent control, taxation and general economic policies.

(3) The index numbers are also used to measure changing purchasing power of the currency, real income, etc.

(4) Index numbers are also used for analysing markets for particular kinds of goods and services.

9.16.3. Construction of a Consumer Price Index

The following are the steps in constructing a consumer price index :

(1) *Decision about the class of people for whom the index is meant.* It is absolutely essential to decide clearly the class of people for whom the index is meant, *i.e.,* whether it relates to industrial workers, teachers, officers, etc. The scope of the index must be clearly defined. For example, when we talk of teachers we are referring to primary teachers, middle class teachers, etc., or to all the teachers taken together. Along with the class of people it is also necessary to decide that geographical area covered by the index. Thus in the example taken above it is to be decided whether all the teachers living in Delhi are to be included or those living in a particular locality of Delhi, say, Chandni Chowk area, Karol Bagh, etc.

(2) *Conducting family budget enquiry.* Once the scope of the index is clearly defined the next step is to conduct a family budget enquiry covering the population group for whom the index is to be designed. The object of conducting a family budget enquiry is to determine the amount that an average family of the group included in the index spends on different items of consumption. While conducting such an enquiry, therefore, the quantities of commodities consumed and their prices are taken into account. The consumption pattern can thus be easily ascertained. It is necessary that the family budget enquiry amongst the class of people to whom the index series is applicable should be conducted during the base period. The Sixth International Conference of Labour Statisticians held in Geneva in 1946 suggested that the period of enquiry of the family budget and the base period should be identical as far as possible.

The enquiry is conducted on a random basis. By applying lottery method some families are selected from the total number and their family budgets are scrutinized in detail. The items on which the money is spent are classified into certain well accepted groups, namely :

(*i*) Food,

(*ii*) Clothing,

(*iii*) Fuel and Lighting,

(*iv*) House Rent, and

(*v*) Miscellaneous.

Each of these groups is further divided into sub-groups. For example, the broad group 'food' may be divided into wheat, rice, pulses, sugar, etc. The commodities included are those which are generally consumed by people for whom the index is meant. Through family budget enquiry an average budget is prepared which is the standard budget for that class of people. While constructing the index only such commodities should be included as are not subject to wide variations in quality and for which regular and comparable quotations of prices can be obtained.

There are several subgroups like cereals, pulses, spices, edible oil, fresh fruits, dry fruits, etc. Each subgroup has large number of items. First index numbers for different subgroups are found, then a composite index number for the group "food" is found with proper weightage (weights are expenditures). Then index number found for the above 5 groups, we may consider them price relatives, are used to find consumer price index using formula for weighted price relatives.

$$\text{Consume Price Index} = \frac{\Sigma WP}{\Sigma W} \text{ or } \frac{\Sigma WI}{\Sigma W}$$

where P or I are index numbers of these groups and W's are expenditure on these groups.

Two methods are used to compute index numbers of subgroups and groups.

9.16.4. Methods of Constructing the Index

After the above-mentioned problems are carefully studied, the index may be constructed by applying any of the following methods :

1. Aggregate Expenditure Method or Aggregative Method, and
2. Family Budget Method or the Method of Weighted Relatives

1. **Aggregate Expenditure Method.** When this method is applied the quantities of commodities consumed by the particular group in the base year are estimated which constitute the weights. The prices of commodities for various groups for the current year are multiplied by the quantities consumed in the base year and the aggregate expenditure in buying those commodities is obtained. In a similar manner the prices of the base year are multiplied by the quantities of the base year and aggregate expenditure for the base period is obtained. The aggregate expenditure of the current year is divided by the aggregate expenditure of the base year and the quotient is multiplied by 100. Symbolically,

$$\text{Consumer Price Index} = \frac{\Sigma p_1 q_0}{\Sigma p_0 q_0} \times 100.$$

This is in fact the Laspeyres method discussed earlier. This method is the most popular method for constructing consumer price index.

2. **Family Budget Method.** When this method is applied the family budgets of a large number of people for whom the index is meant are carefully studied and the aggregate expenditure of an average family on various items is estimated. These constitute the weights. The weights are thus the value weights obtained by multiplying the prices by quantities consumed (*i.e.*, p_0q_0). The price relatives for each commodity are obtained and these price relatives are multiplied by the value weights for each item and the product is divided by the sum of the weights. Symbolically,

$$\text{Consumer Price Index} = \frac{\Sigma PV}{\Sigma V}$$

where, $P = \frac{p_1}{p_0} \times 100$ for each item; V = Value weights, *i.e.*, p_0q_0.

This method is the same as the weighted average of price relatives method discussed earlier.

It should be noted that the answer obtained by applying the aggregate expenditure method and the family budget method shall be the same.

Example 30. *Construct the consumer price index number for 2004 on the basis of 2003 from the following data using (i) the aggregate expenditure method; and (ii) the family budget method :*

Commodity	*Quantity consumed in 2003*	*Units*	*Price in 2003* ₹	*Price in 2004* ₹
A	6 quintal	quintal	5.75	6.00
B	6 "	"	5.00	8.00

C	*1 "*	*"*	*6.00*	*9.00*
D	*6 "*	*"*	*8.00*	*10.00*
E	*4 kg.*	*kg.*	*2.00*	*1.50*
F	*1 quintal*	*quintal*	*20.00*	*15.00*

Solution.

COMPUTATION OF CONSUMER PRICE INDEX NUMBER FOR 2004 (BASE 2003 = 100) BY THE AGGREGATE EXPENDITURE METHOD

Commodity	*Quantities consumed* q_0	*Unit*	*Price in 2003* p_0	*Price in 2004* p_1	p_1q_0	p_0q_0
A	6 qtl.	qtl.	5.75	6.00	36.00	34.50
B	6 "	"	5.00	8.00	48.00	30.00
C	1 "	"	6.00	9.00	9.00	6.00
D	6 "	"	8.00	10.00	60.00	48.00
E	4 kg.	kg.	2.00	1.50	6.00	8.00
F	1 qtl.	qtl.	20.00	15.00	15.00	20.00
					$\Sigma p_1q_0 = 174$	$\Sigma p_0q_0 = 146.5$

$$\text{Consumer Price Index} = \frac{\Sigma p_1q_0}{\Sigma p_0q_0} \times 100 = \frac{2174}{146.5} \times 100 = 118.77.$$

CONSTRUCTION OF CONSUMER PRICE INDEX NUMBER FOR 2004 (BASE 2003 = 100) BY THE FAMILY BUDGET METHOD

Commodities	*Quantities consumed* q_0	*Unit*	*Price in 2003* p_0	*Price in 2004* p_1	$\frac{p_1}{p_0} \times 100$ P	p_0q_0 V	*PV*
A	6 qtl.	qtl.	5.75	6.00	104.34	34.5	3,600
B	6 "	"	5.00	8.00	160.00	30.0	4,800
C	1 "	"	6.00	9.00	150.00	6.0	900
D	6 "	"	8.00	10.00	125.00	48.0	6,000
E	4 kg.	kg.	2.00	1.50	75.00	8.0	600
F	1 qtl.	qtl.	10.00	15.00	75.00	20.0	1,500
						$\Sigma V = 146.5$	$\Sigma PV = 17,400$

$$\text{Consumer Price Index} = \frac{\Sigma PV}{\Sigma V} = \frac{17400}{146.5} = 118.77$$

Thus, the answer is the same by both the methods. However, the reader should prefer the aggregate expenditure method because it is far more easier to apply as compared to the family budget method.

Example 31. *In the construction of a certain Cost of Living Index Number, the following group index numbers were found. Calculate the Cost of Living Index Number by using :*
(i) the weighted arithmetic mean, and (ii) the weighted geometric mean.

Group	*Index Numbers*	*Weights*
1. *Food*	350	5
2. *Fuel and Lighting*	200	1
3. *Clothing*	240	1
4. *House Rent*	160	1
5. *Miscellaneous*	250	2

Solution.

COMPUTATION OF CONSUMER PRICE INDEX USING A.M. AND G.M.

Group	*Index Number* *(I)*	*Weights* *(W)*	*WI*	*log I*	*W log I*
Food	350	5	1750	2·5441	12·7205
Fuel and Lighting	200	1	200	2·3010	2·3010
Clothing	240	1	240	2·3802	2·3802
House Rent	160	1	160	2·2041	2·2041
Miscellaneous	250	2	500	2·3979	4·7958
		$\Sigma W = 10$	$\Sigma WI = 2850$		$\Sigma W \log I = 24{\cdot}4016$

The consumer price index using Arithmetic Mean is

$$P_{01}\text{ (A.M.)} = \frac{\Sigma WI}{\Sigma W} = \frac{2850}{10} = 285$$

Using Geometric Mean, the consumer price index is given by :

$$\log P_{01}\text{ (G.M.)} = \frac{\Sigma W \log I}{\Sigma W} = \frac{24{\cdot}4016}{10} = 2{\cdot}4401$$

$$\Rightarrow \quad P_{01}\text{ (G.M.)} = \text{Antilog } (2{\cdot}4401) = 275{\cdot}4$$

Example 32. *Calculate the Cost of Living Index Number from the following data :*

Items	*Price*		*Weights*
	Base Year	*Current Year*	
Food	30	47	4
Fuel	8	12	1
Clothing	14	18	3
House Rent	22	15	2
Miscellaneous	25	30	1

Solution.

CALCULATIONS FOR COST OF LIVING INDEX NUMBER

Items	*Weights* (*W*)	*Prices*		*Price Relatives*	
		Base Year (p_0)	*Current Year* (p_1)	$P = \frac{p_1}{p_0} \times 100$	*WP*
Food	4	30	47	156·67	626·67
Fuel	1	8	12	150·00	150·00
Clothing	3	14	18	128·57	385·71
House Rent	2	22	15	68·18	136·36
Miscellaneous	1	25	30	120·00	120·00
	$\Sigma W = 11$				$\Sigma WP = 1418{\cdot}74$

$$\text{Consumer price index} = \frac{\Sigma WP}{\Sigma W} = \frac{1418.74}{11} = 128.9$$

Example 33. *An enquiry into the budgets of the middle class families of a certain city revealed that on an average, the percentage expenses in the different groups were:*

Food 45, rent 15, clothing 12, fuel and light 8, miscellaneous 20. The group indices for current year as compared with a fixed base period were 410, 150, 343, 248 and 285 respectively. Calculate the cost of loving index for the current year.

Mr. X was getting ₹ 2,400 in the base period and ₹ 4,300 in the current year. State how much he ought to have received as extra allowance to maintain his former standard of living.

Solution.

CONSTRUCTION OF COST OF LIVING INDEX

Group	*Group Index (I)*	*Weight (W)*	*IW*
Food	410	45	18450
Rent	150	15	2250
Clothing	343	12	4116
Fuel & Light	248	8	1984
Miscellaneous	285	20	5700
		$\Sigma W = 100$	$\Sigma IW = 32{,}500$

$$\text{Cost of Living Index} = \frac{\Sigma IW}{\Sigma W} = \frac{32500}{100} = 325$$

For maintaining same standard of living, Mr. X should earn $\frac{2400 \times 325}{100}$ = ₹ 7,800. So he must receive an extra allowance of ₹ 3500 (*i.e.*, 7,800–4,300).

9.17. PROBLEMS IN THE CONSTRUCTION OF INDEX NUMBERS

Before constructing index numbers a careful thought must be given to the following problems :

1. The purpose of the index. At the very outset the purpose of constructing the index must be very clearly decided—what the index is to measure and why? There is no all purpose index. Every index is of limited and of particular use. Thus, a price index that is intended to measure consumers, prices must not include wholesale prices. And if such an index is intended to measure the cost of living of poor families, great care should be taken not to include goods ordinarily used by middle class and upper-income groups.

The problem of the scope of the index, *i.e.,* the field covered by the index, is linked up with the purpose of the index and the data available. The data available, or rather the lack of it, may necessitate the modification of the purpose.

2. Availability and comparability of data. It is important to keep in mind that, in so far as is possible, data which are used in the construction of an index number must be comparable in the sense that if one wants to compare prices quality should not be changing. Furthermore, the goods or services to which the prices or quantities refer must adhere to uniform definitions that is, rigorous specifications. How to achieve these goals in practice is a problem that has never been solved entirely to everyone's satisfaction.

3. Selection of base period. Whenever index numbers are constructed, a reference is made to some base period. The base period is the period with which comparisons of relative changes are made. It may be a year, month or a day. The index for base period is always taken as 100. Though the selection of the base period would primarily depend upon the object of the index, the following points need careful consideration in the selection of base period:

(i) The base period should be normal one. The period that is selected as base should be normal, *i.e.,* it should be free from abnormalities like wars, earthquakes, famines, booms, depressions, etc. However, at times it is really difficult to select a year which is normal in all respects—a year which is normal in one respect may be abnormal in another. To solve this problem an average of a number of years, say, 3 or 4 (preferable covering one complete cycle), may be taken as the base. The process or averaging will reduce the effect of extremes. Thus the average of the period from 2001 to 2004 may be considered normal whereas no individual year in that span may be considered normal.

(ii) The base period should not be too distant in the past. Since index numbers are helpful in decision-making and economic policies are often a matter of short period, we should not select a base period that is too distant in that past. For example, for deciding increase in dearness allowance at present, there is no advantage in taking 1985 or 1995 as the base ; the comparison should be with the preceding year or the year after which dearness allowance has not been revised.

(iii) Fixed base or chain base. While selecting the base decision has to be made as to whether the base shall remain fixed or not, *i.e.,* whether we have a fixed base or chain base index. In the fixed base method, the year or the period or years to which all other prices are related is constant for all times. On the other hand, in the chain base method the prices of a year are linked with those of the preceding year and not with the fixed year. Naturally the chain base method gives a better picture than what is obtained by fixed base method. However, much would depend upon the purpose of constructing the index.

4. Selection of number or items. Every item cannot be included while constructing an index number and hence one has to select a sample. For example, while constructing a price index it is impossible to include each and every commodity. hence, it is necessary to decide what commodities to include. The commodities should be selected in such a manner that they are representative of the tastes, habits and customs of the people for whom the index is meant. Thus in a consumer price index for working class, items like colour T.V., motor cars, refrigerator, cosmetics, etc., find no place. A decision must also be made on the number of commodities to be included and their qualities. Here we should note that the larger the number of commodities included, the more representative shall be the index but at the same time the greater shall be the cost and the time taken.

5. Price quotations. After the commodities have been selected, the next problem is to obtain price quotations for these commodities. It is a well-known fact that prices of many commodities vary from place to place and even from shop to shop in the same market. It is impracticable to obtain price quotations from all the places where a commodity is dealt with. A selection must be made of representative places and persons. These places should be those which are well-known for trading for that particular commodity. After the places from where the price quotations are to be obtained are decided, the next thing is to appoint some person or institution who can supply price quotations as and when required. Great care must be exercised to see that the price reporting agency is unbiased. In order to check the accuracy of price quotations supplied by an agency is that quotations are obtained from more than one agency. If there is some reliable journal or magazine supplying price quotations then it may be utilised.

6. Choice of an average. Since index numbers are specialized averages, a decision has to be made as to which particular average (*i.e.,* arithmetic mean, median, mode, geometric mean or harmonic mean) should be used for constructing the index. Theoretically speaking geometric mean is the best average in the construction of index numbers because of the following reasons : (*i*) in the construction of index numbers we are concerned with ratios or relative changes and the geometric mean gives equal weights to equal ratio of change; (*ii*) geometric mean is less susceptible to major variations as a result of violent fluctuations in the values of the individual items; and (*iii*) index number calculated by using this average are reversible and, therefore, base shifting is easily possible. The geometric mean index always satisfies the time reversal test.

Despite theoretical justification for favouring geometric mean, arithmetic mean is more popularly used while constructing index numbers. This is for the reason that arithmetic mean is much more simple to compute than the geometric mean. However, wherever possible, in the interest of greater accuracy geometric mean should be preferred. It is gratifying to note that with the growing use of calculating devices, geometric mean is becoming more popular in constructing index numbers.

7. Selection of appropriate weights. The problem of selecting suitable weights is quite important and at the same time quite difficult to decide. The term 'weight' refers to the relative importance of the different items in the construction of the index. All items are not of equal importance and hence it is necessary to devise some suitable method whereby the varying importance or the different items is taken into account. This is done by allocating weights. Thus we have broadly two types of indices — unweighted indices and weighted indices. In the former case, no specific weights are assigned, whereas in the latter case specific weights are assigned to various items. It may be pointed out here that no index is unweighted in strict sense of the term as weights implicitly enter in unweighted indices because we are giving equal importance to all the items and hence weights are unity. It is, therefore, necessary to adopt some suitable method of weighting so that arbitrary and haphazard weights may not affect the results.

8. Selection of an appropriate formula. A large number of formulae have been devised for constructing the index. The problem very often is that of selecting the most appropriate formula. The choice of the formula would depend not only on the purpose of the index but also on the data available. Prof. Irving Fisher has suggested that an appropriate index is that which satisfies time reversal test and factor reversal test. Theoretically, Fisher's method is considered as 'ideal' for constructing index numbers. However, from a practical point or view there are certain limitations of this index which shall be discussed later. As such, no particular formula can be regarded as the best under all circumstances. On the basis of his knowledge of the characteristics of different formulae a discriminating investigator will choose technical methods adopted to his data and appropriate to his purpose.

None of the above problems is simple to solve in practice and the final index is usually the product of compromise between theoretical standards and the standards attainable with the given data.

9.18. MORE EXAMPLES

Example 34. *The following are the index numbers of wholesale prices of a certain commodity based on 1992:*

Year	:	*1992*	*1993*	*1994*	*1995*	*1996*
Index No	:	*100*	*108*	*120*	*150*	*210*

Shift the base to 1994 and obtain the new Index Numbers.

(*B.A. (H), Econ.; Delhi Univ; 1996*)

Solution.

INDEX NUMBERS WITH 1994 AS BASE

Year	*Index Numbers (1992 = 100)*	*Index Numbers (1994 = 100)*
1992	100	$100 \times \frac{100}{120} = 83.33$
1993	108	$108 \times \frac{100}{120} = 90$
1994	120	$120 \times \frac{100}{120} = 100$
1995	150	$150 \times \frac{100}{120} = 125$
1996	210	$210 \times \frac{100}{120} = 175$

Example 35. From the following data, calculate:

(*i*) Quantity index by Marshall-Edgeworth's formulae.

(*ii*) Price index by Bowley's formulae.

Commodities	Expenditure in ₹ Current year	Base year	Quantity in Current year (Kg.)	Price in Base year (₹)
A	75	34	15	8.5
B	40	16	8	3.2
C	25	10	12.5	2.5
D	60	25	10	5
E	70	24	14	8

Solution.

Current year expenditure = p_1q_1 (given)

We calcualate $p_1 = \dfrac{\text{Current year value}}{q_1}$

same way expeidnture in base year = p_0q_0

Thus $q_0 = \dfrac{p_0q_0}{p_0}$

COMPUTATION OF INDEX NUMBERS

Commodities	p_1q_1	q_1	p_1	p_0q_0	p_0	q_0	p_1q_0	p_0q_1
A	75	15	5	34	8.5	4	20	127.50
B	40	8	5	16	3.2	5	25	25.60
C	25	12.5	2	10	2.5	4	8	31.25
D	60	10	6	25	5	5	30	50.00
E	70	14	5	24	8	3	15	112.00
	$\Sigma p_1q_1 = 270$			$\Sigma p_0q_0 = 109$			$\Sigma p_1q_0 = 98$	$\Sigma p_0q_1 = 346.35$

(*i*) Marshall Edgeworth's Quantity Index:

$$Q_{01} = \frac{\Sigma q_1 (p_0 + p_1)}{\Sigma q_0 (p_0 + p_1)} \times 100 = \frac{\Sigma q_1p_0 + \Sigma q_1p_1}{\Sigma q_0p_0 + \Sigma q_0p_1} \times 100$$

$$= \frac{346.35 + 270}{109 + 98} \times 100$$

$$= \frac{616.35}{207} \times 100 = 297.75$$

(*ii*) Bowley's Price Index :

$$P_{01} = \frac{\dfrac{\Sigma p_1q_0}{\Sigma p_0q_0} + \dfrac{\Sigma p_1q_1}{\Sigma p_0q_1}}{2} \times 100 \quad \left[= \frac{L + P}{2}\right]$$

$$= \frac{\dfrac{98}{109} + \dfrac{270}{346.35}}{2} \times 100 = (0.899 + 0.78)\, 50 = 83.95$$

Example 36. *Compute the chain index with 1999 prices as base from the following table giving the average wholesale prices of the commodities A, B and C for the year 2000 :*

	Average wholesale price (in ₹)				
Commodity	*1999*	*2000*	*2001*	*2002*	*2003*
A	20	16	28	35	21
B	25	30	24	36	45
C	20	25	30	24	30

Solution.

COMPUTATION OF CHAIN INDICES

	Price Relatives based on preceding year				
Commodity	*1999*	*2000*	*2001*	*2002*	*2003*
A	100	$\frac{16}{20} \times 100 = 80$	$\frac{28}{16} \times 100 = 175$	$\frac{35}{28} \times 100 = 125$	$\frac{21}{35} \times 100 = 60$
B	100	$\frac{30}{25} \times 100 = 120$	$\frac{24}{30} \times 100 = 80$	$\frac{36}{24} \times 100 = 150$	$\frac{45}{36} \times 100 = 125$
C	100	$\frac{25}{20} \times 100 = 125$	$\frac{30}{25} \times 100 = 120$	$\frac{24}{30} \times 100 = 80$	$\frac{30}{24} \times 100 = 125$
Total of Price Relatives	300	325	375	355	310
Average of Price Relatives	100	108.33	125	118.33	103.33
Chain Index (1999 = 100)	100	$\frac{108.33 \times 100}{100}$ = 108.33	$\frac{125 \times 108.33}{100}$ = 135.41	$\frac{118.33 \times 135.41}{100}$ = 160.23	$\frac{103.33 \times 160.23}{100}$ = 165.57

Example 37. *Reconstruct the following indices using 2000 as the base.*

Year :	*1996*	*1997*	*1998*	*1999*	*2000*	*2001*	*2002*
Index Nos. :	*110*	*130*	*150*	*175*	*180*	*200*	*220*

Solution.

Year	*Index No.*	*Index Number (Base 2000 = 100)*
1996	110	$\frac{100}{180} \times 110 = 61{\cdot}11$
1997	130	$\frac{100}{180} \times 130 = 72{\cdot}22$
1998	150	$\frac{100}{180} \times 150 = 83{\cdot}33$
1999	175	$\frac{100}{180} \times 175 = 97{\cdot}22$
2000	180	100·00
2001	200	$\frac{100}{180} \times 200 = 111{\cdot}11$
2002	220	$\frac{100}{180} \times 220 = 122{\cdot}22$

Example 38. *An index is at 100 in 1981. It rises 4% in 1982, falls 6% in 1983, falls 4% in 1984 rises 3% in 1985. Calculate the index numbers for the five years with 1983 as base.*

Solution. It is given

$P_{81-81} = 100$

$P_{81-82} = 104$ [it rises by 4% from 1981]

$P_{82-83} = 100 - 6 = 94$ [6% decrease from 1982]

$P_{83-84} = 100 - 4 = 96$ [4% decrease from 1983]

$P_{84-85} = 100 + 3 = 107$

Thus we are given "link relatives".

INDEX NUMBERS (BASE 1983 = 100)

Year	*Link Relatives*	*Index Number* (*Base 1981 = 100*)	*Index Number* (*Base 1983 = 100*)
1981	100	100	$\frac{100}{97 \cdot 76} \times 100 = 102 \cdot 32$
1982	104	$\frac{100 \times 104}{100} = 104$	$\frac{100}{97 \cdot 76} \times 104 = 106 \cdot 40$
1983	94	$\frac{94}{100} \times 104 = 97 \cdot 76$	100·00
1984	96	$\frac{96}{100} \times 97 \cdot 76 = 93 \cdot 85$	$\frac{100}{97 \cdot 76} \times 93 \cdot 85 = 96 \cdot 00$
1985	107	$\frac{103}{100} \times 93 \cdot 85 = 96 \cdot 66$	$\frac{100}{97 \cdot 76} \times 96 \cdot 66 = 98 \cdot 88$

Example 39. *From the following data, construct chain base index numbers (Link relatives).*

Items	*Years* 1986	1987	1988	1989	1990
	Prices in ₹				
A	5	8	10	12	15
B	3	6	8	10	12
C	2	3	5	7	10.5

Solution. CALCULATION OF CHAIN BASE INDEX NUMBERS

*PR** → *Items* ↓	*1986*	*1987*	*1988*	*1989*	*1990*
A	100	$\frac{8}{5} \times 100 = 160$	$\frac{10}{8} \times 100 = 125$	$\frac{12}{10} \times 100 = 120$	$\frac{15}{12} \times 100 = 125$
B	100	$\frac{6}{3} \times 100 = 200$	$\frac{8}{6} \times 100 = 133.3$	$\frac{10}{8} \times 100 = 125$	$\frac{12}{10} \times 100 = 120$
C	100	$\frac{3}{2} \times 100 = 150$	$\frac{5}{3} \times 100 = 166.7$	$\frac{7}{5} \times 100 = 140$	$\frac{10.5}{7} \times 100 = 150$
Total of price relatives	300	510	425.0	385	395
CBI	$\frac{300}{3} = 100$	$\frac{510}{3} = 170$	$\frac{425}{3} = 141.7$	$\frac{385}{3} = 128.3$	$\frac{395}{3} = 131.7$

PR* = Price Relatives CBI** = Chain base index number = Link Relatives.

Example 40. *From the following data on retail prices of wheat (in ₹/quintal), construct chain base index numbers. Also construct the chained index numbers and the fixed numbers with 1985 as base year.*

Years	:	*1985*	*1986*	*1987*	*1988*	*1989*	*1990*
Prices	:	*330*	*370*	*385*	*390*	*400*	*425*

Solution. Since it is a single commodity case, therefore, link relatives would be the chain base index numbers and the fixed base index numbers would be equal to the chained numbers.

Year	*Price of Wheat*	*Chain Base Index*	*Chained Index Number (FBI)*
1985	330	100	100
1986	370	$\frac{370}{330} \times 100 = 112.1$	112.1
1987	385	$\frac{385}{370} \times 100 = 104.1$	$\frac{104.1 \times 112.1}{100} = 116.7$
1988	390	$\frac{390}{385} \times 100 = 101.3$	$\frac{101.3 \times 116.7}{100} = 118.7$
1989	400	$\frac{400}{390} \times 100 = 102.6$	$\frac{102.6 \times 118.2}{100} = 121.2$
1990	425	$\frac{425}{400} \times 100 = 106.3$	$\frac{106.3 \times 121.2}{100} = 128.8$

Example 41. *Given below are two price index series. Splice them on the base 1994 = 100. By what per cent did the price of steel rise between 1990 and 1995?*

Year	*Old price index for Steel : (Base 1985 = 100)*	*New price index for Steel : (Base 1994 = 100)*
1990	*141·5*	
1991	*163·7*	
1992	*158·2*	
1993	*156·8*	*99·8*
1994	*157·1*	*100·0*
1995		*102·3*

Solution.

SPLICING OF OLD PRICE INDEX TO NEW PRICE INDEX

Year	*Old price index for Steel : (Base 1985 = 100)*	*New price index for Steel : (Base 1994 = 100)*
1990	141·5	$\frac{100}{157{\cdot}1} \times 141{\cdot}5 = 90{\cdot}07$
1991	163·7	$\frac{100}{157{\cdot}1} \times 163{\cdot}7 = 104{\cdot}20$
1992	158·2	$\frac{100}{157{\cdot}1} \times 158{\cdot}2 = 100{\cdot}70$

1993	156·8	$\frac{100}{157\cdot1} \times 156\cdot8 =$	99·81
1994	157·1		100·0
1995	$\frac{157.1}{100} \times 102.3 = 160.71$		102·3

Hence, the percentage increase in the price of steel between 1990 and 1995 is

$$\frac{102\cdot30 - 90\cdot07}{90\cdot07} \times 100 = 0\cdot1358 \times 100 = 13\cdot58$$

Hence required increase is 13·58%.

Example 42. *In 2003 for working class people wheat was selling at an average price of ₹ 16 per 20 kg., cloth at ₹ 2 per metre, house rent ₹ 30 per house and other items at ₹ 10 per unit. By 2004 cost of wheat rose by ₹ 4 per 20 kg., house rent by ₹ 15 per house and other items doubled in price. The working class cost of living index for the year 2004 (with 2003 as base) was 160. By how much the cloth rose in price during the period ?*

Solution. Let the price of cloth be X in 2004. Applying simple average of price relative method.

Commodity	*Price in 2003* p_0	*Price in 2004* P_1	$P = \frac{p_1}{p_0} \times 100$
Wheat	16	20	125
Cloth	2	X	50 X
House Rent	30	45	150
Miscellaneous	10	20	200
			$475 + 50X = \Sigma P$

$$p_{01} = \frac{\Sigma\left(\frac{p_1}{p_0} \times 100\right)}{N} = \frac{\Sigma P}{N}$$

$$160 = \frac{475 + 50X}{4}$$

$$640 - 475 = 50X$$

$$X = \frac{165}{50} = ₹\ 3.30$$

Hence, increase in price of cloth is by ₹ 1.30 per metre.

Example 43. *The table below shows the average wages in rupees per week of a group of industrial workers during the year 1989-96. The consumer price indices for these years with 1989 as base are also shown :*

Year :	*1989*	*1990*	*1991*	*1992*	*1993*	*1994*	*1995*	*1996*
Average wage of workers (₹) :	*119*	*133*	*144*	*157*	*175*	*184*	*189*	*194*
Consumer Price Index :	*100*	*107.6*	*106.6*	*107.6*	*116.2*	*118.9*	*119.8*	*120.2*

(i) Determine the Real Wage of workers during the years 1989-96 as compared with their wages 1989.

(ii) Determine the purchasing power of rupee for the year 1996 as compared to the year 1989. What is the significance of this result?

Solution. (*i*) $\text{Real Wage} = \dfrac{\text{Money Wage}}{\text{Consumer Price Index}} \times 100$

CALCULATION OF REAL WAGES

Year	*Wages (₹)*	*Consumer Price Index*	*Real Wages*
1989	119	100	$\frac{119}{100} \times 100 = 119$
1990	133	107.6	$\frac{133}{107.6} \times 100 = 123.61$
1991	144	106.6	$\frac{144}{106.6} \times 100 = 135.08$
1992	157	107.6	$\frac{157}{107.6} \times 100 = 145.91$
1993	175	116.2	$\frac{175}{116.2} \times 100 = 150.60$
1994	184	118.9	$\frac{184}{118.9} \times 100 = 154.75$
1995	189	119.8	$\frac{189}{119.8} \times 100 = 157.76$
1996	194	120.2	$\frac{194}{120.2} \times 100 = 161.40$

(*ii*) The purchasing power of rupee $= \dfrac{100}{120.2} = 0.832$ or 83.2 paise.

With a rise in price level always there is a reduction in the purchasing power. Thus, it means a rupee of 1989 worth only 83 paise in 1996. The purchasing power of rupee has decreased by 17% over the period 1989 to 1996.

Example 44. *Construct a Fisher's Ideal Index form the following data and show that it satisfies time reversal and factor reversal tests :*

	2002		*2003*	
Items	p_0	q_0	p_1	q_1
A	10	40	12	45
B	11	50	11	52
C	14	30	17	30
D	8	28	10	29
E	12	15	13	20

Solution. CONSTRUCTION OF FISHER'S IDEAL INDEX

Items	p_0	q_0	p_1	q_1	p_1q_0	p_0q_0	p_1q_1	p_0q_1
A	10	40	12	45	480	400	540	450
B	11	50	11	52	550	550	572	572
C	14	30	17	30	510	420	510	420
D	8	28	10	29	280	224	290	232
E	12	15	13	20	195	180	260	240
					$\Sigma p_1q_0 = 2015$	$\Sigma p_0q_0 = 1774$	$\Sigma p_1q_1 = 2172$	$\Sigma p_0q_1 = 1914$

Fisher's Ideal Index : $P_{01} = \sqrt{\frac{\Sigma p_1 q_0}{\Sigma p_0 q_0} \times \frac{\Sigma p_1 q_1}{\Sigma p_0 q_1}} \times 100$

$$= \sqrt{\frac{2015}{1774} \times \frac{2172}{1914}} \times 100 = 1.135 \times 100 = 113.5$$

Time Reversal Test : The reversal test is satisfied when :

$$P_{01} \times P_{10} = 1$$

$$P_{10} = \sqrt{\frac{\Sigma p_0 q_1}{\Sigma p_1 q_1} \times \frac{\Sigma p_0 q_0}{\Sigma p_1 q_0}} = \sqrt{\frac{1914}{2172} \times \frac{1774}{2015}}$$

$$P_{01} \times P_{10} = \sqrt{\frac{2015}{1774} \times \frac{2172}{1914} \times \frac{1914}{2172} \times \frac{1774}{2015}} = 1$$

Hence time reversal test is satisfied by the given data.

Factor Reversal Test : Factor reversal test is satisfied when :

$$P_{01} \times Q_{01} = \frac{\Sigma p_1 q_1}{\Sigma p_0 q_0}$$

$$Q_{01} = \sqrt{\frac{\Sigma q_1 p_0}{\Sigma q_0 p_0} \times \frac{\Sigma q_1 p_1}{\Sigma q_0 p_1}} = \sqrt{\frac{1914}{1774} \times \frac{2172}{2015}}$$

$$P_{01} \times Q_{01} = \sqrt{\frac{2015}{1774} \times \frac{2172}{1914} \times \frac{1914}{1774} \times \frac{2172}{2015}} = \frac{2172}{1774} = \frac{\Sigma p_1 q_1}{\Sigma p_0 q_0} = V_{01}$$

Hence factor reversal test is satisfied by the given data.

Example 45. *A particular series of consumer price index covers five groups of items. Between 1975 and 1980 the index rose from 180 to 225. Over the same period the price index numbers of various groups changed as follows:*

Food from 198 to 252; clothing from 185 to 205; fuel and lighting from 175 to 195; miscellaneous from 138 to 212; house rent remained unchanged at 150.

Given that the weights of clothing, house rent and fuel and lighting are equal, determine the weights for individual groups of items.

Solution. Let w_1 % be the weight of food, w_2% be the weight of miscellaneous group and w% be the weight of each of the remaining three groups. Therefore we can write $w_1 + w_2 + 3w = 100$ or $w_2 = 100 - w_1 - 3w$.

The given data can be written in the form of table as given below:

Groups	*Weights* W	*Index in 1975 (I_1)*	*Index in 1980 (I_2)*	*1975* WI_1	*1980* WI_2
Food	w_1	198	252	$198\ w_1$	$252\ w_1$
Clothing	w	185	205	$185\ w$	$205\ w$
Fuel & Lighting	w	175	195	$175\ w$	$195\ w$
House Rent	w	150	150	$150\ w$	$150\ w$
Miscellaneous	$100 - w_1 - 3w$	138	212	$138\ (100 - w_1 - 3w)$	$212\ (100 - w_1 - 300)$
Total	100				

For 1975; $\frac{\Sigma WI}{\Sigma W} = \frac{198\,w_1 + (185 + 175 + 150)\,w + 138\,(100 - w_1 - 3w)}{100} = 180$ (given)

or $60w_1 + 96w = 4200$ ...(1)

Further, the consumer price index of 1980 is

$\frac{\Sigma WI}{\Sigma W} = \frac{252w_1 + (205 + 195 + 150)\,w\ 212\,(100 - w_1 - 3w)}{100} = 225$ (given)

or $40w_1 - 86w = 1300$ ...(2)

Solving equations (1) and (2) simultaneously, we get $w = 10$ and $w_1 = 54$

Substituting these values in expression for w_2, we get

$w_2 = 100 - w_1 - 3w = 100 - 54 - 30 = 16$

Example 46. *The sub-group indices of the consumer price index number for urban non-manual employees of an industrial centre for a particular year (with base 2000 = 100) were :*

Food	*200*
Clothing	*130*
Fuel and Lighting	*120*
House Rent	*150*
Miscellaneous	*140*

The weights are 60, 8, 7, 10 and 15 respectively. It is proposed to fix dearness allowance in such a way so as to compensate fully the rise in the price of food and house rent only.

What should be the dearness allowance expressed as a percentage of wage ?

Solution. Let the income of the consumer be 100 rupees. He spent 60 rupees on food and 10 rupees on house rent in 2000. Since the index of food is 200 and the house rent 150 for the particular year for which the data are given, in order to maintain the same consumption standards regarding these two items, he will have to spend ₹ 120 on food and ₹ 15 on house rent. Since the weights of other items are constant, in order to maintain the same standard he will have to spend 120 + 8 + 7 + 15 + 15 = ₹ 165. Hence dearness allowance should be 65 per cent.

Example 47. *Given the following data:*

Year	*Weekly take-home pay (wages)*	*Consumer price index*
1999	*109.50*	*112.8*
2000	*112.20*	*118.2*
2001	*116.40*	*127.4*
2002	*125.08*	*138.2*
2003	*135.40*	*143.5*
2004	*138.10*	*149.8*

(i) What was the real average weekly wage for each year?

(ii) In which year did the employees have the greatest buying power?

(iii) What percentage increase in the weekly wages for the year 2004 is required (if any) to provide the same buying power that the employees enjoyed in the year in which they had the highest real wages.

Solution. (*i*) Real average weekly wage can be obtained by the following formula:

$$\text{Rear wage} = \frac{\text{Money Wage}}{\text{Price Index}} \times 100$$

CALCULATION OF REAL WAGES

Year	*Weekly take-home pay (wages)* ₹	*Consumer price index*	*Real Wages*
1999	109.50	112.8	$\frac{109.5}{112.8} \times 100 = 97.07$
2000	112.20	118.2	$\frac{112.8}{118.2} \times 100 = 94.92$
2001	116.40	127.4	$\frac{116.4}{127.4} \times 100 = 91.37$
2002	125.08	138.2	$\frac{125.08}{138.2} \times 100 = 90.51$
2003	135.40	143.5	$\frac{135.4}{143.5} \times 100 = 94.36$
2004	138.10	149.8	$\frac{138.10}{149.8} \times 100 = 92.19$

(*ii*) The employee has greatest purchasing power (real wages) in year 1999.

(*iii*) Per cent increase in wages in 2004 so that his real wages should become 97.07

$$= \frac{97.07 - 92.19}{92.19} \times 100 = 5.3\%$$

Example 48. *The adjoining table gives the annual income of a person and the general price index number for the period 1988 to 1996. Prepare index number to show the changes in the real income of the person.*

Year	*Annual Income in ₹*	*Price Index Number*
1988	*36,000*	*100*
1989	*42,000*	*120*
1990	*50,000*	*145*
1991	*55,000*	*160*
1992	*60,000*	*250*
1993	*64,000*	*320*
1994	*68,000*	*450*
1995	*72,000*	*530*
1996	*75,000*	*600*

Solution. COMPUTATION OF INDICES OF REAL INCOME

Year (1)	*Annual Income* (*in* ₹) (2)	*Price Index Number* (3)	*Real Income* $(4) = \frac{(2)}{(3)} \times 100$	*Real Income Indices (1988 = 100)* $(5) = \frac{100}{36{,}000} \times (4)$
1988	36,000	100	$\frac{36{,}000}{100} \times 100 = 36{,}000$	100
1989	42,000	120	$\frac{42{,}000}{120} \times 100 = 35{,}000$	$\frac{35{,}000}{36{,}000} \times 100 = 97.22$

1990	50,000	145	$\frac{50,000}{145} \times 100 = 34,482.75$	$\frac{34,482.75}{36,000} \times 100 = 95.78$
1991	55,000	160	$\frac{55,000}{160} \times 100 = 34,375$	$\frac{34,375}{36,000} \times 100 = 95.48$
1992	60,000	250	$\frac{60,000}{250} \times 100 = 24,000$	$\frac{24,000}{36,000} \times 100 = 66.66$
1993	64,000	320	$\frac{64,000}{320} \times 100 = 20,000$	$\frac{20,000}{36,000} \times 100 = 55.55$
1994	68,000	450	$\frac{68,000}{450} \times 100 = 15,111.11$	$\frac{15,111.11}{36,000} \times 100 = 41.97$
1995	72,000	530	$\frac{72,000}{530} \times 100 = 13,589.90$	$\frac{13,589.90}{36,000} \times 100 = 37.75$
1996	75,000	600	$\frac{75,000}{600} \times 100 = 12,500$	$\frac{12,500}{36,000} \times 100 = 34.72$

Example 49. *The consumer price index over a certain period increased from 120 to 215 and the wages of a worker increased from ₹ 1,680 to ₹ 3,000. What is the gain or loss of the worker ?* [Delhi Univ. B.A. (Econ. Hons.), 1997]

Solution. We are given :

Consumer price index in, (say), period I = 120

Consumer price index in (say), period II = 215

The wages of the worker in period I and II are given to be ₹ 1,680 and ₹ 3,000 respectively.

The real wages of the worker in the current period II with respect to the period I as base, are given by :

$$₹\ \frac{120}{215} \times 3,000 = ₹\ 1,674.42$$

Since this wage (₹ 1,674.42) is less than the wages of the worker in the period I (*viz.*, ₹ 1,680), the worker is not better off but worse off by ₹ 5.58 as compared to the period 1.

Example 50. *The consumer price index for a group of workers was 250 in 1994 with 1980 as the base.*

(*i*) *Compute the purchasing power of a rupee in 1994 compared to 1980.*

(*ii*) *At what value of consumer price index would the purchasing power of a rupee be 25 paise ?* [Delhi Univ. B.A. (Econ. Hons.), 1998]

Solution. (*i*) Purchasing power (P.P) of a rupee in 1994 with respect to the base period 1980 is given by :

$$\text{P.P of a rupee} = \frac{100}{\text{Consumer Price Index for 1994 } w.r.t. \text{ base 1980}} \quad ...(*)$$

$$= ₹\ \frac{100}{250} = ₹\ 0.40.$$

This implies that if a person was spending ₹ 0.40 (*i.e.*, 40 paise) to buy a certain basket of goods in 1980, in 1994 he has to spend ₹ 1 to buy the same basket of goods.

(*ii*) If we want the purchasing power of a rupee to be ₹ 0.25 in 1994, then from (*), we get

Consumer price index for 1994 with respect to base 1980

$$= \frac{100}{\text{P.P. of a rupee}} = \frac{100}{0{\cdot}25} = 400.$$

Example 51. (*a*) *Construct the cost of living index number from the table given below .*

Group	*Index for 1998*	*Expenditure*
1. Food	*550*	*46%*
2. Clothing	*215*	*10%*
3. Fuel & Lighting	*220*	*7%*
4. House Rent	*150*	*12%*
5. Miscellaneous	*275*	*25%*

(*b*) *How is the overall index number altered :*

(*i*) *if all the group index numbers are changed in the same ratio ;*

(*ii*) *if all the weights and group indices are changed in the same ratio ;*

(*iii*) *if all the group index numbers are increased by 10 and all the weights doubled ?*

Solution.

COMPUTATION OF COST OF LIVING INDEX NUMBER

Group	*Index* (*I*)	*Expenditure* (*W*)	*W I*
Food	550	46	25300
Clothing	215	10	2150
Fuel & Lighting	220	7	1540
House Rent	150	12	1800
Miscellaneous	275	25	6875
		$\Sigma W = 100$	$\Sigma WI = 37665$

Cost of living index number for 1998 $= \dfrac{\Sigma WI}{\Sigma W} = \dfrac{37665}{100} = 376.65$ ...(*)

(*b*) (*i*) Suppose all the group index numbers are changed in the same ratio, say, *k* so that new group index number becomes *k I*.

Overall cost of living Index No. $= \dfrac{\Sigma W(kI)}{\Sigma W} = \dfrac{k\Sigma WI}{\Sigma W} = 376.65k$ [From (*)]

i.e., Overall index number also changes in the same ratio.

(*ii*) Suppose all the group indices are changed in the same ratio, say, *a* and all the weights are changed in the same ratio, say, *b* then

Overall cost of living Index No. $= \dfrac{\Sigma\,(bW)\,(aI)}{\Sigma bW} = \dfrac{ab\ \Sigma WI}{b\ \Sigma W} = \dfrac{a\Sigma WI}{\Sigma W} = 376.65a$

i.e., Overall index number changes in the same ratio as the group indices.

(*iii*) If all the group index numbers are increased by 10 and all the weights are doubled then

$$\text{Overall cost of living Index No.} = \frac{\Sigma(I + 10)\,.\,2W}{\Sigma 2W} = \frac{2\Sigma\,(WI + 10W)}{2\Sigma W}$$

$$= \frac{\Sigma WI + 10\,\Sigma W}{\Sigma W} = \frac{\Sigma WI}{\Sigma W} + 10 = 376.65 + 10 = 386.65$$

i.e., Overall index number also increases by 10.

EXERCISE 9

1. From the following data compute Fisher's ideal index number:

Commodity	*2003*		*2004*	
	Price	*Quantity*	*Price*	*Quantity*
A	14	32	12	52
B	24	37	11	33
C	17	21	8	44
D	12	27	10	37

[**Ans.** P_{01} = 61.97]

2. Calculate Fisher's and Laspeyre's index number for the following data:

	Base year		*Current year*	
Commodity	*Price*	*Quantity*	*Price*	*Quantity*
A	3.2	20	3.9	22
B	4.8	18	4.9	19

[**Ans.** P_{01} = 110.41, P_{01} = 110.51]

3. Give the following data for a firm, B find average wage and salaries at constant prices (base year 2000):

Year	*Average Wages and Salaries Paid (₹)*	*Consumer Price Index*
2000	5000	100
2001	5670	108
2002	5865	102
2003	6240	104
2004	6820	110

[**Ans.** 5000, 5250, 5750, 6000, 5200]

4. Compute the Fisher price index, P_{01}, for the following data:

Commodity	P_0	Q_0	P_1	Q_1
A	5	4	10	2
B	6	7	8	10
C	4	2	2	8

(*B.A. (H) Econ., Delhi Univ.*)

[**Ans.** P_{01} = 144.17]

5. From the following data, construct Quantity Index Number by (*i*) Fisher's Method; and (*ii*) Marshall-Edgeworth's Method :

	Base Year		*Current Year*	
Commodity	*Price (₹)*	*Quantity (Kgs.)*	*Expenditure (₹)*	*Quantity (Kgs.)*
A	25	40	2,000	50
B	22	18	1,200	30
C	54	16	1,320	44
D	20	40	1,350	45
E	18	30	630	15

[**Ans.** (*i*) 136.85 (*ii*) 134.94]

6. Compute the price index P_{01} using the Marshall Edgeworth formula :

Item	P_0	P_1	Q_0	Q_1
A	20	30	10	12
B	4	4	9	16
C	14	25	17	23

[**Ans.** $P_{01} = 160$]

7. Compute Fisher's Ideal Index and show whether it satisfies Time Reversal test :

Commodity	*Base year*		*Current year*	
	P	*Q*	*P*	*Q*
A	6	50	10	56
B	2	100	2	120
C	4	60	6	60
D	10	30	12	24

8. From the following data calculate Chain Base Index Numbers :

Items	*Prices in Rupees*				
	1986	*1987*	*1988*	*1989*	*1990*
A	5	8	10	12	15
B	3	6	8	10	12
C	2	3	5	7	10.5

[**Ans.** 100, 170, 240.84, 369.07, 406.95.]

9. Calculate the Chain base Index Numbers from the following data:

Commodity	*Prices in Rupees*				
	1991	*1992*	*1993*	*1994*	*1995*
A	2	3	4	2	7
B	3	6	9	4	3
C	4	12	20	8	16
D	5	7	18	11	22

[**Ans.** 100, 197.50, 349.16, 170.70, 352.07.]

10. The following table gives the cost of living index numbers for different groups in their respective weights for the year 1992 (base year : 1982) :

Group	*Cost of Living Index*	*Weight*
Food	525	40
Clothing	325	16
Light and Fuel	240	15
Rent	180	20
Others	200	9

(*i*) Calculate the overall cost of living index number. (*ii*) Mr. Bose got a salary of ₹ 550 in 1982. Determine how much he should have to receive as salary in 1992 to maintain his same standard of living as in 1982.
[**Ans.** (*i*) 352 (*ii*) ₹ 1,936]

11. From the following chain base index numbers, find the fixed base index numbers :

Year	1991	1992	1993	1994	1995
Chain Base Index	80	110	120	90	140

[**Ans.** 80, 80, 105.6, 95.04, 133.06]

12. What is 'base shifting' ? Why does it become necessary to shift the base of index number ? Give an example of the shifting of base of index numbers.

13. Explain, with examples, the shifting and splicing techniques in index numbers.

14. The following are price index numbers (Base 1985 = 100)

Year	1985	1986	1987	1988	1989	1990	1991	1992	1993	1994	1995
Index No.	100	120	122	116	120	120	137	136	149	156	137

Shift the base to 1990 and recast the index numbers.

[**Ans.** 83.33, 100, 101.67, 96.67, 100, 100, 114.17, 113.33, 124.17, 130.00, 114.17.]

15. The following are the index numbers of wholesale prices of a certain commodity based on 1992 :

Year	1992	1993	1994	1995	1996
Index No.	100	108	120	150	210

Shift the base to 1994 and obtain new index numbers.
[**Ans.** 83.33, 90, 100, 125, 175.]

16. The table below shows the average wages in rupees per week of a group of industrial workers during the years 1990-97. The consumer price indices for these years with 1990 as base are also shown :

Year	*Average wage of workers (₹)*	*Consumers Price Index*
1990	119	100.0
1991	133	107.6
1992	144	106.6
1993	157	107.6
1994	175	116.2
1995	184	118.9
1996	189	119.8
1997	194	120.2

(i) Determine the Real wages of workers during the years 1990-97 as compared with their wages in 1990.

(ii) Determine the purchasing power of rupee for the year 1997 as compared to the year 1990. What is the significance of this result?

[Ans. (i) 119, 123.6, 135.8, 145.9, 150.6, 154.8, 157.8, 161.4, (ii) 83.20]

17. Given below are two sets of indices. For the purpose of continuity of record, you are required to construct a combined series with the year 1993 as the base :

Year	*I Set (Price relatives)*	*II Set (Link Relatives)*
1990	100	
1991	120	
1992	125	
1993	150	
1994		110
1995		120
1996		95
1997		105

[Ans. 66.6, 80, 83.3, 100, 110,120, 95, 105]

18. From the following data prove that Fisher's ideal index number satisfies both Time-reversal and Factor-reversal tests:

Commodity	*Base year*		*Current year*	
	Price	*Quantity*	*Price*	*Quantity*
A	6	50	10	60
B	2	100	2	120
C	4	60	6	60

[Ans. P_{01} = 143.04] *[B.A. (H) Econ., Delhi Univ., 1994]*

19. Given the following values:

Year	*A*	*B*
1998	$\Sigma p_0 q_0$ = ₹ 10	
1999	$\Sigma p_1 q_0$ = ₹ 12	
2000	$\Sigma p_2 q_0$ = ₹ 15	
2001	$\Sigma p_3 q_0$ = ₹ 20	$\Sigma p_3 q_3$ = ₹ 25
2002		$\Sigma p_4 q_3$ = ₹ 30
2003		$\Sigma p_5 q_3$ = ₹ 40
2004		$\Sigma p_6 q_3$ = ₹ 45

(i) Calculate two price indices *A* with q_0 as weights and *B* with q_3 as weights.

(ii) Splice the two series so as to make *A* a continuous series.

[Ans. [(i) Index *A* : 100, 120, 150, 200; Index *B* : 100, 120, 160, 180

(ii) 100, 120, 150, 200, 40, 320, 360]

20. From the following chain-base index numbers, find the fixed-base index numbers (changed):

Year	:	2000	2001	2002	2003	2004
Chain Base Indices	:	80	110	120	90	140

(*B.Com. (H), Delhi Univ.*)

[**Ans.** 680, 88, 105.6, 95.04, 133.06]

21. Following are the values:

$\Sigma P_0Q_0 = 425$, $\Sigma P_1Q_0 = 505$, $\Sigma P_1Q_1 = 530$, $\Sigma P_0Q_1 = 470$

Show that Fisher's method, Paasche's and Marshall's method either satisfy time reversal test and factor reversal test or do not satisfy both or one of them.

(*B.Com. (H); Delhi Univ. 1996*)

22. The price index of cosmetics was 110 in 2001 with base at 1995 and 120 in 2002 with 2001 as base. It further increased by 30% in 2003 in relation to the price index of 2002 and decreased by 10% in 2004 as compared to its level in 2003. What is the chain base index number for 2004 with 1995 as base?

[**Ans.** 154.44] (*B.A. (H), Econ.; Delhi Univ.*)

23. A textile worker in the city of Mumbai earns ₹ 3,500 per month. The cost of living index for a particular month is given as 136. Using the following information, find out the amount of money he spent on (*i*) house rent and (*ii*) clothing.

Group	*Expenditure*	*Group Index*
Food	1400	180
Clothing	?	150
House rent	?	100
Fuel and Lighting	560	110
Miscellaneous	630	80

[**Ans.** (*i*) 490 (*ii*) 420]

24. From the following data, construct price index numbers by using the following formulae:

(*i*) Simple aggregative index.

(*ii*) Simple arithmetic average of price relatives index.

(*iii*) Weighted aggregative index with average quantities as weights.

(*iv*) Weighted arithmetic average of price relatives with expenditure in base year as weights.

Items	*Price* (P_0)	*Quantity* (q_0)	*Price* (p_1)	*Quantity* (q_1)
A	10	12	12	15
B	7	15	5	20
C	5	24	9	20
D	16	5	14	5

[**Ans.** 105.3, 114.6, 115.6, 118.8]

□□□

10

Analysis of Time Series

CHAPTER OUTLINE

10.1 INTRODUCTION

One of the most important tasks before economists and businessmen these days is to get estimates for the future. For example, a businessman is interested in finding out his likely sales in the year 2012 or as a long-term planning in 2015 or the year 2020 so that he could adjust his production accordingly and avoid the possibility of either unsold stocks or inadequate production to meet the demand. Similarly, an economist is interested in estimating the likely population in the coming years so that proper planning can be carried out with regard to food supply, jobs for the people, etc. However, the first step in making estimates for the future consists of gathering information from the past. In this connection one usually deals with statistical data which are collected, observed or recorded at successive intervals of time. Such data are generally referred to as 'time series'. Thus when we observe numerical data at different points of time, the set of observations is known as time series. For example, if we observe production, sales, population, imports, exports, etc., at different points of time, say, over the last 5 or 10 year, the set of observations formed shall constitute time series. Hence, in the analysis of time series, time is the most important factor because the variable is related to time which may be either a year, month, week, day, hour or even minute or second.

10.2. TIME SERIES DEFINED

A definition of time series is given below :

"A time series may be defined as a collection of magnitudes, belonging to different time periods, of some variable or composite of variables, such as production of steel, per capital income, gross national product, price of tobacco, or index of industrial production."

—*Ya-Lun-Chou*

It is clear from above definitions that time series consists of data arranged chronologically. Thus if we record the data relating to population per capita income, prices, production, etc., for the last 5, 10, 15, 20 years or some other time period, the series so emerging would be called *time series.*

The problem of time series analysis can best be appreciated with the help of the following example :

The following are the figures of sales of refrigerators of a firm in thousand units :

Year	*Sales of Firm A* ('000)	*Year*	*Sales of Firm A* ('000)
1997	40	2001	43
1998	42	2002	48
1999	47	2003	65
2000	41	2004	42

Set of variable values which vary with time is called "Time Series". Set of values of sales of firm A for different years is an example of time series which is generally denoted by Y so far we had been indicating it X.

If we observe the above series, we find that generally the sales have increased but for two years a decline is also noticed. The statistician, therefore, tries to analyse the effect of the various forces under four broad heads :

(1) Changes that have occurred as a result of general tendency of the data to increase or decrease, known as 'secular movements'.

(2) Changes that have taken place within a period of 12 months as a result of changes in climate, weather conditions, festivals, etc. Such changes are called 'seasonal variations'.

(3) Changes that have taken place as a result of booms and depressions. Such changes are classified under the head 'cyclical variations'.

(4) Changes that have taken place as a result of such forces that could not be predicted like floods, earthquakes, famines, etc. Such changes are classified under the head 'irregular or crratic variations'.

These are called components of time series and shall be discussed in detail.

10.3 UTILITY OF TIME SERIES ANALYSIS

The Analysis of Time Series is of great significance not only to the economist and businessman but also to the scientist, astronomist, geologist, sociologist, biologist, research worker, etc., for the reasons given below :

(1) *It helps in understanding past behaviour.* By observing data over a period of time one can easily understand what changes have taken place in the past. Such analysis will be extremely helpful in predicting future behaviour.

(2) *It helps in planning future operations.* Plans for the future cannot be made without forecasting events and relationship they will have. Statistical techniques have been evolved which enable time series to be analysed in such a way that isolate influences which determines the form of the series. If the regularity of occurrence of any feature over a sufficient long period could be clearly established then, within limits, prediction of probable future magnitude would become possible.

(3) *It helps in evaluating current accomplishments.* The performance can be compared with the expected performance and the cause of variation analysed. For example, if expected sale for 2003 was 10,000 refrigerators and the actual sale was only 9,000, one can investigate the cause for the shortfall in achievement. *Time series analysis will enable us to apply the scientific procedure of "holding other things constant" as we examine one variable at a time.* For example, if we know how much is the effect of seasonality on business we may devise ways and means of ironing out the seasonal influence or decreasing it by producing commodities with complementary seasons.

(4) *It facilitates comparison.* Different time series are often compared and important conclusions drawn therefrom.

However, one should not be led to believe that by time series analysis one can foretell with 100 per cent accuracy the course of future events. After all, statisticians are not foretellers. This could be possible only if the influence of the various forces which affect these series such as climate, customs and traditions, growth and decline factors and the complex forces which produce business cycles would have been regular in their operation. However, the facts of life real that this type of regularity does not exist But this then does not mean that time series analysis is of no value. When such analysis is coupled with a careful examination of current business indicators one can undoubtedly improve substantially upon guestimates (*i.e.,* estimated based upon pure guesswork) in forecasting future business conditions.

10.4 COMPONENTS OF TIME SERIES

It is customary to classify the fluctuations of a time series into four basic types of variations which, superimposed and acting all in concert, account for changes in the series over a period of time. These four types of patterns, movements, or, as they are often called, components or elements of a time series, are :

1. Secular Trend or simply Trend
2. Periodic or Oscillatory Variations
   (*a*) Seasonal Variations
   (*b*) Cyclical Variations

3. Random or Irregular Variations

1. *Secular Trend:* Secular trend or simply trend is the general tendency of the data to increase or decrease or stagnate over a long period of time. Most of the business and economic time series would reveal a tendency to increase or to decrease over a number of years. For example, data regarding industrial production, agricultural production, population, bank deposits, deficit financing, *etc.*, show that, in general, these magnitudes have been rising over a fairly long period. As opposed to this, a time series may also reveal a declining trend, *e.g.*, in the case of substitution of one commodity by another, the demand of the substituted commodity would reveal a declining trend such as the demand for cotton clothes, demand for coarse grains like bajra, jowar, *etc.* With the improved medical facilities, the death rate is likely to show a declining trend, *etc.* The change in trend, in either case, is attributable to the fundamental forces such as changes in population, technology, composition of production, *etc.*

According to A.E. Waugh, secular trend is, *"that irreversible movement which continues, in general, in the same direction for a considerable period of time"*. There are two parts of this definition; (*i*) movement in same direction, which implies that if the values are increasing (or decreasing) in successive periods, the tendency continues; and (*ii*) for a considerable period of time. There is no specific period which can be called as a long period. Long periods are different for different situations. For example, in cases of population or output trends, the long period could be 10 years, 20 years or 30 years. Fig. 1. shows data with increasing tendency and Fig. 2. shows data with decreasing tendency.

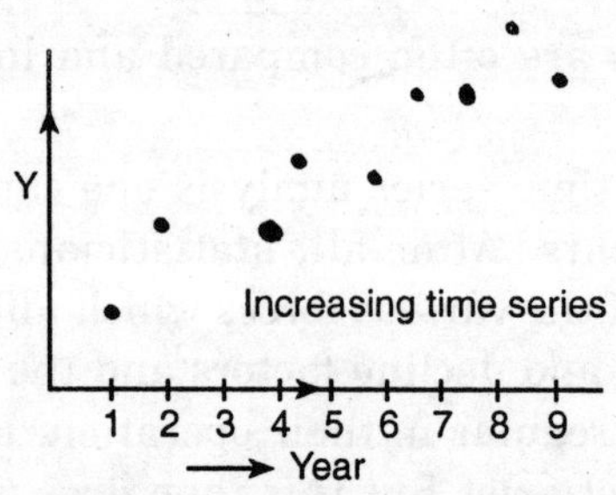

Fig. 1

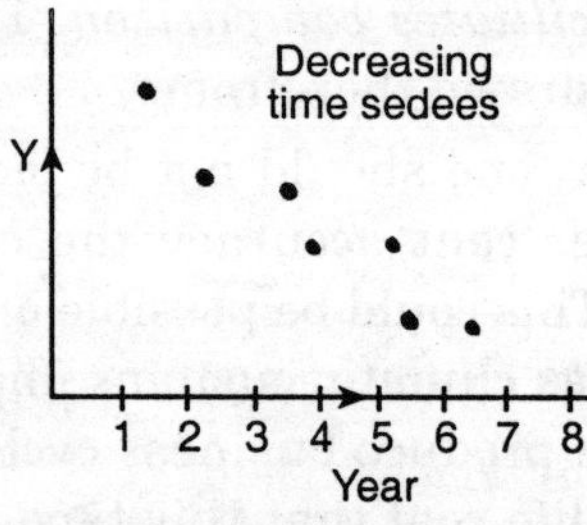

Fig. 2

Objectives of Measuring Trend

There are four main objectives of measuring trend of a time series data :

(*i*) To study past growth or decline of the series. On ignoring the short term fluctuations, trend describes the basic growth or decline tendency of the data.

(*ii*) Assuming that the same behaviour would continue in future also, the trend curve can be projected into future for forecasting.

(*iii*) In order to analyse the influence of other factors, the trend may first be measured and then eliminated from the observed values.

(*iv*) Trend values of two or more time series can be used for their comparison.

2. *Periodic Variations :* These variations, also known as oscillatory movements, repeat themselves after a regular interval of time. This time interval is known as the period of oscillation.

The oscillatory movements are termed as *Seasonal Variations* if their period of oscillation is equal to one year, and as *Cyclical Variations* if the period is greater than one year.

(A) Seasonal Variations

These variations occur within different periods of a year and recur year after year with same pattern. These will be visible in the data only if the data relates to different seasons in a year. These seasons may be quarters or months of a year which will depict quarterly or monthly variations. *e.g.*, if we study sales of woollen garments, cold drinks we see distinct variations increasing and decreasing within a year and pattern shown in a year will be replicated the next year at same points of time.

Suppose a variable depicts increasing trend as shown in Fig. 3. However it depicts seasonal variations which will move around trend values. In case the maximum *Y* occurs (shown as peak *A*) at some point in a year, then next year almost at the same time peak *B* will occur (after a gap of a year) and so on.

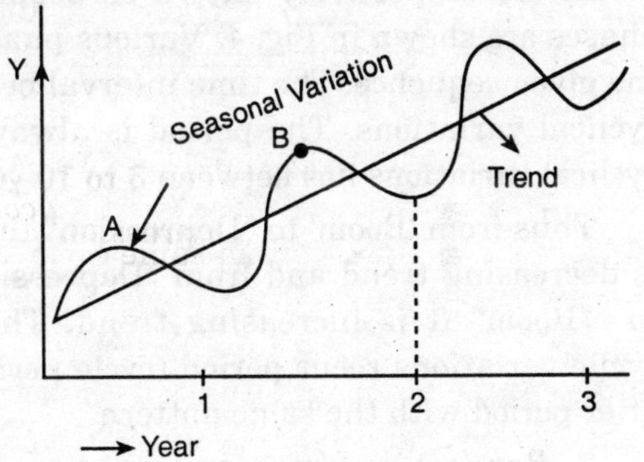

Fig. 3

Although the periodic variations are more or less regular, they may not necessarily be uniformly periodic, *i.e.,* the pattern of their variations in different periods may or may not be identical in respect of time period and size of periodic variations. For example, if a cycle is completed in five years then its following cycle may take greater or less than five years for its completion.

(*a*) *Causes of Seasonal variations*

The main causes of seasonal variations are :

(*i*) Climatic Conditions

(*ii*) Customs and Traditions

(*i*) *Climatic Conditions:* The changes in climatic conditions affect the value of time series variable and the resulting changes are known as seasonal variations. For example, the sale of woolen garments is generally at its peak in the month of November because of the beginning of winter season. Similarly, timely rainfall may increase agricultural output, prices of agricultural commodities are lowest during their harvesting season, *etc.*, reflect the effect of climatic conditions on the value of time series variable.

(*ii*) *Customs and Traditions:* The customs and traditions of the people also give rise to the seasonal variations in time series. For example, the sale of garments and ornaments may be highest during the marriage season, sale of sweets during Diwali, *etc.*, are variations that are the results of customs and traditions of the people.

It should be noted here that both of the causes, mentioned above, occur regularly and are often repeated after a gap of less than or equal to one year.

Objectives of Measuring Seasonal Variations

The main objectives of measuring seasonal variations are :

(*i*) To analyse the past seasonal variations.

(*ii*) To predict the value of a seasonal variations which could be helpful in short-term planning.

(*iii*) To eliminate the effect of seasonal variations from the data.

(*B*) Cyclic Variations

Cyclical variations are revealed by most of the economic and business time series and, therefore, are also termed as trade (or business) cycles. Any trade cycle has four phases which are respectively known as boom, recession, depression and recovery phase. These phases are shown in Fig. 4. Various phases repeat themselves regularly one after another in the given sequence. The time interval between two identical phases is known as the period of cyclical variations. The period is always greater than one year. Normally , the period of cyclical variations lies between 3 to 10 years.

Thus from 'Boom' to "Depression" there is decreasing trend and from "Depression" to "Boom" it is increasing trend. These cyclic variations recur period (cycle period) after period with the same pattern.

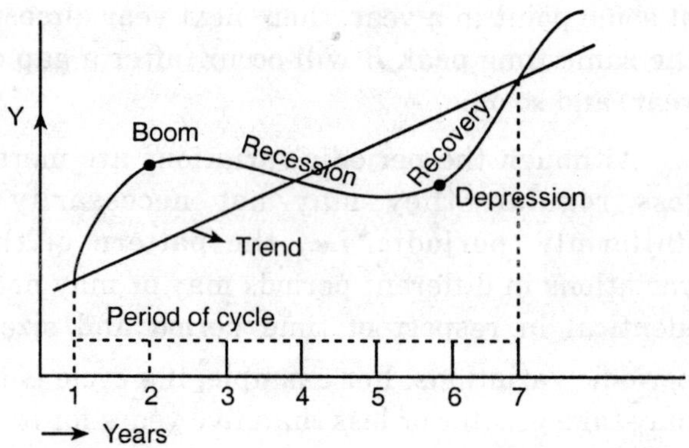

Fig. 4

3. *Random or Irregular Variations:* As the name suggests, these variations do not reveal any regular pattern of movements. These variations are caused by random factors such as strikes, floods, fire, war, famines, *etc.* Random variations is that component of a time series which cannot be explained in terms of any of the components discussed so far. This component cannot be predicted and measured with accuracy.

The four components "Trend", "Seasonal variations", "Cyclic Variations" and "Irregular variations" are represented by letters *T*, *S*, *C* and *I* respectively.

10.5 MODELS FOR DECOMPOSITION OF TIME SERIES

(1) Multiplicative model. In traditional or classical time series analysis, it is ordinarily assumed that there is a multiplicative relationship between these four components, that is, it is assumed that any particular value in a series is the product of factors that can be attributed to the various components. Symbolically,

$$Y = T \times S \times C \times I$$

This model assumes that *Y* and *T* are in absolute magnitude which are measured in the same units and *S*, *C* and *I* are in relative terms.

Example. Suppose trend value (*i.e.*, *T*) is 400 units. Suppose we know that there will be 50% increase due to seasonal effect *i.e.*, seasonal index = 150 in that case $S = \frac{150}{100} = 1.5$. Again if due to cycle, there will be 20% increase *i.e.*, the variable *Y* will be 1.2 times this period then $C = 1.2$. Again if due to irregular variation one estimates that it will tend to decrease Y value by 20% then $I = 0.80$ (= 80%).

This $Y = T \times S \times C \times I$

or $Y = 400 \times 1.5 \times 1.2 \times .8 = 576$ units

Now Y and T are in absolute units and S, C and I are in relative form (ratio).

2. Additive Model. Another approach is to treat each observation of a time series as the sum of these four components. Symbolically,

$$Y = T + S + C + I$$

It is assumed that all the components have same units and such can be added to get Y. Suppose sales due to trend may be 400 crores, seasonal variations are supposed to increase sales by 50 crores, cyclic variation will add 30 crores to sales and irregular variation will tend to decrease sales by 20 crores.

$$Y = T + S + C + I$$

$$= 400 + 50 + 30 - 20 = 460 \text{ crores.}$$

Thus total sales of 460 crores for a period has four components T, S, C and I equal to 400, 50, 30 and – 20 (all in crores) respectively.

10.6 SALIENT FEATURES OF TIME SERIES

(1) Annual time series data will not have seasonal variations as this variation is associated with different periods within a year, which are missing in this case. Thus for annual data the two models are

$Y = T \times C \times I$ (Multiplicative Model)

$Y = T + C + I$ (Addition Model)

(2) Average of annual Y values for a number of years (may be equal to cycle period) will not have cyclic variations also. Because ups and downs for a cycle neutralise each other and cyclic variations also vanish. Also irregular variations will more or less become zero because of many ups and downs within cycle period. Hence $\overline{Y}$ (average of annual Y value for many years will have only trend component. As such $\overline{Y} = T$ (Component).

(3) Time interval and point of time. Though the data will be for an interval (a year extends from 1st Jan. to 31st December, a month may be of 30 days), however we consider data occurs at a point of time which will be exactly at the centre of time interval.

For example if Y_1 & Y_2 are variable values for years 2001 and 2002, we represent it as follows.

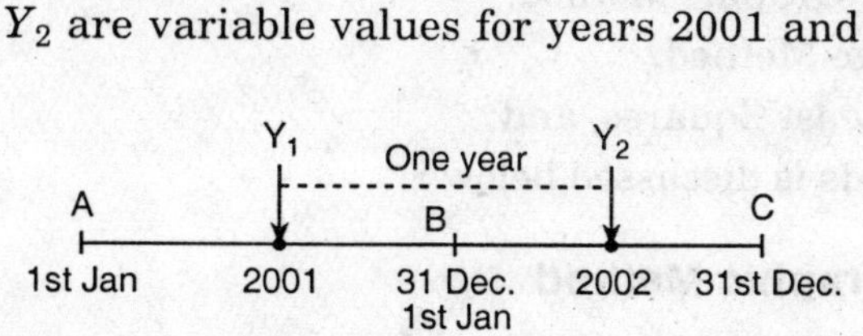

2001 is represented as an interval AB and Y_1 value will be at centre of AB. In case Y value is for two years *i.e.*, for 2001 and 2002.

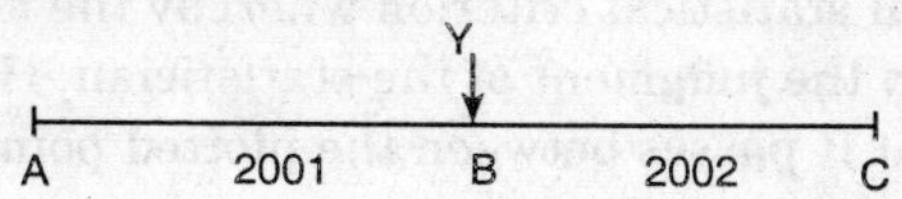

Then Y will be at B (which cannot be described at 2001, as it will mean at the centre of 2001).

Same way if Y_1, Y_2, Y_3 and Y_4 are variable values for 4 quarters of years 2001 then we show this as follows.

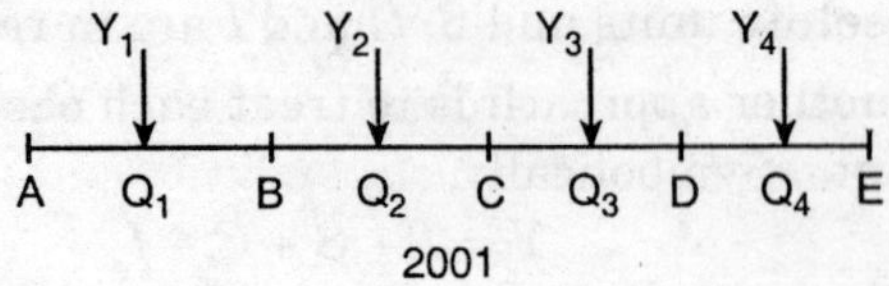

Periods AB, BC, CD and DE represent 4 quarters Q_1, Q_2, Q_3 and Q_4 respectively. Point D may be described as $Q_3 - Q_4$, as it is at the centre of 2 quarters Q_3 and Q_4. Point B may be described as $Q_1 - Q_2$. Thus whether a point is at the centre of year 2001, this point may be described at $Q_2 - Q_3$, 2001 or June—July 2001.

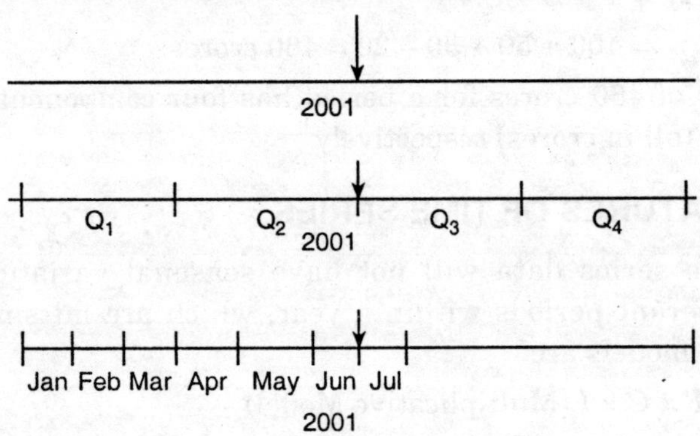

Thus if Y value is for 2001 or $Q_2 - Q_3$, 2001 or June – July, 2001, the reference point of time remains the same.

10.7 MEASUREMENT OF TREND

"Trend" and "Seasonal Variations" are important components and methods to measure the two will be discussed in this chapter. First we proceed to measure trend component of time series.

The following methods are used for measuring trend :

1. The Freehand or Graphic Method,
2. The Semi-average Method,
3. The Method of Least Squares, and

Each of these methods is discussed below :

10.7.1. Freehand or Graphic Method

This is the simplest method of studying trend. Under this method, the given data are plotted on a graph paper and a trend line is fitted to the data just by *inspecting the graph of the series.* There is no formal statistical criterion whereby the adequacy of such a line can be judged and it all depends on the judgment of the statistician. However, as a rough guide the line should be so drawn that it passes between the plotted points in such a manner that the fluctuations in one direction are approximately equal to those in the other direction and that it shows a general movement.

When a trend line is fitted by the freehand method, an attempt should be made to a make it conform as much as possible to following conditions :

1. It should be smooth—either a straight line or a combination of long gradual curves.

2. The sum of the vertical deviations from the trend of the annual observations above the trend line should equal the sum of the vertical deviations from the trend of the observations below the trend line.

3. The sum of the squares of the vertical deviations of the observations from the trend should be as small as possible.

Example 1. *Fit a trend line to the following data by the freehand method :*

Year	*Production of sugar (in million tonnes)*	*Year*	*Production of sugar (in million tonnes)*
1996	*20*	*2001*	*25*
1997	*22*	*2002*	*23*
1998	*24*	*2003*	*26*
1999	*21*	*2004*	*25*
2000	*23*		

The trend line drawn by the freehand method can be extended to predict future values. However, since the freehand cure fitting may be subjective, this method should not be used as a basis for prediction.

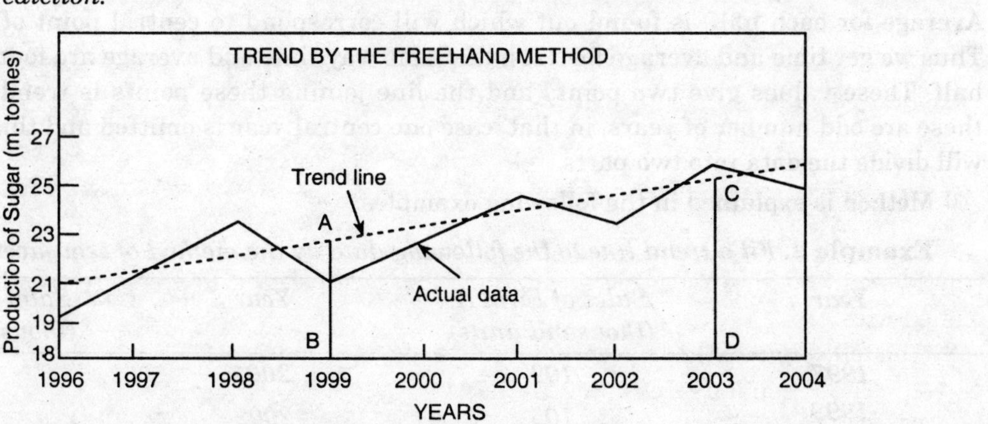

How to use freehand trend line for prediction. e.g., if we want to find trend value for year 1999, it is AB Same way trend value for year 2003 is CD.

10.7.2. Merits and Limitations of the Freehand Method

Merits. 1. This is the simplest method of measuring trend.

2. This method is very flexible in that it can be used regardless of whether the trend is a straight line or curve.

3. The trend line drawn by a statistician experienced in computing trend and having knowledge of the economic history of the concern or the industry under analysis may be

better expression of the secular movement than a trend fitted by the use of a rigid mathematical formula which, while providing a good fit to the points, may have no other logical justification. In fact a specialist of long experience who is familiar with the institutional setting, history and behaviour of the series may well be able manually to fit a trend superior to one derived by mathematical means. Although the freehand method is not recommended for beginners, it has considerable merit in the hands of experienced statisticians and is widely used in applied situations.

Limitations. 1. This method is highly subjective because the trend line depends on the personal judgment of the investigator and, therefore, different persons may draw different trend lines from the same set of data. It must be handled by skilled and experienced people who are well conversant with the history of the particular concern.

2. Since freehand curve fitting is subjective, it cannot have much value if it is used as a basis for predictions.

3. Although this method appears simple and direct, it needs experienced hand to construct a freehand trend.

It is only after long experience in trend fitting that a statistician should attempt to fit a trend line by inspection.

10.7.3. Method of Semi-Averages

The given data is divided into two halves : (1) first half (2) second half. Suppose the data is given for years from 1992 to 2007 (*i.e.,* for 16 years). The first 8 years *i.e.,* from 1992 to 1999 constitute the first half and next 8 years *i.e.,* from 2000 to 2007 constitute second half. Average for each half is found out which will correspond to central point of the interval. Thus we get time and average for 1st half. Same way time and average are found out for 2nd half. These values give two points and the line joining these points is trend line. In case these are odd number of years, in that case one central year is omitted and this central year will divide the data into two parts.

Method is explained in the following examples.

Example 2. *Fit a trend line to the following data by the method of semi-averages :*

Year	*Sales of Firm A (thousand units)*	*Year*	*Sales of Firm A (thousand units)*
1997	*102*	*2001*	*108*
1998	*105*	*2002*	*116*
1999	*114*	*2003*	*112*
2000	*110*		

Solution. The data is for seven years (odd no. of years). The central year's (*i.e.,* 4th year) data is ignored.

Year	*Y*	*Total*	*Av*
1997	102		(Trend value for 1998)
1998	105 →	321	107
1999	114		

2000	110			
2001	108			
2002	116	→	336	112 (trend value of 2002)
2003	112			

Assuming linear trend we plot the points M (1998, 107) and N(2002, 112) and join the two points to get trend line MN as shown. However A is (1997, 102), the given value and similarly B, C, D, E, F and G are other given values.

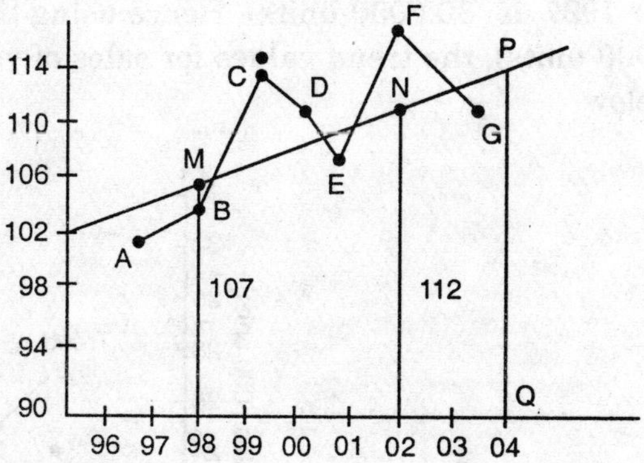

Now we see the trend changes by 112 – 107 = 5 units in 4 years for 1998 to 2002. Thus yearly trend increment is 5/4 = 1.25.

Trend value for 1998 is 107 we indicate this as $T_{98} = 107$. Similarly $T_{02} = 112$ and annual trend increment is $\frac{5}{4} = 1.25$. From this we can find trend value for any year. *e.g.*,

$$T_{05} = T_{02} + 3(1.25) = 112 + 3.75 = 115.75$$

$$T_{96} = T_{98} - 2(1.25) = 107 - 2.5 = 104.5 \text{ and so}$$

we may read T_{97}, T_{98}, T_{02}, T_{05} from the trend line MN also $T_{04} = PQ$..

Example 3. *Apply the method of semi-averages for determining trend of the following data and estimate the value for* 2000 :

Year	:	*1993*	*1994*	*1995*	*1996*	*1997*	*1998*
Sales (thousand units)	:	*20*	*24*	*22*	*30*	*28*	*32*

If the actual figure of sales for 2000 is 35,000 units, how do you account for the difference between the figures you obtain and the actual figures given to you ?

Solution. Here $n = 6$ (even), and hence the two parts will be 1993 to 1995 and 1996 to 1998.

CALCULATIONS FOR TREND BY SEMI-AVERAGES

Year	*Sales (thousand units)*	*3-Yearly Semi-Totals*	*Semi-Average (A.M)*
1993	20		
1994	24	66	$\frac{66}{3} = 22$
1995	22		
1996	30		
1997	28	90	$\frac{90}{3} = 30$
1998	32		

Here the semi-average 22 is to be plotted against the mid-year of first part, *i.e.*, 1994 and the semi-average 30 is to plotted against the mid-year of second part, *viz.*, 1997. The trend line MN is shown in the Fig.

Remark. The trend values for different years can be read from the trend line graph. Alternately, the average increment in value of sales (thousand units) for 3 year from 1994 to 1997 is 30 – 22 = 8 ('000 units). Hence, the yearly increment in sales is (8/3) = 2.667 ('000 units).

Now the trend value of sales for 1994 is the average of first part, *viz.*, 22 ('000 units) and for 1997 is 30 ('000 units). Hence using the fact that the yearly increment in sales is 2.667 ('000 units), the trend values for sales of various year can be obtained as shown in the table below.

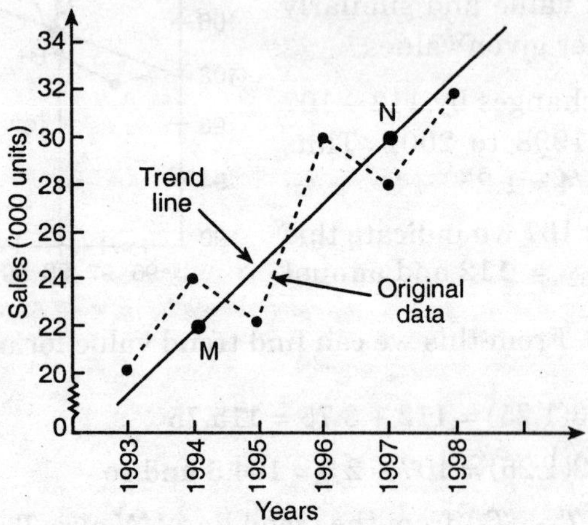

COMPUTATIONS OF TREND VALUES

Year	*Trend Values ('000 units)*	*Year*	*Trend Values ('000 units)*
1993	22 – 2.667 = 19.333	1997	30
1994	22	1998	30 + 2.667 = 32.667
1995	22 + 2.667 = 24.667	1999	32.667 + 2.667 = 35.334
1996	24.667 + 2.667 = 27.334	2000	35.334 + 2.667 = 38.001

Thus the estimated (trend) value for sales in 2000 is 38,001 units. This trend value differs from the given value of 35,000 units because it has been obtained under the assumption that there is a linear relationship between the given time series values which in this case (as is obvious from the graph of the original data) is not true. Moreover, in computing the trend value, the effects of seasonal, cyclical and irregular variations have been completely ignored while the observed values are affected by these factors.

Example 4. *From the following series of annual data, find the trend line by the method of semi-averages. Also estimate the values for 1999.*

Year	:	*1990*	*1991*	*1992*	*1993*	*1994*	*1995*	*1996*	*1997*	*1998*
Actual Value	:	*170*	*231*	*261*	*267*	*278*	*302*	*299*	*298*	*340*

Solution. Here the number of years is 9, *i.e.*, odd. The two middle parts will be 1990 to 1993 and 1995 to 1998, the value for middle year, *viz.*, 1994 being ignored.

TABLE 11.2. CALCULATIONS FOR TREND BY SEMI-AVERAGES

Year	*Actual Value*	*4 Yearly Semi-totals*	*Semi-Average*
1990	170		
1991	231	929	$\frac{929}{4} = 232.25 = 232$ (trend value for 91 – 92)
1992	261		
1993	267		
1994	278		
1995	302		
1996	299	1239	$\frac{1239}{4} = 309.75 = 310$ (trend value for 96-97)
1997	298		
1998	340		

The value 232 is plotted against the middle of the years 1991 and 1992 and the value 310 is plotted against the middle of the years 1996 and 1997. The trend line graph is shown in Fig.

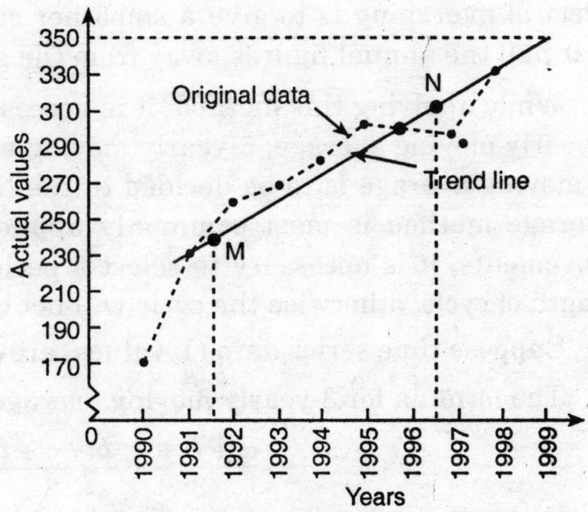

Fig.

From the graph we see that the estimated (trend) value for 1999 is 348.

Aliter. *Trend Value for 1999* : From the calculations in the above table we observe that the increment in the actual value from middle of 1991-92 to the middle of 1996-97, *i.e.*, for 5 years is 310 – 232 = 78. Hence the yearly increment is 78/5. We also find that the average trend value for middle of 1996-97 (1996.5) is 310. Hence the trend value for 1999 is given by

$$310 + \frac{5}{2} \times \frac{78}{5} = 310 + 39 = 349$$

This value differs from the graph value of 348 obtained from the trend line because of the reason given in Example 3 and also because we have obtained the calculations by rounding the decimals.

[**Remark.** Time difference between 1996-97 and 1999 is 2.5 years as 1996-97 may be taken as 1996.5].

10.7.4. Merits and Limitations of the Semi-Average Method

Merits. 1. This method is simple to understand compared to the moving average method and method of least squares (to be discussed later).

2. This is an objective method of measuring trend as everyone who applies the method is bound to get the same result (of course, leaving aside the arithmetical mistakes).

Limitations. 1. This method assumes straight line relationship between the plotted points regardless of the fact whether that relationship exists or not.

2. The limitations of arithmetic average shall automatically apply. If there are extremes in either half or both halves of the series, then the trend line is not a true picture of the growth factor. This danger is greatest when the time period represented by the average is small. Consequently, trend values obtained are not precise enough for the purpose either of forecasting the future values or of eliminating trend from original data.

For the above reasons if the arithmetic average of the data is to be used in estimating the secular movement, it is sometimes better to use moving average than the semi-averages.

10.7.5. Method of Moving Averages

When a trend is to be determined by the method of moving averages, the average value for a number of years (or months, or weeks) is secured, and this average is taken as the normal or trend value for the unit of time falling at the middle of the period covered. The effect of averaging is to give a smoother curve, lessening the influence of the fluctuations that pull the annual figures away from the general trend.

While applying this method, it is necessary to select a period for moving average such as 3-yearly moving average, 6-yearly moving average, 8-yearly moving average, etc. The period of moving average is to be decided in the light of the length of the cycle. Since the moving average method is most commonly applied to data which are characterised by cyclical movements, it is necessary to select a period for moving average which coincides with the length of cycle, otherwise the cycle will not be entirely removed.

Suppose time series data (Y-values) are $a, b, c, d\ e, f, g,$ ..... and so on. Then

The formula for 3-yearly moving average will be :

$$\frac{a+b+c}{3}, \frac{b+c+d}{3}, \frac{c+d+e}{3}, \frac{d+e+f}{3}, \ldots\ldots$$

and for 5-yearly moving average

$$\frac{a+b+c+d+e}{5}, \frac{b+c+d+e+f}{5}, \frac{c+d+e+f+g}{5}, \ldots\ldots$$

Example 5. *Calculate the 5-yearly and 7-yearly moving average for the following data of a number of commercial industrial failures in a country during 1990 to 2005.*

Year	*No. of failures*	*Year*	*No. of failures*
1990	23	1998	9
1991	26	1999	13
1992	28	2000	11
1993	32	2001	14
1994	20	2002	12
1995	12	2003	9
1996	12	2004	3
1997	10	2005	1

Solution.

CALCULATION OF 5-YEARLY AND 7-YEARLY MOVING AVERAGE

Year	No. of failures	5-yearly moving totals	5-yearly moving average	7-yearly moving totals	7-yearly moving average
1990	23	—	—	—	—
1991	26	—	—	—	—
1992	28	129	25.8 (T_{92})	—	—
1993	32	118	23.6 T_{93}	153	21.9 (T_{93})
1994	20	104	20.8	140	20.0 (T_{94})
1995	12	86	17.2	123	17.6
1996	12	63	12.6	108	15.4
1997	10	56	11.2	87	12.4
1998	9	55	11.0	81	11.6
1999	13	57	11.4	81	11.6
2000	11	59	11.8	78	11.1
2001	14	59	11.8	71	10.1
2002	12	49	9.8	63	9.0 (T_{2002})
2003	9	39	7.8 (T_{2003})	—	—
2004	3	—	—	—	—
2005	1	—	—	—	—

As mentioned moving averages are the trend value. Thus in case of 5 yearly moving averages we get trend values for years from 1992 to 2003.

In case of 7 yearly moving averages we get trend values for years for 1993 to 2002.

If the period of moving average is even, say, four-yearly or six-yearly, the moving total and moving average which are placed at the centre of the time span from which they are computed fall between two time periods. This placement is inconvenient since the moving average so placed would not coincide with an original time period. We, therefor, synchronise moving averages and original data. This process is called centering and consists of taking a two-period moving average of the moving average.

Example 6. *Work out the centered 4-yearly moving average for the following data :*

Year	*Tonnage of cargo cleared*	*Year*	*Tonnage of cargo cleared*
1994	*1102*	*2000*	*1452*
1995	*1250*	*2001*	*1549*
1996	*1180*	*2002*	*1586*
1997	*1340*	*2003*	*1476*
1998	*1212*	*2004*	*1624*
1999	*1317*	*2005*	*1586*

Solution.

CALCULATION OF THE CENTERED FOUR-YEARLY MOVING AVERAGE

Year	*Tonnage of cargo cleared*	*4-yearly moving totals*	*4-yearly moving average*	*4-yearly centered moving average*
1994	1102	—	—	—
1995	1250	—		—
	→	4872	1218.00	
1996	1180		→	1231.75
	→	4982	1245.50	
1997	1340		→	1253.87
	→	5049	1262.25	
1998	1212		→	1296.25
	→	5321	1330.25	
1999	1317		→	1356.37
	→	5530	1382.50	
2000	1452		→	1429.25
	→	5904	1476.00	
2001	1549		→	1495.87
	→	6063	1515.75	
2002	1586		→	1537.25
	→	6235	1558.75	
2003	1476		→	1563.37
	→	6272	1568.00	
2004	1624	—	—	—
2005	1586	—	—	—

10.7.6. Merits and Limitations

Merits. 1. This method is simple as compared to the method of least squares.

2. It is a flexible method of measuring trend. If a few more observations are added to the data, the entire calculations are not changed—we only get some more trend values.

3. If the period of moving average happens to coincide with the period of cyclical fluctuations in the data, such fluctuations are automatically eliminated.

4. The moving average has the advantage that it follows the general movements of the data and that its shape is determined by the data rather than the statistician's choice of a mathematical function.

Limitations. 1. Trend values cannot be computed for all the years. The longer the period of moving average, the greater the number of years for which trend values cannot be obtained. For example, in a three-yearly moving average, trend values cannot be obtained for the first year and last year, in five-yearly moving average for the first two years and the last two years, and so on. It is often these extreme years in which we are most interested.

2. Great care has to be exercised in selecting the period of moving average. No hard and fast rules are available for the choice of the period and one has to use his own judgment.

Example 7. *Assume a four-yearly cycle and calculate the trend by the method of moving averages from the following data relating to the production of tea in India :*

Year	*Production (mn. lb)*	*Year*	*Production (mn. lb)*
1995	*464*	*2000*	*540*
1996	*515*	*2001*	*557*
1997	*518*	*2002*	*571*
1998	*457*	*2003*	*586*
1999	*502*	*2004*	*612*

Solution.

CALCULATION OF TREND BY THE MOVING AVERAGE METHOD

Year	*Production (mn. lb)*	*4-yearly moving totals*	*4- yearly moving average*	*4-yearly moving average centered*
1995	464	—	—	—
1996	515	—	—	—
		← 1964	491.00	
1997	518			← 495.75
		← 2002	500.50	
1998	467			← 503.62
		← 2027	506.50	
1999	502			← 511.62
		← 2066	516.50	
2000	540			← 529.50
		← 2170	542.50	
2001	557			← 553.00
		← 2254	563.50	
2002	571			← 572.50
		← 2326	581.50	
2003	586	—	—	—
2004	612	—	—	—

10.7.7. Method of Least Squares

The method is to fit a linear regression of Y on X when X is time *i.e.,*

Y_C (estimated value of Y) $= a + bX$

(The method is already covered in chapter 8. In that chapter X was some variable related to Y. In this case X is a specific variable *i.e.,* time variable).

This method is most widely used in practice. When this method is applied, a trend line is fitted to the data in such a manner that the following two conditions are satisfied :

(1) $\Sigma(Y - Y_c) = 0$

i.e., the sum of deviations of the actual values of Y and the computed values of Y is zero.

(2) $\Sigma(Y - Y_c)^2$ is least,

i.e., the sum of the squares of the deviations of the actual and computed values is least from this line. That is why this method is called the method of least squares. The line obtained by this method is known as the line of '*best fit*'.

The method of least squares can be used either to fit a straight line trend or a parabolic trend.

The straight line trend is represented by the equation

$$Y_c = a + bX$$

where Y_c denotes the trend (computed) value to distinguish it from the actual Y values, a is the Y intercept or the value of the Y variable when $X = 0$, b represents slope of the line or the amount of change in Y variable that is associated with a change of one unit in X variable. The X variable in time series analysis represents time.

In order to determine the value of the constants a and b, the following two normal equations are to be solved :

$$\Sigma Y = Na + b\Sigma X \qquad \ldots(i)$$

$$\Sigma XY = a\Sigma X + b\Sigma X^2 \qquad \ldots(ii)$$

where N represents number of years (months or any other time period) for which data is given.

It should be noted that the first equation is nearly the summation of the given function, the second is the summation after the given function is multiplied by X *i.e.* $XY = aX + bX^2$.

We can measure the variable X from any point of time as origin such as the first year. But the calculations are very much simplified when the mid-point in time is taken as the origin because in that case the negative values in the first half of the series balance out the positive values in the second half so that $\Sigma X = 0$. In other words, the time variable is measured as a deviation from its mean. Since $\Sigma X = 0$, the above two normal equations would take the form :

From (*i*) and (*ii*) we had already found (in chapter 8) :

$$b = \frac{n\,\Sigma XY - \Sigma X\,\Sigma Y}{n\,\Sigma X^2 - (\Sigma X)^2}$$

and $\quad a = \overline{Y} - b\overline{X}$

Here $\quad Y_c = a + b\,X$ is called trend line and in this case we have to specify (*i*) origin year from which X time is measured (*ii*) units of X (*iii*) units of Y.

e.g. $\quad Y_c = a + bX$

origin is 1999, X is in years, Y is annual data

Now if $\quad \Sigma X = 0$ in that case

$$b = \frac{\Sigma XY}{\Sigma X^2}$$

The constant a give the arithmetic mean of Y (*i.e.* $a = \overline{Y}$) and the constant b indicates the rate of change.

It should be noted that in case of odd number of years when the deviations are taken from the middle year, ΣX would always be zero, provided there is no gap in the data series. However, in case of even number of years also ΣX would always be zero if the X origin is placed midway between the two middle years.

Example 8. *Below are given the figures of production (in m. tonnes) of a sugar factory:*

Year	*1998*	*1999*	*2000*	*2001*	*2002*	*2003*	*2004*
Production (in m. tonnes)	*80*	*90*	*92*	*83*	*94*	*99*	*92*

(i) Fit a straight line trend to these figures.

(ii) Plot these figures on a graph and show the trend line.

(iii) Estimate the likely sales of the company during 2005.

Solution : (*i*) FITTING THE STRAIGHT LINE TREND

Year	*Production (in m. tonnes)* Y	*Deviations from middle Year X*	XY	X^2	*Trend Values* Y_c
1998	80	– 3	– 240	9	84
1999	90	– 2	– 180	4	86
2000	92	– 1	– 92	1	88
2001	83	0	0	0	90
2002	94	+ 1	+ 94	1	92
2003	99	+ 2	+ 198	4	94
2004	92	+ 3	+ 276	9	96
$N = 7$	$\Sigma Y = 630$	$\Sigma X = 0$	$\Sigma XY = 56$	$\Sigma X^2 = 28$	$\Sigma Y_c = 630$

The equation of the straight line is: $Y_c = a + bX$.

Since $\Sigma X = 0$

$$a = \frac{\Sigma Y}{N} = \frac{630}{7} = 90; \; b = \frac{\Sigma XY}{\Sigma X^2} = \frac{56}{28} = 2$$

Hence the equation of the straight line trend is

$$Y_c = 90 + 2X.$$

Origin 2001, X in years, Y is annual data.

For $X = -3$, $Y_c = 90 + 2(-3) = 84$

For $X = -2$, $Y_c = 90 + 2(-2) = 86$

For $X = -1$, $Y_c = 90 + 2(-1) = 88$.

Similarly, by putting $X = 0, 1, 2, 3$ we can obtain other trend values. However, since the value of b is constant, only first trend value need be obtained and then if the value of b is positive we may continue adding the value of b to every preceding value. For example, in the above case for 1998 the calculated value of Y is 84. For 1999 it will be $84 + 2 = 86$; for 2000 it will be $86 + 2 = 88$, and so on. If b is negative then instead of adding we will deduct.

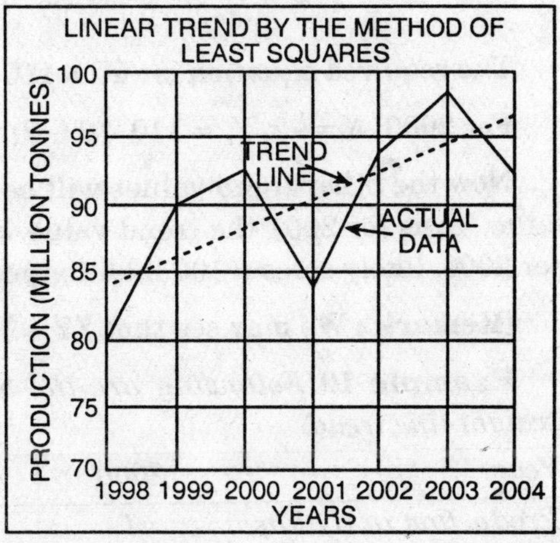

(*ii*) The graph of the above data is given in adjoining figure.

(*iii*) For 2005, X would be + 4. Putting $X = 4$ in the equation

$$Y_{2005} = 90 + 2(4) = 98$$

Hence the likely production for 2005 is 98 m. tonnes.

Example 9. *Apply the method of least squares to obtain the trend equation from the following data :*

Year	*Sales (in lakh tonnes)*	*Year*	*Sales (in lakh tonnes)*
2000	*100*	*2003*	*140*
2001	*120*	*2004*	*80*
2002	*110*		

Also predict the sales for the year 2006.

Solution.

CALCULATION OF TREND VALUES BY THE METHOD OF LEAST SQUARES

Year	Sales Y	Deviations from middle year 2002 X	XY	X^2	Y_c
2000	100	– 2	– 200	4	114
2001	120	– 1	– 120	1	112
2002	110	0	0	0	110
2003	140	+ 1	+ 140	1	108
2004	80	+ 2	+ 160	4	106
$N = 5$	$\Sigma Y = 550$	$\Sigma X = 0$	$\Sigma XY = -20$	$\Sigma X^2 = 10$	$\Sigma Y_c = 550$

The equation of the straight line trend is : $Y_c = a + bX$.

Since $\Sigma X = 0, a = \frac{\Sigma Y}{N} = \frac{550}{5} = 110$ and $b = \frac{\Sigma XY}{\Sigma X^2} = \frac{-20}{10} = -2$

The required equation is : $Y_c = 110 - 2X$. [origin is 2002, X in years, Y is annual data]

For 2000, $X = -2$, $Y_c = 110 - 2(-2) = 114$. *i.e.*, $Y_{2000} = 114$.

Now the other trend values will be obtained by *adding* the value of b from the preceding value. Thus for 2001 the trend value will be 114 – 2 = 112 (since the value of b is negative). For 2006, likely sales = 100 lakh tonnes (since X would be 5 for 2006).

[Remark : We may see that $\Sigma Y = \Sigma Y_c$]

Example 10. *Following are the data of production of computers in a factory. Fit a straight-line trend.*

Year	*2000*	*2001*	*2002*	*2003*	*2004*
Production in (Lakhs)	*4*	*6*	*9*	*10*	*11*

Solution:

Year	Production (Y)	X*	Y^2	X^2	XY	$Y_c = 2.6 + 1.8X$
2000	4	1	16	1	4	4.4
2001	6	2	36	4	12	6.2
2002	9	3	81	9	27	8.0
2003	10	4	100	16	40	9.8
2004	11	5	121	25	55	11.6
Total	40	15	354	55	138	

* origin is 1999

$$b = \frac{n \sum XY - \sum X \sum Y}{n \sum X^2 - (\sum X)^2} = \frac{5\,(138) - 40\,(15)}{5\ (55) -\ (15)^2}$$

$$= \frac{90}{50} = 1.8$$

$$a = \frac{\sum Y}{n} - b\frac{\sum X}{n} = \frac{40}{5} - 1.8\left(\frac{15}{5}\right) = 8 - 5.4 = 2.6$$

Thus trend equation is $Y_c = 2.6 + 1.8\,X$
Origin in 1999, X in years, Y is annual data

[**Note :** Any year can be taken as origin. However if it is taken at the centre, computations will be convenient].

Example 11. *Fit a straight line trend by the method of least squares to the following data and find the trend values :*

Year :	*1998*	*1999*	*2000*	*2001*	*2002*	*2003*
Sale of airconditioners (in lakhs) :	*10*	*13*	*16*	*21*	*24*	*30*

Solution.

FITTING STRAIGHT LINE TREND BY THE METHOD OF LEAST SQUARES

Year	*Sales (in lakhs)*	*Taking deviations from 2000*			Trend V_c
	Y	X	XY	X^2	Y_C
1998	10	− 2	− 20	4	9.143
1999	13	− 1	− 13	1	13.086
2000	16	0	0	0	17.029
2001	21	+ 1	+ 21	1	20.972
2002	24	+ 2	+ 48	4	24.915
2003	30	+ 3	+ 90	9	28.858
$N = 6$	$\Sigma Y = 114$	$\Sigma X = 3$	$\Sigma XY = 126$	$\Sigma X^2 = 19$	$\Sigma Y_c = 114.003$

The equation of the straight line trend is : $Y_c = a + bX$.

Since ΣX is not zero, we use

$$b = \frac{n\Sigma XY - \Sigma X\, \Sigma Y}{n\Sigma X^2 - (\Sigma X)^2} = \frac{6(126) - 3\,(114)}{6\,(19) - (3)^2}$$

$$= \frac{756 - 342}{114 - 9} = \frac{414}{105} = 3.943$$

$$a = \overline{Y} - b\overline{X}$$

$$= \frac{114}{6} - 3.943\ (3/6) = 19 - 1.971$$

$$= 17.029$$

The equation of the straight line trend is :

$$Y_c = 17.029 + 3.943\ X \text{ [origin is 2000, } X \text{ in yeras, } Y_c \text{ is annual data]}$$

$$Y_{1998} = 17.029 + 3.943\ (-2) = 9.143 \text{ [as } X = -2]$$

$$Y_{1999} = 9.143 + 3.943 = 13.086$$

The other trend values can be obtained similarly by adding the value of b to the preceding value.

10.7.8 Merits and Limitations

Merits. 1. This is a mathematical method of measuring trend and as such there is no possibility of subjectiveness.

2. The line obtained by this method is called *the line of best fit* because it is this line from where the sum of the positive and negative deviations is zero and the sum of the squares of the deviation is least, *i.e.*, $\Sigma (Y - Y_c) = 0$ and $\Sigma (Y - Y_c)^2$ least.

Limitations. Mathematical curves are useful to describe the general movement of a time series, but it is doubtful whether any analytical significance should be attached to them, except in special cases.

Hence, mathematical methods of fitting trend are not foolproof—in fact, they can be a source of some of the most serious errors that are made in statistical work. They should never be used unless rigidly controlled by a separate logical analysis. Trend fitting depends upon the judgment of the statistician, and a skillfully made freehand sketch may often be more practical than a refined mathematical formula.

10.8 OPERATIONS ON TREND EQUATIONS

10.8.1. Shifting of Origin of a Trend Equation

If $\qquad Y = a + bX$

(Origin 1985, X in year, Y is annual data) be the trend equation. Trend value for origin *i.e.*, 1985 is a (as $X = 0$) and b is the annual increment. Thus 'a' is the trend value for the base year and 'b' is annual increment.

Let $Y = a + bX$ be the equation of linear trend, with 1985 as the year of origin and unit of X equal to 1 year.

To shift origin of the above equation, say to 1990, we proceed as follows : The associated value of X for 1990 is 5. Thus, the trend for 1990 = $a + 5b$. We know that a linear trend equation is given by Y = trend value in the year of origin + bX. Thus, we can write the trend equation, with origin at 1990, as $Y = a + 5b + bX = a + b\ (X + 5)$. This simples that the required equation can be obtained by replacing X by $X + 5$ in the original trend equation.

Thus it means that if origin is advanced by 5 years we replace X by $X + 5$ in the trend equation $Y = a + bX$

Thus if $Y = a + bX$

(Origin 1985, X in years, Y is annual data) then if origin is advanced by 5 years from 1985 to 1990 if becomes

$$Y = a + b\,(X + 5)$$

(Origin 1990, X in years, Y is annual data) similarly if origin is shifted to 1980 from 1985 *i.e.*, Origin is moved backwards by 5 years.

Then trend equation will be

$$Y_c = a - 5b + bX$$

(Origin is 1985, X in years, Y is annual data)

Suppose trend equation is

$$Y_c = a + bX$$

(Origin is 1985, X in $\frac{1}{2}$ years, Y is annual data)

Shifting origin forward by 5 years (changing origin to 1990) *i.e.*, by 10 half years.

Thus $Y_c = a + b\,(X + 10)$

(origin is 1990, X in $\frac{1}{2}$ years, Y is annual data)

Example 12. *Given the following trend equations:*

(*a*) *$Y = 50 + 3X$, with 1985 as the year of origin and unit of $X = 1$ year. Shift the origin to 1991.*

(*b*) *$Y = 100 + 2.5\,X$, with origin at the middle of 1987 and 1988 and unit of $X = \frac{1}{2}$ year. Shift the origin to (i) 1988 and (ii) 1992.*

Solution.

(*a*) Replacing X by $X + 6$, in the trend equation, we get

$Y = 50 + 3(X + 6) = 68 + 3X$, the required trend equation.

(*b*) (*i*) For shifting origin to 1988 (*i.e.*, middle of 1988), we have to replace X by $X + 1$. (note that $X = 1$ for $\frac{1}{2}$ year)

$\therefore \quad Y = 100 + 2.5(X + 1) = 102.5 + 2.5X$

(*ii*) Replace X by $X + 9$, to get the required equation (From 1987-88 to 1992 we have 9 half years)

$\therefore\ Y = 100 + 2.5(X + 9) = 122.5 + 2.5X$ (Origin is 1992, X in $\frac{1}{2}$ years, Y is annual data)

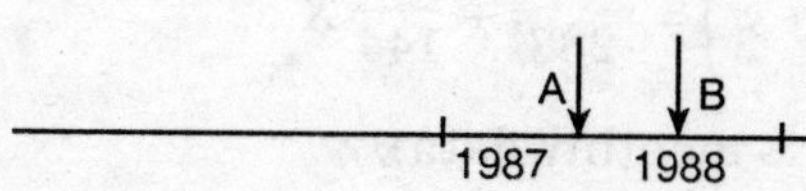

A is 1987-1988 and B is 1988, moving from A to B we move $\frac{1}{2}$ years forward *i.e.*, one unit of X.

From B (1988) to 1992 we move further by 4 years *i.e.*, 8 half years.

10.8.2. Conversion of annual trend equation to monthly trend equation

First trend equation is found from annual data (even if the data is for monthly basis) as there are large variations in monthly data than annual data, as there are seasonal variations in monthly data where as annual data does not have these variations. {Already explained.)

$$\left.\begin{array}{c} Y = T \times C \times I \\ \text{or} \\ Y = T + C + I \end{array}\right\} \text{for annual data}$$

and

$$\left.\begin{array}{c} Y = T \times S \times C \times I \\ \text{or} \\ Y = T + S + C + I \end{array}\right\} \text{for monthly data}$$

Then annual trend equation is changed to monthly trend equation which is used to find estimates of monthly Y values.

Method : Suppose the trend equation is

$$Y = a + bX$$

(Origin is 2004, X in years, Y is annual data). Let we change units of X from years to months *i.e.,* X will now be 12 times the initial value however unit of Y (annual data) remains unchanged, thus b is divided by 12.

Thus $$Y = a + \frac{b}{12}X \quad \text{...(1)}$$

(Origin is 2004, X in months, Y is annual data).

$\left(\frac{b}{12}X \text{ remains same as earlier } bX\right)$.

Now units of Y is changed to average monthly data, dividing (1) by 12.

Thus $Y = \frac{a}{12} + \frac{b}{144}X$

(Origin is 2004, X is in months, Y is monthly data). Now origin is a year which also be changed to a month. As already explained (refer 10.6). reference period year 2004 is same as June-July, 2004.

Thus $$Y = \frac{a}{12} + \frac{b}{144}X$$

(Origin June-July, 2004, X is in months, Y is monthly data)

We may shift origin to July, 2004 by moving forward by half month.

i.e., $$Y = a + \frac{b}{144}\left(X + \frac{1}{2}\right) = \frac{a + b}{288} + \frac{b}{144}X$$

(Origin is July, 2004, X in months, Y is monthly data).

Example 13. *The trend of the annual sales of ABC Co. Ltd. is described by the following equation :*

$$Y_c = 30 + 3.6\,X \text{ (origin 2001, } X \text{ unit} = 1 \text{ year, } Y \text{ unit} = \text{annual sales)}$$

Convert the equation on monthly basis.

Solution. To convert an annual trend equation to monthly basis, the value of '*a*' is divided by 12 and the value of '*b*' by 144. The equation on monthly basis is

$$Y_c = \frac{30}{12} + \frac{3.6}{144} X$$

or $$Y_c = 2.5 + 0.025\, X$$

(Origin June-July, 2001, *X* is in months, *Y* is monthly data).

Example 14. *You are given the following trend equation:*

$Y_c = 280 - 1.8X$, (Origin 2004, X is in years Y unit = annual monthly average sales)

Convert this equation into monthly terms and shift the origin half a month forward.

Solution. (*i*) The given annual trend equation reduced to monthly values will be :

$$Y_c = 280 - \frac{1.8}{12} X$$

$$= 280 - 0.15\, X$$

(origin: 2004; *X* unit = 1 month; *Y* unit = average monthly sales)

(*ii*)Shifting the origin half a month forward : (*i.e.* from June-July, 2004 to July 2004)

$$Y_1 = 280 - 0.15\,(X + 0.5)$$
$$= 280 - 0.15\; X - 0.075$$
$$= 279.925 - 0.15\, X$$

(Origin July, 2004, *X* in months, *Y* is monthly average).

10.9 QUADRATIC OR PARABOLIC TREND EQUATIONS

When the scatter diagram of time series data has any one of two diagrams below.

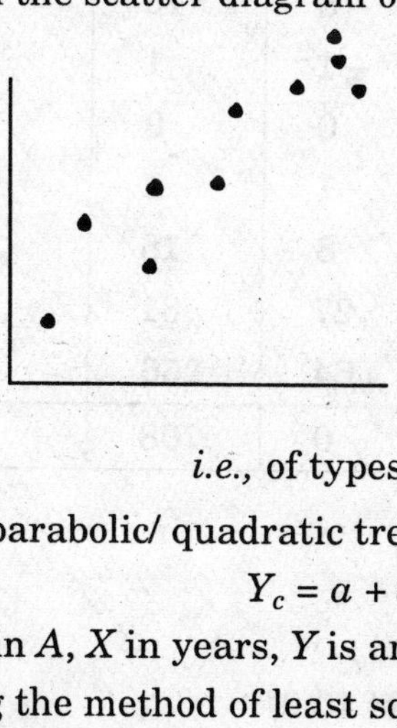

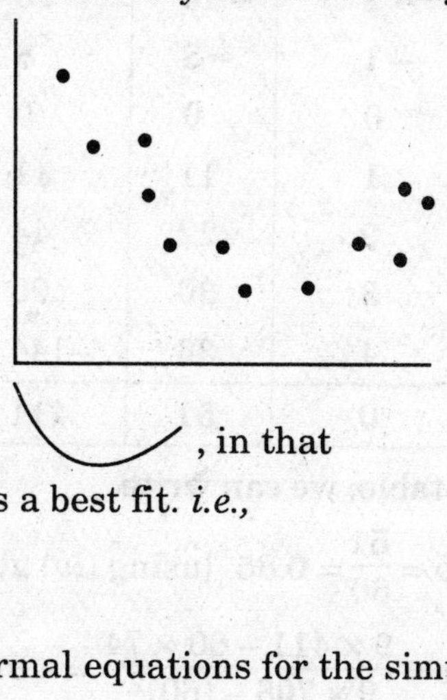

i.e., of types 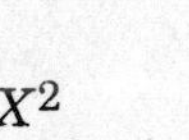 or , in that case parabolic/ quadratic trend equation is a best fit. *i.e.*,

$$Y_c = a + bX + cX^2$$

(Origin *A*, *X* in years, *Y* is annual data)

Using the method of least squares, the normal equations for the simultaneous solution of *a, b,* and *c* are :

$$\Sigma Y = na + b\Sigma X + c\Sigma X^2$$
$$\Sigma XY = a\Sigma X \times b\Sigma X^2 + c\Sigma X^3$$
$$\Sigma X^2Y = a\Sigma X^2 + b\Sigma X^3 + c\Sigma X^4$$

By selecting a suitable year of origin, *i.e.*, define $X = t$ – origin such that $\Sigma X = 0$, the computation work can be considerably simplified. Also note that if $\Sigma X = 0$, then ΣX^3 will also be equal to zero. Thus, the above equations can be rewritten as:

$$\Sigma Y = na + c\Sigma X^2 \quad ...(i)$$

$$\Sigma XY = b\Sigma X^2 \quad ...(ii)$$

$$\Sigma X^2 Y = a\Sigma X^2 + c\Sigma X^4 \quad ...(iii)$$

From equation (*ii*), we get $b = \dfrac{\Sigma XY}{\Sigma X^2}$ ...(*iv*)

Further, from equation (*i*), we get $a = \dfrac{\Sigma Y - c\Sigma X^2}{n}$ ...(*v*)

And from equation (*iii*), we get $c = \dfrac{n\Sigma X^2 Y - (\Sigma X^2)(\Sigma Y)}{n\Sigma X^4 - (\Sigma X^2)^2}$ ...(*vi*)

Thus, equations (*iv*), (*v*) and (*vi*) can be used to determine the values of the constants *a*, *b* and *c*.

Example 15. *Fit a parabolic trend $Y = a + bt + c\,t^2$ to the following data, where t denotes years and Y denotes output (in thousand units).*

t :	*1981*	*1982*	*1983*	*1984*	*1985*	*1986*	*1987*	*1988*	*1989*
Y :	*2*	*6*	*7*	*8*	*10*	*11*	*11*	*10*	*9*

Also compute the trend values. Predict the value for 1990.

Solution.

CALCULATION TABLE

t	*Y*	$X = t - 1985$	*XY*	X^2Y	X^2	X^3	X^4	*Trend Values*
1981	2	– 4	– 8	32	16	– 64	256	2.28
1982	6	– 3	– 18	54	9	– 27	81	5.02
1983	7	– 2	– 14	28	4	– 8	16	7.22
1984	8	– 1	– 8	8	1	– 1	1	8.88
1985	10	0	0	0	0	0	0	10.00
1986	11	1	11	11	1	1	1	10.58
1987	11	2	22	44	4	8	16	10.62
1988	10	3	30	90	9	27	81	10.12
1989	9	4	36	–144	16	64	256	9.08
Total	74	0	51	411	60	0	708	

From the above table, we can write

$$b = \frac{51}{60} = 0.85 \text{ [using (iv) above]}$$

$$c = \frac{9 \times 411 - 60 \times 74}{9 \times 708 - (60)^2} = -0.27 \text{ (using (vi) of 10.9)}$$

$$a = \frac{74 - (-0.27) \times 60}{9} = 10.0$$

[Remark. In case the number of years is odd we easily get $\Sigma X = 0 = \Sigma X^3$ by taking the middle year as origin. The same can be applied if the number of years is even by taking average of two middle years as origin and taking unit of X as $\frac{1}{2}$ year. The method is explained in example below].

Example 16. *The prices of a commodity during 1981-86 are given below. Fit a second degree parabola to the following data. Calculate the trend values and estimate the price of the commodity in 1986.*

Year	:	*1981*	*1982*	*1983*	*1984*	*1985*	*1986*
Price	:	*110*	*114*	*120*	*138*	*152*	*218*

Solution.

No. of years = 6 (even number). Two middle years are 1983 and 1984. The origin is taken average of two years *i.e.,* 1983.5

Let $d = (t - 1983.5)$ years

Now $X = (2\,d)$ half years. Thus unit of X is half year.

CALCULATION TABLE

Year (t)	*Price (Y)*	$X = 2(t - 1983.5)$	XY	X^2Y	X^2	X^4	*Trend Values*
1981	110	– 5	– 550	2750	25	625	114.40
1982	114	– 3	– 342	1026	9	81	109.12
1983	120	– 1	– 120	120	1	1	116.08
1984	138	1	138	138	1	1	135.28
1985	152	3	456	1368	9	81	166.72
1986	218	5	1090	5450	25	625	210.40
	852	0	672	10852	70	1414	

From the above table, we get

$$b = \frac{672}{70} = 9.6,\ c = \frac{6\times10852 - 70\times852}{6\times1414 - (70)^2} = 1.53 \text{ and } a = \frac{852 - 1.53\times70}{6} = 124.15$$

$$\text{Using } b = \frac{\Sigma XY}{\Sigma X^2},\ C = \frac{n\,\Sigma X^2Y - \Sigma X^2\,\Sigma Y}{n\,\Sigma X^4 - (\Sigma X^2)^2},\ a = \frac{\Sigma Y - C\,\Sigma X^2}{n}$$

$\therefore$ The equation of parabolic trend is $Y = 124.15 + 9.6X + 1.53X^2$, with year of origin = 1983.5 or 1st January, 1984 and the unit of $X = \frac{1}{2}$ year.

The calculated trend values are shown in the last column of the above table.

The price of the commodity in 1986 is obtained by substituting $X = 5$, in the above equation.

Thus, $Y = 124.15 + 9.5 \times 5 + 1.53 \times 25 = 210.4$

10.10 FITTING OF EXPONENTIAL TREND

The general form of an exponential trend is $Y = ab^X$, where a and b are constants to be determined from the observed data.

Taking logarithms of both sides, we have $\log Y = \log a + X \log b$.

This is a linear equation in log Y and X and can be fitted in a similar way as done in case of linear trend. Let $A = \log a$ and $B = \log b$, then the above equation can be written as $\log Y = A + BX$.

The normal equations, based on the principle of least squares are

$$\Sigma \log Y = nA + B\,\Sigma X$$

and $$\Sigma X \log Y = A\Sigma X + B\,\Sigma X^2.$$

By selecting a suitable origin, *i.e.*, defining $X = t$ – origin, such that $\Sigma X = 0$, the computation work can be simplified. The values of A and B are given by $A = \frac{\Sigma \log Y}{n}$ and $B = \frac{\Sigma X \log Y}{\Sigma X^2}$ respectively.

Thus, the fitted trend equation can be written as $\log Y = A + BX$

or $$Y = \text{Antilog } [A + BX] = \text{Antilog } [\log a + x \log b]$$

$$= \text{Antilog } [\log a.b^x] = a.b^x.$$

Example 17. *Fit a simple exponential trend to the following data and calculate the trend values. Also estimate the trend for 1992.*

Year	:	*1985*	*1986*	*1987*	*1988*	*1989*
Sales (₹ Crores)	:	*100*	*105*	*112*	*120*	*130*

Solution. CALCULATION TABLE

Year (t)	*Sales (Y)*	$X = t - 1987$	*log Y*	*Xlog Y*	X^2	$^*\log Y_c$	*Trend* = Y_c *Values*
1985	100	– 2	2.0000	– 4.0000	4	1.9955	98.97
1986	105	– 1	2.0212	– 2.0212	1	2.0241	105.71
1987	112	0	2.0492	0.0000	0	2.0527	112.90
1988	120	1	2.0792	2.0792	1	2.0813	120.59
1989	130	2	2.1139	4.2278	4	2.1099	128.80
Total		0	10.2635	0.2858	10		

From the above table, we get

$$A = \frac{10.2635}{5} = 2.0527 \text{ and } B = \frac{0.2858}{10} = 0.0286,\ ^*\log Y_c = A + BX$$

Further, a = antilog 2.0527 = 112.90 and b = antilog 0.0286 = 1.07

Thus, the fitted trend equation is $Y = 112.90(1.07)^x$

Origin : 1987, unit of X = 1 year, Y is annual data.

The trend values, computed by the equation Y = antilog [2.0527 + 0.0286X], are written in the last column of the above table. Further the trend for 1992 is obtained by substituting $X = 5$, in the above equation.

$\therefore$ Y = antilog [2.0527 + 0.0286 × 5] = antilog [2.1957] = 156.93.

Example 18. *Fit an exponential trend $Y = ab^X$ to the following data :*

Census Year (t) :	*1941*	*1951*	*1961*	*1971*	*1981*	*1991*
Population of India (in Crores) :	*31.9*	*36.1*	*43.9*	*54.8*	*68.3*	*84.4*

Predict the population for 2001.

Solution. CALCULATION TABLE

Census Year t	*Population Y*	$X = \frac{(t-1966)}{5}$	*log Y*	*X log Y*	X^2
1941	31.9	– 5	1.5038	– 7.5190	25
1951	36.1	– 3	1.5575	– 4.6725	9
1961	43.9	– 1	1.6425	– 1.6425	1
1971	54.8	1	1.7388	1.7388	1
1981	68.3	3	1.8344	5.5032	9
1991	84.4	5	1.9263	9.6315	25
Total		0	10.2033	3.0395	70

We get $A = \frac{\Sigma \log Y}{n} = \frac{10.2033}{6} = 1.70$

$$B = \frac{\Sigma X \log Y}{\Sigma X^2} = \frac{3.0395}{70} = 0.043$$

a = Antilog (A) = AL (1.70) = 50.12

b = Antilog (B) = AL (0.043) = 1.10

Exponential trend equation is $Y = 50.12\,(1.10)^X$

(Origin 1966, X unit is 5 years, Y = annual value in crores)

Estimated Y *i.e.*, $Y_c = AL\,(A + BX)$

for year 2001, $X = \frac{2001-1966}{5} = 7$

Thus $Y_{2001} = AL\,(1.70 + 0.043 \times 7)$

$= AL\,(2.001) = 100.2$ crores.

10.11 SEASONAL VARIATIONS

If the time series data is in terms of annual figures, the seasonal variations are absent. These variations are likely to be present in data recorded on quarterly or monthly or weekly or daily or hourly basis. As discussed earlier, the seasonal variations are of periodic nature with period equal to one year. These variations reflect the annual repetitive pattern of the economic or business activity of any society. The main objectives of measuring seasonal variations are :

(*i*) To understand their pattern.

(*ii*) To use them for short-term forecasting or planning.

(*iii*) To compare the pattern of seasonal variations of two or more time series in a given period or of the same series in different periods.

(*iv*) To eliminate the seasonal variations from the data. This process is known as *deseasonalisation* of data.

Methods of Measuring Seasonal Variations

The measurement of seasonal variation is done by isolating them from other components of a time series. There are four methods commonly used for the measurement of seasonal variations. These method are :

1. Method of Simple Averages
2. Ratio to Trend Method
3. Ratio to Moving Average Method
4. Method of Link Relatives

Note: In the discussion of the above methods, we shall often assume a multiplicative model. However, with suitable modifications, these methods are also applicable to the problems based on additive model.

10.11.1. Method of Simple Averages

This method is used when the time series variable consists of only the seasonal and random components. The effect of taking average of data corresponding to the same period (say 1st quarter of each year) is to eliminate the effect of random component and thus, the resulting averages consist of only seasonal component. These averages are then converted into seasonal indices, as explained below. If variations due to trend are not there *i.e.,* $T = k$ where k is a constant and Y values will vary around this straight line as shown in the figure.

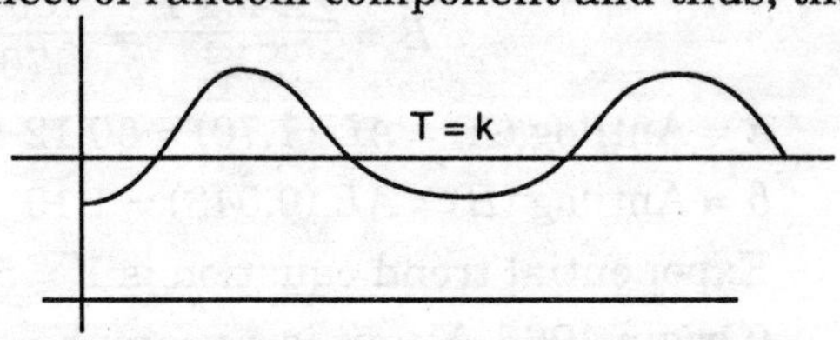

Thus $Y = k \times S \times C \times I$ (multiplicative model) or $Y = k + S + C + I$ (Additive model)

Suppose the seasonal data is quarterly and S_1, S_2, S_3 and S_4 are seasonal effects for four quarters respectively. Suppose $Q_{11}, Q_{12}, Q_{13}, \ldots, Q_{1n}$ are first quarter Y values for n years. Let average of these Y values be

$\overline{Q}_1 = \dfrac{Q_{11} + Q_{12} + Q_{13} + \ldots + Q_{1n}}{n}$. Now $\overline{Q}_1$ will be equal to $k \times S_1$ as C and I components will tend to be eliminated on averaging (refer 10.6 – B) and each of $Q_{11}, Q_{12}, \ldots, Q_{1n}$ will have S_1 component (it is same S_1 for all values)

Thus $\overline{Q}_1 = kS_1$ similarly $\overline{Q}_2 = kS_2$, $\overline{Q}_3 = k\,S_3$ and $\overline{Q}_4 = kS_4$. Now we define

$$\overline{\overline{Q}}\text{(average of averages)} = \frac{\overline{Q}_1 + \overline{Q}_2 + \overline{Q}_3 + \overline{Q}_4}{4}$$

$$= \frac{k\,(S_1 + S_2 + S_3 + S_4)}{4} = k\left(\frac{S_1 + S_2 + S_3 + S_4}{4}\right)$$

$$\overline{\overline{Q}} = k \text{ (as annual data is not impacted by seasonal variations)}$$

Now $\overline{Q}_1 = kS_1 = \overline{\overline{Q}}\, S_1$

$\Rightarrow$ $S_1 = \dfrac{\overline{Q}_1}{\overline{\overline{Q}}} \times 100$ (as in multiplicative model seasonal effect is taken as % changes) similarly $S_2 = \dfrac{\overline{Q}_2}{\overline{\overline{Q}}} \times 100$ and so on. The method is explained in the following example.

Example 19. *Assuming that trend and cyclical variations are absent, compute the seasonal index for each month of the following data of sales (in ₹'000) of a company.*

Year	*Jan*	*Feb*	*Mar*	*Apr*	*May*	*Jun*	*Jul*	*Aug*	*Sep*	*Oct*	*Nov*	*Dec*
1987	*46*	*45*	*44*	*46*	*45*	*47*	*46*	*43*	*40*	*40*	*41*	*45*
1988	*45*	*44*	*43*	*46*	*46*	*45*	*47*	*42*	*43*	*42*	*43*	*44*
1989	*42*	*41*	*40*	*44*	*45*	*45*	*46*	*43*	*41*	*40*	*42*	*45*

Solution. CALCULATION TABLE

Year	*Jan*	*Feb*	*Mar*	*Apr*	*May*	*Jun*	*Jul*	*Aug*	*Sep*	*Oct*	*Nov*	*Dec*
1987	46	45	44	46	45	47	46	43	40	40	41	45
1988	45	44	43	46	46	45	47	42	43	42	43	44
1989	42	41	40	44	45	45	46	43	41	40	42	45
Total	133	130	127	136	136	137	139	128	124	122	126	134
A_i	44.3	43.3	42.3	45.3	45.3	45.7	46.3	42.7	41.3	40.7	42.0	44.7
S.I.	101.4	99.1	96.8	103.7	103.7	104.6	105.9	97.7	94.5	93.1	96.1	102.3

In the above table, A_i denotes the average and *S.I.* the seasonal index for a particular month of various years. To calculate the seasonal index, we compute grand average G, given by $G = \dfrac{\Sigma A_i}{12} = \dfrac{524}{12} = 43.7$. Then the seasonal index for a particular month is given by *S.I.* $= \dfrac{A_i}{G} \times 100$.

Further, $\Sigma S.I. = 1198.9 \neq 11200$. Thus, we have to adjust these values such that their total is 1200. This can be done by multiplying each figure by $\dfrac{1200}{1187.9}$. The resulting figures are the adjusted seasonal indices, as given below :

	Jan	*Feb*	*Mar*	*Apr*	*May*	*Jun*	*Jul*	*Aug*	*Sep*	*Oct*	*Nov*	*Dec*
S.I.	101.5	99.2	96.9	103.8	103.8	104.7	106.0	97.8	94.6	93.2	96.2	102.3

[**Remarks :** Sum of 12 months *S.I's* have to be 1200, because of rounding errors the total is 1198.9 *i.e.,* why adjustment has become necessary. Had we kept *S.I's* 3 places of decimal the difference would have been very small.

Similarly if it is quarterly *S.I.'s* then total will be 400 (each quarters should have index = 100 if seasonal variation are not there, in that case S_1, S_2, S_3, S_4 effects will not be there, as S_1 factor $= \dfrac{100}{100} = 1$.

In case additive model is used then

$$\overline{Q}_1 = k + S_1 \qquad \overline{Q}_2 = k + S_2,\ \overline{Q}_3 = k + S_3,\ \overline{Q}_4 = k + S_4.$$

Now $$\overline{\overline{Q}} = \frac{\overline{Q}_1 + \overline{Q}_2 + \overline{Q}_3 + \overline{Q}_4}{4} = k + \frac{(S_1 + S_2 + S_3 + S_4)}{4} = k$$

as $S_1 + S_2 + S_3 + S_4 = 0$ (in case of additive model). However the method of simple averages is applicable only when $T = k$ (no. variation due to trend).

Thus $$S_1 = \overline{Q}_1 - k = \overline{Q}_1 - \overline{\overline{Q}}$$
$$= A_1 - G \text{ and so on.}$$

Example 20. *Compute the seasonal index from the following data by the method of simple averages.*

Year	*Quarter*	*Y*	*Year*	*Quarter*	*Y*	*Year*	*Quarter*	*Y*
1980	*I*	106	1982	*I*	90	1984	*I*	80
	II	124		*II*	112		*II*	104
	III	104		*III*	101		*III*	95
	IV	90		*IV*	85		*IV*	83
1981	*I*	84	1983	*I*	76	1985	*I*	104
	II	114		*II*	94		*II*	112
	III	107		*III*	91		*III*	102
	IV	88		*IV*	76		*IV*	84

Solution. CALCULATION OF SEASONAL INDICES

Year	*1st Qr*	*2nd Qr*	*3rd Qr*	*4th Qr*	
1980	106	124	104	90	
1981	84	114	107	88	
1982	90	112	101	85	
1983	76	94	91	76	
1984	80	104	95	83	
1985	104	112	102	84	
Total	540	660	600	506	*Total*
A_i	90	110	100	84.33	384.33
$\frac{A_i}{G} \times 100$	93.67	114.49	104.07	87.77	400.00

We have $G = \frac{\Sigma A_i}{4} = \frac{384.33}{4} = 96.08$. Further, since the sum of terms in the last row of the table is 400, no adjustment is needed. These terms are the seasonal indices of respective quarters.

Merits and Demerits

This is a simple method of measuring seasonal variations which is based on the unrealistic assumption that the trend variations are absent from the data. However, we shall see later that this method, being a part of the other methods of measuring seasonal variations, is very useful.

10.11.2. Trend Elimination Methods

Simple Average method is based on an assumption that there are no trend variations which generally does not hold good. As such this method directly is not useful. When this assumption does not hold good, in that case we find trend values for seasonal data and eliminate it from Y values which are known as trend eliminated values.

Trend eliminated values are defined as

$\frac{Y}{T} \times 100$ (in case of multiplicative model) $= S \times C \times T$

and $Y - T$ (in case of additive model) $= C + S + I$

These values *i.e.*, $\frac{Y}{T} \times 100$ or $Y - T$ do not have trend variations and have other components S, C and I. Now seasonal variations are found by using simple average method. Thus the method consists of first finding trend values, eliminating it from Y values and then using simple average method on trend eliminated values. The methods used are named according to the methods used for finding trend and are as follows.

A. Ratio to Trend Method.
(Trend values are obtained by least square method)

B. Ratio to Moving Average Method
(Trend values are obtained by moving average method)

10.11.3. Ratio to Trend Method

Steps. 1. From given seasonal data, annual data is obtained.

2. Annual trend equation is found out.

3. Annual trend equation is converted to seasonal (quarterly or monthly) as required trend equation.

4. Trend values are obtained for the interval.

5. Trend is eliminated using $\frac{Y}{T} \times 100$ or $Y - T$ according as multiplicative or additive model is used respectively.

6. Simple average method is used on values obtained in step 5 to find seasonal variation (seasonal indices in case of multiplicative model).

Method is explained in following examples.

A. Ratio to Trend Method

Example 21. *Assuming that the trend is linear, calculate seasonal indices by the ratio to trend method from the following data:*

QUARTERLY OUTPUT OF COAL IN 4 YEARS (IN THOUSAND TONNES)

Year	*I*	*II*	*III*	*IV*
1982	*65*	*58*	*56*	*61*
1983	*68*	*63*	*63*	*67*

1984	*70*	*59*	*56*	*52*
1985	*60*	*55*	*51*	*58*

Solution. By adding the values of all the quarters of a year, we can obtain annual output for each of the four years. Fit a linear trend to the data and obtain trend values for each quarter.

Year	*Output*	$X = 2\,(t - 1983.5)$	XY	X^2
1982	240	−3	−720	9
1983	261	−1	−261	1
1984	237	1	237	1
1985	224	3	672	9
Total	962	0	−72	20

From the above table, we get $a = \dfrac{962}{4} = 240.5$ and $b = \dfrac{-72}{20} = -3.6$. Since $\Sigma X = 0$ thus $a = \dfrac{\Sigma Y}{n}$ and $b = \dfrac{\Sigma XY}{\Sigma X^2}$. Thus, the trend line is $Y = 240.5 - 3.6X$.

[Origin is 1983 – 1984 (1983.5), X in $\dfrac{1}{2}$ years, Y is annual data] origin may also be written as 1st Jan. 1984.

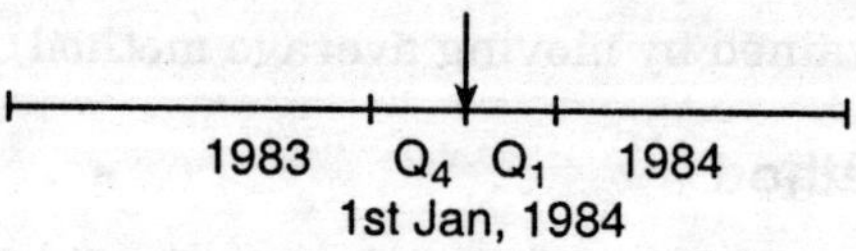

Now changing X to quarters from half years

Annual trend line is $$Y = 240.5 - \frac{3.6}{2}X$$

Quarterly trend line is $$Y = \frac{240.5}{4} - \frac{3.6}{8}X$$
$$= 60.13 - 0.45\,X$$

[Origin is $Q_4 - Q_1$ of 1983–1984, X in quarters, Y is quarterly data]. Let the origin be moved to Q_1, 1984 (moving forward by half quarter] [refer 10.8]

Quarterly trend equation is $$Y = 60.13 - 0.45\left(X + \frac{1}{2}\right)$$
$$= 59.91 - 0.45\,X.$$

[Origin is Q_1, 1984, X in quarters, Y is quarterly data]

Thus trend value for Q_1, 1984 is 59.9, trend value for Q_2, 1984 = 59.9 – 0.45 = 59.45 and so on.

The quarterly trend equation is given by

$Y = \dfrac{240.5}{4} - \dfrac{3.6}{8}X$ or $Y = 60.13 - 0.45X$, Origin : 1st January 1984, unit of X : 1 quarter (*i.e.*, 3 months).

Shifting origin to Q_1, 1984, moving X forward by half quarter we get

$Y = 60.13 - 0.45\,(X + \frac{1}{2}) = 59.9 - 0.45X$, origin I-quarter, unit of X = 1 quarter.

The table of quarterly trend values are given by

Year	I	II	III	IV
1982	63.50	63.05	62.60	62.15
1983	61.70	61.25	60.80	60.35
1984	59.90	59.45	59.00	58.55
1985	58.10	57.65	57.20	56.75

Y Value are :

Year	Q_1	Q_2	Q_3	Q_4
1982	65	58	56	61
1983	68	63	63	67
1984	70	59	56	52
1985	60	55	51	58

The table of Ratio to Trend Values, *i.e.*, $\frac{Y}{T} \times 100$

Years	I	II	III	IV
1982	102.36	91.99	89.46	98.15
1983	110.21	102.86	103.62	111.02
1984	116.86	99.24	94.92	88.81
1985	103.27	95.40	89.16	102.20
Total	432.70	389.49	377.16	400.18
Average	108.18	97.37	94.29	100.05
S.I.	108.20	97.40	94.32	100.08

Simple Av. method is used.

Note: Grand Average, $G = \frac{399.89}{4} = 99.97$ [S.I. for $Q_1 = \frac{A}{G} \times 100 = \frac{108.18}{99.97} \times 100 = 108.20$].

Example 22. *Find seasonal variations by the ratio to trend method, from the following data:*

Year	*I - Qr*	*II - Qr*	*III - Qr*	*IV - Qr*
1975	*30*	*40*	*36*	*34*
1976	*34*	*52*	*50*	*44*
1977	*40*	*58*	*54*	*48*
1978	*54*	*76*	*68*	*62*
1979	*80*	*92*	*86*	*82*

Solution. First we fit a linear trend to the annual totals.

Year	*Annual Totals* (*Y*)	*X*	*XY*	X^2
1975	140	– 2	– 280	4
1976	180	– 1	– 180	1
1977	200	0	0	0
1978	260	1	260	1
1979	340	2	680	4
Total	1120	0	480	10

Now $a = \frac{1120}{5} = 224$ and $b = \frac{480}{10} = 48$

$\therefore$ The trend equation is $Y = 224 + 48X$, origin : 1st July 1977, unit of $X = 1$ year.

The quarterly trend equation is $Y = \frac{224}{4} + \frac{48}{16}X = 56 + 3X$, [origin : 1977, $Q_2 - Q_3$, 1977, X is in quarters, Y is quarterly data]

Shifting the origin to III quarter of 1977, we get

$Y = 56 + 3\left(X + \frac{1}{2}\right) = 57.5 + 3X$ [Origin is Q_3, 1971, X is in quarters, Y is quarterly data]

TABLE OF QUARTERLY TREND VALUES

Year	*I*	*II*	*III*	*IV*
1975	27.5	30.5	33.5	36.5
1976	39.5	42.5	45.5	48.5
1977	51.5	54.5	57.5	60.5
1978	63.5	66.5	69.5	72.5
1979	75.5	78.5	81.5	84.5

Thus trend value for Q_3, 1977 is 57.5 and

Thus trend value for Q_4, 1977 is $57.5 + 3 = 60.5$ and so on.

RATIO TO TREND VALUES $\left(\frac{Y}{T} \times 100\right)$

Year	*I*	*II*	*III*	*IV*
1975	109.1	131.1	107.5	93.2
1976	86.1	122.4	109.9	90.7
1977	77.7	106.4	93.9	79.3
1978	85.0	114.3	97.8	85.5
1979	106.0	117.2	105.5	97.0
Total	463.9	591.4	514.6	445.7
A_i	92.78	118.28	102.92	89.14
S.I.	92.10	117.35	102.11	88.44

Note that the Grand Average $G = \frac{403.12}{4} = 100.78$. Also check that the sum of indices is 400.

10.11.4. (*B*) Ratio to Moving Average Method

Only difference in this method is that trend is obtained by moving average method, (as already explained) all other steps remain the same. The method is explained in the following examples.

Example 23. *Calculate seasonal indices by the 'ratio to moving average method' from the following data :*

Year	*I Quarter*	*II Quarter*	*III Quarter*	*IV Quarter*
1991	*68*	*62*	*61*	*63*
1992	*65*	*58*	*66*	*61*
1993	*68*	*63*	*63*	*67*

Solution. COMPUTATION OF MOVING AVERAGES

Year (1)	*Values* Y (2)	*4-Qtr. Moving Totals* (3)	*4-Qrt. M.A.* (4)	*2-Pd M.T. of col.* (4) (5)	*4-Qrt. M.A. Centred* (6)	*Ratio to M.A. Values* $(7) = \frac{(2)}{(6)} \times 100 = \frac{Y}{T} \times 100$
1991 I Qrt.	68					
II Qrt.	62					
		←254	63.50			
III Qrt.	61			126.25	63.125	$96.63 = \frac{61}{63.125} \times 100$
		← 251	62.75			
IV Qrt.	63			124.50	62.250	$101.20 = \frac{63}{62.250} \times 100$
		← 247	61.75			
1992 I Qrt.	65			124.75	62.375	104.21
		←252	63.00			
II Qrt.	58			125.50	62.750	92.43
		← 250	62.50			
III Qrt.	66			125.75	62.875	104.97
		← 253	63.25			
IV Qrt.	61			127.75	63.875	95.50
		← 258	64.50			
1993 I Qrt.	68			128.25	64.125	106.04
		← 255	63.75			
II Qrt.	63			129.00	64.500	97.67
		← 261	65.25			
III Qrt.	63					
IV Qrt.	67					

COMPUTATION OF SEASONAL INDICES

Year	*Trend Eliminated Values*			
	I Qrt.	*II Qrt.*	*III Qrt.*	*IV Qrt.*
1991	—	—	96.63	101.2
1992	104.21	92.43	104.97	95.50

1993	106.04	97.67	—	—	
Total	210.25	190.10	201.60	196.70	Total
Average	105.13 Q_1	95.05 Q_2	100.80 Q_3	98.35 Q_4	399.33
Seasonal Indices	105.31	95.21	100.97	98.52	400.01

Grand Av. $G = \frac{1}{4}(105.13 + 95.05 + 100.80 + 98.35) = 99.83$

which is less than 400. These indices are, therefore, adjusted to a total of 400 by multiplying each of them by a constant factor :

$$\frac{100}{G} = \frac{100}{99.83} = 1.0017$$

The seasonal indices are given in the last row

As $\text{S.I.} = \frac{\text{Average}}{G} \times 100 = \text{Average} \times \frac{100}{G}$

[**Remark :** There are no moving average values for 1st two and last two quarters and hence trend eliminated values for these quarters are missing].

10.11.5. Interpretation and properties of seasonal indices

(1) Some of monthly indices is 1200 and quarterly indices is 400. Thus if there were no seasonal variation each month or quarter will have same value *i.e.,* 100.

(2) Because of seasonal variation this value of 100 for a season (may be month or quarter) may change and suppose it is 110, then it implies that variable value will increase by 10% from the normal value (trend value) *i.e.,*

$$Y_t = T_t \times S_t = \frac{110}{100} T$$

(3) Suppose quarterly seasonal indices are S_1, S_2, S_3 and S_4, it means that Y values will be in the ratio of $S_1 : S_2 : S_3 : S_4$, if T is same for all quarters otherwise Y values for the 4 Quarters/ will be $\frac{S_1}{100} \times T_1$, $\frac{S_2}{100} T_2$, $\frac{S_3}{100} T_3$ and $\frac{S_4}{100} T_4$ where T_i = Trend value for ith quarter.

Also (1) $S_1 + S_2 + S_3 + S_4 = 400$.

10.11.6. Deseasonalisation of Data

As already pointed out, the objective of studying seasonal variations is : (*i*) to measure them and (*ii*) to eliminate them from the given series. Elimination of the seasonal effects from the given values is termed as *deseasonalisation of the data.* It helps us to adjust the given time series for seasonal variations, thus leaving us with trend component, cyclical and irregular movements. Assuming multiplicative model of the time series, the deseasonalised (seasonality eliminated) values are obtained on dividing the given value by the corresponding indices of seasonal variations.

$$\text{Deseasonalised Data} = \frac{Y}{S} = \frac{TCSI}{S} = TCI$$

Deseasonalisation is specially needed for the study of cyclic component. It also helps businessmen and management executives for planning future production programmes, for forecasting and for managerial control. It also helps in proper interpretation of the data. For example, if the values are not adjusted for seasonality, then seasonal upswings (or downswings) may be misinterpreted as periods of boom and prosperity (or depression) in business.

Remark. In case of absolute seasonal variations (additive model of time series), the deseasonalised values are obtained on subtracting the seasonal variations from the given values. Thus,

$$\text{Deseasonalised Data} = Y - S = (T + S + C + I) - S = T + C + I$$

Example 24. *The quarterly seasonal indices of freight movements on a railway line are given below .*

Quarter	*I*	*II*	*III*	*IV*
Seasonal index	*70*	*110*	*100*	*120*

If the total freight for the first quarter of 1991 is 350,000 tonnes, compute the traffic to be expected in the remaining quarters. (You may assume that there is no trend.)

Solution. We are given that the total freight movements on the given railway line are 3,50,000 tonnes. Under the assumption that there is no trend, the estimated freight for different quarters can be computed as given in the following table.

Quarter	I	II	III	IV
Seasonal index	70	110	100	120
Expected freights (in tonnes)	3,50,000 (Given)	$\frac{3,50,000}{70} \times 110$ = 5,50,000	$\frac{3,50,000}{70} \times 100$ = 5,00,000	$\frac{3,50,000}{70} \times 120$ = 6,00,000

Example 25. *Deseasonalise the following data with the help of the seasonal data given below.*

Month	*Cash Balance ('000) ₹*	*Seasonal Index*
January	*360*	*120*
February	*400*	*80*
March	*550*	*110*
April	*360*	*90*
May	*350*	*70*
June	*550*	*100*

Solution. Deseasonalised values are obtained on dividing the given time series values (*Y*) by the seasonal effect — assuming that the given series data follows multiplicative model of decomposition. We have :

$$\text{Seasonal effect} = \frac{\text{Seasonal Index}}{100} = \frac{\text{S.I.}}{100}$$

Hence, using multiplicative model : $Y = T \times S \times C \times I$;

$$\text{Deseasonalised value} = \frac{Y}{\text{Seasonal effect}} = \frac{Y}{\text{S.I.}} \times 100$$

COMPUTATION OF DESEASONALISED VALUES

Month	Cash balance ('000 ₹) (Y)	Seasonal Index (S.I.)	Deseasonalised Value = $\frac{Y}{S.I.} \times 100$
January	360	120	$\frac{360}{120} \times 100 = 300$
February	400	80	$\frac{400}{80} \times 100 = 500$
March	550	110	$\frac{550}{110} \times 100 = 500$
April	360	90	$\frac{360}{90} \times 100 = 400$
May	350	70	$\frac{350}{70} \times 100 = 500$
June	550	100	$\frac{550}{100} \times 100 = 500$.

10.12 MORE MISCELLABEOUS SOLVED EXAMPLES

Example 26. *Fit a trend line from the following data by using semi-average method.*

Year	*Profits (in '000 ₹)*	*year*	*Profits (in '000 ₹)*
1999	*100*	*2002*	*150*
2000	*120*	*2003*	*130*
2001	*140*	*2004*	*200*

Solution. Fitting of trend line by the method of semi-averages.

Year	*Profits (₹ '000)*	*Average*
1999	100	
2000	120	$\frac{360}{3} = 120$
2001	140	
2002	150	
2003	130	$\frac{480}{3} = 160$
2004	200	

Corresponding to 2000 we will take $Y = 120$ and corresponding to 2003 we will take $Y = 160$ and join two points. This will give the trend line.

We have $T_{2000} = 120$, $T_{2003} = 160$

$$\text{Annual trend increment} = \frac{T_{2003} - T_{2000}}{3}$$

$$= \frac{160 - 120}{3} = 13.33.$$

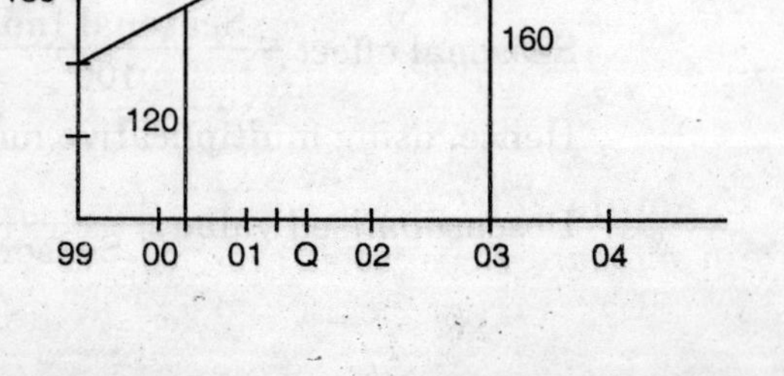

Example 27. *Using three-year moving averages, determine the trend and short-term fluctuations. Plot original and trend values on the same graph paper.*

Year	*Production in '000 tonnes*	*year*	*Production in '000 tonnes*
1995	*21*	*2000*	*22*
1996	*22*	*2001*	*25*
1997	*23*	*2002*	*26*
1998	*25*	*2003*	*27*
1999	*24*	*2004*	*26*

Solution.

CALCULATION OF TREND & SHORT-TERM FLUCTUATIONS

Year	*Production* Y	*3-yearly Totals*	*3-yearly moving average (Trend values)* T	*Short-term fluctuations Additive model* (Y – T)
1995	21	—	—	—
1996	22	66	22.00	0
1997	23	70	23.33	– 0.33
1998	25	72	24.00	+ 1.00
1999	24	71	23.67	+0.33
2000	22	71	23.67	– 1.67
2001	25	73	24.33	+ 0.67
2002	26	78	26.00	0
2003	27	79	26.33	+ 0.67
2004	26	—	—	—

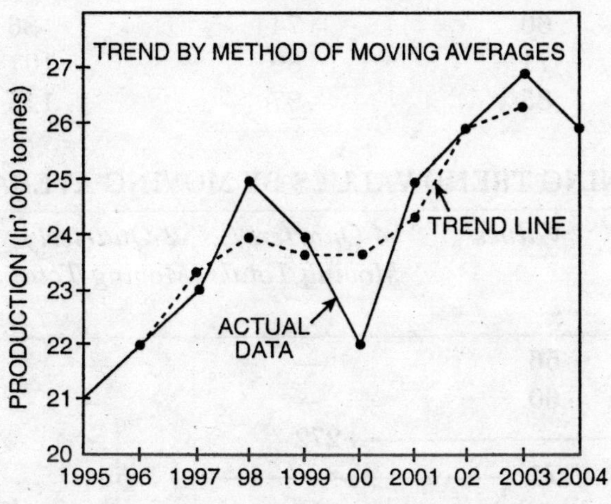

Example 28. *The seasonal indices of the sales of garments of a particular type in a certain shop are given below :*

Quarter	*Jan.-March*	*Apr.-June*	*July-Sept.*	*Oct.-Dec*
Seasonal index	*97*	*85*	*83*	*135*

If the total sales in the first quarter of a year be worth ₹ 15,000 and sales are expected to rise by 4% in each quarter, determine how much worth of garments of this type be kept in stock by the shop-owner to meet the demand for each of three quarters of the year.

Solution. Since the sales are expected to rise by 4% in each quarter, we have:

Expected sales in any quarter = 104% of the value of previous quarter. ...(*)

Taking into account the seasonal index (S.I.) for each quarter we have :

Stock in any quarter = (Expected Sales × S.I.) of that quarter. ...(**)

Using the formulae in (*) and (**), we can find the stock which the shop-owner should keep in the shop to meet the demand for each of the three other quarters of the year as explained below :

Quarter (1)	*Seasonal index S.I. (2)*	*Seasonal effect SI/100 (3)*	*Expected sales (in ₹) T (4)*	*Stock worth (₹)* $(5) = (3) \times (4) = T \times \frac{SI}{100}$
Jan.-March	97	0.97	15,000	14,550
Apr.-June	85	0.85	$\frac{104}{100} \times 15{,}000 = 15{,}600$	13,260
July-Sept.	83	0.83	$\frac{104}{100} \times 15{,}600 = 16{,}224$	13,466
Oct.-Dec.	135	1.35	$\frac{104}{100} \times 16{,}224 = 16{,}873$	22,779

Example 29. *Obtain the trend values for the following quarterly data by the moving averages method :*

	Years			
Quarters	*2001*	*2002*	*2003*	*2004*
I	56	66	72	94
II	60	74	86	120
III	71	89	101	137
IV	85	97	115	155

Solution.

OBTAINING TREND VALUES BY MOVING AVERAGE METHOD

Year	*Quarter*	*Values*	*4-Quarterly Moving Total*	*2-Quarterly Moving Total*	*4-Quarterly Moving Average = T* $5 = 4 \div 8$ *= Trend Value*
2001	I	56	—	—	—
	II	60	—	—	—
			→ 272		
	III	71 →		554	69.25
			→ 282		
	IV	85 →		578	72.25
			→ 296		

2002	I	66		610	76.25
			314		
	II	74		640	80.00
			326		
	III	89		658	82.25
			332		
	IV	97		676	84.50
			344		
2003	I	72		700	87.50
			356		
	II	86		730	91.25
			374		
	III	101		770	96.25
			396		
	IV	115		826	103.35
			430		
2004	I	94		896	112.00
			466		
	II	120		972	121.50
			506		
	III	137	—	—	—
	IV	155	—	—	—

Example 30. *The sale of a company rose from ₹ 60,000 in the month of August to ₹ 69,000 in the month of September. The seasonal indices for these two months are 105 and 140 respectively. The owner of the company was not at all satisfied with the rise of sales in the month of September by ₹ 9,000. He expected much more because of the seasonal index for that month. What was his estimate of sales for the month of September ?*

Solution. The owner of the company was justifiably not satisfied with the rise of sales of ₹ (69,000 – 60,000) = ₹ 9,000 from August to September because on the basis of the seasonal index of September, the estimated sales for September should have been :

$$₹\ \frac{60,000}{105} \times 140 = ₹\ 80,000$$

Thus the actual sales of ₹ 69,000 for September is much below the expected sales and hence the dissatisfaction of the owner is justified.

Aliter. Actual sales for August are ₹ 60,000 and seasonal index for August is 105. Hence the seasonal effect for August is 1.05 and accordingly the expected monthly sales are :

$$₹\ 60,000 \div 1.05 = ₹\ \frac{60,000}{1.05} \text{ (Deceasmalised value)}$$

Seasonal effect for September is 140 ÷ 100 = 1.40 and, therefore, the estimated sales for September are :

$$₹\ \frac{60,000}{1.05} \times 1.40 = ₹\ 80,000$$

Example 31. *On the basis of quarterly sales (in ₹ lakhs) of a certain commodity for the years 1991-95 the following calculations were made :*

Trend :

y = 25.0 + 0.6t, with origin at 1st quarter of 1991,

where t = time units (one quarter), and y = quarterly sales (₹ lakhs).

Seasonal variations :

Quarter	*1st*	*2nd*	*3rd*	*4th*
Seasonal index	*90*	*95*	*110*	*105*

Estimate the quarterly sales for the year 1992 (use multiplicative model).

Solution. Since, in the trend equation :

$$y = 25.0 + 0.6t, \quad \ldots(*)$$

1st quarter of 1991 is origin, we have $t = 0$ for 1st quarter. Further, since time unit is one quarter we have $t = 1, 2,$ and 3 for 2nd, 3rd and 4th quarters respectively of the year 1991.

Hence, the values of t for 1st, 2nd, 3rd and 4th quarters of 1992 are 4, 5, 6 and 7 respectively. Using multiplicative model of time series *i.e.*,

$$y = T \times S \times C \times I,$$

the estimated quarterly sales for the year 1992 are obtained in the Table.

ESTIMATED QUARTERLY SALES FOR 1992

Quarter of 1992	*t*	*Trend Values (T)* (₹ *lakhs*) $T = 25 + 0.6t$	*Seasonal Effect* $S = \frac{\text{Seasonal Index}}{100}$	*Estimated Sales* (₹ *lakhs*) $y_c = (T \times S)$
1	4	$25 + 0.6 \times 4 = 27.4$	0.90	24.66
2	5	$25 + 0.6 \times 5 = 28.0$	0.95	26.60
3	6	$25 + 0.6 \times 6 = 28.6$	1.10	31.46
4	7	$25 + 0.6 \times 7 = 29.2$	1.05	30.66

Example 32. *Using 'Ratio to Trend' method, determine the quarterly seasonal indices for the following data.*

Production of Coal (in Million of Tons)

Year	*1 Qrt.*	*II Qrt.*	*III Qrt.*	*IV Qrt.*
1	*68*	*60*	*61*	*63*
2	*70*	*58*	*56*	*60*
3	*68*	*63*	*68*	*67*
4	*65*	*56*	*56*	*62*
5	*60*	*55*	*55*	*58*

Solution.

COMPUTATION OF LINEAR TREND

Year (*t*)	*Total of quarterly values* *Y (annual)*	$x = t - 3$	x^2	*xy*	*Trend Values (T)* *(Million tons)* $Y_e = T = 61.4 - 1.45x$
1	252	–2	4	504	64.60
2	244	–1	1	244	62.85

3	266	0	0	0	61.40
4	242	1	1	242	59.95
5	224	2	4	448	58.50
	$\Sigma Y = 1228$	$\Sigma X = 0$	$\Sigma x^2 = 10$	$\Sigma xy = -58$	

Let the straight line trend equation be :

$$y = a + bx \qquad \ldots(*)$$

Origin : 3rd Year ; x units : 1 year, and y units : Annual production (in Million tons).

$$b = \frac{\Sigma XY}{\Sigma X^2} = \frac{-58}{10} = -5.8 \text{ [as } \Sigma X = 0]$$

$$a = \overline{Y} = \frac{1228}{5} = 245.6$$

Thus trend equation is $Y_c = 245.6 - 5.8\,X$

(Origin in 3rd year, X in years, Y is annual data)

Converting it to quarterly trend equation

$$Y_c = \frac{245.6}{4} - \frac{5.8}{16}X$$

Origin is $Q_2 - Q_3$, 3rd year, X in quarters, Y is quarterly trend value. Shifting origin to Q_3, 3 rd year (forwarding by $\frac{1}{2}$ quarter)

$$Y_c = 61.4 - 0.36\left(X + \frac{1}{2}\right)$$

$$= 61.22 - 0.36\,X$$

[Origin is Q_3, 3rd year, X in quarters, Y is quarterly data]

Trend value for Q_3, 3rd year = 61.22

Trend value for Q_4, 3rd year = 61.22 – 0.36 = 60.86

Similarly trend values for other quarters are found out and are tabulated below.

COMPUTATION OF SEASONAL INDICES

	Trend Values				*Trend Eliminated Values (Given values as % of Trend values)* $= \frac{Y}{T} \times 100$			
Year	*I Qrt.*	*II Qrt.*	*III Qrt.*	*IV Qrt.*	*I Qrt.*	*II Qrt.*	*III Qrt.*	*IV Qrt.*
1	64.84	64.48	64.12	63.76	104.87	93.05	95.13	98.81
2	63.39	63.03	62.67	62.61	110.43	92.02	89.36	96.29
3	61.94	61.58	61.22	60.86	109.78	102.31	111.07	110.09
4	60.50	60.14	59.78	59.42	107.44	98.10	93.68	104.34
5	59.06	58.70	58.34	57.98	101.59	93.70	87.42	100.03
				Total	534.11	479.81	476.66	509.56
				Average	106.82	95.84	95.33	101.91
				Seasonal Indices	106.85	95.86	95.35	101.94

Sum of seasonal indices = 106.82 + 95.33 + 101.91 = 399.90

G = Grand mean of averages = $\frac{399.90}{4}$

Adjustment factor = $\frac{100}{G} = \frac{400}{399.90} = 1.00025$

Seasonal Indices = $A \times \frac{100}{G}$

S.I. $Q_1 = A_1 \times \frac{100}{G} = 106.82 \times 1.00025$

$= 106.85$

Similarly these are computed for other quarters .

Example 33. *Given the following quarterly sale figures, in thousand of rupees, for the year 1986-1989, find the specific seasonal indices by the method of moving averages.*

Year	*I*	*II*	*III*	*IV*
1986	34	33	34	37
1987	37	35	37	39
1988	39	37	38	40
1989	42	41	42	44

Solution. CALCULATION OF RATIO TO MOVING AVERAGES

Year / Quarter	*Sales*	*4 – Period Moving Total*	*Centred Total*	*4 Period M*	$\frac{Y}{M} \times 100$
1986 I	34		...	...	...
II	33		...	...	...
	→	138			
III	34	→	279	34.9	97.4
	→	141			
IV	37	→	284	35.5	104.2
	→	143			
1987 I	37	→	289	36.1	102.5
	→	146			
II	35	→	294	36.8	95.1
	→	148			
III	37	→	298	37.3	99.2
	→	150			
IV	39	→	302	37.8	103.2
	→	152			
1988 I	39	→	305	38.1	102.4
	→	153			
II	37	→	307	38.4	96.4
	→	154			
III	38	→	311	38.9	97.7
	→	157			
IV	40	→	318	39.8	100.5
	→	161			
1989 I	42	→	326	40.8	102.9
	→	165			
II	41	→	334	41.8	98.1
	→	169			
III	42		...	...	...
IV	44		...	...	...

Trend Eliminated values are = $\frac{Y}{M} \times 1000$

CALCULATION OF SEASONAL INDICES FROM $\frac{Y}{M} \times 100$ VALUES

Year	I	II	III	IV
1986	—	—	97.4	104.2
1987	102.5	95.1	99.2	103.2
1988	102.4	96.4	97.7	100.5
1989	102.9	98.1	—	—
Total	307.8	289.6	294.3	307.9
A_i	102.6	96.5	98.1	102.6
S.I.	102.7	96.5	98.1	102.7

Note that the Grand Average $G = \frac{399.8}{4} = 99.95$. Also check that the sum of indices is 400.

$$\text{SI. for } i\text{th quarter} = A_i \times \frac{100}{G} = A_i \times \frac{100}{99.95}$$

Example 34. *The following table gives the figures of imports of a certain commodity during four years. Determine the seasonal variations using moving average on the assumption that various components are additive.*

Year	*I*	*II*	*III*	*IV*
1988	*22*	*26*	*25*	*27*
1989	*24*	*20*	*29*	*35*
1990	*31*	*27*	*38*	*40*
1991	*41*	*40*	*46*	*48*

Solution.

CALCULATION OF MOVING AVERAGES AND SHORT-TERM FLUCTUATIONS

Year / Quarter	*Imports (Y)*	*4 – Quarter Moving Total*	*Centred Total*	*4 Quarter M.A.*	*Short Term Fluctuations (Y – M.A.)*
1988 I	22		...	...	...
II	26		...	...	...
	→	100			
III	25	→	202	25.2	– 0.2
	→	102			
IV	27	→	198	24.8	2.2
	→	96			
1989 I	24	→	196	24.5	– 0.5
	→	100			
II	20	→	208	26.0	– 6.0
	→	108			
III	29	→	223	27.9	1.1
	→	115			
IV	35	→	237	29.6	5.4
	→	122			
1990 I	31	→	253	31.6	– 0.6
	→	131			
II	27	→	267	33.4	– 6.4
	→	136			

III	38		→	282	35.3	2.7
	→	146				
IV	40		→	305	38.1	1.9
	→	159				
1991 I	41		→	326	40.8	0.2
	→	167				
II	40		→	342	42.8	– 2.8
	→	175				
III	46			...	...	...
IV	48			...	...	...

Seasonal variations are $A_i - G$ (in case of additive model) (ref. 10.11.1 remarks).

Trend eliminated values

	Q_1	Q_2	Q_3	Q_4	
88	—	—	– 0.2	2.2	
89	– 0.5	– 6.0	1.1	5.4	
90	– 0.6	– 6.4	2.7	1.9	
91	0.2	– 2.8	—	—	
Total	– 0.9	– 15.2	3.6	9.5	Total
$A_v = A_i$	– 0.3	– 5.1	1.2	3.2	– 1
$A_i - G = S_i$	– 0.05	– 4.85	1.95	3.45	0

$\sum A_i$ should be zero. In this case $\sum A_i = -1$

$$\Rightarrow \quad G = \frac{\sum A_1}{4} = \frac{-1}{4} = -0.25.$$

Thus we add 0.25 to all values of A_i's .

Example 35. *The quarterly seasonal indices of the sales of popular brand of colour television of a company, in Delhi, are given below:*

Quarter	:	*I*	*II*	*III*	*IV*
Seasonal Index	:	*130*	*90*	*75*	*105*

If the total sales for the first quarter of 2004 is ₹ 6,50,000, estimate the worth of televisions to be kept in store to meet the demand in other quarters. Assume that there is no trend. *(B.A. (H) Econ., Delhi Univ)*

Solution. Since we are given total actual sales in the first quarter, we would lie to find out deseasonalised sale in the first quarter which would form the base for estimating stock in subsequent quarters.

$$\text{Deseasonalised Sales} = \frac{\text{Sales}}{\text{Seasonal index}} \times 100$$

$$= \frac{6,50,000}{130} \times 100 = ₹\,5,00,000$$

Quarters	*Deseasonalised sales T* (1)	*Seasonal index S* (2)	*Estimated stock* $\left(\frac{1 \times 2}{100}\right) = \frac{T \times S}{100}$
II	5,00,000	90	4,50,000
III	5,00,000	75	3,75,000
IV	5,00,000	105	5,25,000

Example 36. *Given the following trend equation :*

$$Y_c = 240 + 3.8\,X$$

(Origin 2001, X unit = 1 year, Y unit = annual production of cement)

Shift the origin to 2003-04.

Solution. 2003-04 implies 1st January, 2004. To shift the origin to 2003–04, origin is to be forwarded by 2.5 years.

Hence required equation shall be :

$$Y_t = 240 + 3.8\,(X + 2.5)$$

$$= 240 + 3.8\,X + 9.5$$

$$= 249.5 + 3.8\,X$$

(Origin 2003-04, X unit = 1 year, Y is annual production).

Example 37. *Given the following trend equation:*

$$Y_c = 148 + 24.4\,X$$

(Origin 2003, X unit = 1 year, Y unit = annual sales of steel)

Obtain the monthly trend equation.

Solution. Since X unit is a year and Y is expressed as annual totals, 'a' shall be divided by 12 and 'b' be 144. Hence the required equation will be :

$$Y_t = \frac{148}{12} + \frac{24.4}{144}X = 12.333 + 0.1694\,X$$

Origin is (June-July 2003, X unit = 1 month, Y unit = monthly sales of steel)

The origin when shifted to July, 2003, *i.e.,* if it is advanced by $\frac{1}{2}$ month. Trend equation will be

$$Y = 12.333 + 0.1694\left(X + \frac{1}{2}\right)$$

$$= 12.418 + 0.1694\,X$$

(Origin July 2003, X is in months, Y is monthly data).

Example 38. *(i) Given the trend equation :*

$$Y_c = 35 + 5X + 3X^2$$

(Origin : 1998, X unit = 1 year) change the origin of the equation to 2004.

(ii) Given the equation $Y_c = 10(1.5)^X$

(Origin : 1998, X unit = 1 year)

Shift the origin (forward) by two years.

(iii) The trend of the annual sales of an Aluminium Company is described by the following equation :

$$Y_c = 12 + 0.7X$$

(Origin : 1998, X unit = 1 year and Y unit = annual production)

Shift the origin to January, 2004 and write the equation on monthly basis.

Solution. (*i*) Since origin is to be shifted from 1998 to 2004, *i.e.,* it is to be forwarded by 6 years. Thus we substitute $X + 6$ in place of X in $35 + 5X + 3X^2$.

Thus $$Y = 35 + 5(X + 6) + 3(X + 6)^2$$
$$= 35 + 30 + 5 + 5X + 3X^2 + 36X + 108$$
$$Y = 173 + 41X + 3X^2$$

(Origin is 2004, X in years, Y is annual data).

(*ii*) For shifting the origin forward by two years, we put $X + 2$ instead of X in the given equation.

The new trend equation is

$$Y_C = 10(1.5)^{X+2}$$
$$= 10(1.5)^2 (1.5)^X = 22.5 (1.5)^X$$

(*iii*) $Y = 12 + 0.7X$

(Origin is 1998, X is in years, Y is annual production)

Converting it to monthly trend equation we get

$$Y = \frac{12}{12} + \frac{0.7}{144} X = 1 + \frac{7}{1440} X$$

(Origin is June-July, 1998, X in months, Y is monthly data) origin is to be shifted to Jan., 2004 from June-July, 1998.

From June-July, 98 to July 98 is	$\frac{1}{2}$ month
July 98 to July 2003 is	$5 \times 12 = 60$ months
July 2003 to Jan. 2004 is	6 months
Total	$66\frac{1}{2}$ months

Thus origin is to be forwarded by 66.5 months. Thus trend equation is

$$Y = 1 + \frac{7}{1440}(X + 66.5)$$
$$= 1 + \frac{133}{2} \cdot \frac{7}{1440} + \frac{7}{1440} X$$
$$= 1 + .323 + \frac{7}{1440} X$$
$$Y = 1.323 + \frac{7}{1440} X$$

(Origin is Jan., 2004, X in months, Y is monthly data).

Example 39. *Calculate seasonal indices by the ratio-to-moving average method from the following data:*

WHEAT PRICE IN RUPEES PER QUINTAL

Year → / *Quarters*	*2001*	*2002*	*2003*	*2004*
Q_1	75	86	90	100
Q_2	60	65	72	78
Q_3	54	63	66	72
Q_4	59	80	85	93

Solution.

CALCULATION OF 4-QUARTERLY CENTERED MOVING AVERAGES

Year	*Quarters*	*Wheat Prices (₹)*	*4-figure moving total*	*4-figure moving average*	*2-figure moving totals*	*Centered 4-quarterly moving average*	*Percentage of centered 4-quarterly moving average col. 2 ÷ col. 6*	
1		2	3	4	5	6	7	
		Y				T	$\frac{Y}{T} \times 100$ = Trend Eliminated values	
2001	Q_1	75						
	Q_2	60						
			248	62.00				
	Q_3	54			126.75	63.375	85.21	$= \frac{54}{63.375} \times 100$
			259	64.75				
	Q_4	59			130.75	65.375	90.25	
			264	66.00				
2002	Q_1	86			134.25	67.125	128.12	
			273	68.25				
	Q_2	65			141.75	70.875	91.71	
			294	73.50				
	Q_3	63			148.00	74.000	85.13	
			298	74.50				
	Q_4	80			150.75	75.375	106.14	
			305	76.25				
2003	Q_1	90			153.25	76.625	117.45	
			308	77.00				
	Q_2	72			155.25	77.625	92.75	
			313	78.25				
	Q_3	66			159.00	79.500	83.02	
			323	80.75				
	Q_4	85			163.00	81.500	104.29	
			329	82.25				
2004	Q_1	100			166.00	83.000	120.48	
			335	83.75				
	Q_2	78			169.50	84.750	92.03	$= \frac{78}{84.750} \times 100$
			343	85.75				
	Q_3	72						
	Q_4	93						

TREND ELIMINATED VALUES

	Q_1	Q_2	Q_3	Q_4		
2001	—	—	85·21	90·25		
2002	128.12	91.71	85.31	106.14		
2003	117.45	92.75	83.02	104.29		
2004	120.48	92.03	—	—		
Total	366.05	276.49	253.54	300.68	Total	G
Averages (A)	122.02	92.16	84.51	100.23	398.92	99.73
SI	122.38	92.41	84.70	100.51	400	

$$SI = A \times \frac{100}{G}$$

Example 40. *Estimate the trend values using the data given below by taking a four-yearly moving average and eliminate the trend:*

Year	*Value*	*Year*	*Value*
1991	*24.1*	*1998*	*45.3*
1992	*25.1*	*1999*	*39.3*
1993	*27.3*	*2000*	*41.3*
1994	*28.3*	*2001*	*42.2*
1995	*28.1*	*2002*	*46.4*
1996	*29.1*	*2003*	*46.6*
1997	*30.1*	*2004*	*49.2*

[*B. Com., Delhi Univ*]

Solution. ESTIMATING AND ELIMINATING THE TREND

Year	*Value* Y	*4-Yearly moving total*	*4-yearly moving average*	*4-Yearly moving average centred* $Y_c = T$	*Elimination of trend based on model* *Multiplicative* $Y/Y_c \times 100$	*Additive* $Y–Y_c$
1991	24.1	—	—	—	—	—
1992	25.1	—	—	—	—	—
		← 104.8	26.20			
1993	27.3			← 26.70	$\frac{27.3}{26.7} \times 100 = 102.25$	0.60
		← 108.8	27.20			
1994	28.3			← 27.70	$\frac{28.3}{27.7} \times 100 = 102.17$	0.60
		← 112.8	28.20			
1995	28.1			← 28.55	$\frac{28.1}{28.55} \times 100 = 98.42$	–0.45
		← 115.6	28.90			
1996	29.1			← 31.03	$\frac{29.1}{31.03} \times 100 = 93.78$	– 1.93
		← 132.6	33.15			

1997	30.1			← 34.55	$\frac{30.13}{4.55} \times 100 = 87.12$	– 4.45
		← 143.8	35.95			
1998	45.3			← 37.48	$\frac{45.3}{37.48}$ 100 = 120.86	7.82
		← 156.0	39.00			
1999	39.3			← 40.51	$\frac{39.3}{40.51} \times 100 = 97.01$	–1.21
		← 168.1	42.02			
2000	41.3			← 42.16	$\frac{41.3}{42.16} \times 100 = 97.96$	– 0.86
		← 169.2	42.30			
2001	42.2			← 43.21	$\frac{42.2}{43.21} \times 100 = 97.66$	– 1.01
		← 176.5	44.12			
2002	46.4			← 45.11	$\frac{46.4}{45.11} \times 100 = 102.86$	1.29
		← 184.4	46.10			
2003	46.6	—	—	—		
2004	49.2	—	—	—		

Example 41. *The seasonal indices of a commodity manufactured by a company for four quarters of a year are respectively 100, 90, 80, and 130. If the total sale in the first quarter is worth ₹ 25,000, how much worth of sale is expected during the whole year ? (Assuming there are no trend variations).*

Solution. EXPECTED SALES IN VARIOUS QUARTERS

Quarter	*Seasonal index (S.I.)*	*Estimated sales (₹)*
I	100	25,000
II	90	22,500
III	80	20,000
IV	130	32,500

$$\text{Estimated sales for 2nd Qtr.} = \frac{\text{Figure for 1st Qtr.}}{\text{S.I. for 1st Qtr.}} \times \text{S.I. for 2nd Qtr.}$$

$$= \frac{25{,}000 \times 90}{100} = 22{,}500$$

$$\text{Estimated sales for 3rd Qtr.} = \frac{\text{Figure for 1st Qtr.}}{\text{S.I. for 1st Qtr.}} \times \text{S.I. for 3rd Qtr.}$$

$$= \frac{25{,}000 \times 80}{100} = 20{,}000$$

$$\text{Estimated sales for 4th Qtr.} = \frac{25{,}000 \times 130}{100} = 32{,}500.$$

Example 42. *The equation for yearly sales (in '000 ₹) of a commodity with 1st July, 1971, as origin is $Y = 91.6 + 28.8X$.*

(i) Determine the trend equation to give monthly trend values with 15th January, 1972, as origin.

(ii) Calculate the trend values for March, 1972 to August, 1972.

Solution.

(*i*) The monthly trend equation with 1st July, 1971, as origin is given by $Y = \frac{91.6}{12} + \frac{28.8}{144}X = 7.63 + 0.2X$, where unit of X is one month.

To shift the origin to 15th January, 1972, we replace X by $X + 6.5$ in the above equation. Note that the associated value of X for 15th January, 1972, is 6.5. Thus, the required equation is $Y = 7.63\ 0.2(X + 6.5) = 8.93 + 0.2X$

(*ii*) Calculation of trend values

Trend value for March, 1972 = 8.93 + 0.2 × 2 = ₹ 9.33

Trend value for April, 1972 = 9.33 + 0.2 = ₹ 9.53

Trend value for May, 1972 = 9.53 + 0.2 = ₹ 9.73

Trend value for June, 1972 = 9.73 + 0.2 = ₹ 9.93

Trend value for July, 1972 = 9.93 + 0.2 = ₹ 10.13

Trend value for August, 1972 = 10.13 + 0.2 = ₹ 10.33.

Example 43. *Calculate the trend values by the method of least squares from the data given below and estimate the sales for the year 2007.*

Year	*2000*	*2001*	*2002*	*2003*	*2004*
Sales of T.V. Sets (in lakhs)	*12*	*18*	*20*	*23*	*27*

Solution.

CALCULATION OF TREND VALUES BY THE METHOD OF LEAST SQUARES

Year	*Sales*	*Taking 2002 as origin*			*Trend values*
	Y	X	XY	X^2	Y_c
2000	12	– 2	– 24	4	13.0
2001	18	– 1	– 18	1	16.5
2002	20	0	0	0	20.0
2003	23	+ 1	+ 23	1	23.5
2004	27	+ 2	+ 54	4	27.0
$N = 5$	$\Sigma Y = 100$	$\Sigma X = 0$	$\Sigma XY = 35$	$\Sigma X^2 = 10$	$\Sigma Y_c = 100$

The equation of the straight line trend is : $Y_c = a + bX$.

Since $\Sigma X = 0$, $a = \dfrac{\Sigma Y}{N} = \dfrac{100}{5} = 20$ and $b = \dfrac{\Sigma XY}{\Sigma X^2} = \dfrac{35}{10} = 3.5$

Thus the equation of the straight line trend is : $Y = 20 + 3.5X$

$Y_{2000} = 20 + 3.5\,(-2) = 13$

$Y_{2001} = 20 + 3.5\,(-1) = 16.5$, etc.

For 2007, X would be + 5.

Hence, $Y_{2007} = 20 + 3.5\,(+5) = 20 + 17.5 = 37.5$

Thus the estimated sales of television sets for the year 2007 is 37.5 lakhs.

Example 44. *Calculate trend values by the method of least squares from the data given below :*

Year	*1996*	*1997*	*1998*	*1999*	*2000*	*2001*	*2002*	*2003*
Sales	*80*	*90*	*92*	*83*	*94*	*99*	*92*	*104*

Plot the data showing also the trend line.

Solution.

FITTING STRAIGHT LINE TREND BY METHOD OF LEAST SQUARES

Years	*Sales* Y	*Deviations from 1999.5*	*Deviations multiplied by 2 X (half years)*	XY	X^2	Y_c
1996	80	– 3.5	– 7	– 560	49	83.0
1997	90	– 2.5	– 5	– 450	25	85.5
1998	92	– 1.5	– 3	– 276	9	88.0
1999	83	– .5	– 1	– 83	1	90.5
2000	94	+ .5	+ 1	+ 94	1	93.0
2001	99	+ 1.5	+ 3	+ 297	9	95.5
2002	92	+ 2.5	+ 5	+ 460	25	98.0
2003	104	+ 3.5	+ 7	+ 728	49	100.5
$N = 8$	$\Sigma Y = 734$			$\Sigma XY = 210$	$\Sigma X^2 = 168$	$\Sigma Y_c = 734$

The equation of the straight line trend is

$$Y = a + bX$$

Since $\Sigma X = 0, a = \dfrac{\Sigma Y}{N} = \dfrac{734}{8} = 91.95, b = \dfrac{\Sigma XY}{\Sigma X^2} = \dfrac{210}{168} = 1.25$

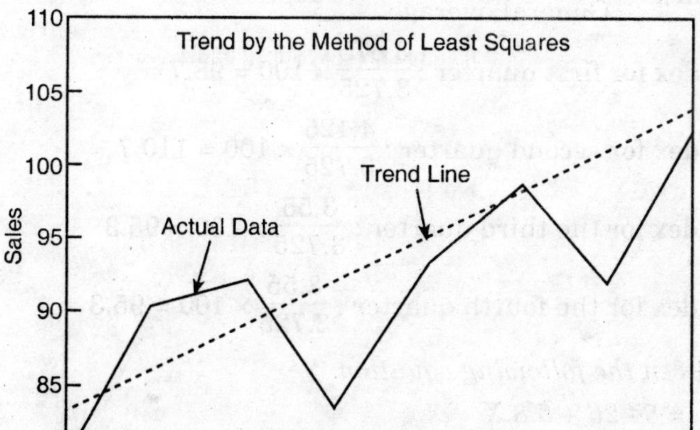

$$Y = 91.75 + 1.25\,X \text{ (Origin is 1999 – 2000, } X \text{ in half years, } Y \text{ is annual data)}$$

$$Y_{1996} = 91.75 + 1.25\,(-7) = 91.75 - 8.75 = 83$$

For finding these annual trend values, double the value of b, *i.e.*, $1.25 \times 2 = 2.5$ and add to the preceding value :

$$Y_{1997} = 83 + 2.5 = 85.5, Y_{1998} = 85.5 + 2.5 = 88 \text{ and so on.}$$

Example 45. *Assuming that trend is absent, determine if there is any seasonality in the data given below :*

Year	*1st Quarter*	*2nd Quarter*	*3rd Quarter*	*4th Quarter*
2002	*3.7*	*4.1*	*3.3*	*3.5*
2003	*3.7*	*3.9*	*3.6*	*3.6*
2004	*4.0*	*4.1*	*3.3*	*3.1*
2005	*3.3*	*4.4*	*4.0*	*4.0*

What are the seasonal indices for various quarters ? [*M. Com., Madurai Kamaraj*]

Solution. COMPUTATION OF SEASONAL INDICES

Year	*1st Quarter*	*2nd Quarter*	*3rd Quarter*	*4th Quarter*
2002	3.7	4.1	3.3	3.5
2003	3.7	3.9	3.6	3.6
2004	4.0	4.1	3.3	3.1
2005	3.3	4.4	4.0	4.0
Total	14.7	16.5	14.2	14.2
Average	3.675	4.125	3.55	3.55
Seasonal index	98.7	110.8	95.3	95.3

Notes for calculating seasonal index

$$\text{The average of averages} = \frac{3.675 + 4.125 + 3.55 + 3.55}{4} = \frac{14.900}{4} = 3.725$$

$$\text{Seasonal Index} = \frac{\text{Quarterly average}}{\text{General average}} \times 100$$

$$\text{Seasonal Index for first quarter} : \frac{3.675}{3.725} \times 100 = 98.7$$

$$\text{Seasonal Index for second quarter} : \frac{4.125}{3.725} \times 100 = 110.7$$

$$\text{Seasonal Index for the third quarter} : \frac{3.55}{3.725} \times 100 = 95.3$$

$$\text{Seasonal Index for the fourth quarter} : \frac{3.55}{3.725} \times 100 = 95.3$$

Example 46. *Given the following equation.*

$$Y_c = 84.26 + 5.8\,X$$

(Origin 2003, X unit = 1 year)

Change the origin (i) to 2001 and (ii) to 1st Jan. 2004

Solution. Shifting origin to 2001.

We are given the equation with 2004 as origin. When we shift the origin to 2001 difference is (2004–2001) = 3. Hence $k = -3$ (negative for the reason that 2001 precedes 2004) [Origin is shifted backward by 3 years]

$$\begin{aligned} Y_t &= a + b\,(X + k) \\ &= 84.26 + 5.8\,(X - 3) = 84.26 + 5.8\,X - 17.4 \\ &= 66.86 + 5.8\,X \end{aligned}$$

[Origin 2001, time unit = 1 year, Y is annual data]

(*ii*) For changing the origin to 1st Jan. 2004, k would be 0.5 (since it is assumed that the origin is the centre of the given year 2003, *i.e.*, 1st July, 2003). The required equation can be obtained easily :

$$
\begin{aligned}
Y_t &= 84.26 + 5.8\,(X + 0.5)\\
&= 84.26 + 5.8\,X + 29\\
&= 87.16 + 5.8\,X
\end{aligned}
$$

(Origin 1st Jan. 2004, X unit = 1 year, Y is annual data)

Example 47. *The seasonal index for a particular consumer good for January is 112.87. Actual demand for January 2004 was 1265 units. Based on this information only, what would be the estimate of sales in 2004 ?*

Solution. S.I. for Jan. is 112.87 (out of total of 1200 for the while year) Jan. Sales are 1265 units. Thus sales for the whole year = $\frac{1265}{112.85} \times 1200 = 13452.$

Example 48. *Fit a parabolic curve of the second degree to the data given below and estimate the value for 2006 and comment on it.*

Year	:	*2000*	*2001*	*2002*	*2003*	*2004*
Sales (in '000 ₹)	:	*10*	*12*	*13*	*10*	*8*

Solution. COMPUTATION OF SECOND DEGREE PARABOLA

Year	*Sales ('000 ₹)* Y	*Origin = 2002* X	XY	X^2	X^2Y	X^4
2000	10	– 2	– 20	4	40	16
2001	12	– 1	– 12	1	12	1
2002	13	0	0	0	0	0
2003	10	+ 1	+ 10	1	10	1
2004	8	+ 2	+ 16	4	32	16
$N = 5$	$\Sigma Y = 53$	$\Sigma X = 0$	$\Sigma XY = -6$	$\Sigma X^2 = 10$	$\Sigma X^2 Y = 94$	$\Sigma X^4 = 34$

The equation of the second degree parabola is : $Y = a + bX + cX^2$, obviously $\Sigma X = 0 = \Sigma X^3$

The values of a, b and c can be determined as follows : [refer 10.9].

$$b = \frac{\Sigma XY}{\Sigma X^2} = \frac{-6}{10} = -0.6$$

$$c = \frac{N\Sigma X^2Y - \Sigma X^2 \Sigma Y}{N\Sigma X^4 - (X^2)^2} = \frac{5 \times 94 - 10 \times 53}{5 \times 34 - (10)^2} = -0.857$$

$$a = \frac{\Sigma Y - c\Sigma X^2}{N} = \frac{53 - (.857 \times 10)}{5} = 8.886$$

∴ Parabolic trend equation is

$$Y = 8.886 - 0.6X - 0.857X^2$$

[Origin is 2002, X is in years, Y is annual data]

EXERCISE 10

1. (*a*) What is meant by time series analysis? Discuss its importance in business.

   (*b*) Explain briefly the different components of time series. Give some illustrations of the use of time series in economic analysis.

2. (*a*) Explain how you would deseasonalise a time series stating the assumptions you would be making.

   (*b*) Explain clearly the meaning of 'Time Series Analysis'. Distinguish between 'Secular Trend' and 'Seasonal Movement' in Time Series.

3. (*a*) Explain briefly the additive and multiplicative models of time series. Which of these models is more popular in practice and why?

   (*b*) Distinguish between ratio to trend and ratio to moving average methods of measuring seasonal variations. Which is better and why?

4. How would you find out the trend value in a time series by the method of least squares?

5. What is secular trend? Point out the significance of its study.

6. Fill in the blanks :

   (*i*) A time series consists of data arranged ......

   (*ii*) Comparable monthly data may be obtained by multiplying each of the values by ......and in a leap year by ......

   (*iii*) The additive model of a time series is expressed as ......

   (*iv*) When the differences between successive observations of series are constant (or nearly so), the......may be an appropriate representation of trend equation.

   (*v*) A polynomial of the form $Y = a + bx + cx^2$ is called ......

   (*vi*) In the trend equation $Y = a + bx$; a is called ...... and b is called ......

   [Ans. (*i*) Chronologically, (*ii*) 30.4167, 30.5, (*iii*) $Y = T + S + C + I$ (*iv*) Arithmetic straight line, (*v*) Second degree equation, (*vi*) Y intercept, slope of the trend line]

7. Fit a straight line trend by the method of least squares and estimate the production in 2006 :

Year	1998	1999	2000	2001	2002	2003	2004
Production	180	190	192	193	194	199	192

   [$Y_c = 190 + 2X$; 200]

8. From the following data, calculate trend by the method of least squares :

Year	1998	1999	2000	2001	2002	2003	2004
Profits (₹ '000)	300	700	600	800	900	700	1000

   [$Y_c = 714.286 + 85.714X$]

9. From the following data fit a Straight Line Trend using Least Squares Methods and plot it on the graph paper :

Year	1997	1998	1999	2000	2001	2002	2003	2004
No. of Accidents:	282	228	185	160	129	90	70	32

[**Ans.** $Y_c = 147 - 34X$]

10. (*a*) Obtain seasonal indices from the following time series by the method of simple averages :

Year	*Quarter* I	II	III	IV
2001	65	58	56	61
2002	68	63	53	67
2003	70	59	56	52
2004	60	55	51	58

[**Ans.** 110.5, 98.74, 90.76, 100]

11. From the following data, calculate the trend value using four-yearly moving average:

Year :	1989	1990	1991	1992	1993	1994	1995	1996	1997
Values :	506	620	1036	673	588	696	1116	738	663

[**Ans.** M.A. Values for 1991 to 1995 respectively are: 719, 738.75, 758.25, 776.375, 793.875]

12. From the following data calculate the 4-yearly moving average and determine the trend values. Find the short-term fluctuations. Plot the original data and the trend on a graph.

Year	*Value*	*Year*	*Value*
1958	50.0	1963	38.1
1959	36.5	1964	32.6
1960	43.0	1965	41.7
1961	44.5	1966	41.1
1962	38.9	1967	33.8

[**Ans.** Tend value:42.1, 40.9, 39.8, 38.2, 38.1, 37.8

Short-term oscillations (assuming multiplicative model):

102.14, 108.80, 97.74, 99.74, 85.56, 110.32]

13. Assume a four-year cycle, calculate the trend by the method of moving average from the following data relating to production of tea in a certain tea estate :

Year	*Production*	*Year*	*Production (Kg.)*
1961	464	1966	540
1962	515	1967	557
1963	518	1968	571

1964	467	1969	586
1965	502	1970	612

[**Ans.** 4-yearly M.A.'s for 1963 to 1968 respectively are :

495.70, 503.60, 511.60, 529.50, 553.00, 572.50]

14. (*a*) What do you understand by deseasonalisation of data ? Explain its uses.

(*b*) The seasonal indices of sale of a firm are as under :

January	106	July	93
February	105	August	89
March	101	September	92
April	104	October	102
May	98	November	106
June	96	December	108

If the firm is expecting total sales of ₹ 42,00,000 during 1996, estimate the sales for the individual months of 1996.

[**Ans.** Estimated sales (in '000 ₹) for January to December are :

371, 367.5, 353.5, 364, 343, 336, 325.5, 311.5, 322, 357, 371, 378]

15. (*a*) The quarterly seasonal indices of the sales of a popular brand of colour television of a company, in Delhi, are given below :

Quarter	:	I	II	III	IV
Seasonal Index	:	130	90	95	105

It the total sales for the first quarter of 1997 is ₹ 6,50,000, estimate the worth of televisions to be kept in store to meet the demand in other quarters. Assume that there is no trend.

[**Hint.** The estimated worth or televisions to be kept in store to meet the demand for the ith quarter is : $\dfrac{\text{Sales of 1st quarter}}{\text{S.I. of 1st quarter}} \times (\text{S.I. of } i\text{th quarter})\ ;\ i = 2, 3, 4$]

[**Ans.** *Quarter*	:	II	III	IV
Inventory to be kept (in ₹)	:	4,50,000	3,75,000	5,25,000]

16. (*a*) Explain the methods of fitting of the quadratic and exponential curves. How would you use the fitted curves for forecasting ?

(*b*) Distinguish between Trend and Exponential Trend.

17. Fit a parabolic curve of second degree to the data given below and estimate the value for 1999 and comment on it :

Years	:	1993	1994	1995	1996	1997
Sales (in '000 ₹)	:	10	12	13	10	8

[**Ans.** $y_c = 12.314 - 0.6x - 0.857x^2$

Trend Values : 10.086, 12.057, 12.314, 10.857, 7.686

(y_c)1999 = – 3.798 (thousand ₹). Since the sales cannot be negative, the given second degree parabolic curve is not a good fit to the given data.]

18. Find a non-linear trend equation from the following three normal equations obtained from the origin 1994 and estimate the value for 1997 :

$10 = 5a + 10b + 30c, \qquad 26 = 10a + 30b + 100c, \qquad 86 = 30a + 100b + 354c.$

[**Hint.** Solving these equations for a, b and c, we shall get ; $a = \frac{38}{35}$, $b = \frac{1}{35}$, $c = \frac{1}{7}$.]

[**Ans.** Trend equation is :

$$Y = \frac{38}{35} + \frac{1}{35}x + \frac{1}{7}x^2 \quad ; \quad \text{Origin : 1994, } (x = X - 1994).]$$

19. The sales of a company in lakhs of rupees for the years 1995 to 1999 are given below:

Year (x) :	1995	1996	1997	1998	1999
Sales (y) :	65	92	132	190	275

Estimate the sales for the year 2000 using an equation of the form $y = a\,b^x$.

[**Ans.** $y = 132.7\,(1.435)^x$; (Origin : 1997) ; $(y_c)_{2000} = 392.127$ (lakh ₹).]

20. Given the following population figures for India, estimate, the population for 1991, using an equation of the form $y = AB^x$.

Census year (X) :	1921	1931	1941	1951	1961	1971	1981
Population (Y) *(in crores)* :	25.1	27.9	31.9	36.1	43.9	54.8	68.5

[**Ans.** $y = 37.83 \times (1.182)^u$; $u = (X - 1951)/10$; $(y_c)_{1991} = 75.7946$ (crores).]

21. Compute the average seasonal movement for the following series :

	Quarterly production			
Year	*I*	*II*	*III*	*IV*
2000	3.5	3.9	3.4	3.6
2001	3.5	4.1	3.7	4.0
2002	3.5	3.9	3.7	4.2
2003	4.0	4.6	3.8	4.5
2004	4.1	4.4	4.2	4.5

[**Ans.** Seasonal Indices using Multiplicative model are 94.06, 105.69, 95.07, 105.18.]

22. On the basis of quarterly sales (in ₹ lakhs) of a certain commodity for the period 2000-2004, the following results were computed:

Trend line : $y = 27.2. + 0.6t$ with origin 1st quarter 2000, t = time units (one quarter) and y = quarterly sales (in ₹ lakhs).

The seasonal indices are:

1st quarter	*2nd quarter*	*3rd quarter*	*4th quarter*
90	95	110	105

Estimate the quarterly sales for the year 2002 assuming that cyclical and irregular movements are absent.

[I Qtr. : 28.8, II Qr. : 30.97, III Qr. : 36.52, IV, Qt. : 35.49]

23. The trend equation for yearly sales of a commodity with 1st July, 2003 as origin is $Y = 96 + 28.8\,X$.

(*i*) Determine the monthly trend equation with January 2004 as origin, (*ii*) Compute the trend values for August 2003 and March 2004. *(B.A. Econ. (H), Delhi Univ.)*

[Ans. (*i*) $Y_{\text{Jan. 2004}} = 9.2 + 0.2X$; (*ii*) $Y_{\text{Aug.2003}} = 8.2 + 0.2X$; $Y_{\text{Mar. 2004}} = 9.6 + 0.2X$]

24. Fit a straight line trend by the method of least squares to the following data:

Year	*Production of TV sets (in '000)*	*Year*	*Production of TV sets (in '000)*
1994	17	2000	35
1995	20	2001	55
1996	19	2002	50
1997	26	2003	74
1998	24	2004	69
1999	40		

Estimate the production for 2009.

[Ans. $Y_c = 39 + 5.8\,X$; $Y_{2009} = 97 + 5.8X$]

25. (*a*) The sale of a reputed organisation rose from ₹ 1,26,000 in the month of August 1993 to ₹ 1,38,000 in the month of September 1993. The seasonal indices for the two months were 105 and 140. The General Manager was not at all satisfied with rise of the sales in the month of September 1993 by ₹ 12,000. He expected much more because of seasonal index for the month. What was his expectations of sales for the month of September 1993 ? *[Delhi Univ. B.Com. (Hons.), 1994]*

[Hint. G.M.'s estimate of sales for Sept. 1993 = ₹ $\dfrac{1,26,000}{105} \times 140$ = ₹ 1,68,000].

(*b*) The sales of readymade garments of a particular brand, of a departmental store rose from ₹ 25,000 in January to ₹ 30,000 in February, the seasonal indices for these months being 105 and 135 respectively. While the sales manager of the store was satisfied with ₹ 5,000 increase, the owner of the store expressed his dissatisfaction. Who is right ? Justify your answer.

[Ans. Expected sales in February should be ₹ $\left(\dfrac{25,000}{105} \times 135\right)$ = ₹ 32142.86. The owner of the store is right].

26. On the basis of quarterly sales in (₹ lakhs) of a certain commodity for the years 1994-95, the following calculations were made :

SEASONAL VARIATIONS

Quarter	I	II	III	IV
Seasonal Index	80	90	120	110

$Y = 20 + 0.5\,X$ with origin : 1st quarter of 1994

X = unit = one quarter ; Y = Quarterly sales (₹ lakhs)

Estimate the quarterly sales for each of the four quarters of 1995, using the multiplicative model. *[Delhi Univ. B.A. (Econ. Hons.), 2000]*

[**Ans.** Estimated quarterly sales for the quarters of 1995 (in ₹ lakh) are

17.60, 20.25, 27.60, 25.85 respectively].

27. A store has an annual trend equation for its sales index as

$$Y_{1997} = 100 + 3X$$

If its December seasonal is 200 and its July seasonal 60, which was a relatively better month for sales, July 2000 when the sales index was at 70 or December 1998 when the index was at 220 ?

[**Ans.** Estimated Sales in December = $(100 + 3 \times 11) \times 2.00 = 266$; Actual sales = 220

Estimated Sales in July = $(100 + 3 \times 6) \times 0.60 = 70.8$; Actual sales = 70].

28. Convert the following into annual trend equation :

$Y = 350 + 3X$; Origin = I – II Quarter, 1986 ; X unit = 1 Quarter ; Y unit = Quarterly Production.]

[**Hint.** $Y = 350 + 3(X + 1) = 353 + 3X$: Origin II – III Quarter 1986.

Annual Trend Equation :

$Y = 4 \times 353 + 4 \times 4 \times 3X = 1412 + 48X$; Origin 1986 ; X unit = 1 Year ; Y = Annual Production.

29. The annual production of a commodity is given ass follows :

Year	:	1990	1991	1992	1993	1994	1995	1996
Production (in tonnes)	:	70	80	90	95	102	110	115

(*i*) Fit a straight line trend by the method of least squares.

(*ii*) Convert the annual trend equation into a monthly trend equation.

[C.A. (Foundation), Nov. 1999]

Ans. (*i*) Y : Production (in tonnes) ; t : Years.

$Y = 94.57 + 7.39\,X$; ($X = t - 1993$ *i.e., Origin* : *1993*)

(*ii*) $Y = 7.88 + 0.05X$

[Origin : 1993 ; x unit = 1 Month ; y unit : Monthly production (in tonnes)].

30. Below are given the annual production (in thousand tons) of a fertilizer factory :

Year	:	1987	1988	1989	1990	1991	1992	1993
Production	:	70	75	90	91	95	98	100

(*i*) Fit a straight line trend by the method of least squares and tabulate the trend values.

(*ii*) Convert the annual trend equation into a monthly trend equation.

[**Ans.** Trend Values : 75.3215, 78.3572, 83.3929, 88.4286, 93.4643, 98.5000, 103.5357]

Linear trend equation is :

$$y_c = 88.4286 + 5.0357x$$

[Origin : 1990 ; x unit = 1 year ; y unit = annual production (in '000 tons)]

Monthly trend equation :

$$y_c = 7.3691 + 0.0357x$$

[Origin : 1990 ; x unit = 1 month ; y unit = Monthly production (in '000 tons)]

31. Trend equation for yearly sales (in '000 ₹) for a commodity with year 1999 as origin is $Y = 81.6 + 28.8X$. Determine the trend equation to give the monthly trend values with January 2000 as origin and calculate the trend value for March, 2000.

[**Ans.** $y_c = 8.1 + 0.2x$; Origin : Middle of January 2000 ; x unit = 1 month; y unit = Average monthly sales ('000 ₹).]

32. The trend equation for certain production is given by $y = 3{,}600 + 288t$, where

y : Annual production in thousand tons ; t : Time with origin, the year 1990 and unit = 1 year.

Estimate the trend value of the production for September 1994.

[I.C.W.A. (Intermediate), June 2000]

[**Hint.** Monthly trend equation is given by :

$$y = \frac{3{,}600}{12} + \frac{288}{144}t = 300 + 2t$$; Origin : 30th June, 1990 ; t : Unit 1 month ; y : Monthly production.

For September 1994 *i.e.,* 15th September, 1994 ; $t = 4 \times 12 + 2.5 = 50.5$.

$\therefore$ Estimated production for 1994 = $360 + 2 \times 50.5 = 401$ thousand tons.]

□□□

11

Probability Theory

CHAPTER OUTLINE

- Classical Definition
- Counting Techniques, Sets (review)
- Statistical of Empirical definition of probability
- Theorems on Probability
- Baye's Theorem

11.1 INTRODUCTION TO PROBABILITY

The study of probability provides a basis for inferential statistics. Inferential statistics involves sample selection, computing sample statistic on the basis of the concerned sample, and then inferring population parameter on the basis of the sample statistic. We do this exercise because population parameter is unknown. We try to estimate the unknown population parameter on the basis of the known sample statistic. This procedure works on uncertainty. By applying some defined statistical rules and procedures (discussed later in this book), an analyst can assign the probability of obtaining a result. To make rational decisions, a decision maker must have a deep understanding of probability theory. This understanding enhances his capacity to make optimum decisions in an uncertain environment. This chapter focuses on the basic concept of probability which will serve as the foundation of probability distribution (discussed in Chapters 12 and 13). A sound knowledge of probability and probability distributions also helps in developing probabilistic decision models.

11.2 CONCEPT OF PROBABILITY

We live in a world dominated by uncertainty. Change is the only permanent phenomenon. We can never predict the nature and directions of change in our lives.

Sometimes change is planned, but more often, change is unplanned. Even in cases of planned change, it is not possible to avoid uncertainty. There is a perceived need to be accurate (up to an extent) and prepared in this uncertain environment. Our need to cope with this unavoidable uncertainty of life has led to the study of **probability theory.** Probability is a concept that we all understand. In our daily life, we use words like chance, possibility, likelihood, and of course, probability. There might have been many occasions when we have said that the chances are 50–50 or there is a 70% chance of India winning the match, and so on. By making these statements, we try to attach some probability of the event happening or not happening. If we look at the wider picture, all these statements are related to the concept of probability. Therefore, there is a general understanding about the concept of probability, but there is a problem in terms of its proper application-oriented understanding.

In simple words, **probability** is the likelihood or chance that a particular event will or will not occur. The theory of probability provides a quantitative measure of uncertainty or likelihood of occurrence of different events resulting from a random experiment, in terms of quantitative measures ranging from 0 to 1. This means that the probability of a certain event is 1 and the probability of an impossible event is 0. In other words, a probability near 0 indicates that an event is unlikely to occur whereas a probability near 1 indicates that an event is almost certain to occur. For example, suppose an event is the success of a new product launched. A probability 0.90 indicates that the new product is likely to be successful whereas a probability of 0.15 indicates that the product is unlikely to be successful in the market. A probability of 0.50 indicates that the product is just as likely to be successful as not.

11.3 BASIC MATHEMATICAL CONCEPTS USED

Before we start with measures of probability, the following mathematical tools used are reviewed.

11.3.1. (*A*) Set

A set is list/collection/group of certain number of well defined and distinct units, units may be numbers, objects, places, etc. All the units are placed within brackets separated by commas. Each unit is an element/a member of the set. Such a set is also referred as "Universal" set.

Examples

1. Set of all natural numbers less than 5 is set [1, 2, 3, 4], Members of set are 1, 2, 3 and 4.

(*B*) "Cardinal" Number of a Finite Set

It is a number which indicates the number of elements in a set *A* and is written as $n(A)$ If $n(A) = 5$ *i.e.* cardinal number of set *A* is five which means that set *A* contains 5 elements.

'Null' sets or 'Empty' set. A set which does not have any element, *i.e.,* no element qualifies to be its member. It is denoted as ϕ or { }.

i.e., (*a*) $\{x/x$ is a natural number and $2 < x < 3\}$

There is no natural number which is greater than 2 and less than 3.

(C) Relations Between 2 Sets

1. "Subset". Set A is called subset of set B if all elements of A belong to B.

Example

Let $A = \{x / x \text{ is natural number less than } 5\} = \{1, 2, 3, 4\}$

and $B = \{x / x \text{ is natural number less than } 7\} = \{1, 2, 3, 4, 5, 6\}$

It is observed that *all element of A belong to B*, hence we say A is subset of B and same fact is described by the relation $A \subseteq B$.

We may also say that A is contained in B or B contains A.

2. "Proper Subset". Set A is said to be "Proper subset" of set B if *all* elements of A belong to B and B has at least one element which does not belong to A. In the above example

$A = \{1, 2, 3, 4\}$ and $B = \{1, 2, 3, 4, 5, 6\}$

Now all elements of A belong to B and B has two elements '5' and '6' which do not belong to A. Thus A is proper subset of B [A is subset of B is also true] which is expressed as

$A \subset B$ or $A \subseteq B$

We may also say that if

$A \subseteq B$ and $n(A) < n(B)$

then A is proper subset of B.

3. "Equal Sets". If $A \subseteq B$ and also $B \subseteq A$ [*i.e.* A and B both sets are subsets of each other] then Set A = Set B *i.e.* sets A and B both have exactly same elements.

Example 1. $A = \{x / x \text{ is natural number less than } 5\} = \{1, 2, 3, 4\}$

Set $B = \{x / x \text{ is natural number less than or equal to } 4\} = \{1, 2, 3, 4\}$

Thus $A \subseteq B$ and $B \subseteq A$

Hence $A = B$.

4. "Equivalent Sets". Sets A and B are equivalent if they contains equal number of elements *i.e.* $n(A) = n(B)$

Let $A = [2, 4, 6, 8, 10]$, $B = [a, e, i, o, u]$

Thus $n(A) = 5$ and $n(B) = 5$

Thus A and B are equivalent.

(D) Venn Diagram

Venn Diagram is a diagram which represents different sets and its element. Universal set S is represented as a rectangle and its subsets are generally represented as circles.

Let $S = \{1, 2, 3, 4, 5, 6\}$, $A = \{2, 4, 6\}$, $B = \{3, 6\}$

then Venn diagram showing all these sets will be as follows :

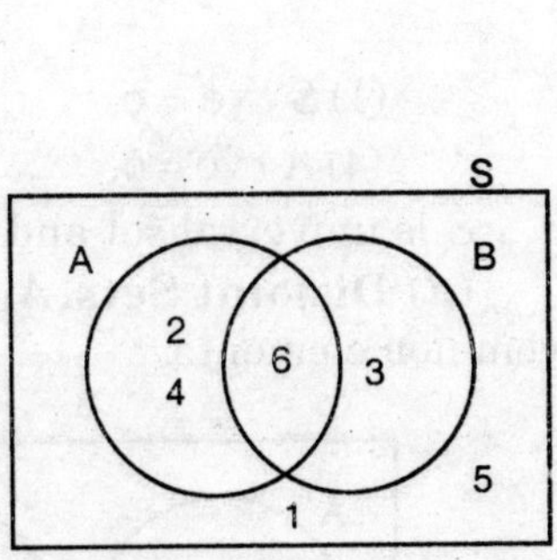

(E) Operations on Sets

(a) Compliment of a Set. If A is subset of universal set S then compliment of A (which is written as A^C or A') is a set of all those elements of S which do not belong to A.

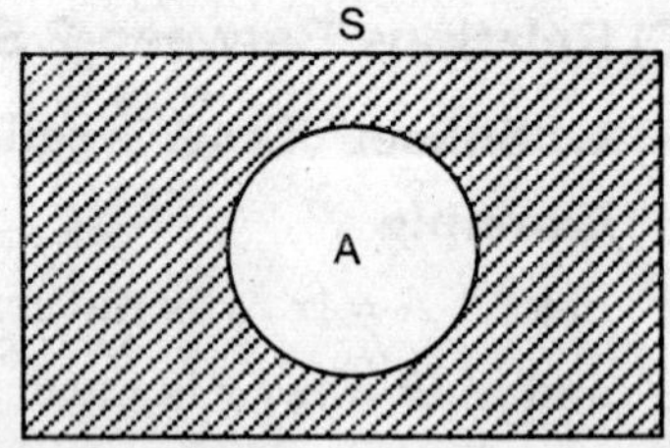

Let $S = \{1, 2, 3, 4, 5\}$ and $A = \{1, 4\}$

then $A^c = A' = [2, 3, 5]$

A^c is shaded are in the Venn diagram.

Thus $S' = \phi$, $\phi' = S$

$(A')' = A, A \cup A' = S, A \cap A' = \phi$

(*b*) Union of 2 Sets. Union of two sets A and B is a third set which is denoted as $A \cup B$ and which is defined as a set containing only those elements which are included either in A or B.

For Example,

If $A = \{2, 4, 6\}, B = \{3, 6\}$

then $A \cup B = \{2, 3, 4, 6\}$ which is shown in Venn diagram below :

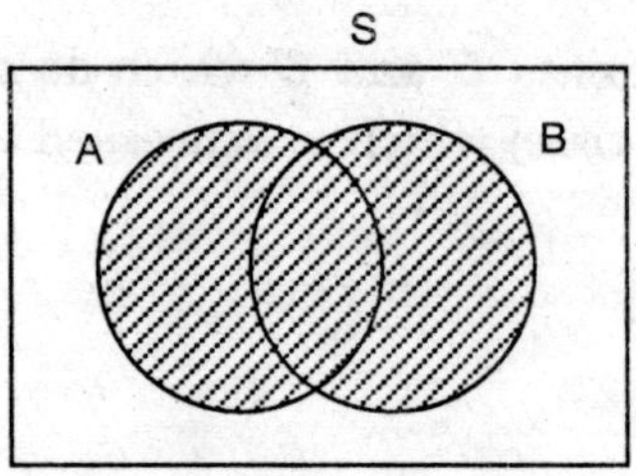

$A \cup B$ = shaded set

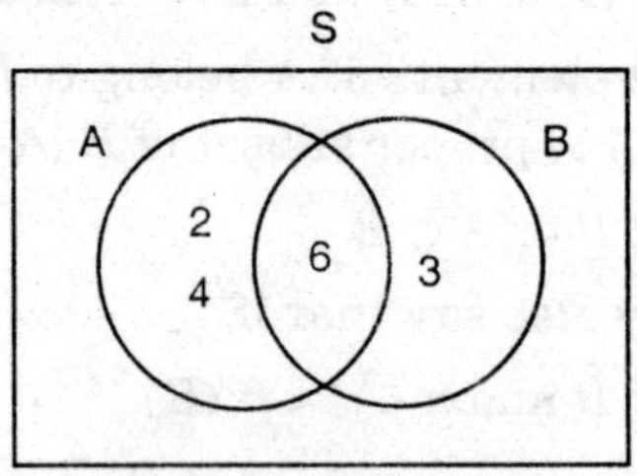

$A \cup B = \{2, 3, 4, 6\}$

Some results on union of sets

(1) $A \cup A = A$ (2) $A \cup S = S$ (3) $A \cup \phi = A$ (4) $A \cup A^C = S$

where S = universal set

(*c*) Intersection of 2 Sets. Intersection of 2 sets A and B is a third set which is denoted by $A \cap B$ and which contains only those elements which are contained in both sets (*i.e.* common elements in both).

If $A = \{3, 6, 7\}, B = \{2, 3, 4, 6\}$

$A \cap B = \{3, 6\}$

Some results on intersection of sets

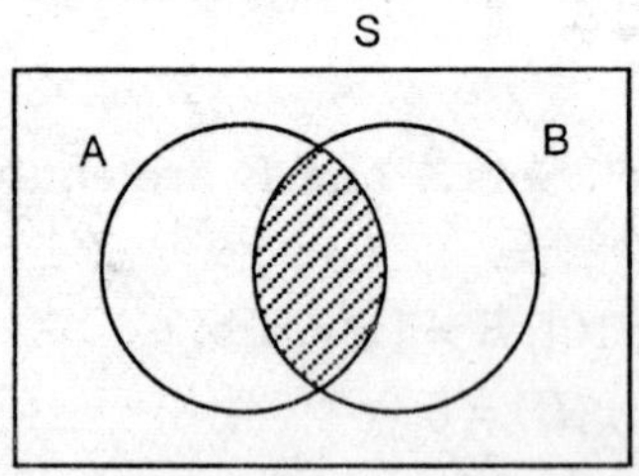

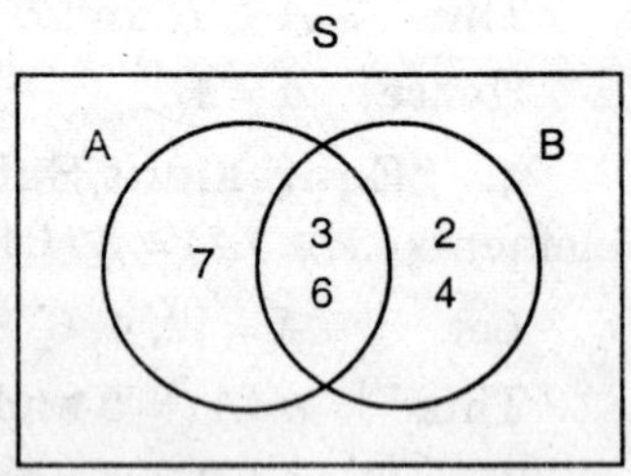

$A \cap B$ = Shaded Area

(1) $S \cap \phi = \phi$, (2) $S \cap A = A$ (3) $A \cap A = A$,

(4) $A \cap \phi = \phi$, (5) $A \cap A^C = \phi$

S is universal set and ϕ is null set.

(*d*) Disjoint Sets. A and B sets are disjoint if $A \cap B = \phi$, *i.e.,* A and B do not have any common elements.

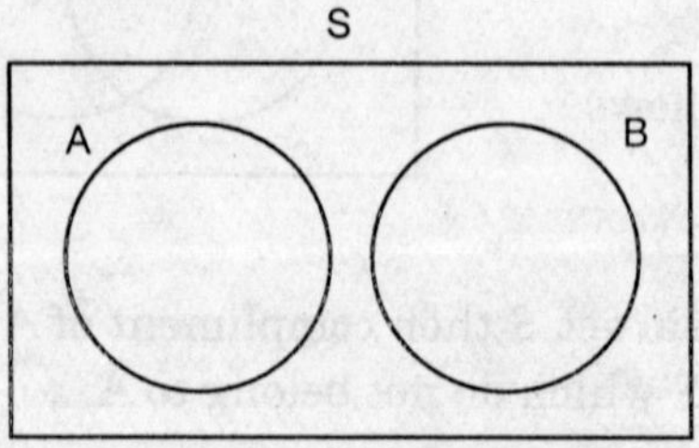

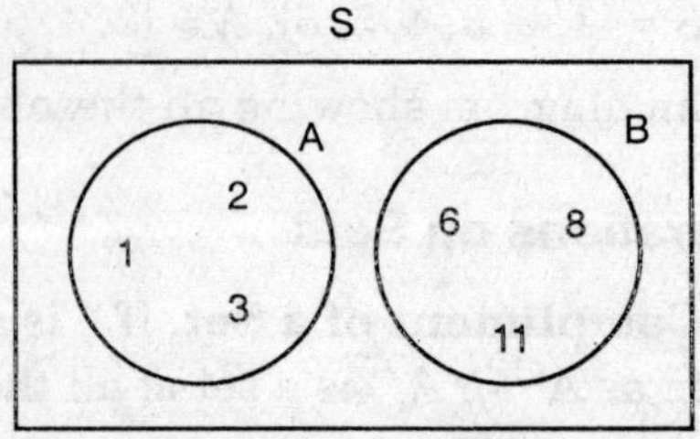

Set A = {1, 2, 3} and B = {6, 8, 11} are disjoint sets as $A \cap B = \phi$

(e) Difference of 2 sets A and B *i.e.* $A - B$ is a third set which contains only those elements of A which are not in B. $A - B = A \cap B^c$

(f) Symmetric Difference. Symmetric difference of 2 sets A and B is denoted by $A \Delta B$ and is defined as

$$A \Delta B = (A - B) \cup (B - A)$$

i.e. $A \Delta B$ is a set of those elements which belong *only to set* A $(= A - B)$ or only to set B $(= B - A)$

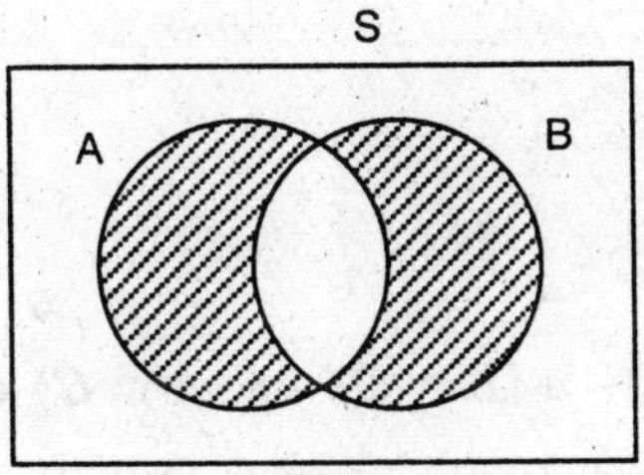

$A \Delta B$

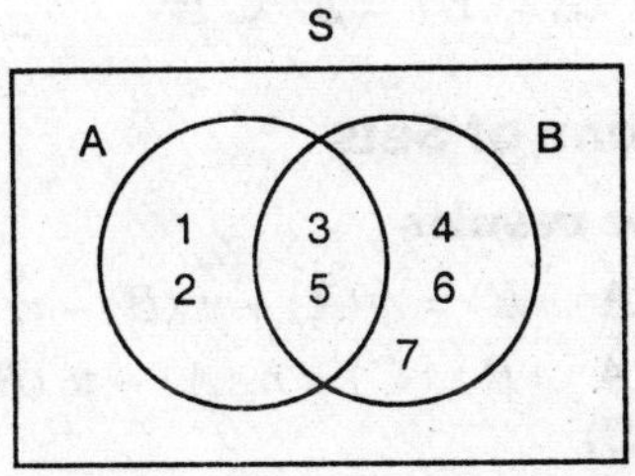

$A \Delta B = \{1, 2, 4, 6, 7\} = (A \cup B) - (A \cap B)$

Thus $A \Delta B = (A - B) \cup (B - A) = (A \cup B) - (A \cap B)$

Example. If $A = \{1, 2, 3, 5\}$ $B = \{4, 3, 5, 6, 7\}$

$A - B = \{1, 2\}$ as elements 1 and 2 belong to A but do not belong to B. Elements 3 and 5 are removed from A to get $A - B$ as 3, 5 belong to B.

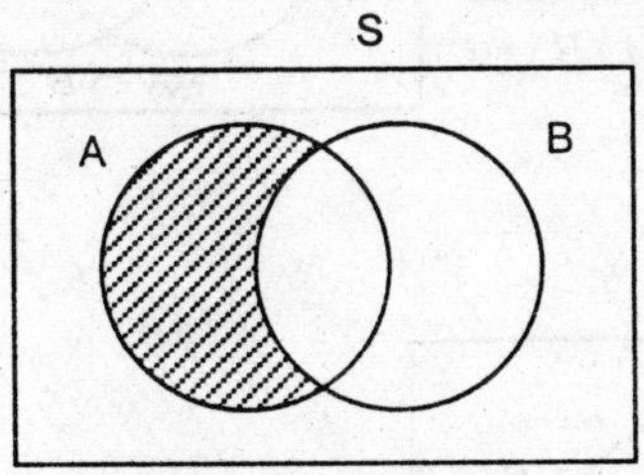

$A - B$ = Shaded Set

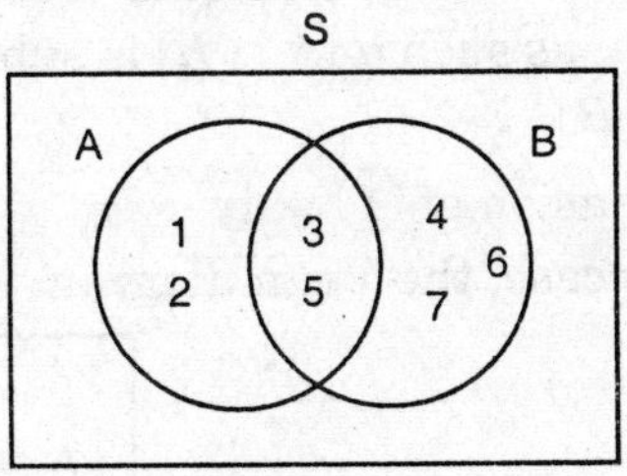

$A - B = \{1, 2\}$

We also see that $A - B = A - (A \cap B)$

$= A \cap B^C$

Similarly $B - A = B - (A \cap B) = B \cap A^C$

Thus we see $A \cup B = (A - B) \cup (B - A) \cup (A \cap B)$ and also all the three sets $A - B$, $B - A$ and $A \cap B$ are disjoint.

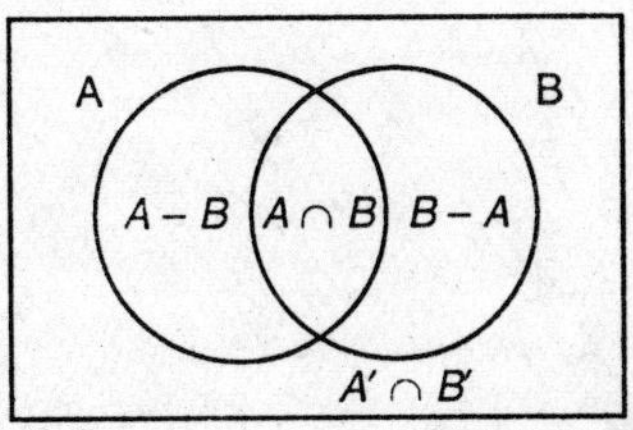

$A' \cap B'$ = set of those elements which are neither in A nor in B.

Also $A = (A - B) \cup (A \cap B)$ and $B = (B - A) \cup A \cap B$

Some results on difference of Sets, $A - A = \phi$, $S - A = A^C$, $A - \phi = A$

Some more Results on Sets

(*i*) $A \cap B \subseteq A$ (*ii*) $A \cap B \subseteq B$

(*iii*) $A \subseteq A \cup B$ (*iv*) $B \subseteq A \cup B$

(*v*) $(A - B) \cup B = A \cup B$ (*vi*) $(A - B) \cap B = \phi$

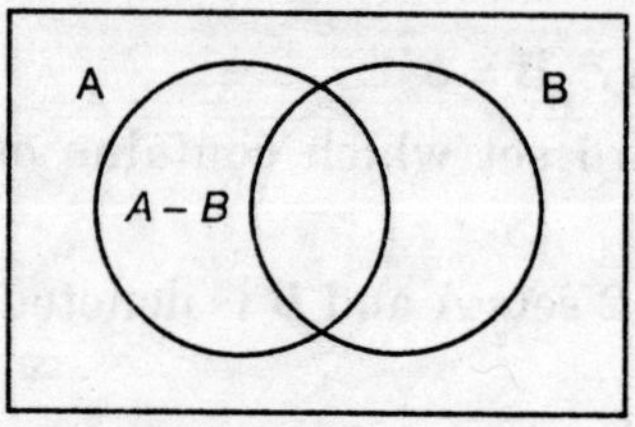

(as $A - B$ and B are 2 disjoint sets)

(*vii*) Demorgan's Law

(*a*) $(A \cup B)' = A' \cap B'$

(*b*) $(A \cap B)' = A' \cup B'$

Applications of Sets

We use results

(1) $n(A \cup B) = n(A) + n(B) - n(A \cup B)$

(2) $n(A \cup B \cup C) = n(A) + n(B) + n(C) - n(A \cup B) - n(B \cap C) - n(A \cap C) + n(A \cap B \cap C)$

(1) is easy to see

as $n(A \cup B) \quad = n(A - B) + n(B)$

$= n(A) - n(A \cap B) + n(B)$

$= n(A) + n(B) - n(A \cap B)$

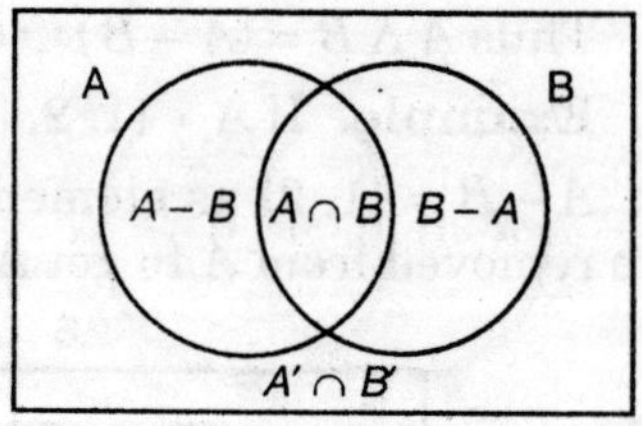

Also we find that elements of $A \cap B$ are counted twice, in A and B both, as such $n(A \cap B)$ is subtracted from $n(A) + n(B)$ to get $n(A \cup B)$.

② is extension of ① only

In this case, the Venn diagram is as follows :

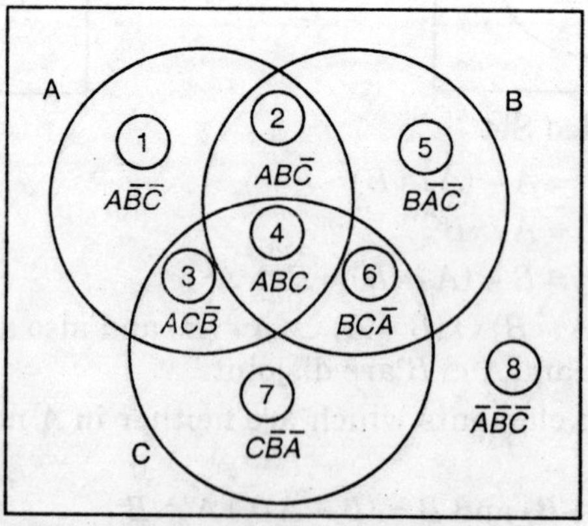

There are 3 sets A, B and C. The region ① indicates the elements which are *only* in A = $A\bar{B}\,\bar{C}$ these elements are not included in any other set) ② + ④ indicates $A \cap B$.

④ indicates $A \cap B \cap C$ (elements common to all 3 sets)

Thus ② will have elements which are A and B both, but are not in C

i.e. ② $= A \cap B \cap C'$ = exactly two of A and B or A and B but not C.

⑤ is only B, ⑦ is only C

④ + ⑥ $= B \cap C$

⑥ $= B \cap C \cap A'$

⑧ $= A' \cap B' \cap C'$ = neither A nor B nor C (none of the three)

11.3.2 Permutations—Combinations

(A) Fundamental Theorems of Counting

(1) **Multiplication Rule.** If one operation can be performed in p ways and corresponding to each one of these p ways, another operation can be performed in q ways, then the two operations together can be performed in $p \times q$ ways.

Example 1. *Anil has 4 pants and 5 shirts, In how many ways can he go to the school with different dress ?*

Solution. Let P_1, P_2, P_3, P_4, be 4 pants and S_1, S_2, S_3, S_4, S_5 be 5 shirts. With P_1 there may be any of S_1, S_2, $S3$, $S4$, S_5, shirts (five). Thus for each pant there are 5 combinations of shirts and there are 4 pants, thus there are 4×5 dress combinations.

The same may be represented as form of boxes. Box 1 represents pant and Box 2 represents shirt. The two boxes are to filled labels indicating pants and shirts.

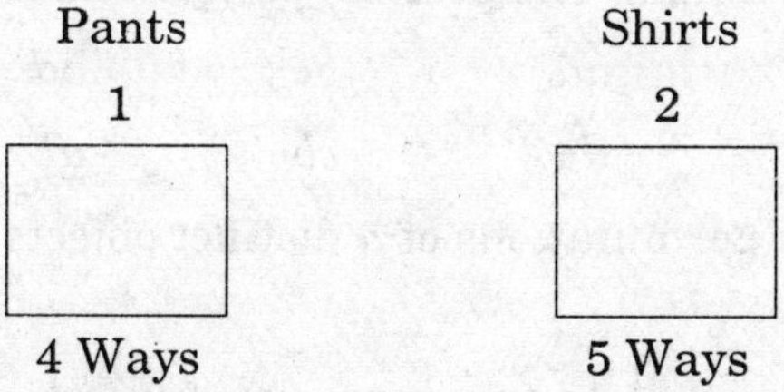

Total number of dresses = $4 \times 5 = 20$.

(2) **Additional Rule.** If one operation can performed in p different ways, and if another operation can be performed in q different ways and if the two operations are mutually exclusive (two operations are said to be mutually exclusive if both cannot happen simultaneously in a single trial) then either of the two operations can be performed is $(p + q)$ ways. (either one or other but not both).

Example 2. *A team consists of 4 boys and 6 girls and other has 6 boys and 5 girls. How many single matches can be arranged between the two teams when a boy plays against a boy and a girl against a girl ?*

Solution. A body can be selected from the 1st team in 4 ways and from the 2nd in 6 ways. Hence no. of single matches between the boys of two teams

$= 4 \times 6 = 24$ ...(A) (Using the Multiplication Rule)

Similarly, no. of single matches between the girls of two teams

$= 6 \times 5 = 30$ ... (B) (Using the Multiplication Rule)

Operations A and B are mutually exclusive (they cannot happen simultaneously in a single trial hence the total no. of single matches that can be arranged between the two teams

$= 24 + 30 = 54$ (Using Additional Rule)

(B) Factorial Notation

We begin by introducing a useful shorthand notation—the *factorial symbol.*

Fro a positive integer n, the symbol $n!$ or $\underline{|n}$ is read n factorial or factorial n and it represents the product of first n positive integers. That is,

$$n! = 1 . 2 . 3 ......n$$
$$= n (n-1)(n-2) ......1$$

For example, $4! = 4 \times 3 \times 2 \times 1 = 24$

(C) Permutations

Definition. A permutation is an ordered arrangement of all or part of a set of objects. More precisely, an ordered arrangement of r objects chosen from n distinct objects is called a **permutation of *n* objects taken *r* a time.**

For example, let us consider the number of permutations that are possible from four letters a, b, c and d taken 2 at a time. The possible permutations are

ab	*ac*	*ad*	*bc*	*bd*	*cd*
ba	*ca*	*da*	*cb*	*db*	*dc*

Notation. The number of permutations of n distinct objects taken r at a time is denoted by ${}^nP_r$ or $P(n, r)$ where

$${}^nP_r = \frac{n!}{(n-r)!\,r!} = n(n-1)(n-2) \ldots (n-r+2)(n-r+1)$$

Thus $\quad {}^8p_3 = 8 \times 7 \times 6 = 336.$

Example 3. *Ten students are participating in a race. In how many ways can the first three prizes be won ?*

Solution. The problem is asking for the number of permutations of 10 students taken three at a time.

$\therefore$ Number of ways in which three prizes can be won by 10 students

$${}^{10}P_3 = 10 \times 9 \times 8 = 720.$$

In case objects are not distinct. Number of permutations of n things out of which p are alike of one kind and q are alike of other kind, by taking all things *i.e.,* ${}^np_n = \dfrac{n!}{p!\,q!}$

Example 4. *In how many ways can the letters of the word "ACCOUNTANT" be arranged. In how many of those, vowels are always together ?*

Solution. *First Part.* The word "ACCOUNTANT" consists of 10 letters of which A, C, N and T each are repeated twice and the remaining letters are all different. Hence number of distinct arrangements of the letters of the word "ACCOUNTANT" is given by

$$\frac{10\,!}{2!\;2!\;2!\;2!} = 2{,}26{,}800$$

Second Part. The word "ACCOUNTANT" has 4 vowels, *viz..*, A, O, U, A of which A is repeated twice. To obtain the number of arrangements in which the 4 vowels are always together, we regard them as tied together, forming only one letter, so that the number of letters to be permuted in the word "ACCOUNTANT" may be taken as to be permuted in remaining 6 + 1 (of 4 vowels). In these 7 letters (leaving vowels), C, N, T are repeated twice and hence can be arranged in $\frac{7!}{2!\;2!\;2!}$ ways.

However, the number of ways in which 4 vowels can be arranged among themselves is $\frac{4!}{2!}$ given by (having 2 A 's)

Hence the total number of arrangements favourable in which all vowels are together is given by

$$\frac{7!}{2!\;2!\;2!} \times \frac{4!}{2!} = 7{,}560.$$

Combination. Selection of a group of object, some or all, out of given number of objects is a combination, *e.g.*, ABC or ACB is one combination (not two).

EACH OF THE COLLECTIONS OBTAINED BY TAKING r ($r \le n$) OBJECTS FROM n DIFFERENT OBJECTS IS KNOWN AS A COMBINATION

The symbol ${}^nC_r$ is used to denote the total number of combinations obtained by taking objects from different objects in each time. An alternative symbol for denoting combination is $\binom{n}{r}$.

The number of combinations of n different objects taken r at a time, i.e., ${}^nC_r$ *is given by*

$${}^nC_r = \frac{\underline{|n}}{\underline{|n}\;\underline{|n-r}} . = \frac{{}^np_r}{r!}$$

Thus $\quad {}^8c_3 = \dfrac{{}^8p_3}{3!} = \dfrac{8 \times 7 \times 6}{3 \times 2 \times 1}$

Also $\quad {}^{10}c_2 = \dfrac{10 \times 9}{2 \times 1}$

11.4 EXPERIMENT

An experiment is a process which produces outcomes. For example, if we toss a fair coin, we may obtain either a head or a tail. So, tossing this fair coin is an experiment which can produce two outcomes, either a head or a tail. Similarly, when we roll a die, six possible outcomes can arise, that is, turning of any of the six numbers 1, 2, 3, 4, 5, 6 on the upper face of the die. An interview to gauge the job satisfaction levels of an employee in an organization is also an experiment because this will produce outcomes.

11.4.1. Sample Space

Set of all possible out comes of an experiment is called sample space and is denoted by S. $n(S)$ denotes the no. of elements (outcomes) in S.

Experiment	Sample Space $=S$	$n(S)$
Tossing a coin	$\{H, T\}$	2
Tossing two coins	$\{HH, HT, TH, TT\}$	4
Rolling a die	$\{1, 2, 3, 4, 5, 6\}$	6
Rolling two dice	$\begin{Bmatrix} 11, 12, 13, \ldots, 16 \\ 21, 22, 23, \ldots, 26 \\ \vdots \\ 61, 62, 63, \ldots, 66 \end{Bmatrix}$	36

11.4.2. An Event

An event is set of all such outcomes which satisfy a given criteria.

e.g., experiment is rolling a die. In that case $S = \{1, 2, 3, 4, 5, 6\}$

Let event E_1 = outcome is multiple of 3 = $\{3, 6\}$, $n(E_1) = 2$

Let event E_2 = outcome is multiple of 2 = $\{2, 4, 6\}$, $n(E_2) = 3$

and event E_3 = outcome is multiple of 5 = $\{5\}$, $n(E_3) = 1$

and event E_4 = outcome is multiple of 7 = ϕ or $\{\ \}$, $n(E_4) = 0$

[as there are no such outcome which is multiple of 7].

11.4.3. "Elementary Event" are such events which have only one outcome. E_3 is an elementary event " Composite Events" are those events which have more than one out come.

Sometimes $n(E)$ is expressed as n_e and $n(S)$ as N.

11.5 PROBABILITY ASSIGNING TECHNIQUES (APPROACHES)

There are three general techniques of assigning probability. These are (1) Classical technique (2) Relative frequency technique and (3) Subjective approach. These three approaches represent the three different concepts of assigning probability.

11.5.1 Classical Definition

This definition, also known as the mathematical definition of probability, was given by J. Bernoulli. With the use of this definition, the probabilities associated with the occurrence of various events are determined by specifying the conditions of a random experiment. It is because of this that the classical definition is also known as 'a priori' definition of probability.

Definition

If n is the number of equally likely, mutually exclusive and exhaustive outcomes of a random experiment out of which m outcomes are favourable to the occurrence of anevent A, then the probability that A occurs, denoted by $P(A)$, is given by :

$$P(A) = \frac{\text{Number of outcomes favourable to } A}{\text{Number of exhaustive outcomes}} = \frac{m}{n} = \frac{n(A)}{n(S)}$$

Various terms used in the above definition are explained below :

1. ***Equally likely outcomes:*** The outcomes of random experiment are said to be equally likely or equally probable if the occurrence of none of them is expected in preference to others. For example, if an unbiased coin is tossed, the two possible outcomes, a head or a tail are equally likely.

2. ***Mutually exclusive outcomes:*** Two or more outcomes of an experiment are said to be mutually exclusive if the occurrence of one of them precludes the occurrence of all others in the same trial i.e. they cannot occur jointly. For example, the two possible outcomes of toss of a coin are mutually exclusive. Similarly, the occurrences of the numbers 1, 2, 3, 4, 5, 6 in the roll of a six faced die are mutually exclusive. No two outcomes can occur simultaneously.

3. ***Exhaustive outcomes:*** It is the totality of all possible outcomes of a random experiment. The number of exhaustive outcomes in the roll of a die are six. Similarly, there are 52 exhaustive outcomes in the experiment of drawing a card from a pack of 52 cards. All those outcomes which constitute sample space are called exhaustive outcomes.

Example 5. *Find the probability of throwing a total of six in a single throw with two unbiased dice.*

Solution. The number of exhaustive cases $n = 36$, because with two dice all the possible outcomes are :

(1, 1), (1, 2), (1, 3), (1, 4), (1, 5), (1, 6),
(2, 1), (2, 2), (2, 3), (2, 4), (2, 5), (2, 6),
(3, 1), (3, 2), (3, 3), (3, 4), (3, 5), (3, 6),
(4, 1), (4, 2), (4, 3), (4, 4), (4, 5), (4, 6),
(5, 1), (5, 2), (5, 3), (5, 4), (5, 5), (5, 6),
(6, 1), (6, 2), (6, 3), (6, 4), (6, 5), (6, 6),

[All these 36 outcomes are considered equi-likely, are mutually exclusive and exhaustive.]

Thus $n(S) = 36$

Out of these outcomes the number of cases favourable to the event A of getting a total of 6 are :

(1, 5), (2, 4), (3, 3), (4, 2), (5, 1). Thus, we have $m = 5 = n(A)$

$$\therefore \quad P(A) = \frac{n(A)}{n(S)} = 5/36$$

Example 6. *What is the probability of obtaining at least one head in the simultaneous toss of two unbiased coins ?*

Solution. The equally likely, mutually exclusive and exhaustive outcomes of the experiment are (H, H), (H, T), (T, H), and (T, T), where H denotes a head and T denotes a tail. Thus, $n(S) = 4$.

Let A be the event that at least one head occurs. This event corresponds the first three outcomes of the random experiment, (H, H), (H, T), (T, H). Thus $n(A) = 3$.

Hence, probability that A occurs, *i.e.*, $P(A) = \dfrac{n(A)}{n(S)} = 3/4$.

Example 7. *A bag contains 15 tickets marked with numbers 1 to 15. One ticket is drawn at random. Find the probability that*

(*i*) *the number of it is greater than 10,*

(*ii*) *the number on it is even,*

(*iii*) *the number on it is a multiple of 2 or 5.*

Solution. Number of exhaustive cases $n = 15$ as $S = \{1, 2, 3, 4, 5, 6, 7, 8, 9, 10, 11, 12, 13, 14, 15\}$

(*i*) Tickets with number greater than 10 are 11, 12, 13, 14 and 15. Therefore, $m = 5$ and hence the required probability of a number greater than 10 $= \dfrac{5}{15}$

(*ii*) Let B = Number is even = $\{2, 4, 6, 8, 10, 12, 14\}$

$n(B) = 7$

$$P(B) = \frac{n(B)}{n(S)} = \frac{7}{15}$$

(*iii*) Let C = No. on it is multiple of 2 or 5 = $\{2, 4, 5, 6, 8, 10, 12, 14, 15\}$

$n(C) = 9$

$$\therefore \quad P(C) = \frac{n(C)}{n(S)} = \frac{9}{15} = 3/5$$

11.5.2. Statistical or Empirical or Relative Frequency Definition of Probability

The scope of the classical definition was found to be very limited as it failed to determine the probabilities of certain events in the following circumstances :

(*i*) When n, the exhaustive outcomes of a random experiment is infinite.

(*ii*) When actual value of n is not known.

(*iii*) When various outcomes of a random experiment are not equally likely.

In addition to the above this definition doesn't lead to any mathematical treatment of probability.

In view of the above shortcomings of the classical definition, an attempt was made to establish a correspondence between relative frequency and the probability of an event when the total number of trials become sufficiently large.

Definition

If an experiment is repeated N times, under essentially the identical conditions and, if, out of these trials, an event A occurs m times, then the probability that A occurs is given by $P(A) = \lim_{N \to \infty} \dfrac{m}{N}$, provided the limit exists.

This definition of probability is also termed as the **empirical definition** because the probability of an event is obtained by actual experimentation.

Although, it is seldom possible to obtain the limit of the relative frequency, the ratio $\dfrac{m}{N}$ can be regarded as a good approximation of the probability of an event for large values of N.

Since $\frac{m}{N}$ is a ratio and (*i*) $n \le N$ (*ii*) $m \ge 0$, *i.e.*, m cannot be negative, therefore the ratio $\frac{m}{N}$ lies between 0 and 1, *i.e.*, $0 \le \frac{m}{N} \le 1$. $\frac{m}{N} = 0$ do not imply that event E does not occur at all. But it implies that its occurrence is so infrequent that for all practical purposes its occurrence can be taken as insignificant and the event E can be regarded as an impossible event. Similarly $\frac{m}{N} = 1$ do not imply that the event always occurs but it simply means that its occurrence is so frequent that for all practical purposes its occurrence can be considered almost certain and the event can be regarded as a certain event.

This approach has the limitation that the computation of the probability requires repetition of an experiment a large number of times which reduces its practical utility in a number of situations specially when the event occurs only once so that the repetitive occurrence under same conditions is not possible. For example, the probability that a particular candidate will win the parliamentary elections from a certain constituency cannot be obtained on the basis of this approach because it is not possible to conduct the elections repeatedly under the same conditions.

Example : A coin is tossed 500 times and was observed that head appears 255 times then

P (head in a toss of a coin) $= \frac{255}{500} = 0.51.$

11.5.3. Subjective Approach (or Personalistic Approach)

The subjective approach is based on the intuition of an individual. Though this is not a scientific approach, it is based on the accumulation of knowledge, understanding, and experience of an individual. This approach is not based on mathematics but its importance in decision making cannot be ignored. Some of the top entrepreneurs always make their decision on the basis of their intuition. Usually there exists a solid base for their intuition in terms of their interaction with the environment, their experience of handling problems, and their talent to predict and forecast the future. Though it might seem that this approach does not have solid grounding, in fact, this approach has some basis in terms of the qualities of individuals discussed above.

In real life there are situations where past data or information related to the problem is unavailable but a decision maker still has to make a decision. The decision maker is left with no alternatives except to rely on his own assessment and analysis. For example, a sales manager wants to promote one of his subordinates out of three. All three subordinates are equal in terms of efficiency, punctuality, selling potential, relationship with the customers, behavioural aspects, and the like. In this kind of situation, the sales manager has to rely on his intuition only which he can use for the promotion of one sales executive out of three. His intuition will help him in selecting the best person of the job.

The main limitation of this approach is the probabilities are based on personal confidence which may vary from person to person depending on one's perception of the situation and past experience. Even when two persons have the same knowledge about the past and the circumstances prevailing in the present, their assessment of probabilities may differ according to personal prejudice and bias. The main advantage of this approach is that it is highly flexible and can be applied to number of situations where the earlier two approaches fail to offer any solution. For example one makes a statement that probability of raining today is 1/5 or getting railway reservation is 30%.

Example 8. *What is the chance of drawing a face card in a draw from a pack of 52 well-shuffled cards?*

Solution. Total possible outcomes $n = 52$.

Since the pack is well-shuffled, these outcomes are equally likely. Further, since only one card is to be drawn, the outcomes are mutually exclusive.

There are 12 face cards, $\therefore m = 12$.

Thus, probability of drawing a face card $= \frac{12}{52} = \frac{3}{13}$.

Example 9. *What is the probability that a leap year selected at random will contain 53 Sundays ?*

Solution. A leap year has 366 days. It contains 52 complete weeks and 2 days. In 52 weeks all days will repeat 52 times as such there must be 52 Sundays as well. The remaining two days of the year could be anyone of the following pairs:

(Monday, Tuesday), (Tuesday, Wednesday), (Wednesday, Thursday), (Thursday, Friday), (Friday, Saturday), (Saturday, Sunday), (Sunday, Monday). Thus, there are seven possibilities out of which last two are favourable to the occurrence of 53rd Sunday.

Hence, the required probability $= \frac{2}{7}$.

Example 10. *If A, B and C are mutually exclusive and exhaustive events, find P (B) if*

$$\frac{1}{3}P(C) = \frac{1}{2}P(A) = P(B)$$

Solution. $\frac{1}{3}P(C) = \frac{1}{2}P(A) = P(B) = k$ (say)

$\Rightarrow \quad P(C) = 3k, P(A) = 2k, P(B) = k$

Since the events A, B, C are mutually exclusive and exhaustive, the sum of the probabilities of their occurrence should be equal to 1

$$\therefore \quad 3k + 2k + k = 1 \quad \Rightarrow \quad k = \frac{1}{6} \quad \Rightarrow \quad P(B) = \frac{1}{6}.$$

Example 11. *A, B and C are bidding for a contract. It is believed that A has exactly half the chance that B has, B in turn, is 4/5th as likely as C to win the contract. What is the probability for each to win the contract ?*

Solution. Let $P(A), P(B), P(C)$ denote the probabilities of winning the contract by A, B and C respectively.

Let $P(C) = k$, then $P(B) = \frac{4}{5}k$, $P(A) = \frac{2}{5}k$. Since one and only one of A, B and C can win the contract, the three events of winning the contract by A, B and C can be taken as mutually exclusive and exhaustive

$$\therefore \quad P(A) + P(B) + P(C) = 1$$

or $\frac{2}{5}k + \frac{4}{5}k + k = 1 \Rightarrow k = \frac{5}{11}$

$$P(A) = \frac{2}{11}, P(B) = \frac{4}{11}, P(C) = \frac{5}{11}.$$

11.6. COMPOUND EVENTS

If A and B are two events then we have two compound events which are based on these two events.

11.6.1. Simultaneous Occurrence of Two Events

A and B is third event which is written as $A \cap B$ [A and B are represented by two set A and B and event $A \cap B$ will be represented by set $A \cap B$].

Example. A die is rolled. We know that sample space $S = \{1, 2, 3, 4, 5, 6\}$. Let us define

Event A = Outcome is multiple of 2 = $\{2, 4, 6\}$

Event B = Outcome is multiple of 3 = $\{3, 6\}$

Thus $A \cap B = \{6\}$. Thus if outcome is 6 that means both events A and B have occurred.

Then $P(A \cap B) \frac{n(A \cap B)}{n(5)} = \frac{1}{6}$

11.6.2. Occurrence of either *A* or *B* or both

This is represented by an event $A \cup B$. Let A and B be two events defined as above

i.e., $A = \{2, 4, 6\}, B = \{3, 6\}$

$$A \cup B = \{2, 3, 4, 6\}$$

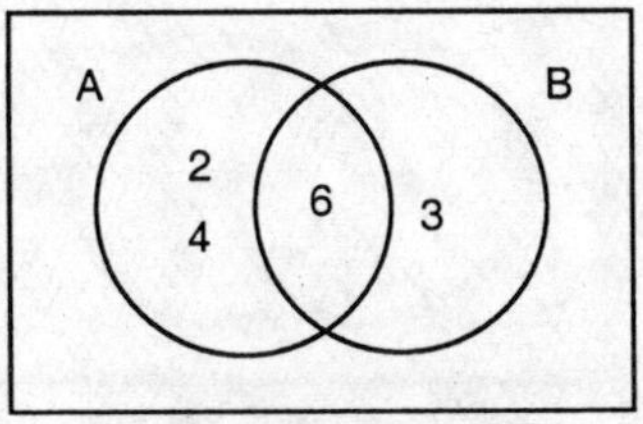

$A \cup B = \{2, 3, 4, 6\}$
$A \cap B = \{6\}$

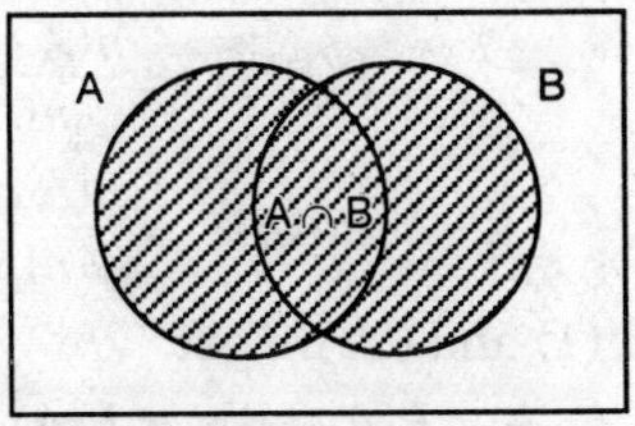

Shaded area $= A \cup B$
$n(A \cup B) = 4$
$n(A \cap B) = 1$

Thus $P(A \cup B) = \frac{n(A \cup B)}{n(S)} = \frac{4}{6}$

and $P(A \cap B) = \frac{n(A \cap B)}{n(S)} = \frac{1}{6}$

[**Note.** If A and B are *M.E.E.* then $A \cap B = \phi = \{\ \}$ = null set

Thus $n(A \cap B) = 0 \Rightarrow P(A \cap B) = 0$.

11.7. CONDITIONAL PROBABILITY OF AN EVENT WHEN ANOTHER EVENT HAS ALREADY OCCURRED

Let A be any event in a sample space S where $P(A) > 0$. The probability than an event B occurs subject to the condition that the event A has already occurred is called the conditional probability of the occurrence of the event B on the assumption that the event A has already occurred (or happened) and is denoted by symbol $P(B / A)$ and read as the probability of B given A. If $P(B / A) = 1$, then occurrence of A implies the occurrence of B.

Example. A die is rolled we known $S = \{1, 2, 3, 4, 5, 6\}$

Let A = multiple of 2 = {2, 4, 6}, $n(A) = 3$

and B = multiple of 3 = {3, 6}, $n(B) = 2$

Event B/A means occurance of B when A has already occurred.

Thus if it is known that A has occurred that means only possible outcomes are {2, 4, 6} (it is not S now) as such sample space has changed from S to A. B/A are only those elements of B which are present in A and which actually represented by $A \cap B$. (Now favourable cases) using theorem on probability.

$$P(B/A) = \frac{\text{No. of favourable outcomes}}{\text{total no. of possible outcomes}} = \frac{n(A \cap B)}{n(A)}$$

We have $A \cap B = \{6\}$, thus $n(A \cap B) = 1$

Thus $P(B/A) = \frac{1}{3}$

Same way $P(A/B) = \frac{n(A \cap B)}{n(B)} = \frac{1}{2}$

$$P(B/A) = \frac{n(A \cap B)}{n(A)} = \frac{\frac{n(A \cap B)}{n(S)}}{\frac{n(A)}{n(S)}} \quad \left[\begin{array}{l}\text{Dividing both numerator} \\ \text{and denominator by } n(S)\end{array}\right]$$

$$= \frac{P(A \cap B)}{P(A)}$$

Thus $$P(B/A) = \frac{n(A \cap B)}{n(A)} = \frac{P(A \cap B)}{P(A)} \qquad ...(1)$$

also $$P(A/B) = \frac{n(A \cap B)}{n(B)} = \frac{P(A \cap B)}{P(B)} \qquad ...(2)$$

From (1) and (2) we get

$$P(A \cap B) = P(A)\, P(B/A) \qquad ...(3)$$

or $$P(A \cap B) = P(B) \,.\, P(A/B) \qquad ...(4)$$

11.8. MUTUALLY EXCLUSIVE EVENTS (M.E.E.)

Events are said to be mutually exclusive if the occurrence of any one of them prevents the occurrence of any other event in the same experiment, *i.e.*,

Mutually exclusive events cannot occur simultaneously in the same experiment.

Examples : (*i*) If a fair coin is tossed, turning up of head or turning up of tail are two mutually exclusive events because if head turns up, then tail cannot turn up in the same experiment and *vice-versa*.

(*ii*) If a fair die is thrown (or **rolled or flipped**) there are 6 mutually exclusive outcomes (simple events) because only one of numbers out of 1, 2, 3, 4, 5 or 6 can show up in the experiment.

Suppose a die is rolled then $S = \{1, 2, 3, 4, 5, 6\}$

and let the three events be as follows.

A = outcome is multiple of 2 = {2, 4, 6}

B = outcome is multiple of 3 = {3, 6}

C = outcome is multiple of 5 = {5}

Obviously events A and C and B and C are two pairs of mutually exclusive events. However B and C are not *M.E.E.* as this pair can occur simultaneously *i.e.*, if '6' occurs as an outcome in that case both B and C had occurred. That is B and C can occur simultaneously.

11.9. COMPLEMENTARY AND EXHAUSTIVE EVENTS

The concept of complementary events always refers to a given space. If an event A contains some points of a sample space, then the event complementary to A will contain the remaining points in that sample space. The complement of an event A is the event 'A does not occur', *i.e.*, the two complementary events are opposite to each other. Complement of A is represented by A' or A^C or $\overline{A}$.

Consider an event A containing $n(A)$ outcomes. Thus complimentof A will have $[n(S) - n(A)]$ outcomes.

$$\text{Hence} \quad P(A^C) = P(\overline{A}) = \frac{n(S) - n(A)}{n(S)} = 1 - \frac{n(A)}{n(S)}$$

$$= 1 - P(A)$$

It is impossible for an event A and its opposite (complement) to occur at the same time, the two complementary events are mutually exclusive. Moreover in a given sample space either event A or its complement must occur, therefore the two complementary events are **exhaustive** also. Hence the complementary events are mutually exclusive and exhaustive, *i.e.*, for any event A.

11.10. INDEPENDENT EVENTS

Two events are said to be independent when the non occurrence or occurrence of any one of them does not affect the probability of the occurrence or non occurrence of the other event, *i.e.*, if A and B are two independent events then the happening of event A will not affect the probability of the happening of event B, *i.e.*, $P(B/A) = P(B) = P(B\overline{A})$ This means that probability of B is not affected whether A has occurred or not.

From 11.7 we have relations (3) and (4) as

$$P(A \cap B) = P(A) \,.\, P(B/A)$$

$$= P(B)\, P(A/B)$$

Also we know that if A and B are independent $P(B/A) = P(B)$ and $P(A/B) = P(A)$, the above two relations give $P(A \cap B) = P(A) \,.\, P(B)$.

(if A and B are independent)

Event A and B are dependent events if $P(A/B) \neq P(A/\overline{B})$

11.11. TWO FUNDAMENTAL THEOREM ON PROBABILITY.

11.11.1. Multiplication Rule of Probability

The probability of simultaneous occurrence (or joint occurrence) of the two events A and B denoted by $P(A \cap B)$ is given by

$P(A \cap B) = P(A)\, P(B/A)$ ....(refer 10.7...(3))

(1) If A and B are mutually exclusive then $P(B/A) = 0$.

thus $P(A \cap B) = 0$

(2) If A and B are independent then $P(B/A) = P(B)$ thus $P(A \cap B) = P(A)\, P(B)$

(3) When A and B are dependent in that case

$$P(A \cap B) = P(A) \,.\, P(B/A)$$

or $$P(A \cap B) = P(B) \,.\, P(A/B).$$

11.12. ADDITION RULE OF PROBABILITY (THEOREM OF TOTAL PROBABILITY)

If A and B are any two events then the probability that at least one of them occurs is denoted by $P(A \cup B)$ and is given by $P(A \cup B) = P(A) + P(B) - P(A \cap B)$.

Proof. $P(A \cup B) = \dfrac{n(A \cup B)}{n(S)}$

$$= \frac{n(A) + n(B) - n(A \cap B)}{n(S)} \text{ (from set theory)}$$

$$= \frac{n(A)}{n(S)} + \frac{n(B)}{n(S)} - \frac{n(A \cap B)}{n(S)}$$

$$= P(A) + P(B) - P(A \cap B) \quad \text{...(1)}$$

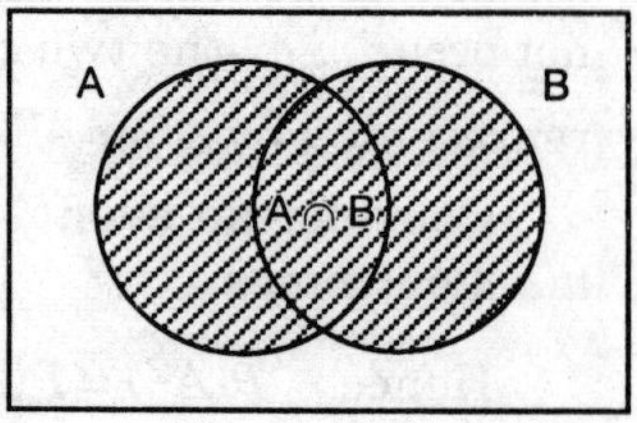

Mutually exclusive events have no sample point common in them, therefore if A and B are two mutually exclusive events then $A \cap B = \phi$, *i.e.*, the intersection of two mutually exclusive events is a null set and in this case $P(A \cap B) = 0$

(*a*) ∴ In case of mutually exclusive events

$$P(A \cup B) = P(A) + P(B)$$

If there are three events A, B, C the probability of the occurrence of at least one of them is given by

$$P(A \cup B \cup C) = P(A) + P(B) + P(C) - P(A \cap B) - P(B \cap C) - P(A \cap C) + P(A \cap B \cap C)$$

If the events are mutually exclusive, then

$$P(A \cup B \cup C) = P(A) + P(B) + P(C)$$ [∵ *If the events are mutually exclusive,* $P(A \cap B) = P(B \cap C) = P(A \cap C) = P(A \cap B \cap c) = 0$]

(*b*) If A and B are Independent Events

In that case $P(A \cap B) = P(A)\, P(B)$

Thus $P(A \cup B) = P(A) + P(B) - P(A)\, P(B)$ ......from (1)

Example 12. *A die is loaded in such a way that the probability of each face is proportional to the number on that face. What is the probability of getting an even number in one throw ?*

Solution. Let the probability of getting $1 = k$ (say)

Then the probability of getting $2 = 2k$ and the probabilities of getting 3, 4, 5 and 6 are $3k$, $4k$, $5k$ and $6k$ respectively.

Since all the events, *i.e.*, getting 1, 2, 3, 4, 5 and 6 are mutually exclusive and exhaustive, we have $k + 2k + 3k + 4k + 5k + 6k = 1 \Rightarrow k = \dfrac{1}{21}$

The probability of getting an even number = $2k + 4k + 6k = 12k = 12 \times \frac{1}{21} = \frac{4}{7}$.

[**Note:** *In example 3, the probability of getting an odd number* = $k + 3k + 5k = 9k = \frac{9}{21} = \frac{3}{7}$.]

Example 13. *Three horses A, B and C are in a race. A is twice as likely to win as B and B is twice as likely to win as C. What are their respective probabilities of winning ? Presume that dead heat is not possible.*

Solution. Let the probability of winning of horse $C = p$. Then the probability of winning of B and A will be $2p$ and $4p$ respectively.

Since the events of the winning of horses are mutually exclusive and exhaustive, we have

$$p + 2p + 4p = 1 \quad \Rightarrow \quad p = \frac{1}{7}$$

$\therefore$ Respective probabilities of winning of A, B, C are $\frac{4}{7}, \frac{2}{7}$ and $\frac{1}{7}$.

Note : *In the above example the events are mutually exclusive because only one horse can win. The events are exhaustive because there is no other horse in the race.*

Example 14. *A die is loaded in such a way that each odd number is twice as likely to occur as each even number. Find*

(i) the probability that the number rolled is a perfect square.

(ii) the probability that the number rolled is a perfect square provided it is greater than 3.

Solution. Let the probability of getting an even number $= p$

Then the probability of getting an odd number $= 2p$

When a die is rolled either an even number will come up or an odd number will come up, *i.e.*, the events 'coming up' of an odd number and 'coming up' of an even number are mutually exclusive and exhaustive.

$$\therefore \quad 2p + p + 2p + p + 2p + p = 1 \quad \Rightarrow \quad p = \frac{1}{9}$$

On a die there are six faces numbered 1, 2, 3, 4, 5, 6 out of which 1 and 4 are perfect squares

$\therefore$ The probability of getting a perfect square

= Probability of getting 1 + Probability of getting 4

$$= \frac{2}{9} + \frac{1}{9} = \frac{1}{3}$$

Probability of getting a perfect square greater than 3

= Probability of getting 4 $= \frac{1}{9}$.

Example 15. *In a certain town, male and female each form 50 per cent of the population. It is known that 20 per cent of the males and 5 per cent of the females are unemployed. A research student studying the employment situation selects an unemployed person at random. What is the probability that the person so selected is (a) male (b) female?*

Solution. The problem gives us the following probabilities as shown in the table below :

UNEMPLOYMENT DATA (in probabilities)

	Unemployed	*Employed*	*Total*
Males	0.100	0.400	0.50
females	0.025	0.475	0.50
Total	0.125	0.875	1.00

(*a*) P [Male/Unemployed] $= P\,(M/U) = \dfrac{p(M \cap U)}{P\,(U)} = \dfrac{0.10}{0.125} = 0.8$

(*b*) P [Female/Unemployed] $= P(F/U) = \dfrac{p(F \cap U)}{P\,(U)} = \dfrac{0.025}{0.125} = 0.2$

Example 16. *A piece of equipment will function only when all the three components A, B and C are working. The probability of A failing during one year is 0.15, that of B failing is 0.05 and that of C failing is 0.10. What is the probability that the equipment will fail before the end of the year ?*

Solution. The probability that component A does not fail during the year = 0.85

The probability that component B does not fail during the year = 0.95

The probability that component C does not fail during the year = 0.90.

Since the events are independent, therefore, the probability that all the three components do not fail $= 0.85 \times 0.95 \times 0.90 = 0.727$.

Hence the probability that the equipment will fail before the end of the year

$$= 1 - 0.727 = 0.273$$

Example 17. *Two computers A and B are to be marketed. A salesman who is assigned the job of finding customers for them has 60% and 40% chances respectively of succeeding in case of computer A and B. The computers can be sold independently. Given that he was able to sell at least one computer, what is the probability that computer A has been sold ?*

(MBA, IGNOU, 2002; MBA, DU, 2002)

Solution. Let event A and B denote that the computer A and B are sold respectively,

Then, $P(A) = 0.60; P(B) = 0.40$

and $P(A \cap B) = P(A).\,P(B) = 0.60 \times 0.40 = 0.24$ [Independent events]

Probability of selling at least one computer is given by

$$P(A \cup B) = P(A) + P(B) - P(A \cap B) = 0.60 + 0.40 - 0.24 = 0.76$$

We are required to find out

$$P(A/A \cup B) = \frac{P\,[A \cap (A \cup B)]}{P\,(A \cup B)} = \frac{P\,(A)}{P\,(A \cup B)} = \frac{0.60}{0.76} = 0.7895.$$

Example 18. *A market survey conducted in four cities pertained to preference for brand A soap. The responses are shown below :*

	Delhi	*Kolkata*	*Chennai*	*Mumbai*
Yes	45	55	60	50
No	35	45	35	45
No opinion	5	5	5	5

(i) *What is the probability that a consumer selected at random preferred brand A ?*

(ii) *What is the probability that a consumer preferred brand A and was from Chennai ?*

(iii) *What is the probability that a consumer preferred brand A given that he was from Chennai ?*

(iv) *Given that a consumer preferred brand A, what is the probability that he was from Mumbai ?* *(MBA, Kumaon Univ., 1999; MBA, Delhi Univ., 2002)*

Solution.

	Delhi (D)	*Kolkata (K)*	*Chennai (C)*	*Mumbai (M)*	Total
Yes	45	55	60	50	210 $n(A)$
No	35	45	35	45	160
No opinion	5	5	5	5	20
Total	$85 = n(D)$	$105 = n(K)$	$100 = n(C)$	$100 = n(M)$	$390 = n(S)$

Let the event A denote that a consumer selected at random preferred brand A.

(i) $$P(A) = \frac{210}{390} = \frac{7}{13} = 0.5385$$

(ii) $$P(A \cap C) = \frac{60}{390} = \frac{2}{13} = 0.1538$$

(iii) $$P(A/C) = \frac{n(A \cap C)}{n(C)} = \frac{60}{100} = 0.6$$

(iv) $$P(M/A) = \frac{n(A \cap M)}{n(A)} = \frac{50}{210} = \frac{5}{21}$$

Example 19. *A die has two of its sides painted red, two black, and other two yellow. If the die is rolled twice what is the probability that the same colour appears both the times.*

Solution. Since there are three colours, the probability that the die shows any particular colour both the times $= \frac{1}{3} \times \frac{1}{3} = \frac{1}{9}$

The required probability $= 3 \times \frac{1}{9} = \frac{1}{3}$. [both can be either red or black or yellow]

Note : When the die is rolled the probability of getting any colour remains the same in each trial.

Example 20. *Two different digits are selected at random from the digits 1, 2, 3, ..., 9. If the sum is odd, what is the probability that 2 is one of the digits selected.*

Solution. A = Sum is odd

Sum can be odd if one of digits is even (*a* out of 2, 4, 6, 8) and the other is odd (out of 1, 3, 5, 7, 9) and it can happen in 5×4 ways.

Let B = one digit is 2 and it can happen in 1×8 ways (one is 2 and the second can be any of remaining 8)

$A \cap B$ = one is 2 and other is any one of odd numbers = 5 [if one is 2 (even) then other has to be odd]

We have to find $P(B/A)$ *i.e.,* if sum is odd what is the probability that one is 2.

Now $$P(B/A) = \frac{n(A \cap B)}{n(A)} = \frac{5}{20} = \frac{1}{4}$$

Example 21. *A problem in statistics is given to three students A, B and C whose chances of solving are* $\frac{1}{2}, \frac{1}{3}, \frac{1}{4}$ *respectively. What is the probability that the problem is solved.*

Solution. the respective probabilities of student A, B and C not solving the problem are $\left(1-\frac{1}{2}\right), \left(1-\frac{1}{3}\right)$ and $\left(1-\frac{1}{4}\right)$ $\left[\text{As } P(A) = \frac{1}{2}, P(\overline{A}) = 1 - P(A) = 1 - \frac{1}{2} = \frac{1}{2}\right]$

It is required to find out $P(A \cup B \cup C) = P$ (at least one solves). We also know that

$$P(A \cup B \cup C) + P(\overline{A} \cap \overline{B} \cap \overline{C}) = 1$$

Thus $P(A \cup B \cup C) = 1 - P(\overline{A})\, P(\overline{B})\, P(\overline{C})$

$= 1 - P(\overline{A})\, P(\overline{B})\, P(\overline{C})$ [events are independent]

$$= 1 - \frac{1}{2} \cdot \frac{2}{3} \cdot \frac{3}{4} = 1 - \frac{1}{4} = 3/4.$$

OR

The problem will be solved if at least one student solves the problem.

Required Probability $= 1 -$ None of the students solves the problem

$$= 1 - \left(1-\frac{1}{2}\right)\left(1-\frac{1}{3}\right)\left(1-\frac{1}{4}\right)$$

$$= 1 - \frac{1}{2} \times \frac{2}{3} \times \frac{3}{4} = \frac{3}{4}.$$

11.13. BAG PROBLEM

Suppose a bag contains 5 white and 4 black balls as shown in the figure (W stands for white and B for black)

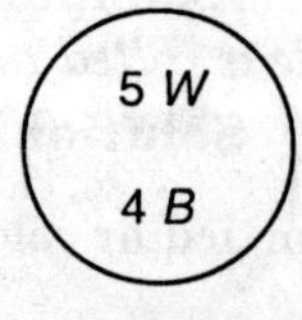

Experiments is that 3 balls are drawn out of any 9.

$n(S) = {}^9c_3 = \frac{9 \times 8 \times 7}{3 \times 2 \times 1} = 84$ [as explained in the beginning of the chapter]

Let event A = 2 balls are white *i.e.,* two are white and one is black.

$n(A) = {}^5c_2 \times {}^4c_1$ $\quad$ [${}^5c_2$ = no. of ways 2 white are taken out of 5 $= \frac{5 \times 4}{2 \times 1} = 10$ and no. of ways in which one black ball is taken out of 4 $= {}^4c_1 = 4$.]

Hence $P(A) = \frac{n(A)}{n(S)} = \frac{{}^5c_2 \times {}^4c_1}{{}^9c_3} = \frac{40}{84} = \frac{10}{21}.$

Example 22. *A library received 20 books including 8 Hindi novels. If 2 of these books are selected at random. What is the probability that none of them is a Hindi novel.*

Solution. The number of ways in which 2 books can be selected from 20 books = ${}^{20}c_2. = n(S)$

A = It is not Hindi novel *i.e.,* these 2 books are out of remaining 12.

$$n(A) = {}^{12}c_2 = \frac{12 \times 11}{2 \times 1} = 66$$

$$n(S) = {}^{20}c_2 = \frac{20 \times 19}{2 \times 1} = 190$$

$$\therefore \quad P(A) = \frac{n(A)}{n(S)} = \frac{66}{190} = \frac{33}{95}$$

Odds in favour and against.

The probability of an event is expressed in other way. Probability of an event A is described as odds in favour of A or odds against A. If out of $n(S) = m + n$ ways we have $n(A) = m$ (outcomes in favour of A) then $n(\overline{A}) = n$ (outcomes against A).

Now $P(A) = \dfrac{m}{m+n}$, we also describe this probability of A as (1) odds in favour of A are m to n (this indicates m outcomes are in favour and n are against it) (2) odds against A are $n : m$ (this mean n outcomes are against A and m are in favour).

[**Note.** The first number indicates favourable outcomes if it is said "odds in favour" and the number indicates outcomes against A if it is written "odds against"].

Example 23. *If* $P(A) = \dfrac{4}{9}$. *Find (a) odds in favour of A (b) odds against A.*

Solution. Since $P(A) = \dfrac{4}{9} \Rightarrow$ 4 outcomes out of 9 are in favour of A and 5 outcomes against it.

(*a*) Thus odds in favour of A are 4 to 5.

(*b*) and odds against A are 5 to 4.

Example 24. *The odds are 9 to 5 against a person aged 50 years living till he is 70 and 8 to 6 against a person aged 60 years living till he is 80. Find the probability that at least one of them will be alive after 20 years.*

Solution. The probability that A will be alive after 20 years is

$P(A) = \dfrac{5}{14}$ or $P(\overline{A}) = \dfrac{9}{14}$ [out comes against A are 9 and in favour are 5]

The probability that B will be alive after 20 years is

$$P(B) = \frac{6}{14} \quad \text{or} \quad P(\overline{B}) = \frac{8}{14}$$

Alternative I : Since the events are independent the chance that both will die is:

$$P(\overline{A}) \times P(\overline{B}) = P(\overline{A} \cap \overline{B}) = \frac{9}{14} \times \frac{8}{14} = \frac{72}{196}$$

Now we know P(at least one is alive) $= P(A \cup B)$

$$= 1 - P(\overline{A} \cap \overline{B}) = 1 - \frac{72}{19} = \frac{124}{196}.$$

Alternative II : The events are not mutually exclusive, hence, probability that at least one of them will be alive after 20 years is

$$P(A \text{ or } B) = P(A) + P(B) - P(A \text{ and } B)$$

$$= \frac{5}{14} + \frac{6}{14} - \left(\frac{5}{14} \times \frac{6}{14}\right)$$

$$= \frac{11}{14} - \frac{30}{196} = \frac{154 - 30}{196} = \frac{124}{196}$$

Example 25. *There are four clerks and three officers in a bank. A committee of 3 is to be formed at random. Find the probability that at least one clerk and at least one officer are included in the committee.*

Solution. Different ways in which the committee can be formed

	Clerks		Officers	Number of ways
	1	+	2	${}^4c_1 \times {}^3c_2 = 4 \times 3 = 12$
or	2	+	1	${}^4c_2 \times {}^3c_1 = 6 \times 3 = 18$

The number of ways in which 3 persons can be selected from 7 persons = ${}^7c_3 = \frac{7 \times 6 \times 5}{3 \times 2 \times 1} =$
35

$$\text{Required Probability} = \frac{12 + 18}{{}^7c_3} = \frac{30}{35} = \frac{6}{7}.$$

Example 26. *Five men in a group of 20 are graduates. If 3 men are picked out of 20 at random (i) what is the probability that all are graduates, and (ii) what is the probability of at least one being graduate ?*

Solution. (*i*) Probability of all graduates

$$= \frac{{}^5C_3}{{}^{20}C_3} = \frac{5 \times 4 \times 3 \times 2}{2 \times 20 \times 19 \times 18} = \frac{1}{114}$$

(*ii*) Probability of at least one graduate :

= 1 – Probability of zero graduates

= 1 – P (all 3 are others)

$$= 1 - \frac{{}^{15}C_3}{{}^{20}C_3}$$

$$= 1 - \frac{91}{228} = \frac{137}{228}$$

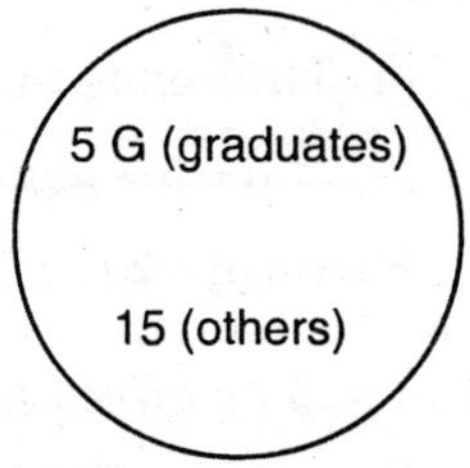

Example 27. *A box contains 3 red and 7 white balls. One ball is drawn at random and in its place a ball of the other colour is put in the box. Now one ball is drawn at random from the box. Find the probability that it is red.*

Solution. (*A*) One ball is drawn from bag one it can be (1) red which is denoted by R_1 or (2) white which is denoted by W_1.

Now if R_1 occurs then contents of bag (1) changes to bag (2) and if W_1 occurs then bag (1) changes to bag (3). Then from (2) or (3) on ball is drawn and let R_2 = that it is red. Thus R_2 occurs after either R_1 or W_1 has occurred.

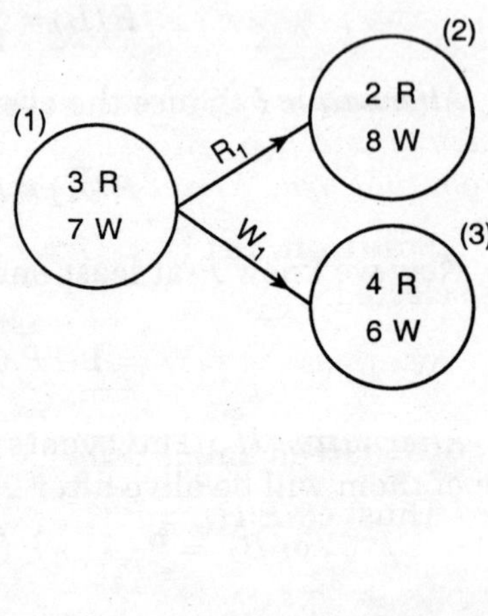

$$P(R_2) = P[(R_1 \cap R_2) \cup (W_1 \cap R_2)]$$

$\therefore$ $P(R_2) = P(R_1 \cap R_2) + P(W_1 \cap R_2)$

[as $R_1 \cap R_2$ and $W_1 \cap R_2$ are MEE]

$$P(R_2) = P(R_1)\, P(R_2/R_1) + P(W_1)\, P(R_2/W_1)$$

$$= \frac{3}{10} \cdot \frac{2}{10} + \frac{7}{10} \cdot \frac{4}{10} = \frac{34}{100} = \frac{17}{50}.$$

Example 28. *An urn A contains 2 white and 4 black balls. Another urn B contains 5 white and 7 black balls. A ball is transferred from the urn A to the urn B. Then a ball is drawn from urn B. Find the probability that it will be white.*

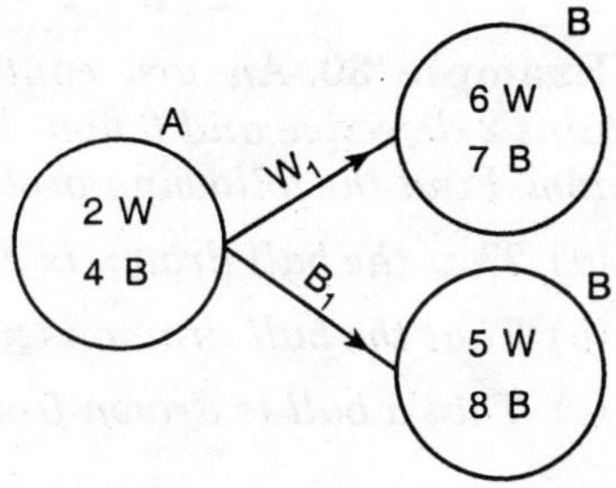

Solution. The ball transferred can either be black or white.

(i) When a white ball is transferred :

Probability of drawing white ball from urn A = $P(W_1)$

$$= \frac{2}{2+4} = \frac{1}{3}.$$

Now urn B has 6 white and 7 black balls. So probability of drawing a white ball from it is = $P(W_2/W_1)$

$$P(W_2/W_1) = \frac{6}{6+7} = \frac{6}{13}. \quad \text{[where } W_2 = \text{white ball from 2nd bag]}$$

∴ Probability of the compound event, transferring a white ball and then drawing a white ball is : = $P(W_1 W_2)$

$$= P(W_1) \,.\, P(W_2/W_1) = \frac{1}{3} \times \frac{6}{13} = \frac{2}{13}.$$

(ii) When black ball is transferred :

Probability of drawing black ball from urn A = $P(B_1)$

$$= \frac{4}{2+4} = \frac{2}{3}$$

Now urn B has 5 white and 8 black balls.

The probability of drawing white ball from it $P(W_2/B_1)$

$$= \frac{5}{5+8} = \frac{5}{13}$$

∴ Chance of the compound event, transferring a black ball and then drawing a white ball from it is = $P(B_1 W_2)$

$$= P(B_1)\, P(W_2/B_1) = \frac{2}{3} \times \frac{5}{13} = \frac{10}{39}$$

The two events are mutually exclusive. Hence the probability of transferring a ball from A to B then drawing a white from second

$$= P(W_1 W_2) + P(B_1 W_2) = \frac{2}{13} + \frac{10}{39} = \frac{16}{39} = 0.41.$$

Example 29. *Urn I contains three green and five red balls. Urn II contains two green, one red and two yellow balls. We select an urn at random and then draw one balls at random from that urn. What is the probability that we obtain a green ball ?*

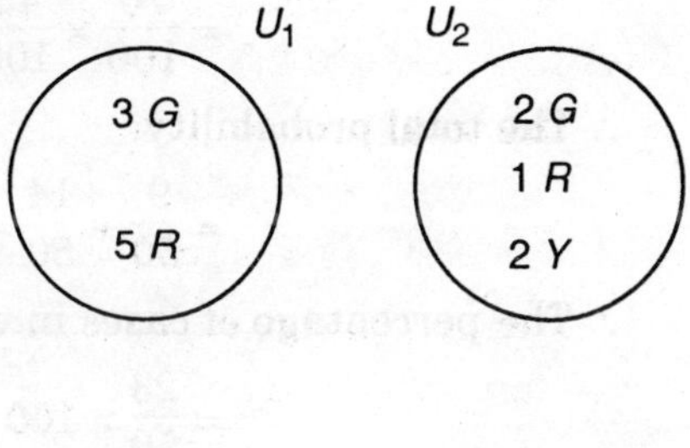

Solution. Let U_1 = Urn I is selected and U_2 = Urn II is selected.

We have $\quad P(U_1) = P(U_2) = \frac{1}{2}$

G = Green ball is drawn. (it can either from U_1 or U_2)

Thus $\quad P(G) = P[(U_1 \cap G) \cup (U_2 \cap G)$

$$= P(U_1 \cap G) + P(U_2 \cap G)$$

$$= P(U_1)\, P(G/U_1) + P(U_2)\, P(G/U_2)$$

$$= \frac{1}{2}\,\frac{3}{8} + \frac{1}{2}\,\frac{2}{5} = \frac{3}{16} + \frac{1}{5} = \frac{15+16}{80} = \frac{31}{80}.$$

Example 30. *An urn contains 4 defective and 8 non-defective balls. A second urn contains 2 defective and 6 non-defective balls. A ball is drawn from one of the urns selected at random. Find the following probabilities :*

(*a*) *That the ball drawn is defective.*

(*b*) *That the ball drawn is non-defective.*

(*c*) *That a ball is drawn from the first urn, given that it was a defective ball.*

Solution. Probability of selecting any urn $= \frac{1}{2} = P(U_1) = P(U_2)$

Let D be defective and $N.D.$ = non defective

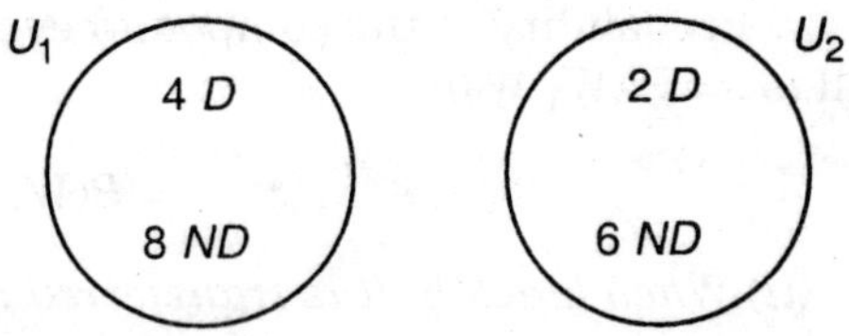

(*a*) $P(U_1 \cap D) = P(U_1)\, P(D/U_1)$

$$= \frac{1}{2}\,\frac{4}{12} = \frac{4}{24}$$

$$P(U_2 \cap D) = \frac{1}{2} \cdot \frac{2}{8} = \frac{1}{8} = \frac{3}{24}$$

$$P(D) = P(U_1 \cap D) + P(U_2 \cap D) = \frac{4}{24} + \frac{3}{24} = \frac{7}{24}.$$

(*b*) $P(N.D.) = P(U_1 \cap ND) + P(U_2 \cap ND)$

$$= \frac{1}{2}\,\frac{8}{12} + \frac{1}{2}\,\frac{6}{8} = \frac{8}{24} + \frac{3}{8} = \frac{17}{24}$$

(*c*) P (the ball is drawn from U_1 given that it was defective)

$$= P(U_1/D) = \frac{P(U_1 \cap D)}{P(D)} = \frac{4/24}{7/24} = \frac{4}{7}.$$

Example 31. *'A' speaks truth in 60 per cent cases and 'B' in 70 per cent cases. In what percentage of cases they likely to contradict each other in stating the same fact ?*

Solution. They will contradict each other only if one of them speaks the truth and the other speaks a lie.

The probability that A speaks the truth and B a lie

$$= \frac{60}{100} \times \frac{30}{100} = \frac{9}{50}$$

The probability that B speaks the truth and A a lie

$$= \frac{70}{100} \times \frac{40}{100} = \frac{14}{50}$$

∴ The total probability

$$= \frac{9}{50} + \frac{14}{50} = \frac{23}{50}$$

∴ The percentage of cases in which they contradict each other

$$= \frac{23}{50} \times 100 = 46\%.$$

Example 32. *Three groups of workers contain 3 men and 1 woman, 2 men and 2 women, and 1 man and 3 women respectively. One worker is selected at random from each group. What is the probability that the group selected consists of 1 man and 2 women?*

Solution. *There are three possible cases*

(*i*) Man is selected from the 1st group and women from 2nd and 3rd groups; ($M_1\ W_2\ W_3$)

or (*ii*) Man is selected from the 2nd group and women from the 1st and 3rd groups; ($W_1\ M_2\ W_3$)

or (*iii*) Man is selected from the 3rd group and women from 1st and 2nd groups. ($W_1\ W_2\ M_3$)

$$P\text{ (one man \& two women)} = P(M_1\ W_2\ W_3) + P(W_1\ M_2\ W_3) + P(W_1\ W_2\ M_3)$$

$$= \frac{3}{4} \times \frac{2}{4} \times \frac{3}{4} + \frac{1}{4}\frac{2}{4}\frac{3}{4} + \frac{1}{4}\frac{2}{4}\frac{1}{4}$$

$$= \frac{18+6+2}{64} = \frac{26}{64} = \frac{13}{32}$$

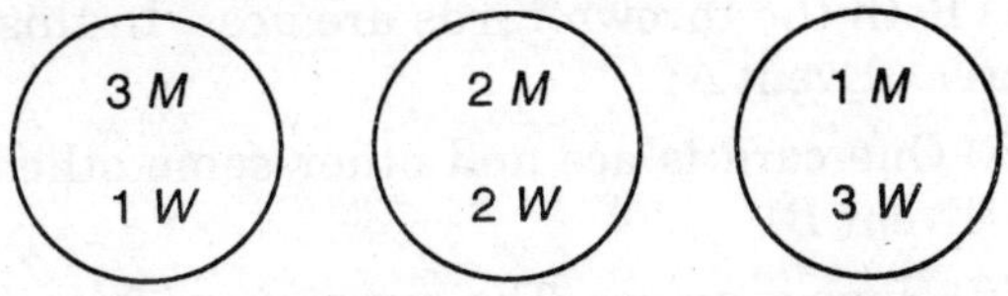

Example 33. *Box 1 contains 2 white and 2 black balls. Box 2 contains 2 white and 1 black ball, one of the boxes is selected at random and one ball is drawn from it. Find*

(*i*) *the probabilities that it turns out to be white*

(*ii*) *it is selected from box I if the ball drawn is white.*

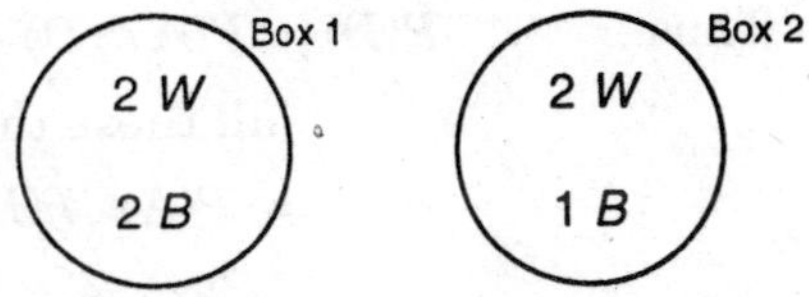

Solution. Let B_1 and B_2 be events that Box 1 and Box 2 are selected. W is event that white ball is taken out from selected box.

Now obviously $P(B_1) = P(B_2) = \frac{1}{2}$

$$P(W/B_1) = \frac{2}{4},\ P(W/B_2) = \frac{2}{3}$$

Now $\quad W$ = (white is drawn from B_1) U (white from B_2)

(*i*)

$$P(W) = P(B_1\,W) + P(B_2\,W)$$

$$= P(B_1)\,P(W/B_1) + P(B_2)\,P(W/B_2)$$

$$= \frac{1}{2}\cdot\frac{2}{4} + \frac{1}{2}\frac{2}{3} = \frac{1}{4} + \frac{1}{3} = \frac{7}{12}$$

(*ii*)

$$P(B_1/W) = \frac{P(B_1 \cap W)}{P(W)} = \frac{\frac{1}{4}}{7/12} = \frac{3}{7}.$$

Example 34. *A candidate is selected for interview for three posts. For the first post there were 3 candidates, for the second 4 and for the third 2. What is the probability that the candidate is selected for at least one post ?*

(Assuming all candidates are equally likely to be selected.)

Solution. P (getting first post) $= \frac{1}{3}$; P(getting second post) $= \frac{1}{4}$; P(getting third post) $= \frac{1}{2}$

P(candidate getting at least one post) = 1 – P(not getting any of the three post) $[P(A \cup B \cup C) = 1 - P(\bar{A} \cap \bar{B} \cap \bar{C})$

$$= 1 - \left(1-\frac{1}{3}\right)\left(1-\frac{1}{4}\right)\left(1-\frac{1}{2}\right) = 1 - \frac{2}{3} \times \frac{3}{4} \times \frac{1}{2} = \frac{3}{4}.$$

Second Method :

$$P(A \cup B \cup C) = P(A) + P(B) + P(C) - P(A \cap B) - P(A \cap C) - P(B \cap C) + P(A \cap B \cap C)$$

$$= \frac{1}{3} + \frac{1}{4} + \frac{1}{2} - \frac{1}{3} \times \frac{1}{4} - \frac{1}{4} \times \frac{1}{2} - \frac{1}{3} \times \frac{1}{2} + \frac{1}{3} \times \frac{1}{4} \times \frac{1}{2}$$

$$= \frac{8 + 6 + 12 - 2 - 3 - 4 + 1}{24} = \frac{18}{24} = \frac{3}{4}.$$

Example 35. *Two cards are randomly drawn from a pack of 52 cards and thrown away. What is the probability of drawn an ace in a single draw from the remaining 50 cards.*

Solution. Three cases are possible

(*i*) Both the thrown cards are aces. In this case the remaining 50 cards will contain only two aces. (Event A)

(*ii*) One card is ace and other some other card. The remaining 50 cards will contain 3 aces. (Event B)

(*iii*) None is an ace. The remaining 50 cards will contain 4 aces. (Event C)

Let D = an ace is drawn (after 2 cards are thrown away)

D occurs after any one of three events A, B and C had occurred. *i.e.*, D occurs either with A or B or C.

Thus $P(D) = P(A \cap D) + P(B \cap D) + P(C \cap D)$

[all these three events $A \cap B, B \cap D$ and $C \cap D$ are *M.E.E.*]

$$= P(A) \,.\, P(D/A) + P(B)\, P(D/B) + P(C)\, P(D/C)$$

$$= \frac{{}^4c_2}{{}^{52}c_2} \cdot \frac{2}{50} + \frac{{}^4c_1 \times {}^{48}c_1}{{}^{52}c_2} \frac{3}{50} + \frac{{}^{48}c_2}{{}^{52}c_2} \cdot \frac{4}{50}$$

$$= \frac{4 \times 3}{52 \times 51} \frac{2}{50} + \frac{4 \times 48 \times 2}{52 \times 51} \cdot \frac{3}{50} + \frac{48 \times 47}{52 \times 51} \times \frac{4}{50}$$

$$= \frac{1}{50\,(51)\,(52)} [24 + 152 + 9024]$$

$$= \frac{10200}{50(51)(52)} = \frac{204}{51 \times 52} = \frac{51}{51 \times 13} = \frac{1}{13}.$$

Example 36. *A can hit a target four times in five shots. B can hit three times in 4 shots, C can hit twice in three shots. They fire a volley i.e., shoot simultaneously what is the probability that exactly 2 shoots hit the target.*

Solution. Let $P(A)$ = Probability that A hits the target $= \frac{4}{5} \Rightarrow P(\overline{A}) = \frac{1}{5}$

$P(B)$ = Probability that B hits the target $= \frac{3}{4} \Rightarrow P(\overline{B}) = \frac{1}{4}$

$P(C)$ = Probability that C hits the target $= \frac{2}{3} \Rightarrow P(\overline{C}) = \frac{1}{3}$

Probability (exactly two shoots hit the target)

$$= P(A)\, P(B)\, P(\overline{C}) + P(A)\, P(\overline{B})\, P(C) + P(\overline{A})\, P(B)\, P(C)$$

$$= \frac{4}{5} \times \frac{3}{4} \times \frac{1}{3} + \frac{4}{5} \times \frac{1}{4} \times \frac{2}{3} + \frac{1}{5} \times \frac{3}{4} \times \frac{2}{3} = \frac{12 + 8 + 6}{60} = \frac{26}{60} = \frac{13}{30}.$$

11.14. BAYE'S THEOREM

The theorem is applicable in a particular situation which is as follows.

A compound event A is made up of few simple events say A_1, A_2, A_3 ... which are exhaustive and mutually executive.

i.e. $A = A_1 \cup A_2 \cup A_3$ ......

and $P(A_i \cap A_j) = 0$ where i, j are any two distinct numbers

Thus $P(A) = P(A_1) + P(A_2) + ...$ ...(1)

D is another event which occurs with any of A_i's and conditional probabilities of D for given occurrence of A_i's are known *i.e.*, $P(D/A_1)$, $P(D/A_2)$ ...... are known.

> **Example.** Let A = student of a degree college
> A_1 = Student of 1st year
> A_2 = Student of 2nd year
> A_3 = Student of 3rd year
> D = passing examination
> Now A_1, A_2, A_3 are M.E.E. and exhaustive
> D occurs with either of A_i's
> $A_1 \cap D$ = student of 1st year who passed.

The situation is represented diagramatically. Sample space is A and A_1, A_2 and A_3 are subsets of A are mutually exclusive.

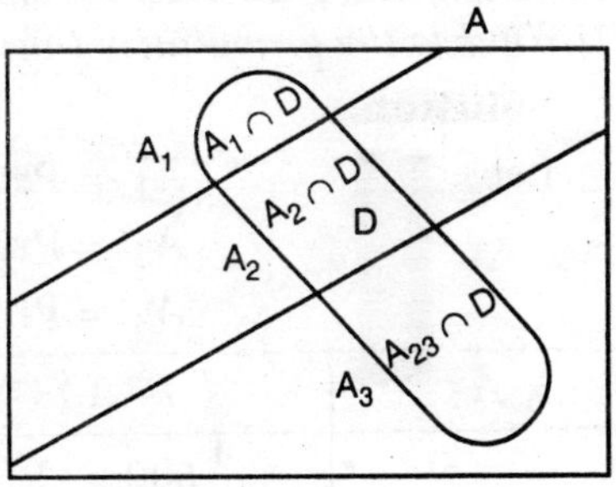

Bayes theorem : An event A occurs in any of mutually exclusive and exhaustive ways like A_1, A_2, A_3 ... $P(A_1), P(A_2)$ ... are known. D is another event which occurs with either of A_i's and $P(D/A_1)$, $P(D/A_2)$ ... are also known. [These conditional probabilities are called priori-probabilities]. We are required to find $P(A_1/D)$, $P(A_2/D)$ ... and so on (known as inverse or posterior probability).

$$P(A_i/D) = \frac{P(A_i) \,.\, P(D/A_i)}{\Sigma\, P(A_i)\, P(D/A_i)}$$

Thus if $i = 2$
$$P(A_2/D) = \frac{P(A_2) \,.\, P(D/A_2)}{P(A_1)\, P(D/A_1) + P(A_2)\, P(D/A_2) + P(A_3)\, P(D/A_3)}$$

The calculations become easier if the given information is put in tabular form

(1) A	(2) $P(A_i)$	(3) $P(D/A_i)$	(4) $P(A_i \cap D) = (2) \times (3)$	(5) $P(A_i/D)$
A_1	$P(A_1)$	$P(D/A_1)$	$P(A_1).\, P(D/A_1) = P(A_1 \cap D)$	$\frac{P(A_1 \cap D)}{P(D)}$
A_2	$P(A_2)$	$P(D/A_2)$	$P(A_2).\, P(D/A_2) = P(A_2 \cap D)$	$\frac{P(A_2 \cap D)}{P(D)}$
A_3	$P(A_3)$	$P(D/A_3)$	$P(A_3).\, P(D/A_3) = P(A_3 \cap D)$	$\frac{P(A_3 \cap D)}{P(D)}$
			$P(D) = \Sigma\; P(A_i \cap D)$	

Information in columns (1), (2) and (3) is known. We know as D occurs with either of A_1's, $P(D) = P(A_1 \cap D) + P(A_2 \cap D) + P(A_3 \cap D)$

Now $P(A_1 \cap D) = P(A_1)\, P(D/A_1)$

$P(A_2 \cap D) = P(A_2)\, P(D/A_2)$ and so we are able to generate column (4) by taking (4) = (2) × (3).

By adding elements of column (4) we get $P(D)$

Thus $$P(D) = \Sigma P(A_i \cap D) = \Sigma P(A_i)\, P(D/A_i)$$

Now $$P(A_i/D) = \frac{P(A_i \cap D)}{P(D)} = \frac{P(A_i)\, P(D/A_i)}{\Sigma P(A_i)\, P(D/A_i)}$$

Each element of column (4) is divided by total of column (4) of get column (5) which lists values of $P(A_1/D)$, $P(A_2/D)$ ......Thus first 3 columns are known (given) only column (4) and (5) are to be generated.

Example 37. *A manufacturing firm produces steel pipes in three plants with daily production volumes of 500, 1,000 and 2,000 units respectively. According to past experience it is known that the fractions of defective output produced by the three plants are respectively at random 0.005, 0.008 and 0.010. If a pipe is selected from a day's total production and found to be defective, find out (i) from which plant for this defective pipe, the probability is highest. (ii) What is the probability that it came from the first plant?*

Solution.

Let A_1 = Production of first plant. D = Defective

A_2 = Production of second plant.

A_3 = Production of third plant.

A	$P(A_i)$	$P(D/A_i)$	$P(A_i \cap D)$	$P(A_i/D)$
A_1	$\frac{500}{3500} = \frac{1}{7}$	$.005 = \frac{5}{1000}$	$\frac{5}{7000}$	$\frac{5}{61}$
A_2	$\frac{1000}{3500} = \frac{2}{7}$	$\frac{8}{1000}$	$\frac{16}{7000}$	$\frac{16}{61}$
A_3	$\frac{2000}{3500} = \frac{4}{7}$	$\frac{10}{1000}$	$\frac{40}{7000}$	$\frac{40}{61}$
			$P(D) = \Sigma = \frac{61}{7000}$	

(*i*) As $P(A_3/D)$ has the highest probability we can say that it is most likely that the defective item has been drawn from the third plant.

(*ii*) The probability that it came from the first plant is given by $P(A_1/D)$ which is 5/61.

Example 38. *Due to turnover and absenteeism at an assembly plant, 20% of the items are assembled by inexperienced employees. Management has determined that customers return 12% of the items assembled by inexperienced employees, whereas only 3% of the items assembled by experienced employees are returned. What is the probability that an item was assembled by an inexperienced employee, given that the item was returned?*

[*ICWA QM June 1995*]

Solution. Let

$P(A_1)$ = Probability that the items selected at random is assembled by an inexperienced employee = 0.2

$P(A_2)$ = Probability that the items selected at random is assembled by an experienced employee = 0.8

Let D by the event that the item is returned.

$P(D/A_1)$ = Probability that the item is returned when it is known that it is assembled by an inexperienced employee.

$P(D/A_2)$ = Probability that the item is returned when it is known that it is assembled by an experienced employee.

$P(A_1/D)$ = Probability that the item is assembled by an inexperienced employee given that the item is returned.

The information put in tabular form

(1) A	(2) $P(A_i)$	(3) $P(D/A_i)$	(4) $P(A_i \cap D)$	(5) $P(A_i/D)$
A_1	$.2 = \frac{2}{10}$	$\frac{12}{100}$	$\frac{24}{1000}$	$\frac{24}{48} = \frac{1}{2} = P(A_1/D)$
A_2	$.8 = \frac{8}{10}$	$\frac{3}{100}$	$\frac{24}{1000}$	$\frac{24}{48} = \frac{1}{2} = P(A_2/D)$
			$\frac{48}{1000} = P(D)$	

[**Note.** Common denominator is kept same as in col. (1) $\frac{2}{10}, \frac{8}{10}$ and in col. (2) $\frac{12}{100}, \frac{3}{100}$ so that in col. (4) the denominator is 1,000 *i.e.* $\frac{24}{1000}, \frac{24}{1000}$ so that additions, division in col. (5) are easy to calculate.]

Example 39. *Suppose that there is a chance for a newly constructed flyover to collapse whether the design is faulty or not. The chance that the design is faulty is 5%. The chance that the flyover collapses if the design is faulty is 95%, otherwise it is 30%. A flyover collapsed. What is the probability that it collapsed because of faulty design ?* [*ICWA QM Dec. 1994*]

Solution. Let D be the event that the flyover collapses. Let A_1 be the event that the design is faulty, A_2 be the event that the design is faultless. Then

$$P(A_1) = \frac{5}{100}, P(A_2) = \frac{95}{100}.$$

Application of Baye's theorem

(1) A	(2) $P(A_i)$	(3) $P(D/A_i)$	(4) $P(A_i \cap D)$	(5) $P(A_i/D)$
(Faulty) A_1	$\frac{5}{100}$	$\frac{95}{100}$	$\frac{475}{10000}$	$\frac{475}{3325} = \frac{19}{133} = \frac{1}{7}$
(Not Faulty) A_2	$\frac{95}{100}$	$\frac{30}{100}$	$\frac{2850}{10000}$	$\frac{2850}{3325} = \frac{6}{7}$
			$\frac{3325}{10000} = P(D)$	$\Sigma P(A_i/D) = 1$

[Note : $\Sigma P(A_i/D) = 1$ always, as entries in column are divided by their sum]

Example 40. *In a test, an examinee either guesses or copies or knows the answer to a multiple choice question with four choices. The probability that he makes a guess is* $\frac{1}{3}$ *and the probability that he copies the answer is* $\frac{1}{6}$. *The probability that his answer is correct given that he copied it, is* $\frac{1}{8}$. *Find the probability that he knew the answer to the question given that he correctly answered it.*

Let A_1 = examinee guesses, A_2 = he copies, A_3 = he knows

D = Answer is correct. Obviously $P(D/A_3) = 1$

i.e., he knows the correct answer, it has to be correct

A	$P(A_1)$	$P(D/A_i)$	$P(A_i \cap D)$	$P(A_i/D)$
A_1	$1/3 = \frac{2}{6}$	$\frac{1}{4} = \frac{2}{8}$	$\frac{4}{48}$	$\frac{4}{29}$
A_2	$1/6 = \frac{1}{6}$	$1/8 = \frac{1}{8}$	$\frac{1}{48}$	$\frac{1}{29}$
A_3	$3/6$	$1 = \frac{8}{8}$	$\frac{24}{48}$	$\frac{24}{29}$
	$\Sigma P(A_i) = 1$		$P(D) = \frac{29}{48}$	

[$P(D/A_1) = \frac{1}{4}$ [as there are 4 choices and he guesses any one]

$P(A_3) = 1 - P(A_1) - P(A_2)$]

Example 41. *Two boxes contain respectively 4 white and 2 black and 1 white and 3 black balls. One ball is transferred from the first box into the second and then one ball is drawn from the latter. It turns out to be black. What is the probability that the transferred ball was white ?*

Solution. Let A_1 be the event that the transferred ball (ball drawn from the first box) is white and A_2 be the event that the transferred ball is black.

$P(A_1) = \frac{4}{6} = \frac{2}{3}$, $P(A_2) = \frac{2}{6} = \frac{1}{3}$

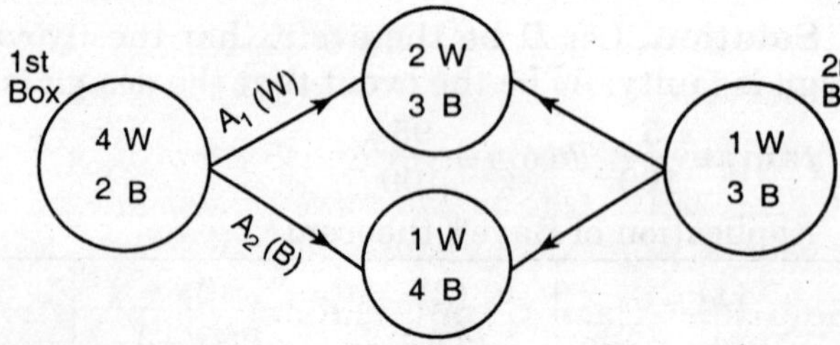

Let D be the event that the ball drawn from the 2nd box (after a ball is transferred from the first box to the second box) is black, then

A	$P(A_i)$	$P(D/A_i)$	$P(A_i \cap D)$	$P(A_i/D)$
A_1	$\frac{4}{6} = \frac{2}{3}$	$\frac{3}{5}$	$\frac{6}{15}$	$\frac{6}{10} = \frac{3}{5}$
A_2	$\frac{2}{6} = \frac{1}{3}$	$\frac{4}{5}$	$\frac{4}{15}$	$\frac{4}{10} = \frac{2}{5}$
			$\frac{10}{15} = P(D)$	

MISCELLANEOUS SOLVED EXAMPLES

Example 42. *In a survey of 100 readers, it was found 40 read magazine A, 15 read magazine B, and 10 read both. What is the probability of a person reading at least one of the magazines ?*

Solution. $P(A) = 0.40 \quad P(B) = 0.15 \quad P(A \cap B) = 0.10$

$$P(A \cup B) = P(A) + P(B) - P(A \cap B) = 0.40 + 0.15 - 0.10 = 0.45.$$

Therefore, the probability that a person read at least one magazine is 0.45.

Example 43. *A bag contains 8 red and 5 white balls. Two successive drawings of 3 balls are made such that (i) balls are replaced before the second trial. (ii) The balls are not replaced before the second trial. Find the probability that the first drawing will give 3 white and the second 3 red balls.*

Solution. (*a*) *When the balls are replaced.*

Total number of balls in the bag = 13

Total number of red balls = 8

3 balls out of 13 can be drawn in ${}^{13}C_3$ ways.

3 white balls can be drawn out of 5 in ${}^{5}C_3$ ways.

3 red balls can be drawn out of 8 red in ${}^{8}C_3$ ways.

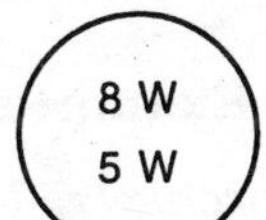

Since balls are replaced before the second draw, the total number of outcomes for both the draws remain the same, *i.e.*, ${}^{13}C_3$.

$$P(A) = \frac{{}^{5}C_3}{{}^{13}C_3} \text{ and } P(B) = \frac{{}^{8}C_3}{{}^{13}C_3}$$

$$P(A \cap B) = P(A) \times P(B) = \frac{{}^{5}C_3}{{}^{13}C_3} \times \frac{{}^{8}C_3}{{}^{13}C_3} = \frac{140}{20449}.$$

(*b*) *When balls are not replaced.* When balls are not replaced, there would be no change in $P(A)$. Also the number of outcomes favourable to event B shall be ${}^{8}C_3$ but on the second draw the total number of outcomes would be ${}^{10}C_3$ (since 3 balls drawn are not replaced).

$$P(B/A) = P(B) = \frac{{}^{8}C_3}{{}^{10}C_3}$$

Hence $$P(A \cap B) = P(A) \times P(B) = \frac{{}^{5}C_3}{{}^{13}C_3} \times \frac{{}^{8}C_3}{{}^{10}C_3} = \frac{7}{429}.$$

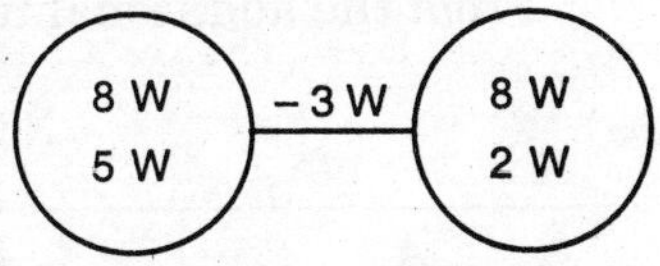

Example 44. *Two urns A and B contain respectively 2 white and 5 black balls, 3 white and 6 black balls. One ball is transferred from A to B and then a ball is drawn from B. Find the probability that it is a white ball.*

Solution. Case 1. Ball transferred in white.

Probability of drawing a white ball from urn A $= \frac{2}{7}$.

After transfer urn B will contain 4 white and 6 black balls. ...(1)

Probability the white ball is transferred from A to B and then white ball is drawn from B $= \frac{2}{7} \times \frac{4}{10} = \frac{8}{70}$

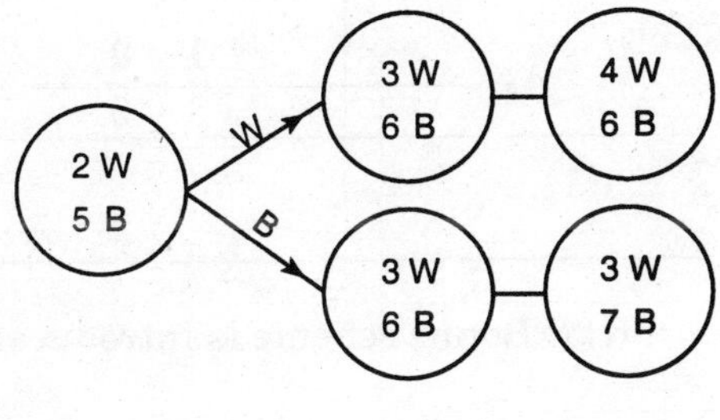

Case 2. Black ball is transferred

Probability of drawing a black ball from urn A $=\frac{5}{7}$, after transfer urn B will have 3 white and 7 black ball.

$$P(W/B) = \frac{3}{10}$$

Thus $P(W \cap B)$ = P(white ball is drawn and ball transferred is back)

$$= \frac{5}{7} \cdot \frac{3}{10} = \frac{15}{70} \quad \text{...(2)}$$

$$P(W) = (1) + (2)$$

$$= \frac{8}{70} + \frac{15}{70} = \frac{23}{70}$$

Example 45. *The probabilities of X, Y and Z becoming managers are* $\frac{4}{9}$, $\frac{2}{9}$ *and* $\frac{1}{3}$ *respectively. The probability that the Bonus Scheme will be introduced if X, Y and Z becomes manager are* $\frac{3}{10}$, $\frac{1}{2}$ *and* $\frac{4}{5}$ *respectively.*

(i) What is the probability that the Bonus Scheme will be introduced; and

(ii) If the Bonus Scheme has been introduced, what is the probability that the manager appointed was X ?

Solution. Let A_1 = the event that X becomes manager

A_2 = the event that Y becomes manager

A_3 = the event that Z becomes manager

and B = the event of Bonus Scheme be introduced either by X, Y or Z.

From the first information :

$$P(A_1) = \frac{4}{9}, P(A_2) = \frac{2}{9}, P(A_3) = \frac{1}{3}$$

From the additional information :

$$P(B/A_1) = \frac{3}{10}, P(B/A_2) = \frac{1}{2}, P(B/A_3) = \frac{4}{5}$$

A	$P(A_i)$	$P(B/A_i)$	$P(A_i \cap B)$	$P(A_i/B)$
A_1	$\frac{4}{9}$	$\frac{3}{10}$	$\frac{12}{90}$	$\frac{12}{46}$
A_2	$\frac{2}{9}$	$\frac{1}{2} = \frac{5}{10}$	$\frac{10}{90}$	$\frac{10}{46}$
A_3	$\frac{1}{3} = \frac{3}{9}$	$\frac{4}{5} = \frac{8}{10}$	$\frac{24}{90}$	$\frac{24}{46}$
			$\Sigma = \frac{46}{90} = P(B)$	

(*i*) P(Bonus scheme is introduced) $= P(B) = \frac{46}{90} = \frac{23}{45}$

(*ii*) P (X is appointed if bonus scheme is introduced)

$$= P(A_1/B) = \frac{12}{46} = \frac{6}{23}.$$

Example 46. *The odds against student X solving a Mathematics problem are 8 : 6 and the odds in favour of student Y solving the same problem are 14 : 16, then*

(*i*) *Find the probability that neither of them is able to solve the problem.*

(*ii*) *Find the probability that the problem will be solved if they both try independently of each other.*

Solution. The probability that student X solves the problem $= \frac{6}{14}$

The probability that student X is not able to solve the problem $= \left(1 - \frac{6}{14}\right) = \frac{8}{14}$

The probability that student Y solves the problem $= \frac{14}{30}$

The probability that student Y is not able to solve the problem $= \left(1 - \frac{14}{30}\right) = \frac{16}{30}$

(*i*) Required Probability $= \left(1 - \frac{6}{14}\right)\left(1 - \frac{14}{30}\right) = \frac{8}{14} \times \frac{16}{30} = \frac{128}{420} = \frac{32}{105}$

[*Events are independent*]

(*ii*) P(Problem is solved) = 1 – P (Problem is not solved)

$$= 1 - \frac{32}{105} = \frac{73}{105}.$$

Example 47. *8 distinguishable marbles are distributed at random into 3 boxes marked as 1,2 and 3. Find the probability that they contain 3, 4 and 1 marbles respectively.*

Solution. Since the first, second...8th marble, each, can go to any of the three boxes in 3 ways, the total number of ways of putting 8 distinguishable marbles into three boxes is 3^8.

[Each marble can be put n any of 3 boxes, .*e.*, in 3 ways. Thus total no. of ways = 3 × 3 × 3 .... 8 times = 3^8].

The number of ways of putting the marbles, so that the first box contains 3 marbles, second contains 4 and the third contains 1, are $\frac{8!}{3!\,4!\,1!}$

$\therefore$ The required probability $= \frac{8!}{3!\,4!\,1!} \times \frac{1}{3^8} = \frac{380}{6561}$.

Example 48. *12 persons are seated at random (i) in a row, (ii) in a ring. Find the probabilities that three particular persons are sitting together.*

Solution. (*i*) 12 persons are seated in row

$n(S) = 12!$

A = particular three persons sit together (considering three persons as 1 person) these can be arranged in a row in 10! 3! ways = $n(A)$

$$\therefore \quad P(A) = \frac{n(A)}{n(S)} = \frac{10!\,3!}{12!} = \frac{6}{12 \times 11} = \frac{1}{22}$$

(*ii*) When they are sitting in a ring.

$$n(S) = (n - 1)! = (12 - 1)! = 11!$$

When 3 person as a group are fixed and the remaining 9 persons can be seated in 9! ways. Those 3 persons can be arranged in 3! ways.

Thus total no. of ways = $n(A)$ = 9! 3!

$$P(A) = \frac{9!\,3!}{11!} = \frac{6}{11 \times 10} = \frac{3}{55}.$$

Example 49. *A and B are two independent events. The probability that both occur simultaneously is* $\frac{1}{6}$ *and the probability that neither occurs is* $\frac{1}{3}$. *Find the probabilities of occurrence of events A and B separately.*

Solution. $P(A \cap B) = \frac{1}{6} = P(A) \times P(B) = xy$ [$\because$ *A and B are independent*] ...(1)

[Let $P(A) = x$, $P(B) = y$]

$1 - P(A \cup B)$ = Probability that neither occurs $= \frac{1}{3} = P(\overline{A})\,P(\overline{B})$

$$\Rightarrow \quad (1 - x)(1 - y) = \frac{1}{3}$$

$$\Rightarrow \quad 1 - (x + y) + xy = \frac{1}{3}$$

$$x + y = 1 - \frac{1}{3} + \frac{1}{6} = \frac{6 - 2 + 1}{6} = \frac{5}{6}$$

$$x = \frac{5}{6} - y$$

Also from (1) $\quad xy = \frac{1}{6}$

$$\left(\frac{5}{6} - y\right) y = \frac{1}{6}$$

$(5 - 6y)\,y = 1$ [Multiplying by 6]

$$6y^2 - 5y + 1 = 0 \quad 6y^2 - 3y - 2y + 1 = 0$$

$$\Rightarrow 3y\,(2y - 1) - (2y - 1) = 0$$

$$\Rightarrow \quad (3y - 1)(2y - 1) = 0 \Rightarrow y = \frac{1}{3}, \frac{1}{2}$$

$$\Rightarrow \quad x = \frac{1}{2}, \frac{1}{3}$$

$$(x, y) = \left(\frac{1}{3}, \frac{1}{2}\right) \text{ or } \left(\frac{1}{2}, \frac{1}{3}\right)$$

$$P(A) = \frac{1}{3} \text{ and } P(B) = \frac{1}{2}$$

or $\quad P(A) = \frac{1}{2}$ and $P(B) = \frac{1}{3}$

Example 50. *A coin is tossed. If it turns up head, two balls will be drawn from urn A ; otherwise two balls will be drawn from urn B. Urn A contains three black and five white balls. Urn B contains seven black and one white ball. In both cases selections are to be made with replacement. What is the probability that urn A is used given that both the balls drawn are black?*

Solution. Probability of getting head or tail $= \frac{1}{2}$.

Let A_1 = getting head, $P(A_1) = \frac{1}{2}$

A_2 = getting tail, $P(A_2) = \frac{1}{2}$

D = Both balls drawn are black.

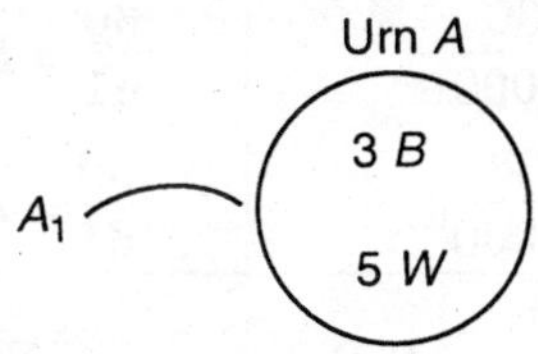

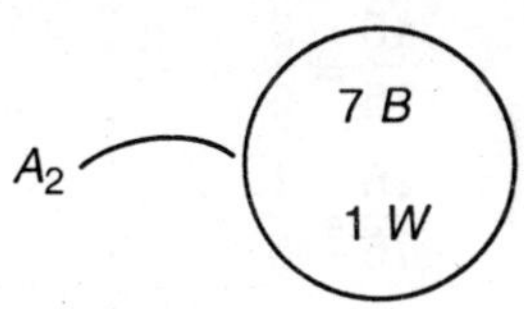

$$P(D/A_1) = \frac{{}^3c_2}{{}^8c_2} = \frac{3 \times 2}{8 \times 7} = \frac{3}{28}$$

$$P(D/A_2) = \frac{{}^7c_2}{{}^8c_2} = \frac{7 \times 6}{8 \times 7} = \frac{3}{4} = \frac{21}{28}$$

To find $P(A_1/D)$; we apply Baye's theorem

A	$P(A_i)$	$P(D/A_i)$	$P(A_i \cap B)$	$P(A_i/D)$
A_1	$\frac{1}{2}$	3/28	$\frac{3}{56}$	$\frac{3}{24} = \frac{1}{8}$
A_2	$\frac{1}{2}$	21/28	$\frac{21}{56}$	$\frac{21}{24}$ = 7/8
			$\Sigma = \frac{24}{56} = P(D)$	

$= P(A_1/D)$

Example 51. *It is given than* $P(A \cup B) = \frac{5}{6}$, $P(A \cap B) = \frac{1}{3}$ *and* $P(B) = \frac{1}{2}$. *Show that A and B are independent events.*

Solution. We have $P(A \cup B) = P(A) + P(B) - P(A \cap B)$

$$i.e., \frac{5}{6} = P(A) + \frac{1}{2} - \frac{1}{3}$$

$$\Rightarrow \quad P(A) = \frac{5}{6} - \frac{1}{2} + \frac{1}{3} = \frac{5 - 3 + 2}{6} = \frac{4}{6} = \frac{2}{3}$$

$$P(B) = \frac{1}{2} \text{ (given)}$$

$$P(A) \, . \, P(B) = \frac{2}{3} \cdot \frac{1}{2} = \frac{1}{3} = P(A \cap B)$$

Hence A and B events are independent.

Example 52. *In a class of 75 students, 15 were considered to be intelligent, 45 as medium and the rest below average. The probability that a very intelligent student fails in a viva-voce examination is 0.005, the medium student failing has a probability of 0.05, and the corresponding probability for a below average student is 0.15. If a student is known to have passed the viva-voce examination, what is the probability that he is below average?*

Solution. Let A_1, A_2 and A_3 be the events that a student is very intelligent, medium and below average respectively and D be the event that a student passes in a viva-voce examination.

Baye's Theorem is to be used

A	$P(A_i)$	$P(D/A_i)$	$P(A_i \cap D)$	$P(A_i/D)$
A_1	$\frac{15}{75}=\frac{1}{5}$	$\frac{5}{1000}=\frac{1}{200}$	$\frac{1}{1000}$	$\frac{1}{61}=P(A_1/D)$
A_2	$\frac{45}{75}=\frac{3}{5}$	$\frac{50}{1000}=\frac{10}{200}$	$\frac{30}{1000}$	$\frac{30}{61}=P(A_2/D)$
A_3	$\frac{15}{75}=\frac{1}{5}$	$\frac{15}{100}=\frac{30}{200}$	$\frac{30}{1000}$	$\frac{30}{61}=P(A_3/D)$
			$\Sigma=\frac{61}{1000}=P(D)$	$\Sigma=1$

Example 53. *Find the probability that*

(*i*) *leap year has 53 Sundays.*

(*ii*) *A non leap year has 53 Sundays.*

(*iii*) *A leap year has 53 Sundays or Mondays.*

(*iv*) *A non leap year has 53 Sundays or Mondays.*

(*v*) *A year chosen at random has 53 Sundays.*

(*vi*) *A year chosen at random has 53 Sundays or Mondays.*

Solution. (*i*) A leap year contains 366 days, *i.e.,* 52 weeks and 2 days*. These two days are consecutive days. Therefore these two days can be

or Sunday	and	Monday	
or Monday	and	Tuesday	
or Tuesday	and	Wednesday	
or Wednesday	and	Thursday	$n(S)=7$
or Thursday	and	Friday	
or Friday	and	Saturday	
or Saturday	and	Sunday	

In the above seven outcomes each day is repeated twice. Therefore the probability for any particular day say Sunday to be repeated 53 times in a leap year $=\frac{2}{7}$.

(*ii*) The probability that a leap year has 53 Sunday or Monday =

P (53 Sundays or 53 Mondays) $= P(A) + P(B) - P(A \cap B)$

$$P(A \text{ or } B) = \frac{2}{7}+\frac{2}{7}-\frac{1}{7}=\frac{3}{7}$$

[both 53 Sundays and 53 Mondays occur in only 1 outcome out of 7] (*iii*) In a non leap year there are 365 days, *i.e.*, 52 weeks and one day which can be any of the seven days in a week. Therefore the probability that a non leap year contains 53 Sunday $= \frac{1}{7}$.

(*iv*) The probability that a non leap year contains 53 Sundays or 53 Mondays.

$$= P\text{ (53 Sundays)} + P\text{ (53 Mondays)}$$

$$= \frac{1}{7} + \frac{1}{7} = \frac{2}{7}.$$

(*v*) The probability that a year chosen at random is a leap year $= \frac{1}{4} = \text{P(L)}$.

The probability that the year chosen at random is not a leap year $= \frac{3}{4}$.

The probability that a year chosen at random is a leap year and contains 53 Sundays $= \frac{1}{4} \times \frac{2}{7} = \frac{2}{28}$

The probability that a year chosen at random is non leap year and contains 53 Sundays $= \frac{3}{4} \cdot \frac{1}{7} = \frac{2}{28}$

Thus P(A year chosen at random has 53 Sundays) $= \frac{2}{28} + \frac{3}{28} = \frac{5}{28}$.

(*vi*) Similarly P that a year is leap year and has 53 Sundays or 53 Mondays)

$= \frac{1}{4} \times \frac{3}{7}$ [see (*ii*)] $= \frac{3}{28}$

P (that a non leap year has 53 Sundays or 53 Mondays)

$$= \frac{3}{4} \cdot \frac{2}{7} \text{ [see (iv)]} = \frac{6}{28}$$

P (year chosen randomly has 53 Sundays or Mondays]

$$= \frac{3}{28} + \frac{6}{28} = \frac{9}{28}.$$

Example 54. *Two digits are selected at random from the digits 1 through 9. If the sum is even, find (1) the probability that their sum is even, (2) If the sum is even, find the probability that both digits are odd.*

Solution. Even digits are 2, 4, 6, 8 and odd digits are 5 = {1, 3, 5, 7, 9}

Probability (that both digits are even and sum is even) $= \frac{^4C_2}{^9C_2} = \frac{3}{18} = P(A_1)$

Probability (that both digits are odd and sum is even) $= \frac{^5C_2}{^9C_2} = \frac{5}{18} = P(A_2)$

Probability of even sum $= P(A_1) + P(A_2)$ $= \frac{3}{18} + \frac{5}{18} = \frac{8}{18} = f(D)$

Probability of odd digits given that sum is even $= \frac{5/8}{8/18} = \frac{5}{18}$

$\therefore P(A_2/D)$

Aliter : We may use Baye's Theorem (only its last 2 columns)

	$P(A_i \cap D)$	$P(A_i/D)$
Both digits are even A_1	$\frac{3}{18}$	3/8
Both digits are odd A_2	$\frac{5}{18}$	5/8
	$\Sigma = 8/18\ P(D)$	

[**Note :** If both digits are even, D occurs with probability one,

Hence $\quad P(A_1 \cap D) = P(A_1) \,.\, P(D/A_1)$

$= P(A_1) \times 1 = P(A_1)$]

Example 55. *A candidate is selected for interview for 3 posts. For the first post there are 3 candidates, for the second there are 4 and for the third there are 2. What are the chances of his getting at least one post ?*

Solution. The probability that the candidate gets at least one post

= 1 – probability that the candidate does not get any post. [As $P(A \cup B \cup C) = 1 - P(\overline{A} \cap \overline{B} \cap \overline{C})$]

Probability that he does not get the first post $= 1 - \frac{1}{3} = \frac{2}{3} = P(\overline{A})$

Probability that he does not get the second post $= 1 - \frac{1}{4} = \frac{3}{4} = P(\overline{B})$

Probability that he does not get the third post $= 1 - \frac{1}{2} = \frac{1}{2} = P(\overline{C})$

Since the events are independent, probability that he does not get any of the three posts

$$P(\overline{A} \cap \overline{B} \cap \overline{C}) = P(\overline{A}) \times P(\overline{B}) \times P(\overline{C}) = \frac{2}{3} \times \frac{3}{4} \times \frac{1}{2} = \frac{1}{4}$$

Hence the probability that the candidate gets at least one post $= 1 - \frac{1}{4} = \frac{3}{4} = P(A \cup B)$.

Example 56. *In a railway reservation office, two clerks are engaged in checking reservation forms. On an average, the first clerk checks 55% of the forms, while the second does the remaining. The first clerk has an error rate of 0.03 and second has an error rate of 0.02. A reservation form is selected at random from the total number of forms checked during a day, and is found to have an error. Find the probabilities that it was checked by first and second clerk respectively.*

Solution. Let A_1 = the event that the form is checked by first clerk.

A_2 = He event that it is checked by second and E = the event that selected form has an error.

$P(A_1) = 0.55 \qquad P(A_2) = 0.45$

$P(E/A_1) = 0.03 \qquad P(E/A_2) = 0.02$

Finding posterior probabilities

A	$P(A_i)$	$P(E/A_i)$	$P(E \cap A_i)$	$P(A_i/E)$
A_1	$.55 = \frac{55}{100}$	$\frac{3}{100}$	$\frac{165}{10000}$	$\frac{165}{255} = P(A_1/E)$
A_2	$.45 = \frac{45}{100}$	$\frac{2}{100}$	$\frac{90}{10000}$	$\frac{90}{255} = P(A_2/E)$
			$\Sigma = \frac{255}{10000}$ P(E)	$\Sigma = 1$

Example 57. *The table of percentages describing the educational level of a factory's 5,000 employees is given below :*

		High School	*Bachelor*	*Master*	*Ph. D*
Male	:	*5%*	*20%*	*12%*	*11%*
Female	:	*18%*	*15%*	*14%*	*5%*

Suppose an employee is chosen at random from the firm's 5,000 employees.

(a) What is the probability that the selected person is a female and a bachelor's degree holder ?

(b) What is the probability that the selected person is a male ?

(c) Given that the selected person is a woman, what is the probability that her highest degree is a master's degree ?

Solution. Let M = Male, Female = F, H = High School, B = Bachelor, Ma = Master, P = Ph.D.

	H	B	Master	Ph.D.	Total
Male	5%	20%	12%	11%	48% (M)
Female	18%	15%	14%	5%	52% (F)
Total	23% (H)	35% (B)	26% (Ma)	16% P	100% (S)

(i) $P(F \cap B) = \frac{n(F \cap B)}{n(S)} = \frac{15}{100}$

(ii) $P(M) = \frac{n(M)}{n(S)} = \frac{48}{100}$

(iii) $P(Ma/F) = \frac{n(Ma \cap F)}{n(F)} = \frac{14}{52}$

Example 58. *The probability of a man hitting a target is* $\frac{1}{4}$. *How many times must be fire so that probability of hitting the target at least one is greater than* $\frac{2}{3}$.

Solution. Suppose he fires n times.

P (not hitting a target in one trial) $= 1 - \frac{1}{4} = \frac{3}{4}$

P (missing the target in all n trials $= \left(\frac{3}{4}\right)^n$

P (hitting at least once) = 1 – P (hitting none) = $1-\left(\frac{3}{4}\right)^n$

Now $\quad 1-\left(\frac{3}{4}\right)^n > \frac{2}{3}$ (given)

$\Rightarrow \quad 1-\frac{2}{3} > \left(\frac{3}{4}\right)^n$

$\Rightarrow \quad \left(\frac{3}{4}\right)^n < \frac{1}{3}$ (we have to find minimum n which satisfies this condition) This can be found by "hit and trial" method.

n	$\left(\frac{3}{4}\right)^n$	
1	$\frac{3}{4}$	$> \frac{1}{3}$
2	$\frac{9}{16}$	$> \frac{1}{3}$
3	$\frac{27}{64}$	$> \frac{1}{3}$
4	$\frac{81}{256}$	$< \frac{1}{3}$

Thus when $n = 4$, $\left(\frac{3}{4}\right)^n < \frac{1}{3}$. Hence $n = 4$.

Example 59. *A company has a security system comprising of four electronic devices (A, B, C and D) which operate independently. Each device has a probability of failure of 0.1. the four electronic devices are arranged so that the whole system operates properly i.e., at least one of A and B functions and at least one of C and D functions.*

Solution. Let $\quad P(A)$ = Probability device A functions successfully then

$P(A) = 1 - 0.1 = 0.9$

Similarly, $\quad P(B) = P(C) = P(D) = 0.9$

$P(A \cup B)$ = At least one of A and B functions successfully

$= P(A) + P(B) - P(A \cap B) = 0.9 + 0.9 - 0.9 \times 0.9$

[*Since the functioning of devices A and B are independent,* $P(A \cap B) = P(A)\,P(B)$]

$= 1.80 - 0.81 = 0.99$

Similarly, $\quad P(C \cup D) = 0.99$

Since all the four devices are independent, the probability of at least one of A and B and at least one of C and D functioning

$= 0.99 \times 0.99 = 0.9801.$

Example 60. *20 per cent of a bank's accounts holders have taken loans from the bank. Among them 90% are males. On the other hand, among the account holders who did not take*

loan 95% are males. An account holder is randomly selected and is found to be a male. What is the probability that he has a loan with the bank ?

Solution. Let A_1 = Loan takers, A_2 = have not taken loan, D = Male

To find posterior probabilities *i.e.*, $P(A_1/D)$

A	$P(A_i)$	$P(D/A_i)$	$P(A_i \cap D)$	$P(A_i/D)$
A_1	$.2 = \frac{2}{10}$	$\frac{90}{100} = \frac{18}{20}$	$\frac{36}{200}$	$\frac{36}{188} = \frac{9}{57} = P(A_1/D)$
A_2	$.8 = \frac{8}{10}$	$\frac{95}{100} = \frac{19}{20}$	$\frac{152}{200}$	$\frac{152}{188} = \frac{38}{47} = P(A_2/D)$
			$\Sigma = \frac{188}{200} = P(D)$	

Thus $P(A_1/D) = \frac{9}{47}$.

Example 61. *The probability that Indian Cricket term wins a test match against English team is 3/5. If Indian and English teams play three test matches, what is the probability that*

(i) India will lose all the test matches ?

(ii) India will win at least one test match ?

Solution. Probability of losing a match is $1 - \frac{3}{5} = \frac{2}{5}$

As the outcome of all the matches is mutually exclusive

Probability of losing all the matches

$$= \frac{2}{5} \times \frac{2}{5} \times \frac{2}{5} = \frac{8}{125}$$

(*ii*) Probability of winning at least one test match = $1 - \frac{8}{125} = \frac{117}{125}$.

Example 62. *A and B throw alternately with a pair of balanced dice. A wins if he throws a sum of six points before B throws a sum of seven points, while B wins if he throws a sum of seven points before a throws a sum of six points. If A begins the game, show that his probability of winning is 30/61.*

Solution. No. of outcomes if 2 dice are thrown = $6 \times 6 = 36$. In a throw of two dice sum of six points can appear in (1, 5), (2, 4), (4, 2), (5, 1) = 5 ways. Sum of 7 points can appear in (1, 6), (2, 5), (3, 4). (4, 3), (5, 2), (6, 1) = 6 ways.

P (throwing a sum of 6) = 5/36

P (throwing a sum of 7) = $\frac{6}{36} = \frac{1}{6}$

The game is as follows : A throws pair of dice and if he throws a sum of 6 he wins and if he does not get sum 6 then B throws two dice, again he wins if he throws 7, otherwise A throws again and game continues till some one wins .

A wins in following ways : either he wins in 1st throw or 3rd throw or 5th throw and so on.

Let A_i = A wins in ith throw and $\overline{A}_i$ =A does not win in ith throw. Same meaning is attached to B_i and $\overline{B}_i$

$$P(\text{A wins}) = P(A_1 \cup \overline{A}_1\, \overline{B}_2\, A_3 \cup \overline{A}_1\, \overline{B}_2\, \overline{A}_3\, \overline{B}_4\, A_5 \,\ldots\ldots\ldots\ldots)$$

$$= P(A_1) + P(\overline{A}_1\, \overline{B}_2\, A_3) + P(\overline{A}_1\, \overline{B}_2\, \overline{A}_3\, \overline{B}_4\, A_5) + \ldots\ldots\ldots$$

$$P(A) = \frac{5}{36} + \left[\frac{31}{36}\frac{5}{6}\right]\frac{5}{36} + \left(\frac{31}{36}\frac{5}{6}\right)\left(\frac{31}{36}\frac{5}{6}\right)\frac{5}{36} + \ldots\ldots\ldots \quad \text{[all are } \mu EE]$$

[As $P(A_i) = \frac{5}{36}$, $P(\overline{A}_i) = 1 - \frac{5}{36} = \frac{31}{36}$

Also $P(B_i) = \frac{1}{6}$, $P(\overline{B}_i) = 5/6$]

$$P(A) = \frac{5}{36}\left[1 + \left(\frac{31}{36}\ \frac{5}{6}\right) + \left(\frac{31}{36}\ \frac{5}{6}\right)^2 + \ldots\ldots\ldots\right]$$

[This is infinite G.P. whose sum $S_\infty = \frac{a}{1-r}$ where a = 1st term, r = common ratio]

$$P(A) = \frac{5}{36}\left[\frac{1}{1-\frac{155}{216}}\right] = \frac{5}{36}\cdot\frac{216}{61} = \frac{30}{61}$$

$B(B) = 1 - P(A)$ [as B wins when A does not win]

$$= 1 - \frac{30}{61} = \frac{31}{61}.$$

EXERCISE 11

1. From a set of 17 cards numbered 1, 2, 3, ..., 16, 17, one is drawn at random. Show that the chance of appearing a number which is divisible by 3 or 7 is $\frac{7}{17}$.
2. Four cards are drawn from a pack of 52 cards. What is the chance that these 4 will contain just one queen ? **[Ans.** $\frac{{}^4c_1 \times {}^{48}c_3}{{}^{52}c_4}$
3. Three screws are drawn at random from a lot of 10 screws containing four defectives. Find the probability that all three screws drawn are non-defective, assuming that screws are drawn
   (*i*) with replacement and (*ii*) without replacement
   $\left[\textbf{Ans. } (i) \left(\frac{6}{10}\right)^3 = .216, (ii0\ \frac{{}^6c_3}{{}^{10}c_3} = \frac{1}{6}\right]$
4. Out of numbers 1 to 100, one is selected at random. What is the probability that it is divisible by 4 or 5 ? **[Ans.** 0.4]
5. A pair of dice is rolled. If the sum of 9 has appeared, find the probability that one of the dice shows 3. $\left[\textbf{Ans. } \frac{1}{2}\right]$

6. The chance of an accident in a factory in a year is 10 in 50 in Mumbai, 10 in 60 in Poona, 10 in 120 in Nagpur. Find the chances that an accident may happen in (*i*) at least one of them (*ii*) all of them. $\left[\textbf{Ans. } (i)\ \frac{7}{18}\ (ii)\ \frac{1}{360}\right]$

7. A's chance of hitting a target is 1/5, B's chance is 1/4 and C's chance is 1/3. If they fire together, find the chance of only one short hitting the target. [**Ans.** 13/30]

8. Three urns contain respectively 6 white and 4 black balls, 8 black and 2 white balls, 10 white and 10 black balls. One urn is selected and one ball is drawn from it which is found to be black. Find the probability that it came from the second urn. $\left[\textbf{Ans. } \frac{8}{17}\right]$

9. A problem in statistics is given to five students *A*, *B*, *C*, *D* and *E*. Their chances of solving it are 1/2, 1/4, 1/5, 1/6 and 1/3. What is the probability that the problem will be solved ? $\left[\textbf{Ans. } \frac{5}{6}\right]$

10. The probability that India wins a cricket test match against Pakistan is given to be 1/3. If India and Pakistan play three test matches, what is the probability that—

(*i*) India will lose all the three test matches ?

(*ii*) India will win at least one test match ? $\left[\textbf{Ans. } (i)\ \frac{8}{27},\ (ii)\ \frac{19}{27}\right]$

11. A bag contain 4 red and 3 blue balls. Two drawings of 2 balls are made. Find the probability that the first drawing gives 2 red balls and the second drawing 2 blue balls, (*i*) if the balls are returned to the bag after the first draw, and (*ii*) if the balls are not returned. $\left[\textbf{Ans. } (i)\ \frac{2}{49}\ (ii)\ \frac{3}{35}\right]$

12. The probability that *A* can solve a problem is 4/5; that *B* can solve it is 2/3; that *C* can solve it is 3/7. If all of them try independently, find the probability that the problem will be solved. $\left[\textbf{Ans. } \frac{101}{105}\right]$

13. There are 4 boys and 2 girls in room No. 1 and 5 boys and 3 girls in room No. 2. A girl from one of the two rooms laughed loudly. What is the probability that the girl who laughed loudly was from room No. 2. $\left[\textbf{Ans. } \frac{9}{17}\right]$

14. Five men in a company of 20 are graduates. If 3 men are picked out at random what is the probability that they are graduates ? What is the probability that at least one is a graduate ? $\left[\textbf{Ans. } \frac{1}{114}, \frac{137}{228}\right]$

15. A lot contains 12 items of which 4 are defective. Three items are drawn at random from the lot one after other (without replacement). Find the probability that all three are non-defective. $\left[\textbf{Ans. } \frac{14}{55}\right]$

16. The odds in favour of one student passing at a test 3 : 7. The odds against another passing at are 3 : 5. What are the probabilities-that (*i*) both pass (*ii*) both fail ? $\left[\textbf{Ans. } \frac{3}{8}, \frac{21}{80}\right]$

17. There are two papers in Economics at a certain examination Paper I and II. The probability that a candidate passes in Paper I is 60% and that he passes in Paper II is 50%. What is the probability that a particular candidate passes only in any one of the two papers ? $\left[\textbf{Ans. } \frac{1}{2}\right]$

18. The chance that in a management Accountant's job an applicant has a post-graduate degree is 30% and that he has had some work experience as Accountant is 70% and that he had both is 20%. Out of 400 applicants, how many applicants would have either a post-graduate degree or some professional experience or both ? [**Ans.** 320]

19. An *X* urn contains 3 white balls and 5 black balls. Another urn *Y* contains 6 white balls and 4 black balls. *A* ball is transferred from the run *X* to the run *Y*. Then a ball is taken from urn *Y*. Find the probability that it will be white. $\left[\textbf{Ans. } \frac{51}{88}\right]$

20. Among 1000 applicant for admission to M.A. Economics Course in a University, 600 applicants were economics graduates and 400 applicants were non-economics graduates; 30 percent of economics graduate applicants and 5 percent of non-economics graduate applicants obtained admission. If an applicant selected at random is found to have been given admission, what is the probability that he/she is an economics graduate ? [**Ans.** 0.9]

21. On an average, 20% of persons going to the handicraft emporium are foreigners, and the remaining 80% are local person. 75% of such foreigners and 50% of such local persons are found to make purchases. If a bundle of purchased items is sent to the cash counter, what is the probability that the purchaser is a foreigner ? $\left[\textbf{Ans. } \frac{3}{11}\right]$

22. A financial analyst feels that the chances are 30% that the price of shares of the company A would rise next week, and 15% that the price of the shares of the company would rise. The two prices are expected to move independent of each other. Find the probability that in the next week.
(*i*) only one company's share price would increase
(*ii*) neither would increase. [**Ans.** 0.36 (*ii*) 0.595]

23. An urn contains 10 counters on which digits 0, 1, 2, ..., 9 are written one digit on each counter, no digit being repeated. A chooses a counter first and then *B* chooses another counter (the first is not replaced). Find the probability that the product of the two digits, chosen is zero. $\left[\textbf{Ans. } \frac{1}{5}\right]$

24. A 6 faced die is so biased that it is twice as likely to show an even number as an odd number when it is thrown. What is the probability that the sum of the two numbers is even ? $\left[\textbf{Ans. } \frac{5}{9}\right]$

25. The foreman in an iron foundary knows that the sand used for moulding iron castings is too dry 5% of the time and too wet 2% of the time. He also knows that the defective castings occur 0.5% of the time when the sand has the correct amount of moisture; 5% of the time when the sand is too dry; and 25% of the time when the sand is too wet. Suppose a casting is selected at random from the batch just produced and is found to be defective. What is the probability that each of the following is true ?

(*i*) The sand was too wet (*ii*) The sand was too dry.

(*iii*) The sand had the correct amount of moisture. $\left[\textbf{Ans.} \frac{100}{243}, \frac{50}{243}, \frac{93}{243}\right]$

26. In a certain town males and females are in equal percentage of the population. It is known that 20 per cent of the males and 5 per cent of the females are unemployed. A research student studying the employment situation selects unemployed persons at random. What is the probability that the person selected is a (*i*) male (*ii*) female ?

$\left[\textbf{Ans.} \frac{4}{5}, \frac{1}{5}\right]$

27. You note that your officer is happy in 60% cases of your calls. You have also noticed that if he is happy, he accedes to you request which a probability of 0.4 whereas if he is not happy, he accedes to your request with a probability 0.1. You call on him one day and he accedes to your request. What is the probability of his being happy ?

$\left[\textbf{Ans.} \frac{6}{7}\right]$

28. A bag contains 5 red and 7 black balls and second contains 4 blue and 3 green balls. A ball is taken out from each bag. Find the probability that (*i*) one ball is red and the other blue, (*ii*) one ball is black and the other green. $\left[\textbf{Ans.} 5/21, \frac{1}{4}\right]$

29. The personnel department of a company has records which show the following analysis of its 200 engineers :

Age	*Bachelor's degree only*	*Master's degree*	*Total*
Under 30	90	10	100
30 to 40	20	30	50
Over 40	40	10	50
Total	150	50	200

If one engineer is selected at random from the company, find :

(*a*) The probability that he has only a bachelor's degree.

(*b*) The probability that he has a master's degree given that he is over 40.

(*c*) The probability that he is under 30 given that he has only a bachelor's degree.

$\left[\textbf{Ans.} \frac{3}{4}, \frac{1}{5}, \frac{3}{5}\right]$

30. A group of 200 persons was classified according to age and sex as given below :

Age in years	*Male*	*Female*	*Total*
Below 30	60	50	110
30 and above	80	10	90
Total	140	60	200

(*i*) What is the probability that a randomly chosen person from this group is a male below 30 years of age ?

(*ii*) What is the probability that a person is below 30 years of age given that he is a male ?

$\left[\textbf{Ans. } \frac{3}{10}, \frac{3}{7}\right]$

31. A bag contains 5 brown and 4 white socks. A man pulls out two socks. The probability that they are of the same colour is

(*i*) 5/108 (*ii*) 1/6 (*iii*) 5/18 (*iv*) 4/9 (*v*) 5/9 **[Ans.** (*iv*)**]**

32. If two dice are thrown, the probability that at least one of the dice shows a number greater than 3 is

(*i*) 1/8 (*ii*) 1/4 (*iii*) 1/2 (*iv*) 3/4 (*v*) 4/5 **[Ans.** (*iv*)**]**

33. If $P(A \text{ or } B) = P(B)$, then

(*i*) A and B must be mutually exclusive (*ii*) A and B must be independent

(*iii*) $P(A) + P(B)$ is the joint probability of A and B

(*iv*) $P(A) = P(B)$ (*v*) Occurrence of A implies occurrence of B **[Ans.** (*v*)**]**

[Hint. Show that $P(B/A) = 1$]

34. If A and B are independent events such that $P(A) = 0.3$, $P(A \cup B) = 0.8$, then $P(B)$ is

(*i*) $\frac{1}{7}$ (*ii*) $\frac{2}{7}$ (*iii*) $\frac{4}{7}$ (*iv*) $\frac{5}{7}$ **[Ans.** (*iv*)**]**

[Hint $P(A \cup B) = .3 + x - .3x$, if $P(B) = x$]

35. If six dice are rolled, then the probability that all show different faces is

(*i*) $\frac{1}{6^6}$ (*ii*) $\frac{6}{6^6}$ (*iii*) $\frac{6!}{6^6}$ (*iv*) none of these **[Ans.** (*iii*)**]**

36. The chance of an accident in a factory in a year in the cities A, B and C are 10 in 50, 10 in 120 and 10 in 60 respectively. The chance that an accident may happen in at least one of them is

(*i*) $\frac{5}{8}$ (*ii*) $\frac{6}{18}$ (*iii*) $\frac{7}{18}$ (*iv*) $\frac{8}{18}$ **[Ans.** (*iii*)**]**

37. A committee of 5 persons is formed from 8 gentlemen and 3 ladies. What is the probability that the committee contains (*i*) exactly 2 ladies, (*ii*) at least one lady ?

$\left[\textbf{Ans. } \frac{4}{11}, \frac{24}{33}\right]$

38. If n persons are seated around a round table, find the probability in no two ways a man has the same neighbours.

$\left[\textbf{Ans. } \frac{1}{2}(n-1)!\right]$

39. Let A, B and C be three events. Write down the following events in usual set notations :

(*i*) A and B occur together, (*ii*) Both A and B occur but not C, (*iii*) all the three events occur, (*iv*) at least one event occur and (*v*) at least two events occur.

[Ans. (*i*) $A \cap B$ (*ii*) $A \cap B \cap \overline{C}$ (*iii*) $A \cap B \cap C$]

40. The records of 400 examinees are given below :

	Educational Qualification			
Score	*B.A.*	*B.Sc.*	*M.Com.*	*Total*
Below 50	90	30	60	180
Between 50 and 60	20	70	70	160
Above 60	10	30	20	60
Total	120	130	150	400

If an examinee is selected at random from this group, find

(*i*) the probability that he is a commerce graduate,

(*ii*) the probability that he is a science graduate, given that his score is above 60 and

(*iii*) the probability that his score is below 50, given that he is B.A. $\left[\textbf{Ans. } \frac{3}{8}, \frac{1}{2}, \frac{3}{4}\right]$

41. A piece of electronic equipment has two essential parts, *A* and *B*. In the past, part *A* has failed 40% of the time; part *B* 50% of the time. Parts *A* and *B* operate independently. Assume that both parts must operate to enable the equipment to function. What is the probability that the equipment will function ? [**Ans.** 0.30]

42. Three groups of workers contain 3 men and 1 women, 2 men and 2 women, and 1 man and 3 women, respectively. One worker is selected at random from each group. What is the probability that the group selected consists of 1 man and 2 women ? [**Ans.** 0.4063]

43. Two sets of candidates are competing for the position on the Board of Directors of a company. The probability is that the first and second sets will win 0.6 and 0.4 respectively. If the first set wins, the probability of introducing a new product is 0.8, and the corresponding probability if the second set wins is 0.3. What is the probability that the new product will be introduced ? [**Ans.** 0.60]

44. (*a*) It is given that $P(A \cup B) = \frac{5}{6}$, $P(AB) = \frac{1}{3}$ and $P(\overline{B}) = \frac{1}{2}$, where $P(\overline{B})$ stands for the probability that event *B* doesn't happen. Determine *P*(*A*) and *P*(*B*). Hence, show that the events *A* and *B* are independent. $\left[\textbf{Ans. } P(A) = \frac{2}{3}, P(B) = \frac{1}{2}\right]$

(*b*) Given $P(A) = 0.5$ and $P(A \cup B) = 0.7$, find *P*(*B*) if :

(*i*) *A* and *B* are independent events;

(*ii*) *A* and *B* are mutually exclusive events ;

(*iii*) $P(A/B) = 0.4$ [**Ans.** 0.4, 0.2, 0.33]

(*c*) Prove that following :

(*i*) If $P(A/B) \geq P(A)$ then $P(B/A) \geq P(B)$

(*ii*) If $P(B/\overline{A}) = P(B/A)$, then *A* and *B* are independent events.

45. *A* can solve 75% of the problems in accountancy while *B* can solve 70% of the problems. Find the probability that a problem selected at random from an accountancy book;

(*a*) will be solved by both *A* and *B*,

(b) will be solved by A or B,

(c) will be solved by one of them. $\left[\textbf{Ans. } 21/40, \frac{37}{40}, \frac{16}{40}\right]$

46. There are three cars, A, B and C. Car A, contains two males, car B contains one male and one female, and car C contains two females. If one of these cars is selected at random, and one person is observed to be male, what is the probability that the other person in that car is male ? $\left[\textbf{Ans. } \frac{2}{3}\right]$

47. A salesman has a 60 per cent chance of marking a sale to each customer. The behaviour of successive customers is independent. If two customers A and B enter, what is the probability that the salesman will make a sale to A or B ? [**Ans.** 0. 84]

48. A factory produces certain type of output by three machines. The respective daily production figures are ; Machine A = 3,000 units; Machine B = 2,500 units; and Machine C = 4,500 units. Past experience shows that 1 per cent of the output produced by machine A is defective. The corresponding fractions of a defectives for the other two machines are 1.2 and 2 per cent respectively. An item is drawn at random from the day's production run and is found to be defective. What is the probability that it comes from the output of (i) Machine A ; (ii) Machine B; and (iii) Machine C ?

[(i) 0.2; (ii) 0.2; (iii) 0.6] [**Ans.** 0.2, 0.2, 0.6]

49. Probability that a man will be alive 25 years hence is 0.3 and the probability that his wife will be alive 25 years hence is 0.4. Find the probability that 25 years hence (i) both will be alive (ii) only the man will be alive (iii) only the woman be alive and (iv) at least one of them will be alive.

50. A convention begins with an evening lecture, attended by 60% of the delegates. The following morning lecture is attended by 10% of the delegates. Seventy per cent of those attending this session had attended the previous evening session.

(i) What is the probability that a randomly selected delegate attended both the sessions ?

(ii) What is the probability that a delegate who attended the evening session also attended the following morning session ?

(iii) What is the probability that a delegate selected at random attended at least one of the two sessions ?

(iv) Are attendances at the two sessions statistically independent ?

51. Mr. Ram speaks the truth in 3 out of 4 times, while Mr. Shyam speaks the truth in 4 out of 5 times. Find the probability that they will contradict each other in stating the same fact. [**Ans.** 0.35]

52. The probability that India wins a cricket test match against Pakistan is, given to be 1/3. If India and Pakistan play six test matches, what is the probability that :

(i) India will lose all the six test matches ?

(ii) India will win at least one test match ? [**Ans.** 0.088, 0.912]

53. Three persons A, B and C are being considered for the appointment as Vice-Chancellor of a university whose chances of being selected for the post are in the proportion 4 : 2 : 3. The probability that A, if selected, will introduce democratisation in the University Structure is 0.3 and the corresponding probabilities for B and C doing the same are respectively 0.5 and 0.8. What is the probability that democratisation would be introduced in the University? [**Ans.** 0.5(1)]

54. 20% of all students at a university are graduates and 80% are undergraduates. The probability that a graduate student is married is 0.5 and the probability that an undergraduate student is married is 0.1. One student is selected at random.

(*a*) What is probability that he is married?

(*b*) What is the probability that he is a graduate if he is found to be married?

$\left[\textbf{Ans. } \frac{9}{50}, \frac{5}{9}\right]$

55. A die is loaded in such a way that each odd number is twice as likely to occur as each even number. Find (*i*) the probability that the number rolled is a perfect square and (*ii*) the probability that the number rolled is a perfect square provided it is greater than 3. $\left[\textbf{Ans. } \frac{1}{3}, \frac{1}{9}\right]$

56. A husband and wife appear in an interview for two vacancies in the same post. The probability of husband's selection is 1/7 and that of wife's selection is 1/5. What is the probability that

(*a*) both of them will be selected,

(*b*) only one of them will be selected, and

(*c*) none of them will be selected? $\left[\textbf{Ans. } \frac{1}{35}, \frac{10}{35}, \frac{24}{35}\right]$

57. A hotel gets cars for its guests from three rental agencies, 20 per cent from agency X, 40 per cent from agency Y and 40 per cent from Z. If 14 per cent of the cars from X, 4 per cent from Y and 8 per cent from Z, need tune-ups, what is the probability that car needing a tune-up is delivered to one of the hotel's guests? $\left[\textbf{Ans. } \frac{19}{250}\right]$

58. The odds against student X solving a Business statistics problem are 8 : 6 and odds in favour of student Y solving the same problem are 14 : 16. (*i*) What is the chance that the problem will be solved if both try? (*ii*) What is the probability that they both, working independently of each other, solve the problem? (*iii*) What is the probability that neither solves the problem? [**Ans.** (*i*) 0.6952; (*ii*) 0.2; (*iii*) 0.3048]

59. There are 100 students in a college class of which 36 boys are studying statistics and 13 girls are not studying statistics. If there are 55 girls in all, find the probability that a boy picked at random is not studying statistics. $\left[\textbf{Ans. } \frac{1}{5}\right]$

60. If pair of dice is thrown, find the probability that

(*i*) the sum is neither 7 nor 11

(*ii*) the sum is neither 8 nor 10

(*iii*) the sum is greater than 12. $\left[\textbf{Ans. } \frac{7}{9}, \frac{7}{9}, 0\right]$

61. Three horses A, B and C are in race. A is twice as likely to win as B, and B is twice as likely to win as C. What are the respective probabilities of winning?

$\left[\textbf{Ans. } \frac{4}{7}, \frac{2}{7}, \frac{1}{7}\right]$

62. 6 teachers, of whom 2 are from science, 2 from arts and 2 from commerce, are seated in a row. What is the probability that the teachers of the same discipline are sitting together ? [**Ans.** $\frac{1}{15}$]

63. (*a*) If $P(A) = 0.5$, $P(B) = 0.4$ and $P(\overline{A} \cup B) = 0.7$, find $P(A/B)$ and $P(A \cup B)$, where $\overline{A}$ is compliment of A. State whether A and B are independent.

[**Ans.** 0.7, 0.5, independent]

(*b*) If $P(A) = \frac{1}{3}$, $P(B) = \frac{1}{2}$, $P(A/B) = \frac{1}{6}$, find $P(B/A)$ and $P(B/\overline{A})$. [**Ans.** $\frac{1}{4}, \frac{1}{8}$]

(*c*) If A, B and C are three mutually exclusive events, find $P(B)$ if
$\frac{1}{3}P(C) = \frac{1}{2}P(A) = P(B)$. [**Ans.** $\frac{1}{6}$]

64. Let A be the event that a business executive selected at random has stomach ulcer and B be the event that he has a heart disease. Interpret the following events:
(*i*) $A^c \cup A$, (*ii*) $A^c \cap A$, (*iii*) $A^c \cap B$, (*iv*) $A \cap B^c$, (*v*) $(A \cap B)^c$

65. A salesman has 80% chance of making a sale to each customer. The behaviour of each customer is independent. If two customers A and enter, what is the probability that the salesman will make a sale to A or B ? [**Ans.** 0.96]

66. A problem in economics is given to 3 students whose chances of solving it are $\frac{2}{3}$, $\frac{3}{4}$ and $\frac{4}{5}$ respectively. What is the probability that the problem will be solved ?

[**Ans.** 59/60]

67. A man and a women appear in an interview for two vacancies in the same post. The probability of man's selection is $\frac{1}{4}$ and that of women's selection is $\frac{1}{3}$. What is the probability that.

(*a*) both of them will be selected ?

(*b*) only one of them will be selected ?

(*c*) none of them will be selected ?

(*d*) at last one of the m will be selected ? [**Ans.** $\frac{1}{12}$, 5/12, $\frac{1}{2}$, $\frac{1}{2}$]

68. What is the chance that a non-leap year selected at random will contain 53 Sundays ? [**Ans.** $\frac{1}{7}$]

□□□

12

Probability Distribution and Mathematical Expectation

CHAPTER OUTLINE

- Random Variable—Defined
- Probability Distribution of a Random Variable
- Expectation and Variance of a Random Variable
- Theorems on Expectation.

12.1 VARIABLE VERSUS RANDOM VARIABLE (R.V.)

Already defined variable, is some measurement which varies from unit to unit of a population. If the variable values are expressed in form of grouped data, it is called frequency distribution.

12.1.1 Random Variable (R.V.)

R.V. is a variable which takes different values with some assigned probabilities which are obtained theortically and not by actual measurement. *e.g.*, number of heads obtained when two unbiased coins are tossed. Immediately we come to know values of the variable are 0, 1 and 2 (number of heads in a toss of 2 coins) and we are able to assign probabilities to these variables values theortically which are as follows :

Now $S = \{HH, HT, TH, TT\}$

Each outcome has some numerical value according to defined variable.

Outcome	*No. of Heads (X)*	*P(X)*
HH	2	$\frac{1}{4}$
HT	1	$\frac{1}{4}$
TH	1	$\frac{1}{4}$
TT	0	$\frac{1}{4}$

Thus X takes values 2,1 and 0 with respective probabilities $\frac{1}{4}$, $\frac{1}{2}$ and $\frac{1}{4}$. Since all the outcomes are exhaustive and mutually exclusive thus $\Sigma P(X) = 1$. thus X variable *i.e.,* no. of heads in throw of 2 coins can be assigned probabilities, it is a random variable.

12.1.2 Discrete Random Variable

In case the variable values of the random variable are discrete *i.e.,* certain specific values, it is called discrete random variable. In the above example variable X is a discrete random variable.

Example. In case a die is rolled, in this case outcomes already have numerical values *i.e.,* 1, 2, 3, 4, 5 and 6 and each is assigned a probability of $\frac{1}{6}$ (assuming an unbiased die). Thus the variable is a discrete random variable.

12.2 PROBABILITY DISTRIBUTION

It is description of how the probabilities are distributed over different values of random variable (It is just like frequency distribution of discrete variable, in place of frequencies we have probabilities for different variable values).

Example 1. *Give the probability distribution of no. of heads in a toss of a 2 unbiased coins.*

Solution.

No. of heads X	*P(X)*
2	1/4
1	2/4
0	1/4

Example 2. *Give the probability distribution of number of dots on upward face when an unbiased die is rolled.*

Solution. Probability distribution of no. of dots on a die.

X No. of dots.	*P(X)*
1	1/6
2	1/6

3		1/6
4		1/6
5		1/6
6		1/6
		$\Sigma P(X) = 1$

12.3 EXPECTATION OF A RANDOM VARIABLE

"Expected Value" or "Expectation of Random Variable" is a measure of central location *i.e.*, "Arithmetic Mean" of a random variable which is generally denote by $E(X)$ or μ which is defined as

$$\mu = E(X) = \Sigma X P(X)$$

[In case of non random variable it is written as $\overline{X}$ and is given as $\overline{X} = \dfrac{\Sigma fX}{\Sigma f}$ where $\dfrac{f}{\Sigma f}$ is relative frequency which is replaced by $P(X)$ in case of random variable].

$\mu = E(X)$ can be obtained only if the probability distribution of a random variable X is known.

Expectations of functions of X

Similarly we may have derived variables from X and their expectations are also defined. *e.g.*

$$E(X + k) = \Sigma(X + k)\, P(X)$$
$$E(X^2) = \Sigma X^2\, P(X)$$
$$E(X^3) = \Sigma X^3\, P(X) \text{ and so on.}$$

Since $P(X^2) = P(X)$ *i.e.*, probability of getting X^2 is same as of getting X.

Example 3. *A random variable X has the following probability distribution :*

X	:	-2	-1	0	1	2
Probability	:	$\frac{1}{6}$	p	$\frac{1}{4}$	p	$\frac{1}{6}$

(i) Find the value of p.

(ii) Calculate E(X + 2) and E(2X²).

Solution. Since the total probability under a probability distribution is equal to unity, the value of p should be such that $\frac{1}{6} + p + \frac{1}{4} + p + \frac{1}{6} = 1$ as $\Sigma P(x) = 1$.

This condition gives $p = \dfrac{5}{24}$.

Probability distribution of variable X is

X	$P(X)$	$X + 2$	$(X + 2)\,P(X)$	$2X^2$	$2X^2\,P(X)$
-2	$\frac{1}{6}$	0	0	8	$\frac{8}{6} = \frac{16}{12}$
-1	5/24	1	5/24	2	$\frac{10}{24} = \frac{5}{12}$
0	$\frac{1}{4}$	2	$\frac{1}{2} = \frac{12}{24}$	0	$0 = 0$

1	5/24	3	$\frac{15}{24}$	2	$\frac{10}{24}=\frac{5}{12}$
2	$\frac{1}{6}$	4	$\frac{4}{6}=\frac{16}{24}$	8	$\frac{8}{6}=\frac{16}{12}$
			$\Sigma=\frac{48}{24}=2$ $\Sigma\,(X+2)\,P(X)$ $=E\,(X+2)$		$\Sigma=\frac{42}{12}=\frac{7}{2}$ $\Sigma 2X^2\,P(X)$ $=E\,(2X^2)$

Thus $E(x+2)=2$, $E(2x^2)=\frac{7}{2}$

Variance of Random Variable

Now we know in case of frequency distribution variance

$$V(X) = \sigma^2 = \frac{\Sigma fX^2}{\Sigma f} - \left(\frac{\Sigma fX}{\Sigma f}\right)^2$$

$$= \Sigma X^2\,P(X) - [X\,P(X)]^2 \qquad \left[\text{replacing } \frac{f}{\Sigma f} \text{ by } P(x)\right]$$

$$= E(X^2) - [E(X)]^2$$

Also $$V(X) = \sigma^2 = \frac{\Sigma f\,(X-\overline{X})^2}{\Sigma f} \qquad [\text{replacing } \overline{X} \text{ by } E(X) \text{ and}$$

$$= \Sigma[X - E(X)]^2\,P(X) \qquad \frac{f}{\Sigma f} \text{ by } P(X)]$$

$$= E\,[X - E(X)]^2$$

12.4 PROPERTIES OF EXPECTED VALUE AND VARIANCE

There are several important properties of expected value and variance which allow computational shortcuts. The results are given without proofs.

1. The expected value of a constant c is equal to the constant.

$$E\,(c) = c \qquad [\text{As } \Sigma C\,P(x) = C\Sigma\,P(x) = C]$$

2. The expected value of the product of a constant c and a random variable X is equal to the constant times the expected value of the random variable.

$$E\,(cX) = cE\,(X)$$

3. The expected value of the sum of a random variable X and a constant c is the sum of the expected value of the random variable and the constant.

$$E\,(X+C) = E\,(X) + c$$

4. The expected value of the product of two independent random variables is equal to the product of their individual expected values.

$$E\,(XY) = E\,(X)\,E\,(Y)$$

5. The expected value of the sum of the two random variables is equal to the sum of their individual expected values.

$$E\,(X+Y) = E\,(X) + E\,(Y)$$

6. The variance of the product of a constant and a random variable X is equal to the constant squared times the variance of the random variable X.

$$\text{Var}(cX) = c^2\,\text{Var}(X)$$

7. The variance of the sum of two independent random variables equal the sum of their individual variances. Also, the variance of the difference of two independent random variable equal the sum of their individual variances.

$$\text{Var}(X + Y) = \text{Var}(X) + \text{Var}(Y) = \text{Var}(X - Y)$$

Example 4. *Anil company estimates the net profit on a new product, it is launching, to be ₹ 3,000,000 during the first year if it is 'successful' ₹ 1,000,000 if it is moderately successful and a loss of ₹ 1,000,000 if it is 'unsuccessful'. The company assigns the following probabilities to first year prospects for the product, successful : 0.15, moderately successful: 0.25, and unsuccessful: 0.60. What are the expected value and standard deviation of first year net profit for the product?*

Solution. The probability distribution of net profit (X) of the new product in the first year is given to be

Profit (in million ₹) X	3	1	–1
Probability $P(X)$	0.15	0.25	0.60

Therefore, expected value of profit is given by

$$\begin{aligned} E(X) &= \Sigma X\,P(X) \\ &= 3 \times 0.15 + 1 \times 0.25 - 1 \times 0.60 \\ &= 0.10 \text{ million ₹} = ₹\ 1{,}00{,}000. \\ E(X^2) &= \Sigma X^2\,P(X) \\ &= 9 \times 0.15 + 1 \times 0.25 + 1 \times 0.6 = 2.20 \text{ million ₹} \\ \text{Var}(X) &= E(X^2) - [E(X)]^2 = 2.20 - (0.10)^2 = 2.19 \\ \text{s.d.} &= \sigma = \sqrt{2.19} = 1.48 \text{ (Million ₹)} \end{aligned}$$

Example 5. *A die is thrown at random. What is the expectation of the number on it ?*

Solution. Let X denote the number obtained on the die. Then X is a random variable which can take any one of the values 1, 2, 3, ..., 6 each with equal probability 1/6. Thus the probability distribution of a number on the die is given below.

X	1	2	3	4	5	6	
$P(X)$	1/6	1/6	1/6	1/6	1/6	1/6	Total
$X(P(X)$	$\frac{1}{6}$	$\frac{2}{6}$	$\frac{3}{6}$	$\frac{4}{6}$	$\frac{5}{6}$	$\frac{6}{6}$	$\frac{21}{6} = \Sigma X\,P(X)$

Thus $E(X) = \Sigma X\,P(X) = \dfrac{21}{6} = \dfrac{7}{2}$.

Example 6. *What is the expected number of heads appearing when a fair coin is tossed three times ? What is its variance.*

Solution. In this case

$$S = \{HHH, \underbrace{HHT, HTH, THH}_{\text{2 heads}}, \underbrace{HTT, THT, TTH}_{\text{one head}}, TTT\}$$

$n(S) = 8$

Probability distribution of no. of heads in three throws of an unbiased coin and computation of $E(X) = \Sigma X\,P(X)$ and $V(X) = E(X^2) - [E(X)]^2$ is given below.

X	$P(X)$	$X\,P(X)$	$X^2\,P(X)$
0	1/8	0	0
1	3/8	3/8	3/8
2	3/8	6/8	12/8
3	$\frac{1}{8}$	3/8	$\frac{9}{8}$
		$\Sigma = \frac{12}{8}$	$\Sigma = \frac{24}{8}$

Thus $E(X) = \Sigma X\,P(X) = \frac{12}{8} = \frac{3}{2}$

$E(X^2) = \Sigma X^2\,P(X) = \frac{24}{8} = 3$

$V(X) = 3 - \left(\frac{3}{2}\right)^2 = \frac{3}{4} = \sigma^2$

$E(X)$ = average no. of heads per throw of 3 coins.

Example 7. *A random variable X is defined as the sum of faces when a pair of dice is thrown. Find the expected value of X.*

Solution. We know

$$\begin{Bmatrix} 11 & 12 & 13 & 14 & 15 & 16 \\ 21 & 22 & \dots & \dots & \dots & 26 \\ \dots & \dots & \dots & \dots & \dots & \dots \\ \dots & \dots & \dots & \dots & \dots & \dots \\ \dots & \dots & \dots & \dots & \dots & \dots \\ 61 & 62 & \dots & \dots & \dots & 66 \end{Bmatrix}$$

We see that total varies from 2 to 12.

Sum	*Outcomes*
2	{11}
3	{12, 21}
4	{13, 31, 22}
—	—
—	—
—	—
—	—
10	{46, 64, 55}
11	{56, 65}
12	{66}

The random variable X denote the sum of points obtained on a pair of dice when thrown. Then, the probability distribution of X is :

X	2	3	4	5	6	7	8	9	10	11	12	Total
$P(X)$	$\frac{1}{36}$	$\frac{2}{36}$	$\frac{3}{36}$	$\frac{4}{36}$	$\frac{5}{36}$	$\frac{6}{36}$	$\frac{5}{36}$	$\frac{4}{36}$	$\frac{3}{36}$	$\frac{2}{36}$	$\frac{1}{36}$	
$X\,P(X)$	$\frac{2}{36}$	$\frac{6}{36}$	$\frac{12}{36}$	$\frac{20}{36}$	$\frac{30}{36}$	$\frac{42}{36}$	$\frac{40}{36}$	$\frac{36}{36}$	$\frac{30}{36}$	$\frac{22}{36}$	$\frac{12}{36}$	$\frac{252}{36}$

Thus $E(X) = \Sigma X\,P(X) = \dfrac{252}{36} = 7$

This implies that if the experiment is repeated several time and sum values are noted we expect the average to be 7.

Example 8. *An urn contains 7 white and 3 red balls. Two balls are drawn together, at random, from this urn. Compute the probability that neither of them is white. Find also the probability of getting one white and one red ball. Hence compute the expected number of white balls drawn.*

Solution. From an urn containing 7 white and 3 red balls, two balls can be drawn in ${}^{10}C_2$ ways. Let X denote the number of white balls drawn. The probability distribution of X is obtained as follows :

$P(X)$ = Probability that neither of two balls is white

= Probability that both balls drawn are red $= \dfrac{{}^3C_2}{{}^{10}C_2} = \dfrac{3 \times 2}{10 \times 9} = \dfrac{1}{15}$

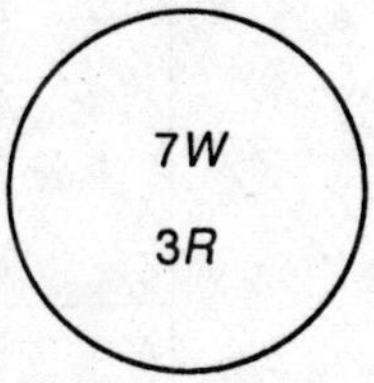

since 2 balls can be drawn out of 3 red balls in ${}^3C_2$ ways.

$P(X = 1)$ = Probability of getting 1 white and 1 red ball

$$= \frac{{}^7C_1 \times {}^3C_1}{{}^{10}C_2} = \frac{7 \times 3 \times 2}{10 \times 9} = \frac{21}{45} = \frac{7}{15}$$

since 1 white ball can be drawn out of 7 white balls in ${}^7C_1$ ways and 1 red ball can be drawn out of 3 red balls in ${}^3C_1$ ways and all these ways can be associated with each other.

$P(X = 2)$ = Probability of getting two white balls $= \dfrac{{}^7C_2}{{}^{10}C_2} = \dfrac{7 \times 6}{2} \times \dfrac{2}{10 \times 9} = \dfrac{21}{45} = \dfrac{7}{15}$

Thus probability distribution of X (no. of white balls) is as follows :

X	$P(X)$	$X\,P(X)$
0	1/15	0
1	7/15	$\frac{7}{15}$
2	$\frac{7}{15}$	$\frac{14}{15}$

$$\Sigma X\,P(X) = \frac{21}{15} = \frac{7}{5}$$

Thus $\quad E(X) = \dfrac{7}{5}$

[Remark : This means that on the average $\frac{7}{5}$ white balls will be obtained per draw if large number of draws are performed].

Example 9. *A dealer of ceiling fans has estimated the following probability distribution of the price of a ceiling fan in the next summer season:*

Price (P)	:	*800*	*825*	*850*	*875*	*900*
Probability (p)	:	*0.15*	*0.25*	*0.30*	*0.20*	*0.10*

If the demand (x) of his ceiling fans follows a linear relation $x = 6000 - 4P$, find expected demand of fans and expected total revenue of the dealer.

Solution. Since P is a random variable, therefore, $x = 6000 - 4P$, is also a random variable. Further, Total Revenue $TR = P.x = 6000P - 4P^2$ is also a random variable.

We need $E(R) = E(6000\,P - 4\,P^2)$

$$= 6{,}000\,E(P) - 4\,E(P^2) = 6000\,E(X) - 4\,E(X^2) \quad \text{... (1)}$$

[replacing P by X]

Probability distribution of X (price) is as follows :

Price X	$P(X)$	$X\,P(X)$	$X^2\,P(X)$
800	0.15	120.00	96,000.00
825	0.25	206.25	170,156.25
850	0.30	255.00	216,750.00
875	0.20	175.00	148,125.00
900	0.10	90.00	81,000.00
		846.25 $\Sigma X\,P(X)$	717,031.25

$$E(P) = E(X) = 846.25 = \text{expected price} \quad \text{...(2)}$$

$$E(R) = 6000\,E(X) - 4\,E(X^2) \quad \text{[from (1)]}$$

$$= 6000\,(846.25) - 4\,(717{,}031.25)$$

$$= 5077500 - 2868125$$

$$= 2209375$$

Now we demand $X = 6000 - 4P$

Expected demand $= E(X) = E(6000 - 4P)$

$$= 6000 - 4\,E(P)$$

$$= 6000 - 4(846.25) \quad \text{[from (2)]}$$

$$= 6000 - 3385 = 2615 \text{ fans}$$

Example 10. *A contractor spends ₹ 3,000 to prepare for a bid on a construction project which, after deducting manufacturing expenses and the cost of bidding, will yield a profit of ₹ 25,000 if the bid is won. If the chance of winning the bid is ten per cent, compute his expected profit and state the likely decision on whether to bid or not to bid.*

Solution. Expenses incurred on preparing the bid = ₹ 3,000.

This will be his loss if the bid is not won by the contractor. Profit if bid is won = ₹ 25,000.

P (Winning the bid) = 10% = 0.10 (Given) ; P (Losing the bid) = 1 – 0.10 = 0.90

∴ Contractor's expected profit

= ₹ [25,000 × 0.10 + (–3,000) × 0.90] = ₹ (2,500 – 2,700) = (–) ₹ 200

Since the contractor's expected profit is negative, he should not bid.

Example 11. *A player tosses two fair coins. He wins ₹5 if 2 heads occur, ₹ 2 if 1 head occurs and ₹ 1 if no head occurs.*

(i) Find his expected gain.

(ii) How much should he pay to play the game if it is to be fair?

Solution. Two fair coins are tossed, the no. of heads obtained vary from 0,1, 2

No. of heads	*Given X*	*P(X)*	*X P(X)*
0 (*TT*)	1	$\frac{1}{4}$	$\frac{1}{4}$
1 {*HT* or *TH*}	2	$\frac{2}{4}$	$\frac{4}{4}$
2 {*HH*}	5	$\frac{1}{4}$	5/4

$$\frac{10}{4} = \Sigma X\,P(X)$$

(i) His expected gain (per throw of 2 coins) = ₹ $\frac{5}{2}$

(ii) Thus he continues to gain and for the game to be fair his expected gain should be zero. Thus he should pay ₹ 5/2 per game. In that case his expected gain will be zero and game will be fair (no gain – no loss game).

Example 12. *The probability that there is at least one error in an accounts statement prepared by A is 0.2 and for B and C they are 0.25 and 0.4 respectively. A, B and C prepared 10, 16 and 20 statements respectively. Find the expected number of correct statements in all.*

Solution. We expected no. of correct statements. The probabilities of account statements to be correct. Let p_1, p_2, p_3 be such probabilities for A, B and C respectively.

	X	P(X)	X P(X)
A	10	.8 (1 – .2)	8
B	16	0.75 (1 – 0.25)	12
C	20	0.6 (1 – .4)	12
	$\Sigma X = 46$		$\Sigma X\,P(X) = 32$

We expect 32 account statements to be correct out of 46.

Example 13. *If the probability that the value of a certain stock will remain the same is 0.46, the probabilities that its value will increase by ₹ 0.50 or ₹ 0.25 per share is 0.14, what is the expected gain per share?*

Solution.

Gain (x)	*Prob. (P)*	*Px*
0	0.46	0
0.5	0.17	0.085
1.0	0.23	0.230
– 0.25	0.14	– 0.035
		$\Sigma Px = 0.28$

Expected gain per share = 28 paise

Example 14. *If a player plays a game of chance where he can win ₹ 1,000 with probability 0.5, win ₹ 500 with probability 0.3 and lose ₹ 3,000 with probability 0.2. What is his expected gain in one play of the game?*

Solution.

Gain X	*P(X)*	*X P(X)*
1000	0.5	500
500	0.3	150
– 3000	0.2	– 600
		50

$= \Sigma X\,P(X) = E(X) = 50$

Example 15. *A box contains 8 tickets, 3 of the tickets carry a prize of ₹ 5 each and the other 5 a prize of ₹ 3 each.*

(*i*) *If one ticket is drawn, what is expected value of the prize ?*

(*ii*) *If two tickets are drawn, what is the expected value of the game ?*

Solution. Let the ticket carrying a prize of 5 be *A* and the ticket carrying a prize of 3 be *B*. So we have 3*A* and 5*B*.

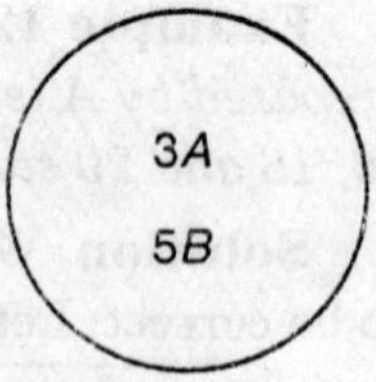

(*i*) One ticket is drawn, it may be *A* or *B* carrying a prize of 5 or 3 respectively

Thus

Ticket	*Price X*	*P(X)*	*X P(X)*
A	5	3/8	15/8
B	3	5/8	15/8

$$\Sigma X\,P(X) = \frac{30}{8} = \frac{15}{4}$$

Expected value of the prize $= \frac{15}{4}$.

(*ii*) When two tickets are drawn then

Tickets	*Price X*	*P(X)*	*X P(X)*
2 A	$2 \times 5 = 10$	$\frac{^3C_2}{^8C_2} = \frac{3}{28}$	30/28
A + B	$5 + 3 = 8$	$\frac{^3C_1 \times {^5C_1}}{^8C_2} = \frac{15}{28}$	120/28
2B	$2 \times 3 = 6$	$\frac{^5C_2}{^8C_2} = \frac{10}{28}$	$\frac{60}{28}$

$\Sigma X\,P(X) = \frac{210}{28} = \frac{105}{14}$

Expected prize = ₹ 105/14.

Example 16. *A survey conducted over the last 25 years indicated that in 10 years the winter was mild, in 8 years it was cold and in the remaining 7 years it was very cold.*

A company sells 1000 woollen coats in a mild year, 1300 in a cold year and 2000 in a very cold year.

You are required to find the yearly expected profit of the company if a woollen coat costs ₹ 1730 and it is sold to stores for ₹ 2480.

Solution. From the given data, we obtain the following probability distribution of the number of woollen coats sold in any winter (year).

Winter	*Probability P (X)*	*No. of woollen coats sold (X)*	*X P (X)*
Mild	$\frac{10}{25}$	1000	$\frac{10}{25} \times 1000 = 400$
Cold	$\frac{8}{25}$	1300	$\frac{8}{25} \times 1300 = 416$
Very cold	$\frac{7}{25}$	2000	$\frac{7}{25} \times 2000 = 560$

Hence, the expected number of woollen coats sold in any year is given by :

$E(X) = \Sigma X\,P(X) = 400 + 416 + 560 = 1376$

Since the cost of a woollen coat is ₹ 1730 and it is sold to the stores for ₹ 2480, the company makes a profit of ₹ (2480 – 1730) = ₹ 750 per coat.

Hence, the yearly expected profit of the company is ₹ 1376 × 750 = ₹ 10,32,000.

Example 17. *From a bag containing 4 white and 6 red balls, three balls are drawn at random.*

(*i*) *Find the expected number of white balls drawn.*

(*ii*) *If each white ball drawn carries a reward of ₹ 4 and each red ball ₹ 6, find the expected reward of the draw.*

Solution. There are 4 white and 6 red balls *i.e.,* 10 balls in the bag.

Three balls can be drawn out of 10 balls in $^{10}C_3$ ways, which gives the exhaustive number of cases.

In a random draw of 3 balls from the bag, the number of favourable cases for getting x white balls and consequently $(3 - x)$ red balls, is given by the principle of counting by :

$$^4C_x \times {^6C_{3-x}} \quad ; \quad x = 0, 1, 2, 3 \qquad n(S) = {^{10}C_3} = \frac{10 \times 9 \times 8}{3 \times 2 \times 1} = 120$$

$\therefore \quad P(X)$ = Probability of drawing x white balls

$$= \frac{{}^4C_x \times {}^6C_{3-x}}{{}^{10}C_3}; \quad x = 0, 1, 2, 3$$

$$\Rightarrow P(X = 0) = \frac{{}^4C_0 \times {}^6C_3}{{}^{10}C_3} = \frac{1 \times 6 \times 5 \times 4 \times 3\,!}{3\,! \times 10 \times 9 \times 8} = \frac{1}{6} = \frac{5}{30}$$

$$P(X = 1) = \frac{{}^4C_1 \times {}^6C_2}{{}^{10}C_3} = \frac{4 \times 15}{120} = \frac{15}{30}$$

$$P(X = 2) = \frac{{}^4C_2\, {}^6C_1}{{}^{10}C_3} = \frac{6 \times 6}{120} = \frac{9}{30}$$

$$P(X = 3) = \frac{{}^4C_3}{{}^{10}C_3} = \frac{4}{120} = \frac{1}{30}$$

Probability distribution of reward is according to 4 possibilities.

	White + Red	*Reward X*	*P(X)*	*X P(X)*
1	0 + 3	18	$\frac{5}{30}$	$\frac{90}{30}$
2	1 + 2	16	$\frac{15}{30}$	$\frac{240}{30}$
3	2 + 1	14	$\frac{9}{30}$	$\frac{126}{30}$
4	3 + 0	12	$\frac{1}{30}$	$\frac{12}{30}$
				$\Sigma = \frac{468}{30}$

Expected reward = $E(X) = \frac{468}{30}$ = 15.60 (rupees).

Example 18. *Two cards are selected at random from a box which contains five cards number 1, 1, 2, 2 and 3. Let x denote the sum of the number. Find the expected value of the sum.*

Solution. Let the cards be *A, B, C, D* and *E* which carry the numbers 1, 1, 2, 2 and 3 respectively. Two cards are drawn simultaneously that mean cards are drawn without replacement (card dawn once will not repeat on the 2nd draw).

The following are possibilities

In terms of cards				*In terms of number*				*In terms of sum*			
AB	*AC*	*AD*	*AE*	11	12	12	13	2	3	3	4
BA	*BC*	*BD*	*BE*	11	12	12	13	2	3	3	4
CA	*CB*	*CD*	*CE*	21	21	22	23	3	3	4	5
DA	*DB*	*DC*	*DE*	21	21	22	23	3	3	4	5
EA	*EB*	*EC*	*ED*	31	31	32	32	4	4	5	5

There are 20 possibilities, so each have probability $= \frac{1}{20}$. 2 appears twice so it has probability $\frac{2}{20}$.

Probability Distribution of sum

X Sum	*P*(*X*)	*X P*(*X*)
2	$\frac{2}{20}$	$\frac{4}{20}$
3	$\frac{8}{20}$	$\frac{24}{20}$
4	$\frac{6}{20}$	$\frac{24}{20}$
5	$\frac{4}{20}$	$\frac{20}{20}$

$\Sigma X\,P(X) = \frac{72}{20} = 3.6 = X\,P(X) = E(X).$

Example 19. *A weighted coin so that* $P\,(H) = \frac{1}{3}$, $P\,(T) = \frac{2}{3}$ *is tossed until head or 5 tails occur. Find the expected number of tosses of the coin.*

Solution. The following are possibilities

H, TH, TTH, TTTH, TTTTH, TTTTT

(last trial is head or all 5 are tails)

No. of trials $X = 1,\quad 2,\quad 3,\quad 4,\quad 5,\quad 5$

$$P(X) = \frac{1}{3},\quad \frac{2}{3}\frac{1}{3},\quad \left(\frac{2}{3}\right)^2\frac{1}{3},\quad \left(\frac{2}{3}\right)^3\frac{1}{3},\quad \left(\frac{2}{3}\right)^4\frac{1}{3},\quad \left(\frac{2}{3}\right)^5$$

Thus Probability distribution of trials (*X*)

X	*P*(*X*)	*X P*(*X*)
1	$\frac{1}{3} = \frac{81}{243}$	$\frac{81}{243}$
2	$\frac{2}{9} = \frac{54}{243}$	$\frac{108}{243}$
3	$\frac{4}{27} = \frac{36}{243}$	$\frac{108}{243}$
4	$\frac{8}{81} = \frac{24}{243}$	$\frac{96}{243}$
5	$\frac{16}{243}$	$\frac{80}{243}$
5	$\frac{32}{243}$	$\frac{160}{243}$

$E(X) = \Sigma X\,P(X) = \frac{633}{243} = \frac{211}{81}$ = expected no. trials need to get the required result.

Example 20. *A die is tossed twice. Getting 'a number greater than 4' is considered a success. Find the mean and variance of the probability distribution of the number of successes.*

Solution. Since the favourable cases for 'getting a number greater than 4' in a throw of a die are 5 and 6, *i.e.*, 2 in all, we have :

Probability of success $(S) = \frac{2}{6} = \frac{1}{3}$ $\Rightarrow$ Probability of failure $(F) = 1 - \frac{1}{3} = \frac{2}{3}$

Let X denote the number of successes. Then, X is a random variable taking the values 0, 1 and 2.

$$P(X = 0) = P(F \text{ and } F) = P(F) \times P(F) = \frac{2}{3} \times \frac{2}{3} = \frac{4}{9}$$

$$P(X = 1) = P(F \text{ and } S) + P(S \text{ and } F) = P(F).\,P(S) + P(S).\,P(F)$$
$$= \frac{2}{3} \times \frac{1}{3} + \frac{1}{3} \times \frac{2}{3} = \frac{4}{9}$$

$$P(X = 2) = P(S \text{ and } S) = P(S)\,P(S) = \frac{1}{3} \times \frac{1}{3} = \frac{1}{9}$$

PROBABILITY DISTRIBUTION AND COMPUTATION OF VARIANCE

X	$P(X)$	$XP(X)$	$X^2P(X)$
0	4/9	0	0
1	4/9	4/9	4/9
2	1/9	2/9	4/9
Total		$\Sigma X\,P(X) = \frac{6}{9}$	$\Sigma X^2\,P(X) = \frac{8}{9}$

Thus Expected $X = E(X)$

$$= \Sigma X\,P(X) = \frac{6}{9} = \frac{2}{3}$$

and $\sigma^2 = \Sigma X^2\,P(X) - (\Sigma X\,P(X))^2$

$$= \frac{8}{9} - \frac{4}{9} = \frac{4}{9}.$$

Example 21. *A random variable X has the following probability distribution :*

X	:	4	5	6	8
$P(X)$	:	0.1	0.3	0.4	0.2

Find $E[X - E(X)]^2$.

Solution. $E[X - E(X)]^2 = \text{Var}(X) = E(X^2) - [E(X)]^2 = \Sigma X^2 P(X) - [\Sigma XP(X)]^2$

$$V(X) = E([X - E(X)]^2$$
$$= 36.3 - (5.9)^2$$
$$= 36.30 - 34.81$$
$$= 1.49$$

x	$P(X) = p$	px	px^2
4	0.1	0.4	0.6
5	0.3	1.5	7.5
6	0.4	2.4	14.4
8	0.2	1.6	12.8
Total	1	$\Sigma px = 5.9$	$\Sigma px^2 = 36.3$

Example 22. *A random variable x has the following probability functions :*

Values of x	0	1	2	3	4	5	6	7
p(x)	0	$2k$	$3k$	k	$2k$	k^2	$7k^2$	$2k^2 + k$

Find the value of k and then evaluate $p(x < 6)$, $p(x \geq 6)$ and $p(0 < x < 5)$. [C.A. May 1991]

Solution. Since total probability is one, $\Sigma p(x) = 1$

or $0 + 2k + 3k + k + 2k + k^2 + 7k^2 + 2k^2 + k = 1$

or $10k^2 + 9k - 1 = 0$ or $(10k - 1)(k + 1) = 0$

$\therefore$ $k = \frac{1}{10}$ [$k \neq -1$ as probability cannot be negative]

Thus probability Distribution of X is as follows.

x	0	1	2	3	4	5	6	7
$p(x)$	0	$\frac{2}{10}$	$\frac{3}{10}$	$\frac{1}{10}$	$\frac{2}{10}$	$\frac{1}{100}$	$\frac{7}{100}$	$\frac{12}{100}$

Hence (*i*) $p(x < 6) = p(0) + p(1) + p(2) + p(3) + p(4) + p(5)$

$$= 0 + \frac{2}{10} + \frac{3}{10} + \frac{1}{10} + \frac{2}{10} + \frac{1}{100} = \frac{81}{100} = 0.81.$$

(*ii*) $p(x \geq 6) = p(6) + p(7)$

$$= \frac{7}{100} + \frac{12}{100} = \frac{19}{100} = 0.19.$$

(*iii*) $p(0 < x < 5) = p(1) + p(2) + p(3) + p(4)$

$$= \frac{2}{10} + \frac{3}{10} + \frac{1}{10} + \frac{2}{10} = \frac{8}{10} = 0.8.$$

Example 23. *A box contains 8 items of which 2 are defective. A man selects 3 items at random. Find the expected number of defective items he has drawn. (Items are drawn with replacement)*

Solution. Probability that an item selected at random is defective $= \frac{2}{8} = \frac{1}{4}$

If getting a defective items is, success then probability of success $= p = \frac{1}{4}$

Probability of failure $= q = 1 - \frac{1}{4} = \frac{3}{4}$

Probability of having no defective items $P(X = 0) = \left(\frac{3}{4}\right)^3 = \frac{27}{64}$ [$= qqq$ (none is non defective)]

Probability of having one defective item $P(X = 1) = 3\left(\frac{3}{4}\right)^2 \frac{1}{4} = \frac{27}{64}$ [$= pqq + qpq + qqp$]

Probability of having two defective items $P(X = 2) = 3\left(\frac{3}{4}\right)\left(\frac{1}{4}\right)^2 = \frac{9}{64}$ [$= ppq + pqp + qpp$]

Probability of having 3 defectives $= P(X = 3) = \left(\frac{1}{4}\right)^3 = \frac{1}{64}$ [$= ppp$]

Expected no. of defectives $= E(X) = \Sigma X\, P(X)$

$$= 0\left(\frac{27}{64}\right) + 1\left(\frac{27}{64}\right) + 2\left(\frac{9}{64}\right) + 3\left(\frac{1}{64}\right)$$

$$= \frac{27+18+3}{64} = \frac{48}{64} = \frac{3}{4}.$$

Example 24. *A bag contains 2 white balls and 3 black balls. Four persons. A, B C and D, in the order named, each draw one ball and do not replace it. The first to draw a white ball receives ₹ 20. Determine their expectations.* [Delhi Univ. B.A. (Econ. Hons.), 1995]

Solution. The box contains 2 white and 3 black balls.

Since *A*, *B*, *C* and *D* draw the ball successively without replacement and the person who first draws the white ball wins, their respective chances of winning are as follows :

P (*A*'s winning) = *P* (*A* draws a white ball in the first draw) $= \frac{2}{5} = 0.4$

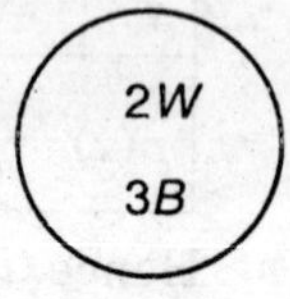

P (*B*'s winning) = *P* (*A* does not get a white ball and in the next draw *B* gets a white ball)

$$= \left(1-\frac{2}{5}\right) \times \frac{2}{4} = \frac{3}{5} \times \frac{2}{4} = 0.3$$ [After A has got black ball]

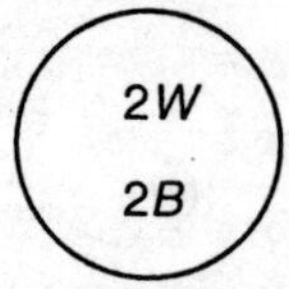

P(*C*'s winning) = *P* [*A* and *B* do not get a white ball in the first two draws and *C* gets the white ball in the 3rd draw]

$$P(BBW) = \left(1-\frac{2}{5}\right) \times \left(1-\frac{2}{4}\right) \times \frac{2}{3} = \frac{3}{5} \times \frac{2}{4} \times \frac{2}{3} = 0.2$$

[as *A* and *B* both has drawn black balls]

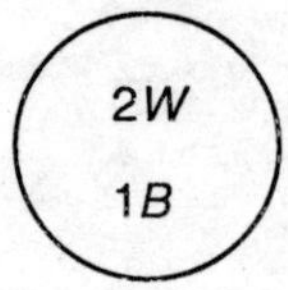

Similarly

$$P(D\text{'s winning}) = \left(1-\frac{2}{5}\right)\left(1-\frac{2}{4}\right)\left(1-\frac{2}{3}\right) \times \frac{2}{2} = \frac{3}{5} \times \frac{2}{4} \times \frac{1}{3} = 0.1$$

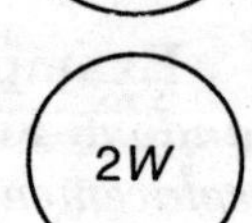

or *P*(*D*'s winning) = 1 – 0.4 – 0.3 – 0.2 = 0.1.

Hence, their respective expectations for a prize of ₹ 20 are :

A's expectation = ₹ 20 × 0.4 = ₹ 8 ; *B*'s expectation = ₹ 20 × 0.3 = ₹ 6

C's expectation = ₹ 20 × 0.2 = ₹ 4 ; *D*'s expectation = ₹ 20 × 0.1 = ₹ 2

Example 25. *Evaluate k if P (X) = k, when x = 1, 2, 3, 4, 5, 6 and = 0 elsewhere, is a probability mass function.*

Find its mean and standard deviation.

Solution. In this case *f*(*x*) is *P*(*x*)

Probability distribution of *X* is as below

X	*P*(*X*)	*P*(*X*)	*X P*(*X*)	X^2 *P*(*X*)
1	*k*	1/6	1/6	1/6
2	*k*	1/6	2/6	4/6
3	*k*	1/6	3/6	9/6
4	*k*	1/6	4/6	16/6
5	*k*	1/6	5/6	25/6
6	*k*	1/6	6/6	36/6
	$\Sigma P(X) = 6k$		$\Sigma XP(X) = 21/6$	$\frac{9}{6} = \Sigma X^2 P(X)$

Now $\Sigma P(X) = 1 \Rightarrow 6k = 1 \Rightarrow k = \frac{1}{6}$

$$E(X) = \Sigma X\, P(X) = \frac{21}{6} = \frac{7}{2}$$

$$V(X) = E(X^2) - [E(X)]^2 = \Sigma X^2 P(X) - [E(X)]^2$$

$$= \frac{91}{6} - \left(\frac{7}{2}\right)^2 = \frac{91}{6} - \frac{49}{4} = \frac{182-147}{12} = \frac{35}{12}.$$

Example 26. *A and B play for a prize of ₹ 3240. If A is to throw a dice first and is to win if he throws 6. If he fails B is to throw and is to win if he throws 6 or 5. If he fails A is to throw again and to win if he throws 6 or 5 or 4 and so on. Find their respective expectations.*

Solution. The probability that A will win in the first throw $= \frac{1}{6} = P(A_1)$

The probability of that A will lose in the first throw $= 1 - \frac{1}{6} = \frac{5}{6} = P(\overline{A}_1)$

$P(B$ throws 5 or 6 at 2nd throw$) = \frac{2}{6} = \frac{1}{3} = P(B_2)$

$P(A$ throws 4 or 5 or 6 in 3rd throw$) = \frac{3}{6} = \frac{1}{2} = P(A_3)$

Same way $P(B_4) = \frac{4}{6} = \frac{2}{3}$ and $P(A_5) = \frac{5}{6}$

and $P(B_6) = \frac{6}{6}$.

Now A may win either at 1st or 3rd or 5th

Throw *i.e.*, $P(A) = P(A_1) + P(\overline{A}_1\, \overline{B}_2\, A_3) + P(\overline{A}_1\, \overline{B}_2\, \overline{A}_3\, \overline{B}_4\, A_5)$

$$= \frac{1}{6} + \frac{5}{6}\cdot\frac{2}{3}\cdot\frac{1}{2} + \frac{5}{6}\cdot\frac{2}{3}\cdot\frac{1}{2}\frac{1}{3}\cdot\frac{5}{6}$$

$$= \frac{1}{6} + \frac{5}{18} + \frac{25}{354} = \frac{54+90+90+25}{324} = \frac{169}{324}$$

and $P(B) = 1 - P(A) = \frac{324-169}{324} = \frac{155}{324}$

A's expected win $= XP(A) = \frac{169}{324} \times 3240 = 1690$

B's expected win $= X\,P(B) = 3240 \times \frac{155}{32400} = 1550.$

EXERCISE 12

1. A box contains 6 tickets. two of the tickets carry a prize of ₹ 5 each, the other four prizes are ₹ 1. (*a*) If one ticket is drawn what is the expected value of the prize ? (*b*) If two tickets are drawn, what is the expected value of the prize ?

   $\left[\textbf{Ans.}\ \frac{7}{3}, \frac{14}{3}\right]$

2. A player tosses a fair die. If a prime number occurs the wins that number of rupees, but if a non-prime number occurs he losses that number of rupees. Determine whether the game is favourable or unfavourable to the player.

[**Ans.** $E(X) = -1/_6$]

3. A player tosses 3 fair coins. He wins ₹ 5 if 3 heads appear, ₹ 3 if 2 heads appear, ₹ 1 if 1 head occurs. On the other hand, he losses ₹ 15 if 3 tails occur. Find the expected gain of the player.

$\left[\textbf{Ans. } \frac{1}{4}\right]$

4. Define mathematical expectation. For the following probability distribution, calculate the mean and the variance of the random variable x.

x	8	12	16	20	24
$p(x)$	$\frac{1}{8}$	$\frac{1}{6}$	$\frac{3}{8}$	$\frac{1}{4}$	$\frac{1}{12}$

[**Ans.** $E(X) = 16$; Var $(X) = 20$.]

5. The probability distribution of a random variable X is given in the adjoining table.

x	–2	3	1
$p(x)$	$\frac{1}{3}$	$\frac{1}{2}$	$\frac{1}{6}$

Find (*i*) $E(2X + 5)$ and (*ii*) $E(X^2)$

[**Ans.** $E(X) = 1$; $E(2X + 5) = 7$; $E(X^2) = 6$.]

6. When two unbiased coins are tossed once, the variance of the number of heads is

(*i*) 1, (*ii*) $\frac{3}{2}$, (*iii*) $\frac{1}{4}$, (*iv*) none of these.

[**Ans.** Var $(X) = \frac{1}{2}$; (*iv*) is the correct answer.]

7. Three coins whose faces are marked 1 and 2 are tossed. what the expectation of the total of numbers on their faces.

[**Hint.** Let $H = 1$, $T = 2$ and $S = \{HHH, HTH, THH, HHT, TTH, THT, HTT, TTT\}$]

$\left[\textbf{Ans. } \frac{9}{2}\right]$

8. If it rains an umbrella sales man earns ₹ 300 per day. and on a fair day he loses ₹ 80 per day. What are his expected earnings if probability of rain is

[**Ans.** 148]

9. Obtain the probability distribution of 'number of sixes' in two tosses of a die. Hence obtain its mean and variance.

Ans.

x	0	1	2
$p(x)$	$\frac{25}{36}$	$\frac{10}{36}$	$\frac{1}{36}$

Mean $= \frac{1}{3}$, Variance $= \frac{5}{18}$

10. If the random variable X assumes only two values 0 and 1, with $P(X = 0) = 3\,P(X = 1)$, then find variance of X.

$\left[\textbf{Ans. } \frac{3}{16}\right]$

11. A die is tossed twice. 'Getting a number less than 3' is termed as success. Obtain the probability distribution and hence the mean and variance of the number of successes.

[**Ans.** Mean = 2/3, Variance = 4/9]

12. The monthly demand for transistors is known to have the following probability distribution :

Demand	(n) :	1	2	3	4	5	6
Probability	(p) :	0.10	0.15	0.20	0.25	0.18	0.12

Determine the expected demand for transistors. Also obtain the variance. Suppose that the cost (C) of producing 'n' transistors is given by the rule, $C = 10{,}000 + 500\,n$. Determine the expected cost.

[**Hint.** Expected demand for transistors is : $E(n) = \Sigma n \times p$.

$E(C) = E[10{,}000 + 500n] = 10{,}000 + 500\,E(n) = 10{,}000 + 500 \times 3.62 = 11.810$].

[**Ans.** $E(n) = 3.62$, $V(n) = 2.22$, $E(c) = 11{,}810$].

□□□

13

Theoretical Distributions : Binomial, Poisson and Normal

CHAPTER OUTLINE

- Theoretical Distributions
- Binomial, Poisson and Numal
- Their Constants, Mean, Variance, Skewness, Kurtosis
- Fitting of Binomial & Poisson
- Applications of the distributions.

13.1 INTRODUCTION

In previous two chapters we have found out probability distributions of certain random variables which were defined differently. $P(X)$ was found out using concept of probability and its theorems. The function $P(X)$ is known as probability mass function. There are some experiments which have certain characteristics, we come across more often and $P(X)$, the probability mass function is obtained using some mathematical function specific to a given characteristic. Such probability distributions are known as "Theoretical Distribution".

In this chapter we take up three univariate probability distribution very commonly used.

(*i*)	Binomial Distribution	(B.D.)
(*ii*)	Poisson Distribution	(P.D.)
(*iii*)	Normal Distribution	(N.D.)

This first two distributions are discrete and third is continuous variable.

13.2 BINOMIAL DISTRIBUTION (B.D)

This distribution is also known as "Bernoulli Distribution" after the name of person, Swiss mathematician James Bernoulli who discovered it in 1700.

SUCCESS AND FAILURE (S AND F).

Occurrence of an event is called "Success" and non occurrence of it is called "Failure".

For example a coin is tossed, getting head is defined success and its non occurrence *i.e.,* getting head is failure. Similarly a die is tossed, let success be getting multiple of 3 *i.e.,* getting 3 or 6 is success $S = \{3, 6\}$ and failure $F = \{1, 2, 4, 5\}$. Thus outcomes of any experiment can be divided into two mutually exclusive and exhaustive events success and failure. We will use p for P(Success) and q for P (Failure) so that $p + q = 1$ (always).

13.3 CONDITIONS NECESSARY FOR A BINOMIAL EXPERIMENT (ASSUMPTIONS IN BINOMIAL EXPERIMENTS)

A process in which each trial (experiment) can result only one of the two states is called *Binomial Process or Bernoulli Process. In a true Binomial Process* the following conditions have to be satisfied :

(*i*) Each trial has only two possible outcomes called *success* and *failure*.

(*ii*) There is a finite number of trials say n in an experiment *e.g.,* if a coin tossed 5 times the experiment consists of 5 trials.

(*iii*) All trials are identical, *i.e.,* the probability of success in each trial is same.

(*iv*) The trials are independent of each other. Independent means that trials do not follow any fixed pattern. The outcome of a particular trial does not affect the outcome of any other trial.

13.4 PARAMETERS OF BINOMIAL DISTRIBUTION

There are only two parameters required to define a Binomial distribution :

(*i*) Number of trials, *i.e.,* n.

(*ii*) Probability of success in each trial, *i.e.,* p which remains constant from trial to trial (Since in Binomial experiment success and failure are mutually exclusive and exhaustive, the probability of success + probability of failure = 1, *i.e.,* if the probability of success is p the probability of failure $= 1 - p = q$ which remains constant from trial to trial).

(*iii*) A binomial probability distribution with parameters n and p is written as $B\,(n, p)$ *i.e.,* $B\,(10, .4)$.

13.5 MATHEMATICAL FORM OF B.D.

Since experiment consists of n trials and each trial results in success (S in short) or failure (F in short). The outcome of an experiment will be sequence of S and F say $S_1F_2S_3S_4F_5$ .... which have certain no. of successes (say r) and $(n - r)$ numbers of F

(where S_3 means getting success in 3rd trial). We say that there are r successes in trials which implies that their are $(n - r)$ failures. Let X be the no. of success in n trials and X will have any value from 0 to n. In this case

$\boxed{P(X = r) = {}^nC_r\, p^r\, q^{n-r}}$ which is known as probability function of "Binomial Distribution".

Proof. Let a particular sequence of r successes and $(n - r)$ failures be as follows.

$$S_1\, S_2\, F_3\, F_4 \ldots\ldots\ldots\ldots S_{n-1}\, F_n \text{ and}$$

$P(S_1\, S_2\, F_3\, F_4 \ldots\ldots\ldots\ldots) = P(S_1)\, P(S_2) \ldots\ldots\ldots P(F_n)$

$= p\, pq \ldots q = p^r\, q^{n-r}$ [there are r p's and $(n - r)q$'s in the product].

Now no. of sequences which has r p's and $(n - r)$ q's are obtained in $\dfrac{n!}{r!\,(n-r)!} = nc_r$ ways and each with probability $p^r\, q^{n-r}$

Therefore $P(X = r) = {}^nC_r\, p^r\, q^{n-r}$

Putting different values for r *i.e.,* 0, 1, 2, ..., n we get the following probability distribution.

13.5.1. Binomial Probability Distribution

Number of successes	*P(X)*
0	${}^nC_0\, p^0\, q^{n-0} = q^n$ $[{}^nC_0 = 1, p^0 = 1]$
1	${}^nC_1\, p^1\, q^{n-1} = np\, q^{n-1}$
2	${}^nC_2\, p^2\, q^{n-2} = \dfrac{n(n-1)}{2} p^2\, q^{n-2}$
3	${}^nC_3\, p^3\, q^{n-3} = \dfrac{n(n-1)(n-2)}{6} p^3\, q^{n-3}$
⋮	⋮
n	${}^nC_n\, p^n\, q^{n-n} = p^n$ $[{}^nC_n = 1]$

13.5.2 Why it is called Binomial Distribution

We know from "Binomial Theorem" that

$(q + p)^n = q^n + {}^nC_1\, q^{n-1}\, p + {}^nC_2\, q^{n-2}\, p^2 + \ldots\ldots\ldots + p^n$ ...(1)

Now from "Binomial Distribution"

We know

$$P(X = 0) = q^n$$
$$P(X = 1) = {}^nC_1\, q^{\,n-1} p$$
$$P(X = 2) = {}^nC_2\, q^{n-2}\, p^2$$
$$\vdots \qquad \vdots$$
$$P(X = n) = p^n$$

Thus we know various terms of binomial expansion represent the various terms of binomial probability distribution.

13.6 CONSTANTS OF BINOMIAL DISTRIBUTION

The following results are obtained from the above probability distribution and which is given below (without proof).

1. Mean = np = Number of trial × Probability of success in each trial = $\Sigma X\, P(X)$
2. Standard Deviation = $\sqrt{npq} = \sqrt{(np)q} = \sqrt{(\text{mean})q}$ = Square root of the product of mean and the probability of failure in each trial
3. Variance = $npq = \sigma^2 = E(X^2) - [E(X)]^2 = \mu_2$
4. Skewness = $\dfrac{q-p}{\sqrt{npq}} = \gamma_1 = \dfrac{\mu_3}{\mu_2^{3/2}}$
5. Kurtosis = $\dfrac{1-6pq}{npq} = \gamma_2$ (Gamma two) = $\dfrac{\mu_4}{\mu_2} = 3$

Example 1. *Suppose that historical sales records indicate that 40 per cent of all customers who enter a discount department store make a purchase. What is the probability that two of the next three customers will make a purchase ?*

Solution. In order to find this probability, we first note that the experiment of observing three customers making a purchase decision has several distinguishing characteristics :

(*i*) The experiment consists of three identical *trials;* each trial consists of a customer of a customer making a purchase decision here $n = 3$.

(*ii*) Two outcomes are possible on each trial : the customer makes a purchase (which we call a *success* and denote as S), or the customer does not make a purchase (which we call a *failure* and denote as F). Thus $p = .4$ and $q = .6$

Using *B.D.* we get

$$P(X=2) = {}^nC_r\, p^r\, q^{n-r} = {}^3C_2\, (.4)^2\, (.6)$$
$$= 3\,(.16)(.6) = 0.288.$$

Example 2. *An unbiased die is tossed three times. Find the probability of obtaining (a) no six, (b) one six, (c) at least one six, (d) two sixes and (e) three sixes.*

Solution. The three tosses of a die can be taken as three repeated trials which are independent. Let the occurrence of six be termed as a success. Therefore, r will denote the number of six obtained. Further, $n = 3$ and $p = \dfrac{1}{6}$.

(*a*) Probability of obtaining no six, *i.e.*,

$$P(r=0) = {}^3C_0\, p^0 q^3 = 1.\left(\frac{1}{6}\right)^0 \left(\frac{5}{6}\right)^3 = \frac{125}{216}$$

(*b*) $P(r=1) = {}^3C_1 p^1 q^2 = 3.\left(\dfrac{1}{6}\right)\left(\dfrac{5}{6}\right)^2 = \dfrac{25}{72}$

(*c*) Probability of getting at least one six $= 1 - P(r=0) = 1 - \dfrac{125}{216} = \dfrac{91}{216}$

(*d*) $P(r = 2) = {}^3C_2 p^2 q^1 = 3.\left(\frac{1}{6}\right)^2\left(\frac{5}{6}\right) = \frac{5}{72}$

(*e*) $P(r = 3) = {}^3C_3 p^3 q^0 = 3.\left(\frac{1}{6}\right)^3 = \frac{1}{216}$

Example 3. *Assuming that it is true that 2 in 10 industrial accident are due to fatigue, find the probability that:*

(*a*) *Exactly 2 of 8 industrial accident will be due to fatigue.*

(*b*) *At least 2 of the 8 industrial accidents will be due to fatigue.*

Solution. Eight industrial accidents can be regarded as Bernoulli trials each with probability of success $p = \frac{2}{10} = \frac{1}{5}$. The random variable r denotes the number of accidents due to fatigue.

(*a*) $P(r = 2) = {}^8C_2\left(\frac{1}{5}\right)^2\left(\frac{4}{5}\right)^6 = 0.294$

(*b*) We have to find $P(r \geq 2)$. We can write

$P(r \geq 2) = 1 - P(0) - P(1)$, thus, we first find $P(0)$ and $P(1)$.

we have $P(0) = {}^8C_0\left(\frac{1}{5}\right)^0\left(\frac{4}{5}\right)^8 = 0.168$

and $P(1) = {}^8C_1\left(\frac{1}{5}\right)^1\left(\frac{4}{5}\right)^7 = 0.336$

$\therefore \quad P(r \geq 2) = 1 - 0.168 - 0.336 = 0.496.$

Example 4. *Four candidates A, B, C and D are contesting for an election. the probabilities that a voter will vote for A, B, C and D respectively are 0.3, 0.1, 0.2 and 0.4. What is the probability that out of 4 voters, three or more will vote for B ?*

Solution. Probability that a voter will vote for $B = 0.1$ = Probability of success for B.

Probability that a voter will not vote for $B = 1 - 0.1 = 0.9$ = Probability of B's failure.

Required Probability = Probability of three successes + Probability of four successes

$= {}^4c_3\, qp^3 + {}^4c_4\, p^4$

$= 4(0.9)(0.1)^3 + (0.1)^4 = 4 \times 0.9 \times 0.001 + 0.0001$

$= 4 \times 0.0009 + 0.0001 = 0.0036 + 0.0001 = 0.0037.$

Example 5. *If the probabilities of having a male or female child are both 0.50, find the probabilities that*

(*a*) *a family's fourth child is their first son;*

(*b*) *a family's seventh child is their second daughter;*

(*c*) *a family's tenth child is their fourth or fifth son.*

Solution. Let $p = P(\text{Male}) = \frac{1}{2}$, $q = P(\text{Female})$

(*a*) The required Probability is the probability that there is no son in the first three children × the Probability the fourth child is son = $qqqp = q^3p$

$$= \left(\frac{1}{2}\right)^3 \times \frac{1}{2} = \frac{1}{16}$$

(*b*) Required Probability = The Probability that there is only one daughter in the first six children and the seventh child is daughter.

$$= P\text{ (5 Males in first 6 children). } P\text{ (Female)}$$

$$= \left[{}^6c_5 \left(\frac{1}{2}\right)^5 \times \frac{1}{2}\right] \times \frac{1}{2} = 6 \times \frac{1}{128} = \frac{6}{128}$$

(*c*) P(family's tenth child is their 4th or 5th son)

$$= P\text{(tenth child is 4th son)} + P\text{(tenth child is 5th son).}$$

$$= P\text{(there are 3 sons in first 9 children). } P\text{(4th son)}$$

$$+ P\text{(there are 4 sons in first 9 children). } P\text{(5th son)}$$

$$= {}^9c_3 \left(\frac{1}{2}\right)^6 \times \left(\frac{1}{2}\right)^3 \times \frac{1}{2} + {}^9c_4 \left(\frac{1}{2}\right)^5 \times \left(\frac{1}{2}\right)^4 \times \frac{1}{2}$$

$$= \frac{9 \times 8 \times 7}{6} \times \frac{1}{1024} + \frac{9 \times 8 \times 7 \times 6}{24} \times \frac{1}{1024}$$

$$= \left[\frac{84}{1024} + \frac{126}{1024}\right] = \frac{210}{1024} = 0.205.$$

Example 6. *A post-graduate student in commerce is trying to decide on the number of firms to which he should apply. Given his work experience and grades, he can expect to receive a job offer from 80% of the firms to which he applies. The student decides to apply to only four firms.*

(*i*) *What is the probability that he received no job offers ?*

(*ii*) *What is the probability that he received more than two offers ?* [DU M.Com. 2008]

Solution. Let p be the probability of receiving a job offer and $q = 1 - p$, the probability of not receiving a job offer, then $p = 0.8$, $q = 1 - 0.8 = 0.2$, $n = 4$.

(*i*) Required Probability $= {}^4c_0\, q^4 p^0 = {}^4c_0\, (0.2)^4 (0.8)^0 = 0.0016$

(*ii*) Required probability $= {}^4c_3\, q^{4-3}\, p^3 + {}^4c_4\, q^{4-4}\, p^4 = P$ (3 or 4 offers)

$$= 4 \times 0.2 \times (0.8)^3 + (0.2)^0 (0.8)^4 = 4 \times 0.1024 + 0.4096$$

$$= 0.4096 + 0.4096 = 0.8192$$

= Probability he received three offers or four offers.

Example 7. *Write down the binomial distribution whose mean is 16 and variance being 4.03.*

Solution. Mean $= np = 16$ ... (1)

Variance $= npq = 4.03$ ... (2)

where n = Number of trials, p = Probability of success in each trial, q = Probability of failure in each trial.

Dividing (2) by (1), we get

$$q = \frac{npq}{np} = \frac{4.03}{16} = \frac{403}{1600}$$

$$p = 1 - q = 1 - \frac{403}{1600} = \frac{1197}{1600}$$

$$n \times \frac{1197}{1600} = 16$$

$$\Rightarrow \qquad n = \frac{16 \times 1600}{1108} = 21.3868 = 21 \text{ (approx.)}$$

Example 8. *The proportion of male and female students in a class is found to be 1 : 2. What is the probability that out of 4 students selected at random with replacement, two or more will be females?*

Solution. Let the selection of a female student be termed as a success. Since the selection of a student is made with replacement, the selection of 4 students can be taken as 4 repeated trials each with probability of success $p = \frac{2}{3}$.

Thus, $$P(r \geq 2) = P(r = 2) + P(r = 3) + P(r = 4)$$

$$= {}^4C_2 \left(\frac{2}{3}\right)^2 \left(\frac{1}{3}\right)^2 + {}^4C_3 \left(\frac{2}{3}\right)^3 \left(\frac{1}{3}\right) + {}^4C_4 \left(\frac{2}{3}\right)^4 = \frac{8}{9}$$

[Note that $P(r \geq 2)$ can alternatively be found as $1 - P(0) - P(1)$.]

Example 9. *The probability of a bomb hitting a target is 1/5. Two bombs are enough to destroy a bridge. If six bombs are aimed at the bridge, find the probability that the bridge is destroyed.*

Solution. Here $n = 6$ and $p = \frac{1}{5}$

The bridge will be destroyed if at least two bomb hit it. Thus, we have to find $P(r \geq 2)$. This is given by

$$P(r \geq 2) = 1 - P(0) - P(1) = 1 - {}^6C_0 \left(\frac{4}{5}\right)^6 - {}^6C_1 \left(\frac{1}{5}\right)\left(\frac{4}{5}\right)^5 = \frac{1077}{3125}.$$

Example 10. *An insurance salesman sells policies to 5 men all of identical age and good health. According to the actuarial tables, the probability that a man of this particular age will be alive 30 years hence is 2/3. Find the probability that 30 years hence (i) at least 1 man will be alive, (ii) at least 3 men will be alive.*

Solution. Let the event that a man will be alive 30 years hence be termed as a success. Therefore, $n = 5$ and $p = \frac{2}{3}$.

(*i*) $$P(r \geq 1) = 1 - P(r = 0) = 1 - {}^5C_0 \left(\frac{2}{3}\right)^0 \left(\frac{1}{3}\right)^5 = \frac{242}{243}$$

(*ii*) $$P(r \geq 3) = P(r = 3) + P(r = 4) + P(r = 5)$$

$$= {}^5C_3 \left(\frac{2}{3}\right)^3 \left(\frac{1}{3}\right)^2 + {}^5C_4 \left(\frac{2}{3}\right)^4 \left(\frac{1}{3}\right) + {}^5C_5 \left(\frac{2}{3}\right)^5 = \frac{64}{81}.$$

Example 11. *Multiple choice test consists of eight questions and three answers to each question (of which only one is correct). If a student answers each question by rolling a balanced die and marking the first answer if he gets 1 or 2, the second answer if he gets 3 or 4 and the third answer if he gets 5 or 6, what is the probability that he will get exactly four correct answers ?*

Solution. Probability that the students marks first answer $= \frac{1}{3}$

Probability that the student marks second answer $= \frac{1}{3}$

Probability that the student marks third answer $= \frac{1}{3}$

Since there is equal probability of marking first, second or third answer, we can presume that the marking made by the student is random. Therefore the probability of any marking being correct $= \frac{1}{3}$

The Probability of success $= \frac{1}{3}$

The Probability of failure $= \frac{2}{3}$

Probability of getting exactly four correct answers $= {}^8c_4 \left(\frac{1}{3}\right)^4 \left(\frac{2}{3}\right)^4$

$$= \frac{8!}{(4!)(4!)} \left[\frac{1}{81} \times \frac{16}{81}\right]$$

$$= \frac{8 \times 7 \times 6 \times 5}{4 \times 3 \times 2 \times 1} \times \frac{16}{81 \times 81} = \frac{70 \times 16}{81 \times 81} = \frac{1120}{6561}.$$

Example 12. *In a Binomial distribution with 6 independent trials, the probabilities of 3 and 4 successes are found to be 0.2457 and 0.0819 respectively. Find the parameters 'p' and 'q' of the Binomial distribution.*

Solution. $P(X = 3) = {}^6C_3\, p^3q^3 = 20\, p^3\, q^3 = 0.\,2457$ ...(1)

$P(X = 4) = {}^6C_4\, p^4q^2 = 15p^4q^2 = .0819$ ...(2)

(1) ÷ (2) we get $\frac{20\, p^3q^3}{15\, p^4q^2} = \frac{0.2457}{0.0819}$

$\Rightarrow \frac{4\, q}{3\, p} = 3 \Rightarrow$

$4q = 9p = 9\,(1 - q) \Rightarrow q = \frac{9}{13} \Rightarrow p = \frac{4}{13}$

Example 13. *The output of a production process is 10 per cent defective. What is the probability of getting exactly two defectives in a sample of five ?*

Solution. Probability that the output is defective = 0.1

Probability that the output is good = 0.9

Required Probability $= {}^5c_2\,(0.9)^3(0.1)^2$

$$= \frac{5!}{(2!)(3!)} \times 0.729 \times 0.01 = 7{\cdot}29 \times 0.01 = 0.0729.$$

Example 14. *The telephone company reports that among 5000 telephones installed in a new subdivision 4000 have push buttons. If 10 people are called at random, what is the probability that exactly 3 will be talking on dial telephones ?*

Solution. Probability that a telephone has a push button $= \dfrac{4000}{5000} = 0.8$

Probability that a telephone is a dial telephone (*i.e.*, Telephone without push button) = 0.2

$$\text{Required Probability} = {}^{10}c_3 (0.8)^7 (0.2)^3$$

$$= \frac{10!}{(7!)(3!)}(0.2097)(0.008) = \frac{10 \times 9 \times 8}{6} \times 0.2097 \times 0.008 = 0.2013.$$

Example 15. *One-fourth of the female freshmen entering a Virginia College are out-of-state students. If the students are assigned at random to the dormitories, 3 to a room, what is the probability that in one room at most 2 of the 3 room-mates are out-of-state students ?*

Solution. Probability that a freshman is out-of-state student $= \dfrac{1}{4} = p$

Probability that a student is not out-of -state student $= 1 - \dfrac{1}{4} = \dfrac{3}{4}$

$$\text{Required Probability} = 1 - {}^3c_3 p^{3*}$$

$$= 1 - {}^3c_3 \left(\frac{1}{4}\right)^3 = 1 - \frac{1}{64} = \frac{63}{64}.$$

Alternative Method

$$\text{Required Probability} = P(x = 0) + P(x = 1) + P(x = 2)$$

$$= {}^3c_0 q^3 + {}^3c_1 pq^2 + {}^3c_2 p^2 q^1$$

$$= \left(\frac{3}{4}\right)^3 + 3\left(\frac{1}{4}\right) \times \left(\frac{3}{4}\right)^2 + 3\left(\frac{1}{4}\right)^2 \times \frac{3}{4} = \frac{27}{64} + \frac{27}{64} + \frac{9}{64} = \frac{63}{64}.$$

Example 16. *How many tosses of a coin are needed so that the probability of getting at least one head is 87.5%.*

Solution. Probability of getting a head $= p = \dfrac{1}{2}$

Probability of getting a tail $= q = \dfrac{1}{2}$

$$P(r) = {}^nC_r q^{n-r} p^r$$

$$P(r \geq 1) = 1 - P(r = 0)$$

$$P(r = 0) = {}^nC_0 (q)^n (p)^0$$

$$= q^n = \left(\frac{1}{2}\right)^n$$

$$P(r \geq 1) = 87.5\% = 0.875$$

$$0.875 = 1 - \left(\frac{1}{2}\right)^n$$

$$0.875 = 1 - (.5)^n$$

$$(.5)^n = 1 - 0.875 = 0.125$$
$$(.5)^n = .5 \times .5 \times .5$$
$$(.5)^n = (.5)^3$$
$$n = 3$$

Hence 3 tosses of a coin are needed to have probability of at least one head equal to 87.5%.

Example 17. *A machine produces on an average 20% defective bolts. A batch is accepted if a sample of 5 bolts taken from that batch contains no defective and rejected if the sample contains 3 or more defectives. In other cases, a second sample is taken. What is the probability that the second sample is required ?*

Solution. Probability of defective bolt $= p = 20\% = \frac{1}{5}$

Probability of non-defective bolt $= q = \frac{4}{5}$

$$n = 5$$

Second sample is taken only when number of defective bolts is either 1 or 2.

Thus, probability of second sample taken $= P(r = 1) + P(r = 2)$

$$= {}^5C_1 \left(\frac{4}{5}\right)^4 \left(\frac{1}{5}\right) + {}^5C_2 \left(\frac{4}{5}\right)^3 \left(\frac{1}{5}\right)^2$$

$$= \frac{5 \times 256}{3125} + \frac{10 \times 64}{3125} = \frac{1280 + 640}{3125}$$

$$= \frac{1920}{3125} = 0.6144.$$

12.7. Fitting of Binomial Distribution. Suppose a random experiment consists of n trials, satisfying the conditions of Binomial distribution and suppose this experiment is repeated N-times. Then the frequency of r successes is given by the formula.

$$N \times p(r) = N \times {}^nC_r\, p^r q^{n-r}\ ;\ r = 0, 1, 2, \ldots, n.$$

We may say that this is expected frequency of r-successes in N trials.

Putting $r = 0, 1, 2, \ldots, n$ we get the expected or theoretical frequencies of the Binomial distribution, which are given in the table.

No. of Successes (r)	*Expected or Theoretical Frequencies N. p(r)*
0	$N \cdot q^n$
1	$N \cdot {}^nC_1 q^{n-1} p$
2	$N\, {}^nC_2\, q^{n-2} p^2$
$\vdots$	$\vdots$
n	$N \cdot p^n$

If p, the probability of success which is constant for each trial, is known, then the expected frequencies can be obtained easily as given in the table. However, if p is not known and if we want to fit a binomial distribution to a given frequency distribution, we first find the mean of the given frequency distribution by the formula $\bar{x} = \Sigma fx / \Sigma f$ and equate it to np, which is the mean of the binomial probability distribution, Hence, p can be estimated by the relation

$$np = \bar{x} \quad \Rightarrow \quad p = \frac{\bar{x}}{n}$$

Then $q = 1 - p$. With these values of p and q, the expected or theoretical Binomial frequencies can be obtained by using the formulae as given in the table.

Example 18. *(a) 8 coins are tossed at a time, 256 times. Find the expected frequencies of successes (getting a head) and tabulate the results obtained.*

(b) Also obtain the value of the mean and standard deviation of the theoretical (fitted) distribution.

Solution. In the usual notations, we are given : $n = 8, N = 256.$

$$p = \text{Probability of success (head) in a single throw of a coin} = \frac{1}{2}$$

$$\therefore \quad q = 1 - p = \frac{1}{2}$$

Hence, by the Binomial probability law, the probability of r successes in a toss of 8 coins is given by :

$$p(r) = {}^nC_r p^r q^{n-r} = {}^8C_r \left(\frac{1}{2}\right)^r \left(\frac{1}{2}\right)^{8-r}$$

$$= {}^8C_r \left(\frac{1}{2}\right)^8 = \frac{1}{256}\,{}^8C_r \quad \ldots(*)$$

Hence, in 256 throws of 8 coins, the frequency of r successes is :

$$f(r) = N.\,p(r) = 256 \times \frac{1}{256}\,{}^8C_r = {}^8C_r;\ r = 0, 1, \ldots, 8.$$

EXPECTED BINOMIAL FREQUENCIES

No. of heads	*Expected Frequencies*
0	${}^8C_0 = 1$
1	${}^8C_1 = 8$
2	${}^8C_2 = 28$
3	${}^8C_3 = 56$
4	${}^8C_4 = 70$
5	${}^8C_5 = 56$
6	${}^8C_6 = 28$
7	${}^8C_7 = 8$
8	${}^8C_8 = 1$

Thus, the expected (theoretical) frequencies are obtained as shown.

(*b*) For the theoretical distribution (Binomial distribution),

$$\text{Mean} = np = 8 \times \frac{1}{2} = 4 \quad ; \quad s.d. = \sqrt{npq} = \sqrt{8 \times \frac{1}{2} \times \frac{1}{2}} = \sqrt{2} = 1.4142$$

Example 19. *Out of 320 families with 5 children each, what percentage would be expected in have (i) 2 boys and 3 girls, (ii) at least one boy ? Assume equal probability for boys and girls.*

Solution. Probability of a boy $= p = \frac{1}{2}$

Probability of a girl $= q = \frac{1}{2}$

(we need out of 5 children), $n = 5$

(*i*) Probability of 2 boys and 3 girls in a family of 5.

$$r = 2, n - r = 5 - 2 = 3$$

$$p(r) = {}^nc_r q^{n-r} p^r$$

$$p(r = 2) = {}^5C_2 \left(\frac{1}{2}\right)^3 \left(\frac{1}{2}\right)^2 = \frac{10}{32}$$

Expected number of families with 2 boys and 3 girls: (out of 320 families)

$$N[P\,(r)] = 320 \times \frac{10}{32} = 100$$

Percentage of families expected to have 2 boys and 3 girls = $\frac{10}{32} \times 100 = 31.25\%$

(*ii*) Probability of at least one boy = 1 – probability of no boy.

$$P(r = 0) = {}^5C_0 \left(\frac{1}{2}\right)^5 \left(\frac{1}{2}\right)^0 = \frac{1}{32}$$

$$P(r \geq 1) = 1 - \frac{1}{32} = \frac{31}{32}$$

Percentage of families expected to have a least one boy = $\frac{31}{32} \times 100 = 96.875\%$

Expected number of families with at least one boy:

$$= 320 \times \frac{31}{32} = 310.$$

Example 20. *In a binomial distribution consisting of 5 independent trials, probabilities of 1 and 2 successes are 0.4096 and 0.2048. Find the parameter 'p' of the distribution.*

Solution. $n = 5$, $P(r = 1) = 0.4096$, $P(r = 2) = 0.2048$

$$P(r) = {}^nC_r\, q^{n-r}\, P^r$$

$$P(r = 1) = {}^5C_1\, q^4 p = 5q^4 p$$

$$P(r = 2) = {}^5C_2\, q^3 p^2 = 10q^3 p^2$$

$$\frac{P(r = 2)}{P(r = 1)} = \frac{10q^2p^2}{5q^4p} = \frac{0.2048}{0.4096} \quad \text{(given)}$$

$$\Rightarrow \quad \frac{2p}{q} = \frac{0.2048}{0.4096}$$

$$\Rightarrow \quad \frac{2p}{q} = \frac{1}{2}$$

$$\Rightarrow \quad 4p = q$$

$$\Rightarrow \quad 4p = 1 - p$$

$$\Rightarrow \quad 5p = 1$$

$$\Rightarrow \quad p = \frac{1}{5}.$$

Example 21. *Six dice are thrown 729 times. How many times do you expect 3 dice to show 5 or 6.*

Solution. Six dice are thrown ⇒ $n = 6$.

A die has to show 5 or 6 (= success)

$$p = \frac{2}{6} = \frac{1}{3},\ q = \frac{2}{3}$$

Now 6 dice thrown should show 3 successes

$$P(X = 3) = {}^6C_3\, p^3 q^3 = 20 \left(\frac{1}{3}\right)^3 \left(\frac{2}{3}\right)^3 = \frac{160}{729}$$

If this experiment is repeated 729 times we expect 3 success = $\frac{160}{729} \cdot 729 = 160$ times.

Example 22. *Bring out the fallacy, if any, in the following statement :*

(*a*) *The mean of a binomial distribution is 15 and its standard deviation 5.*

(*b*) *Find the binomial distribution whose mean is 6 and variance 4.*

Solution. (*a*) Mean of binomial distribution is np and standard deviation $\sqrt{npq}$.

Given $np = 15$ and $\sqrt{npq} = 5$

Since $\sqrt{npq} = 5, npq = 25$

$$q = \frac{npq}{np} = \frac{25}{15} = 1.67$$

Since q is $P(F)$ which cannot exceed 1. But in this question q is greater than 1, *i.e.*, 1.67 which is not possible. The statement is, therefore, wrong.

(*b*) We are given :

$$np = 6 \qquad \ldots(i)$$

$$npq = 4 \qquad \ldots(ii)$$

Dividing (*ii*) by (*i*), we have

$$q = \frac{4}{6} = \frac{2}{3} \text{ and } p = 1 - \frac{2}{3} = \frac{1}{3}$$

Substituting the value of p in (*i*)

$$n\frac{1}{3} = 6$$

$$\Rightarrow \qquad n = 6 \times 3 = 18$$

Hence the required binomial distribution is

$$(q+p)^n = \left(\frac{2}{3} + \frac{1}{3}\right)^{18}. \quad \text{or} \quad X \text{ is a } B\left(18, \frac{1}{3}\right)$$

Example 23. *If the probability of a defective bolt is 0.1 find (a) the mean, and (b) the standard deviation of defective bolts in a total of 900. Also calculate skewness and kurtosis.*

Solution.

(*a*) Mean = np = 900 (0.1) = 90, *i.e.*, we can expect 90 bolts to be defective

(*b*) Variance = npq = 900 (0.1) (0.9) = 81

Hence the standard deviation = $\sqrt{81} = 9$

$$\text{Skewness} = \frac{q-p}{\sqrt{npq}} = \frac{0.9 - 0.1}{9} = .089$$

$$\text{Kurtosis} = \frac{1 - 6pq}{npq} = \frac{1 - 6(0.1)(0.9)}{81} = 0.006 = .006$$

The distribution is slightly *Leptokurtic*.

Example 24. *The probability that an evening college student will be graduate is 0.4. Determine the probability that out of 5 students (a) none, (b) one, and (c) at least one will be graduate.*

Solution. Here $p = 0.4$, $q = 0.6$. Applying the Binomial distribution

$$p(r) = {}^nc_r q^{n-r} p^r$$

(*a*) Probability that none will graduate

$= {}^5C_0\,(0.6)^5\,(0.4)^0$

$= 0.0777$ or 0.08

(*b*) Probability that one will be graduate

$= {}^5C_1\,(0.6)^4\,(0.4)^1$

$= 0.2590$ or 0.26.

(*c*) Probability that at least one will be graduate = 1 – (probability that none will be graduate)

$= 1 - 0.0.08 = 0.92$.

Example 25. *If on an average 9 ships out of 10 arrive safely to ports, find the mean and standard deviation of ships returning safely out of a total of 500 ships.*

Solution. Probability of safe arrival or $p = \frac{9}{10} = 0.9$

$\therefore \quad q = 1 - p = 1 - 0.9 = 0.1$

Mean number of ships returning safely is given by

$m = np = 500 \times 0.9 = 450$

Standard deviation will be given by :

$\sqrt{npq} = \sqrt{500 \times .9 \times .1} = 6.71$

Hence the mean and standard deviation of ships returning safely is respectively 450 and 6.71.

Example 26. *The mean and variance of a binomial distribution are 3 and 2, respectively. Find the probability that the variate takes values (i) less than or equal to 2, (ii) greater than or equal to 7.*

Solution. If n and p are the parameters of the binomial distribution, then, we are given :

Mean $= np = 3$ ...(*i*) and Variance $= npq = 2$ ... (*ii*)

Dividing (*ii*) by (*i*), we get

$$\frac{npq}{np} = \frac{2}{3} \quad \Rightarrow \quad q = \frac{2}{3} \quad \Rightarrow \quad p = 1 - q = 1 - \frac{2}{3} = \frac{1}{3}$$

Substituting in (*i*), we get $n \times \frac{1}{3} = 3 \quad \Rightarrow \quad n = 3 \times 3 = 9$

Let X be $B\,(n, p)$ variate where $n = 9$ and $p = \frac{1}{3},\, q = \frac{2}{3}$

$$\therefore \quad P(X = r) = {}^nC_r\, p^r\, q^{n-r} = {}^9C_r \left(\frac{1}{3}\right)^r \left(\frac{2}{3}\right)^{9-r} \quad ; r = 0, 1, 2, \ldots, 9 \qquad \text{...(iii)}$$

(*i*) the probability that the variable takes the value less than or equal to 2 is given by :

$$P(X \le 2) = P(X = 0) + P(X = 1) + P(X = 2)$$

$$= {}^9C_0 \left(\frac{2}{3}\right)^9 + {}^9C_1 \left(\frac{1}{3}\right)\left(\frac{2}{3}\right)^8 + {}^9C_2 \left(\frac{1}{3}\right)^2 \left(\frac{2}{3}\right)^7 \qquad \text{[From (iii)]}$$

$$= \left(\frac{2}{3}\right)^7 \left[\left(\frac{2}{3}\right)^2 + 9 \times \frac{1}{3} \cdot \frac{2}{3} + \frac{9 \times 8}{2!} \cdot \left(\frac{1}{3}\right)^2\right]$$

$$= \left(\frac{2}{3}\right)^7 \left[\frac{4}{9} + 2 + 4\right] = \frac{58}{9} \times \left(\frac{2}{3}\right)^7$$

(*ii*) Required probability is :

$$P(X \geq 7) = P(X = 7) + P(X = 8) + P(X = 9)$$

$$= {}^9C_7 \left(\frac{1}{3}\right)^7 \left(\frac{2}{3}\right)^2 + {}^9C_8 \left(\frac{1}{3}\right)^8 \left(\frac{2}{3}\right) + {}^9C_9 \left(\frac{1}{3}\right)^9$$

$$= \left(\frac{1}{3}\right)^7 \left[\frac{9 \times 8}{2!}\left(\frac{2}{3}\right)^2 + 9 \times \frac{1}{3} \cdot \frac{2}{3} + 1. \left(\frac{1}{3}\right)^2\right]$$

$$= \frac{1}{2187}\left[\frac{9 \times 8}{2} \times \frac{4}{9} + 2 + \frac{1}{9}\right] = \frac{1}{2187}\left(16 + 2 + \frac{1}{9}\right) = \frac{1}{2187} \times \frac{163}{9}$$

$$= \frac{163}{19683}.$$

Example 27. *If the probability of a defective bolt is 1/10, find (i) the mean ; (ii) variance ; (iii) moment coefficient of skewness; (iv) kurtosis, for the distribution of defective bolts in a total of 400.*

Solution. In the usual notations, we have : $n = 400, \quad p = \frac{1}{10} = 0.1, \quad q = 1 - p = 0.9$

According to Binomial probability law :

(*i*) Mean = $np = 400 \times 0.1 = 40$;

(*ii*) Variance = $npq = 400 \times 0.1 \times 0.9 = 36$.

(*iii*) The moment coefficient of skewness

$$\gamma_1 = \frac{q-p}{\sqrt{npq}} = \frac{0.9 - 0.1}{\sqrt{36}} = \frac{0.8}{6} = \frac{2}{15} = 0.134$$

(*iv*) Coefficient of kurtosis is given by :

$$\gamma_2 = \frac{1 - 6pq}{npq} = \frac{1 - 6 \times 0.1 \times 0.9}{36} = \frac{0.46}{36} = 0.013 = .013$$

Remark. Since $r_1 \neq 0$, the distribution is not symmetrical. But since it is nearly zero, it is moderately asymmetric and γ_2 is also nearly zero hence distribution is platykurtic.

Example 28. *A multiple choice test consists of 8 questions with 3 answers (of which only one is correct). A student answers each question by rolling a balanced die and checking the first answer if he gets 1 or 2, the second answer if he gets 3 or 4 and the third answer if he gets 5 or 6. To get a distinction, the student must secure a least 75% correct answers. If there is no negative marking, what is the probability that the student secures a distinction?*

Solution.

Probability of getting correct answer = $p = \frac{1}{3}$

Probability of getting incorrect answer = $q = 1 - \frac{1}{3} = \frac{2}{3}$

$n = 8$

The minimum number of questions a student is supposed to answer correctly to get at least 75% marks

$$= 8 \times 75\% = 8 \times \frac{3}{4} = 6 \text{ questions.}$$

Probability of getting at least 75% marks :

$$P(r = 6) + P(r = 7) + P(r = 8) = {}^8C_6\left(\frac{2}{3}\right)^2\left(\frac{1}{3}\right)^6 + {}^8C_7\left(\frac{2}{3}\right)\left(\frac{1}{3}\right)^7 + {}^8C_8\left(\frac{1}{3}\right)^8$$

$$= \frac{28\times 4}{6561} + \frac{8\times 2}{6561} + \frac{1}{6561} = \frac{112+16+1}{6561}$$

$$= \frac{129}{6561} = 0.0197.$$

Example 29. *For a binomial distribution, the mean = 5 and standard deviation = 2. Obtain the p.m.f. of the distribution. Hence find the probability of a non-zero value of this distribution.*

Hint. $np = 5, \sqrt{npq} = 2, npq = 4, \frac{npq}{np} = q = \frac{4}{5}, p = 1 - q = \frac{1}{5}$

$q = \frac{4}{5}, p = \frac{1}{5}, n = 25$

$$P(X) = \text{p.m.f.} = {}^{25}c_x\left(\frac{4}{5}\right)^{25-x}\left(\frac{1}{5}\right)^x$$

Probability of non-zero value $= [1 - P(X = 0)] = 1 - {}^{25}c_0\left(\frac{4}{5}\right)^{25} = 1 - \left(\frac{4}{5}\right)^{25}.$

Example 30. *A random variable X is binomially distributed with mean 4 and standard deviation $\sqrt{2.4}$. Find the probability that more than half the trials are successes.*

Solution. $np = 4, \sqrt{npq} = \sqrt{2.4}$

$$npq = 2.4 \Rightarrow q = \frac{2.4}{4} = 0.6, p = 1 - q = 1 - 0.6 = 0.4$$

$$np = 4 \Rightarrow n \times 0.4 = 4 \Rightarrow n = 10$$

More than half the trials are successes ⇒ successes are more than 5, *i.e.*, 6, 7, 8, 9 or 10

$$\text{Required probability} = \sum_{x=6}^{10} {}^{10}c_x\, q^{10-x} p^x$$

$$= {}^{10}c_6 (0.6)^4 (0.4)^6 + {}^{10}c_7 (0.6)^3 (0.4)^7 + {}^{10}c_8 (0.6)^2 (0.4)^8 + {}^{10}c_9 (0.6)(0.4)^9 + {}^{10}c_{10} (0.4)^{10}.$$

Example 31. *It is observed that 80% of television viewers watch 'Balika Vadhu' programme. What is probability that at least 80% of the viewers in a random sample of five watch this programme ?*

Solution. If viewing the programme is a success then

$p = \frac{80}{100} = 0.8, q = 1 - 0.8 = 0.2$

80% of 5 = 4. Therefore we are to find the probability that 4 or 5 viewers watch the programme.

$$\text{Required Probability} = {}^5c_4 (0.2)^{(5-4)} (0.8)^4 + {}^5c_5 (0.8)^5$$

$$= 5 \times 0.2 \times (0.8)^4 + (0.8)^5$$

$$= (0.8)^4 (1 + 0.8) = 0.4096 \times 1.8 = 0.73728.$$

Example 32. *The probability that a bulb will fail before 100 hours is 0.2. Bulbs fail independently. If 15 bulbs are tested for life lengths. What is the probability that the number of failures before 100 hours does not exceed 1 ?*

Hint. $p = 0.2, q = 1 - 0.2 = 0.8$

Required Probability = $P(0) + P(1) = {}^{15}c_0 (0.8)^{15} + {}^{15}c_1 (0.8)^{14} (0.2)$.

Example 33. *The incidence of occupational disease in an industry is such that the workers have a 20% chance of suffering from it. What is the probability that out of six workers*

(*a*) *4 or more will contract disease ?*

(*b*) *2 or more will contract disease ?*

Solution. Probability that a worker suffers from the disease = 0.2 = Probability of success

Probability that a worker does not contract the disease = 1 – 0.2 = 0.8

(*a*) Required Probability $= {}^6c_4 (0.8)^2(0.2)^4 + {}^6c_5 (0.8)(0.2)^5 + {}^6c_6 (0.2)^6 = P(X = 4) + P(X = 5) + P(X = 6)$

$$= 15 \times 0.64 \times 0.0016 + 6 \times 0.8 \times 0.00032 + 0.000064$$

$$= 0.01536 + 0.001536 + 0.000064 = 0.01696.$$

$$P(2 \text{ or more}) = 1 - P(0) - P(1)$$

$$= 1 - (0.8)^6 - {}^6c_1 (0.8)^5 \times 0.2 = 1 - 0.262144 - 0.393216 = 0.344964.$$

EXERCISE 13.1

1. If the probability of male birth is 0.5, then the probability that in a family of 4 children there will be at least 1 boy, is

   (*i*) $\frac{4}{16}$, (*ii*) $\frac{4}{16}$, (*iii*) $\frac{11}{16}$, (*iv*) $\frac{15}{16}$.

   [**Ans.** (*iv*).]

2. From the past experience a stock broker finds that 70% of the telephone calls he receives during the business hours, are orders and the remaining are for other business. What is the probability that out of first 8 telephone calls during a day —

   (*i*) exactly 5 calls are order calls ?

   (*ii*) at least 6 are order calls ?

   [**Ans.** (*i*) 0.2542 (*ii*) 0.5515.]

3. An oil exploration firm finds that 5% of the test wells it drill, yield a deposit of natural gas. If the firm drills 6 wells, what is the probability that

   (*i*) exactly 2 wells, (*ii*) at least one well, yield gas ?

   [**Ans.** (*i*) 0.0305 (*ii*) $1 - (0.95)^6 = 0.2649$.]

4. A manufacturing process turns out articles that, on the average, are 10% defective. Compute the probability of 0, 1, 2 and 3 defective articles that might occur in a sample of 3 articles.

   [**Ans.** 0.729, 0.243, 0.027, 0.001.]

5. Under what conditions can a binomial distribution be applied? The incidence of occupational disease in an industry is such that workmen have a 20% chance of

suffering from it. What is the probability that out of six workmen, 4 or more will contact the disease?

[**Ans.** 0.017]

6. A binomial random variable satisfies the relation $9P(X = 4) = P(X = 2)$ for $n = 6$. Find the value of the parameter p.

Hint : $P(X = 2) = {}^6C_2 p^2 q^4$ *etc.*

$\left[\textbf{Ans. } \frac{1}{4}\right]$

7. If a die is thrown 6 times, calculate the probability that :

(*i*) a score of 3 of less occurs on exactly 2 throws;

(*ii*) a score of more than 2 occurs on exactly 3 throws;

(*iii*) a score of 5 or less occurs at least once;

(*iv*) a score of 2 or less occurs on at least 5 throws.

[**Hint.** Use binomial distribution with $n = 6$ and a different value of p in each case.]

$\left[\textbf{Ans. } \frac{15}{64}, \frac{160}{729}, \frac{46655}{46656}, \frac{13}{729}\right]$

8. On an average 2% of the population in an area suffers from T.B. What is the probability that out of 5 persons chosen at random from this area, at least two suffer form T.B. (Simplification is not necessary.)

[**Ans.** $1 - (0.98)^4 \times 1.08$.]

9. Assuming that it is true that 2 in 10 industrial accidents are due to fatigue, find the probability that —

(*i*) *exactly* 2 of 8 industrial accidents will be due to fatigue.

(*ii*) *at least* 2 of 8 industrial accidents will be due to fatigue.

[**Ans.** (*i*) ${}^8C_2 (0.2)^2 (0.8)^6$, (*ii*) $1 - (0.8)^7 \times 2.4$]

10. The probability that a secretary will not put the correct postage on a letter is 0.20. Find the probability that this secretary will not put the correct postage —

(*i*) on 3 of 9 letters, (*ii*) on at least 3 of 9 letters. (*iii*) on at the most 3 of 9 letters.

[**Ans.** (*i*) $84(0.2)^3 (0.8)^6$ (*ii*) $1 - [(0.8)^9 + 9(0.2)(0.8)^8 + 36(0.2)^2 (0.8)^7]$

(*iii*) $(0.8)^9 + 9 (0.2) (0.8)^8 + 36 (0.2)^2 (0.8)^7 + 84 (0.2)^3 (0.8)^6$]

11. It if known from the past experience that 80% of the students in a school do their home work. Find the probability that during a random check of 10 students

(*i*) all have done their home work,

(*ii*) at the most 2 have not done their home work,

(*iii*) at least one has not done the home work.

[**Hint :** Take $n = 10$ and $p = 0.8$.]

[**Ans.** 0.1074, 0.6678, 0.8926]

12. Take 100 sets of 10 tosses of an unbiased coin. In how many cases do you expect to get (*i*) 6 heads and 4 tails and (*ii*) at least 9 heads?

[**Hint :** Use binomial distribution with $n = 10$ and $p = 0.5$.]

[**Ans.** 20.5, 1.1]

13. In a binomial distribution consisting of 5 independent trials, the probabilities of 1 and 2 successes are 0.4096 and 0.2048 respectively. Find the probability of success.
[**Hint :** Use the condition $P(1) = 2P(2)$.]
[**Ans.** 0.2]

14. For a binomial distribution, the mean and variance are respectively 4 and 3. Calculate the probability of getting a non zero value of this distribution.
[**Hint :** Find $P(r \neq 0)$.]

$\left[\textbf{Ans. } 1 - \left(\frac{3}{4}\right)^{16}\right]$

15. From past weather records, it has been found that, on an average, rain falls on 12 days in June. Find the probability that in a given week of June :
(*i*) the first 4 days will be dry and the remaining three days wet ;
(*ii*) there will be rain on alternate days ; (*iii*) exactly 3 days will be wet.

$\left[\textbf{Ans. } (i) \left(\frac{3}{5}\right)^4 \cdot \left(\frac{2}{5}\right)^3; \quad (ii) \left(\frac{2}{5}\right)^3 \cdot \left(\frac{3}{5}\right)^3; \quad (ii)\ {}^7C_3 \left(\frac{2}{5}\right)^3 \left(\frac{3}{5}\right)^4\right]$

16. If on an average, 1 ship in every 10 is sunk, find the chance that out of 5 ships expected, at least 4 will arrive safely.
[**Ans.** $1.4 \times (0.9)^4 = 0.9185$.]

17. The incidence of occupational disease, in an industry is such that the workmen have a 20% chance of suffering from it. What is the probability that out of six workmen, 4 or more will contract the disease ?

$\left[\textbf{Ans. } \frac{53}{3125} = 0.0169.\right]$

18. An insurance salesman sells policies to five men, all of identical age and good health. According to the actuarial tables, the probability that a man of this particular age will be alive 30 years hence is $\frac{2}{3}$. Find the probability that in 30 years (*i*) all five men, (*ii*) at least one man, (*iii*) at most three men, will be alive.

$\left[\textbf{Ans. } (i) \left(\frac{2}{3}\right)^5 = \frac{32}{243}; \quad (ii)\ 1 - \frac{1}{3^5} \quad (iii)\ 1 - \left[{}^5C_4 \left(\frac{2}{3}\right)^4 \left(\frac{1}{3}\right) + {}^5C_5 \left(\frac{2}{3}\right)^5\right]\right]$

19. Write down the mean and variance of a binomial distribution with armatures n and p. If the mean and variance are 4 and 8/3 respectively, find the values of n and p. State whether it is symmetric for these values ?
[**Hint :** Binomial distribution is symmetric when $p = 0.5$.]

$\left[\textbf{Ans. } 12, \frac{1}{3}, r_{10}\right]$

20. 20% of the bolts produced by a machine are defective. Obtain the probability distribution of the number of defectives in a sample of 5 bolts chosen at random.
[**Ans.** $p(x) = {}^5C_x \cdot (1/5)^x (4/5)^{5-x}$; $x = 0, 1, 2, 3, 4, 5$.]

21. Four coins are tossed simultaneously. What is the probability of getting (*i*) 2 heads and 2 tails, (*ii*) at least two heads, and (*iii*) at least one head.

$\left[\textbf{Ans. } (i) \frac{3}{8}, \quad (ii) \frac{11}{16}, \quad (iii) \frac{15}{16}.\right]$

22. What do you understand by Binomial distribution ? What are its features ?
Three perfect coins are tossed together. What is the probability of getting at least one head ?
[**Ans.** 7/8]

23. An accountant is to audit 24 accounts of a firm. Sixteen of these are of highly-valued customers. If the accountant selects 4 of the accounts at random, what is the probability that he chooses at least one highly-valued account ?
[**Ans.** 80 / 81]

24. Eight coins are thrown simultaneously. Show that the probability of obtaining at least 6 heads is 37 / 256.

25. The average percentage of failures in a certain examination is 40. What is the probability that out of a group of 6 candidates, at least 4 passed in the examination ?
[**Ans.** 0.54432.]

26. The probability of bomb hitting a target is 1/5. Two bombs are enough to destroy a bridge. If six bombs are aimed at the bridge, find the probability that the bridge is destroyed.
[**Hint.** $n = 6, \quad p = 1/5$.
The bridge is destroyed if at least two of the bombs hit it. Hence the required probability that bridge is destroyed is given by

$$p(2) + p(3) + p(4) + p(5) + p(6) = 1 - [p(0) + p(1)] = 1 - \frac{2048}{3125} = 0.345.]$$

[**Ans.** 0.345]

27. A multiple choice test consists of 8 questions with three answers to each question (of which only one is correct). A student answers each question by rolling a balanced die and checking the first answer if he gets 1 or 2, the second answer if he gets 3 or 4, and the third answer if he gets 5 or 6. To get a distinction, a student must secure at least 75% correct answers. If there is no negative marking, what is the probability that the student secures a distinction ?

$\left[\textbf{Hint.} \text{ Let } X : \text{Number of correct answers. Then } X - B\left(n = 8, p = \frac{1}{3}\right).\right]$

[**Ans.** Required probability = $P(X \geq 75\% \text{ of } 8) = P(X \geq 6) = 0.0197$].

28. Past surveys show that 40% of the officers at the certain industry own cars. Suppose six officers are selected at random from this industry (with replacement).

(*a*) What is the probability that exactly four will own cars ?

(*b*) What is the probability that at least one will own a car ?

(*c*) What is the theoretical mean of the probability distribution under consideration ?

[**Ans.** (*a*) 0.1382, (*b*) 0.9533, (*c*) 2.4]

29. A machine produces an average of 20% defective bolts. A batch is accepted if a sample of 5 bolts taken from that batch contains no defective and rejected if the sample contains 3 or more defective. In other case, a second sample is taken. What is the probability that the second sample is required ?

$\left[\textbf{Ans.} \left(\frac{1}{5}\right)^5 [{}^5C_1 \times 4^4 + {}^5C_2 \times 4^3] = 0.6144.\right]$

30. The probability of a man hitting the target is $\frac{1}{4}$.

(*a*) If he fires 7 times, what is the probability that he hits the target :

(*i*) at least once (*ii*) at least twice ?

(*b*) How many times must he fire so that the probability of his hitting the target at least once is greater that 2/ 3 ?

[**Ans.** (*a*) (*i*) $1 - (3/4)^7$ (*ii*) $1 - (3/4)^7 - 7.(1/4).(3/4)^6$
(*b*) $n = 4$.]

13.8 POISSON DISTRIBUTION (P.D.)

Poisson distribution is a discrete probability distribution and is very widely used in statistical work. It was originated by a French mathematician. Simeon Denis Poisson (1781 – 1840), in 1837. Poisson distribution may be expected in cases where the chance of any individual event being a success is small. The distribution is used to describe the behaviour of rare events such as the number of accidents on road, number of printing mistakes in a book, etc. and has been called "the law of improbable events". In recent years the statisticians have had a renewed interest in the occurrence of comparatively rare events, such as serious floods, accidental release of radiation from a nuclear reactor, and the like.

Poisson distribution is a limiting form of Binomial Distribution under conditions as follows :

(*i*) Number of trials n is very large *i.e.*, $n \to \infty$

(*ii*) Probability of success in a trial (= p) is very small *i.e.*, $p \to 0$

(*iii*) np is a finite number generally denoted by m or λ. Under the conditions.

$$P(X = r) = \lim_{\substack{p \to 0 \\ n \to \infty}} {}^nC_r\, p^r\, q^{n-r} \simeq \frac{e^{-m}\, m^r}{r!} \text{ where } np = m$$

[$\simeq$ stands for approximately equal to]

13.9. SHAPES OF POISSON DISTRIBUTION

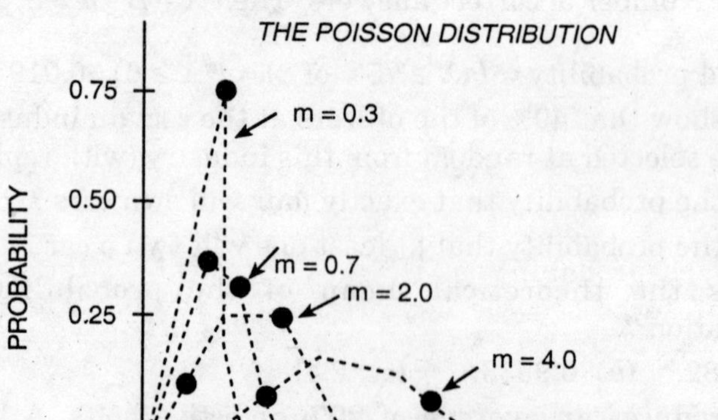

The Poisson distribution is defined as :

$$P(X = r) = \frac{e^{m}\, m^r}{r\,!}$$

where $r = 0, 1, 2....$

$e = 2.7183$ (the base of natural Logarithms)

m = the mean of the Poisson distribution, *i.e.*, np or the average number of occurrences of an event.

The Poisson distribution is a discrete distribution with a single parameter m. As m increases, the distribution shifts to the right. This is illustrated in the above diagram for 4 values from $m = 0.3$ to $m = 4.0$.

The Poisson distribution can frequently be used to approximate the binomial distribution under the following conditions:

(*i*) number of trials, *i.e.*, n, is indefinitely large, *i.e.*, $n \to \infty$,

(*ii*) p, *i.e.*, the probability of success for each trial indefinitely small, *i.e.*, $p \to 0$, and

(*iii*) $np = m$ (say) is finite.

In practice, the Poisson distribution may be used in place of the Binomial distribution, where $n \geq 20$ and $P \leq 0.1$.

13.10 POISSON DISTRIBUTION—PROBABILITY DISTRIBUTION

Like binomial distribution, the variate of the Poisson distribution is also a discrete one, *i.e.*, it takes only integral values. The probabilities of 0, 1, 2.... successes are given by the successive terms of the expansion

$$e^{-m}\left(1 + m + \frac{m^2}{2!} + \frac{m^3}{3!} \;......+ \frac{m^r}{r!} \;......+\right)$$

This can be written in tabular form as follows :

No. of successes (x)	*Probabilities* $p(x)$	*No. of successes* (x)	*Probabilities* $p(x)$
0	e^{-m}	4	$\frac{m^4 e^{-m}}{4!}$
1	me^{-m}	⋮	⋮
2	$\frac{m^2 e^{-m}}{2!}$	r	$\frac{m^r e^{-m}}{r\,!}$
3	$\frac{m^3 e^{-m}}{3!}$	⋮	⋮

The above table gives probabilities. If we want to know the expected number of occurrences for different successes, we have to multiply each term by N, *i.e.*, the total number of observations.

13.11 CONSTANTS OF THE POISSON DISTRIBUTION

Since p is very small in case of Poisson distribution, the value of q is almost equal to 1. The constants of the Poisson distribution can thus be easily obtained by putting 1 in place of q in the constants of the binomial distribution and $np = m$.

The various constants of the Poisson distribution are : (which are obtained from constants of *B.D.*)

B.D.	*P.D*
Mean np	m
Variance npq	m
Skewness $(\gamma_1) = \dfrac{q-p}{\sqrt{npq}}$	$\dfrac{1}{\sqrt{m}}$ $[q = 1, p = 0, np = m]$
Kurtosis $(\gamma_2) = \dfrac{1-6\,pq}{npq}$	$\dfrac{1}{m}$ $[p = 0, q = 1]$

13.13 ROLE OF THE POISSON DISTRIBUTION

The Poisson distribution is used in practice in a wide variety of problems where there are infrequently occurring events with respect to time, area, volume or similar units. Some practical situations in which Poisson distribution can be used are given below :

(1) it is used in quality control statistics to count the number of defects of an item,

(2) in biology to count the number of bacteria,

(3) in physics to count the number of particles emitted from a radioactive substance,

(4) in insurance problem to count the number of casualties.

(5) in waiting-time problems to count the number of incoming telephone calls or incoming customers.

(6) number of traffic arrivals such as trucks at terminals, aeroplanes at airports, ships at docks, and so forth.

(7) in determining the number of deaths in a district in a given period say a year by a rare disease.

(8) the number of typographical errors per page in typed material, number of death as a results of road accidents, etc.,

(9) in problems dealing with the inspection of manufactured products with the probability that any one piece is defective is very small and lots are very large.

(10) to model the distribution of the number of persons joining a queue (a line) to receive a service or purchases of a product.

In general, the Poisson distribution explains the behaviour of these discrete variates where the probability of occurrence of the event is small and the total number of repetitions are sufficiently large.

Example 34. *The mean of the Poisson distribution is 2.25. Find the other constants of the distribution.*

Solution. We are given mean or $m = 2.25$.

$$\sigma = \sqrt{m} = \sqrt{2.25} = 1.5$$

$$\mu = m = 2.25 = \text{variance}$$

$$\gamma_1 = \frac{1}{\sqrt{m}} = \frac{1}{\sqrt{2.25}} = \frac{1}{1.5} = \frac{2}{3} \text{ (Skewness)}$$

$$\gamma_2 = \frac{1}{m} .444 = 0.444 \text{ (Kurtosis)}$$

Example 35. *For a Poisson variate X, calculate P (X > 0), if it is known that*

$$4P\,(X = 4) = 5P(X = 5)$$

Solution. $4P(X = 4) = 5P(X = 5)$

$$\Rightarrow \quad \frac{4e^{-m} m^4}{4!} = \frac{5e^{-m} m^5}{5!} = \frac{5e^{-m} m^5}{5 \times 4!}$$

$$\Rightarrow \quad 4e^{-m} m^4 = e^{-m} m^5 \Rightarrow m = 4$$

$\therefore$ Required Probability $= 1 - e^{-m} = 1 - e^{-4}$. $[= 1 - P(X = 0)]$

Example 36. *Assuming that on an average 1% of the output in a factory making certain part of an article are defective and that 200 units are in a package. Find the probabilities that (i) At most 2 defectives (ii) At least 2 defectives may be found in the package. (e^{-2} = 0.1353).*

Solution. Mean $= 200 \times \frac{1}{100} = 2 = m$

Probability (at most 2 defectives)

= Prob. (no defective) + Prob. (one defective) + Prob. (two defectives)

$$= e^{-m} + me^{-m} + \frac{m^2}{2} e^{-m}, \text{ where } m = 2$$

$$= e^{-2} [1 + 2 + 2] = 5e^{-2} = 5 \times 0.1353 = 0.67667$$

Probability (at least two defectives)

= 1 – Prob. (no defective) – Prob. (one defective)

$$= 1 - e^{-m} - me^{-m} = 1 - e^{-m}(1 + m) = 1 - e^{-2}(1 + 2) \quad [\because m = 2]$$

$$= 1 - 3e^{-2} = 1 - 3 \times 0.1353 = 0.5939.$$

Example 37. *If the expectation of a Poisson variable is 1, then find P (X > 1).*

Solution. $E(X) = m = 1$ [*Given*]

$$P(X > 1) = P(X = 2) + P(X = 3) + \ldots$$

$$= 1 - P(X = 0) - P(X = 1)$$

$$= 1 - e^{-m} - me^{-m} = 1 - e^{-m}(1 + m)$$

$$= 1 - e^{-1}(1 + 1) \quad [\because m = 1]$$

$$= 1 - 2e^{-1}.$$

Example 38. *An oil exploration firm finds that 5% of the test wells it drills, yield a deposit of natural gas. If the firm drills 6 wells, what is the probability that.*

(*i*) *exactly 2 wells,*

(*ii*) *at least one well yield gas ?*

Solution. Probability that a well will yield a deposit of natural gas = 0.05

Since the probability is small we may use Poisson distribution.

Here $m = 0.05 \times 6 = 0.3$

Probability that exactly two wells yield a deposit of natural gas

$$= \frac{e^{-0.3}(0.3)^2}{2!}$$

Probability that at least one well will yield a deposit of natural gas

$$= 1 - P(0) = 1 - e^{-0.3}.$$

Example 39. *The average number of custom arrivals per minute at a super bazaar is 2. Find the probability that during one particular minute (i) exactly 3 customers will arrive, (ii) at the most two customers will arrive, (iii) at least one customer will arrive.*

Solution. It is given that $m = 2$. Let the number of arrivals per minute be denoted by the random variable r. The required probability is given by

(i) $P(r = 3) = \dfrac{e^{-2} \cdot 2^3}{3!} = \dfrac{0.13534 \times 8}{6} = 0.18045$

(ii) $P(r \leq 2) = \sum_{r=0}^{2} \dfrac{e^{-2} \cdot 2^r}{r!} = e^{-2}\left[1 + 2 + \dfrac{4}{2}\right] = 0.13534 \times 5 = 0.6767$

(iii) $P(r \geq 1) = 1 - P(r = 0) = 1 - \dfrac{e^{-2} \cdot 2^0}{0!} = 1 - 0.13534 = 0.86464$

Example 40. *An executive makes, on an average, 5 telephone calls per hour at a cost which may be taken as ₹ 2 per call. Determine the probability that in any hour the telephone calls cost (i) exceeds ₹ 6, (ii) remains less than ₹ 10.*

Solution. The number of telephone calls per hour is a random variable with mean = 5. The required probability is given by

(i) $P(r > 3) = 1 - P(r \leq 3) = 1 - \sum_{r=0}^{3} \dfrac{e^{-5} \cdot 5^r}{r!}$ [as cost exceeds ₹ 6 $\Rightarrow$ calls must be more than 3]

$= 1 - e^{-5}\left[1 + 5 + \dfrac{25}{2} + \dfrac{125}{6}\right] = 1 - 0.00678 \times \dfrac{236}{6} = 0.7349$

(ii) $P(r \leq 4) = \sum_{r=0}^{4} \dfrac{e^{-5} \cdot 5^r}{r!} = e^{-5}\left[1 + 5 + \dfrac{25}{2} + \dfrac{125}{6} + \dfrac{625}{24}\right] = 0.00678 \times \dfrac{1569}{24} = 0.44324.$

[number of calls will be less than 5]

Example 41. *A company produces electric toys. The probability that an electric toy is defective is 0.01. What is the probability that a shipment of 300 toys will contain exactly 5 defectives?*

Solution. Since n is large and p is small, Poisson distribution is applicable. The random variable is the number of defective toys with mean $m = np = 300 \times 0.01 = 3$. The required probability is given by

$$P(r = 5) = \frac{e^{-3} \cdot 3^5}{5!} = \frac{0.04979 \times 243}{120} = 0.10082.$$

Example 42. *Given that the switchboard of consultant's office receives on the average 0.9 calls per minute. Find the probabilities that*

(i) In a given minute there will be at least one incoming call.

(ii) Between 10.00 AM and 10.02 AM there will be exactly 2 incoming calls.

(iii) During an interval of 4 minutes there will be at most 3 incoming calls.

Solution. (i) $1 - e^{-0.9}$ [$P(X \geq 1) = 1 - P(X = 0) = 1 - e^{-m}$]

(ii) Here $m = 0.9 \times 2 = 1.8$ [average no. of calls in 2 minutes]

Required Probability $= \dfrac{e^{-1.8}(1.8)^2}{2!} = P(X = 2)$

(iii) $m = 0.9 \times 4 = 3.6$ [average no. of calls per 4 minutes]

Required probability $= P(X = 0) + P(X = 1) + P(X = 2) + P(X = 3)$

$$= e^{-3.6} + e^{-3.6}(3.6) + \frac{e^{-3.6}(3.6)^2}{2!} + \frac{e^{-3.6}(3.6)^3}{3!}$$

$$= e^{-3.6}\left[1 + 3.6 + \frac{(3.6)^2}{2} + \frac{(3.6)^3}{6}\right]$$

Example 43. *In a town, on an average 10 accidents occur in a span of 50 days. Assuming that the number of accidents per day follow Poisson distribution, find the probability that there will be three or more accidents in a day.*

Solution. The random variable denotes the number accidents per day. Thus, we have $m = \frac{10}{50} = 0.2$. The required probability is given by

$$P(r \geq 3) = 1 - P(r \leq 2) = 1 - e^{-0.2}\left[1 + 0.2 + \frac{(0.2)^2}{2!}\right] = 1 - 0.8187 \times 1.22 = 0.00119.$$

Example 44. *A car hire firm has two cars which it hire out every day. The number of demands for a car on each day is distributed as a Poisson variate with mean 1.5. Calculate the proportion of days on which neither car is used and the proportion of days on which some demand is refused.* [$e^{-1.5} = 0.2231$]

Solution. When both car are not used, $r = 0$

$\therefore$ $P(r = 0) = e^{-1.5} = 0.2231$. Hence the proportion of days on which neither car is used is 22.31%.

Further, some demand is refused when more than 2 cars are demanded, *i.e.*, $r > 2$

$$\therefore P(r > 2) = 1 - P(r \leq 2) = 1 - \sum_{r=0}^{2} \frac{e^{-1.5}(12.5)^r}{r!} = 1 - 0.2231\left[1 + 1.5 + \frac{(1.5)^2}{2!}\right] = 0.1913$$

Hence the proportion of days is 19.13%.

Example 45. *One hundred car radios are inspected as they come off the production line and number of defects per radio set is recorded below :*

No. of Defects	0	1	2	3
No. of Radio Sets	79	18	2	1

Estimate the average number of defects per radio and expected frequencies of 0, 1, 2 and 3 defects assuming Poisson distribution. [*D.U. MBA 1999*]

Solution.

$$\text{Mean} = \frac{0 \times 79 + 1 \times 18 + 2 \times 2 + 3 \times 1}{79 + 18 + 2 + 1}$$

$$= \frac{18 + 4 + 3}{100} = 0.25$$

Expected frequency for 0 defect $= e^{-0.25} \times 100$

Expected frequency for 1 defect $= me^{-m} \times 100 = 0.25 \times e^{-0.25} \times 100$

Expected frequency for 2 defects $= \frac{m^2 e^{-m}}{2!} \times 100 = \frac{(0.25)^2 e^{-0.25}}{2} \times 100$ and so on.

Example 46. *A firm produces articles of which 0.1 percent are usually defective. It packs them in cases each containing 500 articles. If a wholesaler purchases 100 such cases, how many cases are expected to be free of defective items and how many are expected to contain one defective item?*

Solution. The Poisson variate is number of defective items with mean

$$m = \frac{1}{1000} \times 500 = 0.5$$

Probability that a case is free of defective items

$P(r = 0) = e^{-0.5} = 0.6065$. Hence the number of cases having no defective items = 0.6065 × 100 = 60.65

Similarly, $P(r = 1) = e^{-0.5} \times 0.5 = 0.6065 \times 0.5 = 0.3033$. Hence the number of cases having one defective item are 30.33.

Example 47. *If r is a Poisson variate such that P(r) = P (r + 1). What is mean and standard deviation of variable 'r'.*

Solution. $P(r) = P(r + 1) \Rightarrow \frac{e^{-m} m^r}{r!} = \frac{e^{-m} m^{r+1}}{(r+1)!}$

$\Rightarrow \quad 1 = \frac{m}{r+1} \quad \Rightarrow \quad m = (r + 1) = \text{mean}$

Now $\sigma^2 = (r + 1)$ that standard deviation $= \sqrt{r+1}$.

Example 48. *One fifth per cent of the blades produced by a blade manufacturing factory turn out to be defective. The blades are supplied in packets of 10. Use Poisson distribution to calculate the approximate number of packets containing no defective, one defective and two defective blades respectively in a consignment of 1,00,000 packets.* $[e^{-102} = 0.9802]$

Solution. $P = \frac{1}{5}\% = \frac{1}{500}$, $n = 10$, $m = np = \frac{10}{500} = 0.02$

$$P(X = 0) = e^{-m} = e^{-0.02} = .9802$$

(*a*) The probability that a packet of 10 blades will have no defective = 0.9802

Thus out of 1,00,000 packets, no. of packets which do not have any defective.

$= 1{,}00{,}000 \times 0.9802 = 98020$

(*b*) $P(X = 1) = e^{-m}\, m = \frac{1}{50}\, e^{-.02} = \frac{0.9820}{50}$

Expected frequency $= 1{,}00{,}000 \times \frac{0.9820}{50}$

$= 1960.4 = 1960$

(*c*) $P(X = 2) = e^{-m} \frac{m^2}{2} = e^{-0.02} \times \left(\frac{1}{50}\right)^2 \cdot \frac{1}{2}$

Expected frequency $= 1{,}00{,}000 \times \frac{1}{5000} \times 0.9820$

$= 19.64 = 20.$

Example 49. *If X is a Poisson variate such that P(X = 2) = 9P(X = 4) + 90P(X = 6), find the mean and variance of X.*

[Hint : Mean = Variance]

Solution. $P(X = 2) = 9\, P(X = 4) + 90\, P(X = 6)$

$$\frac{e^{-m} m^2}{2} = 9 \frac{e^{-m} m^4}{24} + 90 \frac{e^{-m} m^6}{720} \quad [\text{as } 6! = 720]$$

$$1 = \frac{9\,m^2}{12} + \frac{900}{360}\,m^4 \left[\text{Dividing both sides by } \frac{e^{-m}\,m^2}{2}\right]$$

$$= \frac{3}{4}\,m^2 + \frac{m^4}{4}$$

$\Rightarrow \quad 4 = 3m^2 + m^4$ or $m^4 + 3m^2 - 4 = 0$

$\Rightarrow \quad m^4 + 4m^2 - m^2 - 4 = 0$

$m^2\,(m^2 + 4) - (m^2 + 4) = 0$

$\Rightarrow \quad (m^2 + 4)\,(m^2 - 1) = 0 \Rightarrow m^2 - 1 = 0$

as $m^2 + 4$ is not equal to 0.

$\Rightarrow \quad m = 1$ (m cannot be – ve]

mean = variance = 1.

Example 50. *Suppose that a local appliances shop has found from experience that the demand for tubelights is roughly distributed as Poisson with a mean of 4 tubelights per week. If the shop keeps 6 tubelights during a particular week, what is the probability that the demand will exceed the supply during that week ?*

Solution. Demand exceeds supply (which is 6) means that demand $X > 6$ *i.e.*,

$X = 7, 8, 9, 10, \ldots\ldots\ldots$

Now $P(X > 6) = 1 - P(X \le 6)$

$$= 1 - e^{-m}\left[1 + m + \frac{m^2}{2} + \frac{m^3}{6} + \frac{m^4}{24} + \frac{m^5}{120} + \frac{m^6}{720}\right]$$

$$= 1 - e^{-m} \sum_{r=0}^{6} \frac{m^r}{r!}$$

$$= 1 - e^{-4} \sum_{r=0}^{6} \frac{4^r}{r!} \quad \text{[as } m = 4 \text{ is given]}.$$

Example 51. *Assuming that the probability of a fatal accident in a factory during a year is 1/1200, calculate the probability that in a factory employing 300 workers, there will be at least two fatal accidents in a year. [Given $e^{-0.25} = 0.7788$].*

Solution. $p = \dfrac{1}{1200}$, $n = 300$

$$m = np = \frac{300}{1200} = 0.\,25$$

$P(\text{at least 2 accidents}) = P(X \ge 2)$

$$= 1 - [P(X = 0) + P(X = 1)]$$

$$= 1 - e^{-m}\,(1 + m) = 1 - e^{-0.25}\,(1 + 0.25)$$

$$= 1 - 0.7788\,(1.25) = 1 - 0.9735$$

$$= 0.0265.$$

Example 52. *Certain mass-produced articles of which 0.5 per cent are defective, are packed in cartons each containing 100 articles. What proportion of cartons are free from defective articles, and what proportion contain 2 or more defectives? [Given $e^{-0.5} = 0.6065$].*

Solution. $\quad n = 100,\ p = \dfrac{.5}{100} = \dfrac{5}{1000} = \dfrac{1}{200}.$

$$m = np = 100 \times \frac{1}{200} = 0.5$$

$$P(X = r) = \frac{e^{-m}\, m^r}{r\,!}$$

$$P(X = 0) = e^{-0.5} = 0.6065 \text{ (given)}$$

$$P(X = 1) = e^{-m} \times m = 0.6065 \times 0.5 = 0.30325$$

The probability of a carton with 2 or more defectives = $1 - [P(X = 0) + P(X = 1] = 0.0903$

Therefore the proportion of cartons free from defective articles is 60.65% or 61% and with 2 or more defectives is 9% (approx).

Example 53. *Between the hours of 2 and 4 p.m. the average number of phone calls per minute coming into the switchboard of a company is 2.5. Find the probability that during one particular minute there will be no phone call at all. (Given $e^{-2} = 0.13534$ and $e^{-.5} = 0.60650$).*

(I.C.W.A., 1982; C.A.. 1983)

Solution. This is a problem of Poisson distribution.

$$P(r) = \frac{e^{-m}\, m^r}{r\,!}\ ;\ P(0) = e^{-2.5}$$

$e^{-2} = 0.13534$ and $e^{-0.5} = 0.60650$

$\therefore\ e^{-2.5} = .13534 \times 60650 = 0.0821 \quad [e^{-2.5} = e^{-2} \times e^{-0.5}]$

Hence the probability that during one particular minute there will be no phone call at all = 0.0821.

EXERCISE 13.2

1. If 2 per cent of electric bulbs manufactured by a certain company are defective, find the probability that in a sample of 200 bulbs,

   (*i*) less than 2 bulbs, (*ii*) more than 3 bulbs, are defective. [Given $e^{-4} = 0.0183$]

   [**Ans.** (*i*) 0.0915, (*ii*) 0.5669.]

2. (*a*) In a certain manufacturing process, 5% of the tools produced turn out to be defective. Find the probability that in a sample of 40 tools, atmost 2 will be defective. (Given $e^{-2} = 0.135$)

   [**Ans.** 0.675.]

3. (*b*) In a town 10 accidents took place in 50 days. Assuming that number of accidents per day follows Poisson distribution, find the probability that there will be at least three accidents per day (given $e^{-0.2} = 0.8187$)

   $\left[\textbf{Hint. } \lambda = \text{Average number of accidents per day} = \frac{10}{50} = 0.2\right]$

   [**Ans.** $1 - e^{-0.2}(1 + 0.2 + 0.02) = 0.0012$.]

4. If the probability that an individual suffers a bad reaction from an injection of a given serum is 0.001, determine the probability that out of 2000 individuals:

   (*i*) exactly 3; and; (*ii*) more that two individuals, will suffer a bad reaction. ($e^{-2} = 0.13534$)

   [**Hint.** $m = np = 2000 \times 0.0a01 = 2$]

   $\left[\textbf{Ans. } (i)\ \frac{4}{3} e^{-2} = 0.1801 \qquad (ii)\ 1 - 5e^{-2} = 0.3245.\right]$

5. The number of arrivals of telephone calls at a switch board follows a Poisson process at an average rate of 8 calls per 10 minutes. The operator leaves for a 5 minutes tea break. Find the probability that (*a*) at the most two calls go unanswered and (*b*) 3 calls go unanswered, while the operator is away.

   [**Hint :** $m = 4$, $e^{-4} = 0.1832$]

   [**Ans.** 0.2381, 0.1954]

6. What probability model is appropriate to describe a situation where 100 misprints are distributed randomly throughout the 100 pages of a book? For this model, what is the probability that a page observed at random will contain (*i*) no misprint, (*ii*) at the most two misprints, (*iii*) at least three misprints?

   [**Hint :** The average number of misprint per page is unity. $e^{-1} = 0.36788$]

   [**Ans.** 0.3679, 0.9198, 0.0802]

7. If the probability of getting a defective transistor in a consignment is 0.01, find the mean and standard deviation of the number of defective transistors in a large consignment of 900 transistors. What is the probability that there is at the most one defective transistor in the consignment?

   [**Hint :** The average number of transistors in a consignment is $900 \times 0.01 = 9$]

   [**Ans.** 9, 3, 0.0012]

8. In a certain factory turning out blades, there is a small chance 1/500 for any one blade to be defective. The blades are supplied in packets of 10. Use Poisson distribution to compute the approximate number of packets containing no defective, one defective, two defective, three defective blades respectively in a consignment of 10,000 packets.

   [**Hint :** The random variable is the number of defective blades in a packet of 10 blades.]

   [**Ans.** 9802, 196, 2, 0]

9. A manufacturer of cotter pins knows that 2% of his product is defective. If he sells cotter pins in boxes of 200 and guarantees that not more than-5 pins will be defective, what is the probability that a box will fail to meet the guaranteed quality? [Given $e^{-4} = 0.0183$]

   [**Ans.** $P(X > 5) = 1 - P(X \le 5) = 0.2155.$]

10. A cigarette company wants to promote the sales of Brand *A* cigarettes with special advertising campaign. Fifty out of every 1000 cigarettes are rolled up in gold foil and randomly mixed with the regular (special king-sized mentholated) cigarettes. The company offers to trade a new package of cigarettes for each gold cigarette a smoker finds in a package of Brand *A*. What is the probability that buyers of Brand *A* will find 0, 1, 2, 3, ..., gold cigarettes in a single pack of 10 ?

    $\left[\textbf{Hint.}\ X:\ \text{No. of gold cigarettes found in a pack of 10. Then } X \sim P\left(m = np = 10 \times \frac{50}{1000} = 0.5\right).\right]$

    [**Ans.** The probabilities of 0, 1, 2, 3 and 4 gold cigarettes are respectively : 0.6065, 0.3033, 0.0758, 0.0126 and 0.0016.]

11. A manufacturer of pins knows that on an average 5% of his product is defective. He sells pins in boxes of 100, and guarantees that not more than 4 pins will be defective. What is the probability that a box will meet the guaranteed quality ? ($e^{-5} = .0067$).

$$\left[\textbf{Ans. } e^{-5}\left[1+5+\frac{25}{2!}+\frac{125}{2!}+\frac{125}{3!}+\frac{625}{4!}\right] = 0.0067 \times 65.37 = 0.438.\right]$$

12. Lots of 400 wall-clocks are purchased by a retailer. The retailer inspects sample of 20 clocks from each lot and returns the lot to the supplier if there are more than two defectives in the sample. Suppose a lot containing 30 defective clocks is received by the retailer what is the probability that it will be returned to the supplier?

$$\left[\textbf{Hint : } n = 20 \text{ and } p = \frac{30}{400}\right]$$

[**Ans.** 0.1912]

13. A manufacturer knows that 0.3% of items produced in his factory are defective. If the items are supplied in boxes, each containing 250 items, what is the probability that a box contains (*i*) no defective, (*ii*) at the most two defective items?

$$\left[\textbf{Hint : } m = \frac{0.3}{100} \times 250 = 0.75.\right]$$

[**Ans.** 0.4724, 0.9596]

14. A random variable r follows Poisson distribution, where $P(r = 2) = P(r = 3)$. Find (*i*) $P(r = 0)$, (*ii*) $P(1 \leq r \leq 3)$.

[**Hint :** $P(1 \leq r \leq 3) = P(r = 1) + P(r = 2) + P(r = 3)$.]

[**Ans.** 0.0498, 0.5976]

13.13 NORMAL DISTRIBUTION

13.13.1 Introduction

The distribution discussed so far, *viz.*, Binomial distribution and Poisson distribution, are discrete probability distributions, since the variables under study were discrete random variables. Now we confine the discussion to continuous probability distributions which arise when the underlying variable is a continuous one.

Normal probability distribution or commonly called the *normal distribution* is one of the most important continuous theoretical distribution in Statistics. Most of the data relating to economic and business statistics or even in social and physical sciences conform to this distribution. Normal distribution has been used in wide variety of practical applications of random variables like heights weights, test scores, amount of rainfall etc. It is widely used in statistical inferences, which will be taken up in chapters which follows.

The normal distribution was first discovered by English Mathematician De-Moivre (1667-1754) in 1733 who obtained the mathematical equation for this distribution while dealing with problems arising in the game of chance. Normal distribution is also known as Gaussian distribution (Gaussian Law of Errors) after Karl Friedrich Gauss (1777-1855) who used this distribution to describe the theory of accidental errors of measurements involved in the calculation of orbits of heavenly bodies. Today, normal probability model is one of the most important probability models in statistical analysis.

13.14 PROBABILITY MASS FUNCTIONS (p. m. f.) AND PROBABILITY DENSITY FUNCTION (p.d.f.)

In case of discrete probability distribution we have probability mass function or simply probability function $f(x)$ or $P(x)$ which describes probabilities for different countable values of random variable X.

In case of continuous variable we have infinite values of X in any interval, however small it may be. Suppose we know that X variable lies between 1 and 6. Now even we take an interval of 2.1 to 2.01, there are infinite variable values in this interval however we know that $P(2.1 \leq X \leq 2.01)$.

Thus probability for any particular point in this interval will be very very small and is taken as zero. Thus $P(X = k) = 0$ for any value of k (for a continuous variable).

13.15 PROBABILITY DENSITY FUNCTION OF CONTINUOUS VARIABLE

While defining probability (relative frequency method) we see that probability distribution is analogous to frequency distribution. If number of observations are very large the relative frequency becomes probability. Thus relative frequency curve will give us probability distribution. If we consider relative frequency curve of grouped continuous data, it will become smoother as the sample size increase and number of classes is increased. This smooth curve of relative frequencies is called the density curve and if there exists a function which defines the density curve, it is called "Probability Density Function"—(*p.d.f.*).

13.15.1 Properties of Probability Density Function

Let X be a continuous random variable taking values on the interval $[a, b]$ then a function $f(x)$ will be "Probability Density Function" (*p.d.f.*) if it satisfies the following properties

(1) $f(x) \geq 0$ for all x in $[a, b]$

(*ii*) if c and d *belong to* $[a, b]$ and $d > c$ then $P(c \leq X \leq d)$ = shaded area = area under the curve, x – axis and two vertical lines $x = c$ and $x = d$ which also is equal to $\int_c^d f(x)\,dx$.

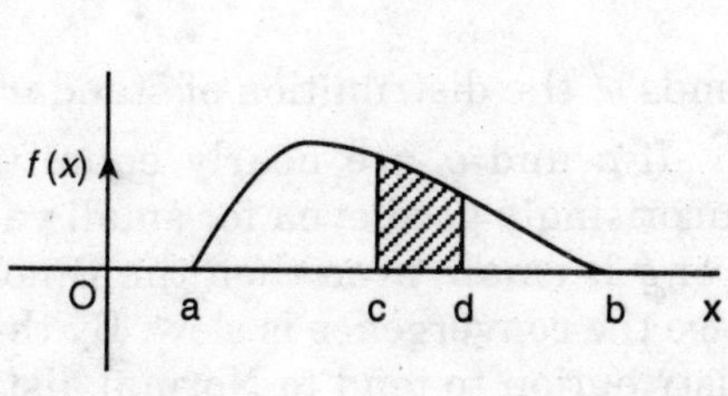

(*iii*) Total area between the curve and x-axis = 1.

(*iv*) $P(X = k) = 0$ for all values of k.

13.16 PROBABILITY DENSITY FUNCTION OF NORMAL DISTRIBUTION

If X is a continuous random variable following normal probability distribution with mean μ and standard deviation σ, then its probability density function (p.d.f.) is given by

$$f(x) = \frac{1}{\sqrt{2\pi}.\,\sigma}\, e^{-\frac{1}{2}\left(\frac{x-\mu}{\sigma}\right)^2}, \; -\infty < x \leq \infty \quad ...(1)$$

or

$$f(x) = \frac{1}{\sqrt{2\pi}.\,\sigma}\, e^{-\frac{(x-\mu)^2}{2\sigma^2}}, \; -\infty < x < \infty \quad ...(2)$$

where π and e are the constants given by

$$\pi = \frac{22}{7}, \qquad \sqrt{2\pi} = 2.5066$$

and $e = 2.71828$ [The base of the system of Natural logarithms.]

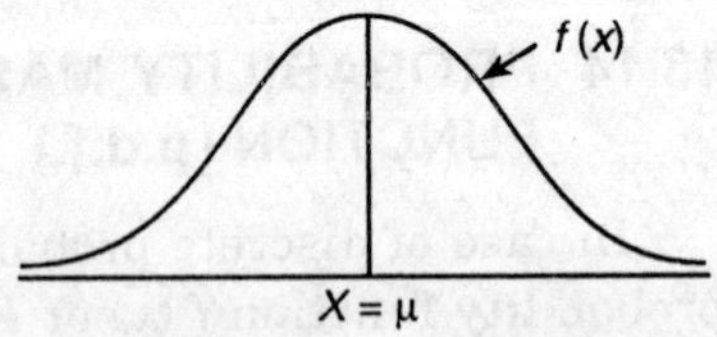

Normal Probability Curve

Its shape and position depend on μ (mean) and σ (standard deviation). Thus μ and σ are parameters of normal distribution.

We express normal distribution with mean μ and standard deviation σ as

$$X \cap N(\mu, \sigma)$$

[The random variable X is distributed normaly with mean = μ and s.d. = σ]

Standard Normal Variable

It is a normal distribution with mean = 0 and $\sigma = 1$

i.e. $X \cap N(0,1)$. Then X is known as Standard Normal variate.

13.17 RELATION BETWEEN BINOMIAL AND NORMAL DISTRIBUTIONS

Normal distribution is a limiting case of the binomial probability distribution under the following conditions :

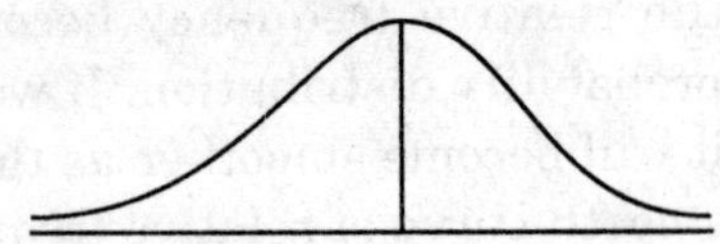

(*i*) n, the number of trials is indefinitely large, *i.e.*, $n \to \infty$.

(*ii*) Neither p nor q is very small.

We know that for a binomial variate X with parameters n and p,

$$E(X) = np \text{ and } \operatorname{Var}(X) = npq$$

De-Moivre proved that under the above two conditions, the distribution of standard normal variate

$$Z = \frac{X - E(X)}{\sigma_x} = \frac{X - np}{\sqrt{npq}},$$

tends to the distribution of standard Normal variate stated above.

If p and q are nearly equal (*i.e.*, p is nearly 1/2), then the normal approximation is surprisingly good even for small values of n. However, when p and q are not equal, *i.e.*, when p or q is small, even then the Binomial distribution tends to normal distribution but in this case the convergence is slow. By this we mean that if p and q are not equal then for Binomial distribution to tend to Normal distribution we need relatively larger value of n as compared to the value of n required in the case when p and q are nearly equal. Thus, the normal approximation to the Binomial distribution is better for increasing values of n and is exact in the limiting case as $n \to \infty$.

13.18 PROPERTIES OF NORMAL DISTRIBUTION

It has the following properties :

1. The graph of $p(x)$ is the famous bell shaped curve as shown in the fig. The top of the bell is directly above the mean (μ).

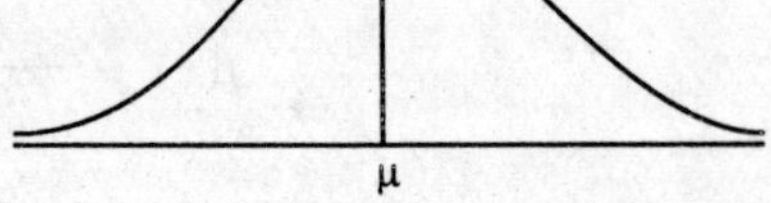

2. The curve is symmetrical about the line $X = \mu$, *i.e.*, it has the same shape on either side of the line $X = \mu$.

This is because the equation of the curve $p(x)$ remains unchanged if we change x to $-x$.

3. Since the distribution is symmetrical, mean, median and mode coincide. Thus,

$$\text{Mean} = \text{Median} = \text{Mode} = \mu$$

4. Since Mean = Median = μ, the ordinate at $X = \mu$, divides the whole area into two equal parts. Further, since total area under normal probability curve is 1, the area to the right of the ordinate as well as to the left of the ordinate at $X = \mu$ is 0.5.

5. Also, by virtue of symmetry, the quartiles are equidistant form median (μ), *i.e.*,

$$Q_3 - Md = Md - Q_1 \quad \Rightarrow \quad Q_1 + Q_3 = 2Md = 2\mu$$

6. Since the distribution is symmetrical, the moment coefficient of skewness is given by:

$$\beta_1 = 0 \quad \Rightarrow \quad \gamma_1 = 0$$

7. The value of $\rho(X)$ is always non-negative for all values of X, *i.e.,* the whole curve lies above X axis.

8. The points of inflexion (the point at which curvature changes) of the curve are at $X = \mu \pm \sigma$.

9. Since the distribution is symmetrical, all odd ordered central moments are zero.

10. The coefficient of kurtosis $\beta_2 = \dfrac{\mu_4}{\mu_2{}^2} = \dfrac{3\sigma^4}{\sigma^4} = 3.$ *i.e.,* $\gamma_2 = 0$

11. Area properties.

The area under the normal curve is distributed by its standard deviation in the following manner:

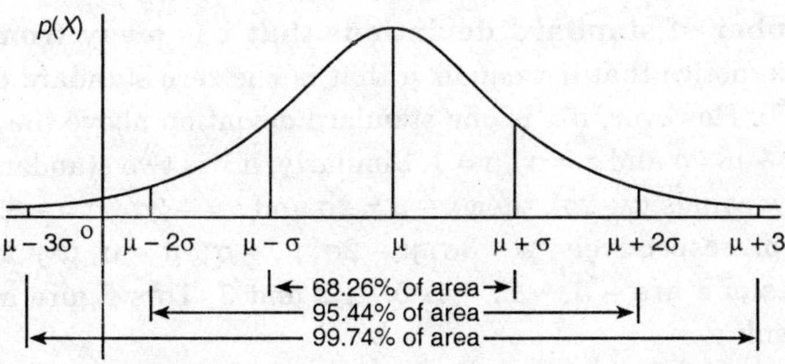

(*i*) The area between the ordinates at $\mu - \sigma$ and $\mu + \sigma$ is 0.6826. This implies that for a normal distribution about 68% of the observations will lie between $\mu - \sigma$ and $\mu + \sigma$.

(*ii*) The area between the ordinates at $\mu - 2\sigma$ and $\mu + 2\sigma$ is 0.9544. This implies that for a normal distribution about 95% of the observations will lie between $\mu - 2\sigma$ and $\mu + 2\sigma$.

(*iii*) The area between the ordinates at $\mu - 3\sigma$ and $\mu + 3\sigma$ is 0.9974. This implies that for a normal distribution about 99% of the observations will lie between $\mu - 3\sigma$ and $\mu + 3\sigma$. This result shows that, practically, the range of the distribution is 6σ although, theoretically, the range is from $-\infty$ to ∞.

13.19 PROBABILITY OF NORMAL VARIATE IN AN INTERVAL

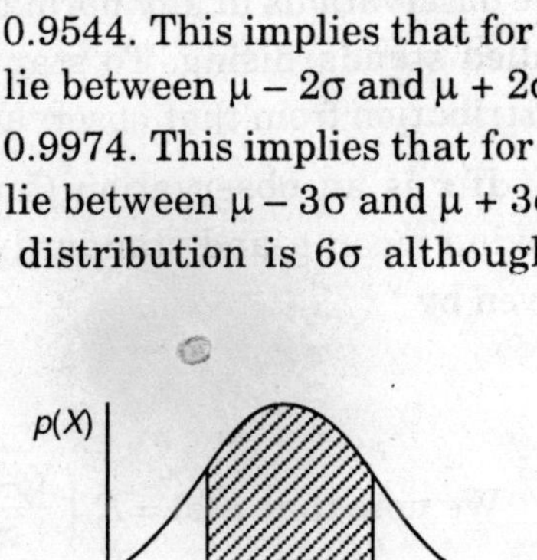

Let X be a normal variate distributed with mean μ and standard deviation σ, also written in abbreviated form as $X \cap N(\mu, \sigma)$. The probability of X lying in the interval (X_1, X_2) is given by shaded area in the figure.

$$P(X_1 \le X \le X_2) = \int_{X_1}^{X_2} \frac{1}{\sigma\sqrt{2\pi}} e^{-\frac{1}{2}\left(\frac{X-\mu}{\sigma}\right)^2} dX$$

In terms of figure, this probability is equal to the area under the normal curve between the ordinates at $X = X_1$ and $X = X_2$ respectively.

Note : *It may be recalled that the probability that a continuous random variable takes a particular value is defined to be zero even through the event is not impossible.*

The computation of $P(x_1 \le X \le x_2)$ for different normal curves will require that either we make use of integrals calculus, or we construct separate probability tables for each normal curve. The first alternative is beyond our scope. The second alternative is not practicable as preparing separate probability tables for every normal curve will indeed be impossible. Therefore, we would like to have one table of normal curve areas that applies to all normal curves. There is such a table, and we can use it by thinking in terms of how many standard deviations a value of interest is from the mean. Specifically, consider a random variable x that is normally distributed with mean μ and standard deviation σ. Then the random variable Z defined as under

$$z = \frac{x-\mu}{\sigma}$$

expresses the number of standard deviations that x is away from the mean μ. To understand this idea, notice that if x equals μ that is x is zero standard deviations from μ), then $z = (\mu - \mu)/\sigma = 0$. However, if x is one standard deviation above the mean (that is, if x equals $\mu + \sigma$), then $x - \mu = \sigma$ and $z = \sigma / \sigma = 1$. Similarly, if x is two standard deviations below the mean (that is, if x equals $\mu - 2\sigma$), then $x - \mu = 2\sigma$ and $z = -2\sigma / \sigma = -2$. Figure illustrates that for values of x of, respectively, $\mu - 3\sigma$, $\mu - 2\sigma$, μ, $-\sigma$, $\mu + \sigma$, $\mu + 2\sigma$ and $\mu + 3\sigma$, the corresponding values of z are -3, -2, -1, 0, 1, 2 and 3. This figure also illustrates the following general result :

In fact all normal distributions are same if we measure each observation in terms of number of standard deviations it is away from the mean. Taking the measurements of all the observations in any normal distribution in terms of standard deviations from the mean is called standardising. To standardise any value (or observation) subtract the mean of the distribution from that observation and then divide by the standard deviation.

If x is an observation (any point on the horizontal axis) from a normal distribution having mean μ and standard deviation σ, then the standardised value of x denoted by z is given by

$$z = \frac{x-\mu}{\sigma}$$

We note that $E(z) = E\left(\frac{X-\mu}{\sigma}\right) = \frac{1}{\sigma}[E(X) - \mu] = 0$

and $Var(z) = Var\left(\frac{X-\mu}{\sigma}\right) = \frac{1}{\sigma^2} Var(X-\mu) = \frac{1}{\sigma^2} Var(X) = 1$

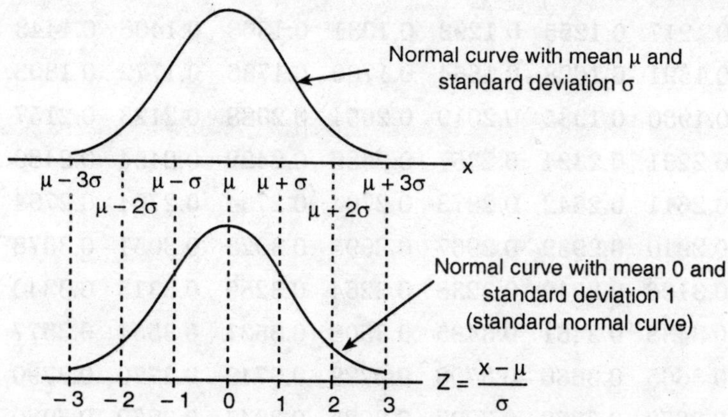

If X is Normally Distributed with Mean μ and Standard Deviation σ, then $Z = \frac{X - \mu}{\sigma}$ is Normally Distributed with Mean 0 and Standard Deviation 1

Thus if $X \cap N(\mu, \sigma)$ then $\frac{X - \mu}{\sigma} = Z \cap N(0, 1)$.

Thus we conclude that if X is a normal variate with mean μ and standard deviation σ, then $z = \frac{X - \mu}{\sigma}$ is a normal variate with mean zero and standard deviation unity. Since the parameters of the distribution of z are fixed, it is a known as *standard normal distribution* (*s.n.d.*). Further, z is termed as a *standard normal variate* (*s.n.v.*).

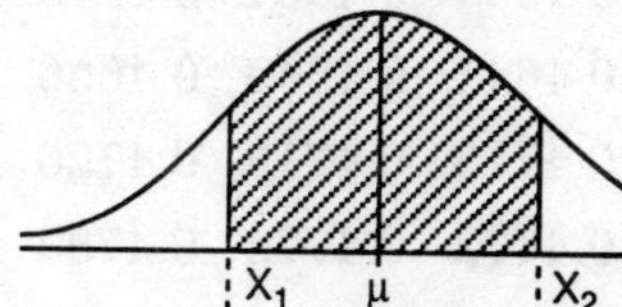

Fig. 1

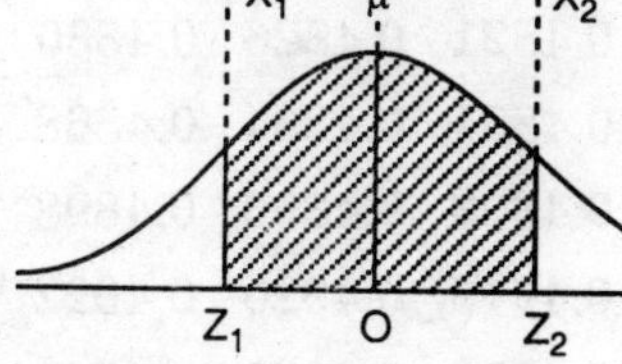

Fig. 2

It is obvious from the above that the distribution of any normal variate X can always be transformed into the distribution of standard normal variate z. This fact can be utilised to evaluate the integral given above.

$$P(X_1 \le X \le X_2) = \text{Shaded Area in Fig. 1.}$$

We can write $P(X_1 \le X \le X_2) = P\left[\left(\frac{X_1 - \mu}{\sigma}\right) \le \left(\frac{X - \mu}{\sigma}\right) \le \left(\frac{X_2 - \mu}{\sigma}\right)\right]$

$= P(z_1 \le z \le z_2)$ $\left[\text{where } z_1 = \frac{X_1 - \mu}{\sigma} \text{ and } z_2 = \frac{X_2 - \mu}{\sigma}\right]$ = shaded area in Fig. 2

In terms of figure, this probability is equal to the area under the standard normal curve between the ordinates at $z = z_1$ and $z = z_2$. Since the distribution of z is fixed, the probabilities of z lying in various intervals are tabulated in the form of a table. These tables can be used to get the desired probability.

The value of $P(0 \le z \le k)$, for all + ve values of k, are tabulated in a table given below.

z	0.00	0.01	0.02	0.03	0.04	0.05	0.06	0.07	0.08	0.09
0.0	0.0000	0.0040	0.0080	0.0120	0.0160	0.0199	0.0239	0.0279	0.0319	0.0359
0.1	0.0398	0.0438	0.0478	0.0517	0.0557	0.0596	0.0636	0.0675	0.0714	0.0753
0.2	0.0793	0.0832	0.0871	0.0910	0.0948	0.0987	0.1026	0.1064	0.1103	0.1141

0.3	0.1179	0.1217	0.1255	0.1293	0.1331	0.1368	0.1406	0.1443	0.1480	0.1517
0.4	0.1554	0.1591	0.1628	0.1664	0.1700	0.1736	0.1772	0.1808	0.1844	0.1879
0.5	0.1915	0.1950	0.1985	0.2019	0.2054	0.2088	0.2123	0.2157	0.2190	0.2224
0.6	0.2257	0.2291	0.2324	0.2357	0.2389	0.2422	0.2454	0.2486	0.2517	0.2549
0.7	0.2580	0.2611	0.2642	0.2673	0.2704	0.2734	0.2764	0.2794	0.2823	0.2852
0.8	0.2881	0.2910	0.2939	0.2967	0.2995	0.3023	0.3051	0.3078	0.3106	0.3133
0.9	0.3159	0.3186	0.3212	0.3238	0.3264	0.3289	0.3315	0.3340	0.3365	0.3389
1.0	0.3413	0.3438	0.3461	0.3485	0.3508	0.3531	0.3554	0.3577	0.3599	0.3621
1.1	0.3643	0.3665	0.3686	0.3708	0.3729	0.3749	0.3770	0.3790	0.3810	0.3830
1.2	0.3849	0.3869	0.3888	0.3907	0.3925	0.3944	0.3962	0.3980	0.3997	0.4015
1.3	0.4032	0.4049	0.4066	0.4082	0.4099	0.4115	0.4131	0.4147	0.4162	0.4177
1.4	0.4192	0.4207	0.4222	0.4236	0.4251	0.4265	0.4279	0.4292	0.4306	0.4319
1.5	0.4332	0.4345	0.4357	0.4370	0.4382	0.4394	0.4406	0.4418	0.4429	0.4441
1.6	0.4452	0.4463	0.4474	0.4484	0.4495	0.4505	0.4515	0.4525	0.4535	0.4545
1.7	0.4554	0.4564	0.4573	0.4582	0.4591	0.4599	0.4608	0.4616	0.4625	0.4633
1.8	0.4641	0.4649	0.4656	0.4664	0.4671	0.4678	0.4686	0.4693	0.4699	0.4706
1.9	0.4713	0.4719	0.4726	0.4732	0.4738	0.4744	0.4750	0.4756	0.4761	0.4767
2.0	0.4772	0.4778	0.4783	0.4788	0.4793	0.4798	0.4803	0.4808	0.4812	0.4817
2.1	0.4821	0.4826	0.4830	0.4834	0.4838	0.4842	0.4846	0.4850	0.4854	0.4857
2.2	0.4861	0.4864	0.4868	0.4871	0.4875	0.4878	0.4881	0.4884	0.4887	0.4890
2.3	0.4893	0.4896	0.4898	0.4901	0.4904	0.4906	0.4909	0.4911	0.4913	0.4916
2.4	0.4918	0.4920	0.4922	0.4925	0.4927	0.4929	0.4931	0.4932	0.4934	0.4936
2.5	0.4938	0.4940	0.4941	0.4943	0.4945	0.4946	0.4948	0.4949	0.4951	0.4952
2.6	0.4953	0.4955	0.4956	0.4957	0.4959	0.4960	0.4961	0.4962	0.4963	0.4964
2.7	0.4965	0.4966	0.4967	0.4968	0.4969	0.4970	0.4971	0.4972	0.4973	0.4974
2.8	0.4974	0.4975	0.4976	0.4977	0.4977	0.4978	0.4979	0.4979	0.4980	0.4981
2.9	0.4981	0.4982	0.4982	0.4983	0.4984	0.4984	0.4985	0.4985	0.4986	0.4986
3.0	0.4987	0.4987	0.4987	0.4988	0.4988	0.4989	0.4989	0.4989	0.4990	0.4990

13.20 HOW TO READ THE TABLE

Suppose we want to find $P(0 \le Z \le 1.64)$.

We see the z column, below this we look for 1.6 (value of z upto one decimal). In the row corresponding to 1.6 we look for value below 0.04 which is 0.4495. Thus $P(0 \le z \le 1.64) = 0.4495$. In this row we find $P(0 \le Z \le 1.60) = 0.4452$.

$P(0 \le Z \le 1.61) = 0.4463$ and $P(0 \le Z \le 1.62) = 0.4474$ and so on.

How to find the $P(X_1 \le X \le X_2)$

(1) X_1 and X_2 are converted to Z_1 and Z_2 as follows $Z_1 = \dfrac{X_1 - \mu}{\sigma}$, $Z_2 = \dfrac{X_2 - \mu}{\sigma}$.

Now the variable X (Normal Variable) is converted to Z (Standard Normal Variate)

Thus $P(X_1 \le X \le X_2) = P(Z_1 \le Z \le Z_2)$.

(2) Since table gives probabilities $P(0 \le Z \le k)$ for + ve values of k, however we make use of symmetry of the curve to find probabilities like $P(-1 \le Z \le 0) = P(0 \le Z \le 1)$ *i.e.*, area between – 1 and 0 is same as between 0 and 1.

(3) We have $P(0 \le Z \le 3.09) = 0.4990$. (from the table)

therefore $P(Z \ge 3.09) = 0.5 - 0.4990 = 0.001$ which is very small and may be taken equal to 0.

Example 54. *Find P(0.6 ≤ Z ≤ 0.8) [both values of Z are + ve)*

Solution. We may write $P(0.6 \le Z \le 1.8)$

$= P(0 \le Z \le 1.8) - P(0 \le Z \le 0.6)$

$= 0.4641 - 0.2257 = 0.2384$. [using tables]

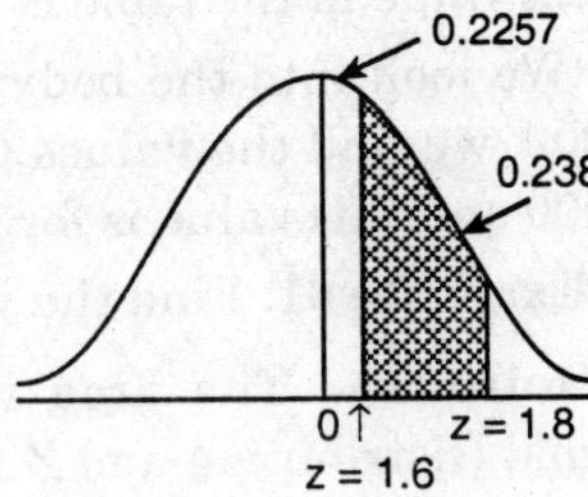

Example 55. *Find P(– 1.8 ≤ Z ≤ – 0.6) i.e., both values of Z are – ve.*

Solution. Because of symmetry

$P(-1.8 \le Z \le -0.6) = P(0.6 \le Z \le 1.8)$

$= 0.4641 - 0.2257$

$= 0.2384$.

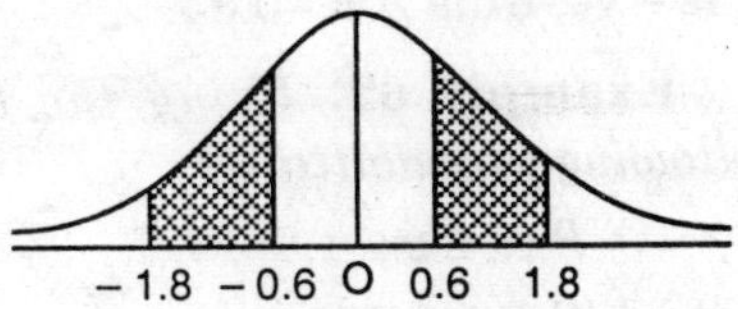

Example 56. *Find P(– 0. 6 ≤ Z ≤ 1.8) (one is – ve and other + ve)*

Solution. $P(-0.6 \le Z \le 1.8)$

$= P(-0.6 \le Z \le 0) + P(0 \le Z \le 1.8)$

$= 0.2257 + 0.4641$

$= 0.6898$.

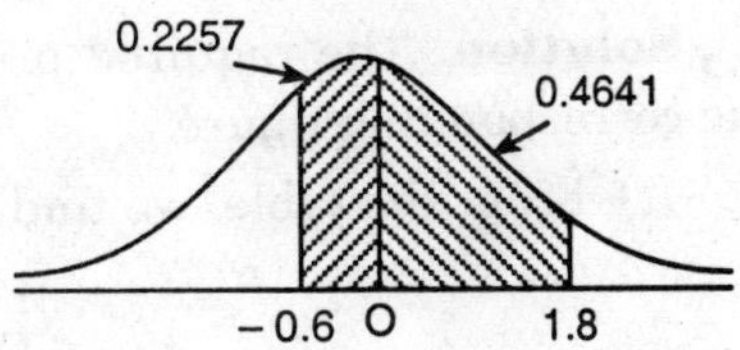

Example 57. *Find P(Z ≥ 1.8).*

Solution. $P(Z \ge 1.8)$

$= 0.5 - P(0 \le Z \le 1.8)$ [Area on right of $Z = 0$ is 0.5]

$= 0.5 - 0.4641 = 0.0359$.

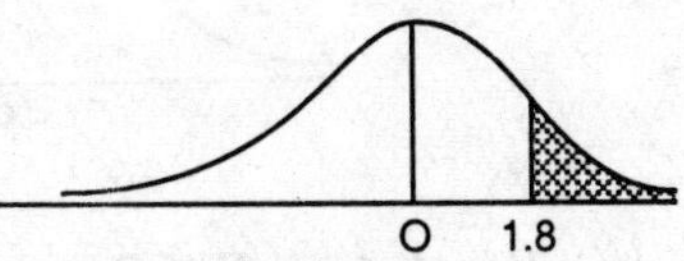

Example 58. *Find P(Z ≥ – 1.8).*

Solution. $P(Z \ge -1.8)$

$= P(-1.8 \le Z \le 0) + 0.5$

$= P(0 \le Z \le 1.8) + 0.5$

$= 0.4641 + 0.5 = 0.9641$.

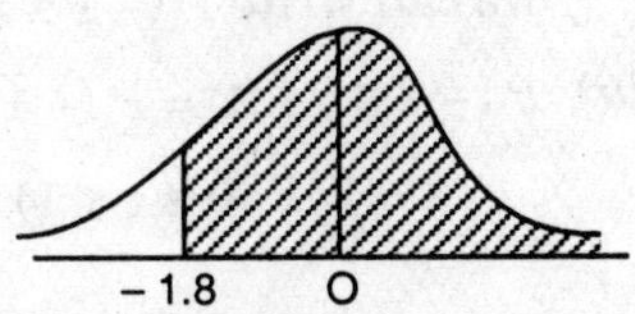

Example 59. *Find P(Z ≤ 1.8)*

Solution. $P(Z \le 1.8)$

$= 0.5 + P(0 \le Z \le 1.8)$

$= 0.5 + 0.4641 = 0.9641$.

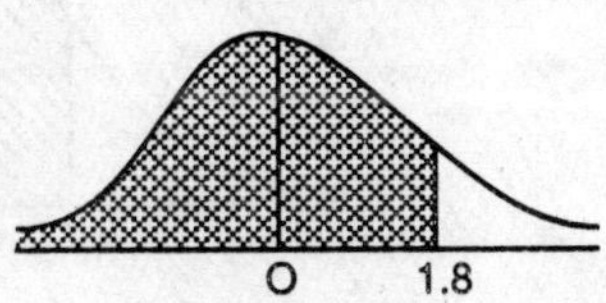

13.20.1 At times we may be given the area under the normal curve and asked to determine the corresponding value of Z.

Example 60. *Find a Z which is such that area to its right is 0.2000.*

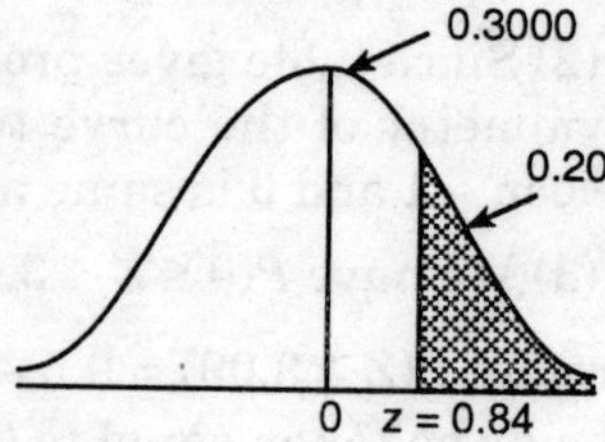

Solution. As it is seen from the figure the z values will have to correspond to an entry of 0.3000 in the table and the closest value in the table is $z = 0.84$.

[We look into the body of table and look for entry close to 0.3000, we find the values 0.2995 and 0.3023, 0.2995 is close to 0.3000 and this value is for $z = 0.84$].

Example 61. Find the value of Z such that area to its left is 0 . 2000

Solution. The area is in the left tail of Standard Normal Distribution and Z must be – ve.

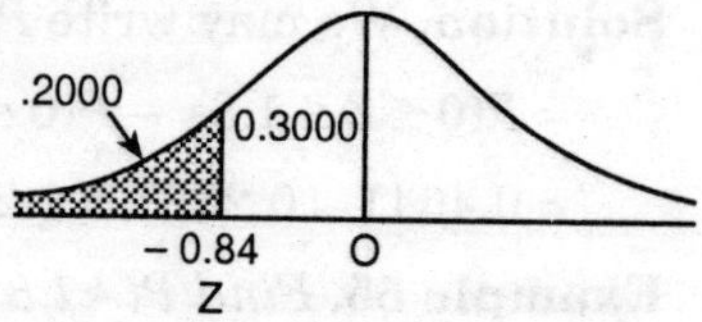

Thus area between 0 and Z is 0.3000 and from tables we find corresponding to area 0.3000, Z value is 0.84. Since it is – ve, thus $Z = -0.84$.

Example 62. *Using the table of areas under the standard normal curve, find the following probabilities :*

(*i*) $P(0 \le z \le 1.3)$ (*ii*) $P(-1 \le z \le 0)$ (*iii*) $P(-1 \le z \le 2)$

(*iv*) $P(z \ge 1.54)$ (*v*) $P(|z| > 2)$ (*vi*) $P(|z| < 2)$

Solution. The required probability, in each question, is indicated by the shaded are of the corresponding figure.

(*i*) From the table, we find $P(0 \le z \le 1.3) = 0.4032$.

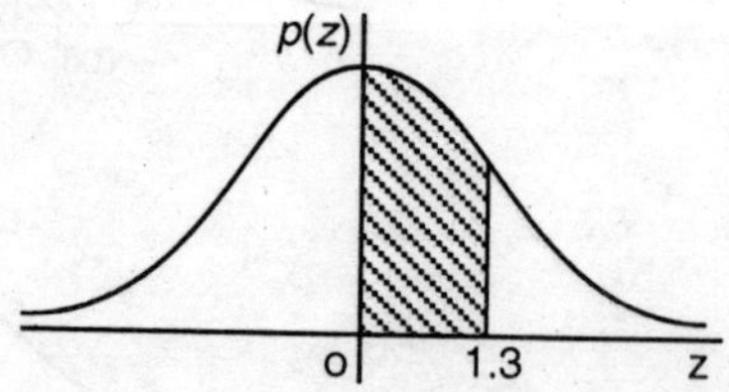

(i)

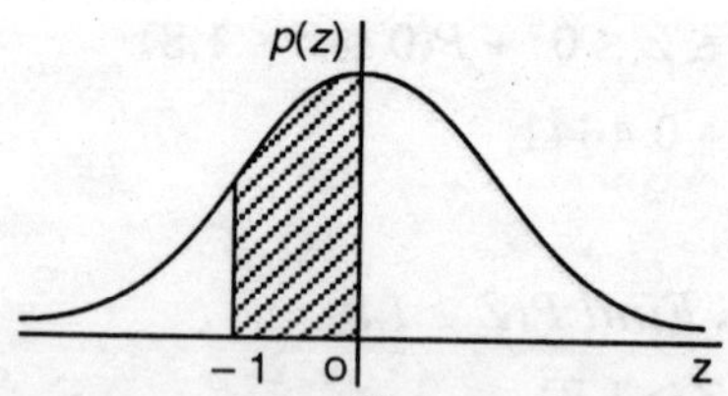

(ii)

(*ii*) $P(-1 \le z \le 0) = P(0 \le z \le 1)$, because the distribution is symmetrical. From the table, we can write $P(-1 \le z \le 0) = P(0 \le z \le 1) = 0.3413$.

(*iii*) $P(-1 \le z \le 2) = P(-1 \le z \le 0) + P(0 \le z \le 2)$

$$= P(0 \le z \le 1) + P(0 \le z \le 2) = 0.3413 + 0.4772 = 0.8185.$$

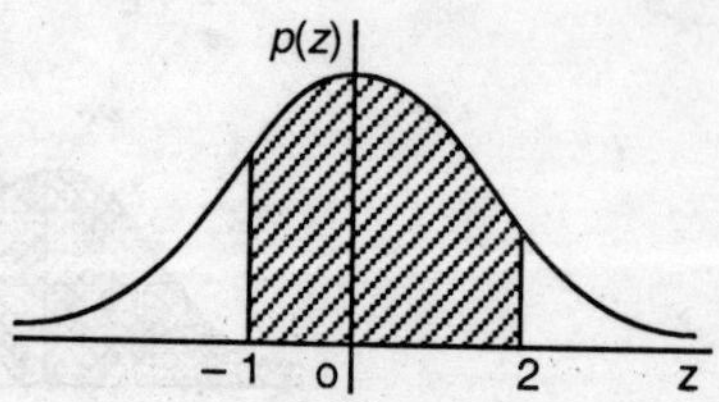

(iii)

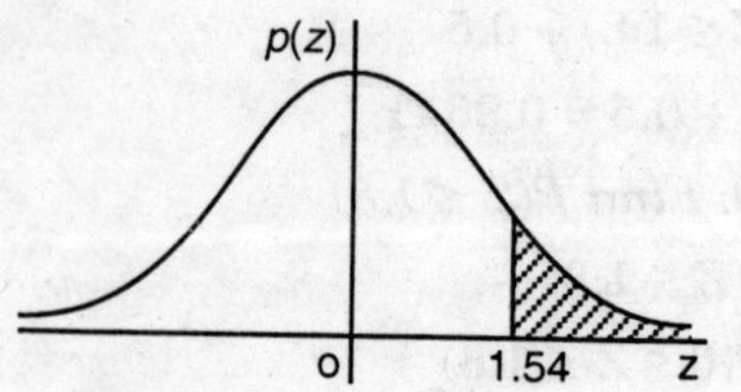

(iv)

(*iv*) $P(z \geq 1.54) = 0.5000 - P(0 \leq z \leq 1.54) = 0.5000 - 0.4382 = 0.0618.$

(*v*) $P(|z| > 2) = P(z > 2) + P(z < -2) = 2P(z > 2) = 2[0.5000 - P(0 \leq z \leq 2)]$

$= 1 - 2P(0 \leq z \leq 2) = 1 - 2 \times 0.4772 = 0.0456.$

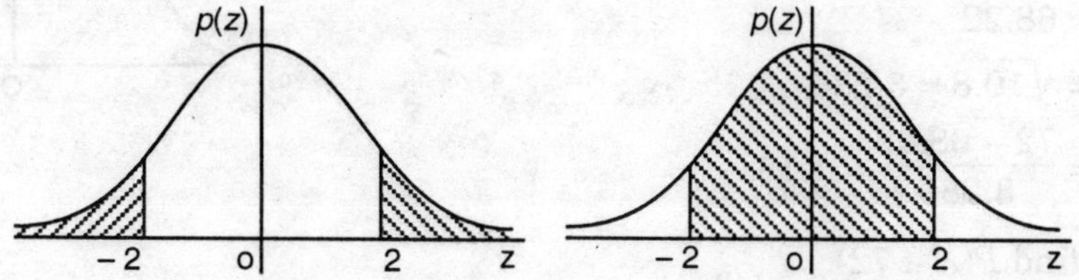

(v) (vi)

(*vi*) $P(|z| < 2) = P(-2 \leq z \leq 0) + P(0 \leq z \leq 2) = 2P(0 \leq z \leq 2) = 2 \times 0.4772 = 0.9544.$

Example 63. *Determine the value or values of z in each of the following situations:*

(*a*) *Area between 0 and z is 0.4495.* (*b*) *area to the left of z = 0.1401*

(*c*) *Area between – ∞ to z is 0.6103.*

Solution.

(*a*) On locating the value of z corresponding to an entry of area 0.4495 in the table of areas under the normal curve, we have $z = 1.64$. We note that the same situation may correspond to a negative value of z. Thus, z can be 1.64 or – 1.64.

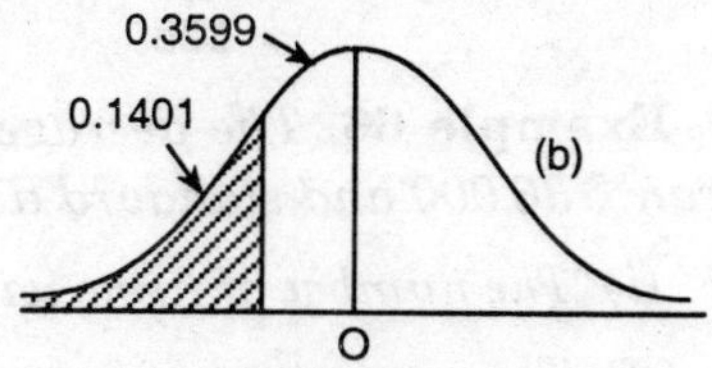

(*b*) Since the area between $-\infty$ to z is < 0.5, z will be negative. Further, the area between z and $0 = 0.5000 - 0.1401 = 0.3599$. On locating the value of z corresponding to this entry in the table, we get $z = -1.08$.

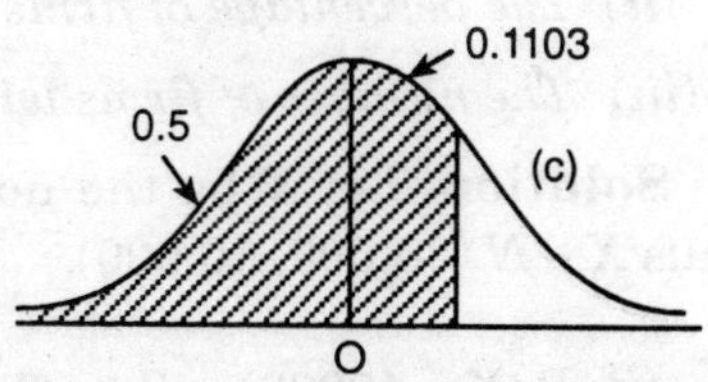

(*c*) Since the area between $-\infty$ to $z > 0.5000$, z will be positive. Further, the area between 0 to $z = 0.6103 - 0.5000 = 0.1103$. On locating the value of z corresponding to this entry in the table, we get $z = 0.28$.

Example 64. *A normal curve has* $\overline{X} = 20$ *and* $\sigma = 10$. *Find the area between* $x_1 = 15$ *and* $x_2 = 40$.

Solution. $z_1 = \dfrac{X - \overline{X}}{\sigma} = \dfrac{15 - 20}{10} = -0.50$; $z_2 = \dfrac{40 - 20}{10} = +2.0$

Consulting the table we find the areas corresponding to $Z = 0.5$ and $Z = 2$ are 0.1915 and 0.4772 respectively and thus the desired area between $x_1 = 15$ and $x_2 = 40$ is $(0.1915 + 0.4772) = 0.6687$ as shown in the figure.

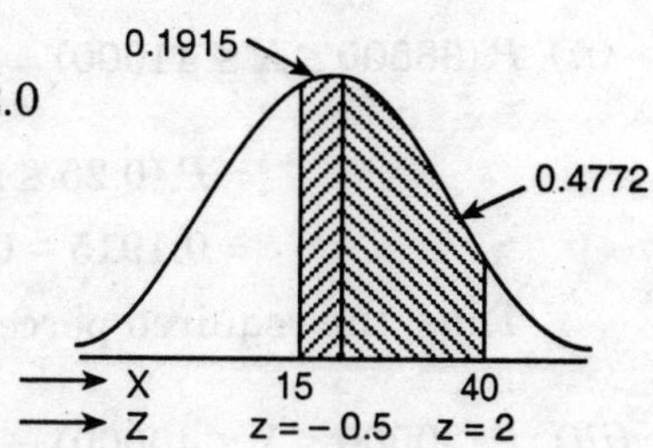

Example 65. *Assume the mean height of soldiers to be 68.22 inches with a variance of 10.8 inches. How many soldiers in a regiment of 1,000 would you expect to be over 6 feet.*

Solution. Assume the distribution of height is normal.

Standard normal variate or $z = \dfrac{X - \overline{X}}{\sigma}$

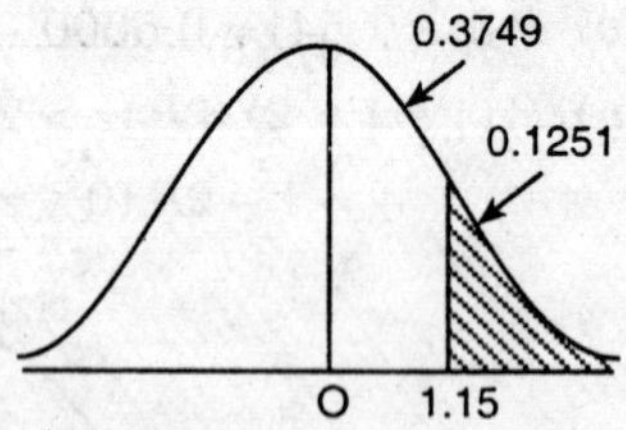

Here $X = 12 \times 6 = 72$ inches

$\overline{X} = 68.22$

$\sigma = \sqrt{10.8} = 3.286$

$z = \dfrac{72 - 68.22}{3.286} = 1.15.$

Required to find $P(X \geq 72)$

$= P(Z \geq 1.15)$

$= 0.5 - P(0 \leq Z \leq 1.15)$

$= 0.5 - 0.3749 = 0.1251$

This is the probability that a soldier is more than 6 feet. Now out of 1000 how many such soldiers are there

$= 1000 \times 0.1251 = 125.1$

$= 125.$

Example 66. *The average monthly sales of 5,000 firms are normally distributed with mean ₹ 36,000 and standard deviation ₹ 10,000. Find:*

(*i*) *The number of firms with sales of over ₹ 40,000.*

(*ii*) *The percentage of firms with sales between ₹ 38,500 and ₹ 41,000.*

(*iii*) *The number of firms with sales between ₹ 30,000 and ₹ 40,000.*

Solution. Let X be the normal variate which represents the monthly sales of a firm. Thus $X \sim N$ (36,000, 10,000).

(*i*) $P(X > 40000) = P\left(z > \dfrac{4000 - 36000}{10000}\right) = P(z > 0.4)$

$= 0.5000 - P(0 \leq z \leq 0.4) = 0.5000 - 1.1554 = 0.3446$

Thus, the number of firms having sales over ₹ 40,000

$= 0.3446 \times 5000 = 1723$

(*ii*) $P(38500 \leq X \leq 41000) = P\left(\dfrac{38500 - 36000}{10000} \leq z \leq \dfrac{41000 - 36000}{10000}\right)$

$= P(0.25 \leq z \leq 0.5) = P(0 \leq z \leq 0.5) - P(0 \leq z \leq 0.25)$

$= 0.1915 - 0.0987 = 0.0987$

Thus, the required percentage of firms $= 0.0987 \times 100 = 9.87\%$.

(*iii*) $P(30000 \leq X \leq 40000) = P\left(\dfrac{300 - 36000}{10000} \leq z \leq \dfrac{40000 - 36000}{10000}\right)$

$= P(-0.6 \leq z \leq 0.4) = P(0 \leq z \leq 0.6) + P(0 \leq z \leq 0.4)$

$= 0.2258 + 0.1554 = 0.3812$

Required number of firms = 0.3812 × 5000
= 1906.

Example 57. *You are incharge of rationing in a State affected by food shortage. The following reports were received form investigators :*

Daily calories of food available per adult during current period.

Area	*Mean*	*S.D.*
A	*2,000*	*350*
B	*1,750*	*100*

The estimated requirement of an adult is taken at 2,500 calories daily and the absolute minimum of 1,000. Comment on the reported figures and determine which area in you opinion needs more urgent attention.

Solution.

Area A	*Area B*
Mean ± 3 σ	Mean ± 3 σ
2,000 ± (3 × 350)	1,750 ± (3 × 100)
Between 950 and 3,050 calories	Between 1,450 and 2,050 calories

Since the estimated requirement is a minimum of 1,000 calories, area *A* needs more urgent attention because there are people here who are getting less than 1,000 calories.

In group *A* calorie intake varies from 950 to 3050. As such there as some persons who do not get base minimum required and in Area *B* everybody is getting more than bare minimum.

Example 68. *In a distribution exactly normal, 7% of the items are under 35 and 89% are under 63. What are the mean and standard deviate of the distribution?*

Solution. Since 7% of items are under 35, 43% are between $\overline{X}$ and 35. Similarly the percentage of term between $\overline{X}$ and 63 in 39%.

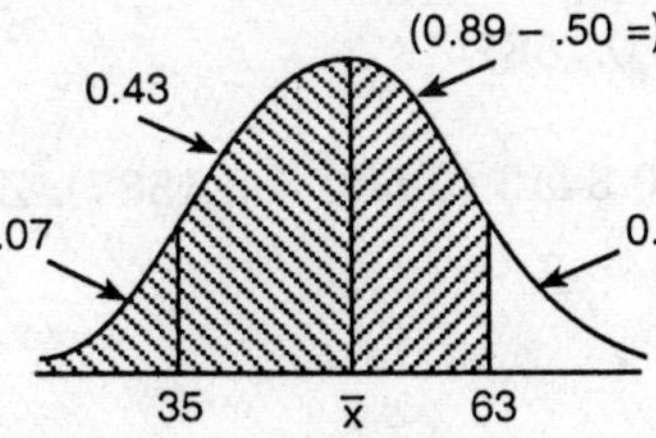

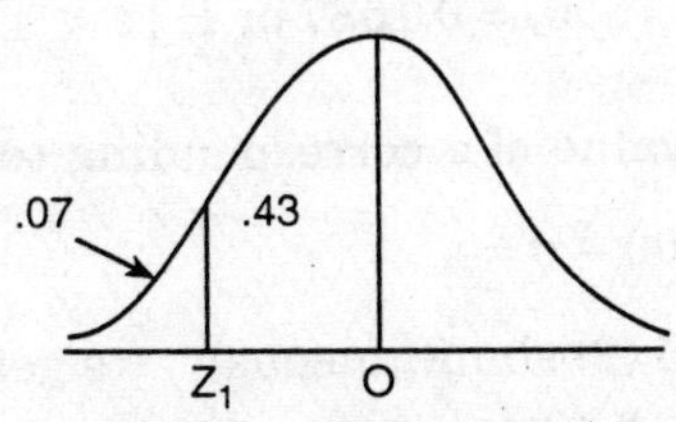

The standard normal variate corresponding to 0.43 (43%) is 1.48. [As area to the left of Z_1 is 0.07 thus Z_1 = – 1.48 see example 60]

Thus $Z_1 = \dfrac{35 - \overline{X}}{\sigma} = -1.48$ ...(*i*)

The standard normal variate corresponding to area 0.39 (39%) is 1.23 [As area between 0 & *Z* is 0.39]

$Z_2 = \dfrac{63 - \overline{X}}{\sigma} = +1.23$ ...(*ii*)

From (*i*) and (*ii*)

$1.48\,\sigma - \overline{X} = -35$

$1.23\,\sigma + \overline{X} = 63$

On adding these equations, we get

$$2.71\,\sigma = 28$$

$$\therefore \quad \sigma = \frac{28}{2.71} = 10.33$$

$$\overline{X} = 1.48 \times 10.33 + 35 \quad \text{[From (i)]}$$

$$\therefore \quad \overline{X} = 50.3$$

Hence the mean of distribution is 50.3 and $\sigma = 10.33$.

Example 69. *In a large institution, 2.28% of employees have income below ₹ 4,500 and 15.87% of employees have income above ₹ 7,500 per month. Assuming the distribution of income to be normal, find its mean and standard deviation.*

Solution. Let the man and standard deviation of the given distribution be μ and σ respectively.

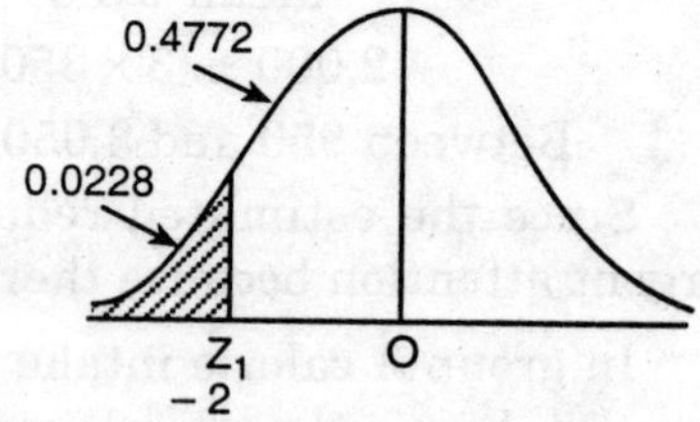

It is given that $P(X < 4500) = 0.0228$ or $P\left(z < \frac{4500 - \mu}{\sigma}\right)$ $= 0.0228$

or $P(Z < Z_1) = 0.022$ where $Z_1 = \frac{4500 - u}{\sigma}$

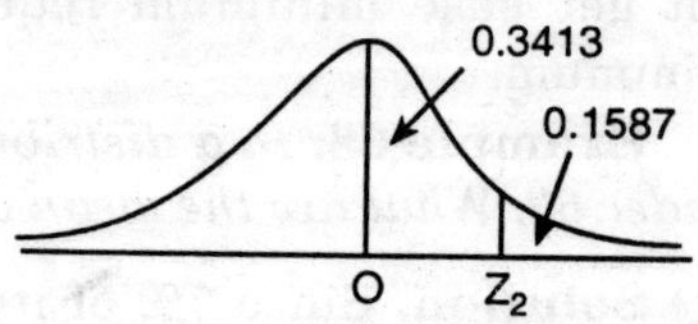

Z_1 is – ve and z value corresponding to area 0.4772 is $2 \Rightarrow Z_1 = -2$

$$\frac{4500 - \mu}{\sigma} = -2 \text{ or } 4500 - \mu = -2\sigma \qquad \ldots(1)$$

Similarly, it is also given that

$$P(X > 7500) = 0.1587 \text{ or } P\left(z < \frac{7500 - \mu}{\sigma}\right) = 0.1587$$

Locating the value of z corresponding to an area 0.3413 (0.500 – 0.1587), $Z_2 = 1$. Thus

$$\frac{7500 - \mu}{\sigma} = 1 \text{ or } 7500 - \sigma = \mu \qquad \ldots(2)$$

Solving (1) and (2) simultaneously, we get

$$\mu = ₹\,6{,}500 \text{ and } \sigma = ₹\,1{,}000.$$

Example 70. *Marks in an examination are approximately normally distributed with mean 75 and standard deviation 5. If the top 5% of the students get grade A and the bottom 25% get grade F, what mark is the lowest for A and what mark is the highest for F ?*

Solution. Let A be the lowest mark for grade A and F be the highest mark for grade F. From the given information, we can write

$$P(X \geq A) = 0.05 \text{ or } P\left(z \geq \frac{A - 75}{5}\right) = 0.05$$

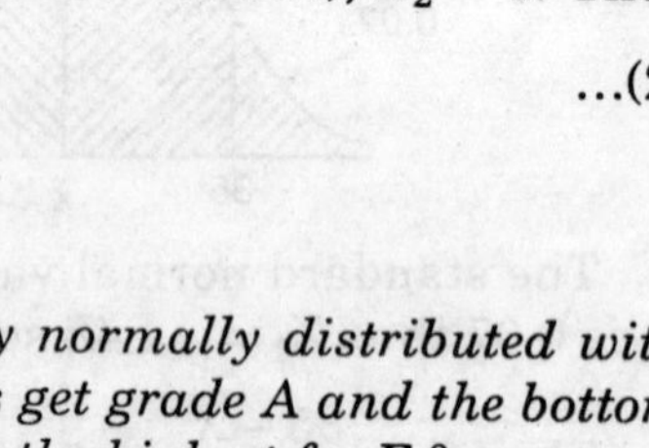

On locating the value of z corresponding to an area 0.4500 (0.5000 – 0.0500), we can write $z_1 = \frac{A - 75}{5} = 1.645 \Rightarrow A = 83.225$

Further, it is given that

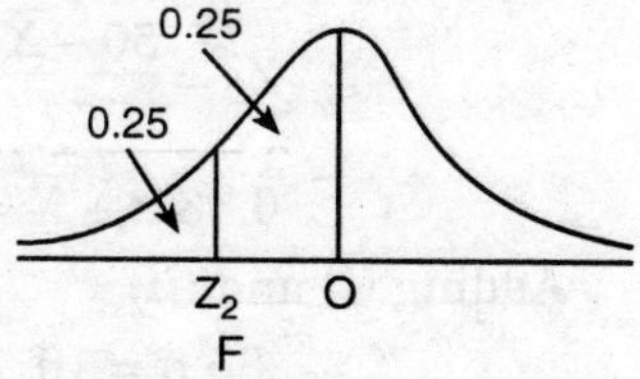

$P(X \leq F) = 0.25$ or $P\left(z \leq \dfrac{F-75}{5}\right) = 0.25$

On locating the value of z corresponding to an area 0.2500 (0.5000 – 0.2500), we can write $z_2 = \dfrac{F-75}{5} = -0.675 \Rightarrow F =$ 71.625.

Example 71. *The mean inside diameter of a sample of 200 washers produced by a machine is 5.02 mm and the standard deviation is 0.05 mm. The purpose for which these washers are intended allows a maximum tolerance in the diameter of 4.96 to 5.08 mm, otherwise the washers are considered as defective. Determine the percentage of defective washers produced by the machine on the assumption that diameters are normally distributed.*

Solution. Let X = diameter of washers, it is given $X \cap N$ (5.02, 0.05) P(washer is good, within tolerance limit) = $P(4.96 \leq X \leq 5.08)$.

$= P\left(\dfrac{4.96-5.02}{0.05} \leq Z \leq \dfrac{5.08-5.02}{0.05}\right) = P(-1.2 \leq Z \leq 1.2)$

$= 2P(0 \leq Z \leq 1.2) = 2\,(0.3849)$ [from tables]

$= 0.7698$

P (washer is defective) = 1 – 0. 7698 = 0 .2302.

Example 72. *The following table gives frequencies of a variate X between certain limits.*

X	*Frequency*
Less than 40	30
4 or more but less than 50	33
50 or more	37
	100

The distribution is exactly normal. Find the average and standard deviation of X.

Solution. Probability of X being less than 40 :

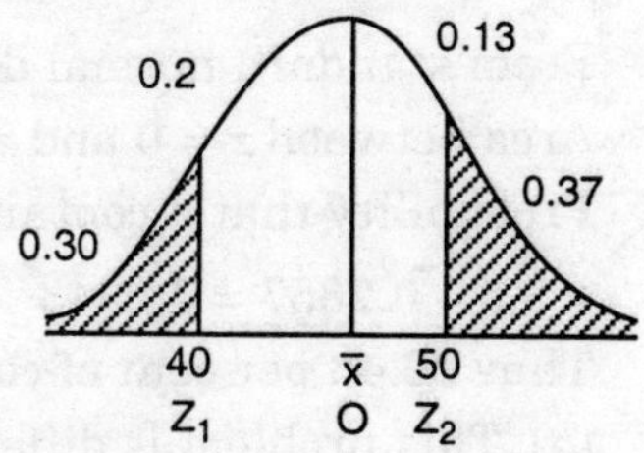

$P(X < 40) = \dfrac{30}{100} = 0.30$

Probability of X being more than 50 :

$P(X > 50) = \dfrac{37}{100} = 0.37$

From the table the z value corresponding to 0.2 or 20% area is 0.52.

From the table the z value corresponding to 0.13 or 13% area is 0.33.

For proportion of area 0.2 :

$z = \dfrac{X - \overline{X}}{\sigma}$

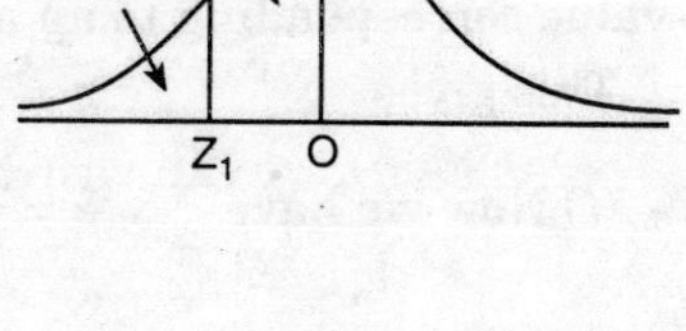

Hence $\quad Z_1 \simeq \dfrac{40 - \overline{X}}{\sigma} = -0.52$ (Z_1 is – ve)

$0.52\,\sigma - \overline{X} = -40 \qquad \ldots(i)$

For proportions of area 0.13, $Z_2 = 0.33$

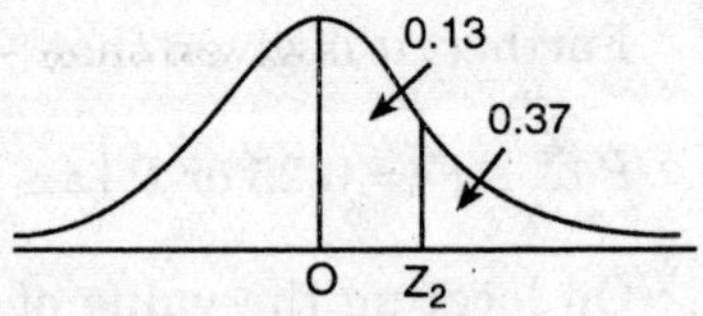

$$Z_2 = \frac{50 - \overline{X}}{\sigma} = 0.33$$

$$0.33\,\sigma + \overline{X} = 50 \quad \ldots(ii)$$

Adding (*i*) and (*ii*)

$$.85\,\sigma = 10$$

$$\sigma = \frac{10}{.85} = 11.76$$

Putting the value in (*i*)

$$0.52 \times 11.76 - \overline{X} = -40$$

$$6.1152 - \overline{X} = -40$$

$$6.1152 + 40 = \overline{X}$$

$$46.12 = \overline{X}$$

Example 73. *The finance department of a pharmaceutical company is concerned that the ageing machinery on its production line is causing losses by putting too much on average of a certain product into each container. A heck on the line shows that the mean amount being put into a container is 499.5 ml, with a standard deviation of 0.8 ml.*

(a) Adopting a normal distribution, what percentage of containers will contain more than the notional contents of 500 ml ?

(b) There are two courses of remedial action available : one would reduce the mean amount inserted (leaving the standard deviation unaltered), while the other would reduce the standard deviation (mean unaltered). If the manager wishes to reduce the percentage of containers containing over 500 ml to 10 per cent, how could this be achieved by reducing (i) the mean; and (ii) the standard deviation amount inserted ?

Solution. (*a*) $\mu = 499.5$, $\sigma = 0.8$

When $x = 500$, $z = \dfrac{500 - 499.5}{0.8} = 0.63$

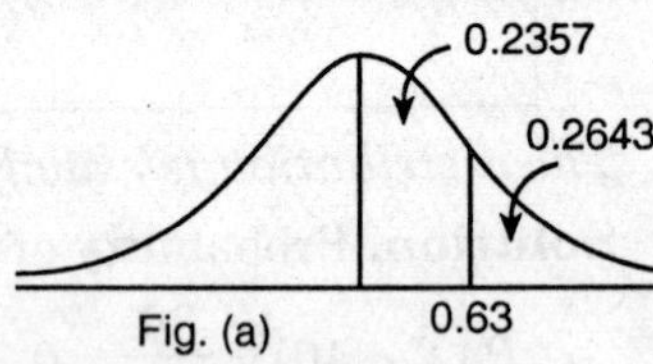

Fig. (a)

From standard normal distribution area tables,

Area between $z = 0$ and $z = 0.63$ is 0.2357

Probability that a container contains more than 500 ml

$= 0.5 - 0.2357 = 0.2643$

Thus 26.43 per cent of containers have contents over 500 ml.

(*b*) This problem is different from the earlier ones : we now know the probability (10 per cent = 0.1) and we need to 'work backwards' to find a new value for :

(*i*) μ (*ii*) σ

Figure (*b*) shows the standard normal distribution, with the upper 10 per cent of area shaded. To find the unknown *z*-value marked, we must look through the body of the table to find the *z*-value corresponding to an area of 0.4.

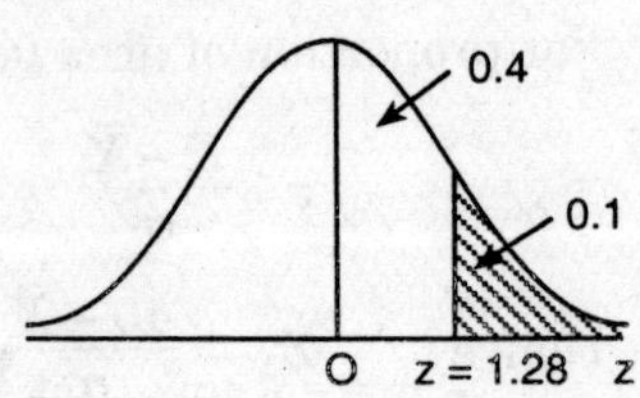

Fig. (*b*)

This gives $z = 1.28$ (approx.)

(*i*) Now we have $z = \dfrac{x - \mu}{\sigma}$ (when σ is fixed)

So, using the value of z we have found

$$1.28 = \frac{500 - \mu}{0.8} \Rightarrow 1.28 \times 0.8 = 500 - \mu \Rightarrow \mu = 499$$

Hence reducing the mean input to 499.0 ml would reduce the percentage of containers with over 500 ml to 10 per cent.

(*ii*) Similarly, if we regard μ as fixed at 499.5 and change σ; we get

$$1.28 = \frac{500 - 499.5}{\sigma} \Rightarrow 1.28\sigma = 0.5 \Rightarrow \sigma = 0.39$$

Thus the standard deviation input must be reduced to 0.39 ml to achieve the reduction to 10 per cent of container with contents over 500 ml.

Example 74. *In a certain examination, the percentage of passes and distinctions were 46 and 9 respectively. Assuming the marks to be distributed normally, determine the average marks obtained by the candidates, the minimum pass and distinction marks being 40 and 75 respectively.*

Also, determine, what should have been the minimum qualifying marks for admission to re-examination of the failed candidates, had it been desired that the best 25% of them should be given another opportunity of being examined.

Solution. (*i*) Given

$P(X > 40) = 0.46$ (46%)

and $P(X > 75) = 0.09$ (9%)

The above data when displayed through a normal curve, they will appear as in figure (*a*) and (*b*).

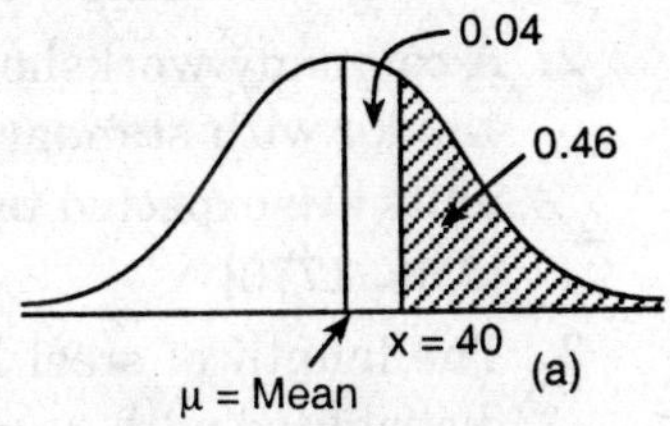

(a)

From the area of a normal curve it is seen that an area of 0.04 is enclosed when Z = 0.105 and that an area of 0.41 (*i.e.*, 0.04 + 0.37 or 0.5 – 0.09) is enclosed when Z = 1.340625.

Thus $Z = 0.105$, when $X = 40$

and $Z = 1.340625$, when $X = 75$

we have $Z = \dfrac{X - \mu}{\sigma}$

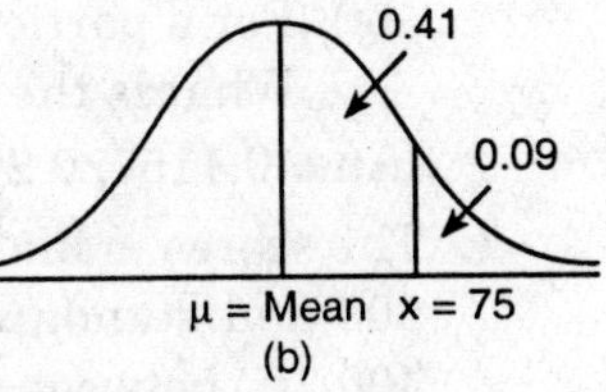

(b)

Thus, $0.1 = \dfrac{40 - \mu}{\sigma}$

$\Rightarrow$ $0.1\,\sigma = 40 - \mu$ ...(1)

Again $1.34 = \dfrac{75 - \mu}{\sigma}$

$1.34\,\sigma = 75 - \mu$ ...(2)

(2) – (1), $(1.34 - 0.1)\,\sigma = 35$

$\Rightarrow$ $\sigma = \dfrac{35}{1.33} = 26$

and $u = 37.4$ [from (*i*)]

Now we know that percentage of students who failed = 54% [= 100 – 46]

25% of these should be given chance to reexamination

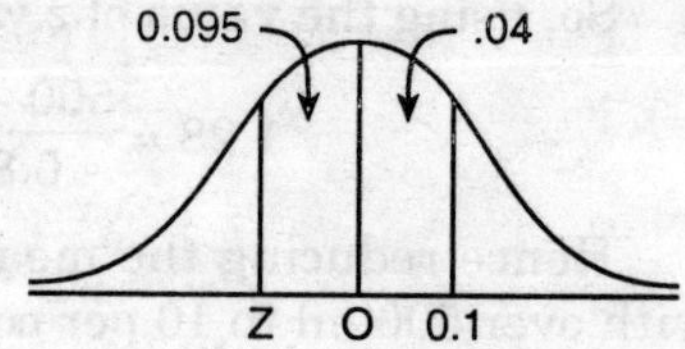

i.e., $54 \times \frac{25}{100} = 13.5\% = 0.135$

Thus area between Z and 0.1 should be 0.135 whereas area between 0 and 0.1 is .04. Thus Z must be on left side of 0 and area between Z and 0 will be 0.135 – 0.04

= 0.095 and looking in the table we find $Z = -0.24$

We need in X for this value of $Z = -0.24$

$$-0.24 = \frac{X-\mu}{\sigma} = \frac{X-37.4}{26}$$

$$X = 37.4 - 26\,(0.24)$$

$= 37.4 - 6.24 = 31.16$. *i.e.,* students who score between 31 and 40 qualify for reexamination.

EXERCISE 13.3

1. The income of a group of 10,000 persons was found to be normally distributed with mean ₹ 1,750 p.m. and standard deviation of ₹ 50, show that of this group 95% had income exceeding ₹ 1,668 and only 5% had income exceeding ₹ 1,832.
2. A company workshop produces 2,000 units per day. The average weight of units is 130 kg with standard deviation of 10 kg. Assuming Normal distribution, how many units are expected to weigh less than 142 kg ?
   [**Ans.** 1770]
3. The length of steel I beam made by the Smokers City Steel Company is normally distributed with $\mu_x = 25.1$ feet and $\sigma_x = 0.25$ foot.
   (*a*) What is the probability a steel beam will be less than 24.8 feet long ?
   (*b*) What is the probability a steel beam will be more than 25.25 feet long ?
   (*c*) What is the probability a steel beam will between 24.9 and 25.7 feet long ?
   (*d*) What is the probability a steel beam will be between 24.6 and 24.9 feet long ?
   (*e*) For a particular application, any beam less than 25 feet long must be scrapped. What is the probability a beam will have to be scrapped ?
   [**Ans.** 0.1157, 0.2743, 0.7799, 0.7891, 0.3446]
4. The scores made by candidates in a certain test are normally distributed with mean 500 and standard deviation 100. What per cent of candidates receive (*i*) less than 400, (*ii*) between 400 and 600?
   [**Ans.** (*i*) 15.86%, (*ii*) 68.26%]
5. A certain automatic screw manufacturing machine produces on the average one slotless screw among every 100 screws. If the screws are packed in boxes of 300, what percentage of these boxes would you expect to have (*i*) no slotless screw, and (*ii*) at least one slotless screw ?
   [**Ans.** (*i*) 4.98%, (*ii*) 95.02%]
6. In an examination 15% of the candidates go first class (60% marks or above) while 40% failed (securing below 40%). Assuming the marks to be normally distributed, estimated the mean and standard deviation.
   [**Ans.** $\mu = 43.88$, $\sigma = 15.5$]

7. The weekly wages of 2,000 workers in a factory are normally distributed with a mean of ₹ 200 and a variance of 400. Estimate the lowest weekly wages of the 197 highest paid workers and the highest weekly wages of the 197 lowest paid workers.
[**Ans.** 225.80, 174.20]

8. Among 10,000 random digits, in how many cases do we expect that the digit 3 appears at the most 950 times. (The area under the standard normal curve for z = 1.667 is 0.4525 approximately.)
[**Hint :** $\mu = 10000 \times 0.10$ and $\sigma^2 = 1000 \times 0.9$]
[**Ans.** 475]

9. Marks obtained by certain number of students are assumed to be normally distributed with mean 65 and variance 25. If three students are taken at random, what is the probability that exactly two of them will have marks over 70 ?
[**Hint :** Find the probability (p) that a student gets more than 70 marks. Then find ${}^3C_2 p^2 q$, where $p = P\,[x \geq 70]$.
[**Ans.** 0.0636]

10. Steel rods are manufactured to a specification of 20 cm length and are acceptable only if they are within the limits of 19.9 cm and 20.1 cm. If the lengths are normally distributed, with mean 20.02 cm and standard deviation 0.05 cm, find the percentage of rods which will be ejected as
(*i*) undersize and (*ii*) oversize.
[**Ans.** 0.8%, 5.5%]

11. (*a*) Discuss the importance of the Normal distribution.
(*b*) Daily electricity power consumption in a large office block is normally distributed with a mean of 10,000 kilowatts and a standard deviation of 2,000 kilowatts. What is the probability that the consumption of electricity on a given day is :
(*i*) Greater than 13,000 kilowatts (*ii*) less than 8,000 kilowatts
(*iii*) between 7,500 and 14,000 kilowatts ?
[**Ans.** 0.0668, 0.1587, 0.8716]

12. Applicants for a certain jobs are given an aptitude test. Past experience shows that the scores form the test are normally distributed with a mean of 60 points and a standard deviation of 12 points. What percentage of candidates would be expected to pass the test if a minimum score of 75 is required ?
[**Ans.** 0.1056]

13. The weekly wages of 200 workers are normally distributed. Its mean and standard deviation are ₹ 140 and ₹ 10 respectively. Estimate the number of workers whose weekly wages will be, (*i*) between ₹ 120 and ₹ 130, (*ii*) more than ₹ 170, and (*iii*) less than ₹ 165.
[**Ans.** (*i*) 272, (*ii*) 3, (*iii*) 1988]

14. A company, that sells 5000 batteries in a year, guarantees them for a life of 24 months. Life of batteries is estimated to be approximately normal with mean equal to 34 months and standard deviation of 5 months. Find the number of batteries that will have to be replaced under the guarantee.
[**Ans.** 114]

15. The marks of the students in a class are normally distributed with mean 70 and S.D. of 5. If the instructor decides to give '*A*' grade to the top 15% of the class, how many marks a student must get to be able to get '*A*' grade ?

[**Ans.** 73.15]

16. A complex television component has 1,000 joints by a machine which is known to produce on an average one defective in forty. The components are examined and the faulty soldering corrected by hand. If the components requiring more than 35 corrections are discarded, what proportion of the components will be thrown away?

[**Hint** : Use Poisson approximation to normal distribution.]

[**Ans.** 2.28%]

17. The average number of units produced by a manufacturing concern per day is 355 with a standard deviation of 50. It makes a profit of ₹ 150 per unit. Determine the percentage of days when its total profit per day is (*i*) between ₹ 457.50 and ₹ 645.00, (*ii*) greater than ₹ 628.50.

[**Hint :** Find the probabilities of producing 457.50/150 to 645/150 units etc.

[**Ans.** 77.45%, 2.28%]

18. A tyre manufacturing company wants 90% of its tyres to have a wear life of at least 40,000 kms. If the standard deviation of the wear lives is known to be 3,000 kms, find the average war life that must be achieved by the company. Assume that the wear life of tyres is normally distributed.

[**Hint :** $P\left(\frac{40000-\mu}{3000} > z_0\right) = 0.90$

[**Ans.** 43840 Kms.]

19. The average time required to perform job A is 85 minutes with a standard deviation of 16 minutes, and the average time required to perform job B is 110 minutes with a standard deviation of 11 minutes. Assuming normal distributions, what proportion of the time will job A take longer than the average job B, and what proportion of the time will job B take less time than the average job A ?

[**Ans.** 0.0594, 0.0116]

20. The number of days which guests stay at a large resort is a random variable having approximately a Normal distribution with the mean μ = 8.5 and the standard deviation σ = 2.2. Among 1,000 guests, how many can be expected to stay at the resort anywhere form 5 to 10 days, inclusive ?

[**Ans.** 784.2]

21. The head of the complaint department of a department store knows from experience that the number of complaints he receives per eight-hour day is a random variable with the mean μ = 33.4 and the standard deviation σ = 5.5. Assuming that the distribution of the number of complaints has roughly the shape of a Normal distribution, find the probabilities that he will receive

(*a*) more than 40 complaints
(*b*) at least 40 complaints
(*c*) at most 30 complaints
(*d*) less than 30 complaints.

[**Ans.** 0.0985, 0.1335, 0.2981, 0.2389]

22. The mean marks on a final examination was 72 and the standard deviation was 9. The top 10% of be students are to receive A's. What is the minimum marks a student must get in order to receive an A?
[**Ans.** 83.52]

23. Given a normal distribution with $\mu = 50$ and $\sigma = 10$, find x_1 and x_2 so that 13% of the area is to the left of x_1 and 4% of area to the right of x_2.
[$x_1 = 38.7$, $x_2 = 67.5$]
[**Ans.** 38.7, 67.5]

24. After an airplane has discharged its passengers, it takes crew *A* an average of 15 minutes ($\sigma = 4$ min.) to complete its task of handling baggage and loading food and other supplies. Crew *B* fuels the plane and does maintenance checks, taking an average of 16 minutes ($\sigma = 2$ min.) to complete its task. Assume that the two crews work independently and their times, to complete the tasks, are normally distributed. What is the probability that both crews will complete their tasks soon enough for the plane to be ready for take off with in 20 minutes?
[**Hint :** $P(A).\ P(B) = P(AB)$.]
[**Ans.** 0.874]

25. An automobile company buys nuts of a specified mean diameters μ A nut is classified as defective if its diameter differs form μ by more than 0.2 mm. The company requires that not more than 1% of the nuts may be defective. What should be the maximum variability that the manufacturer can allow in the production of nuts so as to satisfy the automobile company ?
[**Hint :** Find S.D.
[**Ans.** 0.078]

26. The probability that a hand-made biscuit has a weight less than 15 grams is 0.4. What is the probability that more than 65 biscuits are below 15 grams in weight out of a lot of 150 biscuits purchased by a consumer?
[**Hint :** Use normal approximation to binomial.]
[**Ans.** 0.2266]

27. A standard I.Q. test produces normally distributed results with a mean of 100 and a S.D. of 15 A class of high school science students is grouped homogeneously by excluding students with I.Q. in scores either the top 5% or the bottom 5%. Find the lowest and the highest possible I.Q. scores of students remaining in the class.
[**Ans.** 75.3, 124.7]

28. 10 per cent of all values of a Normal distribution are between 90 and 90 is the maximum value. Assuming the all values are within four S.D.s of the mean, find μ and σ.
[**Ans.** 82.64, $\sigma = 1.84$]

29. Suppose we begin with a population of normally distributed values with mean of zero an S.D. of 1 and we add 5 to every score. If a value is randomly selected form this modified population. Find the probability that it is between 4 and 7.
[**Ans.** 0.8185]

□□□

14

Sampling and Sampling Distributions

CHAPTER OUTLINE

- Data Collection—Census and Sampling Methods
- Various Sampling Techniques
- Parameter and Statistic
- Sampling Distribution of a Statistic
- Examples of Sampling Distributions—Standard Normal, Student's *t*, Chi-Square (χ^2) and Snedecor's F—Distributions.

14.1. METHODS OF DATA COLLECTION

The need for adequate and reliable data is ever increasing for taking wise decisions in different fields of human activity and business is no exception to it. There are two ways in which the required information may be obtained :

1. Complete enumeration survey or census method, and
2. Sampling method.

Census Method. In the census method we resort to 100% inspection of the population and enumerate each and every unit of the population. In the sample method we inspect only a selected representative and adequate fraction (finite subset) of the population and after analysing the results of the sample data we draw conclusions about the characteristics of the population.

The census method seems to provide more accurate and exact information as compared to sample enumeration as the information is collected from each and every unit of the population. Moreover, it affords more extensive and detailed study. For instance, the population census conducted by the Government of India every 10 years collects information not only about the population but also obtains data relating to age, marital status, occupation, religion, education, employment, income, property, etc. The census method has its obvious limitations and drawbacks given below :

(*i*) The complete enumeration of the population requires lot of time, money, manpower and administrative personnel. As such this method can be adopted only by the government and big organisations who have vast resources at their disposal.

(*ii*) Since the entire population is to be enumerated, the census method is usually very time consuming. If the population is sufficiently large, then it is possible that the processing and the analysis of the data might take so much time that when the results are available they are not of much use because of changed conditions.

Remark. *When to use Census Method* ? Census method is recommended in the following situations :

(*a*) If the information is required about each and every unit of the population, there is no way but to resort to 100% enumeration.

(*b*) In any manufacturing process in industry, 100% enumeration should be taken recourse to under the following conditions :

(*i*) The occurrence of a defect may cause loss of life or serious casualty to personnel.

(*ii*) A defect may cause serious malfunction of the equipment.

It may also be desirable to carry out complete census if,

(*i*) *N*, the lot size is small and

(*ii*) the incoming lot quality is poor or unknown.

The effort, money and time required for carrying out complete enumeration will generally be extremely large, and, in many cases, cost may be so prohibitive that the very idea of collecting information by this method may have to be dropped. The choice, then ,may be either no data or data through the sampling method. Unless the information is required for each and every unit in the domain of study, the sampling technique is generally used to obtain the information.

Sample Method. The sample method has a number of distinct advantages over the complete enumeration method. Prof. R.A. Fisher sums up the advantages of sampling techniques over complete census in just four words : *Speed, Economy, Adaptability and Scientific Approach*. A properly designed and carefully executed sampling plan yields fairly good results, often better than those obtained by the census method. We now summarise the merits of the sample method over the census method.

1. *Speed, i.e., less time*. Since only a part of the population is to be inspected and examined, the sample method results in considerable amount of saving in time and labour. There is saving in time not only in conducting the sampling enquiry but also in the processing, editing and analysing the data. This is a very sensitive and important point for the statistical investigations where the results are urgently and quickly needed.

2. *Economy, i.e., Reduced Cost of the Enquiry*. The sample method is much more economical than a complete census. In a sample enquiry, there is reduction in the cost of collection of the information, administration, transport, training and man hours. Although, the labour and the expenses of obtaining information per unit are generally large in a sample enquiry than in the census method, the overall expenses of a sample survey are relatively much less, since only a fraction of the population is to be enumerated. This is particularly significant in conducting socio-economic surveys in developing countries with budding economies who cannot afford a complete census because of lack of finances.

3. *Administrative Convenience.* A complete census requires a very huge administrative set up involving lot of personnel, trained investigators and above all the co-ordination between the various operating agencies. On the other hand, the organisation and administration of a sample survey is relatively much convenient as it requires less personnel staff and the field of enquiry is also limited.

4. *Reliability.* In the census, the sampling errors are completely absent. If the non-sampling errors are also absent the results would be 100% accurate. (For sampling and non-sampling errors see § 15.9.] On the other hand, a sample enquiry contains both sampling and non-sampling errors. In spite of this weakness, a carefully designed and scientifically executed sample survey gives results which are more reliable than those obtained from a complete census. This is because of the following reasons :

(*a*) It is always possible to ascertain the extent of sampling error and degree of reliability of the results. Even the desired degree of accuracy can be achieved through sampling using different devices.

(*b*) The non-sampling errors such as due to measuring and recording observations, inaccuracy or incompleteness of informations, location of units, non-response or incomplete response, training of investigators, interpretation of questions, bias of the investigators, etc., are of a more serious nature in a complete census. In a sample survey these errors can be effectively controlled and minimised by

(*i*) employing highly qualified, skilled and trained personnel,

(*ii*) imparting adequate training to the investigators for conducting the enquiry,

(*iii*) better supervision,

(*iv*) using more sophisticated equipment and statistical techniques for the processing and analysis of the relatively limited data.

Lastly, follow-up work in case of non-response or incomplete response can be effectively undertaken in a sample survey than in a census. The effective reduction of the non-sampling errors in a sample survey more than compensates the errors in the estimates due to sampling procedure and thus provides relatively more accurate and reliable results. The efficiency of the sampling procedure lies in the fact that quite often the accuracy of the results of a complete census is ascertained by using some type of sampling check procedure.

5. *Greater Scope.* It appears that there is possibility of obtaining detailed information only in a complete census where each and every unit in the population is enumerated. But in practice because of our limitations in any statistical enquiry in terms of time, money and man hours and because of the fact that sampling procedure results in considerable savings in time, money and labour, it is possible to obtain more detailed and exhaustive information from the limited few units selected in the sample. Obviously, it is relatively easy to collect information on, say, 25 questions from each of 100 units selected in the sample than to obtain the information on, say, 10 questions from each of 1,000 units in the population. Moreover, complete enumeration is impracticable, rather inconceivable if the enquiry requires highly trained personnel and more sophisticated equipment for the collection, processing and analysis of the data. The sampling procedure is more readily adaptable than census for statistical investigations.

6. *Infinite and Hypothetical Population.* If the population is infinite or too large, then sampling procedure is the only way of estimating the parameters of a population. For instance, the number of fish in the sea or the number of wild elephants in a dense forest can be estimated only by sampling method.

Similarly, in case of hypothetical population, as for example in the problem of throwing a die or a coin several times.

CENSUS VERSUS SAMPLING—RELIABILITY

14.2. SAMPLING AND NON-SAMPLING ERRORS

The inaccuracies or errors in any statistical investigation, *i.e.,* in the collection, processing, analysis and interpretation of the data may be broadly classified as follows :

(*i*) *Sampling Errors* and (*ii*) *Non-Sampling Errors.*

14.2.1. Sampling Errors

In a sample survey, since only a small portion of the population is studied, its results are bound to differ from the census results and thus have a certain amount of error. This error would always be there, no matter that the sample is drawn at random and that it is highly representative. This error is attributed to fluctuations of sampling and is called *sampling error*. Sampling error is due to the fact that only a subset of the population (*i.e.,* sample) has been used to estimate the population parameters and draw inferences about the population. Thus, sampling error is present only in a sample survey and is completely absent in census method.

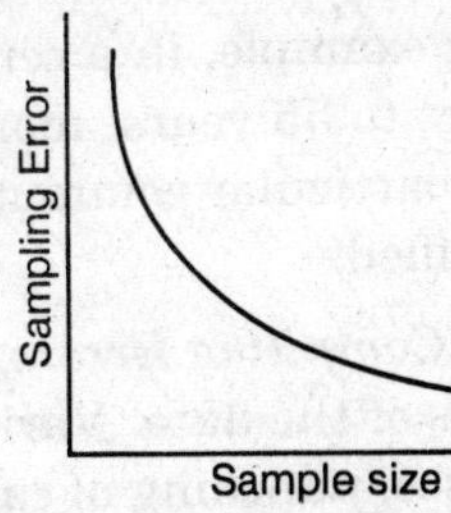

It is also established that sampling errors are reduced by increasing sample size. Larger the sample size, smaller are the sampling errors. In fact if sample size becomes as large as population size, then it is census method, and sampling error is zero.

14.2.2. Non-Sampling Errors

Non-sampling errors are not attributed to chance and are a consequence of certain factors which are within human control. In other words, they are due to certain causes which can be traced and may arise at any stage of the enquiry, *viz.,* planning and execution of the survey and collection, processing and analysis of the data. Non-sampling errors are thus present both in census surveys as well as sample surveys. Obviously, non-sampling errors will be of large magnitude in a census survey than in a sample survey because they increase with the increase in the number of units to be examined and enumerated. It is very difficult to prepare an exhaustive list of all the sources of non-sampling errors. We enumerate below some of the important factors responsible for non-sampling errors in any survey (census or sample).

1. Faulty planning, including vague and faulty definitions of the population or the statistical units to be used, incomplete list of population-members (*i.e.*, incomplete frame in case of sample survey).

2. Vague and imperfect questionnaire which might result in incomplete or wrong information.

3. Defective methods of interviewing and asking questions.

4. Vagueness about the type of the data to be collected.

5. Exaggerated or wrong answers to the questions which appeal to the pride or prestige or self-interest of the respondents. For example, a person may over-state his education or income or understate his age or he may give wrong statements to safeguard his self-interest.

6. Personal bias of the investigator.

7. Lack of trained and qualified investigators and lack of supervisory staff.

8. Failure of respondents' memory to recall the events or happenings in the past.

9. *Non-response and Inadequate or Incomplete Response.* Bias due to non-response results if in a house-to-house survey the respondent is not available in spite of repeated visits by the investigator or if the respondent refuses to furnish the information. Incomplete response error is introduced if the respondent is unable to furnish information on certain questions or if he is unwilling or even refuses to answer certain questions.

10. *Improper coverage.* If the objects of the survey are not precisely stated in clear cut terms, this may result in

(*i*) the inclusion in the survey of certain units which are to be excluded, or

(*ii*) the exclusion of certain units which were to be included in the survey under the objectives.

For example, in a census to determine the number of individuals in the age group, say, 15 years to 55 years, more or less serious errors may occur in deciding whom to enumerate unless particular community or area is not specified and also the time at which the age is to be specified.

11. *Compiling Errors, i.e.,* wrong calculations or entries made during the processing and analysis of the data. Various operations of data processing such as editing and coding of the responses, punching of cards, tabulation and summarising the original observations made in the survey are a potential source of error. Compilation errors are subject to control *through verification, consistency checks, etc.*

12. *Publication Errors.* Publication errors, *i.e.,* the errors committed during presentation and printing of tabulated results are basically due to two sources. The first refers to the mechanics of publication-the proofing error and the like. The other, which is of a more serious nature, lies in the failure of the survey organisation to point out the limitations of the statistics.

Remark. In a census, sampling error is completely absent so that the total error is non-sampling error. A sample survey, on the other hand, contains both sampling and non-sampling errors. As pointed out earlier, in a sample survey non-sampling errors can be effectively controlled by :

(*i*) Employing qualified and trained personnel for the planning and execution of the survey ;

(*ii*) Using more sophisticated statistical techniques and equipment for the processing and analysis of the data.

(*iii*) Providing adequate supervisory checks on the field work.

(*iv*) Pre-testing or conducting a pilot survey.

(*v*) Through editing and scrutiny of the results.

(*vi*) Effective checking of all the steps in the processing and analysis of the data.

(*vii*) More effective follow up of non-response cases.

(*viii*) Imparting thorough training to the investigators for efficient conduct of the enquiry.

Moreover, the sampling error in a sample survey can be minimised by taking an adequately large sample selected by an appropriate sampling plan.

Though in sampling.

Total error = sampling error + non sampling error ...(1)

And in case of census,

Total error = non sampling error ...(2)

However, non sampling errors are significantly smaller in (1) than in (2). Thus total error in (2) is generally larger than total error in (1).

14.3. PRINCIPLES OF SAMPLING

The fact that the characteristics of the sample (sample statistics) provide a fairly good idea about the population characteristics (population parameters) is borne out by the theory of probability. We discuss below some important laws which form the basis of the sampling theory.

14.3.1. Law of Statistical Regularity

This law has its origin in the mathematical theory of probability. In the words of L.R. Conner, "*The law of statistical regularity lays down that a group of objects chosen at random from a larger group tends to possess the characteristics of that large group (universe)*". According to King "*the law of statistical regularity lays down that the moderately large number of items chosen at random from a large group are almost sure on the average to possess the characteristics of the large group*.

The principle of statistical regularity impresses upon the following two points :

(*i*) *large sample size.* Logically, it seems that as the sample size increases, the sample is more likely to reveal the true characteristics of the population and thus provide better estimates of the parameters. It is known that the reliability of the sample statistic as an estimate of the population parameter is proportional to the square root of the sample size n. But due to certain limitations in terms of time, money and manpower, it is not always possible to take very large samples. Moreover, the effort and cost of drawing large samples might outlive the utility of the sample study as against the complete enumeration (census).

(*ii*) *Random selection*. The sample should be selected at random from the population. By random selection we mean a selection in which each and every unit in the population has an equal chance of being selected in the sample.

If a sample is selected such that the above two conditions are satisfied, then it will depict the true characteristics of the population fairly accurately and can be used for drawing valid inferences about the population. For example, if we are interested in studying the average height of the students in Delhi University, then it is not desirable to resort to 100% enumeration of the students in the university. A fairly adequate sample of the students from each college may be selected at random and the average height of the students selected in the samples may be computed. Since the sample is random, it would be representative of the population and the average so obtained will not differ much from the true value.

14.3.2 Principle of Inertia of Large Numbers

This principle is a corollary of the principle of statistical regularity. It is of great significance in the theory of sampling. It states that, other things being equal, larger the size of the sample, more accurate the results are likely to be. This is because large numbers are more stable as compared to small ones. The difference in the aggregate result is likely to be insignificant when the number in the sample is large, because when large numbers are considered, the variations in the component parts tend to balance each other and, therefore, the variation in the aggregate is insignificant. For example, if a coin is tossed 10 times, we should expect an equal number of heads and tails, i.e., 5 each. But since the experiment is tried a small number of times, it is likely that we may not get exactly 5 heads and 5 tails. The result may be combination of 9 heads and 1 tail, or 8 heads and 2 tails, or 7 heads and 3 tails etc. If the same experiment is carried out 1,000 times, the chance of getting 500 heads and 500 tails would be very high, i.e.. the results would be very near to 50% heads and 50% tails. The basic reason for such likelihood is that the experiment has been carried out a sufficiently large number of times and possibility of variations in one direction compensating for others in a different direction is greater. If at one time we get continuously 5 heads, it is likely that at other times we may get continuously 5 tails, and so on, and for the experiment as a whole, the number of heads and tails may be more or less equal. Similarly, if it is intended to study the variation in the production of rice over a number of years and data are collected from one or two States only, the result would reflect large variation in production due to the favourable or unfavourable factors in operation. If, on the other hand, figures of production are collected for all the States in India, it is quite likely that we find little variation in the aggregate. This does not mean that the production would remain constant for all years. It only implies that the changes in the production of the individual States will be counterbalanced and reflect small variation in production for the country as a whole.

14.4. MERITS OF SAMPLING METHOD

The sampling method has the following merits over the complete enumeration survey method:

1. *Less time*. Since the sample is a study of part of the population, considerable time and labour are saved when a sample survey is carried out. Time is saved not only in collecting

data but also in processing it. For these reasons, a sample provides more timely data in practice than a census.

2. *Less cost.* The amount of effort and expenses involved in collecting information is always greater per unit of the sample than a complete census, the total financial burden of a sample survey is generally less than that of a complete census. This is because of the fact that in sampling, we study only a part of the population and the total expense of collecting data is less than that required when the census method is adopted. This is a great advantage particularly in an underdeveloped economy where much of the information would be difficult to collect by the census method for lack of adequate resources.

3. *More reliable results.* Although the sampling technique involves certain inaccuracies owing to sampling errors, the result obtained is generally more reliable than that obtained from a complete count. There are several reasons for it. *First,* it is always possible to determine the extent of sampling errors. *Secondly,* other types of errors to which a survey is subjected, such as inaccuracy of information, incompleteness of returns, etc., are likely to be more serious in a complete census than in a sample survey. This is because more effective precautions can be taken in a sample survey to ensure that the information is accurate and complete. Moreover, it is possible to avail of the services of experts and to impart thorough training to the investigators in sample survey which further reduces the possibility of errors. Follow-up work can also be undertaken much effectively in the sampling method. Indeed, even a complete census can only be tested for accuracy by some type of sampling check.

4. *More detailed information.* Since the sampling technique saves time and money, it is possible to collect more detailed information in a sample survey. For example, if the population consists of 1,000 persons in a survey of the consumption pattern of the people, the two alternative techniques available are as follows:

(*a*) We may collect the necessary data from each one of the 1,000 persons through a questionnaire containing, say, 10 questions (census method), or

(*b*) We may take sample of 100 persons (*i.e.,* 10% of population) and prepare a questionnaire containing as many as 100 questions. The expenses involved in the latter case would almost be the same as in the former, but it will enable many times more information to be obtained.

5. *The destructive nature of certain tests.* Many tests are of destructive nature. Steel plates, wires and other similar products often must have a certain minimum tensile strength. To ensure that the product meets the minimum standard, a relatively small sample is selected. Each piece is stretched until it breaks, and the breaking point (usually measured in pounds) is recorded. Obviously, if all the wires or all the plates were tested for tensile strength, none would be available for sale or use. And for the same reason, only a sample of photographic film is selected to determine the quality of all the film produced, only a few seeds are tested for germination prior to planting season and only a few chalks out of a certain lot are tested for ascertaining the breaking strength.

14.5. LIMITATIONS OF SAMPLING

Despite the various advantage of sampling, it is not altogether free from limitations. Some of the precautions involved in sampling are given below :

(*i*) A sample survey must be carefully planned and executed, otherwise, the results obtained may be inaccurate and misleading. Of course, even for a complete count care must be taken but serious errors may arise in sampling, if the sampling procedure is not perfect.

(*ii*) Sampling generally requires the services of experts, if only for consultation purposes. In the absence of qualified and experienced persons, the information obtained from sample surveys cannot be relied upon. A shortage of experts in the sampling field is a serious hurdle in the way of reliable statistics.

(*iii*) At times, the sampling plan may be so complicated that it requires more time, labour and money than a complete count. This is so if the size of the sample is a large proportion of the total population and if complicated weighted procedures are used. With each additional complication in the survey, the chances of errors multiply and greater care has to be taken which, in turn, means more time and labour.

(*iv*) If the information is required for each and every unit in the domain of study, a complete enumeration survey is necessary.

14.6. METHODS OF SAMPLING

When a sample is required to be reflected from a population, it is necessary to decide which method should be applied. The various methods of sampling or sampling designs can be grouped under the heads as random sampling and non-random sampling. Random sampling is also referred to as probability sampling, since, if the sampling process is random, the laws of probability can be applied; thus the pattern of sampling distribution needed to interpret and evaluate a sample is provided. A non-random sample is selected on a basis other than probability considerations such as expert judgment, convenience or some other criteria. The most important aspect of non-random sampling worth noting is that it is subjected to sampling variability but there is no way of knowing the pattern of variability in the process.

We shall now discuss some of the various sampling methods under two separate headings as follows:

A. Random sampling methods:

(*i*) Simple Random Sampling

(*ii*) Stratified Sampling

(*iii*) Systematic Sampling

(*iv*) Multi-stage Sampling

14.6.1. Simple Random Sampling

Simple random sampling is considered to be the purest form of **probability sampling.**

In simple random sampling, each element in the entire population has an **equal chance** of being selected into the sample and every possible sample of given size (say n elements) drawn from specified population (or universe) has a known and equal probability of being selected, *i.e.,* every combination of n population elements is just as likely to occur as any other combination of n units.

In simple random sampling the probability of selecting any element in a sample

$$= \frac{\text{Sample size}}{\text{Population size}}$$

and the equal probability of selecting each sample of size n

$$= \frac{1}{\text{Number of possible random samples}}$$

For example, take the population of four elements B, C, D, E. The possible samples of size 2 are BC, BD, BE, CD, CE, DE *i.e.*, there are six samples.

In these six samples each element occurs three times. Therefore, the probability of selecting each element $= \frac{3}{6} = \frac{1}{2}$. This is also equal to $\frac{\text{Sample size}}{\text{Population size}} = \frac{2}{4} = \frac{1}{2}$.

i.e., $P(B) = P(C) = P(D) = P(E) = \frac{1}{2}$

and the probability of selecting each sample is $\frac{1}{6}$, *i.e.*,

$$P(BC) = P(BD) = P(BE) = P(CD) = P(CE) = P(DE) = \frac{1}{6}$$

In general, we can drawn $^{N}C_n = \frac{N!}{n!(N-n)!}$ number of samples of size n from a population of size N.

Random sample can be drawn either by lottery method or by random numbers.

But no element is repeated in the sample.

Advantages

1. The technique is easily understood and the survey's data results can be generalized to defined target population with a pre-specified margin of error.
2. Simple random samples allow the researcher to gain unbiased estimates of the population's characteristics.
3. This method basically guarantees that every sampling unit of the population has a known and equal chance of being selected, no matter the actual size of the sample, resulting valid representation of the defined target population.

Disadvantages

1. The primary disadvantage of simple random sampling is the difficulty of obtaining a complete current and accurate listing of the target population element.
2. Simple random sampling requires that all sampling units be identified. For this reason simple random sampling often works best for small populations or those where computer derived lists are available.

14.6.2. Stratified Random Sampling

In simple random sampling, the population to be sampled is treated as homogeneous and the individual elements are drawn at random from the whole universe. But many times the population is heterogeneous with respect to the characteristic or variable under study and simple random sampling fails to depict the true characteristics of the population under study. In such cases we use stratified sampling to obtain more efficient results. In stratified sampling, target population is divided into smaller subgroups and to ensure that the sample maintains the required precision of the total population, representative samples must be drawn from each of the smaller population groups (i.e., each stratum). Drawing a stratified random sample involves following basic steps :

1. In stratified sampling, the population which is to be sampled is divided into homogeneous groups in such a way that there is homogeneity **within the groups** and heterogeneity **between the groups** and these homogeneous groups (subgroups of population) are called **strata**. These homogenous groups are **mutually exclusive** and exhaustive. Various strata are (*a*) non overlapping (mutually exclusive), i.e., each and every unit in the population belongs to one and only one strata, (*b*) exhaustive, *i.e.*., the whole population is covered by these strata.
2. A sample of specified size is selected from each strata by random sampling methods.
3. Samples from each stratum area combined into a single sample of the target population.
4. Simple random samples without replacement are drawn from each strata, *i.e.*, no number is repeated.

As shown in figure population S is divided into 5 strata. From each stratum a sample is drawn randomly. Let the population be divided into k strata having units $N_1, N_2, N_3, \ldots, N_k$ units and samples of sizes $n_1, n_2, \ldots, n_k$ are drawn respectively, such that $N_1 + N_2 + \ldots\ldots + N_k = N$ (population size) and $n_1 + n_2 + \ldots\ldots + n_k = n$ (total sample size). Various criteria is used to find $n_1, n_2, \ldots\ldots n_k$.

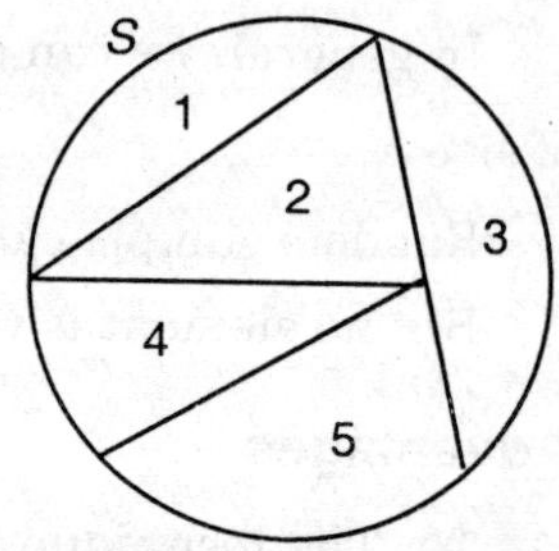

One method is proportional allocation which means $\frac{n_1}{n} = \frac{N_1}{N}$ *i.e.* $n_1 = \frac{n}{N} N_1$ and $n_2 = \frac{n}{N} N_2$ and so on (n and N both are constants).

Proportional stratification yields a sample that represents the population with respect to the proportion in each stratum in the population. This procedure is satisfactory if there is no great difference in variation from stratum to stratum. But, it is certainly not the most efficient procedure, especially when there is considerable variation in different strata. This indicates that in order to obtain maximum efficiency in stratification, we should assign greater representation to a stratum with a large variation and smaller representation to one with small variation For instance, in conducting an all-India survey of the market of a new product, all the States of India may be taken as strata. If the potential consumers of a given State are 10 per cent of all the consumers, but according to our information the product in that State is bound to have a market, we may take, say, 1 per cent or 2 per cent of our sample from that State. If, however, the outcome of another State is highly doubtful we may decide to give it a much greater representation in the sample from its relative size. A sample, thus obtained is a disproportionate stratified sample. Disproportionate stratified sampling also includes procedures of taking an equal number of items from each stratum irrespective of its size.

Merits. 1. Since the population is first divided into various strata and then a sample is drawn from each stratum there is little possibility of any essential group of the population being completely excluded. A more representative sample is thus secured. Stratified sampling is frequently regarded as the most efficient system of sampling.

2. Stratified sampling ensures greater accuracy. The accuracy is maximum if each stratum is so formed that it consists of uniform or homogeneous items.

3. As compared to random sample, stratified samples can be more concentrated geographically. Thus, the time and expense of interviewing may be considerably reduced

Limitations. 1. Utmost care must be exercised in dividing the population into various strata. Each stratum must contain, as far as possible, homogeneous items as otherwise the results may not be reliable. However, this is a very difficult task and may involve considerable time and expense.

2. The items from each stratum should be selected at random. But, this may be difficult to achieve in the absence of skilled sampling supervisors and a random selection within each stratum may not be ensured.

14.6.3. Systematic Sampling

Systematic sampling is used when the complete and upto date list of the sampling units is available and the units of the population to be sampled are ordered in a specific manner, *e.g.,* the arrangement of names in a telephone directory is in an alphabetical order and can be used for selecting a sample of telephone subscribers by the systematic sampling method.

14.6.4. Steps to select a systematic sample

1. Find the sampling interval by the formula :

   $$\text{Sampling interval or skip interval} = \frac{\text{Number of units in the population}}{\text{Desired sample size}}$$

   For instance, if the researcher wants a sample of 100 to be drawn from a defined target population of 1,000, the skip interval would be 10(1,000/100).
2. Select a random number between 1st unit and the sampling interval figure. This identifies the first element on the universe list to be included in the sample. In above example number from 1 to 10 is selected at random. Let it be 6. 1st unit of the sample is 6th unit in the list.
3. Add the sampling interval to the serial number of the random number selected in Step 2. Total gives the serial number of the second element in the universe list to be included in the sample. Thus in above example 2nd unit will be (6 + 10) 16th.
4. Other elements are obtained similarly. Similarly the serial numbers of units (in the example above) included in the sample are 26th, 36th and so on.

There are two important considerations when using systematic random sampling :

1. The natural order of the defined target population list should not be related to the characteristic being studied.
2. The skip interval must not correspond to a **systematic change in the target** population. For example, if a skip interval of 7 were used in sampling daily sales or invoices from a retail store and Tuesday was randomly selected as the starting point, we would end up with a data from the same day every week which may not give true

picture of the overall sales performance because the results are based on the sale figures which are collected on each Tuesday only. If in a certain area the sampled houses are all corner houses the sample will not represent the population.

Advantages

Systematic sampling is frequently used because, it done correctly, it is a relatively easy way to draw a sample while ensuring randomness. The availability of lists and the shorter time required to draw a sample versus simple random sampling makes systematic sampling an attractive, economical method for researchers.

Disadvantages

1. The greatest weaknesses of systematic random sampling is that there may be some hidden patterns in the data that are not found by the researcher. This could result in a sample that is not truly representative.
2. Here, the researcher must know exactly how many sampling units make up the defined target population. In research situations, where the size of the target population is extremely larger or unknown, identifying the true number of units is very difficult.
3. Sometimes sampling error is more in this type of sampling.

14.6.5. Multi-stage Sampling

As the name implies, this method refers to a sampling procedure which is carried out in several stages. The population regarded as made up of a number of first stage sampling units, each of which is made of a number of second stage units, etc. At first, the first stage units are sampled by some suitable method, such as random sampling. Then, a sample of second stage units is selected from each of the selected first stage units again by some suitable method which may be the same or different from the method employed for the first stage units. further stages may be added as required. The procedure may be illustrated as follows :

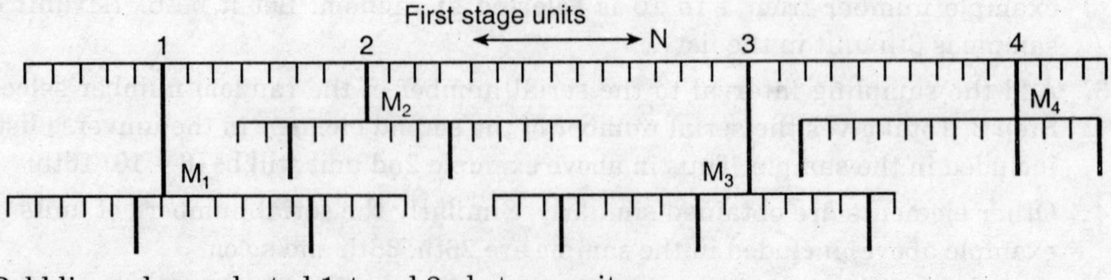

Bold lines show selected 1st and 2nd stage units.

The figure illustrates that 4 (suppose) 1st stage units out of given N 1st stage units are selected. Let these selected units have M_1, M_2, M_3 and M_4 2nd stage units. Out of these M_1, M_2, M_3 and M_4, 2nd stage units (suppose) 2, 2, 3 and 3, 2nd stage units are selected randomly.

Suppose, we want to take a sample of 5,000 households from the State of U.P. AT the first stage, the State may be divided into a number of districts and a few districts selected at random. At the second stage, each selected district may be sub-divided into a number of villages and a sample of villages may be taken at random. At the third stage, a number of households may be selected from each of the villages selected at the second stage. In this way, at each stage, the sample size becomes smaller and smaller.

Merits. Multi-stage sampling introduces flexibility in the sampling method which is lacking in other methods. It enables existing divisions and sub-divisions of the population to be used as units at various stages, and permits the field work to be concentrated and yet large area to be covered. Another advantage of the method is that sub-division into second stage unit (*i.e.,* the construction of the second stage frame) need be carried out for only those first stage units which are included in the sample. It is, therefore, particularly valuable in surveys of underdeveloped areas where no frame is generally sufficiently detailed and accurate for sub-division of the population into reasonably small sampling units.

Limitations. However, a multi-stage sample is in general less accurate than a sample containing the same number of final stage units which have been selected by some suitable stage process.

14.7. NON-PROBABILITY SAMPLING DESIGNS

Sampling techniques used to select elements from the population by any mechanism that does not involve a random selection process are called **non-random** sampling techniques. Since chance is not used to select items from the samples, these techniques are non-probability techniques and are *not desirable for use in gathering data to be analysed by the methods of inferential statistics.* Sampling error cannot be determined objectively for these sampling techniques. Three non-random sampling techniques are discussed here : Convenience Sampling, Judgment Sampling and Quota Sampling.

14.7.1. Convenience Sampling

As the name implies, convenience sampling (or accidental sampling) is a method in which samples are drawn at the convenience of the researcher or interviewer, when the study is being conducted. For example mall-intercept interviewing of individuals at shopping malls or other high-traffic areas is a common method of generating a convenience sample. The assumptions are that the target population is homogenous and the individuals interviewed at the shopping mall are similar to the overall defined target population with regard to the characteristic being studied. In reality, these is no way to accurately assess the representativeness of the sample. Given the self-selection and the voluntary nature of participating in the data collection process associated with convenience sampling, researchers should, but rarely do, give serious consideration to the extremely important issue of non-response error.

Advantages

Convenience sampling allows a large number of respondents (*e.g.,* 150-200) to be interviewed in a relatively short time. For this reason, it is commonly used in the early stages of research (*i.e.,* construct and scale measurement development as well as protesting activities of questionnaire designs).

Disadvantages

1. The major disadvantage of convenience samples is that the raw data and results are not generalizable to the defined target population with any measure of precision.
2. It is not possible to measure the representativeness of the sample, because sampling error estimates cannot be accurately determined.

14.7.2. Judgment Sampling/Subjective/Purposive sampling

In this method of sampling, the choice of sample items depends exclusively on the judgment of the investigator. In other words, the investigator exercises his judgment in the choice of sample items and includes those items in the sample which he thinks are most typical of the population with regard to the characteristics under investigation. For example, if a sample of ten students is to be selected from a class of sixty for analysing the spending habits of students, the investigator would select 10 students who, in his opinion, represent the class.

Disadvantages

This method, though simple, is not scientific because the results may be considerably affected by the personal prejudice or bias of the investigator. Thus, judgment sampling involves the risk that the investigator may establish foregone conclusions by including those items in the sample which conform to his preconceived notions. For example, if an investigator holds the view that the wages of workers in a certain establishment are very low, and if he adopts the judgment sampling method, he may include only those workers in the sample whose wages are low and thereby establish his point of view which may be far from the truth.

Advantages

Even though the principles of sampling theory are not applicable to judgment sampling, this method is often used in solving many types of economic and business problems such as :

(*i*) Judgment sampling is used when size of sample is small. In such a case, simple random simple may miss the more important elements, whereas judgment selection would certainly include them in the sample.

(*ii*) In solving everyday business problems and making public policy decisions, executives and public officials are often pressed for time and cannot wait for probability sample designs. Judgment sampling is then the only practical method, since estimates can be made available quickly that will enable businessmen and governmental officials to arrive at solutions to their urgent problems that are better than decisions made without any statistical data.

(*iii*) Judgment sampling may be used to conduct pilot studies. In any case, the reliability of sample results in judgment sampling depends on the quality of the sampler's expert knowledge or judgment. If it is good and is carefully and skillfully applied, judgment samples may be expected to be representative and to yield valuable results. On the other hand, when a sample is obtained with poor judgment, serious bias will be present.

The success of this method depends upon the excellence in judgment. If the individual making decisions is knowledgeable about the population and has good judgment, then the resulting sample may be representative, otherwise the inference based on the sample may be erroneous. It may be noted that even if a judgment is reasonably representative, there is no objective method for determining the size or likelihood of sampling error. This is a big defect of the method.

14.7.3. Quota sampling

Quota sampling is special kind of judgment sampling. In this case, population is subdivided into certain groups and number of units to be sampled is fixed (Quota) in each subgroup.

For example, if an enquiry is to be conducted in an area the researcher may fix that sample should have 50% housewives, 25% children under age of 16 years and remaining 25% should have college students. Determining sample sizes for different subgroups may be subjective may be based on some secondary information.

Advantages

The greatest advantage of quota sampling is that the sample generated contains specific subgroups in the proportions desired by researchers. In those research projects that require interviews, the use of quotas ensures that the appropriate subgroups are identified and included in the survey. The quota sampling method may eliminate or reduce selection bias on the part of the field workers.

Disadvantages

An inherent limitation of quota sampling is that the success of the study will again be dependent on subjective decisions made by the researchers. As a non-probability sampling method, it is incapable of measuring the true representativeness of the sample or accuracy of the estimate obtained. Therefore, attempts to generalize the data results beyond those respondents who were sampled and interviewed become very questionable and may misrepresent the given defined target population.

14.8. PARAMETER AND STATISTIC

Suppose we have a population of size N and variable values are $X_1, X_2, \ldots\ldots, X_N$ (using capital X for population values) and suppose a sample of n units is drawn with variable values $x_1, x_2, \ldots, x_n$ (using small x for sample values). N is population size and n is sample size.

Parameter. A parameter is function of population values say $f(X)$. Examples of parameters are $\frac{\Sigma X}{N}, \frac{\Sigma X^2}{N}$ etc.

$$\frac{\Sigma X}{N} = \frac{X_1 + X_2 + \ldots\ldots + X_N}{N} = \mu \text{ (population mean)} \qquad \ldots(1)$$

$$\text{Let } V_2 = \frac{\Sigma X^2}{N} = \text{2nd moment about 0} = \frac{X_1^2 + X_2^2 + \ldots\ldots + X_N^2}{N} \qquad \ldots(2)$$

$$\sigma^2 = \text{population variance} = \frac{\Sigma(X-\mu)^2}{N} = \frac{(X_1-\mu)^2 + (X_2-\mu)^2 + \ldots\ldots + (X_N-\mu)^2}{N} \qquad \ldots(3)$$

These are 3 examples of parameters.

Statistic. A "statistic" is function of sample value, *i.e.* $f(x)$

e.g. $\overline{X}$ = sample mean = $\dfrac{\Sigma x}{n} = \dfrac{x_1 + x_2 + ... + x_n}{n}$ ...(4)

Similarly $\dfrac{\Sigma x^2}{n} = \dfrac{x_1^2 + x_2^2 + x_3^2 + ... + x_n^2}{n}$ = sample 2nd moment about 0.

$$S^2 = \frac{\Sigma(x - \overline{X}^2)}{n} = \frac{(\overline{x}_1 - \overline{X})^2 + (x_2 - \overline{X})^2 + ... + (x_n - \overline{X})^2}{n}$$

$$s^2 = \frac{\Sigma(x - \overline{X})^2}{n-1} = \frac{(x_1 - \overline{X})^2 + (x_2 - \overline{X})^2 + ... + (x_n - \overline{X})^2}{n-1}$$

These are 4 examples of statistic.

14.9. SAMPLING DISTRIBUTION

From definition we see that a parameter is a constant for a given population whereas statistic will vary from sample to sample (As statistic is function of sample values which depends on the units included in the sample).

Suppose a sample of n units is selected from a population consisting of N units using simple random sampling with replacement (repetition of units in the sample is allowed). There are N^n such samples possible (As first unit is selected in N ways, 2nd units also is selected in N ways and so on. Using fundamental theorem of counting, no. of possible samples is N^n). Each sample gives one $\overline{X}$ and as such there are N^n values of possible $\overline{X}$'s (all may not be distinct) each value of $\overline{X}$ will have same probability $\dfrac{1}{N^n}$ for its occurrence. Thus $\overline{X}$ will have probability distribution "Probability Distribution" of a Statistic is known as "Sampling Distribution" of that "Statistic".

Similarly if sample selection is with sample random sampling without replacement in that case there are N_{C_n} possible samples as such there are as many $\overline{X}$'s and each has a probability of occurrence $\dfrac{1}{N_{C_n}}$.

Example 1. *Let N = 4 be the number of units in the population say A, B, C and D. Let the variable values be 2, 3, 5, 6 (i.e.* $X_1 = 2$, $X_2 = 3$, $X_3 = 5$ *and* $X_4 = 6$*). Find sampling distribution of* $\overline{X}$ *and its expectation when a sampleof 2 units is drawn.*

Solution. Now parameter, population mean $\mu = \dfrac{2 + 3 + 5 + 6}{4} = 4$

Suppose a sample of 2 units is taken with simple random sampling without replacement (*srswor*). The table below shows the ${}^4C_2 = 6$ possible samples and the "Statistic" $\overline{X}$.

Sr. No.	*Sample*	*Sample Values*	*Sample Mean* $\overline{X}$	$P(\overline{X})$
1	*AB*	2, 3	2.5	$\frac{1}{6}$
2	*AC*	2, 5	3.5	$\frac{1}{6}$
3	*AD*	2, 6	4.0	$\frac{1}{6}$

4	*BC*	3, 5	4.0	$\frac{1}{6}$
5	*BD*	3, 6	4.5	$\frac{1}{6}$
6	*DC*	5, 6	5.5	$\frac{1}{6}$

Sampling distribution of $\overline{X}$ is as follows :

$\overline{X}$	$P(\overline{X})$	$\overline{X}\, P(\overline{X})$
2.5	1/6	$\frac{5}{12}$
3.5	1/6	$\frac{7}{12}$
4.0	2/6	$\frac{16}{12}$
4.5	1/6	$\frac{9}{12}$
5.5	1/6	$\frac{11}{12}$

Now $E(\overline{X}) = \Sigma\overline{X}\, P(\overline{X}) = \frac{48}{12} = 4\ (= \mu)$.

4.10. ESTIMATING "PARAMETER" BY A "STATISTIC"

If we are interested to know a parameter and collection of data by census method is not feasible, (for reasons already stated) it is not possible to get value of parameter.

Very often, the value of various parameters are unknown and these are estimated by the corresponding statistic. For example, sample mean $\overline{X}$ is used as an estimator of population mean μ, sample standard deviation s is used as an estimator of population standard deviation σ, where $s^2 = \frac{\Sigma(X - \overline{X})^2}{n - 1}$ etc. The difference between a statistic and the corresponding parameter is known as *sampling error.* For example the sampling error in estimation of μ by $\overline{X}$ is $\overline{X} - \mu$. It may be noted that the sampling error is an error caused by pure chance factors.

We state this fact by saying that $\overline{X}$ (sample mean) is an estimate of μ (population mean). From the table above we find that sample means ($\overline{X}$'s) vary around population mean $\mu = 4$.

14.10.1. Unbiased Estimate

In case of a parameter θ is estimated by a statistic t such that $E(t) = \theta$, then t is called unbiased estimate of θ.

In above example, $t = \overline{X}$ and $\theta = \mu$ we have shown that $E(\overline{X}) = \mu = 4$, thus $\overline{X}$ is unbiased estimate of μ.

It can be established theoretically that $\overline{X}$ based on n sampled units, sample selected with *srswr or srswor* for any population of size N is an unbiased estimate of μ (Proof is omitted). If the probability distribution of a population is known, we are able to find sampling distribution of a statistic theoretically using concepts of theoretical statistics (which are out of scope of this book) and we will be using only the results.

14.11. STANDARD ERROR (S.E.) OF A STATISTICS

Sampling distribution of a statistic will have its own constants, mean and variance (and standard deviation).

Standard deviation of sampling distribution of a statistic is known as its standard error. Thus standard error is a specific standard deviation (of a sampling distribution).

Remarks :

1. The standard deviation of a statistic is termed as *standard error.* The standard error of $\overline{X}$, to be written in abbreviated form as *S.E.* $\overline{X}$), is equal to $\frac{\sigma}{\sqrt{n}}$, when sampling is with replacement and it is equal to $\frac{\sigma}{\sqrt{n}} \cdot \sqrt{\frac{N-n}{N-1}}$, when sampling is without replacement. (Result without proof).
2. *S.E.* $(\overline{X})$ is inversely related to the sample size.
3. Their term $\sqrt{\frac{N-n}{N-1}}$ is termed as finite population correction (*fpc*). We note that *fpc* tends to become closer and closer to unity as population size becomes larger and larger.
4. As a general rule, *fpc* may be taken to be equal to unity when sample size is less than 5% of population size, *i.e.*, $n < 0.05\,N$.

APPLICATIONS OF STANDARD ERROR

1. Standard error is used to test whether the difference between the sample statistic and the population parameter is significant or due to sampling fluctuations. Standard error gives us an idea of the error we might be making if we were to use a sample statistic instead of population parameter.
2. Standard error is used to find the precision of the sample estimate of a population. If a statistic θ is used to estimate the parameter, then the

$$\boxed{\text{Precision of } \theta = \frac{1}{\text{Standard error of } \theta}}$$

e.g. S.E. of mean $= \frac{\sigma}{\sqrt{n}}$

$$\text{Precision of mean} = \frac{1}{\frac{\sigma}{\sqrt{n}}} = \frac{\sqrt{n}}{\sigma}$$

$$\Rightarrow \sqrt{n} = \sigma \times \text{Precision of mean}$$

$$\Rightarrow n = \sigma^2 \times (\text{Precision of mean})^2$$

For a given population σ is constant.

∴ Sample size varies directly as square of precision of mean, *i.e.,* if the precision is doubled, the sample size becomes 4 times.

14.12. SOME IMPORTANT SAMPLING DISTRIBUTIONS

We have some important and widely used sampling distributions which are as follows :

1. Standard Normal Distribution—Z Distribution.
2. Student '*t*' Distribution
3. Chi (pronounced as 'Kye') Square Distribution
4. Snedecor's F-Distribution.

14.13. Z-SAMPLING DISTRIBUTION

14.13.1. Sampling Distribution of a Sample Mean $\overline{X}$

If parent population, from where sample is drawn, follows normal distribution with mean μ and standard deviation σ *i.e.* if $X \cap N(\mu, \sigma)$ then

(*i*) $\overline{X} \cap N\left(\mu, \dfrac{\sigma}{\sqrt{n}}\right)$ in case sample of size n is taken with replacement.

(*ii*) $\overline{X} \cap N\left(\mu, \dfrac{\sigma}{\sqrt{n}}\sqrt{\dfrac{N-n}{N-1}}\right)$ in case sample is take without replacement.

Example 2. *Construct a sample distribution of the sample mean for the following population when random samples of size 2 are taken from it (a) with replacement and (b) without replacement. Also find the mean and standard error of the distribution in each case.*

Population Unit	:	*1*	*2*	*3*	*4*
Observation	:	22	24	26	28

and show that

$E(\overline{X}) = u$ *and* $V(\overline{X}) = \dfrac{\sigma^2}{n}$ *(in case of srswr),* $V(\overline{X}) = \dfrac{N-n}{N-1}\dfrac{\sigma^2}{n}$ (in cvase of *srswor*)

Solution. The mean and standard deviation of population are :

$$\mu = \frac{22 + 24 + 26 + 28}{4} = 25 \text{ and}$$

$$\sigma = \sqrt{\frac{(22)^2 + (24)^2 + (26)^2 + (28)^2}{4} - (25)^2} = \sqrt{5} = 2.236 \text{ respectively.}$$

(*a*) When random samples of size 2 are drawn, we have $4^2 = 16$ samples, shown below :

Sample No.	*Sample Values*	$\overline{X}$
1	22, 22	22
2	22, 24	23
3	22, 26	24
4	22, 28	25
5	24, 22	23
6	24, 24	24
7	24, 26	25

8	24, 28	26
9	26, 22	24
10	26, 24	25
11	26, 26	26
12	26, 28	27
13	28, 22	25
14	28, 24	26
15	28, 26	27
16	28, 28	28

Since all the above sampels are equally likely, therefore, the probability of each value of $\overline{X}$ is $\frac{1}{16}$. Thus, we can write the sampling distribution of $\overline{X}$ as given below :

$\overline{X}$	22	23	24	25	26	27	28	*Total*
$P(\overline{X})$	$\frac{1}{16}$	$\frac{2}{16}$	$\frac{3}{16}$	$\frac{4}{16}$	$\frac{3}{16}$	$\frac{2}{16}$	$\frac{1}{16}$	1

The mean of $\overline{X}$, *i.e.*,

$$\mu_{\overline{X}} = E(\overline{X}) = 22 \times \frac{1}{16} + 23 \times \frac{2}{16} + 24 \times \frac{3}{16} + 25 \times \frac{4}{16} + 26 \times \frac{3}{16} +$$

$$27 \times \frac{2}{16} + 28 \times \frac{1}{16} = 25$$

Further, $S.E. (\overline{X}) = \sigma_{\overline{X}} \sqrt{E(\overline{X})^2 - [E(\overline{X})]^2}$, where

$$E(\overline{X})^2 = \frac{1}{16}(22^2 + 23^2 \times 2 + 24^2 \times 3 + 25^2 \times 4 + 26^2 \times 3 + 27^2 \times 2 + 28^2) = 627.5$$

Thus, $\sigma_{\overline{X}} = \sqrt{627.5 - 25^2} = \sqrt{2.5}$ which is equal to $\frac{\sigma}{\sqrt{n}}$ as $\frac{\sigma}{\sqrt{n}} = \sqrt{\frac{5}{2}} = \sqrt{2.5}$.

(*b*) When random samples of size 2 are drawn without replacement, we have ${}^4C_2$ samples, shown below :

Sample No.	*Sample Values*	$\overline{X}$
1	22, 24	23
2	22, 26	24
3	22, 28	25
4	24, 26	25
5	24, 28	26
6	26, 28	27

Since all the sample are equally likely, the probability of each value of $\overline{X}$ is $\frac{1}{6}$. Thus, we can write the sampling distribution of $\overline{X}$ as

$\overline{X}$	23	24	25	26	27	*Total*
$p(\overline{X})$	$\frac{1}{16}$	$\frac{1}{6}$	$\frac{2}{6}$	$\frac{1}{6}$	$\frac{1}{6}$	1

Further, $\mu_{\overline{X}} = E(\overline{X}) = \dfrac{1}{6}[23 + 24 + 25 \times 2 + 26 + 27] = 25$

To find $S.E.\ (\overline{X})$, we first find $E(\overline{X}^2)$ given by

$$E(\overline{X}^2) = \frac{1}{6}[23^2 + 24^2 + 2 \times 25^2 + 26^2 + 27^2] = \frac{3760}{6} = 626.67.$$

Thus, $\sigma_{\overline{X}} = \sqrt{626.67 - 25^2} = \sqrt{1.67} = 1.292$

Alternatively, $\sigma_{\overline{X}} = \sqrt{\dfrac{N-n}{N-1} \cdot \dfrac{\sigma^2}{n}} = \sqrt{\dfrac{4-2}{3} \times \dfrac{5}{2}} = \sqrt{1.67} = 1.292$

Thus, $V(\overline{X}) = \dfrac{N-n}{N-1}\dfrac{\sigma^2}{n} = 1.67$

$$SE(\overline{X}) = \sqrt{1.67} = 1.29.$$

Example 3. *The income of a group of workers is distributed normally with mean ₹ 1,500 and standard deviation ₹ 800. If a random sample of 64 workers is taken from this group, determine*

(i) the sampling distribution of mean,

(ii) the probability that the sample mean will lie between ₹ 1,200 and 1,600, and

(iii) the percentage of sample having their means greater than ₹ 1,700.

Solution. Given $u = 1{,}500$, $\sigma = 800$, $X \cap N(1500, 800)$

$n = 64$

(i) We know $\overline{X} \cap N\left(\mu, \dfrac{\sigma}{\sqrt{n}}\right)$ *i.e.* $SE_{\overline{X}} = \dfrac{\sigma}{\sqrt{n}} = \dfrac{800}{\sqrt{64}} = 100$

$\cap N(1500, 100)$

(ii) $P(1200 \le \overline{X} \le 1600) = P\left(\dfrac{1200-1500}{100} \le Z < \dfrac{1600-1500}{100}\right)$

$= P(-3 \le Z \le 1)$

$= 0.4987 + 0.3413$

$= 0.8400$

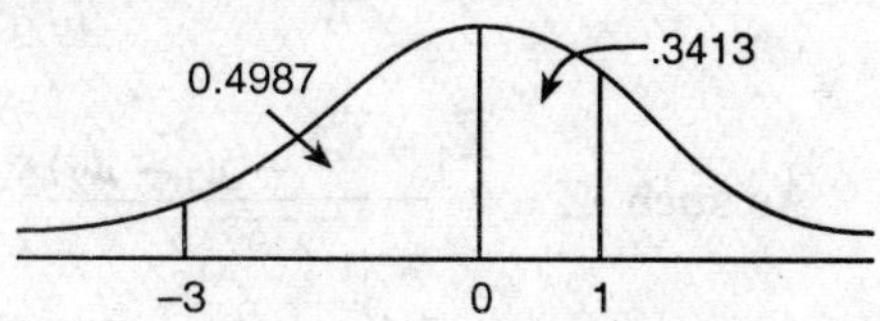

(iii) $P\left(\overline{X} \ge 1700\right) = P\left(Z \ge \dfrac{1700-1500}{100}\right)$

$= P(Z \ge 2)$

$= 0.5 - 0.4772$

$= 0.0228$

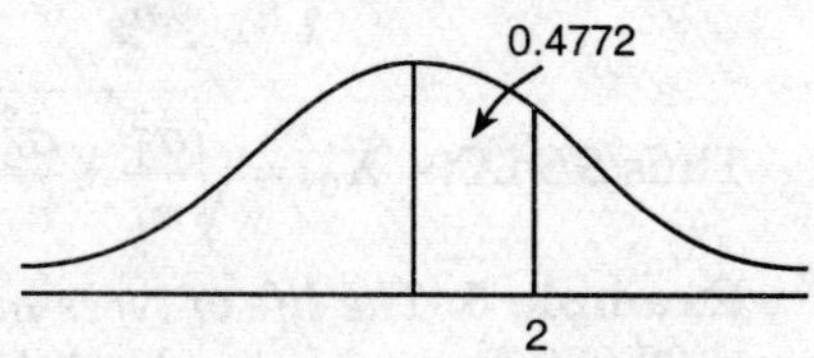

$0.0228 = (0.0228 \times 100)\%$

$= 2.28\%$

Example 4. *Consider a population of 6 units with values 1, 2, 3, 4, 5, 6. A sample of size 2 (without replacement) is drawn and $\overline{x}$ is sample mean. Find $E(\overline{x})$ and $V(\overline{x})$ through population parameters.*

Solution. We know $E(\bar{x}) = \mu$ (population mean) and $V(\bar{x}) = \frac{N-n}{N-1}\frac{\sigma^2}{n}$. We find μ and σ^2 for population with values 1, 2, 3, 4, 5 and 6.

X	$(X-\bar{X})^2$	$(X-\bar{X})^2$
1	$(2.5)^2$	6.25
2	$(1.5)^2$	2.25
3	$(.5)^2$	0.25
4	$(.5)^2$	0.25
5	$(1.5)^2$	2.25
6.	$(2.5)^2$	6.25
$\Sigma X = 21$ $\bar{X} = \frac{21}{6} = 3.5$		17.50 $\Sigma(X-\bar{X})^2$

$$\mu = \bar{X} = 3.5$$

$$\sigma^2 = \frac{\Sigma(X-\bar{X})^2}{N}$$

$$= \frac{17.50}{6} = 2.92$$

$$N = 6,\ n = 2$$

Thus $E(\bar{X}) = \mu = 3.5,\ V(\bar{X}) = \frac{N-n}{N-1}\frac{\sigma^2}{n} = \frac{6-2}{6-1}\frac{2.92}{2} = \frac{5.84}{5} = 1.17.$

14.13.2. Sampling Distribution of Difference of Two Sample Means (Samples are drawn independently from two populations)

Let X_1 and X_2 be the variables from two populations such that

$X_1 \cap N(\mu_1, \sigma_1)$ and $X_2 \cap N(\mu_2, \sigma_2)$

Now $\bar{X} \cap N\left(\mu_1, \frac{\sigma_1}{\sqrt{n_1}}\right)$ and $\bar{X}_2 \cap N\left(\mu_2, \frac{\sigma_2}{\sqrt{n_2}}\right)$

Where n_1 and n_2 are sample sizes from the two populations.

Thus $\bar{X}_1 - \bar{X}_2 \cap N\left(\mu_1 - \mu_2, \sqrt{\frac{\sigma_1^2}{n_1} + \frac{\sigma_2^2}{n_2}}\right)$

As such $Z = \dfrac{\bar{X}_1 - \bar{X}_2 - (\mu_1 - \mu_2)}{\sqrt{\frac{\sigma_1^2}{n_1} + \frac{\sigma_2^2}{n_2}}}$

Thus $SE(\bar{X}_1 - \bar{X}_2) = \sqrt{\frac{\sigma_1^2}{n_1} + \frac{\sigma_2^2}{n_2}}$.

Example 5. *The life of tyres manufactured by a company A is distributed normally with mean 32,000 kms and standard deviation 8,000 kms and of that manufactured by company B is distributed normally with mean 30,000 kms and standard deviation 5,000 kms. If 100 tyres of company A and 81 tyres of company B are selected at random, determine the sampling distribution of the difference between mean life of tyres.*

Solution. $\mu_1 = 32{,}000 \quad \sigma_1 = 8{,}000,\ n_1 = 100$

$\mu_2 = 30{,}000 \quad \sigma_2 = 5{,}000,\ n_2 = 81$

$$SE\,(\overline{X}_1 - \overline{X}_2) = \sqrt{\frac{\sigma_1^2}{n_1} + \frac{\sigma_2^2}{n_2}} = \sqrt{\frac{(8000)^2}{100} + \frac{(5000)^2}{81}} = 974$$

$$\mu_1 - \mu_2 = 2000$$

$$\Rightarrow \quad \overline{X}_1 - \overline{X}_2 \cap N\,(2000,\, 974).$$

14.3.3. Sampling Distribution of Proportion

We talk of population proportion or sample proportion, if the characteristics under study is an attribute. An attribute is a quality characteristic which cannot be measured quantitatively, *e.g.*, beauty, honesty, intelligence, colour, habit, etc. In a number of situations, it may not be possible to measure the characteristic under study yet it may be possible to classify the given population into various classes w.r.t. the given attribute. If we classify the population into only two classes w.r.t. an attribute, the classification is termed as *dichotomous classification* and if the population is divided into more than two classes, it is termed as *manifold classification*. Here we shall confine our attention to the cases where the population can be classified only into two mutually exclusive and exhaustive classes, say, C or C' according as the given unit possesses or does not processes the attribute respectively. Which can be observed only as attributes by classifying an item as good or bad; defective or non-defective, *i.e.,* conforming to specifications or not ; honest or dishonest; employed or unemployed and so on.

Let us consider a population consisting of N units and let the number of units possessing the attribute under study be 'n', say. Then in a dichotomous classification, the number of units which do not possess the given attribute is $(N - n)$.

Then

P = Proportion of units (in the population) possessing the given attribute = n/N

Q = Proportion of population units which do not possess the given attribute

$$= \frac{N-n}{N} = 1 - \frac{n}{N}$$

$$\Rightarrow \quad Q = 1 - P$$

In sampling theory, the possession of an attribute by a sampling unit is termed as a *success* and non-possession as a *failure.* Therefore, P and Q may be interpreted as representing the proportion of successes and failures respectively in the population.

If there are 10 girls in a class of 30 students then P = proportion of girls in the class = $\dfrac{10}{30}$ and $Q = \dfrac{20}{30}$.

Let us take a simple random sample without replacement (srswor) of size n from this population. If m is the number of units possessing the given attribute in the sample, then define :

p = Proportion of sampled units possessing the given attribute = $\dfrac{m}{n}$

q = Proportion of units (in the sample) which do not possess the given attribute.

$$\therefore \quad p + q = 1 \quad \Rightarrow \quad q = 1 - p$$

In sampling theory, m is termed as the number of successes and p is the proportion of successes and $q = 1 - p$, is the proportion of failure in the sample.

We shall now given some important results in SIMPLE RANDOM SAMPLING WITHOUT REPLACEMENT from a finite population.

Sample proportion 'p' is an unbiased estimate of the population proportion P i.e.,

$$E(p) = P$$

Thus, the sample proportion '*p*' can be used as an estimate for population proportion *P* *i.e.,* $\hat{P} = p$.

In srswor,

$$\text{Var}(p) = \frac{N-n}{N-1} \cdot \frac{PQ}{n} \quad \Rightarrow \quad S.E.(p) = \sqrt{\frac{N-n}{N-1} \cdot \frac{PQ}{n}}$$

In case of simple RANDOM SAMPLE WITH REPLACEMENT (*srswr*) or in case of sampling from an *infinite* population, *i.e.,* $N \to \infty$, we can approximate $N - 1$ by N. Hence

$$\text{Var}(p) \simeq \frac{N-n}{N} \cdot \frac{PQ}{n} = \left(1 - \frac{n}{N}\right)\frac{PQ}{n} = \frac{PQ}{n} \quad \left(\text{ignoring } \frac{n}{N} \text{ which will be very small}\right)$$

Example 6. *A random sample of 500 pineapples was taken from a large consignment and 65 of them were found to be bad. Show that the Standard Error of the proportion of bad ones in a sample of this size is 0.015 and deduce that the percentage of bad pineapples in the consignment almost certainly lies between 8.5 and 17.5.*

Solution Here $n = 500$.

Number of bad pineapples in the sample = 65

$\therefore \quad p$ = Proportion of bad pineapples in the sample $= \frac{65}{500} = \frac{13}{100} = 0.13$

$\Rightarrow \quad q = 1 - p = 1 - 0.13 = 0.87$

The standard error of proportion of bad pineapples in the sample is given by : $S.E.(p) = \sqrt{PQ/n}$

where *P* is the population proportion of bad pineapples in the whole consignment. Since *P* is not known, we use its unbiased estimate provided by the sample proportion *p*. Thus

$$\text{Est. } [S.E.(p)] = \sqrt{\frac{pq}{n}} = \sqrt{\frac{0.13 \times 0.87}{500}} = \sqrt{\frac{0.1131}{500}} = \sqrt{0.0002262} = 0.015$$

The most probable limits for the population proportion of bad pineapples using 3σ limits *i.e.* $p \pm 3\, SE(p)$

$$p \pm 3\sqrt{\frac{pq}{n}} = 0.130 \pm 3 \times 0.015 = 0.130 \pm 0.045 = (0.085 \text{ and } 0.175)$$

Hence the percentage of bad pineapples in the consignment lies almost surely between the limits 8.5 and 17.5.

Example 7. *There are 500 mangoes in a basket out of which 80 are defective. If obtaining a defective mango is termed as a success, determine the mean and standard error of the proportion of successes in a random sample of 10 mangoes, drawn (a) with replacement and (b) without replacement.*

Solution. It is given that $P = \frac{80}{500} = \frac{4}{25}$. Therefore, $E(p) = P = \frac{4}{25} = .16$

(*a*) *S r s w r*

$$SE\,(p) = \sqrt{\frac{PQ}{n}} = \sqrt{\frac{.16 \times .84}{10}} = .116$$

(*b*) *S r s w o r*

$$SE\,(p) = \sqrt{\frac{N-n}{N-1}}\sqrt{\frac{PQ}{n}} = \sqrt{\frac{500-10}{500-1}}(0.116) = .99 \times 0.116 = 0.115.$$

It is also observed is p follows a normal distribution as follows.

$$p \cap N\,(P, SE(p)]$$

Thus $Z = \dfrac{p - P}{SE(p)}$

where p, P and $SE(p)$ has usual meaning and values as described.

14.13.5. Sampling Distribution of Difference of Proportions

If p_1 and p_2 are the sample proportions in large and independent random samples of sizes n_1 and n_2 respectively from infinite populations with proportions P_1 and P_2, then

$$E(p_1 - p_2) = E(p_1) - E(p_2) = P_1 - P_2$$

(Since samples are independent)

$$\text{Var}\,(p_1 - p_2) = \text{Var}\,(p_1) + \text{Var}\,(p_2) = \frac{P_1Q_1}{n_1} + \frac{P_2Q_2}{n_2}$$

Hence, for large samples,

Thus $$p_1 - p_2 \cap N\left[(P_1 - P_2), \sqrt{\frac{P_1Q_1}{n_1} + \frac{P_2Q_2}{n_2}}\right]$$

and $$Z = \frac{(p_1 - p_2) - E(p_1 - p_2)}{\text{S.E.}\,(p_1 - p_2)} \cap N(0, 1)$$

$\Rightarrow$ $$Z = \frac{(p_1 - p_2) - (P_1 - P_2)}{\sqrt{\dfrac{P_1Q_1}{n_1} + \dfrac{P_2Q_2}{n_2}}} \cap N(0, 1).$$

Example 8. *On the basis of past experience it is observed that 2 machines A and B produce 5% and 10% defectives. If a sample of 100 units from machine A and of 200 units from machine B. What is the probability that the difference in two sample proportions* p_1 *and* p_2 *of defectives is greater or equal to 0.01.*

Solution. We know $P_1 = .05$, $P_2 = 0.10$

$n_1 = 100$, $n_2 = 200$.

Now $$p_1 - p_2 \cap N\left(P_1 - P_2, \sqrt{\frac{P_1Q_1}{n_1} + \frac{P_2Q_2}{n_2}}\right)$$

$$P_1 - P_2 = .05 - 0.10 = -0.05$$

$$\frac{P_1Q_1}{n_1} + \frac{P_2Q_2}{n_2} = \frac{0.05 \times 0.95}{100} + \frac{0.10 \times 0.90}{200}$$

$$= 0.000475 + .000450 = 0.000925$$

$$SE_{(p_1-p_2)} = \sqrt{0.000925} = 0.0304$$

This $p_1 - p_2 \cap N(-0.05, 0.0304)$

Now $P(p_1 - p_2 > .01) = P\left[Z > \dfrac{.01 - (-0.5)}{0.0304}\right]$

$= P(z > 1.97) = 0.0244$ (using tables)

14.14. STUDENT '*t*' DISTRIBUTION

In 14.13.1. it is stated that if a population variate X is normally distributed with mean μ and variance σ^2 then $\overline{X} \cap N\left(\mu, \dfrac{\sigma}{n}\right)$ (if sampling is with replacement with any sample size or if sampling is without replacement and n is large). However, if σ^2 is not known then it is estimated by s^2 where $s^2 = \dfrac{\Sigma(X-\overline{X})^2}{n-1}$ (such that $E(s^2) = \sigma^2$ *i.e.* s^2 is unbiased estimate of σ^2) in that case sampling distribution of $\overline{X}$ is such that $\dfrac{\overline{X}-\mu}{s/\sqrt{n}}$ follows a sampling distribution known as Student '*t*' Distribution with $n - 1$ degrees of freedom (n is sample size).

The t distribution was derived in 1908 by W.S. Gosset who was an employee in an Irish Brewery. The brewery did not permit its employees to publish their research work. To get over this restriction, Gosset got his work on t distribution published under the pen name *Student.* That is why t distribution is commonly known as *Student t* distribution.

Gosset's distribution is derived on the assumption that the sampled population is normally distributed. However, it can be shown that t distribution holds good even for populations possessing bell-shaped distribution.

The density function of t distribution is not being given here. Nor is it required because the 't' values for different values of $v = n - 1$ and the corresponding areas under the t distribution curve are available to us in a tabulated form in sufficient details.

Carefully observe the two t distribution curves, one for $v = 5$ and the other for $v = 20$, drawn against the standardized Z normal distribution curve, as in Fig. 1. A comparison of these t curves with standardized Z curve brings out some of the essential properties of the t distribution.

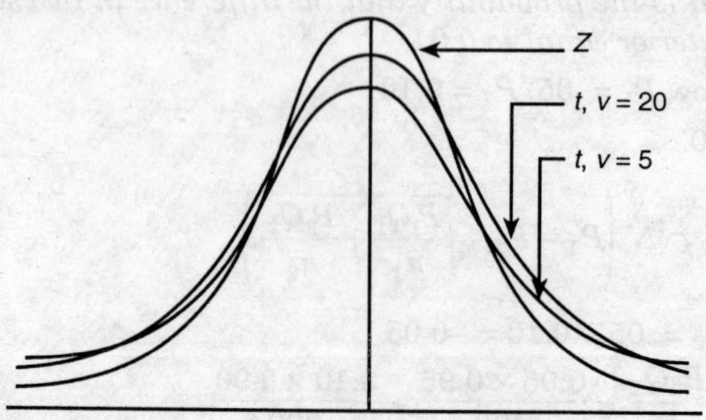

Fig. 1. The t Distribution for $v = 5$ and $v = 20$, Compared with Z Distribution

A part of table which gives few values of '*t*' for given probabilities is produced below :

α = Area in Right Tail, 2α = Area in Two-Tails Combined

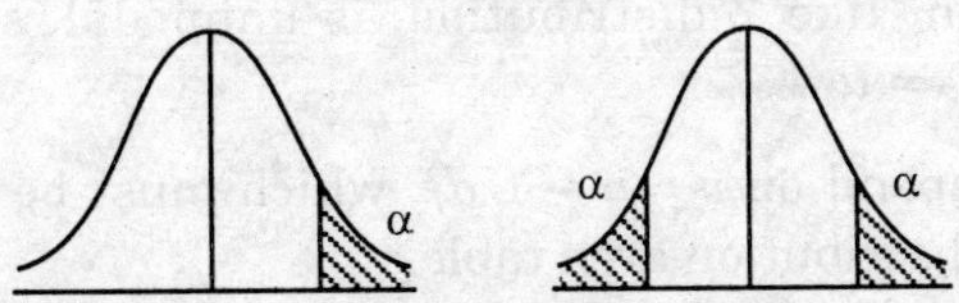

Degree of Freedom	Area in One Tail					
	0.25	0.10	0.05	0.025	0.01	0.005
	Area in Two-Tails Combined					
	0.50	0.20	0.10	0.05	0.02	0.01
1	1.000	3.078	6.314	12.706	31.821	63.657
2	0.816	1.886	2.920	4.303	6.965	9.925
3	0.765	1.638	2.353	3.182	4.541	5.841
4	0.741	1.533	2.132	2.776	3.747	4.604
5	0.727	1.476	2.015	2.571	3.365	4.032
6	0.718	1.440	1.943	2.447	3.143	3.707
7	0.711	1.415	1.895	2.365	2.998	3.499
8	0.706	1.397	1.860	2.306	2.896	3.355
9	0.703	1.383	1.833	2.262	2.821	3.250
10	0.700	1.372	1.812	2.228	2.765	3.169
11	0.697	1.363	1.796	2.201	2.718	3.106

Thus $P(t_5 > 0.727) = 0.25$ (see row against 5)

$P(t_7 > 1.895) = 0.05$ (see row against 7 and see probability above 1.895). This we express as $t_{7,.05} = 1.895 \Rightarrow P(t_7 > 1.895) = .05$.

In general if t_{n-1}, $\alpha = a \Rightarrow P(t_{n-1} > a) = \alpha$

The table gives values of t_{n-1} such that area in the right tail beyond that value is probability α. Since it is symmetrical distribution we can have value of '*t*' such that area on left of it is also α. For example if $P(t_7 > 1.895) = .05$

then also $P(t_7 < -1.895) = .05$

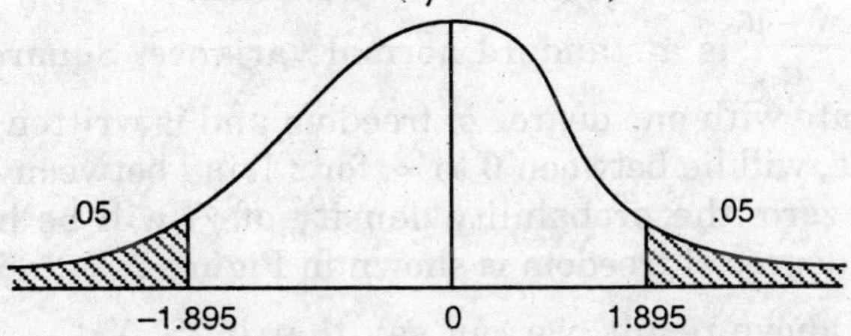

Thus just above 1.895 in a row against 7 their are two value 0.05 (single tail area) and 0.10 (two tailed area).

14.14.1. Properties of '*t*' distribution

More important among the various properties may be stated as follows :

(*i*) The t distribution, like Z distribution, is unimodal, symmetric about mean 0. Its values vary from $-\infty$ to $+\infty$.

(*ii*) The 'ψ' values depend on $v = n - 1$ *df*, which must be known to obtain the desired areas from the t distribution area table.

(*iii*) The t distribution has no mean for $n = 2$ (or $v = n - 1 = 1$), and no variance for $n \leq 3$ or $v \leq 2$. However, for $v > 1$ its mean

$$\mu = E(T) = 0,$$

and for $v > 2$ its variance

$$V(T) = \frac{v}{v - 2}.$$

(*iv*) As against the Z distribution mean 0 and variance 1, the t distribution is more variable since its variance as $V(T) = v/(v - 2)$ must always be greater than 1. This is because while the Z values vary from sample to sample owing to the changes in the sample mean $\overline{X}$ alone, the variations in 't' values are due to changes both in $\overline{X}$ and $\hat{\sigma}$.

(*v*) The variance of t distribution approaches 1 as the sample size n tends to increase. In general, for $v \geq 30$, its variance is approximately the same as that of the Z distribution. In other words, the t distribution is approximately normal for $n > 30$. Thus $t_{n-1, \alpha}$ is approximated to z_α where z_α is value such that $P(z \geq z_\alpha) = \alpha$.

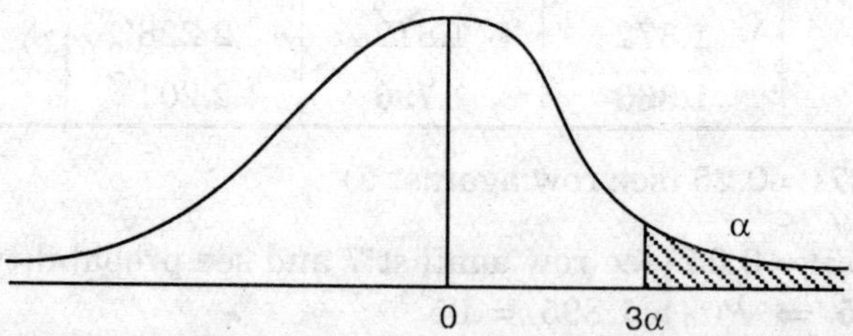

Since we know that $z_\alpha = 1.64$ for $\alpha = .05$ (as $P(z > 1.64) = .05$) thus we take $t_{35, .05} = 1.64$. As 't' tables generally give values upto t_{30}.

14.15. CHI-SQUARE (χ^2) DISTRIBUTION

We know that if X is a random variate distributed normally with mean μ and standard deviation σ, then $z = \frac{X - \mu}{\sigma}$ is a standard normal variance. Square of z, *i.e.*, $z^2 = \frac{(X - \mu)^2}{\sigma^2}$ is distributed as χ^2-variate with one degree of freedom and is written as χ_1^2. Further, the value of χ_1^2, a squared value, will lie between 0 to ∞, for z lying between $-\infty$ to ∞. Since most of the z-values are close to zero, the probability density of χ^2 will be highest near zero. The χ^2 distribution with one degree of freedom is shown in Figure 2.

Generalising the above result, we can say that if $X_1, X_2, \ldots\ldots X_n$ are n independent normal varieties each with mean μ_i and standard deviations σ_i, $i = 1, 2, \ldots n$, respectively, then the sum of squares $\Sigma z_i^2 = \Sigma \frac{(X_i - \mu_i)^2}{\sigma_i^2}$ is a χ^2 variate with n degrees of freedom, *i.e.*, χ_n^2.

Thus, we can say that χ_n^2 *is sum of squares of n independent standard normal variate.*

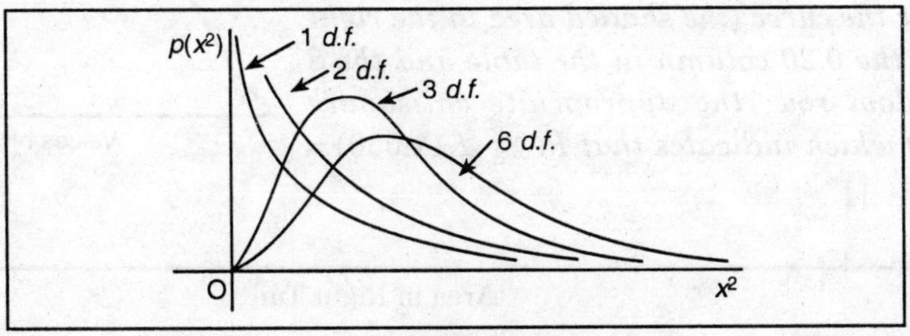

Figure 2

Features of χ^2 Distribution

1. The distribution has only one parameter, *i.e.*, number of degrees of freedom or *d.f.* (in abbreviated form) which is a positive integer.
2. We may note that as the *d.f.* increases, the height of the probability density function decreases. The distribution is positively skewed and the skewness decreases as *d.f.* increases. For large values of *d.f.*, the distribution approaches normal distribution. The curves for various d.f. are shown in figure 20.1.
3. The mean of χ_n^2, *i.e.*, $E(\chi_n^2) = n$ and its variance = $2n$, where $n = d.f.$

14.15.1. Sampling distribution of $s^2 = \frac{\Sigma(X - \overline{X})^2}{n-1}$

It has been established (stated without proof) that $\frac{\Sigma(X - \overline{X})^2}{\sigma^2}$ or $\frac{(n-1)\,s^2}{\sigma^2}$ follows χ_{n-1}^2 (χ^2 with $n - 1$ degrees of freedom).

14.15.2. If O_i stands for observed frequencies for ith outcome obtained under an experiment repeated N times and E_i are the corresponding expected frequencies in N trials (according to given Theory), then $\sum_{i=1}^{n} \frac{(O-E)^2}{E}$ follows χ_{n-1}^2 (there are n possible outcomes in an experiment).

For example : If a die is tossed 600 times ($N = 600$) which gives frequencies for 6 possible ($n = 6$) outcomes 1, 2, 3, 4, 5, 6. Let O_1 be number of times 1 appears, O_2 frequency of 2 occurring and so on then $\chi_5^2 = \frac{(O_1 - E_1)^2}{E_1} + \frac{(O_2 - E_2)^2}{E_2} + \ldots\ldots + \frac{(O_6 - E_6)^2}{E_6}$.

However in this case $E_1 = E_2 = E_3 = E_4 = E_5 = E_6 = \frac{600}{6} = 100$.

14.15.3. χ^2-tables

The χ_{n-1}^2 tables are given in the same pattern as '*t*' tables. For given probabilities 'α' the value of χ_{n-1}^2 are tabulated where α is the area in right tail of the distribution A part of χ^2-table is reproduced here.

Area in the Right Tail of Chi-square (χ^2) Distribution

Example : *In a chi-square distribution with 8 degrees of freedom to find the chi-square value for 0.20 of the area under the curve (the shaded area in the right tail) look under the 0.20 column in the table and the 8 degrees of freedom row, the appropriate chi-square values is 11.030 which indicates that* $P(\chi^2_8 \geq 11.030) =$ 0.20.

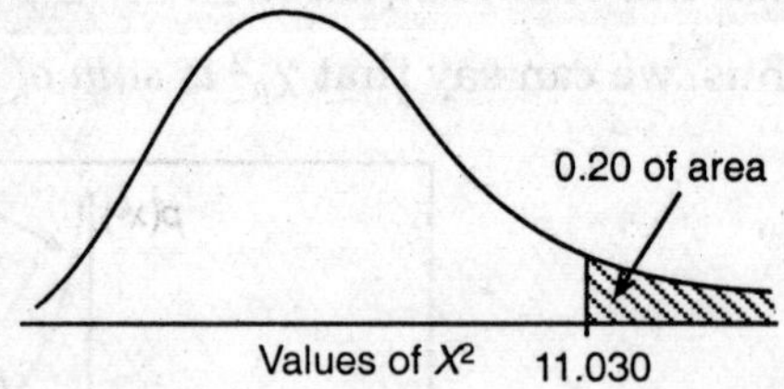

Degree of Freedom	Area in Right Tail									
	0.99	0.975	0.95	0.90	0.800	0.20	0.10	0.05	0.025	0.01
1	0.00016	0.00098	0.00398	0.0158	0.0642	1.642	2.706	3.841	5.024	6.635
2	0.0201	0.0506	0.103	0.211	0.446	3.219	4.605	5.991	7.378	9.210
3	0.115	0.216	0.352	0.584	1.005	4.642	6.251	7.815	9.348	11.345
4	0.297	0.484	0.711	1.064	1.649	5.989	7.779	9.488	11.143	13.277
5	0.554	0.831	1.145	1.610	2.343	7.289	9.236	11.070	12.833	15.086
6	0.872	1.237	1.635	2.204	3.070	8.558	10.645	12.592	14.449	16.812
7	1.239	1.690	2.167	2.833	3.822	9.803	12.017	14.067	16.013	18.475
8	1.646	2.180	2.733	3.490	4.594	11.030	13.362	15.507	17.535	20.090

Same if $\alpha = 0.10$ and degrees of freedom for a χ^2 distribution is 6. We look under the column 0.10 and figure under this column in a row corresponding to 6 is 10.645 which is expressed as $\chi^2_{6,\ .05} = 10.645$ and which means that $P(\chi^2_6 \geq 10.645) = .05$.

14.16. SNEDECOR'S F-DISTRIBUTION

Let there be two independent random samples of sizes n_1 and n_2 from two normal populations with variances σ_1^2 and σ_2^2 respectively. Further, let $s_1^2 = \dfrac{1}{n_1 - 1}\Sigma(X_{1i} - \overline{X}_1)^2$ and $s_2^2 = \dfrac{1}{n_2 - 1}\Sigma(X_{2i} - \overline{X})^2$ be the estimates of variances of the two populations *i.e.* σ_1^2 and σ_2^2.

Then F-statistic is defined as

$$F = \frac{\dfrac{s_1^2}{\sigma_1^2}}{\dfrac{s_2^2}{\sigma_2^2}} \text{ with } n_1 - 1, n_2 - 1 \text{ degrees of freedom which is also written as}$$

$$F_{(n_1 - 1,\, n_2 - 1)}$$

The necessary assumption for this statistic are

(1) The samples are drawn by sample random sampling

(2) The samples are independently drawn

(3) The parent population from which samples are drawn are normal.

Special case :

If both parent populations have same variance, *i.e.,* if $\sigma_1^2 = \sigma_2^2$ then

$$F_{n_1-1,\, n_2-1} = \frac{s_1^2}{s_2^2}$$

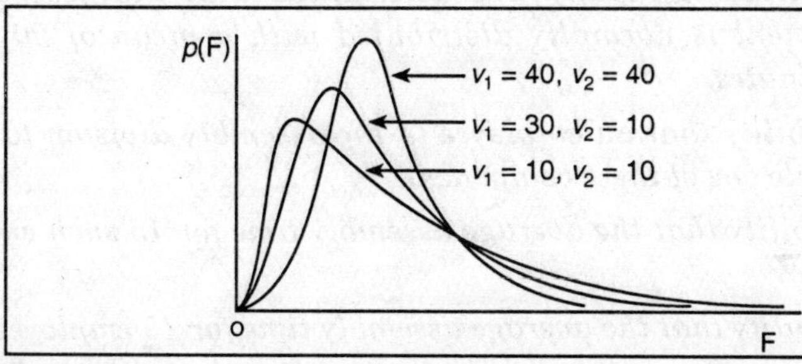

Features of *F*-distribution

1. This distribution has two parameters v_1 (= $n_1 - 1$) and v_2 (= $n_2 - 1$).
2. For large values of V_1 and V_2, the distribution approaches normal distribution.

14.16.1. Tables of 'F' Distribution

'*F*' distribution is already two way distribution, column for *d.f.* of numerator and rows for *d.f.* (degrees of freedom) of denominator, separate tables are prepared for different α.

Values of *F* for *F* distributions with 0.05 for the Area in the Right Tail]

Example : *In an F distribution with 15 degrees of freedom for the numerator and 6 degrees of freedom for the denominator, to find the F value for 0.05 for the area under the curve look under the 15 degrees of freedom column and across the 6 degrees of freedom row, the appropriate F value is 3.94*

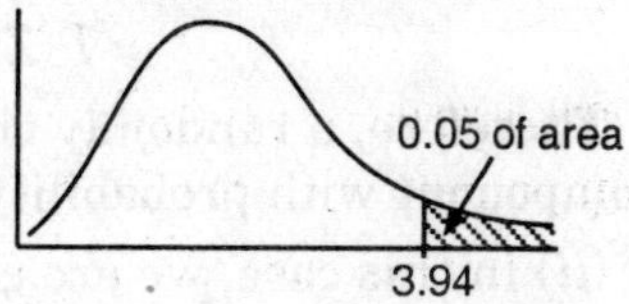

d.f. for Denominator	Degrees of Freedom for Numerator																		
	1	2	3	4	5	6	7	8	9	10	12	15	20	24	30	40	60	120	∞
1	161	200	216	225	230	234	237	239	241	242	244	2465	248	249	250	251	252	253	254
2	18.5	19.0	19.2	19.2	19.3	19.3	19.4	19.4	19.4	19.4	19.4	19.4	19.4	19.5	19.5	19.5	19.5	19.5	19.5
3	10.1	9.55	9.28	9.12	9.01	8.94	8.89	8.85	8.81	8.79	8.74	8.70-	8.66	8.64	8.62	8.59	8.57	8.55	8.53
4	7.71	6.94	6.59	6.39	6.26	6.16	6.09	6.04	6.00	5.96-	5.91	5.86	5.80	5.77	5.75	5.72	5.698	5.66	5.63
5	6.61	5.79	5.41	5.19	5.05	4.95	4.88	4.82	4.77	4.74	4.68	4.62	4.56	4.53	4.50	4.46	4.43	4.40	4.37
6	5.99	5.14	4.76	4.53	4.39	4.28	4.21	4.15	4.10	4.06	4.00	3.94	3.87	3.84	3.81	3.77	3.74	3.70	3.67
7	5.59	4.74	4.35	4.12	3.97	3.87	3.79	3.73	3.68	3.64	3.57	3.51	3.44	3.41	3.38	3.34	3.30	3.27	3.23
8	5.32	4.46	4.07	3.84	3.69	3.58	3.50	3.44	3.39	3.35	3.28	3.22	3.15	3.12	3.08	3.04	3.01	2.97	2.93
9	5.12	4.26	3,.86	3.63	3.48	3.37	3.29	3.23	3.18	3.14	3.07	3.01	2.94	2.90	2.86	2.83	2.79	2.75	2.71
10	4.96	4.10	3.71	3.48	3.33	3.22	3.14	3.07	3.02	2.98	2.91	2.85	2.77	2.74	2.70	2.66	2.62	2.58	2.54
11	4.84	3.98	3.59	3.36	3.20	3.09	3.01	2.95	2.90	2.85	2.79	2.72	2.65	2.61	2.57	2.53	2.49	2.45	2.40
12	4.75	3.89	3.49	3.26	3.11	3.00	2.91	2.85	2.80	2.75	2.69	2.62	2.54	2.51	2.47	2.43	2.38	2.34	2.30
13	4.67	3.81	3.41	3.18	3.03	2.92	2.83	2.77	2.71	2.67	2.60	2.53	2.46	2.42	2.38	2.34	2.30	2.25	2.21
14	4.60	3.74	3.34	3.11	2.96	2.85	2.76	2.70	2.65	2.60	2.53	2.46	2.39	2.35	2.31	2.27	2.22	2.18	2.13

If we want to look for $F_{5,\, 10\, (\alpha\, =\, .05)}$, first we get a table which is prepared for α = 0.05 (as given above). Since *d.f.* of numerator is 5, under column captioned 5 we look for number in row corresponding to 10 (*d.f.* for denominator) and that number is 3.33. Thus $F_{5,\, 10,\, .05} = 3.30$ which means that $P(F_{5,\, 10} \geq 3.30) = 0.05$.

14.17. MORE SOLVED EXAMPLES

Example 9. *An electrical company has determined that the assembly time for a particular electric component is normally distributed with a mean of 20 minutes and a standard deviation of 3 minutes.*

(*i*) *What is the probability that an employee in the assembly division takes longer than 22 minutes assemble one of these components ?*

(*ii*) *What is the probability that the average assembly time for 15 such employees exceeds 22 minutes.*

(*iii*) *What is the probability that the average assembly time for 15 employees in between 19 and 22 minutes ?*

Solution. (*i*) /The random variable X here is the assembly time for a component. It is assumed to a normal random variable, with $\mu = 20$ minutes and $\sigma = 3$ minutes. We wish to determine $P(X > 22)$. Standardizing this variable we obtain

$$Z = \frac{X - 20}{3} = \frac{22 - 20}{3} = 0.67$$

$$P(X > 22) = P\left[\frac{X-20}{3} > \frac{22-20}{3}\right]$$

$$= P(Z > 0.67) = 0.5 - 0.2486 = 0.2514 \quad [P(0 < Z < 0.67) = 0.2486$$

Therefore, a randomly chosen employee will require longer than 22 minutes to assemble a component with probability 0.25 (approx.)

(*ii*) In this case, we are concerned with the *average* time for employees, not an individual employee. Since the S.D. of the population is given we know the curve describing $\overline{X}$ (an average of 15 employees) is normal with mean = $\mu_{\overline{X}} = \mu = 20$ minutes.

and $\quad$ Standard error $= \mu_{\overline{X}} = \dfrac{\sigma}{\sqrt{n}}$

$$= \frac{3}{\sqrt{15}} = 0.77 \text{ minutes}$$

Thus $\overline{X} \cap N(20, 077)$

Thus $\quad P(\overline{X} > 22) = P\left(Z > \dfrac{22-20}{0.77}\right)$

$$= P(Z > 2.6)$$

$$= 0.5 - 0.4953 - 0.0047$$

(*ii*) $P(19 \le \overline{X} \le 22) = P\left(\dfrac{19-20}{0.77} \le Z \le \dfrac{22-20}{0.77}\right)$

$$= P(-1.3 \le Z \le 2.6)$$

$$= P(-1.3 \le Z \le 0) + P(0 \le Z \le 2.6)$$

$$= 0.4032 + 0.4953 = 0.8985.$$

Example 10. *A market research firm conducts telephone surveys with a 40% historical response rate. What is the probability that in a new sample of 400 telephone numbers, at least*

150 individuals will cooperate and respond to the questions ? In other words, what is the probability that the sample proportion will be at least 150/400 = .375 ?

Solution. Population proportion $P = 0.40$

$$SE_{(p)} = \sqrt{\frac{PQ}{n}} = \sqrt{\frac{0.40 \times 0.60}{400}} = 0.0245$$

Thus $p \cap N(0.40, 0.0245)$

$$P(p > 3.75) = P\left(Z > \frac{0.375 - 0.40}{0.0245}\right)$$

$$= P(Z \geq 1.02) = 0.5 - 0.3461 = 0.1539.$$

Example 11. *The distribution of weekly wages of workers in Mumbai and Kanpur are assumed to be normal with the following parameters :*

Mumbai : mean wages 490 and standard deviation 140.

Kanpur : Mean wages 480 and standard deviation 130.

If two independent random samples of 1,600 and 900 workers respectively from Mumbai and Kanpur are selected, find :

(i) Sampling distribution of the difference of average weekly wages of workers of Mumbai and Kanpur.

(ii) What is the probability that the above difference is less than or equal to zero ?

Solution. *(i)* Using X_1 for Mumbai and X_2 for Kanpur. Given $X_1 \cap N(490, 140)$ and $X_2 \cap N(480, 130)$

Thus $\overline{X}_1 - \overline{X}_2 \cap N\left(\mu_1 - \mu_2, \sqrt{\frac{\sigma_1^2}{n_1} + \frac{\sigma_2^2}{n_2}}\right)$.

$n_1 = 1600, \; n_2 = 900$

Thus $\frac{\sigma_1^2}{n_1} + \frac{\sigma_2^2}{n_2} = \frac{(140)^2}{1600} + \frac{(130)^2}{900} = 12.25 + 2.86 = 15.11$

$\mu_1 - \mu_2 = 490 - 480 = 10$

$\therefore \quad \overline{X}_1 - \overline{X}_2 \cap N(10, 3.9)$

(ii) $P(\overline{X}_1 - \overline{X}_2) \leq 0) = P\left(Z \leq \frac{0 - 10}{3.9}\right)$

$$= P(Z \leq -2.59)$$

$$= 0.5 - .4952 = 0.0048.$$

Example 12. *The electric light tubes of manufacturer A have mean life time of 1,400 hours with a standard deviation of 200 hours, while those of manufacture B have a mean life time of 1,200 hours with a standard deviation of 100 hours. If random samples of 125 tubes of each brand are tested, what is the probability that brand A tubes would have a mean life time which is at least (i) 160 hours more than the brand B tubes, (ii) 250 hours more than the brand B tubes ?*

Solution. Let X_1 and X_2 represent the lives of two brands A and B given $X_1 \cap N(1400, 200)$, $X_2 \cap N(1200, 100)$

$n_1 = 125,\ n_2 = 125,\ \mu_1 = 140,\ \mu_2 = 1200,\ \sigma_1 = 200,\ \sigma_2 = 100$

(*i*) To find $P(\overline{X}_1 - \overline{X}_2 \geq 160)$

We know $\overline{X}_1 - \overline{X}_2 \cap N\left(\mu_1 - \mu_2, \sqrt{\frac{\sigma_1^2}{n_1} + \frac{\sigma_2^2}{n_2}}\right)$

Now $\mu_1 - \mu_2 = 1400 - 1200 = 200.$

$\frac{\sigma_1{}^2}{n_1} + \frac{\sigma_2{}^2}{n_2} = \frac{(200)^2}{125} + \frac{(100)^2}{125} = 320 + 80 = 400$

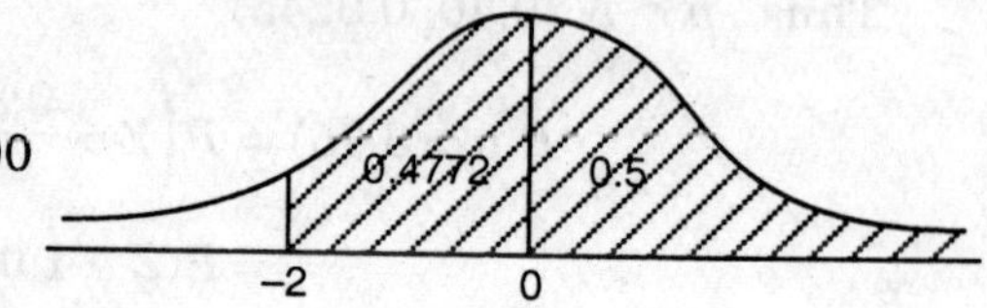

Thus $\overline{X}_1 - \overline{X}_2 \cap N\,(200, 20)$

Thus $P(\overline{X}_1 - \overline{X}_2 \geq 160) = P\left(Z \geq \frac{160 - 200}{20}\right)$

$= P(Z \geq -2)$

$= 0.9772$

(*ii*) $P(\overline{X}_1 - \overline{X}_2 \geq 250)$

$= P\left(Z \geq \frac{250 - 200}{20}\right) = P(Z \geq 2.5)$

$= 0.5 - 0.4938 = 0.0062.$

Example 13. *Assume the population mean is μ = 3 and the population standard deviation is σ = 1.2 hours. Suppose a sample of 50 teens will be used to monitor television viewing time. Let $\overline{x}$ denote the sample mean viewing time.*

(*a*) *Show the sample distribution of $\overline{x}$.*

(*b*) *What is the probability the sample mean will be within ± .25 hours of the population mean ?*

Solution. Given that $X \cap N(3, 1.2)$, $n = 50$

(*a*) Thus $\quad \overline{X} \cap N\left(3, \frac{1.2}{\sqrt{50}}\right)$

$\overline{X} \cap n\ (3, 0.17)$ (Sampling distribution of $\overline{X}$)

(*b*) $\quad P(3 - 0.25 \leq \overline{X} \leq 3 + 0.25)$

$= P(2.75 \leq \overline{X} \leq 3 + 3.25)$

$= P\left(\frac{2.75 - 3}{0.17} \leq Z \leq \frac{3.25 - 3}{0.17}\right)$

$= P(1 - 1.47 \leq Z \leq 1.47)$

$= 2\ P(0 \leq Z \leq 1.47)$

$= 2\ (0.4292) = 0.8584.$

Example 4. *A random sample of 10 observations is to be taken from a normal population with variance equal to 16. What is the probability of obtaining a sample with variance greater than 20 ?*

Solution. It is given that sample variance > 20

i.e. $$\frac{\Sigma(X-\overline{X})^2}{10} > 20 \qquad [n = 10]$$

$$\Rightarrow \quad \Sigma(X-\overline{X})^2 > 200$$

$$\chi^2_{n-1} = \frac{\Sigma(X-\overline{X})^2}{\sigma^2} > \frac{200}{16} \qquad [\text{as } \sigma^2 = 16]$$

We are required to find $P(\chi_9^2 > 12.5)$

Now from the tables we find that $P(\chi_9^2 > 12.242) = 0.20$

Thus $P(\chi_9^2 > 12.5)$ is approximately equal to 0.20 (it will be little less than 0.20)

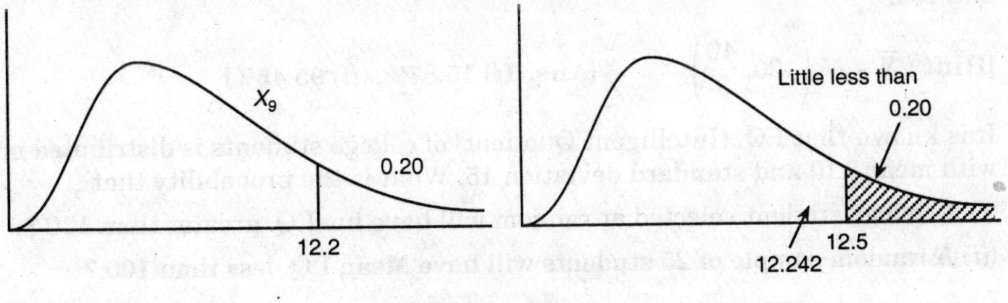

EXERCISE 14

1. Explain the concept of sampling distribution of a statistics.
2. Find the mean and standard error of sample mean in (*a*) Simple random sampling with replacement, (*b*) Simple random sampling without replacement.
3. Distinguish between :
   (*a*) Parameter and Statistic.
   (*b*) Sampling distribution and Probability distribution.
   (*c*) Standard deviation and Standard error.
4. (*a*) Distinguish between sampling with replacement and sampling without replacement. How many random samples of size n can be drawn from a population consisting N items if the sampling is done (*i*) with replacement, (*ii*) without replacement ?
   (*b*) What is the variance of the sample mean if sampling is done (*i*) with replacement (*ii*) without replacement ?
   (*c*) Under what conditions do the answers in (*b*) approach each other ?
5. If X_i $(i = 1, 2, ..., n)$ are n independent normal varieties with respective mean μ_i and standard deviation σ_i, then show that the variate $u = \Sigma X_i$ is normally distributed with mean $\Sigma\mu_i$ and variance $\Sigma\sigma_i^2$.
6. Write short notes on :
   (*i*) χ^2-distribution (*ii*) t-distribution (*iii*) F-distribution.
7. A readymade shirt manufacturer sells the defective shirts at a discount. According to reports of his supervisors, the manufacturer has estimated that 10% of the

manufactured garments are defective. If a sample of 60 shirt is taken at random from a large lot of shirts, what is the probability that :

(*i*) It contains at the most 4 defective shirts ?

(*ii*) It contains at least 9 defective shirts ?

[Hint : $p \sim n\left(0.1, \sqrt{\frac{0.1 \times 0.9}{60}}\right)$

[Ans. : (*i*) 0.1949, (*ii*) 0.1003]

8. If a large number of independent random samples, each of size 64, are drawn from a normal population with mean 120 and standard deviation 40, find the percentage of samples that are expected to have their means (*i*) greater than 125, (*ii*) between 110 and 130.

[Hint : $\overline{X} \sim N\left(120, \frac{40}{8}\right)$ **[Ans.** (*i*) 15.87%, (*ii*) 95.45%]

9. It is known that I.Q. (Intelligent Quotient) of college students is distributed normally with mean 110 and standard deviation 15. What is the probability that :

(*i*) A college student selected at random will have his I.Q. greater than 130 ?

(*ii*) A random sample of 25 students will have Mean I.Q. less than 100 ?

[Hint : Mean I.Q. $\sim N\left(110, \frac{15}{\sqrt{25}}\right)$ **[Ans.** (*i*) 0.0918, (*ii*) 0.0004]

10. A researcher reports survey results by stating that the standard error of the mean is 20. The population standard deviation is 500.

(*a*) How large as the sample used in this survey ?

(*b*) What is the probability that the point estimate was within ± 25 of the population mean ?

[Ans. : (*a*) 625, (*b*) 0.7888]

11. As of June 1, 2001, 30.5% of individual investors were bullish on the stock market short term. Answer the following questions assuming a sample of 200 individual investors is used.

(*a*) Show the sampling distribution of *p*, the sample proportion of individual investors who are bullish on the market short term.

(*b*) What is the probability that the sample proportion will be within ± .04 of the population proportion ?

(*c*) What is the probability that the sample proportion will be within ± .02 of the population proportion ?

[Ans. (*a*) Normal with $E(p) = 0.305$ and $\sigma_p = 0.0326$. (*b*) 0.7814 (*c*) 0.4582]

12. The average annual salary for federal government employees in Indiana is $41,749. Use this figure as the population mean and assume the population standard deviation is σ = $5000. Suppose that a random sample of 50 federal government employees will be selected from the population.

(*a*) What is the value of this standard error of the mean ?

(*b*) What is the probability that the sample mean will be more than \$41,979 ?

(*c*) What is the probability the sample mean will be within \$1000 of the population mean?

(*c*) How would the probability in part (*c*) change if the sample size were increased to 100 ?

[**Ans.** (*a*) 707 (*b*) 0.50 (*c*) 0.8414 (*d*) 0.9544]

13. If X_1, X_2, X_3 is a simple random sample of size three from a large population with mean 5 and variance 4, evaluate the expected value and standard error of the statistics $T = (2X_1 + X_2 - 3X_3)$.

[**Ans.** 0, $2\sqrt{14}$]

15. The diameter of a component produced on a semi-automatic machine is known to be distributed normally with mean of 10 mm and a standard deviation of 0.1 mm. If we pick up a random sample of size 25, what is the probability that the sample mean will be between 9.95 and 10.05 mm ?

[**Ans.** 0.9876]

16. It is known that 10% of the bolts manufactured by a factory are defective. If a random sample of 100 bolts is chosen at random from a day's production, construct the sampling distribution of (*i*) the number of defective bolts, (*ii*) the proportion of defective bolts.

[**Ans.** (*i*) $N(10, 3)$, (*ii*) $N(0.10, 0.03)$

17. The mean and standard deviation of per capita consumption of wheat in rural and urban areas of Delhi are estimated to be 450 gms, 75 gms and 410 gms, 100 gms respectively. Assuming that the per capita consumption of wheat is distributed normally, construct the sampling distribution of the difference between two sample means obtained from random samples of sizes 80 and 60 from rural and urban populations respectively.

[**Ans.** 40 gms, 15.39 gms]

□□□

15

Statistical Inference– Estimation and Testing of Hypothesis

CHAPTER OUTLINE

- Statistical Inference
- Estimation — Point and Interval
- Confidence interval using normal, t and χ^2 distributions
- Testing of Hypothesis
- Significance of a mean, difference of means
- Using Z and t distribution

15.1 MEANING OF THE STATISTICAL INFERENCE

Statistical Inference refers to the process of selecting and using a sample statistic to conclude about the parameter of a population from which the sample is drawn. It deals with following two type of problems:

1. Problem of Estimation. This problem arises when no information is available about the parameters of the population from which the sample is drawn. Statistics obtained from the sample are used to estimate the unknown parameter of the population from which the sample is drawn.

2. Problem of Test of Hypothesis (or Test of Significance). This problem arises when some information is available regarding the values of parameters of the population from which the sample is drawn and it is required to test how far this information about the population parameter is tenable in the light of the information provided by the sample.

15.2 MEANING AND TWO WAYS OF ESTIMATION

Meaning-in the context of statistics, an estimation is a statistical technique of estimating unknown population parameters from the corresponding sample statistic.

TWO ways- A population parameter can be estimate in two ways:

1. Point Estimation, and
2. Interval Estimation

15.2.1 Point Estimation

Meaning - It provided a single value of a statistic that is used to estimate an unknown population parameter.

Estimator - The statistic which is used to obtain a point estimate is called estimator.

Estimate - The value of statistic is the estimate.

Example - If sample mean ($\overline{X}$) is used for estimating the parameter, population mean (μ), then $\overline{X}$ is called as estimator and the value of $\overline{X}$ is called an estimate. The estimator $\overline{X}$ will be unbiased if $E(\overline{X}) = \mu$ (the parameter).

A **Point estimate** is a sample statistic used to estimate a population parameter. For example suppose a company wants to estimate the mean age of buyers of high definition televisions. They select a random sample of say 50 recent purchasers, determine the age of each purchaser and compute the mean which comes to 38 years. This sample means (38) is an estimate of average of buyers or we say the point estimate of the parameter (mean age of all buyers in the population) is 38. However this point estimate is not unique and will vary from sample to sample.

15.2.2 Interval Estimation and Confidence Interval

Using point estimation, it is possible to provide a single quantity as an estimator of a parameter. Any point estimator, even if it satisfies all the characteristics of a good estimator, has a limitation that it provides no information about the magnitude of errors due to sampling. This problem is taken care of by the method of interval estimation, that gives a range of the estimator of the parameter.

In above example $\overline{X} = 38$ is an estimation of μ, it does not mean that population mean μ is 38. However we know that population mean will be around 38 or we may say that μ will lie between $38 - k_1$, and $38 + k_2$ and we are able to specify values of k_1 and k_2. For example we may say, on the basis of $\overline{X} = 38$, that μ lies between 30 and 50 (*i.e.* 38 – 8 and 38 + 12). In general we may say that μ lies between $\overline{X} - k_1$ and $\overline{X} + k_2$ (where k_1 and k_2 are to be specified). This sort of estimation is called interval estimate. We may specify this interval with some confidence which will be expressed in terms of probability known as confidence level and this confidence level (indicated as C) should be very close to 1 (may be .90, .95, .98 or .99) so that it will be very likely that parameter lies in the interval.

Given a random sample of n observations $X_1, X_2, \ldots\ldots X_n$, we can find two values l_1 and l_2 such that the probability of population parameter θ lying between l_1 and l_2 is (say) C. Using symbols, we can write $P(l_1 \leq \theta \leq l_2) = C$.

Such an interval is termed as a *Confidence Interval* for θ and the two limits l_1 and l_2 are termed as *Confidence* or *Fiducial Limits.* The percentage probability or confidence is termed as *Level of Confidence* or *Confidence Coefficient* of the interval. For example, if we say that confidence level C for an interval is 100 % or $C = 1$ This level of confidence implies that if a large number of random samples are taken from a population and confidence interval are constructed for each, then 100 % of these intervals are expected to contain the population parameter θ. Alternatively, a 100 % confidence interval implies that we are 100 % confident that the population parameter θ lies between l_1 and l_2.

As compared to point estimation, the interval estimation is better because it takes into account the variability of the estimator in addition to its single value and thus, provides a range of values. Unlike point estimation, interval estimation indicates that estimation is an uncertain process.

Calculation of Confidence Limits - The calculation of confidence limits is based on the knowledge of sampling distribution of an appropriate statistic which estimates parameter.

15.2.3 Use of Normal Sampling Distribution

Example 1. Construct 95% and 99% confidence intervals for mean of a normal population.

Solution.

Let $X_1, X_2, \ldots, X_n$ be a random sample of size n from a normal population with mean μ and standard deviation σ.

We know that sampling distribution of $\overline{X}$ is normal with mean μ and standard error $\frac{\sigma}{\sqrt{n}}$. Therefore, $z = \frac{\overline{X} - \mu}{\sigma / \sqrt{n}}$ is a standard normal variate.

From the tables of areas under standard normal curve, we find

$$P[-1.96 \le z \le 1.96] = 0.95 \text{ or } P\left[-1.96 \le \frac{\overline{X} - \mu}{\sigma / \sqrt{n}} \le 1.96\right] = 0.95 \qquad \ldots (1)$$

The inequality $-1.96 \le \frac{\overline{X} - \mu}{\sigma / \sqrt{n}}$ can be written as

$$-1.96 \frac{\sigma}{\sqrt{n}} \le \overline{X} - \mu \text{ or } \mu \le \overline{X} + 1.96 \frac{\sigma}{\sqrt{n}} \qquad \ldots (2)$$

Similarly, from the inequality $\frac{X - \mu}{\sigma / \sqrt{n}} \le 1.96$, we can write

$$\mu \ge \overline{X} - 1.96 \frac{\sigma}{\sqrt{n}} \qquad \ldots (3)$$

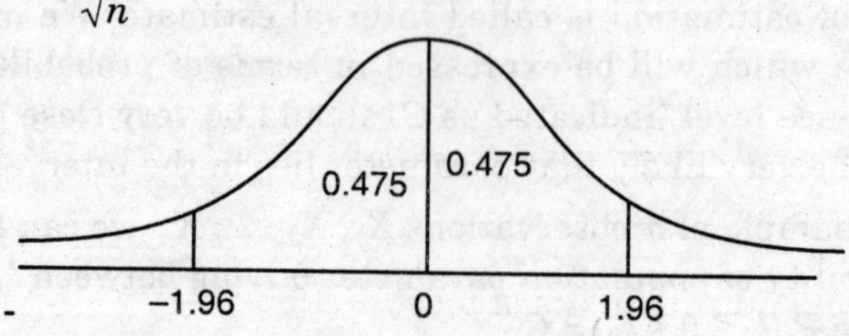

Combining (2) and (3), we get

$$\bar{X} - 1.96\frac{\sigma}{\sqrt{n}} \le \mu \le \bar{X} + 1.96\frac{\sigma}{\sqrt{n}}$$

Thus, we can write equation (1) as

$$P\left(\bar{X} - 1.96\frac{\sigma}{\sqrt{n}} \le \mu \le \bar{X} + 1.96\frac{\sigma}{\sqrt{n}}\right) = 0.95$$

This gives us a 95% confidence interval of the parameter μ. The lower limit of μ is $\bar{X} - 1.96\frac{\sigma}{\sqrt{n}}$ and the upper limit is $\bar{X} + 1.96\frac{\sigma}{\sqrt{n}}$. The probability of μ lying between these limits is 0.95 and therefore, this interval is also termed as 95% confidence interval for μ.

In a similar way, we can construct a 99% confidence interval for μ

$$P\left(\bar{X} - 2.58\frac{\sigma}{\sqrt{n}} \le \mu \le \bar{X} + 2.58\frac{\sigma}{\sqrt{n}}\right) = 0.99$$

[as $P(-2.58 \le Z \le 2.58) = 0.99$ from standard normal table]

Thus, the 99% confidence limits for μ are $\bar{X} \pm 2.58\frac{\sigma}{\sqrt{n}}$.

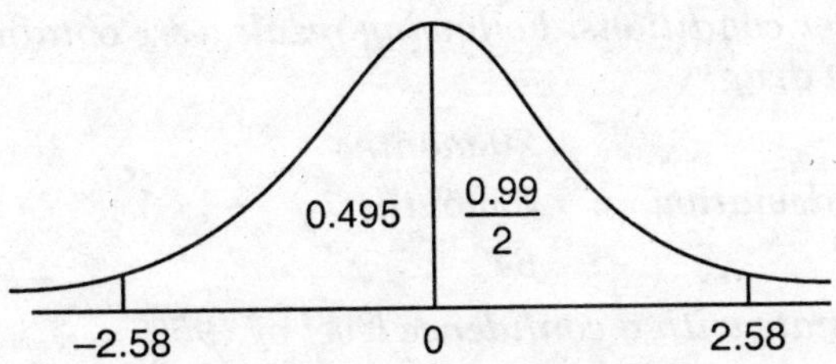

Example 2. *Confidence Interval for Population Proportion*

Obtain the 95% confidence limits for the proportion of successes in a binomial population.

Solution. Let the parameter P denote the proportion of successes in population. Further, p denotes the proportion of successes in a sammple of n (≥ 50) trials. We know that the sampling distribution of p will be approximately normal with mean P and standard error

$$\sqrt{\frac{P(1-P)}{n}} = \sqrt{\frac{PQ}{n}} \text{ i.e. } p \cap N\left(P, \sqrt{\frac{PQ}{n}}\right)$$

Since p is not known, therefore, its estimator p is used in place of P to estimate the standard error of p, *i.e.,* $S.E.(p) = \sqrt{\frac{p(1-p)}{n}}$.

Thus, the 95% confidence interval for p is given by

$$P\left(p - 1.96\sqrt{\frac{p(1-p)}{n}} \le P \le p + 1.96\sqrt{\frac{p(1-p)}{n}}\right) = 0.95$$

This gives the 95% fiducial limits of p as $p \pm 1.96\sqrt{\frac{p(1-p)}{n}}$.

Example 3. *In a newspaper article of 1600 words in Hindi, 64% of the words were found of be of Sanskrit origin.*

Assuming that the simple sampling conditions hold good, estimate the confidence limits of the proportion of Sanskrit words in the writer's vocabulary. (using 100% confidence level).

Solution. Let P be the proportion of Sanskrit words in the writer's vocabulary. The corresponding proportion in the sample is given as $p = 0.64$.

$$\therefore\ S.E.(p) = \sqrt{\frac{0.64 \times 0.36}{1600}} = \frac{0.48}{40} = 0.012$$

We know that almost whole of the distribution lies between 3σ limits. Therefore, the confidence interval is given by

$$P[p - 3S.E.(p) \le p \le P + 3S.E.(p)] = 0.9973$$

Thus, the 99.73% confidence limits of P are 0.604 (= 0.64 – 3 × 0.012) and 0.676 (= 0.64 + 3 × 0.012) respectively.

Hence, the proportion of Sanskrit words in the writer's vocabulary are between 60.4% to 67.6%.

Example 4. *A pharmaceutical company wants to estimate the mean life of a particular drug under typical weather conditions. Following result were obtained from a simple random sample of 64 bottles of the drug:*

Sample mean	:	*20 months*
Population standard deviation	:	*3 months*
sample size	:	*64*

Find an interval estimate with a confidence level of 95%

Solution. $S.E(\overline{X}) = \dfrac{\sigma}{\sqrt{n}} = \dfrac{3}{\sqrt{64}} = \dfrac{3}{8}$

At 95% confidence level

$$-1.96 \le Z \le 1.96 \quad \text{where } Z = \frac{\overline{X} - \mu}{\frac{\sigma}{\sqrt{n}}}$$

or $$-1.96 \le (20 - \mu) \times \frac{8}{3} \le 1.96$$

or $$20 - 0.734 \le \mu \le 20 + 0.734$$

or $$19.264 \le \mu \le 20.734$$

15.3 CONFIDENCE LIMITS OF Z FOR CERTAIN GIVEN CONFIDENCE LEVELS

Confidence level	*Z – values*
0.90	± 1.645
0.95	± 1.96
0.98	± 2.33
0.99	± 2.58
almost sure level	± 3

15.4 ESTIMATE OF POPULATION VARIANCE (σ^2)

Sample variance which is denoted by S^2 is given by $S^2 = \dfrac{\Sigma (x-\overline{x})^2}{n}$ ...(1)

It was shown (proof not given) that

$$E(S^2) = \frac{n-1}{n}\sigma^2$$

Thus $$E\left(\frac{n}{n-1}S^2\right) = \sigma^2 \quad \text{...(2)}$$

Now $$\frac{n}{n-1}S^2 = \frac{n}{n-1}\,\frac{\Sigma (x-\overline{x})^2}{n} = \frac{\Sigma (x-\overline{x})^2}{n-1}$$

which will be denoted by s^2 *i.e.*

$$s^2 = \frac{\Sigma (x-\overline{x})^2}{n-1}$$

Thus from (2) $E(s^2) = \sigma^2$.

or we may say $\hat{\sigma}^2 = s^2$ (*i.e.* unbiased estimate if σ^2 is s^2).

In case n is large $\dfrac{n}{n-1}$ is close to 1 and using approximation from (2) we may say that $E(S^2) = \sigma^2$ (in case of large samples). However $E(s^2) = \sigma^2$ (in case of samples of any size whether large or small).

15.5. ESTIMATES OF DIFFERENT PARAMETERS, SAMPLING DISTRIBUTIONS OF WHOSE ESTIMATORS FOLLOW STANDARD NORMAL (Z) DISTRIBUTION

15.5.1 Estimation of Population Mean (μ)

In the following situations, sample mean $\overline{X}$ is an unbiased estimate of population mean μ and interval estimate of μ is $\overline{X} \pm Z_c\, SE(\overline{X})$ where Z_c is value of Z for a given level of confidence = C.

(A) In case of large samples (when n > 30 the sample size is considered to be large)

(1) When sampling is with replacement

(*a*) $\text{SE}(\overline{X}) = \dfrac{\sigma}{\sqrt{n}}$ when σ is known

(*b*) $\text{SE}(\overline{X}) = \dfrac{s}{\sqrt{n}}$ when σ is not known and σ^2 is estimated by $s^2 = \dfrac{\Sigma(X-\overline{X})^2}{n-1}$.

(2) When sampling is by s. r. s. wor (simple random sampling without replacement)

$$\text{SE}(\overline{X}) = \frac{\sigma}{\sqrt{n}}\sqrt{\frac{N-n}{N-1}}, \text{ when } \sigma \text{ is known}$$

$$\text{SE}(\overline{X}) = \frac{s}{\sqrt{n}}\sqrt{\frac{N-n}{N-1}}, \text{ when } \sigma \text{ is not known.}$$

(B) In case of small samples

$\text{SE}(\overline{X}) = \dfrac{\sigma}{\sqrt{n}}$, when σ is known and parent population follows normal distribution.

Notes : (1) In case of (A) parent population may be normal or may not be normal. (2) The factor $\sqrt{\dfrac{N-n}{N-1}}$ may be ignored if either N is infinite or n is relatively small compared to N (when n is less than 5% of N) (3) when n is small and σ is not known. Then sampling distribution of $\overline{X}$ is not normal and follows 't' distribution which is discussed in a later section.

Example 6. *A random sample of 460 ball bearing chosen at random from a very large consignment is found to have a mean diameter of 0.450 inches, with a standard deviation of 0.58 inches. Determine (i) 95% and (ii) 99% confidence interval of mean diameter of the ball bearings in the consignment .* [*D.U.M. Com. 2001*]

Solution.

(*i*) Here $n = 460, \overline{X} = 0.450, \sigma = 0.058$, at 95% confidence $z = \pm 1.96$

μ lies between $\overline{X} \pm Z_c \dfrac{\sigma}{\sqrt{n}}$

i.e. μ lies between $0.450 \pm 1.96 \dfrac{0.058}{\sqrt{460}}$

i.e. μ lies between 0.450 ± 0.0053

i.e. μ lies between 0.4447 and 0.4553

(*ii*) For 99% Confidence interval, $Z_{.99} = 2.58$

Confidence interval for μ is $0.450 \pm 2.58 \dfrac{0.058}{\sqrt{460}}$ or $0.450 \pm .0069$

i.e., μ lies between 0.4431 and 0.4569 with 99% confidence level.

Example 7. *A random sample of size 65 was taken to estimate the mean annual income of 1,000 families and the mean and S.D. were found to be ₹ 6,300 and ₹ 9.5 respectively. Find a 95% confidence interval for the population mean.* [*CA Foundation May 1996*]

Solution. Since the population is finite, *i.e.*, $N = 1{,}000$, we will apply finite population correction factor. $\overline{X} = 6300$, sample SD $= s = 9.5, n = 65$

$$\text{S.E.}_{\overline{x}} = \frac{s}{\sqrt{n}}\sqrt{\frac{N-n}{N-1}} = \frac{9.5}{\sqrt{65}}\sqrt{\frac{1{,}000-65}{1{,}000-1}}$$

At 95% level of confidence

$$z = \pm 1.96$$

$$\pm 1.96 = \frac{6{,}300-\mu}{\dfrac{9.5}{\sqrt{65}}\sqrt{\dfrac{1{,}000-65}{1{,}000-1}}} = \frac{6{,}300-\mu}{\dfrac{9.5\times 0.9674378}{\sqrt{65}}} = \frac{6{,}300-\mu}{\dfrac{9.2}{8.06}} = \frac{(6{,}300-\mu)}{1.14}$$

Confidence interval for

$$\mu = 6{,}300 \pm 1.96 \times 1.14 = 6{,}297.76. \text{ and } 6302.2344.$$

Example 8. *Kitchencare Products Ltd. has a sales force of 561 sales persons. The sales manager of the company wants to know the estimated interval within which the average commission paid to its salespersons over the last year falls. A sample of 49 sales persons are taken and the average is found to be ₹ 48,000. The standard deviation of the sample is ₹ 4,200.*

You are required to find out a 95% confidence interval for the average commission in the last year.

Solution. Given :

$n = 49,$

$\overline{x} =$ ₹ 48,000, S.D. = ₹ 4,200, N = 561

The population is finite and sampling fraction $\frac{n}{N} = \frac{49}{561} = 0.0873 > 0.05$. So, the standard error of the sampling distribution of mean has to be calculated by using finite population correction factor along with the standard formula of standard error of mean. Further the standard deviation of population is not known. So, the standard deviation of sample is to be used as an estimate of the population standard deviation.

$\therefore$ Standard error of mean $= \frac{s}{\sqrt{n}}\sqrt{\frac{N-n}{N-1}}$ where, s = S.D. = 4,200

(in place of σ, s is used)

$$= \frac{4{,}200}{\sqrt{9}}\sqrt{\frac{561-49}{561-1}} = 573.71$$

$$Z = \frac{x-\mu}{S.E.}$$

At 95% level of confidence, $Z = \pm 1.96$

$\Rightarrow$ Confidence Interval for $\mu = 48{,}000 \pm 573.71 \times 1.96 = 48{,}000 \pm 1{,}124.$

$=$ from 46875 to 49124.

15.5.2. Estimation of Difference of two Population means

It was shown earlier that $\overline{X}_1 - \overline{X}_2 \cap N\left(\mu_1 - \mu_2, \sqrt{\frac{\sigma_1^2}{n_1} + \frac{\sigma_2^2}{n_2}}\right)$

where a sample of n_1 units is taken from one population whose mean is μ_1, and S.D. = σ_1 and $\overline{x}_1$ is sample mean. For 2nd population the corresponding values are n_2, μ_2, σ_2 and $\overline{X}_2$. The confidence interval for $\mu_1 - \mu_2$ is given as follows.

Thus $(\overline{X}_1 - \overline{X}_2) - Z_c \text{ SE } (\overline{X}_1 - \overline{X}_2) \le \mu_1 - \mu_2 \le (\overline{X}_1 - \overline{X}_2) + Z_c \text{ SE } (\overline{X}_1 - \overline{X}_2)$

where S.E. $(\overline{X}_1 - \overline{X}_2) = \sqrt{\frac{\sigma_1^2}{n_1} + \frac{\sigma_2^2}{n_2}}$

Example 9. *400 women shoppers are chosen at random is market A which gave average food expenditure of ₹ 250 with S.D. of ₹ 40. A sample of 400 shoppers in market B gave corresponding figures as ₹ 220 and 55 respectively.*

Find 95% confidence interval for $\mu_1 - \mu_2$.

Solution.

$$\text{S.E. } (\overline{X}_1 - \overline{X}_2) = \sqrt{\frac{\sigma_1^2}{n_1} + \frac{\sigma_2^2}{n_2}}$$

Now σ_1^2 and σ_2^2 are replaced by sample variances S_1^2 and S_2^2 as sample sizes are large.

$$\text{S.E. } (\overline{X}_1 - \overline{X}_2) = \sqrt{\frac{S_1^2}{n_1} + \frac{S_2^2}{n_2}}$$

given $S_1^2 = (40)^2 = 1600$

$S_2^2 = (55)^2 = 3025$

$n_1 = 400, n_2 = 400$

$$= \sqrt{\frac{1600}{400} + \frac{3045}{400}} = \sqrt{\frac{4625}{400}} = \frac{68}{20} = 3.4$$

Now $\mu_1 - \mu_2$ lies between $(\overline{X}_1 - \overline{X}_2) \pm 1.96 \text{ SE } (\overline{X}_1 - \overline{X}_2)$

i.e. between $(250 - 220) \pm 1.96\ (3.4)$

i.e. between $30 \pm 1.96\ (3.4)$

i.e. between 30 ± 6.66

Thus $\mu_1 - \mu_2$ lies between 23.34 and 36.66 with Confidence level of 0.95.

15.5.3. Interval Estimation of Population Proportion (= *P*) obtained from sample proportion (= *p*).

As already given in previous chapter sample proportion $p \cap N\left(P, \sqrt{\frac{PQ}{n}}\right)$.

Where $\text{SE}(p) = \sqrt{\frac{PQ}{n}}$ (in case x is large and population size is infinite)

However from a finite population of size N, $\text{SE}(p) = \sqrt{\frac{N-n}{N-1}\frac{PQ}{n}}$

However if P and Q $(= 1 - P)$ are not known they are replaced by p (= sample proportion) and q $(= 1 - p)$. Thus

$$\text{SE}(p) = \begin{cases} \sqrt{\dfrac{pq}{n}}, & n \text{ is large and population is infinite} \\ \sqrt{\dfrac{N-n}{N-1}\dfrac{pq}{n}}, & n \text{ is large and population size is finite } N \end{cases}$$

Thus confidence interval at confidence level c for P is $p \pm Z_c\ \text{SE}(p)$.

Example 10. *A random sample of 500 pineapples was taken from a large consignment and 65 of them were found to be bad. Show that the Standard Error of the proportion of bad ones in a sample of this size is 0,015 and deduce that the percentage of bad pineapples in the consignment almost certainly lies between 8.5 and 17.5.*

Solution (*a*) Here $n = 500$.

Number of bad pineapples in the sample = 65

$$\therefore \quad p = \text{Proportion of bad pineapples in the sample} = \frac{65}{500} = \frac{13}{100} = 0.13$$

$$\Rightarrow \quad q = 1 - p = 1 - 0.13 = 0.87$$

The standard error of proportion of bad pineapples in the sample is given by : S.E (p) =. $\sqrt{PQ/n}$ where P is the population proportion of bad pineapples in the whole consignment. Since P is not known, we use its unbiased estimate provided by the sample proportion p. Thus

$$\text{Est. [S.E. (p)]} = \sqrt{\frac{pq}{n}} = \sqrt{\frac{0.13 \times 0.87}{500}} = \sqrt{\frac{0.1131}{500}} = \sqrt{0.0002262} = 0.015$$

The most probable limits (99.73% confidence limits) for the population proportion of bad pineapples are :

$$p \pm 3\sqrt{\frac{pq}{n}} \quad = \; 0.130 \pm 3 \times 0.015 = 0.130 \pm 0.045 = (0.085 \text{ and } 0.175)$$

Hence the percentage of bad pineapples lies in the consignment lies almost surely between the limits 8.5 and 17.5.

15.5.4. Confidence interval for $P_1 - P_2$ (Difference of two population proportions)

The logical estimation of $P_1 - P_2$ may be taken as $p_1 - p_2$ (difference of sample proportions) based on large independent samples taken from the two populations). We consider the sample sizes large enough if $n_1 P_1$, $n_1 Q_1$, $n_2 P2$ and $n_2 Q_2$ are all greater than 5. (where $Q_1 = 1 - P_1$ and $Q_2 = 1 - P_2$). In that case sampling distribution of $P_1 - P_2$ can be approximated by a normal distribution as given.

$$p_1 - p_2 \cap N\left[(P_1 - P_2), \sqrt{\frac{P_1 Q_1}{n_1} + \frac{P_2 Q_2}{n_2}}\right]$$

Thus interval estimate of $P_1 - P_2$ is

$$(p_1 - p_2) \pm Z_c \sqrt{\frac{p_1 q_1}{n_1} + \frac{p_2 q_2}{n_2}}$$

(as P_1, Q_1, P_2 and Q_2 are unknown and are replaced by p_1, q_1, p_2 and q_2 respectively)

Example 11. *Out of 100 rebuilt engines from Repair Engines 28 failed within 28 month warranty and a sample of 150 rebuilt engines by Freed Mothers 48 failed during 12 month warranty period. Both type of engines were run under similar conditions. Find 95% confidence interval for difference of P_1 and P_2 where P_1 and P_2 are proportions in the two populations.*

Solution. Let p_1 and p_2 be the sample proportions from the two populations.

$$\text{Now } p_1 = \frac{28}{100} = .28 \text{ and } p_2 = \frac{48}{150} = 0.32$$

Now $p_1 - p_2 \cap N\left(P_1 - P_2, \sqrt{\frac{P_1Q_1}{n_1} + \frac{P_2Q_2}{n_2}}\right)$

Since P_1 and P_2 are not known we use p_1 and p_2 in their place.

Thus $\sqrt{\frac{P_1Q_1}{n_1} + \frac{P_2Q_2}{n_2}} = \sqrt{\frac{p_1q_1}{n_1} + \frac{p_2q_2}{n_2}}$

$$= \sqrt{\frac{(.28)(0.72)}{100} + \frac{(0.32)(0.68)}{150}} = 0.059$$

Confidence interval for $P_1 - P_2$ (95% level)

$= (p_1 - p_2) \pm 1.96 \text{ SE } (p_1 - p_2)$

$= (0.28 - 0.32) \pm 1.96 (.059)$

$= -0.04 \pm 0.117 =$ from -0.157 to 0.77.

15.6. ESTIMATION OF POPULATION MEAN (= μ) USING '*t*' DISTRIBUTION

As already mentioned in 15.5 (B) when n is small and σ is not known (if n is large σ is not known, sampling distribution of $\overline{X}$ still follows Z distribution after σ is replaced by its estimate s.) it is already established that $\frac{\overline{X} - \mu}{\frac{s}{\sqrt{n}}}$ follows t – distribution with $n - 1$ degrees of freedom and μ is will lie between $\overline{X} \pm t_{n-1,c} \frac{s}{\sqrt{n}}$.

15.6.1 When to use Z or *t*

We usually employ the standard normal distribution when the sample size is at least 30. We should, strictly speaking, base the decision whether to use z or t on the basis whether σ is known or not. When σ is known, we use z; when it is not, use t. The rule of using z when the sample is 30 or more is based on the fact that the t-distribution approaches the normal distribution as the sample size increases. When the sample reaches 30, there is little difference between the z and t values, so we may ignore the difference and use z. We will show this when we discuss the details of the t distribution and how to find values in a t distribution. Fig. below summarizes the decision-making process.

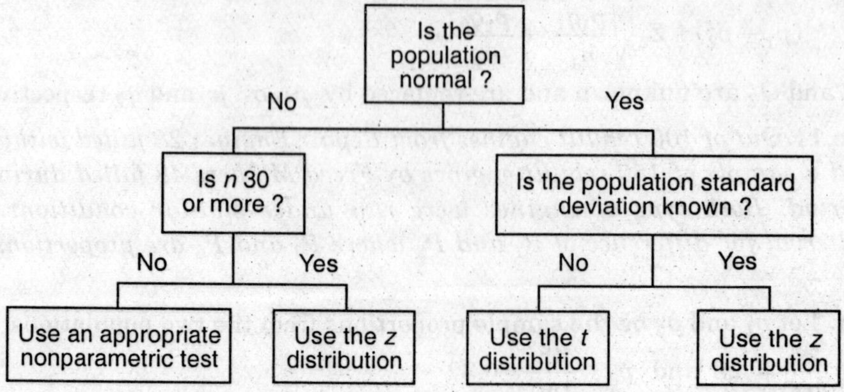

Determine when to use the Z Distribution or the t Distribution.

Example 12. *A researcher wants to estimate time firm put in by managers in a company. 18 managers were sampled and the extra time they work extra in a specific week was observed as follows (in hours).*

6	*21*	*17*	*20*	*7*	*0*	*8*	*16*	*29*
3	*8*	*12*	*11*	*9*	*21*	*25*	*15*	*16*

Construct a 90% confidence interval to estimate extra work put in per week in the industry.

Solution. We known $n = 18$ and $\overline{X}$ from the data is obtained. In order to estimate μ we need $s^2 = \frac{\Sigma (x - \bar{x})^2}{n-1}$, which are obtained as under.

X	$d = X - 14$	d^2
6	–8	64
21	7	49
17	3	09
20	6	36
7	–7	49
0	–14	196
8	–6	36
16	2	04
29	15	225
3	–11	121
8	–6	36
12	–2	04
11	–3	09
9	–5	25
21	7	49
25	11	121
15	1	01
16	2	04
	$\Sigma d = -8$	$\Sigma d^2 = 1038$

We have

$$s^2 = \frac{\Sigma (x - \bar{x})^2}{n-1}$$

$$= \frac{n}{n-1} \frac{\Sigma (x - \bar{x})^2}{n}$$

$$= \frac{n}{n-1}\left[\frac{\Sigma x^2}{n} - \left(\frac{\Sigma x}{n}\right)^2\right]$$

$$= \frac{n}{n-1}\left[\frac{\Sigma d^2}{n} - \left(\frac{\Sigma d}{n}\right)^2\right]$$

$$= \frac{18}{17}\left[\frac{1038}{18} - \frac{64}{324}\right]$$

$$= \frac{1}{17}\left[1038 - \frac{64}{18}\right]$$

$$= 60.8$$

$$s = \sqrt{60.8} = 7.8$$

$$\overline{X} = A + \frac{\Sigma d}{n} = 14 - \frac{8}{18}$$

$$= 13.56.$$

Degree of freedom = 17

From t-distribution we find $t_{n-1, c} = 1.74$ (using tables)

Thus 90% confidence interval for μ is

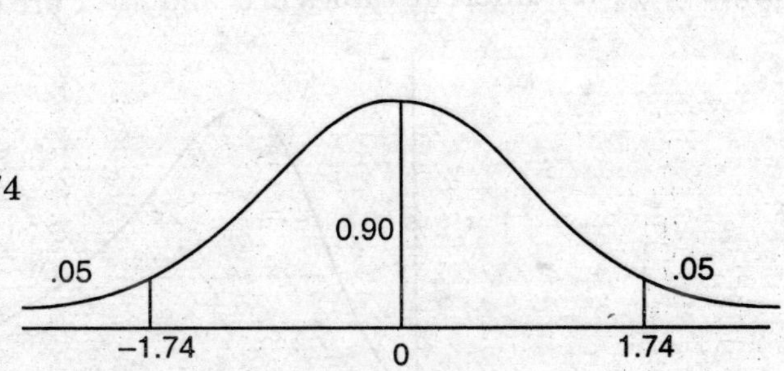

$$\overline{X} - t_{17, .90} \frac{s}{\sqrt{n}} \le \mu \le \overline{X} + t_{17, .90} \frac{s}{\sqrt{n}}$$

i.e. $13.56 - 1.74 \frac{7.8}{\sqrt{18}} \leq \mu \leq 13.56 + 1.74 \frac{7.8}{\sqrt{18}}$

i.e. $13.56 - 3.20 \leq \mu \leq 13.56 + 3.20$

i.e. $10.36 \leq \mu \leq 16.76.$

The point estimate for this problem is 13.56 hours, with an error of ± 3.20 hours. The researcher is 90% confident that the average amount of extra time accumulated by a manager per week in this industry is between 10.36 and 16.76 hours.

15.7. USE OF χ^2 FOR ESTIMATION OF σ^2 (POPULATION VARIANCE) FROM s^2

The following was discussed in previous chapter.

The sample variance

$$s^2 = \frac{\Sigma(x_1 - \bar{x})^2}{n - 1}$$

is the point estimator of the population variance σ^2. In using the sample variance as a basis for making inferences about a population variance, the sampling distribution of the quantity $(n - 1)\, s^2/\sigma^2$ is helpful. This sample distribution is described as follows.

Sampling Distribution of $(n - 1)s^2/\sigma^2$

Whenever a simple random sample of size n is selected from a normal population, the sampling distribution of

$$\frac{(n-1)s^2}{\sigma^2}$$

has a chi-square distribution with $n - 1$ degree of freedom.

The figure below shows some possible forms of the sampling distribution of $(n - 1)s^2/\sigma^2$.

Tables of areas or probability are readily available for the chi-square distribution. Since the sampling distribution of $(n - 1)s^2/\sigma^2$ is known to have a chi-square distribution whenever a simple random sample of size n is selected from a normal population, we can use the chi-square distribution to develop interval estimates and conduct hypothesis tests about a population variance.

We will use the notation χ^2_a to denote the value for the chi-square distribution that provides an area or probability of a to the right of the χ^2_a value as shown in figure below and values of χ^2_a for different values of a and $n - 1$ are given in the table which follows.

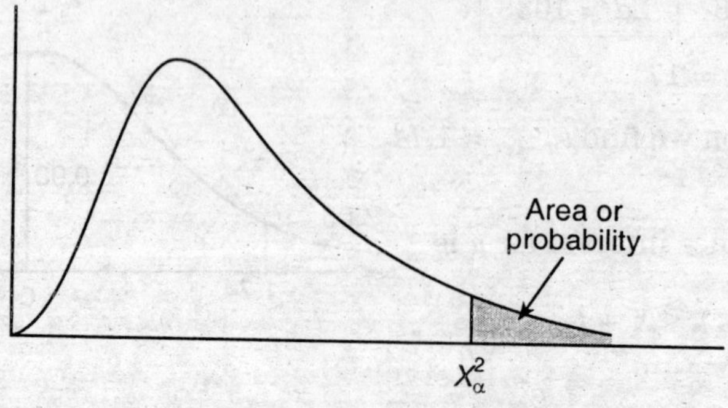

Degree of	Area in Upper Tail							
Freedom	.99	.975	.95	.90	.10	.05	.025	.01
1	.000	.001	.004	.016	2.706	3.841	5.024	6.635
2	.020	.051	.103	.211	4.605	5.991	7.378	9.210
3	.115	.216	.352	.584	.6.251	7.815	9.348	11.345
4	.297	.484	.711	1.064	7.779	9.488	11.143	13.277
5	.554	.831	1.145	1.610	9.236	11.070	12.832	15.086
6	.872	1.237	1.635	2.204	10.645	12.592	14.449	16.812
7	1.239	1.690	2.167	2.833	12.017	14.067	16.013	18.475
8	1.647	2.180	2.733	3.490	13.362	15.507	17.535	20.090
9	2.088	2.700	3.325	4.168	14.684	16.919	19.023	21.666
10	2.558	3.247	3,940	4.865	15.987	18.307	20.483	23.209
11	3.053	3.816	4.575	5.578	17.275	19.675	21.920	24.725
12	3.571	4.404	5.226	6.304	18.549	21.026	23.337	26.217
13	4.107	5.009	5.892	7.041	19.812	22.362	24.736	27.688
14	4.660	5.629	6.571	7.790	21.064	23.685	26.119	29.141
15	5.229	6.262	7.261	8.547	22.307	24.996	27.488	30.578
16	5.812	6.908	7.962	9.312	23.542	26.396	28.845	32.000
17	6.408	7.564	8.672	10.085	24.769	27.587	30.191	33.409
18	7.015	8.231	9.390	10.865	25.989	28.869	31.526	34.805
19	7.633	8.907	10.117	11.651	27.204	30.144	32.852	36.191

Suppose $n - 1 = 19$ (degrees of freedom) and confidence interval is 0.95 then χ^2 values bordering central 95% area are given below.

A CHI-SQUARE DISTRIBUTION WITH 19 DEGREE OF FREEDOM

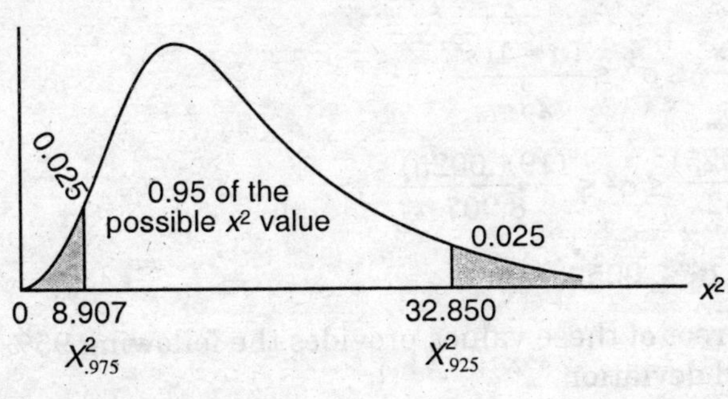

For a 0.95 confidence interval thus

$$\chi^2_{0.975} \le \chi^2 \le \chi^2_{0.025}$$

i.e. $$\chi^2_{.975} \le \frac{(n-1)s^2}{\sigma^2} \le \chi^2_{.025} \quad ...(1)$$

In effect, expression (1) provides an interval estimate in that .95, or 95%, of all possible values for $(n - 1)s^2/\sigma^2$ will be in the interval $\chi^2_{.975}$ to $\chi^2_{.025}$. We now need to do some algebraic manipulations to develop an interval estimate for the population variance σ^2. Working with the leftmost inequality in expression (1), we have

$$\chi^2_{.975} \leq \frac{(n-1)s^2}{\sigma^2} \quad \ldots(1)$$

Thus

$$\sigma^2 \chi^2_{.975} \leq (n-1)s^2$$

or
$$\sigma^2 \leq \frac{(n-1)s^2}{\chi^2_{.975}} \quad \ldots(2)$$

Performing similar algebraic manipulations with the rightmost inequality

i.e.
$$\frac{(n-1)s^2}{\chi^2_{.025}} \leq \sigma^2 \quad \ldots(3)$$

The results of expressions (2) and (3) can be combined to provide

$$\frac{(n-1)s^2}{\chi^2_{.025}} \leq \sigma^2 \leq \frac{(n-1)s^2}{\chi^2_{.975}} \quad \ldots(4)$$

Because expression (1) is true for 95% of the $(n-1)s^2/\sigma^2$ values, expression (4) provides a 95% confidence interval estimate for the population variance σ^2.

Example 13. *Radii of 20 screws was noted down and s^2 for these 20 values were found to be 0.0025. Find 95% confidence of σ (population standard deviation) of radii of all screws in the population.*

Solution. Since σ^2 is to be estimated from s^2 and $s^2 = 0.0025$ is a point estimate of σ^2.

Now for $n - 1 = 19$, for confidence interval of 0.95 we find $\chi^2_{0.025} = 8.907$ and $\chi^2_{0.975} = 32.852$ for 19 degrees of freedom. Also we have

$$\frac{(n-1)\,s^2}{\chi^2_{0.025}} \leq \sigma^2 \leq \frac{(n-1)\,s^2}{\chi^2_{0.975}}$$

$$\frac{(19)(.0025)}{32.852} \leq \sigma^2 \leq \frac{(19)(.0025)}{8.907}$$

or
$$.0014 \leq \sigma^2 \leq .0053$$

Taking the square root of these values provides the following 95% confidence interval for the population standard deviation.

$$.0380 \leq \sigma \leq .0730$$

15.8. TEST OF HYPOTHESIS

A hypothesis is a preconceived idea about the nature of population or about the value of its parameters. The statement like the distribution of heights of students of a university is normally distributed, the number of road accidents per day in Delhi is 10, *etc.*, are some examples of a hypothesis.

The test of hypothesis is a procedure by which we test the validity of a given statement about a population. This is done on the basis of a random sample drawn from it and sampling distribution of statistic estimating the parameter.

15.8.1 Null Hypothesis

Meaning – Null hypothesis is the assumption which we wish to test and whose validity is tested for possible rejection on the basis of sample information. It asserts that there is no significant difference between the sample statistic (e.g. Mean ($\overline{X}$), Standard Deviation (S), Proportion in a Sample (p)) and population parameter (e.g. Mean (μ), Standard Deviation (σ), Proportion of Population (P)) and the difference if any, is due to chance and has arisen out of sampling fluctuations.

Symbol – It is denoted by H_0.

Acceptance – The acceptance of null hypothesis implies that we have no evidence to believe otherwise and indicates that the difference is not significant and is due to sampling fluctuations.

Rejection. Rejection of H_0 implies that it is highly unlikely (*i.e.* probability is very small) to get a result as given by sample if H_0 is true.

Significant Difference – The difference is said to be significant one when it is more than what is expected theoretically with a given probability.

Example – The null hypothesis may be that the population mean (μ) is 50 and is set up as follows:

$$H_0 : \mu = 50$$

15.8.2 Alternative Hypothesis

Meaning – Alternative hypothesis is the hypothesis which differs from the null hypothesis. It is not tested.

Symbol – It is denoted by H_1.

Acceptance – Its acceptance depends on the rejection of the hypothesis.

Rejection – Its rejection depends on the acceptance of the null hypothesis.

Example – If population mean is assumed to be 50, an alternative hypothesis may be one of the following three:

$$H_1 : \mu \neq 50, \qquad H_1 : \mu > 50, \qquad H_1 : \mu < 50$$

H_0 and H_1 are mutually exclusive statement in the sense that both cannot hold good simultaneously. Rejection of one implies the acceptance of the other.

15.8.3 Level of Significance

Meaning – Level of significance is the maximum probability of rejecting the null hypothesis when it is true.

Symbol – It is usually expressed as % and is denoted by symbol α (*called 'Alpha'*)

Usefulness – It is used as a guide in decision-making. It is used to indicate the upper limit of the size of the critical rejection.

Example – 5% level of significance implies that there are about 5 chances in 100 of rejecting the H_0 when it is true or in other words, we are about 95% confidence that we will make a correct decision.

Note: Customarily, 5% or 1% level of significance is taken. Unless otherwise stated in the question, the author advises the students to consider 5% level of significance.

Example : If we have H_0, $\mu = 50$ and H_1, $\mu \neq 50$. Now we take a sample of size n and find $\overline{X}$. We know that $\overline{X} \cap N\left(50, \frac{\sigma}{\sqrt{n}}\right)$ [assuming n is large or the parent population is normal]. Thus $Z = \dfrac{\overline{X} - 50}{\frac{\sigma}{\sqrt{n}}}$ (This value of Z is obtained assuming H_o; $\mu = 50$ is true).

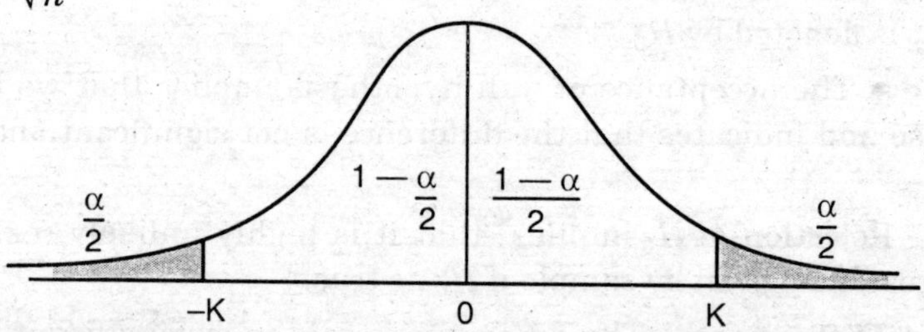

From Z distribution we know that it is unlikely (*i.e.* probability is small) for Z to lie in the shaded region. We specify this shaded region according to specified small value α (called level of significance). It also says that probability is large for Z to lie in the unshaded areas and that probability is $1 - \alpha$ (which earlier we had referred as level of confidence). Each shaded area, in this case, on either side should be equal and each be equal to $\frac{\alpha}{2}$. As Z is symmetrical, the unshaded areas on either side of central line is $\frac{1-\alpha}{2}$. For specified α, we are able to find two values $-k$ and k which separate shaded areas from unshaded and which are known as "Critical Values" and the value of a sampling distribution (as Z in this case) is called "Test Statistic". If computed values of Z lies between $-k$ and k, then there is no reason for us to doubt H_0 (Null Hypothesis).

15.8.4 Test Statistic

Meaning – Test statistic refers to a function of sample observations (*i.e.* statistic) whose computed value determines the final decision regarding acceptance or rejection of null hypothesis (H_0).

Critical Region or Rejection Region

Meaning – Critical region is the region which corresponds to a pre-determined level of significance. The set of values of the test statistic which leads to rejection of the null hypothesis is called region of rejection *or* Critical Region of the test. Conversely, the set of values of the test statistic which leads to the acceptance of H_0 is called Region of acceptance.

Critical Value – Critical value is that value of statistic which separates the critical region from the acceptance region. It lies at the boundary of the regions of acceptance and rejection.

Size of Critical Region – The probability of rejecting a true null hypothesis is called as size of critical region.

Usefulness of Test Statistic and Critical Region – It is used as a guide in decision making regarding acceptance *or rejection* of H_0. If the value of the test statistic falls in the critical region, the null hypothesis is rejected. If the value of the test statistic does not fall in the critical region, the null hypothesis is accepted.

Types of Test Statistics

Test-Statistic	*Used for*
(*i*) Z-test	For test of hypothesis involving large sample *i.e.* > 30
(*ii*) *t*-test	For test of hypothesis involving small sample *i.e.* ≤ 30 and if σ is unknown.
(*iii*) x^2-test	For testing the discrepancy between observed frequencies and expected frequencies without any reference to population parameter.
(*iv*) *F*-test	For testing the population variance.

15.8.5 Rejection of Null Hypothesis

Example. Suppose a sample of 100 bulbs gives average life of bulbs $\overline{X}$ hrs. (assuming life of a bulb follows normal distribution with S.D. = 150 hrs.)

Let $H_0,\quad \mu = 1600$

$$\text{Now we know that SE }(\overline{X}) = \frac{\sigma}{\sqrt{n}} = \frac{150}{10} = 15$$

$$\text{Thus } \overline{X} \cap N(1600, 15),\ Z = \frac{\overline{X} - 1600}{15}$$

$$\text{From normal distribution Z it is known that } P\left(-2 \le \frac{\overline{X} - 1600}{15} \le 2\right) = 0.9544$$

or $\quad P\,(1600 - 2 \times 15 \le \overline{X} \le 1600 + 2 \times 15) = 0.9544$

or $\quad P\,(1570 \le \overline{X} \le 1630) = 0.9544$

This result shows that the likelihood of getting a random sample of size 100, from the given population, with mean lying between 1570 and 1630 hours is 95.44% or equivalently, the likelihood of getting a random sample having its mean either less than 1570 or more than 1630 hours is only 4.56%. Thus, a random sample with its mean lying outside these limits is highly unlikely under the assumption that null hypothesis is true.

However, if the mean computed from the drawn sample is found to lie outside these limits, it may imply that either null hypothesis is false or the rare event, with probability = 4.56%, has occurred.

Thus, if we decide to reject the null hypothesis whenever the computed sample mean fall outside the above limits, the probability of our decision being wrong is only 4.56% or 0.0456.

15.8.6. Two Types of Error

The decision of acceptance or rejection of a null hypothesis is made on the basis of a sample from a population and hence, an element of uncertainty is always involved in making such decisions. Two types of errors are likely to be committed in the procedure of testing a hypothesis. These are *Type I* and *Type II* errors. Type I error is committed when a true null hypothesis is rejected. The probability of this error is termed as the *Level of Significance* of the test and will be denoted by α. The probability of committing an error is also termed as its size. Note that size of type I error, is = α = 0.0456, in the above example.

Contrary to this, type II error is committed when a false null hypothesis is accepted. The probability of type II error is denoted by β.

	Accept H_0	*Reject* H_0
H_0 is true	No error	Type I error (Probability = α)
H_0 is not true	Type II error (probability β)	No error

Type II Error

To understand the meaning of type II error, we assume that the true value of μ is 1620 instead of the hypothesised value of 1600 hours (Refer previous example of 15.8.5). If the standard deviation is same

Since we tend to accept H_0 (μ = 1600) if $1570 \le \overline{X} \le 1630$. But actually $\mu = 1620$

Thus $\beta = P(1570 \le \overline{X} \le 1630)$ when $\overline{X} \cap N$ (1620, 15)

$$= P\left(\frac{1\,570 - 1620}{15} \le Z \le \frac{1330 - 1620}{15}\right)$$

$$= P(-3.33 \le \ge \le 0.67) = 0.4996 + 0.2486 = 0.7482$$

15.8.7 Two Tailed Versus Single Tailed Test

(*a*) Two Tailed Test

The specification of the critical region for a test depends upon the nature of the alternative hypothesis and the value of α. For example, $H_1 : \mu \ne \mu_0$, this implies that μ may be less or greater than μ_0. Thus, the critical region is to be specified on both tails of the curve with each part corresponding to half of the value of α. A test having critical region at both the tails of the probability curve is termed as a *two tailed test.*

In this case test statistic is $Z = \dfrac{\overline{X} - \mu_0}{SE(\overline{X})}$, distribution of Z is given below for α= .05.

Thus if μ actually much smaller than assumed value μ_0 then $\overline{X}$ is likely to be small compared to μ_0 and we get high negative value of Z.

For this same reason if μ much larger than μ_0 (assumed value) then $\overline{X}$ is also expected to be large compared to μ_0 and thus Z will have large positive value. Thus rejection regions are in both tails of the distribution and critical values for α = 0.05 are ± 1.96.

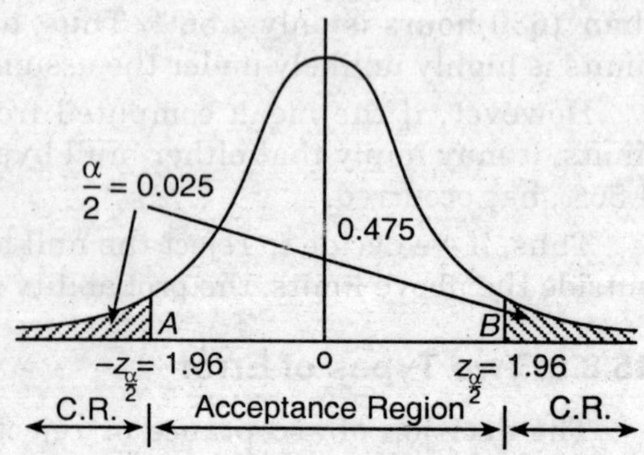

(b) Single Tailed Tests

(i) Right Tailed Test

Suppose H_1 is $\mu > \mu_0$ (this is case when we certainly know that if $\mu \neq \mu_0$ then it must be $\mu > \mu_0$ and possibility of $\mu < \mu_0$ is ruled out).

Thus in this case if H_0 is not true then Z must lie in the right tail of Z-distribution and the area for $\alpha = 0.05$ is only on the right of critical value which has area for $\alpha = 0.05$ and for this critical value of Z is 1.645 (For the same value of $\alpha =$ 0.05 critical values for two tailed test were ± 1.96).

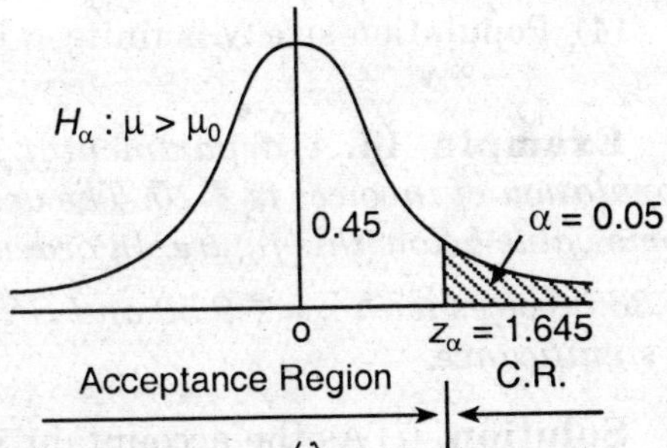

(i)

(ii) Left Tailed Test

Suppose H_1 is $\mu < \mu_0$ (and this will be case when we know that if $\mu \neq \mu_0$, then it must be less than μ_0) then in this case critical region will be in the left tail of Z distribution (in this case if H_1 is true $\overline{X}$ will be small compared to assumed value μ_0). Thus critical value in this case is $Z = -1.645$ and if compared value of $Z = \dfrac{\overline{X} - \mu_0}{SE\,(\overline{X})}$ is less than – 1.645 we have reasons to accept H_1 *i.e.* $\mu < \mu_0$.

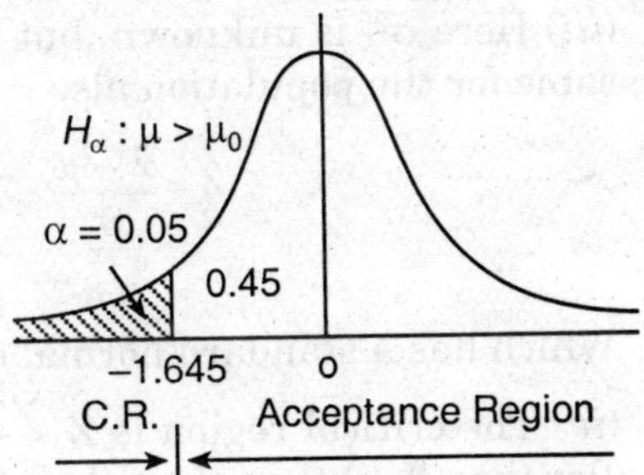

(ii)

15.9. TESTS WHEN TEST STATISTICS IS Z-VARIATE

15.9.1. Critical values of Z for different values of confidence level C are reproduced again.

Confidence Level *C*	*Significance Level* $\alpha = 1 - c$	*Critical values of Z (two tailed)*
0.90	0.10	± 1.645
0.95	0.05	± 1.96
0.98	0.02	± 2.33
0.99	0.01	± 2.58
Nearly 1.00	0.00 (al most)	± 3.00

15.9.2 Test for Assumed Mean of a Population

We know that $\overline{X} \cap N\left(\mu, \dfrac{\sigma}{\sqrt{n}}\right)$ in the following cases

(1) Population is normal, σ is known, $n \geq 2$

(2) Population is not normal and is infinite σ is known, n is large.

(3) Population is not normal, and is infinite, σ is not known and is replaced by *s*, *n* is large.

(4) Population size *N* is finite, σ is replaced by $\sigma\sqrt{\dfrac{N-n}{N-1}}$, *n* is large.

Example 14. *A departmental manager believes that the average value of a large population of invoices is ₹ 10. The accountant, however, disagrees with him and believes it is some value below this figure. In order to test his belief the accountant takes a random sample of 36 invoices with* $\overline{x}$ *= ₹ 9.50 and* S^2 *= ₹ 4.00. Formulate and perform a test at the 0.05 level of significance.*

Solution. (*i*) As the accountant specifically wishes to show that the mean invoice value is less than ₹ 10, we set up a non-tailed test.

$H_0 : \mu = 10, H_1 : \mu < 10$ (It should be either 10 or less than 10, according to question, as such H_1 is $\mu < 10$)

(*ii*) $\alpha = 0.05$

(*iii*) Here σ^2 is unknown, but as *n* is large, σ^2 for the sample *i.e.*, S^2 can be taken to be the same for the population also

$$Z = \frac{\overline{x} - \mu}{\frac{S}{\sqrt{n}}}$$

Which has a standard normal distribution.

(*iv*) The critical region is $Z < -1.645$, as illustrated in given figure. Clearly if $\overline{x}$ is much smaller than ₹ 10 then the value of *Z* will fall in the critical region.

(*v*) $$Z = \frac{9.50 - 10.00}{\frac{2}{\sqrt{36}}} = -1.5$$

(*vi*) As the value of Z does not fall in the critical region we do not have enough evidence to reject the manager's claim.

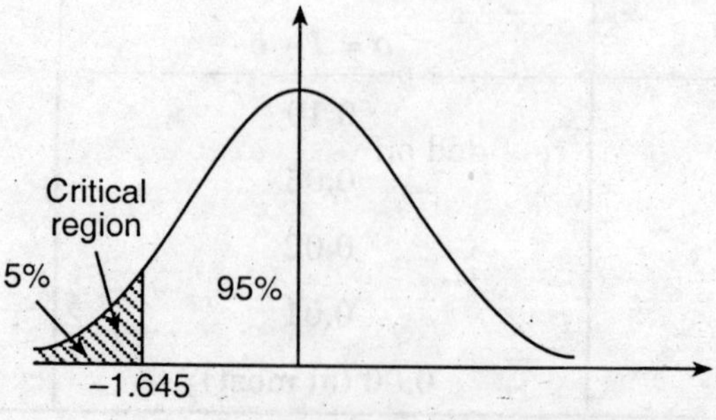

Example 15. *An aircraft manufacturer needs to buy aluminum sheets of 0.05 inches in thickness. Thinner sheet would not be appropriate and thicker sheets would to too heavy. The aircraft manufacturer takes a random sample of 100 sheets with mean width equal to 0.048 and S.D. equal to 0.01 inches. Should the aircraft manufacturer buy the aluminum sheets from his supplier if he wants to make the decision at*

(i) 5% level of significance ?

(ii) 1% level of significance ? [D.U.B.A. (Hons.), 1995]

Solution. Let the Null hypothesis be H_0 that he should buy. *i.e.* $H_0, = \mu = 0.05$

Alternative hypothesis H_1 that he should not buy. *i.e.* $H_1, \mu \neq 0.05$

We should apply two tailed test because the manufacturer does not want more deviation on either side.

$$Z = \frac{\overline{X} - \mu_0}{\text{S.E. of mean}} = \frac{.048 - 0.05}{\frac{\sigma}{\sqrt{n}}} = \frac{0.002 \times 10}{0.01} = -2$$

The critical values of Z at 5% level of significance for two tailed test = ± 1.96 and at 1% level of significance it is ± 2.58.

∴ The manufacturer can accept the sheets at 1% level of significance and reject at 5% level of significance.

Example 16. *An index fund manager complied comprehensive data on weekly returns from the stock market index for the last 10 years. On studying the data, he found that the index provided a weekly return of 0.4% on an average with a standard deviation of 0.35% during the 10-year period and a return of 0.32% with a standard deviation of 0.45% in the last nine months. He wants to find out whether the average weekly return from the index has declined from its long-term average. Help him in finding out the same using the test of hypothesis. Assume a level of significance of 5% and show the rejection region in a diagram. You may also assume that long-term average weekly returns from the index follow a normal distribution.*

Solution. In this case $H_0, \mu = 0.4$

H_1 $\mu < 0.4$ (Has μ declined from μ = 0.4%)

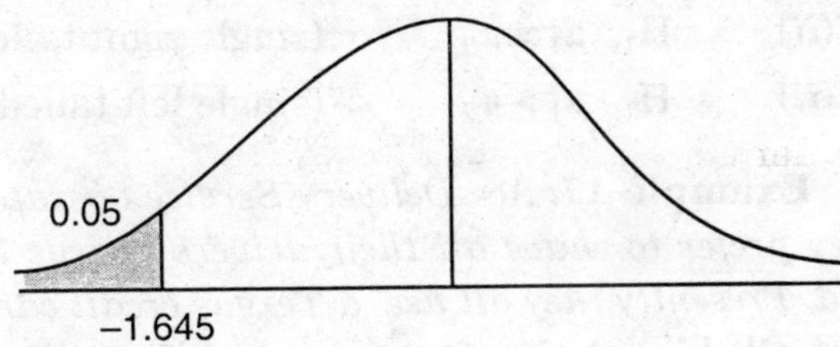

(This if left tailed Test)

$\alpha = 0.05$, critical

Values of $Z = -1.645$

Also given $\sigma = 0.35$

$\overline{X} = 0.32, \quad s = 0.45$

$n = \frac{270}{7}$ weeks (Time period is 9 months = 270 days)

= 39 weeks (rounded off to nearest integer)

Now since σ is known, knowledge of $s = 0.45$ is irrelevant.

$$Z = \frac{\overline{x} - \mu}{\text{S.E.}} = \frac{0.32 - 0.4}{\frac{0.35}{\sqrt{39}}} = \frac{-0.08 \times \sqrt{39}}{0.35} = -1.42742$$

This calculated value of Z does not lie in the rejection region, H_0 is not rejected. Thus average weekly wage has not declined.

15.9.3. Testing Equality of Means of Two Populations

In case means of two populations is assumed to be equal then H_0, $\mu_1 = \mu_2$ (though each one is not known. In this case two independent samples from two populations are drawn. Let the informations (sample and population) be as follows.

	Population I	Population II
Sample mean	$\overline{X}_1$	$\overline{X}_2$
Sample size	n_1	n_2
Population variance	σ_1^2	$\sigma_2{}^2$

As already covered in this chapter

$$\overline{X}_1 - \overline{X}_2 \cap N\left[(\mu_1 - \mu_2), \sqrt{\frac{\sigma_1^2}{n_1} + \frac{\sigma_2^2}{n_2}}\right]$$

$$\cap N\left(0, \sqrt{\frac{\sigma_1^2}{n_1} + \frac{\sigma_2^2}{n_2}}\right) \quad [\text{according to } H_0 \text{ as } \mu_1 = \mu_2 \Rightarrow \mu_1 - \mu_2 = 0]$$

$$\text{Thus compute } Z = \frac{(\overline{X} - \overline{X}_2) - 0}{\sqrt{\frac{\sigma_1^2}{n_1} + \frac{\sigma_2^2}{n_2}}} = \frac{\overline{X}_1 - \overline{X}_2}{\sqrt{\frac{\sigma_1^2}{n_1} + \frac{\sigma_2^2}{n_2}}}$$

Tests:—

In case alternative hypothesis is

(*i*) H_1, $\mu_1 \neq \mu_2$ (Two tailed values of Z are used as critical values)

(*ii*) H_1, $\mu_1 > \mu_2$ (single right tailed value is used as critical value)

(*ii*) H_1, $\mu_1 > \mu_2$ (single left tailed values is used as critical value)

Example 17. *Ace Delivery Service operates a fleet of delivery vans in the Houston area. They prefer to have all their drivers charge their gasoline using the same brand of credit card. Presently they all use a Texgas credit card. Ace management has decided that perhaps Quik-Chek, a chain of convenience stores that also sell gasoline but does not accept credit cards, is worth investigating. A random sample of gas prices at 35 Texgas stations and 40 Quik-Chek stores in the Houston area is obtained. The cost of 1 gallon of regular gasoline is recorded; the data are summarized:*

Sample 1 (Texgas)	***Sample 2 (Quik-Chek)***
$n_1 = 35$	$n_2 = 40$
$\overline{x}_1 = \$1.48$	$\overline{x}_2 = \$1.39$
$s_1 = \$0.12$	$s_2 = \$0.10$

Test at 95% if the gasoline at the Quik-Chek store was less expensive than at Texgas.

Solution. Here, μ_1 represents the average price at all of the Texgas stations and μ_2 is the average price at the Quik-Chek stores in the area. It is to be investigated whether $\mu_2 < \mu_1$? Or, put another way, is $\mu_1 > \mu_2$? Use a significance level of 0.05.

Step 1 : *Define the hypothesis* : The question is whether the data support the claim that $\mu_1 > \mu_2$, so we put this statement in alternative hypothesis.

H_0: $\mu_1 = \mu_2$ (Texgas less expensive or the same)

H_1: $\mu_1 > \mu_2$. Quik-Chek is less expensive)

Step 2 : *Define the test statistic* : This is the statistic that you evaluate using the sample data. Its value will either support the alternative hypothesis or it will not. The test statistic for this situation is given by equation

$$Z = \frac{\overline{X}_1 - \overline{X}_2}{\sqrt{\frac{\sigma_1^2}{n_1} + \frac{\sigma_2^2}{n_2}}}$$

Step 3 : Using $\alpha = 0.05$, the corresponding value of $Z_{0.05} = 1.645$

$\therefore$ reject H_0 if calculated $Z > 1.645$

(since it is right tailed test)

Since σ_1^2 and σ_2^2 are not known, these are explaced by s_1^2 and s_2^2 respectively.

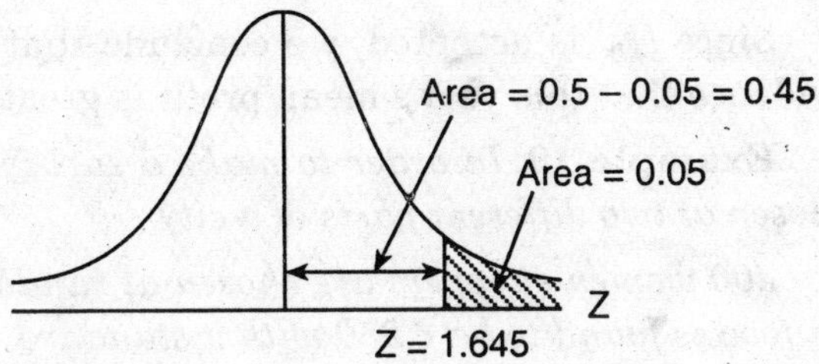

Step 4 : Evaluate the test statistic and carry out the test.

$$Z = \frac{\overline{X}_1 - \overline{X}_2}{\sqrt{\frac{\sigma_1^2}{n_1} + \frac{\sigma_2^2}{n_2}}} = \frac{\overline{X}_1 - \overline{X}_2}{\sqrt{\frac{s_3^2}{n_1} + \frac{s_2^2}{n_2}}} = \frac{1.48 - 1.39}{\sqrt{\frac{(0.12)^2}{35} + \frac{(0.10)^2}{40}}} = \frac{0.09}{0.0257} = 3.50 = Z$$

As Z (calculated) lies in the critical region we reject H_0 ; μ_1 is significantly larger than μ_2. Therefore, we claim that $\mu_1 > \mu_2$.

Step 5 : *State a conclusion* : We conclude that the Quik-Chek stores *do* charge less for gasoline (on the average) than do the Texgas stations. If the locations of these stores are equally convenient to Ace Delivery Service, buying gas for Quik-Chek appears to be a money-saving alternative.

Example 18. *The sales manager of a company asserts that the mean profit per car for this year μ_1 is greater that mean profit for last year μ_2. In as much as detailed accounting is the sales manager determine this profit for random samples of 35 cars sold this year and 35 sold last year. Perform a hypothesis test at the 5 per cent level if this year's sample has a mean of $\bar{x}_1$ = \$350 and a standard deviation s_1 = \$ 25, and last year's sample has a mean of $\bar{x}_2$ = \$ 340 and a standard deviation of s_2 = \$30.*

Solution. The sales manager's contention is that this year's mean μ_1 is greater than last year's mean μ_2 that is, that $\mu_1 > \mu_2$ or $\mu_1 - \mu_2 > 0$. Hence, the hypothesis are

1. $H_0 : \mu_1 - \mu_2 = 0$ $H_1 : \mu_1 - \mu_2 > 0$

The alternative hypothesis has the > sign; so that test is a right-tail test with critical value of $Z_{0.05} = 1.64$. (for $\alpha = 0.05$)

2. Hence we will reject H_0 if calculated $Z > 1.645$.

Using $n_1 = n_2 = 35$, $s_1 = 25$ and $s_2 = 30$, we compute the sample standard error of the difference between means,

$$s_{\bar{x}_1 - \bar{x}_2} = \sqrt{\frac{s_1^2}{n_1} + \frac{s_2^2}{n_2}} = \sqrt{\frac{(25)^2}{35} + \frac{(30)^2}{35}} = 6.60$$

Now, $\bar{x}_1 = 350$ and $\bar{x}_2 = 340$, we compute

$$Z = \frac{\bar{x}_1 - \bar{x}_2}{s_{\bar{x}_1 - \bar{x}_2}} = \frac{350 - 340}{6.60} = 1.51$$

Therefore

The calculated Z, 1.51 is less than 1.64. Hence, we do not reject H_0.

Since H_0 is accepted, we conclude that the sales manager did not produce convincing evidence that this year's mean profit is greater than last year's mean profit.

Example 19. *In order to make a survey of the buying habits, two markets A and B are chosen at two different parts of a city.*

400 women shoppers are chosen at random in market A. Their average daily expenditure on food is found to be ₹ 250 with a standard deviation of ₹ 40. The figures are ₹ 220 and ₹ 55 respectively in the market B where also 400 women shoppers are chosen at random. Test at 1% level of significance whether the average daily food expenditures of the two populations of shoppers are equal.

Solution. Let X and Y denote the daily expenditure (in ₹) of women on food in two markets A and B respectively. There in usual notations we are given :

$n_1 = 400$, $\bar{x} = 250$, $s_x = 40$ $\Rightarrow$ $s_x^2 = 1,600$

$n_2 = 400$, $\bar{y} = 220$, $s_y = 55$ $\Rightarrow$ $s_y^2 = 3.025$

Null Hypothesis. $H_0, \mu_x = \mu_y$.

Alternative Hypothesis. $H_1 : \mu_x \neq \mu_y$ (two-tailed).

Level of significance. $\alpha = 1\% = 0.01$, Critical values of $Z = \pm 2.58$

Test Statistic. Since sample are large, under H_0.

$$Z = \frac{\bar{x} - \bar{y}}{\sqrt{\frac{\sigma_x^2}{n_1} + \frac{\sigma_y^2}{n_2}}} = \frac{\bar{x} - \bar{y}}{\sqrt{\frac{s_x^2}{n_1} + \frac{s_y^2}{n_2}}} \quad \text{[because } \hat{\sigma}_x^2 = s_x^2 \text{ and } \hat{\sigma}_y^2 = s_y^2 \text{ for large samples.]}$$

$$Z = \frac{250 - 220}{\sqrt{\frac{1600}{400} + \frac{3025}{400}}} = \frac{30 \times 20}{\sqrt{4625}} = \frac{600}{68.01} = 8.82$$

Since $Z = 8.82$, is much greater than 2.58, the significant value of Z at 1% level of significance, it is highly significant. Hence, the data are inconsistent with the null hypothesis and we conclude that the average daily expenditures of two populations of shoppers in markets A and B differ significantly.

Example 20. *An investigation of the relative merits of two kinds of flashlight batteries showed that a random sample of 100 batteries of brand A lasted on the average 36.5 hours with a standard deviation of 1.8 hours, while a random sample of 80 batteries of brand B lasted on the average 36.8 hours with a standard deviation of 1.5 hours. Use a level of significance of 0.05 to test whether the observed difference between the average life times is significant.*

Solution. Let X and Y denote the life (in hours) of the flashlight batteries of brands A and B respectively. Then, in the usual notations we are given.

$n_1 = 100$, $\bar{x} = 36.5$, $s_x = 1.8$ $\Rightarrow$ $s_x^2 = 3.24$

$n_2 = 80$, $\bar{y} = 36.8$, $s_y = 1.5$ $\Rightarrow$ $s_y^2 = 2.25$

Null Hypothesis. $H_1 : \mu_x \neq \mu_y$, *i.e.*, there is no significant difference between the average life times of the two brands of flashlight batteries.

Alternative Hypothesis.. $H_1 : \mu_x \neq \mu_y$ (two-tailed)

Level of significance. $\alpha = 0.05$ (Critical values of $Z = \pm 1.96$)

Test Statistic. Under H_0, the test statistic is

$$Z = \frac{\bar{x} - \bar{y}}{\sqrt{\frac{s_x^2}{n_1} + \frac{s_y^2}{n_2}}} \quad \text{[Since samples are large, } \sigma_1^2 \text{ and } \sigma_x^2 \text{ are replaced by } s_1^2 \text{ and } s_2^2\text{]}$$

$$Z = \frac{36.5 - 36.8}{\sqrt{\frac{3.24}{100} + \frac{2.25}{80}}} = \frac{-0.3}{\sqrt{0.0324 + 0.0281}} = \frac{-0.3}{0.0605} = \frac{-0.03}{0.2460} = 1.2195$$

Since $|Z| = 1.2195$ is less than 1.96, the value of Z is not significant at 5% level of significance. This implies that the data do not provide us any evidence against the null hypothesis (H_0) which may, therefore, be accepted. Hence we conclude that $\mu_x = \mu_y$ *i.e.*, there is no significant difference between the average life times of the two brands A and B of the flashlight batteries.

Example 21. *The mean height of 50 male students who showed above average participation in college athletics was 68.2 inches with a standard deviation of 2.5 inches : while 50 male students who showed no interest in such participation had a mean height of 67.5 inches with a standard deviation of 2.8 inches. Test the hypothesis that male students who participate in college athletics are taller than other male students.*

Solution. Let X denote the height (in inches) of the male students who showed above average participation in college athletics and Y denote the height of the students who showed no interest in athletic participation. Then we are given.

$n_1 = 50$, $\bar{x} = 68.2$, $s_x = 2.5$ $\Rightarrow$ $s_x^2 = 2.25 = \hat{\sigma}_x^2$

$n_2 = 50$, $\bar{y} = 67.5$, $s_y = 2.8$ $\Rightarrow$ $s_y^2 = 7.84 = \hat{\sigma}_y^2$

since the samples are large.

Null Hypothesis. $H_0 : \mu_x = \mu_y$ *i.e.*, there is no significant difference between the mean heights of the male students who participate and who do not participate in college athletics.

Alternative Hypothesis. $H_1 : \mu_x > \mu_y$ (Right-tailed)

Level of significance. $\alpha = 0.05$.

Test Statistic. Under H_0, the test statistic is (since the sample are large):

$$Z = \frac{\bar{x} - \bar{y}}{\sqrt{\frac{s_x^2}{n_1} + \frac{s_y^2}{n_2}}} \sim N(0, 1)$$

$$Z = \frac{68.2 - 67.5}{\sqrt{\frac{6.25}{50} + \frac{7.84}{50}}} = \frac{0.7}{\sqrt{0.1250 + 0.1568}} = \frac{0.7}{\sqrt{0.2818}} = \frac{0.7}{0.5308} = 1.3188$$

Since the calculated value of Z is less than 1.645 (Right-tailed test), it is not significant at 5% level of significance. Hence the data are consistent with the null hypothesis and we conclude that average height of the male students who participate in college athletics is same as the average height of the other male students in the college.

15.9.4. Testing for Proportion of an Attribute in a Population

Now population proportion (P) is defined as $\frac{M}{N}$ for an attribute if in a population of size N their are M units which are having an attribute and same way sample proportion (p) is defined as $\frac{m}{n}$ if in a sample of n units, m units have their particular attribute.

As described earlier $p \cap N\left(P, \sqrt{\frac{PQ}{n}}\right)$, and in that case $\frac{p-P}{\sqrt{\frac{PQ}{n}}}$ will follows Z distribution. Thus if H_0 is $P = P_0$ (some specified value then calculated $Z = \frac{p - P_0}{\sqrt{\frac{P_0 Q_0}{n}}}$ then we compare this calculated values of Z with critical value and test the hypothesis accordingly.

Example 22. *A die was thrown 9000 times and of these 3220 yield a 3 or 4. Can the die be regarded as unbiased?*

Solution. In the usual notations, we are given $n = 9000$

The observed proportion of successes (getting 3 or 4) in 9000 throws of die is given by:

$$p = \frac{3220}{9000} = 0.3578$$

We set up the *null hypothesis* H_0 *that the die is unbiased, i.e.,* under H_0,

$$H_0 \,;\; P = \text{Population proportion of successes}$$

$$= P\,[\text{Getting 3 or 4 in throw of an unbiased die}] = \frac{2}{6} = \frac{1}{3}$$

$$\Rightarrow \quad Q = 1 - P = 1 - \frac{1}{3} = \frac{2}{3}$$

Alternative Hypothesis is $H_1 : P \neq \frac{1}{3}$ (two-tailed). [*i.e.* the die is biased]

Under the null hypothesis, $\left(H_0 : P = \frac{1}{3}\right)$, the test statistic is :

$$Z = \frac{p - E(p)}{S.E.\,(p)} = \frac{p - P}{\sqrt{PQ/n}} \quad \text{[since the sample is large.]}$$

$$S.E.\ (p) = \sqrt{\frac{P_0 Q_0}{n}} = \sqrt{\frac{\frac{1}{3} \cdot \frac{2}{3}}{9000}} = \frac{1}{90\sqrt{5}}$$

$$Z = \frac{\frac{322}{900} - \frac{1}{3}}{\frac{1}{90\sqrt{5}}} = \frac{22}{900} \times 90\sqrt{5} = \frac{22 \times \sqrt{5}}{10} = 4.95$$

Since $|Z|$ is greater than 3, it is significant (at all levels of significance). Hence, the null hypothesis is rejected and we conclude that the die is certainly biased. In other words, the given data are not consistent with the hypothesis that the die was unbiased.

Example 23. *In a random sample of 400 persons from a large population, 120 are females. Can it be said that males and females are in the ratio 5 : 3 in population? Use 1% level of significance ?*

Solution. We are given :

$$n = 400 \text{ and } X = \text{No. of females in the sample} = 120$$

$$p = \text{Observed proportion of females in the sample} = \frac{120}{400} = 0.3$$

Null Hypothesis. The males and females in the population are in the ratio 5 : 3, *i.e.*,

$$H_0 : P = \text{Proportion of females in the population} = \frac{3}{8} = P_o$$

$$\Rightarrow \qquad Q_0 = 1 - P = \frac{5}{8}$$

Alternative Hypothesis : $H_1 : P \neq \frac{3}{8}$ (Two-tailed).

Level of significance. $\alpha = 0.01$

Test Statistic. Under H_0, the test statistic is

$$Z = \frac{p - E(p)}{S.E.(p)} = \frac{p - P_0}{\sqrt{\frac{P_0 Q_0}{n}}}$$

$$\frac{P_0 Q_0}{n} = \left(\frac{3}{8} \times \frac{5}{8}\right) \frac{1}{400} = \frac{3.}{64 \times 80} = \frac{3.}{64 \times 16 \times 5}$$

$$\sqrt{\frac{P_0 Q_0}{n}} = \frac{13}{8 \times 4 \times \sqrt{5}} = \frac{1}{32}\sqrt{0.6}$$

$$\therefore \qquad Z = (p - p_0)\frac{1}{\sqrt{\frac{P_0 Q_0}{n}}} \left(\frac{3}{10} - \frac{3}{8}\right)\frac{32}{\sqrt{0.6}} = \frac{-6}{80} \cdot \frac{32}{\sqrt{0.6}}$$

$$\therefore \qquad = -3.12$$

The significance value of Z at 1% level of significance for a two-tailed test in 2.58. Since calculated $|Z|$ is greater than 2.58, it is significant at 1% level of significance. Hence, the null hypothesis H_0 is rejected and we concluded that the males and females in the population are not the ratio 5 : 3.

Example 24. *A manufacture claimed that at least 95% of the equipment which he supplied to a factory conformed to specifications. An examination of a sample of 200 pieces of equipment revealed that 18 were faulty. Test this claim at a significance level of (i) .05 (ii) .01.*

Solution.

In the usual notations, we are given $n = 200$,

$$X = \text{No. of pieces conforming to specifications in the sample} = 200 - 18 = 182$$

$$\therefore \quad p = \text{Proportion of pieces conforming to specifications in the sample} = \frac{182}{200} = 0.91$$

Null Hypothesis. $H_0 : p = 0.95$, *i.e.*, the proportion of pieces conforming to specifications in the lot is 95%.

Alternative Hypothesis : $H_1 : P < 0.95$ (Left-tailed alternative).

It will suffice to test $H_0 : P = 0.95 \Rightarrow Q_0 = 1_0 - P = 0.05$

Level of significance. (*i*) $\alpha = 0.05$ (*ii*) $\alpha = 0.01$.

Test Statistic. Under H_0, the test statistic is

$$Z = \frac{p - E(p)}{S.E.\,(p)} = \frac{p - P}{\sqrt{PQ/n}} \sim N(0, 1), \text{ since sample is large.}$$

$$\therefore Z = \frac{0.91 - 0.95}{\sqrt{0.95 \times 0.05/200}} = \frac{-0.04}{\sqrt{0.00237}} = \frac{-0.04}{0.0154} = -2.6$$

(*i*) *Significance at 5% level of significance.* Since the alternative hypothesis is one-sided (left-tailed), we shall apply left-tailed test for testing significance of Z. The significant value of Z at 5% level of significance for left-tail test is – 1.645. Since computed value of Z – 2.6 is less than –1.645, we say Z is significant (as it lies in the critical region) and we reject the null hypothesis at 5% level of significance. Hence, the manufacturer's claim is rejected at 5% level of significance.

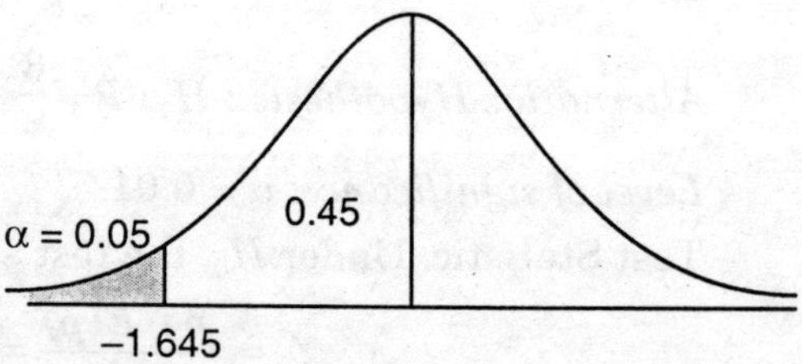

Now calculated $Z = -2.6$, this lies in rejection region ($\alpha = 0.01$ critical value is – 2.33). Even at 1% level of significance the manufacturer's claim is rejected.

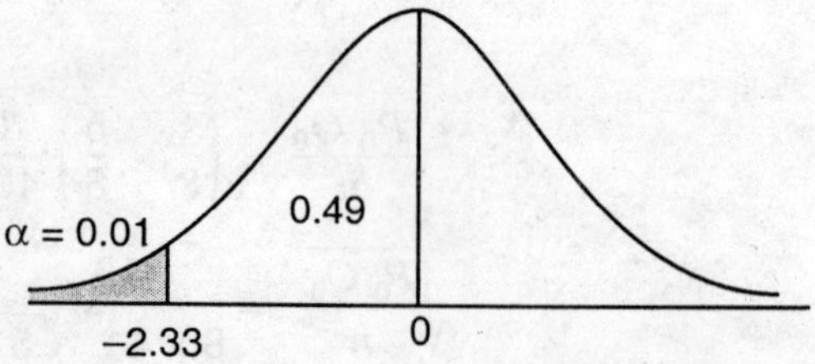

15.9.5. Testing Significance of Difference of Proportions of two Populations

Two independent samples from two populations with population proportions as P_1 and P_2 are drawn. Sample sizes are n_1 and n_2 and sample proportions are p_1 and p_2.

We have $\quad p_1 \cap N\left(P_1, \sqrt{\frac{P_1 Q_1}{n_1}}\right)$

and $$p_2 \cap N\left(P_2, \sqrt{\frac{P_2 Q_2}{n_2}}\right)$$

Thus $$p_1 - p_2 \cap N\left(P_1 - P_2, \sqrt{\frac{P_1 Q_1}{n_1} + \frac{P_2 Q_2}{n_2}}\right)$$

However H_0 in this case is $P_1 = P_2$ (Two population proportions are equal) and P_1 and P_2 are not known. In that case.

$$p_1 - p_2 \cap N\left(0, \sqrt{\frac{P_1 Q_1}{n_1} + \frac{P_2 Q_2}{n_2}}\right)$$

Let $P_1 = P_2 = P$ and thus $Q_1 = Q_2 = Q$.

Thus $\text{SE}(p_1 - p_2) = \sqrt{PQ\left(\frac{1}{n_1} + \frac{1}{n_2}\right)}$. We estimate P (and thus Q also) by pooling the two samples.

We had estimate of $P_1 = p_1 = \frac{m_1}{n_1}$ $(\Rightarrow m_1 = n_1 P_1)$

and estimate of $P_2 = p_2 = \frac{m_2}{n_2}$ $(\Rightarrow m_2 = n_2 P_2)$

Thus by pooling two samples estimate of P

$$= \hat{P} = \frac{m_1 + m_2}{n_1 + n_2} = \frac{n_1 p_1 + n_2 p_2}{n_1 + n_2}$$

Thus $$\text{SE}(p_1 - p_2) = \sqrt{\hat{P}\hat{Q}\left(\frac{1}{n_1} + \frac{1}{n_2}\right)}$$

Where $$\hat{P} = \frac{n_1 p_1 + n_2 p_2}{n_1 + n_2}$$

Now $(p_1 - p_2) \cap N\left(0, \sqrt{\hat{P}\hat{Q}\left(\frac{1}{n_1} + \frac{1}{n_2}\right)}\right)$ [under H_0]

Thus test statistic $$Z = \frac{(p_1 - p_2) - 0}{\sqrt{\hat{P}\,\hat{Q}\left(\frac{1}{n_1} + \frac{1}{n_2}\right)}} = \frac{p_1 - p_2}{\sqrt{\hat{P}\,\hat{Q}\left(\frac{1}{n_1} + \frac{1}{n_2}\right)}}$$

Then we use normal way of testing.

Example 25. *To test the effectiveness of the approach and layout of two direct-mail brochures, a marketing manager mailed out 150 copies of each brochure and recorded the number of responses generated by each. There were 30 responses generated by the first brochure and 10 generated by the second. Can the marketing manager conclude that the first brochure is more effective ? Let $\alpha = 0.05$.*

Solution. Here we want to test the hypothesis H_0. $P_1 = P_2$ against $H_0 : P_1 > P_2$, where P_1 is the proportion of responses that will be generated from a nationwide mailing of the first brochure and P_2 is the proportion of responses generated by the second brochure. (It is right tailed test)

We have, $p_1 = \dfrac{30}{150} = 0.200, \; p_2 = \dfrac{10}{150} = 0.067$

$$\hat{P} = \frac{m_1 + m_2}{n_1 + n_2}$$

$$= \frac{30 + 10}{300} = \frac{40}{300}, \; \hat{Q} = 1 - \frac{40}{300} = \frac{260}{300}$$

Also, $s^2_{p_1 - p_2} = \dfrac{40}{300}\left(\dfrac{260}{300}\right)\left(\dfrac{1}{150} + \dfrac{1}{150}\right)$

$$= 0.001541$$

$$s_{p_1 - p_2} = 0.0392$$

Our calculated Z is

$$Z = \frac{p_1 - p_2}{s_{p_1 - p_2}} = \frac{0.133}{0.0392} = 3.40$$

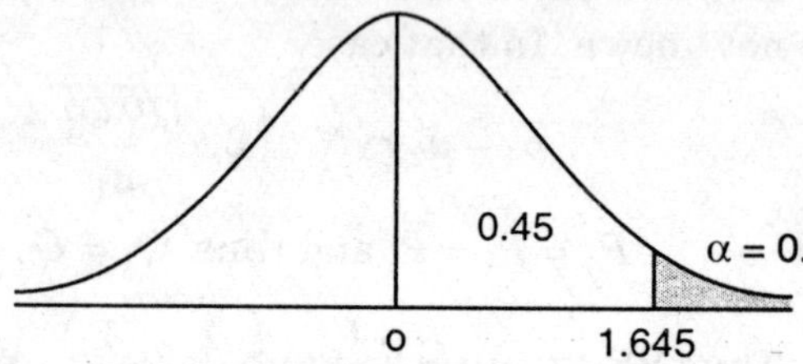

The critical region in this test is $Z_{0.05}$ for one tailed test = 1.645. Since calculated $Z > Z_{0.05} = 1.645$, we reject the null hypothesis and conclude that the first brochure is more effective in generating responses.

Example 26. *A brick-making firm makes its bricks by two different processes. In samples of 200 bricks from the first process and 300 bricks from the second process, 20 of the first type broke during baking in the kiln and 45 of the second type broke in the kiln. Test the hypothesis that the kiln breaking rates are the same against the alternative hypothesis that they are different. Let α be 0.02.*

Solution. For this problem we have the following :

$H_0 : P_1 = P_2$

$H_a : P_1 \neq P_2$ (Two tailed test)

Critical values of Z distribution are ± 2.33

$$p_1 = \frac{20}{200} = 0.10, \; p_2 = \frac{45}{300} = 0.15$$

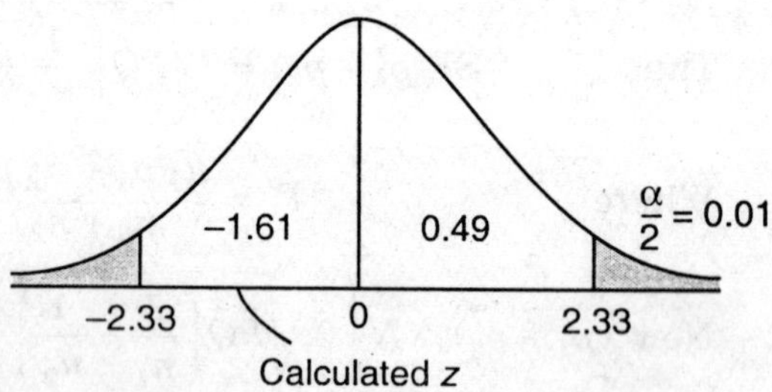

The pooled value of $\hat{p}$ the best estimate of the breakage rate in the two populations, assuming these rates are equal, is

$$\hat{P} = \frac{20 + 45}{200 + 300} = \frac{65}{500} = 0.13$$

Then $s^2_{p_1 - p_2} = (0.13)(0.87)\left(\dfrac{1}{200} + \dfrac{1}{300}\right) = 0.000943$

And finally, $s_{(p_1 - p_2)} = \sqrt{0.000943} = 0.031$

$$Z = \frac{p_1 - p_2}{s_{(p1 - p2)}} = \frac{0.10 - 0.15}{0.031} = -1.61$$

Since this value is not within the rejection region, we cannot reject the null hypothesis that the breakage rates of the two processes are the same.

Example 27. *A company has the head office at Kolkata and a branch at Mumbai. The personnel director wanted to know if the workers at the two places would like the introduction of a new plan of work and a survey was conducted for this purpose. Out of a sample of 500* *workers at Kolkata, 62% favoured the new plan. At Mumbai, out of a sample of 400 workers, 41% were against the new plan. Is there any significant difference between the two groups in their attitude towards the new plan at 5% level ?*

Solution. Let p_1 and p_2 denote the sample proportion of workers favouring the new plan at Kolkata and Mumbai respectively. Then in the usual notations, we are given :

$$n_1 = 500, \quad p_1 = 0.62$$
$$n_2 = 400, \quad p_2 = 0.59$$

Null Hypothesis. We set up the null hypothesis that the population proportion of workers favouring the new plan in Kolkata and Mumbai is same, *i.e.*,

$$H_0 : P_1 = P_2 = P, \text{ (say)}.$$

In other words, there is no significant difference between the two groups in their attitude towards the new plan.

Alternative Hypothesis. $H_1 : P_1 \neq P_2$ (two-tailed).

Level of significance. $\alpha = 0.05$.

Test Statistic. Under H_0, the test statistic is (since the sample are large),

$$Z = \frac{p_1 - p_2}{\sqrt{PQ\left(\frac{1}{n_1} + \frac{1}{n_2}\right)}}$$

where $$\hat{P} = \frac{n_1 p_2 + n_2 p_2}{n_1 + n_2} = \frac{500 \times 0.62 + 400 \times 0.59}{500 + 400}$$

$$= \frac{310 + 236}{900} = \frac{546}{900} = 0.607$$

$$\Rightarrow \quad \hat{Q} = 1 - \hat{P} = - 0.607 = 0.393$$

$$\therefore \quad Z = \frac{0.62 - 0.59}{\sqrt{0.607 \times 0.393\left(\frac{1}{500} + \frac{1}{400}\right)}} = \frac{0.03}{\sqrt{0.2386 \times (0.002 + 0.0025)}}$$

$$= \frac{0.03}{\sqrt{0.001074}} = \frac{0.03}{0.0328} = 0.9155$$

The significant value of Z for two-tailed test at 5% level of significance is 1.96. Since, the calculated value of Z is less than 1.96, it is not significant. Hence, H_0 may be accepted at 5% level of significance and we may conclude that there is no significant difference in the two groups in their attitudes towards the new plan.

Example 28. *A machine puts out 16 imperfect articles in a sample of 500. After the machine is overhauled, it puts out 3 imperfect articles in a batch of 100. Has the machine improved ?*

Solution.

We are given $n_1 = 500$, and $n_2 = 100$.

p_1 = Proportion of defectives in the 1st sample $= \frac{16}{500} = 0.032$

p_2 = Proportion of defectives in the 2nd sample (after overhauling of machine).

$$= \frac{3}{100} = 0.030$$

Null Hypothesis. $H_0 : P_1 = P_2$, *i.e.,* there is no significant difference in the machine before overhauling and after overhauling. In other words, the *machine has not improved after overhauling.*

Alternative Hypothesis. $H_1: P_2 < P_1$ or $P_1 > P_2$ (Right Tailed)

(*i.e.*, the machine has improved after overhauling).

Level of Significance. $\alpha = 0.05$

Test Statistic. Under H_0, since the samples are large, the test statistic is :

$$Z = \frac{p_1 - p_2}{S.E.(p_1 - p_2)} = \frac{p_1 - p_2}{\sqrt{\hat{P}\hat{Q}\left(\frac{1}{n_1} + \frac{1}{n_2}\right)}} \quad ...(*)$$

where $\hat{P} = \frac{n_1 p_1 + n_2 p_2}{n_1 + n_2} = \frac{16 + 3}{500 + 100} = \frac{19}{600} = 0.032$

$\Rightarrow$ $\hat{Q} = 1 - \hat{P} = 0.968$

$$\text{S.E. } (p_1 - p_2) = \sqrt{0.032 \times 0.968\left(\frac{1}{500} + \frac{1}{100}\right)} = \sqrt{0.031 \times \frac{(1+5)}{500}} = \sqrt{\frac{0.186}{500}}$$

$$= \sqrt{0.000373} = 0.0193$$

Substituting in (*), $Z = \frac{0.032 - 0.030}{0.0193} = \frac{0.002}{0.0193} = 1.04$

Since $Z < 1.645$ (Right-tailed test), it is not significant at 5% level of significance. Hence, we may accept the null hypothesis and conclude that the machine has not improved after overhauling.

15.10 USE OF *t*-DISTRIBUTION FOR CERTAIN TESTS

15.10.1. Test for Significance of Population Mean

In case a sample of size n is drawn which gives sample mean $\overline{X}$ from a normal population with mean μ and whose S.D. σ is not known then $\frac{\overline{X} - \mu}{s/\sqrt{n}}$ is known as t-statistic which follows t-distribution with $(n - 1)$ degrees of freedom where $s^2 = \frac{\Sigma(X - \overline{X})^2}{n - 1}$ (s^2 is estimate of σ^2, has already been discussed in 15.4).

Also $\frac{s^2}{n} = \frac{\Sigma(X - \overline{X})^2}{n - 1} \cdot \frac{1}{n} = \frac{\Sigma(X - \overline{X})^2}{n} \cdot \frac{1}{n - 1} = \frac{S^2}{n - 1}$

Thus $\frac{\overline{X} - \mu}{\frac{s}{\sqrt{n}}} = \frac{\overline{X} - \mu}{\frac{S}{\sqrt{n - 1}}}$ $\left[\text{where } S^2 = \frac{\Sigma(X - \overline{X})^2}{n}\right]$

Conditions for the use of *t*-Test

t-test is used when :

1. the sample size is 30 or less

2. the variance of the population is unknown
3. the sample is random sample
4. the population is normal and selection of items is independent.

Properties of *t*-Distribution

1. The variable *t*-distribution ranges from $-\infty$ to $+\infty$.
2. It is symmetrical.
3. Its mean is zero.
4. Its variance is > 1 but approaches 1 as the sample size become large.
5. Its standard deviation is $\sqrt{\dfrac{n}{n-2}}$ and $n > 2$.
6. If n is large it is close to Z-distribution.
7. Thus t-statistic $\dfrac{x-\mu}{\dfrac{s}{\sqrt{n}}}$ can be taken as Z-distribution when n is large

   (This property has already been used).

   Also we know that $(\Sigma(X-\overline{X})^2 = \Sigma X^2 - \dfrac{(\Sigma X)^2}{n} = \Sigma d^2 - \dfrac{(\Sigma d)^2}{n}$ $\left[\text{where } d = X - A\right]$

   Thus $s^2 = \dfrac{1}{(n-1)}\left[\Sigma X^2 - \dfrac{(\Sigma X)^2}{n}\right] = \dfrac{1}{n-1}\left[\Sigma d^2 - \dfrac{(\Sigma d)^2}{n}\right]$

Critical values (for two tailed or single tailed *t*-values) are similarly found as in case of *Z*-distribution which are tabulated for different degrees of freedom ($n-1$).

Example 29. *A fertilizer mixing machine is set to give 4 kg of nitrate for every quintal bag of fertilizers. Five 100 kg bags are examined. The percentages of nitrate are: 2, 6, 4, 3, 1. Is there reason to believe that the machine is defective?*

Solution.

Step 1 → $H_0 : \mu_1 = 4, H_1 : \mu \neq 4$

Step 2 → *Calculation of Mean and Standard Deviation.*

Let us take assumed mean = 3

X	$d = X - 3$	d^2	
2 6 4 3 1	− 1 + 3 + 1 0 − 2	1 9 1 0 4	$\overline{X} = A + \dfrac{\Sigma d}{n} = 3 + \dfrac{1}{5} = 3.2$ $s^2 = \dfrac{1}{n-1}\left[\Sigma d^2 - \dfrac{(\Sigma d)^2}{n}\right]$ $= \dfrac{1}{4}\left[15 - \dfrac{1}{5}\right] = \dfrac{74}{20} = 3.7$ $s = \sqrt{3.7} = 1.93.$
$\Sigma X = 16$	$\Sigma d = +1$	$\Sigma d^2 = 15$	

$$\text{Calculated } t_{n-1} = \frac{\overline{X} - \mu_0}{\dfrac{s}{\sqrt{n}}} = \frac{(3.2 - 4)\sqrt{5}}{1.93} = \frac{-0.8 \times \sqrt{5}}{1.93} = -0.92$$

Degree of freedom (ν) = $n - 1 = 5 - 1 = 4$, for $\nu = 4$, $t_{0.05} = 2.78$ (from tables) *Interpretation* : Since the computed value of t is less than the table value of t, we accept H_0 and conclude that the population mean is 4 *i.e.*, the data do not indicate that the machine is defective.

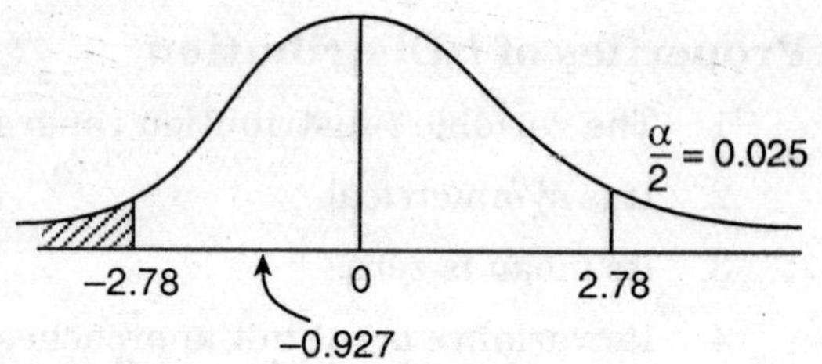

Example 30. *A random sample of heights of 20 students gave a mean of 68 inches with S.D. of 3 inches. Test the hypothesis that mean height in population is 70 inches under the assumption that the heights are normally distributed. Also construct a 95% confidence interval for the population mean.*

Solution. We have to test $H_0 : \mu_1 = 70$ against $H_0 : \mu_1 \neq 70$.

It is given that $n = 20$, $\overline{X} = 68$ and $S = 3$.

$$\text{SE}(\overline{x}) = \frac{s}{\sqrt{n}} = \frac{s}{\sqrt{n-1}} = \frac{3}{\sqrt{19}} = 0.688$$

$$\text{Thus calculated } i.e., t_{\text{cal},\,19} = \frac{68 - 70}{0.688} = -2.906.$$

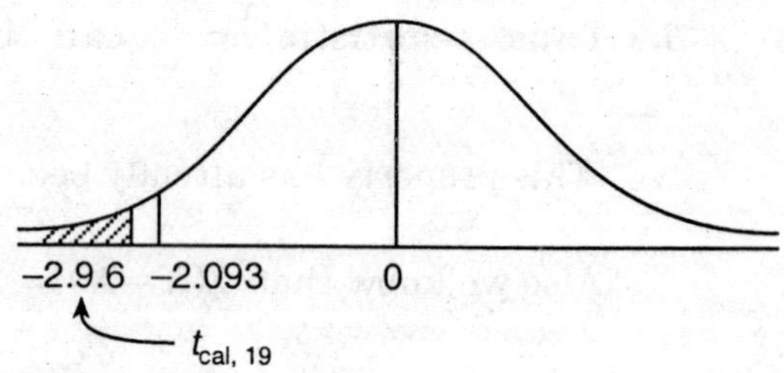

Critical values of $t_{0.05,\,19} = \pm 2.093$

Since $t_{cal} = -2.093$ lies in the critical region, H_0 is rejected.

15.10.2. Test for Equality of Two Population Means

Now suppose we randomly select small independent sample from two populations and do not know the population variance σ_1^2 and σ_2^2. We can obtain a statistic having a t-distribution if we assume that the population variances σ_1^2 and σ_2^2 are equal. Denoting the common value of these variances of σ^2, it follows that

$$SE(\overline{x}_1, \overline{x}_2) = \sqrt{\frac{\sigma_1^2}{n_1} + \frac{\sigma_2^2}{n_2}} = \sqrt{\frac{\sigma^2}{n_1} + \frac{\sigma^2}{n_2}} = \sqrt{\sigma^2\left(\frac{1}{n_1} + \frac{1}{n_2}\right)} = \sigma\sqrt{\left(\frac{1}{n_1} + \frac{1}{n_2}\right)}$$

Because we are assuming that $\sigma_1^2 = \sigma_2^2 = \sigma^2$, we do not need separate estimates of σ_1^2 and σ_2^2. Instead, we combine the results of the two independent random samples to compute a single estimate of σ^2. This estimate is called the **pooled estimate** of σ^2, and it is a weighted average of the two sample variances s_1^2 and s_2^2 with their respective degrees of freedom as weights. Denoting the pooled estimate as s_p^2, it is computed using the formula

$$s_p^2 = \frac{(n_1 - 1)s_1^2 + (n_2 - 1)s_2^2}{(n_1 - 1) + (n_2 - 1)} = \frac{(n_1 - 1)s_1^2 + (n_2 - 1)s_2^2}{n_1 + n_2 - 2} = \frac{\Sigma(X - \overline{X}_2 + \Sigma(Y - \overline{Y})^2}{n_1 + n_2 - 2}$$

Where X and Y values denote sampled values from two samples.

Using s_p^2 the estimate of $\sigma_{x_1 - x_2}$ is $\sqrt{s_p^2\left(\frac{1}{n_1}+\frac{1}{n_2}\right)}$

and we form the statistic $t = \dfrac{(\bar{x}_1 - \bar{x}_2) - (\mu_1 - \mu_2)}{\sqrt{s_p^2\left(\frac{1}{n_1}+\frac{1}{n_2}\right)}} = \dfrac{\bar{x}_1 - \bar{x}_2}{\sqrt{s_p^2\left(\frac{1}{n_1}+\frac{1}{n_2}\right)}}$ $\left[\text{under } H_0,\ \mu_1 = \mu_2\right]$

It can be shown that, if we have randomly selected independent samples from two normally distributed populations having equal variances, then the sampling distribution of the statistic is a t-distribution having $(n_1 + n_2 - 2)$ degrees of freedom.

Example 31. *A production supervisor at a major chemical company must determine which of two catalysts, catalyst XA-100 or catalyst ZB-200, maximizes the hourly yield of a chemical process. In order to compare the mean hourly yields obtained by using the two catalysts, the supervisor runs the process using each catalyst for five one-hour periods. The resulting yields (in pounds per hour) for each catalyst, along with the means and the variances of the yields, are given in the following table. Assuming that all other factors affecting yields of the process have been held as constant as possible during the test runs, it seems reasonable to regard the five observed yields for each catalyst as a random sample from the population of all possible hourly yields for the catalyst.*

Yields of a Chemical Process	*Obtained Using two Catalysts*
Catalyst XA-100 $= X_1$	*Catalyst ZB-200* $= X_2$
801	752
814	718
784	776
836	742
820	763
$\bar{x}_1 = 811$	$\bar{x}_2 = 750.2$
$s_1^2 = 386$	$s_2^2 = 484.2$

Determine if there is any significant difference in the mean yield of XA-100 and ZB-200.

Solution. In order to compare the mean hourly yields obtained by using catalysts XA-100 and ZB-200, suppose we wish to test

$$H_0 : \mu_1 - \mu_2 = 0$$

which says the mean hourly yields obtained by using the two catalysts do not differ, versus

$$H_1 : \mu_1 - \mu_2 \neq 0$$

which says there is a difference between these mean hourly yields.

$$\text{Pooled estimate of S.D.} = s_p^2 = \frac{(n_1 - 1)s_1^2 + (n_2 - 1)s_2^2}{n_1 + n_2 - 2}$$

$$= \frac{(5-1)(386) + (5-1)(484.2)}{5+5-2} = 435.1$$

Thus $$\text{SE}(\bar{x}_1 - \bar{x}_2) = \sqrt{s_p^2\left(\frac{1}{n_1}+\frac{1}{n_2}\right)}$$

$$= \sqrt{435.1\left(\frac{1}{5}+\frac{1}{5}\right)} = \sqrt{174.04} = 13.2$$

Thus $$t_{\text{cal}} = \frac{\overline{X}_1 - \overline{X}_2}{\text{SE}(\overline{X}_1 - \overline{X}_2)} = \frac{811 - 750.2}{13.2} = 4.6.$$

Since α is not mentioned we assume $\alpha = 0.05$

$$t_{.05, 5+5-2} = t_{0.05,\,8} = 2.306 \text{ (Table value)}$$

Since t_{cal} lies in the rejection region we reject H_0 *i.e.*, we reject $\mu_1 = \mu_2$.

Example 32. *A group of 5 patients treated with medicine A weigh 42, 39, 48, 60, 41 kg. A second group of 5 patients treated with medicine B weight 38, 42, 48, 67, 40 kg. Do the two medicines differ significantly with regard to their effect in increasing weight?*

Given the following:

Degree of freedom	*5*	*8*	*9*	*10*
Value of t at 5% level	*2.57*	*2.31*	*2.26*	*2.23*

Solution.

Step 1 → We set $H_0: \mu_1 = \mu_2$, $H_1: \mu_1 \neq \mu_2$

Step 2 → Since both the samples are small and independent, student *t*-statistic is to be used.

Step 3 → *Calculation of means and combined standard deviation of both the samples.*

X_1	$X_1 - \overline{X}_1 = X_1 - 46$	$(X_1 - \overline{X}_1)^2$	X_2	$X_2 - \overline{X}_2 = X_2 - 47$	$(X_1 - \overline{X}_1)^2$
42	− 4	16	38	− 9	81
39	− 7	49	42	− 5	25
48	+ 2	4	48	+ 1	1
60	+ 14	196	67	+ 20	400
41	− 5	25	40	− 7	49
$\Sigma X_1 = 230$	$\Sigma(X_1 - \overline{X}_1) = 0$	$\Sigma(X_1 - \overline{X}_1) = 290$	$\Sigma X_2 = 235$	$\Sigma(X_2 - \overline{X}_2) = 0$	$\Sigma(X_2 - \overline{X})^2 = 556$

$$\overline{X}_1 = \frac{\Sigma X_1}{n_1} = \frac{230}{5} = 46, \overline{X}_2 = \frac{\Sigma X_2}{n_2} = \frac{235}{5} = 47$$

$$s_p = \sqrt{\frac{\Sigma(X_1 - \overline{X}_1)^2 + \Sigma(X_2 - \overline{X}_2)^2}{n_1 + n_2 - 2}}$$

$$= \sqrt{\frac{290 + 556}{5 + 5 - 2}} = \sqrt{105.75} = 10.283$$

Step 4 → $t_{cal} = \dfrac{\overline{X}_1 - \overline{X}_2}{s_p\sqrt{\dfrac{1}{n_1}+\dfrac{1}{n_2}}} = \dfrac{\overline{X}_1 - \overline{X}_2}{s_p\sqrt{\dfrac{n_1+n_2}{n_1 n_2}}}$

$$= \frac{46-47}{10.283}\cdot\sqrt{\frac{25}{10}} = \frac{-1}{61.283}\sqrt{2.5} = -0.154$$

Step 5 → Degrees of freedom = 5 + 5 − 2 = 8

$t_{.05, 8} = \pm 2.31$. (table value)

Step 6 → Interpretation; since $t_{cal} = 0.154$ lies within ± 2.31 (*i.e.*, it lies in acceptance region) we conclude that the medicines *A* and *B* do not differ significantly with regard to their effect in increasing weight.

15.10.3. Testing Equality of Means for Dependent Samples (Paired *t*-test)

In this case two variable values are measured on each unit of a sample taken once. Let *X* and *Y* be the two variable measured on each unit.

In this case $\mu_x = \mu_y$ *i.e.* $\mu_x - \mu_y = 0$

$\Rightarrow$ $\mu_{x-y} = 0$ or $\mu_d = 0$ [where $d = x - y$]

Where $d = x - y$ is a variable obtained from two variables x and y.

Using the test as given in 15.10.1 we get

$$t_{cal,\, n-1} = \frac{\overline{d} - \mu_d}{\dfrac{s_d}{\sqrt{n}}} \quad \text{where } \overline{d} = \frac{\Sigma d}{n}$$

$$s_d^2 = \frac{1}{(n-1)}\left[\Sigma d^2 - \frac{(\Sigma d)^2}{n}\right] \quad \text{or} \quad \frac{s_d}{\sqrt{n}} = \sqrt{\frac{\Sigma(d-\overline{d})^2}{n(n-1)}}$$

Thus we get *t*-statistic with $(n - 1)$ degrees of freedom. Then we test the significance of this t_{cal} as explained earlier. The method is explained in examples which follow.

Example 33. *A certain medicine was given to each of the 5 patients. The results are given below.*

	I	*II*	*III*	*IV*	*V*
Weight before medicine	42	39	48	60	41
Weight after medicine	38	42	48	67	40

Test whether there is any change in weight after the medicine at 5% level of significance. Given the following:

Degrees of freedom	4	5	8	9	10
Value of t at 5% level	2.78	2.57	2.31	2.26	2.23

Solution.

Step 1 → We set $H_0 : \mu_x = \mu_y$, $H_1 : \mu_x \neq \mu_y$ (*X* is weight before and *Y* is weight after)

Step 2 → *Since both the samples are small and dependent (paired). t-test based on paired observations is to be used.*

Step 3 → *Calculation of d, $\bar{d}$, d^2 and s_d*

Before X	*After Y*	$d = y - x$	d^2
42	38	–4	16
39	42	+3	9
48	48	0	0
60	67	+7	49
61	40	–1	1
$n = 5$		$\Sigma d = 5$	$\Sigma d^2 = 75$

Step 4 → Calculate $s_d^2 = \dfrac{\Sigma(d - \bar{d})^2}{n-1} = \dfrac{1}{n-1}\left[\Sigma d^2 - \dfrac{(\Sigma d)^2}{n}\right] = \dfrac{1}{4}\left[75 - \dfrac{25}{5}\right] = 17.5$

Step 5 → Compute $t_{n-1} = \dfrac{\bar{d} - 0}{\sqrt{\dfrac{s_d^2}{n}}}$ $\left[\text{since } H_0 \text{ is } \mu_d = 0\right]$

Computed $t_4 = \dfrac{\frac{5}{5} - 0}{\sqrt{\dfrac{17.5}{5}}} = \dfrac{1}{\sqrt{3.5}} = \dfrac{1}{1.87} = 0.53.$

Step 6 → New $t_{4,\,0.05} = \pm\, 2.78$ (as given in the table)

Thus calculated value to t lies within ± 2.78, as such there is no evidence to reject H_0. Thus we conclude that medicine has no effect to increase weight.

Example 34. *Productivity (units produced per day) for a random sample of 10 workers was recorded before and after training. The following data pairs were obtained; the first number in each pair is the "before" output and the second is the "after" output : (54, 60); (56, 59); (50, 57); (52, 56); (55, 56); (52, 58); (56, 62); (53, 55); (53, 54); (60, 64). Perform a hypothesis test at the 1 per cent level to determine if mean productivity is greater after training than before training.*

Solution. Let X = Output before and Y = output after H_0, $\mu_x = \mu_y$ *i.e.*, $\mu_{y-x} = 0$ or $\mu_d = 0$ $[d = y - x]$

We to test whether $\mu_y > \mu_x \Rightarrow \mu_d > 0$

Thus H_i, $\mu_d > 0$ (right tailed test).

The test is one-tailed with $\alpha = 0.01$. There are $n = 10$ observations; so the number of degrees of freedom is

$$df = n - 1 = 10 - 1 = 9$$

From table $t_{9,\,0.01} = 2.82$. Hence,

2. Reject H_0 if calculated $t > 2.82$

To compute t, we need $\bar{d}$ and s_d. The following table shows the computations of the sample differences d, their mean $\bar{d}$ and s_d.

Computations for Paired Samples

Worker	Units produced per day Before X	After Y	d = Y – X Differenced (after minus before)	$d-\bar{d}$	$(d-\bar{d})^2$
1	54	60	6	2	4
2	56	59	3	–1	1
3	50	57	7	3	9
4	52	56	4	0	0
5	55	56	1	– 3	9
6	52	58	6	2	4
7	56	62	6	2	4
8	53	55	2	– 2	4
9	53	54	1	– 3	9
10	60	64	4	0	0
			$\Sigma d = 40$ $\bar{d} = 4$		$(\Sigma d - \bar{d})^2 = 44$

The sample standard deviation of the d's is

$$s_d = \sqrt{\frac{\Sigma(d-\bar{d})^2}{n-1}} = \sqrt{\frac{44}{10-1}} = 2.21$$

Now we can compute the standard error of $\bar{d}$,

$$\text{S.E} = s_{\bar{d}} = \frac{s_d}{\sqrt{n}} = \frac{2.21}{\sqrt{10}} = 0.699$$

Then, Sample $t = \frac{\bar{d}}{s_{\bar{d}}} = \frac{4}{0.699} = 5.72$

The sample t = 5.72, exceed the value of t = 2.82 observed from table.

Hence, we reject H_0.

We conclude that after training productivity is greater than before-taking productivity.

15.11 USE OF χ^2 (CHI-SQUARE) FOR TESTING HYPOTHESIS

χ^2-distribution is explained in 15.7. It is used to test significance of population variance and to test whether an assumed frequency distribution of a population is valid or not.

15.11.1. Testing Hypothesis regarding standard deviation of a population

It has been shown in earlier chapter that

$$\frac{\Sigma(x-\bar{x})^2}{\sigma^2} = \frac{ns^2}{\sigma^2}$$ follows χ^2-distribution with $(n-1)$ degrees of freedom when $n \le 30$.

15.11.2. Use of χ^2-distribution for testing significance of variance. Thus

H_0, $\sigma^2 = \sigma_0^2$ (σ_0^2 is some assumed value)

H_1, $\sigma^2 \neq \sigma_0^2$ or $\sigma^2 < \sigma_0^2$ or $\sigma^2 > \sigma_0^2$

Example 35. *A random sample of 20 bulbs from a large lot revealed a standard deviation of 150 hours. Assuming that the life of bulbs follow normal distribution, test the hypothesis that the standard deviation of the population is 130 hours.*

Solution. $n = 20$, $s = 150$

We have to test $H_0 : \sigma = 130$ against $H_a : \sigma \neq 130$ (two tailed test).

The test statistics, under H_0 is $\chi^2_{cal} = \dfrac{20 \times 150^2}{130^2} = 26.63.$ $\left[\chi^2 = \dfrac{ns^2}{\sigma_0^2}\right]$

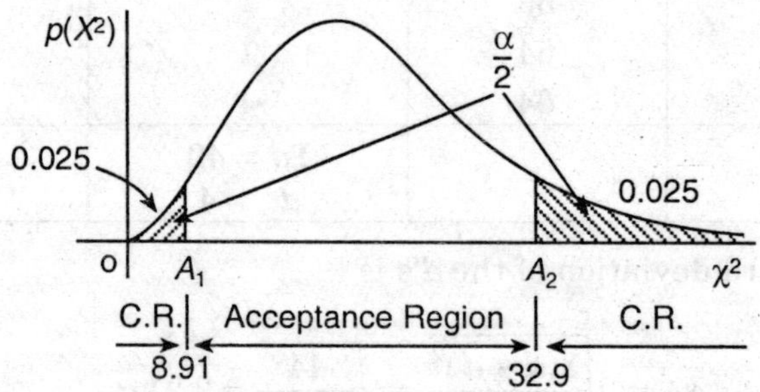

From the table of χ^2 at 5% level of significance and 19 degrees of freedom, the critical values are $A_1 = 8.91$ and $A_2 = 32.9$. In the figure A_1 is corresponding to $\chi^2_{0.975}$ and A_2 coresponding to $\chi^2_{0.025}$ [which indicates areas to the right of A_1 and A_2 respectively]. Since χ^2_{cal} lies within these two values, (*i.e.,* it lies in acceptance region) there is no evidence to reject H_0. Thus $\sigma =$ 130 is accepted.

Example 36. *The standard deviation of a random sample of 25 units, taken from a normal population with $\sigma = 8.5$, was calculated to be 10.8. Test the hypothesis that the observed value of standard deviation is significantly higher than the population standard deviation:*

Solution. We have to test $H_0 : \sigma = 8.5$ against $H_a : \sigma > 8.5$. (one tailed test)

The test statistic is $\chi^2_{cal} = \dfrac{25 \times 10.8^2}{8.5^2} = 40.36.$

χ^2 from tables at 5% level of significance and 24 *d.f.* is 36.4. Since this value is less than the calculated value, H_0 is rejected. Thus, the observed value of standard deviation is significantly higher than 8.5.

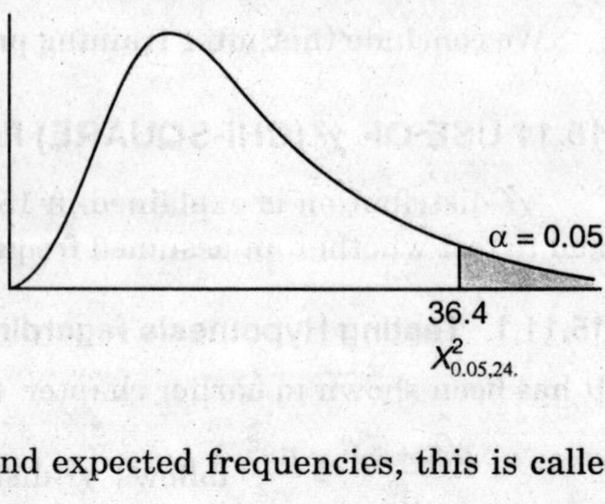

15.11.2. Uses of χ^2 Test

1. To test the discrepancies between observed and expected frequencies, this is called **goodness of fit**.

2. To determine the association between two or more attributes, *i.e.*, to decide whether observed differences among more than two sample proportions can be attributed to chance.

15.11.3. Testing of Goodness-of-Fit

The Chi-square goodness-of-fit test compares the ***expected*, or theoretical,** *frequencies* of categories from a population distribution to the *observed,* or actual, *frequencies* from a distribution to determine whether there is a difference between what **was expected and what was observed.**

Formula is used to compare a Chi-square goodness-of-fit test

$$\chi^2 = \sum_{i=1}^{n} \frac{(O_i - E_i)^2}{E_i} = \frac{(O_1 - E_1)^2}{E_1} + \frac{(O_2 - E_2)^2}{E_2} + \ldots + \frac{(O_n - E_n)^2}{E_n}$$

$$df = n - 1 - C$$

where $O_1, O_2, \ldots O_n$ = Observed frequencies of variable values

$E_1, E_2, \ldots E_n$ = Corresponding expected frequencies

n = number of categories

C = number of parameters being estimated from the sample data to get expected frequencies.

The test loses one degree of freedom because the total number of expected frequencies must equal the number of observed frequencies. That is, the observed total taken from the sample is used as the total for the expected frequencies ($\Sigma O_i = \Sigma E_i$). In addition, in some instances a population parameter, such as λ, μ, or σ, is estimated from the sample data to determine the frequency distribution of expected values. Each time this estimation occurs an additional degree of freedom is lost. As a rule, **if a uniform distribution is being used as the expected distribution or if an expected distribution of values is** *given,* $k-1$ degrees of freedom are used in the test. In testing to determine whether an observed distribution is Poisson, the degrees of freedom are $k-2$ because an additional degree of freedom is lost in estimating λ *i.e.*, mean. In testing to determine whether an observed distribution is normal, the degrees of freedom are $k-3$ because two additional degrees of freedom are lost in estimating μ and σ from the observed sample data.

Important : In this case only right tail is used for given level of significance as if all O_i's exactly equal to E_i's, χ^2 will be O, as such extreme left value of $\chi^2 = 0$ indicates acceptance of H_0.

Example 37. *The theory predicts that the proportion of beans in the four groups A, B, C and D should be 11 : 4 : 3 : 2. In an experiment it was observed that the number of four group A, B, C and D are 1,070, 430, 330, 170. Does the result of the experiment support theory ? (Value of the Chi-square at 5% level of significance and 3, 4 and 5 degrees of freedom are 7.815, 9.488 and 11.070 respectively.)* *[ICWA Dec., 1998]*

Solution. The Null hypothesis H_0 is that the result of the experiment fits well the theory *i.e.*, four categories have frequencies in the ratio 11 : 4 : 3 : 2. Alternative hypothesis H_1 is that the result of the experiment does not fit well the theory.

The expected frequencies (E) can be computed as follows :

Total No. of beans = 1,070 + 430 + 330 + 170 = 2,000.

O_A = Observed No. of beans in Gr. A = 1,070

E_A = Expect No. of beans in Gr. A $= 2{,}000 \times \frac{11}{20} = 1{,}100$;

$O_B = 430,\ E_B = 2{,}000 \times \frac{4}{20} = 400,\ O_C = 330,\ E_C = 2{,}000 \times \frac{3}{20} = 300$

$O_D = 170,\ E_D = 2{,}000 \times \frac{2}{20} = 200.$

$$\chi^2 = \frac{(O_A - E_A)^2}{E_A} + \frac{(O_B - E_B)^2}{E_B} + \frac{(O_C - E_C)^2}{E_C} + \frac{(O_D - E_D)^2}{E_D}$$

$$= \frac{(-30)^2}{1{,}100} + \frac{(30)^2}{400} + \frac{(30)^2}{300} + \frac{(-30)^2}{200} + \frac{900}{1{,}100} + \frac{900}{400} + \frac{900}{300} + \frac{900}{200}$$

$$= 0.8182 + 2.25 + 3 + 4.5 = 10.5682 > 7.815, \text{ since } \chi^2_{0.05;3} = 7.815$$

(Table value)

It has 4 classes and hence *d.f.* = 4 – 1 = (*n* – 1).

Hence, H_0 is rejected at 5% level of significance.

Example 38. *A die is thrown 120 times with the following results :*

Face	1	2	3	4	5	6
Frequency	16	30	22	18	14	20

Test the hypothesis that the die is unbiased.

(Given : $\chi^2_{0.05;5} = 11.07,\ \chi^2_{0.05;6} = 12.59$). *[ICWA June 2000]*

Solution. Null hypothesis : The dice is biased = H_1

Alternate hypothesis : The dice is biased = H_1

Face	*1*	*2*	*3*	*4*	*5*	*6*
Observed Value	16	30	22	18	14	20
Expected Value	20	20	20	20	20	20
$O - E$	– 4	10	2	– 2	– 6	0
$(O - E)^2$	16	100	4	4	36	0
$\frac{(O-E)^2}{E}$	$\frac{16}{20}$	$\frac{100}{20}$	$\frac{4}{20}$	$\frac{4}{20}$	$\frac{36}{20}$	0

[According to H_0 all the numbers 1 to 6 are equally likely and each will occur $\frac{120}{6} = 20$ times *i.e.,* each class has expected frequency = 20]

$$\chi2 = \Sigma\frac{(O-E)^2}{E} = \frac{16 + 100 + 4 = 4 + 36 + 0}{20} = \frac{160}{20} = 8$$

At 5 *d.f.*, the tabulated value of $\chi2$ = 11.07.

Since, the calculated value is less than the tabulated value, the Null hypothesis is accepted, *i.e.,* the die is unbiased.

Example 39. *A survey of 320 families each having 5 children the following distribution was observed.*

No. of boys	5	4	3	2	1	0
No. of families	14	56	110	88	40	12

Is the result consistent with the hypothesis that male and female births are equilikely

Solution. $H_0,\ p = \frac{1}{2}$ where p = Prob. that child is a boy

$H_1,\ p \neq \frac{1}{2}$

The distribution is binomial with $n = 5, p = \frac{1}{2}$

Where $P(x = r) = {}^nc_r\, p^r\, q^{n-r}$

No. of Boys X	*P (X)*	*Expected frequency in 320 families = E.*
5	${}^5c_5\left(\frac{1}{2}\right)^5\left(\frac{1}{2}\right)^5 = \frac{1}{32}$	10
4	${}^5c_4\left(\frac{1}{2}\right)^4\frac{1}{2} = \frac{5}{32}$	50
3	${}^5c_3\left(\frac{1}{2}\right)^3\left(\frac{1}{2}\right)^2 = \frac{10}{32}$	100
2	${}^5c_2\left(\frac{1}{2}\right)^2\left(\frac{1}{2}\right)^3 = \frac{10}{32}$	100
1	${}^5c_1\left(\frac{1}{2}\right)^1\left(\frac{1}{2}\right)^4 = \frac{5}{32}$	50
0	${}^5c_0\left(\frac{1}{2}\right)^0\left(\frac{1}{2}\right)^5 = \frac{1}{32}$	10
		Total 320

Computation of χ^2

Class (no. of boys)	O_i	E_i	$(O_i - E_i)^2$	$\frac{(O_i - E_i)^2}{E_i}$
5	14	10	16	1.60
4	56	50	36	0.72
3	110	100	100	1.00
2	88	100	144	1.44
1	40	50	100	2.00
0	12	10	4	0.40

Calculated $\chi^2 = \Sigma \frac{(O-E)^2}{E} = 7.16$

$d.f. = n - 1 = 6 - 1 = 5$

Table value $\chi^2_{0.05,\,5} = 11.07$

Since χ^2_{cal} is less than the table value, there is no evidence to reject H_0.

15.11.4. Test for Independence of two attributes

Let the population be classified according to two attributes, example of which is as follows.

2 × 2 Contingency Table

	Employed E	*Unemployed (U)*	*Total*
Males *M*	(*ME*)	(*MU*)	(*M*)
Females *F*	(*FE*)	(*FU*)	(*F*)
Total	(*E*)	(*U*)	*N*

Let sample of *N* individual have (*E*) employed and (*U*) Unemployed persons. Also it has (*M*) males and (*F*) females. Out of (*M*) males it has (*ME*) employed males and (*MU*) unemployed males. Same way (*FE*) and *F*(*U*) represents employed females and unemployed females.

Thus $(E) + (U) = N = (M) + (F)$

Also $(ME) + (MU) = M$ and $(FE) + (FU) = F$

Now if employment is independent of sex of a person which will be H_0 in that case ratio employed males to males should be equal ratio employed to total no. of persons *i.e.*,

$\frac{(ME)}{(M)} = \frac{(E)}{N}$. Thus according to H_0 expected no. of males employed *i.e.*, *E* (*ME*) be given as

$$E(ME) = \frac{(E)\,(M)}{N}$$

Also $E\,(MU) = M - E\,(ME)$

and $E(FE) = (E) - E\,(ME)$. Thus we have the following information

	Employed E	*Unemployed U*	*Total*
Males *M*	*E* (*ME*)		(*M*)
Females *F*			(*F*)
	(*E*)	(*U*)	*N*

Note: M stand for males and (*M*) stands for no. of males.

The remaining expected frequencies in 3 empty cell are obtained by differences.

The procedure is explained in the following example.

$$\text{Expected frequency of any cell} = \frac{\text{Its raw total} \times \text{its column total}}{\text{Grand Total}}$$

Observed Frequencies

	C_1	C_2	*Total*
R_1	f_{11}	f_{12}	(R_1)
R_2	f_{21}	f_{22}	(R_2)
	(C_1)	(C_2)	*N*

$$E(f_{11}) = \frac{(R_1)(C_1)}{N}.$$

Expected frequencies of remaining cells in this case are found by difference (when marginal totals (R_1), (R_2), (C_1) and (C_2) remaining same as in observed frequencies.

Degree of freedom for $\chi^2 = \Sigma\frac{(O-E)^2}{E}$ in case of contingency table is $(r-1)(C-1)$ where r = no. of rows c = no. of columns. Then *d.f.* in case of 2 × 3 table for χ^2 is = (2 – 1) (3 – 1) = 2.

15.11.5. Alternative Method of Finding χ^2 directly from observed frequencies (this method is applicable only in case of 2 × 2 contingency table)

Observed Frequencies

	A_1	A_2	Total
B_1	a	b	$a+b$
B_2	c	d	$c+d$
Total	$a+c$	$b+d$	N

$$\chi_1^2 = \frac{N(ad-bc)^2}{(a+b)(c+d)(a+c)(b+d)}.$$

Example 40. *In a survey of 200 girls of which 40% were intelligent, 60% had uneducated fathers, while 20% of the unintelligent girls had educated fathers. Do these figures support the hypothesis that educatd fathers have intelligent girls? Test at 5% level of significance.*

Solution. *Setting up the hypothesis* as follows

H_0 : No association exists between educated fathers and intelligent girls.

H_1 : Association exists between educated fathers and intelligent girls.

The information given is tabulated in the form of 2 × 2 contingency table.

	Intelligent girls	*Unintelligent girls*	*Total*
Educated fathers		(24)	
Uneducated fathers			(120) (60%)
	(80) (40%)	120	(200)

The remaining observed frequencies are found by differences. Frequencies in circles were given.

Observed Frequencies (*O*)

	Intelligent girls	*Unintelligent girls*	*Row Total*
Educated fathers	56	**24**	80
Uneducated fathers	24	96	**120**
Column Total	**80**	120	200

Now $E(f_{11}) = \frac{80 \times 80}{200} = 32 \quad \left[= \frac{\text{Row Total} \times \text{Column Total}}{N}\right]$

Thus we have, table of expected frequencies, as follows.

Expected frequencies (E)

	Intelligent girls	*Unintelligent girls*	*Row Total*
Educated fathers	$\frac{80 \times 80}{200} = 32$	$\frac{80 \times 120}{200} = 48$	80
Uneducated fathers	$\frac{120 \times 80}{200} = 48$	$\frac{120 \times 120}{200} = 72$	120
Column Total	80	120	200

Calculation of x^2

O	E	O – E	$(O - E)^2$	$(O - E)^2/E$
56	32	24	576	18
24	48	– 24	576	12
24	48	– 24	576	12
96	72	24	576	8
				$50 = \chi^2$

$d.f. = (r = 1)(c - 1) = (2 - 1) = 1$

Table value of χ^2 for degrees of freedom at 5% level of significance is 3.84.

Decision : Since the value of χ^2 is greater than the table value of χ^2, we reject H_0 and conclude that an association exists between educated fathers and intelligent girls.

Alternative Direct Method of Calculating the value of x^2

Observed Frequencies

	A_1	A_2	Total
B_1	*a* 56	*b* 24	$a + b$ 80
B_2	*c* 24	*d* 96	$c + d$ 120
Total	80 $a + c$	120 $b + d$	200 *N*

$$\chi^2 = \frac{(ad - bc)^2 N}{(a + b)(c + d)(a + c)(b + d)} = \frac{\left[(56 \times 96) - 24 \times 24\right]^2 200}{(80)(120)(80)(120)} = 50$$

Example 41. *Two researchers adopted different sampling techniques while investigating the same group of students to find the number of students falling in different intelligence level. The results are as follows:*

Number of Students in each Level

Researcher	*Below average*	*Average*	*Above average*	*Genius*	*Total*
X	137	164	152	147	600
Y	32	57	56	35	180
Total	169	221	208	182	780

Required : Would you say that the sampling techniques adopted by the researchers are significantly different ?

Solution. *Null hypothesis* H_0 : Sampling techniques of two researchers do not differ significantly.

Calculation of the expected values.

Expected frequencies for X calculated using the formula $\frac{R \times C}{N}$ and expected frequencies for Y are found out by difference = Total X frequencies as shown below.

X	Y	*Total*
$\frac{600 \times 169}{780} = 130$	169 – 130 = 39	169
$\frac{600 \times 221}{780} = 170$	221 – 170 = 57	221
$\frac{600 \times 208}{780} = 160$	48	208
$\frac{600 \times 182}{780} = 140$	42	182
Total 600	180	780

Calculation of χ^2

(*O*)	(*E*)	(*O* – *E*)	$(O-E)^2$	$(O-E)^2/E$
137	130	+ 7	49	0.377
164	170	– 6	36	0.212
152	160	– 8	64	0.400
147	140	+ 7	49	0.350
32	39	– 7	49	1.256
57	51	+ 6	36	0.706
56	48	+ 8	64	1.333
35	42	– 7	49	1.167
780	780			$\chi^2 = 5.801$

Degree of freedom = $(r-1)(c-1) = (2-1)(4-1) = 3$.

For $v = 3$ and $p = .05$, the critical value of $\chi^2 = 7.815$

Decision : Since the computed value of x^2 is less than the table value, we accept H_0 and conclude that there is no significant difference in the sampling techniques used by the two researchers.

15.12. USE OF 'F' TEST

15.12. Testing Equality of Variances of two Populations

In 14.16 it is shown that $\frac{s_1^2}{s_2^2}$ follows F-distribution with $n_1 - 1$, $n_2 - 1$ degrees of freedom if two independent samples of sizes n_1 and n_2 are drawn from two populations of equal variances where s_1^2 and s_2^2 has usual meaning *i.e.*, $s_1^2 = \dfrac{\Sigma (X_1 - \overline{X}_1)^2}{n_1 - 1}$ and $s_2^2 = \dfrac{\Sigma (X_2 - \overline{X}_2)^2}{n_2 - 1}$. In case α is the small area in the right tail of F-distribution and corresponding to this value of α the tabulated value is k for F_{n_1-1, n_2-1} which means that

$P(F_{n_1-1, n_2-1} \geq k) = \alpha$ [see 14.16]

However for F_{n_1-1, n_2-1} values for α area in the left tail are not tabulated. Using properties of F-distribution we may use only right tail for $\frac{\alpha}{2}$ area if we keep larger value out of s_1^2 and s_2^2 as numerator.

Thus $F_{n_1-1, n_2-1} = \dfrac{s_1^2}{s_2^2}$ if $s_1^2 > s_2^2$

or $F_{n_2-1, n_1-1} = \dfrac{s_1^2}{s_2^2}$ if $s_2^2 > s_1^2$

and their use only $\frac{\alpha}{2}$ area right tail (If it is the two tailed test for α level of significance)

Example 42. *A standardised test in general knowledge was given to 10 girls and 16 boys seeking admission to a management programme. The girls obtained an average of 80 marks with a standard deviation s_1 = 16 marks. the boys got an average of 70 marks with a standard s_2 = 9 marks. Does the sample information support the contention that boys and girls do not differ in terms of the variance in their marks in the test ? Use 0.10 level of significance and assume the two populations to be normally distributed.*

Solution. Letting σ_1^2 and σ_2^2 be the population variances of the marks obtained by girls and boys, respectively, we have the following.

$$\begin{bmatrix} H_0 : \sigma_1{}^2 = \sigma_2{}^2 \\ H_0 : \sigma_1{}^2 \neq \sigma_2{}^2 \\ \alpha = 0.10. \end{bmatrix} \qquad \text{Given} \qquad \begin{matrix} s_1{}^2 = 16^2 = 256 \\ s_2{}^2 = 9^2 = 81 \end{matrix} \qquad \begin{matrix} n_1 = 10 \\ n_2 = 16 \end{matrix}$$

Since it is 2 tailed test we use $\frac{\alpha}{2} = 0.05$ for right tailed only (keeping larger values of s_1^2, s_2^2 as numerator).

Thus $F_{10-1, 16-1} = \dfrac{s_1^2}{s_2^2} = \dfrac{256}{81} = 3.16$

Now table value for $F_{.05\,(9,\,15)}$ = 2.59.

Since calculated value F = 3.16 is greater than tabulated value of F, H_0 is rejected and conclude that the two populations differ in terms of their variances.

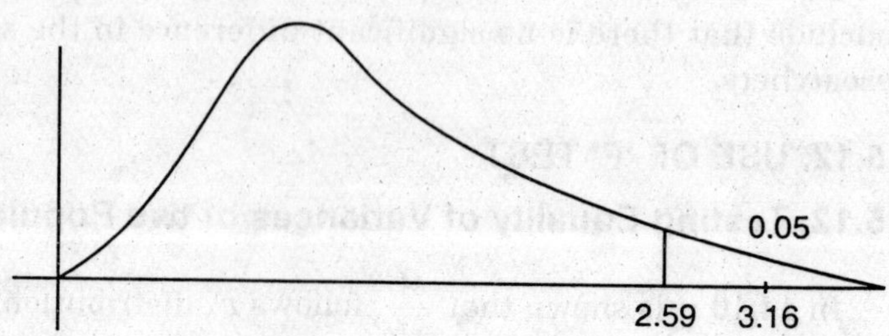

15.12.2. Testing for Equality of Means of more than Two Populations (One way Classification)

With usual notation we are required to test $\mu_1 = \mu_2 = \mu_3 \ldots = \mu_4$. That is means of all k populations are equal with H_1 that not all means are equal (out of k means some may be equal or all may be different).

Our testing procedure is to find out difference among the sample means which is done by investigating variances.

As the procedure focuses on analysis of variances, we call it **analysis of variance.** (ANOVA)

15.12.3. Definition of Analysis of Variance

The technique implies the analysing or breaking up of variance into portions arising from specified sources and the testing of whether these portions are significantly different.

The analysis of variance is based on the following **assumptions** :

1. The sample are independently (or randomly) drawn from the populations.
2. All the populations from which samples have been drawn are normally distributed.
3. The variances of all the populations are equal.
4. The samples drawn are with simple random samples.
5. Null hypothesis is taken as **'population means are equal'.**

In this method, the total variance is splitted into two parts :

1. Variance between the sample (or groups).
1. Variance within the sample (or groups).

15.12.4. To Break sum of Squares in Different Components

Suppose we have 3 populations (groups) here $K = 3$ and samples have been drawn independently of sizes n_1, n_2 and n_3 respectively and the observed values of sampled units are given as below :

Observed 1 – 4 Values

	Population 1	Population 2	Population 3	
	X_{11}	X_{21}	X_{31}	
	X_{12}	X_{22}	X_{32}	
	X_{13}	X_{23}	X_{33}	
	$\vdots$	$\vdots$	$\vdots$	
	$X_1 n_1$	$X_2 n_2$	$X_3 n_3$	Grand Total
Total	$T_1 = \sum_{i=1}^{n_1} x_{1i}$	T_2	T_3	$T = T_1 + T_2 + T_3$
Sample size	n_1	n_2	n_3	$n = n_1 + n_2 + n_3$
Sample means	$\overline{X}_1$	$\overline{X}_2$	$\overline{X}_3$	$\overline{\overline{X}} = \frac{T}{n}$

We define total sum of squares (TSS) $= \Sigma (X - \overline{\overline{X}})^2$

X values are for all n $(= n_1 + n_2 + n_3)$ units.

SSB (sum of squares between)

$$= \text{Sum of squares of deviations between samples} = \sum_{i=1}^{k} n_i (\overline{X}_I - \overline{\overline{X}})^2$$

$$= n_1 (\overline{X}_1 - \overline{\overline{X}})^2 + n_2 (\overline{X}_2 - \overline{\overline{X}})^2 + n_3 (\overline{X}_3 - \overline{\overline{X}})^2 + \cdots$$

K = Number of groups

n_i = Sizes of the ith sample = Number of items in the ith sample

$\overline{X}_i$ = Mean of the ith sample

$\overline{\overline{X}}$ = Grand mean of sample means.

By dividing SSB by $k - 1$ [(*i.e.*, number of groups – 1 = degree of freedom] we get means square between the samples.

$MSSB$ = Mean square between samples

$$= \frac{SSB}{K - 1} = s_b^2.$$

Sum of the squares of the variations within the samples (SSW) or sum of the squares due to errors (SSE) = Sum of the squares of the deviations of the various items (or values) from the mean values of the respective samples.

Steps to Calculate SSW

1. Calculate Sample means $\overline{X}_1, \overline{X}_2, \overline{X}_3, \cdots \overline{X}_K$ of all the K samples.
2. Find the deviations of the various items of K samples from the maean values of their respective samples.
3. Square all the deviations obtained in Step 2 and find the total of these squared deviations.

   This is equal to SSW or SSE.

$$SSW = \underbrace{\Sigma(X_{ij} - \overline{X}_1)^2}_{\text{SS within 1st-group}} + \underbrace{\Sigma(X_{2j} - \overline{X}_2)^2}_{\text{SS within 2nd-group}} + \underbrace{\Sigma(X_{3j} - \overline{X}_3)^2}_{\text{SS within 3rd -group}} + \cdots$$

where X_{1i}^* denotes the elements in the first sample, X_{2i} the elements in 2nd sample and so on.

Mean square within the sample = MSW or MSE $= \dfrac{SSW}{\text{Degree of freedom}} = \dfrac{SSW}{n - k} = s_w^2.$

It is also estabilished that $TSS = SSB + SSW$.

Thus we have to calculate any two and third will be found out from the above result.

Also MSW and MSB both are estimates of σ^2 the common variance of all groups under H_0 as such

$$F = \frac{MSB}{MSW} \text{ or } \frac{MSW}{MSB} \text{ (which ever is greater than 1).}$$

Thus in order to test H_0, we test the significance of F for a given α.

15.12.5. Short cut method for Computing Values for ANOVA

Coding Method

We make X_{ij} values small by using deviation method *i.e.,* we find $d_{ij} = X_{ij} - A$ (thus replacing X_{ij} by d_{ij} for all computations).

Also it is established that $SSB = \Sigma n_i \left(\overline{X}_2 - \overline{\overline{X}}\right)^2$

$$= n_1 \left(\overline{X}_1 - \overline{\overline{X}}\right)^2 + n_2 \left(\overline{X}_2 - \overline{\overline{X}}\right)^2 + n_3 \left(\overline{X}_3 - \overline{\overline{X}}\right)^2$$

$$= \frac{T_1^2}{n_1} + \frac{T_2^2}{n_2} + \frac{T_3^2}{n_3} - \frac{T^2}{n} \qquad \text{(without proof)}$$

Also SST (Total SS) $= \Sigma(X_{ij} - \overline{\overline{X}})^2$

$$= \Sigma X_{ij}^2 - \frac{T^2}{n} \quad \left(\frac{T^2}{n} \text{ is called correction factor}\right)$$

Thus in short we calculate

$$SST = \Sigma X_{ij}^2 - \frac{T^2}{n}$$

$$SSB = \frac{\Sigma T_i^2}{n_i} - \frac{T^2}{n}$$

$$SSW = SST - SSB.$$

F value is calculated from following ANOVA Table.

Source of error	*SS Sum of squares*	*d.f.*	*M.S.S mean SS*	*F*
Between	SSB	$k-1$	$\frac{SSB}{k-1} = s_b^2$	$\frac{s_b^2}{s_w^2}$ or $\frac{s_w^2}{s_b^2}$
within or error	SSW	$n-k$	$\frac{SSW}{n-k} = s_w^2$	
Total	SST	$n-1$		

Thus $F_{k-1, n-k} = \frac{s_b^2}{s_w^2}$ or $F_{n-k, k-1} = \frac{s_w^2}{s_b^2}$

One of these which is greater than 1 is computed and then it is tested as right tailed test for $\frac{\alpha}{2}$ level of significance (if the original test is two tailed with α level of significance).

Example 43. *A company wants to test whether its three salesmen A, B and C have the same selling ability. Their records of sales (in ₹ '000) during various weeks of the last month are given in the following table:*

Sales men	*1st week*	*2nd week*	*3rd week*	*4th week*
A	16	21	18	25
B	22	20	15	26
C	25	24	16	20

Prepare an analysis of variance table and test the hypothesis that the mean sales per week of all the salesmen are equal.

Solution. The null hypothesis to be tested is $H_0 : \mu_1 = \mu_2 = \mu_3$, where μ_1, μ_2 and μ_3 denote the mean sales per week by the salesmen *A, B* and *C* respectively.

(a) Direct Method

X_{ij} Values			X_{ij}^2			Total
A	*B*	*C*	*A*	*B*	*C*	
16	22	25	256	484	625	1365
21	20	24	441	400	576	1417
18	15	16	324	225	256	805
25	26	20	625	676	400	1701
$T_1 = 80$	$T_2 = 83$	$T_3 = 83$			Total	$5288 = \Sigma X_{ij}^2$
$\frac{T_1^2}{n_1} = \frac{(80)^2}{4} = 1600$	$\frac{T_2^2}{n_2} = \frac{(83)^2}{4} = 1722.25$	$\frac{T_3^2}{n_3} = \frac{(85)^2}{4} = 1806.25$	(Here $n_1 = 4 = n_2 = n_3$) $n = n_1 + n_2 + n_3 = 12$			

$$T = 40 + 83 + 85 = 248, \quad \frac{T^2}{n} = \frac{(248)^2}{12} = 5125.33$$

$$\text{Now } SST/TSS = \Sigma X_{ij}^2 - \frac{T^2}{n} = 5288 - 5125.33 = 162.67$$

$$SSB = \frac{T_1^2}{n_i} + \frac{T_2^2}{n_2} + \frac{T_3^2}{n_3} - \frac{T^2}{n}$$

$$= 1600 + 1772.25 + 1806.25 - 5125.33 = 3.17$$

$$SSW = SSE = TSS - SSB = 162.67 - 3.17 = 159.50$$

Analysis Variance Table

Source of Variation	*Sum of Squares*	*d.f.*	*Mean S.S.*	*F*
Between Salesmen	*BSS* = 3.17	2	$s_b^2 = \frac{3.17}{2} = 1.585$	$F_{9,2} = \frac{17.72}{1.585} = 11.2$
Within Salesmen	*ESS* = 159.50	9	$s_w^2 = \frac{159.50}{9}$ 17.72	
Total	*TSS* = 162.67	11		

Table value for $F_{0.05\,(9.2)} = 19.8$

Such calculated value of *F* is less than the tabulated value, hence H_0 is not rejected.

Thus salemen do not differ significantly on the basis of average sales per week.

Alternative Method of calculations for ANOVA

X_{ij}			Coding $di_j = X_{ij} - 20$			d_{ij}^2			
A	B	C	A	B	C	A	B	C	Total
16	22	25	–4	2	5	16	4	25	45
21	20	24	1	0	4	1	0	16	17
18	15	16	–2	–5	–4	4	25	16	45
25	26	20	5	6	0	25	36	0	61
	Total		0	3	5				$168 = \Sigma d_{ij}^2$
			T_1	T_2	T_3				

$T = 0 + 3 + 5 = 8 \qquad \frac{T^2}{n} = \frac{64}{12} = 5.33.$

$\therefore \quad SST = \Sigma d_{ij}^2 - \frac{T^2}{n} = 168 - 5.33 = 162.67$

$SSB = \Sigma \frac{T_i^2}{n_i} - \frac{T^2}{n} = \frac{0 + 9 + 25}{4} - 5.33 = 3.17$

Example 44. the following table gives the yield of a hybrid variety of wheat; in quintals per acre, from 17 trial plots of land treated with four types of fertilisers.

Treatments with Fertilizer

A	B	C	D
24	31	39	38
39	25	41	32
35	26	33	35
	21	40	34
		45	26

Test whether there is any significant difference in the mean yield of wheat due to difference in fertiliser application.

We have to test $H_0 : \mu_A = \mu_B = \mu_C = \mu_D$, where μ_A, μ_B, μ_C and μ_D denote the mean yield per acre due to fertiliser *A, B, C* and *D* respectively.

On subtracting 33 from every observation, the given table can be rewritten as

Treatments with Fertilizer $d_{ij} = X_{ij} - 33$				d_{ij}^2				
A	B	C	D	A	B	C	D	Total
–9	–2	6	5	81	04	36	25	146
6	–8	8	–1	36	64	64	01	165
2	–7	0	2	04	49	0	04	57
	–12	7	1	—	144	49	01	194
		12	–7	—	—	144	49	193
$T_1 = -1$	$T_2 = -29$	$T_3 = -33$	$T_4 = 0$				Total	755

From the above table, we can write

$$\Sigma\Sigma d_{ij}^2 = 755, \frac{T_1^2}{n_1} = \frac{1}{3}, \frac{T_2^2}{n_2} = \frac{29^2}{4} = \frac{841}{4}, \frac{T_3^2}{n_3} = \frac{1089}{5}, \frac{T_4^2}{n_4} = 0, \frac{T^2}{n} = \frac{9}{17}$$

$$T = -1 - 29 + 33 = 3$$

$$\frac{T^2}{n} = \frac{9}{17} = 0.53$$

Thus $$TSS = 755 - \frac{9}{17} = 754.47 \quad \left[\Sigma\Sigma d_{ij}^2 - \frac{T^2}{n}\right]$$

$$BSS = \frac{1}{3} + \frac{841}{4} + \frac{1089}{5} - \frac{9}{17} = 427.85 \quad \left[\frac{T_1^2}{n_1} + \frac{T_2^2}{n_2} + \frac{T_3^2}{n_2} + \frac{T_4^2}{n_4} - \frac{T^2}{n}\right]$$

$$ESS = TSS - BSS = 754.47 - 427.85 = 326.62$$

Analysis of Variance Table

Source of Variance	*S.S.*	*d.f.*	*M.S.S.*
Between Treatment	427.85	3	$s_b^2 = \frac{427.85}{3} = 142.62$
Within Treatment	326.62	13	$s_w^2 = \frac{326.62}{13} = 25.12$
Total	754.47	16	

From the above table, we have

$$F = \frac{142.62}{2512} = 5.68 > 3.41$$ [The critical of F for 3,13 *d.f* and $\alpha = 0.05$ is 3.41]

Thus, H_0 is rejected at 5% level of significance.

15.12.3 Two Way Analysis of Variance

The example 44. a number of plots were treated with 4 different varieties of of fertilisers. We have assumed no variations due to plots (*i.e.* all the plots give same yield and yields vary only to different responses to different fertilisers). However if we take plot-variations into account also, then we may test two hypothesis simultaneously

(1) H_{0_1}, $\mu_1 = \mu_2 = \mu_3 = \mu_4$ (*i.e.* all 4 varieties of fertilisers are equally effective.

(2) H_{0_2}, $m_1 = m_2 = m_3 =$ (*i.e.* all plots give some mean out put without fertilisers). In that case data required have to be in the following format.

Fertilisers → *Plots* ↓	A	B	V	D	*Total (row)*
I	X_{11}	X_{12}	X_{13}	X_{14}	T_{10}
II	X_{21}	X_{22}	X_{23}	X_{24}	T_{20}
III	X_{31}	X_{32}	X_{33}	X_{34}	T_{30}
Total Column	T_{01}	T_{02}	T_{03}	T_{04}	

$T_{.j}$ = Total for j th column (fertilisers)

$T_{i.}$ = Total for i th row (plot)

In that case *SSB* are two (*i*) SSB (columns) and (*ii*) *SSB* (rows). Which are calculated in the same way as done for single classification

$$SSB \text{ (row)} = \frac{\Sigma T_{i.}^2}{m} - \frac{T^2}{mn}$$

where each row has got m entries.

$$SSB \text{ (row)} = \frac{\Sigma T_{i.}^2}{m} - \frac{T^2}{mn}$$

where each column has got n entries and total number of observations are mn.

In this case*SST* = *SSB* (columns) + *SSB* (rows) + *SSE* (error sum of squares)

Then we get two values of *F* (one for columns and one for rows)

$$i.e. \quad F \text{ (columns)} = \frac{MSSB \text{ (columns)}}{MSSE}$$

$$F \text{ (rows)} = \frac{MSSB \text{ (rows)}}{MSSE}$$

Where *MSSB* (columns) stands for mean sum

$$\text{of square (between columns)} = \frac{SSB \text{ (columns)}}{d.f.}$$

and similarly other *MSSB* (rows) and *MSSE* are defined. The following examples illustrate the procedure.

Example 45. Set-up a two way Anova table for the following per hectare yield for 4 varieties of yield of wheat on 3 plots :

Plot of Land	*Yield*			
	A	*B*	*C*	*D*
I	3	4	6	6
II	6	4	5	3
III	6	6	4	7

Test at 0.05 significance level whether means over plots and means of yields for different fertilisers are equal.

Solution.

H_0, $\mu_1 = \mu_2 = \mu_3$ (μ_1, μ_2, μ_3 are mean yields for plots)
$m_1 = m_2 = m_3 = m_4$ (m_i in the mean yield for i th fertiliser.

H_i, all means over plots are not equal
all means over fertiliser are not equal.

First, the given information is listed in a table with row, column and grand totals as follows:

Plot of Land	*Yield*					
	A	*B*	*C*	*D*	*Total*	
I	3	4	6	6	19	$T_{1\cdot}$
II	6	4	5	3	18	$T_{2\cdot}$
III	6	6	4	7	23	$T_{3\cdot}$
Total	15	14	15	16	60	T
	$T_{\cdot 1}$	$T_{\cdot 2}$	$T_{\cdot 3}$	$T_{\cdot 4}$		

Where $T_{1\cdot}$ $T_{2\cdot}$ and $T_{3\cdot}$ are row tables for 3 rows and $T_{\cdot 1}$, $T_{\cdot 2}$, $T_{\cdot 3}$ and $T_{\cdot 4}$ are 4 column Totals. n = no. of rows = 3 and m = no. of columns = 4.

$$\text{Correction factor} = \frac{T^2}{mn} = \frac{(60)^2}{12} = 300.$$

$$\text{Sum of square between columns } (SSC) = \frac{15^2}{3} + \frac{14^2}{3} + \frac{15^2}{3} + \frac{16^2}{3} - 300 = 0.67 \qquad \left[\Sigma \frac{T_{\cdot j}^2}{n} - \frac{T^2}{mn}\right]$$

$$\text{Sum of square between rows } (SSR) = \frac{19^2}{4} + \frac{18^2}{4} + \frac{23^2}{4} - 300 = 3.5 \qquad \left[\Sigma \frac{T_{i\cdot}^2}{m} - \frac{T^2}{mn}\right]$$

$$\text{Total sum of squares } (SST) = (9 + 36 + 36 + 16 + 16 + 36 + 36 + 25 + 36 + 9 + 49) - 300$$

$$= 20$$

$$\text{Error sum square} = SST - (SSR + SSC = 15.83$$

ANOVA Table

Source of error	*SS*	*d.f.*	*MSS*	*F* ratio
Columns	$SSC = 0.67$	$m - 1 = 3$	$MSSC = \frac{0.67}{3} = 0.22$	$\frac{MSSE}{MSSC} = \frac{2.64}{0.22} = 12 = F_{(6,3)}$
Rows	$SSR = 3.50$	$n - 1 = 2$	$MSSR = \frac{3.50}{2} = 1.75$	$\frac{MSSE}{MSSR} = \frac{2.64}{1.75} = 1.5 = F_{(6,2)}$
Error	$SSE = 15.83$	$(m-1)(n-1) = 6$	$MSSE = \frac{15.83}{6} = 0.64$	
Total	20	$mn - 1 = 11$		

Table value for $\alpha = 0.05$ $\quad F_{(6,\,3)} = 8.94$, $F_{(6,\,2)} = 19.3$

Since Calculated $F_{(6,\,3)} = 12$ is greater than tabulated value 8.94 for $F_{(6,\,3)}$, hence we reject their part of H_0 which says means over different columns (fertilisers) are equal. Since calculated value of $F_{(6,\,2)} = 1.5$ is less than tabulated value of 19.3 for $F_{(6,\,2)}$ we accept H_0 regarding equality of means over rows (plots).

Example 46. *The following data represent the sale (₹ '000) per month of three brands of a toilet soap allocated among three cities:*

Cities→ *Brands↓*	*A*	*B*	*C*
I	12	48	30
II	42	54	57
III	9	42	21

Test whether (i) the mean sales of the three brands are equal and (ii) the means sales of the toilet soap in each city are equal.

Solution. We have to test $H_0: \mu_1 = \mu_2 = \mu_3$, where μ_i denotes mean sale of brand *i*, and $H_0: m_1 = m_2\ m_3$, where m_i denotes mean sale of soap in city *j*.

$$T_{.1} = 12 + 42 + 9 = 63,\ T_{.2} = 48 + 54 + 42 = 144,\ T_{.3} = 30 + 57 + 21 = 108$$

$$T_{1.} = 12 + 48 + 30 = 90,\ T_{2.} = 42 + 54 + 57 = 153,\ T_{3.} = 9 + 42 + 21 = 72$$

$$T = 63 + 144 + 108 = 315$$

$$TSS = 12^2 + 48^2 + 30^2 + 42^2 + 54^2 + 57^2 + 9^2 + 42^2 + 21^2 - \frac{315^2}{9} = 2538$$

$$\frac{\text{(Between cities) } CSS}{\text{(Columns)}} = \frac{63^2 + 144^2 + 108^2}{3} - \frac{315^2}{9} = 12123 - 11025 = 1098$$

$$\frac{\text{(Between brands) } RSS}{\text{(rows)}} = \frac{90^2 + 153^2 + 72^2}{3} - \frac{315^2}{9} = 12231 - 11025 = 1206$$

$$\text{error sum of squares } = ESS = 2538 - 1098 - 1206 = 234$$

	A	*B*	*C*	
I	12	48	30	$T_{1.} = 90$
II	42	54	57	$T_{2.} = 153$
III	9	42	21	$T_{3.} = 72$
	63 $T_{.1}$	144 $T_{.2}$	108 $T_{.3}$	$T = 315$

Analysis of Variance Table

Source of Variation	*Sum of Squares*	*d.f.*	*Mean S.S.*	*F Value*
Between Cities	*CSS* = 1098	2	549	$F_c = \frac{549}{58.5} = 9.4 = F_{2,,4}$
Between Brands	*RSS* = 1206	2	603	$F_r = \frac{603}{58.5} = 10.3 = F_{2,,4}$
Error	*ESS* = 234	4	58.5	
Total	TSS = 2538	8		

The value of *F* from table for 2, 4 *d.f.* at 5% level of significance is 6.94. Thus, both the null hypotheses are rejected.

We conclude (*i*) Mean sales of all brands are not equal (*ii*) Mean Sales of all toilet soaps are not equal.

Miscellanous Examples

Examples 47. *In a college entrance examination taken by 2,000 students, the average marks scored by 36 randomly selected boys was 72 with S.D. of 8 while the average score of a sample of 36 girls was 75 with a S.D. of 10. Test the hypothesis that girls fare better in competitice examination.* [D.U. B.A. (Hons.) Eco.]

Solution. Null hypothesis : Boys and girls fare equal. → $\mu_g = \mu_b$ [g stands for girl and b for boy]

Alternative Hypothesis : Girls are better than the boys. ⇒ $\mu_g > \mu_b$ (right tailed test.)

$$Z = \frac{\overline{X}_1 - \overline{X}_2}{\sqrt{\frac{\sigma_1^2}{n_1} + \frac{\sigma_2^2}{n_2}}} = \frac{75 - 72}{\sqrt{\frac{64}{36} + \frac{100}{36}}} = \frac{3}{\frac{1}{6}\sqrt{164}} = \frac{3 \times 6}{12.8} = 1.4 < 1.645$$

At 5% level of significance the table value of z is 1.645 because it is a one tailed test.

Since the calculated value is less than the table value, the null hypothesis is accepted *i.e.*, boys and girls perform equally well.

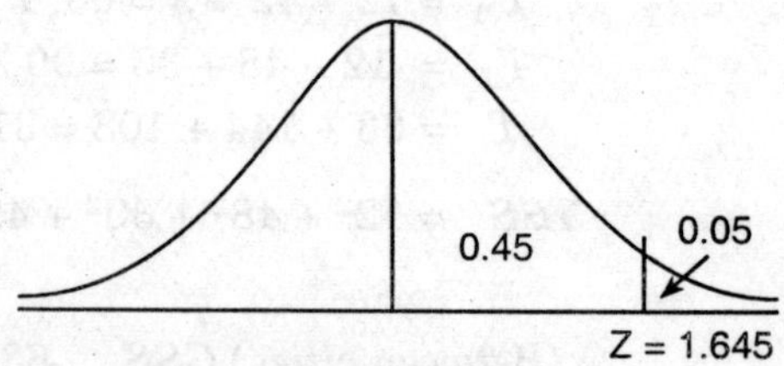

Example 48. *The manufacturer of a spot remover claims that his product removes at least 90% of all spots. What can be concluded about his claim at the level of significance α = 0.05, if the spot remover removed only 174 of the 200 spots chosen at random from the spots on clothes brought to a dry cleaning establishment?*

Solution. We have to test $H_0 : P = 0.90$ against $H_a : P < 0.9$. (it is needed to reject the claim)

It is given that $p = \frac{174}{200} = 0.82$ and $n = 200$.

$$\therefore \quad z_{cal} = (0.82 - 0.90)\sqrt{\frac{200}{0.9 \times 0.1}} = -3.77 \qquad \left[(p - p_0)\sqrt{\frac{n}{p_0 Q_0}}\right]$$

Since this value is less than – 1.645, H_0 is rejected at 5% level of significance. Thus, the sample evidence does not support the claim of the manufacturer.

Example 49. *470 heads were obtained in 1,000 throws of an unbiased coin. Can the difference between the proportion of heads in sample and their proportion in population be regarded as due to fluctuations of sampling?*

Solution. We have to test $H_0 : P = 0.5$ against $H_a : P \neq 0.5$.

It is given that $p = \frac{470}{1000} = 0.47$ and $n = 1000$.

$$\therefore \quad z_{cal} = |0.47 - 0.50| \sqrt{\frac{1000}{0.5 \times 0.5}} = 1.897.$$

Since this value is less than 1.96, the coin can be regarded as fair and thus, the difference between sample and population proportion of heads are only due to fluctuations of sampling.

Example 50. *In a random sample of 600 persons from a large city, 450 are found to be smokers. In another sample of 900 persons from another large city, 450 are smokers. Do the data indicate that the cities are significantly different with respect to the prevalence of smoking? Let the level of significance be 5%.*

Solution. We have to test $H_0 : P_1 = P_2$ against $H_a : P_1 \neq P_2$.

It is given that $n_1 = 600,\ n_2 = 900$

$$\therefore \quad p_1 = \frac{m_1}{n_1} = \frac{450}{600} = 0.75 \text{ and } P_2 = \frac{m_2}{n_2} = \frac{450}{900} = 0.50$$

The pooled estimate of p, *i.e.*, $p = \dfrac{450 + 450}{600 + 900} = 0.6$

$$\text{Thus,} \quad z_{cal} = |0.75 - 0.50| \sqrt{\frac{600 \times 900}{0.6 \times 0.4 \times 1500}} = 9.682 \quad \left[= (p_1 - p_2)\sqrt{\frac{n_1 n_2}{p(1-p)(n_1+n_2)}} \right]$$

This value is highly significant, therefore, H_0 is rejected. Thus, the given samples indicate that the two significantly different with regard to the prevalence of smoking.

Example 51. *A company is considering two different television advertisements for the promotion of a new product. Management believes that advertisement A is more effective than advertisement B. Two test market areas with virtually identical consumer characteristics are selected; advertisement A is used in one area and advertisement B is used in the other area. In a random sample of 60 customers who saw the advertisement A, 18 tried the product. In a random sample of 100 customers who saw advertisement B, 22 tried the product. Does this indicate that advertisement A is more effective than advertisement B, if a 5% level of significance is used?*

Solution. We have to test $H_0 : P_A = P_B$ against $H_a : P_A > P_B$.

It is given that $n_A = 60,\ n_B = 100$

$$\text{Thus,} \quad p_A = \frac{18}{60} = 0.30 \text{ and } p_B = \frac{22}{100} = 0.22$$

Also, the pooled estimate of p, *i.e.*, $p = \dfrac{18 + 22}{160} = 0.25$

$$\therefore \quad z_{cal} = (0.30 - 0.22)\sqrt{\frac{60 \times 100}{0.25 \times 0.75 \times 160}} = 1.131$$

Since this value is less than 1.645, there is no evidence against H_0 at 5% level of significance. Thus, the sample information provides no indication that advertisement A is more effective than advertisement B.

Example 52. *A money market mutual fund manages a ₹ 100 crores fund invested in money market securities. It has assessed it average daily cash needs as 10% of the corpus to meet the redemptions pressure even in difficult times. Last 100 days average was found to be 10.08% of the corpus. The experience of mutual fund manager has revealed the standard deviation of average daily cash balance as ₹ 30 lakhs.*

(i) He wants to find out whether or not his last 100 days average cash balance is within the limits of 10% at a level of significance of 5%. How can you help him?

(ii) What is the action that the fund manager should take based on the result obtained in (a) above ?

Solution. (*i*)

σ = ₹ 30 lakh = ₹ 0.3 crores [crore is taken as unit]

$n = 100$

$\bar{x} = 0.1008 \times 100$ = ₹ 10.08 crores

$H_0 : \mu$ = ₹ 10 crores [10% of 100 crores]

$H_1 : \mu \neq$ ₹ 10 crores

α : 0.05 level of significance

$$S.E. = \frac{\sigma}{\sqrt{n}} = \frac{0.3}{\sqrt{100}} = ₹\ 0.03 \text{ crores}$$

The acceptance region is $\mu \pm 1.96$ S.E. that is $10 \pm 1.96 \times 0.03 = (9.9412 \text{ to } 10.0588)$ as the sample mean 10.08 falls outside this region. H_0 is rejected, which means that his cash balance is not within the limits at a significance level of 5%.

(*ii*) He should bring down his daily cash balance in order to avoid the loss to forego investment opportunities.

Example 53. *A manufacturer needs to buy acrylic sheets of 5 mm thickness. Thinner sheets would not be appropriate and thicker sheets would be too heavy. He took a random sample of 100 sheets from a supplier and found that their average thickness was 3.8 mm with a standard deviation of 1 mm. Should he buy the sheets from the supplier if he wants to make a decision at:*

(*i*) *5% level of significance;*

(*ii*) *1% level of significance ?* [*D.U. B.A.* (*Hons.*) *Eco. 2006*)

Solution.

$H_0 : \mu = 5$

$H_1 : \mu \neq 5$

Here $\bar{x} = 3.8,\ \sigma = 1,\ n = 100$

Test variate standard is normal given by

$$Z = \frac{\bar{x} - \mu}{\sigma / \sqrt{n}}$$

$$Z \text{ (calculated)} = \frac{3.8 - 5}{\frac{1}{10}} = 12$$

Which is significance both at 5% level ($|z| = 1.96$) and 1% level $|z| = 2.57$ for two tailed test.

Hence, H_0 is rejected. So he should not buy them.

Example 54. *The shelf life of milk packaged by a manufacturer is normally distributed with a mean of 10 days and S.D. of 2 days. The manufacturer claims that introduction of a new technique in the packaging process can increase the shelf life of milk. A sample of 16 milk packets produced by the new process tested and the mean shelf life of the sample is found to be 11 days.*

Is the manufacturer claim justified at 5% level of signficance.

[D.U. B.A. (Hons.) Eco. 2007)

Solution.

H_0; Null hypothesis. The life has not improved. *i.e.* $\mu = 10$

H_i; Alternate Hypothesis; $\mu > 10$ (The life has improved).

Since S.D. of the population σ is given we use Z-test

$$Z = \frac{X-\mu}{\frac{\sigma}{\sqrt{n}}} = \frac{11-10}{\frac{2}{\sqrt{16}}} = \frac{1}{2} \times 4 = 2 > 1.645$$

The table value of Z at 5% level of significance for one tailed test is 1.645.

Since the calculated value is more than the table value we may conclude that the life has improved.

Example 55. *Measurement performed on random samples of two kinds of cigarettes yielded the following results on their nicontine content (in mgs)*

Brand A : 21.4, 23,6, 24.8, 22.4, 26.3

Brand B : 22.4, 27.7, 23.5, 29.1, 25.8

Assuming that the nicontine content is distributed normally, test the hypothesis that brand B has a higher nicontine content than brand A.

Solution. We have to test $H_0 : \mu_A = \mu_B$ against $H_a : \mu_A < \mu_B$. (left tailed-test)

Note that the rejection of H_0 would imply that brand B has a higher nicotine content than brand A.

The means of the two samples are

$$\overline{X}_A = \frac{21.4 + 23.6 + 24.8 + 22.4 + 26.3}{5} = 23.7$$

and

$$\overline{X}_B = \frac{22.4 + 27.7 + 23.5 + 29.1 + 25.8}{5} = 25.7$$

Also $\Sigma(X_{Ai} - \overline{X}_A)^2 = 14.96$ and $\Sigma(X_{Bi} - \overline{X}_B)^2 = 31.30$

The pooled estimate of σ is $s = \sqrt{\frac{14.96 + 31.30}{5+5-2}} = 2.40 \left[s_p^2 = \frac{\Sigma(X_{Ai} - \overline{X}_A)^2 + \Sigma(X_{Bi}\ \overline{X}_B)^2}{n_1 + n_2 - 2} \right]$

Thus, the test statistic is $t_{cal} = \frac{(23.7 - 25.7)}{2.40} \times \sqrt{\frac{5\times5}{5+5}} = -1.318 = \frac{\left(\overline{X}_A - \overline{X}_B\right)}{s_p\sqrt{\frac{1}{n_1} + \frac{1}{n_2}}}$

The critical value of t at 5% level of significance and 8 *d.f.* is – 1.86. Since t_{cal} is greater than this value, it lies in the region of acceptance and hence, there is no evidence against at 5% level of significance. Thus, the nicotine content in brand B is not higher than in brand A.

Example 56. *A ramdom sample of size 65 was taken to estimate the mean annual income of 1,000 families and the mean and S.D. were found to be ₹ 6,300 and ₹ 9,5 respectively. Find a 95% confidence interval for the population mean.*

[CA Foundation May 1996]

Solution. Hence $n = 65$, $\overline{X} = 6300$, $s\,(= \hat{\sigma}) = 9.5$

Since the population is finite, *i.e.*, 1,000, we will apply finite population correction factor.

$$S.E.\ (\overline{X}) = \frac{\sigma}{\sqrt{n}}\sqrt{\frac{N-n}{N-1}} = \frac{9.5}{\sqrt{65}}\sqrt{\frac{1{,}000-65}{1{,}000-1}} = 1.14$$

At 95% level of confidence

$$z = \pm 1.96$$

μ lies between $\overline{X} \pm Z_C\ SE\ (\overline{X})$

i.e. $6300 \pm 1.96\ (1.14)$

i.e. 6300 ± 2.30

Thus $6297.70 \le \mu \le 6302.30.$

Example 57. *Two types of batteries are tested for their length of life and the following data are obtained:*

	No. of Sample units	*Mean life in hours*	*Variance*
Type A	9	600	121
Type B	8	640	144

Is there significant diference between the means of two batteries at 5% level of significance?

Given the following:

Degree of freedom	15	16	121
Value of t at 5% level	2.13	2.12	2.11

Solution.

Step 1 → We set $H_0:\ \mu_1 = \mu_2,\ \ H_1:\ \mu_1 \ne \mu_2$

Step 2 → Since both the samples are small and independent, Fisher's t statstic is to be used.

Step 3 → *Calculation of combined standard deviation* :

$$n_1 = 9,\quad n_2 = 8,\quad S_1^2 = 121,\quad S_2^2 = 144$$

$$S_p = \sqrt{\frac{(n_1-1)S_1^2 + (n_2-1)S_2^2}{n_1+n_2-2}}$$

$$= \sqrt{\frac{(9-1)\,121 + (8-1)\,144}{9+8-2}} = \sqrt{\frac{1976}{15}}$$

$$= \sqrt{131.733} = 11.4778$$

Step 4 → $$t = \frac{|\overline{X}_1 - \overline{X}_2|}{S_p} \times \sqrt{\frac{n_1 n_2}{n_1+n_2}} = \frac{|600-640|}{11.478} \times \sqrt{\frac{9\times 8}{9+8}}$$

$$= \frac{40}{11.478} \times 2.058 = \frac{82.32}{11.478} = 7.172$$

Step 5 → Degrees of freedom = 9 + 8 – 2 = 15

Step 6 → For ν = 15, table value of t at 5% level = 2.13

Step 7 → ***Interpretation:*** Since the computed value of t (i.e. 7.172) is greater than the table value of t (i.e. 2.13), we reject H_0 and conclude that there is significant difference between the means of the two batteries at 5% level of significance.

Example 58. *The mean height of 50 male students who showed above average participation in college athletics was 68.2 inches with a standard deviation of 2.5 inches ; while 50 males students who showed no interest in such participation had a mean height of 67.5 inches with a standard deviation of 2.8 inches. Test the hypothesis that male students who participate in college athletics are taller than other male students.*

Solution. Let X denote the height (in inches) of the male students who showed above average participation in college athletics and Y denote the height of the students who showed no interest in athletic participation. Then we are given:

$$n_1 = 50, \quad \bar{x} = 68.2, \quad s_x = 2.5 \quad \Rightarrow \quad s_x{}^2 = 6.25 = \hat{\sigma}_x^2$$

$$n_2 = 50, \quad \bar{y} = 67.5, \quad s_y = 2.8 \quad \Rightarrow \quad s_x{}^2 = 7.84 = \hat{\sigma}_y^2$$

since the samples are large.

Null hypothesis. $H_0 : \mu_x = \mu_y$ *i.e.,* there is no significant difference between the mean heights of the male students who participate and who do not participate in college athletics.

Alternative Hypothesis. $H_1 : \mu_x > \mu_y$ (Right-tailed).

Level of significance. $\alpha = 0.05$

Test Statistic. Under H_0, the test statistic is z (since the samples are large) :

$$Z = \frac{\bar{x} - \bar{y}}{\sqrt{\frac{s_x^2}{n_1} + \frac{s_y^2}{n_2}}} \qquad \left[\sigma_1^2 \text{ and } \sigma_2^2 \text{ are replaced by } s_x^2 \text{ and } s_y^2 \right]$$

$$Z = \frac{68.2 - 67.5}{\sqrt{\frac{6.25}{50} + \frac{7.85}{50}}} = \frac{0.7}{\sqrt{0.1250 + 0.1568}} = \frac{0.7}{\sqrt{0.2818}} = \frac{0.7}{0.5308} = 1.3188.$$

Since the calculated value of Z is less than 1.645 (Right-tailed test). It is not siginficant at 5% level of significance. Hence the data are consistent with the null hypothesis and we conclude that average height of the male students who participate in college athletics is same the average height of the other male students in the college.

Example 59. *Ace Delivery Service operates a fleet of delivery vans in the Houston area. They prefer to have all their drivers charge their gasoline using the same brand of credit card. Presently they all use a Texgas credit card. Ace management has decided that perhaps Quik-Chek, a chain of convenience stores that also sells gasoline but does not accept not credit cards, is worth investigating. A random sample of gas prices at 35 Texgas stations and 40 Quik-Chek stores in the Houston area is obtained. The cost of 1 gallon of regular gasoline is recorded; the data are summarized:*

Sample 1 (Texgas)	***Sample 2 (Quik-Chek)***
$n_1 = 35$	$n_2 = 40$
$\bar{x}_1 = \$1.48$	$\bar{x}_2 = \$1.39$
$s_1 = \$0.12$	$s_2 = \$0.10$

Test at 95% if the gasoline at the Quik-Chek store was less expensive than at texgas.

Solution. Here, μ_1 represents the average price at all of the Texgas stations and μ_2 is the average price at the Quik-Chek stores in the area. Is $\mu_2 < \mu_1$? Or, put another way, is $\mu_1 < \mu_2$? Use a significance level of 0.05.

Step 1: *Define the hypothesis*: The question is whether the data support the claim that $\mu_1 < \mu_2$, so we put this statement in alternative hypothesis.'

$H_0 : \mu_1 \leq \mu_2$ (Texgas is less expensive or the same)

$H_a : \mu_1 > \mu_2$ (Quik-Chek is less expensive)

The equals sign goes into H_0 for a one-tailed test. In other words, the case where $\mu_1 = \mu_2$ is contained in the null hyppothesis.

Step 2: *Define the test statistic* : This is the statistic that you evaluate using the sample data. Its value will either support the alternative hypothesis or it will not. The test statistic for this situation is given by equation.

$$Z = \frac{\overline{X}_1 - \overline{X}_2}{\sqrt{\frac{\sigma_1^2}{n_1} + \frac{\sigma_2^2}{n_2}}}$$

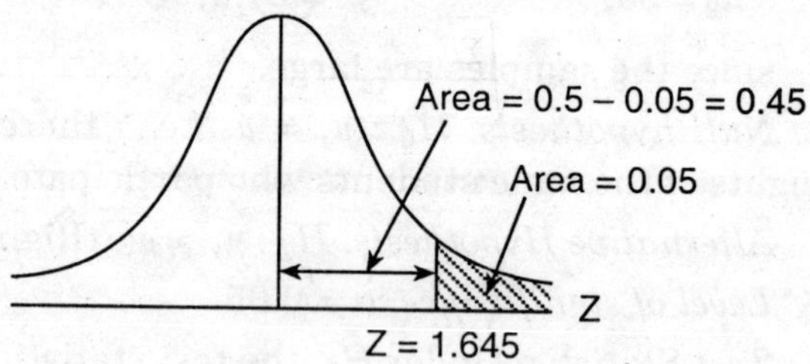

Step 3: Using α = 0.05, the corresponding value of $Z_{0.05}$ = 1.645

Reject H_0 if tabulated $Z > 1.645$

Step 4: Evaluate the test statistic and carry out the test.

$$Z = \frac{\overline{X}_1 - \overline{X}_2}{\sqrt{\frac{\sigma_1^2}{n_1} + \frac{\sigma_2^2}{n_2}}} \approx \frac{\overline{X}_1 - \overline{X}_2}{\sqrt{\frac{s_1^2}{n_1} + \frac{s_2^2}{n_2}}} = \frac{1.48 - 1.39}{\sqrt{\frac{(0.12)^2}{35} + \frac{(0.10)^2}{40}}}$$

$$= \frac{0.09}{0.0257} = 3.50 = Z$$

Because 3.50 > 1.645, we reject H_0 ; $\overline{x}_1$ is siginficantly larger than $\overline{x}_2$. Therefore, we claim that $\mu_1 > \mu_2$.

Step 5: *State a conclusion :* We conclude that the Quik-Chek store *do* charges less for gasoline (on the average) than do the Texgas stations. If the locations of these stores are equally convenient to Ace Delivery Service, buying gas for Quik-Chek appears to be a money-saving alternative.

Example 60. *Eleven students of B.Com. (Hons) were given a test in economic analysis. They were imparted a month's special coaching and a second test was held at the end of it. The result were as follows :*

Student No.	:	1	2	3	4	5	6	7	8	9	10	11
Marks in 1st Test	:	36	40	36	34	46	32	38	46	40	38	42
Marks in 2nd Test	:	40	44	40	40	46	40	34	48	38	44	36

Do the marks give an evidence that the students have benefited by extra coaching?

Solution. This is case of dependent sample and n = 11 (t = test) is to be used on $d = x - y$.

We have to test $H_0 : \mu_1 = \mu_2$ against $H_a : \mu_1 \neq \mu_2$. [*i.e.*, $H_0 ; \mu_d = 0$, $H_1 , \mu_d \neq 0$]

We have to test $H_0 : \mu_1 = \mu_2$ against $H_a : \mu_1 \neq \mu_2$.

Note that H_0 implies that students have not benefited by the extra coaching.

Let X_1 and X_2 denote the marks in 1st and 2nd tests respectively and $d = X_1 - X_2$

Calculation of $\bar{d}$ and s_d

Student No.	1	2	3	4	5	6	7	8	9	10	11	Total
d_i	– 4	– 4	– 4	– 6	0	– 8	4	– 2	2	– 6	6	– 22
d_i^2	16	16	16	36	0	64	16	4	4	36	36	244

Now $\Sigma d = -22$, $\bar{d} = \frac{-22}{11} = -2$ $\Sigma d^2 = 244$

$$s_d = \sqrt{\frac{\Sigma d^2 - n\bar{d}^2}{n-1}} = \sqrt{\frac{244 - 11(4)}{10}} = \sqrt{20}$$

$$t = \frac{\bar{d} - 0}{\sqrt{\frac{s^2}{n}}} = \frac{-20}{\sqrt{\frac{20}{11}}} = \frac{-2}{\sqrt{1.82}} = 1.48$$

The value of t at 5% level of significance and 10 *d.f.* is 2.228. Therefore, the sample information provides no evidence that students have benefited by extra coaching.

Examle 61. *A sample analysis of examination results of 200 M.B.A.'s was made. It was found that 46 students had failed. 68 secured a third division, 62 secured a second division and the rest were placed in the first division. Are these figures commensurate with the general examination result which is in the ratio of 2 : 3 : 3 : 2 for the various categories, respectively ? (Given : Table value of chi-square for 3 d.f. at 5% level of significance is 7.81).*

Solution . H_0: The students in various categories are distributed in the ratio 3 : 3 : 2.

The expected number of students, under the assumption that H_0 is true, are :

expected number of failures $= \frac{2}{(2+3+2)} \times 200 = 40.$

expected number of third divisionsers $= \frac{3}{10} \times 200 = 60.$

expected number of second divisionsers $= \frac{3}{10} \times 200 = 60$ and

expected number of first divisionsers $= \frac{2}{10} \times 200 = 40.$

Thus, we have $\chi^2 = \frac{(46-40)^2}{40} + \frac{(68-60)^2}{60} + \frac{(62-60)^2}{60} + \frac{(24-40)^2}{40} = 8.44$

Since this value is greater than the tabulated value, 7.81, for 3 *d.f.* and 5% level of significance, H_0 is rejected.

Example 62. *In a recent diet survey, the following results were obtained in an Indian city :*

No. of families	*Hindus*	*Muslims*	*Total*
Tea takers	1236	164	1400
Non-tea takers	564	36	600
Total	1800	200	2000

Discuss whether there is any siginficant difference between the two communities in the matter of taking tea? Use 5% level of significance.

Solution. The null hypothesis to be tested can be written as H_0: There is no difference between the two communities in the matter of taking tea.

H_{ij} It is not so i.e., there is dependence of tea taking and religion.

Direct formula for computing χ^2 is $= \dfrac{N\,(ad - bc)^2}{(a + b)\,(c + d)\,(a + c)\,(b + d)}$

	A_1	A_2	*Total*
B_1	a	b	$a + b$
B_2	c	d	$c + d$
Total	$a + c$	$b + d$	N

Using the direct formula, we have $\chi^2 = \dfrac{2000\,(1236 \times 36 - 164 - 564)^2}{1400 \times 1800 \times 200 \times 600} = 15.24$

The value of χ^2 from table for 1 *d.f.* and 5% level of significance is 3.84. Since the calculated value is greater than the tabulated value, H_0 is rejected.

Example 63. *Calculated the expected frequencies foy the following data presuming the two attributes, viz., condition of home and condition of child as independent.*

		Condition of Home	
		Clean	***Dirty***
Condition of Child	*Clean*	70	50
	Fairly Clean	80	20
	Dirty	35	45

Use Chi-square test at 5% level of state whether the two attributes are independent.

(Table values of Chi-square at 5% for 2 d.f. is 5.991 and for 3 d.f. is 7.815 and for 4 d.f is 9.488)

Solution. An expected frequency E, correponding to each cell in the table will be given by

$$E = \frac{\text{Row total} \times \text{Column total}}{\text{Grand total, } i.e., \text{ Sample size}}$$

We form the table of expected frequencies with the help of the above rule and write the expected frequencies in each cell within brackets.

Expected value of $(r-1)(c-1)$ cells are found and the rest can be obtained by difference.

Condition of Child	*Condition of Home*		
	Clean	*Dirty*	*Total*
Clean	$70 \leftarrow O$ $\frac{185 \times 120}{300} = 74\ E$	$50 \leftarrow O$ 46 E	120
Fairly Clean	$80 \leftarrow O$ $\frac{185 \times 100}{300} = 61.67 = 62$	$20 \leftarrow O$ 38 *E*	100
Dirty	$35 \leftarrow O$ 49 *E*	$45 \leftarrow O$ 31 *E*	80
Total	185	115	300

O and *E* denote observed expected frequencies.

Let us set the Null and the Alternate hypothesis as follows :

H_0. No association exists between the attributes, *i.e.*, the two attributes are independent.

H_1. An association exists between the attributes.

$$\chi^2 = \Sigma \frac{(O_i - E_i)^2}{E_i} = \frac{(70-74)^2}{74} + \frac{(50-46)^2}{46} + \frac{(80-62)^2}{62} + \frac{(20-38)^2}{38} + \frac{(35-49)^2}{49} + \frac{(45-31)^2}{31}$$

$$= 0.2162 + 0.3478 + 5.226 + 8.526 + 4.00 + 6.322 = 24.638$$

Degree of freedom = $(3-1)(2-1) = 2 \times 1 = 2$.

Since the computed value is more than the table value, $\chi^2_{2,0.05} = 5.991$ as such Null hypothesis is rejected.

Example 64. *To test the effectiveness of the approach and layout of two direct-mail brochures, a marketing manager mailed out 150 copies of each brochure and recodred the number of responses generated by each. There were 30 responses generated by the first brochure and 10 generated by the second. Can the marketing manager conclude that the first brochure is more effective ? Let* $\alpha = 0.05$.

Solution. Here we want to test the hypothesis $H_0 : p_1 = p_2$, against $H_a : p_1 > p_2$, where $p_1$is the proportion of responses that will be generated from a nationwide mailing of the first brochure and p_2 is the proportion of responses generated by the second brochure. We have

$$p_1 = \frac{30}{150} = 0.200 \quad p_2 = \frac{10}{150} = 0.067$$

$$p = \frac{m_1 + m_2}{n_1 + n_2}$$

$$= \frac{30 + 10}{300} = \frac{40}{300} = p$$

Also, $s^2_{p_1-p_2}{}^* = \frac{40}{300}\left(\frac{260}{300}\right)\left(\frac{1}{150}+\frac{1}{150}\right) = 0.001541$ $\quad {}^*s_{p_1-p_2} = \sqrt{pq\left(\frac{1}{n_1}+\frac{1}{n_2}\right)}$

$s_{p_1-p_2} = 0.0392$

Our calcuated Z is $Z = \frac{p_1 - p_2}{s_{p_1-p_2}} = \frac{0.133}{0.0392} = 3.40$

The critical region in this test is $Z_{0.05}$ for one tailed test = 1.645. Since calculated $Z > Z_{0.05} = 1.645$, we reject the null hypothesis and conclude that the first brochure is more effective in generating responses.

Example 65. *A brand of matches is sold in boxes on which it is claimed that the average contents are 40 match sticks. A check on 5 boxes giave the following results 41, 39, 37, 40, 38.*

(i) Test the manufacturer's claim keeping the interests of both the manufacturer and the customer in mind

(ii) As a customer test the manufacturer's claim .

Solution.

(*i*) Sample Mean = $\frac{41+39+37+40+38}{5} = 39$

Interest of the manufacturer and customer will be kept in view if we examine the sample for two tailed test.

$$t_{n-1} = \frac{\bar{x}-\mu}{S.E.\ (\bar{x})} = \frac{x-\mu}{s/\sqrt{n}}$$

$$\text{Sample S.D. } (s) = \sqrt{\frac{n}{n-1}}\sqrt{\frac{\Sigma x^2}{n} - \left(\frac{\Sigma x}{n}\right)^2}$$

$$= \sqrt{\frac{5}{4}}\sqrt{\left[\frac{(41)^2+(39)^2+(37)^2+(40)^2+(38)^2}{5} - (39)^2\right]}$$

$$= \sqrt{\frac{5}{4}}\sqrt{\frac{1681+1521+1369+1600+1444}{5} - 1521}$$

$$= \sqrt{\frac{5}{4}}\sqrt{1523-1521} = \sqrt{\frac{5}{4}}(1.4142) = 1.5811$$

$$t = \frac{39-40}{\frac{1.5811}{\sqrt{4}}} = \frac{2}{1.5811} = 1.264$$

At 5% level of significance, the value of t for two tailed test for 4 *d.f.* is 2.776. Since the calculated value is less than 2.776, we may accept the manufacturer's claim that the average content is 40 matches.

(*ii*) From the point of the customer, we must go for one tailed test. For one tailed test the value of t at 5% level of significance for 4 *d.o.f.* is 2.132. Even in this case the manufacturer's claim is justified.

Example 66. *Two independent samples of sizes 10 and 12 from two normal populations have their mean square deviations about their respective means equal to 12.8 and 15.2 respectively. Test the equality of variances of the two populations.*

Solution. We have to test $H_0 : \sigma_1 = \sigma_2$ against $\sigma_1 \neq \sigma_2$.

It is given that $S_1^2 = 15.2$, $S_2^2 = 12.8$, $n_1 = 12$ and $n_2 = 10$.

The unbiased estimates of respective population variances are

$$s_1^2 = \frac{12}{11} \times 15.2 = 16.58 \text{ and } s_2^2 = \frac{10}{9} \times 12.8 = 14.22 \qquad \left[s_1^2 = \frac{n}{n-1} S_2^2 \right]$$

Thus, $$F_{cal} = \frac{16.58}{14.22} = 1.166 \qquad \left[F = \frac{s_1^2}{s_2^2} \right]$$

The value of F from tables at 5% level of significance with 11 and 9 *d.f.* is 3.10. Since this value is greater than F_{cal}, there is no evidence against H_0.

Example 67. *A random sample of 100 items taken from a large batch of articles contain 5 defective items. (a) Set up 96 per cent confidence limits for the proportion of defective items in the batch. (b) If the batch contains 2,669 items, set up 95% confidence interval for the propurtion of defective items.*

Solution. In usual notations, we have

$$n = 100 \text{ ; Number of defectives in the sample} = 5$$

$$\therefore \quad p = \text{Proportion of defectives in the sample} = \frac{5}{100} = 0.05$$

$$q = 1 - p = 0.95$$

Hence an estimate of Standard Error of p is given by :

$$S.E.(p) = \sqrt{\frac{pq}{n}} = \sqrt{\frac{0.05 \times 0.95}{100}} = \sqrt{0.000475}$$
$$= 0.02179 \simeq 0.022 \text{ (approx)}.$$

From the tables of normal probability curve, we find that

$P(-205 \leq Z \leq 2.05) = 0.96 \Rightarrow P(|Z| \leq 2.05) = 0.96$

Hence, the significant value of Z at confidence coefficience 96% is 2.05. Hence 96% confidence limits for the population proportion of defectives are :

$p \pm 2.05\ S.E.(p) = 0.05 \pm 2.05 \times 0.022 = 0.050 \pm 0.045 = (0.005, 0.095)$

(*b*) If $N = 2669$. then 95% considence limits for P are given by

$$p \pm 1.96\ S.E.(p) = p \pm 1.96 \sqrt{\frac{(N-n)pq}{(N-1)n}}$$

$$= 0.050 \pm 1.96 \times \sqrt{\frac{(2669-100) \times 0.05 \times 0.95}{2668 \times 100}}$$

$$= 0.050 \pm 1.96 \times \sqrt{\frac{122.0275}{266800}} = 0.050 \pm 1.96 \times \sqrt{0.0004618}$$

$$= 0.050 \pm 1.96 \times 0.0215 = 0.050 \pm 0.042$$

$$= (0.008, 0.092).$$

Example 68. *A manufacturer manufactures battery powered AM/FM ratio sets that include the required batteries. This unit uses a smaller battery, and four suppliers (brands) of this battery are being considered. Past experience has indicated that the battery lifetimes are normally distributed. The supervising inspector of incoming quality wants to know whether there is any difference among the average lifetimes of the four battery brands. Twenty-four batteries (six of each brand) are placed on a test device that slowly drains the battery power and records the battery lifetime. The following data (in hours) were obtained :*

	Brand 1	Brand 2	Brand 3	Brand 4
	41	32	35	33
	35	37	30	27
	48	46	24	36
	40	53	26	35
	45	41	28	27
	52	43	31	25
Total (T)	261	252	174	183
Average ($\overline{X}$)	43.5	42.0	29.0	30.5
Variance (s^2)	37.1	52.8	15.2	22.3

The four sample averages are $\overline{x}_1 = 43.5$, $\overline{x}_2 = 42.0$, $\overline{x}_3 = 29.0$ and $\overline{x}_4 = 30.5$. Brands 1 and 2 appear to be outlasting brands 3 and 4. In other words, it appears that there is a significant betwee-group variation. But do these sample means provide sufficient evidence to reject H_0: $\mu_1 = \mu_2 = \mu_3 = \mu_4$, where each μ_1 represents the average of all lifetimes for brand i ? Use the ANOVA procedure to answer this question with $\alpha = 0.05$.

Solution. The requirements for this analysis are (i) the sample were obtained randomly and independently from each of the four populations, and (*ii*) the battery lifetimes for each brand follow a normal distribution with a *common variance*, say σ^2.

$$BSS\text{ (factor)} = \left[\frac{T_1^2}{n_1} + \frac{T_2^2}{n_2} + \frac{T_3^2}{n_3} + \frac{T_4^2}{n_4}\right] - \frac{T^2}{n}$$

Here $n = n_1 + n_2 + n_3 + n_4 = 24$, and

$$T = \Sigma X = T_1 + T_2 + T_3 + T_4$$

$$= 261 + 252 + 174 + 183 = 870$$

Therefore, *BSS* (factor) = *SSC* = Sum of the squares between the columns

$$= \frac{261^2}{6} + \frac{252^2}{6} + \frac{174^2}{6} + \frac{183^2}{6} - \frac{870^2}{24}$$

$$= 32{,}565 - 31{,}537.5 = 1{,}027.5$$

$$SS \text{ (total)} = SST = \sum X^2 - \frac{T^2}{n} = [41^2 + 35^2 + \ldots + 27^2 + 25^2] - \frac{870^2}{24}$$

$$= 33{,}202 - 31{,}537.5 = 1{,}664.5$$

$$SS \text{ (error)} = SSE = SS \text{ (total)} - SS \text{ (factor) or } SSC = 1{,}644.5 - 1{,}027.5 = 637$$

The ANOVA table for this analysis follows :

Source	*df*	*SS*	*MSS*	*F*
Factor	$k - 1 = 3$	1,027.5	$\frac{1{,}027.5}{3} = 342.5$	$\frac{342.5}{31.85} = 10.75 = F^*_{3,20}$
Error	$n - k = 20$	637	$\frac{637}{20} = 31.85$	
Total	23	1,664.5		

The computed F-value from the ANOVA table is $F^* = 10.75$. Since $\alpha = 0.05$, we use Table to find that $F_{0.05,3,20} = 3.10$. Comparing these two values, $F^* = 10.75 > 3.10$, so we reject H_0.

We conclude that the average lifrtimes for the four brands are not the same. Our results indicate that the brand factor *does* have a significant effect on battery lifetime.

Example 69. *WARTA, the Warren Area Regional Transit Authority, is expanding bus service from the suburb of Starbrick into the central business district of Warren. There are four routes being considered from Starbrick into downtown Warren : via U.S. 6, via the West end via the Hickory Street Bridge, and via Rte. 59. WARTA conducted test runs to determine if there is a difference in the mean travel times along the four routes. The travel times, in minutes, along each of the four routes are given below :*

Travel Time from Starbrick to Warren (Minutes)

Driver	*U.S. 6*	*West end*	*Hickory St. Bridge*	*Rte. 59*
Piper	18	20	20	22
Sanders	21	22	24	24
McLain	20	23	25	23
Hammons	25	21	28	25
Hoffman	26	24	28	25

At the 0.05 significance level, can it be concluded that there is a diffrerence among the four routes ? Is there a difference among the drivers ?

Solution. There is two way classification as such

H_0 ; [Mean travel times of all 5 drivers are equal
Mean travel times for all 4 routes are equal]

H_1 ; [Mean travel times for at least 2 drivers differ
Mean travel times for at least 2 routes differ]

Calculations Needed for Two-Way Anova

Driver	Travel Time, by Route (Minutes)					
	U.S. 6	West End	Hickory St. Bridge	Rte. 59	Row Sum, B_r	
Piper	18	20	20	22	80	
Sanders	21	22	24	24	91	
McLain	20	23	25	23	91	
Hammons	25	21	28	25	99	
Hoffman	26	24	28	25	103	Total
Column total, T.	110	110	125	119		464
Sum of squares	2,466	2,430	3,169	2,839		10,904
Number of Units (n_i)	5	5	5	5		

$$\text{Sum of squares (Columns) } SSC = \Sigma\frac{T_{.j}^2}{n} - \frac{T^2}{mn}$$

$$= \left[\frac{(110)^2}{5} + \frac{(110)^2}{5} + \frac{(125)^2}{5} + \frac{(119)^2}{5}\right] - \frac{(646)^2}{20} = 32.4$$

$$\text{Sum of squares (rows) } SSR = \left[\frac{(80)^2}{4} + \frac{(91)^2}{4} + \frac{(91)^2}{4} + \frac{(99)^2}{4} + \frac{(103)^2}{2}\right] - \frac{(464)^2}{20} = 78.2$$

$$SST = \Sigma X^2 - \frac{\Sigma X^2}{N} = 10{,}904 - \frac{(464)^2}{20} = 139.2$$

$$SSE = SST - SSC - SSR$$

$$= 139.2 - 32.4 - 78.2 = 28.6$$

Anova Table

Source of Variation	*(1) Sum of Squares*	*(2) Degrees of Freedom*	*(3) Mean Square (1)/(2)*	*F*
Columns	32.4	3	10.8	$\frac{10.8}{2.38} = 4.54 = F_{(3,12)}$
Rows	78.2	4	19.55	$\frac{19.55}{2.38} = 8.21 = F_{(4,12)}$
Error	28.6	12	2.38	
Total	139.2			

Table value for $\alpha = 0.05$

$F_{(3,12)} = 3.49$

$F_{(4,12)} = 3.26$

Thus both H_0's are rejected as calculated values of F exceed the corresponding table values for $\alpha = 0.05$

EXERCISE

1. Explain the concept of significance in tests of hypothesis. Describe, briefly, the procedure of testing hypothesis.
2. Distinguish between a null hypothesis and an alternative hypothesis. Use an example to explain the nature of null and alternative hypothesis in cases of one and two tailed tests.
3. Distinguish between:
   (*i*) Confidence interval and confidence limits.
   (*ii*) Type I and Type II errors.
   (*iii*) Critical region and the region of acceptance.
   (*iv*) Level of significance.
4. Define and explain Type I and Type II errors for a simple null and alternate hypothesis using a sketch of the distribution. How are these errors affected by an increase in the sample size ?
5. A manufacturer of TV tubes has for many years used a process giving a mean tube life of 4700 hours and a standard deviation of 1460 hours. A new process is tried to see if it will increase the life significantly. A sample of 100 new tubes gave a mean life of 5000 hours. Is the new process better than the old at the 1 per cent level of significance ?

   [**Ans.** No]
6. A manufacturer claimed that at least 95% of the equipment that it supplied to a factory conformed to specifications. An examination of a sample of 200 pieces of equipment revealed that 18 were faulty. Test this claim at significance levels of (*a*) 1% and (*b*) 5%.

   [**Ans.** Claim is rejected at both levels]
7. Random samples of 200 bolts manufactured by machine *A* and of 100 bolts manufactured by machine *B* showed 19 and 5 defective bolts, respectively. Test the hypotheses (*a*) that the two machines are showing different qualities of performance and (*b*) that machine *B* is performing better than *A*. Use the 5% significance level.
   [**Ans.** (*a*) No (*b*) Machine *B* is not better than *A*].
8. Given a sample mean of 83, a sample standard deviation of 12.5, and a sample size of 22, test the hypothesis that the value of the population mean is 70, against the alternative that it is more than 70. Use the 2.5% significance level.

   [**Ans.** $\mu > 70$]
9. A television documentary on overeating claimed that Americans are about 10 pounds over-weight on average. To test this claim, eighteen randomly selected individuals were examined, and their average excess weight was found to be 12.4 pounds, with a sample standard deviation of 2.7 pounds. At a significance level of 1%, is there any reason to doubt the validity of the claimed 10 pound value ?

   [**Ans.** Claim is rejected]

10. A car retailer thinks that a 40,000 miles claim for tire life by the manufacturer is too high. She carefully records the mileage obtained from sample of 64 such tires. The mean turns out to be a 38,500 miles. The standard deviation of the life of all tires of this type has previously been calculated by the manufacturer to be 7,600 miles. Assuming that the mileage is normally distributed, determine the largest significance level at which we should accept the manufacturer's mileage claim, that is, at which we would not conclude the mileage is significantly less than 40,000 miles.

[**Ans.** $Z = 1.58$, 5.71%]

11. A sample of eight workers in a cloth manufacturing company gave the following figures for the amount of time (in minutes) needed to mount a collar on a shirt : 10, 12, 13, 9, 8, 14, 10 and 11. At the 5% level of significance, would it be justified in saying that the mean time to mount a collar is more than 10 minutes ?

[**Ans.** No]

12. In a sample of 400 oranges from a large consignment, 40 were considered bad. Estimate the percentage of defective oranges in the whole consignment and assign the limits within which the percentage would probably lie ?

[**Ans.** 10%, 0.055 – 0.145]

13. The Inflato Tyre Company wishes to determine the average mileage of its new *PQ* tyres. A random sample of 49 tyres gives a mean of 25,000 miles with a standard deviation of 2,450 miles. Find a 90% confidence interval for the true mean mileage.

[**Ans.** 2442.25 – 25575.75]

14. A random sample of 64 men, from a population with known standard deviation of height of 2.4 inches, gives a mean height of 69.8 inches. Find a 90% confidence interval for μ, the mean height of men population.

[**Ans.** 69.31 – 70.29]

15. A life insurance company has 1,500 policies averaging ₹ 2,000 on lives at the age 30. From the past experience table, it is found that out of 1,00,000 alive at the ago of 30; 99,000 are alive at age 31. Find the lower and the upper value of the amount that the company will have to pay out in insurance during the year.

[**Ans.** 6879 – 53121 as pliers between .00226 and .01774]

16. In a city 350 out of 600 persons were found to be vegetarian. On the basis of this data, can we say that majority of the population in the city is vegetarian ?

[*C.A. (Foundation), Nov., 1999*]

[**Ans.** $H_0 : \; P = \frac{1}{2}, \; H_1 : \; P > \frac{1}{2}, Z = 4.165 > 1.645$. Highly significant. Reject H_0.

Majority of the population in the city is vegetation].

17. In random samples of 600 and 1000 men from two cities 400 and 600 men are found to be smokers. Do the data indicate that the populations are significantly different in the percentage of smoking at 5% level of significance, after calculation of standard error of difference between proportion of smokers in the samples from two cities ?

[Given $P(Z > 1.96) = 0.025$ when Z follows $N(0, 1)$].

[I.C.W.A. (Intermediate), June 1998]

[**Ans.** $H_0 : P_1 = P_2$; $H_1 : P_1 \neq P_2$ (Two tailed).

$SE(p_1 - p_2) = \frac{1}{40}$; $Z = 2.67$; Significant.]

18. In a certain district *A*, 450 persons were considered regular consumers of tea out of a sample of 1000 persons. In another district *B*, 400 were regular consumers of tea out of a sample of 800 persons. Do these facts reveal a significant difference between the two districts as far as tea drinking habit is concerned ? Use 5% level.

[**Ans.** $H_0 : P_1 = P_2$; $H_1 : P_1 \neq P_2$. $|Z| = 2.08$; Significant at 5% level.]

19. In a sample of 600 students of a certain college 400 are found to use dot pens. In another college, from a sample of 900 students, 450 were found to use dot pens. Test whether the two colleges are significantly different with respect to the habit of using dot pens. (Null and alternative hypothesis should be stated clearly).

[**Ans.** $H_0 : P_1 = P_2$; $H_1 : P_1 \neq P_2$; $|Z| = 6.4885$; Significant.]

20. On the basis of their total scores, 200 candidates of a civil service examination are divided into two group, the upper 30 per cent and the remaining 70 per cent. Consider the first question of this examination. Among the first group, 40 had the correct answer, whereas among the second group, 80 had the correct answer. On the basis of these results, can one conclude that the first question is no good at discriminating ability of the type being examined here ?

[**Ans.** $H_0 : P_1 = P_2$; $H_1 : P_1 \neq P_2$; $Z = 1.26$; No Significant.]

21. In a year there are 956 births in a town *A*, of which 52.5% were males, while in towns *A* and *B* combined, this proportion in a total of 1.406 births was 0.496. It there any significant difference in the proportion of male births in the two towns ?

[**Ans.** $H_0 : P_1 = P_2$; $H_1 : P_1 \neq P_2$; $Z = .3.37$, Significant.]

22. A machine produced 20 defective articles in a batch of 400. After overhauling, it produced 10 defectives in a batch of 300. Has the machine improved ?

[**Ans.** $H_0 : P_1 = P_2$; $H_1 : P_1 > P_2$; $|Z| = 1.103$; No Significant.]

23. From the past record of 100 sales, selected at random, the manager of a super bazaar computed the average sales per customer as ₹ 50 with a standard deviation of ₹ 20. Test the hypothesis that the mean sales per customer are not less than ₹ 60. Assume the distribution of sales to be normal.

[**Hint** : *Use one-tailed test.*]

[**Ans.** $Z = -5$, $\mu < 60$].

24. A radio shop sells, on an average, 200 radios per day with a standard deviation of 50 radios. After an extensive advertising campaign, the management will compute the average sales for the next 25 days to see whether an improvement has occurred. Assume that the daily sales of radios is normally distributed.

(*i*) Write down the null and alternate hypothesis.

(*ii*) Test the hypothesis at 5% level of significance if $\overline{X} = 216$.

(*iii*) How large must $\overline{X}$ be in order that the null hypothesis is rejected at 5% level of significance ?

[**Hint** : *Use one-tailed test.*]

[**Ans.** $Z = 1.6$, $\overline{X} > 216.4$].

25. Nine readings have been taken of a certain measurement and from these it has been found that $\Sigma X = 108$ and $\Sigma X^2 = 1584$. Construct a 95% confidence interval for population mean and test the hypothesis that the population means is 9 units.

[**Hint** : *Use one-tailed test.*]

[**Ans.** 7.388 – 16.612, accepted].

26. Given is the following information:

	No. of items	Sample Mean	Population S.D.
Sample I	36	₹ 180.00	₹ 4.00
Sample II	50	₹ 177.50	₹ 5.60

Calculate the standard error of the difference between two sample means and state at 5% level of significance whether the difference is statistically significant?

[**Hint** : *Use two tailed standard normal test.*

[**Ans.** 1.035, $Z = 2.415$].

27. The following data show that the cost per square foot of floor area concerning randomly selected 7 schools and 5 office blocks from those completed during the period 1984 to 1989:

Building Type	:	*Cost per sq. ft*						
School	:	28	31	26	27	23	38	37
Office Blocks	:	37	42	34	37	35		

Can we conclude that the mean cost per sq. ft. is same for the two type of buildings?

[**Hint** : *Use two tailed-test.*]

[**Ans.** $t = 1.46$].

28. A population consists of numbers 2, 3, 6, 8, 11.

Enumerate all possible samples of size 2 which can be drawn from the population without replacement and show that the mean of the sampling distribution of the sample means is equal to the population mean. Calculate the variance of the sample distribution of the sample mean and show that it is less than the population variance. [*D.U. B.A. (Hons.) Eco. 2000*]

29. Suppose it is known from experience that the standard deviation of 100 kg package of sugar made by a certain sugar mill is 2 kg. To check whether packaging is under control on a given data a random sample of 64 packages in selected and the mean weight is found to be 99kg. Would you accept or reject the Null hypothesis $\mu = 100$ against the Alternate hypothesis $\mu \neq 100$ at 0.01 level for significance.

[*D.U. B.A. (Hons.) Eco. 2000*]

30. Of the patients admitted consecutively to a hospital, every fifth one is treated by a new therapy and the remainder by the old therapy. 20% of the patients treated by the new therapy die while 30% die out of those treated by the old therapy. Test at 5% level of significance whether the difference in the fatality is more than occurrence by chance?

[**Hint** : *Let there be 500* patients admitted for treatment.

[**Ans.** $\chi^2 = 3.97$]

31. 50 students selected at random from 500 students enrolled in a computer crash program were classified according to age and grade points giving the following data :

Grade Point	*Age (in years)* 20 *and under*	21 – 30	*above* 30
Upto 5.0	3	5	2
5.1 – 7.5	8	7	5
7.6 – 10.0	4	8	8

Test at 5% level of significance the hypothesis that age and grade points are independent.

[**Hint** : *Calculate* χ^2 *and test its significance*, $\chi^2 = 2.875$].

32. A sample of 100 tyres is taken from a lot. The mean life of tyres is found to be 39,350 kilometres with a standard deviation of 3.260 km. Could the sample come from a population with mean life of 40,000 kilometres?

Also obtain 99% confidence limits within, which the mean life of tyres is expected to lie. [*Delhi Univ. B.A. (Econ. Hons.). 1996*]

[**Ans.** $H_0 : \mu = 40{,}000$ km. $H_1 : \mu \neq 40.000$ km. $|Z| = 1.99 > 1.96$

Significant at 5% level of significance H_0 rejected. **99% limits per** μ. (39,350 ± 841.04) km = (38508.92, 40191.08) km.]

33. From the following table test whether the colour of the sons' eyes is associated with that of the fathers'.

Eye colour of father	*Eye color sons* Not light	*Light*	*Total*
Not light	230	148	378
Light	151	471	622
Total	381	619	1000

The value of $\chi^2_{0.05} = 3.84$ for $\nu = 2$, 7.82 for $\nu = 3$.

[**Ans.** $\chi^2 = 132.26$. Highly significant. Hence colour of sons' eyes is associated with that of fathers'.]

34. The following data show the weekly production of 10 employees before change (X_1) and after change (X_2) in the production techniques.

Employee	*A*	*B*	*C*	*D*	*E*	*F*	*G*	*H*	*I*	*J*
(X_1)	24	26	20	21	23	30	32	25	23	23
(X_2)	26	26	22	22	24	30	32	26	24	25

Test whether there is any significant increase in average production due to change in the production technique. Let the level of significance be 1%.

[**Hint** : *Use one tailed paired t-test.*

[**Ans.** $t = 3.873$].

35. A normal population is supposed to have a mean of 3 cms and a S.D. of 2.31 cms. A sample of 900 members is found to have a mean of 3.24 cms. Can it be regarded as a simple random sample drawn from this population?

[**Hint** : *The sample can be regarded as simple random sample from the population only if there is no evidence against the* $H_0 : \mu = 3.00$.

[**Ans.** $Z = 3.12$].

36. An I.Q. test was administered to 10 men before and after they were trained. The results are given below:

S. No.	:	1	2	3	4	5	6	7	8	9	10
I.Q. Before training	:	167	124	157	155	163	154	156	168	133	143
I.Q. After training	:	170	138	158	158	156	167	168	172	142	138

Test whether there is any change in I.Q. after the training program?

[**Hint** : *Use paired t-test.* $t = 2.039$].

37. A toothpaste manufacturing company conducted a survey and found that it could sell only 60 tubes on an average per month per shop. Immediately, the company advertised heavily in several media and after three months again conducted a survey and found that the mean sales was 72 tubes with a S.D. of 10 tubes in sample of 20 shops. Can it be concluded that the advertisment is effective?

[**Hint** : *Use one tailed test.*

[**Ans.** $t = 5.23$].

38. Four varieties of rice were grown on each of the four beds of three identical plots. The output (in quintals) of different varieties are given in the following table:

Plot	*Varieties of Rice* A	B	C	D
I	19	27	30	27
II	24	15	15	18
III	20	23	25	30

Test whether the mean yield of different varieties of rice are significantly different.

[**Ans.** $F = 3.7$].

39. The data regarding life (in '00 hours) of three types of bulbs manufactured by a company are given in the following table. Test the hypothesis that mean life of bulbs of different types are same.

Type of Bulbs						
	A	16	18	19		
	B	14	13	15	20	
	C	18	17	19	21	21

[**Ans.** $F = 2.97$].

40. The Amit Merchandising Company wishes to test whether its three salesmen *A, B* and *C* tend to make sales of the same size or whether they differ in their selling ability as measured by the average size of their sales. During the last week there have been 14 sale calls. A made 5 calls, B made 4 calls and C made 5 calls. The weekly sales (in ₹) recorded for the three salesmen are given below. Perform the analysis and give your conclusions.

A : 300, 400, 300, 500, 0; *B* : 600, 300, 300, 400; *C* : 700, 300, 400, 600, 500.

[**Ans.** $F = 1.83$].

41. A buyer of electric bulbs bought 50 bulbs of brands *A* and *B* each. Upon testing these bulbs, it was found that brand *A* had a mean life of 1282 hours with a standard deviation of 80 hours, where as brand *B* had a mean life of 1208 hours with a standard deviation of 94 hours. Can the buyer be reasonably certain that mean life of bulbs of brand *A* differ by more than 50 hours as compared to that of brand *B*.

$$\left[\textbf{Ans. } Z = 1.375 = \frac{(\overline{X}_1 - \overline{X}_2) - 50}{SE(\overline{X}_1 - \overline{X}_2)}\right].$$

42. To test the effect of fertilisers on rice production, 24 plots of equally fertile land, were chosen. Only half of them were treated with fertilisers. The mean yield on untreated plots was 4.8 quintals with *S.D.* of 0.5 quintal while on treated plots it was 5.1 quintals with *S.D.* 0.36 quintal respectively. Can we conclude that the use of fertilisers causes a significant improvement in production ?

[**Ans.** $t = -1.62$]

43. A chemical extraction plant processes sea water to collect sodium chloride and magnesium. From scientific analysis, sea water is known to contain sodium chloride, magnesium and other elements in the ratio 62 : 4 : 34. A sample of 200 tonnes of extracted mineral has resulted in 130 tonnes of sodium chloride and 6 tonnes of magnesium. Are these data consistent with the scientific model? Use 0.05 as the level of significance.

[**Ans.** $\chi^2 = 1.026$].

44. The appearance of 2 or 3 on a die is counted as a success. Five dice are thrown 729 times and the following results are observed :

No. of successes :	0	1	2	3	4	5
Frequency :	45	195	237	132	81	39

Are the results consistent with the belief that all the dice are unbiased?

[**Hint** : *Fit a binomial distribution by taking* $n = 5$ *and* p 1/3.

[**Ans.** $\chi^2 = 555.47$ expected frequencies are 96, 240, 240, 120, 30, 3].

45. A test was given to 5 students chosen at random from the M.Com. class of each of the three universities in Bihar. Their scores were found as follows:

University			*Scores*		
A	90	70	60	50	80
B	70	40	50	40	50
C	60	50	60	70	60

Perform analysis of variance and show if there is any significant difference between the scores of students in the three universities.

[Himachal Pradesh Univ. M.Com., 1998]

[**Ans.** F (Universities) $= 3.33 \sim F(2, 12)$; Not significant]

There is no significant difference between the score of students in the three universities.]

46. A manufacturer of machine parts is considering one of the 4 machines currently in the market. The following is the daily output on 5 randomly selected days for each machine :

Machine I	72	56	68	65	60
Machine II	62	70	66	64	78
Machine III	68	72	74	70	66
Machine IV	64	72	68	68	58

Do the five machine have an equal output rate? Use $\alpha = 0.01$

[**Ans.** F (Machine) = 1.06, not significant.

Yes, the five machines have an equal output rate.]

47. A survey is commissioned by the Government of Ruritania to test whether men and women have different views on capital punishment, by asking the question: Are you in favour of capital punishment ? In a sample survey of 800 men there were 536 replies of 'yes', and in a sample of 700 women there were 427 replies of 'yes'. By ignoring the problem of 'don't know', test at 1% level if there is a significant difference in attitude due to sex.

[**Hint :** *Use two tailed test.*

[**Ans.** $Z = 2.418$].

□□□

16

Statistical Decision Theory

CHAPTER OUTLINE

- Different Types of decision problems
- Decision problem in terms of decision alternatives, states of nature and payoffs.
- Payoff and regret tables to analysis decision problems.
- Non-probabilistic decision making criteria such as maximax criterion, maximin criterion, minimax regret criterion, and so on.
- Decision under risk, expected payoff criterion
- Decision under certainty expected value of perfect information
- Decision tree approach in decision making.

16.1. INTRODUCTION

A businessman has to operate in an atmosphere of uncertainty and has to select the best course out of several alternative courses of action that may be available to him. In earlier days decisions were made mainly on personal judgement. However, these days judgement is combined with several quantitative techniques and the best action is arrived at in a given situation.

In any organisation the main function of the executive is to make decisions. The organisation is faced with several types of decision problems such as : Should a new product be introduced in the market? How many units of a product should be produced? How many units of a products should be marketed? How many units of a particular machine part or raw materials should be kept in stock? The decision-maker has to face such endless problems. In each so such decision-making problems, there are certain common elements which are called ingredients of decision problems. These ingredients are :

16.2. INGREDIENTS OF DECISION PROBLEM

16.2.1 Alternative Actions

The process of decision-making involves the selection of a single act from among a set of alternative acts. Decision is needed in a problem situation where two or more alternative courses of action are available, and where only one of these actions can be taken. Obviously, if there is only one course of action available, no decision is required since that action must be taken in order to solve the problem. For the sake of simplicity the possible actions are symbolised by a_1, a_2, a_3, ... etc. The totality of all possible actions is called *action space* denoted by A (a_1, a_2, a_3). The decision procedure involves selecting among the alternatives a single course of action that can actually be carried out. If such a course of action is selected that cannot be carried out in the existing situation and circumstance, it will tantamount to waste of time and resources. Quite often the objective of precision is to select an act which will accomplish some pre designated purpose. The decision taken may be regarded as satisfactory or not depending upon whether it has helped in the attainment of the objective.

16.2.2 States of Nature

In all decision problems 'uncertainty' is found to be the common element. When the outcome of some action is not known in advance, the outcome is said to be uncertain. When there are many possible outcomes of an event (also called *states of nature*), one cannot predict with certainty what will happen– it is only in terms of probabilities we may be able to talk. It is a general term which is used to encompass all those factors beyond the control of the decision-maker that affect the outcome of his decision. The various states of nature (outcomes) are symbolised by s_1, s_2, ... etc. Totality of all outcomes is called nature space or state space symbolised by S. If an action leads to three outcomes s_1, s_2, and s_3 then we write :

$$S = \{s_1, s_2, s_3\}$$

For example if a student is preparing for an examination he has several alternative actions before him e.g. (1) He study exhaustively (2) He makes selective study (3) He study only few important chapters (4) He prepares answers to questions from last 5 years questions papers.

After he had selected one alternative he may confront with the following states of nature (1) The question paper was very difficult (2) It was very simple (3) The paper had mostly questions from last 5 years papers (4) It had very few questions from last 5 years question papers and so on.

16.2.3 Payoff Table

A number of consequences result for each action under different conditions, the condition being various states of nature. In general if there are m possible actions and n admissible states of nature, the consequences will be $m \times n$ in number. In practical situations, particularly in business and economic problems consequences can be expressed in terms of money and utility.

The consequences may be evaluated in several ways such as :

(*i*) in terms of profits,

(*ii*) in terms of costs, and

(*ii*) in terms of opportunity losses.

In most decision problems the expected monetary value is used as a decision criterion. When consequences are evaluated in terms of profits they are called payoffs. A payoff table is prepared and it shows the relation between all possible states of nature, all possible actions and the values associated with the consequences. A specimen of payoff table is given below :

State of Nature \ Action	a_1	a_2	a_3	a_4
S_1	p_{11}	p_{12}	p_{13}	p_{14}
S_2	p_{21}	p_{22}	p_{23}	p_{24}
S_3	p_{31}	p_{32}	p_{33}	p_{34}

In the example there are 4 alternative actions and 3 states of nature.

Example 1. *Four types of toys T_i (i = 1, 2, 3, 4) are produced. The choice of item of production will depend on contribution to profit. The fixed and variable costs in each are as follows :*

Types	*Fixed Cost (₹)*	*Variable Cost (₹)*
T_1	1,00,000	5
T_2	1,60,000	4
T_3	3,00,000	3
T_4	5,00,000	2

The likely demand D_i (i = 1, 2, 3) for each in four situations are as follows :

		Units
D_1	Light	25,000
D_2	Moderate	1,00,000
D_3	Heavy	1,50,000

If price of each type is ₹ 10 the Pay-off from each will be calculated as follows :

Solution. In this case there are 4 possible actions for producing one out of given 4 types, T_1, T_2, T_3, or T_4. and there are 3 likely states of nature corresponding to each likely demand which is not under control of decision maker.

Pay-off Profit = Sales Revenue from the stimated demand—Total variable cost—Fixed cost

For example, T_1D_1 or the Pay-off in case of T_1 toy with D_1 = 25000 demand level will be ₹ 10 (25,000) – ₹ 1,25,000 — ₹ 1,00,000 = 25,000 = 25 thousand.

Similarly for T_1D_2 (*i.e.* Toy is T_1 and demand is D_2 = 1,00,000.

Thus net profit = 10 (1,00,000) – 1,00,000 – 5 (1,00,000) = 4,00,000

[Revenue – F.C. – Total variable cost]

= 400 thousands.

The Pay-off for all other cells is calculated in the same manner and are tabulated as follows :

Pay-off Table *(figures in thousand rupees)*

	T_1 (A_1)	T_2 (A_2)	T_3 (A_3)	T_4 (A_4)
D_1 (S_1)	25	–10	–125	– 300
D_2 (S_2)	400	440	400	300
D_3 (S_3)	650	740	750	700

(negative figures indicate losses)

16.2.4. Opportunity Loss Table or Regret Table

Opportunity Loss or Regret is defined as the difference between the best possible Pay-off which could have been released if we had the information about the state of nature which was going to occur and the realized Pay-off. This difference which measures the magnitude of the loss incurred by not selecting the best alternative is also known as **opportunity loss*** for **opportunity cost.** The method to get O.L. Table or regret Table from payoff table is explained in the example which follows.

Example 2. *Prepare O.L. Table (Regret table) from payoff table given in example 1.*

In case of state of nature S_1, the maximum payoff is 25. The had it been known before hand that S_1 is going to occur one should have taken action A_1 (which gives a max. profit of 25 thousand). Now if A_1 was taken there is no opportunity loss but if A_2 was taken there is opportunity loss of 25–(1–10) = 35 *(i.e., loss because A_2 was taken in place of A_1) similarly O.L.'s for A_3 and A_4 are (25 – (–125) and [25–(300)] respectively. Thus O.L.'s in case of S_1 are as follows :*

	A_1	A_2	A_3	A_4
S_1	0	35	150	325

Similarly had it been known that S_2 was going to occur best course would have been A_2 which gives maximum payoff of 440 thousands as such regret for S_2 would be

	A_1	A_2	A_3	A_4
S_2	440– 400	440 – 440	440 – 400	440 – 300

Thus *O.L.* Table would be

	A_1	A_2	A_3	A_4
S_1	0	35	150	325
S_2	40	0	40	140
S_3	100	10	0	50

16.3. DECISION MAKING

Given the payoff matrix or regret table for a decision problem, the process of decision making depends upon the situation under which the decision is being made. These situations can be classified into three broad categories : (*a*) Decision making under uncertainty and (*b*) Decision making under risk (*c*) Decision making under certainty.

16.3.1. Decision Making Under Uncertainty

(*a*) On the basis of payoff table

A situation of uncertainty arises when there can be more than one possible consequences selecting any course of action. In terms of the payoff matrix if the decision maker selects A_1, his payoff can be X_{11}, X_{12}, etc., depending upon which state of nature S_1, S_2, S_3, *etc.*, is going to occur. A decision problem, where a decision maker is aware of various possible states of nature but has insufficient information to assign any probabilities of occurrence to them, is termed as *decision making under uncertainty.*

There are a variety of criteria that have been proposed for the selection of an optimal course of action under the environment of uncertainty. Each of these criteria make an assumption about the attitude of the decision maker.

Maximin Criterion

This criterion, also known as the *criterion of pessimism,* is used when the decision maker is pessimistic about nature. Maximin implies the *maximisation of minimum payoff.* The pessimistic decision maker locates the minimum payoff for each possible course of action and the maximum of these minimum payoffs is identified and the corresponding course of action is selected. This is explained in the following example:

Example 3. *Let there be a situation in which a decision maker has three possible alternatives* A_1, A_2, and A_3, *where the outcome of each of them can be affected by the occurrence of any one of the four possible events* S_1, S_2, S_3 and S_4. *The monetary payoffs of each combination of* A_i *and* S_i *are given in the following table:*

Payoff Matrix

Events → *Action* ↓	S_1	S_2	S_3	S_4	*Min. Payoff*	*Max. Payoff*	
A_1	27	12	14	26	12	27	A_1
A_2	45	17	35	20	17	45	A_2
A_3	52	36	29	15	15	52	A_3

Solution. Since 17 is maximum out of the minimum payoffs, the optimal action is A_2 (maximum out of the minimum payoffs) on the basis of maximin criteria.

Maximax Criterion

This criteria, also known as the *criteria of optimism,* is used when the decision maker is optimistic about future. Maximax implies the *maximisation of maximum payoff.* The optimistic decision maker locates the maximum payoff for each possible course of action. The maximum of these payoffs is identified and the corresponding course of action is selected. The optimal course of action in the above example, based on this criterion, is A_3. (Maximum out of maximum payoff's is 52 for A_3 (Maximax criterion).

(b) On the basis of regret table

Regret Criterion

This criterion focuses upon the regret that the decision maker might face from selecting a particular course of action. Regret is defined as the difference between the best payoff we could have realised, if we know which state of nature was going to occur, and the actual realised payoff. This difference, as such measures the magnitude of the loss incurred by not selecting the best alternative, is also known *opportunity loss* or the *opportunity cost*.

The regret criterion is based upon the minimax principle, *i.e.,* the decision maker tries to minimise the maximum regrets from different actions. Thus, the decision maker selects the maximum regret for each of the actions and out of these the action which corresponds to the minimum regret is regarded as optimal.

For each action maximum regret is found out and find minimum of these maximum values. The action corresponding to this minimum is the action to be taken on the basis of minimax regret criterion. The regret table of example 2 is reproduced below.

	A_1	A_2	A_3	A_4
S_1	0	35	150	325
S_2	40	0	40	140
S_3	100	10	0	50
maximum regret	100	35	150	325

↑

Minimum out of maximum (Minimax value)

This minimax value of regret table is 35 corresponding to action A_2. Thus action A_2 is recommended on the basis of this criteria.

Thus under uncertainty a rational decision maker will use Maximin criteria on payoff's and minimax criteria on regret (*O.L.*) values to decide upon optimal course of action.

Example 4. *A baker produces a certain type of special pastry at a total average cost of ₹ 3 and sells it at a price of ₹ 5. This pastry is produced over the weekend and is sold during the following week; such pastry being produced but not sold during a week's time are totally spoiled and have to be thrown away. According to past experience the weekly demand for these pastries is never less than 78 or greater than 80. You are required to formulate action space, payoff table and loss table and find optimal action in each case.*

Solution. It is clear from the problem given that the manufacturer will not produce less than 78 and more than 80 pastries. Thus there are three courses of action open to him.

a_1 = produce 78 pastries

a_2 = produce 79 pastries

a_3 = produce 80 pastries

Thus the action space is A (a_1, a_2, a_3).

The state of nature is the weekly demand for pastries. There are three possible states of nature, *i.e.*,

s_1 = demand is 78 pastries

s_2 = demand is 79 pastries

s_3 = demand is 80 pastries

The uncertainty element in the problem is the weekly demand. The bakery profits are conditioned by the weekly demand. Cell values of payoff table are computed as follows :

Let supply be m units and demand be n units. If $n \geq m$, all m units are sold and each units gives a profit of (5 – 3) = ₹ 2 and profit in that case is $2m$.

If $m > n$ then n units are sold to give a profit of $2n$ and $(m - n)$ are left which result in a loss of $3(m - n)$. Thus net profit in this case is $2n - 3(m - n)$.

Let $P(m, n)$ indicates profit when supply is m units and demand is n units then

$$P(m, n) = \begin{cases} 2m & m \leq n \\ 2n - 3(m - n) & \text{when } m > n \end{cases}$$

Thus $P(79, 80) = 2(79) = 158 \quad (\text{as } m \leq n)$

$P(80, 79) = 2(79) - 3(80 - 79) = 155 \quad [\text{as } m > n]$

Thus payoff matrix is

Action Supply / State of nature = Demand	a_1	a_2	a_3
	78	79	80
S_1 (78)	156	153	150
S_2 (79)	156	158	155
S_3 (80)	156	158	160
Minimum payoff	156	153	150

Using maximin criteria optimal action is A_1 that he should have supply of 78 units.

Loss table is obtained by subtracting each payoff under one event from the maximum payoff of that event. The loss table corresponding to the given payoff is given below.

Action Supply / State of nature = Supply	a_1	a_2	a_3
	78	79	80
S_1 (78)	156 – 156 = 0	156 – 153 = 3	156 – 150 = 6
S_2 (79)	158 – 156 = 2	158 – 158 = 0	158 – 155 = 3
S_3 (80)	160 – 156 = 4	160 – 158 = 2	160 – 160 = 0
maximum regret	4	3 ↑ minimum	6

Thus optimal action on the basis of minimax regret is A_2 *i.e.,* he should have supply of 79 units.

16.3.2 Decision Making Under Risk

In case of decision making under uncertainty the probabilities of occurrence of various states of nature are not known. When these probabilities are known or can be estimated, the choice of an optimal action, based on these probabilities, is termed as decision making under risk.

The choice of an optimal action is *an action with maximum Expected Monetary Value (EMV) or minimum Expected Opportunity Loss (EOl) or Regret.*

It may be pointed out that sometimes a distinction is made between decision-making under "risk" and decision-making under *"uncertainty'*. When probabilities of state of nature is unknown, but objective or empirical data is available so that the decision-maker can use these data to assign probabilities to the various states of nature the procedure is generally referred to as decision-making under 'risk'.

Example 4. *The payoffs (in ₹) of three Acts A_1, A_2 and A_3 and the possible states of nature S_1, S_2, and S_3 are given below :*

Acts → *State of nature ↓*	A_1	A_2	A_3
S_1	– 20	– 50	200
S_2	200	– 100	– 50
S_3	400	600	300

The probabilities of the states of nature are 0.3, 0.4 and 0.3 respectively. Determine the optimal act using payoff and regret tables.

Solution.

Computation of Expected Monetary Value

	S_1	S_2	S_3	
$P(S)$	0.3	0.4	0.3	$EMV = \Sigma X\, P(X)$
A_1	– 20	200	400	$-20 \times 0.3 + 200 \times 0.4 + 400 \times 0.3 = 194$ (Maximum EMV)
A_2	– 50	– 100	600	$-50 \times 0.3 + 100 \times 0.4 + 600 \times 0.3 = 125$
A_3	200	– 50	300	$200 \times 0.3 - 50 \times 0.4 + 300 \times 0.3 = 130$

From the above table, we find that the act A_1 is optimal.

The problem can alternatively be attempted by finding minimum EOL, as shown below:

Computation of Expected Opportunity Loss

	S_1	S_2	S_3	
$P(S)$	0.3	0.4	0.3	*EOL*
A_1	220	0	200	$220 \times 0.3 + 0 \times 0.4 + 200 \times 0.3 = 126$ (Minimum *E.O.L.*)
A_2	250	300	0	$250 \times 0.3 + 300 \times 0.4 + 0 \times 0.3 = 195$
A_3	0	250	300	0×0.3 $250 \times 0.4 + 300 \times 0.3 = 190$

This indicates that the optimal act is again A_1.

[Expectation of a random variable is discussed in Chapter 12. $E(x) = \Sigma x\ P(x)$]

16.3.3 Decision Under Laplace Principle

Laplace Principle

Laplace Principle is based on the fact that if we are uncertain about the happening of the various events, then equal probability may be assigned to each event. Under this assumption, the expected value of Pay-off for each act (strategy) is determined and the act with the highest expected value is adopted. If the Pay-offs are in terms of costs, we choose the strategy with the lowest expected cost. Under this principle the expected monetary value (*E.M.V.*) of any act is exactly the average of all payoffs for that act.

Example 5. A *person wants to invest in one of three alternative investment plans : stocks, bonds or a savings account. It is assumed that the person wishes to invest all of the funds in one plan. The conditional Pay-offs of the investments are based on three potential economic conditions : accelerated, normal or slow growth. The Pay-off matrix is given below.*

Alternative	*Economic Conditions (States of Nature)*		
Investment	*Accelerated Growth*	*NormalGrowth*	*Slow Growth*
Stocks	₹ 10,000	₹ 6,500	– ₹ 4,000
Bonds	8,000	6,000	1,000
Savings	5,000	5,000	5,000

Determine the best investment plan using each of the following criteria :

(*i*) *Laplace* (*ii*) *Maximin* (*iii*) *Maximax*

[*ICWA Dec. 1997*]

Solution

(*i*) **Laplace criterion :**

$$\text{Average of stock} = \frac{1}{3}[10{,}000 + 6{,}500 + (-4{,}000)] = ₹\,4{,}167 \text{ (approx.)}$$

= Expected profit of stocks.

$$\text{Average of bonds} = \frac{1}{3}(8{,}000 + 6{,}000 + 1{,}000) = ₹\,5{,}000$$

= Expected profit of bonds.

Average of savings $= \frac{1}{3}(5{,}000 + 5{,}000 + 5{,}000) = ₹\,5{,}000$

= Expected profit of savings.

Since the expected profit for bonds and savings is the same, investment can be made either in bonds of in savings.

Note. In Laplace criteria, equal probabilities are attached to all states of nature.

(*ii*) **Maximin criterion :**

Investment	*Minimum Pay-offs (₹)*
Stocks	– 4,000
Bonds	1,000
Savings	5,000

Now maximum out of minimum is 5,000. Therefore, investment should be made in savings.

(*iii*) **Maximax criterion :**

Investment	*Maximum Pay-offs (₹)*
Stocks	10,000
Bonds	8,000
Savings	5,000

Now maximum of maximums is ₹ 10,000. So investment should be made in stock.

Example 7. *A company is trying to manufacture a new type of toy. The company is attempting to decide whether to bring out a full, partial or minimal product line. The company has three levels of product acceptance and has estimated their probability of occurrence. Management will make the decision on the basis of maximizing the expected profit from the first year of production. The relevant data are shown in the following table where first years profits in thousand rupees are given :*

Table 16.1 : The Pay-off Matrix

Act		*State of Nature →*	*Good*	*Fair*	*Poor*
Product Line		*Probability*	*0.2*	*0.4*	*0.4*
Full	A_1		*90*	*60*	*– 15*
Partial	A_2		*80*	*65*	*– 10*
Minimal	A_3		*60*	*50*	*0*

(*i*) *What is the optimum product line and its expected profit ?*

(*ii*) *What is the optimum value of expected opportunity loss and the optimum course of action?* *[I.C.W.A. (Intermediate), June 1998]*

Solution. Let us define the following acts :

A_1 : *Full product line,* A_2 : *Partial product line,* A_3 : *Minimal product line*

(*i*) To find the optimum product line, we'll use *EMV* criterion. We have

$$EMV(A_1) = 0.2 \times 90 + 0.4 \times 60 + 0.4 \times (-15) = 36$$
$$EMV(A_2) = 0.2 \times 80 + 0.4 \times 65 + 0.4 \times (-10) = 38$$
$$EMV(A_3) = 0.2 \times 60 + 0.4 \times 50 + 0.4 \times 0 = 32$$

Since *EMV* is maximum for Act A_2, therefore by the *EMV* criterion, the act A_2 : 'Partial Product Line' is the optimum act and its expected profit is

$$EMV(A_2) = 38 \text{ thousand rupees or ₹ } 38{,}000$$

(*ii*) To find the optimum value of expected opportunity loss, it is first necessary to find the opportunity loss table which is obtained by using the following two-step procedure :

(*a*) Find the maximum payoff for each state of nature. We have

maximum payoff (S_1: Good) = 90

maximum payoff (S_2: Fair) = 65

maximum payoff (S_3: Poor) = 0

(*b*) The opportunity loss table is constructed, column by column, by subtracting each value from the maximum value in its column. The resulting opportunity loss table in shown in table 16.2.

Table 16.2 : The Opportunity Loss Table

Act	State of Nature		
Product Line	S_1 : Good (0.2)	S_2 : *Fair* (0.4)	S_3 : *Poor* (0.4)
A_1 : *Full*	90 – 90 = 0	65 – 60 = 5	0 (– 15) = 15
A_2 : *Partial*	90 – 80 = 10	65 – 65 = 0	0 (– 10) = 10
A_3 : *Minimal*	90 – 60 = 30	65 – 50 = 15	0

$$EOL(A_1) = 0.2 \times 0 + 0.4 \times 5 + 0.4 \times 15 = 8$$
$$EOL(A_2) = 0.2 \times 10 + 0.4 \times 0 + 0.4 \times 10 = 6$$
$$EOL(A_3) = 0.2 \times 30 + 0.4 \times 15 + 0.4 \times 0 = 12$$

Since *EOL* is minimum for Act A_2, therefore by the *EOL* criterion, the act A_2: 'Partial Product Line', is the optimum act. The optimum value of expected opportunity loss is :

$$EMV(A_2) = 6 \text{ thousand rupees or ₹ } 6{,}000.$$

Note. The reader may note that the *EMV* criterion and the *EOL* criterion result in the same optimum act.

Example 8. *A manufacturing company is faced with the problem of choosing from four products to manufacture. The potential demand for each product may turn out to be good, satisfactory or poor. The probabilities estimated for each type of demand are given below.*

Probability of Type of Demand

Product	*Good*	*Satisfactory*	*Poor*
A	0.60	0.20	0.20
B	0.75	0.15	0.10
C	0.60	0.25	0.15
D	0.50	0.20	0.30

The estimated profit or loss under different states of demand in respect of each product may be taken as :

Product	₹	₹	₹
A	40,000	10,000	11,00
B	40,000	20,000	– 7,000
C	50,000	15,000	– 8,000
D	40,000	18,000	15,000

Prepare the expected value table and advise the company about the choice of the product to manufacture. [*Delhi Univ. B.Com.* (*H*) *2009*]

Solution. The expected value table is prepared as shown in Table 16.3.

Table 16.3 : Expected Value Table

Product	A			B			C			D		
Type of Demand	*Profits* (*'000 ₹*) *Col. 1*	*Prob. Col. 2*	*Col.1 × Col. 2 Col. 3*	*Profits* (*'000 ₹*) *Col. 4*	*Prob. Col. 5*	*Col. 4 × Col. 5 Col. 6*	*Profits* (*'000 ₹*) *Col. 7*	*Prob. Col. 8*	*Col. 7 × Col. 8 Col. 9*	*Profits Col. 10*	*Prob* (*'000 ₹*) *Col. 11*	*Col. 10 × Col. 11 Col. 12*
Good	40	0.60	24	40	0.75	30	50	0.60	30	40	0.50	20
Satis-factory	10	0.20	2	20	0.15	3	15	0.25	3.75	18	0.20	3.6
Poor	1	0.20	0.2	– 7	0.10	– 0.7	– 8	0.15	– 1.20	15	0.30	4.5
EMV			26.2			32.3			32.55			28.1

Since *EMV* is maximum for 'Product *C*, hence company is advised to manufacture 'Product *C*'.

Example 9. *A fruit wholeseller buys cases of strawberries for ₹ 200 each and sells them for ₹ 500 each. Any case left would at the end of the day have a salvage value of only ₹ 50. An analysis of past sales record reveals the following probability distribution for the daily number of cases sold :*

Daily Sales :	10	11	12	13
Probability :	0.15	0.25	0.40	0.20

What is the optimum stock action for the fruit seller? [*Delhi Univ. B.Com.* (*H*) *2005*]

Solution. Here, the number of cases of strawberries purchased (or stocked) daily is an *act* and the daily demand of the cases is an *event, i.e.*, state of nature. Since the cost price of each case of strawberry is ₹ 200 and its selling price is ₹ 500, the fruit seller makes a profit of ₹ 300 on each case sold. However, if a case is not sold, it has a salvage value of ₹ 50 at the end of the day and hence the fruit seller would incur a loss of ₹ (200 – 50) or ₹ 150 on each case unsold at the end of the day.

Conditional Payoffs

Let m = no. of cases bought (or stoked) by the fruit seller

n = no. of cases demanded per day

Then the fruit seller profit, *i.e.*, conditional payoff $P(m, n)$ can be obtained as explained below :

Case 1. *$n \geq m$, i.e., the demand is more than the stock*

In this case, all the stocked costs are sold out and hence the conditional payoff is given by

$$P(m, n) = ₹\ 300\ m, \quad n \geq m \qquad \ldots(1)$$

Case 2. *$n \geq m$, i.e., the demand is less than the stock*

In this case only n cases of strawberries are sold out and the remaining $(m, - n)$ cases are left unsold. Hence, at the end of the day, the fruit seller's profit is given by

$$P(m, n) = ₹\ [300n - 150\ (m - n)] \quad n < m \qquad \ldots(2)$$

Using (3), we can obtain the payoffs resulting from all possible stock/demand combinations. The payoffs are shown in Table below.

The Payoff Table

Event (No. of cases demanded)	Act (No of cases stocked)			
	10	11	12	13
10	3000	2850	2700	2550
11	3000	3300	3150	3000
12	3000	3300	3600	3450
13	3000	3300	3600	3900

(*i*) To determine the optimum stock action, we apply the expected payoff criterion. The expected payoff (or expected monetary value) for any stock action is given by

EMV (for any stock action) = Σ(Probability × Conditional payoff)

the summation being taken over a particular state of nature.

$\therefore$ *EMV* (Act : 10 cases) = ₹ [0.15 × 3000 + 0.25 × 3000 + 0.40 × 3000 + 0.20 × 3000]
= ₹ 3000

EMV (Act : 11 cases) = ₹ [0.15 × 2850 + 0.25 × 3300 + 0.40 × 3300 + 0.20 × 3000]
= ₹ 3232.50

EMV (Act : 12 cases) = ₹ [0.15 × 2700 + 0.25 × 3150 + 0.40 × 3600 + 0.20 × 3600]
= ₹ 3352.50

EMV (Act : 13 cases) = ₹ [0.15 × 2550 + 0.25 × 3000 + 0.40 × 3450 + 0.20 × 3900]
= ₹ 3292.50

Since *EMV* is maximum for the act "Stock 12 cases", therefore according to the *EMV* criterion, the optimum act is "stock 12 cases". Thus the fruit seller should stock 12 cases of strawberries each day in order to get the best expected daily profit which is ₹ 3352.50.

16.4. DECISION UNDER PERFECT INFORMATION

(*a*) On the Basis of Payoff's

The optimal stock action by the fruit seller in the preceding example was to stock 12 cases each day in order to get the highest possible average daily profit under the conditions given. This stock action was obtained under uncertainty using the expected payoff criterion.

Now suppose that the fruit seller in the preceding Example 9 could remove all uncertainty from his problem by obtaining complete and accurate information about the future, called the *perfect* information. This does not mean that sales would not vary from 10 to 13 cases per day. Sales would still be 10 cases per day 15 percent of the time, 11 cases 25 percent of the time, 12 cases 40 percent of the time, and 13 cases 20 percent of the time. However, with perfect information, the retailer would know in advance how many cases were going to be called for a particular day.

Under these circumstances, the fruit seller would stock today the exact number of cases buyers will want tomorrow. When sales were going to be 10 cases, the fruit seller would stock exactly 10 cases, thus realizing a profit of ₹ 3000. For sales of 11 cases, the fruit seller would stock 11 cases and realize a profit of ₹ 3300, and so on.

Table shows the conditional profit table with perfect information that is applicable to the fruit seller's problem.

Conditional Profit Table with Perfect Information

Event	Act (*No. of cases stocked)*			
(No. of cases demanded)	10	11	12	13
10 (0.15)	3000	–	–	–
11 (0.25)	–	3300	–	–
12 (0.40)	–	–	3600	–
13 (0.20)	–	–	–	3900

Knowing the size of the marked in advance for a particular day, the fruit seller chooses the stock action that will maximize his profits.

We can now compute the expected profit with perfect information (*EPPI*), also referred to as expected value under perfect information (*E.V.P.I.*). To find the expected profit with perfect information, we multiply the conditional profit that is maximum for each state of nature by the probability of the state and then summing these products. Symbolically,

EPPI = Σ (Conditional profit that is maximum for a state × Probability of the state), the summation being taken over different states of nature.

In our example, the fruit seller expected profit with perfect information is:

$$EPPI = 0.15 \times 3000 + 0.25 \times 3300 + 0.40 \times 3600 + 0.20 \times 3900 = ₹\ 3495$$

This means that the fruit seller can earn average daily profits of ₹ 3495 if he has perfect information about the future. However, his best expected daily profit without the perfect information was ₹ 3352.50 as calculated earlier in Example 9. The difference between these expected values is called the *expected value of perfect information*. Symbolically,

$$EVPI = EPPI - \max EMV$$

The expected values of perfect information in the case of fruit seller is :

$$EVPI = ₹\ 3495 - ₹\ 3352.50 = ₹\ 142.40$$

The *EVPI* of ₹ 142.50 is the maximum amount the fruit seller would be willing to pay, per day, for a perfect predictor, because that is the maximum amount by which he can increase his expected daily profit.

(*b*) On the basis of Opportunity Loss

In this case we minimise *O.L.* on the basis of perfect information and for a given state of nature the best act will give *O.L.* = 0 (for all states of nature). Hence expected *O.L.* under perfect information = *O*. As such gain due to perfect information will be minimum *E.O.L.* (as we are able to reduce minimum *EOL* to *O* under perfect information.)

As such *EVPI* (expected value of perfect information) = gain due to perfect information = Minimum *EOL*.

Example 10. *Payoffs of three acts A, B and C and state of nature X, Y and Z are given below:*

Payoff (in ₹)

State of Nature	*Acts*		
	A	*B*	*C*
X	– 20	– 50	200
Y	200	– 100	– 50
Z	400	600	300

The probabilities of the states of nature are 0.3, 0.4 and 0.3. Calculate (*i*) *EMV* and (*ii*) *EVPI.*

Solution. (*i*) Calculating *EMV*

***EMV* Table**

State of Nature	*Probability*	*Acts*		
		A	*B*	*C*
X	0.3	– 20 × 0.3 = – 6	– 50 × 0.3 = – 15	200 × 0.3 = 60
Y	0.4	200 × 0.4 = 80	– 100 × 0.4 = – 40	– 50 × 0.4 = – 20
Z	0.3	400 × 0.3 = 120	600 × 0.3 = 180	300 × 0.3 = 90
	E.M.V.	194	125	130

The highest *EMV* is ₹ 194; therefore Act *A* is optimal.

(ii) *EPPI* = Σ (Maximum payoff of each state of nature × corresponding Probability of that state of nature)

(Max. *X*) *P* (*x*)

State of Nature *X* : 200 × 0.3 = 60
State of Nature Y : 200 × 0.4 = 80
State of Nature *Z*: 600 × 0.3 = 180
EPPI ₹ 320

Therefore, *EVPI* = *EPPI* – Maximum *EMV*
= ₹ 320 – ₹ 194 = ₹ 126.

Example 11. *Miss A is planning to attend a convention in Honolulu and she must send reservation for her room immediately. The convention is so large that the activities are held partly in Hotel X and partly in Hotel Y and Miss A does not know whether the particular session she wants attend will be held at Hotel X or Hotel Y. She is planning to stay only one night which would cost her ₹ 6,600 at Hotel X and ₹ 6,240 at Hotel Y and it will cost her extra ₹ 600 for taxi fare if she stays at the wrong hotel.*

(*A*) *Miss A feels that odds are 3 : 1 that the Session she wants to attend will be held at Hotel X. Where should she make her reservation so as to minimise her expected cost.*

(*B*) *If she feels that the odds are 1 : 5 that the Session she wants to attend will be held at Hotel X, where should she make her reservation so as to minimise her expected cost.*

Solution. There are two actions.

$A_1 \rightarrow$ She stays at *X*, $A_2 \rightarrow$ she stays at *Y* . There are two states of nature (1) S_1 session — will be held at *X* (2) S_2 – session will be held at *Y*.

(A) Payoff table.

If she stays at *X* (1) session is at *X* cost of session is 6600 (2) session is at *Y* cost of session is 6600 + 600 = 7200.

Same way if stays at *Y* costs are 6240 + 600 (when session at *X*) and 6240 (when session is at *Y*.

Payoff Table (Cost to be paid)

P(s)	Acts (Stay) / Sates of Nature (session)	$A_1(X)$	$A_2(Y)$
$\frac{3}{4}$	S_1 (*X*)	6600	6840
$\frac{1}{4}$	S_1 (*Y*)	7200	6240
	EMV (Cost)	6750 $\left[6600 \times \frac{3}{4} + 7240\left(\frac{1}{4}\right)\right]$	6690 $\left[6840 \times \frac{3}{4} + 6240 \times \frac{1}{4}\right]$

Minimum *EMV* (cost in this case) = 6690 at *X*.

Thus she should try reservation at *X* first.

(B) Payoff (cost) in this case are shown as follows :

Payoffs (Costs)

Sates of Nature (session)	*Acts (Stay)*	*Pay offs (Costs)* *P(s)*	$A_1(X)$	$A_2(Y)$
S_1	*X*	$\frac{1}{6}$	6600	6840
S_2	*Y*	$\frac{5}{6}$	7200	6240
		EMV	7100 $6600 \times \frac{1}{6} + 7240 \times \frac{5}{6}$	6340 $6840 \times \frac{1}{6} + 62040 \times \frac{5}{6}$

Thus she should try reservation at *Y* first.

Example 12. *Each unit of a product produced and sold yields a profit of ₹ 50 but a unit produced not sold results in a loss of ₹ 30. The probability distribution of the number of units demanded is as follows :*

No. of units demanded	0	1	2	3	4
Probability	0.20	0.20	0.25	0.30	0.05

How many unit be produced to maximise the expected profits ? Also calculate EVPI.

[*D.U. B.Com. (Hons.) 2002*]

Solution. Given : Profit for units produced and sold = ₹ 50

Loss for units produced and not sold = ₹ 30

If m be supply and n be demand and $P(m, n)$ be the profit when supply is m and demand is n

Thus $P(m, n) = \begin{cases} 50\,m \text{ when } m \le n \text{ (all } m \text{ units are sold)} \\ 50\,n - 30\,(m - n) \text{ when } m > n \text{ then } n \text{ units are sold and } (m - n) \text{ are unsold.} \end{cases}$

Payoff Table

Demand ↓	Production (acts)										
		A_1		A_2		A_3		A_4		A_5	
State of Nature (S)	*P* (*S*)	0 *X*	*X P* (*S*)	1 *X*	*X P* (*S*)	2. *X*	*X P* (*S*)	3 *X*	*X P* (*S*)	4 *X*	*X P* (*S*)
$0 - S_1$	0.2	0	0	– 30	– 6	– 60	– 12	– 90	– 18	– 120	– 24
$1 - S_2$	0.2	0	0	50	10	20	4	–10	– 2	– 40	– 8
$2 - S_3$	0.25	0	0	50	12.50	100	25	70	17.50	40	10
$3 - S_4$	0.3	0	0	50	15.00	100	30	150	45	120	36
$4 - S_5$	0.05	0	0	50	2.50	100	5	150	7.50	200	10
EMV			0		34		52		50		24

Maximum payoff is for A_3 (production = 2 units) as optimal course of action is to produce 2 units.

***EPPI* Table**

Demand	*Probability P(X)*	*Max. Pay-off*	*XP (X)*
0 —— S_1	0.2	0	$0 \times 0.2 = 0$
1 —— S_2	0.2	50	$50 \times 0.2 = 10$
2 —— S_3	0.25	100	$100 \times 0.25 = 25$
3 —— S_4	0.30	150	$150 \times 0.30 = 45$
4 —— S_5	0.05	200	$200 \times 0.05 = 10$
Total			*EPPI* = 90

∴ EVPI = 90 – 52 = ₹ 38.

Example 13. *A retailer wants to determine the number of units to be stocked, during a particular season. Given that*

(*a*) *Cost price of the production in a season is ₹ 12.*

(*b*) *Selling price of the production in a season ₹ 18.*

(*c*) *Cost of holding an item beyond the season ₹ 1.*

(*d*) *Bargain price after the season is ₹ 9.*

(*e*) *The probability distribution of demand based on past data is as follows:*

Units Demanded :	7	8	9	10	11
Probability :	0.2	0.2	0.25	0.15	0.2

Solution. When Demand = Supply, Profit = ₹ 18 – ₹ 12 = ₹ 6, Loss = 12 + 1 – 9 = ₹ 4 (cost + holding cost – bargain price)

Thus $P(m, n)$ = Profit when supply is m and demand is n

$= 6\,m \quad m \le n$ (as all m units will be sold)

$= 6\,n - 4\,(m - n)$ when $m > n$, n will be sold and $(m - n)$ be unsold

Payoff Table

State of nature		Probability	Supply (m) 7	8	9	10	11
Demand (n)	7	0.20	(7 × 6) = 42	(7 × 6) – 4 = 38	(7 × 6) – (9 – 7) × 4 = 34	(7 × 6) – (10 – 7) × 4 = 30	(7 × 6) – (11 – 7) × 4 = 26
	8	0.20	42	8 × 6 = 48	(8 × 6) – (9 – 8) × 4 = 44	(8 × 6) – (10 – 8) × 4 = 40	(8 × 6) – (11 – 8) × 4 = 36
	9	0.25	42	48	(9 × 6) = 54	(9 × 6) – (10 – 9) × 4 = 50	(9 × 6) – (11 – 9) × 4 = 46
	10	0.15	42	48	54	10 × 6 = 60	(10 × 6) – (11 – 10) × 4 = 56
	11	0.20	42	48	54	60	11 × 6 = 66

E.M.V. for different acts.

Act of stocking 7 units: 42 × 0.2 + 42 × 0.2 + 42 × 0.25 + 42 × 0.15 + 42 × 0.20 = ₹ 42.

Act of stocking 8 units: 38 × 0.2 + 48 × 0.2 + 48 × 0.25 + 48 × 0.15 + 48 × 0.20 = ₹ 46.

Act of stocking 9 units: 34 × 0.2 + 44 × 0.2 + 54 × 0.25 + 54 × 0.15 + 54 × 0.20 = ₹ 48.

Act of stocking 10 units: 30 × 0.2 + 40 × 0.2 + 50 × 0.25 + 60 × 0.15 + 60 × 0.20 = ₹ 47.5.

Act of stocking 11 units: 26 × 0.2 + 36 × 0.2 + 46 × 0.25 + 56 × 0.15 + 66 × 0.20 = ₹ 45.5.

Since, *EMV* is highest when 9 units are stocked, the retailer should maintain 9 units.

16.4.1. Cost of Uncertainty

This concept is similar to the concept of *EVPI*. Cost of uncertainty is the difference between the *EOL* of optimal action and the *EOL* under perfect information.

Given the perfect information, the decision maker would select an action with minimum opportunity loss under each state of nature. Since minimum opportunity loss under each state of nature zero, therefore,

EOL under certainty = 0× 0.3 + 0 × 0.4 + 0 × 0.3 = 0.

Thus, the cost of uncertainty = *EOL* of optimal action = *EVPI*

Example 14. *A group of students raise money each year by selling souvenirs outside the stadium of a cricket match between teams A and B. They can buy any of three different types of souvenirs from a supplier. Their sales are mostly dependent on which team wins the match. A conditional payoff (in ₹) table is as under:*

Types of Souvenir →	*I*	*II*	*III*
Team A wins	1200	800	300
Team B wins	250	700	1100

(i) Construct the opportunity loss table.

(ii) Which type of souvenir should the students buy if the probability of team A's winning is 0.6?

(iii) Compute the cost of uncertainty.

Solution.

(*i*) The opportunity Loss Table

Actions →	*Types of Souvenir bought (acts)*		
Events ↓	*I*	*II*	*III*
Team A wins	0	400	900
Team B wins	850	400	0

(*ii*) *EOL* of buying type *I* Souvenir $= 0 \times 0.6 + 850 \times 0.4 = 340$

EOL of buying type *II* Souvenir $= 400 \times 0.6 + 400 \times 0.4 = 400$

EOL of buying type *III* Souvenir $= 900 \times 0.6 + 0 \times 0.4 = 540$

Since the *EOL* of buying Type *I* Souvenir is minimum, the optimal decision is to buy Type I Souvenir.

(*iii*) Cost of uncertainty = *EOL* of optimal action = ₹ 340

16.5. DECISION TREES

A **decision tree** is a graphic model of a decision problem – whereby the sequence of alternate courses of action, states of nature, likely outcomes of various action/state combinations along with the conditional monetary values attached to these outcomes are depicted as if they are branches and sub-branches of a 'horizontal tree'. Decision tree provide a useful tool in making decisions concerning investments, project management, personnel and new-product strategies. These trees are especially helpful when a sequence of decisions are required to be made at different stages.

Constructing Decision Tree

A decision tree is constructed starting from left and moving towards right. It is very important to maintain the proper time sequence when constructing a decision tree. The time in a decision tree flows from left to right. The following standard symbols are used to construct a decision tree.

Standard symbols are used drawing a decision tree

(*i*) A square (□) is used to represent a *decision point* or *decision node* at which the decision maker has to decide about one of the various acts or alternatives available to him.

(*ii*) Each act or alternative is shown as a line, representing a branch of the tree emanating from the square.

(*iii*) A *circle* (○) is used to represent a *chance event* or *chance node* at which various events or states of nature are represented by lines, which depict the sub-branches of the tree emanating from the circle.

(*iv*) Each branch of the tree (corresponding to each act or strategy) has as many sub-branches as the number of events or states of nature.

(*v*) Along the branches/sub-branches are also shown the probabilities of various states of nature and the payoffs or each combination (S_i, A_j) ; $i = 1, 2 \ldots m; j = 1, 2, \ldots, n$ along with the *EMV* or *EOL* for each act.

(*vi*) As a branch can sub-branch again, we obtain a tree like structure which represents the various steps in a decision problem.

Illustration. The problem of carrying an umbrella on any day in rainy season can be represented diagrammatically by a decision tree given below.

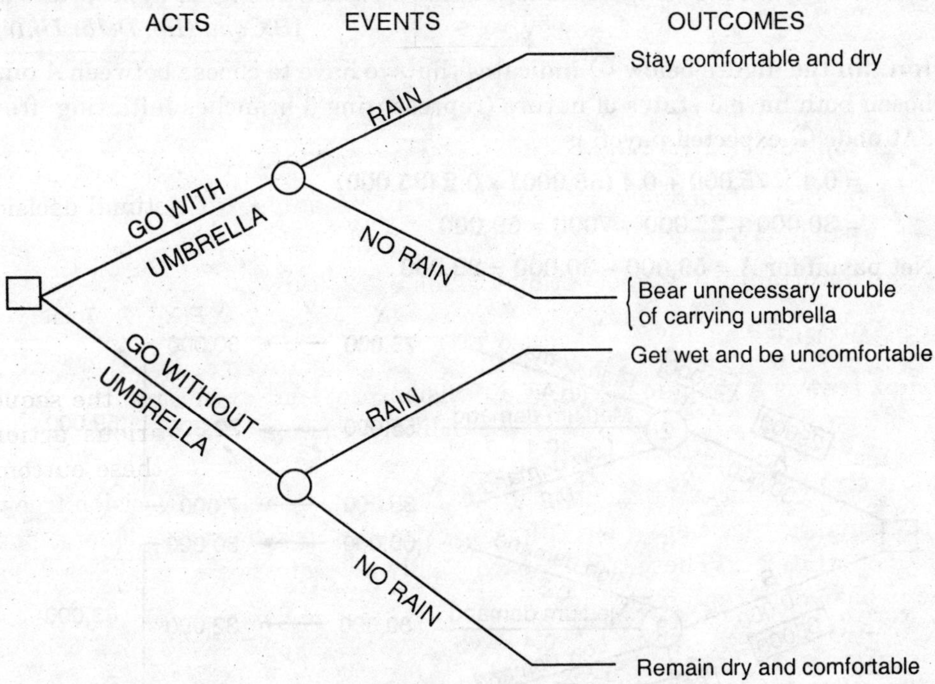

Figure 16.1 : Decision Tree

Analyzing a Decision Tree : Roll-back Technique

A decision tree can be analyzed using a technique, called the **roll-back technique.** The procedure in this technique starts from the rightmost column of the tree (*i.e.,* from the top of the tree) and moves back to the left one column at a time to the root of the tree. Thus in this roll-back technique, by working from right to left, we make the future decisions first and then roll them back to become part of the earlier decisions. There are two rules directing this roll back procedure :

1. If we are analyzing a chance node (circle), we calculate its expected payoff by multiplying the expected payoff of each branch emanating from the node by the probability of that branch and then summing these products.
2. If we are analyzing a decision node (square), we compare the expected payoff of its branches and choose the alternative whose branch has the largest expected payoff. We record the choice on the decision tree by inserting a double dash as a barrier to those branches which have been rejected.

Example 15. *A businessman has two independent investments A and B available to him but he lacks the capital to undertake both of them simultaneously. Investment A requires capital of ₹ 30,000 and investment B ₹ 50,000. Market survey shows: high, medium and low demands with corresponding probabilities of 0.4, 0.4 and 0.2 respectively in case of investment A and 0.3 , 0.4 and 0.3 for investment B. Returns from investment A are ₹ 75,000, ₹ 55,000 and ₹ 35,000 and corresponding figures for investment B are likely to be ₹ 100,000, ₹ 80,000 and ₹ 70,000 for high, medium and low demand respectively.*

What decision should the company take? Decide by constructing an appropriate decision-tree. [B.Com. (H), Delhi Univ., 2007]

Solution. In the figure below ① indicates that we have to choose between A and B, if A or B is chosen both have 3 states of nature (representing 3 branches initiating from nodes ② and ③. At node ② expected payoff is

$$= 0.4 \times 75{,}000 + 0.4\,(55{,}000) + 0.2\,(35{,}000)$$

$$= 30{,}000 + 22{,}000 + 7000 = 59{,}000$$

Thus Net payoff for A = 59,000 – 30,000 = 29,000

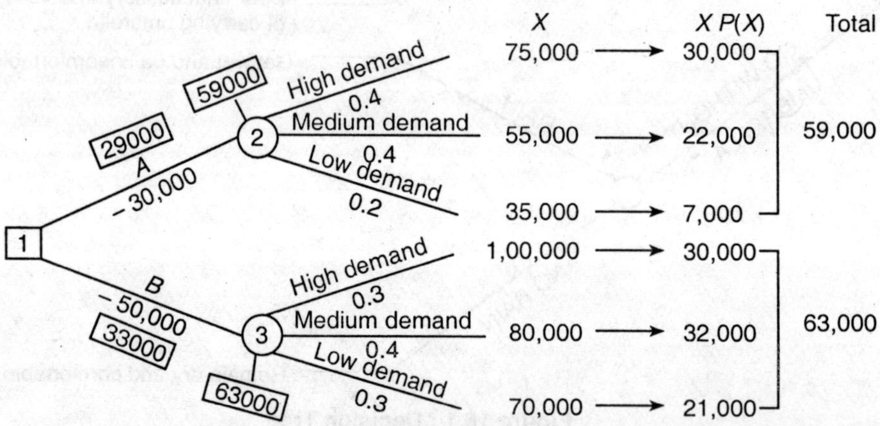

Expected net profit for investment A $= 0.4 \times 75{,}000 + 0.4 \times 55{,}000 + 0.2 \times 35{,}000 - 30{,}000$
= ₹ 29,000

Expected net profit for investment B $= 0.3 \times 100{,}000 + 0.4 \times 80{,}000 + 0.3 \times 70{,}000 - 50{,}000$
= ₹ 33,000

Since the expected net profit for investment B is more than A, the businessman should invest in B.

Example 16. *A Finance Manager is considering drilling a well. In the past, only 70% of wells drilled were successful at 20 metres depth in that area: Morever on finding no water at 20 metres, some persons in that area drilled it further upto 25 metres but only 20% struck water at that level. The prevailing cost of drilling is ₹ 500 per metre. The Finance Manager estimated that in case he does not get water in his own well, he will have to pay ₹ 15000 to buy water from outside for the same period of getting water from the well. The following decisions are considered :*

(*i*) Do not drill any well.

(*ii*) *Drill upto 20 metres, and*

(*iii*) *If no water if found at 20 metres, drill-further upto 25 metres.*

Draw an appropriate decision tree and determine the Finance Manager's optimal strategy.

Solution. The decision tree based on the given information has been depicted in figure.

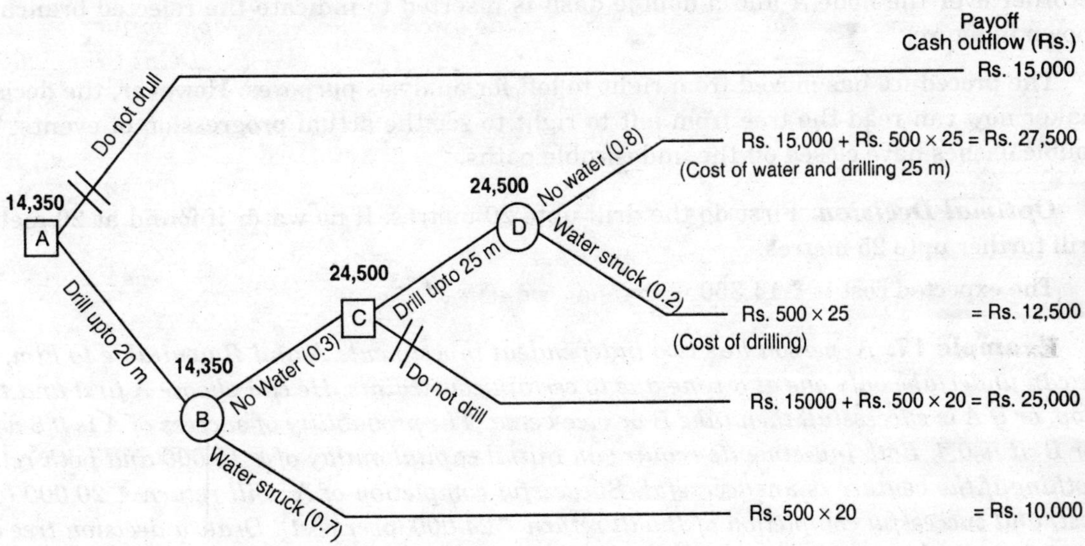

1st decision square is *A* and second one is at *C*. According roll back technique we have to take decision at *C* (whether to drill further 25 metres).

We begin by considering the rightmost node, namely, the chance node *D* and calculate its expected cost by multiplying the cost of each branch by the probability of that branch and then summing these products. Thus expected cost for node *D* is calculated as :

$$(\text{node } D) = 0.8 \times 27{,}500 + 0.2 \times 12{,}500 = ₹\ 24{,}500$$

This expected cost then is placed above this node *D*, as shown in figure. Next, we move one column to the left, which consists of a decision node *C*. For decision node *C*, compare the expected cost of its branches and choose the alternative whose branch has the smallest expected cost. Thus, at node *C*,

Drill alternative has expected cost = ₹ 24,500

Do not drill alternative has expected cost = ₹ 25,000

∵ 24,500 < 25,000 so choose the drill alternative.

The expected payoff of this chosen alternative is recorded in boldface over its decision node *C*, as shown in figure. The chosen alternative is also indicated by inserting a double dash for the rejected branch.

Next, moving one more column to the left brings us to chance node *B*. The expected payoff for node *B* is:

EC. (node *B*) = 0.3 × 24,500 + 0.7 × 10,000 = ₹ 14,350,

which is recorded over this node in Fig.

Finally, we move left to node A, a decision node. For this node, we find that

Drill alternative has $E.C.$ = ₹ 14,350

Do not drill alternative has $E.C.$ = ₹ 15,000

Since 14,350 < 15,000, so choose drill alternative. This expected cost of ₹ 14,350 is recorder over the node A and a double dash is inserted to indicate the rejected branch, as shown in figure.

The procedure has moved from right to left for analysis purposes. However, the decision maker now can read the tree from left to right to see the actual progression of events. The double dashes have closed off the undesirable paths.

Optimal Decision. First do the drill upto 20 metres. If no water if found at 20 metres, drill further upto 25 metres.

The expected cost is ₹ 14,350

Example 17. *A person has two independent investments A and B available to him, but he can undertake only one at a time due to certain constraints. He can choose A first and then stop, or if A is successful, then take B or vice-versa. The probability of success of A is 0.6 while for B it is 0.4. Both investments require an initial capital outlay of ₹ 10,000 and both return nothing if the venture is unsuccessful. Successful completion of A will return ₹ 20,000 (over cost) and successful completion of B will return ₹ 24,000 (over cost). Draw a decision-tree and determine the best strategy.* [B.Com. (H), Delhi Univ., 2007]

Solution.

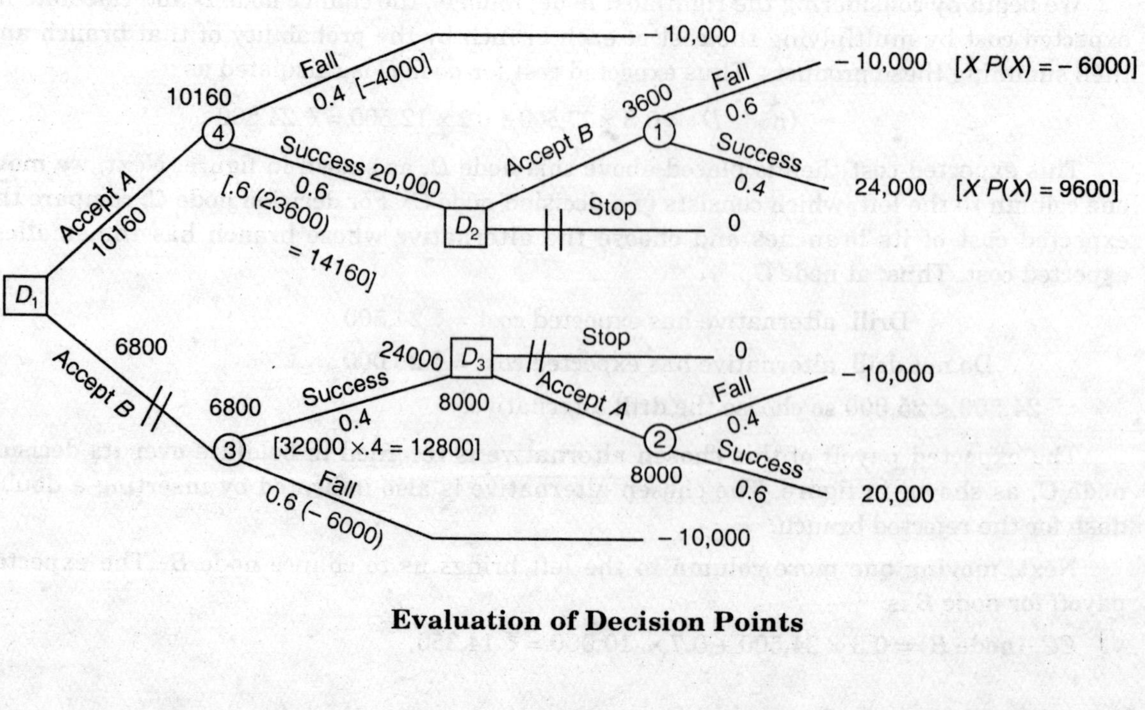

Evaluation of Decision Points

	Decision Point	*Outcome*	*Probability*	*Conditional values*	*Expected value*
D_3	(*i*) Accept *A* (2)	Success Failure	0.6 0.4	20,000 – 10,000	12,000 – 4,000 8,000
	(*ii*) Stop	—	—	—	—
D_2	(*i*) Accept *B* (1)	Success Failure	0.4 0.6	24,000 – 10,000	9,600 – 6,000 3,600
	(*ii*) Stop	—	—	—	—
D_1	(*i*) Accept *A*, then *B*	Success Failure	0.6 0.4	20,000 + 3,600 – 10,000	14,160 – 4,000 10,160
	(*ii*) Accept *B*, then *A*	Success Failure	0.4 0.6	24,000 +8,000 –10,000	12,800 – 6,000 6,800

EMV is highest when he accepts investment *A* and on success invests money in *B*.

Example 18. *A manufacture of leather goods must decide whether to expand his plant capacity now or wait at least another year. His advisors tell him that if he expands now and economic conditions remained good, there will be a profit of ₹ 1,64,000 during the next year. If he expands now and there is recession, there will be a loss of ₹ 40,000. If he waits at least another year and economic conditions remain good, there will be a profit of ₹ 80,000 and if he waits at least another year and there is a recession, there will be a small profit of ₹ 8,000. What should the manufacturer decide to do if he wants to minimise the expected loss during the next year and he feels that the odds are 2 : 1 that there will be recession.*

Solution.

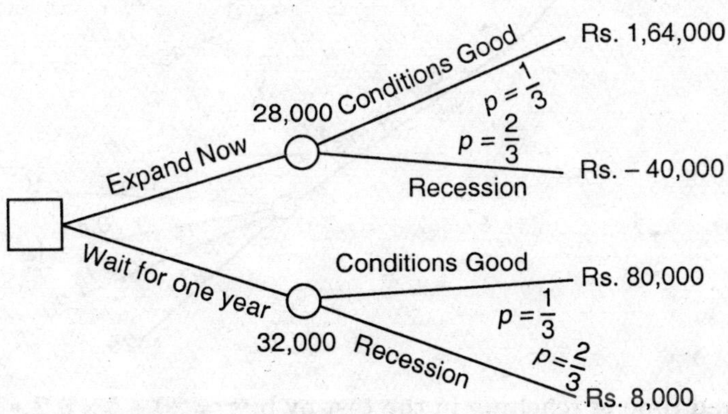

$$\text{Expected profit if expanded now} = 1{,}64{,}000 \times \frac{1}{3} - 40{,}000 \times \frac{2}{3} = ₹\ 28{,}000$$

$$\text{Expected profit if waited for one year} = \frac{80{,}000}{3} + \frac{8{,}000 \times 2}{3} = ₹\ 32{,}000$$

Since the expected profit is more if he waits for one year thus decision is that he should wait for a year.

Example 19. *(a) Sameer lives off compus and has just missed the bus that could have taken him to campus for his 10 a.m. test. It is now 09.45 a.m. and Sameer has several options available to get him to campus : Waiting for the next bus, walking, riding his bike or driving his car. The bus is scheduled to arrive in 10 minutes, and it will take Sameer exactly 20 minutes to get to his test from the time he gets on the bus. However, there is 0.2 chance that the bus will be 5 minutes early, and 0.3 chance that the bus will be 5 minutes late.*

If Sameer walks, there is 0.8 chance he will get to his test in 30 minutes, and 0.2 chance he will get there in 35 minutes. If Sameer rides his bike, he will get to the test in 25 minutes with probability 0.5, 30 minutes with probability 0.4, and there is 0.1 chance of a flat tyre causing him to take 45 minutes.

If Sameer drives his car to campus, he will take 15 minutes to get campus, but the time needed to park his car and get to his test is given below.

Time of park and arrive (in min.)	10	15	20	25
Probability	0.30	0.45	0.15	0.10

Assuming that Sameer wants to minimise his expected late time in getting to his test, draw the decision tree and determine his best option. [AIMA June 1997]

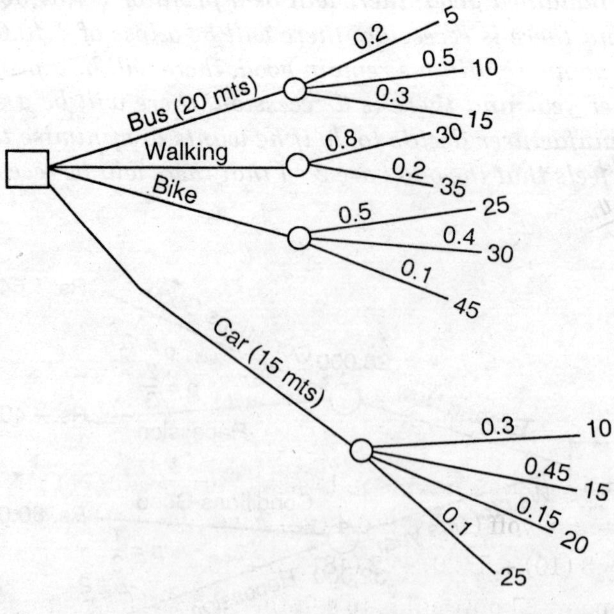

Expected time of reaching in the test by bus $= 20 + 5 \times 0.2 + 10 \times 0.5 + 15 \times 0.3$

$= 20 + 1 + 5 + 4.5 = 30.5$ mts.

Expected time of reaching in the test by walking $= 30 \times 0.8 + 35 \times 0.2 = 31$ mts.

Expected time of reaching in the test by bike $= 25 \times 0.5 + 30 \times 0.4 + 45 \times 0.1$

$= 12.5 + 12 + 4.5 = 29$ mts.

Expected time of reaching in the test by car $= 15 + 10 \times 0.3 + 15 \times 0.45 + 20 \times 0.15 + 25 \times 0.1$

$= 15 + 3 + 6.75 + 3 + 2.5 = 30.25$ **mts.**

Since the expected time by bike is minimum, Sameer should go by bike.

Example 20. *Acme Limited is a cosmetic manufacturing company. During a research survey the company came across a chemical which can be developed as a shampoo for clearing dandruff. Another company P and D in similar business has offered to buy the rights of the chemical for ₹ 5,00,000. Development of the product and the market is the responsibility of P and D company. Acme feels that it can develop the product and market also. Development cost is estimated to be around ₹ 7,50,000 and the probability of successful development of the shampoo is considered to be 50%. If development is successful, many companies will try to buy the rights to marketing the shampoo. Acme believes that there is 0.40 probability that it could receive ₹ 28,00,000 for rights and 0.6 probability that they may get only ₹ 20,00,000. Another option after the successful development of the shampoo would be to launch the product themselves. The possible returns for this option will be ₹ 10,00,000, ₹ 20,00,000 and ₹ 48,00,000 with probabilities of 0.3, 05 and 0.2 respectively.*

(a) *Draw the tree diagram showing all possible actions and their economic effects.*

(b) *Identify the optional plan of action for Acme Ltd.*

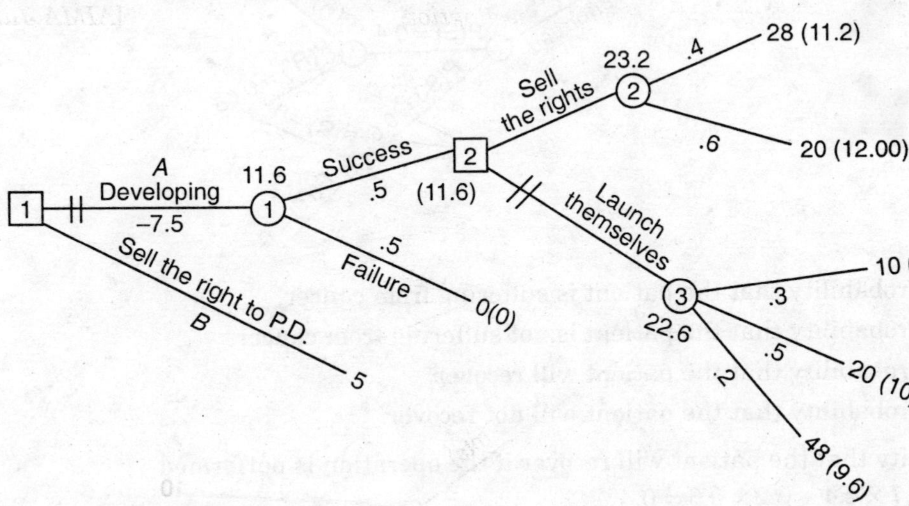

Payoffs are shown in lakhs. Figures in brackets are product of payoff and its probability.

At node ② expected payoff (*E. P.*) = 0.4 (28) + 0.6 (20) = 23.2.

At note ③ *E.P.* = .3 (10) +.5 (20) + .2 (48) = 3 + 10 + 9.6

Thus at decision point 2 optimal is to sell the rights. Thus option ③ is closed.

At node ① *E.P* = 0.5 (23.2) + 0.5 (0) = 11.6

Thus *E.P.* for *A* = 11.6 – 7.5 (developing expenditure) = 4.1

For branch *B* payoff is 5

Out of *A* and *B*, *B* is optimal option.

Thus the company should sell the rights.

Example 21. *There is 40% chance that a patient admitted to the hospital, is suffering from cancer. A doctor has to decide whether a serious operation should be performed or not. If the patient is suffering from cancer and the serious operation is performed, the chance that he will recover, is 70% otherwise it is 35%. On the other hand, if the patient is not suffering from cancer and the serious operation is performed, the chance that he will recover is 20%, otherwise it is 100%. Assume that recovery and death are the only possible results.*

Construct an appropriate decision tree.

What decision should the doctor take? [ICWA QM June 1995]

Solution.

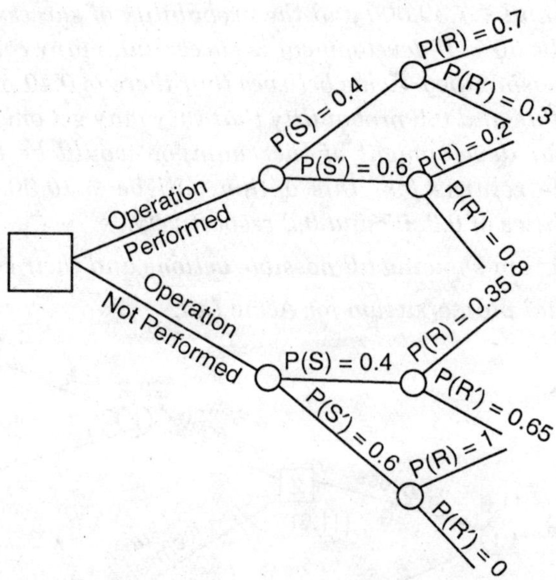

$P(S)$ = Probability that the patient is suffering from cancer.

$P(S')$ = Probability that the patient is not suffering from cancer.

$P(R)$ = Probability that the patient will recover.

$P(R')$ = Probability that the patient will not recover.

Probability that the patient will recover if the operation is performed

$= 0.7 \times 4.4 + 0.2 \times 0.6 = 0.4$

Probability that the patient will recover if the operation is not performed

$= 0.35 \times 0.4 + 1 \times 0.6 = 0.74$

Since the doctor should be interested in the recovery of the patient, he should not performed the operation.

EXERCISE 16

1. A company is contemplating the introduction of a revolutionary new product with new packaging to replace the existing product at much higher price (S_1) or a moderatele changing the composition of the existing product with a new packaging

at a small increase in price to or a small change in the composition of existing except the word 'New' with a negligible increase in price (S_3). The three possible states of nature of events are (*i*) high increase in Sales (P_1), (*ii*) no change in Sales (P_2) and (*iii*) decrease in sales (P_3). The marketing department of the company worked out the pay-offs in terms of yearly net profits for each of the strategies for these events (expected sales). This is represented in the following table :

State of Nature / Strategies (action)	Pay-off (in '000 ₹)		
	P_1	P_2	P_3
S_1	700	300	150
S_2	500	450	100
S_3	300	300	300

Which strategy should the executive concerned choose on the basis of

(*i*) Maximin Criterion (*ii*) Maximax Criterion

(*iii*) Minimax Regret Criterion ? [*C.A. Foundation June,* 1994]

[**Ans.** S_3, S_1, S_1]

2. A physician purchases a particular vaccine on Monday of each week. The vaccine must be used within the week following, otherwise it becomes worthless. The vaccine costs ₹ 2 per dose and the physician charges ₹ 4 per dose. In the past 50 weeks, the physician has administered the vaccine in the following quantities :

Doses per Week	*Number of Weeks*
20	5
25	15
50	25
60	5

On the basis of EMV, find how many doses the physician must purchase each week to maximise his profits. [*D.U. B. Com. (Hons.)* 2002]

[**Ans.** 50 Doses].

3. (*a*) Explain briefly the "Statistical Decision Theory".

[*Delhi Univ. B. Com. (H)* 1999, *2007*]

(*b*) List the different ingredients of "Statistical Decision Theory".

[*Delhi Univ. B. Com. (H) 2003*]

4. Explain briefly statistical decision theory. What are the ingredients of a decision problem? [*Delhi Univ. B. Com. (H) 2008*]

5. Distinguish between Payoff Table and Regret Table giving suitable example.

[*Delhi Univ. B. Com. (H)* 1996, *1997*]

6. (*a*) What is EVPP. How is it calculated? [*Delhi Univ. B. Com. (H) 2000*]

(*b*) Explain the concept of decision-making under risk. What is there a need for expected value of perfect information? How is it calculated?

[*Delhi Univ. B. Com. (H)* 2003]

7. Given the following payoff of a factory owner :

States of Nature ↓	Actions Pay off (in '000 ₹)			Probability
	Do not expand	*Acts Expand 200 units*	*Expand 400 units*	
High demand	300	500	600	0.5
Medium demand	250	300	500	0.3
Low demand	200	– 100	– 300	0.2

Obtain the optimal strategy by using (*a*) *EMV* criterion, and (*ii*) *EOL* criterion.

Is the conclusion same in both the cases ? Explain why ?

[**Ans.** (*a*) Act : *Do not expand* *Expand 200 units* *Expand 400 units*

EMV ('000 ₹) : 265 320 90

Optimal act is to expand the plant by 200 units.

(*b*) Expand the plant by 200 units.

8. The following payoff table is given :

PAYOFF TABLE

Acts	Events			
	E_1	E_2	E_3	E_4
A_1	40	200	– 200	100
A_2	200	0	200	0
A_3	0	100	0	150
A_4	– 50	400	100	0

Suppose that the probability of the events of this table are $P(E_1) = 0.20$, $P(E_2) = 0.15$, $P(E_3) = 0.40$, $P(E_4) = 0.25$. Calculate the expected payoff and the expected loss of each action.

[*C.A. (Foundation), May 1997*]

[**Ans.** $EMV(A_2) = 120$: Maximum *EMV* ; $EOL(A_2) = 120$: Minimum *EOL*. In each case, A_2 is the optimal act.]

9. A factory produces 3 varieties of fountain pens. The fixed and variable costs are given below :

	Fixed Cost	*Variable Cost (per unit)*
Type 1	₹ 2,00,000	₹ 10
Type 2	₹ 3,20,000	₹ 8
Type 3	₹ 6,00,000	₹ 6

The likely demands under three situations are given below :

	Unit
Demand Poor	25,000
Demand Moderate	1,00,000
Demand High	1,50,000

If the price of each type is ₹ 20 per unit, prepare the payoff table after showing the necessary calculations.

If it can produce only one of the three varieties, which one should be produced, given that the probabilities of poor, moderate and high demand are 0.2, 0.3 and 0.5 respectively.

[**Ans. PAYOFF TABLE (IN '000 ₹)**

Event	*Acts (Pens)*		
(Demand)	A_1: *Type 1*	A_2: *Type 2*	A_3: *Type 3*
Poor	50	– 20	– 250
Moderate	800	800	800
High	1,300	1,480	1,500

EMV (A_1) = ₹ 900 thousand ;

EMV (A_2) = ₹ 1,000 thousand ;

EMV (A_3) = ₹ 940 thousand.

⇒ Act A_2 : 'Produce type 2 of fountain pens' is the optimal act.

10. The management is faced with the problem of choosing one of the products for manufacturing. The potential demand for each product may turn out to be good; fair or poor. The probability matrix after market research for the three products was as follows:

	State of Nature		
Acts	*Good*	*Fair*	*Poor*
Product A	0.75	0.15	0.10
Product B	0.60	0.30	0.10
Product C	0.50	0.30	0.20

The profits that the management can make for different levels of markets acceptability of the products are as follows :

	Profit (in ₹) if market is		
Acts	*Good*	*Fair*	*Poor*
Product A	35,000	15,000	5,000
Product B	50,000	20,000	Loss of 3,000
Product C	60,000	30,000	20,000

Calculate EMV for each act advise the management about the best choice of the product. [*Delhi Univ. B.Com. (H)* 2005 *(C.C.)*]

[**Ans.** EMV (*A*) = 29,000, EMV (*B*) = 35,700 EMV (*C*) = 43,000

'Product *C*' is the best choice.]

11. A group of volunteers of a service organisation raises money each year by selling articles outside the stadium after a football match between Team *X* and *Y*. They can buy any of the three different types of gift articles from a dealer. Their sales are mostly dependent on which team wins the match. A conditional payoff table is as under :

	Types of gift articles		
	I	II	III
Team X wins	₹ 1000	900	600
Team Y wins	₹ 400	500	800

(i) Construct the opportunity loss table, and

(ii) Which type of gift article should the volunteers buy if the probability of Team X's winning is 0.8? [Delhi Univ. B.Com. (H) 2003]

[**Ans.** (i) **OPPORTUNITY LOSS TABLE**

	Types of gift articles		
	I	II	III
Team X wins	0	100	400
Team Y wins	400	300	0

(ii) Type I]

12. A shopkeeper of some highly perishable type of fruit sees that the daily demand X of this fruit in his area has the following probability distribution :

Daily demand (in dozen) :	6	7	8	9
Probability :	0.1	0.3	0.4	0.2

He sells fruits for ₹ 10 a dozen while he buys each dozen at ₹ 4. Unsold fruits in a day are traded on the next day at ₹ 2 per dozen. Assuming that he stocks the fruits in dozen, how many should he stock so that his expected profit will be maximum?

[**Ans.** 8 dozen]

13. A stockist of a particular commodity makes a profit of ₹ 30 on each sale made within the same week of purchase, otherwise he incurs a loss of ₹ 30 on each item. The data on the past sales are given below :

No of items sold within the same week :	5	6	7	8	9	10	11
Frequency :	0	9	12	24	9	6	0

(i) Find out the optimum number of items the stockist should buy every week in order to maximize the profit.

(ii) Calculate the expected value of perfect information.

[C.A. (Foundation) May, 1996]

[**Ans.** (i) 8 (ii) EVPI = ₹ 25.50.]

14. A magazine vendor has assigned the following probabilities to the demand for a weekly magazine :

Copies demanded :	1	2	3	4
Probability :	0.4	0.3	0.2	0.1

A copy of the magazine sells for ₹ 7 and costs ₹ 6. An unsold copy can be returned for ₹ 5. How many copies of the magazine should the vendor buy so that his expected profit will be maximum?

[**Ans.** 2 copies].

15. An engineering firm has installed a machine costing ₹ 4 lakhs and is in the process of deciding on an appropriate number of a certain spare parts required for repairs. The spare parts cost ₹ 4,000 each but are available only if they are ordered now. In case the machine fails and no spares are available, the cost to the company of mending the plant would be ₹ 18,000. The plant has an estimated life experience with similar machines, as follows :

No. of failures during 8 yearly period	:	0	1	2	3	4	5	6 +
Probability	:	0.1	0.2	0.3	0.2	0.1	0.1	0

Ignoring any discounting for time value of money, determine the following :

(*a*) The optimal number of units of the spare part on the basis of (*i*) minimax principle, (*ii*) minimin principle, (*iii*) Laplace principle, and (*iv*) expected cost principle.

(*b*) The expected number of failures in the 8-year period.

(*c*) The regret table, and the optimum choice on the basis of least expected regret criterion.

(*d*) *EVPI.* (*Poona Univ. M.B.A., 1996*)

[**Hint.** Define :

Act A_j : Number of spare parts is j ; $j = 0, 1, 2, ..., 5, 6 +$.

State of nature S_i : Number of failure is i ; $i = 0, 1, 2, ..., 5, 6 +$.

If S denotes the number of spares and F denotes the number of failures, then according to the conditions of the problem, the cost function (C) in Rupees is given by :

$$\left.\begin{aligned} C &= 4{,}000\, S & ; \quad & F \le S \\ &= 4{,}000\, S + 18{,}000\, (F - S) & ; \quad & F > S \end{aligned}\right\} \qquad ...(*)$$

States of Nature (No. of failures)	*Probability*	*Opportunity Cost (in '000 ₹) Act (No. of Spares)*						*Regret Values (in '000 ₹) Act (No. of Spares)*					
		A_0 (0)	A_1 (1)	A_2 (2)	A_3 (3)	A_4 (4)	A_5 (5)	A_0 (0)	A_1 (1)	A_2 (2)	A_3 (3)	A_4 (4)	A_5 (5)
S_0 (0)	0.1	0	4	8	12	16	20	0	4	8	12	16	20
S_1 (1)	0.2	18	4	8	12	16	20	14	0	4	8	12	16
S_2 (2)	0.3	36	22	8	12	16	20	28	14	0	4	8	12
S_3 (3)	0.2	54	40	26	12	16	20	42	28	14	0	4	8
S_4 (4)	0.1	72	58	44	30	16	20	56	42	28	14	0	4
S_5 (5)	0.1	90	76	62	48	34	20	72	56	42	28	14	0
Expected cost		41.4	29.2	20.6	17.4	17.8	20	Expected regret :					
								32.2	20	11.4	8.2	8.6	10.8

Note Bold figures are the minimum cost for each state of nature and are required to calculate ECPI.

[**Ans.** (*a*) (*i*) 5, (*ii*) Nil (0), (*iii*) 4 (*iv*) 3.

(*b*) Expected number of failures in the 8-year period (from the given probability distribution of number of failures) is given by :

$0 \times 0.1 + 1 \times 0.2 + 2 \times 0.3 + 3 \times 0.2 + 4 \times 0.1 = 0 + 0.2 + 0.6 + 0.6 + 0.4 + 0.5 = 2.3.$

(*c*) Regret table is given above.

Min (*EOL*) = Min (Expected Regret) = ₹ 8.2 thousand

$\therefore A_4$: Number of spares = 4, is the optimal act.

(*d*) *EVPI* = Minimum (Expected Cost) – *ECPI*

$= 17.4 - (0 \times 0.1 + 4 \times 0.2 + 8 \times 0.3 + 12 \times 0.2 + 16 \times 0.1 + 20 \times 0.1)$ = ₹ 8.2 ('000).]

16. Each unit of a product produced and sold yields a profit of ₹ 50, but a unit produced but not sold results in a loss of ₹ 30. The probability distribution of the number of units demanded is as follows :

No. of units demanded	:	0	1	2	3	4
Probability	:	0.20	0.20	0.25	0.30	0.05

How many units be produced to maximize the expected profits ? Also calculate EVPL. [*Delhi Univ. B.Com. (H) 2001, 2003*]

[**Ans.** 2 units, *EVPI* = 038]

17. A TV dealer finds that the cost of holding a TV in stock for a week is ₹ 50. Customers who cannot obtain new TVs immediately tend to go to other dealers and he estimates that for every customer who cannot get immediate delivery he loses an average of ₹ 200. For one particular model of TV, the probabilities of demand of 0, 1, 2, 3, 4 and 5 TVs in a week are 0.05, 0.10, 0.20, 0.30, 0.20 and 0.15 respectively.

(*i*) How many televisions per week should the dealer order ? Assume that there is no time lag between ordering and delivery.

(*ii*) Compute *EVPI.*

(*iii*) The dealer is thinking of spending on a small market survey to obtain additional information regarding the demand levels. How much should he be willing to spend on such a survey ? [*Delhi Univ. M.B.A., Nov.* 1997]

[**Hint.** Let m be the number of televisions stored (stocked) and n be the number of televisions demanded per week. Then the according to the conditions of the problem, the conditional cost function (C) in Rupees is given by :

$$\left.\begin{aligned} C &= 50m + 200\,(n - m) \quad ; \quad n \geq m \\ &= 50m \quad ; \quad n > m \end{aligned}\right\} \qquad \ldots(*)$$

Using (*), we can compute the cost matrix for different combinations of (*m, n*), each ranging from 0 to 5. We shall finally get :

m	:	0	1	2	3	4	5
Expected Cost	:	590	450	330	250	230	250

Ans. (*i*) Optimal decision is to stock $m = 4$, televisions per week.

(*ii*) *EVPI* = Minimum (Expected cost) – *ECPI*]

18. A newspaper distributor assigns probabilities to the demand for a magazine on any day as follows :

Copies demanded	:	11	12	13	14
Probability	:	0.4	0.3	0.2	0.1

A copy of the magazine sells for ₹ 7 and costs ₹ 6. The distributor can return the unsold copies of magazine for ₹ 5 each. How many copies of magazine should he order for the next day? Use EMV criterion to answer the question? Also calculate EVPI. [*Delhi Univ. B.Com. (H)* 2005 (*C.C.*)]

[**Ans.** 12 copies, EVPI = 0.80]

19. The demand for a seasonal product is given below :

Demand	:	40	45	50	55	60	65
Probability	:	0.10	0.20	0.30	0.25	0.10	0.05

The product costs ₹ 60 per unit and sells at ₹ 80 per unit. If the units are not sold within the season, they will have no market value.

(*i*) Determine the optimum number of units to be produced using EMV criterion.

(*ii*) Calculate EVPI and interpret it.

(*iii*) Prepare the 'Regret Table' and using EOL criterion, obtain the optimal act.

(*iv*) Compare the conclusions in (*i*) and (*iii*).

[**Ans.** 45 units, *E.V.P.I* = ₹ 160, 45 units].

20. The following payoff table is given.

Acts	*Events* E_1	E_2	E_3	E_4
A_1	40	200	– 200	100
A_2	200	0	200	0
A_3	0	100	0	150
A_4	– 50	400	100	0

Suppose that the probability of the events of this table are $P(E_1) = 0.20$, $P(E_2) = 0.15$, $P(E_3) = 0.40$, $P(E_4) = 0.25$. Calculate the expected payoff and the expected loss of each action. [*C.A. Foundation, May* 1997]

[**Ans.** EMV (A_1) = – 17, EMV (A_2) = 120, EMV (A_3) = 37.5, EMV (A_4) = 90

EOL (A_1) = 234.5, EOL (A_2) = 97.5, EOL (A_3) = 165, EOL (A_4) = 127.5

Act A_2 is the optimal (best) act.

21. Amar Company is currently working with a process which after paying for materials, abour, etc., brings a profit of ₹ 12,000. The following alternatives are made available to the company :

(*i*) The company can conduct research (R_1) which is expected to cost ₹ 10,000 having 90% chances of success. If it proves a success, the company gets a gross income of ₹ 25,000.

(*ii*) The company can conduct research (R_2) which is expected to cost ₹ 8,000 having a probability of 0% success, the gross income will be ₹ 25,000.

(*iii*) The company can pay ₹ 6,000 as royalty for a new process which will bring a gross income of ₹ 20,000.

(*iv*) The company continues the current process.

Because of limited resources, it is assumed that only one of the two types of research can be carried but at a time.

Use decision tree analysis to locate the optimal strategy for the company.

[C.A. (Foundation), May 1994]

[**Ans.** — Pay royalty for new process, $EMV = 4{,}000$]

22. The Oil India Corporation is considering whether to go for an offshore oil drilling contract to be awarded in Bombay High. If they bid, value would be ₹ 600 million with 65% chance of gaining the contract. They may set up a new drilling operation or move already existing operation, which has proved successful, to new site. The probability of success and expected returns are as follows :

Outcome	*New Drilling Operation*		*Existing Operation*	
	Probability	*Expected Revenue (₹ million)*	*Probability*	*Expected Revenue (₹ million)*
Success	0.75	800	0.85	700
Failure	0.25	200	0.15	350

If the Corporation do not bid or lose the contract, they can use ₹ 600 million to modernize their corporation. This would result in a return of either 5% or 8% on the sum invested with probabilities 0.45 and 0.55 (Assume that all costs and revenue have been discounted to present value).

(*i*) Construct a decision tree for the problem showing clearly the courses of action.

(*ii*) By applying an appropriate decision criterion recommend whether or not the Oil India Corporation would bid the contract.

[**Hint.** The decision tree based on the given information in the problem is depicted in the following figure :

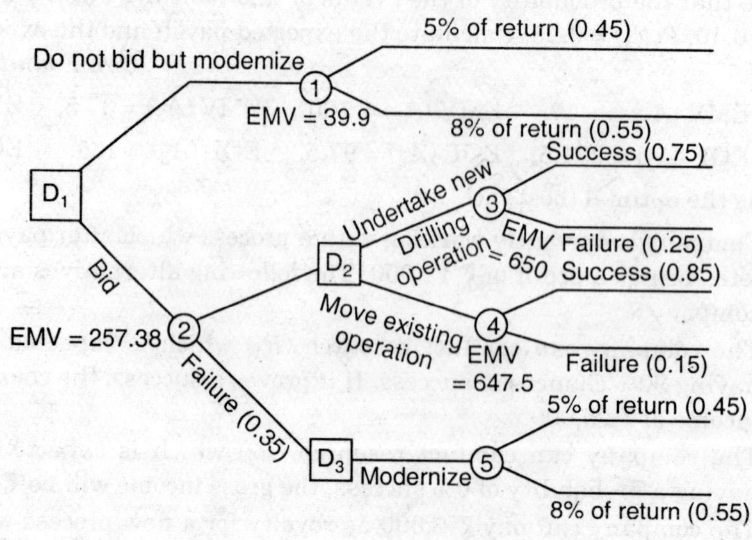

Since EMV at node 2 is highest, therefore the best decision at node D_2 is to decide for bid and if successful establish a new drilling operation.]

23. Matrix Company is planning to launch a new product, which can be introduced initially in Western India or in the entire country. If the product is introduced initially in Western India or in the entire country. If the product is introduced only in Western India, the investment outlay will be ₹ 12 million. After two years, Matrix can evaluate the project to determine whether it should cover the entire country. For such expansion it will have to incur an additional investment of ₹ 10 million. To introduce the product in the entire country right in the beginning would involve an outlay of ₹ 20 million. The product, in any case, will have a life of 5 years, after which the plant will have zero net value.

If the product is introduce only in Western India, demand would be high or low with the probabilities of 0.8 and 0.2 respectively and annual cash inflow of ₹ 4 million and ₹ 2.5 million respectively.

If the product is introduced in the entire country right in the beginning the demand would be high or low with probabilities of 0.6 and 0.4 respectively and annual cash inflows of ₹ 8 million and ₹ 5 million respectively.

Based on the observed demand in Western India, if the product is introduced in the entire country the following probabilities would exist for high and low demand on an all India basis:

Western India	*Whole Country*	
	High Demand	*Low Demand*
High demand	0.90	0.10
Los demand	0.40	0.60

The hurdle applicable to this project is 12 per cent.

(*a*) Set up a decision tree for the investment situation.

(*b*) Advice Matrix Company on the investment policy it should follow.

Support your advice with appropriate reasoning. [*ICWA, June* 1990]

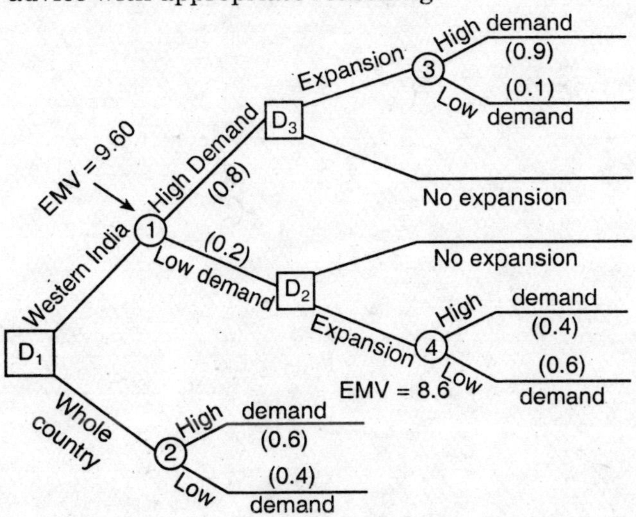

EMV at node 2 is highest (= 14). Thus decision is to launch the product in whole country].

□□□